LUTHERANISM: FROM WITTENBERG TO THE U.S.A.

LUTHER, THE REFORMATION, AND LUTHERANISM IN AMERICA

A CONSERVATIVE PERSPECTIVE

By Arthur J. Clement

LUTHERANISM: FROM WITTENBERG TO THE U.S.A.
Luther, The Reformation, and Lutheranism in America
A Conservative Perspective

About the cover: "The City of Wittenberg seen from the Elbe,"
drawing from the travel album of Count Palatine Ottheinrich (1536),
University Library Würzburg. Image source: Wikimedia Commons.

Library of Congress Card
Lutheran News, Inc.
684 Luther Lane
New Haven, MO 63068
Published 2012
Printed in the United States of America,
Lightning Source, Inc.
LaVergne, TN, USA 37086
ISBN 978-0-9644799-9-9

Acknowledgements

Arthur J. Clement worked for many years, almost until shortly before his death in 2011, on *Lutheranism From Wittenberg to the U.S.A.* This was his magnum opus.

Luke Otten, managing editor of *Christian News*, made the arrangements to have this book published. Naomi Finck and Mary Zastrow set the type in 2008.

As the 500th anniversary of the Reformation approaches in 2017, publication of *Lutheranism From Wittenberg to the U.S.A.* is part of the program of *Christian News* to work for a 21st Century Reformation and an updated 21st Century Formula of Concord which reaffirms the Formula of Concord of 1580 and speaks to such contemporary issues as evolution, historical criticism of the Bible, abortion, birth control, sex outside marriage, and homosexuality.

Lutheran Hour speaker, Walter A. Maier, wrote in the November, 1933 *Walther League Messenger* on the 450th birthday of Martin Luther:

"We repeat, the appeal to American Protestantism is: 'BACK TO LUTHER!' And if this be a battle cry that is to summon the latent forces of a complacent laity to action; if it be the rallying summons to a spiritual crusade for Christ; if it means the splitting of the church into two groups, one liberal and unbelieving, and the other conservative and faithful unto death; if it requires the breaking of conventionalities, the banishment of pulpit Judases, then we still repeat the cry: 'BACK TO LUTHER!'"

TABLE OF CONTENTS

PREFACE

The purpose of this volume is, of course, to provide the reader with an overview of the intriguing history of Lutheranism in America, a history which began close to 400 years ago on this great nation's Eastern Seaboard. Long before this nation was officially formed, Lutherans were here as colonists, helping to tame and inhabit the vast wilderness that lay before them. And when the colonists were driven by developing circumstances to form their own independent nation, Lutherans played an important part in helping to bring this about, for large numbers fought in the War of Independence. And after the war, Lutherans were counted among the statesmen who ruled the newly formed nation. When timber needed to be cut from virgin forests to build the towns and cities that would dot the nation, much of it was felled by Lutheran lumberjacks. When minerals needed to be dug from the earth, many of the miners who did the digging were Lutherans. Lutheran farmers helped to supply the young nation with food and raw materials. Lutherans designed, built and operated machinery. Lutherans established and conducted businesses. Lutherans helped to lead the way in education and in maintaining institutions of charity and mercy. Lutherans were among the pioneers who expanded the frontier and helped to settle villages, towns and cities in widely scattered places. Lutherans joined the fight to preserve the nation and to end slavery. Whenever our nation has been threatened, Lutherans have been on hand to help defend it. Lutherans have contributed much to the establishment and development and preservation of this nation, both as skilled and unskilled as well as professional and non-professional citizens—men and women.

The people who brought Lutheranism to America came from all over Europe and from Scandinavia as well. From the mid-nineteenth to the early twentieth century, wave after wave of immigrants came to these shores, many of whom were at least nominally Lutheran. Religious and economic oppression in their homeland urged many of these Lutherans to emigrate to America in order to experience freedom and enjoy a better life. A fascinating drama unfolds before the eyes of the reader as he or she delves into the stories of transplanted people and transplanted Lutheranism. Adding much intensity to the drama are the personalities and spiritual bearings of those who provided spiritual guidance to their fellow Lutherans in a new country. Some of these men were hierarchical, some were pietists. Some emphasized lay ministry and were suspicious of the pastoral office. Some were orthodox to their finger tips, while others were Lutheran in name only. Some could best be described as wolves in sheep's clothing. There were those who did much good on the religious scene, while others did much damage. Lutheran congregations and synods were also formed that were anything but Lutheran. Indeed, some Lutheran congregations could better be described as Reformed or as Methodist. Sadly, many Lutherans succumbed to the enticement of the religious sects that dotted the scene. For example, not a few Lutherans were lost to the

Mormon Church.

Large numbers of the Lutheran immigrants did not remain with their Christian faith, let alone their Lutheranism. The deplorable conditions encountered in America, especially on the frontier, made it easy for those who were less spiritual to make excuses for not practicing their faith. Bad feelings rooted in the oppression they experienced from the state church in their homeland, plus the lack of Lutheran churches and Lutheran pastors where the Lutheran immigrants settled, and finally, the rigors of life and the isolation that cut them off from fellow Lutherans and even fellow Christians, all too often crowded out the faith they may have once had.

Nevertheless, in spite of all this, there were those Lutherans who kept the faith and struggled heroically to practice it. They built churches and schools and went to great lengths and made sacrifices in order to obtain pastors, to organize congregations, and even to form church bodies or synods. Their's is a heartwarming story.

Disagreements in doctrine and practice sometimes plagued the Lutheran church bodies, sometimes tearing them apart. And when that happened, new church bodies often took form. Unionism—fellowship with heterodox churches—was, and still is, a powerful temptation to Lutherans to end their so-called isolation and join the much touted "mainstream" of the Protestant community. But, as this history clearly shows, unionism results in a much watered down Lutheranism, and a significant loss of scriptural orthodoxy.

This volume scans the Lutheran scene as it has presented itself here in America. But what is Lutheranism? Why was it important that Lutheranism be established in America? What does it have to offer—especially confessional, orthodox Lutheranism? To help the reader to review and thus appreciate better this "thing" called Lutheranism, a brief history of the founder and of the founding of Lutheranism—as well as its spread to European countries and to Scandinavia—is given at the beginning of this volume.

Because this history of Lutheranism in America is given from a conservative, confessional perspective, much space is provided to cover doctrinal controversies, which controversies are approached from the standpoint of each individual body that was involved. And for the reason that this volume looks at Lutheranism in America from a conservative, confessional perspective, extra space is given to the conservative, confessional synods or church bodies—even though the amount of coverage may seem out of proportion to their size and generally recognized importance. This is especially true in regards to the Wisconsin Evangelical Lutheran Synod (WELS)—now the largest of the conservative Lutheran bodies (not counting the Lutheran Church-Missouri Synod, which is recognized as both conservative and moderate). Also, the Evangelical Lutheran Synod (ELS), the Church of the Lutheran Confession (CLC). The Lutheran Church-Missouri Synod, which has an especially fascinating history and has historically occupied a leadership role in conservative Lutheranism here in America, also receives thorough coverage.

One of the things that should stand out very clearly as one reads this historical overview of Lutheranism in America, is the degree to which a church body's orthodoxy and polity can change from one era to the next, even from one generation to the next. Also we see the impact that the theology and practice of a church's leaders—who embody either orthodoxy or heterodoxy, conservatism or liberalism—has on the church body or synod they lead. A case in point is the Lutheran Church-Missouri Synod (LCMS). When this synod no longer was led by a Walther or a Pieper—i.e. by scripturally orthodox men like these—the synod suffered in its orthodox character. It floundered. It simply yielded some of the conservative stand that had been a beacon to generations of Lutherans, guiding them to rock solid Christianity and to Lutheran orthodoxy. Another case in point is the doctrinal slide experienced by the American Lutheran Church (ALC) as the leadership changed over the years. The old doctrinal conservatism gave way to the new theology of modernism and the historical criticism kind of Bible interpretation, which is now the prevailing theology in Lutheranism in America (and in the world).

The reader will probably come to the conclusion that Lutheranism is itself in great peril. And it is. The conservative, confessional Lutheran bodies comprise the last outpost of orthodox Lutheranism in America, and considerably so also on the world scene of Lutheranism. Perhaps the reader may even recognize in this volume the call to Lutherans to move away from neo-Lutheranism and modernism and return to sound, scriptural orthodoxy, both in teaching and in polity. That, of course, is our hope.

Arthur J. Clement

Introduction

A TIME OF EXPLORATION AND DISCOVERY

The Reformation (also called the German Reformation), which resulted in the establishing of the Lutheran Church, took place as explorers and adventurers from Europe were making discoveries and establishing settlements in the New World. In 1507, twenty-four years after the birth of German Reformer Martin Luther, the name America was given to land discovered in the New World. This discovery is credited to a Catholic, an Italian sea captain named Christopher Columbus. Strangely, at the time of his death in 1506 Columbus was not aware of what he had accomplished. His several voyages, including the final one in 1503, were aimed at finding the sea passage that would lead to China or to India.

A Catholic monk persuaded Queen Isabella of Spain to act upon Columbus' dreams of exploration. From his studies and travels Columbus was convinced that the world is round, not flat as was generally thought. This meant that men ought to be able to sail west from Spain and finally arrive in China and India, which lay to the east. While testing out his theory, Columbus landed on a small island in the Bahamas on October 12, 1492, and claimed the land for his queen. He thought that he had reached the Indies. In subsequent voyages, Columbus explored the coasts of Central America, Venezuela, and other spots along the Caribbean. Everywhere he landed, this pioneer explorer took possession of the land in the name of Catholic Spain.

It has, of course, been firmly established that the Vikings, perhaps led by Leif Ericson himself, settled in North America around 1,000 A.D. Remains of their camp have been found near the Strait of Belle Isle on the Northern tip of the Island of New Foundland. However, Columbus has left us a chronicle of his voyages and discoveries. Thus he helped to lay out courses across the great Ocean Sea (the Atlantic) that others were able to follow, thereby enabling further exploration and exploitation of the New World.

IN EUROPE ONE CHURCH

At the time of the discovery of the New World in 1492, there was—as far as Christianity is concerned—only Catholicism in Europe. The Great Schism which occurred in the Christian Church in 1054 divided the Church into Roman Catholicism in the West and the Greek Orthodox Church in the East. Nurtured by the Schism, the doctrine of papal supremacy was recognized by the Western Church but was not accepted by the Eastern Church. The voyages of discovery to the Western Hemisphere were made at a time when Roman Catholicism held sway not only in the western part of Europe but in the English Isles and the Scandinavian countries as well. All religious teachings which dared to differ with the teachings of Catholicism were branded as heresy and rooted out by the papacy, using imprisonment, torture, confiscation of property, and even death. In

1

these endeavors the Church of Rome was closely allied with the secular powers.

The need was felt for the reformation of the Church in order to release men's consciences from papal oppression and suppression; to reestablish the Church on the basis of Holy Scripture; and to turn the members of the clergy—high and low—from the rampant immorality, worldliness, and secularism with which they had become so deeply imbued. John Wyclif (1320-1384) had been a leader of such a reform movement, a movement that spread over England and even to areas of the Continent. Among other things, Wyclif stood for justification of the sinner alone through faith in Christ and regarded the Bible as the only source of religious truth. In England, in 1401, heresy of which Wyclif was accused was made punishable by death, and his movement was suppressed by an iron fist. Years after Wyclif's death, he was tried and condemned to death by the Church and his bones were dug up and burned.

John Hus (1369-1415) led a reform movement in Bohemia, and the nation followed him. However, Hus was eventually summoned before the Council of Constance, having been assured by the Emperor (with agreement by the pope) of safe conduct. This disciple of Wyclif was thrown into prison, tried, and summarily condemned as a heretic by the Church. He was taken to a field near the city and burned alive at the stake. The promise of safe conduct was but a ruse to enable the Church to destroy Hus.

Girolama Savonarola (1452-1498) was a Dominican monk who reformed the city of Florence, Italy. He was a bold preacher of repentance and made the rulers and even the pope objects of his scathing rebukes. He taught that salvation can be attained only by God's grace through Christ Jesus, and that good works can be attained only by a heart regenerated with faith in Christ. Savonarola became entrenched in politics and thus erred by confusing church and state. When political affairs turned against him, the Reformer began to lose favor with the people, who tired of his constant intrusion into their private lives. The pope placed the monk under the ban and the city of Florence under the interdict. One day a fanatical mob took Savonarola prisoner. He was tortured, tried, condemned, hanged, and burned. This Reformer met his end six years after the first successful voyage of discovery made by Columbus. Permanent successful reform would not come until the great movement by Martin Luther in Germany.

THE LINE OF DEMARCATION

An Italian adventurer, Amerigo Vespucci, claimed around the turn of the sixteenth century to have journeyed to a northern coast of what we now know to be South America. He reported seeing a coastline that was so long that it seemed more like the edge of a continent than the coastline of an island. In 1507 the mapmaker Martin Waldseemuler designed a map of the New World which incorporated such a body of land and placed Amerigo's name on it.[1] The Latin of Amerigo is Americus. In spite of Amerigo Vespucci's claims, the burden of interest in the New World at first lay with the Portugese and the Spaniards, not with the Italians. In 1498 a

2

Portugese, Vasco da Gama, succeeded in reaching India by sailing around Africa and then eastward across the Indian Ocean, thereby discovering the route to India others had sought but failed to find. Still, Spain's discoveries in the New World, which it was hoped would bring much commerce to Spanish merchants, were made six years before the Portugese sailed to India. In order to protect Spain's claims in the New World from Portugal's aspirations, Spain appealed to the pope to act as arbiter. And so it was that in 1493 Pope Alexander VI established the Line of Demarcation for Spain and Portugal, which line the two kings finally agreed to abide by. This line was established 100 leagues west of the Cape Verde Islands and was to run from pole to pole. Later it was moved 270 leagues further west of the Islands. Heathen lands east went to Portugal; heathen lands to the west went to Spain. The line granted the eastern portion of what is now known as Brazil to the Portugese, who later officially claimed it. While the eastern bulge of South America went to the Portugese, the rest of the Continent of South America was finally conquered by Spaniards, with Roman Catholicism established as the official religion.

PROTESTANTISM BECOMES FIRMLY ESTABLISHED IN NORTH AMERICA

It is of great interest to note that the discovery and exploration of the New World coincided to a great extent with the life of the Church's greatest Reformer, Martin Luther. By the time that successful attempts of colonization were made in the seventeenth century, the Reformation had become an established reality in much of Europe and in England and the Scandinavian countries. Though Catholic countries were the first to send out explorers, the actual settling of the Continent of North America was to a far greater extent the work of Protestants, including Lutherans. In fact, Protestants in great numbers came as settlers to American's shores.

But with early exploration and settlement in the New World carried on chiefly by Catholic countries, things could have taken a different turn as far as the religious makeup of the early colonies in America is concerned. However, the intervention of one nation in particular prevented this from occurring. That North America today is not Catholic is due under God to Protestant England, which became Protestant as a result of Luther's reform movement in Germany and the efforts of other reformers to establish his doctrine in England. The Spaniards ruled the waves until the English "Dragon," Sir Francis Drake, changed the balance of power in favor of England. Drake was responsible for preventing Spain's conquest of North America. He successfully raided Spanish ships along American Coasts and finally, in 1588, defeated the Spanish Aramada. In that year, Catholic Spain sent the Invincible Aramada to invade Protestant England, but it met with disastrous defeat from Drake and the weather. This was the true turning point in Spain's heretofore claim to be ruler of the sea. The defeat of the Aramada made successful English colonization in America possible. Eventually, in 1667, Protestant England took America from the Dutch Re-

3

formed rulers and clergy. About one hundred years later, in 1760, England took Canada from France. England gave religious freedom to the American Colonies, a freedom which was not enjoyed even in Protestant countries in Europe, for there was much persecution under the State Churches—including the Lutheran State Church—in Europe and Scandinavia.

It is a significant fact of history that the Protestant Church, a result of the life and work of Martin Luther and other reformers, was on hand to have a crucial impact on the settlement and development of North America. What Martin Luther taught from Holy Scripture was brought to America and planted here by vast numbers of Lutherans who migrated to these shores from all over Europe and Scandinavia. Lutheranism, as well as other Protestant denominations, played an important part in the founding, expansion, and refining of this nation.

After a brief but comprehensive review of the Reformer's life and the founding and spread of Lutheranism, we will give our attention to the fascinating and exciting story of the journey made by Lutheranism from Wittenberg, Germany, to other European countries, to Scandinavia, to England, and finally also to America, where it has been planted from border to border and from shore to shore.

Footnotes for Introduction
1 Johanna Johnston and James L. Steffenson, *The Universal History of the World, Vol. 8, Reformation and Exploration* (Golden Press, New York, 1966 by Western Publishing Company, Inc. and Librairie Hachette), p. 679.

CHAPTER ONE

MARTIN LUTHER THE REFORMER

BIRTH OF THE REFORMER

The man for whom the Lutheran Church is named was born in Eisleben, Germany, on November 10, 1483. The infant son of Hans Luder and his wife Margaretha Ziegler was baptized the following day and given the name Martin in honor of the saint of the day. (Martin Luther changed the spelling of the last name to Luther, which spelling will be used here also for his family and other relatives.) Martin Luther came from humble peasant stock, and all his life he proudly recounted the fact that his ancestors were farmers. He never lost his love for the town of his birth and, coincidently, died there sixty-three years later. The religious world of Europe at the time Luther entered it was Roman Catholic, with the pope at Rome regarded as the spiritual leader of all Christendom. The Luthers too were devoted Catholics and taught this religion to Martin and their six other children.

A GLIMPSE OF THE PAPACY OF LUTHER'S TIME

History shows that the papacy reached its lowest ebb during Martin Luther's time.[1] A cursory examination of the lives of the popes of this era certainly bears this out. Most of the popes were brilliant-minded men who, while they possessed a high degree of intelligence, were nevertheless spiritually lacking. They were interested mainly in worldly and secular pursuit and displayed little interest in religion.

Martin was born during the reign of Pope Sixtus IV (1471-1484). This

5

pope completely secularized the papacy and was addicted to avarice, nepotism (he removed others from office to make room for his relatives), and simony. Sixtus was a plotter and a tyrant, who aimed to make himself the master of Central Italy. He introduced the Inquisition and used it to persecute the Jews in Spain. Even children as young as twelve years of age (girls included) were tortured on the rack. Nor were elderly men and women spared. Sixtus also persecuted the Waldensians. In 1476 Sixtus established indulgences for souls in purgatory.

Innocent VIII (1484-1492), according to some reports, blessed his celebate life with offspring. He strengthened the inquisition in Spain and stirred up crusades against the Waldensians. Innocent interfered in the political matters of several countries. Some of the darkest deeds of the papacy occurred during his tenure.

Alexander VI (1492-1503) was mentally gifted and morally bankrupt. He had, according to reports, several children out of wedlock. The lowest depth of all papal history was reached during his reign. Alexander had a depraved son, Cesare Borgia, whom he aided in committing heinous crimes, including the possible murder of more than one hundred people. It was rumored that Alexander was not even a Christian and believed simply nothing. He stands out as "the vilest monster of his age." This is the pope whom Savonarola defied. According to Machiavelli, Alexander "never did anything but deceive men."

Julius II (1504-1514) was known as the "warrior pope," and his reign has been called the "Pontificate Terrible," because of the wars he conducted and fought in. For ten years he urged the Italians on in their battle to rid their country of foreign soldiers. Deeply involved in international politics, Julius made league with Germany and France, but later joined the Venetians against France. This pope established the Church with its holdings as one of the five great powers in Italy. He spent much of his time in the pursuits of a secular prince, including, of course, the waging of war. Julius founded the Holy League and was a patron of art; among other things he saw to the painting of the ceiling in the Sistine Chapel. Julius occupied the papal chair when Luther as a monk journeyed to Rome. However, at the time of Luther's visit, Julius was in northern Italy waging war with the French.

Leo X (1515-1521) was the play boy pope, and occupied the papal chair during the earliest stage of the Reformation. Leo was a Medici (an old and powerful Italian family) and therefore possessed the contacts and influence that helped to further his ambitions. He was made a priest at age six, a cardinal at thirteen, and pope at thirty-seven. His life embodied the philosophy "Let us enjoy the papacy since God has given it to us." In 1517, the year Luther nailed his Ninety-five Theses to the door of the Castle Church in Wittenberg, Leo created 39 cardinals for the return favor of 500,000 ducats. Leo closed his eyes to the pressing need of reform and did not understand the seriousness of Luther's verbal attacks on the abuses in Roman Catholicism. Luther found it impossible to deal with Leo when he became bound by his conscience and Holy Scripture to accuse the papacy of error. Leo finally excommunicated Luther and branded him as a heretic and an outlaw and sought his death.[2]

LUTHER'S CHILDHOOD WAS CLOSELY TIED TO RELIGION

The year following Martin Luther's birth, his parents moved to Mansfeld, where he then lived from 1484 to 1497. Things improved economically and socially for the family while living in Mansfeld. Hans Luther was a miner and by much hard work and frugality he was able to go into business for himself by buying a smeltery. He also became one of the town counselors.

Martin's father and mother conducted a strict household and did not hesitate to punish their son severely for any infraction of the rules. While Hans Luther was faithful in his prayer life, it was the piety of young Martin's mother which especially made a lasting impression on him.

Martin Luther's elementary schooling started in Mansfeld. His teachers were outstanding for their eagerness to punish the lads, and the Reformer later described them as "usually unskilled and as cruel as the hangman." In the course of his schooling the students were told to forget about their baptism. If they wanted spiritual help they were to go to the saints. Later in life Luther related that had he died as a child he would have died without the comfort of baptism or of having Christ as his Savior. In his youth he knew Jesus only as an angry Judge, popularly pictured sitting on a rainbow. His personal relationship to God and to Christ was one of terror and dread rather than of joy, peace, and hope.

At Magdeburg there was a Latin school conducted under the auspices of the Franciscan order of monks. Luther was sent to this school, which lay about sixty miles north of Mansfeld, but studied there not quite a year. Later in his life Luther remarked about a bit of visual education that he received at Madgeburg from a church window. Pictured was a ship sailing to heaven. In this ship were the monks and priests. Outside the ship were the lay people, to whom the monks and priests threw ropes. Thus the laity were pictured as being saved from eternal damnation by the graces extended to them by the clergy in the sacraments (which only the clergy have the authority to administer). The scene in the church window served as a striking reminder of the separation of the clergy and laity, and how much the laity are indebted to the clergy of the Church.

THE BEGGAR

From 1498 to 1501 Martin attended a school in Eisenach conducted by St. George's Church. Around Easter time he suddenly appeared in Mansfeld and was immediately sent on to school in Eisenach. Some historians conclude that Hans Luther sent Martin there in order to receive economic aid from relatives, which aid did not materialize. Others reason that by this time Hans Luther was probably well enough off to support his son at St. George's. At any rate, it was customary for the students to beg for their bread. Begging was not disgraceful for it afforded the people opportunities to give alms and thus earn merit with God – so it was thought. Luther's life had its hardships as well as its joys and pleasures at Eisenach.

A kind, soft-hearted woman, Frau Cotta, became attracted to this sad-faced young man who sang so well in church. She took Martin into her home and provided him a room. Frau Cotta's maiden name is thought to have been Schalbe, and it is reported that the Schalbe family fed Luther. The generosity of these two families brought about a change in the young man. Not only did he display a jovial nature, his musical talent was also given a boost.

HIGHER EDUCATION FOR LUTHER

On July 17, 1501, the eighteen year old Luther entered the University of Erfurt. By this time his father was financially secure and desired to provide his son with a good education. Erfurt was considered one of the better schools of Germany and was highly regarded by Martin himself, who had a keen mind and intended to achieve all the secular knowledge that he could. However, up to this time he had not yet found peace with God; he had not yet come to trust in Jesus Christ alone as his Savior from sin. The Church of the Middle Ages did not emphasize the Gospel and thus didn't urge the people to put full trust in Christ their Savior nor to take comfort in the cross as Christ's means of making full and complete payment for all their sins. A long and difficult inner struggle lay ahead for this young student. While he had in mind to achieve worldly knowledge, he also sought to gain insight into a philosophy that would quiet his inner disturbance and give him the peace of soul and mind which he did not yet experience. This was am impelling motive for his entry into the university. Martin's father felt strongly that his son should be a lawyer and make a name for himself.

Studying law finally had little interest for Luther, but he did come across a book that immediately attracted his attention. Here at Erfurt he came across a complete Bible for the first time in his life. He was amazed to learn that the Bible is such a large volume. Prior to this time he had been acquainted only with the pericopes, selected Scripture passages to be read on appointed days. In the Old Testament Luther read First Samuel 2:6ff. – the story of Hannah, the mother of Samuel – and exclaimed, "That book is written for me!"

In 1502 Luther received the Bachelor of Arts degree, studying particularly Aristotle and philosophy. This degree entitled him to teach to some extent at the University of Erfurt. In this same year the University of Wittenberg was founded. Frederick the Wise, Elector of Saxony, who later served Luther well as his faithful friend and protector, played an important role in the university's funding. Wittenberg would become Luther's home, and the university would afford him a permanent place of labor.

During the Easter holiday in 1504 a mishap occurred to Luther that could have resulted in his death. On his way home to Mansfeld he accidentally stuck himself with his rapier when it came loose. An artery had been cut and the wound bled profusely. Had it not been for the intervention of a physician who was called to the scene Luther would no doubt have bled to death. During the night the wound opened and began to bleed again, whereupon he repeated a prayer made to the Virgin Mary following the accident: "O Mary, help me!" Sadly, as Luther later recounted, had he died he would have departed this world trusting in the name of Mary instead of Christ. This incident could only add to the deep concern his soul felt regarding his relationship with God and add urgency to his quest to find the way to become acceptable to his divine Judge.

On January 26, 1505, Luther acquired his Masters of Arts degree, which entitled him to lecture in philosophy at Erfurt. However, in a few months another event would occur to Luther that would profoundly alter the course of his life, and in such a way, that he would impact the world for all time to come.

TO THE MONASTERY – FRIAR AUGUSTINE

While Hans Luther dreamed of his son becoming a great lawyer, God had other plans for him. During the first half of 1505 Martin Luther remained and lectured at Erfurt. However, his soul was meanwhile undergoing terrible conflicts and terrors regarding his sins. He kept searching for peace with God but couldn't find it. Luther's contemporaries could not relate to the constant ordeal that he was going through, for they simply did not experience the inner struggles that so profoundly affected him. Constant questioning went on in his soul regarding his sins, for Luther was an extremely honest and thoughtful individual. But all his learning, instead of answering his questions, just "made hell hotter."

It was during this time that Luther must have been giving some thought to entering the monastery as a means to bring peace to his soul. It was thought that monks lived close to God and were especially holy since they deprived themselves of the comforts and pleasures of this world, while dedicating themselves to prayer and acts of service. Certain events took place in Luther's life around this time that helped to persuade him to flee the world and enter the sheltered and holy life provided by the monastery. Bear in mind that the plague hovered over Europe like a black cloud causing a great number of deaths. Even Luther's family was affected. We recall the incident of the year before when Luther almost bled to death on the way to his home in Mansfeld. Then too one of Luther's close friends was murdered, an occurrence that deeply shocked and saddened him. But the event that served Luther as the final deciding factor to cause him to enter the monastery and become a monk occurred on July 2, 1505, near Stod-

9

dernheim. On his return trip to the university from home, Luther was suddenly engulfed in a violent thunder storm. A bolt of lightening struck nearby almost hitting him. Thereupon he made a vow to the patron saint of miners, Saint Anne, that he would enter the monastery if she would protect him. This second brush with death was evidently the defining moment that drew from Luther's lips the vow to embark on a career in the Church.

Luther visited the Augustinian cloister in Erfurt and talked to the monks there about his decision. The date of Luther's entry was set for July 17. No great secrecy surrounded his decision to become a monk. During the two-week interval that existed between his Stotternheim experience, when he was nearly struck by lightening, and his entry into the cloister at Erfurt, Luther shared his decision with his friends, sold his law books, informed his parents, and made preparations for a farewell party in the Georgenburse, where he lived.[3] Luther's friends reacted with shock and dismay at his announcement, and tried to dissuade him. When Hans Luther received his son's letter informing him that he intended to become a monk, also requesting the father's permission, Hans Luther was furious. In fact, he was so angry and resentful over Martin's intentions to enter the cloister that he wrote him a letter in which he cut him off completely from all "paternal grace and favor." His mother and relatives informed him that they would have nothing more to do with him. But then a second letter arrived from Martin's father allowing him to become a monk. It was a decision the elder Luther made "with reluctance and sadness."[4]

On July 16 Luther held a party for his closest friends, who the following day would lead him into the monastery, called the "Black Cloister" (so named from the black attire of the monks.)[5] Luther had sent some of his things (e.g. his master's ring) home, and other personal effects were distributed among his friends.

Upon entering the cloister, Luther gave up his baptismal name and instead was called Augustinus. As a monk, Luther fled from the sinful world and took the three-fold vow of chastity, poverty, and obedience. In his mind and soul Luther nourished the hope that he could earn special favors from God by his life as a monk. He later confessed: "I made the vow for the salvation of my soul. I entered the spiritual state for no other reason than to serve God and please him in eternity."[6] Luther would remain a member of the Augustinian Order of Hermits for almost twenty years (1505-1524); ultimately he was released from his monastic vows by Vicar Staupitz.

Even though Luther entered the cloister he remained a member of the faculty of Erfurt University and on occasion was called upon to lecture there. He was, of course, also a student at the cloister. At first his studies, like those at the university, were in the realm of philosophy, but eventually theological studies were included in his curriculum. So began the new theological studies which would make him a Doctor of Theology.[7] Upon entering the cloister Luther was given a Bible bound in red leather. This book would profoundly influence and shape Luther's personal beliefs and theology, which in turn would bring about the Lutheran or German Reformation.

The first year at the cloister served as the novitiate for Luther and the other novices. During this time they learned to show humility and prove their sincerity, not only by faithfully following the routine of the cloister but also by carrying out the meanest, lowliest tasks. These included such things as serving as doorkeepers, scrubbing floors, and even begging food.

Two things later lightened Luther's load. First, arrangements were made so that he could continue as a professor, and second, the provincial head of the Augustinian order, John Staupitz, was much impressed by Luther and envisioned him occupying his own chair in the University of Wittenberg at a later date. And so, Staupitz brought his influence to bear on the cloister in behalf of Luther. Furthermore, he encouraged his protégé to read the Bible, and made it possible for him to do so. Staupitz proved to be Luther's reliable friend, confidant, and support. Luther later remarked, "I owe everything to Staupitz."[8]

O WRETCHED MAN!

As was previously mentioned, Luther entered the cloister because of what he felt was his wretched spiritual condition. His sins tormented him night and day, year upon year. "(T)he basis of his struggle lay in his anxiety to render an angry God gracious unto him."[9] During this terrifying time of torment and struggle Luther lacked faith in his Savior Jesus Christ. Instead of accepting by faith Jesus' gracious invitation, "Come to me, all you who are weary and burdened, and I will give you rest," Luther tried to bear the burden of saving himself by his good works and sacrifices. He saw in Jesus only a stern and terrifying Judge, rather than a loving, caring Savior, who sacrificed himself on the cross to save sinners. Simply put, Luther was not a Christian at this time in his life. Later he had this to say in a sermon:

I ALWAYS WALKED AROUND IN A DREAM AND REAL IDOLATRY, FOR I DID NOT BELIEVE IN CHRIST BUT BELIEVED HIM TO BE NOTHING ELSE THAN A STERN AND TERRIBLE JUDGE, AS ONE PAINTS HIM SITTING ON A RAINBOW. FOR THIS REASON I SOUGHT OTHER INTERCESSORS, MARY AND THE SAINTS AND MY OWN GOOD DEEDS AND MERITS OF FAITH. ALL THIS I DID NOT DO FOR MONEY OR POSSESSIONS, BUT FOR GOD'S OWN SAKE; YET, IT WAS ALL A FALSE RELIGION AND IDOLATRY BECAUSE I DID NOT KNOW CHRIST AND I DID NOT SEEK TO DO THESE THINGS THROUGH AND IN HIM.[10]

Not until Luther learned to look in faith to Jesus Christ as the one and only source of righteousness for sinners – thus trusting in Jesus' merit and in Jesus' suffering and death on the cross in behalf of sinners – did he find peace with God.

(I) HAD DEPARTED FROM THE FAITH, AND I COULD NOT MAKE MYSELF BE-LIEVE ANYTHING BUT THAT I HAD OFFENDED GOD, WHOM I WOULD HAVE TO MAKE FAVORABLE AGAIN THROUGH MY GOOD WORKS. BUT THANK GOD WE AGAIN HAVE HIS WORD, WHICH PICTURES AND PORTRAYS CHRIST AS OUR RIGHTEOUSNESS.[11]

In his zeal to excel in works and self-induced suffering and privation by which he hoped to placate an angry God and earn merit from him, Luther permanently damaged his health. The cold he endured in his unheated cell almost killed him. And to what avail! Luther even selected twenty-one saints to whom he appealed for help, three each day. He regarded the Virgin Mary as occupying the highest position among the saints. He was so deeply troubled by feelings of guilt that he frequently approached his fellow monks to hear his confession. He was told that if he still had sins not yet absolved there was purgatory. But at times Luther was actually directed to the Gospel for comfort, and he was reminded that in the Creed, which he confessed, God commands us both to hope and to believe.

Luther feared to partake of the Lord's Supper, for he felt himself unworthy and thus had to drive himself to commune. Staupitz did much to comfort his young monk, although he and the others never really knew the terrors of conscience that Luther experienced. Since Staupitz was grooming his young friend for the professorship at the new little Wittenberg University, he remained close to Luther in his mental and spiritual battles. When Luther became troubled about his eternal election, the vicar pointed out to him that his election was due to Christ. The vicar also used humor to lift Luther's spirits.

During this time, when Luther was experiencing such terrible inner struggles and confusion, the building of St. Peter's Cathedral in Rome was begun (1506). Significantly, the means devised to help fund this magnificent, costly structure would later have a great impact on Luther's thinking and propel him into a world-shaking confrontation with certain teachings and practices of Roman Catholicism.

In the following year (1507), Luther was ordained to the priesthood and entitled to read his first mass. Since this was a red-letter day for the new priest, he invited his father to attend the service. By this time Hans Luther had gotten over much of his anger over his son's decision to become a monk, and wrote back a friendly reply. He would come to the service if a day could be chosen that would be convenient for him. His wishes were granted and so Hans Luther, in the company of some relatives from Mansfeld, journeyed to Erfurt to help the new priest celebrate the occasion. The elder Luther even brought a sizeable monetary gift for the monastery to help pay the cost of the festivities.

According to Roman Catholic teaching, Luther, a priest, was given power in the mass to turn the bread and wine of the Lord's Supper into the body and blood of Christ (transubstantiation), and offer up Christ anew in an unbloody sacrifice for the sins of both the living and the dead. This was such a great responsibility that if the officiant did not complete the mass he was subject to the Church's ban. This almost happened to Luther, for he became so nervous that someone had to help him. Afterwards, at the banquet held in is honor, Luther recounted the terrifying thunderstorm that engulfed him at Stotternheim, which then led to his decision to become a monk. Luther regarded it as a divine call from heaven. Hans Luther, however, was not impressed and replied: "Would that it may not have been a mere illusion or deception." A little later, pressing the matter further, the father went on to ask his son in front of the monks and guests:

"Have you not read that you should honor your father and your mother?"[12] These remarks made a deep and lasting impression on the new priest.

Luther did not find the peace he was searching for in the cloister. He often said to himself, "Look, you are still envious, impatient, impassionate. It profits you nothing, O wretched man, to have entered this sacred order." In the meantime God was preparing something better for this monk.

TO WITTENBERG

Wittenberg was a small, rather unremarkable city located about seventy miles east and sixty miles north of Erfurt. Surprisingly, it boasted a new university, established by Elector Frederick the Wise in 1502. Staupitz had been asked to choose men for professorships at this little, rather humble institution of higher learning. And so it happened that Luther was brought to Wittenberg to teach in 1508, a move that was so sudden even his friends were not aware of it. He began his teaching duties by lecturing on Aristotle, but also continued his personal studies in scholastic theology, attending lectures several times a week. He had other duties as well. (Scholasticism involved a kind of theology taught in the schools in a condensed form that looked to human reason to find answers rather than to the Bible.) On March 9, 1509, Luther received his Bachelor of the Bible degree, and with it the obligation to carry on another course of lectures on chapters of the Bible. In the fall of 1509 Luther passed his examination on the Sentences of Peter Lombard. (Lombard, a Scholastic, was one of the formulators of Catholicism's sacramental theology, which Luther later openly and vigorously attacked.)

Luther also preached. However, he neither volunteered for this duty nor did he desire it. In fact, he was opposed to it. Staupitz made the decision for Luther and wouldn't be talked out of it. The reluctant preacher started his work in a small ramshackle chapel in a compound of the cloister. But though the surroundings were humble, nevertheless brother Martin got off to a good start. Large numbers of people attended his services and spoke well of his efforts. One learned man, touched by his sermons, opined: "This friar will confound all doctors, bring a new doctrine, and reform the Church, for he stands on the writings of the prophets and apostles and relies on the words of Christ."[13]

As suddenly as Luther was brought to Wittenberg, so suddenly he was called back to Erfurt (October 1509). There he lectured for about a year on the *Sentences* of Peter Lombard. This was also the year of the birth of John Calvin (July 10) in Noyon of North France. Calvin became Europe's second greatest Reformer, working during the final years of Luther's life as his contemporary.

THE PILGRIM TO ROME

Between the fall of 1510 and the spring of 1511 Luther and an older monk were sent by Staupitz as emissaries to Rome. A controversy had arisen between two groups of the Augustinians, the conservatives and the liberals. A need for reform was felt and definite efforts were put forth to bring the liberals into line. However, these efforts were not very success- ful, and seven cloisters refused to see eye to eye with Staupitz. Among them was the cloister at Erfurt. An appeal was made by the dissenting cloisters to the archbishop, and when this was refused the dissenters ap- pealed to Rome. While the vicar wanted to unite the two factions, the seven dissenting cloisters wanted to be heard in their objections and rights. And so it was that John von Mecheln and brother Luther were sent to Rome to lay the matter before the pope. Luther went along mainly as a companion to von Mecheln on this long, wearisome journey traveled on foot; however, he also went for personal reasons. He viewed the journey as a pilgrimage to the Holy City, hoping it would help him find peace for his soul affording him the merit he needed in order to be on good terms with God.

While the two monks were in Rome action on the appeal moved slowly, leaving them with time on their hands. In fact, they did not get to meet with the pope, or even see him, for he was in northern Italy at the time. In Luther's zeal he rushed madly about, visiting the shrines, viewing the relics, making confession, saying mass, and attending church services. He visited the seven principal churches of Rome in one day while fasting – a very fatiguing endeavor. While brother Martin wanted to make confession of his sins in order to unburden his conscience, he came upon priests who didn't even know how to hear confession.[14] Luther crawled up the twenty- eight steps of the *Scala Sancta*, praying an "Our Father" for his grandfa- ther, Heine Luther, on each step. (The *Scala Sancta* were supposedly the holy steps that Jesus had to ascend to enter Pilate's Judgment Hall.) Rome taught that one could free a soul from purgatory by going up the steps on hands and knees. But upon reaching the top the thought came to Luther: "Who knows whether it is true?" In his excited pilgrim's tour of Rome, Luther read masses at various altars to release souls of friends and rela- tives from purgatory. He rushed through churches and catacombs – under- ground burial crypts – in order to earn all the indulgences that were available. (The catacombs contained the remains of countless thousands of early Christians and martyrs.) Luther was eager to feast his eyes on all the magnificent world-famous shrines that existed in Rome.[15]

All in all, however, Luther came away from Rome disappointed and dis- illusioned. He was shocked by the extravagant and frivolous life-style of the clergy, especially that of the hierarchy. He was dismayed by the lax church life and the immorality of the people. To serious-minded Luther the levity with which the masses were rendered was an intolerable condition. What Luther sadly discovered in Rome was that church life there had in many ways become a business transaction.[16] As Luther matured, he passed harsh judgment on what he saw and experienced in Rome. The claims that were made regarding the relics and shrines which he saw in Rome, he later labeled as things that had been "invented with stinking lies."[17] He later conjectured that if there is a hell, then Rome is built on top of it.

LUTHER DEVELOPS

After his return in spring, 1511, the Erfurt professor took his second examination and received the Sententiarius Degree, which entitled him to lecture on the first and second books of Peter Lombard's *Sentences*. Later in 1511, evidently on his own volition, but with Staupitz' approval, Luther went back to Wittenberg and took his third examination, receiving the Baccalaureus Formatus. This entitled him to lecture on the last two books of Peter Lombard. His degrees were confined solely to Scholasticism. Later on Luther turned away from this type of theology, which had as one of its features the attempt to prove dogmatic concepts, not from the Bible but from human reason, thus following the philosophy of Aristotle. In regards to justification, Scholastic Theology emphasized human merit. Right standing with God is to be achieved by man by his good works, which are made possible by God's infused grace – thus a joint divine, human endeavor.* In October 1512 Luther took the examination for the Licentiatus Degree, which entitled him to lecture on Scholastic Theology in general. Two weeks later he also passed his examination for Doctor of the Bible. This degree represented a definite obligation on Luther's part, for it was a mandate compelling him to teach and defend the Bible. He remained a professor of Biblical Theology until his death in 1546. Later on, when he was belabored by his enemies, who attempted to crush him, it was also the obligation that accompanied this degree that gave him the courage to uphold the truths of the Bible.

Following his return to Wittenberg, Luther probably began his work with a series of lectures on Genesis, 1512-1513. From 1512 to the time of his death he delivered a series of lectures covering just 13 books of the Bible, lecturing usually twice a week.[17] From August 1513 to October 1515, the professor lectured on the Psalms.

In 1514 Luther began to preach in the Town Church, often several times a week. Due to the illness of Priest Simon Heinz, the city council requested him to assist with the preaching and hearing of confessions. The following year his work load was increased even further when he was made district vicar, responsible for the welfare of ten or eleven convents in Meissen and Thuringia.

The Reformer's theological development started with his lectures on the Psalms, and it was early on in these lectures that his Christian conversion came about, in what is referred to as the Tower Discovery. This occurred sometime either in 1513 or 1514 and was the event that rescued Luther from his awful fears of damnation by opening his eyes to see the gift of eternal salvation which God freely bestows to sinners through the Savior, our Lord Jesus Christ. His discovery involved learning the truth, finally, about two highly significant expressions found in the Bible: "the righteousness of God" and "justification." For many years Luther had been terrified by the expression "the righteousness of God." Originally, he thought of this righteousness as "'formal or active' righteousness in which God proves Himself righteous in that He punishes the sinner as an unrighteous person."[18] Therefore Luther thought of the "righteousness of God" as being

15

connected to God's anger and to his power and intent to bring terrible suffering upon everyone who is not righteous like he is. Sadly, Luther had determined in his own mind that God is not a God of love but a God of anger and hate, and he felt that he could not love a God like that. The result was that Luther's life had become filled with the frustration of trying to do enough good works to merit the approval of God as he pictured him. Until Luther discovered the truth concerning "justification," he regarded it in the Roman Catholic sense, as an inner change worked in the sinner by God's grace which is infused in the sinner through the Sacrament of Penance. With the help of infused grace the sinner is thus able to do works that merit God's approval.

But, as Luther reported, God took pity on him and enabled him to finally learn the truth. The Reformer was sitting in his cell in the tower of the cloister, preparing his lecture on the Psalms. He opened his Bible to Romans chapter one, verse seventeen, to check once again the words "the righteousness of God." There Luther read the words of St. Paul: "For in the gospel a righteousness from God is revealed, a righteousness that is by faith from first to last, just as it is written; 'the righteous will live by faith.'" (NIV) Finally, Luther was able to comprehend what he described as "the inner connection between the two expressions, 'The righteousness of God is revealed in the gospel' and 'The just shall live by faith.'"

Here is Luther's testimony:

THEN I BEGAN TO COMPREHEND THE "RIGHTEOUSNESS OF GOD" THROUGH WHICH THE RIGHTEOUS ARE SAVED BY GOD'S GRACE, NAMELY, THROUGH FAITH; THAT THE "RIGHTEOUSNESS OF GOD" WHICH IS REVEALED THROUGH THE GOSPEL WAS TO BE UNDERSTOOD IN A PASSIVE SENSE IN WHICH GOD THROUGH MERCY JUSTIFIES MAN BY FAITH, AS IT IS WRITTEN, "THE JUST SHALL LIVE BY FAITH." NOW I FELT EXACTLY AS THOUGH I HAD BEEN BORN AGAIN, AND I BELIEVED THAT I HAD ENTERED PARADISE THROUGH WIDELY OPENED DOORS. . . AS VIOLENTLY AS I HAD FORMERLY HATED THE EXPRESSION "RIGHTEOUSNESS OF GOD," SO I WAS NOW AS VIOLENTLY COMPELLED TO EMBRACE THE NEW CONCEPTION OF GRACE AND, THUS, FOR ME, THE EXPRESSION OF THE APOSTLE REALLY OPENED THE GATES OF PARADISE.[19]

And so, the "righteousness of God" connected to the expression "justified by faith," came to mean simply the non-imputation of guilt to the sinner who believes in Jesus Christ the Savior. Or, to say it another way: God himself declares the repentant, believing sinner not guilty, that is, righteous. God bestows on the sinner full forgiveness for all his sins, which then leaves the sinner righteous in God's sight. The consequence of Luther's Tower Discovery was that "he realized for the first time that justification did not presuppose some inner change in man or inner healing, as had been formerly taught; now he knew it was something outside of man, the belief in Christ's atoning death, that liberated man from the bondage of sin and death."[20]

This monk who had been tormented for so long by his sins finally found the righteousness that truly avails before God, righteousness that is in every way a precious and free gift from God, whom Luther came to picture, not as a stern Judge but as a merciful heavenly Father whose innermost being is love.[21]

At this time, Luther did not fully understand St. Paul's gospel message in his letter to the Romans. This would not occur until 1520. From 1512 to 1520 Luther's theology underwent a critical evolution from Catholicism to Lutheranism. In this evolution Luther had to discover the God of the Bible, and to do this he had to master the original languages of the Old and New Testaments, the Hebrew and the Greek.[22] The amazing thing is that Luther taught these languages to himself; and so well did he accomplish this that he was capable of later giving the Bible – the Old and New Testaments – to his beloved German people in their own language.

In spite of all the help and encouragement that Dr. Staupitz afforded Luther, the vicar was not able to direct his monk to the true biblical, gospel meaning of the words grace, righteousness of God, and justification. The sad fact was that Staupitz believed that man can not be saved by divine mercy alone but that the merit of Christ must somehow be completed by the merit of the individual. Still, we owe Dr. Staupitz this, that he encouraged Luther to read and study the Bible, and chose him to fill the chair he vacated, which was to lecture on books of the Bible. It was Luther's intense study of God's Word that finally liberated him from the chains of darkness that had bound his mind and soul for so long and made possible the Lutheran or German Reformation.

THE INDULGENCE TRAFFIC

Soon after Luther went to Wittenberg, Pope Leo X ascended the throne in Rome. He reigned from 1513 until his death in 1521. In 1517 Leo did something that would profoundly influence Luther to take a public stand against the abuses that were rampant in the Roman Church. Leo issued a bull that granted plenary or full indulgence to any person who would donate money for the building of St. Peter's Cathedral in Rome. This indulgence promised forgiveness of all sins and removal of all punishment in purgatory. (Pope Leo, the play-boy, loved living life as though it was one long carnival, spending money recklessly and entertaining wildly.[23] St. Peter's Cathedral was an example of his lavish life-style and expensive, even extravagant, tastes). Leo conceived the idea of a plenary indulgence, to be granted to contributors, as a means to refill his coffers, which his squandering ways had emptied. He gave the license to sell indulgences in Germany to Albert Hohenzollern, the bishop of Brandenburg and Magdeburg, who was recently appointed also archbishop of Mainz. Albert's cut from the indulgence sale would enable him to pay off a large debt he owed to the Fugger Bank. He had borrowed ten thousand ducats to pay Leo for privileges Leo had granted him. Half of the proceeds from sales in Germany was to go to Albert and half to the building of St. Peter's Cathedral. The new arch bishop subsequently hired John Tetzel, a Dominican monk, to sell indulgences for him.

John Tetzel was an ingenious rascal, who worked out an unscrupulous but very effective system of selling Rome's wares. He would enter a city with drums banging, bells ringing, and other clamor in order to attract the people's attention. After setting up a large red cross in front of the high altar of the cathedral or church, Tetzel extolled the virtues of his wares. A large chest was placed near the cross to receive the money from the sales. Pointing to the red cross, he would announce: "This cross has as much efficacy as the cross of Christ . . . . I would not exchange my privileges for those of St. Peter in heaven, for I have saved more souls by my indulgences than the apostle did by his sermons. . . At the very instant the money rattles at the bottom of the chest, the soul escapes from purgatory and flies to heaven!"

Elector Frederick the Wise would not allow Tetzel to operate in his territory; he had his own indulgence sale in connection with the thousands of relics that were displayed in the Castle Church each year on All Saints Day (November 1). With the pope's blessing, indulgences were granted to the pious folk who viewed the Elector's relics and made the required contributions. In fact, by visiting the Castle Church it was possible to receive indulgences that would grant a total reduction of time spent suffering in purgatory by 1,902,202 years, 270 days! Both the Castle Church and the university were supported by this indulgence sale.[24]

Luther was incensed by Tetzel's actions and claims. In the conversion which Luther had experienced he came to trust in Christ alone as his Savior. Any sinner who repents of his sins and trusts in Jesus Christ takes personal possession of the forgiveness and salvation Jesus purchased by his own merit and his own suffering and death on the cross. No one needs to, and no one can, purchase forgiveness. Certainly then, the Church has no business selling forgiveness. We need to bear in mind that at this juncture we can't say that Luther was against the sale of all indulgences. He believed that indulgences could only remit the penalties assigned by the Church in the Sacrament of Penance. Luther was certain that no indulgence can grant forgiveness. Still, this is exactly what the papal bull granting this special indulgence, sold by Tetzel, claimed to bestow on the buyer.

The whole system of indulgence sales militated against St. Paul's theme of "Justification by faith in Christ alone." A brief review of Rome's teaching concerning indulgences is in order here.

THE CONTRITE SINNER MUST CONFESS TO THE PRIEST, AT LEAST ONCE A YEAR, EVERY MORTAL SIN, OF WHICH HE BECOMES CONSCIOUS AFTER EXAMINING ALL THE FOLDS AND RECESSES OF HIS CONSCIENCE, TOGETHER WITH THE CIRCUMSTANCES UNDER WHICH IT WAS COMMITTED. . .AFTER CONFESSION THE PRIEST PRONOUNCES ABSOLUTION, WHICH IS NOT "A BARE DECLARATION OF THE GOSPEL," BUT A JUDICIAL ACT, BY WHICH THE PENITENT IS RECONCILED TO GOD AND FREED FROM ETERNAL, THOUGH NOT FROM TEMPORAL PUNISHMENT [PUNISHMENT OF LIMITED DURATION]. TO REMOVE TEMPORAL PUNISHMENT, THE PRIEST IMPOSES WORKS OF SATISFACTION (SUCH AS FASTING, PRAYER, ALMS) THE DOING OF WHICH RENDERS SATISFACTION TO GOD AND REMOVES TEMPORAL PUNISHMENT, WHICH, HOWEVER, MAY FURTHER BE REMOVED BY OTHER MEANS[E.G. INDULGENCES].[25]

Again,

IT IS TO BE NOTED THAT, ACCORDING TO ROMAN DOCTRINE, ABSOLUTION ABSOLVES ONLY FROM ETERNAL PUNISHMENT. EVEN AFTER ABSOLUTION THE PENITENT IS SUPPOSED TO REMAIN SUBJECT TO TEMPORAL PUNISHMENTS FOR HIS SINS AT THE HANDS OF GOD. TO ESCAPE THESE PUNISHMENTS, HE MUST DO THE WORKS OF SATISFACTION ENJOINED BY THE PRIEST, EARN INDULGENCES, ETC.[26]

There follows, then this teaching of Rome:

THOSE WHO DIE IN A STATE OF GRACE, BUT HAVE NOT FULLY ABSOLVED, IN THIS LIFE, THE TEMPORAL PUNISHMENTS REMAINING AFTER ABSOLUTION, MUST SUFFER FOR THEM AFTER DEATH IN THE FIRES OF PURGATORY, BEFORE THEY CAN GO TO HEAVEN. THE LENGTH OF SUFFERING DEPENDS ON THE AMOUNT OF UNEXPIATED SIN. THE TIME CAN, HOWEVER, BE SHORTENED THROUGH THE ASSISTANCE OF THE LIVING (BY PRAYERS, MASS, INDULGENCES).

We can only conclude that the doctrine of purgatory. . . .

. . . .LED TO A DENIAL OF THE ALL-SUFFICIENT SATISFACTION OF CHRIST AND TO THE SUBSTITUTION OF MAN-INVENTED WORKS AS A MEANS OF SATISFYING THE JUSTICE OF GOD.[27]

And so, to understand Rome's teaching concerning indulgences, we must first understand that she makes a distinction between "mortal" sins, that is, sins of a much graver nature than others and which require the Sacrament of Penance, and sins that are lighter in character, called "venial" sins. Venial sins do not entail the degree of wrong that is true of mortal sins and do not require the Sacrament of Penance. (The same kind of sin may be either mortal or venial, depending on the degree of wrong that is committed. For example, the sin of stealing can be either mortal or venial depending on the amount stolen and the circumstance involved.)

Rome teaches that when Jesus Christ died on the cross he took care of the guilt and eternal punishment of mortal sins. The guilt of venial sins is taken care of by the sinner's good works. Though Jesus suffered to save sinners from eternal punishment, nevertheless temporal punishment for sins still remains for the sinner to endure. However, he can relieve himself of this temporal punishment by doing good works, including the works of satisfaction imposed by the priest. In most cases the sinner has not sufficiently paid for his mortal sins and their temporal punishment at the time he dies, therefore, he must be kept out of heaven for a time. Rome teaches that at this point he is too good for hell but not yet good enough for heaven; therefore he must still suffer for his sins, but not eternally. This temporal suffering takes place in purgatory, located midway between heaven and hell, where the soul suffers excruciating pain, similar to the suffering of the damned in hell, until every last bit of punishment has been endured. This may take a relatively short time or it may go on for hundreds and even thousands of years. Time spent suffering in purgatory can be shortened and even completely eliminated through indulgences, which tap into the treasury of superfluous works compiled by Christ and the saints.

We will now further illustrate the matter of indulgences by setting up a practical example. As a believer in Jesus Christ, Mr. Roman Catholic is not assured of heaven. He has merely stepped on the bottom rung of the ladder leading to heaven, for Christ took care of only the guilt of Mr. R.C.'s mortal sins and their eternal punishment. This leaves Mr. R.C. with the chore of making satisfaction for the temporal punishment God imposes. To make it possible for Mr. R.C. to do good works and thereby make satisfaction to God, God infuses his grace into Mr. R.C., actually giving him the power to do good and thereby save himself from temporal punishment for both his mortal and venial sins. This infusion of grace into Mr. R.C. to help him accomplish his acts of penance occurs when he hears that his mortal sins are forgiven.

All of this is connected to the Sacrament of Penance, which itself consists of three things: (1) for Mr. R.C. to confess his mortal sins, after careful reflection, to a priest; (2) for the priest to pronounce absolution or forgiveness, if he thinks that Mr. R.C. is sincere, and (3) for the priest to prescribe good works (acts of penance) that Mr. R.C. is to perform in order to shorten his time of suffering in purgatory. But there is more.

Mr. R.C. does not have to depend solely upon his own good works and sacrifices in order to obtain salvation; there is the doctrine of indulgences. Simply put: Indulgences are commutations of penance.[28] Rome teaches that one drop of Jesus' blood would have been sufficient to pay for people's sins. However, the Savior shed a torrent of blood more than enough. An infinite treasure of merit is contained in that extra blood to which treasure the papacy has the key. The Church, through its priesthood, can dispense merit from the treasure for reasonable cause (usually money) for either full or partial remission of the temporal punishment imposed due to sin. And there is still more. Great saints, such as Mary and Joseph; the great apostles, such as Peter and Paul; and other great Christians, such as St. Jerome and St. Augustine, did more works than they needed. These super works are also on tap for the church to dispense to its people through indulgences. "The superfluous credits were stored in a treasury placed by God at the disposal of the popes and capable of transfer to those whose sins were in the arrears."[29]

Such a system was bound to suffer abuse, with extraordinary claims being made for indulgences. For example: "Indulgences were being used [in Luther's time] not only for the mitigation of penalties, including release from purgatory, but also for the forgiveness of sins."[30]

Furthermore, many had come to think of indulgences as a substitute for true sorrow over sin. They came to be regarded as a quick and easy fix for the guilt and punishment that had been incurred, even making it unnecessary to make confession to a priest. Thus indulgences promoted complacency rather than contrition.[31] Indulgences rested on the merits of saints, rather than promoting good works in the sinner himself (which good works God looks for in the Christian as a fruit of his faith). In 1516 Martin Luther charged that the saints, upon whose merits indulgences rested, were sinners too and had no merit before God.

As we can plainly see, the Church of Rome does not teach that Mr. R.C. is justified before God alone through his faith in Jesus Christ, but is justified partly by his good works, or by the good works of others credited to

20

him. In fact, "The Roman Church denies that men are justified before God only through faith in the merit of Christ." The Council of Trent, Sess. VI, can. 11, 12 states:

> IF ANY ONE SAYS THAT MEN ARE JUSTIFIED, EITHER BY THE SOLE IMPUTA-
> TION OF THE JUSTICE OF CHRIST OR BY THE SOLE REMISSION OF HIS SINS,
> TO THE EXCLUSION OF THE GRACE AND THE CHARITY WHICH IS POURED
> FORTH IN THEIR HEARTS BY THE HOLY GHOST AND IS INHERENT IN THEM,
> OR EVEN THAT THE GRACE WHEREBY WE ARE JUSTIFIED IS ONLY THE FAVOR
> OF GOD: LET HIM BE ACCURSED [DAMNED TO HELL]. . . . IF ANY ONE SAITH
> THAT JUSTIFYING FAITH IS NOTHING ELSE BUT CONFIDENCE IN THE DIVINE
> MERCY, WHICH REMITS SINS FOR CHRIST'S SAKE, OR THAT THIS CONFIDENCE
> ALONE IS THAT WHEREBY WE ARE JUSTIFIED, LET HIM BE ACCURSED.[32]

Thus Rome refuses to allow its adherents to trust in the all-sufficient merits of Christ alone.[33]

LUTHER RESPONDS TO THE SALE OF INDULGENCES – THE NINETY-FIVE THESES

Luther discovered that the sale of indulgences had engendered among his parishioners the very attitude he had warned against: that a person can obtain an indulgence—perhaps by buying it outright—and therefore has no need to repent before God for his sins. Even though the Elector of Saxony prohibited Tetzel from crossing the river into Saxony with his wares, Tetzel was not without customers. People flocked across the river to buy indulgences from him. Luther's reaction at first was mild, for he wanted to learn more about the situation. But then Luther's own congregation also bought indulgences and in the confessional told him so. When he refused to absolve their sins because of their willful neglect to live more God-pleasing lives, they showed their priest that they had already been absolved by buying Tetzel's indulgences. This so rankled Luther that he decided "to put a hole in Tetzel's drum." Luther knew from the Scripture that a Christian must be truly sorry for his sins. God expects repentance to come from the heart. Furthermore, good works will naturally follow genuine repentance and faith. Good works are evidence of faith. In fact, without faith in Christ the sinner cannot even do works that are good in the sight of God.

At this point, Luther felt certain that Tetzel was acting contrary to the wishes of the pope, who surely must have been ignorant of the things Tetzel was saying and doing. Furthermore, there were many factors regarding indulgences and their sale that Luther wanted to clear up; he wanted more information. Therefore, in order to show up Tetzel for his objectionable actions and for the outlandish claims that he was making, and to obtain the information he sought regarding the sale of indulgences, Luther drew up Ninety-five Theses or propositions which he intended to serve as points for debate among university professors. In order that all might read these points and become interested in the debate, Luther nailed the Theses to the town bulletin board, one of the heavy wooden doors of the Castle

Church.

On October 31, 1517, this Wittenberg monk struck hammer blows which resounded around the world. He began a chain of events which became the great watershed for Christianity. The posting, and subsequent spread of the Ninety-five Theses across Europe and Scandinavia and the English Isles, would culminate in the Lutheran (or German) Reformation of the Church and the founding of Protestantism. Other Reformers would accompany Luther on the arduous and dangerous journey back to the Scripture, the Word of God. The Ninety-five Theses and the furor that they caused marked the beginning of Luther's break with Rome. However, it was not until the Leipzig Debate in 1519 that Luther realized the full extent of his departure from Roman Catholicism.[34] As time went on, Luther came to realize that Rome could not be pulled away from its errors and that a new Evangelical Christianity had to be built.[35] God had chosen a long, dangerous, and difficult road for Martin Luther to travel in order to restore God's truth to the Church and to the world.

Luther's Ninety-five Theses begin with this introduction:

OUT OF LOVE AND ZEAL FOR THE ELUCIDATION OF TRUTH, THE FOLLOWING THESES WILL BE DEBATED AT WITTENBERG, THE REVEREND FATHER MARTIN LUTHER, MASTER OF ARTS AND SACRED THEOLOGY, PRESIDING. HE BEGS THAT THOSE WHO CANNOT BE PRESENT AT THE ORAL DISCUSSION WILL COMMUNICATE THEIR VIEWS IN WRITING. IN THE NAME OF OUR LORD JESUS CHRIST. AMEN.

The Theses speak of repentance:

(1) OUR LORD AND MASTER JESUS CHRIST IN SAYING: "REPENT YE," ETC., INTENDED THAT THE WHOLE LIFE OF BELIEVERS SHOULD BE PENITENCE.

The Theses, while cautiously accepting indulgences, hits hard at their abuse:

(20) THEREFORE THE POPE, WHEN HE SPEAKS OF PLENARY [FULL] REMISSION OF ALL PENALTIES, DOES NOT MEAN SIMPLY OF ALL, BUT ONLY OF THOSE IMPOSED BY HIMSELF.

(21) THUS THOSE PREACHERS OF INDULGENCES ARE IN ERROR WHO SAY THAT BY THE INDULGENCES OF THE POPE A MAN IS LOOSED AND SAVED FROM ALL PUNISHMENT.

(32) THOSE WHO BELIEVE THAT THROUGH LETTERS OF PARDON THEY ARE MADE SURE OF THEIR OWN SALVATION WILL BE ETERNALLY DAMNED ALONG WITH THEIR TEACHERS.

(36) EVERY CHRISTIAN WHO FEELS TRUE COMPUNCTION OVER HIS SINS HAS PLENARY REMISSION OF PAIN AND GUILT, EVEN WITHOUT LETTERS OF INDULGENCE.

(37) EVERY CHRISTIAN, WHETHER LIVING OR DEAD, HAS A SHARE IN ALL THE BENEFITS OF CHRIST AND OF THE CHURCH, GIVEN HIM BY GOD, EVEN WITHOUT LETTERS OF INDULGENCE.

(43) CHRISTIANS SHOULD BE TAUGHT THAT UNLESS THEY HAVE SUPERFLUOUS WEALTH, THEY ARE BOUND TO KEEP WHAT IS NECESSARY FOR THE USE OF THEIR OWN HOUSEHOLDS AND BY NO MEANS LAVISH IT ON INDULGENCES.

(47) CHRISTIANS SHOULD BE TAUGHT THAT WHILE THEY ARE FREE TO BUY INDULGENCES THEY ARE NOT COMMANDED TO DO SO.

(66) THE TREASURE OF INDULGENCES ARE NETS WHEREWITH THEY [THE PRIESTS] NOW FISH FOR THE MEANS OF MEN.

In his Theses Luther actually began to question and even attack the power of the pope. Thus the Wittenberg monk was pictured by contemporary artists standing before the church door writing his Ninety-five Theses with a feather pen so long that the end of it reached all the way to Rome and knocked the pope's crown from his head!

(5) THE POPE HAS NEITHER THE WILL NOR THE POWER TO REMIT ANY PENALTIES EXCEPT THOSE WHICH HE HAS IMPOSED BY HIS OWN AUTHORITY OR BY THAT OF THE CANONS.

(56) THE TREASURES OF THE CHURCH, WHENCE THE POPE GRANTS INDULGENCES, ARE NEITHER SUFFICIENTLY NAMED OR KNOWN AMONG THE PEOPLE OF CHRIST.

(81) THIS LICENSE IN THE PREACHING OF PARDONS MAKES IT NO EASY THING, EVEN FOR LEARNED MEN, TO PROTECT THE REVERENCE DUE TO THE POPE AGAINST THE CALUMNIES OR, AT ALL EVENTS, THE KEEN QUESTIONING OF THE LAITY.

(82) FOR INSTANCE: WHY DOES NOT THE POPE EMPTY PURGATORY FOR THE SAKE OF MOST HOLY CHARITY AND OF THE SUPREME NECESSITY OF SOULS—THIS BEING THE MOST JUST OF ALL REASONS—IF HE REDEEMS AN INFINITE NUMBER OF SOULS FOR THE SAKE OF THAT MOST PERISHABLE THING, MONEY, TO BE SPENT ON BUILDING A BASILICA—THIS BEING A VERY SLIGHT REASON?

Luther emphasized the Gospel of Jesus Christ as the treasure of the Church:

(55) THE MIND OF THE POPE CANNOT BUT BE THAT IF INDULGENCES, WHICH ARE A VERY SMALL MATTER, ARE CELEBRATED WITH SINGLE BELLS, SINGLE PROCESSIONS, AND SINGLE CEREMONIES, THE GOSPEL, WHICH IS A VERY GREAT MATTER, SHOULD BE PREACHED WITH A HUNDRED BELLS, A HUNDRED PROCESSIONS, AND A HUNDRED CEREMONIES.

(62) THE TRUE TREASURE OF THE CHURCH IS THE HOLY GOSPEL OF THE GLORY AND GRACE OF GOD.

(94) CHRISTIANS SHOULD BE EXHORTED TO STRIVE TO FOLLOW CHRIST, THEIR HEAD, THROUGH PAIN, DEATH, AND HELL;

(95) AND THUS TO ENTER HEAVEN THROUGH MANY TRIBULATIONS RATHER THAN IN THE SECURITY OF PEACE.

THE EFFECT OF LUTHER'S NINETY-FIVE THESES

Of course, Luther would mature over the years in his knowledge of Scripture, his understanding of the doctrine of salvation, and in his stand on scriptural truths. The Ninety-five Theses were only a mild beginning. In fact, when Luther posted the Theses on the church doors for the public to read, he did not mean that they should be taken as his declarations of truth. Rather, his intentions were to engender discussion and debate, through which he hoped to learn the truth. However, the fact is that the Theses were generally regarded as Luther's declarations of truth as he saw it, and this perception of the Theses brought Luther both fame and friends, as well as outspoken enemies. Many regarded the Theses as the beginning of a long-needed reform of the Church. In two weeks they were printed and scattered throughout Germany. Within a month they were found all over Europe. The printing press, which had been in existence for only about three-quarters of a century,[36] proved to be a powerful and indispensable aid to Luther and to other Reformers. It is intriguing that the invention of movable type printing should occur in Germany* in such close proximity with the Lutheran (German) Reformation.

At first, Pope Leo was not alarmed concerning Luther's Ninety-five Theses, for he tended to regard their composition and posting as a "mere monkish squabble." Meanwhile, many, even from afar, wrote to Luther encouraging him. Soon, opposition began to mount against him in the Church. At first, Luther thought that the pope was on his side, but later discovered that he actually sided with Tetzel and was angry with his Wittenberg monk. The pope finally realized that what was taking place in Wittenberg, Germany, was no monkish squabble after all, but a serious threat to his authority. He then set the wheels in motion to suppress Luther. Of course, behind the pope's determination to silence Luther also lay the fact that his Ninety-five Theses had all but stopped the sale of indulgences, a chief source of revenue for Rome.

Among those who opposed Luther was one John Eck, professor of theology at Ingolstadt University. He attacked Luther in his pamphlet called *Obelisks* (named for the little dagger-shaped figures used in ancient writings to call attention to questionable passages). Luther gave Eck's *Obelisks* a similar treatment by countering with his own *Asterisks*.

In April 1518, at a meeting at Heidelberg of the Augustinian monasteries, Dr. Staupitz, on request by the pope, asked Luther to be silent regarding indulgences. Luther, however, defended his views. Returning to Wittenberg, he published a carefully written defense to answer all opponents. The book was titled *Resolutions*. It was a point by point defense of his Theses. The die was cast!

On August 17, 1518, Luther received Pope Leo's orders to come to Rome. Had he obeyed the pope's summons he surely would have been burned at the stake as a heretic. Meanwhile, Elector Frederick the Wise came to Luther's side. He admired his talented Wittenberg professor and set about to place safeguards around him. Back in Rome the pope, because he needed Frederick's support and even wanted him as the new head of the Holy Roman Empire, canceled his summons to have Luther stand before him. Upon the advice of Cardinal Cajetan, the papal representative to Germany, the pope commanded that Luther be tried at Augsburg. Having assurance of safe conduct from Emperor Maximilian, Luther journeyed to Augsburg. At first Cajetan tried to conjol Luther into saying one Latin word: *Revoco*—"I recant." Luther boldly and steadfastly refused. The three day meeting in October 1518 ended in hot debate. Luther was threatened but again stood firm. Realizing the danger to his life, he slipped quietly out of Augsburg by night.

Cajetan next tried to have Frederick arrest Luther and deliver him to Rome, but the Elector refused, since he was not convinced that Luther was a heretic. When this latest effort to snare Luther failed, the pope issued a bull referring to statements of certain monks about indulgences and condemned them as heretical.

Next, the pope decided to send von Miltitz, a Saxon, to talk to Frederick. He was to use flattery, but if that failed he was to place Saxony under the interdict. He also carried with him a ban against Luther. However, Miltitz found the Germans to be three out of five on Luther's side, so he decided to use diplomacy. The outcome was that Luther agreed to be silent. We could well call this decision on the part of Luther "the low point of the Reformation." He was willing at this point to let the whole thing "bleed to death."

THE LEIPZIG DEBATE

One of Luther's fellow professors at Wittenberg, Andreas Bodenstein von Karlstadt (commonly referred to simply as Carlstadt), came forth with a set of theses against Dr. Eck who, prior to 1517, had begun a pen pal relationship with Luther. Eck answered Carlstadt's theses with some of his own in which he promoted the doctrine of papal supremacy. In his theses Eck made the mistake of attacking Luther, thus breaking the silence which both men had agreed upon. Luther reciprocated, replying to Eck with an outspoken attack against papal supremacy. There was no precedent for such an attack on the pope. The battle lines had been drawn. Eck felt that he had to debate with Luther. As a ruse he challenged Dr. Carlstadt to a debate in Leipzig for the summer of 1519. However, it was plain to Luther that Eck's real intention was to debate with him, and not with Carlstadt. Therefore he accompanied Carlstadt to Leipzig with the express intention of "crossing swords with Eck."

From June 27 to July 3 the debate was between Eck and Carlstadt, but from July 4 to July 13 the antagonists were Eck and Luther. Eck pounced on Luther and pointed out that his views were much like those of the Bohemian Hus, who had been burned at the stake for his heresies. In spite of this connection which Eck made between Hus and Luther, the Wittenberg monk let it be known ever so plainly that he stood firmly on Scripture and even dared to point out that councils and even popes can, and indeed have, erred. The council which condemned Hus to death was a case in point as far as Luther was concerned. Luther had studied the writings of the Bohemian Reformer and was impressed by much that he read. Furthermore, Luther maintained that Scripture alone is infallible.

When Luther nailed his Ninety-five Theses on the church door he still considered himself a good Catholic and continued to pledge his allegiance to the pope. He did not fully realize the gulf that now existed between himself and Rome. The Leipzig Debate was an important crisis in Luther's theological development for he saw much more clearly how far he had ventured from the Church's accepted teachings. At Leipzig Luther had been maneuvered by Eck into taking a definite, public stand against papal supremacy and to cast his lot alone with Scripture as the sole authority in matters of doctrine and practice. By this time Luther saw the Church as a fellowship of believers, not as a clergy-dominated institution; and this fellowship of believers has Christ as its head, not the pope. Luther and everyone else could now see that reconciliation with the papacy was not possible; Rome could not be pulled from her false teachings. Casting off the yoke of Rome was inevitable, and the brewing storm, which a few months before had quieted to a lull, was beginning to blow itself into a mighty tempest. No doubt many felt that Eck had won the Leipzig Debate, and yet it served to strengthen Luther's followers and also won him new friends. He was more than ever the champion of the common people. He had broken off the shackles of the priesthood that had bound them, and he had accomplished this by emphasizing that the individual sinner has direct access to God through Christ. For Luther himself – as we have noted – the debate clearly revealed the issues that were involved and put spur to Luther's own theological development. It set the course for the Lutheran or German Reformation.

THE STORM RAGES

Back at Wittenberg the Reformer took up the pen, which to his dying day would serve him as a mighty weapon to expose and attack error and to defend the truth. Though Luther developed rapidly as a Bible theologian, still it was not until the late 1520's that his theology was full-blown Lutheranism.[37] As he carried on the incredibly difficult task to which the Lord had called him, Luther's pen and the printing press combined to lay the foundations for a new evangelical Christianity that the world so sorely needed. It is interesting to note that an average of only about forty books a year were printed in Germany up to the time Luther nailed his Ninety-five Theses to the church door. But then, Luther's own output was often greater than this. Of the 208 books published in Germany in 1520, 133 of them were authored by Luther. The Reformer found writing an easy task, especially when he was angry about something that merited his attention. He reported, "I have a swift hand and a quick memory. . . .When I write, it just flows out; I do not have to press and squeeze."[38]

From August to November 1520 the Reformer published three books to make clear his stand on the controverted issues.

(1) ADDRESS TO THE CHRISTIAN NOBILITY OF THE GERMAN NATION CONCERNING THE REFORM OF THE CHRISTIAN ESTATE. LUTHER URGED THE GERMAN PEOPLE TO STAND FOR THEIR NATIONAL RIGHTS AND SHOWED THEM THEY HAVE THE RIGHT TO CAST OFF THE YOKE OF THE PAPACY. IN FACT, LUTHER DEALT A TERRIBLE BLOW TO THE POPE. HE EVEN SUGGESTED THE POSSIBILITY THAT THE POPE AND HIS FOLLOWERS WERE WICKED MEN AND NOT TRUE CHRISTIANS AND LACKED TRUE UNDERSTANDING.

(2) TWO MONTHS LATER CAME THE TREATISE ON THE BABYLONIAN CAP-

TIVITY OF THE CHURCH. LUTHER LIKENED THE CAPTIVITY OF THE IS-
RAELITES IN BABYLON UNDER KING NEBUCHADNEZZAR TO THE WAY ROME
HELD THE PEOPLE CAPTIVE WITH HER MAN-MADE DOCTRINE OF THE SEVEN
SACRAMENTS. ROME HAD CORRUPTED THE TWO SACRAMENTS OF BAPTISM
AND THE LORD'S SUPPER, WHICH CHRIST GAVE TO THE CHURCH AND ARE
DEPENDENT ON CHRIST'S WORD, AND ADDED FIVE OTHERS TO SUIT HER PUR-
POSES. ROME TAUGHT THAT THE SACRAMENTS "WERE THE ONLY CHANNELS
OF GOD'S SAVING GRACE AND THAT ONLY PRIESTS COULD ADMINISTER
THEM."[39] LUTHER POINTED OUT THAT "THERE IS NO SUCH THING AS A
PRIESTHOOD WITH SPECIAL POWERS GIVEN BY ORDINATION." INSTEAD,
EVERY CHRISTIAN IS A PRIEST. ORDAINED PRIESTS ARE SIMPLY CHOSEN
FROM AMONG THE CHRISTIANS AND PERFORM THEIR DUTIES IN THE NAME
OF THE CHRISTIANS WHO CHOSE THEM.[40]
(3) TREATISE ON CHRISTIAN LIBERTY. IN THIS SIMPLE, SUBDUED LITTLE
TRACT LUTHER LAYS OUT THE REAL MEANING OF FAITH AND POINTS UP THE
CHRISTIAN LIFE THAT THE BELIEVER WILL LIVE OUT OF GRATITUDE FOR THE
LIBERTY THAT HE HAS FOUND IN CHRIST. "A CHRISTIAN MAN IS A PER-
FECTLY DUTIFUL SERVANT OF ALL, SUBJECT TO ALL."[41]

These treatises were intended to satisfy the curious and remove all
doubts as to where Luther stood.

THE FINAL BRIDGE IS BURNED

In May 1520 Luther published a little book titled *On Good Works*. Here
he brings out that man is justified by faith alone, and that the believer will
serve God out of this faith. He strikes out against the monastic system to
which he himself had fled years earlier, hoping to offer the sheltered life
of the cloister as a means to obtain good standing with God. But Luther
now denigrates the life of deprivation and asserts that it is not a meritori-
ous work in God's eyes. Instead of extolling the monastic life, Luther
points out that every one must serve God in his every day occupation.

Meanwhile Luther also *read* books. One of them, on the works of the Bohemian Hus, Luther devoured with complete relish. Since Hus had seen
the same errors in Rome as Luther himself, he therefore regarded himself
as a disciple of Hus.

Back in Rome, Pope Leo was not about to let Luther have the final word.
On June 15, 1520, Leo signed the bull of excommunication against Luther.
The bull listed forty-one propositions purported to be Luther's, and condemned them as "heretical or scandalous, or false or offensive to pious ears,
or seducing to simple minds, and standing in the way of the Catholic faith."
Faithful Catholics were called upon to burn Luther's books. Luther was ordered not to preach any more, and all followers of the heretic were to recant
publicly in a period of sixty days or themselves be treated as heretics. The
government was ordered to seize Luther and his followers and imprison
them. The interdict would be placed over any town or district that afforded
him shelter.

Eck himself brought the bull back to Germany; but drawing it up and getting people to publish it were two different matters. The Germans were aligned to such an extent on Luther's side that scarcely anyone was willing publish the bull.

Luther answered the papal bull with his *Against the Execrable Bull of Antichrist*. The Reformer had been granted sixty days to repent of all he had said and done against the Church, but this only made him stand firmer in his teachings. Luther actually called upon the pope to retract and to punish Dr. Eck.

At Wittenberg the faculty refused to post the bull and instead posted their own notice on December 10, 1520, that at nine o'clock "the godless books of the papal constitutions and scholastic theology will be burned according to the ancient and apostolic usage, inasmuch as the boldness of the enemies of the Gospel has waxed so great that they have cast the godly, evangelical books of Dr. Luther into the fire." On this date the sixty days of grace, allowed by the bull for Luther to recant, expired. The pious youth were urged to attend the burning, calling it the time to expose the Antichrist.

At the appointed hour Luther, members of the faculty, students, and many citizens gathered at the spot where a heap of fagots was kindled. When the blaze was high enough, Luther threw on a group of papal writings. Finally, he consigned a copy of the bull of excommunication to the flames, saying, "Because you have vexed the Holy One of God let the everlasting fire consume you!" This was serious, even deadly, business; Luther had burned the final bridge behind him. With pen, and now with fire, he had defied the pope. He had refused to turn back.

BEFORE THE TRIBUNAL

Luther's friends were surprised by the boldness of his action, and now there was more cause than ever to fear for the good Doctor's life. The pope, of course, was furious and on January 3, 1521, formally excommunicated Luther and declared him an outlaw. In his move against the Reformer, the pope received help from the new Emperor, Charles V. Elector Frederick had decided against becoming Emperor of the Holy Roman Empire and instead threw his weight to Charles, King of Spain. Subsequently, during the Leipzig Debate Charles had been elected Emperor. The new ruler was a good Catholic and had no sympathy for Luther's theology or for the bold stand that he had taken in opposing and defying the pope. Since Luther had been placed under the Church's ban, Charles was determined to punish him as a heretic. The great Imperial Diet was scheduled to open in Worms, Germany, in January 1521. The German constitution, which Charles was required to sign, stipulated that no German should be tried outside of Germany and that no German should be outlawed without a hearing. A determined minority of the Diet pushed for Luther to be heard, and the Emperor finally agreed to summon him before the Council of German rulers.

For weeks much maneuvering and intrigue were carried on behind the scenes regarding the matter of Luther appearing before the Diet. On the one hand there were those – the minority – who felt that Luther should have his writings and teachings examined by a group of experts, and that Luther should be given a hearing. Luther himself, in his *Offer and Protest*, had earlier requested a hearing, that is, an examination of his teachings in the light of Holy Scripture. Subsequently both the Reformer and his Elector requested a hearing before unprejudiced experts under protection of the Diet.[42] However, the last thing that Rome's representatives wanted was for Luther to be given the chance to defend his writings and teachings on the basis of the Scripture. Rome's thinking was that Luther had already been condemned as a heretic by the Church; the only issue that needed to be settled was whether Luther was willing to recant, or not. Finally, on March 26, 1521, Luther received the Emperor's summons to appear in Worms before the Diet. However, the summons said nothing about recanting.[43] Luther was informed that the Emperor and the empire wanted him to inform them about his teachings and books. Luther was assured of the imperial safe-conduct, which allowed him twenty-one days' grace. [44] The twenty year old Emperor promised to abide by his word. Encouraged by the Emperor's promise of safety, Luther decided in favor of appearing before the Diet. Naturally, his friends tried to dissuade him, but he was determined to go. Secretly, he felt that he would not see Wittenberg again, but the Emperor's promise of an inquiry into his doctrines and books was the compelling force in Luther's decision.

On the Tuesday after Easter, April 2, Luther, together with three companions, climbed into a small wagon loaned by a goldsmith and began the long journey to Worms. A small shed built on the wagon afforded the travelers a degree of shelter. The papal representatives, upon learning that Luther was coming to Worms, tried different schemes in order to frighten him and thus keep him away. Nevertheless, Luther was determined to appear before the Diet, even if it cost him his life. Wherever the Reformer appeared on his journey, old and young alike poured out of their homes and businesses to see him. After all, Luther was the man who had set himself against the pope and the whole world.[45] The authorities of the towns and cities through which Luther passed tended to treat him with honor. The papal nuncio reported that Luther was received everywhere enthusiastically by the people so that his journey was like a triumphal march. Meanwhile, Elector Frederick sent word to Luther not to come, for he could not protect him. Furthermore, Luther's case had already been decided; he had been condemned. The Reformer could not be frightened away. He wrote back: "Even if there were as many devils in Worms as there are tiles on the roofs, I would enter anyway."[46]

On Tuesday, April 16, in the morning, Luther arrived in Worms, heralded by the town watchman with trumpet blasts. In his procession were about one hundred men on horses. A crowd of about two thousand citizens turned out to see the Reformer. However, the next day, when Luther appeared before the Diet, things did not go well. Appearing before men of very high rank, headed by Charles V himself, Luther quickly found that their true purpose in summoning him to Worms was to determine whether or not he was willing to recant. Luther was asked two questions: "First, are you willing to confess that the books which have been circulated under your name are yours?" Lying on the table before him were twenty books. After the titles were read, Luther answered that the books were his. "Second, are you ready to renounce these books or part of them?" To this question, since it involved faith, salvation, and the Word of God, Luther requested time to give the matter due consideration. He humbly begged the Emperor for time to think, that he might answer without violence to the Word of God or peril to his soul. Luther was granted twenty-four hours to ponder his answer. Naturally, the papal party was not pleased. Rome's representatives wanted the Emperor to be swift and brief in his dealings with Luther; yes, to condemn and punish him as a heretic, and not grant him a hearing. But since Luther's request was a fair one, the princes and councilors of the Emperor agreed to give him time, but only twenty-four hours, to think things over. Then the Emperor dismissed him.

Luther meditated and prayed all through the night. Finally, at four o'clock in the afternoon on the next day he was led back to the Episcopal palace to give his answer. Such a large crowd had gathered to witness Luther's final appearance that a large room in the palace had been chosen for the assembly of dignitaries. It was a weary, but valiant and determined thirty-seven year old Reformer that stood before the Diet. No longer the timid and awed man of the day before, Luther set about to answer the question posed to him earlier, and to do so with the stalwart resolution of a man willing to die, if need be, for the Savior whom he loved and for the Word of God, which he believed to be without error. When asked again if he was ready to retract all or part of his books, Luther spoke in German for about ten minutes, explaining why he could not retract what he had written; and he also entreated the Emperor, the princes, and all persons there to refute him from the Bible. If he were so refuted he would recant and be the first to throw his books in the fire.[47] When he had finished he was asked to repeat his address – which was spoken freely, not read – in Latin. This he did.

When Luther was informed that he could not expect a disputation, but that he should give a straightforward, honest, unambiguous, unreserved answer whether he will retract his books and the errors contained in them or not, Luther responded in Latin with an answer that has resounded loudly and clearly down through the centuries. "Unless I am convinced by the testimonies of the Holy Scriptures or evident reason (for I believe neither in Pope nor councils alone, since it has been established that they have often erred and contradicted themselves), I am bound by the Scriptures adduced by me, and my conscience has been taken captive by the Word of God, and I am neither able nor willing to recant, since it is neither safe nor right to act against conscience. God help me. Amen." Given strength by the Lord he served, the hero of faith had stood firm.

INTO HIDING

Emperor Charles V finally added his condemnation of Luther to that of Pope Leo X. But God protected his servant. While Luther's enemies were busy preparing the formal document to condemn him as outlaw and heretic, Luther's friends were formulating a plan of their own for his safe keeping. Luther was informed that the Emperor was left with no recourse but to begin to prosecute him as a heretic. He was given a safe-conduct which was to last twenty-one days. Luther was to return home and not preach, teach, or write on the way.[48] Secretly, Luther was given a message from the Elector that he would be "put up" somewhere as he journeyed back to Wittenberg. Frederick, who made the arrangement to keep Luther safe from his enemies, left it up to his councilors how the plan for Luther's safety would be carried out. He didn't even want to know where Luther would be hidden away.[49]

On the morning of April 26 Luther started on his journey homeward, accompanied by his friends. However, Luther did not arrive in Wittenberg. Soon rumors were flying that his party had been set upon in the forest and Luther had been snatched away. One rumor even purported that Luther's body had been found in a silver mine with a dagger through it. The great painter Albrecht Duerer of Nuremberg wrote in his diary: "O God, if Luther is dead, who can expound the Holy Gospel to us?"

But Luther was not dead. At one point on his journey home, Luther was advised to take an alternate route and to use a visit with his relatives in and around Mőhra as a pretext for the change in itinerary. The Reformer, with two of his four companions, stopped over in Mőhra. The other two continued to travel the main highway. They knew nothing of the plan to spirit Luther into hiding. On May 4 Uncle Heinz and other Luthers (or Luders) accompanied Luther for a ways and then turned back toward home. Soon afterwards, five horsemen were seen sweeping out of the forest. The horsemen reigned up in front of the driver of the wagon, pointing crossbows at him. They roughly demanded to know if he was driving Luther. The Reformer was then rudely pulled down from the wagon and swiftly dragged down the road. He had to run as fast as he could to keep up. But when the party of kidnappers were out of sight they stopped and revealed their identity to Luther. They mounted him on a horse and finally, after traveling a back and forth route to deliberately hide their tracks, they arrived at the Wartburg Castle very late in the evening. Luther was given a hearty welcome, assigned out-of-the-way quarters, and instructed to let his tonsure grow out. He was also to sport a knight's beard. The monk was dressed in a knight's clothing and given the name Junker (Knight) George. And so it was that Frederick, in his grave concern for Luther's safety had his beloved professor kidnapped and hidden away in a place his councilors chose – the Wartburg, located some two miles south of Eisenach. Here Luther lived for ten months in disguise while the storm which had erupted at Worms quieted.

While Luther was hiding away he worked tirelessly at his studies. His greatest achievement was the completion of the first draft of his translation of the New Testament into German. (Later, Luther, with the help of a few scholars, translated the Old Testament into German and published the entire German Bible in 1534.) Luther took great pains in translating, for he wanted the prophets and apostles to speak the language of the common people so that each could study God's Word on his own and learn the truth. Luther quickly realized that if the Reformation of the Church was to succeed the people had to be able to read the Bible in their own tongue and then compare what it says with the teachings of the Church. Of course, Rome didn't want the people to read the Bible, and punished severely, even with torture and death, those who dared to make God's Word available in the vernacular. Luther also realized that the people must have an accurate translation and worked tirelessly to accomplish this. He would sometimes seek for two, three, or four weeks for a single word to translate the Hebrew. There is strong evidence that William Tyndale, in making his monumental English translation of the Bible, consulted Luther's German translation. Furthermore, Luther's translation "made him, in fact, the father of a uniform literary German, for his Bible was widely distributed, read, and understood by all who spoke German in any dialect. Many of the expressions from his Bible became a part of the common idiom of the German people."[50]

THE REFORMER RETURNS
TO WITTENBERG

Luther's disappearance created a void that others tried to fill. . . .with disastrous results. In fact, affairs in the Lutheran camp were in a tumult. In their zeal to reform the Church, Dr. Carlstadt and his followers were going too far too fast; they were trying to work reforms with force, and this engendered open violence. They misrepresented Luther and were threatening the Reformation. Carlstadt "became the leader of a movement which was bent upon the destruction of all religious forms traditionally associated with the Roman mode of worship. [Carlstadt] and his followers particularly despised the presence of images in the churches.[51] As a result; open rebellion and mob rule took the place of the rule by the Word of God. Churches were desecrated, statues were toppled, and works of art were destroyed.

Earlier, before his appearance before the Diet of Worms, Luther made it clear that he did not want anyone "to contend for the Gospel with violence and bloodshed. The world was overcome through the Word, through the Word the church was saved, through the Word it will be restored."[52] Luther was deeply concerned by the uproar the fanatics were causing. On December 4 he came secretly into Wittenberg and unrecognized, stayed five days. He recorded his concerns and impressions in a document which he later released from the Wartburg: *Admonition to All Christians to Beware of Riot and Rebellion.* Aware that things were not quieting down in Wittenberg, Luther decided to come out of hiding and return to his pulpit

32

and the university – against the will of Elector. Preaching eight sermons in as many days, Luther mastered the tumult and restored order in Wittenberg.

The Reformer did not need to go into hiding again for the rest of his life. As long as he stayed in Saxony he was under the protection of the Elector. Furthermore, the feeling of the German people for Luther was so great that neither pope nor council nor Emperor could touch him.

The years from 1519 to 1522 were great, momentous ones. It was a time of exploration and the completion of the greatest sea voyage ever made. One of the five ships commanded by Captain Ferdinand Magellan sailed around the world, a feat never before accomplished. This voyage opened the way for exploration of the far corners of the earth. But while Magellan was fighting hunger, thirst, disease, savages, and mutiny, our Wittenberg monk fought the greatest battle of all, and won! Martin Luther had defied pope, Emperor, and councils; he had defied bans and burned bulls. He had succeeded in restoring the Gospel of Jesus Christ to the world, which had all but lost it. And he gave the precious Word of God, the foundation of the Christian faith, back into the hands of the people, and in their own language. He brought freedom to souls enslaved and oppressed by the tyranny of Rome and her errors. The German Reformer succeeded to do all this only because God through his manifold blessings enabled him to succeed. The name "Lutheran", by the way, was first applied to Luther and his followers by John Eck in sarcasm on July 4, 1519 at the Leipzig Debate. It was next used by Pope Leo X in the bull of excommunication of January 3, 1521, to stigmatize Luther and his followers as heretics and separatists from the Church. The name was accepted by the German Reformation as a badge of honor.[53]

Up to the time of his death Luther remained a prodigious writer. His gift to his countrymen of the German Bible has been mentioned. The Reformer also wrote poems and hymns. Some of these were inspired by the martyrdom suffered by his faithful followers in other parts of the empire, stalwart Christians to whom Rome refused the right to believe and live as Lutherans or Protestants.

In 1524 Luther published the first Lutheran hymnal, a small booklet of eight hymns, four of which were Luther's own. As time passed, Luther wrote and revised many more hymns. Before 1529, Luther wrote his finest and best loved hymn, *Ein' Feste Burg* (A Mighty Fortress). Based on Psalm 46, it is the battle hymn of the Reformation. Giving people beautiful hymns was an important tool in the Reformation. The great Cajetan, who was stymied at Augsburg in his dealings with the Reformer, later had to admit, "By his songs he has conquered us." Luther's hymns spread far beyond the bounds of Germany. Indeed, he was the father of the gospel hymn and was called the "Nightingale of Wittenberg."

From Luther's prolific pen came an immense store of writings over the years, whose volume simply overwhelms us. There were many treatises and letters that were written to clarify his stand or to answer those who sought his counsel, not a few of whom were princes. The Reformer wrote many sermons (he feared entering the pulpit without a prepared manuscript) and authored exegetical works in which he sought to put out a plain and simple – and often lively – explanation of scriptural truths. It was the reading of Luther's "Preface to Romans" at the Moravian meeting in London that led to the conversion of John Wesley, the founder of Methodism (1738).

LUTHER THE EDUCATOR

The Reformer was dedicated to the immensely important but difficult task of educating the children as well as the scripturally illiterate adults of his time. In 1524 he addressed an *Appeal to the Councilors of All Cities in German Lands to Establish and Maintain Christian Schools*. No doubt Luther's greatest work for the religious education of the youth was his *Small Catechism*, which he published in 1529. The same year he also published his *Large Catechism*, aimed at the adult reader.

A SUMMARY OF OUTSTANDING EVENTS

Space does not permit us to pursue in detail the post-Reformation life of the Reformer. Instead, we will close our brief study of Luther and the Reformation by listing a few of the more important events and their dates.

June 13, 1525 – Luther received his greatest helper when he married a former nun, Catherina von Bora. And so, the evangelical parsonage was founded. The Elector gave Luther and his bride the Black Cloister in Wittenberg and one hundred gold pieces for a wedding present. The Luthers were blessed by God with six children: Hans, Elizabeth, Magdalena, Martin, Paul, and Margaret.

October 30 to November 5, 1529 – Luther met with the Swiss Reformer, Ulrich Zwingli (1484-1531), for the purpose of settling their differences. Known as the Marburg Colloquy, this meeting accomplished agreement in all things but the Lord's Supper. Here the Reformers went their separate ways. Zwingli refused to take the word "is" literally in Christ's words "this is my body which is given for you." Luther insisted on a literal interpretation of Christ's words; thus he taught what is referred to as "the real presence of Christ's body and blood in the Sacrament of the Altar." Luther finally wrote with his finger in the dust on the table, *"Hoc est corpus meum"* (This is my body). He then told Zwingli, "You have a different spirit from us." The two Reformers remained parted in their ways.

June 25, 1530, at Augsburg – When the Elector of Saxony received the Emperor's summons to a diet, the Elector requested Luther and three of his co-workers to deliberate concerning articles of faith and practice. The *Torgau Articles* resulted. Melanchthon then used them as a guide and subsequently prepared a statement of the Lutheran position, which became known as the *Augsburg Confession*.

34

The *Confession* was read on June 25 and later was signed by a number of Lutheran rulers. This was the first creed drawn up by Christians in the Middle Ages. Luther could not be present at Augsburg because he was under the ban, and his life would have been in jeopardy outside Saxony; therefore he remained at Coburg where he was safe. The *Augsburg Confession* was accepted by Luther with some reservations on his part. The Catholics attacked the *Augsburg Confession* with a document read on August 3 to the Papalist estates. Melanchthon set about preparing an *Apology of the Augsburg Confession*. When he completed this document, which was a refutation of the Catholic response as well as a defense and amplification of the original *Augsburg Confession*, it was published as a private document. Both Confessions treat the fundamental doctrines of Christianity and have as their central theme, justification by God's grace through faith in Christ. Luther endorsed the *Apology*. The *Augsburg Confession* and the *Apology* were signed at Smalcald in 1537.[54] "In Germany the *Augsburg Confession* became the confessional basis of the Smalcald League 1532 and was adopted by nearly all the Evangelicals within fifteen years after its presentation."[55] To this day, confessional Lutherans throughout the world subscribe to the *Unaltered Augsburg Confession* and the *Apology*.

1534 – The entire Bible, Old and New Testaments, was published in the German language by the Reformer.

1537 – Acting on the request of Elector John, Luther produced his own articles of faith, known as the *Smalcald Articles*. They were so named because they were presented at the Diet of the Princes at Smalcald in February. (Luther's *Large* and *Small Catechisms*, both of which appeared in 1529, also present his views on the fundamental teachings of Scripture, and were included along with the *Smalcald Articles* in the *Lutheran Book of Concord 1580*.)

Special note: Martin Luther's father died in 1530 and his mother in 1531.

THE PRICELESS TREASURES FOR
WHICH WE OWE UNDER GOD TO MARTIN LUTHER
THE REFORMER

Martin Luther was an instrument in God's hands to bring about the much needed Reform of the Church. We shall always revere his name for all that God accomplished through him. A foremost emphasis of Luther was that the Bible is the inspired and inerrant Word of God and therefore the one source of doctrine and practice that God has given. From the Bible or Holy Scripture we learn that most wonderful and comforting doctrine, that God with his grace has done all that is necessary for man's eternal salvation. While man cannot and need not work, sacrifice, barter for, or buy God's forgiveness and acceptance, God, through the life and death and resurrection of his Son Jesus Christ, has provided the whole world of sinners with forgiveness and salvation. The sinner who trusts in Jesus Christ benefits personally from this forgiveness and salvation. Through his faith alone he is justified, that is, he is declared righteous or sinless in God's sight; thus he is made an eternal beneficiary of the merits of Jesus Christ. And so, the three greatest blessings of the Reformation headed by Martin Luther can be summed up thus: *Sola Scriptura* (Scripture Alone), *Sola Gratia* (Grace Alone), *Sola Fide* (Faith Alone).

Luther gave the Scripture to the people in their beloved German language. He gave the Church Christian hymns thereby giving the people voice in the worship services. In doing so he made the Lutheran Church into the Singing Church. Luther knocked down the wall separating the clergy from the laity, and restored the scriptural truth that each believer is a priest with direct access to God through Jesus Christ, without the mediation of a priesthood or of dead saints. Luther placed the public preaching of God's Word from the pulpit at the center of the worship service.

Luther reformed the liturgy used in public worship, casting out everything that was offensive to God and contrary to Scripture, but retaining everything that is not offensive and which lends dignity, beauty, instruction, and sincere worshipfulness to the service.

Luther rejected the papacy and the councils and broke off the shackles of man-made teachings, laws, and traditions with which Rome unscripturally bound people's consciences. Popes and councils can and do err, he maintained, and proved it. Luther taught that Scripture alone determines true doctrine and allowable practice; God alone can claim our spiritual allegiance.

Luther brought back the true meaning and use of the sacraments and also their true number. There are not seven sacraments as Rome teaches, but only two: Baptism and the Lord's Supper. The sacraments are means of grace – presentations of the Gospel – through which the Holy Spirit bestows God's forgiveness, and thus engenders and strengthens faith in the hearts of the recipients. The Reformer gave the communion cup back to the laity and taught correctly the doctrine of the real presence of Christ in the Lord's Supper. He emphasized genuine repentance and humble, sincere faith.

Luther established the evangelical parsonage and did away with the requirement of clergy celibacy.

Luther placed good works in their right position, showing from Scripture that they proceed from a heart in which true faith in Christ dwells. Good works are then the result and not the cause of salvation. Indeed, good works are the proofs of faith that God looks for in the lives of all who profess to be his Christians. Recall what was stated regarding the Sacrament of Penance and regarding Rome's teachings concerning indulgences and purgatory.

THE END COMES – PEACE AT LAST

The hero of the German Reformation was not a well man. In fact, the final six years of his life were fraught with illness. The torture and discipline and deprivation that his body endured in the monastery – years of living in an unheated cell, years of improper rest and nourishment, years of self-denial – all did permanent damage to his health. In addition, Luther was grossly overworked and overburdened in his role of Reformer, professor, and parish pastor. Then too he was continually sought out for consultations and advice. Even today we marvel at his work load as well as his accomplishments. Of great courage and strong will, but possessing poor health, Luther often suffered severe attacks of prolonged illness. At times his friends and family feared for his life. For years before the end finally came, Luther stated his readiness and willingness to die. In fact, he looked forward to death as a pleasant relief.

The princes of Mansfeld became involved in a bitter family quarrel. Although in a weak and sickly condition, and against his own better judgment, Luther made the arduous journey in the company of his two sons to Eisleben, the town of his birth, where he settled the dispute on February 17, 1546. During the day Luther's sons and close friends noticed his fatigue and urged him to rest. That evening the Reformer began to complain of sharp pains in his chest. He was given a hot bath and medicine and slept quietly for an hour. He awakened and went to an adjoining bedroom and fell asleep again. Very early in the morning he awakened, once more experiencing sharp pains in his chest. Measures were taken to make him comfortable and he again fell asleep. When he awakened he experienced an even more severe attack of pain. After that he grew steadily weaker. Realizing that his end was near, and in spite of his weak condition, Luther recited Bible passages and continually commended his soul to God. Luther was asked: "Venerable father, are you willing to die in the name of the Christ and the doctrine which you have preached?" To this he answered a resolute "Yes" that was heard by everyone in the room.[56] Shortly afterward, Luther fell asleep, not to awaken again to life in this world.

A funeral service was held for the Reformer in Eisleben in St. Andrew's Church, only a few blocks from where he had been born. On February 20, upon the request of Luther's prince, John Frederick, his body was escorted in a funeral procession from Eisleben and brought to Wittenberg. All along the route sorrowing people gathered to honor the Reformer. On February 22 his body finally entered Wittenberg. Funeral services were held in the Castle Church, which was filled to capacity. Thousands turned out to pay their respects to Germany's most famous citizen and the Church's hero of the faith. Luther was buried in the floor of the church where he preached, near the pulpit, and there his bones rest to this day.[57]

> If God had not been on our side
> And had not come to aid us.
> Our foes with all their pow'r and pride
> Would surely have dismayed us,

For we, his flock, would have to fear
The devil's wolves, both far and near,
Who rise in might against us.

Their furious wrath, did God permit,
Would surely have consumed us,
And as a deep and yawning pit
With life and limb entombed us.
A hellish storm would o'er us roll
From Satan, who desires our soul
And seeks to overwhelm us.

Blest be the Lord, who foiled their threat
That they could not devour us.
Our souls, like birds, escaped their net;
They could not overpow'r us.
The snare is broken – we are free!
Our helper and our strength is he
Who made the earth and heavens.[58]

Footnotes for Chapter One

1 E.G. Schwiebert, *Luther and His Times,* (Saint Louis, MO: Concordia Publishing House, 1950), p. 29.

2 Information regarding the popes listed was gathered from the following sources: Schwiebert, *Luther and His Times,* pp. 28-30, 190, 305. Erwin L. Lueker, Editor in Chief, *Lutheran Cyclopedia,* (Saint Louis, MO: Concordia Publishing House), p. 831. James L. Steffensen, The Universal History of the World, Vol. 7, (Golden Press, New York, NY, 1966, Western Publishing Co., Inc., & Libraire Hachette), p. 570. Reginald W. Deitz, W. Kent Gilbert, Editor, Luther and the Reformation, (Muhlenberg Press, Philadelphia, PA, 1953), p. 18

3 Schwiebert, *Luther and His Times,* p. 138

4 Heinrich Boehmer, *Road to Reformation.* (Philadelphia, PA: Muhlenberg Press, 1946), Translated by John W. Doberstein and Theodore G. Tappert, p. 37.

5 Schwiebert, *Luther and His Times,* p. 138.

6 W.G. Polack, *The Story of Luther.* (Saint Louis, MO: Concordia Publishing House, 1931, 1934, 1941), pp. 22, 23.

7 Schwiebert, *Luther and His Times,* p. 148.

8 Schwiebert, *Luther and His Times,* p. 170.

9 Schwiebert, *Luther and His Times,* p. 154.

10 Schwiebert, *Luther and His Times,* p. 155.

11 Schwiebert, *Luther and His Times,* p. 154.

12 Schwiebert, *Luther and His Times,* p. 148.

13 Polack, *The Story of Luther,* p. 28.

14 Boehmer, *Road to Reformation,* p. 62.

15 Boehmer, *Road to Reformation,* p. 65

16 M.A. Kleeberg & Gerhard Lemme, *In the Footsteps of Martin Luther* (Saint Louis, MO: Concordia Publishing House, translated by Erich Hopka), p. 20.

* James Edward McGoldrick, *Luther's English Connection,* (Northwestern Publishing House, Milwaukee, WI, 1979), p. 118.

17 Schwiebert, *Luther and His Times,* p. 282.

18 Schwiebert, *Luther and His Times*, p. 286.

19 Schwiebert, *Luther and His Times*, p. 286.

20 Schwiebert, *Luther and His Times*, p. 288.

21 Schwiebert, *Luther and His Times*, p. 290.

22 Schwiebert, *Luther and His Times*, p. 280, 281.

23 Reginald W. Deitz, W. Kent Gilbert, Editor, *Luther and the Reformation* (Muhlenberg Press, Philadelphia, PA, 1953), p. 18.

24 Deitz and Gilbert, *Luther the Reformation* pp. 46,47.

25 Erwin L Lueker, Editor in Chief, *Lutheran Cyclopedia* (Concordia Publishing House, Saint Louis, MO, 1954), p. 802

26 Lueker, *Lutheran Cyclopedia*, p. 550.

27 Lueker, *Lutheran Cyclopedia*, p. 874.

28 Lueker, *Lutheran Cyclopedia*, p. 506.

29 Roland H. Bainton, *The Reformation of the Sixteenth Century*, (Beacon Press, Boston, MA, 1952), p. 13.

30 Bainton, *The Reformation of the Sixteenth Century*, p. 37.

31 Bainton, *The Reformation of the Sixteenth Century*, p. 37.

32 Lueker, *Lutheran Cyclopedia*, p. 1138.

33 Lueker, *Lutheran Cyclopedia*, p. 1139.

34 Schwiebert, *Luther and His Times*, p. 282.

35 Schwiebert, *Luther and His Times*, p. 282.

* Johann Gutenberg of Germany developed movable type printing between 1440 and 1450. The earliest definitely dated specimen of such printing was an indulgence granting plenary absolution in return for a contribution to the war with the Turks. The indulgence was printed in 1454.

36 J.A. Hamerton, Editor, *Universal World History*, Vol. Six (Wm. H. Wise & Co, New York, NY, 1937), pp. 1798, 1799.

37 Schwiebert, *Luther and His Times*, p. 282.

38 Deitz, *Luther and the Reformation*, p. 52.

39 Deitz, *Luther and the Reformation*, p. 55.

40 Deitz, *Luther and the Reformation*, p. 55.

41 Deitz, *Luther and the Reformation*, p. 55.

42 Boehmer, *Road to Reformation*, p. 406.

43 Boehmer, *Road to Reformation*, p. 399.

44 Boehmer, *Road to Reformation*, p. 399.

45 Boehmer, *Road to Reformation*, p. 401.

46 Boehmer, *Road to Reformation*, p. 404.

47 Boehmer, *Road to Reformation*, p. 413.

48 Boehmer, *Road to Reformation*, pp. 426, 247.

49 Boehmer, *Road to Reformation*, pp. 426, 247.

50 M.A. Kleeberg & Gerhard Lemme, *In the Footsteps of Martin Luther*, p. 34.

51 James Edward McGoldrick, *Luther's English Connection* (Northwestern Publishing House, Milwaukee, WI 1979), pp. 85, 86.

52 M.A. Kleeberg & Gerhard Lemme, *In the Footsteps of Martin Luther*, p. 36.

53 Lueker, *Lutheran Cyclopedia*, pp. 605, 606.

54 Lueker, *Lutheran Cyclopedia*, pp. 630-632.

55 Lueker, *Lutheran Cyclopedia*, p. 632.

56 Schwiebert, *Luther and His Times*, pp. 749, 750.

57 Schwiebert, *Luther and His Times*, pp. 751, 752.

58 Martin Luther; tr. *The Lutheran Hymnal* (Saint Louis, MO: Concordia Publishing House, 1941), alt.; Christian Worship (Northwestern Publishing House, Milwaukee, WI, 1993), #202.

LUTHER TODAY
What Would He Do or Say?
ABOUT

Roman Catholic Church
Orthodox Church
W. C. C.
N. C. C
U. C. C.
Disciples of Christ
Episcopal Church
Presbyterian Church
United Methodist
Baptists
Lutheran Church
Charismatics
Truth and Doctrine
God
Deity of Christ
Virgin Birth
Justification
Vicarious Satisfaction
Resurrection
The Pope

*Luther's Theology
Forgotten Relic or Lived
Reality?*

Abortion
Immortality
Creation
Evolution
Homosexuality
A Just War
Church & State
Jews
Millennialism
Israel
Bible Translations
Marriage
Music
Muslim
Worship
Work
Death
Family
Children
21st Century
Reformation
Heaven and Hell

HERMAN OTTEN, EDITOR

The American Luther
CFW Walther
1811-1887

Theologian, Pioneer, Author

Dr. C.F.W. Walther
First President of The Lutheran Church-Missouri Synod. Leading Lutheran theologian, referred to by many as "The American Luther". President from 1847-1850; 1864-78

" . . . justifying and saving faith has that God for its object who raised Christ from the dead." Christian Dogmatics II, p. 321)

Francis Pieper
1852-1931

Francis Pieper
President of The Lutheran Church-Missouri . Synod from 1899-1911. Author of the three volume Christian Dogmatics long used as a standard textbook in the Seminaries of the LCMS.

Kurt Marquart
Teacher of the Church

The Book of Concord

Dr. Kurt Marquart
"The Walther and Pieper of the Lutheran Church-Missouri Synod today."

CHAPTER TWO

THE LUTHER REFORMATION IN GERMANY

THE SMALCALD LEAGUE – TEMPORARY TRUCE BETWEEN THE LUTHERANS AND THE CATHOLICS

Even though Catholics heard the Lutherans' Confession at Augsburg in 1530, the Diet of Augsburg nevertheless demanded that the Lutherans retract all their accusations made against the Romanists and submit absolutely to the Imperial and papal authorities. Emperor Charles V even threatened war against the Lutherans, which threat he later carried out in the Smalcald War.

In 1531 the Smalcald League was established in Germany, which bound together a group of Lutheran powers who pledged to come to each other's aid in the event of being attacked for the sake of the Lutheran faith. Persuaded by the formidable front displayed by the League, Charles made a formal truce with the Lutherans in 1532, just two years after the Lutherans read their Confession at Augsburg. By 1540 practically all of Northern Germany was officially Lutheran. In fact, it seemed possible for the Reformation to drive Catholicism completely out of the land.

LUTHER'S SMALCALD ARTICLES

Pressured by Charles, Pope Paul III, in June 1536, ordered a Church Council to open at Mantua, Italy, on May 23, 1537. And the purpose of convening the Council? In the pope's own words: The purpose was "the utter extirpation of the poisonous, pestilential Lutheran heresy." As far as receiving a fair hearing from this prejudiced Council, things did not bode well for the Lutherans.[1] "Toward the close of the year 1536, the Elector John Frederick of Saxony asked Luther to write an ultimatum which was to be considered by the Lutherans at their meeting at Smalcald, in February 1537. He complied with this request, and this document is now known as the *Smalcald Articles*."[2]

While Luther was at Smalcald he became very ill and had to leave for home while the convention was still in session. (Luther was so ill that he felt that death might take him. A bumpy wagon ride dislodged kidney stones and no doubt saved his life.) Though the *Articles* were not officially adopted – for several reasons, including Luther's absence – they were, nevertheless, signed by forty-four leading Lutheran theologians.[3] Luther wrote no other doctrinal confession per se. "The *Smalcald Articles*... were to be a summary of Luther's main teachings against the papal party. They have been fitly called Luther's last will and testament with regard to his doctrine."[4]

THE SMALCALD WAR – THE DEFEAT OF THE LEAGUE BRINGS ON THE AUGSBURG INTERIM

Various discussions were held in 1540 and 1541 between the Lutherans and the Catholics, but with no result, as far as the pope and Emperor were concerned. The Catholic side finally recognized that force was the only tool that could be employed successfully to put down the Reformation that was sweeping the country. "In December 1545 the pope was obliged to summon a Council at Trent, an Italian city although nominally in Germany."[5] The Emperor hoped to use the Council to reunite the religious factions by forcing them to agree to a compromise. However, the pope would allow no doctrinal concessions to the Protestants, who not only refused to abide by the decisions of the permanent majority in the Council, but also made the decision not to be represented at Trent. This action by the Lutherans gave the pope and Imperial forces reason to go to war against them. Meanwhile, Luther was graciously called to his heavenly home.[6]

On "June 26, 1546, four months after Luther's death, Pope and Emperor entered into a secret agreement to compel the Protestants by force of arms to acknowledge the decrees of the Council of Trent, and to return to the bosom of the Roman Church. . . .The Pope promised to assist the Emperor with 200,000 Krontaler, more than 12,000 Italian soldiers, and quite a number of horsemen."[7] Other sources of revenue were also placed by the pope at the Emperor's disposal.

The Smalcald War, so-named because it was directed against the Smalcald League, was quickly and easily won by the Catholic forces, for some of the Lutheran princes put up no resistance, taking a neutral attitude instead. A large factor in the defeat of the Lutherans was the treacherous behavior of Duke Maurice of Saxony, a talented military leader. His selfish political ambitions induced him to make a secret agreement with the Emperor. Maurice wanted to rule Saxony in the place of his cousin, John Frederick, the Elector. And so, having been promised territory and the Electoral hat, Maurice turned traitor to the Lutheran cause and joined the Imperial and papal forces against the League, even fighting against his own cousin, John Frederick. The Smalcald League was defeated at Muehlberg on April 24, 1547. Southern Germany and most of Northern Germany had been conquered. Elector Frederick and Landgrave Philip of Hesse – Duke Maurice's father-in-law were captured, imprisoned, and treated shamefully. Though Elector Frederick was condemned to die, his life was spared under the condition that he resign his office and allow Duke Maurice to succeed him as the Elector of Saxony. Frederick was also to remain in prison as long as the Emperor willed it.

What was to become of the Evangelical cause? The next move by the Catholics actually answered this question in favor of the Lutherans, although terribly hard days were still ahead for them. A quarrel arose between the pope and the Emperor. Fearing that his own temporal power would be threatened by the Emperor achieving an absolute victory, the pope withdrew his troops, formed a new alliance with the French King and adjourned the Council from Trent to Bologna, thus placing it completely under Italian control. The pope had effectively dissolved the Council and would not reassemble it. The Emperor then took matters into his own hands and went ahead with his own reformation of the Church in his Empire. Charles instructed two papal bishops and a third party, John Agricola, a Lutheran, to draft a set of reform laws – the Augsburg Interim – which Charles meant to be imposed on everyone, including the conquered Lutherans. (Agricola was a court preacher at Brandenburg. Though Agricola had been a co-worker of Luther, nevertheless the Reformer had, since 1540, refused further communication with him, "owing to his insincerity and duplicity.")[8] The Interim was meant to govern the Church until the Catholic Council could meet again at Trent to decide the issues involving the Lutherans. The Augsburg Interim was proclaimed the law of the Empire on May 15, 1548.[9]

The Interim sacrificed Luther's doctrine of Justification by Faith in Jesus Christ, imposed the use of Catholic ritual, required adherence to the doctrine of Seven Sacraments and the doctrine of Transubstantiation. There were other concessions that the Interim required of the Lutherans.

In Southern Germany the Italian and Spanish troops of Emperor Charles V rigidly enforced the Interim with brute force. If a pastor refused to introduce the Interim he was deposed. Some pastors were banished, imprisoned, even executed. Magistrates who did not cooperate were treated as rebels. Many pastors, together with their families, became fugitives. There was much passive resistance to the Interim on the part of the Lutherans. Many city churches, for example, stood empty as the people silently protested it.[10]

In Northern Germany there was more than passive resistance to the Interim. In city after city it was rejected. Some rulers let it be known that they would rather give their blood than accept the Interim. The "Interim before long became a dead letter throughout the greater part of Germany."[11] Though the Council of Trent was reassembled in 1551-1552 by the new pope, Julius III, the Emperor found his efforts to unite the two religious factions a failure, for the Interim was opposed by Catholics and Lutherans alike. Charles also ran into political opposition from some German princes who were not happy to learn that he had made plans to give the Hapsburgs permanent possession of the Imperial crown. Had the Augsburg Interim been successful, it would have resulted in a Reformed-Catholic Church in Germany and the destruction of Lutheranism. By the grace of God this did not come to pass.

THE LEIPZIG INTERIM – MELANCHTHON COMPROMISES AND THE LUTHERANS WAVER

Maurice of Saxony did not like the Augsburg Interim. "What's more, he knew that trying to enforce it in both his old and new territories would meet determined resistance and cause great unrest among his subjects."[12] After careful consideration, Maurice notified the Emperor on May 18 that he was unable to introduce the Augsburg Interim at that time. Shortly thereafter he gave instructions to the Wittenberg and Leipzig theologians to produce a compromise to be substituted for the Augsburg Interim, that would be more favorable to his subjects.[13] Though the new or substitute Interim was the product of a group of eight theologians, headed by Melanchthon, still it was Melanchthon who was chiefly responsible for its formulation.

The Leipzig Interim, which modified the original Interim, was drawn up in November 1548 and made the law of the land in Saxony in December at Leipzig – hence its name. But the Leipzig Interim was hated even more intensely by some Lutherans than the original one. After all, though it was prepared by Lutherans under the leadership of the very one who was looked upon as the logical successor of Luther to guide the Reformation now that he was gone, the Interim was full of compromises to Catholicism. Among other things, it compromised the doctrine of Justification by Faith and pledged the clergy to obey the pope and to participate once again in several Roman Catholic ceremonies, which rituals were terribly offensive to strict Lutherans. Included was the Corpus Christi celebration, which the Lutheran Church rightfully labeled as nothing short of idolatry. Melanchthon regarded the Catholic ceremonies as adiaphora – things which the Bible neither commands nor rejects and are therefore neutral in character. Yet these ceremonies or rituals were clearly marks of the Roman Church and for that reason identified those who participated in them as followers of Rome. The Lutheran theologian, Flacius, declared: "Nothing is an adiaphoron in case of confession and offense." And so, the so-called adiaphora, which Melanchthon regarded as acceptable items of compromise, were found to be highly objectionable and offensive to the strict Lutherans.

Why did Melanchthon do such a thing? Why did he compromise so severely and unscripturally to the Church of Rome? Bear in mind that the discussion which the Lutherans had with the Catholics in 1540 and 1541 already revealed Melanchthon's tendency to compromise. In the later years of his life, Luther on several occasions had scolded Melanchthon for the direction his theology was taking. Melanchthon was a gentle, shy individual; Luther was the opposite. Melanchthon tended to yield under pressure, especially when he feared for his life or felt the threat of war. Luther, on the other hand, was a very brave-hearted, strong-willed person, who felt an unshakable allegiance to God's Word and to the cause of the Lutheran Reformation. He did not yield under pressure but stood firm on the issues he believed in.

Even while the *Augsburg Confession* was becoming firmly rooted in Germany, Melanchthon, who was its author, was busy revising it, moving ever closer to the Reformed position. In 1540 Melanchthon came out with the *Variata* or *Altered Augsburg Confession*. In this document great concessions were made in the article on the Lord's Supper. True Lutherans subscribe, not to the *Variata*, but to the *Unaltered Augsburg Confession* (U.A.C.) of 1530.

With the crushing defeat of the Smalcald League in the spring of 1547, followed the next spring by the Augsburg Interim, which caused further havoc and suffering on the Lutheran scene, Melanchthon was no doubt compelled to a great extent by fear – also for his own life – to have a large part in framing a compromise document, the Leipzig Interim that so many Lutherans found even more obnoxious than the original Interim. No doubt, Melanchton also acted as he did because he geniunely believed that there existed the possibility of reaching an understanding with the Romanists, which would then ensure peace.[14] Due to his part in framing this Interim, Melanchthon was repudiated altogether by the strict Lutherans as Luther's successor in leading the Reformation.

MAURICE OF SAXONY COMES TO THE AID OF THE LUTHERAN CAUSE – THE PEACE OF PASSAU

Three years after the Augsburg Interim, chafing from being branded as a traitor, renegade, apostate, and even as a Judas who sold out his fellow Lutherans for an Electorate – but angry also at the Emperor for not keeping his promises and for the shameful treatment his father-in-law, Philip of Hesse, was receiving in prison, and fully aware that he could not enforce the Leipzig Interim – Maurice, the turncoat, decided to change sides again. Maurice became the leader of a conspiracy of German princes against the Hapsburgs, who had placed Charles V on the throne. Thus he hoped to redeem himself. In 1552 Maurice gathered an army, with orders to punish Magdeburg for its resistance to the Augsburg Interim. However, he suddenly turned his army southward and attacked the Emperor at Innsbruch, almost capturing him. After two months of war against the Catholic forces, Maurice had Germany at his feet. Charles was forced to negotiate the Treaty of Passau.[15] The Peace of Passau (June 1552) restored the religious situation to its status in 1545. Thus the Catholics lost all they had gained through the Smalcald War.

In 1556 Charles, a beaten man, abdicated and placed all German matters in the hands of his brother Ferdinand. He had not succeeded in thwarting the Lutheran Reformation, or in putting down its "heresy," and he had not reformed the German Catholic Church, which he had attempted to do through the Augsburg Interim.

THE PEACE OF AUGSBURG

The religious Peace of Augsburg of 1555 was actually a compromise, but it did grant Lutherans relative religious liberty. It recognized the right of both Lutheranism and Catholicism to exist in the Holy Roman Empire. However, Calvinism and Anabaptism were excluded. Furthermore, each state in Germany was to choose between the two religions. A Catholic prince did not have to tolerate Lutherans, and a Lutheran prince did not have to tolerate the Catholics. Without making it a part of a formal agreement, it was understood that where there was a majority of the other religion present in the state, the followers would be allowed to worship in their own way. If the followers were in the minority they would be allowed to emigrate. This was an improvement over the Edict of Worms, enforced by the Diet of Speyer, 1529; religious liberty was given to Catholic minorities in Lutheran lands but was not granted to Lutheran minorities in Catholic lands. "Against the invidiousness of this arrangement the evangelicals protested: hence the origin of the name Protestant."[16]

The Lutheran territories were more numerous than those that were Catholic, and also more populous. But following the compromise the Lutherans were prohibited by law to reach across Catholic boundaries. The Church of the Reformation was effectively divided up into a number of Lutheran State Churches, with the rulers providing for their maintenance and support.

CONTROVERSIES ARISE BETWEEN THE
LUTHERAN THEOLOGICAL GROUPS

Not only were the Lutherans involved in controversy with the pope and the Emperor, a storm of controversy broke upon the Lutherans themselves. The controversies occurred mainly between 1548 and 1577 – after Luther's death – but one controversy came about almost twenty years before the Reformer died. The controversies took place mainly between the followers of Melanchthon (the Philippists) and the Gnesio (True) Lutherans. However, Flacius, who was the leader of the Gnesio Lutherans, became so extreme in some of his views that he caused a faction to break away from his group and subsequently form a third or Middle Party. It was this group that later solved things with the help of the princes.

Briefly, then, the Lutheran controversies can be listed as follows:

(1) The Adiaphoristic Controversy (1548-1555). Some Lutherans defended Melanchthon's Leipzig Interim, which made concessions to the Catholics, while others opposed it. The defenders maintained that the concessions "demanded of the Lutherans were mere ceremonies, or adiaphora [neither commanded nor forbidden by God], which could be accepted by them."[17] A bitter controversy ensued. Recall Flacius' warning: "Nothing is an adiaphoron in case of confession and offense."

(2) The Majoristic Controversy (1551-1562). George Major with others defended Melanchthon's phrase that good works are necessary to salvation. Loyal Lutherans opposed the phrase, since it was easily misunderstood. Good works are necessary. However, good works are not necessary to salvation – since man is saved by God's grace through faith – but rather are necessary proofs of faith. In this way Lutherans explain the importance of good works in the life of the Christian.

(3) The Synergistic Controversy (1555-1560). Melanchthon and his followers held that man by his own natural powers cooperates in his conversion. Loyal Lutherans opposed this teaching, maintaining instead that God alone converts man, who is by nature spiritually dead, thus bringing him to faith. (Synergism means to work together.)

(4) The Flacian Controversy (1560-1575). Flacius erred in maintaining that original sin is the very substance of man, that it belongs to his very nature, instead of being accidental to him. Some Lutherans taught that original sin is "only a slight, insignificant blot or blemish on man's nature."[18] Most Lutherans, of whatever stripe, opposed these teachings.

(5) The Osiander and the Stancarian Controversy (1549-1566). Involved was the issue of how Christ is our righteousness. Osiander taught that Christ is our righteousness only according to his divine nature. Stancarus taught that Christ is our righteousness only according to his human nature. These two theologians were opposed by practically all Lutherans, who taught that Christ is our righteousness according to both natures. The error of these two theologians caused considerable trouble in the Church.

(6) The Antinomistic Controversy (1527-1556). (Anti-nomos literally means "against the law.") Various false views of the Law and the Gospel were put forth among the Lutherans and were defended by some and opposed by others. What part does God's Law have in the life of the Christian? What place does it have in the Church? What is the relationship between the Law and the Gospel? There were Lutherans who taught falsely that God's Law has no place in the Church and denied both the use of the Law as a mirror revealing man's sins and as a rule to guide his conduct.

(7) The Crypto-Calvinistic Controversy (1560-1574). The followers of Melanchthon (the Philippists) dishonestly attempted to replace Luther's doctrine of the Lord's Supper and the majesty of Christ's human nature,

with Calvin's teachings on these points. True Lutherans everywhere opposed the Philippists.

(8) Christ's descent into hell was also the subject of controversy. At what point did the Savior descend into hell? Did he do so only in his human nature or in both natures? The correct Lutheran view prevailed, which is that Jesus Christ the God-Man, risen from the dead and in his glorified state, went into hell to proclaim the victory.

(9) The Calvinistic doctrine that faith once implanted in the heart could never be lost was also a cause of confusion and controversy among Lutherans. And there were other issues that also confronted the Lutherans. [19, 20]

These controversies were all settled by various articles of the *Formula of Concord* (1577).

A FINAL LUTHERAN CONFESSION: THE FORMULA OF CONCORD

The *Formula of Concord* is the only Lutheran Confession that was written and adopted after Luther's death. In 1537 the *Apology of the Augsburg Confession* – prepared by Melanchthon in 1530 – was signed at Smalcald along with the *Augsburg Confession* also prepared in 1530. The *Apology* was a refutation of the *Catholic Confutation*. In time, a need was felt for a new Lutheran Confession, which would answer the questions not answered by the *Augsburg Confession* and which would settle the disturbing controversies that had arisen among the Lutherans. It should be noted here that the ill will that these controversies at times caused between the Gnesio-Lutherans and the Philippists deeply disturbed the German rulers. Philippists were sometimes driven from the Lutheran Church and forced into the Calvinist Camp, thus losing the protection of the Peace of Augsburg – to cite an example. The new confession had to be true to the fundamental teachings of Luther, while avoiding the extremism of Flacius on the one hand, and the Philippists on the other.

There were two men, especially, to whom we are indebted for the new confession, which would serve as the peace formula for the Lutheran Church in Germany – the document which would be known as the *Formula of Concord*. One was Jacob Andreae (1528-1580). This theologian, who was in the service of the Elector of Saxony, was deeply devoted to promoting peace and Lutheran unity. The other man, Martin Chemnitz (1522-1586) has been called "the prince of the Lutheran divines of his age and, next to Luther, the greatest theologian of our Church."[21]

Acting upon the request of Duke Julius of Brunswick, who in 1567 ordered them to draw up peace formulas, Andreae and Chemnitz held their first meeting the following year and produced two documents: the *Brunswick Church Order* and the *Corpus Doctrinae Iulium*, which included all the Lutheran Confessions which had been written up to that time. After the 1568 meeting with Chemnitz, which produced the two peace formulas, Andreae, armed with the formulas, personally attempted to establish peace between the Philippists and the Gnesio-Lutherans. However, his efforts met with only disappointment and failure, for the Philippists refused to repudiate their Calvinistic tendencies. (It should be noted that Philip Melanchthon, whose writings the Philippists placed ahead of those of Luther, had been dead since the spring of 1560.) The recalcitrant behavior of the Philippists convinced Andreae to travel the route of establishing harmony among the Gnesio or True Lutherans, instead of attempting to bring the Philippists back to the Lutheran position on the controverted doctrines.[22]

In 1572 Andreae wrote and delivered a work titled *Six Christian Sermons*, concerning the troubles that had plagued the Lutherans over nearly a quarter of a century. Andreae's work was revised, with the help of Chemnitz and other theologians, into the *Swabian Concord* or *Tuebingen Book*. This document was accepted by the churches in Swabia. The *Swabian Concord* was further revised by Chemnitz and Chytraeus for approval by the churches in Saxony. The revised document was called the *Swabian-Saxon Concord*. On the basis of criticisms that were offered, this document also underwent revision.[23]

In 1574 Elector August of Saxony became fully aware that he had been deceived by his Wittenberg theologians, who were, in fact, Crypto-Calvinists, not Lutherans. He ended the dishonest rule of the Philippists[24] and threw his full weight to the cause of a truly Lutheran union. A meeting of theologians was called at his behest at the Maulbronn Cloister by Count George Ernest of Henneberg. This meeting produced another confession, the *Maulbronn Formula*, which was adopted.

A group headed by Nicholas Selnecker of Wittenberg, Jacob Andreae of Tuebingen, Martin Chemnitz of Brunswick, and Chytraeus of Rostock – the most important Lutheran theologians of the later part of the sixteenth century – along with Christoph Koerner of Frankfurt and Andreas Musculus, met at Torgau for a month in the spring of 1576. There the *Torgau Book* was formulated on the basis of the *Swabian-Saxon Concord* and the *Maulbronn Formula*. Elector August of Saxony sent the *Torgau Book* to the various Lutheran lands for comments and criticism. Later, the responses that were received were examined and weighed by three of the six men responsible for the *Torgau Book*, who then revised the book accordingly. The three – Chemnitz, Andrea, and Selnecker – carried on the revision work at the cloister in Bergen in March of 1577. Still another revision took place in May with the help of the other three theologians who had worked on the original *Torgau Book*. Their efforts culminated in what was called the *Bergen* (or *Bergic*) *Book*. Today, it is known as the *Solid* or *Thorough Declaration*. [25, 26]

Thus, the document that came to be known as the *Formula of Concord* went through several revisions before its final form. On May 28, 1577, "the long form of agreement" known as the *Solid Declaration*, was adopted. A shorter, less comprehensive version, known as the *Epitome (Summary)*, was prepared by Andreae especially for use in the congregations. These two forms comprise the confession known as the *Formula of Concord*, a truly monumental doctrinal and confessional work by Martin Luther's successors, who, following in the footsteps of the great Reformer, were God's instruments in defending, preserving, and expounding divine truth; also in restoring peace and harmony to the Church.

THE BOOK OF CONCORD

While the *Formula of Concord* was overwhelmingly accepted by the majority of Lutheran States in Germany as the answer to the questions raised by the controversies within the Lutheran Church, it was deemed best to include with it the previous Confessions, which focused on the controversy between the Lutherans and the Catholics. Both the Lutheran princes and the theologians saw the need to compile a Body of Doctrine that would be acceptable to all Lutherans everywhere, that would settle the theological controversies dividing the Lutheran Church, and that would also "define Lutheranism as against Catholicism and Calvinism."[27]

The entire collection of confessional statements was put together in what is called the *Book of Concord*. The German edition was published officially on June 25, 1580 – the Fiftieth Anniversary of the reading of the *Augsburg Confession* before Emperor Charles V. The *Book of Concord* contains the following Creeds and Confessions: the three *Ecumenical Creeds* (*Apostles, Nicene, Athanasian*); the *Unaltered Augsburg Confession* (1530); the *Apology (Defense)* of the *Augsburg Confession* (1530); *Luther's Small* and *Large Catechisms* (1529); *Luther's Smalcald Articles* (1537) and *Tract*; the *Formula of Concord* (1577).

The *Book of Concord* became a legal document signed by fifty-one princes, thirty-five cities, and more than eight thousand members of the Lutheran clergy and other congregational representatives. The publication and acceptance of the *Book of Concord* marked the doctrinal completion of the Lutheran Church.[28] The Peace of Augsburg marked its political completion. True Lutherans accept the Lutheran Confessions because they are a true exposition of God's Word, not insofar as they agree with God's Word – as some maintain. To this day, the prerequisite to ordaining a candidate to the ministry of the Evangelical Lutheran Church is his **full** subscription to the *Book of Concord* of 1580.

Footnotes for Chapter Two

1 John Theodore Mueller, *The Lutheran Confessions* (Professor of symbolics, Concordia Theological Seminary, Saint Louis, Mo – a tract), p. 20

2 John Theodore Mueller, *The Lutheran Confessions*, p. 20.

3 John Theodore Mueller, *The Lutheran Confessions*, p. 20.

4 John Theodore Mueller, *The Lutheran Confessions*, p. 21

5 Lars P. Qualben, St. Olaf College, *A History of the Christian Church*, (Thomas Nelson and Sons, New York, NY, 1942), p. 279.

6 Lars P. Qualben, *A History of the Christian Church*, p. 279.

7 F. Bente, *Concordia Triglotta – Historical Introduction*, (Concordia Publishing House, Saint Louis, MO, 1921), p. 94.

8 F. Bente, *Concordia Triglotta*, p. 95.

9 F. Bente, *Concordia Triglotta*, p. 95.

10 F. Bente, *Concordia Triglotta*, p. 96.

11 F. Bente, *Concordia Triglotta*, p. 96.

12 James A. Fricke, *Formula of Concord – A Study Guide for Bible Classes*, (Northwestern Publishing House, Milwaukee, WI 53226-3284, 1979), p. 7.

13 F. Bente, *Concordia Triglotta*, p. 98.

14 F. Bente, *Concordia Triglotta*, p. 99.

15 Erwin L. Lueker, Editor-in-Chief, *Lutheran Cyclopedia*, (Concordia Publishing House, Saint Louis, MO 63118-3968), p. 662.

16 Roland H. Bainton, *The Reformation of the Sixteenth Century*, (Beacon Press, Boston, MA, 1952), pp. 148, 149.

17 John Theodore Mueller, *The Lutheran Confessions,* p. 26.

18 John Theodore Mueller, *The Lutheran Confessions,* p. 26.

19 Lars P. Qualben, *A History of the Christian Church*, pp. 282, 283.

20 F. Bente, *Concordia Triglotta*, p. 103.

21 James A. Fricke, *Formula of Concord,* p. 11.

22 James A. Fricke, *Formula of Concord,* p. 11, 12.

23 James A. Fricke, *Formula of Concord,* p. 12.

24 Erwin L. Lueker, *Lutheran Cyclopedia*, p. 634.

25 James A. Fricke, *Formula of Concord*, pp. 13, 14.

26 Erwin L. Lueker, *Lutheran Cyclopedia*, p. 634.

27 Lars P. Qualben, *A History of the Christian Church*, p. 284.

28 Lars P. Qualben, *A History of the Christian Church*, p. 284.

CHAPTER THREE

REFORMATION OUTSIDE GERMANY

SWITZERLAND

ULRICH ZWINGLI WORKS REFORMS

The Two most important names in connection with the Protestant Reformation of Switzerland are Ulrich Zwingli (1484-1531) and John Calvin (1509-1564). There were several other men who were personally dedicated to the task of reforming the Church in Switzerland, but the names of these two Reformers stand out with special prominence.

One year after Luther attacked the sale of indulgences in Germany, Ulrich Zwingli followed the German Reformer's example and attacked their sale in Switzerland. Luther's bold act of burning the papal bull of excommunication in 1520 was a powerful stimulus to Zwingli, who then attacked the Church of Rome with unabated fury.

Zwingli became a parish priest in Glarus in 1506. From 1516 to 1518 he served as people's priest at Einsiedeln, a very important Catholic shrine. Early in 1519 Zwingli was elevated to the position of great minister at Zürich. . . At Einsiedeln, Zwingli had become a preacher of the gospel of Christ and through his preaching gained a large following. Erasmus (a leading humanist of his time) once estimated that there were 200,000 persons in Swiss Cantons who no longer adhered to the See of Rome because of the influence of Zwingli and his gospel preaching. By the time Zwingli took up his position at Zürich he was convinced that a thorough moral ref-

53

ormation was needed in the Church. While serving as a chaplain of Swiss armies in campaigns in Northern Italy, Zwingli saw much moral decay, and this struck him as being especially serious, since it was happening on the pope's home soil.

Between the years 1519 and 1533 Zwingli studied Luther's works and was deeply influenced by them. He did not, however, profess to be a disciple of Luther, nor did he admit to bringing the Lutheran Reformation into his home country. Various reforms were begun at Zűrich and spread elsewhere. In 1523 the city council required preachers to base their sermons on Holy Scripture. This decision by the council actually stemmed from an attempt by the Catholics to silence the Reformer. Zwingli defended his principles so well at the Zűrich Disputation of 1523 that the city council sided with him. Images were abolished in the churches, the clergy were allowed to marry, and in 1525 the Catholic mass was abolished and replaced with a simple service in which the Lord's Supper was celebrated. There were other reforms that were introduced. For example, the command prohibiting the eating of meat during Lent was repudiated and religious houses were discontinued. Zwingli's ideals for Reformation were actually built into laws passed by the city council.

Eventually the Catholic cantons went to war against the Reformed cantons in a violent attempt to stop the Reformation. After the two sides battled to a draw, the First Peace of Cappel was drawn up in 1529. This agreement allowed the Reformed cantons to keep their religion and allowed the Catholic cantons to refuse to have the Reformation introduced within their boundaries.

While Zwingli's Reformation had some things in common with Luther's German Reformation – a prime example being the elevation of the gospel of Jesus Christ to its rightful place as mankind's only means to be saved from sin and inherit eternal life, and this through faith along – there were important differences. Zwingli depended on the secular powers to agree on the changes to be made in the Church, and then officially order these changes for the Church. Luther's Reformation did not depend upon enforcement by civil authorities. Another area of difference was the treatment given to church ornamentation, musical instruments, religious symbols and the like. Zwingli removed these from the churches, while Luther left things alone that were not wrong in themselves. A chief difference between the Reformers involved the Lord's Supper. Luther believed in the Real Presence of Christ's body and blood in the Sacrament of the Altar, accepting at face value the Lord's words; "This is my body (concerning the bread) and this is my blood of the New Testament (concerning the wine)." Zwingli believed and taught that the bread and wine merely represent the body and blood of the Lord, which are far removed from the Lord's Supper.

Now then, Philip of Hesse wanted very much for the Swiss and German Protestants to unite and therefore arranged a meeting at the Marburg Castle in 1529 between Zwingli and Luther in order to discuss their differences. After three days of discussion it was clear that the two sides could not be brought together in agreement regarding Christ's words "This is my body, this is my blood." There was another important area of disagreement between the two sides regarding the Lord's Supper. Zwingli did not agree with Luther that this sacrament is a sign given by God whereby he confirms his promise of forgiveness of sins through Christ. To the Zwinglians the Lord's Supper is merely an affirmation of faith on the part of the celebrants. Zwingli allowed his human reason to help him formulate his doctrinal confessions, instead of simply relying on the words of Scripture. The two Reformers went their separate ways. "Luther gave Zwingli the hand of peace and charity, but not of fellowship."[1] Later, when the Lutherans presented their *Augsburg Confession* to the Emperor at Augsburg, Germany, they repudiated any connection with the Swiss Reformer.

Though Luther withheld the hand of fellowship from Zwingli, the latter's efforts to bring about Reformation of the Church and thus an acceptance of his teachings among his own Swiss countrymen met with great success. ". . .Zwingli. . . .no longer stood alone in Switzerland. Brave, devoted friends had been at work in various places and the strongholds of the papacy fell one after another."[2] This included Bern, the most powerful of the cantons. Tragically, Zwingli became more and more involved in the affairs of government, mingling Church and State. Meanwhile the Forest Cantons, which stubbornly remained Catholic, formed an alliance with Austria, "the archenemy of the Reformation."[3] Antagonism developed between the Forest Cantons and the Reformed Cantons, with finally erupted into civil war. The Forest Cantons attacked the territory of Zurich with overwhelming strength. The forces of Zurich were defeated at Cappel, October 11, 1531. During the battle Ulrich Zwingli was slain. The breach between the Lutheran and Reformed sides, which became apparent at Marburg, has never been healed. In fact, through the Reformation efforts of Zwingli's successor the breach was widened.

JOHN CALVIN: EUROPE'S
SECOND-GREATEST REFORMER

After Zwingli's death the main scene of Swiss Protestant Reform changed from Zurich to Geneva. The reason for this change was a man named John Calvin, a Frenchman by birth. Born July 10, 1509 in Noyon, Picardy, France, of an aristocratic family, he grew up to become not only the second most important leader of the Protestant cause, who brought the Reformation to much of the European Continent, he also had tremendous influence on the political development of the world, an influence still felt today.[4]

At first it seems that Calvin, a highly intellectual individual, was destined for the priesthood. However, a bitter experience endured with the Catholic Church by his father changed the direction of Calvin's life. His father decided that he should study law. Eventually Calvin found that his life's interest was not in the law, although later, as a Reformer, he would become deeply involved with both the formulation and enforcement of civil as well as church law. While studying in Paris, Calvin, a humanist, connected up with the Protestant cause, thus becoming familiar with Lutheranism. By 1533 he was converted to Protestantism. Twice, Calvin was forced to flee from Paris because of his Protestant connection. His second flight from Paris, which occurred late in 1534, brought him to Basel, Switzerland, the home of a close friend, who was also associated with the Protestant movement.

During his stay in Basel Calvin published his *Institutes of the Christian Religion*. It was an extraordinary accomplishment. This classic exposition of Calvin's personal theology established him as a theologian of the first rank.[5] His *Institutes* was a dogmatic work which thoroughly presents Reformed doctrine, and was intended to be a defense of the French King, Francis I.[6] Calvin's *Institutes*, though giving evidence of Luther's influence, also reveal important differences in the doctrines held by the Lutheran and Reformed bodies. Calvinism differs from Lutheranism in several important areas, including Predestination, Worship Forms, the Lord's Supper, the power of the State in Church matters, the Sovereignty of God, and the gospel as the Means of Grace. Calvinists tend to regard the Bible more as a set of divine rules that must be followed than as the book wherein God presents himself to mankind as a merciful, forgiving, loving God. "There existed. . . a distinct difference between the two Reformers characterized by Calvin's predominantly formal and legalistic approach to Christianity in contrast to Luther's warm and evangelical spirit. 'Luther stresses the glory of God's love; Calvin stresses God's love of glory'."[7] Luther depended on the power of the Word of God to accomplish God's purpose, whereas Zwingli and Calvin – like the Church of Rome – depended to a great extent on the power of the State to accomplish God's purpose and the Church's aims. Thus there is a dangerous and even tyrannical intermingling of Church and State in Calvinism that even calls on the police agencies of civil governments to enforce religious beliefs and laws, and to punish dissidents.

While passing through Geneva, Calvin was persuaded by Farel, the Protestant preacher, to remain there and help make Geneva a Protestant city. Calvin did so and became more or less a dictator for the Protestant cause. Using his *Confession of Faith* as a creed-test, he determined those who accepted the Protestant faith, as well as those who did not. Those who refused to be Protestants were banished, while others – a large number – who were zealous for the Protestant cause, were allowed in. The citizens were closely watched for infractions of the laws. Punishment, including banishment and even death, was applied to those who broke the laws of the Church and remained incorrigible. In the case of excommunicated persons, the civil magistrates were to take over the matter from the Church in order to try and work a change of sentiment in the person. In cases where they did not succeed they were to administer the proper punishment.

Soon, Calvin's oppressive tactics reminded the citizens of previous oppressors, with the result that his reputation came into disrepute. What made matters even worse was the fact that the people were being oppressed by someone who was not even Swiss, that foreigner they sneeringly called "the Frenchman." And so, Calvin was forced to leave Geneva. For several years he pastored the French Protestant Church in Strassburg. He also married. Then, because things were going badly in Geneva, Calvin was invited back. He returned in September 1541. Calvin demanded, and received, complete authority to lead Geneva as a theocracy. Geneva became a Puritan State, the "City of God." The civil code framed by Calvin made Geneva a Republic, which served from that time on as the center of the Reformed Church. Within four years after Calvin's return, 58 people were executed and many others were banished.

Calvin's influence spread throughout Switzerland. From his base in Geneva, Calvin's doctrine spread out into all parts of Europe. "Calvin's influence went out far beyond the confines of Geneva. Through his school in Geneva, to which men were attracted from all parts and which supplied many countries with ministers, the seed of Calvinism was carried far afield. In the southwestern part of Germany, from where we have the [HEIDELBERG CATECHISM], in the Netherlands, in England, among the Scotch and the Irish Presbyterians, through the work of John Knox and others, Calvinism spread. The French Huguenots, the Puritans, the Dutch settlers brought it to our shores. And we need but read the stories of Puritan New England, of Dutch New Amsterdam, to see a repetition of what happened in Geneva under Calvin's rule."[8] Regarding this last statement: for example, recall that Mary Dyer, a Quaker, was hanged on the Boston Common in 1660 while in pursuit of religious liberty. The Puritans, who were Calvinist extremists, abhorred any deviation. Many of the tyrannical laws which held sway in the early American Colonies were founded on Calvin's principles. Through the years Calvinism has been softened, as indeed it needed to be.

John Calvin died on May 27, 1564. However, his name, like that of Martin Luther, remains very much alive today throughout much of the world. We will meet up again with Calvin and his Reformed Church when we review the history of Lutheranism in America.

FRANCE

Cruel means were used by the Catholics to suppress the Reformation movement in France. Still, in spite of this persecution, large numbers of people, especially in Southern France, joined the movement.

THE INFLUENCE OF LUTHER AND CALVIN

Luther was the chief reformatory influence in this country. Nevertheless, Calvin through his *Institutes*, which he wisely published in the French language, did much to organize the French Protestants. In 1559 the Protestant Churches of France held a synod in Paris and adopted the *Gallic Confession*, which was drawn up by Calvin. While the Protestants in France were partly Lutheran, partly Calvinists, they became known about this time as Huguenots. In 1559 there was forty established Protestant congregations and more than two thousand preaching stations. Naturally, due to the influence of Calvin and his *Institutes*, Geneva became the training place for the Protestant ministers of France.

PERSECUTION OF THE
PROTESTANT CHURCH BY ROME

The French Protestant Church was divorced from the state since the Catholic government was totally intolerant of it. Several wars of religion were fought by the Catholics and Protestants between the years 1562 and 1593. But Protestantism was dealt a crushing blow by the horrific massacre of St. Bartholomew, August 24, 1572. The plot to massacre all the Huguenots in France was hatched by Catherine de Medici and authorized by both the King and the Roman Catholic leaders. When the antiHuguenot element among the populace was unleashed against the Protestants, Admiral Coligny, the man behind Frency Protestantism, was the first to be murdered. Though the massacre centered in Paris, with thousands of Protestants slaughtered, including men, women, children, and even babies, it soon spread throughout France. The final toll of victims has been estimated to be between 25,000 and 100,000. Blood literally flowed in the gutters of the streets. Upon hearing of the slaughter Pope Gregory XIII was jubilant and began a celebration. Among other things, he had a *Te Deum* (God, we Praise You) sung in St. Peter's Cathedral and ordered a medal to be struck commemorating this Roman "victory." Two of these medals are extant. The author has viewed the one owned by the Lutheran Church-Missouri Synod, and kept in the historical archives at Concordia Seminary, St. Louis, Missouri. According to the reverse side of the medal the massacre was a service pleasing to God!

In 1598, Henry IV–who vacillated between Catholicism and Protestantism–in order to further his political aims, issued the Edict of Nantes. The edict recognized Catholicism as the official religion of the kingdom but also stipulated that no one was to be molested or annoyed because of his Protestant faith. Protestant worship was restricted to the bounds it occupied in 1597. Elsewhere, especially in Paris, it was forbidden. This edict, unpopular with both sides, remained the religious law of the land until it was revoked on October 22, 1685, by Louis XIV, who was determined to break the back of Protestantism in France. The King's action forced thirty to forty thousand Huguenots to flee their homeland. However, two million members of the Reformed Church remained. According to the *Lutheran Cyclopedia*, there were no congregations for these Protestants, except in the wilderness. On May 14, 1724, the last great law against the Protestants was issued by Louis XV, and this law enforced the most oppressive measures of Louis XIV. Far from attracting the Huguenots to Catholicism, it drove them further away.[9] "After 1760 the principles of toleration began to prevail, and Louis XVI in November 1788 published an edict of toler-

58

ance, which restored to the French Protestants their religious liberty."[10] In the seventeenth century, Lutherans in German districts conquered by France (for example, Alsace) were guaranteed their religious liberty, and these eventually coalesced into one Evangelical Lutheran Church of France.[11]

THE NETHERLANDS

JOHN CALVIN IS THE GUIDING LIGHT

The writings of Luther and his bold stand against the papacy had long been influences in the Netherlands. Again, as in other places, confusion reigned among the Protestants. But eventually, Calvin's *Institutes* became the guidebook for Protestants. As a result the influence of men like Luther and Zwingli began to fade. The Reformed faith of Calvin became the chief influence, resulting in the formation of the Reformed Church of the Netherlands (the Dutch Calvinists). In 1561 the *Belgic Confession* was drawn up by Guido De Bres. Ten years later the organization of the Reformed Church in the Netherlands was complete.

THE INFLUENCE OF WESSEL, ERASMUS, AND LUTHER

John of Wessel (d. 1479) had connection to Erfurt, Worms, and Mainz in Germany, and to Basel in Switzerland. He was a theologian who anticipated some of Luther's doctrines and also some of Zwingli's. Along with others he attacked the authority of the pope and of the councils, and other Roman doctrines as well. He was tried for heresy and recanted.

Erasmus (1466-1536) was a Hollander, who lived during Luther's time and sympathized with many points of Luther's doctrines. But due to his vacillating ways he did not serve the cause of the Reformation as he might have. Luther finally turned against Erasmus.

Luther's writings were published as early as 1518 in the Netherlands. By 1521 a special Inquisition was organized to put a stop to Luther's heresy. The first Lutheran martyrs in the world were put to death in this Inquisition, being burned alive at the stake at Antwerp in 1523. Lutheranism in the Netherlands became adulterated with old false doctrines and after 1540 it became increasingly Calvinistic in certain areas, and even Anabaptist (a movement which rejected infant baptism and placed little stress on the Lord's Supper).

THE GREAT PROTESTANT REVOLT

Reformation between 1560 and 1570 in the Netherlands was Revolution. Beginning with the year 1567, Philip II of Spain, through the Duke of Alva, tried to wipe out Protestantism. This persecution resulted in so many deaths and exiles that it has been compared to the Roman persecutions of the Christians in the first three centuries. The year 1572 marked the beginning of the great revolt by the Protestants. The following year William of Orange placed himself at its head. William was counseled by Philip van Marnix, the genius of the Dutch Revolution, who had succeeded in organizing the Protestants in Holland into a Calvinistic Church.

The Revolution was a success. As a result, the Netherlands were equally divided into two sections. The southern province of the Lowlands – later known as Belgium – remained subject to Spain and was Catholic. The Northern provinces became United Netherlands, where the state religion was Calvinism. However, extensive toleration of other Protestants, especially Lutherans and Anabaptists, was granted.

SCOTLAND

A COUNTRY RIPE FOR REFORMATION

The Roman Catholic Church in Scotland was in a terrible state of blight and deterioration. E.F. Haertel writes in his essay on John Knox that half of the wealth of the land was owned by the Church, the Bible was unknown, the sacrifice of the Mass replaced Christ's sacrifice on the cross, the priests lived scandalously corrupt lives and their ignorance was beyond belief. He also points out that the country swarmed with ignorant, vicious monks, who robbed the poor people even of their means of subsistence. Church services were neglected and the church buildings were rarely used for divine purposes. At the same time the people were sorely oppressed by Church laws. The author quotes John Knox, who relates in his *Historie* that a husband and wife, accused along with others of eating a goose on a Friday (when meat was prohibited), were condemned without mercy to be executed. The husband was hanged and the wife, with a nursing infant tied to her breast, was drowned.[12]

A student of Martin Luther, named Patrick Hamilton, tried to bring the gospel to Scotland, but on February 28, 1528, was burned alive at the stake for his efforts. The books of Martin Luther and other German Reformers, along with Tyndale's English New Testament, were popular with the Scottish people. An early Reformer, named George Wishart, preached the gospel in Scotland and on March 1, 1546, was burned at the stake.[13]

Scotland found an outspoken, fearless, and stern Protestant Reformer in John Knox, who was in sympathy with George Wishart. Knox, a Catholic priest, became convinced that the Roman Church is "the synagog of Satan," and the pope is the man of sin that Scripture warns against. Knox openly preached against the pope and even administered the Lord's Supper according to Reformed customs. Knox was under the influence of the Swiss Reformers and so the Protestant Church in Scotland developed along Reformed lines rather than Lutheran.

For a period of nineteen months, Knox was a prisoner of the French, who came to the aid of Mary Stuart against a group of Protestant conspirators with whom Knox associated. During this time he was chained to an oar in a French galley, where he came close to dying. Following his release, Knox served as a minister in England and there he helped to found English Puritanism. Later, he had to leave England to save his life during the pro-Catholic reign of Mary Tudor (Bloody Mary) and made his way to Geneva. Later, in 1555, when it was safe to do so, Knox returned to Scotland. He and other followers of the Reformed way resolved to meet henceforth as Reformed congregations, completely separating themselves from the Roman mass. Author Haertel makes the observation that by this act the organization of a Reformed Scottish Church had begun.[14] Knox traveled and preached with much success. For three years he pastored a congregation in Geneva and so was absent from Scotland. But in 1559 Knox returned for the final time to Scotland. Later, the Reformer drew up *The Confession of the Faith and Doctrine Believed and Professed by the Protestants of the Realm of Scotland.* On August 17, 1560, this Calvinistic Confession of faith was adopted by the Scottish Estates, to whom had been granted the authority to settle religious questions in the absence of Queen Mary in France. This was the first presentation of Scotch Presbyterian doctrine. In December 1567 the Parliament or Scottish Estates took the step that established the Reformed Church constitutionally in Scotland by ratifying the actions taken back in 1560. By the year 1570 – after Mary, Queen of the Scots had unsuccessfully tried to reinstate Catholicism – the Presbyterian Church was fully and firmly established.

John Knox died on November 24, 1572. Knox's Reformation practiced a strict puritanical kind of Calvinism. Like Zwingli and Calvin, Knox confused Church and State, relying on civil government to enforce religious rules and decrees. True to Calvinsim, Knox aimed at establishing the state as a "City of God." His emphasis was very much on the Law of Moses and lacked tenderness and sweetness of the Gospel which, on the other hand, was Luther's emphasis. Knox taught that whatever is not commanded by God in the Scripture must be forbidden in the Church. Luther's philosophy was that whatever is neither commanded nor forbidden by God in Scripture is then a matter of Christian liberty. The stern features of Knox Presbyterianism, too, showed up later on the religious and governmental policies and practices of the early American Colonies.

ENGLAND

THE IMORTANCE OF MARTIN LUTHER'S
TEACHINGS AND OF BIBLE TRANSLATIONS

The Protestant Reformation in England was not so easily or so swiftly accomplished as it was in some countries. John Wyclif had begun to prepare England for Reformation already in the fourteenth century. He opposed the pope's meddling in English affairs of Church and State. He also wrote many tracts against Roman errors. Like Martin Luther after him, he translated the Bible into the language of the people (1382). Wycliff died in 1384 without leaving the Church of Rome. However, his teachings were branded as heresy and years later he was tried, condemned, and excommunicated in *absentia*. His bones were dug up and burned.

Luther's Reformation writings were important in England almost immediately, and as the German Reformation progressed, Wittenberg attracted Englishmen like Robert Barnes and William Tyndale, who were eager to learn from the Reformer, and carried much of his doctrine back to England. Luther's teachings were discussed by students at both Cambridge and Oxford. Lutheranism gained a steady foothold in the hearts of the English people. Nothing, however, helped the Reformation movement in England more than the translation of the Bible into the language of the people, for it is the Sword of the Spirit, which moves hearts yearning for peace and salvation to receive with faith the gospel of Christ. The natural result of the gospel in men's hearts was to move them to cast off the Catholic yoke, which falsely bound consciences to man-made traditions and customs and to the false gospel of salvation by works. In 1525 Tyndale published an English translation from the Greek at Worms, Germany. This translation, while it helped to bring about Tyndale's death in 1536 by the forces of Rome, nevertheless did much to further the Reformation in both England and Scotland.

KING HENRY VIII AND
THE PROTESTANT REFORMATION

At times, in order to further his personal ambitions as well as his political aims, Henry was friendly toward the Protestants in other countries, and often used the services of Robert Barnes as his personal messenger and a kind of ambassador of good will. Barnes frequently carried messages between Henry and Martin Luther in regards to the King's plans to divorce his wife. Author Neelak Tjernagel in his book *Henry VIII and the Lutherans* claims that the formative and determinative religious influence during Henry VIII's reign was that of Martin Luther and German Lutheranism. Tjernagel makes the point that all the theologians and scholars who were most important in the English Reformation in Henry VIII's reign had touched Wittenberg (Luther's home base) directly or indirectly. They were all imbued with Lutheranism, but Robert Barnes, more than any other single Reformer, gave England a Lutheran theology.[15]

Author James Edward McGoldrick, who has studied the writings of the early English Reformers in great depth, makes this observation toward the conclusion of his book, *Luther's English Connection*: "In appraising the enduring influence of Lutheran concepts in England, one must travel the paths first walked by Barnes and Tyndale. True, no English denomination of great size was to call itself the Lutheran Church, but the doctrinal content of Anglican theology bears unmistakable evidence of Lutheran teachings. A careful study of such documents as the *Ten Articles* (1536), the *Bishops' Book* (1537), and the *Thirteen Articles* (1538) supports this conclusion. Cranmer's *Book of Common Prayer* also borrowed heavily from Lutheran sources [i.e. Luther's Catechisms, liturgies and litanies]."[16] The bald fact is that many of the fundamental doctrines of the Anglican Church are plainly Lutheran in character.

Many Englishmen favored Luther's doctrine, and changes were made after a time in the Catholic Church in England. For example, monasteries and relic worship were discontinued. At the end of Henry's reign the majority of the people of Southeastern England, including London, were Lutherans. But the rest of the population were mostly Catholic.

Henry himself – though at times friendly toward the Lutheran Reformation in order to further his own causes – still considered himself a good Catholic, even after he had Parliament pass the *Act of Supremacy*, which replaced the pope of Rome with the King of England as the supreme head of the Church. It is interesting to note that Henry executed many of his fellow Catholics, who would not recognize his supremacy. What the King really wanted was a Reformed Catholic Church that was national in character, and strictly under royal control.[17] By the *Six Articles* passed by Parliament, Henry forbade the teaching of Protestant doctrine in England. The *Articles* were later repealed under the rule of Henry's son, Edward VI. Finally, Henry would not tolerate Lutheranism in England. Still, he had his son trained in the faith of the Reformers.

AFTER HENRY VIII,
PROTESTANTISM'S GAINS AND LOSSES

Edward VI, who succeeded his father as King in 1547, was sympathetic to the Protestant cause. A limited freedom of the press was allowed, which brought to England the work of Protestant theologians. Between 1550 and 1553, England pretty much parted ways with Roman Catholicism. As the Reformation in England stepped up its conquests under Edward, changes were made in worship forms and in the doctrines of the Church of England. In 1549 Parliament made the use of the *Book of Common Prayer* obligatory. Little by little Catholic worship forms were dropped or replaced. The *Forty-two Articles* of Thomas Cranmer (1489-1556), drawn up in 1553, were adopted.

However, under Edward's successor, Mary Tudor (Bloody Mary), Protestantism lost much of the ground it had gained during the few years of Edward's reign. Edward died in 1553. In his book *The Church in History* Kuiper reports that Mary, a strong Catholic, "set the clock of the Reformation in England back at least twenty-five years." It is an act of God's mercy that her reign lasted only five years, but during that time laws passed against Catholicism and in favor of Protestantism were repealed, and persecution of Protestant leaders commenced on a grand scale. Mary was responsible for the known deaths of almost 300 persons, including Cranmer, Archbishop of Canterbury, who could not save his life in spite of vacillating between Rome and Reform. Mary had strong ties to Catholic Spain through her affiliations with Emperor Charles V and his son Philip II, and finally, her marriage to Philip. Mary also sought to make England once again subject to the supreme rule of the Roman pontiff, and thus relinquished the royal supremacy of England invoked by her father, Henry VIII. However, she was opposed in this by the Lords and the Commons. Bishops and other clergy who refused to return to Catholic worship were either removed from office or put to death.[18]

Mercifully, Queen Mary died in 1558 and was succeeded by Elizabeth I, Henry's daughter by Ann Boleyn. During Elizabeth's reign, from 1558 to 1603, Protestantism was again in favor in England, especially for the political expedience it offered. In 1559 Parliament passed a new law which once-for-all ended papal power over the Church of England. Romanism was outlawed. In the same year Parliament also passed a law requiring that all public worship be conducted according to the *Revised Prayer Book* of 1552. In 1563 the *Forty-Two Articles* were reduced to the *Thirty-Nine Articles*, which became and remain the official creed of the Church of England. These *Thirty-Nine Articles* of the Elizabethan settlement "were and remain Lutheran." [19]

CHARACTERISTICS OF THE CHURCH OF ENGLAND, NOW PROTESTANT (ANGLICAN)

"In the second half of the sixteenth century, the tide of non-Lutheran Protestant influence from the Continent, especially from Switzerland and the Rhineland, rose significantly in England. Consequently, Zwinglian and Calvinistic religious ideas gained a large following during the reigns of Edward VI and Elizabeth I. The foundations of Anglican Protestantism, however, had been laid by an earlier generation of Reformers, and prominent among them were the two men who represented Luther's English connection, Robert Barnes and William Tyndale."[20]

Like the Lutheran Church, the Anglican Church seeks to preserve in the worship service as many of those elements in the old rites and ceremonies as are in accord with Scripture. In fact, Elizabeth, while ordering the Church to use the *English Book of Prayer*, also ordered the clergy to perform most of the old Roman ceremonies.[21] While this did not set well with the Puritans, it pleased the majority of Englishmen. The Anglican Church today is part Lutheran, part Calvinistic, part Catholic.

SCANDINAVIA – DENMARK

Practically the whole populations of the Scandinavian countries became Lutheran. By 1540 almost all of Northern Germany was officially Lutheran, which of course, gave great impetus to the Lutheranizing of the Scandinavian countries. The most important conquest of nations by the Lutheran Reformation outside of Germany was in the four Scandinavian countries.

EARLY ATTEMPTS OF REFORM

Between 1520 and 1523, Christian II of Denmark tried without success to bring the Lutheran Reformation into Denmark. He even attempted to have Luther come to Denmark. The King's aim at Lutheranism for his country was, sad to say, highly political, since it appeared to be a convenient means to overpower the Catholic bishops, confiscate Church property and add revenues to his faltering treasury. A law was passed forming a State Church headed by the King, but the revolution of 1523 brought it to naught, and the King was exiled.

LUTHERANISM SUCCEEDS

The new King, Frederick I (1523-1533), was wise. In sympathy with the Reformation movement, he allowed Lutheran preachers to spread the new doctrines while not enforcing the old heresy laws against them. The Diet of Odensea in 1527 decreed equal toleration of the Lutherans.

The Danish Lutheran, Hans Tausen (1494-1561), led the work of preaching Luther's doctrines, and beginning with the year 1530, the Reformation spread very rapidly among all classes of people.

Frederick I was admitted into the Smalcald League in 1532, thus becoming a part of the German Lutheran alliance, which was formed to present a unified defense against attack by Catholic forces. Under Frederick's successor, Christian III, the Reformation was completed in Denmark. He was a strong Lutheran and had been present at the Diet of Worms in 1521.

In 1536 the Catholic bishops were deposed, their property was confiscated, and the King was made head of the church organization. Seven new bishops (at first called superintendents) were ordained by a Lutheran preacher, John Bugenhagen, who was imported from Wittenberg to set up church law for Denmark along Lutheran lines. The Catholic religion was abolished by law.

The Church in Denmark was not forced upon the people, but was simply recognized as the faith that had come about in the kingdom through the Reformers. The Church was national. The bishops were appointed by the King. The Church was under royal patronage and under control of the King.

SCANDINAVIA – NORWAY

BERGEN: THE CENTER OF THE LUTHERAN REFORMATION

The Lutheran faith became established in Norway after taking over in Denmark. To review the political situation: Denmark, Norway and Sweden were united by the Union of Calmar in 1397 and ruled by one King. Denmark dominated the union. Sweden broke away from the union in

1523, but Norway continued to be united with Denmark until 1814. From 1814 to 1905 Norway was united with Sweden under the Swedish crown and then, in 1905, declared her independence and elected her own King. Now then, the bishops of the Norwegian Catholic Church had opposed the succession of Christian III to the throne of Denmark in 1533. After he was firmly in control in his home country Christian proceeded to put down resistance in Norway. After driving out the Catholic bishops, Lutheran bishops were appointed in their place. And so, Norway became Lutheran as the result of subjugation to the crown of Denmark.

At the beginning, Bergen was the center of the Reformation movement in Norway. Though at first opposed by the Catholic bishop there, Lutheranism, under protection of, and promotion by, the government, triumphed. The bishop had to retreat and left the city in 1535. After this fateful year Lutheranism met no serious opposition in Bergen. The Catholic Church was actually opposed by the nobility as they carried out the wishes of the crown. As the Reformation spread out from Bergen, the nobility again acted as influence in its favor. By 1540 the Lutheran Reformation was formally established in Norway.

SCANDINAVIA – SWEDEN

THE PETRI BROTHERS

Olavus Petri (1493-1552) brought the Reformation to Sweden about 1520. He had spent some years at the University of Wittenberg (1516-1519). His brother, Laurentius Petri (1499-1573), also studied at Wittenberg. During their stay in Germany, the brothers became ardent followers of Luther and his doctrine. Olavus returned to Sweden and in 1520 was ordained a deacon and made head of the regional Cathedral School. Olavus' office in the school, and also his permission to preach, gave him the opportunity to introduce Lutheran doctrine. And so, the Reformation in Sweden had its beginning when Olavus Petri assumed his duties. Olavus converted his arch deacon, Laurentius Andreae, to Lutheranism, who then became the second important Swedish Reformer.

SWEDISH POLITICS AND ECONOMICS

Politics and economics influenced the Lutheran Reformation also in Sweden. In 1520 Sweden, under Gustavus Vasa, began to revolt against Denmark. In 1523 he was elected King of Sweden, thus breaking from the Union of Calmar, that dated back to 1397. The new King badly needed money to pay the debts incurred by the revolt. What and whom could he tax, since two-thirds of Swedish land was owned by the Church, and the secular nobility claimed almost all the remaining land? To top it off, these two land-owning groups demanded tax exemption.

Prior to this time the King had already shown interest in the work of the

Petri brothers. When Laurentius Andreae, their co-worker, advised the King at a diet in 1523 to place the Catholic Church and its wealth immediately under the control of the crown by introducing the Lutheran Reformation, Gustavus took to the suggestion. The three Reformers were given positions of honor: Andrea became chancellor of Sweden, Laurentius Petri was made professor at Upsala. Later, in 1531, he was made the first Lutheran Bishop of Upsala. Olavus was placed as deacon-preacher in St. Nicholas Church of Stockholm.

King Gustavus proceeded slowly in setting the Reformation in place lest he rile the peasants, who were strongly entrenched in Catholicism. In 1527 the Swedish Diet at Westeras adopted a new Church law, which provided for a Reformation of the Church in the kingdom along the lines suggested by Luther in his *Open Letter to the Christian Nobility of the German Nation*. Previous to this, the King had already declared that all wealth of the Church must be at the King's disposal, and that holding back contributions to the royal treasury by the bishops constituted treason. However, after the decree of 1527 the King had legal basis for action against the bishops. Property was confiscated and bishops who fled were replaced with new ones consecrated by Peter Magnusson of Westeras, who had been consecrated by the pope. The apostolic succession was – theoretically, at least – maintained.

CONSERVATIVE LITURGICAL REFORM

Lutheranism enjoyed freedom in Sweden in this period of transition. Catholic bishops sought to have the Lutherans silenced, but without success. Olavus Petri was the strong guiding light of the Reformation all this while, until 1539.

A distinctive feature of Petri's Reformation involved religious forms and usages. While the Reformation in Germany and elsewhere sought to remove all of the Roman features that were objectionable, Petri (Swedish for Peterson) removed as little from Roman forms as possible, with the result that liturgical reform and development were held along conservative lines.

COMPLETION OF THE ORGANIZATION OF
THE LUTHERAN CHURCH IN SWEDEN

King Gustavus died in 1560. Afterwards there was an attempt to establish Calvinism in Sweden, and for a long time it was a strong influence. There was also an attempt to take Sweden back to the Church of Rome. But in 1593 the last brick was laid in the wall of Swedish Lutheranism when a synod adopted the *Augsburg Confession* as its doctrinal standard and chose *Luther's Catechism* as its handbook of religious instruction. In 1526 a Swedish translation of the New Testament was published – Olavus Petri probably being the chief translator. And so, the people could finally examine God's Word for themselves to determine which side was teaching God's truths. In 1529 a *Swedish Church Book* or *Manual*, followed by the *Swedish Mass* (Order of Service), were put into print.

SCANDINAVIA – FINLAND

THE LUTHERAN REFORMATION: A NATURAL RESULT

Finland had become a Catholic state in 1229 under the English Dominican, Thomas of Upsala. The spread of the Reformation to Finland was a natural result of its success in Sweden. Finland was a dependency of Sweden; therefore the Church in Finland, like the Church in Sweden, was a national institution. After 1528 the Bishop of Finland was obliged to swear allegiance to the Swedish King.

Michael Agricola was the hero of the Finnish Reformation. Agricola was one of eight students sent to study under Luther and Melanchthon at Wittenberg. Of interest is the fact that they were sent there by a Catholic bishop, Martin Skytte who, though he was Catholic, was favorably disposed to the Lutheran Reformation. When Agricola returned from his studies bearing Luther's recommendation, he became Bishop Skytte's assistant. Pietari Sarkilahti, who had been converted to Lutheranism while studying in Central Europe, had directed attempts between 1516 and 1522 to abolish the evils of Catholicism and establish Lutheranism. But it was Agricola, later ordained Bishop of Turku, who was the shining light of the Lutheran Reformation in Finland. An important vehicle of the Lutheran Reformation has always been the preparation of Scripture, prayers and hymns in the language of the people. Agricola accomplished this task for Finland, preparing an *ABC Book* in 1542, a lengthy prayer book (770 pages) in 1544, a translation of the New Testament in 1548, followed in 1549 by an Agenda (a book of church rites). He thus earned the title: "Father of Finnish Literature." After the *Augsburg Confession* was adopted in 1593 by Sweden-Finland, only the Lutheran religion was tolerated.

Footnotes for Chapter Three

1 L. Buchheimer, Editor, *Great Leaders and Great Events – Historical Essays on the Field of Church History*, (Concordia Publishing House, Saint Louis, MO), p. 285.

2 L. Buchheimer, *Great Leaders and Great Events*, pp. 285, 286.

3 L. Buchheimer, *Great Leaders and Great Events*, pp. 286, 287.

4 L. Buchheimer, *Great Leaders and Great Events*, p. 288.

5 Erwin L. Lueker, *Editor in Chief, Lutheran Cyclopedia*, (Concordia Publishing House, Saint Louis, MO, 1954), p. 155.

6 L. Buchheimer, *Great Leaders and Great Events*, p. 292.

7 Erwin L. Lueker, *Lutheran Cyclopedia*, p. 156.

8 L. Buchheimer, *Great Leaders and Great Events*, p. 296.

9 Lueker, *Lutheran Cyclopedia*, pp. 385, 386.

10 Lueker, *Lutheran Cyclopedia*, p. 386.

11 Lueker, *Lutheran Cyclopedia*, p. 386.

12 L. Buchheimer, *Great Leaders and Great Events*, pp. 312, 313.

13 L. Buchheimer, *Great Leaders and Great Events*, p. 312.

14 L. Buchheimer, *Great Leaders and Great Events*, p. 317.

15 Neelak Tjernagel, *Henry VIII and the Lutherans – A Study of Anglo-Lutheran Relations from 1521 to 1547*, (Concordia Publishing House, Saint Louis, MO, 1965), pp. 250, 251, 252.

16 James Edward McGoldrick, *Luther's English Connection*, (Northwestern Publishing House, Milwaukee, WI 53226-3284, 1979), p. 200.

17 Lars P. Qualben, *A History of the Christian Church*, (Thomas Nelson and Son, New York, NY, 1942), p. 322.

18 Lars P. Qualben, *A History of the Christian Church*, pp. 324, 325.

19 Neelak Tjernagel, *Henry VIII and the Lutherans*, p. 253.

20 J.E. McGoldrick, *Luther's English Connection*, p. 200.

21 Johanna Johnston/James L. Steffensen, *The Universal History of the World, Vol. 8*, (Golden Press, New York, NY, 1966 Western Publishing Co.), p. 665.

CHAPTER FOUR

EARLIEST TRACES OF LUTHERANISM IN THE WESTERN HEMISPHERE

LUTHERANS IN WELSERLAND (VENEZUELA)

Columbus discovered Venezuela on August 1, 1498 while making the third of his four voyages to America. Settlement of Venezuela began in 1527 with the building of the town of Coro. In 1528 Emperor Charles V gave this portion of South America, which he called his little Venice, to Bartholomew Welser, to whom he owed such a large sum of money that he was unable to repay it. The Welsers, a company of bankers and traders, renamed it Welserland. They appointed Ambrosius Ehinger as manager and sent four hundred Spaniards from Andalusia to settle their colonial empire. In 1528 the Welsers empowered Hieronymous Walther of Leipzig to send out thirteen miners from their Saxon Erzgebirge. In 1529 a second group of miners, twenty-four in number, set out. In time, hundreds of Augsburgers were settled in Venezuela or Welserland. Most Augsburgers were Lutherans. In fact, there is evidence that already by 1532 the entire colony had accepted the Lutheran faith. The Catholic monastic order of Dominicans was sent to Welserland for missionary purposes but could not function because "the Germans had all become adherents of the new Lutheran doctrine." Lutherans also settled early on in other South American countries. A note of special interest is that Heliodorus Eobanus, the

71

son of one of Martin Luther's best friends, became one of the founding fathers of Rio de Janeiro, and Ulrich Schmidt, another Lutheran, helped to found Buenos Aires.[1]

After the Counter Reformation and the establishment of the Inquisition, most Lutherans returned to Germany. Those who stayed on in South America were either put to death or converted to Catholicism. The Welsers left Emperor Charles' "little Venice" after fewer than thirty years, for the work there was more difficult than they had envisioned. By the end of the 1550's the Lutherans were gone from South America. Attention turned to North America, with Lutherans settling in Florida.[2]

THE EXTERMINATION OF
THE LUTHERANS IN FLORIDA

Persecution of the Protestants or Hugeunots in France brought increasing numbers of these Frenchmen to the New World, where the French were already leaders in trade. Admiral Coligny, who had adopted the Hugeunot faith in 1557 while he was a prisoner of Spain and later became joint leader of the movement with Prince de Conde, decided to establish a place of religious freedom for the French Protestants. In 1562 Coligny sent out two ships under Jean Ribault, filled with co-religionists, to find a haven of refuge from persecution at Port Royal, Florida. A second expedition landed the same year and built Fort Caroline, five miles up the St. Johns River. Captain Ribault took possession of the coastal strip of Florida for France. In 1565 Ribault set out for Florida with a third expedition of seven vessels and six hundred persons.

When King Philip II of Spain (son of Charles V) heard about the French settlements in Florida, he was furious. Recall that the Line of Demarcation, drawn by Pope Alexander VI, had given North America to the Spaniards, who then claimed the right to control Florida and much of the North American Continent. King Philip soon undertook the extermination of the Protestants in the New World, for he didn't want a "nest of heretics" in his Spanish Domain. To do the work of exterminating the "heretics", King Philip chose an ardent Catholic and fierce persecutor of Protestants – a truly ruthless individual – by the name of Pedro Menedez de Aviles.

Many Hugeunots had been brought in to settle Fort Caroline. In August 1565 Captain Ribault finally arrived with his third expedition of additional Hugeunots and supplies for the Fort. But who were these people who were migrating from France to the New World? According to author Walter G. Tillmanns, writing in his article, "the First American Martyrs," quoted by *Liberty* magazine, these settlers were Lutherans. He claims that they were recognized in France in 1561 as "adherents of the *Augsburg Confession.*" However, their Lutheranism was mixed with Calvinism, so it was not the pure variety of the strict German Lutherans.[3]

On September 4, 1565, when Menedez arrived off the coast of Florida near Fort Caroline with a squadron of five vessels and a contingent of men, he found that Ribault had already arrived with his settlers and supplies. Due to low tide Menendez was unable at first to sail up to the French fleet, but later, during the night, he was able to approach his enemy. With a bullhorn in hand Menedez demanded to know who they were and what they were doing there. He further demanded to know whether the settlers were Catholic or Lutherans. Someone boldly answered, "We are all Lutherans and subjects of the King of France." Then Menendez revealed the reason for his own presence, announcing that he had been sent by the King of Spain to kill all Lutherans. The Catholics would be allowed to live and stay in Florida, but not the French Lutherans.

Instead of attacking the Protestants right then and there, Menendez moved down the coast and secured his fleet in the harbor of St. Augustine. The French followed intent on destroying the Spanish fleet. However, a sudden violent storm wrecked the French ships. Menendez later marched his troops back to Fort Caroline, which he attacked in the night and slaughtered 140 French Lutherans. Twenty-six Frenchman escaped and made their way back to Europe and informed the Continent of the massacre. Menendez went on with his bloody work. He turned south to find and dispatch the French survivors of the wrecked ships. When he discovered them he carried out his murderous intent on each group of Lutherans after they confessed their Christian faith and chose to remain true to their Lutheran Confession. By night 111 Lutherans had been put to death. Through October, Menendez journeyed up and down the coast of Florida looking for stray Frenchmen, whom he then killed. Author Tillmanns informs us that more than 900 Lutherans had been killed in Florida by Reformation day (October 31) of 1565. He also adds this interesting bit of information: Menendez tacked to each body an inscription that stated that the victims had died "not as Frenchmen but as Lutherans" (non por Francese, sino por Lutheranos).[4] Tillmanns also reminds us that these murders perpetrated against the Lutherans or Hugeunots in Florida mark the bloodiest religious massacre ever perpetrated on North American soil. Thus was closed the first chapter of Protestant persecution in the Western Hemisphere, a chapter which had its tragic sequel in the shedding of the blood of the Protestant martyrs back home in France.

In 1572 the boiling pot of Catholic hatred toward the Protestants boiled over, producing the Massacre of Saint Bartholomew. The adherents of Rome committed wholesale slaughter of the Hugeunots in France, beginning in Paris but soon spreading throughout the country. During this unspeakably cruel and indiscriminate slaughter Admiral Coligny, the Hugeunot leader, was assassinated. Already under Francis I, beginning in 1545, Protestantism was severely oppressed.

Finally, the French colonies in the New World were Catholic and were established partly for the purpose of propagating the Catholic religion. Many of the most enthusiastic and daring French explorers were Catholic priests. It would require a half-century to pass in order for Lutherans to again settle in the New World (in New Amsterdam). Even then they would not be completely free of persecution. Strangely enough, persecution would befall the Lutherans for a time from their fellow Protestants.

THE FIRST LUTHERAN PASTOR IN THE WESTERN HEMISPHERE – LUTHERANS IN NOVA DANIA, 1619-1620 (NEW DENMARK, NORTH CANADA)

The *Dagbog* or Ship's Log of Captain Jens Erikson Munck of Copenhagen, in 1624, contains the earliest reference to a Lutheran minister in North America. The Danish King sent out two ships under Captain Munck in 1619 to find the Northwest Passage. Munck went ashore on September 7, 1619 on what is now known as Fort Churchill, Manitoba, taking possession of the country in the name of the King. Bear in mind that the Mayflower, which brought the celebrated Pilgrims to America, did not arrive until November 1620. The chaplain of Munck's expedition was Rasmus Jensen, the first Lutheran pastor in North America. On Christmas Day, "we had preaching and communion; and after preaching we offered something to the pastor – some gave white fox furs for the pastor to line his gown. . . ." However, scurvy took hold of the men and on February 20, 1620, Pastor Jensen died and was buried in the frozen North. In July 1620 Captain Munck took the smaller of the two ships and with the two surviving sailors set sail, arriving in Denmark in September of the same year.

EUROPE HAS AN EYE ON AMERICA

WHAT DREW THE EUROPEANS TO AMERICA

Starting in the early 1600's governments of Europe had their eye on America and encouraged those of their citizens who possessed adventurous hearts to settle here. Four reasons can be given for their zeal to colonize America: (1) Empires in the New World fulfilled the European rulers' desire for power. It simply was easier to colonize America than to wage war in Europe. Colonization of America became a race for power. (2) The new land held out promise of wealth, which the rulers wanted to appropriate for themselves. (3) To some extent at least, a need was felt to plant the Christian religion in America, although much of the religion that was brought here at the beginning was Catholicism or extreme kinds of Protestantism. (4) There were economic considerations. It was envisioned that the colonists would ship home to the Continent a rich supply of raw materials at low cost and then in turn would depend on manufactured goods from the mother country.

SPANISH AND FRENCH SETTLEMENTS

The Spaniards settled in North America ahead of the French, establishing St. Augustine in Florida in 1565. (This is the oldest permanent white settlement in the United States.) Quebec was not settled by the French until 1608, and Montreal was not founded until 1642. Both Spain and France sent out missionaries, who not only preached and established churches, but also made important exploratory discoveries for the mother countries.

DUTCH ATTEMPTS AT COLONIZATION

Henry Hudson, while working for the Dutch East India Company, established Dutch claims along the River named for him. Like the French, the Dutch were interested in fur-trading. They also divided up the land and brought over farmers to work it. The Dutch first came to Manhattan Island in 1623, building the town of New Amsterdam on land purchased from the Indians. A Dutch Reformed Church was organized here, but many other religions, including Lutheranism, came to be represented. A settlement was later established at Fort Orange (Albany). Colonies were placed along the Hudson River and southward to the Delaware River. Naming their colony after their mother country, the Dutch called it New Netherland. The colony never attracted large numbers of settlers; consequently, it remained weak.

The Dutch did not fare well in their ability to stand up to the English, who very soon outnumbered them. What little foothold the Dutch had was finally lost to the English, who claimed that the land under the Dutch colony was rightfully theirs, since it was their own John Cabot who had discovered it. When the Dutch and English back home went to war, the Dutch colony at New Netherland was claimed by the English King, who in turn gave it as a gift to his brother, the Duke of York, after whom the land was renamed. England's claims to the land were bolstered by a fleet of ships sent to New Amsterdam. Peter Stuyvesant, a very unpopular governor with his people, was forced to surrender to the English Crown . At first the English tried to enforce worship according to the teachings of the Church of England, but unsuccessfully. The Dutch too had tried to mix Church and State, having attempted to implant their Calvinist Reformed religion by force in people's hearts, as we shall see in another chapter. As a result Lutherans suffered persecution from their fellow Protestants.

ENGLAND SUCCEEDS IN
PLANTING STRONG COLONIES

Although England too became interested in America, her first several attempts to colonize failed. One of the most celebrated failures was the attempt by Sir Walter Raleigh to establish a colony on Roanoke Island (North Carolina) 1585. A fortune was spent and lost there. The first attempt failed when the settlers were driven back to England by starvation and hostile Indians. The second attempt failed too, when the colonists disappeared without a trace, the fabled "Lost Colony." Eventually, rich merchants of London formed the London Company for the purpose of furnishing transportation to and from America for the colonists and their produce. The name was later changed to the Plymouth Colony. In 1607 the company gathered and sent out its first group of colonists. Upon landing, they built the Jamestown settlement. This colony was almost a disaster like the others, but assistance and additional people sent over from England finally enabled it to survive, and with it, England's roots in America.

The English colonies were Protestant. Many of the English settlers came to America for the sake of their religion; they wanted to practice it in peace. For example: there was a group of Englishmen who had left the Church of England, earning for themselves the name Separatists. Often called Pilgrims, they had gone to Holland in order to enjoy freedom of worship. Later, they decided to settle in America, and in 1620 they landed at the place where Plymouth, Massachusetts, stands today.

In 1628 some Puritans — so named because they sought to purify religion by very strict adherence to the Mosaic Law — settled at Salem, Massachusetts. In another two years Boston was founded by a larger group of Puritans. For many years people other than Puritans were discouraged from living in this part of New England, for the Puritans did not grant freedom of worship.

Maryland was formed out of a grant given to an English Catholic, George Calvert, to whom the King of England owed a sum of money. Calvert died before he could establish a colony which would grant religious asylum to Catholics who were persecuted in England. His son, who inherited the grant, did build such a colony, and since he granted religious liberty to all religions, many Protestant settlers were also attracted to Maryland. Ultimately Protestants formed the majority.

Colonies in Connecticut were eventually formed by settlers who were embittered by the harsh Puritanical laws and penalties in Massachusetts. Some English colonies were established primarily for the purpose of having a place to worship where Church and State were kept separate, and where religious liberty was a right guaranteed to all people. Roger Williams, who was banished by the Puritans in Massachusetts, founded such a colony, which later became known as Rhode Island.

William Penn established a colony in America to grant religious freedom to all who pursued it. This land, now constituting the States of Pennsylvania and Delaware, was given him by the government of England as payment of a debt owed to his father. In 1681, with the arrival of a group of Quakers, a "holy experiment" was begun that established equal rights and freedom in regards to religion. The following year, Penn himself arrived in America and brought others with him. Philadelphia was established as the capital. Penn advertised his colony in Europe, with the result that in time many non-English settlers arrived. Lutherans who migrated to America came in greatest numbers to Pennsylvania, subsequently causing it to become an important center of Lutheranism in colonial times.

The last English colony to be established was Georgia. In 1733 James Oglethorpe founded the town of Savannah. Since religious freedom was given to all, many people, of various nationalities, were attracted there.

By this time England had a chain of colonies down the Eastern Cost of America, from Maine to Georgia.

LUTHERANISM ARRIVED BY WAY OF THE SWEEDES

A commercial company of Swedes settled on land south of the Dutch colony. In 1638, fifteen years after the Dutch landed on Manhattan Island, the Swedes built Fort Christiana (Christina) on the Delaware River. Later, they built other trading posts and forts. But the Dutch resented this Swedish infringement on what was considered Dutch soil, so Peter Stuyvesant captured the fort from the Swedes in 1655. However, nine years later the English seized New Netherlands and thus gained New Sweden as their colony. Part of it was named for the English explorer, Lord de la Warr and hence was called Delaware. Many Fins had gone to Sweden to live. These, together with true Swedish stock, migrated to America. The Swedes and the Finns brought the Lutheran Church with them, and also the first regular Lutheran clergyman, Pastor Reorus Torkillus.

LUTHERANISM IN THE WEST INDIES AND IN GUYANA

Before we close the chapter we can make mention of two other areas in the Western Hemisphere which early on attracted Lutheran settlers. In the 17th century Lutheranism was permanently established in the West Indies. Danes and other Europeans settled on this group of islands, which then the Danes governed for two and a half centuries. A long succession of Danish pastors were sent from the homeland to serve the colonists' spiritual needs. The islands did not turn out to be a worthwhile investment of money and manpower, so Denmark sold them to the United States in 1917 for $25 million. They were renamed the Virgin Islands.

There was also a settlement of Dutch and German Lutherans in Berbice, present-day Guyana (located in the northern part of South America). Though granted permission by the government of the Netherlands to have Lutheran services, these Lutherans often suffered neglect; but then in 1890 Lutherans in Pennsylvania undertook the spiritual care of these people.[5]

Footnotes for Chapter Four

1 Walter G. Tillmanns, *The First American Mrtyrs*, (Liberty, November – December, 1969, a reprint from the Lutheran Standard, November 2, 1965, pp. 7, 8), P. 16.

2 Tillmanns, *The First American Martyrs*, p. 16.

3 Tillmanns, *The First American Martyrs*, p. 18.

4 Tillmanns, *The First American Martyrs*, p. 19.

Note: For additional information regarding the religious persecution under Pedro Menendez refer to:

Tee Loften Snell, *The Wild Shores, America's Beginnings*, (The National Geographical Society, 1974), pp. 42-53.

5 Theodore G. Tappert, *The Lutherans in North America*, Part 1, chapter 1 (Fortress Press, Philadelphia, PA, 1975), p. 4.

CHAPTER FIVE

NEW SWEDEN

THE FIRST SWEDISH COLONY

In 1609, Henry Hudson sailed up the river now named for him. Since he was employed by the Dutch India Company at the time, the Dutch subsequently lay claim to all the territory from the Connecticut River to the Delaware, calling it New Netherland. The year was 1614. Later, in 1623, Nassau was established on the eastern shore of the Delaware.

King Gustavus Adolphus of Sweden was interested in establishing Swedish colonies in America, and also planned to send missionaries to evangelize the Indians; however, his tragic death in battle during the Thirty Years' War prevented him from doing so. Nevertheless, King Adolphus' plans were later carried out. William Usselinx organized the New Sweden Company to expedite Swedish migration to America. Preparations for a Swedish colony were carried out by Axel Oxenstierna, and finally, under the leadership of Peter Minuit (who formerly worked for the Dutch), the first Swedish colony was established.

The Kalmar Nykel and the Fogel Grip anchored March 28, 1638, on the tributary of the Delaware named Miquas Kill (now Christina Creek). On March 29 a treaty was made with the Indians and a seventy mile strip of land was purchased along the western bank of the Delaware River. Minuit established Fort Christina two miles west of the Delaware at what is now Wilmington, acting out of deference to both the Dutch and the English. The first colony was conducted as an experiment. Peter Minuit, its leader, later perished at sea, and for almost two years the little colony, which was composed of only twenty-three persons, was alone. However, on April 17, 1640, the Kalmar Nykel arrived with a second load of colonists. With this group came the first resident pastor in the United States, Reorus Torkillus. Services were at first held in one of the cabins built by Minuit, and later, in 1641 or '42 a chapel was erected.

MORE SWEDISH
SETTLEMENTS AND PREACHERS

In November 1641 Herr Christopher arrived on the third voyage of the Kalmar Nykel to gain experience. He had charge of the colonists outside of Fort Christina, while Pastor Torkillus ministered to the people of the Fort. Pastor Christopher returned to Sweden two years later. Pastor Torkillus died in an epidemic four years after he began his work in America.

The Dutch partners in the New Sweden Company became discouraged after Minuit's death and lack of profit and therefore sold out to the Swedes, who then reorganized the venture. Oxenstierna induced various undesirables, along with forest-dwelling Finns to migrate to America. After five years Fort Christina was still a small colony, compromised of about one hundred settlers, who were unhappy to be there. And then John Printz arrived on the scene as governor of New Sweden. Printz, the son of a Lutheran minister was a huge man, whom the Indians nicknamed "Big Belly." He was an energetic man, who set about to get things done.[1]

Two sections of the instructions given Governor Printz are of special interest: (1) He should try to gain the confidence of the Indians and convert them. (2) He was to introduce proper worship according to the *Unaltered Augsburg Confession*, the Council of Upsala, and the ceremonies of the Swedish Church. The Swedes (and of course the Finns with them) were not to molest the Reformed Dutch. The Council of Upsala in 1593 had declared that the Bible is the "sole rule of faith," and that its doctrines were set forth correctly by the three Christian Symbols (Creeds) and the *Unaltered Augsburg Confession*.

Two clergymen came with Governor Printz in 1643 to convert the heathen: John Campanius and Israel Fluviander, the nephew of Printz. Seeing that Fort Christina did not give the Swedes control of the Delaware, Printz built Fort Elsborn in 1643 on the east shore of this important river. He placed Pastor Fluviander there as chaplain of the garrison the same year. After seven months Fluviander transferred to New Sweden and later, after Pastor Torkillus' death, served Christina until his return to Sweden in 1647.

The governor transferred the seat of government to Tinicum Island (9 miles southwest of Philadelphia) where he built Fort Nya Goetteborg and a residence, Printzhof. The two-story log residence for Governor Printz was actually a mansion, the finest dwelling for many miles around. No doubt a chapel was also erected. It is reported that a bell from Sweden hung there until the fire of 1645 destroyed the residence and chapel.

After Pastor Torkillus' death in 1643, Pastor Campanius served alone. A well-educated man, he translated Luther's Catechism into the Indian language in 1648. This was the first book ever to be translated into an Indian tongue. This work predated that of John Elliot, a Congregationalist who, after studying the Indian language for seven years, published an Indian Catechism, which then became the first book to be printed in that language. Elliot also translated some of the Bible into the Indian language. Campanius' catechism was not published until 1696.

Pastor Campanius' ministry was an active one. He lived at Upland (Chester, Pennsylvania) halfway between Tinicum and Christina. He could reach all the churches of New Sweden – Tinicum, Christina, Cranhook and Wicaco (Philadelphia) – by canoe. In 1647 he requested his recall, listing four reasons. Thus, after serving as pastor and missionary in America for about six years, Campanius returned to his mother country, embarking on the Swan in May of 1648. The same ship had brought his successor, Lars Karlson Lock at the beginning of the same year. John Campanius died in 1683. Two years before he left the American scene, plans for a new church building at Tinicum were drawn up. Logs and clapboards were purchased from the English. The belfry was set apart from the church. Silver cloth draped the altar. The church was dedicated in September 1646. The congregation held to the regular order of service which the Church of Sweden used.

TROUBLE WITH THE NEIGHBORS

After 1648 the Swedes were able to pay more attention to New Sweden, but the previous year had brought autocratic Peter Stuyvesant to be governor of New Netherland. The Dutch, who had previously built Fort Nassau, in 1651 built Fort Casimir. They also had a blockhouse on the Schuykill until 1647.

The English maintained a fort at Varkens Kill (Salem, New Jersey) 1641-43, and a blockhouse on Province Island in 1642.

The Swedes had sent out and landed eight expeditions between 1638 and 1648. The failure of the ninth expedition in 1649 with Pastor Nertunius was an encouraging sign to the Dutch, who were feeling the presence of the Swedes in the West. Dutch and Swedish relations became more strained. At this time there were about two hundred Swedish settlers.

When he was building Fort Casimir, Stuyvesant landed two hundred soldiers. More trouble loomed for the Swedes. The Dutch under Governor Stuyvesant, continued to make settlements in New Sweden. Governor Printz of New Sweden appealed for help to the mother country but none came. In October 1653, after failing to hear from Sweden, John Printz left the country, having placed his son-in-law, Johan Papegoja, in charge. The tenth expedition from Sweden – headed by John Rising and numbering 350 passengers – sailed in 1654 on the Oernen. Pastor Nertunius served as chaplain. On May 20th the ship arrived at Fort Elfsborg. The next day, Trinity Sunday, the ship proceeded to Fort Casimir, landed twenty soldiers and took the garrison, which then took an oath of allegiance to Sweden.

The fort was renamed Trefaltighet. Papegoja gladly yielded his command to John Rising.

Naturally, Stuyvesant was furious over the capture of Fort Casimir, but later the opportunity presented itself for him to get back at the Swedes. When the Swedish ship Gyll Haj (Golden Shark), sailing via Porto Rico, passed the Delaware and landed at New Amsterdam, Stuyvesant notified Governor Rising that he would keep the ship until Fort Casimir (renamed Trefaltighet) was returned to the Dutch. However, Rising did not act upon Stuyvesant's threat. His refusal to surrender, plus reports of encroachments of Swedes in Dutch territory moved the Dutch government in Holland to act. Two hundred men with thirty-six cannon sailed from Holland in May 1655. Six more ships were fitted out at New Amsterdam. Following a solemn service the fleet moved out on Sunday, September 4th. The Dutch sailed to Fort Trefaltighet and by the following Saturday it was flying the Dutch flag under its old Dutch name, Casimir.

Later, on September 25, 1655, Rising also surrendered Fort Christina to the Dutch. The colonists who wished to remain were required to take an oath of allegiance to Holland, while the others were given free transportation back to Sweden. Article 7 of the surrender read: "Those Swedes and Finns who wish to remain of their own free will in order to gain their livelihood in this country shall enjoy the right to remain with the *Augsburg Confession* and to have a person among them who shall be able to instruct them in its doctrine."

LARS LOCK, AMERICA'S
ONLY LUTHERAN PASTOR

Prior to surrender to the Dutch, Lars Lock was stationed at Christina; Peter Hjort, "a worldly and spiritually poor preacher," was stationed at Fort Trefaltighet; and Pastor Nertunius was stationed at Upland (Chester). Support of the pastors was encouraged by Governor Rising. He suggested to the people that they tithe their grain and cattle, "one-half for salaries and one-half for the erection and support of a school building and church."

After the Swedes' surrender to the Dutch, Pastors Nertunius and Hjort accompanied Rising back to Sweden, leaving Lars Lock behind to look after the spiritual welfare of the remaining colonists. Lock, who was from Finland, was then the only Lutheran preacher in the American Colonies. He lived at Upland and served as pastor from 1648 to 1688. (The last years of his life were difficult for Lock, who was incapacitated and unable to get around to his parishioners.)

In 1669 Lars Lock began to conduct services in the blockhouse at Wicaco, north of the Schuylkill where southern Philadelphia is now located. Thus it was that when William Penn selected the site for the present city of Philadelphia in 1682, he chose the site where stood a Swedish village and the Lutheran Church founded by Lock.

At times the life of Pastor Lars Lock was fraught with troubles. For one thing his temper brought him into conflict with Dutch authorities. And there were troubles in his marriage: his wife deserted him, eloping with an agent of the vice-governor. Lock married again but some were unhappy with his choice of a wife. And he was accused of breaking into his own house, which his former wife had locked up when she deserted him. Lock found himself in trouble when he married a couple without the will and consent of the parents and without publishing the bans. There were indications of opposition against his ministry by the Dutch Reformed Church, which of course was closely allied with the governing powers. Furthermore, in 1669, Lock was among those who were accused of leading a movement to return the country to Sweden. He was fined 600 and 800 gulden. But while Lock was not on good terms with the government or the Reformed Church, he was however held in esteem by his parishioners.

Abelius Zetskorn, who was sent over as a replacement for Pastor Gutwasser, who had been banished by the Dutch from New Amsterdam, was sent to Delaware to minister to the German and Dutch Lutherans at New Amstel in order to satisfy their desire for a pastor. New Amstel was in danger of being taken over by the English. Lock ordained Zetzkorn in 1663. When the two pastors found that they could not agree on some matters, Lock retained the north field and Zetzkorn served the one in the south.

Before the end of 1663 the West India Company yielded all of New Sweden to Amsterdam, but the following year the English took possession. Under English rule religious freedom was granted upon the taking of an oath. The immigration of Swedes and Finns was encouraged by the government.

TWO CONSECRATED LAYMEN
HOLD THE CHURCH TOGETHER

In 1667 a new church was built at Cranhook near the confluence of the Delaware River and Christina Creek. This church served the southern field, while Tinicum Church (1646) served the northern field. In 1669 Lock was joined by Pastor Jacob Fabritius – another misfit – who was then licensed to carry on pastoral duties. Lock served to the north and Fabritus to the south. The latter had commended himself to the Lutherans in Amsterdam for pastoral work in America, and after arriving in the Colonies in 1669 was licensed by the governor for the ministry. He began his work in New York but within a year his congregation complained about his strange conduct. In 1671 the new pastor, Bernard Arnzius was installed as Fabritius' successor, who then moved to the Delaware. Arnzius served until his death in 1691. Fabritius served the congregations of Philadelphia and Tinicum, Pennsylvania, on the upper Delaware, and Lock concentrated his ministry to the congregations on the lower Delaware – Wilmington and new Castle, Delaware. Lock was chronically plagued with ill health. After a time, Fabritius again found himself in trouble, both with the law (for conduct unbecoming a minister) and with his congregations, whose parishioners complained that he didn't preach to them in Swedish – a language he was slow to learn – but rather in German. Still, less than a decade later the people commended him for pure doctrine and for leading an exemplary life. Regarding Fabritius' pastorate in Philadelphia: This small settlement had developed to the extent that it proposed to erect a blockhouse to serve as a church and a place of refuge. This occurred under the rule of Governor Printz. When Fabritius began his ministry here he thus became the first pastor of the first church in present Philadelphia.

In 1685 Pastor Fabritius became blind, and yet, after the death of Lars Lock in 1688, he served the whole parish with the assistance of two outstanding laymen: Karl Christoph Springer and Andreas Bengsten, who served as readers in the churches. When Pastor Fabritius died in 1696 these two laymen were largely responsible for maintaining the Lutheran Church on the Delaware. They conducted the services and read sermons to the people.

A DEARTH OF LUTHERAN PASTORS

Pastor Fabritius retired from the ministry in 1691, the same year that Pastor Arnzius died. It would be another six years before the American Colonies would once again have active Lutheran pastors on the scene. Furthermore, it can be noted that for almost ten years the Lutherans on the Delaware were without adequate pastoral care. The two laymen mentioned above pleaded with the Lutheran Consistory in Amsterdam for pastors, but no help came. A nephew of Governor Printz, Andreas Printz, while traveling through the New World stumbled upon his Swedish countrymen and reported their condition to King Charles XI. In answer to official inquiry, Karl Springer (one of the lay readers) wrote in 1693 that there were 919 Lutherans on the Delaware and requested two pastors together with Swedish Bibles, catechisms, and other essential books. It should be noted that several earlier requests had been sent to Sweden, but with no results.

Finally, however, help did come. Adreas Rudman, Eric Tobias Bjorch, and Jonas Aureen Bhosen – supplied with thirty Bibles, six postils, two agendas, and one hundred hymnals, plus other books – arrived at Philadelphia, June 29, 1697. But it took intervention on the part of Sweden's King to bring this about. Pastor Rudman took charge of the upper field, shepherding the Lutherans in Philadelphia, while Pastor Bjork took charge of the lower field, being stationed at Wilmington. Pastor Aureen eventually went to Maryland to work among the Indians. From this time, the Church in Sweden considered the Swedish congregations in America as missions. Later on, Pastor Rudman served the Lutherans on the Hudson for more than a year, but then, due to ill health, went into semi-retirement, returning to Philadelphia.

Though the Lutheran Church suffered many setbacks, especially through shortages of properly trained and consecrated clergy, and while there was much to be desired on the church scene, nevertheless the Swedes as a people managed to establish themselves firmly in the colony. William Penn, the proprietor of the colony (1683) thought highly of the Swedes and gave them seats in councils of the colony. The Church territory was organized under provosts, who were to supervise it under the direction of the Church in Sweden. The first provost was A. Sandel, 1702.

The Swedes built some fine church buildings in the years following the arrival of the new pastors. One of these buildings – now Trinity Church – is located at Wilmington, Delaware. The other is Gloria Dei – built at Wicaco or Philadelphia and known as "old Swedes." For many years these churches were the finest and largest public buildings in America. Sad to report, they are no longer Lutheran, for the congregations were assimilated by the Episcopal Church.

THE SWEDISH LUTHERAN CHURCH DISINTEGRATES

THE CAUSE OF DISINTEGRATION

Several reasons have been given for the failure of the Swedish Lutheran Church to establish a firm and lasting foothold in America in the colonial period: (1) The peculiar relation of the American churches to the State Church of Sweden. The State Church regarded the Swedish Church in America as a perpetual missionary outpost, instead of as a Lutheran Church that had been transplanted. (2) Lack of self-government. (3) Lax discipline. (4) Short pastorates. The pastors for the most part regarded themselves as temporary missionaries waiting for more advantageous placement back in the home country. (5) Association with the Episcopalians. (6) Lack of juvenile training.

THE SWEDISH LUTHERANS AND THE EPISCOPALIANS

The Swedish State Church looked upon the Anglican (Episcopal) Church as a sister Church. Hence the Episcopalians were looked upon as brothers. Pastor Rudman, for example, served for over a year as Episcopalian pastor in Philadelphia. In 1737 Pastor Dylander of Gloria Dei served the Episcopalians as well as the Lutherans. Bear in mind that the Episcopalian Church had been established in America for a long time, having come to Virginia in 1607. The pastors of both denominations were on very friendly terms, which was evidenced in their exchanging of pulpits and in carrying on other acts of fellowship.

A failure on the part of the Swedish pastors was that they did not strive to learn English. However, the young people became fluent in the language of the nation that came to rule the American Colonies and therefore were attracted to the worship services of the Episcopal Church. The Swedes had no systematic training of the youth in the colonies and there were no Christian Day Schools. It is no wonder then that so many of the Swedish young people grew up outside the Swedish Lutheran Church.

From 1742 to 1846 the absorption of the Swedes by the Episcopal Church was common place. In 1742 Penn's Neck resolved that all services were to be conducted according to the *Common Service*, which is the service book of the Episcopal Church. We note that after 1789 there was no longer support given to the Episcopal Church in America by the mother Church, because the Colonies had broken away from England through the War for Independence.

By 1846 all the Swedish Lutheran Churches had become Episcopalian except the one located at Swedeville on the Schuylkill. This congregation still remains. But the New Sweden area, once Lutheran, now is the grave-yard of early American Lutheranism. The Augustana Synod (which will be reviewed later) – not organized until 1860 – gathered the largest number of Swedish immigrants into a Lutheran synod and kept them intact.

Footnotes for Chapter Five

1 Tee Loften Snell, *The Wild Shores: America's Beginnings*, (The National Geographical Society, 1974), p. 138.

CHAPTER SIX

LUTHERANISM IN NEW NETHERLAND, PENNSYLVANIA, MARYLAND, VIRGINIA, AND GEORGIA

THE SETTLING OF NEW NETHERLAND – LUTHERANISM COMES TO MANHATTEN

In 1609 Henry Hudson sailed up the river that is named for him, as far as the present city of Albany. He was followed by Henrich Christiansen who, from 1611 to 1614, opened the Hudson Valley for the Dutch, claiming all the territory between the Connecticut and the Delaware Rivers. He called it New Netherland. In 1613 Christiansen built the first dwelling for white men on Manhattan Island. New Netherland later came to be known as New York.

In 1614 the Dutch government gave the right of commerce and trade, as well as the authority to carry on mission work in the new territory, to the West India Company. This firm was organized in 1602 and was early engaged in the fur trading business. Between 1623 and 1624 the West India Company brought over to America about thirty families, whom they landed on Manhattan Island. Later, in 1626, Peter Minuit placed a settlement called New Amsterdam on the island, and this became the capital of the American Dutch Colony.

The Dutch Reformed Church was the official Church of the colony, with

Lutherans at first tolerated because of Lutheran communities in the old country. In fact, the Lutherans had helped their fellow countrymen establish the Dutch colony, since some Lutherans came to America with the early settlers.

Fort Orange or Albany was established in 1618. In 1623 Peter Minuit bought Manhattan Island from the Indians for an equivalent of $24. There he built Fort Amsterdam. (An interesting side note: According to Paul Aurandt in his book *Destiny*, Minuit paid the Canarsie Indians for Manhattan Island, but the Canarsies didn't own the island. They were only visiting there at the time. Their home was actually in what we know today as Brooklyn.)[1]

The patroon system was inaugurated which gave to the patroons or stockholders of the India Company a portion of land sixteen miles along the Connecticut River. The patroons were given this land because they were willing to bring over fifty families at their own expense and settle them in the new country. These people were not only owners but also rulers of their estates. During the Thirty Years' War in Europe, men from Northern Germany who were employed in Amsterdam, Holland, came to America and took employment on the estates of the patroons near Albany. Some of them became tradesmen and merchants on Manhattan Island. By 1653 there were about 150 Lutheran families in the colony out of a total population of 2,000 persons.

A few names that we should take note of: Jonas Bronck, a Lutheran, arrived in 1638. His name is perpetuated in the Bronx Borough of New York City. Laurens Andriesen lent the use of his home, located on the present site of Trinity Episcopal Church, to serve as the first Lutheran Church in New York. The Lutherans were formally recognized as a group in 1642. Jonas Michaelius was not a Lutheran but a Reformed clergyman and had the distinction of being the first pastor in the colony. The first church was built by the Reformed in 1633. Lutherans are believed to have settled along the Hudson River at least as early as 1637.

In 1648 the Church of the Unaltered *Augsburg Confession* on Manhattan Island was formed. This Lutheran congregation sent a delegation to the Lutheran Consistory in Amsterdam, Holland, requesting a pastor. These Lutherans had originated from a number of European countries, but by living in the Netherlands for a while they had learned to communicate in the Dutch language. A pastor was not forthcoming and the following year a request was again made for Lutheran pastoral care.

TROUBLE WITH THE REFORMED CHURCH

In 1647 Peter Stuyvesant was made governor of the Dutch Colony. Because of his narrow-minded, autocratic, stubborn ways, he was not very popular with the people, and became even less so with the Lutherans. Through the governor and certain Reformed clergymen – who were rabid in their Reformed views – the Lutheran Church eventually met with severe opposition. Again in 1653 the Lutherans petitioned Holland for a pastor, and in the same year petitioned the West India Company, stressing the fact that the Lutherans in America ought to enjoy the same freedom as the Lutherans do in Holland. A copy of both petitions was handed to Governor Stuyvesant, who maintained that in accordance with his oath he could tolerate only the Reformed religion. However, he was willing to grant religious liberty if the government were so inclined. The petition that was dispatched to Holland was entrusted to Paulus Schrick, but the same ship upon which he sailed also carried a petition from the Reformed domines (pastors) on Manhattan to the Classis or Synod of Amsterdam to frustrate the plans of the Lutherans. The Classis gave the petition to the West India Company, telling them to turn down the Lutheran request. In 1654 the Lutheran Consistory of Amsterdam resolved to aid the Manhattan congregation to secure a pastor and addressed the request to the West India Company on their behalf. However, the Company resolved not to permit a Lutheran pastor in Manhattan. The West India Company informed Governor Stuyvesant of their action and recommended that in the future he not accept similar petitions. The following year, in a display of preferential treatment, the Jews received permission to live and worship in Manhattan because of their support of the Company. Thus, while the Jews could worship according to their beliefs, the Lutherans could not.

PROTESTANTS PERSECUTED
BY PROTESTANTS

Up to this time, the Lutherans had been holding services with "reading, prayer and singing." After 1656 even this was forbidden by formal placard, which imposed a fine of 100 pounds upon him who conducted the service and 25 pounds upon anyone who attended. As a result many Lutherans endured hardship for the sake of their religious convictions. Some were even committed to prison on account of this unfair law. Stuyvesant, meanwhile, was rebuked by the directors of the Company for his severity.

The Reformed Classis of Amsterdam, not having heard from Manhattan since 1653, concluded that the Lutherans had abandoned their intentions and admonished the domines to employ all diligence to frustrate all further plans of the Lutherans. However, a short time later the Classis learned that the Lutherans had again requested privilege of public exercise of religion, and four weeks later learned that the directors of the West India Company had given consent to the Lutheran request. The logic in giving their consent seems to be this: If the Jews could worship, so could the Lutherans. Accordingly, on October 24, 1656, the Lutherans in New Amsterdam again requested Stuyvesant for permission for public worship, basing their request on the fact that their friends in Holland had secured permission for them from the West India Company. Governor Stuyvesant was rather taken aback but ordered that the Lutherans should be content with family worship until he had received further information.

THE CASE OF PASTOR GUTWASSER

On April 3, 1657, the Lutheran Consistory in Amsterdam extended a call to John Ernestus Gutwasser, who held the degree of Master of Sacred Theology. He was called to serve in New Netherlands and was ordained April 10th in the Lutheran Church at Amsterdam. But on July 6th of the same year, after Gutwasser arrived at New Amsterdam, the Reformed domines registered protest with the burgomasters of New Amsterdam, stating six reasons why the authorities should not permit Gutwasser to remain in America. When asked by the council of burgomasters why he had come, Pastor Gutwasser replied that he had been sent by the Lutheran Consistory to minister to the Lutherans. His case was then referred to Stuyvesant. In the meanwhile Gutwasser was not permitted to preach or hold services. The Dutch domines in a letter to the Classis stated: "In the meantime, however, we have the snake in the bosom."

Friends of Gutwasser were successful in hiding him at a farmer's house and supported him with $2.40 a week. However, after a time the idle pastor became ill and had to be brought to New Amsterdam for treatment. The authorities ordered that as soon as he recovered he was to be sent back to Holland. But according to the letters of the trouble-making Megapolensis and Drisius in 1659, Gutwasser had begun to hold meetings and to preach. He was arrested several times, and after battling overwhelming odds returned to Holland on June 19, 1659.

THE LUTHERANS PETITION
FOR ANOTHER MINISTER

Undaunted by the government's actions against Pastor Gutwasser, the congregations of New Amsterdam – Manhattan, Long Island, Fort Orange, and colonies around – again petitioned to have their own Lutheran pastor. The petition was signed with seventy signatures. The Dutch West India Company urged the Manhattan domines to make concessions to the Lutherans. The domines, however, insisted that the Lutherans use a form of baptism which required the parents to acknowledge the doctrine taught in the Reformed Church to be the correct one. As it turned out, it was not the Lutherans who yielded. The domines finally consented to the Lutherans using their own baptismal formulary.

On July 20, 1659 the Lutherans sent a letter to the Lutheran Consistory at Amsterdam asking for another pastor, while at the same time the Classis of Amsterdam pleaded with the directors of the Company to prohibit the conventicles or privately held services of the Lutherans in New Amsterdam. Governor Stuyvesant again placarded the town forbidding all services except that of the Reformed Church, at a fine of 50 gulden for the first, 100 gulden for the second, and 200 gulden for the third offense – certainly, not small amounts. The English Quaker, John Browne, refusing to pay the fine, was sent to Holland for punishment. This caused the directors of the Company to once again rebuke Stuyvesant.

On October 12, 1662, Abelius Zetskorn – a ministerial candidate – landed and began to minister to the Lutherans. Governor Stuyvesant, however, made him go to the Swedes in the Dutch settlement of New Amstel on the Delaware. There he was ordained by Lars Lock in 1663.

FREEDOM TO WORSHIP
COMES WITH THE ENGLISH

By 1663 the Lutherans began to weaken; hence a Dutchman by the name of Hendrick Bosch addressed the Consistory in his own name for help for the Lutherans. In 1664 New Netherland was taken by the English. In the same year Charles II of England gave the New Netherland territory to his brother, James, the Duke of York. James subsequently sent an expedition out under Col. R. Nicholls, to whom the Dutch in New Netherlands surrendered, since they no longer supported Governor Stuyvesant. Article 8 of the Surrender granted the Dutch inhabitants freedom of conscience in worship and in church discipline. Fearing that they were not included, the Lutherans petitioned Col. Nicholls for a special charter, which was granted December 6, 1664. This charter, which specifically granted freedom to practice the Lutheran faith, is still in existence.

Two days after the granting of the charter the Lutherans issued a call for a pastor. After calling two men in vain, the Amsterdam Consistory commissioned Jacob Fabritius (whom we have already mentioned), who then arrived in New York in February 1669. A house that had once been, among other things, a tavern, was acquired by the Lutheran congregation for a church. The members of the congregation became dissatisfied with Fabritius, whom they found to lack tact and discretion and to have odd ways. Fabritius left for the South River and eventually married the widow of a tavern keeper. His successor, Bernhardus Arenzius, arrived in August 1671. He was able to smooth out the difficulties in the congregation and was given a regular pastoral call. An unsuccessful attempt was made to induce the Swedes to help the Lutherans in New York build a church building.

In 1673 the Hudson River region was again in the hands of the Dutch. New York was changed to New Orange. Fortunately, the Lutherans were permitted to have their own church services. When the city was prepared to meet a siege, the Dutch tore down their church, since it stood in the way of the cannon fire. But the Lutherans were given replacement property just inside the new wall. The deed for this property, dated May 22, 1674, is the oldest deed for Lutheran property in America. On this piece of ground a small wooden church and parsonage were built in 1674.

Pastor Arenzius served Manhattan and Albany, where a church had been built in 1674. It is reasonable to assume that he also served the Lutherans at Loonenburgh (Athens, NY) and Hackensack (Teaneck, NJ) and that he ministered to other scattered groups of Lutherans along the Hudson, and in New Jersey. Arenzius was an uncompromising Lutheran and continued working in New York until his death in 1691.

NO LUTHERAN PASTOR

For more than ten years there was no Lutheran pastor on the Hudson. Though the New York Lutherans appealed to the Lutheran Consistory at Amsterdam in 1696 and again in 1700, no pastor was sent. Rumors of the church building program on the Delaware reached the New York Lutherans, who then addressed a letter to Pastor Andrew Rudman in September 1701, requesting him to serve them. Pastor Rudmam had arrived in 1697 along with Eric Bjork to shepherd the Lutherans on the Delaware, having been sent over to America by the Church in Sweden. A second appeal reached Rudman from the New York Lutherans in March of the following year. Having installed Andreas Sandel as his successor on July 7th, Rudman left for New York and there found matters in a chaotic condition.

Having been weakened by a yellow fever attack in 1703, and no longer physically capable of such a vast parish, Rudman decided to secure the services of a young German theologian who had been attending his services at Wicaco. He then returned to Philadelphia, where he went into semi-retirement. His able successor, Justus Falkner, was one of two brothers. The older brother, Daniel, had come to America in 1694 and had established himself in the backwoods near Germantown, Pennsylvania. In 1703 he organized the first permanent German Lutheran congregation in Pennsylvania, at Hannover or Falkner's Swamp. Justus Falkner had studied theology at Leipzig and Halle, finally coming to America in 1700, where he too lived in the backwoods. When the call was extended to him he was at first hesitant to accept, but finally was persuaded through reassuring letters from Rudman to enter the ministry.

Justus Falkner was ordained in Gloria Dei Church on November 24, 1703. This was probably the first ordination service of a Lutheran clergyman in America. Pastor Falkner went to New York to take over his work in December of the same year. Of all the pastors that had served the Lutherans in America up to this time, Justus Falkner was by far the most able and devoted. The New York parish was very large, extending thirty miles south of Perth Amboy (near Brunswick, NJ) north to the Mohawk Valley, and west to the Raritan River. Pastor Falkner was notably conscientious regarding indoctrination. He was opposed to all unionism, that is, to uniting with heterodox churches for religious worship and fellowship. In 1708 he published the first book to appear from a Lutheran pastor in the United States. It was titled: *Thorough Instruction Concerning Chief Articles of the True, Pure, Saving Christian Doctrine*. After faithfully serving Lutherans of various nationalities, Pastor Falkner died in 1723.

THE GERMAN IMMIGRATION
TO NEW YORK

Until now, the Lutherans in New York were chiefly Dutch. However, under Joshua Kochertal, a Lutheran pastor from Landau, Bavaria, a strong German migration to America began. Bear in mind that unlike the

English, the Dutch, the Swedes, and the French, the Germans were not officially in the business of establishing colonies in America. After the Thirty Years' War (1618 – 1648), Louis XIV invaded the Palatinate or German State along the Rhine River and persecuted the Protestants. From ten to twenty Germans living in Palatinate in the cities of Hesse, Baden, and Wuerttemberg came to London, having received permission to emigrate to the New World. Queen Anne favored them. Pastor Kochertal made arrangements already in 1704 in London to emigrate with a group of Germans to America. Finally, in 1708 he sailed with 53 souls to New York. These Germans were actually bond servants of the English and settled on the right bank of the Hudson, where Newburg is now located. Each member of the group received a grant of 50 acres, and the congregation, as such, received 500 acres.

Pastor Kochertal returned to England in 1709 to fetch another group, leaving the New York settlers in charge of Justus Falkner. In 1710 he embarked in 11 ships with 3,000 souls; however, 800 of these died while enroute. Each of the survivors of the trip received forty acres at the foot of the Catskills, about 100 miles north of New York. Settling on both sides of the Hudson, they called their settlements East and West Camp. Kochertal lived at West Camp, serving this congregation and the Schohari Valley until his death, December 27, 1719. Pastor Falkner took over Kochertal's work, but the grossly overworked pastor suffered the loss of his health and died in 1723 at the age of fifty-one years.

ENGLISH CRUELTY TO THE GERMANS

The English governor, Hunter, was very cruel to the Germans. Taskmasters were placed over them to force the people to make tar, even though Hudson trees were not really suitable for this purpose. A mutiny occurred in 1712 with the result that fifty families left for the Mohawk Valley, where they obtained land from the Indians and founded the Schoharie congregation. Two prominent laymen among them will be remembered. They were John Konrad Weiser and his son of the same name. The latter became the father-in-law to Henry Muhlenberg, who is called the "Patriarch of the Lutheran Church in America." We will learn more of him in the next chapter.

To obtain clear title to the land, Weiser went to England, but was maltreated and unsuccessful in his venture. Instead of seeing the queen, he landed in jail. As a result of his failure, 33 families left Schoharie and settled in Tulpenhocken, Pennsylvania in 1723. Reports of the unjust treatment of the Germans in New York circulated in Germany so that the main stream of immigrants was diverted to Pennsylvania, with Philadelphia becoming the chief port of entry.

The successors of Pastor Kochertal were: Justus Falkner, until 1723; Daniel Falkner, until 1725; William C. Berkenmeyer, until 1742; and Peter N. Sommer, until 1788. Pastor Sommer preached in 13 other settlements and baptized 84 Indians. He died in 1795.

TROUBLE WITH CLERGY PRETENDERS

After Pastor Kochertal's death no permanent pastor was available. John Sybrand of New York offered to travel to Europe at no expense to find a pastor and make a selection tour. He was then dispatched in 1723, carrying letters to the Consistory in Amsterdam from the New York congregation. In the meantime John van Dieren, a clergy pretender (he was neither ordained nor called) ingratiated himself with the New York Lutherans. As a result, in the spring of 1725 a document with twenty signatures was sent to Amsterdam canceling the call they had extended through John Sybrand. (Clergy pretenders also were sometimes called "vagabond preachers" for they roamed around here and there preaching and performing official acts for whatever money they could obtain for their services. The pretenders have even been called "freebooters", the inference being that they plundered the unsuspecting congregations by ingratiating themselves on the people for purely material gain.)

John Sybrand was successful in his venture. From the Council in Hamburg, the King of Denmark, and friends in Holland came substantial contributions. The Consistory obtained W.C. Berkenmeyer, a ministerial candidate from Hamburg, for work in New York. He was ordained in Amsterdam in May 1725. In England the document signed the same year canceling his call finally reached him. However, since the Consistory had not cancelled his call, he continued to New York, where he soon succeeded in having the pretender ousted. Van Dieren continued his agitation in other Lutheran congregations until Berkenmeyer, in a tract in 1728, exposed him.

Sadly, John Sybrand ultimately proved a disappointment. No results of his collections were felt in America. Furthermore, he presented a bill to the New York congregation which exceeded his actual expenses by $600.

On June 29, 1729, New Trinity Church was dedicated in New York. However, New York was not the extent of young Pastor Berkenmeyer's work. His parish, in fact, was huge, stretching for 150 miles; included were 14 congregations. These were: New York, Albany, Loonenburg, Hackensack, Raritan, Clavernack, Newton, West Camp, Tar Bush, East Camp, Rheinbeck, Scenectady, Coxsackie, and the Schoharie Valley. Here he baptized the infant daughter of Konrad Weiser, Jr., who 18 years later became the wife of the illustrious Henry M. Muhlenberg.

In order to put a stop to the religious activities of the clergy tramps such as John van Dieren and John Spahler, who had stolen a number of congregations from Berkenmeyer, the latter endeavored to have Sweden appoint a consistory in America. He also petitioned the King of England to legislate against all clergymen who could not obtain approval of said consistory. This consistory was never established; furthermore, the plan itself was not practical. And it was not the duty of government to dabble in the matter of clergy pretenders, who stepped in to fill the large voids that were created when the Church in the home country failed to provide adequate pastoral care to the immigrant churches. In the end, van Dieren and Spahler had to withdraw from the field.

CONTINUED SCARCITY
OF LUTHERAN PASTORS

In 1731 Berkenmeyer moved to Loonenburg (Athens, NY) to counteract the activities of van Dieren, who at that time still presented a problem. This move by Berkenmeyer worked additional hardships and hence a new parish was formed in New York and vicinity. The choice of a pastor for the new parish was given to Dr. Gerdes of the London Consistory. The congregation promised to support the pastor by offering a dwelling, heat, light, and accidentals. Candidate Michael Christian Knoll was ordained in London and sent to America, arriving in December 1732. John August Wolf came in 1734 to labor in New Jersey. Wolf was from Hamburg, Germany. The congregations he was called to serve had been under the care of Pastor Daniel Falkner, who was growing old and feeble. The congregations at first had sought help from the Swedes but were refused. With the arrival of Wolf, there were then three Lutheran pastors serving in New York and New Jersey – far too few shepherds for so many flocks of sheep. As it turned out, many Lutherans had little or no contact with a legitimate pastor, who had been properly trained and ordained.

Meanwhile a need was felt for closer contact between the congregations that had been established. In the Hudson Valley, a "fraternity of congregations" was organized in 1735. This is sometimes referred to as the first Lutheran synod in America. Notably, its first and only convention was held at Raritan, August 20, 1735, at which nine congregations, represented by delegates, and the three pastors, were in attendance. One of the chief reasons for meeting was to consider complaints against Pastor Wolf. In question were his charges for ministerial acts, his sermons, his moral conduct, and also his neglect of school and confirmation classes. This meeting did not develop into a true synod and no further meetings were held.

In time, more pastors arrived, but still the fields of labor were far more extensive than could be shepherded properly by the total number of those laboring on the American scene. A newcomer, Pastor Peter Sommer made Schoharie the center of his activity. Knoll was pastor at New York and also served Quassaick (Newburgh) and Hackensack, New Jersey. The English settlers filtered in and in 1750 dispossessed the Germans here of their property. Pastor Knoll continued in New York under increasing difficulties, due to the fact that he was to preach Dutch to a German congregation. Finally, he lost control and resigned in 1750. Some of the Germans split off and formed a new congregation. Knoll then went to Athens as successor to Berkenmeyer.

In the next chapter we will learn more of the German immigration and of the reinforcing of the Lutheran Church in America by such men as Henry M. Muhlenberg.

THE SALZBURGERS

Before we close this chapter we will make brief mention of an isolated case of German immigration which occurred in the southern part of the colonies at the time when immigrants were filing into New York.

BANISHMENT FOR BEING LUTHERAN

The Lutheran Reformation took swift hold in Salzburg, a province of Austria. However, in 1588 Archbishop Dietrich gave the Protestants the choice of coming back to Roman Catholicism or of leaving the country. Many left. After a time it appeared that Protestantism had been wiped out; however, the truth of the matter was that it continued in secret. According to the Treaty of Westphalia in 1648, the Protestants should have been granted the right to their religious convictions, but the archbishop would not tolerate them. The *Lutheran Cyclopedia* reports: "In the midst of winter (1685) a decree of banishment was issued, and groups of exiles, torn from their children, to say nothing of the loss of their property, wandered over the snow-clad mountains to Ulm, Augsburg, and other cities. The last edict of banishment was issued in 1731 on the pretext that the Protestants were fomenting sedition and rebellion. William I of Prussia received 20,000 fugitives, while a small number found refuge in the Colony of Georgia in the New World."[2] These Lutherans were faced with a terrifying decree orchestrated by the Catholic archbishop, who was also ruler of the province. He let it be known that he would rather have weeds than Protestants in his domain. The Protestants must return to the Catholic Church, or they must leave Salzburg. However, in the event that they chose to leave the country they would be required to leave their property as well as their young children behind. The year was 1731. The Lutherans had already been slapped with fines for not attending Catholic mass and for not abstaining from eating meat on Friday (cf. 1 Timothy 4:1-3). Lutheran leaders had been arrested and other means were also used to persecute these children of the Reformation to discourage them from practicing their faith. About 30,000 Lutherans refused to bow to the demands of the Church of Rome and chose banishment instead, having taken the oath of salt at Schwartzbach in August 1731. In winter the exiles marched northward across the mountains. Their plight attracted attention all over Europe. Wherever they marched on Protestant soil they were well received. Their religious zeal made a deep impression on the people who saw them.

Pastor Urlsperger of Augsburg became interested in the welfare of the exiles, thousands of whom settled in northern Europe. He interceded in their behalf to Pastor Ziegenhagen in London, who then interested the Society for the Promotion of Christian Knowledge, in the Salzburgers' plight. It so happened that in 1733 General James E. Oglethorpe founded Savannah, Georgia. Oglethorpe was interested in providing a sanctuary in Georgia for English debtors and "for the distressed Salzburgers and other Protestants."[3] The S.P.C.K. volunteered to provide transportation for 91 Salzburgers to Georgia, using money collected from Protestants in Europe. The 91 Salzburgers who were chosen to receive free transportation to

America sailed from Rotterdam, and after enduring a dangerous passage, arrived in Charleston in 1734. Others followed, so that a group of about 1,200 Salzburgers were dispatched to Georgia. The first contingent to reach Charleston, traveled on from there to Savannah, where they arrived March 10, 1734. These Lutherans proceeded on upstream, toward the northwest, for 25 miles to establish a colony on the banks of the Savannah River. There they erected a monument of stones and named the colony Ebenezer (Stones of Help). Two years later the settlement moved two miles east and was called New Ebenezer. Jerusalem Church was built in 1767. Each household received 50 acres. The colonists proved to be very industrious, well-organized people, who succeeded in farming in an area of poor soil and climate. They also produced wood products, among other things. By the time of the War for Independence, there were about 1000 Salzburgers living in Georgia – in Ebenezer and other parts. The War and the ever-moving frontier helped to cause the decline of the colony at Ebenezer. Finally, only the church was left to mark the place where the colony once existed.

THE FIRST ORPHANS' HOME IN NORTH AMERICA

With help from Europe, the Salzburgers in Georgia erected the first orphanage in America. Those who were cared for were not only orphans but also half-orphans as well as other children. Forsaken adults were also welcomed. George Whitefield, the founder of Calvinistic Methodism, and well-known evangelist, was greatly impressed when he visited the institution.

In summary: Georgia Colony, which was established as a place of refuge for those who were politically oppressed, became the haven of religious refuge for the Salzburgers, who brought with them a zealous faith, and intense work ethic, and a caring heart for the underprivileged and the suffering.

GERMAN LUTHERANS IN PENNSYLVANIA, MARYLAND AND VIRGINIA

PENNSYLVANIA

The Germans were surpassed only by the English in settling and developing our country in colonial times. The first permanent German settlement in North America was at Germantown, Pennsylvania during the period of August 20 to October 24, 1683. The settlers were Mennonites, and their leader was Franz Daniel Pastorius, who bought 5350 acres from William Penn and later purchased 22,377 acres more. Pastorius was the first to protest against slavery, which this protest dates to April 18, 1688. The Germans built the first paper mill in America in 1690, and Christopher Sauer established the first newspaper and printed the first German

Bible in America in 1743.

To the Mennonites – a sect springing out of the Anabaptist movement – must be added the Moravians, who founded Bethlehem and Nazareth. The Moravians were people in Bohemia and Moravia who followed the teachings of John Huss. The Moravians in Germany were influenced very much by the confessions of the Lutheran Church.

In 1747 Pennsylvania had 120,000 inhabitants, of whom 72,000 were Germans, who then accounted for three-fifths of the population. Benjamin Franklin wrote in 1753: "Of the six printing houses in the province two are entirely German, two are half German, and but two are entirely English. The signs in our streets have inscriptions in both languages, and in some places only German. In short, unless the stream of their importation could be turned from this to other colonies, they will soon outnumber us, that all advantages we have will not, in my opinion, be able to preserve our language, and even our government will become precarious." About 40,000 of these Germans were Lutherans.

Many of the Germans were redemptionists. The transportation of these people was paid for by persons in the American Colonies. Subsequently the immigrants had to redeem themselves by working for their benefactor until their entire dept was paid off. One-half to two-thirds of all German colonists to America between 1720 and 1775 came as indentured servants or redemptionists.[4]

The first German Lutheran Church service in Germantown is said to have been conducted by H.B. Koester, who arrived in 1694 with forty families. However, he had apocalyptic ideas and finally united with the Episcopalians, founding Christ Episcopal Church in Philadelphia. He later returned to Germany.

Daniel Falkner, who emigrated with Koester, organized the first German Lutheran congregation at Falkner's Swamp (New Hannover) in 1703. Daniel's brother, Gerhard, went to Virginia. Pastor J.C. Schulz arrived in Philadelphia in September 1732. A Lutheran Church was founded at New Providence, with the first entries in the church register dating back to 1729. A sort of union between New Hanover, Providence, and Philadelphia was brought about in 1734.

MARYLAND

The Swedish Lutherans settled here as early as 1645. However, the Germans did not come until 1727. Under Pastor Stoever, Jr., the Germans organized a congregation at Monocacy Valley in 1734. Stations were established at York, Frederick, and Baltimore. Pastors Hausheal and Kirschner were among the very early Lutheran pastors in Maryland.

The offer of cheap land by the proprietor of Maryland induced many Germans to settle here. Baltimore grew the swiftest and had the largest concentration of German Lutherans.

VIRGINIA

The Lutheran Church entered Virginia through the Shenandoah Valley and established the first congregation at Hebron in 1717. Gerhard Henkel was the first Lutheran pastor. While he was stationed at New Hannover, Pennsylvania, he and Pastor Stoever, Sr. served Hebron. The famous Henkels established the first Lutheran printing house in North America, at Newmarket.

A considerable amount of migration by the German Lutherans from Pennsylvania resulted in the establishing of several Lutheran congregations.

Footnotes for Chapter Six

1 Paul Aurandt, *Destiny*, (Bantom Books, Inc., New York, NY 10103, 1983 by Paulynne, Inc.), pp. 125, 126.

2 Erwin L. Lueker, Editor in Chief, *Lutheran Cyclopedia*, (Concordia Publishing House, Saint Louis, MO, 1954), p. 942.

3 E. Clifford Nelson, Editor, *The Lutherans in North America*, (Fortress Press, Philadelphia, PA, 1973), p. 34.

4 E. Clifford Nelson, *The Lutherans in North America*, p. 26.

* * *

Appendix

"America's Oldest Lutheran Church Celebrates Tercentenary"
Story on page one of the December 28, 1964 Lutheran (now Christian) News reported:

NEW YORK (December 6) St. Matthew Evangelical Lutheran Church celebrated its 300th Anniversary here today. St. Matthew, the oldest Lutheran Church in America, received its charter from Richard Nicolls, first English governor in New York, on December 6, 1664.

Dr. Oswald C. J. Hoffmann, regular speaker for the International Lutheran Hour and assistant pastor of St. Matthew form 1948 to 1963, was the guest preacher today for the second in a series of four Tercentenary celebrations.

Justus Falkner, Henry Melchoir Muhlenberg, first president of the oldest Lutheran Synod in America, Frederick Augustus Conrad Muhlenberg, Johann Christoph Kunze, Justus Ruperti, Johann Heinrich Sieker and Adloph Wismar, were among those who served as pastors of St. Matthew congregation.

Conservative In Doctrine

St. Matthew left the liberal Lutheran New York Ministerium in 1885 and joined the Evangelical Lutheran Synod of Missouri, Ohio and other states. A book published by the congregation commemorating the Tercentenary states: "The 'ancient Lutheran Church' in New York had been more conservative in doctrine and practice than the majority of Lutheran churches in the East. Even when religious life was at a low stage and rationalism and unionism held full sway, most of its preachers had been more faithful to the confessions of the church than their contemporaries. But the man who, in God's gracious providence, was to bring the oldest Lutheran church in America back to the Old Lutheran standards in all respects was Pastor Johann Heinrich Sieker. . .

"As a result of Pastor Sieker's outstanding testimony to the truth in sermons and article in Zeuge der Wahrheit the congregation left the New York Ministerium and, in 1885, joined the Evangelical Lutherans Synod of Missouri, Ohio, and other states.

Sound Lutheranism

"Now came the dawn of Saint Matthew's greatest power and usefulness—the congregation developed unprecedented strength under influence of God's Word, as preached by a man of such towering personality as Pastor Sieker. The strength was not merely numerical and financial it was a strength based on a foundation of spiritual knowledge and faith and love; Saint Matthew's in no small measure contributed to the growth of sound Lutheranism in New York, New Jersey, New England and on Long Island through its large donations towards the building of mission churches. . .

"The Christian training of the young played a prominent part in the ministry of Pastor Sieker. A separate school building was erected . . in 1879. . . The building had accommodations for some 300 pupils and housed both the church school and academy. Pastor Sieker and all of his assistants taught daily in the school, instructing the higher grades in religion. By the middle of the 80's the Sunday School numbered between 1,700 and 1,800 pupils. . . .

". . . There would be little challenge to any claim by Saint Matthew that it had no equal among Lutheran Churches in its support of missions and charities; and there is no argument at all about the reasons behind this support—evangelical appeals of Pastor Sieker and the Christian generosity of his members."

Many Nationalities

St. Matthew Lutheran Church moved to its present location when it merged with Messiah Lutheran Church in 1945. Rev. Alfred W. Trinklein, who began serving Messiah as its pastor in 1935, has remained as pastor through Messiah's merger with St. Matthew. A new school, representing the merged congregations, was dedicated in 1946. In 1952 the 200th anniversary of the founding and continuous operation of St. Matthew Lutheran School was celebrated. Dr. John W. Behnken, president of the Lutheran Church-Missouri Synod was preacher at the observance. In 1957 the congregation dedicated its present church building.

In 1953 Pastor Trinklein reported that racial and national groups represented in the congregation included: "German, Polish, Greek, Norwegian, Rumanian, Dutch, Irish, Slovak, Puerto Rican, Danish, Yugoslav, Syrian, English, Russian, Persian, Estonian, French, Japanese, Scotch,

Czech, Negroes, Finnish, Lithuanian, Chinese, Hungarian, Italian, Latvian, Swiss, Jews, Austrian, Spanish, Swedish, Armenian, Belgian."

The final celebration marking the 300th Anniversary will be on October 3, 1965 with Dr. Oliver Harms, president of The Lutheran Church-Missouri Synod, as guest preacher.

* * *

Thanks in part to Dr. Oswald Hoffmann, St. Matthew was served by a line of leading liberals such as John Tietjen, John Damm, and Ralph Klein who became professors at Concordia Seminary, St. Louis and later Seminex. St. Matthew teacher, Robert Schnabel, became president of Concordia College, Bronxville and then Valparaiso University. Herman Otten, Sr., the father of the editor of *Christian News*, was often president of St. Matthew. Today, St. Matthew has sold its property and its present pastor says it has about 30 members.

The historical record shows that Otten and not Tietjen, who was a vicar at St. Matthew, followed in the former conservative tradition of St. Matthew.

John Tietjen preached at a graduation at St. Matthew in 1955 while he was attending Union Seminary. Tietjen later maintained that Jews who died without saving faith in Jesus Christ could still go to heaven on the basis of their good life while Otten insisted that those who died without saving faith in Jesus Christ are lost.

Official Lutheran Church-Missouri Synod publications seldom mention Otten, *Christian News*, or any of its publications, including An American Translation of the Bible. Among CPH publications are *A Seminary in Crisis,* by Paul Zimmerman, published by the LCMS's CPH in 2009. It says nothing about the 860 page *Christian Handbook on Vital Issues* which *Christian News* sent to all delegates to the LCMS's 1973 convention. The book included documentation showing that the liberal majority at Concordia Seminary were promoting liberal theology. The 1973 convention in resolution 3-09 declared that the seminary majority's "Faithful to Our Calling, Faithful to Our Lord" contained "false doctrine running counter to the Holy Scriptures, the Lutheran Confessions, and the synodical stance and for that reason cannot be tolerated in the Church of God, much less be excused and defended (FC, SD, Preface,9)."

Seminex professor, Frederick Danker, who became the Evangelical Lutheran Church's leading Greek and New Testament scholar, wrote in his *No Room in the Brotherhood – The Preus-Otten Purge of Missouri* (Clayton Publishing House, 1977):

"Herman Otten, editor of *Christian News*, unofficial director of the Synod's decision-making process, and defined as 'a 20th century Jeremiah' by one of his adherents, called for the reelection of his Chief of Staff, J.A.O. Preus. Pre-writing even some of the resolutions, he defined hard-core heresy as maintenance of the following;

"1. Moses did not write the first five books of the Bible.

"2. Isaiah did not write chapters 40-66.

"3. Almah in Isaiah 7:14 need not be translated 'virgin' and does not refer to the Virgin Mary.

"4. The Book of Jonah does not relate historic fact.

"5. The sixth-century prophet Daniel did not write Daniel."

In 1965 Christian News sent Otten's Baal or God to all LCMS congregations and convention delegates. The second printing of this book has this statement on the back cover:

"Of all the religious papers and publications I receive, I rank Christian News among the finest. Herman Otten is an apologist of our time the like of which is difficult to find" (Editor, Guidelines For Today).

"Christian News is a religious weekly unlike any other in the world. Crammed with news articles, columns of comment, and book reviews photo-reproduced, as well as much original material, this Lutheran paper has the polemical fervor of a lost age of religious controversy." "Otten is largely ecumenical by adhering to an ecumenical thing" (National Catholic Register).

"For the *Christian News* is now without doubt the most influential publication in the (Lutheran Church-Missouri Synod." "It is an impressive record. Concerns which had been generated when the editor was still a student have almost all been validated by convention resolution: affirming a six day creation, a historical Jonah, an inerrant Scripture, Adam and Eve are real historic persons, etc. (*Lutheran Campus Pastor*).

"Somebody should rise and publicly thank Herman Otten for his brave fight. We all were sometimes not fully agreed with him. He has made blunders. But why was it left to a young pastor to speak where others should have spoken?" Dr. Hermann Sasse, one of the leading theologians of the Twentieth Century.

"But when historians assess power and influence in Missouri (Lutheran Church-Missouri Synod) in the '60s, no man right or left will be more important than journalist Herman Otten. Before the ink was dry on his final exams at Concordia, St. Louis in the late '50s, Otten was accusing his professors of heresies ... Although he was to influence the mighty Missouri Synod as much as any individual, he never became a certified minister. He liked his independence..." James Adams, religion editor of the *St. Louis Post-Dispatch* in his *Preus of Missouri*, Harpers, 1977

"Tough in print, but likeable enough in person" (*Christianity Today*).

"Feared firebrand of The Lutheran Church." "Tough in print, Otten is warm and friendly in person" (*St. Louis Globe Democrat*).

Rev. John Hannah, president of the American Lutheran Publicity Bureau wrote in the Fall, 2012 *Lutheran Forum* in a series "On the Fiftieth Anniversary of the Opening of Vatican II:

"Fifty years ago Christianity was at a crossroads. For example, in 1962 the Lutheran Church-Missouri Synod elected its first new president in twenty-seven years. John W. Behnken, who had led through World War II and beyond, retired and was replaced by Oliver Harms. Also in, 1962 Herman Otten launched *Christian News*, the single most influential medium the LCMS has ever known."

James Burkee, chairman of the faculty of Concordia University Wisconsin wrote in his *Power, Politics, and the Missouri Synod - A Conflict That Changed American Christianity* (Fortress, 2011, Foreword, by Martin E. Marty) under a photo showing Otten speaking to students at an LCMS college:

"Herman Otten Jr. founded conservative tabloid *Christian News* following his rejection by Concordia Seminary. He shaped Missouri conservatism with an impact magnified by his freedom from church oversight. Otten was the most significant figure in modern LCMS history."

Otten has often said that his former St. Louis seminary roommate, Kurt Marquart, was far more significant.

CHAPTER SEVEN

HENRY MELCHIOR MUHLENBERG: THE PATRIARCH OF THE LUTHERAN CHURCH IN AMERICA

EVENTS LEADING TO HIS COMING TO AMERICA

AN ATTEMPT TO SECURE PASTORS THROUGH THE UNIVERSITY OF HALLE

The Swedes in New Sweden had depended upon the State Church to supply them with pastors. The Lutherans in New Netherland looked to the Lutheran Consistory at Amsterdam for pastors and devotional materials. The Germans who came over and settled in Pennsylvania and the states to the south, at first depended upon missionaries sent over from Europe to serve them. Eventually, the Germans came to depend upon the mission school conducted by August Francke at the University of Halle in Germany to supply them with Lutheran pastors.

Under the influence of Philipp Jacob Spener (1635-1705), the new Prussian University of Halle became a stronghold of the Pietistic Movement, which became established in religious thinking in the late 17th and early 18th centuries. Spener was a leader of the more moderate degree of pietism.

[THERE WERE THOSE WHO] FELT THAT THE DOCTRINE OF JUSTIFICATION HAD BEEN STRESSED IN AN ONE-SIDED WAY, AT THE EXPENSE OF SANCTIFICATION, SO THAT THE FRUITS OF FAITH WERE OFTEN NOT APPARENT AND THE CONGREGATIONAL LIFE WAS CHARACTERIZED BY A DEAD FORMALISM. IN COMBATING THIS SITUATION A REFORMED LEAVEN WAS ADDED TO THE LUTHERAN [WORSHIP SERVICE], SO THAT THE FINAL RESULT WAS AN EMOTIONALISM WHICH DEPRECATED THE POWER OF THE MEANS OF GRACE AS SUCH AND STRESSED SPIRITUAL EXERCISES AS BEING MORE IMPORTANT. PHILIP JACOB SPENCER OF FRANKFURT BECAME A LEADER IN THE PIETISTIC MOVEMENTS, ESPECIALLY BY ESTABLISHING HIS CONVENTICLES. . . .GROUPS IN WHICH THE PIOUSLY INCLINED COULD EXERCISE THEMSELVES IN FORMS OF CHRISTIAN CONDUCT, ESPECIALLY BY AN EMOTIONAL REFLECTING ON INNER EXPERIENCE. PIETISM SPONSORED CHIEFLY THREE FUNDAMENTAL ERRORS: (1) THE CONCEPT PIETY IS SEPARATED FROM THE MEANS OF GRACE AND THUS PLACED IN A FALSE RELATION TO RELIGION AND SALVATION; (2) THE CONCEPT ORTHODOXY IS MISUNDERSTOOD AND MISAPPLIED, SO THAT INDIFFERENTISM WITH REGARD TO NORMATIVE INFORMATION FROM HOLY WRIT IS UNDERESTIMATED; (3) THERE IS ERRONEOUS TEACHING ON THE CONCEPTS SPIRIT AND FLESH. OUT OF THESE ERRORS GREW A CONTEMPT FOR THE MEANS OF GRACE, AN UNDERESTIMATION OF THE OFFICE OF THE CHRISTIAN MINISTRY, MIXTURE OF SANCTIFICATION AND JUSTIFICATION, CHILIASM, A FALSE MYSTICISM, AND A GENERAL SCHISMATIC ATTITUDE.[1]

From the University of Halle, now a center for the Pietistic movement, came pastors, teachers, and foreign missionaries, as well as highly educated, influential laymen, who then served Lutheran churches all over Europe. It was to Professor August Hermann Francke and his missionary school at Halle that the Lutherans in Philadelphia, in 1732, petitioned for a pastor. In fact, a pastor and two lay delegates were sent over to Germany, not only to secure laborers but also to collect money for mission work in Pennsylvania.

The delegates found Francke willing to send a pastor. But since America was under English rule he also felt it wise to communicate with Pastor Ziegenhagen of London, who was head of the Lutheran Church in England. Ziegenhagen insisted, among other things, that the Germans in Pennsylvania guarantee a salary for the pastor. Francke sent an application blank back to Philadelphia with the order that a regular call be issued by the Lutherans, with transportation costs and salary provided. Today, these things are routinely included in the calls our Lutheran congregations issue to pastors. But back then, the Germans in Pennsylvania balked at this demand and stated that they would not pledge a salary. They even complained that a written call implies mistrust, and recommended that the bishop ought not concern himself too much about material matters. (A little later we will include a portion of this letter, which was read by Francke to Muhlenberg.)

The collection by the delegates amounted to a fair sum of money, but it was retained in Germany by the church authorities. Thereupon the Philadelphia congregation suggested that the collected funds be used to send over a pastor for one year and to buy land to support pastors and teachers. However, Professor Francke replied that he could not promise anything since the Lutherans in Pennsylvania would not commit themselves. This made the Pennsylvania Germans indignant. They finally petitioned Pastor Bolzius in Georgia for a pastor, but in vain. They felt that Francke in Halle and Ziegenhagen in London, by their demands, lacked confidence in God.

COUNT NICHOLAS LUDWIG VON ZINZENDORF AND THE MORAVIANS

Counted among the Germans in Pennsylvania were the Moravians, organized by Zinzendorf (1700-1760) into colonies (e.g. Bethlehem, PA). His indifference toward doctrinal formulas and confessions of faith had earlier brought him into discredit with the Lutheran Church and the government of Saxony. Having been exiled from Saxony, he later came to America and began to work among the German Protestants here in the New World (1741-1743). However, he was opposed by the University of Halle. Zinzendorf lived at Germantown, traveled extensively, and preached his first sermon in a Reformed Church in Germantown. This interesting character vacillated between Lutheran and Reformed theology. At one time he conducted a conference in his house with Adventists, Baptists, Mennonites, Lutherans, and Reformed ministers.

The Lutherans in Philadelphia requested his services, and so he preached and administered the Lord's Supper, and because he did these things, he was called a Lutheran. Zinzendorf distinguished himself with the self-appointed title of "Inspector of all Lutheran Congregations in Pennsylvania." His vacillating between the Lutheran and Reformed camps can be seen in the fact that while he edited a Lutheran catechism, he also consecrated Reformed pastors and issued a Reformed catechism. (History repeats itself, for this same vacillating can be seen today in the practice of liberal Lutheran pastors joining with other Protestants in Ministerial Unions, exchanging pulpits, and holding special joint services – at times even with non-Christian religions and sects. Within most Lutheran bodies are those who participate in the modern charismatic movement, which actively promotes fellowship with all those who claim to have experienced Holy Spirit baptism, regardless of their doctrinal stand.)

Zinzendorf tried to organize his adherents into a Moravian Church in Philadelphia in 1742. Besides, he had eight conferences for the purpose of uniting churches and personally formulated the principles. His ambition was to organize all German Protestants into one large denomination. But the longer he labored, the worse affairs grew. Finally, because of increasing dissension, Zinzendorf and his adherents separated from the others and organized a congregation, calling themselves Lutheran. The disorder increased when a deposed Lutheran pastor, Johann Krafft arrived from Germany and ingratiated himself with a number of Pennsylvania Lutherans. He pretended to be a superintendent of the congregations in Pennsylvania and endeavored to organize a consistory under his control. This struggle for power by certain members of the clergy could only lead to confusion among the people and to the subsequent deterioration of the Lutheran Church.

When Francke in Halle heard of the activities of Zinzendorf, and especially of his attempt to unite the various Protestant groups, he got in touch with Ziegenhagen in London, whereupon the two men decided that something had to be done to save the Lutheran Church from total destruction in America. And so begins the Muhlenberg saga – the story of a gifted and dedicated preacher who, with God's help, did much to preserve and to plant the Lutheran Church in America and to bring order out of chaos.

MUHLENBERG:
THE MAN WHO WAS SENT TO SALVAGE
LUTHERANISM IN AMERICA

THE MAN AND THE TIMES

Lutheran historian, Abdel Ross Wentz, calls Muhlenberg "the right man in the right place at the right time." Muhlenberg is described by Wentz as "a fervent Christian and a firm Lutheran, strong in body and trained in mind, endowed with unusual tact and adaptability, a trained scholar who brought to the task broad vision and talent for practical affairs."[2]

Henry Melchior Muhlenberg was born at Eimbeck, Hanover, Germany on September 6, 1711, and died at the age of 76 on October 7, 1787, in Pennsylvania, after laboring here in America for 45 fruitful years. His father was a shoemaker and his mother was the daughter of an army officer.[3] During his youth, Heinrich or Henry attended private schools. Later, at the age of 24, he entered the University of Goetingen (1735). Muhlenberg later claimed that it was during his first year at Goetingen that he was converted to Christianity. After the deaths of his father, family friends – influential people – assured his continuing education. During his time at Goetingen, Muhlenberg taught clavichord for a year in the Harz Mountains and later earned his doctorate in theology. Early on, he became very much interested in mission work and therefore conducted his final studies at Halle University, the center for the Pietistic Movement. While at Halle he taught a variety of theological subjects, and also taught for 15 months at the Halle Orphanage school. Muhlenberg was chosen to be a missionary to India, but eventually someone else was sent in his place. From 1739 to 1741 Muhlenberg pastured the Country Church of Grosshennersdorf,

Upper Silesia, near Hernnhut.

While Muhlenberg was a staunch confessional Lutheran, his Lutheranism was nevertheless tinged with the Pietism advanced by the University of Halle. Thus he stressed to some extent personal feeling and religious experience, a characteristic of Pietism. Muhlenberg also at times showed a spirit of ecumenicity, which continues on today in a segment of Lutheranism that has its roots in the area of his labors. While in Germany, Muhlenberg published his only book, in 1741, a defense of Pietism against B. Mentzer. Some Lutheran pastors on the American scene were quite scornful of Muhlenberg and his fellow pietists.

On September 6, 1741, while visiting Professor Francke, Muhlenberg, who was celebrating his 30th birthday, was informed at the dinner table that God was calling him to go to America. Francke read the letter from the two delegates from America on the salary question. The letter is quite interesting:

WE ARE SURPRISED THAT YOU INSIST ON A SALARY FOR THE PASTOR WHOM WE HOPE TO GET, SINCE WE HAVE REPEATEDLY DESCRIBED TO YOU THE POVERTY OF OUR CONGREGATIONS. OUR PEOPLE ARE NOT IN A POSITION TO MAKE ANY DEFINITE SALARY PROMISES; NEITHER SHOULD A PASTOR BE MORE CONCERNED ABOUT THE WOOL THAN ABOUT THE SOULS OF THE FLOCK. TO INSIST ON A DEFINITE SALARY FOR OUR PASTOR WOULD SET ASIDE TRUST IN GOD, AS THOUGH A CALL WERE OF NO MORE VALUE THAN THE ALMIGHTY DOLLAR. A BISHOP SHOULD NOT BE DESIROUS OF FILTHY LUCRE. IT IS NOT OUR INTENTION TO LET OUR PASTOR STARVE. WE SHALL SUPPORT HIM AS WELL AS WE CAN. ON THE OTHER HAND, WE WANT A PASTOR WHO TAKES AN INTEREST IN US, NOT FOR REASONS OF MONEY BUT BECAUSE HE IS CONCERNED ABOUT OUR SOULS. WE LIVE IN A LAND WHERE MINISTERS CANNOT EXPECT TO LIVE IN A GRAND STYLE OR TO LEAD A PARADISIACAL EXISTENCE. BUT FOR ANY MINISTER WHO REGARDS HIMSELF AS A SERVANT OF CHRIST THERE WILL BE ENOUGH TO LIVE ON.

After some thought, Muhlenberg replied that he would go. Francke and Ziegenhagen agreed to call him for three years. His call was to the three vacant congregations in Pennsylvania – New Hanover, Philadelphia, and New Providence (usually referred to as The Trappe).

In December, Muhlenberg preached his farewell sermon and then left for England. King George II of England was from the House of Hanover, and his royal chaplain was a German, who then had Muhlenberg preach in German at the royal chapels of the Savoy and St. James.[4] Muhlenberg, a Hanoverian, was recognized by the Hanoverian Consistory, and made his journey to America under the protection of King George II, who was also King of Hanover. After a sea voyage of 14 weeks and 4 days – a voyage beset by hostile frigates, pirates, hurricanes, seasickness, scurvy, and overcrowded living conditions, Muhlenberg arrived at Charleston, South Carolina, September 24, 1742. As a favor to his Halle superiors, the young preacher visited the Lutheran colony of Ebenezer in Georgia before continuing northward to Pennsylvania. He finally arrived in Philadelphia on November 25, 1742, alone and friendless, unknown and unwelcomed.

At the time that Muhlenberg came to America, the colonial era was beginning to fade out. Eventually it would disappear entirely and be replaced with nationalism. The colonies were destined to become an independent nation. A new era was dawning for the Colonies and, hopefully, also for the struggling Lutheran Church. The Lutheran Church in America sorely needed the leadership of a man of Muhlenberg's character, demeanor, learning, broad vision, and many abilities (e.g. as a planter of churches, organizer, arbiter, and restorer of peace). He quickly showed himself to be the man for the times. Later, his work of organizing the Lutheran congregations into a larger unit (a ministerium or synod) paralleled the federal union of the American Colonies into the American Republic.[5]

The Lutheran situation in the Colonies at this time: There were Lutherans in Delaware, New York, Pennsylvania, New Jersey, Georgia, Virginia, Maryland, North and South Carolina. Among the genuine Lutheran pastors there were the following: In New York, Berkenmeyer and Knoll. In New Jersey, Wolf (who did not prepare sermons and later had to resign). In Pennsylvania, John Casper Stoever, Jr. (an untiring missionary for over 50 years). In Virginia, Klug. Among the Swedes, Dylander in Philadelphia, and Tranberg in Christina. In Georgia, Gronau and Bolzius. Among the vagabonds or pretenders who had ingratiated themselves in congregations, there were: Krafft and Schmit in Pennsylvania; Van Dieren in New York. There were also others.

ONE PASTOR TOO MANY

After his visit to the Salzburgers in Georgia, Muhlenberg had to travel by sloop to Philadelphia. A man whom Muhlenberg was told to contact informed him that the Philadelphia congregation had split and now had two pastors, Count Zinzendorf and another man, who had arrived recently from Germany. Muhlenberg journeyed to New Hanover the next day to visit his parish there, but when he showed them his call, they told him they already had a minister, Pastor Schmidt. They suggested a division of the parish and to have it served by both pastors. Muhlenberg's answer to this proposal was: "I have a call to this congregation and I am going to preach here Sunday."

Come Sunday morning, both pastors arrived, put on their gowns, and sat together in the first pew. At the beginning of the service Muhlenberg leaned over and whispered to Schmidt: "I'm going to preach my introductory sermon today." Schmidt gave his consent and Muhlenberg preached. Afterwards there was dissent among the people as to which man to keep.

On Monday, Muhlenberg went to his third parish, Providence. He presented his call to the elders, who then informed him that they too had a pastor. Since they had not received a pastor right away from Germany, they had engaged the services of Pastor Krafft. It was suggested that he and Krafft settle the matter between them. The next day Muhlenberg returned to Philadelphia and on the following day he met Pastor Krafft. The latter coldly asked him if he did not know that he was superintendent of the Lutheran churches in Pennsylvania. Krafft thought that Muhlenberg should first have talked to him before he proceeded to visit the parishes. But Muhlenberg defended himself and concluded by saying: "In the meanwhile I shall preach in Philadelphia Sunday." On the first Sunday, he preached in a stable in Philadelphia and also in Gloria Dei Church. Afterwards, Krafft tried to get him to take over another parish, but Muhlenberg stood by his three calls, which were to New Hanover (36 miles from Philadelphia), Providence (26 miles from Philadelphia), and to Philadelphia itself. Soon a fourth congregation, located in Germantown, was added to his parish labors. Muhlenberg centered his work in Trappe or Providence and obtained a home there.

THE STABILIZING EFFECT OF MUHLENBERG

The man chosen for the times met with very discouraging conditions and many hardships; still, he labored on faithfully, energetically, and with success. When Muhlenberg began his work in America he was the only Lutheran pastor in the middle colonies. The congregations were few and weak. In the winter time he journeyed through dense forests and swamps. Sometimes it took hours to travel only a few miles. He once wrote: "When there is only one hook in the house, everything is hung on it until it bends and finally breaks. So it is with me." As to the salary issue: New Hanover supplied him with the use of a horse. Providence gave him nothing, and Philadelphia did not give him enough to pay his rents. However, he was given produce from the farms. He once wrote: "One man brings me a sausage, another a piece of meat, a third brings a chicken, and a fourth, a loaf of bread."

Muhlenberg was considered a good preacher, and spoke in German, English, or Dutch as the occasion and circumstance called for. He did considerable work among the Indians, who also respected his speaking skills. They named him "Gachswungarorachs or "The Preacher-whose-words-cut-through-hard-hearts-like-a-saw-through-a-gnarled- tree."[6] Infact, Muhlenberg doomed the future of the clergy pretenders, the religious tramps, who posed as Lutheran pastors, by outshining them in preaching and in missionary and pastoral work. To Count Zinzendorf, who caused him much trouble as he went about his missionary labors, Muhlenberg spoke especially plain words: "I do not acknowledge you as a Lutheran, much less a minister." This exchange took place in 1748.*

Muhlenberg did not use his pulpit to further a political agenda or foster social reform. His single-minded purpose in being a minister was reflected in his personal motto, *Ecclesia plantanda* – "The church must be planted"; and he labored tirelessly to do just that, traveling from New York to Georgia, gathering the scattered Lutherans into congregations. Beside each church he built a school house for training the youth. He made conciliatory trips to New York and New Jersey, to Maryland and to Georgia, to restore unity and life to dysfunctional congregations or to restore peace between the pastor and the congregation. He was the general advisor to a large number of Lutheran Churches in America, and was the general counselor and stabilizer of Lutheranism in the colonies.

Muhlenberg reported regularly and voluminously to Halle. His reports were printed and circulated widely. As a result, men and money arrived in America. Through Muhlenberg's efforts quite a few pastors were brought to America. One of the most interesting of these was John Christopher Hartwick, an eccentric wandering bachelor, who arrived in New York in 1746. Hartwick did work in New York, Pennsylvania, Maryland, Virginia, and New England. Before he died he willed his estate for the purpose of establishing a seminary. Thus Hartwick Seminary was later founded. Muhlenberg personally trained one man after another for the ministry, being aided in this work by his intimate friend and adviser, Charles Magnus Wrangel. The first Lutheran pastor to be born, educated, and ordained here in America – Jacob van Buskirk – was instructed by Muhlenberg.

There was a pressing need for native-born clergy, and Muhlenberg recognized this need early on in his labors. Germany simply could not supply all the pastors that the influx of German immigrants called for. With the establishing of Hartwick Seminary in New York in 1797, the immediate need to fill new pulpits as they sprang up was better met. By 1771 there were well over 100 Lutheran congregations in America, many of which Muhlenberg had a hand in forming; and 81 of these congregations were in one way or another under his supervision. In spite of gains made in providing Lutheran congregations with qualified Lutheran pastors, nevertheless when Muhlenberg died in 1787 there were still not more than 40 Lutheran ministers of any kind in America. So much work and yet so few men to carry it out! Historian Abdel Wentz estimates that at the outbreak of the Revolutionary War, 75,000 of the 120,000 Germans in the Pennsylvania Colony were Lutherans, yet only a fraction had been gathered into congregations.[8]

THE FIRST SYNOD AND FIRST
CONGREGATIONAL CONSTITUTION

Through hard, diligent work and personal sacrifice, Muhlenberg was able to dedicate several new church buildings. Among them was Augustus Church at Trappe, named for Augustus Francke of Halle. Augustus Church was built in 1743 at a cost of $898.92, and still stands. It is used occasionally for special services and remains the oldest unaltered Lutheran church in America, perhaps in the Western Hemisphere. It was used for a hospital during the Revolutionary War and was visited by George Washington.

In 1748 Muhlenberg organized the first Lutheran synod. Participating were 6 pastors and 24 lay delegates representing 10 congregations. The group was called the Conference of the United Congregations. In 1760, the United Congregations grew into the Evangelical Lutheran Ministerium of North America. In 1792, the title read "Pennsylvania," rather than "North America." By this time a second Lutheran Synod had been formed, the Ministerium of New York (1786), formally organized by Muhlenberg's son-in-law, John Christopher Kunze.

In 1762, Muhlenberg formulated a congregational constitution of St. Michael's Church of Philadelphia. This constitution became a model for the Lutheran Churches in America. (The State Churches in Europe did not have such constitutions.)

MORE ABOUT THE MAN AND HIS FAMILY

Henry Melchior Muhlenberg was a highly educated man, who had been trained in medicine as well as theology, for the University of Halle offered both disciplines to the students. Thus Muhlenberg prescribed medicines and treated his members' ailments in addition to providing spiritual care. Wentz states that many Lutheran pastors were able to combine medicine with their prayers.[9]

A gifted musician, Muhlenberg helped to develop a hymn book and to formulate a liturgy for use in the worship services.

Henry Muhlenberg was not only famous in his own right as the Patriarch of the Lutheran Church in America; he was well-known also for his offspring, which have been called "a family illustrious in Church and State." In April 1745, Henry married Anna Mary Weiser, daughter of Conrad Weiser, well-known Indian agent, of whom it was said that he continually waged peace. Henry and Mary were blessed with three sons, all of whom were ordained to the Lutheran ministry and all became famous.

The oldest son, John Peter Gabriel (1746-1807) is best remembered for his part in the Revolutionary War. One notable Sunday he preached a sermon on Ecclesiastes 3:1-8, which ends with "A time for war and a time for peace." After the benediction, according to one account, he disappeared into the sacristy and a little later came out dressed in the uniform of a regimental colonel, the 8th Virginia Regiment. General Washington himself had made the request which resulted in Pastor Peter Muhlenberg being given the rank of colonel. (The Muhlenberg family friends included George Washington, Benjamin Franklin, and James Madison.) The pastor, now in the army, went outside the church and while a drum continued to beat, he proceeded to enroll a large number of men from his parish for the army. He and his men saved the day at Brandywine and penetrated the farthest of four columns into the British line at Germantown. They were at Valley Forge, too, which was located just over the ridge from the elder Muhlenberg's Trappe Church. Finally, when the victorious charge was made against the British at Yorktown that ended the War for Independence, Peter Muhlenberg led that charge. Later, he was a United States senator and also held other posts. He was Vice-president of Pennsylvania, with Benjamin Franklin as President. Statues honor Peter in Philadelphia and in Statuary Hall in the United States capitol.

A second son of Henry and Mary Muhlenberg, Frederick Augustus Conrad (1750-1801) was for a time pastor in New York and Pennsylvania. He entered political life and was a member of the Continental Congress. Frederick was present when the Declaration of Independence was read. He became Speaker of the Pennsylvania Assembly. From 1789 to 1797 Frederick served in the congresses elected under the Constitution. As Speaker of the House, he and John Adams, who was the vice-president of the United States and also President of the Senate, signed the first ten amendments to the Constitution, commonly known as the Bill of Rights. Frederick was the first and third Speaker of the House of Representatives.

A third son of Henry and Mary Muhlenberg, Gotthilf Henry Ernestus (1753-1815), labored his lifetime as pastor to Trinity Church, Lancaster, Pennsylvania. He was a writer and a botanist, who classified 100 new species of plants and grasses. He was considered the greatest botanist of his day in both America and Europe and was called the American Linnaeus.[10] (Carolus Linnaeus [1707-1778] invented a new method of cataloguing plant species.) Ernestus Muhlenberg's name has been given to many of the plants he discovered.

THE FINAL YEARS

Henry Melchior Muhlenberg lived his personal motto: "The Church must be planted." In doing so, Muhlenberg's health and strength paid a heavy price. In 1776 he moved to Providence where he owned his own home. In 1779 his parish retired him with a pension of 50 lbs ($200) a year. Upon his protest, his congregation rescinded its resolution, thus enabling him to resign. He then received a pension of 100 lbs. In 1782 he compiled a hymnal, which was printed in 1786. He received the degree of Doctor of Divinity from the Pennsylvania Academy in 1784.

The Patriarch of the Lutheran Church in America died on October 7, 1787, and was buried just outside the walls of the church in Trappe (Providence) near the altar. He had reached the age of 76 years. The bodies of his wife and one of his sons later joined him.

This man gave much to both the Lutheran Church in America and to the new nation itself. His rare talents, strong faith, perseverance, and dedication to the task at hand were indeed needed by the struggling Lutheran Church. Muhlenberg's imprint remained on the Lutheran Church in America for generations to come – for good as well as for bad. For while he must be credited with keeping the Lutheran Church in the Colonies from disintegrating, and credited with stabilizing the Lutheran Church – as well as planting it over a wide area – his shortcomings due to his training in Pietism at Halle are also recognized, and these too impressed themselves even on future congregations and synods. Still, the sum of the matter, finally, is that Henry Muhlenberg remains to this day one of the most important and influential men in the history of American Lutheranism, a recognition not shared by many.

Footnotes for Chapter Seven

1 Erwin L. Lueker, Editor-in-Chief, *Lutheran Cyclopedia*, (Concordia Publishing House, Saint Louis, MO 63118-3968, 1954), pp. 818, 819.

2 Abdel Ross Wentz, *A Basic History of Lutheranism in America*, (Muhlenberg Press, Philadelphia, PA, 1955), p. 38.

3 T.J. Kleinhans, "Muhlenberg, The Right Man in the Right Place at the Right Time," p. 5, A magazine article, its reference has been lost.

4 Kleinhans, A magazine article, p. 5.

5 Wentz, *A Basic History of Lutheranism in America*, p. 38.

6 Inez Steen, *The March of Faith*, (Augsburg Publishing House, Minneapolis, MN, 1939), p. 91.

*Lutheran historian, Conrad Bergendoff, informs us that Zinzendorf had been reared as a Lutheran and educated at Halle. A personal love of Jesus was for Zinzendorf the supreme teaching of Scripture. He welcomed a colony of Bohemian Brethren on his estate in Silesia, in Herrnhut. Because he thought of the love of Jesus being present in all churches, Zinzendorf was willing to overlook the difference that existed among them and endeavored to bring them all together – a consuming idea with him. Over his lifetime, Zinzendorf sent out over 200 missionaries in diaspora teams to places near and far. Sometimes there was open opposition – including from governments – toward Zinzendorf and his message. After being expelled from Saxony, he was made a Moravian bishop in Berlin in 1737. Out of his movement came a new church, "Unity of the Brethren," with congregations in Europe and America. Zinzendorf finally failed to bring about a new church throughout the earth. He is the author of two enduring hymns: "Jesus, Thy Blood and Righteousness," and "Jesus, Lead Thou on."[7]

7 Conrad Bergendoff, *The Church of the Lutheran Reformation*, (Concordia Publishing House, Saint Louis, MO 63118-3968, 1967), pp. 165, 166.

8 Wentz, *A Basic History of Lutheranism in America*, p. 44.

9 Wetz. *A Basic History of Lutheranism in America*, p. 57.

10 Steen, *The March of Faith*, pp. 91, 92.

CHAPTER EIGHT

THE FIRST LUTHERAN SYNODS

THE PENNSYLVANIA MINISTERIUM

THE UNITED CONGREGATIONS

In order to stabilize the congregations in Pennsylvania, Muhlenberg, together with five other pastors and ten congregations, organized the Pennsylvania Synod. At first, it was called the United Congregations or the United Pastors. The synod was the outgrowth of the United Congregations which formed Muhlenberg's original parish. It was Pastor John Christian Schulz, temporarily stationed in America, who organized into a single parish the three congregations which called Muhlenberg. The name was later broadened in scope to include not only the three congregations served by Muhlenberg but also those who served by his co-workers.

While the need was felt for an organization of congregations to help bring stability to them, there were other compelling reasons as well for a general organization. Among them were these: (1) to counteract the activity of the Moravians, (2) to present a united front against the Reformed and other denominations, (3) to establish a basis of cooperation among the Lutherans.

The synod was organized August 15, 1748, at Philadelphia. Among the delegates was Peter Koch, who represented the Swedish laity. Pastor

115

Muhlenberg presided. Not all the German pastors were invited to this meeting. Muhlenberg pointed out that they could have no fellowship with the uninvited pastors because they accused Muhlenberg and his co-workers of being pietists, without cause; they have neither been sent to America to minister, nor have they an external call; they are not willing to observe the same Church Order, but each prefers the ceremonies of his home. According to Muhlenberg's experience with these men, they "care for nothing but their bread; and, finally, these pastors are under no Consistorium, and do not give account of their official doings.¹

At the Organization meeting, lay delegates were called upon to give an account of the efficiency of their pastors. There was also an inquiry into school conditions. A new liturgy for use in the churches was proposed. The adoption of a constitution had to wait until much later, 1781.

A MINISTERIUM

Seven annual meetings were held, the last one at New Hanover in 1754. Since only the clergy possessed the right to vote in the meetings, the first synod was actually a ministerium. This is also borne out by one of the earliest designations for the organization: ministerium of North America. It is interesting to note here that in the mid-eighteen hundreds, when the Missouri Synod – a leading Lutheran synod in America – was organized, it came close to being designated a Ministerium. The Loehe men, as we shall learn in another chapter, wanted a unity of pastors, but C.F.W. Walther, who became the synod's first president, emphasized that it should be an organization of congregations, with the laymen having the right to vote.

After lying dormant for six years, the United Congregations was revived in 1760 by Provost Wrangel and Pastor Henry Muhlenberg and gained permanent existence under the name Evangelical Lutheran Ministerium of Pennsylvania. In 1918 it became a part of the United Lutheran Church in America (ULCA) and in 1961 it became a member of the federation called the Lutheran Church of America (LCA). Still later it became a member of the federation called the Evangelical Lutheran Church of America (ELCA), the largest Lutheran body in North America, and there it takes its place to this day. By the mid-twentieth century there were 509 pastors, 568 congregations, and 176,166 communicants in the Pennsylvania Ministerium.

DIFFICULT CONDITIONS

Because of the great distances involved, and poor traveling conditions, congregations and pastors often found it difficult to fellowship. By 1800, the Pennsylvania Ministerium had congregations in Maryland, Virginia, North Carolina, South Carolina, Georgia, Kentucky, Tennessee, Western Pennsylvania, and the Ohio Territory. Because the congregations were so widely scattered, making travel difficult and expensive, District Conferences were set up for the congregations to enable those that were widely scattered to come together in their own districts for fellowship and to take

116

care of needs arising in their midsts.[2] It is estimated that by 1765 there were about 133 congregations in the colonies, scattered from Georgia to Upper New York. Congregations established on the frontier had to rely to a great extent on so-called "independent preachers", with no synodical affiliation. This added to their isolation.

There were other difficulties encountered by congregations and by pastors. In 1754 a memorandum signed by Muhlenberg, Brunholta, and Handschu was sent to London and Halle revealing deplorable conditions experienced by the Lutherans in America. Lack of interest on the part of the European Church was emphasized. At this time three dangers were cited as threatening the inner life of the congregations: (1) the wealthy in the parish assumed the right to rule; (2) worthless men had been introduced into the ministry; (3) the new freedom in America was being abused and misused by the immigrants. The picture drawn in the memorandum was very dark.

Muhlenberg's work in Pennsylvania was interrupted by a two-year stint in New York, where the language question had forced Pastor Knoll to resign in 1750. Prior to this, some Germans had withdrawn from Trinity Church and organized Christ Church. In August 1750 Muhlenberg and his father-in-law, C. Weiser, sailed up the Hudson to settle difficulties in Pastor Hartwick's congregation at Rheinbeck, New York. At the request of the Dutch congregation there, Muhlenberg spent 1751 and 1752 with them, preaching Dutch in the morning, German in the afternoon, and English in the evening. Although he was unable to reunite Trinity and Christ Churches, Muhlenberg secured for them Pastor Weygand from Raritan, who continued to preach in three languages, thus pacifying the language groups. Muhlenberg continued his role of supervisor, visiting the congregations on the Raritan in 1758 and 1759.

Muhlenberg's work bore much fruit. In 1771 he reported that there were seventy large and small parishes in Pennsylvania and neighboring provinces. In 1774 he went to Georgia, by order of the authorities in Europe, to establish peace in the congregation at New Ebenezer. And so, he spent much time and energy traveling the width and length of the colonies, laboring where there were difficulties to overcome, new churches to be established, or where a word of encouragement needed to be given. We might say that Muhlenberg served in the capacity of chairman of the Ministerium, visiting elder, chairman of the mission board, missionary, historian, goodwill ambassador, and supervisor – all rolled into one.

A SYNODICAL CONSTITUTION

Following the Swedish provost Wrangel's encouragement to revive the dormant synod, which was accomplished in 1760, the synod or ministerium was reorganized along better lines, and the elements of a synodical constitution were formulated. Finally, by 1781 a constitution was recorded in the minutes. The name given to the synod was the Evangelical Ministerium in North America. It was the first synodical constitution in America and served until 1840. According to the constitution the pastors were pledged to the Word of God and the Lutheran Confessions. Only ordained pastors had the right of suffrage in doctrinal matters. Ordination was performed only by resolution of the synod. The constitution prescribed that a certain liturgy must be used by the congregations. It furthermore introduced the custom of requiring ministerial candidates to preach trial sermons; also the custom of announcing to the pastor one's intention to commune. The constitution stipulated that the public examination of catechumens was to last 1 ½ hours. Failure to attend three consecutive meetings of synodical sessions canceled membership, unless valid excuse was given.

By 1767 there were forty pastors in the synod. The name was changed to the Annual Ministerium of the United Churches, and, as already noted, the name was finally changed to the Evangelical Lutheran Ministerium of Pennsylvania.

MUHLENBERG'S IMPRINT

Henry Melchior Muhlenberg's personal motto, "The Church Must Be Planted," was a guiding light in his own ministry. He dedicated his life to sowing the Lutheran Church in America, from New York to Georgia, and he did it in several ways as we have seen. No doubt one of the most significant and long-felt ways that he planted the Church was through the founding and organizing and reorganizing of the first Lutheran synod in America. He helped to unite congregations and pastors for common work and common goals. Muhlenberg brought order out of chaos.

The synod or ministerium which Muhlenberg founded, and which he served as a guding light for so many years, declared its independence from the European Churches. This declaration of independence began a new era of Lutheranism in America. With it, Lutheranism took on a new vitality.

THE NEW YORK MINISTERIUM

BRINGING IT ABOUT

The New York pastors, Berkenmeyer, Knoll, and others – except Hartwick – did not participate in the organization and meetings of the Pennsylvania Ministerium because of the manifested pietism in this body. Still, a need for a synodical body was felt. During the years 1773 and 1774 an attempt was made to establish a separate synod in New York. However, the Revolutionary War delayed further efforts to accomplish the project. Finally, formal organization of the New York Ministerium was master-minded by Henry Muhlenberg's son-in-law, John Christopher Kunze, in 1786. The second Lutheran synodical body was organized at Albany, New York, by Pastor Kunze, assisted by Pastor H. Moeller (Albany) and J.S. Schwerdefeger (Fellstrom), and two lay delegates. While Pastors Moeller, Schwerdefeger, and Kunze had held themselves aloof from the Pennsylvania Ministerium, eight of the eleven pastors in the New York territory took no part in the organization of this new Ministerium. A second meeting of the New York Ministerium was not held until 1792. This synod amounted to a duplication of the Pennsylvania Ministerium and adopted the constitution of that body in 1792.

Mention has been made of the fact that a group of Germans left Trinity Church in New York and formed a new congregation, Christ Church, in 1749. Frederick Muhlenberg, a son of Henry, served Christ Church from 1773 until 1776, when he fled before the British. For a time J. Weygand served the Dutch congregation (Trinity) from 1753 to 1770. Pastor Houseal, his successor, conducted the last service in Dutch in 1771. In 1776, General Howe of the British, with about 20,000 troops, sailed to New York. The fires that were set destroyed Trinity Church. The documents, however, were rescued by the pastor.

In 1783, the two New York congregations reunited, with J.C. Kunze as their pastor. Prior to this, Kunze conducted a Lutheran Seminary at Philadelphia, from 1773 to 1776, and then served as professor of philosophy and oriental languages in the University of Pennsylvania. Within six months after coming to New York, Pastor Kunze confirmed 87 persons. He placed particular stress on the English language and also trained young men for the English ministry. He published *The Rudiments of the Shorter Catechism of Dr. Martin Luther* in 1785, and the *First English Lutheran Hymnal* in 1795. Though an advocate of English Lutheranism, Kunze was not a staunch Lutheran. At his funeral in 1807, the Reformed pastor, J. Runkel, delivered the sermon.

FRIENDLY WITH THE EPISCOPALIANS

At a convention at Rheinbeck in 1797, Dr. Kunze introduced the following interesting resolution: "RESOLVED, that on account of the intimate relation subsisting between the English Episcopalian and the Lutheran Churches, the identity of their doctrine, and the near approach of their church discipline, this consistory will never acknowledge a newly erected Lutheran church in places where the members may partake of the services of the said Episcopal Church." For the sake of expediency this resolution was rescinded several years later.

WATERED DOWN LUTHERANISM

A pupil of Dr. Kunze, G. Strebeck, was called to preach English at Christ Church. Instead, he organized an English Lutheran Church and in 1804, with a part of his English flock, united with the Episcopal Church. In New York the Lutherans tended toward union with the Episcopalians. The English congregation which remained, then called a former Presbyterian pastor, who was later succeeded by a former Methodist. In 1810 the entire

119

congregation followed Pastor Strebeck into the Episcopal Church.

A man who was destined to do the cause of confessional Lutheranism in America much harm became the second president of the New York Ministerium and served in this capacity for 21 years. Dr. F.H. Quitman (1760-1850) was a determined protagonist of German Rationalism, having come under its pervasive influence after it crept into Halle and other German universities. Rationalism seeks to make the divine revelation of God's Word agree with human reason and logic, even if this means denying express scriptural teachings. Rationalism led to Deism, which amounts to no more than a general acknowledgement of the existence of God, while denying the diety of Jesus Christ. Rationalism and Deism teach that God is operative in the universe only through natural means.

It is no wonder then that Quitman, in his revised edition of Kunze's catechism (published by approval of the New York Ministerium), denied several fundamental doctrines of Scripture. In 1806 he published a Lutheran hymnal containing the union formula for distributing Holy Communion. This formula supposedly agrees with either Lutheran or Reformed teaching. In it the pastor recites to the congregation the words: "Christ our Lord *says*, This is my body. . . Christ our Lord says, This is my blood." The individual communicant may then understand these words in the light of his church's teaching. Dr. Quitman also wrote some rationalistic prayers to the "Great Father of the Universe." In 1817 he published several sermons on the 300th Anniversary of the Reformation. In them he established reason and revelation as the true source of religious knowledge.

The Rationalism of Quitman became firmly entrenched in the New York Ministerium and was protected by the Constitution of 1816, which stated: "We establish it as a fundamental rule of this association that the person to be ordained shall not be required to take any other engagement than this, that he will faithfully teach, as well as perform other ministerial duties, and regulate his walk and life according to the Gospel of our Lord Jesus Christ as contained in the Holy Scriptures, and that he will observe this constitution while he remains a member of the Ministerium." Doctrinal discussions were permitted on the floor of synod with the express proviso: ". . . .that the fundamental principle of Protestantism, the right of free research, be not infringed upon." Eventually, a younger evangelical element saved the day for Lutheranism in the New York Ministerium.[3]

The spirit of Rationalism, which gained such a foothold in the New York Ministerium and was so antagonistic toward Scripture and the Lutheran Confessions (1580), was also at the time rearing its ugly head in the Pennsylvania Ministerium. Just five years after the death of the Ministerium's patriarch, Henry Muhlenberg, this – the first synod in America which gathered Lutherans together – revised its constitution, striking out all references to the Confessions of the Lutheran Church. This spirit of weakened confessionalism never left the Pennsylvania Ministerium, as subsequent chapters will reveal.

Growth for the New York Ministerium was slow. By 1807 there were 14 pastors enrolled in America. Canadian efforts to enroll pastors in the Ministerium failed. In New York, the Lutherans there tended toward union with the Episcopalians.

There were definite problems that threatened the Lutheran Church and impaired its progress early in the history of the new republic. Historian Abdel Wentz lists especially three problems: (1) Rationalism, which was brought to America by such men as Dr. Fred Henry Quitman. (2) Unionism, stemming from religious indifference brought on by rationalism shattering the Lutheran Confessions. Unionism brought on the decline of denominational consciousness. (Unionism in the form of united congregations, union hymnals, liturgies, etc.) (3) The language problem – staying with the German language, when the tendancy of the young people was to adopt English. Thus many sought membership in Presbyterian, Methodist, and Episcopalian churches, driven there by the desire to have their religion presented to them in English.[4]

LUTHERANS IN SOUTH CAROLINA

LUTHERANISM WAS NOT AN ENDURING FORCE

In 1735 colonists from Germany and Switzerland settled in Orangeburg, South Carolina. J.U. Giessendanner was the first resident pastor, arriving in 1734 with the immigrants, but died the following year. He was succeeded by his nephew, who was ordained by the Presbyterians and then, in 1748, by the Bishop of London. That ended Orangeburg Lutheranism.

Pastor Bolzius of the Salzburgers (Georgia), conducted the first Lutheran service at Charleston in 1734. Later, in 1755, Pastor Friedrichs organized St. John's congregation. In 1778 Pastor Christian Streit began to serve this congregation, having served for a year as chaplain of the Eighth Regiment of the American forces in the Revolutionary War. His congregation was a "model of Christian unity," for it consisted of Lutherans, German Reformed, and Catholics. Later, when their pastor resigned, the congregation was satisfied with Episcopal services.

By 1788 there were nine Lutherans and six Reformed German congregations in South Carolina. These had united in 1787 as an evangelical body under the name of Church Union of the German Protestant Churches in the State of South Carolina. At the convention of 1788 all Lutheran pastors pledged themselves upon the symbolical books of the Lutheran Church. However, the Constitution also read: "The intention of this union is not that any members should deny his own confession." A directorium consisting of the ministers and two laymen was established with the provision that it was to rule as long as a majority of the 15 congregations supported it. This directorium had charge of all church affairs; for example: admission, dismissal, examination, ordination, new churches and schools. The local congregation, by majority rule, chose its own catechism and agenda.

The synod's last meeting was held in 1794. By 1804 the ministers who had organized this union body were all dead, save one. The congregations became easy prey to the Methodists and Baptists. As H. George Anderson points out: Those synods that were too small to survive a sharp drop in membership soon disappeared, as was the case in both Carolinas.[5] Later, in 1824, a successful synod was formed.*

THE NORTH CAROLINA SYNOD

GENUINE LUTHERANISM WAS CONSPICIOUSLY ABSENT

Lutherans from Pennsylvania settled in Rowan and Mecklenburg Counties early in the 18th century. In 1771 congregations in these counties sent a delegation to England, Holland, and Germany requesting assistance. The result was that a pastor and a teacher were sent. The years 1787 and 1788 brought a total of three more pastors. However, genuine Lutheranism was not represented among them. This state of confessional and doctrinal deterioration was attested by the fact that in 1794 Pastor R.J. Miller pledged himself to the *Thirty-Nine Articles* of the Episcopal Church.

The congregations served by Pastor Arends, Miller, Storch, and Paul Henkel organized themselves as the Synod of Salisbury on May 2, 1803. After a time, Lutheran congregations in South Carolina and Virginia, as well as in Tennesee, came to be represented in the synod, which eventually took the name Synod of North Carolina. The article of the Constitution defining the synod made no mention of the Lutheran Confessions. At a meeting held in 1804, a Reformed minister administered communion. (In New York, Pastor Kunze promoted union of the Reformed and Lutheran churches. These two main bodies of Protestantism built common church buildings and schools. Franklin College, Lancaster, Pennsylvania [1787], was a joint Lutheran-Reformed endeavor). Cooperation between the two Protestant bodies was common also in the Carolina's. However, distinctive doctrines and practices of the Methodists – perfectionism and awakenings – caused Lutherans to shy away from them. On the other hand, Lutherans even helped to train Reformed ministers, and taught Reformed confirmation classes, using the Heidelberg Catechism.[6] Philip Henkel was commissioned to make a trial at revivalism, a type of church meeting commonly used by the Methodists or followers of the Wesley's. (People were mightily stirred up emotionally in order to bring about conversion.) While many Lutheran laymen were lost to Methodism and its emotionalism, nevertheless there were Lutheran pastors who strongly opposed it. In 1804 the Moravian, G. Schober, was ordained by order of the North Carolina Synod. He had no formal ministerial training. Also indicative of a weakened Lutheranism was the fact that the meeting of 1816 was held, upon invitation, in a Reformed Church.

A year later, in 1817, which was the 300th year anniversary of the Reformation, the North Carolina Synod became more demonstrative concerning Lutheranism and declared that it would continue to bear the Lutheran name. Generally speaking the tercentenary was celebrated in the congregations of the various synods in the company and fellowship of their Reformed counterparts. A result of the tercentenary was a series of efforts to bring about a general union of the Lutheran and Reformed churches.[7] Eventually, however, the plans and hopes for union were dropped. Mention should be made of Pastor G. Schober and the jubilee book that he authored for the tercentenary. The Convention of 1817 resolved to approve it and put it into print. This volume, titled simply *Luther*, was "in reality a plea for a general assembly of all Protestant denominations to which the several churches would send official delegates."[8] The ex-Moravian in the spirit of the times and not in the true spirit of the Reformation approved union of the various Protestant Churches in America, despite their doctrinal differences, which he tended to overlook as unimportant. Schober wrote: "I have carefully examined the doctrine of the Episcopal Church, have read many excellent articles of the Presbyterians, know the doctrines of the Methodists, and am acquainted with the doctrine of the Baptists, as far as they receive and adore Jesus as the Savior. Among all classes of those who adore Jesus as God, I find nothing of importance which could prevent a cordial union." Thus the goal of the leadership of the synod was the forming of a national church.

THE UNTIMELY SYNOD

In 1819 Pastor Gottlieb Schober, Secretary of the North Carolina Synod, was given a seat and the right to vote at the meeting of the Pennsylvania Ministerium. Pastor Schober was present for the purpose of urging the Ministerium to develop and adopt a plan for a central organization for the Lutheran synods in America. The result was that the Pennsylvania Ministerium invited all other Lutheran bodies to attend a general convention at Baltimore. It was at this Baltimore meeting that the idea for the General Synod, organized the following year in Maryland, definitely took shape. The idea to form a central body of Lutheran synods had been fostered by some since 1811, when the subject was broached by Pastors Storch and Schober.

To enable the North Carolina Synod to attend the sessions at Baltimore, the officers autocratically convened the body five weeks before the time fixed by the Constitution. This meeting became known as the "Untimely Synod." It ultimately led to a rupture within the synod's ranks and to the formation of the Tennessee Synod. When the North Carolina Synod participated in organizing the General Synod in 1820, the dissatisfied parties – which included the Henkels (David, Paul, Philip) – held a synod meeting of their own at Buffalo Creek at the time specified by the Constitution and ordained candidate Bell as well as David Henkel. Henkel had been charged with teaching transubstantiation (Catholicism's doctrine) because he preached the Lutheran doctrine of the Real Presence of Christ's body and blood with the bread and wine in the Lord's Supper. As a result he had been degraded to the rank of catechist for six months.

Of President Storch, the Henkels reported: "We have written evidence that, when a paper was read at said 'Untimely Synod' containing the statement that the human nature of Jesus Christ had been received into the divine nature and therefore He possessed all the divine attributes, Storch declared that he could not believe this. And when it was stated that this is the teaching of the Scriptures, Storch answered, 'Even if five hundred Bibles should say so, I would not believe it'"

The regular meeting of the North Carolina Synod at Lincolnton in 1820 was marked by painful scenes and altercations, with the final breach occurring between the majority (who resolved to unite with the General Synod), and the minority (who refused to recognize the leaders as Lutherans and opposed union with the General Synod). The General Synod – the first federation of Lutheran Synods in America – was organized on October 22, 1820, at Hagerstown, Maryland. In this federation or central synodical body, the North Carolina Synod (1803) was joined together with the Pennsylvania Ministerium (1748), the New York Ministerium (1786), and the Synod of Maryland and Virginia (1820). (It should be mentioned that the congregations of the North Carolina Synod located in South Carolina requested and received permission in 1824 to establish their own synod* due to the negative effect which the controversy over the General Synod was having among the people.)

The North Carolina Synod at first was so small that it ceased to exist – for all practical purposes – between annual conventions, and the elected officers had duties only for the actual session.[9] In *The Lutherans in North America*, the observation is made that the early synods were primarily concerned with seeing that the Church was adequately supplied with qualified clergymen, and business at conventions consisted of reading and replying to letters received from congregations and pastors. The author points out that congregations either wanted a pastor or wanted to get rid of one, while the clergy either wanted to be admitted to the synod or complained that their congregations argued too much and paid too little.[10]

THE SYNOD OF VIRGINIA AND MARYLAND

EARLY HISTORY

Henry Muhlenberg, in the year 1754, sent an appeal to London and to Halle for pastors for this great territory. He wrote of the thousands of Lutherans who were scattered through North Carolina, Virginia, and surrounding territories.

Twelve Lutheran Palatinate families who had escaped the Indian Massacre of New Bern in 1710, found refuge in Virginia and were given homes by Governor Spottwood in Spottsylvania County. Probably Gerhard Henkel was the first pastor. Many years later they were served by Caspar Stoever, Sr., a famous missionary. After Stoever died (while on a collection trip to Europe), George Klug offered his services, arriving in 1736. This was the beginning of Hebron Church, Madison County, Virginia.

Many of the enterprising Germans of Pennsylvania went into the Shenandoah Valley. Their numbers were swelled by immigrants arriving from Germany. In 1772 Peter Muhlenberg, son of the Patriarch Henry Muhlenberg, was sent to Woodstock to serve the German Lutherans there. In order to be a licensed minister in Virginia, which was under English rule, and thus be able to perform legal marriages, Peter had to be re-ordained in the Episcopal Church by the Bishop of London. Peter became acquainted with George Washington and Patrick Henry when he settled in Virginia. They became good friends. At that time, Washington was a surveyor, planter, and statesman. Muhlenberg became an ardent supporter of Patrick Henry's spirit against English rule. In December 1775 the House of Delegates of Virginia, in view of Peter's training with the dragoons in Germany, appointed him Colonel of the Eighth Virginia Regiment. This regiment was made up mostly of German Lutherans. As we have already learned, in the middle of January 1776 Pastor Muhlenberg said farewell to his pulpit and congregation and set off on a brilliant military career. The historian, George Bancroft (Quoted from Fink) points out: "The command of another regiment was given to the Lutheran minister, Peter Muhlenberg, who left the pulpit to form out of his several congregations one of the most perfect battalions in the army." Muhlenberg distinguished himself in many fields of battle, in recruiting soldiers, and in training them. Before the war closed he was elevated to Major General, and after the war, until his death, he served his country as a statesman. He served both as vice-president of Pennsylvania under Benjamin Franklin and as a member of congress. After Peter Muhlenberg joined the army, a succession of pastors took charge of the Woodstock congregation. Among them were Pastors Wildbahn, Goering, Kurtz, and J.N. Schmucker (1805).

John Abraham Lidenius was the first Lutheran minister born in America, Jacob van Buskirck was the second, while Christian Streit and Peter Muhlenberg tied for third place. Streit came from Pennsylvania in 1785 and served the Winchester church until 1812. He was a hard worker and a good leader. The church building, begun in 1764, was not completed until two years after Streit came to Winchester. A Latin document laid in the cornerstone of this church is of special interest, for it contained the following sound declaration of faith: "This temple is dedicated to the Triune God and the Lutheran Religion; all sects, whatever their names may be, departing from or not fully agreeing with the Evangelical Lutheran Religion, shall forever be excluded from it." Streit instructed candidates for the Lutheran ministry in his own home.

In August County, with a population made almost completely of Germans, the Koiners, a large family which originally came from Wuerttemberg, established a Lutheran Church. It was known as "Koiners' Church."

Of particular importance in New Market, Virginia, was the home of the Henkels. Paul Henkel, the most famous, and grandson of Gerhard, was born in North Carolina in 1754 and died in 1825. Licensed and ordained by the Pennsylvania Ministerium, Paul did much traveling in Virginia, North and South Carolina, Tenessee, Kentucky, Ohio, and Indiana. He was the greatest missionary of the Lutheran Church in America following the Revolutionary War and during the first part of the nineteenth century. The printshop which he established at New Market was the oldest

125

Lutheran Publishing House in the United States. Established in 1806, it was located in Henkel's home. Paul Henkel gave to America truly Lutheran books including the complete *Lutheran Book of Concord*. This occurred at a time when the Lutheran Church, as a whole, was drifting away from confessional Lutheranism. The *Book of Concord* published by Henkel was the first English edition printed in America.

Five of Paul Henkel's six sons became Lutheran pastors. Succeeding generations of Henkels also produced Lutheran pastors, and so it can be said that for nearly two centuries the Henkel family produced a conservative influence on the Lutheran Church in America. The *Lutheran Cyclopedia* points out that the Henkels were "earnest preachers, tireless missionaries, faithful educators, and zealous publicists." Though somewhat unionistically inclined, the Henkels became increasingly free from the prevailing doctrinal indifference and arrived at a clearer understanding of Lutheran truths. And this took place at a time when all existing Lutheran synods were fast moving in the opposite direction. The Henkel's loyalty to Lutheranism led to the organization of the Tennessee Synod in 1820. The plan for this synod was first conceived by Paul's son, Philip, of Green County, Virginia. Paul Henkel also took part in organizing the Ohio Synod in 1818, and served as secretary.

ORGANIZING THE SYNOD OF
MARYLAND AND VIRGINIA

Beginning in 1793, the pastors in Maryland and Virginia – members of the Pennsylvania Ministerium – met together in a conference called The Special Conference of the Evangelical Lutheran Preachers and Delegates in the State of Virginia. By 1809 there were 49 organized congregations in Virginia. It is noteworthy that the pastors and delegates from these congregations showed much interest in Christian schools. The conference of 1815 urged every preacher to make provision for a German Lutheran school in each of his congregations.

On October 11, 1820, these Special Conferences led to the organization of the Synod of Maryland and Virginia at Winchester, Virginia. Ten pastors and nine delegates formed the new synod. Prominent men were Dr. D. Kurtz, D.F. Schaeffer, and Charles Porterfield Krauth, Sr. There were 18 schools in operation in the parishes at this time.

In 1829 the Synod of Maryland and Virginia spawned a new synod, when eight pastors amicably withdrew and formed the separate Virginia Synod. The original synod continued simply as the Maryland Synod.

THE TENNESSEE SYNOD

THE "HENKEL" SYNOD

The Tennessee Synod has always been a small body, but also interesting, instructive, and important. The more conservative group of the North Carolina Synod met at Cove Creek, July 17 to 19, 1820, to organize the new synod. Present were: J. Zink of Virginia, Paul Henkel of Virginia, Adam Miller of Tennessee, Philip Henkel of Tennessee (with whom the idea originated), George Esterly of Tennessee, and David Henkel of North Carolina. The result was called the "Henkel" Synod for the reason that the Henkels were the ones who took the first steps in its organization. The Tennessee or "Henkel" Synod was a Lutheran body which, oddly enough for that period of time, was organized as the result of a protest against prevailing liberalism in doctrine and practice among the majority of pastors and congregations. Often enough in the history of the Lutheran Church, it has been a small minority of pastors and congregations who have courageously held up the Bible and the Lutheran Confessions for the Church to follow and cling to.

The Tennessee Synod at first was determined to remain a German body, reasoning that true Lutheranism is best preserved in the tongue in which it was originally presented. The Tennessee pastors, especially the Henkels, were earnest students of Luther. Solomon was manager of the printery at New Market, and although he was not a pastor, was quoted as saying, "A week ago Mr. York was here bringing with him Luther's works. They are bound in 13 folio volumes and cost $100 [a large sum in that day]. I purchased the books." From the Henkel publishing house came forth sound Lutheran books and pamphlets. They also printed text books for use in the Christian schools. Sermons by Luther, Arndt, and others were also printed and distributed. Some of these also came to be translated into English and sold to the English-speaking public.

OSTRACIZED!

Because of their Lutheranism, the men of Tennessee Synod were avoided, despised, and ostracized by their opponents. The "Henkelites," it was said, had been convicted of error at the "Quarreling Synod," and were false Lutherans. They had been excluded from the synod, and hence had no authority to serve as clergymen. The "Quarreling Synod" was a name given to the meeting of the North Carolina Synod at Lincolnton, North Carolina in 1820, following the "Untimely Synod" of 1819. It was at the 1820 meeting that the majority – who were liberal and wanted to unite with the General Synod – and the minority – who vehemently opposed such union – split from each other. The Henkels of the minority declared that they could not have fellowship with people who were given to false teaching regarding Baptism and the Lord's Supper, and who rejected the doctrines of the *Augsburg Confession*. After much wrangling the two parties split. But because of the sharp contention present between the two groups, the synod has been called the "Quarreling Synod" or "*Streitsynode*" (German).

In the eyes of the North Carolina Synod the Tennessee Synod was not lawful, because its clergymen were not to be considered true pastors. As late as 1826 Henry A. Muhlenberg remarked that the Tennessee Synod had as yet not been recognized as a synod by the other Lutheran groups.

THE OHIO SYNOD

THE CHURCH ON THE
MOVE WESTWARD

There was a strong westward migration after the Revolutionary War, much of it to Ohio, which became a state in 1803. Immigrants from Pennsylvania and Virginia had come west and settled in Fairfield, Montgomery, Columbiana, Stark, and Jefferson Counties. By 1814 there were 60 Lutheran congregations and 37 church buildings in Ohio. The frontier kept moving westward at a fast pace, and with it came more Lutheran congregations and church buildings.

The Lutherans appealed to the Pennsylvania Ministerium for spiritual care, with the result that in 1805 Pastor Forster arrived at Fairfield County, and Pastor J. Stauch arrived at Combiana County. In 1812 there were twelve pastors active in the present State of Ohio, of whom three extended their activities into western Pennsylvania, and one into western Virginia. Among them was Paul Henkel.

In order to discuss and arrange their work the pastors organized a special conference in 1812 in Pastor Weygand's house, Washington County, Pennsylvania. This conference had the right to license, but not to ordain clergymen. The name given to it was the Ohio Conference of the Pennsylvania Ministerium. Because of distance, and also for other considerations, the petition was made to the Pennsylvania Ministerium in 1816 to organize the Ministerium of Ohio. This was accomplished on September 14, 1818, at Sommerset, Ohio. In 1826 this synod called itself The Evangelical Lutheran Synod of Ohio and Neighboring States. The president was J. Stauch; the secretary was Paul Henkel. Of Paul Henkel it is reported that he traversed all Ohio in a two-wheeled cart.[11]

AN OUTLINE OF THE COMPLEX
HISTORY OF THE OHIO SYNOD

The subsequent history of this synod is interesting, especially in this way: it demonstrates how established synods branch out, how new synods are formed from the old, and how larger amalgamations are brought about.

1820 – When on October 22 the Convention to organize the General Synod was held, neither the Ohio nor the Tennessee Synod sent delegates. The Ohio Synod was fearful of the hierarchy dictating to the individual synods and that English would become the language of the federation.[12] The Ohio Synod never did join the General Synod.

1830 – The Ohio Synod began its own seminary at Canton, Ohio, and the following year moved it to Columbus.

1831 – The Ohio Synod is divided into districts.

1832 – The two synods, Ohio and Tennessee, published and distributed thousands of copies of *Luther's Catechism* (many included the *Augsburg Confession*).

1833 – The synod came to be called The Joint Synod of Ohio.

1836 – Ohio adopted the resolution: ". . . . this Synod strictly adheres to the *Augsburg Confession* and admits no one to membership in its body who shall deny any part thereof, and that all congregations within its synodical boundaries be advised to receive no one as a teacher who does not fully adhere to the *Confession*."[13]

1836 – The English Synod of Ohio was formed out of one of the districts.

1840 – This synod became independent of the Joint Synod and joined the General Synod (organized 1820).

1842 – Ohio published the *Lutheran Standard*, committed to the *Augsburg Confession*.

1844 – Organization of the Synod of Miami by pastors of the English Synod and others working in southern Ohio. Miami joined the General Synod in 1845.

1847 – Organization of the Wittenberg Synod when pastors in northwestern part of Ohio withdrew from the English Synod.

1857 – A new English District of the Joint Synod of Ohio was formed.

1858 – The English Synod of Ohio became the Synod of East Ohio.

1867 – The new English District of the Joint Synod of Ohio joined the more conservative federation formed that same year, the General Council. It took its membership out of the Joint Synod and became the District Synod of Ohio.

1920 – The four synods – East Ohio, Wittenberg, Miami, and District Synod of Ohio – merged into one body, forming the Ohio Synod of the United Lutheran Church in America (ULCA).

A SURVEY OF
LUTHERANISM TO 1820

STATISTICS

By the end of 1820 there were six Lutheran Synods operating in America. The following statistics are for the year 1825.

(1) PENNSYLVANIA MINISTERIUM (1748): 58 clergy; 20 candidates; 235 congregations; 225 schools; 26,884 communicants. (2) NEW YORK MINISTERIUM (1786): 21 clergy; 6 candidates; 31 congregations; no schools; 2,258 communicants. (3) NORTH CAROLINA SYNOD.* (1803): 17 clergy; 3 candidates; 51 congregations; no schools; 2,443 communicants. (4) OHIO SYNOD (1818): 22 clergy; 3 candidates; ? congregations* 51 schools; 5,229 communicants. (5) MARYLAND AND VIRGINIA SYNOD+ (1820): 22 clergy; 3 candidates; 75 congregations; 25 schools; 5,696 communicants. (6) TENNESSEE SYNOD (1820): 6 clergy; ? candidates; ? congregations; ? schools; ? communicants.

The Pennsylvania Ministerium was the leading group, although the Tennessee Synod was most nearly Lutheran.

SCHOOLS

By the close of the Revolutionary War, public, tax-supported schools had become widely accepted in New England and were called District Schools. The Lutherans, on the other hand, showed much interest in maintaining their own parish schools. As a rule, wherever German Lutheranism was established, the cry for schools was heard; however, the Swedes were rather weak regarding parish schools. The Germans took note of this neglect among the Swedes, and the Pennsylvania Ministerium minutes of 1962 record: "In the Swedish congregations the schools have for several generations been regrettably neglected. Dr. Wrangel, however, has started an English school in one of his congregations, in which the Lutheran catechism is read in an English translation."

The Salzburgers of Georgia had two schools, both taught originally by the pastors. The Palatinates (who settled in New York along the Hudson), on arrival in 1710, built a church and school. Likewise schools sprang up among the Lutherans in North Carolina, Virginia, Tennessee, and Ohio.

TIME FOR THE LUTHERAN
CHURCH TO WAKE UP

The greatest obstacle to the spread and healthy growth of the Lutheran Church in America was the dearth of well-trained, able, and truly Lutheran pastors and teachers. A serious mistake was made in neglecting to establish seminaries for the training of congregational workers qualified to work in American surroundings.

The growing indifferentism and deterioration of the Lutheran ministry, as well as of the Lutheran congregations, was a necessary consequence of the neglect to provide for suitable pastors and teachers. This in turn resulted in inadequate service by incompetent or heterodox ministers. The doctrinal aberrations were due, in part, to the fact that a number of the Lutheran clergy had received training at Princeton and other non-Lutheran schools. (The training of Lutheran clergy in schools dedicated to liberal theology remains to this day a blight on segments of the Lutheran Church.) Furthermore, for many decades the evil practice of licensing candidates for the ministry was maintained. The candidates were made to serve for a time under a license. Later, after receiving a call into the holy ministry, they were ordained. The men who were licensed were often lacking in sufficient preparatory education.

The German trained clergy had been augmented by such as had been tutored by pastors in America. Hartwick Seminary in New York, established and opened in 1815, was limited in its services to train pastors. The ministers who came to America from Germany toward the close of the eighteenth century were in many instances not adapted to their surroundings, which were rapidly becoming English, the language commonly used. Often both pastors and congregations refused to yield to the popular English language. Furthermore, the universities in Germany in which the pastors had been educated had fallen prey to Rationalism and so could hardly be called Christian, let alone Lutheran.

Very early in his career, Henry M. Muhlenberg considered the matter of training a native or indigenous ministry. He suggested it to the Ministerium in 1769. A school begun by L.C. Kunze had to close during the Revolutionary War when funds dried up. The hopelessness of the situation was revealed in a letter by Helmuth to the Ministerium in 1784: "Brethren, we are living in a sad time. My heart weeps over the awful decay of Christendom. I readily acknowledge my share of the guilt that God seems to hide His countenance from us, permitting the doors to stand wide open for the spirit of lies (Rationalism) to enter and destroy the vineyard of the Lord. You will learn from the report from Halle how the swine are uprooting the garden of Christ in Germany. . . . Another thing dearest brethren, how shall we in the future supply our congregations with pastors? Where shall we find ministers to meet our need, which will increase from time to time? From Germany? Possibly a secret Arian, Socinian, or Deist? For over there everything is full of this vermin. God forbid! We ourselves must put our hands to the plow. God will call us to account for it, and will let our children suffer for it, if we do not wake up, and hazard something for the weal of immortal souls."

DRY ROT IN THE LUTHERAN CHURCH

To overcome the problem of properly educating pastors, Franklin College was established at Lancaster, Pennsylvania, in partnership with the German Reformed. Lutheran pastors were on the board of trustees. The college later became the exclusive property of the Reformed. The historian Bente remarks that the opening of Franklin College was the beginning of the end of true Lutheranism.

Until 1827 there were only ten preachers who had been produced by Lutheran seminaries in the United States. There was a constant shortage of properly trained, capable pastors to meet the needs of the influx of immigrants and to keep up with the fast westward moving frontier. Already in the second decade of the nineteenth century a period writer estimated that there were 650 Lutheran congregations in the United States. And there were an additional 10 congregations and preaching stations in Canada.[14] A result that was inevitable from the continual dearth of properly trained Lutheran pastors was doctrinal deterioration. Already in 1792 the confession of the Lutheran symbols was omitted in the new constitution of the Pennsylvania Ministerium. The New York Ministerium, under the influence of Quitman, became rationalistic; yet the Pennsylvania Ministerium made no protest and did not sever its connection with this group. Rather, the Pennsylvania Ministerium, in a measure, opened the door to Rationalism by regarding the German language as more important than adhering to the Lutheran Confessions. Protection against both Rationalism and the English language was sought in the German language; hence it was logical for the German *Lutherans* to tie in with the German *Reformed* and the German *Moravians*. Thus the German language, not the

131

Lutheran Confessions, was held as the important basis for religious union, as well as protection against Rationalism and the viewed threat which the English language posed.

The utter degeneration of the Pennsylvania Ministerium was evidenced from the new *Agenda* which was to be introduced in all congregations from 1818 on into the future. In the confirmation rite, the *Agenda* struck out the confirmand's confession to remain faithful to the Lutheran Church; instead it incorporated the union formula (Lutheran – Reformed). The formula for ordination no longer demanded of the candidate for the holy ministry that he adhere to the Lutheran Confessions.

In 1812 the *Evangelische Magazin* appeared "under the auspices of the German Evangelical Lutheran Synod" with the avowed purpose not to represent Lutheranism but to bolster the German language and oppose the introduction of the English language. It also solicited literary contributions and subscriptions from the non-Lutheran brethren.

In view of the celebration of the Reformation Jubilee in 1817, the Pennsylvania Ministerium resolved, "that the German Reformed, Moravian, Episcopal, and Presbyterian Churches be invited by our president to take part with us in the festival of Reformation."

From 1817 to 1825 prominent men of the Pennsylvania Ministerium considered and advocated plans for an "organic union of our Church in this country with the Reformed Church." According to the historian Jacobs, the Pennsylvania Ministerium left the General Synod in 1823 in order to further union with the Reformed, and to have a joint college with them.

Now then, what has been stated about the un-Lutheran outlook and conduct of the Pennsylvania Ministerium was true in almost the same measure of the New York Ministerium, the North Carolina Synod, the Maryland and Virginia Synod. The only exception was the Tennessee Synod. The Ohio Synod was to some extent more Lutheran than the mother synod.

Such, in brief, were the conditions in 1820, when the first federation of synods, the General Synod, was organized.

Footnotes for Chapter Eight

1 Richard C. Wolf, *Documents of Lutheran Unity in America*, (Fortress Press, Philadelphia, PA, 1966), p. 25.

2 Wolf, *Documents of Lutheran Unity*, p. 49.

3 Abdel Ross Wentz, *A Basic History of Lutheranism in America*, (Muhlenberg Press, Philadelphia, PA, 1955), p. 74.

4 Wentz, *A Basic History of Lutheranism in America*, pp. 73-77.

5 E. Clifford Nelson, Editor, *The Lutherans in North America*, (Fortress Press, Philadelphia, PA, 1975). P. 87.

6 Nelson, *The Lutherans in North America*, p. 91.

7 Wentz, *A Basic History of Lutheranism in America*, pp. 96, 97.

8 Wentz, *A Basic History of Lutheranism in America*, pp. 96.

* The Synod of South Carolina

9 Nelson, *The Lutherans in North America*, p. 87.

10 Nelson, *The Lutherans in North America*, p. 87, 88.

11 Wentz, *A Basic History of Lutheranism in America*, p. 71.

12 Wentz, *A Basic History of Lutheranism in America*, p. 79.

13 Wentz, *A Basic History of Lutheranism in America*, p. 135.

* In 1824, members of the North Carolina Synod living in South Carolina requested and received permission to form a new synod due to controversy over the General Synod having a negative impact on the congregations – hence, South Carolina Synod.

* Recall that six years earlier, in 1814, there were 60 congregations in Ohio.

+ In 1829, the pastors and congregations in Virginia withdrew to form the Virginia Synod. Later, in 1842, six pastors left this body to form the Ministerium of Southwest Virginia.

14 Nelson, *The Lutherans in North America*, p. 106.

CHAPTER NINE

THE GENERAL SYNOD-1820

THE FIRST LUTHERAN FEDERATION

THE NEED WAS FELT FOR A FEDERATION OF SYNODS

A Synod here. . . . a synod there, could perhaps describe the formation of Lutheranism in America. While the Methodists and Episcopalians were strong in consolidating congregations into general bodies, the Lutheran congregations were gathered into various synods, with boundaries of language, customs, theology, geography, distance, and even personalities to divide them.

The danger was always present of Lutherans being absorbed by the Reformed groups. There was also a crying need to establish a theological seminary to handle the training of future pastors for the Lutheran ministry. Requests were not being directed to the old country for pastors, nor were any pastors being provided from there. Still, maintaining a seminary seemed to lie in a federation of synods. Furthermore, wouldn't evangelism itself be made simpler through a consolidation of Lutherans?

THE "PROPOSED PLAN"
(*"Plan Entwurf"*)

The idea for a federation of Lutheran synods came up in the North Carolina Synod in 1811 when pastors Storch and Schober discussed establishing a better intersynodical fellowship through a general Lutheran administrative body. At its meeting at Harrisburg in 1818, the Pennsylvania Ministerium gave evidence of being in favor of a closer connection of

135

the various synods. When the Ministerium met at Baltimore in 1819, Pastor Gottlieb Schober was present with his Proposed Plan (*Plan Entwurf*). Several theologians were appointed as a committee to confer with Schober as they gave consideration to his proposal. The Proposed Plan which was submitted had to its discredit some hierarchical tendencies. For example: UNTIL THE FORMAL PERMISSION AND CONSENT HAS BEEN GRANTED BY THE GENERAL SYNOD NO NEW ESTABLISHED BODY SHALL BE RECOGNIZED BY US AS A MINISTERIUM AND NO ORDINATION PERFORMED BY IT AS VALID. . . . THE GENERAL SYNOD HAS THE RIGHT, WITH THE CONSENT OF THE MAJORITY OF THE SPECIAL SYNODS, TO INTRODUCE NEW BOOKS FOR GENERAL USE OF THE CHURCHES AS WELL AS TO MAKE RECOMMENDATIONS IN LITURGY. While no confessional paragraph was included and no mention was made of the Bible, the following restriction was posted: THE GENERAL SYNOD HAS NO POWER TO MAKE OR DEMAND ANY CHANGES WHATEVER IN THE DOCTRINES OF FAITH ADOPTED HERETOFORE AMONG US.* The pronounced purpose of the plan was for the individual synods to transfer their rights to this central body and that everything be thus centered in the General Synod. The tendency was also evident to make the new organization one of ministers.

The Proposed Plan was adopted by the Pennsylvania Ministerium by a vote of 42 to 8. The Ministerium also resolved to have 600 copies of the Plan printed and distributed.

SOME SYNODS HOLD BACK

In 1819 the Ohio Synod adopted the Proposed Plan ". . . . in the expectation that such a union of pastors would be more effective in the advancement of the kingdom of Christ." However, this synod changed its mind at Canton, Ohio in 1820, because ". . . . by adopting the Plan Entwurf we would transfer many of our rights upon delegates to the General Synod, and we are convinced from Church History that in this way the papacy was established." Of Article Five, which made ordination dependant on permission from the General Synod, the Ohioans concluded: "We cannot but judge that this Article is more in accord with papacy than with the teachings of the apostles." And so, the Ohio Synod resolved not to send a delegate, but to wait until it had opportunity to study the new Constitution.

The New York Ministerium considered the Proposed Plan at a meeting at Rheinbeck in 1819. The reporting committee stated that "several of the principles of the *Plan Entwurf* do not agree with the spirit of the Constitution of the New York Ministerium," meaning, of course, the hierarchical sections. The Ministerium resolved not to join the movement for a central synod, as it was proposed by the Pennsylvania Ministerium.

The North Carolina Synod, as we have already seen, suffered a split on account of the proposed General Synod. Its officers had autocratically convened the Synod five weeks early to enable its members to attend the meeting scheduled to be held in Baltimore in 1819. In protest of this "Untimely Synod" and of the "Synod of Strife" the following year, a group split off and formed the Tennessee Synod. The remaining North Carolina Synod adopted the Proposed Plan on May 28, 1820, by a vote of 15 to 6.

The Tennessee Synod, as could be expected, rejected the Proposed Plan in toto. But due to the testimonials and objections of the Henkels in particular, the hierarchical features of the Plan were somewhat toned down in the Constitution adopted in 1820.

Finally, only two synods favored forming a central body – the Pennsylvania Ministerium and the North Carolina Synod. The Pennsylvania Ministerium resolved to appoint delegates and declared that if three-fourths of the established synods adopted the new Constitution, to consider the General Synod established. A meeting of the delegates a Hagerstown, Maryland, was proposed for October 22 to 24, 1820.

The Prospects for a central body were brightened before the general meeting took place. Although the New York Ministerium had opposed the idea, the matter was reconsidered by the pastors after the close of the synodical sessions, who then resolved to send delegates. A new, but small synod, The Synod of Maryland and Virginia, was organized in 1820 and also brightened the prospects for a central body, for they appointed Dr. Kurtz and two laymen as delegates.

HAGERSTOWN, MARYLAND, OCTOBER 22 TO 24, 1820

The following synods were represented: Pennsylvania Ministerium, New York Ministerium, North Carolina Synod, Maryland and Virginia Synod. The chairman was Dr. Kurtz and the secretary was Henry A. Muhlenberg of Reading. It was resolved to vote according to synods, with each synod entitled to one vote.

Of interest is the fact that the Constitution adopted by the representatives contained no confessional paragraph. Also, the hierarchical tendency, though toned down, still remained. All books and writings, liturgical forms, and so forth, had to be approved by the General Synod before they could be published for public use. On the other hand, the General Synod could propose new books or writings for general or special public use. An example of how hierarchical the General Synod was, is shown by the report of the Gettysburg Seminary (1827), which begins with the words: "In presenting to the *Supreme Judicatory of the Lutheran Church in America* an account of the progress. . . ."

THE CONSTITUTION OF 1829

Certain interesting observations can be made:
(1) Absolute obedience
IF A CONGREGATION HERETOFORE CONNECTED WITH A SYNOD SHOULD REFUSE TO OBEY THE RESOLUTIONS OF THAT SYNOD OR THE PRECEPTS OF THIS CONSTITUTION, IT SHALL BE EXCLUDED FROM THE CONNECTION WITH THAT SYNOD AS LONG AS ITS DISOBEDIENCE LASTS, AND WITHOUT SPECIAL PERMISSION FROM THE PRESIDENT NEITHER ANY OTHER SYNOD NOR A

137

LUTHERAN PASTOR OR CANDIDATE SHALL SERVE HER.

(2) Doctrine

NO GENERAL SYNOD SHALL BE ALLOWED TO INTRODUCE SUCH ALTERNA-TIONS IN MATTERS PERTAINING TO THE FAITH OR MODE OF PUBLISHING THE GOSPEL OF JESUS CHRIST AS MIGHT IN ANY WAY TEND TO BURDEN THE CONSCIENCES OF THE BRETHREN IN CHRIST.

(3) Indifferentism

THE GENERAL SYNOD SHALL GIVE ADVICE OR OPINION WHEN COMPLAINTS SHALL BE BROUGHT BEFORE THEM BY WHOLE SYNODS OR CONGREGATIONS OR INDIVIDUALS CONCERNING DOCTRINE OR DISCIPLINE. THE GENERAL SYNOD, HOWEVER, SHALL BE EXTREMELY CAREFUL THAT THE CONSCIENCE OF THE MINISTERS IS NOT BURDENED WITH HUMAN LAWS AND THAT NO ONE BE OPPRESSED BY REASON OF DIFFERENCE OF OPINION OR *NON-FUNDAMEN-TAL* DOCTRINES.

(4) Unionism

THE GENERAL SYNOD SHALL BE SEDULOUSLY AND INCESSANTLY REGARD-FUL OF THE CIRCUMSTANCES OF THE TIMES AND OF EVERY RISE AND PROGRESS OF UNITY OF SENTIMENT AMONG CHRISTIANS IN GENERAL IN ORDER THAT BLESSED OPPORTUNITIES TO PROMOTE CONCORD AND UNITY MAY NOT PASS BY NEGLECTED AND UNAVAILING.

Lutheran historian R.C. Wolf notes that the desire for union with other denominations, which was strong among Lutherans in the first quarter of the nineteenth century, gradually lessened. He further points out that there was an increased sense of Lutheran identity in doctrine and worship, in varying degree, in the Muhlenberg strand of Lutheranism in the middle decades of the nineteenth century.[1] In 1833, a special committee was appointed by the General Synod to study the aspects of the proposed union with the Reformed and to study the merits, the difficulties and the specific basis involved to achieve union. No definite conclusions were reached after two years and the committee upon their request was discharged.[2]

The lack of a confessional platform for the General Synod was evidently an intentional omission – at least it was regarded as such by some, e.g. the Tennessee Synod. Schober urged recognition of the *Augsburg Confession* but failed to accomplish this. Though the Tennessee Synod vigorously protested against the General Synod, because neither the Bible nor the *Augsburg Confession* had been mentioned in the Constitution, the General Synod remained silent. Dr. Kurtz, president, stated in 1852: "We admit that the General Synod never formally or by express resolution repudiated or abandoned the doctrinal basis." However, when was a doctrinal basis ever established? The Tennessee Synod gave a very searching critique of the Constitution. (See R.C. Wolf's *Documents of Lutheran Unity in America*, pp. 74-77 for this critique.)

THE FIRST REGULAR CONVENTION

At the Hagerstown meeting it was resolved to have the chairman convene meeting of the General Synod at Frederick, Maryland, as soon as three of the synods adopted the proposed Constitution. Meanwhile, committees were appointed to draw up plans for a Lutheran Seminary, to arrange for a mission institute, and to create a fund for the support of widows, pastors, and others.

While the Constitution was rejected by the New York Ministerium, the Ohio Synod, and the Tennessee Synod, it was accepted by the other three, meeting at Hagerstown: the Pennsylvania Ministerium, the North Carolina Synod, and the Maryland and Virginia Synod. At the Frederick, Maryland, meeting in October 1821, twenty delegates were present. Thus, this general or central body that was destined to exist into the next century had a rather humble beginning. In 1823 the Pennsylvania Ministerium, which had provided the greatest impetus for the federation, withdrew from the General Synod. The Ministerium feared centralization of authority, and its constituent congregations feared infringements on their liberties (especially the congregations in the rural areas considered the General Synod to be "an aristocratic spiritual congress" that would impose the horrors of an ecclesiastical despotism on them.)[3] These congregations were also vocal against establishing theological seminaries, which they considered to be useless and costly, a reason to tax the farmers.[4] Furthermore, the Ministerium long cherished union with the Reformed Church and feared that the General Synod would interfere with its plans for union. In fact the Ministerium resolved, "To desire solely the accomplishment of the future union with the Reformed Church. . . . ."[5] It would be another thirty years before the Ministerium would again join the General Synod.

The withdrawal of the Pennsylvania Ministerium was a devastating loss to the General Synod and many thought that it would fail to survive, but survive it did. The original requirement of three member synods for the General Synod's existence was met when a third synod was organized to meet this requirement. A group of congregations west of the Susquehanna River seceded from the Pennsylvania Ministerium in protest of its withdrawal from the General Synod. The new group organized in September 1825 and chose the name Synod of West Pennsylvania. Later on two more synods were formed out of this group. In 1842 the congregations to the west withdrew and formed the Allegheny Synod. And in 1855 another group withdrew and formed the Synod of Central Pennsylvania. The Allegheny Synod joined the General Synod.

A PERIOD OF GROWTH

During the initial years of the federation's existence, it was due chiefly to the exertions of Samuel Simon Schmucker, then only 25 years old, that the General Synod survived. During the years 1831 to 1864 a large number of district synods joined the General Synod, so that by 1860 this central body accounted for two-thirds of the 164,000 Lutheran Communicants living in America. (1) HARTWICK SYNOD: Organized in 1830 in Schoharie, New York, by the Western Conference of the New York Ministerium. Its members desired greater opportunities to participate in revivalism. Embraced fifteen counties in central New York. Acknowledged the *Augsburg*

Confession and joined the General Synod in 1831. (2) SOUTH CAROLINA SYNOD: Organized in 1824 by six pastors and five laymen, and joined the General Synod in 1835. Dr. John Bachman was the leading spiritual. (3) NEW YORK MINISTERIUM: Organized in 1786 and finally joined the General Synod in 1837. (4) SYNOD OF VIRGINIA: Organized in 1828 by eight pastors who amicably withdrew from the Synod of Maryland and Virginia. Two laymen helped to form the synod. Confessed the *Augsburg Confession* and joined the General Synod in 1839. (5) SYNOD OF THE WEST: Organized in 1833 and embraced Kentucky, Indiana, Illinois, and Missouri. Friedrich Conrad Dietrich Wyneken, who became a leading spiritual in the Missouri Synod, was a member until 1845. The Synod of the West joined the General Synod in 1841. In 1846 it divided into three parts: Synod of the Southwest (Kentucky and Tennessee), Synod of Illinois, and Synod of the West (Indiana). (6) EAST OHIO SYNOD (ENGLISH SYNOD): Organized in 1836, it was a liberal body, joining the General Synod in 1841. (7) EAST PENNSYLVANIA SYNOD: Organized in 1842 by nine pastors withdrawing from the Pennsylvania Ministerium. Advocated the use of the English language, revivals, and greater liberty in worship forms. It joined the General Synod in 1843. (8) SOUTHWEST VIRGINIA SYNOD: Organized in 1843 and joined the General Synod the same year. (9) ALLEGHENY SYNOD: Organized in 1842 by pastors of the West Pennsylvania Synod, and joined the General Synod in 1843. (10) MIAMI SYNOD: Organized in 1844. Located in Ohio, it joined the General Synod in 1845. (11) ILLINOIS SYNOD: Organized in 1846, joining the General Synod in 1848. After 1867 the greater part joined the Illinois District of the Missouri Synod. (12) WITTENBERG SYNOD: Organized in 1847. Located in Ohio, it joined the General Synod in 1848. (13) OLIVE BRANCH SYNOD OF INDIANA: Organized in 1848. It joined the General Synod in 1850. (14) PENNSYLVANIA MINISTERIUM: Organized in 1748. Joined the General Synod in 1820, left in 1823, rejoined in 1853. (15) TEXAS SYNOD: Organized in 1851 by six pastors from St. Chrischona and joined the General Synod in 1853. (16) SYNOD OF NORTH ILLINOIS, IOWA, AND WISCONSIN: Joined the General Synod in 1853. (17) PITTSBURG SYNOD: Organized in 1845. Known as the "Mission Synod," it joined the General Synod in 1853. (18) Kentucky Synod and Central Pennsylvania Synod: Organized in 1852 and joined the General Synod in 1855. (19) SYNOD OF NORTHERN INDIANA: Organized in 1855 and joined the General Synod in 1857. (20) SYNOD OF IOWA: organized in 1852 and joined the General Synod in 1857. (21) SYNOD OF SOUTHERN ILLINOIS: Organized in 1856 and joined the General Synod in 1857.

HOLDING OUT THE HAND OF FELLOWSHIP

The General Synod, conceived in unionistic spirit, continued so. The minutes of 1827 read: THE FOLLOWING GENTLEMEN WERE PRESENT AND ADMITTED AS ADVISORY MEMBERS: THE REV. MR. HELFENSTEIN OF PHILADELPHIA, DELEGATE FROM THE BIBLE SOCIETY OF THAT CITY AND THE REV. MR. VAN DER SLOOT, DELEGATE FROM THE GENERAL SYNOD OF THE REFORMED CHURCH.

The subject of publishing a new hymnbook adapted to the use of both Lutheran and Reformed congregations was discussed, but the General Synod decided against it since the joint hymnbook for both Lutheran and Reformed services had been introduced in a large number of congregations and had considerable merit.

The minutes of 1829 stated: MINISTERS, REGULAR MEMBERS OF OTHER SYN-ODS OR OF SISTER CHURCHES [SECTARIAN DENOMINATIONS] WHO MAY BE PRESENT OR APPEAR AS DELEGATES OF SUCH BODIES, MAY BE RECEIVED AS ADVISORY MEM-BERS, BUT HAVE NO VOTE IN ANY DECISION OF THE SYNOD. At Hagerstown in 1837, a Presbyterian, an Episcopalian, a German Reformed member, and a Methodist were received as advisory members. At Charlestown in 1850, delegates were appointed to the German Reformed, the Presbyterian, the Cumberland Presbyterian, and the Congregational Churches. At Dayton, Ohio, in 1855, 16 sectarian ministers were seated as advisory members. At Lancaster, Pennsylvania, in 1862, the delegate to the German Reformed Church reported being. . . MOST KINDLY RECEIVED BY THAT BODY AND WAS CHARGED BY THE SAME TO RETURN ITS CORDIAL SALUTATIONS TO THIS SYNOD WITH THE HOPE ON THE PART OF OUR GERMAN REFORMED BRETHREN THAT THE PRESENT FRATERNAL CORRESPONDENCE BETWEEN OUR CHURCHES, TWIN-SISTERS OF THE REFORMATION, MAY NEVER BE INTERRUPTED. At Philadelphia, in 1845, the General Synod. . . . CORDIALLY APPROVES OF THE PRACTICE WHICH HAS HITHERTO PREVAILED IN OUR CHURCHES OF INVITING COMMUNICANTS IN REGU-LAR STANDING IN EITHER CHURCH [LUTHERAN OR REFORMED] TO PARTAKE OF THE SACRAMENT OF THE LORD'S SUPPER IN THE OTHER, AND OF THE DISMISSION OF CHURCH MEMBERS, AT THEIR OWN REQUEST, FROM THE CHURCHES OF THE ONE TO THOSE OF THE OTHER DENOMINATION.

In 1846 Schmucker, Kurtz, and Morris of the General Synod attended the World's Convention at London where they united with 800 ministers of 50 different denominations in founding the Evangelical Alliance, which assumed the ecumenical motto: "We are One Body in Christ." The purpose of the Alliance was not to unify in doctrine, but to make for closer fellow-ship, thus hoping to draw together in closer unity all evangelical Chris-tians. The General Synod was represented at the conferences that were held by this Alliance.

In his book *A Century of Grace* (a history of the Lutheran Church – Mis-souri Synod), Walter A. Baepler made this terse but revealing observation of the General Synod: ITS LEADERS WERE AVOWED ENEMIES OF THE LUTHERAN CONFESSIONS. THEY DENOUNCED THE LUTHERAN DOCTRINES OF BAPTISM, THE LORD'S SUPPER, ABSOLUTION AND THE PERSONAL UNION OF THE TWO NATURES OF CHRIST. THEY LOVED THE DOCTRINES OF THE REFORMED CHURCH, CHAMPI-ONED THE REVIVAL, AND ADVOCATED A UNION WITH THE SECTS.[6]

The General Synod was severely attacked by Friedrich Wyneken, at that time a member of the Synod of the West. He later severed his connection with the General Synod and joined the Missouri Synod, later becoming its second president. While on a trip to Germany, Wyneken attacked the fed-eration in a German Church paper, accusing it of assuming the form of a "serpent seeking to destroy the Church." He also labeled it as "Methodis-tic" and pointed out that it was promoting a union of Lutheran and Reformed Churches. Finally, when the General Synod would not defend its doctrine and practice against his charges, Wyneken withdrew.

BREAK UP

In 1860 the Scandinavians withdrew because of the admission of the Melanchthon Synod, which was committed to the Definite Platform, a document prepared by Samuel Simon Schmucker and intended to be a substitute for the *Augsburg Confession*.

In 1864 the un-Lutheran Franckean Synod was received. This action resulted two years later in a disruption of the General Synod at Fort Wayne, Indiana. The Pennsylvania Ministerium, the Synods of Illinois, Minnesota, and Texas, and the English Synod of Ohio, together with a large part of the Pittsburgh Synod, left the General Synod and organized the General Council (1867).

With the nation embroiled in Civil War between the North and the South, it was inevitable that division occur also in the Church. In 1863 the Southern synods – North Carolina, South Carolina, Virginia, and Southwestern Virginia – withdrew from the General Synod and organized their own General Synod of the Confederate States.

IMPROVEMENT AND WEAKNESSES

The York resolution in 1864 made the *Augsburg Confession* its doctrinal base. In 1895 the General Synod spoke of the *Unaltered Augsburg Confession* "as throughout in perfect consistence with God's Word." In 1901 the General Synod dropped the distinction between fundamental and so-called non-fundamental doctrines. In 1909 it withdrew its objections to the secondary symbols of the Book of Concord, and in 1913 it approved, at Atchison, Kansas, all the symbols of the Lutheran Church. Still, there was a breakdown of doctrinal discipline within the federation. Members in the Masonic Lodge were not disciplined; rather, membership in the Lodge was openly tolerated both for the clergy and the laity. UnLutheran practice was continued by individuals without official censure.

On the other hand, the federation's action of taking a more definite stand on the Lutheran Confessions made it possible for it to merge with the General Council and the United Synod of the South in 1918 to form the United Lutheran Church in America.

THE LEADERS

(1) The first that should be named is Samuel Simon Schmucker (1799-1883), the author of forty-four books and pamphlets and perhaps the most influential man in the General Synod. He was not merely unionistic, he was a pronounced Reformed theologian who rejected many distinctive

142

Lutheran doctrines. A student of Helmuth, who had trained several men for the ministry (Lutheranism is indebted to him for supplying early Lutheran pastors), Schmucker also studied at Princeton. He served as pastor at New Market, Virginia, and was professor of theology at Gettysburg. From 1864 until 1873 he devoted himself to writing, and was the author of most of the organic documents of the General Synod. In England he was lauded as the "Father" of the Evangelical Alliance. (2) Benjamin Kurtz (1795-1865) conducted his ministry in Maryland and Pennsylvania and served as editor of the *Lutheran Observer* (1833-1863). He was an ardent advocate of new measures such as revivals, Sabbath observance, and temperance reforms. He favored the liberal "American Lutheranism" movement and violently opposed every effort at Lutheranizing and confessionalizing the General Synod. (3)Samuel Sprecher (1810-1905) was a brother-in-law of Schmucker and his supporter. He insisted that the General Synod refuse admission to such as adhered to the Lutheran symbols and their doctrines. Later, he was influenced to a great extent by the Missouri Synod and retracted much of his stand. Still, he was not completely cured of his Reformed subjectivism. (4) James Allen Brown (1821-1882) served as professor at Gettysburg (1864-1879). He was conservative, an opponent of Schmucker, and editor of the *Lutheran Quarterly*. (5) Charles Philip Krauth (1797-1867) first studied medicine, then theology under D.H. Schaeffer. Served as professor at Gettysburg (1833-1867) and was the exponent of mild confessionalism, pleading for peace and mutual toleration. The father of Charles Porterfield Krauth, he became the leading spirit in establishing the General Synod. (6) E.F. Schaeffer (1807-1879). Pastored in Maryland, Pennsylvania, New York, and Ohio. Was professor at Columbus, Gettysburg, and Philadelphia. (7) J.G. Morris (1803-1895). Founded the *Lutheran Observer* in 1831. Was pastor in Baltimore and Lutherville, Maryland. He was noted as a pulpit orator and writer. (8) Charles Porterfield Krauth (1823-1883). According to C.F.W. Walther (Missouri Synod) Krauth was "the most eminent man in the English Church of this country, a man of rare learning, a noble man and without guile." Until 1861 he served congregations at Baltimore, Shepherdstown, Virginia, and others, including a Reformed congregation in the absence of its pastor. He also served in Pittsburg and Philadelphia, and in 1861-1864 was editor of the *Lutheran and Missionary*. He was professor of Dogmatics at Philadelphia Seminary in 1864. He was the leading spirit in establishing the General Council (which was the result of a decided move toward Lutheran confessionalism). He was president of the General Council (1870-1880). In 1868 he was appointed professor of philosophy at the University of Pennsylvania, but retained his chair at the seminary. He was also the author of many books, chief of which was *The Conservative Reformation and its Theology*. It must also be recognized that during his early years he was unionistically inclined.

Ministerial education until 1815 and for a period after this date was chiefly of a private nature. Classes began to be taught at Hartwick Seminary in 1797, before any buildings were up. Various attempts to establish seminaries in Pennsylvania, in North Carolina and in Tennessee proved futile – including joint attempts with the Reformed Church. In many cases the parsonages furnished the ministerial candidates and their training. F.D. Schaeffer instructed his four sons, Paul Henkle his five sons. Among the younger men S.S. Schmucker was particularly zealous for the training of the clergy. His efforts to save the General Synod from dissolving in 1823 were prompted chiefly by his desire to have the Church establish her own seminary. He kept the matter always before the Synod. In 1825 the General Synod adopted the plan to open a seminary, appointed time for the opening, selected Chucker as professor, chose a board of directors, opened a subscription list, selected canvassers and appointed Pastor Kurtz to go to Europe to secure books for the library, and also endowments. "In this Seminary shall be taught, in the German and English languages, the fundamental doctrines of the Sacred Scriptures as contained in the *Augsburg Confessions*. The Seminary opened with its one professor at Gettysburg in 1826. Ten students were enrolled. Southern Theological Seminary, Columbia, South Carolina, was opened in 1830. Hamma Divinity School, Springfield, Ohio, was opened in 1845 and later became a part of the United Lutheran Church in America (ULCA). Susquehanna University, Selinsgrove, Pennsylvania, opened in 1858 and later became a coeducational college under the United Lutheran Church in America.

In 1835 the Central Missionary Society of the Evangelical Lutheran Church in the U.S. was formed at Mechanicsburg, Pennsylvania by private members. A similar society connected with the Pennsylvania Ministerium worked in harmony with the Central Missionary Society. Being a private venture, the Central Missionary Society later had to cease its work due to lack of funding. In 1845 the Home Missionary Society of the General Synod was organized with auxiliaries in the district synods. Through this agency many new district synods were established. In 1869 this society transferred all its funds and interests to the General Synod. In 1837 the Foreign Missionary Society of the Evangelical German Churches in the U.S. was organized. It was to serve both the Lutherans and the Reformed. The Pennsylvania Ministerium was represented, but the Reformed and the Moravians refused to join and so the name was changed to the Foreign Mission Society of the Evangelical Lutheran Church in the U.S.A. Dr. Rhenius' work in India was supported. (The General Synod had begun to support mission work in India already in 1821.) In 1840 C.F. Heyer was appointed missionary to India. In 1857 he retired from the India field and devoted himself to home mission work in Minnesota. Later, when Pastor Heyer was 77 years old, he returned to India. However, he died four years later in America. It is noteworthy that while he was a missionary in Minnesota, Pastor Heyer led the way in forming the Minnesota Synod, which later became a district of the Wisconsin Synod.

In 1869 the General Synod assumed responsibility for the work of the

Foreign Missionary Society in India and in Liberia, Africa, and appointed a Mission Board. In 1853 a Church Extension Society was organized to grant loans to missions. In 1869 it turned its work over to the General Synod. Until that year, the General Synod did no mission work as a synod.

In eleemosynary work Dr. W.A. Passavant was the leader. He began with a hospital at Pittsburgh in 1849, an orphanage at the same place and at Rochester. With the help of Lutheran Sisters from Kaiserwerth, Germany, Passavant founded hospitals in Milwaukee, Chicago, and Jacksonville, Illinois. He established orphanages at Mt. Vernon, Germantown, and Boston.

Over the years several church papers were published, some in English, some in German. None of the early publications lasted more than six years. But others attained permanent status. (*Note the diagram of the General Synod*)

Footnotes for Chapter Nine

* Compare to R.C. Wolf's *Documents of Lutheran Unity*, pp. 56, 57; Doc. #24

1 Richard C. Wolf, *Documents of Lutheran Unity in America*, (Fortress Press, Philadelphia, PA, 1966), pp. 84, 85.

2 Wolf, *Documents of Lutheran Unity in America*, p. 84.

3 Abdel Ross Wentz, *A Basic History of Lutheranism in America*, (Muhlenberg Press, Philadelphia, PA, 1955), p. 81.

4 Wentz, *A Basic History of Lutheranism in America*, p. 81.

5 Wolf, *Documents of Lutheran Unity in America*, p. 83.

6. Walter A. Baepler, *A Century of Grace*, (Concordia Publishing House, Saint Louis, MO 63118-3968, 1947), pp. 5,6.

CHAPTER TEN

THE GENERAL COUNCIL-1867

SITUATIONS AND EVENTS LEADING TO THE FORMATION OF THE GENERAL COUNCIL

THE FLOOD OF IMIGRANTS

The period from 1830 onward, toward the final decades of the nineteenth century, saw a strong influx of German immigrants, of whom many were Lutherans.

$$
\begin{array}{l}
1820 - 1830. \ldots 6{,}761 \\
1831 - 1840. \ldots 152{,}454 \\
1841 - 1850. \ldots 434{,}636 \\
1851 - 1860. \ldots 951{,}669 \\
1861 - 1870. \ldots 787{,}468
\end{array}
$$

These German immigrants settled in the heart of the Mississippi Valley, but also in New York and Pennsylvania. Many of the immigrants were Catholic, but a greater number were Lutheran. Wentz points out that fortunately for the Church, those who came at the beginning of the great immigration were stoutly loyal to the Lutheran confessions. This was the start of a completely different branch of Lutheranism in America, and this branch would have a good effect on the Muhlenberg descendants, helping to firm up the confessional reaction that those Lutheran bodies had begun to experience.[1] A deep Lutheran confessionalism was especially displayed by those German immigrants who founded the Missouri Synod, which became the brightest guiding light for confessional Lutheranism for decades to come. We shall cover this territory thoroughly in a separate chapter containing the history of this, the largest Lutheran synod in America (not counting the merger January 1988 creating the Evangelical Lutheran Church in America).

And so, as a result of this mounting tide of German Lutherans, stoutly confessional in character, a confessional reaction from within and without was felt by the General Synod. This reaction was also helped to some extent by the influx from Scandinavian countries. In the late 1830's the Norwegians settled across the Mississippi in northeastern Iowa. By 1843 immigrants from Norway numbered 1,600 a year, but this increased still further after 1847, when America received more than 4,000 Norwegians annually.

Tragically, not all Lutherans migrating from Germany helped to swell the numbers in the Lutheran congregations in America. In the year 1825 there were about 45,000 Lutherans enrolled in the congregations. Many of the German Lutheran immigrants that came after this year did not join existing congregations, nor did they help to begin new churches in the wilderness regions in which they settled. Instead many led a haphazard, aimless, and uninvigorated spiritual existence. Too often, the hard work of clearing the wilderness and of putting bread and potatoes on the table sapped strength and time from these immigrants, so that they did not concern themselves with feeding upon the Bread of Life. Missionary Friedrich Wyneken in one of his reports describes the sad religious plight of the German pioneers in forests and upon prairies thus: EITHER SINGLY OR IN SMALL GROUPS OUR BRETHREN GO INTO THE FOREST WITH THEIR WOMEN AND CHILDREN. IN MANY CASES THEY HAVE NO NEIGHBORS FOR MILES AROUND, AND EVEN IF THEY HAVE SUCH NEAR BY, THE DENSE FOREST SO SEPARATES THEM THAT THEY LIVE IN IGNORANCE OF EACH OTHER. COME NOW, READER, AND ENTER THE SETTLEMENTS AND LOG HUTS OF YOUR BRETHREN! HUSBAND, WIFE, AND CHILDREN MUST WORK HARD TO FELL THE GIANT TREES, TO CLEAR THE VIRGIN FORESTS, TO PLOW, TO SOW, AND TO PLANT, FOR THEIR PITTANCE OF MONEY RUNS LOW OR IS ALREADY GONE. BREAD MUST BE PROCURED; BUT THIS CAN BE GOTTEN ONLY FROM THE GROUND WHICH THEY TILL. IN THEIR LOG HUTS A STRANGE SIGHT MEETS GERMAN EYES; THERE ALMOST EVERYTHING IS WANTING THAT YOU WOULD CONSIDER ABSOLUTELY NECESSARY IN THE LINE OF FURNITURE. EVERYTHING IS PRIMITIVE, AND THERE IS NO THOUGHT OF COMFORT. SHOES AND CLOTHING WEAR OUT, AND THE WINTER IS AT HAND. SMALL WONDER, THEN, THAT EVERYBODY WORKS IN ORDER TO SUPPORT THIS BODY AND LIFE. NO DIFFERENCE IS MADE BETWEEN SUNDAY AND WEEKDAY, ESPECIALLY SINCE NO CHURCH BELL CALLS THEM TO THE HOUSE OF GOD, AND NO NEIGHBOR IN HIS SUNDAY OUTFIT ARRIVES TO CALL FOR HIS FRIEND. IT IS NOT TO BE WONDERED AT THAT THE PIONEER'S TIRED LIMBS SEEK THEIR COUCH WITHOUT PRAYER; EVEN THE PRAYER AT MEALTIME HAS LONG SINCE BEEN BANISHED BY THE LAPSE INTO UNBELIEF OR RECENT TROUBLE. ALAS, BIBLE AND HYMNAL ALSO IN MANY CASES HAVE BEEN LEFT IN THE OLD COUNTRY, AS THE PEOPLE, UNDER THE INFLUENCE OF RATIONALISM, HAD LOST THE TASTE FOR THEM. NO PREACHER ARRIVES TO ROUSE THEM FROM THEIR CARNAL THOUGHTS AND PURSUITS, AND THE SWEET VOICE OF THE GOSPEL HAS NOT BEEN HEARD FOR A LONG TIME. Wyneken pointed out that a person GETS ACCUSTOMED TO LIVING WITHOUT CHURCH, DIVINE SERVICE, AND SCHOOL; THE EXTERNAL LIFE FASCINATES MORE AND MORE; ONE IS EVER MORE ABSORBED BY TEMPORAL AFFAIRS AND FINALLY FINDS IT CONVENIENT TO BE NO

LONGER DISTURBED OR REPROVED BY THE TRUTH.[2]

Nor were the German Lutheran immigrants wholly unaffected by the course and godless way of life which was so often present on the ever-moving frontier. Wyneken himself was deeply shocked and dismayed by the open and course immorality which he witnessed in America, a way of life many immigrants succumbed to.

Neither did all Norwegian Lutherans who immigrated contribute to the building up of the Lutheran Church in America. Wentz points out: THE SPIRITUAL CONDITION OF THESE IMMIGRANTS REFLECTED THE WIDE VARIETY OF RELIGIOUS POINTS OF VIEW FLOURISHING IN NORWAY AT THE TIME. ALONGSIDE OF CONFESSIONALISM, STATE CHURCH LOYALTY, AND INDIFFERENCE, THERE WERE ELEMENTS OF RATIONALISM, PIETISM, PURITANISM, ANTI-CLERICALISM, QUAKERISM, AND MORMONISM.[3]

In spite of the conglomeration of unLutheran beliefs among the Norwegians, a Norwegian Lutheran synod with a confessional platform was finally organized in 1853, and was called the Norwegian Evangelical Lutheran Church in America. Begun by Pastor Dietrichson, the synod was finally fully organized under Herman Preuss, who was strictly orthodox. But prior to the organization of this synod the Evangelical Lutheran Church of North America marked its beginning in 1846. This loose organization effected by Elling Eielson came to be known as the Eielson Synod.

According to Wentz, SWEDISH IMMIGRATION DURING THIS PERIOD, BECOMING SIGNIFICANT IN THE 1840'S, BROUGHT TO AMERICA LESS VARIETY OF FAITH AND PRACTICE THAN THE NORWEGIAN. THE SWEDES KEPT IN CLOSER TOUCH WITH THE AMERICANIZED PART OF THE LUTHERAN CHURCH.[4]

The Finns who came to America continued in the lines they knew best: mining, logging, and farming. Large numbers of them settled in Michigan's Upper Peninsula. The first Finnish Lutheran congregations were organized in 1867 at Hancock and Calumet in Michigan's Upper Peninsula.

OPPOSITION TO POSITIVE LUTHERANISM

The rising tide of positive Lutheranism aroused opposition in some of the older bodies, culminating in what is commonly called "American Lutheranism." Its chief representatives were Pastors Samuel Simon Schmucker, Benjamin Kurtz, and Samuel Sprecher. The chief contention of the proponents of "American Lutheranism" was that the Lutheran Church in America can have a national development only by adjusting itself to its environments. This in fact amounted to making concessions to the revivalistic and puritanical spirit of the surrounding denominations. The new movement was essentially Calvinistic, Methodistic, Puritan, indifferent toward truly Lutheran doctrine, and unionistic (willing to extend church fellowship to non-Lutherans). It was anything but Lutheran! In Volume 2 of his history of Lutheranism, Bente points out: "AMERICAN LUTHERANISM", ACCORDING TO SCHMUCKER, WAS NOT LUTHERANISM IN SYMPATHY WITH AMERICAN INSTITUTIONS AND THE ENGLISH LANGUAGE, BUT ABOLITION OF THE LUTHERAN SYMBOLS AND REJECTION OF THE LUTHERAN DOCTRINES (ABSOLUTION, THE REAL PRESENCE OF CHRIST IN THE LORD'S SUPPER, BAPTISMAL REGENERATION, ETC.) IN FAVOR OF THE CORRESPONDING RE-

FORMED TENETS AND THE NINE ARTICLES OF THE EVANGELICAL ALLIANCE.[5] Quoting from the 1873 *Lehre and Wehre*, Bente reported: SO-CALLED AMERICAN LUTHERANISM IS BUT A NEW EDITION OF ZWINGLIANISM, WHICH, IN A DISHONEST FASHION, APPROPRIATES THE LUTHERAN NAME. THE MORE ONE AGREES WITH ZWINGLI AND DISAGREES WITH THE SIXTEENTH CENTURY LUTHERANISM, THE MORE GENUINE AN AMERICAN LUTHERAN HE IS.[6]

Schmucker, who had rallied the General Synod from dissolution in 1823 and who had once been considered a conservative among Lutherans, was unable to accept the strict Lutheranism which by 1850 was on the upswing in the General Synod under the influence of the conservatives. Schmucker's "conservative Lutheranism" no longer appeared as conservative; instead, he led the way for a strong liberal element, bent on turning back the confessional tide. His rise to the position of a liberal leader made following him and those on his side unacceptable to the conservative Lutherans. They could see that Schmucker denied and assailed every doctrine distinctive to Lutheranism, and that men like Kurtz ridiculed what was most sacred to Luther and thus most prominent in the Lutheran Confessions.

THE DEFINITE PLATFORM

While the confessional basis recommended by the General Synod to the district synods was "that the fundamental doctrines of the Word of God are taught in a manner *substantially correct* (emphasis added) in the doctrinal articles of the *Augsburg Confession*," great liberties were taken with the words "fundamental" and "substantially correct" and also with the term "doctrinal." To give a definite pledge to the General Synod, Dr. Baugher, a conservative, proposed in 1844 that the Maryland Synod prepare an "Abstract of Doctrines and Practices of the Evangelical Lutheran Church in America." However, the report of the committee appointed to the task was inspired by the liberal Kurtz and subsequently rejected, because it modified Lutheran doctrines or omitted or rejected all distinctive points.

The next year this matter was referred to the General Synod. Consequently, S.S. Schmucker was made the chairman of a committee to frame "A clear and concise view of the doctrines and practices of the Lutheran Church in America." But the General Synod was no longer following the leadership of Schmucker; hence his report was rejected. In 1853 the Pennsylvania Ministerium, which had been making forward confessional strides, again joined the General Synod. Likewise, the conservative Synods of North Illinois (org. 1851) and Texas (org. 1851) joined.

The advocates of "American Lutheranism" unexpectedly published anonymously a small pamphlet titled *Definite Synodical Platform*. This pamphlet was actually written by Schmucker, who urged its adoption upon all the synods connected with the General Synod. The idea was that the *Definite Synodical Platform* should serve as the doctrinal basis of the General Synod. It was drawn up with the purpose of counteracting the confessional Lutheran movement arising out of the west, particularly in the Missouri Synod. The *Platform* charged the *Augsburg Confession* with five specific errors: (1) The approval of

150

the ceremonies of the Mass. (2) Private confession and absolution. (3) Denial of the divine obligation of the Christian Sabbath [i.e. Sunday]. (4) Baptismal regeneration. (5) The real presence of the body and blood of the Savior in the Eucharist.[7] The articles are purged of all condemnatory sections. Even the deniers of the Trinity are not rejected. The *Apostles Creed* is relieved of the Phrase "He descended into hell." *The Athanasian Creed* is omitted and the rest of the Lutheran Symbols rejected on account of their length and alleged errors.

A STORM OF CONTROVERSY OVER
THE DEFINITE SYNODICAL PLATFORM

Schmucker wanted very much to unite Christendom in America. To bring about a union of the Protestant Churches in America, he was not only willing to sacrifice distinctive Lutheran teachings but even to demand that some of them be retracted. His attitude was that of the true ecumenist of modern times – to discover the areas of doctrinal agreement, and emphasize these, and make these the basis of uniting the Churches, at the same time refraining from publicizing the differences which exist between them. Schmucker was willing to label the differences in doctrine as "teachings distinctive to a particular denomination," rather than as doctrines which should divide the Protestant Churches.

Instead of uniting Lutherans with other Protestants, Schmucker's attempts at an ecumenical movement succeeded in dividing Lutherans. Through the adverse reaction which set in, which amounted to a storm of controversy over his *Platform*, it became even more evident who the conservative Lutherans were, and who were in the liberal camp. This was true not only in the General Synod, but outside the Synod as well, for the reaction against the *Platform* was voiced by Church leaders who were avowed Lutherans – men like C.F.W. Walther, who founded the Missouri Synod. (This ultra conservative body was formed in Perry County, Missouri, south of St. Louis, in 1847.) Walther's cry was, "Back, back to Luther, ye Lutherans!" H.J. Mann wrote in 1856, "The Platform controversy will, in the end, prove a blessing. The conservative party will arrive at a better understanding. In ten years Schmucker has not damaged himself so much in the public opinion as in the one last year."[8] One theologian observed, "The principal effect of the *Definite Platform* was to open the eyes even of the indifferent and undecided ones, and to cause them to reflect and to realize the ultimate designs of the men at the helm of the General Synod."[9] Even many men who had sympathy toward "American Lutheranism" had only rebuke for the *Definite Synodical Platform*. It is of special note that Samuel Sprecher, who helped to sponsor the *Platform*, later, in 1891, a few years prior to his death and having come under the influence of the Missouri Synod, disavowed the modifications that were made to the Lutheran creed.[10]

While a number of smaller synods endorsed the *Platform* (East Ohio, Wittenburg, and Olive Branch) the older and larger synods firmly opposed it. In 1856 the Pennsylvania Ministerium condemned the *Platform*, and the New

York Ministerium instructed its delegates to vote against it. How the wind was blowing is indicated by the fact that representatives from the Pennsylvania Ministerium and the New York Ministerium participated in the Free Evangelical Lutheran Conferences (1856 – 1859), which were proposed, advocated, and led by the leading voice for true and sound Lutheranism in America, C.F.W. Walther of the Missouri Synod.[11]

STRIFE WITHIN THE GENERAL SYNOD

The convention of the General Synod in 1857 took no formal action regarding Schmucker or the *Definite Platform,* nor towards the synods that had endorsed the *Platform.* It more than tolerated the theology advocated by Schmucker's controversial pamphlet. While Schmucker later acknowledged being the author of the *Platform*, Doctors Sprecher and Kurtz zealously sponsored it. Sprecher later disavowed the Platform, as mentioned above. Dr. Kurtz withdrew from the Maryland Synod when it tended toward conservative doctrine, and helped to organize the unLutheran Melanchthon Synod, whose doctrinal standards were mainly those of the Evangelical Alliance; its confessional basis was that of the *Platform*. This synod was accepted into the General Synod in 1859. This disturbed the Scandinavian element in the General Synod, who feared that this body might not remain doctrinally sound. And it later served as a reason for their withdrawing – along with the Synod of Northern Illinois – and in founding their own body, the Augustana Synod, in 1860.[11]

The Franckean Synod was organized in 1837 by four members of the Hartwick Synod. These men were abolitionists who, when the Hartwick Synod declined to come out publicly against slavery, separated themselves and formed their own synod. They adopted a resolution calling slavery, as it exists in America, a sin. The men of the Franckean Synod had abandoned the *Augsburg Confession* entirely and instead adopted a *Declaration of Faith*, which "does not maintain and declare the doctrine of the Trinity or that the three persons constitute the Deity. It does not declare or admit the divinity of Jesus Christ." In 1864 the Franckean Synod applied for admission to the General Synod. After spirited debate, the Franckean Synod was accepted into membership by a vote of 90 to 40, whereupon the delegation of the Pennsylvania Ministerium withdrew from the sessions of the General Synod in order to report to the Ministerium at its approaching convention. While the delegation of the Pennsylvania Ministerium did not regard its act as constituting withdrawal from the General Synod – and the Ministerium itself did not so regard it – others did.

In this same meeting of the General Synod, a resolution was adopted that denied that the *Augsburg Confession* contains errors, thus endeavoring to fortify its conservative position. However, this did not satisfy some, who felt that the Franckean Synod should have made a positive declaration over against the *Augsburg Confession* before being admitted to the General Synod.

THE WITHDRAWAL OF FIVE DISTRICT SYNODS
TO FORM A SOUTHERN GENERAL BODY

Another split in the ranks of the General Synod was occasioned by the Civil War and the issue of slavery. By the time the Synod met in Lancaster in 1862, only one delegate south of the Potomac River was present. When Civil War broke out between the North and the South, the Lutheran synods came to the support of their own respective governments. Thinking that the South would emerge from the war as a separate nation, the Southern synods set about to organize their own General Synod in May 1863. Later, their organization became known as the United Synod in the South. Thus five district synods were withdrawn from the old General Synod to form a new one in the South: North Carolina, South Carolina, Virginia, Western Virginia, and Georgia – a total of 217 congregations and 146 ministers.

THE WITHDRAWAL OF THE
PENNSYLVANIA MINISTERIUM

The largest loss to the General Synod, however, was occasioned by the withdrawal of the Pennsylvania Ministerium. What brought this on? For one thing, there was the seminary question, which proved to be vexatious. Dr. Schmucker had resigned from Gettysburg Seminary in February 1864. Many conservatives desired C.P. Krauth, Jr. as his successor. But the demand for German-speaking pastors was growing more insistent, thus reviving the old desire for a seminary at Philadelphia. This resulted in the establishing of Philadelphia Seminary in 1864, with C.P. Krauth, Jr. as a professor. Dr. C.W. Schaeffer of Gettysburg was also made a professor at the new seminary. The removal of one professor from Gettysburg, and the withdrawal of many students, occasioned bitter feelings. The representatives of the Pennsylvania Ministerium, who came as usual to attend the meeting of the Board of Directors of Gettysburg, were told that they had no place there. Literary war broke out between Krauth and Brown, who was the new head of Gettysburg Seminary. Open attacks against the Pennsylvania Ministerium were initiated by members of the General Synod.

When the General Synod met at Fort Wayne, Indiana, in 1866, the atmosphere was charged. The Pennsylvania Ministerium sent a delegate, yet both sides expected rupture. While the purely German element in the Ministerium was determined to leave the general body, the left wing delegates of the General Synod were of a mind to oblige the Germans and consequently were vocal in their desire to exclude the Pennsylvania Ministerium, if possible.

The president of the General Synod, Dr. Sprecher, was a leftist. He rejected the credentials of the Pennsylvania Ministerium delegates, declaring that this synod was "in a state of practical withdrawal from the governing functions of the Synod." When attention was called to the Ministerium's reservations of 1853 – which implied the right to secede – Sprecher replied that such reservations were not in the minutes of the General Synod and therefore could not be recognized. Sprecher's decision was upheld by the majority of synods present. On this technicality, and against the protests from other synods, the Pennsylvania delegation was excluded from the election of officers and other business.

Dr. Brown was elected the new president. While he desired to preserve the unity of the General Synod and keep the Pennsylvania Ministerium, he nevertheless endeavored to annul the reservations of that body made in 1853. Various compromise arrangements were proposed, but they all foundered on the General Synod's insistence that the Pennsylvania Ministerium give up its 1853 reservations, and the Ministerium's refusal to do so. Hence the delegation withdrew, and the rupture was complete. A few weeks later, at its 119th convention, the Ministerium withdrew from the General Synod, since it claimed it had been unjustly deprived of its rights. Furthermore, it was convinced of the impossibility "to harmonize the conflicting opinions and factions within the General Synod."

The Ministerium of New York, the Pittsburg Synod, the English Synod of Ohio, the Illinois Synod, and the Minnesota Synod followed the example of the Pennsylvania Ministerium. The final result of this impasse between synods was that instead of encompassing two-thirds of the Lutherans in America, the General Synod had been reduced in size to only about one-fourth of the total Lutheran membership.

REALIGNMENT OF SYNODS

IN THE STATE OF OHIO

On November 3, 1920, a merger took place of the Wittenberg Synod, the East Ohio Synod, the Miami Synod, and the District Synod of Ohio, forming the Ohio Synod of the United Lutheran Church in America.

IN THE STATE OF VIRGINIA

On March 17, 1922, the Synod of Virginia (1839), the Synod of Southwest Virginia (1842), and the Holston Synod (1860), merged into the Synod of Virginia.

IN THE STATE OF PENNSYLVANIA

On May 22, 1924, The Synod of Central Pennsylvania merged with the Susquehannah Synod, finally adopting in 1932 the name, the Susquehannah Synod. In 1938 the Central Pennsylvania Synod was organized from the Synod of West Pennsylvania, the Synod of East Pennsylvania, the Allegheny Synod, and the Susquehannah Synod. In 1919 the Pittsburg Synods of the General Council and the General Synod reunited.

IN THE STATE OF NEW YORK AND THE
TERRITORY OF NEW ENGLAND

In 1908 there was the merger of the Hartwick Synod, the Franckean Synod, and the Synod of New York and New Jersey, forming the New York Synod.

IN THE STATE OF ILLINOIS

In 1897 there occurred the merger of the Central Illinois Synod and the Synod of Southern Illinois to form the Synod of Central and Southern Illinois. Later, after the formation of the United Lutheran Church in America in 1918, this synod merged with the Northern Illinois Synod and parts of the Chicago Synod to form the new Illinois Synod.

THE FORMATION OF THE GENERAL
COUNCIL – 1867

THE PENNSYLVANIA MINISTERIUM:
THE INITIATOR OF UNION

In a short while after formally withdrawing from the General Synod, the Pennsylvania Ministerium issued a call to all Lutheran synods acknowledging the *Unaltered Augsburg Confession* to participate in the organization of a new body "on a truly Lutheran basis." The convention took place at Reading, Pennsylvania, December 12 – 14, 1866. Thirteen Synods were represented:
> Pennsylvania, Ministerium
> English District of Ohio
> Wisconsin Synod
> Joint Synod of Ohio
> Michigan Synod
> Pittsburgh Synod
> Minnesota Synod
> Norwegian Synod
> Iowa Synod
> Missouri Synod
> Synod of Canada
> New York Ministerium

The Scandinavian Evangelical Lutheran Augustana Synod, while not represented by a delegate, did send a letter.

MOVING TOWARD UNION

To begin discussions leading to union, Charles Porterfield Krauth, who was then the leading conservative in the Pennsylvania Ministerium, presented a set of theses on the *Fundamental Principles of Faith and Church Policy*. Of particular interest are sections 2, 5, and 6.

> Section 2: THE TRUE UNITY OF A PARTICULAR CHURCH, IN VIRTUE OF WHICH MEN ARE TRULY MEMBERS OF ONE AND THE SAME CHURCH, AND BY WHICH ANY CHURCH ABIDES IN REAL IDENTITY, AND IS ENTITLED TO A CONTINUATION OF HER NAME, IS UNITY OF (IN) DOCTRINE AND FAITH AND IN THE SACRAMENTS, TO WIT: THAT SHE CONTINUES TO TEACH AND TO SET FORTH, AND THAT HER TRUE MEMBERS EMBRACE FROM THE HEART, AND USE, THE ARTICLES OF FAITH AND THE SACRAMENTS AS THEY WERE HELD AND ADMINISTERED, WHEN THE CHURCH CAME INTO BEING AND RECEIVED A DISTINCTIVE NAME.
>
> Section 5: THE UNITY OF THE EVANGELICAL LUTHERAN CHURCH. . . . DEPENDS UPON HER ABIDING IN ONE AND THE SAME FAITH, IN CONFESSING WHICH SHE OBTAINED HER DISTINCTIVE BEING AND NAME, HER POLITICAL RECOGNITION AND HER HISTORY.
>
> Section 6: THE *UNALTERED AUGSBURG CONFESSION* IS BY PRE-EMINENCE THE CONFESSION OF THAT FAITH. THE ACCEPTANCE OF ITS DOCTRINES AND THE AVOWAL OF THEM WITHOUT EQUIVOCATION OR MENTAL RESERVATION MAKE, MARK AND IDENTIFY THAT CHURCH WHICH ALONE IN THE TRUE, ORIGINAL, HISTORICAL AND HONEST SENSE IS THE EVANGELICAL LUTHERAN CHURCH.[12]

These theses, which made the *Unaltered Augsburg Confession* the basis for Lutheran union, and which declared "that the other Confessions of the Evangelical Lutheran Church, inasmuch as they set forth none other than its system of doctrine and articles of faith, are of necessity pure and Scriptural," were adopted by all thirteen synods. Thus was agreement reached on a definition of what truly is Lutheran.

After the approval of the theses, a resolution was made that the first session of the General Council of the Evangelical Lutheran Church of America be called, if the Fundamental Principles were adopted by ten synods. The first session of the new body was held at Fort Wayne, Indiana, November 20 – 26, 1867. There were representatives of thirteen synods. In the list posted above, the Norwegian Synod and the Missouri Synod withdrew from the movement; their places being taken by the Augustana Synod and the Illinois Synod. The only synod failing to ratify the *Fundamental Principles of Faith and Church Polity* was the Joint Synod of Ohio. All except this synod and the Iowa Synod resolved to form the General Council of the Evangelical Lutheran Church in America. And so, a union of diverse languages, cultures, and customs was accomplished to serve as a welcome alternative to the old General Synod. Still, it was not a general body that appealed to everyone.

SYNODS WHICH DECLINED TO JOIN THE GENERAL COUNCIL OR DID NOT REMAIN AS MEMBERS

(1)   IOWA SYNOD: Its representatives declared before the close of the Fort Wayne session that though their synod had adopted the Constitution, they could not unite with the new body on account of its stand on pulpit – altar –

156

Lodge fellowship. Still, the privilege of the floor was accepted and freely exercised by Iowa until the merger of 1918. This merger of the General Synod, the General Council, and the United Synod in the South formed the United Lutheran Church in America. In 1875 the so-called Galesburg Rule was adopted by the General Council. It states: "The rule which accords with the Word of God and with the Confessions of our Church is: Lutheran pulpits for Lutheran ministers only; Lutheran altars for Lutheran communicants only." This rule, having been adopted, the Iowa Synod then declared that confessional scruples no longer prevented her from organic union with the Council. However, the union was not consummated because the anti-unionistic construction which Iowa put on the Galesburg Rule was disavowed within the General Council and was never really officially acknowledged and approved by the body. Therefore, on the one hand Iowa took the Rule for what it seemed to say – no unionism to be permitted with other church bodies, while the General Council on the other hand tried to make exceptions which would be allowed under various circumstances, especially to be decided at the discretion of the individual pastor.

(2) THE JOINT SYNOD OF OHIO: The synod did not adopt the new Constitution. It declined to enter because of the noncommittal attitude on the part of the Council regarding Chiliasm (the imaginary one thousand year reign of Christ on earth which various Protestant denominations believe that Christians can expect), pulpit and altar fellowship, and the Lodge (should Lodge membership be allowed?) Regarding this last point, it should be noted that the Council was quite lax regarding the Lutherans – especially those in the East – who joined lodges. The question regarding pulpit fellowship, altar fellowship, lodge membership, and Chiliasm became known as the "Four Points."

(3) WISCONSIN SYNOD: While this synod did actually join the Council in 1867, it separated the following year because of the Four Points, and after being persuaded by the Missouri Synod to withdraw from the Council. While the Pittsburgh Convention in 1868 answered the Four Points, some were dissatisfied with the answer. While Chiliasm, in a way was condemned, in another way it was left open. While lodgery was condemned, the question of pulpit and altar fellowship was not explicitly answered. And so, the Wisconsin Synod felt there was too much tendency toward liberalism regarding these important questions or points. In 1872 the Wisconsin Synod became a member of the Synodical Conference, a truly conservative federation of Lutheran synods.

(4) MICHIGAN SYNOD: Organized in 1860, this synod joined the General Council in 1867 but left the Council twenty years later and joined the Synodical Conference, becoming finally a district of the Wisconsin Synod. Michigan's representatives for several years petitioned the General Council regarding its laxness.

(5) MINNESOTA SYNOD: This synod joined the General Council in 1867 but left this body in 1871 and also became a member of the Synodical Conference, which was organized in 1872. In 1917 a complete merger was made of the Michigan, Minnesota, and Wisconsin Synods.

(6) TEXAS SYNOD: This Southern synod joined the Council in 1868 and left it in 1895, entering the Iowa Synod as the Texas District.

(7) CANADA SYNOD: While remaining with the General Council, it went on

record as being opposed to exceptions to the rule regarding pulpit-altar fellowship. It joined the United Lutheran Church in America in 1918.

SYNODS WHICH JOINED THE
GENERAL COUNCIL AFTER ITS ORGANIZATION

(1) CHICAGO SYNOD: Organized in 1871, it joined the Council in the same year under the name Indiana Synod. This synod was the result of mission work done through the General Council. It later changed its name to the Chicago Synod in 1896. Please note that the Indiana Synod of that era is not to be confused with a later synod organized under the same name in 1920, formed by a merger of the Olive Branch Synod (1848) with a portion of the Chicago Synod comprised of twenty-five congregations. In the same year, the Chicago Synod divided two other ways, one part helping to form the Illinois Synod of the ULCA and one the Michigan Synod of the ULCA.

(2) SYNOD OF THE NORTHWEST: This synod was also the result of extensive mission work coming out of the English Home Mission Board of the General Council. While the English-speaking congregations were formed from the Swedish population in the territory of the Augustana Synod, they did not join this synod but rather, in 1891, formed the Synod of the Northwest as a district of the General Council. Due to offense caused to the Augustana Synod, it was not received into the General Council until 1893, where it remained until 1918, becoming a part of the merger which formed the ULCA.

(3) GERMAN EV. LUTHERAN SYNOD OF MANITOBA AND THE NORTHWEST TERRITORIES: Commonly known as the Manitoba Synod, it was organized in 1897 and joined the Council. In 1947 the name was changed to the Evangelical Lutheran Synod of Western Canada. It entered the ULCA in 1918.

(4) PACIFIC SYNOD: This Synod was organized in 1901 by ten pastors who lived west of the Missouri River. With the acquisition of this synod, the General Council was extended in its territory from the Atlantic to the Pacific. The Pacific Synod became a part of the ULCA in 1918.

(5) Synod of New York and New England: When it was organized in 1902, the English-speaking pastors and congregations forming this new synod were already members of the General Council, retaining this membership when they withdrew from the New York Ministerium, which had retained its German character.

(6) NOVA SCOTIA SYNOD: One of the smallest of synods, it was organized in 1903 after an affiliation with the Pittsburgh Synod which went back to 1874. From the year of its organization until its entry into the ULCA in 1918, it was a member of the General Council.

(7) EVANGELICAL LUTHERAN SYNOD OF CENTRAL CANADA: Organized in 1909, this synod was formed by a group of English-speaking congregations which withdrew from the Synod of New York and New England. It later became a member of the General Council and finally, in 1818, a member of the ULCA.

A STATISTICAL ANALYSIS OF LUTHERANISM AT THE TIME THE GENERAL COUNCIL WAS FORMED

In 1868 the following statistics applied:

GENERAL SYNOD (ORG. 1820): 610 pastors; 1108 congregations; 87,123 communicants.

GENERAL SYNOD OF THE EVANGELICAL LUTHERAN CHURCH IN THE CONFEDERATE STATES OF AMERICA (ORG. 1863). [IN 1866 IT BECAME THE GENERAL SYNOD OF THE EVANGELICAL LUTHERAN CHURCH OF THE SOUTH. IN 1878 IT BECAME THE GENERAL SYNOD SOUTH.]: 120 pastors; 214 congregations; 17,112 communicants.

GENERAL COUNCIL (ORG. 1867): 575 pastors; 1101 congregations; 144,716 communicants.

ALL OTHER SYNODS: 582 pastors; 997 congregations; 128,254 communicants.

CONFESSIONAL BASIS – EMPHASIS ON *THE AUGSBURG CONFESSION*

The General Council accepted and acknowledged "the doctrine of the *Unaltered Augsburg Confession* in its original sense as throughout in conformity with the pure truth of which God's Word is the only rule." It also declared that "the other Confessions of the Evangelical Lutheran Church, inasmuch as they set forth none other than its system of doctrine and articles of faith, are of necessity pure and scriptural. . . . and that all of them are with the *Unaltered Augsburg Confession* in the perfect harmony of the one and the same scriptural faith." Article 10 was weak, for according to it the General Council was made responsible, not for the actual conditions within the synods but only for the official attitude and deliverances of such synods. Though the confessional basis of the General Council was irreproachable, the Council was nevertheless imbued with a spirit of indifferentism and unionism, though of a finer grade than that prevailing in the General Synod.

The real grievance, as also expressed by other synods, was not that weak members were lagging behind in Lutheran doctrine and practice, but that many of the leaders and her periodicals occupied an unLutheran position. Regarding the "Four Points," the General Council during its subsequent history never rose above the Fort Wayne level. At the Convention held there in 1867, the Council referred the matter of the Four Points – initiated by the Iowa and Ohio Synods – to the member synods for consideration "until such time as. . . we shall be enabled throughout the whole General Council and all its churches, to see eye to eye in all details of practice and usage. . ." There were differences of opinion, as well as of practice, among the members of the General Council over the issues raised by the Four Points. And yet it was the general feeling of that body that disagreement on these issues did not stand in the way of uniting the Lutherans. The Pittsburgh Declaration of 1868 was meant to clear up the Four Points. It stated: "No man shall be admitted to our pulpits, whether of the Lutheran name or any other, of whom there is just reason to doubt whether he will preach the pure truth of God's Word as taught in the Confessions of our church." Also: Heretics and fundamentally false teachers are to be excluded from the Lord's table." But the Chicago Convention, in 1870, explained: ". . . .that the term fundamental errorists refers to those who willfully, wickedly, and persistently desert in part or in whole the Christian faith, especially of the Lutheran Church, and thus overturn or destroy the foundation in them confessed, and who hold, defend, and extend these errors in the face of the admonitions of the church, and to the leading away of men from the path of life." This explanation of "fundamental errorists" had been offered to answer the charge of the Minnesota Synod at the 1869 Convention that the Council's declaration of 1868 had been unclear. But again, its declaration was ambiguous.

THE AKRON AND THE GALESBURG RULES

The declaration of 1870 was explained by C.P. Krauth at Akron, Ohio, in 1872 thus: (1) THE RULE IS: LUTHERAN PULPITS FOR LUTHERAN MINISTERS ONLY. LUTHERAN ALTARS FOR LUTHERAN COMMUNICANTS ONLY. (2) THE EXCEPTIONS TO THE RULE BELONG TO THE SPHERE OF PRIVILEGE, NOT OF RIGHT. (3) THE DETERMINATIONS OF THE EXCEPTIONS TO BE MADE IN CONSONANCE WITH THESE PRINCIPLES, BY THE CONSCIENTIOUS JUDGMENT OF PASTORS AS CASES ARISE. The Iowa Synod delegates asked the General Council to make Krauth's explanation its own, and since the rule was formally adopted at the meeting in Akron it became known as the "Akron Rule."

In 1875 at Galesburg, Illinois, the Council urged all pastors and congregations to conform their practices to the principles laid down at Akron, stating: THE RULE WHICH ACCORDS WITH THE WORD OF GOD AND WITH THE CONFESSIONS OF OUR CHURCH IS: LUTHERAN PULPITS FOR LUTHERAN MINISTERS ONLY, AND LUTHERAN ALTARS FOR LUTHERAN COMMUNICANTS ONLY. THIS THEN BECAME KNOWN AS THE "GALESBURG RULE."

While the leaders of the General Council were outspoken in their endeavors to avoid interdenominational fellowship, individual members were known to have been guilty of such transgressions.

ON THE LODGE ISSUE

Regarding secret societies, we note the resolution of 1868: ALL CONNECTIONS WITH INFIDEL AND IMMORAL ASSOCIATIONS WE CONSIDER AS REQUIRING THE EXERCISE OF PROMPT AND DECISIVE DISCIPLINE, AND AFTER FAITHFUL AND PATIENT ADMONITION AND TEACHING FROM GOD'S WORD, THE CUTTING OFF OF PERSISTENT AND OBSTINATE OFFENDERS FROM COMMUNION OF THE CHURCH UNTIL HE ABANDONS THEM AND SHOWS THEM REPENTANCE.* However, this official declaration remained a dead letter! Wrote the Pilger in 1875: TESTIMONY AGAINST SECRET SOCIETIES WILL BRING LITTLE RESULTS SO LONG AS THE CHURCH LOOKS ON IT WITH SILENCE, WHILE PASTORS OF THE CHRISTIAN CHURCHES ARE MEMBERS OF ANTI-CHRISTIAN LODGES; those who are rebuked laugh at Synod's resolution. *The Lutheran*, in 1866, declared that excommunication because of membership in a secret society has never been an official demand of the General Council. At the Convention of the Pennsylvania Ministerium in 1917, a petition signed by 13 members was presented to amend the Constitution by striking out the lodge paragraph. No action was taken.

OTHER ABERRATIONS

Further departure from the true doctrinal position of the Lutheran Confessions was evidenced in the toleration of Chiliasm; the Sunday Question (for some took the Reformed position of requiring that Sunday be the Sabbath observance); Synergism or the teaching that sinful man is able to cooperate with the Holy Spirit to bring about conversion; and in general, liberalism.

EDUCATION AND BENEVOLENCES

(1) INSTITUTIONS OF HIGHER LEARNING:
Philadelphia Seminary (est. 1866). Later moved to Mt. Airy, Pennsylvania.
Chicago Seminary, Maywood, Illinois (est. 1891).
Kropp Seminary, Schleswig, Germany (est. 1882). Was used by the Canada Synod until it was forced by World War I to establish its own.
Muhlenberg College, Allentown, Pennsylvania (est. 1848).
Wagner College, Rochester, New York (est. 1883). Was later transferred to Statan Island.
Thiel College, Greenville, Pennsylvania (est. 1870).
Luther College, Waterloo, Ontario, Canada (est. 1911). It took the place of Kropp Seminary in Germany.
Luther College, Saskatoon, Saskachewan, Canada (est. 1919).
(2) INSTITUTIONS OF BENEVOLENCE:
Wartburg Orphanage, Mount Vernon New York.
Mary J. Drexel Mother-House for Nurses, Philadelphia.
Lutheran Immigrant House, New York, New York.

THE MERGER OF 1918 FORMING THE ULCA

On November 14, 1918, the General Council entered a merger with the very bodies with whom it once was in conflict: the General Synod (1820), the General Synod South (1863). Several Free Lutheran Diets were held, beginning in 1898, followed by a series of general conferences, beginning in the same year. These were followed by doctrinal discussions, beginning in 1907. Finally, all these efforts toward achieving union resulted in the formation of the United Lutheran Church in America. The ULCA will be treated in another chapter.

REALIGNMENTS OF SYNODS

IN NEW YORK

In 1918 the New York Synod, the New York Ministerium, and the New York and New England Synod merged to form the United Synod of New York, becoming finally the Synod of New York and New England.

IN OHIO

In 1818 a group of congregations of the Pennsylvania Ministerium in Ohio formed an independent synod, keeping itself out of the General Synod. In 1831 it was divided into districts, and after 1833 it was known as the Joint Synod of Ohio. In 1840, when the Joint Synod joined the General Synod, the English Synod of Ohio (a district synod) was independent, becoming in 1858 the Synod of East Ohio. Two other offshoots of this synod were: the Wittenberg Synod and the Synod of Miami. In 1857 a new English District of the Joint Synod was formed, and ten years later it joined the General Council (1867) and changed its name the District Synod of Ohio. And so, four Ohio synods were connected up with the General Synod (Joint Synod of Ohio, East Ohio, Wittenberg, and Miami), while the District synod of Ohio connected up with the General Council.

Later, when all of these Ohio synods joined the merger forming the United Lutheran Church in America (ULCA) in 1918, they themselves merged in 1920 to form one body, the Synod of Ohio. See the following diagram of the General Council.

Footnotes for Chapter Ten

1 Abdel Ross Wentz, *A Basic History of Lutheranism in America*, (Muhlenberg Press, Philadelphia, PA, 1955), p. 115.

2 Theodore Graebner, *Church Bells in the Forest – A Story of Lutheran Pioneer Work on the Michigan Frontier 1840-1850*, (Concordia Publishing House, Saint Louis, MO 63118-3968, 1944), pp. 9-11.

3 Wentz, *A Basic History of Lutheranism in America*, p. 123.

4 Wentz, *A Basic History of Lutheranism in America*, p. 127.

5 Frederick Bente, *American Lutheranism* (2 vols.), (Concordia Publishing House, Saint Louis, MO 63118-3968, 1919).

6 Bente, *American Lutheranism*.

7 Richard C. Wolf, *Documents of Lutheran Unity in America*, (Fortress Press, Philadelphia, PA, 1966), pp. 43, 44.

8 Bente, *American Lutheranism*, Vol. 2.

9 Bente, *American Lutheranism*, Vol. 2.

10 E Clifford Nelson, Editor, *The Lutherans in North America*, (Fortress Press, Philadelphia, PA, 1975), p. 226.

11 Wentz, *A Basic History of Lutheranism in America*, pp. 142, 143.

12 Wolf, *Documents. . . .*, pp. 144, 145; Doc. #63.

* Wolf, *Documents. . . .*, p, 163; Doc.

CHAPTER ELEVEN

THE UNITED SYNOD
IN THE SOUTH

A NATION DIVIDED

The United States of America became a nation divided over the questions of slavery and of states' rights. When Abraham Lincoln (February 12, 1809 to April 14, 1865) – a prairie lawyer from Springfield, Illinois – was elected president, the people in the Northern and Southern parts of the country were galvanized to follow their respective loyalties: the people in the North, to the cause of preserving the Union; those in the South, to the cause of having their own separate and independent nation. As a potential Republican Party nominee, and later, as the party's candidate for the Office of President, Lincoln made it clear where he stood on the two greatest issues facing the nation: he was against slavery, and he was against allowing the Southern States to secede. Lincoln felt that the Union must be preserved intact, even if it required the use of military force. It came, then, as no surprise, when the ill feeling of the people in the South toward the North came to a head when Lincoln won the electoral vote.

Alarmed and dismayed that Lincoln was elected, South Carolina – already in 1860 – withdrew from the Union. Mississippi, Florida, Alabama, Georgia, Louisiana, and Texas followed suite. Feelings in favor of abolition and for preserving the Union ran especially strong in North Carolina – compared with the other southern states – nevertheless, she took her stand with her Southern counterparts the following year. These states met at Montgomery, Alabama on February 4, 1861. A Constitution for the new Southern nation, called the Confederate States of America, was drawn up and Jefferson Davis was appointed to serve as temporary president. These events took place even before Lincoln's inauguration on March 4, 1861. Thus, when Lincoln took the oath of office he was immediately faced with the crucial question: Does a state or a group of states have the right to withdraw from the Union? Lincoln's answer was that "no state upon its own mere motion can lawfully get out of the union."[1] In his Inaugural Address, Lincoln specifically addressed the South in these words: "In your hands, my dissatisfied fellow countrymen, and not in mine, is the momentous issue of civil war ... The government will not assail you ... You have no oath registered in Heaven to destroy the government, while I shall have the most solemn one to 'preserve, protect, and defend it.'"[2]

President Lincoln's strategy was to wait for the South to act. As it turned out, he did not have long to wait. On April 12, 1861, at four o'clock in the morning, the Confederate States of America let the entire nation know where they stood. By firing its cannon on Fort Sumpter – a Federal property located in Confederate territory at the mouth of Charleston Harbor in south Carolina – the Confederacy clearly announced its resolve to be an independent nation. The booming sound of the big guns signaled that civil war between the North and the South had begun. The first battle of the Civil War was fought only about 25 miles from Washington, D.C., along a stream in Virginia called Bull Run. The first victory went to the Confederate army, and many more victories after that one. Still, the North finally prevailed, and after four bloody years General Robert E. Lee surrendered to General Ulysses S. Grant at Appomattox Courthouse, Virginia. The Union had been preserved (or restored) at a horrible cost to both sides, and the Negro slaves were emancipated. Slavery had been abolished throughout the Union..

A CHURCH DIVIDED

The Mason-Dixon line not only divided the nation, it divided the Lutheran Church (and no doubt other church bodies as well) into two camps. The Northern Lutherans showed their loyalty to the Federal government, while the Southern Lutherans rallied behind the Confederacy. As America approached the middle of the nineteenth century, many in the North were openly speaking out against the evils of slavery, some even calling it a sin. But while people in the North were demanding that slavery be abolished, the opinion commonly expressed in the South was that slavery would eventually die out of itself, being at the time, however an "economic necessity."

Division was also felt in the Church. Churchmen in the North were speaking of the "sin of slavery" while churchmen in the South rose up in defense of slavery. In the North, the Lutheran writer against slavery was Dr. Passavant. His counterpart in the South, who spoke and wrote eloquently in defense of slavery, was Dr. Bachman. Did Lutherans own slaves? Some did. Many others did not. Historian Abdel Ross Wentz informs us that when the colonies became independent, Pennsylvania – the leading state for Lutheran settlement – in 1780 led in promoting emancipation for the slaves. Many Lutherans took part in the American Colonization Society, organized in 1816 to settle liberated Negroes in Liberia, Africa. Lutherans put out efforts to Christianize and educate slaves, preparing them for that time when they would be set free.[3]

After South Carolina's secession in 1860, the issue of slavery was thrust before everyone, including the Lutheran Christians, and it became more and more difficult to maintain neutrality on the issues. The Franckean Synod, though tiny in numbers, determined to make its voice heard among the Lutherans in its attack on slavery. Formed in 1837 by a small group of pastors and laymen who withdrew from the Hartwick Synod when that body failed to pronounce against slavery, the Franckean Synod increased its agitation among the Lutherans as the nation became more and more embroiled in the slavery controversy. A few smaller synods showed agreement with its cause by adopting resolutions against slavery. Wentz informs us that many Lutherans made a distinction between slavery as an evil – having to do with human relationships – and slavery as a downright sin against God. Far fewer Lutherans lived in the South, so there were few Lutherans there who owned slaves. Their view of slavery was a practical one.[4] Slavery was seen by many as an economic necessity. The South was mainly agrarian, and slaves were needed, for example, to help in the cotton fields of the large plantations. The Southern Lutherans resented the attempts of Northerners to tell Southerners how to run their affairs. And they resented the inferences of the Northern Lutherans that there was something lacking in the morality and Christianity of their Southern counterparts. The Southern Lutherans were especially offended and incensed by the aggressive actions of the Franckean Synod. Sentiment against Northern abolitionists ran high among the Southern Lutherans. When Civil War broke out, the Lutherans in the North sided with the Union, while the Lutherans in the South pledged their allegiance to the Confederacy. North and South, the Lutherans did not break rank but united with their neighbors. Many Lutherans were killed or wounded, fighting to preserve the Union and to emancipate the slaves. Southern Lutherans lost their lives in defense of the Confederacy. In 1862 the president of the North Carolina Synod commented at the meeting of the Synod in Rowan County, North Carolina: "Many of our parishioners, who at the commencement of the present ecclesiastical year stood at our altars, and whom we followed in our prayers, and to whom we imparted our affectionate counsel, have fallen in defense of our homes, our lives, and our earthly all, while we have mourned the departure of so many loved ones at home."[5]

Still, when all is said and done, the slavery issue, and the schisms resulting within a church body from it – as the book *The Lutherans in North America* points out – did not affect the Lutherans as much as other Protestant denominations.[6] One result of the institution of slavery in the South was that many German and Scandinavian immigrants (among whom were many Lutherans)

165

avoided the South and Southwest and chose to settle in the Midwest instead.

AFTER WAR BREAKS OUT, OFFENSIVE RESOLUTIONS ARE PASSED

Lutheran synods passed resolutions supporting the cause of their respective governments. And so, the war that wracked the nation, wracked the Church also. When the General Synod met in 1862 at Lancaster, Pennsylvania, the Southern synods were unable to send delegates. Resolutions were then adopted by the Convention that were to prove very offensive to the Southern Lutherans.

RESOLVED, THAT IT IS THE DELIBERATE JUDGMENT OF THIS SYNOD, THAT THE REBELLION AGAINST THE CONSTITUTIONAL GOVERNMENT OF THIS LAND IS MOST WICKED IN ITS INCEPTION, UNJUSITIFIED IN ITS CAUSE, UNNARTURAL IN ITS CHARACTER, INHUMAN IN ITS PROSECUTION, OPPRESSIVE IN ITS AIMS AND DESTRUCTIVE IN ITS RESULTS TO THE HIGHEST INTERESTS OF MORALITY AND RELIGION.

RESOLVED, THAT, IN THE SUPPRESSION OF THIS REBELLION AND IN THE MAINTENANCE OF THE CONSTITUTION AND THE UNION BY SWORD, WE RECOGNIZE AN UNAVOIDABLE NECESSITY AND A SACRED DUTY...

RESOLVED, THAT WHILE WE RECOGNIZE THIS UNHAPPY WAR AS A RIGHTEOUS JUDGMENT OF GOD, VISITED UPON US BECAUSE OF INDIVIDUAL AND NATIONAL SINS ... WE NEVERTHELESS REGARD THIS REBELLION AS MORE IMMEDIATELY THE NATURAL RESULT OF THE CONTINUANCE AND SPREAD OF DOMESTIC SLAVERY IN OUR LAND...

RESOLVED, THAT THIS SYNOD CANNOT BUT EXPRESS ITS MOST DECIDED DISAPPROBATION OF THE COURSE OF THOSE SYNODS AND MINISTERS, HERETOFORE CONNECTED WITH THIS BODY, IN THE OPEN SYMPATHY AND ACTIVE CO-OPERATION, WHICH THEY HAVE GIVEN TO THE CAUSE OF TREASON AND INSURRECTION ...[7]

These were powerfully strong words of rebuke toward the Southern Lutherans, and were very offensive to them. They deeply resented being called "rebels" and "traitors" and having their cause condemned. And, of course, these offensive resolutions were tied in with a pledge of loyalty to President Lincoln and the Northern cause, expressed in unmistakably clear terms.

WITHDRAWAL OF THE SOUTHERN SYNODS AND FORMATION OF THEIR OWN GENERAL BODY

In 1862 the North Carolina Synod resolved that all Lutheran Churches in the Confederate states "withdraw and dissolve all connection with the Northern General Synod." On May 15, 1862, a meeting of Southern Lutherans was held at Salisbury, North Carolina, with the view of establishing a Southern General Synod, but because of small attendance only a committee was formed and given the task of preparing a constitution and also the Basis for a Constituting Convention. This convention was held the following year, May 20, 1863.

The following synods were present: North Carolina Synod, South Carolina Synod, Virginia Synod, Southwest Virginia Synod, and the small Georgia Synod (org. 1860 at Concord, North Carolina). These synods, having withdrawn from the General Synod North, immediately showed themselves in favor of establishing their own general synod. John Bachman (1790-1874) of Charleston, South Carolina, was elected the first president. At their Constituting Convention, the Southern Lutherans stated their grievances against their Northern counterparts thus:

> So far as sympathy and harmony of action is concerned, the Northern and Southern portions of our Church have for years been divided. The prevailing spirit of the Northern portion is a spirit of fanaticism, which has been nurtured and intensified until ... it permeates all their religious, social , and political relations. On the other hand, the spirit of the Southern portion is that of conservatism. We claim for ourselves nothing beyond that which reason and God's Word allow. While we have always cheerfully conceded to the Northern Church the right to judge for themselves in matters of conscience, we at the same time have demanded that this privilege be extended to us. But how often it has been denied!... And now, that a cruel and sanguinary war is waged against us by the Government of the United States...so far from uttering a word of remonstrance or protesting against its continuance, the Northern Church has actually gloried in these scenes of blood and carnage, and, by a formal resolution, declared it to be the duty of the Government to prosecute this war even to our subjugation. It is under such circumstances, and for these reasons, we renounce them as brethren; and it becomes us this day to make our separation from them final and complete. In taking so grave and decisive a step, we call God to witness that we are influenced neither by malice nor revenge, but by the teachings of His own Word, which requires that we withdraw ourselves "from every brother that walketh disorderly," and from "men of corrupt minds and destitute of the truth," while at the same time we believe that the peace and prosperity of our Southern Church will be thereby promoted.[8]

The Constitution of the General Synod of the Evangelical Lutheran Church in the Confederate States of America, adopted in 1863, stated the body's acceptance of the Old and New Testaments as the Word of God and only infallible rule of faith and practice, and held that the *Apostles Creed, Nicene Creed,* and *Augsburg Confession* contain the fundamental doctrines of the Sacred Scriptures, which the body receives and adopts as the exponents of the faith. Section 3 of Article II is of particular interest: "Inasmuch as there has always been, and still is, a difference of construction among us with regard to several articles of the *Augsburg Confession*; therefore we, acting in conformity with the spirit and time honored usage of our Church, hereby affirm that we allow the full and free exercise of private judging in regards to those articles."[9]

According to historian R.C. Wolf, the General Synod South (this name adopted in 1878 is often used by writers instead of other designations, due to its simplicity) took on a doctrinal position already in 1863 which the General Synod North did not reach until 1913. At that time the original General Synod strengthened its doctrinal position when it stated that it holds the Canonical Scriptures of the Old and New Testaments as the Word of God and the only infallible rule of faith and practice. The General Synod North furthermore stated that it receives and holds the *Unaltered Augsburg Confession* as a correct exhibition of the faith and doctrine of the Synod as it is founded on the Word. The other Lutheran Symbols were regarded "as expositions of Lutheran doctrine of great historical and interpretative value..."[10]

After the Civil War, the Southern Lutherans decided not to return to the General Synod North but to maintain a separate existence. The South's peculiar problems, as well as the dissension within the General Synod North and the latitudinarianism that was observed in that body discouraged the Southern Lutherans from rejoining the Northern body. It bothered the General Synod South that the General Synod North gave the impression that Lutherans do not differ in any important matters from other denominations. This attitude of acceptance of doctrinal differences among church bodies was labeled "latitudinarianism." In 1866 the Southern General body underwent another name change to the General Synod South.[11]

THE THREE GENERAL BODIES ARE SHUNNED BY THE CONSERVATIVE SYNODS FORMING A FOURTH FEDERATION: THE SYNODICAL CONFERENCE

In 1871 the synods that were planning on forming a larger association, the Synodical Conference (i.e. the synods of Missouri, Wisconsin, Minnesota, and Michigan), gave reasons why they were unable to join any of the general bodies already in existence:

THE GENERAL SYNOD [I.E. NORTH] CLINGS ... TO THE LUTHERAN NAME BUT IT ACTUALLY LACKS COMPLETELY THE ESSENCE AND CHARACTER WHICH CORRESPONDS TO THAT NAME ... IT IS NOTORIOUS THAT NOT ONLY DOES THE GENERAL SYNOD NOT CONSIDER DISTINCTIVE DOCTRINES IMPORTANT, BUT PRACTICALLY NO ONE WITHIN IT CONFESSES THE DISTINCTIVE DOCTRINES OF THE LUTHERAN CHURCH, MUCH LESS TEACHES THEM PUBLICLY. Then, after noting some of its failures, the proponents of a Synodical Conference go on to state: THUS THIS WORTHLESS, HOLLOW AND DECEASED CHURCH BODY ... EXISTS TO THE DISGRACE AND SHAME OF OUR DEAR CHURCH. Turning to the General Synod South, the proponents of the Synodical Conference recognize a different spirit in this Southern body than in the old General Synod North: WE HAVE ALSO BEEN GLAD TO SEE... INDIVIDUAL VOICES WITHIN IT SERIOUSLY URGE FAITHFUL ADHERENCE TO THE DOCTRINE OF OUR LUTHERAN CHURCH ... WE MUST CONFESS OPENLY THAT THE SPIRIT OF THESE SOUTHERN LUTHERANS, DESPITE THEIR WEAKNESSES, ON THE WHOLE APPEAR TO US MUCH MORE HONEST, SINCERE AND SERIOUS THAN THAT OF THE NORTHERN AMERICAN LUTHERANS... AT LEAST A BEGINNING HAS BEEN MADE IN THE DISCIPLINE OF CHURCH DOCTRINE. But then other negative features of the General Synod South are reviewed, which then are reasons the synods involved in establishing the

THE SOUTHERN GENERAL BODY REACHES OUT TO THE OTHER GENERAL BODIES

The General Synod South faced the possibility of dissolution following the loss of the North Carolina Synod in 1871 and the Holston Synod in 1872.. Therefore the president, J.A. Brown, suggested that the membership consider union with the other general bodies. It was not feasible to join with the Synodical Conference (org. 1872), because of its confessional and doctrinal stand with which the Southern body was not in sympathy, but especially regarding the "Four Points." It appeared more propitious to join either the General Synod North or the General Council. So, in 1876 the General Synod South approached both bodies, seeking closer relationship among the three. There were exchanges of delegates culminating in the General council's proposal in 1895 of holding a "General Conference" of Lutherans.[13]

Meanwhile, in 1877 and 1878, Lutheran Diets were held, constituting open forums for individuals to express themselves as free agents, representing no one but themselves. The General Conference of Lutherans that was later proposed in 1895 by the General Council was not to be like the Lutheran Diets. Rather, it was to involve official representatives of the Lutheran bodies, with the purpose "to prepare the way for a better understanding and a more harmonious co-operation among the Lutherans in the bodies" which participated.[14]

Before this General Conference of Lutherans was held, the Southern Lutheran body participated in a merger. The Tennessee Synod had called for a "Diet" to discuss means of forming a more satisfactory Southern general body. Having obtained a good response to this suggestion, the first Diet was held in Salisbury, North Carolina, in 1884. In addition to the synods which were members of the General Synod South (which officially took this name in 1878), the Synods of North Carolina and Tennessee as well as the Holston Synod participated. A second Diet was held in 1886 in Roanoke, Virginia. By the time this Diet was held the participating synods had ratified the constitution and the Basis for a more General Union. The General Synod South then merged with the North Carolina Synod, the Tennessee Synod and the Holston Synod into The United Synod of the Evangelical Lutheran Church in the South, finally becoming simply the United Synod in the South. The synods involved in addition to the three mentioned above were: the Synods of South Carolina, Virginia, West Virginia, Georgia, and Mississippi. Thus the whole stand of Muhlenberg Lutheranism in the South was finally joined together in a general body.

THE TENNESSEE SYNOD TAKES A STAND FOR CONSERVATIVE LUTHERANISM

At first, after joining the United Synod in the South, the Tennessee Synod declined to participate in the United Synod's missionary and educational activities because of that body's refusal to take an official stand on the "Four Points."

(chiliasm, or a supposed 1,000 year reign of Christ on earth; secret societies; pulpit fellowship with non-Lutherans; and altar fellowship with non-Lutherans constituted the "Four Points.") The Tennessee Synod opposed the teaching of some that Christ will appear on earth again before the Judgment and reign visibly for 1,000 years. Tennessee was also opposed to allowing membership in secret societies like lodges, and was opposed to pulpit and altar fellowship with non-Lutherans. Recall the Galesburg (Illinois) rule that specified Lutheran pulpits for Lutheran pastors only and Lutheran altars for Lutheran communicants only. It wasn't until 1900 that the United Synod in the South by official resolution took a conservative stand on the issues involved, which then the Tennessee Synod could endorse.[15]

UNITING THE MUHLENBERG STRAND OF LUTHERANISM, NORTH AND SOUTH, IN ONE BODY

As was mentioned earlier, the General Synod South, in 1876, approached the two other general bodies (not including the Synodical Conference [org. 1872]), seeking closer relationship among the three. Delegates were exchanged, and finally, in 1895 the General Council proposed holding a "General Conference" of Lutherans (mentioned earlier), the aim of which was "better understanding and a more harmonious cooperation among the Lutherans in the bodies' who participated. Thus began a series of Conferences, beginning in 1898, with all three general bodies represented. Conferences in 1902 and 1904 followed. These Conferences produced cooperation in preparing the *Common Service* and resulted in increased cooperation in such things as foreign and home missions, training of deaconesses and youth work.

It was the General Synod South which, as early as 1876, initiated discussions with the other two general Lutheran bodies about "a greater uniformity in our Books of Worship." Later, in 1882, the General Synod South went so far as to suggest a common hymnal. Eventually, the implementing of the General Synod South's suggestions for working together in the field of publications produced, in 1917, the *Common Service Book*. The *Common Service Book* had been published already in 1888. Here was an example where cooperation in the field of publications helped to prepare the participating Lutheran bodies for full church union.

The Conferences also affected the doctrinal statements of the General Synod North, statements in which this body took its stand on Scripture, the *Augsburg Confession*, and the other symbols of the Lutheran Church, thus bringing its doctrinal and confessional basis on par with those of the other two general bodies.[16]

The next impetus toward union came in 1914 from the North Carolina Synod, which urged the United Synod in the South to try to unite all three bodies of the Muhlenberg tradition. The next year the General Synod and the General Council authorized negotiations with the purpose of seeking union with the other general bodies. When the Joint Committee for the Celebration of the

170

Quatercentenary of the Reformation met on April 18, 1917, the call went out for union of the three bodies. During the year the Constitution for the United Lutheran Church in America (ULCA) was drawn up and was accepted by all constituent synods of the three uniting bodies, except the Augustana Synod (Swedish), which withdrew from the General Council so it could continue its independent existence, since the ULCA was to be a union, not a federation. This was a friendly separation.[17] We will look further into the United Lutheran Church in America in a separate chapter. For now, suffice it to repeat the historian's observation, that the union of the three general bodies was not staunchly Lutheran.[18] The United Lutheran Church in America was officially organized on November 14, 1918 at Trinity Lutheran Church in New York City. At the time that the United Synod in the South merged into the ULCA it consisted of eight synods, 262 pastors, 494 congregations, and 55,473 confirmed members.[19]

EDUCATIONAL FACILITIES AND MISSIONS

(1) EDUCATIONAL FACILITIES:
Theological Seminary (est. 1830), Columbia, South Carolina.
Colleges: Newberry, South Carolina (est. 1832 by South Carolina Synod). Roanoke, Roanoke, Virginia (est. 1842 by the Virginia Synod). Lenoir-Rhyne (est. 1891 by the Tennessee Synod).
(2) MISSIONS:
Home Missions
Foreign Mission in Japan (carried on jointly with the General Council).[20]
See the next page for a diagram of The United Synod in the South.

Footnotes for Chapter Eleven

1 Irwin Shapiro, Editor, *The Universal History of the World*, Vol. 12, (Golden Press, New York, NY, 1966 by Western Publ. Co., Inc. and Librairie Hachette), p. 998.

2 Frank Freidel, *Our Country's Presidents*, (The National Geographic Society, Washington, D.C., 1965, 1967, 1970, 1972, 1973, 1975, 1977, 1979, 1981, Ninth Ed.), P. 1004.

3 Abdel Ross Wentz, *A Basic History of Lutheranism in America*, (Muhlenberg Press, Philadelphia, PA, 1955), p. 162

4 Wentz, *A Basic History of Lutheranism in America*, pp. 164, 165

5 E. Clifford Nelson, Editor, *The Lutherans in North America*, (Fortress Press, Philadelphia, PA, 1975), pp. 244, 245

6 Nelson, *The Lutherans in North America*, p. 242

7 Richard C. Wolf, *Documents of Lutheran Unity in America*, (Fortress Press, Philadelphia, PA, 1966), pp. 119,120; Doc. #47.

8 Wolf, *Documents of Lutheran Unity in America*, pp. 121, 122; Doc. #48

9 Wolf, *Documents of Lutheran Unity in America*, p. 123; Doc. #51

10 Wolf, *Documents of Lutheran Unity in America*, p. 267; Doc. #116.

11 Wolf, *Documents of Lutheran Unity in America*, p. 125.

12 Wolf, *Documents of Lutheran Unity in America*, pp. 191, 192; Doc. #87

13 Wolf, *Documents of Lutheran Unity in America*, p. 259.

14 Wolf, *Documents of Lutheran Unity in America,* p. 259

15 Nelson, *The Lutherans in North America*, pp. 331, 332

16 Nelson, *The Lutherans in North America*, pp. 259, 260.

17 Nelson, *The Lutherans in North America*, p. 269

18 Nelson, *The Lutherans in North America*, p. 260.

19 Erwin L. Lueker, Editor in Chief, *Lutheran Cyclopedia*, (Concordia Publishing House, Saint Louis, MO 63118-3968, 1954), p. 1103.

20 Lueker, *Lutheran Cyclopedia*, p. 1103.

CHAPTER TWELVE

THE UNITED LUTHERAN CHURCH IN AMERICA 1918-1962

THREE GENERAL BODIES AT ODDS WITH ONE ANOTHER

In the last three chapters we reviewed the history of three of the four general bodies or federations of Lutheran synods that were organized in the nineteenth century in the United States. These were: the General Synod (org. 1820), the United Synod in the South (org. 1863), and the General Council (org. 1867). These federations brought together Lutheran bodies of the Muhlenberg strain, and were of German heritage.

In our review of these bodies we were made aware of serious divisions that occurred in Muhlenberg Lutheranism, divisions that were at times fraught with bitterness and verbal attacks (oral and written) on one another. These attacks were occasioned not only by the Civil War with its polarizations on the questions of slavery and of states' rights, but also by differences among them in regards to doctrine and practice.

Of the three federations, the original general body, the General Synod, was the most unLutheran, the most liberally inclined, having quickly tossed aside the Lutheran confessional standards of Lutheranism's patriarch, Henry Melchior Muhlenberg, after his death. The General Synod, especially due to its attachment to S.S. Schmucker's "American Lutheranism," deserved the least to bear the Lutheran name. Clergymen in its midst made open attacks against the Lutheran Symbols, which amounted to open attacks against Lutheranism and even against Scripture itself. To a great extent, Schmucker's American Lutheranism was more Reformed and Methodistic than Lutheran. Though some improvements were made over the years to the doctrinal basis of the General Synod, nevertheless these improvements too often served as merely a façade of orthodoxy, for many in the General Synod failed to carry out what had been put on paper. That the confessional movement in the General Synod in the early twentieth century was more or less a formal affair, with the liberal element openly denouncing the new confessional resolutions, can be seen for example, in this statement in the *Lutheran Church Worker and Observer,* September 12, 1918 (a couple of months prior to the merger that formed the United Lutheran Church in America): OUR BODY BREATHES THE FREE ATMOSPHERE OF AMERICA, AND IS NOT SO LEGALISTIC AND PURITANICAL AS TO THINK THAT EVERY PERSON WHO OFFENDS MUST BE BROUGHT BEFORE THE JUDGMENT BAR OF THE CHURCH FOR DISCIPLINE.[1] Another case in point is Dr. Delk (died, 1940), who denied the inspiration of the Holy Scriptures and fellowshipped with Reformed Jews in a Jewish Temple. Dr. Delk was a trustee of Lutheran Theological Seminary.

The United Synod in the South was, to a great extent, a product of the times. The questions of slavery and of states rights that divided the nation North and South were also basic issues involved in the organizing of the United Synod in the South (the name it finally gave itself). Bitter reaction to offensive resolutions made by the General Synod in convention, which involved the Southern states and Southern Lutherans, did much to alienate the Southern pastors and congregations. Upon withdrawing from the General Synod, the Southern synods quickly established their own federation in 1863 under the name The General Synod of the Evangelical Lutheran Church in the Confederate States of America. From its inception the United Synod in the South possessed a declared confessional basis that wasn't reached by the General Synod until the second decade of the twentieth century.

As historian Abdel Ross Wentz has pointed out, the General Council (which organized as a protest to the unLutheran doctrine and practice of the General Synod): NEVER CHANGED "THE FUNDAMENTAL PRINCIPLES OF FAITH" THAT IT HAD ADOPTED WHEN IT WAS ORGANIZED. THE DOCTRINAL POSITION ASSUMED IN THOSE PRINCIPLES WAS THE DISTINGUISHING MARK OF THE GENERAL COUNCIL THROUGHOUT THE FIFTY YEARS OF ITS LIFE. IT ASSERTED THAT THE UNALTERED AUGSBURG CONFESSION IS BY "PRE-EMINENCE" THE CONFESSION OF THE LUTHERAN FAITH, BEING "THROUGHOUT IN CONFORMITY WITH THE PURE TRUTH OF WHICH GOD'S WORD IS THE ONLY RULE," THAT THE OTHER CONFESSIONS OF THE BOOK OF CONCORD ARE IN PERFECT HARMONY WITH THE AUGSBURG CONFESSION, AND THAT THE CONFESSIONS IN ORDER TO BE A BOND OF UNION MUST BE UNDERSTOOD IN THE SAME SENSE BY THOSE WHO SUBSCRIBE TO THEM. THUS THE CONFESSIONAL BASIS OF THE GENERAL COUNCIL WAS VERY CLEAR AND VERY DEFINITE FROM THE BEGINNING, AND NO PARTY WITHIN THE BODY EVER CALLED IT INTO QUESTION. AS A DOCTRINAL POSITION IT MIGHT HAVE FURNISHED THE BASIS FOR A UNION OF ALL THE MORE CONSERVATIVE LUTHERAN BODIES IN AMERICA.[2] However, as Wentz also points out, the General Council had to deal with wide differences of opinion concerning the doctrinal teachings of the Confessions, and this especially in matters of practice. This kept ultraconservative Missouri Synod out of the General Council, and caused the other conservative synods in the Middle West (e.g. the Wisconsin Synod) who were members of the Council, to withdraw. The General Council's application of the Four Points was too mild to suit the more orthodox Lutheran synods.[3]

THREE GENERAL BODIES GRAVITATE TOWARD EACH OTHER – HOW IT HAPPENED

1872 – The North Carolina Synod withdraws from the United Synod in the South, which then faces the possibility of dissolution. President J.A. Brown suggests that the United Synod in the South consider union with other general bodies. Because the Synodical Conference (organized the same year) is too staunchly conservative for the members of the United Synod in the South, it is more plausible to seek union with the General Synod and the General Council.

1873 – The General Synod proposes an interchange of delegates.

1876 – Overtures are made by the United Synod in the South to the General Synod and the General Council, seeking closer relationship through a greater uniformity among the three bodies "in our Book of Worship." The General Council complies in 1879 and the General Synod followed suite in 1881.

1877 & 1878 – Lutheran Diets are held to afford an open forum to individuals, who represent only themselves and not their church bodies. Those who participated in these Diets found that they were not as far apart as they had supposed.

1882 – The United Synod in the South suggests to the other two bodies that the three work together to formulate a common hymnal.

1883 – The Luther Society of New York City is formed as an association of laymen without regard to synodical affiliation, with a goal to celebrate the Reformation each year. Later, it would be the laymen who in 1917 would push especially hard for merger of the three general bodies.[4]

1887 – The work of the Joint Committee to formulate a new liturgy is adopted, and in 1888 two editions of the *Common Service* are adopted, (Later, in 1917 the *Common Service Book*, both a service book and hymnal, is produced).

1893 – The Young People's Lutheran Association becomes "The Luther League." According to Wentz the League spread over all the general bodies "and trained the rising generations of church members in Lutheran unity."[5] Various other organizations and societies also help to give the membership of the three bodies a feeling of cordiality that takes union of the three bodies for granted.[6]

1895 – The three bodies begin to exchange fraternal visitors. The General Synod sends Dr. Owen as the first Fraternal Visitor to the General Council, which reciprocated through Dr. Seiss. The General Council proposes a "General Conference" of Lutherans, who will represent their respective church bodies. The Conference will have the purpose "to prepare the way for a better cooperation among the participating bodies."[7]

1898 – The first General Conference of Lutherans in America is held. All three bodies participate. Doctrine as well as practical work of the church is discussed. The atmosphere is congenial. Historian Eugene L. Fevold reports that the differences which appeared cut across synodical lines. The understood purpose of the Conferences was not to plan for merger – regarded as premature – but to promote understanding. (Henry Eyster Jacobs, who gave the opening remarks at the first Conference stated: "We are here not for the purpose of projecting any plans for the ultimate unification of the Church . . . We are here to treat of the great principles we profess to hold in common . . ."[8] This meeting is called the First General Conference of Lutherans in America.

1902 & 1904 – Two more General Conferences of Lutherans are held.

1907 – An interchange is begun between the General Council and the General Synod regarding differences of doctrine. This resulted, in 1911, in the differences being removed by constitutional amendment of the General Synod.

1909 – The General Council's Committee on Arbitration (appointed, 1895) and its Commission on Practical Cooperation which followed, are consolidated as the Home Mission Arbitration Commission. This Commission is to work with a similar Commission of the General Synod to reduce friction in the home mission enterprises of the two bodies.[9] Wolf informs us that there was increasing cooperation in the work of foreign and domestic missions, deaconess training, youth work, and other practical aspects of their activities. This increase in cooperation in these areas parallels the cooperation among the three bodies in preparing the *Common Service*.[10] Also in 1909 the General Council sends visitors to the General Synod and to the United Synod in the South, inviting them to cooperate in a "Worthy celebration" of the approaching Quadri-Centennial of the Reformation in 1917. This invitation is accepted by both bodies.

1913 – The General Synod amends its Constitution to bring the doctrinal basis section up to par with those of the General Council and the United Synod in the South. It recognizes the Old and New Testaments as the Word of God and only infallible rule of faith and practice. It declares that it "receives and holds the *Unaltered Augsburg Confession* as a correct exhibition of this faith and doctrine or our church as founded upon the Word. . . it also recognizes the *Apology of the Augsburg Confession,* the *Smalkald Articles,* the *Small Catechism of Luther,* the *Large Catechism of Luther,* and the *Formula of Concord* as expositions of Lutheran doctrine of great historical and interpretative value. . ."[11]

1914 – The Carolina Synod proposes that the United Synod in the South press for organic union with the other two general bodies. However, the United Synod in the South concludes at the time that the obvious fact is that present historical developments do not justify any hope of a union of the general bodies in the near future. Therefore this Southern general body does not concur with North Carolina's resolution, but continues to cherish the hope of union of Lutheran forces some day. It resolves to appoint a commission to consult with commissions from the other two bodies to discuss a "federation." The three Eastern general bodies appoint committees for the Reformation celebration to take place in 1917. These then organize as the Joint Committee on the Celebration of the Quadri-Centennial of the Reformation. Offices are opened in Philadelphia with an executive secretary. The first meeting is held at Atlantic City. A resolution is presented that the celebration should be marked by the union of the three general bodies in 1917. However this motion is considered premature.

1915 – In response to the United Synod in the South's overture, the General Synod empowers its Committee on Practical Cooperation and Fraternal Conference to enter negotiation for union "with such general body or bodies looking toward union with the General Synod and such other general body or bodies." The General Council appoints a Commission on Lutheran Unity to officially receive proposals regarding greater unity.[12] And so, in this year both the General Synod and the General Council, in response to the South's overture authorize negotiations "looking toward union" with other general bodies.

A second meeting of the Reformation Quadri-Centennial Commission is held in Pittsburgh and is attended by the presidents of the Iowa Synod and the Joint Synod of Ohio. Dr. Schmauk is a member of the Commission and a leading conservative theologian in the General Council. At first, Dr. Schmauk looks with disfavor on the proposed union, due to his conservatism. When his influence begins to wane he goes along with the others. In fact, he becomes one of the chief promoters of the merger movement. He would later help to organize the National Lutheran Council in 1918. The Honorable John L. Zimmerman, a well-known layman in the General Synod, authors the merger resolutions which result in the formation of the United Lutheran Church in America (ULCA). Dr. Morehead represents the Southern churches.

1916 – The United Synod in the South recognizes the trend toward unification of the three bodies, and states that it "stands ready to contribute its share towards unity of fellowship in word and sacrament on the basis of the common faith which we confess." The Southern body resolves that a Commission on Federation be continued, and this Commission be authorized to arrange for a series of conferences, beginning in 1917, with participation by chosen representatives of those Lutheran bodies "as will participate with us in definite co-operation and constructive work."[13]

1917 – On April 18 at Philadelphia, the last meeting of the Reformation Quadri-Centennial Commission is held. The lay members propose merger. The following resolution, which had been passed the previous night before a gathering of eight laymen, is read: RESOLVED, THAT THIS GATHERING REQUEST THE JOINT LUTHERAN COMMITTEE TO ARRANGE A GENERAL MEETING OF LUTHERANS TO FORMULATE PLANS FOR THE UNIFICATION OF THE LUTHERAN CHURCH IN AMERICA. This resolution reveals a strong desire among the lay delegates for merging the three general bodies. The resolution is signed by J. L. Zimmerman, who explains that the merger will include taking over all church property of individual synods. H. Clarence Miller presents a plan of the merger. (A financier, Mr. Miller became the first and long-time treasurer of the United Lutheran Church serving in that capacity until 1943). The Doctrinal Basis of the United Lutheran Church in America was written by Dr. Henry Eyster Jacobs, who was professor and religious editor. Dr. Jacob's resolution is accepted, which reads: BELIEVING THAT THE TIME HAS COME FOR THE MORE COMPLETE ORGANIZATION OF THE LUTHERAN CHURCH IN THIS COUNTRY, WE PROPOSE THAT THE GENERAL SYNOD, THE GENERAL COUNCIL, AND THE UNITED SYNOD IN THE SOUTH, TOGETHER WITH ALL OTHER BODIES ONE WITH US IN OUR LUTHERAN FAITH, BE UNITED AS SOON A POSSIBLE IN ONE GENERAL ORGANIZATION TO BE KNOWN AS THE UNITED LUTHERAN

CHURCH IN AMERICA. The die is cast. The presidents of the three general bodies, who by this time are cooperating with one another on a regular basis, concur with the resolution and are asked to appoint a committee to prepare a statement of faith and form a Constitution for the new Church. At once, they begin to draw up a merger plan. A Constitution is drafted within two months, and before November all three bodies in convention approve it, and in this order: The General Synod at Chicago, June 20-27; the General Council at Philadelphia, October 24; the United Synod in the South at Salisbury, North Carolina, November 6. The three bodies pass nearly identical enabling acts while approving the proposed Constitution, and direct its submission to the District Synods, heartily recommending its adoption. (In spite of the proliferation of membership in secret societies, especially in the General Synod – or perhaps because of it – no mention of secret societies is made in the Constitution). Finally, the Constitution is ratified by every one of the 46 District Synods in the prescribed manner, except the Augustana Synod, which formally, in a friendly fashion, withdraws from the General Council on November 12, 1918. (The reasons advanced by the Augustana Synod for being aloof to the merger were not of a doctrinal nature chiefly, but were of national character. Augustana wanted to retain its national identity and its independence, since what was being contemplated was a full merger, not a federation. We need to bear in mind that the Augustana Synod was the only organized body of Lutherans in the United States and Canada of Swedish origin, and as such had succeeded in maintaining its national heritage, which it wanted very much to preserve. Not once did the Augustana Synod undergo schism in its rank. It should also be noted that the Augustana Synod had fears that the new body would sink to the level of the General Synod doctrinally). The Evangelical Synod of Iowa and Other States takes a stand similar to the Augustana Synod. (Though this German synod did not join the General Council officially, it nevertheless maintained friendly relations with the Council and was represented in an advisory capacity at its meetings. Furthermore, Iowa's foreign mission work was carried on in former years in connection with the Council). When the Evangelical Synod of Iowa and Other States expresses itself through Dr. Reu, who voted at the Philadelphia Convention on October 24, 1917, he is the only advisory delegate to vote against the merger, pointing to the fact that the General Synod at its last convention had chosen as president Dr. Tressler, a Mason of high degree. Dr. Reu also states that the consummation of the merger will practically mean the abandonment of the Council's position on pulpit/altar fellowship and on lodge membership. (Though the Council had the Galesburg Rule – Lutheran pulpits for Lutheran ministers – exceptions were made. Then too, under prevailing circumstances, non-Lutherans were allowed at the communion rail. While the Council made good Lutheran pronouncements over against secret societies, these were not always carried out in practice, thus a reminder of the reasons Ohio and Iowa had for not joining the General Council. Dr. Reu's comment may be read in the Lutheran Standard, August 4, 1917). [The reader should be aware that there was another Iowa Synod, a body organized in 1854 by seven pastors of various synodical backgrounds. It joined the General Synod in 1857 and in 1918 became a part of the United Lutheran Church. It remained rather small. The larger Iowa Synod joined in 1930 with the Ohio and

178

Buffalo Synods to form the American Lutheran Church].

1918 – On the Day of Armistice in Europe, November 11th, each general body holds a meeting in New York City, concludes its individual business, and adjourns, in order to join in the First Convention of the United Lutheran Church in America. From the very beginning, enthusiasm runs high and historian A. R. Wentz is able to report that this new body "became immediately one of the most potent forces in American Christianity."[14]

With the merger of the three general bodies finally consummated at Trinity Lutheran Church in New York City on November 14th the new body chose its first officers. President: Dr. F.J. Knubel of the New York Synod (General Synod); Secretary: Dr. M.G. Scherer of the South Carolina Synod (United Synod in the South); Treasurer: Dr. E.C. Miller of the Pennsylvania Ministerium (General Council).

STATISTICS AT TIME OF ORGANIZATION

The United Lutheran Church in America embraced 45 District Synods, 10 theological seminaries, 17 colleges, and 6 academies. (The merged bodies continued to exist legally until no property rights were imperiled). There were 3,747 pastors and 758,000 communicants.

General Synod. . . . . 364,000 members.
General Council . . . . 340,000 members.
United Synod in the South . . . . 54,000 members.

The product of the three-way merger was outnumbered by about 50,000 communicant members by the Synodical Conference – a federation, not a merger – at its formation in 1872. But in a short time the United Lutheran Church outnumbered the Missouri Synod alone, which was the largest body within the Conference. The United Lutheran Church went on to become America's largest Lutheran body (for its time).

MEMBER SYNODS

Each of the member bodies was made up of smaller governing bodies or district synods, whose boundaries were often fixed by geographical factors. The following synods joined the United Lutheran Church either as charter members or as assimilated bodies. Unless otherwise noted, the synods were charter members: (1) SYNOD OF CALIFORNIA (org. 1891); (2) SYNOD OF CANADA: The result of mission work in Ontario by the Pittsburgh Synod. In 1853 the Canada Conference was formed. In 1861 it became the Synod of Canada. Merged with Synod of Central Canada. (3) CARIBBEAN EV. LUTHERAN SYNOD (org. 1952 – member ULCA same year). (4) CENTRAL PENNSYLVANIA SYNOD (org. 1938). Formed by a merger of the Synod of West Pennsylvania of 1825, the East Pennsylvania Synod of 1842, the Allegheny Synod of 1842, and the Susquehanna Synod – itself a merger in 1923 of the Susquehanna Synod and the Central Pennsylvania Synod, calling itself in 1923 the Susquehanna Synod of Central Pennsylvania, finally changing its name in 1932 to the Susquehanna Synod. All were members of the ULCA since 1918. (5) FLORIDA SYNOD (org. 1928); member of ULCA same year. (6) GEORGIA-ALABAMA SYNOD (org. 1860). Until

1930 was known as the Synod of Georgia. (7) ICELANDIC SYNOD (org. 1885). This synod, which granted suffrage to women, joined the ULCA in 1942. (8) ILLINOIS SYNOD OF THE UNITED LUTHERAN CHURCH (org. 1920). Formed by a merger of: Northern Illinois Synod, Southern Illinois Synod, Central Illinois Synod, and parts of the Chicago Synod. All were members of the ULCA since 1918. (9) INDIANA SYNOD (org. 1920). Formed by a merger of the Olive Branch Synod of 1848 with a portion of the Chicago Synod of 1835. Known at first as the Synod of Indiana but changed its name to the Chicago Synod in 1871. Both were members of the ULCA since 1918. (10) IOWA SYNOD (org. 1854). To be distinguished from the Evangelical Lutheran Synod of Iowa and Other States, also commonly referred to as the Iowa Synod. This synod in 1930 merged with Ohio and Buffalo to form the American Lutheran Church (ALC). (11) SYNOD OF KANSAS (org. 1868). (12) KENTUCKY-TENNESSEE SYNOD (org. 1934). Member of the ULCA the same year. It was an offshoot of the Indiana and Ohio Synods. (13) MARYLAND SYNOD (org. 1820). (14) MICHIGAN SYNOD (org. 1920). Formed by a merger of the Northern Indiana Synod and portions of the Chicago Synod lying in Michigan. These synods were members of the ULCA since 1918. This synod is to be distinguished from the other synod of the same name, organized in 1840, suffered division, and later rejoined, becoming a district synod of the Wisconsin Synod. (15) SYNOD OF THE MIDWEST (org. 1890). Organized originally under the name German Synod of Nebraska, but changed its name in 1937 to the Synod of the Midwest. Organized by German-speaking pastors of the Nebraska Synod. A member of the ULCA 1918. (16) MISSISSIPPI SYNOD (org. 1855). (17) NEBRASKA SYNOD (org. 1871). This synod is to be distinguished from the Nebraska Synod that became a district synod of the Wisconsin Synod in 1904, being given this designation at that time. (18) SYNOD OF NEW JERSEY (org. 1950). Formed of congregations in the State of New Jersey which were members of the New York Synod, the Pennsylvania Ministerium, and the Central Pennsylvania Synod. These synods were members of the ULCA from 1918. (19) UNITED EV. LUTHERAN SYNOD OF NORTH CAROLINA (org. 1921). Formed by a merger of the North Carolina Synod of 1803 and the Tennessee Synod of 1820 – both members of the United Synod in the South since 1886. Both were members of the ULCA since 1918. (20) SYNOD OF THE NORTHWEST (org. 1891). (21) UNITED SYNOD OF NEW YORK (1929). Later, the Synod of New York and New England. Formed by a merger of the New York Ministerium of 1786, the New York and New England Synod of 1902, and the New York Synod of 1908 – itself a merger of the Hartwick and Franckean Synods – and the Synod of New York and New Jersey. All were members of the ULCA from 1918. (22) NOVA SCOTIA SYNOD (org. 1903). (23) OHIO SYNOD (org. 1920). Formed by a merger of the congregations which had belonged to the East Ohio Synod of 1836, the Miami Synod of 1844, the Wittenberg Synod of 1847, and the District Synod of Ohio of 1857. These bodies had split off the Joint Synod of Ohio of 1833. These synods were members of the ULCA since 1918. (24) THE PACIFIC SYNOD (org. 1901). (25) PENNSYLVANIA MINISTERIUM (org. 1748). (26) PITTSBURGH SYNOD (org. 1845). (27) ROCKY MOUNTAIN SYNOD (org. 1891). (28) SLOVAK EV. LUTHERAN ZION SYNOD (org. 1919). Joined the ULCA in 1920. (29) SYNOD OF SOUTH CAROLINA (org. 1824). (30) TEXAS SYNOD (org. 1851). (31) LUTHERAN SYNOD OF VIRGINIA (org. 1922). Formed by a merger of the Virginia Synod of 1829, the Southwestern Virginia Synod of 1842, and the Holston Synod of 1860. All were members of the ULCA from 1918. (32) WARTBURG SYNOD (org. 1876). (33) SYNOD OF WESTERN CANADA (org. 1897). Organized originally as the Manitoba Synod, changing its name in 1947. (34) SYNOD OF WEST VIRGINIA (org. 1912).[15]

FURTHER REALIGNMENTS AND AFFILIATIONS

The Synod of the Central States (org. 1954) was formed from the Kansas, Nebraska, and Midwest Synods. In addition to the synods listed above, the following church bodies affiliated with the United Lutheran Church and were represented at conventions but had no vote. They were missions of the United Lutheran Church: The Andhra Evangelical Lutheran Church, India; the Evangelical Lutheran Church, Japan; the Evangelical Lutheran Church, British Guiana; the United Evangelical Lutheran Church, Argentina; the Evangelical Lutheran Church, Liberia.

PUBLICATIONS

In 1919 *The Lutheran Church Worker and Observer, The Lutheran Church Visitor*, and the *Lutheran* were consolidated into a new weekly paper, *The Lutheran*, with Dr. G.W. Sandt serving as editor. The theological journal was named *The Lutheran Quarterly*. The publishing house: United Publishing House, Philadelphia, Pennsylvania – with branches in New York, Pittsburgh, Chicago, and Columbia, South Carolina.

MISSIONS

The United Lutheran Church conducted missions in Japan, Argentina, British Guiana, China, India, Liberia, and Malaya. The Board of American Missions performed work among the Germans and English, Magyars, Slovaks, Italians, Letts, Finns, Russians, Poles, Indians, Negroes, and Jews. The Inner Mission Board was charged with welfare work and with work among the deaf-mutes.

EDUCATIONAL INSTITUTIONS - *SEMINARIES*

(1) HARTWICK SEMINARY, New York City, New York (1797). (2) COLUMBIA, South Carolina (1830). (3) SUSQUEHANNA UNIVERSITY, Selingsgrove, Pennsylvania (1858). (4) MAYWOOD, Maywood, Illinois (1891). (5) FREEMONT, Freemont, Nebraska (1893). (6) SEATTLE, Seattle, Washington (1911). (6) SASKATOON, Saskatoon, Saskatchewan (1826). (7) GETTYSBURG, Gettysburg, Pennsylvania (1826). (8) SPRINGFIELD, Springfield, Ohio (1845). (9) PHILADELPHIA, Mount Airy, Pennsylvania (1864). (10) MINNEAPOLIS, Minneapolis, Minnesota (1921). (11) LINCOLN, Lincoln, Nebraska (1913). (12) WATERLOO, Waterloo, Ontario (1911).

EDUCATIONAL INSTITUTIONS –
SENIOR COLLEGES

(1) WAGNER MEMORIAL, Staaten Island, New York. (2) SUSQUEHANNA UNIVERSITY, Selingsgrove, Pennsylvania. (3) THIEL COLLEGE, Greenville, Pennsylvania. (4) LENOIR-RHYNE, Hickory, North Carolina. (5) WEIDNER INSTITUTE, Mulberry, Indiana. (6) MIDLAND COLLEGE, Freemont, Nebraska. (7) LUTHER WOMEN'S COLLEGE, Washington, D.C. (8) GETTYSBURG COLLEGE, Gettysburg, Pennsylvania. (9) MUHLENBERG COLLEGE, Allentown, Pennsylvania. (10) ROANOKE COLLEGE, Salem, Virginia. (11) NEWBERRY COLLEGE, Newberry, South Carolina. (12) WITTENBERG COLLEGE, Carthage, Illinois. (13) CARTHAGE COLLEGE, Carthage, Illinois. (14) HARTWICK COLLEGE, Oneonta, New York.

REACHING OUT TO A LARGER FELLOWSHIP

A consistent characteristic of the United Lutheran Church in America was its willingness, even eagerness, to participate with others in forming larger circles of fellowship. The lack of total doctrinal agreement, and agreement in practice, was not a deterrent to this endeavor of reaching out to others. The ULCA became a member of the Lutheran World Federation and the National Lutheran Council. The ULCA was a charter member of the National Council of the Churches of Christ in the United States of America. The ULCA was also a member of the World Council of Churches, which in fact it helped to organize. In performing its works of charity, the ULCA participated in the Lutheran World Relief Program.

The ULCA devoted considerable time at its conventions to interchurch relations, studying each venture separately on its own merit. It declined to support the Interchurch World Movement and the Lord's Day Alliance, also declining to join the Federal Council of Churches. However, it maintained a "consultative" relationship with the Council, which included participation in joint projects on a selective basis. "All other Lutherans roundly condemned the Federal Council as a modernistic organ of social-gospel interests."[16]

The ULCA, unlike the other Lutheran bodies, looked for areas where it could maintain cordial relationships with non-Lutherans without compromising Lutheran principles. The *Washington Declaration* (1920) was formulated to serve as the basis for co-operation with non-Lutheran bodies, and in it can be found the ULCA teaching on Church unity. The *Declaration* pointed out that each religious group "shall define its relationship to other groups which also claim the name of Church, as well as to other groups and organizations which do not bear that name," and to do it in "the spirit of catholicity," thus . . . (1) TO DECLARE UNEQUIVOCALLY WHAT IT BELIEVES CONCERNING CHRIST AND HIS GOSPEL. . . (2) TO APPROACH OTHERS WITHOUT HOSTILITY, JEALOUSY, SUSPICION, OR PRIDE . . . (3) TO GRANT CORDIAL RECOGNITION OF ALL AGREEMENTS WHICH ARE DISCOVERED [BETWEEN ITSELF AND OTHERS]. . . (4) TO CO-OPERATE WITH OTHER CHRISTIANS IN WORKS OF SERVING LOVE . . . INSOFAR AS THIS CAN BE DONE WITHOUT SURRENDER OF ITS INTERPRETATION OF THE GOSPEL, WITHOUT DENIAL OF CONVICTION, AND WITH-

OUT SUPPRESSION OF ITS TESTIMONY AS TO WHAT IT HOLDS TO BE THE TRUTH.[17]

Concerning co-operative movements among the Protestant Churches, the ULCA declared: THAT IT IS OUR EARNEST DESIRE TO CO-OPERATE WITH OTHER CHURCH BODIES IN ALL SUCH WORKS AS CAN BE REGARDED AS WORKS OF SERVING LOVE . . . . PROVIDED, THAT SUCH CO-OPERATION DOES NOT INVOLVE THE SURRENDER OF OUR INTERPRETATION OF THE GOSPEL, THE DENIAL OF CONVICTION, OR THE SUPPRESSION OF OUR TESTIMONY TO WHAT WE HOLD TO BE THE TRUTH...[18]

And under this same section titled "Concerning Co-operative Movements Among the Protestant Churches," the ULCA declared: THAT, HOLDING THE FOLLOWING DOCTRINES AND PRINCIPLES, DERIVED FROM THE HOLY SCRIPTURES, TO BE FUNDAMENTAL TO THE CHRISTIAN MESSAGE, WE PROPOSE THEM AS A POSITIVE BASIS OF PRACTICAL CO-OPERATION AMONG THE PROTESTANT CHURCHES . . . WE DO NOT REGARD THEM AS A SUMMARY OF LUTHERAN DOCTRINE, OR AS AN ADDITION TO, A SUBSTITUTE FOR, OR A MODIFICATION OF THE CONFESSIONS OF OUR CHURCH; NOR DO WE PROPOSE THEM AS AN ADEQUATE BASIS FOR AN ORGANIC UNION OF THE CHURCHES, BUT . . . A CRITERION BY WHICH . . . TO DETERMINE OUR ATTITUDE TOWARD PROPOSED MOVEMENTS OF CO-OPERATION. THERE FOLLOWS NINE CRITERIA, WHICH ARE HERE GIVEN IN A SHORTENED VERSION: (1) THE FATHERHOOD OF GOD, REVEALED IN HIS SON JESUS CHRIST, AND THE SONSHIP BESTOWED BY GOD, THROUGH CHRIST, AND HIS REDEMPTION OF THE WORLD BY HIS LIFE AND DEATH AND RESURRECTION, AND HIS LIVING PRESENCE IN HIS CHURCH. (3) THE CONTINUED ACTIVITY OF GOD THE HOLY SPIRIT AMONG MEN . . . (4) THE SUPREME IMPORTANCE OF THE WORD OF GOD AND THE SACRAMENTS OF BAPTISM AND THE LORD'S SUPPER, AS THE MEANS THROUGH WHICH THE HOLY SPIRIT TESTIFIES OF CHRIST AND THUS CREATES AND STRENGTHENS FAITH. (HERE A CONFESSION OF FAITH IN THE REAL PRESENCE IN THE LORD'S SUPPER IS STATED)... (5) THE AUTHORITY OF THE PROPHETIC AND APOSTOLIC SCRIPTURES OF THE OLD AND NEW TESTAMENTS, AS THE ONLY RULE AND STANDARD BY WHICH ALL DOCTRINES AND TEACHERS ARE TO BE JUDGED. (6) THE REALITY AND UNIVERSALITY OF SIN, AND THE INABILITY OF MEN, BECAUSE OF SIN, TO ATTAIN RIGHTEOUSNESS OR EARN SALVATION THROUGH THEIR OWN CHARACTER OR WORKS. (7) THE LOVE, AND THE RIGHTEOUSNESS, OF GOD, WHO FOR CHRIST'S SAKE BESTOWS FORGIVENESS AND RIGHTEOUSNESS UPON ALL WHO BELIEVE IN CHRIST. (8) THE PRESENT EXISTENCE UPON EARTH OF THE KINGDOM OF GOD, FOUNDED BY HIS SON JESUS CHRIST, NOT AS AN EXTERNAL ORGANIZATION, BUT AS A SPIRITUAL REALITY AND AN OBJECT OF FAITH. (9) THE HOPE OF CHRIST'S SECOND COMING, TO BE THE JUDGE OF THE LIVING AND THE DEAD...[19]

There follows a series of three limitations to entering into any co-operative movement or organization: (1) any co-operative movement or organization which denies any of the above doctrines or principles; (2) any organization or movement which limits the participants in their confession of truth or their testimony against error. . . . (3) co-operative movements or organizations whose activities lie outside the proper sphere of Church activity. . . .[20] In each case the *Washington Declaration* would prohibit co-operation in the enterprise by the ULCA.

THE DOCTRINE AND PRACTICE OF
THE UNITED LUTHERAN CHURCH DISPLAYED
LIBERAL LUTHERANISM

Especially due to the deeper confessional spirit of the synods in the Midwest, the ULCA had many fine things to say in its doctrinal statements. The *Lutheran Cyclopedia* reports:

ACCORDING TO THE SECOND ARTICLE OF ITS CONSTITUTION, THE ULCA RECEIVES AND HOLDS THE CANONICAL SCRIPTURES OF THE OLD AND NEW TESTAMENTS AS THE INSPIRED WORD OF GOD AND AS THE ONLY INFALLIBLE RULE AND STANDARD OF FAITH AND PRACTICE, ACCORDING TO WHICH ALL DOCTRINES AND TEACHERS ARE TO BE JUDGED. IT ACCEPTS THE THREE ECUMENICAL CREEDS AS IMPORTANT TESTIMONIES DRAWN FROM THE HOLY SCRIPTURES AND REJECTS ALL ERRORS WHICH THEY CONDEMN. IT RECEIVES AND HOLDS THE *UNALTERED AUGSBURG CONFESSION* AS A CORRECT EXHIBITION OF THE FAITH AND DOCTRINE OF THE EV. LUTHERAN CHURCH, FOUNDED UPON THE WORD OF GOD; AND ACKNOWLEDGES ALL CHURCHES THAT SINCERELY HOLD AND FAITHFULLY CONFESS THE DOCTRINES OF THE *UNALTERED AUGSBURG CONFESSION* TO BE ENTITLED TO THE NAME OF EVANGELICAL LUTHERAN. IT RECOGNIZES THE APOLOGY OF THE *AUGSBURG CONFESSION*, THE *SMALCALD ARTICLES*, THE *LARGE AND SMALL CATECHISMS* OF LUTHER, AND THE *FORMULA OF CONCORD* AS IN HARMONY OF ONE AND THE SAME SCRIPTURAL FAITH.[21]

However, in contravention of its own doctrinal statements, a liberal approach to doctrine and practice was allowed both clergy and laity. Doctrine and practice not in harmony with the Lutheran Confessions were allowed, which in many ways nullified the ULCA's bold confession. One area was the doctrine of Holy Scripture. A great many pastors of the ULCA did, in fact, reject the Verbal Inspiration and the Inerrancy of the Scriptures. Halfway though the history of this body, the *Lutheran Church Quarterly* reported: "It is, of course, no secret that Verbal Inspiration is not taught in some of the seminaries of the United Lutheran Church."[22]

The ULCA's liberal stand on Holy Scripture had a very negative impact on the discussions which it attempted to carry on with the Missouri Synod in the 1930's. In fact, the discussions between these two Lutheran bodies began and ended with the doctrine of biblical authority. The Missouri Synod insisted that biblical authority rests on its verbal inspiration and consequent inerrancy. The ULCA Commission, however, maintained that the Bible is authoritative because it communicates God's saving message or the Word of God.[23] In 1938 Missouri's Committee on Lutheran Union reported to the Synod that in two meetings with representatives of the ULCA, the theologians of that body "were not able to come to an agreement with our committee on the fundamental doctrine of inspiration. . ."[24] Missouri finally accused the ULCA of denying that the Bible is the Word of God, and the discussions broke off at this point. (Note: For an interesting parallel to he ULCA doctrine of Inspiration and Inerrancy, refer to the history of the Missouri Synod, to the stand taken by the moderate faction of that synod in the 1970's regarding this controverted doctrine).

The ULCA's discussions with the American Lutheran Church (ALC) accomplished little more. Again, discussions bogged down on the subject of Verbal Inspiration. Discussions broke off in 1939. The ULCA adopted its *Baltimore Declaration* (1938), and the ALC adopted its *Sandusky Declaration* (1938). Following are some pertinent statements from the *Baltimore Declaration:*

(1)   ... WE ALSO ACCEPT THE TEACHING OF THE WHOLE LUTHERAN CHURCH THAT THE SCRIPTURES HAVE THIS UNIQUE AUTHORITY [I.E. AS ONLY RULE AND STANDARD FOR JUDGING DOGMAS AND TEACHERS], BECAUSE THEY ARE THE WORD OF GOD.

(2)   BOTH IN THE SCRIPTURES AND IN THE CONFESSIONS OF THE CHURCH, THIS TERM "WORD OF GOD" IS USED IN MORE THAN ONE SENSE.

(3)   WE BELIEVE THAT, IN ITS MOST REAL SENSE, THE WORD OF GOD IS THE GOSPEL, I.E. THE MESSAGE CONCERNING JESUS CHRIST, HIS LIFE, HIS WORK, HIS TEACHING, HIS SUFFERINGS AND DEATH, HIS RESURRECTION AND ASCENSION FOR OUR SAKES, AND THE SAVING LOVE OF GOD THUS MADE MANIFEST IN HIM. *(Note: In stating that the Word of God is the Gospel, a distinction is made between the Gospel, which tells us of Jesus, and the Scriptures, which contain information on various topics: history, geography, etc. Thus the liberal faction in Lutheranism is willing to speak of the gospel of salvation as inerrant, but that the rest of Scripture may contain error, for it is not regarded as verbally inspired by God. This liberal, modernistic slant on biblical authority later became a prime issue in the 1970's in the great controversy within the Missouri Synod).*

(4)   WE BELIEVE THAT, IN A WIDER SENSE, THE WORD OF GOD IS THAT REVELATION OF HIMSELF WHICH BEGAN AT THE BEGINNING OF HUMAN HISTORY, CONTINUED THROUGHOUT THE AGES, AND REACHED ITS FULLNESS AND COMPLETION IN THE LIFE AND WORK OF JESUS CHRIST, OUR LORD. ... WE BELIEVE THAT THIS REVELATION WAS GIVEN TO MEN CHOSEN AND INSPIRED BY GOD HIMSELF TO INTERPRET THE HISTORICAL EVENTS IN WHICH GOD MADE HIMSELF KNOWN.

(5)   WE BELIEVE THAT THE WHOLE REVELATION OF GOD TO MEN WHICH REACHED COMPLETION IN CHRIST . . . IS FAITHFULLY RECORDED AND PRESERVED IN THE HOLY SCRIPTURES, THROUGH WHICH   A L O N E IT COMES TO US. WE THEREFORE ACCEPT THE SCRIPTURES AS THE INFALLIBLE TRUTH OF GOD <u>IN ALL MATTERS THAT PERTAIN TO HIS REVELATION AND OUR SALVATION</u>. (EMPHASIS ADDED). WE ALSO BELIEVE THAT THE SCRIPTURES ARE NOW, AND WILL BE FOR ALL TIME TO COME, GOD'S REVELATION OF HIMSELF. AND BECAUSE HE CONTINUES TO MAKE HIMSELF KNOWN THROUGH THEM, WE BELIEVE THAT THE SCRIPTURES ALSO ARE THE WORD OF GOD.

(6)   WE BELIEVE THAT, AS GOD'S REVELATION IS ONE AND HAS ITS CENTER IN JESUS CHRIST, SO THE SCRIPTURES ALSO ARE A UNITY, CENTERING IN THE SAME LORD AND CHRIST. THEREFORE WE BELIEVE THAT THE WHOLE BODY OF THE SCRIPTURES IN ALL ITS PARTS IS THE WORD OF GOD. *(Note: This statement does <u>not</u> make the claim that all of Scripture is verbally inspired by God and therefore inerrant throughout).*

(7)   WE BELIEVE THAT THE WHOLE BODY OF THE SCRIPTURES IS INSPIRED BY GOD. GOD'S SAVING TRUTH, WHICH COMES TO US THROUGH THE SCRIPTURES, AND NOT OTHERWISE, IS GOD'S OWN REVELATION OF HIMSELF. THE WRITERS

185

OF THE SCRIPTURES HAVE BEEN HIS AGENTS IN ITS TRANSMISSION. THE POWER TO RECEIVE AND RECORD IT HAS BEEN BESTOWED BY HIM. THE ACT OF GOD, BY WHICH THIS POWER WAS CONFERRED, WE CALL BY THE SCRIPTURAL NAME OF INSPIRATION.

WE DO NOT VENTURE TO DEFINE THE MODE OR MANNER OF THIS INSPIRATION. . . .

THE SCRIPTURES ARE GOD'S TESTIMONY TO HIS SON, WHO IS THEIR CENTER . . . THEY ARE GOD'S WORD, THE MEANS THOUGH WHICH GOD LEADS US TO FAITH IN CHRIST. . . . AND IN OUR FAITH WE SEE THEIR TESTIMONY AS GOD'S OWN. THUS WE KNOW THAT THEY COME FROM HIM, ARE INSPIRED BY HIM, AND ARE GOD'S WORD.

(8) WE BELIEVE THAT THE SCRIPTURES ARE: THE SPRING FROM WHICH THE SAVING POWER OF GOD CONTINUOUSLY FLOWS INTO THE LIVES OF MEN; THE ONLY SOURCE OF TRULY CHRISTIAN DOCTRINE; AND THE ONLY RULE AND NORM FOR CHRISTIAN FAITH AND LIFE.[25]

No clear-cut statement concerning Verbal Inspiration of Holy Scripture is made in the *Baltimore Declaration*. The Word of God is reduced to the Gospel content, the Gospel being the vehicle by which God reveals himself to men. The wording of the *Declaration* cannot be considered as supporting either Verbal Inspiration or the Inerrancy of Scripture. On the other hand the wording would allow a wide range of latitude in interpreting portions of the Scripture such as the miracle accounts and the historical accounts. This allows modern critics of the Bible to legitimately call into question the accuracy of such accounts and to even deny the supernatural occurrences recorded in God's Word. In fact, in 1938 the ULCA Union Commission reported that its members could not accept Missouri's theory of Verbal Inspiration and the statement that the Scriptures are "the infallible truth in all their words, even in those 'which treat of historical, geographical, and other secular matters."[26, 27]

In 1939 Dr. F. H. Knubel of New York City, a member of the New York Synod (General Synod) of the ULCA announced that his Church body would never accept a fundamentalist interpretation of Inerrancy. However, he suggested that the ULCA might agree that the books of the Bible, taken together, "constitute a complete, errorless, unbreakable whole of which Christ is the center." This compromise, by the way, was accepted by the Joint Meeting (ULCA – ALC), which then gave rise to the *Pittsburgh Agreement*.[28] In 1940 the ALC accepted the *Agreement* but declined fellowship with the ULCA because it was wary of that body's intention of living up to the *Agreement*. The ULCA also accepted the *Pittsburgh Agreement* officially, but qualified its acceptance with the statement that where there seemed to be a disagreement between the *Agreement* and its own earlier *Declarations* (*Washington*, 1920; *Savannah*, 1934; *Baltimore*, 1938), these were to have priority.

When it came to the subject of doctrinal discussions, the ULCA's presentation was more vague than that of the old-line confessional Lutherans. The ULCA was moving toward Neo-Lutheranism, and in that frame of mind did not see the need to go beyond its own three *Declarations*, nor did it regard total agreement in every doctrine as prerequisite to Lutheran union. The ULCA claimed an "allowable latitude" in doctrinal questions.

In regards to the doctrine of conversion, the teaching of synergism (that man helps or co-operates in his own conversion; that man's will is free to accept as well as to reject Christ) enjoyed widespread acceptance.

As to the doctrine of God's Election of the Christians, we find that theologians within the ULCA were not united in their teaching. The doctrine was offered by some that God's election of the individual to salvation is conditioned by man's own action when the Gospel is preached to him. The Missouri Synod's teaching of Election has always been that God's election of the individual to salvation is from beginning to end the act of God's grace, which in no way depends on anything that God may or may not see in the person.

While the ULCA in its statements taught that the sinner is justified by faith, thus making God's grace the cause of justification and salvation, nevertheless, through its practice it contended at times against its own statements on Justification. It did this by tolerating membership in non-Christian organizations such as the religious lodges. Many of its pastors also belonged to lodges (especially those who were members of the General Synod). At one time, the number of pastors holding lodge membership was set at about 200. This matter will be taken up further in our study of the Lutheran Church in America (LCA).

Also in the doctrine of the church, the ULCA differed extensively both in teaching and practice from the conservative side of Lutheranism, especially the Synodical Conference. The ULCA's practice of pulpit and altar fellowship, and of participating in general religious bodies which do not subscribe to the Lutheran Confessions, has been roundly condemned as *unionism* by the conservatives. The ULCA excused its fellowship with groups that teach error, by claiming that such practice was being done out of common love for Christ. Recall that the *Baltimore Declaration of 1920* expressed an earnest desire to cooperate with other church bodies in all such works as can be regarded as works of serving love through which the faith of Christians finds expression.

THE GENERAL SYNOD BROUGHT ITS LIBERAL DOCTRINE AND PRACTICE INTO THE MERGER

The General Council through its fraternal delegate had gotten its point across to the General Synod that there could be no closer relationships between the two bodies unless changes were made by the Synod. And so, in its Conventions of 1909, 1911, and 1913 the General Synod complied with all of the General Council's requests made in 1907.

IT AFFIRMED THE BIBLE TO BE THE WORD OF GOD AND INCORPORATED THE PLEDGE TO THE UNALTERED AUGSBURG CONFESSION AND ACKNOWLEDGEMENT OF THE OTHER CONFESSIONAL WRITINGS INTO ITS CONSTITUTION. THAT ACTION NOT ONLY PAVED THE WAY FOR EVENTUAL MERGER BUT ALSO PLACED ALL LUTHERANS IN AMERICA, FOR THE FIRST TIME, ON VIRTUALLY THE SAME CONFESSIONAL BASIS.

OTHER DIFFERENCES BETWEEN THESE TWO BODIES REMAINED TO THE MOMENT OF MERGER BUT SEEMED TO CAUSE NO GREAT DIFFICULTIES. THE GENERAL COUNCIL'S OFFICIAL POSITION BARRED NON-LUTHERANS FROM COMMUNING OR PREACHING IN LUTHERAN SERVICES EXCEPT IN THE MOST UNUSUAL CIRCUM-

STANCES; IT OFFICIALLY DISAPPROVED OF MEMBERSHIP BY PASTORS AND LAY-
MEN IN SECRET SOCIETIES WITH RELIGIOUS CEREMONIES; IT DISCOURAGED PAR-
TICIPATION IN GENERAL PROTESTANT COOPERATIVE VENTURES. THE GENERAL
SYNOD ALLOWED FREEDOM TO THE INDIVIDUAL CONSCIENCE ON INTERCOMMU-
NION AND MEMBERSHIP IN SECRET SOCIETIES, AND WAS MORE READY TO CON-
SULT AND COOPERATE WITH NON-LUTHERANS. BUT THE GENERAL COUNCIL,
ASSURED OF THE GENERAL SYNOD'S GROWING APPRECIATION FOR THE STAN-
DARDS OF HISTORIC LUTHERANISM, DID NOT INSIST THAT THE SYNOD'S POSITION
HAD TO BE IDENTICAL WITH THE COUNCIL'S ON THESE QUESTIONS. ON MOST
COUNTS, THE POSITION OF THE UNITED SYNOD SOUTH WAS CLOSE TO THAT OF
THE GENERAL COUNCIL.[29]
NO REFERENCE WAS MADE IN THE CONSTITUTION TO THE POTENTIALLY TROU-
BLESOME MATTER OF SECRET SOCIETIES OR RELATIONSHIPS WITH NON-LUTHER-
ANS. AN INVITATION IN THE CONSTITUTION'S PREAMBLE FOR ALL LUTHERAN
SYNODS IN AMERICA TO UNITE WITH THE NEW CHURCH ON THIS BASIS WAS RE-
GARDED BY ITS FRAMERS AS A GREAT CONTRIBUTION TO FURTHER UNITY BUT BY
THE MORE CONSERVATIVE SYNODS AS AN ARROGANT AFFRONT.[30]

THE ULCA: A HELP OR A STUMBLING BLOCK TO LUTHERAN UNION?

No other Lutheran body in its history pushed the cause of Lutheran union
more than the United Lutheran Church. And yet, by its very nature as a
widely-recognized liberal body, it caused a stumbling block to such union, as the
above comment illustrates. By its movement toward Neo-Lutheranism (a
movement away from the *Lutheran Formula of Concord*) the ULCA succeeded
in alienating the large segment of conservative and confessional Lutherans.
For example, critics of the ULCA merger in the Missouri Synod, "branded
many writers and teachers in the United Lutheran Church as 'modernists' and
'liberalists' because they did not accept the theory of verbal inspiration. They
were particularly disturbed because the constitution of the United Lutheran
Church leaves to the constituent synods (close to 50) the discipline of ministers
for heresy, for lodgery, and for 'unionism,' evils that the Missourians find rampant in the United Lutheran Church. . . "The Missourians furthermore concluded that "factions characterize the United Lutheran Church, and lines of
cleavage run horizontally, vertically, and diagonally through the entire body."[31]
    Still, after several years of negotiation with three other branches of
Lutheranism, the ULCA was brought together in merger with the Augustana
Lutheran church (Swedish), the American Evangelical Lutheran Church (Danish), and the Suomi Synod (Finnish). The new body, which afterwards was divided geographically into synods, was given the name the Lutheran Church in
America (LCA). This history will be reviewed in a later chapter. Thus a merger
of the German Muhlenberg strain of Lutheranism with Scandinavian
Lutheranism was finally achieved.

Footnotes for Chapter Twelve
1 *The Lutheran Church Worker and Observer*, September 12, 1918 (further information, not

available).

2 Abdel Ross Wentz, *A Basic History of Lutheranism in America*, (Muhlenberg Press, Philadelphia, PA, 1955), pp. 240,241.

3 Wentz, *A Basic History of Lutheranism in America*, p. 241.

4 Wentz, *A Basic History of Lutheranism in America*, p. 281.

5 Wentz, *A Basic History of Lutheranism in America*, p. 281.

6 Wentz, *A Basic History of Lutheranism in America*, p. 282.

7 Wentz, *A Basic History of Lutheranism in America*, p. 280.

8 Richard C. Wolf, *Documents of Lutheran Unity in America*, (Fortress Press, Philadelphia, PA, 1966), p. 265; doc. #115.

9 Wentz, *A Basic History of Lutheranism in America*, p. 281.

10 Wolf, *Documents of Lutheran Unity in America*, pp. 259, 260.

11 Wolf, *Documents of Lutheran Unity in America*, pp. 266, 267.

12 Wolf, *Documents of Lutheran Unity in America*, pp. 266, 267.

13 Wolf, *Documents of Lutheran Unity in America*, p. 268.

14 Wentz, *A Basic History of Lutheranism in America*, p. 283.

15 Erwin L. Lueker, Editor-in-Chief, *Lutheran Cyclopedia*, (Concordia Publishing House, Saint Louis, Mo 63118-3968, 1954), pp. 1086-1094.

16 E. Clifford Nelson, Editor, *The Lutherans in North America*, (Fortress Press, Philadelphia, PA, 1975), p. 441.

17 Wolf, *Documents of Lutheran Unity in America*, pp. 349, 350; Doc. #148

18 Wolf, *Documents of Lutheran Unity in America*, p. 351; Doc. #148.

19 Wolf, *Documents of Lutheran Unity in America*, pp. 352, 353; Doc. #148.

20 Wolf, *Documents of Lutheran Unity in America*, p. 353.

21 Lueker, *Lutheran Cyclopedia*, pp. 1084, 1085.

22 *The Lutheran Quarterly*, V. 10, 1937, p. 196. Quoted in *A Catechism of Differences*, (Northwestern Publishing House, Milwaukee, WI, 1950).

23 Nelson, *The Lutherans in North America*, p. 468.

24 Wolf, *Documents of Lutheran Unity in America*, p. 377; Doc. #156.

25 Wolf, *Documents of Lutheran Unity in America*, pp. 357-359; Doc. #150.

26 Wentz, *A Basic History of Lutheranism in America*, P. 355.

27 Wolf, *Documents of Lutheran Unity in America*, p. 377; Doc. #156.

28 Wolf, *Documents of Lutheran Unity in America*, p. 379; Doc. #157.

29 Nelson, *The Lutherans in North America*, pp. 374, 375.

30 Nelson, *The Lutherans in North America*, p. 376.

31 Wentz, *A Basic History of Lutheranism in America*, p. 351.

Ch
CHAPTER THIRTEEN

THE NORWEGIANS
LAND OF THE NORSEMEN -
AN HISTORICAL SURVEY

FOR CENTURIES, SHARED RULERS

After 1380, Norway and Denmark shared a common ruler, who reigned from Copenhagen, Denmark. Still, Norway was an independent nation. Much later, in 1814, the National Constitution was drawn up and Norway became aligned with Sweden in a comparable partnership, sharing a common sovereign. This arrangement lasted until 1905. On June 7th of that year, Norway declared its union with Sweden dissolved, and an agreement to this effect was signed on October 26, 1905, making Norway completely independent from her Scandinavian neighbors. Almost one month later, Prince Carl of Denmark was elected King by popular election. He accepted, and became King Haakon VII. The Kingdom of Norway is one of the most ancient in the world.

The Democratic Constitution or *Grundlov*, bearing the original date of May 17, 1814, and many times amended, vests the legislative power in the *Storting*, which represents the sovereign power of the people. The executive branch of the government is headed by the Prime Minister and his Cabinet. All meetings of the Cabinet are presided over by the King. He does not, however, have the power to vote.

In Norway considerable authority is exercised by provincial or municipal governments. The country is divided into districts, each of which has an executive functionary. The country is also divided into many urban and rural municipalities, each having extensive local self-government.

The State Church is entirely subordinate to the *Storting* and the King, as "Supreme Bishop," who exercises his authority through the Ministry of Ecclesiastical Affairs.

THE CASTE SYSTEM IN NORWAY

Wealthy business men, government men, and the clergy as well, were included in the upper class and therefore dominated in the Norwegian caste system. Most Norwegians lived on the farm and thus the farmworkers far outnumbered the upper class. Through the caste system, Denmark had an influence on Norway, for most upper class people were either Danes or were from families originating out of Denmark.

The 1814 Constitution of Norway granted dominant representation in the parliament to the rural areas of the country. After decades the farmers were thus able to become the dominate element in the parliament and upset upper class control of the nation.[1]

THE CASTE SYSTEM AND THE EMIGRATION

The first Norwegian emigrants left the old country in 1825, arriving in New York harbor on October 9th. Their voyage from Stavanger took fourteen weeks. These forty-six Norsemen were only a tiny beginning of a migration that would bring hundreds of thousands of their fellow countrymen to these shores. In fact, by 1920 a total of more than 2,000,000 Scandinavians had come. Some motives for leaving Norway were religious, as we shall see, but mainly they had to do with economics, with the caste system playing no little part in the waves of Norwegian immigrants that broke on these shores. First, the caste system built up a resentment against the foreign influence wielded by the upper class, most of whom were Danes. Secondly, the farmers harbored resentment toward the aristocracy. Fees, high taxes and debts were laid upon the farmers. They also had to act inferior before the upper class. Thirdly, there was, and still is in Norway little tillable land. Yet many Norwegians nurtured a deep desire to own some of God's good earth and till it for themselves. And so, many men who could never rise above being farm servants in Norway, looked westward to America, where lay their hope of some day owning their own farms.

THE GREAT EMIGRATION

After 1865, and the end of America's Civil Way, a sizeable portion of Norway's population emigrated. Only Ireland, and later, Italy, excelled Norway in number of emigrants compared with the total population of the country. In the one hundred year period beginning with 1825, more than three-quarters of a million Norwegians left their homeland for America. These came mainly from the farming class, especially from the "small" farmers, and from farm laborers. "The largest number of Scandinavian immigrant didn't stay in the seaboard cities but went to the Midwest. This was perfectly natural, for their background was rural, and the trade they knew was farming. An exception were the 260,000 Finns 'who came primarily from the lowest ranks of society.' They were recruited to mine the copper in Michigan, the iron in Wisconsin, and the coal in Pennsylvania."[2] The author, Ben Maddow, adds: "What they all had in common was poverty."

There were three waves of emigrants: (1) post-Civil War, (2) the 1880's, (3) the beginning of the twentieth century. But even as late as the 1920's a goodly number of America's immigrants came from Norway. Migration from Norway was held back during the remainder of the 1870's, following the 1873 panic. The second and largest wave of Norwegian immigrants came in the 1880's and extended in to the '90's. The immigrations brought great mission opportunities to the Norwegian Church.

The Lutherans among the Norwegian immigrants were divided in their religion. Various segments of Norwegian Lutheranism could be called "State Church Traditionalism," "pietistic Haugeanism," "Grundtvigianism," or Johnsonian "orthodox Pietism." Several years intervened between the time when the first Norwegian colonies were established in America, in the Midwest, and the arrival of the first Lutheran pastor ordained by the Church of Norway.

RELIGIOUS ISSUES IN NORWAY

HAUGENISM:
OPPOSITION BY CHURCH AND STATE

Pietism and conventicles developed in Norway in the eighteenth century. The closing of that century brought inroads of rationalism among the clergy. However, men like Hans Nielson Hauge (1771-1824) counteracted this liberal movement, for they had a strong distaste for the spiritual lethargy which they witnessed in their homeland due to combining the State Church with at least some degree of rationalism. Responding to an inner calling to preach, Hauge went on to cover much of Norway, working to convict people of sin and awaken faith. His aim was to produce repentance and conversion, as well as Christian obedience. Thus, what he hoped for was an experiential Christianity in the people, which would combat what he felt to be dead orthodoxy in the Church of Norway. As a result of Hauge's work there was a resurgence of Pietism, with its emphasis on the Christian life. Hauge preached, counseled, and guided, and as a result a national revival began. The Haugeans taught:

VITAL CHRISTIAN EXPERIENCE IS MORE IMPORTANT THAN CORRECTNESS OF

DOCTRINE OR CONFORMITY TO RELIGIOUS RITES AND PRACTICES. A SEPARATED, SANCTIFIED LIFE IS EVIDENCE OF SUCH LIVING EXPERIENCE. WORSHIP SHOULD BE SIMPLE AND INFORMAL, SINCE THE DANGER OF DEAD FORMALISM ACCOMPANIES A LITURGICAL EMPHASIS. SPIRITUAL REVIVAL AND CHRISTIAN NURTURE SHOULD BE PROMOTED THROUGH THE USE OF EVANGELISTIC (SERVICES) AND PRAYER MEETINGS. LAY ACTIVITY, PARTICULARLY IN THE FORM OF LAY PREACHING AND PUBLIC WITNESSING, IS TO BE ENCOURAGED.[3]

In Norway, church government took on the Episcopal form, with the pastors and bishops receiving their appointments from the King. The 1814 Constitution declared Lutheranism to be the official religion, and the King the protector of the Lutheran Faith. The laymen had very little voice in the affairs of the Church. It is little wonder that the immigrants sometimes brought with them deep-seated dissatisfaction with some of the features of the State Church. Some of the leaders among the Lutheran immigrants were outspoken advocates of democratic congregational life and organization, and at the same time were critical of State Church polity. It is of interest to note that Sven Oftedal and Georg Sverdrup, who later became leaders of the Lutheran Free Church in America, were among the leaders of a free church system in Norway. But it was here in America that their democratic ideals for congregational life and organization could be realized without fear of government intervention.

Men like Hans Nielson Hauge who opposed the inroads of rationalism in the State Church worked to get their message across to their fellow Norwegians as lay preachers. Their meetings, held apart from the regular services conducted by the duly appointed clergy, were termed conventicles. However, Hauge remained loyal to the State Church. His Pietistic movement, known as "Haugeanism," became particularly strong in the first part of the nineteenth century. However, he was not without his problems. And the persecution which Hauge suffered showed both the power of the clergy in the State Church as well as the lack of religious liberty, especially the lack of freedom to hold gatherings outside the auspices of the official Norwegian Church. The following information was gathered from an article appearing in the 1964 issue of *Liberty*, a magazine devoted to religious freedom. A condensation of "Scandinavia's Thorn in the Flesh":

HANS NIELSON HAUGE WAS NOT A PREACHER, BUT HE FELT CALLED TO PREACH, AND FOR THESE EFFORTS HE GOT HIMSELF IN TROUBLE WITH THE LAW. NOT ONLY DID HE PREACH HIMSELF, BUT TRAINED OTHER LAY PREACHERS AND SENT THEM OVER THE COUNTRYSIDE.

IN THE SCANDINAVIAN COUNTRIES THERE WAS A LAW WHICH FOR SEVENTY YEARS BEFORE HAUGE'S TIME, HAD FORBIDDEN LAYMEN TO INITIATE RELIGIOUS MEETINGS. ONLY THE CLERGY WERE TO QUOTE FROM THE BIBLE OR TO EXPLAIN IT, AND ONLY THE CLERGY COULD CALL PEOPLE TOGETHER FOR RELIGIOUS MEETINGS.

HAUGE, HOWEVER, WAS A TROUBLED MAN — TROUBLED BY THE LACK OF SPIRITUALITY IN HIS OWN COUNTRYMEN, TROUBLED BY THE LACK OF ABILITY ON THE PART OF THE STATE CHURCH THROUGH ITS PREACHERS TO CORRECT THE PROBLEM. HE FELT THE NEED FOR SPIRITUAL RENEWAL, AND STRENGTHENING. AND HE FELT CALLED BY GOD TO PREACH TO HIS NEIGHBORS TO HELP BRING THIS ABOUT.

HE STARTED TO HOLD MEETINGS IN HIS OWN HOME. IN THESE MEETINGS HE TOOK THE LOVE OF GOD IN THE GOSPEL AND ATTEMPTED TO SHOW THE PRACTICAL EFFECTS THAT IT SHOULD HAVE IN THE DAILY LIFE OF A CHRISTIAN. WHILE HIS NEIGHBORS SEEMED TO APPRECIATE HAUGE'S EFFORTS, THE LOCAL LUTHERAN PASTOR DID NOT. HE ORDERED HAUGE TO STOP. HAUGE INSISTED ON CONTINUING HIS LAY MINISTRY.

WHEN THE LOCAL PASTOR PETITIONED HIS BISHOP TO TAKE ACTION, THE BISHOP FELT IT BEST NOT TO INTERFERE DIRECTLY WITH THE MEETINGS BUT RATHER TO DISCOURAGE HAUGE'S WORK BY SHOWING CONTEMPT BOTH FOR THE MAN AND HIS MEETINGS. BUT NEITHER HAUGE NOR HIS MEETINGS WERE ILL-TREATED BY THE PEOPLE. HIS WORK FLOURISHED. MANY FOUND THEMSELVES STIRRED BY THE ENTHUSIASTIC ZEAL OF HAUGE, WHEREAS THEY HAD NOT BEEN SO TOUCHED BY THE COLD AND SPIRITLESS PREACHING OF THE STATE CHURCH.

THEN IT FINALLY HAPPENED. IN 1797, ON CHRISTMAS DAY, WHILE CONDUCTING A DEVOTIONAL SERVICE IN THE HOME OF RELATIVES IN GLEMMEN, NORWAY, THE LOCAL PARISH PASTOR INTRUDED, ACCOMPANIED BY SEVERAL SOLDIERS. HAUGE WAS TAKEN TO JAIL AT FREDRICKSTAD. THE ACTION BY THE CLERGY WAS ILL-ADVISED AND STIRRED UP A HORNET'S NEST OF UNFAVORABLE CRITICISM. EVEN THE COUNTRY GOVERNOR WAS CRITICAL OF THE PASTOR'S ACTION. WITH FRIENDS WORKING ON HIS SIDE, AND PUBLIC OPINION IN HIS FAVOR, HAUGE WAS FREED AFTER SPENDING A MONTH IN JAIL.

LIKE ST. PAUL, TIME SPENT IN JAIL ONLY WHET HAUGE'S APPETITE FOR SHARING THE GOSPEL WITH HIS NEIGHBORS. HE WENT NEXT TO KRISTIANIA (NOW OLSO) AND SUBSEQUENTLY WAS ARRESTED WHILE PREACHING IN A HOME. HE WAS SOON RELEASED, BUT A WEEK LATER WAS RE-ARRESTED AND RETURNED TO HIS OWN VILLAGE OF TUNE.

WITH HIS PERSONAL MINISTRY BECOMING MORE AND MORE DIFFICULT, HAUGE SOUGHT TO GET THE JOB DONE BY TRAINING OTHERS TO HELP HIM. HE HAD THEM LABOR IN THE EASTERN PART OF NORWAY WITH ITS RURAL DISTRICTS. AS THESE LAYMEN WANDERED ABOUT GATHERING PEOPLE INTO GROUPS TO TEACH FROM THE BIBLE, THEY WERE SOMETIMES ACCEPTED, OTHER TIMES REJECTED. THEY WERE NOT ONLY CALLED NAMES, BUT THREATENED WITH JAIL. UNDAUNTED, THESE LAYMEN, HAUGEAN TRAINED, CONTINUED TO PREACH, AND AS A RESULT WERE BROUGHT BACK BY AUTHORITIES TO THEIR HOME PLACES. ONE NAME GIVEN TO HAUGE'S MEN WAS "LOAFERS," A THING WHICH INCENSED HAUGE, FOR HE REGARDED HIS PREACHERS AS HONEST MEN WHO INTENDED TO KEEP THE LAWS OF THE COUNTRY AND THE COMMANDMENTS OF GOD. HIS PUBLIC STATEMENTS WARNED THE CLERGY THAT HE HAD NO INTENTION OF GIVING UP.

ON THE WAY TO BERGEN HAUGE WAS ARRESTED, KEPT FOR THREE DAYS IN JAIL ON A FALSE CHARGE AND THEN RELEASED.

SOMETHING WAS STIRRING IN SCANDINAVIA. A RELIGIOUS REVIVAL, HELPED ALONG BY ACTIVITIES OF LAYMEN LIKE HAUGE AND HIS GROUP – AS WELL AS BY OTHERS – WAS BEING FELT THROUGHOUT SCANDINAVIA. BUT WHERE THERE WAS THE SPIRIT OF REVIVAL THERE WAS ALSO THE SPIRIT OF PERSECUTION. WAY TO THE NORTH, IN TRONDHEIM, ONE OF HAUGE'S LAY PREACHERS WAS ARRESTED AS A RESULT OF OPPOSITION STIRRED UP BY THE CLERGY AND THE PRESS. HAUGE AND ANOTHER MAN, ANGERED BY THE ARREST, LASHED OUT AT HIS OPPONENTS. THE PRESS QUOTED HIM, AND SO ONCE AGAIN HIS REPUTATION PRECEDED HIS APPEARANCE. THE TWO MEN FOUND THEMSELVES IN JAIL IN TRONDHEIM. ON THE BASIS OF THE "FORBIDDEN MEETING" LAW, THEY WERE KEPT IN JAIL FOR TWO MONTHS BEFORE BEING SENT HOME.

HAUGE DECIDED TO USE A NEW APPROACH. HE WOULD PRINT CHRISTIAN LITERATURE: GOSPEL TRACTS AND A BOOK, *TEACHING OF SIMPLICITY*. THESE HE HAD WRITTEN HIMSELF, AND PRODUCED ON PRESSES IN DENMARK. TO DISTRIBUTE THEM, HAUGE BECAME A MERCHANT SEAMAN, SECURING A SHIP AND SAILING THE COAST, SELLING CORN AND DISTRIBUTING HIS LITERATURE. AT ONE PLACE POLICE CONFISCATED ALMOST 500 OF HIS BOOKS. NOT DISCOURAGED HAUGE WENT FAR ABOVE THE ARCTIC CIRCLE WITH HIS LITERATURE.

BUT OPPOSITION MOUNTED. ON OCTOBER 25, 1804, HE WAS ARRESTED AT EIKER, NORWAY, AND LATER TRANSFERRED TO KRISTIANIA. THERE HE WAS NOT EVEN ALLOWED TO HAVE VISITORS. IN FACT, FOR TWO YEARS, HE WAS ALLOWED NEITHER TO READ OR WRITE. OTHERS HAD TO CARRY ON THE WORK IN HIS ABSENCE. FOR A TIME HAUGE WAS LET OUT OF PRISON WHEN DURING THE WAR IN EUROPE HE OFFERED HIS SERVICES TO HIS GOVERNMENT TO HELP MAKE SALT FROM SEA WATER, SINCE THE SUPPLY OF SALT HAD BEEN CUT OFF. AFTER A COUPLE OF YEARS HE WAS RETURNED TO HIS CELL WHEN HIS SERVICES WERE NO LONGER NEEDED. (BISHOP PEDER HANSEN WAS THE COMPLAINANT IN THE CASE.)

FINALLY, IN 1813 HE WAS MADE TO APPEAR IN COURT. SIX HUNDRED WITNESSES WERE CALLED TO TESTIFY AGAINST HIM. THREE CHARGES DEALING WITH THE FORBIDDEN MEETING LAW, USING INSULTING, OFFENSIVE EXPRESSIONS AGAINST THE TEACHING PROFESSION AND SOMETIMES AGAINST CIVIL AUTHORITY, AND MAKING STATEMENTS WHICH COULD MISLEAD THE UNEDUCATED AND UNDERMINE THEIR FAITH, WERE THE GROUNDS OF HIS CONVICTION. BUT THE TWO-YEAR SENTENCE METED OUT TO HAUGE WAS NOT UPHELD BY THE SUPREME COURT, AND HAUGE WAS RELEASED UPON THE PAYING OF A FINE (BY FRIENDS). HAUGE, HOWEVER, WAS NOW A PHYSICALLY BROKEN MAN, AND DIED A FEW YEARS LATER, IN 1824. IT HAS BEEN SAID THAT "NO SINGLE PERSON AFFECTED THE RELIGIOUS LIFE IN NORWAY MORE POSITIVELY THAN DID HAUGE." [4]

What then was Haugeanism? Very briefly: "Haugeanism then, was a pietistic, experience-centered, grass-roots movement within the Lutheran Church of Norway...Hauge's theology was Lutheran orthodoxy, interpreted in a pietistic spirit."[5] Hauge's critics point to the fact that the doctrine of grace suffered from too strong an emphasis on obedience to the law of God, at the expense of the gospel. He has been criticized too for minimizing the importance of the sacraments. Still, Hauge's influence on the people helped to bring the lower class into active participation in government and even to change the balance of power.

GISLE JOHNSON
(1822-1894)

Gisle Johnson, who was responsible for the so-called Johnsonian Awakening in Norway, was a theological professor at the University of Oslo. He had much influence on both clergy and laity. "In Gisle Johnson the pietistic and orthodox traditions were combined. His position was that of 'orthodox Pietism'"[6] Johnson stressed Christian life experience and warned of dead formalism, while urging the need of adherence to a conservative Lutheran doctrinal position. Unlike Hauge, Johnson was highly theologically trained. Johnson and his co-worker, Caspari, were hostile toward Grundtvigianism, which itself was hostile toward the Pietism of the Johnsonians and Haugeans.

While Johnson was in favor of lay preaching, he limited its use to genuine need – emergency situations, such as pastoral shortages – and bound himself by Article XIV of the *Augsburg Confession,* which limits public preaching to those "regularly" called.

ELLING EILSEN
(1804-1883)

Eielsen was a lay evangelist, who traveled in Norway, Sweden, and Denmark. Later, in 1843, after emigrating to America, Eielsen was ordained, becoming the first Norwegian Lutheran pastor in America. Eielsen represented the Lutheran "low-church" view and stressed Pietism and Puritanism.[7]

N.S.F. GRUNDTVIG
(1783-1872)

Bishop Grundtvig was a Danish theologian who had some influence on Norwegian minds. He felt that he had made a "matchless discovery" in 1825, namely, that the *Apostles Creed*, not the Bible, is the ultimate authority for the Church. As a result, Grundtvig forsook his close ties with the Bible. Some of his followers (known as Grundtvigians) taught the possibility of conversion after death. Wilhelm Andreas Werels (1797-1866), a pastor in Oslo, was the leader of Grundtvigianism in Norway. Grundtvig believed that through the *Apostles Creed* God comes to the Christian, reborn through Baptism. He believed that the renunciation of sins, together with the *Apostles Creed*, had been the Church's Confession, given it from the Lord's own mouth after his resurrection. Through the person's baptism, the Confession becomes the true Word of life for the believer. Grundtvig also taught that the Lord's Supper was an act of Christ and that "only at the washing [Baptism] and at the table [Lord's Supper] do we hear God's Word to us." Grundtvig regarded the Bible as a glorious book of instruction which was indispensable for the Church, but on the other hand he did not believe that the Bible gives life. He regarded conversion as unnecessary (for Baptism itself supplies all necessary spiritual strength). The Ten Commandments, according to Grundtvig, should be left out of the Catechism, since they were only Jewish laws. He rejected also the concept of man's total corruption in his nature.

Two former associates of Grundtvig – Herslev and Stenersen, both professors at the new university at Oslo (the first Norwegian university, established in 1811) – determined to stand against rationalism and to bring back Biblicism to the Church of Norway.

OPPOSING RELIGIOUS FORCES IN NORWAY

Strong opposing forces were at work in the Lutheran scene in Norway. There was the State Church and its clergy versus those who were involved in lay preaching. There were those who desired freedom to choose a religious movement other than the State Church versus those who practiced religious intolerance. There was Pietism, which fostered a rigorously controlled life and opposed being involved in such pastimes as drinking and cardplaying and participation in the crudities and excesses of the peasant life. There was the staid State Church versus the revivalistic spirit of such men as Johnson, Hauge, and Eielsen. Among the opposing religious forces in Norway were those who pushed for church reform (as in the 1840's) and those who would rather leave things as they were. There was Rationalism versus Biblicism. In the 1870's there existed the influence of scientific Rationalism (e.g. the evolutionary theory) on the one hand, while biblical criticism began to be strongly felt in Norway on the other hand. These movements produced outspoken criticism of traditional Christianity. And then, in the 1880's some tried to push the pendulum the other way by introducing religious revival in western Norway, often laying down a barrage of bitter criticism of the clergy and the State Church.

RELIGIOUS SUPPRESSION IN
NORWAY DOWN TO MODERN TIMES

The experience of Hans Nielsen Hauge was a sad chapter in the history of Norway. Church and State combined to bring much suffering to a man who dared to teach and preach as a layman, thereby conducting religious meetings outside the auspices of the clergy, the official administrators of the law and gospel. Perhaps the reader is not aware that even in modern times complete religious freedom has not been available in Norway. We would like to quote from an article which appeared in *Liberty* magazine in 1971, authorized by Tryge Leivestad, Associate Justice of the Supreme Court of Norway (at the time the article was written). The article is titled:

"Corpses and Closed Doors Tell Their Tale of Religious Suppression in Norway." Justice Leivestad pointed out the following:

- Norway was an absolutely closed country for all other religions and denominations besides the State Church until 1845.
- Norway's first emigrants were Quakers, who were hounded out of the country. (Not all the "Sloopers," as those first 46 emigrants were called, were Quakers. Several were at least Quakers in interest and sympathy, and Lars Larsen, the leader, was probably officially a Quaker. Others in the group of "Sloopers" who sailed on the sloop *Restauration* had come under the influence of Haugeanism.)
- Norway was among the last to allow Jesuits to enter the country.
- Jews were banned from Norway until 1851.
- Mormons were persecuted and punished for "unlawful" religious exercises until 1880.
- The Salvation Army in its infancy in Norway often suffered abuse (from rowdy mobs, theologians and the police). Justice Leivestad made this assertion:

WE HAVE NEVER HAD FULL RELIGIOUS LIBERTY, DO NOT HAVE IT NOW, AND WILL NOT HAVE IT IN THE NEAR FUTURE BECAUSE THE MAJORITY OF THE PEOPLE DON'T WANT TO PERMIT IT. WHAT LIBERTY WE DO HAVE, WE OWE MORE TO HUMANISM AND INDIFFERENCE THEN TO A PHILOSOPHICAL OR SCRIPTURAL COMMITMENT BY THE CHURCH.

On the books today in Norway are laws denying religious liberty: Section 5 of the law regulating dissenters has this sentence: "Religious services or religious meetings which cannot be called worship must not be held behind closed doors." (In spite of the fact that many organization are allowed to hold meetings behind closed doors.)

The laws concerning Sunday rest have clearly been written to aid the State Church. The example is given by Justice Leivestad showing how a member of the State Church can work in the iron works on Sunday, but a Seventh Day Adventist barber could not open his shop in the same day.

The Justice goes on to make the following observation: IN NORWAY, STATE AND CHURCH HAVE ALWAYS BEEN CLOSELY CONNECTED, EVEN IN HEATHEN TIMES. WHEN CHRISTIANITY CAME TO THE COUNTRY, IT WAS SUPPORTED BY THE KING'S POWER. AT THE OLDEST CHRISTIAN COURTS OF JUSTICE IN THE ELEVENTH CENTURY, THE CHURCH WAS UNDER THE STATE'S JURISDICTION. THE KING EMPLOYED BISHOPS, AND THE LAWS OF THE CHURCH WERE VOTED LIKE ANY OTHER LAWS. TO BELIEVE "WRONG" AND "ERRONEOUS" DOCTRINES AND TO NEGLECT RELIGIOUS DUTIES WERE CRIMES.

THE REFORMATION WAS INTRODUCED BY COMMAND FROM THE KING WITHOUT REGARD TO WHAT THE PEOPLE WANTED. SO WAS THE EVANGELISTIC LUTHERAN RELIGION INTRODUCED BY FORCE. THE PEOPLE HAD NO SAY. AND WITH A STRONG HAND, THE STATE RESTRICTED ALL OTHER TEACHINGS FOR THREE HUNDRED YEARS. EVEN WHEN OTHER CHRISTIAN CONFESSIONS WERE ADMITTED AFTER 1845, THEY WERE MORE PERMITTED THAN RECOG-

NIZED.

IN THE POST-REFORMATION PERIOD, APOSTASY FROM THE DOCTRINES OF THE STATE CHURCH — ESPECIALLY ESPOUSAL OF POPERY — WAS A CRIME. ALL "STRANGE" RELIGION AND DOCTRINE WERE STRICTLY FORBIDDEN.

AN EARLY NORWEGIAN CRIMINAL CODE BEGAN WITH A CHAPTER ABOUT ERRONEOUS DOCTRINES, BLASPHEMY, AND WITCHCRAFT. CONVERSION TO OTHER FAITHS WAS THREATENED WITH SEVERE PUNISHMENT. A DECREE OF 1701 ASKED POLICE TO MAKE SURE NO STRANGE RELIGION WAS PERMITTED. IN 1771 THE UNITED BRETHREN — THE OLDEST SO-CALLED SECT IN OUR COUNTRY — WERE PERMITTED TO ENTER THE NATION. BUT ENTER WAS ABOUT ALL. THEY WERE NOT PERMITTED TO EVANGELIZE OR PROSELETIZE. NO ONE ELSE COULD ATTEND THEIR MEETINGS. . . .IF MEMBERS OF A STRANGE RELIGION MARRIED MEMBERS OF THE STATE CHURCH, THEIR CHILDREN AUTOMATICALLY BELONGED TO THE STATE CHURCH.

OF THE ELEVEN MAXIMS FOR THE CONSTITUTION VOTED IN 1814, THE EIGHTH READ: "THE EVANGELICAL LUTHERAN RELIGION SHALL BE THE RELIGION OF THE RULER AND THE STATE. ALL RELIGIOUS SECTS ARE GIVEN LIBERTY TO EXERCISE THEIR RELIGION, BUT JEWS ARE NOT PERMITTED TO ENTER THE KINGDOM."

THE SECTION ON RELIGIOUS LIBERTY — PARAGRAPH 2 — WAS CHANGED TO THIS WORDING: "ALL CHRISTIAN RELIGIOUS SECTS ARE GIVEN LIBERTY TO EXERCISE THEIR RELIGION, BUT JEWS AND JESUITS ARE STILL EXCLUDED FROM ADMITTANCE TO THE KINGDOM. MONASTIC ORDER SHALL NOT BE PERMITTED."

Justice Leivestad gave this stinging appraisal of the situation of religious liberty in Norway: AS THE MINORITY IN THE CHURCH COMMISSION OF 1908 SADLY RECORDED, PARLIAMENT HAD LITTLE UNDERSTANDING OF THE IMPORTANCE OF RELIGIOUS LIBERTY — A JUDGMENT THAT TODAY VALIDLY COULD BE REPEATED AGAINST NOT ONLY PARLIAMENT, BUT ALSO STATE CHURCHMEN AND NORWEGIANS IN GENERAL. WE HAVE NEVER FELT WARMLY FOR RELIGIOUS LIBERTY.

The justice informs us that during a period of imprisonment in England, some Norwegians had been deeply moved by the kind treatment given them by Quakers. As a result a number of them came home as converts. They were soon persecuted by ministers and authorities. The justice reports how Quakers were to be persecuted under the law: A RELIGIOUS COMMISSION — THE FIRST SUCH — APPOINTED IN 1817 PROPOSED THAT QUAKERS BE GIVEN PERMISSION TO LIVE ONLY IN CERTAIN AREAS. THEY WOULD BE FREE FROM OATH AND MILITARY SERVICE AND OF PAYING TAX TO THE CHURCH. INSTEAD THEY WOULD HAVE TO PAY A DUTY TO THE STATE. . .THEY WOULD BE FORBIDDEN TO TEACH THEIR DOCTRINES: A MAN COULD NOT BECOME A QUAKER UNTIL HE WAS THIRTY AND HAD FINISHED MILITARY SERVICE; A WOMAN WOULD HAVE TO WAIT UNTIL SHE WAS TWENTY, AND (WOMEN) COULD NOT VOTE OR BE ELECTED TO OFFICE. . .QUAKERS CONTINUED TO BE PERSECUTED UNTIL THEY BECAME OUR FIRST EMIGRANTS, DRIVEN FROM THE COUNTRY IN SEARCH OF RELIGIOUS FREEDOM.

A third religious commission led to a more liberal law regarding

Christians who are not members of the State Church (this law dates to 1845): IT INTRODUCED FREE PUBLIC RELIGIOUS EXERCISE FOR ALL CHRISTIAN BODIES AND GAVE THEM LIBERTY TO ORGANIZE THEIR OWN CHURCHES WITH ELDERS AND MINISTERS. IT ALSO OPENED THE WAY TO LEAVE THE STATE CHURCH WITHOUT BECOMING MEMBERS OF ANY DENOMINATION.

The battle for religious freedom continued: PUBLIC OFFICERS TO BE ELECTED IN 1880 WOULD NO LONGER HAVE TO BE MEMBERS OF THE STATE CHURCH. THE RESTRICTION WAS REMOVED FOR JUDGES IN 1892 AND FOR COUNTRY GOVERNORS IN 1894. UNTIL 1889, CITY SCHOOL TEACHERS HAD TO BELONG TO THE STATE CHURCH. IN 1915, COUNTRY SCHOOL TEACHERS WERE PERMITTED TO BELONG TO A DISSENTING CHURCH, BUT THEY COULD NOT TEACH RELIGION CLASSES. Since 1935 members of the Free Lutheran Church are allowed to teach such classes.

NOT UNTIL 1956 WAS THE RESTRICTION AGAINST JESUITS REPEALED. Repealing the law was necessary, for in 1948 Norway agreed to the 1948 United Nations Declaration of Human Rights.

Justice Leivestad further pointed out: THE DISSENTER LAW OF 1891 DID NOT SECURE RELIGIOUS RIGHTS FOR OTHERS THAN CHRISTIANS, JEWS, AND UNITARIANS. PERSECUTION OF OTHER RELIGIOUS BODIES DID NOT CEASE UNTIL MAY 1, 1905, WHEN THE PRESENT PENAL LAW WAS ADOPTED AND OTHER RELIGIOUS PENALTIES REPEALED.

BUT EVEN TODAY, WHEN ALL RELIGIOUS BODIES SUPPOSEDLY HAVE RELIGIOUS LIBERTY, THERE IS NOT LEGAL EQUALITY. THE STATE CHURCH STANDS IN A CLASS ALL BY ITS OWN. IT IS CLEARLY PRIVILEGED LEGALLY, FINANCIALLY, AND SOCIALLY. MEMBERS OF THE STATE CHURCH MUST EDUCATE THEIR CHILDREN IN THE DOCTRINES OF THE STATE. ALL RELIGIOUS TEACHERS IN PUBLIC SCHOOLS MUST BELONG TO THE STATE CHURCH OR HOLD THE SAME DOCTRINES. LEADING SCHOOL ADMINISTRATORS MUST BELONG TO THE STATE CHURCH.

IN SECOND-CLASS STATUS COME SOME CHRISTIAN DENOMINATIONS, JEWS, AND UNITARIANS WHO CAN FORM SO-CALLED "ORDERED DISSENTER" CHURCH. . .IN CLASS NUMBER THREE COME THE RELIGIOUS BODIES NOT PERMITTED TO FORM "ORDERED CHURCHES" BECAUSE THEY ARE NOT JUDGED TO BE CHRISTIAN, OR BECAUSE THEY CANNOT FOR OTHER REASONS MEET THE DEMANDS OF THE DISSENTER LAW. THESE GROUPS – WHICH INCLUDE MORMONS, JEHOVAH'S WITNESSES, CHRISTIAN SCIENTISTS, BUDDHISTS, MOHAMMEDANS, AND HUMANIST ORGANIZATIONS – HAVE NO PUBLIC LEGAL STATUS IN NORWAY. THAT IS, THEY MAY OPERATE BUT CANNOT PERFORM THE PUBLIC FUNCTIONS PERMITTED THE STATE CHURCH AND SECOND-CLASS GROUPS. MEMBERS MUST PAY TAXES TO SUPPORT THE STATE CHURCH.

Among his closing remarks, Justice Leivestad wrote: I REGRET THAT NORWEGIAN HISTORY, AS IT APPLIES TO RELIGIOUS LIBERTY, CANNOT BE REWRITTEN. OUR LAWS SHOW IN MANY WAYS THAT WE DO NOT YET HAVE A PROPER CONCEPTION OF RELIGIOUS LIBERTY. THAT THEY ARE YET ON THE BOOKS SHOWS THAT TRADITION HAS NARROWED OUR VISION AND MADE US APATHETIC OF HUMAN RIGHTS"[8]

CHRISTIAN WORK IN NORWAY

In 1842 the Norwegian Mission Society was established. The second half of the century witnessed the establishment or organizations and institutions to carry on Christian work. In 1868 the Norwegian Lutheran Foundation was formed for mission work, devotional activities, inner mission work, and for assisting ministerial students. After the establishment of the University of Oslo in 1811, Norway's Lutheran pastors were thenceforth trained there.

EARLY NORWEGIAN
SETTLEMENTS IN AMERICA

With the arrival of the tiny sloop *Restauration* in New York harbor on October 9, 1825, Norwegian immigration had begun. This small group of forty-six Norwegians, who had set sail from Stavanger, was met in America by Cleng Peerson, who made arrangements for land in upstate New York, near Rochester, with the majority forming a colony on the site that had been secured. This "Kendall Settlement" grew very little and finally disappeared after a few years, for in the following decade almost the entire settlement relocated in northern Illinois, forming the "Fox River Settlement" about seventy miles southwest of Chicago.

By 1840, several original Norwegian settlements were staked out in Illinois and Wisconsin. Besides the Fox River settlement there were those in northern Illinois and southern Wisconsin (Jefferson Prairie, Muskego, Rock Prairie or Lutheran Valley, and Koshkonong—all in Wisconsin).

Footnotes for Chapter Thirteen

1 Eugene L. Fevold, *The Lutheran Free Church – A Fellowship of American Congregations 1897-1963*, (Augsburg Publishing House, Minneapolis, MN, 1969), p. 5.

2 Ben Maddow, *A Sunday Between Wars – The Course of America Life from 1865 to 1917*, (W.W. Norton and Company, New York, NY, London, 1979), p. 180.

3 Fevold, *The Lutheran Free Church*, p. 20.

4 Adrian Krogstad, *Liberty*, November-December, 1964, pp.24,25,28. (By permission.)

5 Fevold, *The Lutheran Free Church*, p. 9.

6 Fevold, *The Lutheran Free Church*, p. 11.

7 E. Clifford Nelson and Eugene L. Fevold, *The Lutheran Church Among Norwegian-Americans, Vol 1*, (Augsburg Publishing House, Minneapolis, MN 55415, 1960), p. 72

8 Tryge Leivestad, "Corpses and Closed Doors," *Liberty*, A Magazine of Religious Freedom, May/June 1971 (6840 Eastern Avenue, NW Washington, D.C., 20012), pp. 14-18. By permission.

CHAPTER FOURTEEN

THE NORWEGIANS
NORWEGIAN LUTHERANISM
COMES TO AMERICA

PIONEER LEADERS OF NORWEGIAN
LUTHERANISM IN AMERICA

ELLING EIELSEN
(1804 - 1883)

The peasant life in Norway was marked by crudities and excesses (e.g. brawling and alcohol abuse). Eielsen, a lay evangelist who traveled extensively, was much disturbed by this intolerable condition and tried to push the pendulum in the other direction. He criticized the negligence on the part of the clergy to take note of, and to speak out against, the unspiritual lifestyle of the peasants. This failure on the part of the clergy turned Eielsen against them and against the State Church system. When Eielsen was arrested in Denmark he determined to go to America where he could enjoy freedom of religious expression. He came to the Fox River Settlement located near Chicago, Illinois, and there he built a church. Perhaps the first Norwegian sermon in America was delivered by Eielsen to a group of immigrants at Chicago, September 22, 1839, in the home of an English woman.

Eielsen was an unflagging worker. He even traveled – possibly walked part of the way – from Illinois to New York to get the English version of the Catechism. Norwegian parents insisted on the use of English. He went again later to have copies of Pontoppidan's explanation of the Catechism printed, and walked the entire distance back to Fox River.

Lutherans around Fox Lake, Illinois, shared Eielsen's anti-clericalism, for they came from an area in Norway where the people had extremely low church attitudes. But around Muskego, Wisconsin, located southwest of Milwaukee, the Norwegians had retained some affection for the Lutheran Church order and for Lutheran pastors. Eielsen did not fare well when he tried to become the leader at Muskego too. The recognized leaders of the settlement at Muskego were Søren Bache, Johansen, and Even Heg. They were laymen who had been committed to the Haugean Lay Movement back in Norway. These and other pioneers in and around the settlement were exposed to the work of Eielsen who, though hard at work in the Fox River settlements in Illinois, nevertheless often visited the settlement on the shore of Wind Lake in Wisconsin.

But even though these three community "leaders" and the majority of Norwegians living in the area belonged to a group called "Hauge's Friends," Eielsen – an exponent of the same trend – was not able to gain them on his side. No doubt his rugged individualism and his legalistic, often negative speech and ways, cooled his reception among the Norwegians at Muskego, a group which had become alienated from the established State Church in Norway. Much of the Norsemen's resentment toward the State Church centered in the clergy, some of whom espoused a questionable theology. But the Muskego Norwegians also disapproved of the ecclesiastical setup, which many recognized as being a virtual caste system.

Eielsen was for unrestricted lay activity in the affairs of the church--preaching and public praying--without a call to do so. Eielsen went further than Haugeanism and injected a vehement negativism, characterized by speaking out against the clergy. Furthermore, his worship services and meetings lacked orderliness and churchly behavior. It should be pointed out that Haugeanism was found throughout Norwegian Lutheranism in America. Some of the synods that came into being, including the Eielsen Synod, expressly perpetuated the Haugean movement in America. Recall that Haugeanism taught simplicity of worship, rather than ritualism and formalism, and made extensive use of the laymen of the church.

In Norway, lay preaching was done within the framework of the Norwegian Church, which then performed the official acts and kept records. In effect, little churches were formed within the big local churches. In the process a certain orderliness was maintained (which was lacking in Eielsen's work). But things were different in America. There was no organized church at first; therefore the Haugeans found it necessary to call someone to be their pastor. Their choice to be their first minister was Claus Lauritz Clausen, an unordained teacher with an eye to ordination. Clausen had been trained in theology. Meanwhile Eielsen too sought ordination.

In the mid-1840s Eielsen was joined by two young men who were sympathetic to his views. Intending to be pastors, these men prevailed on Eielsen to organize a synod. This was quite an accomplishment, considering Eielsen's disdain for orderliness. These young men felt the need for some kind of organization, reflecting to a degree their exposure to Pastor Dietrichson, a churchly pastor imbued with State Church ideals.

PETER ANDREAS RASMUSSEN
(1829 - 1898)

Rasmussen arrived in America in 1850, having come to teach immigrant children. In 1853 and '54 he attended the Practical Seminary of the Missouri Synod at Fort Wayne, Indiana. In 1854 he began his ministry at Lisbon, Illinois. Rasmussen's education under the Missouri Synod later led him to criticize Eielsen's teachings. For example, it became clear to him that he and Eielsen did not share the same doctrine of the Church. By the time the Eielsen Synod (org. 1846) convened in 1856, Rasmussen had found it impossible to work with Eielsen, and open strife between them developed over the constitution which Eielsen had drawn up. The latter's personality only added to the conflict. Rasmussen led half of the delegation out of the synod. Though Rasmussen was a follower of Hauge, nevertheless his Missouri Synod education, as well as his respect for the leadership of that synod, helped bring him to the decision to join the Norwegian Synod in 1862, whose doctrinal views paralleled those of Missouri. Besides being a pastor, Rasmussen was an editor, publisher, and author. As time went on, his feelings toward the Missouri Synod changed so that he finally joined the "anti-Missourian" forces.

CLAUS LAURITZ CLAUSEN
(b. Denmark, 1820; came to Norway, 1841; d. 1892)

At first the Norwegian Lutherans at Muskego, Wisconsin, gathered for worship in Even Heg's hayloft. This layman performed baptisms and led the people in worship and Christian fellowship. Into the circle of worshipers at Muskego, came Clausen, a Danish school teacher who had been persuaded by a wealthy and influential lumberman in Norway, Tollef Bache (father of Søren), to emigrate to Wisconsin. Theologically trained, Clausen came to America as a teacher, but with a desire to be ordained. Upon his arrival in Wisconsin, Claus Clausen began his teaching duties, but twenty-six days later he was drafted by the Muskego group to serve as their pastor. This was accomplished by a formal petition signed by seventy Norwegian immigrants. He accepted this mandate and was ordained October 18, 1843, following examination by Pastor Krause, who served German Lutherans in Milwaukee. Before the ordination, a formal call letter was issued by the Norwegians and sent to Krause. The date of this letter, September 13, 1843, has been referred to by historians as the birth date of the Norwegian Lutheran Church in America. Clausen was ordained in a haymow, which served as a church. It is interesting to note that the congregation to be served by Clausen was Norwegian, Clausen himself was a Dane, and the man who ordained him was German. Clausen was sympathetic to Grundvigianism, but the congregation was Haugean oriented.

The Norwegian's newly ordained pastor was a respected man in high circles in Denmark, and was accepted by the circle of Hauge's Friends in Norway. Clausen had come under the influence of Grundtvigian theology while in Denmark. Unlike Eielsen, Clausen did not divorce himself from the ways of the Church of Norway. Furthermore, he was often bothered with a feeling of insecurity resulting from his lack of a thorough theological training. Pioneer life in Wisconsin in those days was fraught with peril, with sickness and death intruding as unwelcome but frequent visitors to Clausen's parish work. Lack of proper housing, sanitation, and safe drinking water, together with the general hardships of carving out a farmstead in the wilderness—all contributed to the high mortality rate among the settlers. In one day Pastor Clausen performed eight funerals, and in one certain month, thirty-two. But the record came on New Years Day, 1884, when there were seventeen burials on a single day.

A church, the first to be built by the Norwegians in America solely for worship purposes, was constructed in Muskego in 1844.* However, it was not dedicated until March 13th of the following year. In the meantime, two log churches were constructed for the eastern and western parishes in Koshkonong Prairie, which were dedicated in December, 1844, and in January, 1845.

Clausen's energies were shared by his congregation with other Norwegian settlements which he visited and for whom he held services and administered the sacraments. Two and a half years later, Clausen became pastor of a congregation at Rock Prairie, where his work gained him many friends.

Clausen and Eielsen, though living close to one another did not get along. Eielsen did not take kindly to the fact that Clausen in his methods and mannerisms was churchly, for he gave his approval to traditional ecclesiastical vestments and adhered to the liturgy of the *Church Book of Norway*. Eielsen also was outspoken against ordination – seeing in it the old caste system – so he criticized Clausen's plan to seek ordination. However, Eielsen later changed his thinking and sought ordination for himself. Because of the outstanding differences between the two men, Eielsen refused to recognize Clausen as his brother in fellowship. Thus a breach had been formed in Norwegian-American Lutheranism.

Later, Clausen came under the influence of Pastor J.W.C. Dietrichson, who arrived on the scene at Muskego. Dietrichson's penchant for "following the book" had its effect on Clausen. He issued a manifesto in which he decreed a reorganization of the church at Muskego, declaring among other things:

THE DANO-NORWEGIAN CHURCH RITUAL OF 1685, WITH LATER AMENDMENTS AND ORDINANCES NOW IN FORCE IN NORWAY, MUST BE THE ABSOLUTE NORM OF CONSTITUTION BOTH FOR PASTOR AND PARISH. THE ENTIRE ECCLESIASTICAL ORGANIZATION OF THE CONGREGATION MUST REST THEREUPON AND BE IN CONCORDANCE THEREWITH; MOREOVER, ALL DIVINE SERVICES, PUBLIC AND PRIVATE, INCLUDING THE ADMINISTRATION OF THE SACRAMENTS AND OTHER PASTORAL OFFICES, MUST BE EXECUTED PUNCTILIOUSLY IN ACCORDANCE WITH THE PRECEPTS OF THE RITUAL, UNLESS SPECIFIC REASONS NECESSITATED OMITTING OR CHANGING CERTAIN NON-ESSENTIAL MATTERS.[1]

Clausen also legislated private confession, declaring that all must see him at his house the day before the Lord's Supper.

Clausen's manifesto met with bitter resentment from the Norwegians. As a result he had to revise and modify his program of reorganization. While this modified program did gain some acceptance, the hornet's nest that had been stirred up continued to buzz, and the result was that Clausen finally had to move his ministry westward in the mid part of 1846. He was followed at Muskego by Pastor Hans Andreas Stub, whose ministry by comparison was peaceful and fruitful. His stay was also longer. As the time approached to organize a larger church body, the leaders at Muskego, because of their alienation from Pastor Clausen, remained aloof from the movement. Two pastors who later served Muskego, Rasmussen and Thalberg, remained at odds with the leaders of the Norwegian Synod on the issue of the layman's place in the church's program. And so, the Muskego settlement remained an island, with the currents of Lutheranism flowing around it. For many years the Muskego Lutherans failed to become a part of any synodical organization.

We shall close our discussion of Pastor Clausen on a positive note: "Clausen was a shepherd who kept close to his people. In addition to serving several frontier parishes, he held positions of synodical leadership, served as a military chaplain during the Civil War, for a time was a newspaper editor, and led a colonizing expedition from Wisconsin to northern Iowa."[2]

JOHANNES WILHELM CHRISTIAN DIETRICHSON
(1815 - 1882; d. in Norway)

J.W.C. Dietrichson came from an aristocratic Danish family which had moved to Norway. He emigrated to America, arriving in New York City on July 8, 1844. His attempts to do mission work there were met with very little interest in organizing a Lutheran congregation. He then set out for Wisconsin, finally finding his way to Muskego, where he stayed for a time as a guest in the home of Pastor Clausen and his wife. In his officious manner, Dietrichson examined the background of the ordinations of the two men already at work: "Clausen's was validated, Eielsen's
was questioned. Of course, this procedure did not set well with 'Hauge's Friends.'" It reminded them too much of the State Church of Norway, which they had learned so intensely to distrust and dislike, and which they had so vehemently criticized.

Pastor Dietrichson came to America with the distinct purpose in mind of not only organizing congregations and thus providing for the spiritual welfare of the many Norwegian immigrants, but also, if he could, to lay the foundations for a permanent church establishment here.

After consulting with Clausen, Dietrichson chose to go on to Koshkonong Prairie, about fifty miles west of Muskego. He found five separate settlements there. Dietrichson was well received and immediately held divine services. After investigating the field, he concluded that Koshkonong prairies were most suitable for mission work and to serve as the center of his activities. On October 13 a congregation was organized at Koshkonong. Thirty families, plus some single persons, joined. Soon came the erection of the two log church buildings mentioned earlier.[3]

A main part of Dietrichson's mission was to project the order, organization, principles and practices of the old Church of Denmark and Norway here in America. The new Church would thus have its roots in the old. But Dietrichson also brought to America a tension which he invoked among the Norwegians, who saw in him an extension of attitudes, systems, rituals and teachings from which they had separated when they became a lay-oriented movement, no longer following the State Church and its clergy.

Dietrichson was asked by the people at Koshkonong, Wisconsin, to be their pastor, but he deferred on this until he could visit the other Norwegian settlements. However, he finally settled at Koshkonong. His log cabin became as one man wrote, his "palace" from which "he set about to order and rule the whole realm of Norwegian American Lutherans."⁴ Dietrichson showed a great energy for building churches, making missionary journeys, and for instructing people in Lutheranism. He subscribed the people to the ritual of the Church of Norway. At one point Dietrichson journeyed back to Norway to give his report on conditions on the frontier, but returned to America because he could find no one to take over his work.

The Church of Norway had not given the immigrants a heritage of stewardship training and so, in lieu of regular collections, the church members were taxed their fair share of the running expenses. It goes without saying that the Norwegian immigrants, as did others who came out of a State Church system, had to redo their thinking and learn to support their churches by practicing direct, individual Christian stewardship. But this was only one of many problems which pioneer Norwegian pastors like Dietrichson had to deal with.

Our man was a man of order. He drafted constitutions both for congregations and for a synod. In a congregational constitution which he drew up, it was stipulated that the pastor should be called by the congregation and boards elected by the congregation.

Pastors Clausen and Dietrichson, along with a new pastor, H.A. Stub (came to America in 1848) agreed to hold a constituting convention for a synod for the summer of 1849. Letters to all congregations were sent out. However, this venture failed because the people were suspicious of Dietrichson, in whom many saw a tendency toward Norwegian episcopacy, from which they had fled in coming to America. Of the three pastors, only Dietrichson was able to be present, and of the laymen, only a handful showed up. And yet, while this was an unsuccessful attempt to organize Norwegian Lutheranism, another try in 1853 was successful, and Dietrichson's constitution served well in drawing up the basic document at that time. Pastor Clausen served as the first president of the synod.

Before the Norwegian Synod could be organized, Dietrichson left America for his native land that he loved so well, never to return. This occurred in 1850. It can be said that no other person had influenced Norwegian Lutheranism in America as this man. He insisted on order and discipline and a clergy-oriented system as well as a ritualistic churchliness at a time when lay-preaching and low church form were acceptable among many Norwegian Lutherans. Pastor Adoph Bredesen said of Dietrichson in his address at the Fiftieth Jubilee in Koshkonong in 1894:

. . . . HIS LABORS WERE EXTENDED OVER A PERIOD OF BARELY FIVE YEARS .
. . . BUT TO JOHANNES DIETRICHSON BELONGS THE HONOR OF BEING THE FIRST

208

NORWEGIAN LUTHERAN MINISTER IN AMERICA [I.E. ORDAINED IN NORWAY IN THE NORWEGIAN LUTHERAN CHURCH] AND WITH ALL HIS SHORTCOMINGS AND MISTAKES, WHATEVER THEY WERE, HE DESERVES TO BE REMEMBERED WITH RESPECT AND GRATITUDE. ALL OVER SOUTHERN WISCONSIN AND NORTHERN ILLINOIS HE TRAVELED, IN WINTER AND SUMMER ALIKE, WITH HIS SINGLE HORSE AND ROAD-WAGON OR SLEIGH. ROADS OR NO ROADS, THROUGH SNOW DRIFTS, OR THROUGH MORASSES AND PATHLESS FORESTS, OR OVER ENDLESS AND TRACKLESS PRAIRIES, WITH NO GUIDE SAVE A COMPASS, HE ALWAYS MANAGED TO REACH THE WIDELY SCATTERED SETTLEMENTS. DIETRICHSON BRAVELY BORE HARDSHIPS, TRIALS, ANNOYANCES AND DOWNRIGHT PERSECUTION, THAT WOULD HAVE DRIVEN A MEEKER OR LESS DEVOTED MAN IN DESPAIR FROM THE FIELD. . . HE DID NOT LONG ABIDE WITH US, BUT HE DID A GREAT AND BLESSED WORK, AND THE RESULTS OF HIS LABORS REMAIN UNTO THIS DAY.[5]

Ultimately, in Norway, Dietrichson left the ministry and became a postmaster. His stubbornness and unyielding attitude kept him in constant trouble in his congregations and he ultimately sought another way of life. Still, he was a trailblazer and his memory is honored for that.

HERMAN AMBERG PREUS
(1825-1894)

Pastor H.A. Preus emigrated from Norway in 1851. He became an important contributor of Lutheran confessionalism and anti-Grundtvigianism on the American scene. He was described in his time as "orthodox to his finger tips." He was one of the organizers of the Norwegian Synod. In a meeting at Muskego, Wisconsin, in 1862, Pastor Clausen stepped down and Pastor Preus was elected to take his place as the second president of the synod. His leadership was so well received that he was re-elected at every subsequent meeting as long as he lived. Rev. A. Breese said of Preus, "If any man, before all others, deserves to be designated the patriarch of our church in America, that man is Herman Amberg Preus."[7] Preus also served as a president of the Synodical Conference and was the one who proposed that the Conference involve itself with mission work among the Negroes in the South. He was also a writer and editor.

Preus, like H.M. Muhlenberg before him – the patriarch of German Lutheranism in America – was an untiring worker in the capacity of pastor, missionary, and leader.

BESIDES SERVING THE THREE CONGREGATIONS WHICH HAD CALLED HIM AS THEIR PASTOR, PREUS MADE MANY MISSIONARY JOURNEYS TO SETTLEMENTS WHICH WERE WITHOUT PASTORS. HE THUS PREACHED AT NUMEROUS PLACES IN A RADIUS OF 50 MILES AND SOMETIMES EVEN AT PLACES LOCATED 100 MILES FROM HIS HOME. DURING THIS PIONEER PERIOD PREUS, OFTEN FOR WEEKS AT A TIME, CONDUCTED SERVICES EVERY DAY, INSTRUCTED THE CHILDREN AND PERFORMED OTHER MINISTERIAL ACTS. BEING ENDOWED WITH AN IRON CONSTITUTION HE WAS ABLE TO BEAR UP UNDER THE STRAIN. BY AND BY FOUR MORE CONGREGATIONS WERE ADDED TO HIS ORIGINAL CHARGE. HIS QUALIFICATIONS SOON GAVE HIM A PROMINENT POSITION IN THE LUTHERAN CHURCH IN AMERICA.[8]

JACOB AALL OTTESEN
(1825-1904)

J.A. Ottesen came from a family of clergymen. He was called to a parish of three organized congregations in and around Manitowoc, Wisconsin, and eight or ten mission stations along Lake Michigan from Green Bay to Sheboygan. Ottesen traveled as much as thirty to fifty miles a day on horseback but also traveled on foot. "As a result of these strenuous journeys, Ottesen contracted chronic rheumatism, which worked havoc with the nerves in his legs, so that it was difficult for him to walk or stand long. Because of this Ottesen was often forced to sit in the pulpit when delivering his sermons."[9]

Ottesen was a deeply pious man. A pastor who served as assistant and lived in his home for two years wrote of him: "He is pastor the whole day. . . .. During the time I lived in his home, I did not hear a single discordant note, not an irritable word from him or any member of his family, still less a bitter or quarrelsome word. To me he stands as one of the greatest and best gifts to the Norwegian people in this country.[10]

Ottesen was one of the founders of the Norwegian Synod, and the first to ally himself with the Missouri Synod. He became a close life-long friend of Dr. Walther, the founding father of the Missouri Synod. The last 31 years of his parish ministry were spent at the large Koshkonong parish. A good friend of education, he helped establish and maintain Luther College at Decorah, Iowa, and the seminary at Madison. He encouraged young men for the ministry.

ULRIK VILHELM KOREN
(1826-1910)

His ancestry too included ministers; some of these were from the long distant past. After graduation from the university, Koren taught school, but this didn't satisfy him. After hearing about the urgent need for pastors in America he became filled with the desire to serve a parish among the Norwegian emigrants there. Having firmly made up his mind to do this, Koren announced his willingness to accept a call to one of the new parishes being formed in America. He accepted a call to settlements in several counties in northeastern Iowa.[11] "As the only Norwegian pastor west of the Mississippi (and the first), Koren was almost constantly traveling between various settlements in northeastern Iowa and southeastern Minnesota. About twenty parishes in the Norwegian Synod were later formed out of his original field . . . With the special gifts with which he was endowed, it is only natural that Koren's services would be in demand not only in his own parish, but in the Synod at large. In 1855, at the first convention of the Synod which he attended, he was elected Secretary. From 1861 until his death he was a member of the 'Church Council.' For many years he was Vice President of the Synod. When the Synod was divided into districts in 1876, he became President of the Iowa district and served until 1894, when he at the death of Pastor H.A. Preus became general President of the Synod. As such he served until his death in 1910."[12]

Pastor Koren served the parish at Washington Prairie, Iowa for close to sixty years. Besides being a faithful pastor and a recognized leader in the Norwegian Synod, he also procured the campus for Luther College, Decorah. In the pre-destination controversy he was "the chief champion of the true Lutheran doctrine of Conversion and Election." He received the Doctor of Divinity Degree from Concordia Seminary, St. Louis, Missouri.[13]

SUMMARY OF THE NORWEGIAN SYNODS

At this juncture it might be helpful to the reader to have a simple overview of the Norwegian synodical groups that were eventually established in America. At Jefferson Prairie, Wisconsin, two Norwegian Lutheran bodies were formed. One of these, the Evangelical Lutheran Church in America – the Eielsen Synod – was organized in 1846 and has the distinction of being the first Norwegian synodical organization in America. The other synod was organized in 1853 as the Norwegian Evangelical Lutheran Church in America – the Norwegian Synod – in Luther Valley.* In 1860 the Scandinavian Augustana Synod was organized by Scandinavians (both Swedes and Norwegians) who left the Northern Illinois Synod. Ten years later, the Norwegian element split into groups forming, in 1870, the Norwegian Augustana Synod and the Norwegian-Danish Evangelical Lutheran Conference. In 1874 the Hauge Synod was formed from the Eielsen Synod, which body, though greatly reduced in size, continued its existence. In 1890 a merger of the Norwegian-Augustana Synod and the Norwegian-Danish Evangelical Lutheran Conference, together with the Anti-Missourian Brotherhood (an offshoot from the Norwegian Synod under the leadership of Prof. F. A. Schmidt), produced the United Norwegian Church. Later, in 1897, a group which had left the Conference in 1893, established the Lutheran Free Church. In 1917 a merger of most of the Norwegian Lutherans took place (excluding the Eielsen Synod and an element of the Norwegian Synod) and took the name, the Norwegian Lutheran Church of America – later, the Evangelical Lutheran Church (ELC). A small group of the Norwegian Synod, who refused to join the merger in 1917, continued on as the Norwegian Synod, later calling themselves the Evangelical Lutheran Synod (ELS). A small group of Norwegians who did not participate in the 1890 union became known as the Lutheran Brethren. Later, most of the Norwegian Lutherans found themselves in a larger merger, having crossed national lines to become a part of The American Lutheran Church (TALC), and later still, the Evangelical Lutheran Church in America(ELCA). The Eielsen Synod, the Evangelical Lutheran Synod, and the Lutheran Brethren have excluded themselves from these mergers.

THE LANGUAGE QUESTION
AMONG THE NORWEGIANS

Like the Germans, the Norwegians too experienced conflicting feelings regarding language change. On the one hand English was often looked upon with suspicion as the carrier of the disease of doctrinal error. But many saw the handwriting on the wall, and it was in English, not Norwegian. After all, the infant Norwegian Church had to mature in an English-speaking society. Finally, it was the second and third generations of Norwegians in America who forced the use of English. This is the language they wanted to speak and have spoken to them. Great losses were experienced by the Norwegian-speaking Lutheran churches when the second and third generations, through their regular contact with English-speaking people, were pulled from their old heritage into new associations, which included Lutheran as well as non-Lutheran English-speaking churches. The schools provided by the Norwegians for their children more quickly used the English language than did the congregations. The transition to English was further helped along through the issuing of English publications by the various synods. "On the eve of the 1917 merger, about one in every four or five services were conducted in English. On the other hand, teaching of religious instruction was about half-and-half, language-wise."[14]

While the merger of 1917 began in Norwegian, and Norwegian continued to be the popular tongue for some time, nevertheless there were proponents of change to English and in some areas this change was being made. For example, the seminary offered bilingual courses and even courses taught only in English.

But Americanization of the Norwegian church through adoption of the English language was not the only adjustment to the American scene which the church was forced to make. The church had to learn to do its work in ways and manners most effective in an American setting.

EDUCATION IN THE NORWEGIAN SYNODS

The Norwegians loved education. The historian notes that by the turn of the century, the Norwegians had parochial schools and secondary schools. On the college level there were five such institutions, and on the professional level, there were three normal schools and four theological seminaries. The academies or secondary schools were not to remain a permanent fixture among the Norwegians (as they have, for example, in the Missouri and Wisconsin Synods). The view finally prevailed that this type of education should come from public schools. The Great Depression of the thirties was of no little aid to this view, as was also the attitude of "Americanization" – the desire to be identified with America. While the founder of the Eielsen Synod was himself strongly in favor of Christian education and of maintaining schools, his synod evidently was not. Failure upon failure is recorded in his synod's attempt to have its own schools.[15]

The doctrinally conservative Norwegian Synod, with its interest in Christian education, promoted congregational parochial schools. This group of Norwegians had little respect for government-operated public schools. The clergy of the Norwegian Synod were influenced by the teachings and practices of the Missouri Synod. Thus the clergy felt the need for a thorough religious education for the youth, and felt that this must accompany the secular education of the children. This education had to be administered as a matter of course in a church school. While there was widespread ill feeling among the clergy toward American public schools, this attitude was not generally shared by the laymen.

On the whole, the parochial school did not go over well among the Norwegians who occupied the pews; therefore congregations quite often conducted special classes for school children, for example, summer classes in place of maintaining parochial schools. Academies were quite widespread and were as a rule organized by a private corporation. In some cases they were conducted by parishes and even by private individuals. Not a few of the schools have since gone out of existence. Normal schools for training teachers for both parochial and public schools were also in operation among the Norwegian Lutherans.

WORKS OF CHARITY AND INSTITUTIONS OF MERCY

The number of institutions of mercy established by Norwegians – both officially as synodical projects, and independently – comprise a rather noteworthy list. There can be no doubt that the Norwegians were vitally interested in the plight of orphans, the aged, and the care of the sick. This inner mission program grew out of, and was nurtured by, Norwegian Lutheran Pietism, and these charities were aimed at saving souls.[16]

WORSHIP FORMS IN THE NORWEGIAN LUTHERAN CHURCHES

A polarization of views regarding worship forms among the Norwegian Lutheran churches in America was reminiscent of the differing views regarding these forms existing in the churches in Norway. The Norwegian Synod promoted a liturgical worship patterned after the old liturgy enjoined by royal decree in the old country. It was held as dear and beneficial.

The Eielsen Synod, the Hauge's Synod, and the Lutheran Free Church naturally considered organized worship, or following a prescribed liturgy, to be a formalism hindering the Holy Spirit in His work. (They considered the Spirit's work as being characterized by spontaneity).

The United Church possessed a great degree of allegiance to the formal liturgy of the traditional church, but did give license to prayer meetings and evangelistic services. The worship service form which the Norwegian Synod and the United Synod used in the twentieth century was the one introduced in 1887 and presented to the Norwegian Church by royal decree. This was longer and more formal than the liturgy, which had been greatly eroded, first by Pietism and later by rationalism, in the early part of the 1800s. the shorter, eroded liturgy was used by the Norwegian immigrants when they first arrived in America, and continued to be used to the time of the acceptance of the new liturgy in 1887.

The Haugean Synod emphasized prayer, preaching of repentance (evangelistic sermons), personal Christian living by regenerate church membership. The Haugeans, by the way, did not use public absolution in the communion service, lest unrepentant sinners receive false comfort and actually come as unworthy communicants.

213

HOME MISSION WORK
AMONG THE NORWEGIANS

Norwegian migration to the United States slowed greatly at the end of the 1800s, and picked up again as the country entered the twentieth century. Only then, the immigrants were forced to settle on land farther to the west and north. And so, the Norwegians came to the Dakotas, Montana, and the Pacific Northwest, pushing northward also into the wilderness of northern Minnesota and across the border into Canada. As with the German synods in the Midwest, so the Norwegians had to emphasize home missions in order to attempt to keep up with the ever expanding need for new churches, pushing forth into new frontiers where there were as yet no established churches to serve the immigrants. Not only were immigrants pushing westward in pursuit of land, even established families were uprooting themselves – at times in large numbers – to take up the trek westward and northward.

Of the various Norwegian groups, it was primarily the Norwegian Synod and the United Church that carried on home missions on the Eastern Seaboard in order to accommodate especially the immigrants who were settling in and around New York State. Chicago became a center of Norwegian mission activity also. By the time of the 1917 merger, the mission frontier had expanded westward and added new districts to the merging bodies. Some of these districts covered vast geographic areas, with only sparse populations.

In Canada, Saskatchewan became the most Norwegian of the provinces.[17] Norwegians also settled in Manitoba and Alberta, as well as British Columbia. Of the 1917 merger synods, the United Norwegian Lutheran Church had been by far the most active in establishing congregations in Canada.[18]

Between 1890 and 1916, approximately 430 Norwegian Lutheran congregations of all synods, including the Lutheran Free Church, were organized in Canada. In addition about 120 preaching stations had been established.[19] However, many more congregations and preaching stations were begun but were later either dissolved or consolidated with others. The author of volume 2 of *The Lutheran Church Among Norwegian-Americans* makes the interesting observation that already before 1890, 2,629 congregations and preaching places were started, and by 1916 there was a total of 6,764.[20]

Try as it would, the Norwegian Lutheran Church couldn't come close to keeping up with the Norwegian settlement of the West and the North. And so, by 1914 only about one-fourth of the Norwegian population belonged to a Norwegian Lutheran congregation. The greater mission thrust was, of course, from the Norwegian Synod; yet the combined efforts of all Norwegian groups could not keep pace with the ever-increasing Norwegian immigration. As in the German synods, the basic need was for more pastors, and since Norway couldn't furnish the full number that was needed, it became imperative that Norwegian seminaries be established on American soil. Except for the Norwegian Synod, the Norwegian groups made use of laymen in the mission field.

The synods were not all alike in organizing for mission work. In the Norwegian Synod each district president was also responsible for missions in his territory. In the Hauge Synod and the United Church, mission committees dealt with the mission endeavors. New congregations were aided in building churches through the set-up known quite generally among Lutherans as the Church Extension Fund. More will be said on the subject of home missions in connection with a study of the individual synods.

FOREIGN MISSION WORK BY THE NORWEGIANS

The period from 1890 to 1917 witnessed much mission fervor, and as a result each of the synods embarked upon their own foreign mission program. By the time of the 1917 merger, there were flourishing missions in China, Madagascar, and Zululand in South Africa. Some of the missionary work was done through the two mission societies based in Norway: the Norwegian Mission Society and the Schreuder (Skruder) Mission Society.

When the Norwegians became interested in China as a mission field, a group of pastors and laymen of the Hauge Synod, in 1890, formed what was simply called the Mission Society, with membership not restricted by synodical lines. In 1894 the Hauge Synod cut connections with the Society, having decided to work in China officially as a synod. However, the China Society received its chief impetus from the United Church, and in 1903 it was officially taken over by that body.

THE PEOPLE DIVIDED

The author of Volume 1 of *The Lutheran Church Among Norwegian-Americans*, makes the pointed observation that the three sections of Norwegian Lutheranism in America were all internally divided: THE LOW-CHURCH GROUP HAD AN EXTREME AND MODERATE WING – THE EIELSEN SYNOD AND HAUGE'S SYNOD. THE "MIDDLE-WAY" HAD, IN ADDITION TO AUGUSTANA AND CONFERENCE WINGS, TWO SHARPLY OPPOSED GROUPS IN THE CONFERENCE – THE OLD SCHOOL AND THE NEW SCHOOL. FINALLY, THE NORWEGIAN SYNOD, HITHERTO UNITED, FOUND ITSELF BITTERLY DIVIDED INTO MISSOURIANS AND ANTI-MISSOURIANS.[21]

We will view this aspect of Norwegian Lutheranism in America further as we study the histories of the individual synods.

Footnotes for Chapter Fourteen

*The sturdy oak log church built at Muskego was two-story, seating parishioners in a gallery. The log church, when supplanted by a larger one of stone, was moved to the campus of Luther Theological Seminary in St. Paul, MN.

1 *Norsemen*, pp. 13,14.

2 Eugene L. Fevold, "Trailblazers for the Church," *Lutheran Brotherhood/BOND*, June 1975, p. 7

3 George M. Orvick, *Our Great Heritage - - A Popular History of the Ev. Lutheran Synod*, pp. 4,5.

4 E. Clifford Nelson - Eugene L. Fevold, *The Lutheran Church Among Norwegian-Americans*, Vol. 1, (Augsburg Publishing House, Minneapolis, MN, 1960), P. 102.

5 Orvick, *Our Great Heritage*, p.6.

6 Nelson - Fevold, *The Lutheran Church Among Norwegian-Americans*, Vol. 1, p. 155

7 Orvick, *Our Great Heritage*, p. 16

8 Orvick, *Our Great Heritage*, p. 16.

9 Orvick, *Our Great Heritage*, p. 17

10 Orvick, *Our Great Heritage*, p. 18

11 Orvick, *Our Great Heritage*, p. 19.

12 Orvick, *Our Great Heritage*, p. 20.

13 Erwin L. Lueker, Editor in chief, *Concordia Cyclopedia*, (Concordia Publishing house, saint Louis, MO 63118-3968, 1954), p. 559

*Technically, the synod was first organized at Koshkonong, Wisconsin, in 1850 at a meeting poorly attended. It was strongly influenced by Grundtvigianism. The synod was dissolved in 1852 under the leadership of H.A. Preus and reorganized in 1853.

14 Nelson-Fevold, *The Lutheran Church Among Norwegian-Americans*, Vol. 2, p. 103

15 Nelson-Fevold, *The Lutheran Church Among Norwegian-Americans*, Vol. 2, p. 113

16 Nelson-Fevold, *The Lutheran Church Among Norwegian-Americans*, Vol. 2, p. 112.

17 Nelson-Fevold, *The Lutheran Church Among Norwegian-Americans*, Vol. 2, p. 91

18 Nelson-Fevold, *The Lutheran Church Among Norwegian-Americans,* Vol. 2, p. 91

19 Nelson-Fevold, *The Lutheran Church Among Norwegian-Americans*. Vol. 2, p. 92

20 Nelson-Fevold, *The Lutheran Church Among Norwegian-Americans*, Vol. 2, p. 92.

21 Nelson-Fevold, *The Lutheran Church Among Norwegian-Americans*, Vol. 1, p. 238.

CHAPTER FIFTEEN

THE NORWEGIANS
THE SMALL EARLY GROUPS

HAUGE'S SYNOD 1846 – 1917
EIELSEN SYNOD 1876 –
NORWEGIAN AUGUSTANA 1870 – 1890
CONFERENCE 1870 - 1890
LUTHERAN BRETHREN 1900 –
(Reference also to the Scandinavian Augustana Synod 1860-1870)

THE EVANGELICAL LUTHERAN
CHURCH IN AMERICA

(EIELSEN SYNOD, HAUGE'S SYNOD)

THE FOUNDER

A brief story of the life of Elling Eielsen has already been told in the previous chapter. Eielsen and Haugeanism had much in common. Both promoted lay-preaching and lay-praying in the church. Eielsen himself had started out as a lay preacher in Norway. While Haugeanism was a lay-led movement that was found in all the Norwegian Lutheran churches in America, Eielsen went further than Haugeanism and injected vehement negativism, a negativism man-

217

ifested in speaking out against the clergy, and a lack of orderliness or churchly behavior in services and meetings. Hauge was much more sympathetic toward the established Church of Norway than was Eielsen. Even though Haugeanism was at its height in Norway at the time of the emigrations, Eielsen's methods and personality succeeded in alienating him from a large segment of the Norwegian immigrants, and later, even from his own synod.

In the mid-forties, Eielsen was joined by two young men who were sympathetic to his views and intended to be pastors. These men later prevailed on Eielsen to organize a synod. They felt the need for some kind of organization, and their exposure to Pastor Dietrichson had taught them that there was in fact something good to be said for organizing the church, at least to some degree. And so, those who were friendly to Eielsen, the low church lay preacher, formed the Evangelical Lutheran Church in America (popularly called Eielsen's Synod or the Eielsen Synod, also the Ellingian Synod, with its name later in the '70s changed to Hauge's Synod).

TOO MUCH THE WORK OF ONE MAN: DISORDER AND SEPARATION

On April 13 and 14, 1846, Eielsen dictated a constitution for the Church which was accepted by the membership. It was full of shortcomings and omissions. One of its peculiarities made proof of conversion a condition of membership.[1] Eielsen's Synod was simply too much the work of one man, too much injected with the personality and reasoning of one man, who no doubt had more than his share of pride and stubbornness. The result was that Eielsen habitually promoted his own ideas and condemned those of others. Three different times groups separated from his synod. Co-workers labeled his work, "laxity and disorder."

TROUBLE FOR EIELSEN – DEPARTURE TO THE FRANKEAN SYNOD

In 1848, at Middle Point, Illinois, charges were brought against Eielsen during the Convention. As a result he walked out of the meeting. Pastors Andrewson and Anderson, former colleagues, turned against him and brought the Eielsen group into the Franckean Synod, a liberal body. They agreed to union with this group as long as this Eastern synod continued to conduct itself according to God's Word and to rightly teach God's way. They also insisted on using Pontoppidan's explanation of Luther's Catechism, which action gained them much criticism from various sides.

Among the things disdained by the Franckean Synod were the renunciation of the devil and the confession of faith at Baptism; also the confession of sins with accompanying absolution spoken by the pastor at Holy Communion. The members of the Franckean Synod regarded the sacraments only as symbolic of God's grace and not as means of grace – thus denying that the sacraments in fact seal God's forgiveness to the sinner. Anderson and Andrewson were happy to be rid of the ritual imposed by the Norwegian agenda books. They saw in those who followed the Norwegian Lutheranism influenced by Pastor Dietrich-son and men like him, a people who had the orthodox doctrine, but not the orthodox spiritual life of a converted child of God. They saw widespread drunkenness and vulgarity and worldliness. On the other hand, Anderson and Andrewson insisted on the "pure life." They associated reckless Christian living with attendance at church services which were well organized and ritualistic. However, two years later, Anderson began to be disenchanted by the lack of doctrinal forthrightness in the Franckean Synod, and by a wishy-washy view of the Bible and its teachings prevalent there.

SCANDINAVIAN AUGUSTANA SYNOD

At this time, two men entered the scene; Dr. W.A. Passavant of the more conservative party of the General Synod, and Pastor L.P. Esbjørn, a Swede who served as a pastor in Andover, Illinois, and was new to America. Dr. Passavant urged the formation of a Lutheran Scandinavian synod which would amount to a sort of compromise, neither being the orthodoxy of the "Old Lutherans" nor the "New Lutherans" of the Franckeans. However, Pastor Esbjørn wanted to establish a more conservative synod, one based on the *Augsburg Confession*. A decade later, the Scandinavian Augustana Synod was formed.

Meanwhile, a division within the Synod of Illinois was made which allowed the formation of the Evangelical Lutheran Synod of Northern Illinois (org., Cedarville, Illinois, September 1851). Anderson and Esbjørn joined. Andrewson also joined and was ordained during the convention. Up to this time he was preaching under license from the Franckean Synod. Northern Illinois was heavily Scandinavian. In 1860 this Scandinavian movement in Northern Illinois became, as mentions above, the Scandinavian Augustana Synod. Ten years later three synods emerged from it; a Swedish Augustana Synod, the Norwegian Danish Augustana Synod, and the Conference for the Norwegian Danish Evangelical Lutheran Church in America.

HAUGE'S EVANGELICAL LUTHERAN SYNOD & THE CONTINUATION OF THE OLD EIELSEN SYNOD

In 1875 the Eielsen Synod was reorganized, producing Hauge's Norwegian Evangelical Lutheran Synod (Hauge's Synod). Each party — the followers of Hauge and the followers of Eielsen – charged the other with misconduct toward Lutheran doctrine or spirit. A New Constitution had been accepted which toned down much of Eielsen's "Old Constitution," and even went so far as to allow the use of the Norwegian ritual of 1685. The controversy over the change in the Constitution concerned the question of membership in congregations. "Eielsen held that members must have proof of conversion for membership, while the others insisted that acceptance of the Christian faith and a moral life were sufficient."[2] At the time, Eielsen's Synod had 7,500 members in 59 congregations, which were served by twenty-four pastors.

THE OLD EIELSEN SYNOD IS KEPT OPERATING

Eielsen was himself removed from the Hauge's Synod, for the membership recognized that he had broken from them, still pledging his faithfulness to the Old Constitution. Eielsen accused Hauge's Synod of "high churchism" and false doctrine. He and a handful of followers kept the old Eielsen Synod going, using the old name, the Evangelical Lutheran Church in America, and, of course, using also the Old Constitution as the basis. Eielsen died on January 10, 1883. To the time of his death, Eielsen had his followers, and much of his time was taken up wielding the cudgels of criticism against those who did not follow his leadership or say, "Amen," to his philosophy. He was a pompous individual, who considered himself to be the sole representative of the truth among the Norwegian Lutherans in America.

The Eielsen Synod remained the tiniest of the Norwegian groups in America. Eighty years after Eielsen's exclusion from the Hauge's Synod, his own group had only twelve congregations, five pastors, and 1600 members – represented mostly in Minnesota and Wisconsin. The synod maintained no schools of its own and supported mission work among the Indians in southern Wisconsin. Its decline over the years was steady. Relatively few – and these were mostly older members – were left in its congregations.

HAUGE'S SYNOD AND OTHER NORWEGIAN LUTHERANS

In the Hauge's Synod interest arose to study the possibility of union with the Norwegian Augustana Synod (org. 1870). Interest in this direction was promoted by the laity, not so much by the clergy, many of whom listed reasons for not uniting. The Haugean pastors resented the Augustana Synod's connection with the General Council (org. 1867). Finally, the question of union negotiations between Hauge's Synod and the Norwegian Augustana Synod was settled when the Haugeans installed a certain professor (Weenaas) at their Red Wing Seminary, against the protest of the Augustana Synod. Union between the two groups had to wait for almost three decades, when both became a part of the 1917 merger of Norwegian synods. More of this history will be given later when we consider in detail the history of the merger.

MISSION WORK, HOME AND FOREIGN

Hauge's Synod found that Minnesota and the Dakotas held a special appeal as a home mission frontier, for in the final decade of its separate existence, more than half its pastors were ministering in these states. Of course, Hauge's Synod lacked the financial resources of the Conference and the Norwegian Synod for underwriting mission work. Hauge's Synod organized the Norwegian Evangelical Lutheran China Mission Society in 1890 and sent two missionaries to China. "So greatly did mission interest in this synod increase during the eighties that Hauge's Synod emerged as one of the most enthusiastic supporters of foreign missions among Norwegian Lutheran Synods."[3]

THE SCANDINAVIAN
AUGUSTANA SYNOD
1860 – 1870
(Swedish and Norwegian)

ROOTS IN THE NORTHERN ILLINOIS SYNOD

In 1851 the Evangelical Lutheran Synod of Northern Illinois was organized at Cedarville, Illinois, by eight pastor and six laymen who were former members of the unorthodox Franckean Synod. There formed within this synod two Scandinavian conferences. On the east side (the Chicago area) was the Norwegian Conference, and on the west side (bounded by the Mississippi River) was the Swedish or Mississippi Conference. Three years after the Synod's organization two-thirds of its members were Scandinavian.

Led by Paul Anderson, formerly of the Hauge Synod and later of the Franckean Synod, and by L. P. Esbjörn, a Swede, the Scandinavians in the Synod of Northern Illinois pushed for the establishment of Illinois State University at Springfield.* However, the liberal spirit of "American Lutheranism" – which championed the "revival" and the spirit of ecumenicity with other Protestant Churches, and even attacked the *Augsburg Confession* – found its way into the Springfield school. Strife arose between the Scandinavian professor, Esbjörn, and others on the faculty. He finally resigned, taking almost all of the Scandinavian students with him.

THE "SCANDINAVIAN REVOLUTION"

There followed what has been termed the "Scandinavian Revolution," a break with the Synod of Northern Illinois that resulted in the formation in 1860 of the Scandinavian Augustana Synod. The Scandinavian Conferences of the Synod of Northern Illinois took Esbjörn's side in the Springfield matter and appointed him along with Paul Anderson and layman A.N. Testal, to draw up a constitution for a new synod. By midyear things were ready and the Scandinavian Augustana Synod was organized. The word "Augustana," testified to the concern that the group had for the teachings of the *Augsburg Confession* at the same time denouncing "American Lutheranism," – a term denoting the liberal unLutheran movement that had gained a strong foothold in the country. "American Lutheranism" not only minimized the *Augsburg Confession,* through its leader, S.S. Schmucker, it purported to find errors in it. Those who took up membership in the Scandinavian Augustana Synod were glad to be free of what Esbjörn labeled, a "Methodistic-rationalistic cover under the spurious names of evangelization, Americanization, American Lutheranism, American principles, etc., etc."[4]

Sixteen Swedish and nine Norwegian pastors, together with fourteen lay delegates representing thirty-six Swedish congregations (3,747 communicants), and thirteen Norwegian congregations (1,220 communicants), formed the new synod.[5] The new body resolved to open a school, to be called Augustana Seminary, at Chicago. Esbjørn was to continue on as professor. Later, the school was moved to Paxton, Illinois. A more thorough history of the school is given in the chapter detailing the Augustana Synod, Swedish. Difficulty was encountered over the question of which language to use in the classroom, Norwegian or Swedish. The result was that the Norwegian group decided to establish their own seminary. The language issue eventually caused a division in the synod itself, with the language groups parting peaceably in midyear 1870 at Andover, Illinois. Meanwhile, the Norwegians established their seminary at Marshall, Wisconsin. It was given the name Augsburg Seminary, as distinguished from Augustana Seminary.

THE NORWEGIAN-DANISH AUGUSTANA SYNOD
(1870 – 1890)

(THE NORWEGIAN AUGUSTANA SYNOD)

When the Norwegians finally separated from the Swedes in 1870 at Andover, Illinois, it was evident in various ways that the Norwegians were not totally united. The Norwegian pastors were divided regarding the use of the Norwegian-Danish Ritual. Newer, younger pastors brought with them from the old country a closer adherence to liturgical form. Older pastors resented this as "alien liturgical emphasis."[6]   There was also the question as to when the Norwegian-Danish Augustana Synod came into being. A few felt that the new synod did not begin at Andover when the separation took place, for the action taken by the group did not include complete organization. The differences and uncertainties that existed in the synod led to the decision to negotiate with Pastor Clausen to see if he would join the new group, for it was felt that the leadership of men like Clausen was needed. With his churchly ways, Clausen would fit in well with the younger element among the clergy. Some thought that the older men lacked the spirit and polish of churchmanship. Clausen was present when a conference was held in August 1870. The Danish pastor proposed a constitution that he had written, and with some modification it was adopted by the conference. Clausen's constitution called for the organization of a conference rather than a synod. The constitution gave membership to pastors, professors, and lay delegates but not to congregations. His constitution also proposed the traditional Danish-Norwegian confessional writings as the doctrinal basis for the conference, in place of the *Book of Concord (1580)*.

AN UNUSUAL PROCEDURE – A NEGATIVE REACTION

The newly, loosely organized Norwegian-Danish Augustana Synod was dissolved at the end of the conference, and the membership then joined together with Clausen and a young pastor named Gjeldaker to meet as the Conference for the Norwegian Danish Evangelical Lutheran Church in America. When officers were elected, Clausen became president.

What happened at St. Ansgar, Iowa, was highly unusual. A synod was dissolved and a new one formed at a special conference which was not even called for that purpose. Furthermore, the clergy were the dominating force, for few lay delegates were present. It is little wonder, then, that when news of this strange and highly questionable action by the conference reached the grass roots, many were astonished and deeply troubled. As it turned out, the negative reaction of the congregations to the St. Ansgar conference meant that the Norwegian-Danish Augustan Synod was not yet dead. Encouraged by the negative response by the congregations to the conference's arbitrary action, the president, O.J. Hatlestad, announced an Extra-ordinary Convention to be held at Jefferson Prairie, Wisconsin, to which all who intended to remain in the Norwegian Danish Augustana Synod were urged to attend. The meeting was to include pastors and congregational delegates. Six pastors and fourteen lay delegates showed. This meeting, held October 5-12, 1870, declared the action of the St. Ansgar meeting which had dissolved the synod, to be null and void. A constitution written by President Hatlestad was adopted and the group declared itself to be the lawful continuation of the Norwegian group which had separated from the Swedes at Andover, Illinois. While there was some feeling toward joining the General Council (org. 1867), the synod decided not to take this step.

Once again, the antagonism of some individuals against the use of traditional forms of worship was deeply felt, although it was becoming apparent that differences of opinion in this area were something for both sides to live with and not split ranks over.

AFTER PARTING WITH THE SWEDES, A DIVISION REMAINED AMONG THE NORWEGIANS

There were two distinct parties of Norwegian Lutherans who had once belonged to the Northern Illinois Synod. And there were distinct personality clashes that point up this division. Furthermore, in some instances, pompous individuals demanded to be recognized as leaders, even though they did not actually bear a call to lead. Sadly, these men imposed their ideas as well as their personalities on the church to its detriment.

SUMMARY OF THE NORWEGIAN AUGUSTANA SYNOD

At first, named in 1870, the Norwegian-Danish Augustana Synod in America, it later became simply the Norwegian Augustana Synod. Some important points to consider about this synod are these: (1) This group remained small. (2) It had the Haugean spirit which promoted lay-activity in the church. (3) Most pastors had no formal theological training. They were influenced by the Haugean awakening in Norway. Even its presidents at first were lay-preachers. (4) The synod was low church, non-liturgical, but finally came to be tolerant of each other's views. (5) Pietism was strong. This movement emphasized conversion experience followed by refraining from what was recognized by them to be worldly or sinful pursuits – card playing, dancing, and drinking alcohol. (6) This group, though it adopted a new constitution (Hatlestad's) in 1870, finally rejected it, and the old original Augustana Constitution was recognized as being in force. The group claimed, after all, to be the rightful continuation of the Augustana (Norwegian) Synod. (7) The synod showed interest in, and promoted a union of, the Lutheran Churches though it failed to join the General Council. The synod worked for union with the Norwegian-Danish Conference, and this union came about in 1890. It also tried to establish friendly relations with Hauge's Synod.

MISSIONS

On the home mission front the territory to cover was vast, the workers few. It is interesting that in 1884 one pastor was given responsibility to minister to Norwegians in Idaho, Montana, Oregon, Utah, and Washington. As far as foreign mission work was concerned, most of the efforts of the synod were at first directed to the General Council's mission in India. Later, monies were to a great extent redirected to the Norwegian Mission Society. Also, some interest was shown in the support of missions to the Jews and the Norwegian Synod's Indian missions.

THE NORWEGIAN-DANISH EVANGELICAL LUTHERAN CONFERENCE
(1870 – 1890)
(Became in 1884 The Norwegian Lutheran Conference)

QUESTIONABLE BEGINNINGS

Like the Norwegian Augustana Synod, the Norwegian-Danish Evangelical Lutheran Conference (known simply as the Conference) was organized in 1870. Both came out of the Scandinavian Augustana Synod that year. Twenty years later these two Norwegian groups rejoined, forming the United Norwegian Lutheran Church. But before this occurred, the Danish element in the Conference separated (1884) to form their own group, the Danish Evangelical Lutheran Church Association.

As we have already learned, the Conference was brought about when a group, meeting with Pastor Clausen at St. Ansgar, Iowa, adopted a constitution proposed by him and voted to dissolve the newly organized Norwegian-Danish Augustana Synod. However, some of the membership reacted negatively to this arbitrary action and resolved to continue the Norewegian-Danish Augustana Synod. The group that formed the Conference was accused on all sides of causing an illegitimate birth. The Norwegian Synod (with whom the group did not get along) took the men to task, accusing them of wrong-doing, especially in declaring the Norwegian-Danish Augustana Synod disbanded and resolving themselves into existence as the Conference in Augustana's place.

CHURCH GOVERNMENT

The Conference changed a very important point in Clausen's original constitution. The change afforded membership to *congregations* and not just to pastors, professors, and lay delegates. The Conference was not a synod but only a conference. Decisions reached by the Conference meetings were binding upon a congregation only if approved by it. There was no Church Council to carry on the business of the Conference between meetings, for the Conference stood against centralization of authority. In lieu of such a body, the president especially, carried the burden of the affairs of the body. The Norwegian Synod, on the other hand, had a more centralized church government carried on through a Church Council. Member congregations of the Conference were divided into districts, but not for governmental purposes.

DOCTRINE

The Conference was not as dogmatic in its doctrinal position as the Norwegian synod, the Missouri Synod, and the Wisconsin Synod. The members blamed the Norwegian Synod for getting their super-orthodoxy from its association with the Missouri Synod. The group of Norwegians and Danes who formed the Conference wanted neither super-orthodoxy nor doctrinal indifferences. And they did not want the self-righteousness of those who stressed Christian life over doctrine. Still, they allowed individuals in their own midst to wield authority over them in other ways. The theology and practice of this group could be termed "middle-of-the-road."

A strong leader was found in Pastor Weenas, who taught (some years all alone) on the Augsburg faculty and was anti-Missourian. Weenas, who allowed that there were open questions in theology, represented the younger group of theologians. His views were to a great extent an attack on the theological views of the older element of the Norwegian pastors, who leaned toward the theology of the unwavering Norwegian Synod. This latter body characterized the Conference after its first decade, as its largest and worst adversary. The confessional basis of the Conference was *Luther's Small Catechism*, the *Three Ecumenical Creeds*, and the *Augsburg Confession*.

THE "NEW SCHOOL" VERSUS THE "OLD SCHOOL"

The leadership of Professor Weenaas waned as Professor Oftedal and Professor Sverdrup became powerful figures. Both were men looking for a fight. They were quick to attack the Norwegian Synod and what was termed in their circles as "Wisconsinism" or "Norwegian Missourianism." The attack of the

225

young professors on the Norwegian Synod caused much dismay in the Conference even among those who had little love for this orthodox group. The result was that Oftedal caused schism within the Conference, with the "Old School" and the "New School" being at odds. The Old School leaders were: Claus L. Clausen, Johann A. Bergh, Botolph Gjeldaker, followed by Nils C. Brun, and Nils E. Broe. Oftedal's attack had been made in the form of printed, public denunciation of the Norwegian Synod, and the Missourianism found among Norwegians. This brief document was titled "Public Declaration."

There were no serious doctrinal differences between the Old and New Schools, but there existed difference in *emphasis* in doctrine, and there were personality clashes. In 1882, the "Declaration of the Thirty" was signed by a group of men who protested a new and alien emphasis that had been introduced in the Conference by Oftedal's "Public Declaration." The signers did not like the indifference toward doctrinal discussions, nor the new and peculiar concept of congregational freedom that was introduced. They wanted the Conference to repudiate the "Declaration."

The New School justified the divisions in the Norwegian Church by pointing out that each side has its special task to perform. The Old School deplored the divisions, even calling them sinful and advocated movements for the purpose of uniting the opposing parties. The New School did not want to hold Free Conferences and was opposed to having doctrinal discussions. The Old School men were willing to have doctrinal theses, discussions, and conferences.

Both parties within the Conference continued to grow, with the New School having control of Augsburg School. After the United Church was formed in 1890, the radical group refused to turn over control of the institution to the new United Church and somewhat later, in 1897, formed a body of its own, the Lutheran Free Church ("Friends of Augsburg").

STRIFE IN THE CONFERENCE OVER AUGSBURG COLLEGE
(Refer to chapter, Lutheran Free Church)

The cause of strife can be traced to the presence of Oftedal, Sverdrup, and Gunnerson, who were accused by the Old School of introducing an "alien spirit."[7] They implemented a new program of education which was a wide departure from the old Norwegian school system. They also stressed congregational freedom and personal Christianity. Their motto became "free congregations in a free church, and a free church in a free people." And all this in the midst of American Freedom![8]

President Weenaas, who felt his influence rapidly deteriorating, stated his fears that his colleagues were transforming the Conference into a party – a church party – more evil and shameful than any other in Norwegian American Lutheranism.[9] Disappointed by what was happening in the Conference, and saddened by the loss of his wife, Weenaas later returned to Norway.

Tension remained in the faculty. Sverdrup and Oftedal, by their arbitrariness alienated themselves from the other two faculty members, who then did not retain their positions in the school. One went into a parish and the other man resigned. The remaining members of the faculty were the leaders of the

New School party. Augsburg Seminary had become their institution.

A financial crisis which plagued the institution was to a great extent alleviated when Prof. Oftedal, on his own, inaugurated a collection among the congregations. $5,000 was ultimately donated or subscribed to an endowment fund. The arbitrary method by which this was done angered the Old School and charges were brought against the New School. At the same time, it was becoming apparent that the New School had succeeded in gaining the confidence and backing of a majority of the Conference. "By 1883, the Old School had largely been defeated."[10] The school, the religious journal, the congregations themselves, were in the hands of the New School party.

The power base for the two professors was their vocal Anti-Missourian sentiment, their emphasis on congregational freedom, their democratic approach with emphasis on "the people," and with it the right of lay-preaching. The Danes of the Conference – Old School adherents – left the Conference and formed their own group in 1884: The Danish Evangelical Church Association in America. This association merged two years later with other Danes to form the United Evangelical Lutheran Church.

MORE STRIFE

The friction between the Old School and the New School, once a roar, was reduced to a whisper. On the surface, internal peace seemed to be present. But then came 1890 and the formation of the United Norwegian Church. Old antagonists again came to the fore, ready to do battle. Professor Sverdrup insisted on the essential freedom of the congregation, arguing that there must be no papal type authority over it. He maintained that it is the right of every congregation to use the Word and sacraments . . . to organize themselves, to choose their own officers and pastors (which pastors are servants, not rulers, who are not to stand in the way of gifts of grace in the congregation by regulating or suppressing lay ministries in the congregation). Prof. Sverdrup held that a church body was only a union of free congregations. Yet he taught that the church body was not merely advisory, but the organ through which the Church does its work.[11] He felt that a strictly advisory body – an all-talk-but-no-action-body, as we might label it – was a luxury the Church could hardly afford. This was contrary to the old spirit of the Conference. (Note once again avoidance of the word "synod," as used by other groups that were more closely knit and with more central authority).

The Old School very much disliked Prof. Sverdrup's doctrine and withheld allegiance to the body's decisions, influenced as they were by the New School men, who were in control. The Old School wanted a Church in which the pastoral office was well-defined and regulated, an office which could develop and supervise the talents and efforts of the laity. While opposed to the "scholastic orthodoxy" of the Missouri Synod, the Old School did, however, want distinct presentation of Bible doctrine.

The New School minimized the pastoral office to the point where the pastor had no more authority than anyone else. As to doctrine, its presentation in any form seemed distasteful to them.

LITURGY

Congregational autonomy was maintained in liturgical matters and congregations were allowed to use the Ritual of the Church of Norway, with some modification.

MISSION WORK

In the area of Home Missions, Minnesota and the Dakotas held a special appeal to the men of the Conference, who also showed an interest in the West Coast (Washington). Beginning in the 1870's, the Conference channeled its mission monies into the Norwegian Mission Society. In the eighties it authorized the commissioning of a missionary to Madagascar to work through the Society. It should be noted that the missionary, J. R. Hogstad, was the first Norwegian American Lutheran to go as a missionary to a foreign land. Pastor Hogstad was a graduate of Augsburg Seminary and was ordained in 1887. The Conference was then the first American Lutheran body to send out a foreign missionary. [12]

Another interesting aspect of Norwegian foreign mission work was the mission to the Jews – the Zion Society for Israel – carried on by the Conference. Efforts were directed to Jews in Russia, in eastern United States, in Chicago, and in Minneapolis.

EDUCATION

The Conference maintained Augsburg College, Minneapolis, Minnesota, founded in 1868.

MERGER

Beginning in 1885, joint meetings were held between the Norwegian Lutheran groups. The Anti-Missourian Brotherhood, consisting of men who had left the Norwegian Synod in 1886 and were without affiliation, pressed for a union of Norwegian synods. Later the Norwegian Synod cooled toward the idea of a union of Norwegian Lutheran Churches and dropped out of the joint meetings. In June 1890 the Norwegian Augustana Synod, the Norwegian Lutheran Conference, and the Anti-Missourian Brotherhood merged to form the United Norwegian Church.

THE CHURCH OF THE LUTHERAN BRETHREN
(1900 -)

This small but steadily growing Norwegian Lutheran Church was organized at Milwaukee, Wisconsin, in 1900 by a group of eight Norwegian pastors and five congregations who had been members of the United Norwegian Church. They were of the opinion that no one should be allowed church membership who had not undergone a conscious experience of conversion. In this respect they had much in common with the ideas of Eielsen and with the founders of the Lutheran Free Church. Strict discipline and a pure life, as well as lay participation, are matters emphasized strongly among the Brethren.

In outstanding ways the Brethren differ from the mainstream of Lutheranism in America. Upon entering their buildings the visitor sees no altar. In the service he hears no liturgy. No pastor is seen wearing clerical garb. The visitor would not witness confirmation of young people. Though they are instructed in the faith, each must wait for acceptance into communicant membership until he has had a personal experience of conversion, or awakening, which he can actually refer to. In the church services free prayer and testimony are much used. Pastors do not pronounce absolution of sins. Communion is received at the pews.

The president is head of the church which uses a combination of Congregational and Presbyterian elements in its governing functions. The Brethren's first spiritual leader was K.O. Lundeberg, who sought to gain only true Christians for the church.[13] The strength of the Lutheran Brethren is found in the upper Midwest.

Though small in numerical strength, the Brethren have shown a large heart for missions, especially foreign missions. The Brethren established missions in West Africa (the Sudan), Formosa, and Japan. It has co-operated with the National Lutheran Commission for Soldiers' and Sailors' Welfare. It remained aloof from the merger forming the Norwegian Lutheran Church of America in 1917.

The Brotherhood operates a high school, academy and seminary at Fergus Falls, Minnesota. The Lutheran Bible School, which is now located at Fergus Falls, is one of the first Lutheran Bible Schools in America (1903). An Old People's Home is operated at Sauk Center, Minnesota.

After the first half-century of its existence, the Church of the Lutheran Brethren numbered 54 pastors, 53 congregations, and almost 4,000 members, who raised about $200,000 annually for their church's work, a higher average than the other Lutheran groups at that time. Statistics for 1973 showed the following: 119 ordained pastors, of whom 80 were active, serving congregations; 91 congregations; 8,700 baptized members; 5,225 communicant members, and $410,000 contributed to the work of the church at large. By the mid 1990s this body had 200 congregations in the Midwest and on both coasts. There were about 13,000 baptized members and about 225 ordained pastors.

It has not been unusual for this small Lutheran body to allocate nearly half the total church budget for world missions. Its periodical is *Faith and Fellowship*. Joseph H. Levang wrote a diamond jubilee history (1980) titled, *The Church of the Lutheran Brethren*. Published at Fergus Falls, MN.

Footnotes for Chapter Fifteen

1 Erwin L. Luecker, Editor in Chief, *Lutheran Cyclopedia*, (Concordia Publishing House, Saint Louis, MO 63118-3968, 1954), p. 331.

2 Omar Bonderud – Charles Lutz, Editors, *America's Lutherans*, (reprinted from One Magazine), A chapter titled, "The Little Norse," by J.A.O. Preus, Jr., (The Wartburg Press, Columbus, Ohio, 1955), p. 51.

3 E. Clifford Nelson – Eugene L. Fevold, *The Lutheran Church Among Norwegian-Americans*, Vol. 1, (Augsburg Publishing House, Minneapolis, MN 55415, 1960), p. 289.

*Later, this institution became Concordia Theological College and Seminary, owned and operated by the Missouri Synod until the mid 1970s, when it was sold to the State of Illinois and the seminary was moved to Fort Wayne, Indiana.

4 Nelson-Fevold, *The Lutheran Church Among Norwegian-Americans,* p. 196.

5 Nelson-Fevold, *The Lutheran Church Among Norwegian-Americans*, p. 197.

6 Nelson-Fevold, *The Lutheran Church Among Norwegian-Americans*, p. 201.

7 Nelson-Fevold, *The Lutheran Church Among Norwegian-Americans*, p. 226.

8 Nelson-Fevold, *The Lutheran Church Among Norwegian-Americans*, p. 228.

9 Nelson-Fevold, *The Lutheran Church Among Norwegian-Americans*, p. 229.

10 Nelson-Fevold, *The Lutheran Church Among Norwegian-Americans,* p. 233.

11 Nelson-Fevold, *The Lutheran Church Among Norwegian-Americans*, p. 235

12 Nelson-Fevold, *The Lutheran Church Among Norwegian-Americans*, p. 286.

13 Lueker, *Lutheran Cyclopedia*, p. 606.

CHAPTER SIXTEEN

THE NORWEGIANS
THE NORWEGIAN
EVANGELICAL LUTHERAN
SYNOD OF AMERICA
(NORWEGIAN SYNOD)
1853-1917

INTRODUCTION

The Norwegian Evangelical Lutheran Synod of America was the second attempt to organize the Norwegian Lutheran immigrants who were pouring into this country about the middle of the nineteenth century. The first synodical body was that formed by Pastor Elling Eieslen in 1846.

The migration of Norwegians to this country began in earnest about the time of other great migrations from such countries as Germany and Ireland. Thus the year 1840 found a goodly number of Norsemen leaving the steep mountains and deep Fjords of the old country with high hopes of gaining firm footholds in the frontier region of Wisconsin, Minnesota, Iowa, the Dakotas, and as far west as Montana. As was true of the German immigration, so also of the influx of Norwegians, many Lutherans were involved, and these were uprooted from their churches, from the public preaching of the Word and from the care of a pastor. These were transplanted to a completely new and strange, often hostile, environment where, more often than not, they could not be greeted by established churches and pastors. And so, this lack of spiritual care reaped its toll on the hearts and lives of the immigrants. Many were lost altogether from their Christian moorings. Others took up membership in the religious sects.

We recall how the people in Germany were stirred by the lack of German-speaking pastors in America who could give the Bread of Life to the great numbers of immigrants who had chosen to leave the home land. German mission societies tried to fill this need. The people back home in Norway also felt a sense of duty toward the spiritual needs of their fellow Norsemen transplanted to America. Lutheran pastors were thus sent to help establish the Norwegian Lutheran church on the frontier.

FORMING A SYNOD

The name of Claus Lauritz Clausen (born in Denmark, November 3, 1820) stands out with special importance among the early Norwegian pastors in America. He was a teacher and a lay-preacher, who came to Norway from Denmark in 1841 and two years later was sent by a wealthy and influential lumberman to America. He was ordained in the Norwegian settlement at Muskego, Wisconsin, the same year of his arrival (1843).

Another name that stands out prominently is that of J.W.C. Dietrichson (1815-1882), who arrived in America in 1844. His coming to this country was also sponsored by a layman in Norway. Dietrichson became a leader of the Norwegians at Koshkonong, Rock County, Wisconsin.

Others, including H.A. Preus, also came from Norway to serve various Norwegian congregations springing up in Wisconsin and northern Illinois. Further mention of these leaders has been made in the chapter, "Norwegian Lutheranism Comes To America."

Many of the Norwegians who had come to America were at first cold toward the idea of organizing congregations into larger fellowship groups, and so the work of establishing a Norwegian Lutheran synod proceeded slowly. Early plans for a synod failed because of suspicion on the part of the laymen. But the arrival of more pastors on the scene made it seem a propitious time to attempt once more the organizing of congregations into a Norwegian Lutheran synod. A series of inter-congregational meetings was finally held, beginning in 1849, and these meetings resulted, already in 1850, in the formation of the Norwegian Evangelical Lutheran Synod of America. However, the synod got off to a very rocky beginning and was reorganized in 1853, the date usually recognized for its organization. In its original formation the synod was influenced by Grundtvigian principles.

In 1851, the election of officials was held. Clausen was elected superintendent and A .C. Preuss, vice-superintendent. A Church Council was also elected, which included laymen. However, the congregations were somewhat adverse to adopting the constitution, since they feared clergy-dominance. Also to be considered was the fact that late arrivals of new pastors from Norway in 1851 uncovered differences of opinion regarding the constitution, which in one of its paragraphs smacked of Grudtvigianism. They objected to the expression that church doctrine is revealed through God's Word in our baptismal covenant as well as in the canonical books of the Old and New Testaments. Grundvigianism placed the candidate's confession of the *Apostolic Creed* at Baptism, above the Bible as source of Christian doctrine. However, in 1851 H. A. Preus arrived on the scene from Norway. Described as "orthodox to his finger tips,"[1] he became an important contributor of Lutheran confessionalism and anti-Grundtvigianism on the American scene. In a meeting at Muskego, Wisconsin, in February 1852, Clausen stepped down and Preus was elected president. Three new pastors were received. The enactment of the 1851 Constitution was declared null and void. The offending Grudtvigian expression in paragraph two of the proposed constitution was struck over the objection of Clausen.

One year later, in 1853, the synod was re-organized at Luther Valley, Wisconsin, as the Norwegian Evangelical Lutheran Church in America. At the Constituting Convention held in October, six pastors together with lay delegates from seventeen congregations, were present. This body came to be called simply the Norwegian Synod, and more often than not, "The Synod." The Muskego congregation, pastored by H. A. Stub, did not join the Norwegian Synod, fearing hierarchy within the body. Clausen meanwhile had moved to Iowa.

Pastor Dietrichson had come to America with the distinct purpose in mind of not only organizing congregations, but also to lay the foundation for a permanent church establishment in this country. Dietrichson and Clausen were the original "guiding lights" for this group of Norwegian Lutherans. While their first attempt (in 1851) to establish a synod, for all practical purposes failed, the second attempt under the new leadership of H. A. Preus in 1853 was successful. A constitution written by Dietrichson served well in drawing up the basic document for the fledgling synod. Besides the ecumenical creeds, only the *Augsburg Confession* and *Luther's Small Catechism* were specified as basic statements of faith for all members to adhere to. Dietrichson did not himself take part in the final organization of the Norwegian Synod, for he returned to Norway in 1850. But the spirit which he imparted to Norwegian Lutheranism in America remained to be a strong influence on the Norsemen who had come. The Synod's motto was, "It is Written." From the beginning, the Norwegian Synod determined to be orthodox Lutheran in character.

At the time of its organization in 1853, the Norwegian Synod had six pastors and thirty-eight congregations, numbering around 11,400 souls. The Synod grew fairly rapidly in size. By the beginning of the 1880's the Synod counted 193 pastors and 143,885 souls scattered in 723 congregations. Later, due to the election controversy and a resultant split in its ranks, the Synod shrank to 138 pastors serving about 94,000 souls in 512 congregations. However, by the time it celebrated its diamond jubilee, the Synod had just about regained the strength it had before the split.

For more than a generation, the Norwegian Synod, whose pastors were university trained in Norway, dominated the scene. However, the Synod eventually lost its pre-eminence. Dispute within itself was a reason.

THE NORWEGIAN SYNOD
AND THE MISSOURI SYNOD

Because of its orthodox Lutheran character, the Norwegian Synod found it-self doctrinally in accord with the Missouri Synod, and also came to use the St. Louis Seminary for training its pastors. A Norwegian professorship was estab-lished at this seminary, while plans were also developed for the Synod to es-tablish its own school. Pastor Lauritz Larsen was placed on the faculty by the Norwegians.

LAY INVOLVEMENT

The Norwegian Synod's government lay in a Church Council, which in-cluded both clergy and laymen. For a time the new synod met with controversy over the question of lay-preaching. The Haugean influence, of course, was still in evidence in some of the Norwegians. Those who came to America as trained pastors under the established church system were against lay-preaching. On one side were those who even regarded public praying by a laymen a sin. On the other side, the feeling was held that over-much stress was made of the rights of the clergy and that each Christian as a member of the priesthood of believers inherits the function to sacrifice (pray) and teach, in becoming a Christian.

It was Prof. C.F.W. Walther of the Missouri Synod who settled the issue for both sides in the dispute. His suggestion to the Norwegians embraced three points regarding the ministry: (1) It belongs to the universal priesthood (all be-lievers). (2) It is the special office of the ministry in the congregation. (3) It is conditioned by necessity which knows no law (an emergency ministry). This suggestion was acceptable to both sides, and as a result three pastors who had formerly held themselves aloof now joined the Norwegian Synod.

THE SLAVERY ISSUE: A DIVISIVE FORCE

The Norwegians differed with the leaders of the Missouri Synod on the issue of slavery. Dr. Walther could see many references in the Bible which would give slavery other than sinful status. The Norwegians, however, were dead-set against it. No doubt, too many bitter memories of the class system of the old country, and the lowly status of the Norwegian peasant could still be recalled. The Eielsen Synod's Constitution spoke of "the fearful side of the slave traffic." The Norwegians settled above the Mason Dixon Line, and many joined the Federal forces to show their agreement with President Lincoln's position.

But then came the disturbing news that some of the Norwegian pastors, es-pecially who had connection with the Missouri Synod (e.g. Prof. L. Larsen), did not share the same condemnatory spirit of slavery so hotly expressed among the Norwegians. Thus the biblical question of slavery came to be raised. Fur-thermore, the Norwegians, suspicious of the Saxons down in Missouri from the beginning, were calling for separation from that branch of American Lutheranism.

The slavery issue, together with the issue of the Norwegians having their own school, came up in the synodical convention. There was argument to the effect that slavery per se is not condemned as a sin in Scripture. However, the strong anti-slavery element was concerned about slavery as it existed in this democracy and as a question that was now dividing the country in a bloody contest. As the convention drew to a close a sharp difference of opinion between the clergy and the laymen was evidenced. The pastors had united in signing a statement in which they declared that slavery itself is not a sin, and yet an evil, and a punishment from God. Under certain conditions they also stated that they would work for abolition of slavery. Clausen later rescinded his acceptance of this statement, and this action caused the controversy to break with full force in the Norwegian Synod. At issue was the consideration of slavery in the light of the spirit of Christianity. During the Civil War, Clausen even became a chaplain of a Wisconsin regiment made up mainly of Norwegians.

After the war between the states had reunited the North and the South, the slavery controversy flared up again and, as a result, those not in agreement with the majority of the synod's pastors – those who did not call the owning of slaves in itself a sin – severed their connections with the Synod. Their position that slavery cannot be considered anything but sin had been strengthened by European theologians whose opinion they had sought. And so, the Synod suffered the first of two serious schisms that were to divide its forces within a single generation. Later, the election controversy – long and bitter – would rend the church asunder.

The slavery issue among the Norwegians caused some to have bitter feelings toward the Missouri Synod, and even to call for the two synods to go their separate ways. Still more antagonism would be generated in the election controversy, when a group calling themselves the Anti-Missourian Brotherhood (not a synod) would raise vocal attacks against the Missouri Synod and its leadership, accusing it of false doctrine.[2]

CHURCH GOVERNMENT

In the revision of the Synod's Constitution in 1868, the name was changed to the Synod for the Norwegian Evangelical Lutheran Church. The congregations were also given autonomy in matters of discipline, and the Synod was designated as being only advisory in congregational affairs.

In government, the Synod had a Church Council consisting of three pastors and an equal number of laymen, and this Council governed in synodical matters between synodical conventions, and carried out the resolutions enacted by the Synod. It also supervised finances, examined candidates for the ministry and arbitrated in disputes.

In 1876 the constitution was again revised. The Synod was divided into districts for more efficient government.

ATTITUDES TOWARD DOCTRINE, AND LITURGICAL REFORM

The pastors of the Norwegian Synod considered purity of doctrine a must, and they did not hesitate to point out doctinal indifference in other Lutheran circles. The pastors of the Norwegian Synod were unyielding in their orthodoxy and required complete unity in order to have church fellowship or union. Thus the Synod remained aloof from other Norwegian groups, since it was felt that these held to doctrinal error.

Certain ties were maintained with the traditional. The liturgical forms and the vestments of the Dano-Norwegian Church were rigorously adhered to. Keep in mind that the Norwegians in the Eielsen's Synod abhorred these forms and vestments, since in their way of thinking such practice made religion an external matter and robbed it of its spiritual nature.

EDUCATION

As has already been pointed out in the chapter, NORWEGIAN LUTHERANISM COMES TO AMERICA, the parochial school did not go over among the Norwegians. While the clergy of the Synod desired such schools and entertained ill-feelings for the American public schools, the laymen in general did not share their feelings. Instead of maintaining parochial schools, the Synod chose the route of establishing schools of higher learning. Luther College, Decorah, Iowa, became a strong and permanent fixture in the Norwegian Synod, with Prof. Lauritz Larsen as the president. A private school known as St. Olaf, was established by men of the Synod in Northfield, Minnesota. Later, St. Olaf College was located here. It is interesting to note that the president and the local pastor were both anti-Missourian during the election controversy and established an anti-Missourian seminary on the campus.

For many years, the Norwegian Synod depended upon the Missouri Synod to train its pastors at the St. Louis Seminary. But because this arrangement really was not wholly satisfactory, a "practical" seminary, known as Luther Seminary, was begun at Madison, Wisconsin, in 1876. The seminary had somewhat of a precarious existence over the years. Friction which arose among faculty members between anti-Missourians and pro-Missourian forces was resolved only when Prof. F. A. Schmidt, the leading protagonist, resigned in 1885. Later, the seminary was transferred to Minneapolis. Finally, it was moved to St. Paul, but eventually–as a result of the merger of 1917 – it amalgamated with the seminaries of the other union bodies to form Luther Theological Seminary of St. Anthony Park, St. Paul.

PUBLICATION

The publication of the Norwegian Synod bore the name *Evangelical Lutheran Church Times*.

MISSION WORK

HOME MISSIONS

Eleven years after its founding , the Norwegian Synod, in 1864, began a home mission program to be carried out under synodical supervision. By 1871 it could be reported that mission work was supported as far east as New York, as far west as California. And in Kansas, Indiana, Texas, Illinois, Dakota, and Minnesota in the Midwest and the South. There soon followed expansion in some areas, and entry into completely new fields in the Pacific Northwest. Entry in the last decade of the century was gained in Massachusetts, New Jersey, Colorado, Montana, Idaho, and Canada (Montreal). The Synod also gave its financial support to the Negro work carried on in the south by the Synodical Conference. Seamen's missions (both east and west and in Galveston, Texas), classified as immigrants' missions, were also conducted by the Synod.

FOREIGN MISSIONS

Early interest in foreign missions found an outlet by supporting the Norwegian Mission Society, an independent mission effort in Norway. Norwegians from all groups supported it, although its acceptance among the pastors of the Norwegian Synod was suspect, since it smacked of religious unionism. For a time the Synod was officially affiliated with the Norwegian Mission Society but its official acceptance cooled somewhat when the liberal Conference became an affiliate. In its early foreign mission work, the Synod included work among the Indians in Wisconsin and among Norwegians in Australia. Already in 1894 the Synod commissioned an Alaskan missionary, and in 1900 it embarked on what at first was a short-lived medical mission program in Japan (1900-02). After that, the Synod (in 1912) went to China with the Gospel. In bringing about the merger of the Synod, the United Church, and the Hauge's Synod in 1917, the three Chinese missions, which had been carried on separately by the three bodies, were merged into one.

CHARITABLE INSTITUTIONS – SPECIAL MINISTRIES

The Norwegians were slow in establishing institutions of mercy but later showed great zeal in such ventures. At Wittenberg, Wisconsin, Pastor Homme of the Norwegian synod ventured forth on his own with an orphanage and also cared for the aged. In 1886 he was caring for 64 children and 11 aged people. But his institutions also provided a mission school for Indian children, and provided a normal school as well.[3] His institution received wide support among the Norwegians. Pastor Homme became anti-Missourian and after his death the United Church took over his institutions. The Norwegian Synod, following Homme's departure, established its own official orphanage at Madison, Wisconsin.

REACHING OUT TO OTHERS: EXPLORING UNION POSSIBILITIES THROUGH GENERAL CONFERENCES

While the Norwegian Synod stated its desire for union of the Norwegians, others did not share its conviction that doctrinal theses had to be prepared and studied – a Missouri Synod trait – by which theses each body could judge the sincerity of the others in their subscription to the Lutheran Confessions. Early in the history of the Norwegian Lutherans in America, conferences were held by Norwegian Synod pastors with others, but such gatherings did not move the Norwegian groups closer to union.

In 1870 a call went out from the ranks of the Norwegian Synod to explore union possibilities of all who regarded themselves as Lutherans. But this joint meeting turned out to be a meeting attended only by men from the Synod. At issue was the Synod's denial of the existence of "open questions." It considered that granting such a premise would open the flood gates of unionism and doctrinal indifference. On the other side (the Conference) it was felt that subscription to the Lutheran confessions was sufficient. That simply holding up the old confessions and pointing to them as adequate statements of truth was all that was necessary for church union, and that any more than this would promote sectarianism.

A general conference was held at Decorah, Iowa, in 1871 between the Norwegian Synod and the Conference. The atmosphere was a friendly one, and yet it was evident that there was not a meeting of minds on the question of the relation of Scripture and the Lutheran Confessions.

In 1872 another general conference was held. Open hostilities surfaced at this meeting. Professor Oftedal's "Public Declaration" was presented, which attacked the Norwegian Synod. This document, while doing nothing to ease tensions, did succeed in establishing out in the open the points of difference between the thinking of the Norwegian synod pastors and those of the Conference. Discussions between the bodies slowed to a halt.

REGIONAL MEETINGS

The president of the Synod's Minnesota District, in 1877 proposed regional doctrinal conferences. The idea took hold and nine such meetings were held, with representatives in attendance not only from the Synod and the Conference, but from the Hauge's Synod as well. These meetings were concluded before the 1878 Convention of the Synod. In his report to the convention, District President Muus stated that there was some hope for the Hauge's Synod but the Conference was still imprisoned in error.'The reader may refer back to the chapter, THE SMALL, EARLY GROUPS, for a review of the situation. However, in two short years the bitterness disappeared as each Norwegian group took a more serious look at themselves and also at the others. Pastors and laymen were becoming worried that the decade of strife between Lutherans was having an adverse effect upon the evangelism outreach. Turned off toward their own church, forever embroiled in controversy, Norwegian Lutherans were being lost to sectarian churches. Furthermore, division and strife among the Norwegians resulted in a proliferation of Lutheran congregations in the same community. It was like cutting up a star fish, for each piece severed from the body grew a whole new body. When factions causing open schism arose in a congregation, each part of the original group became a new, separate congregation.

VOICES IN THE SYNOD CALLING FOR UNION

Pastor P. A. Rasmussen of the Norwegian Synod – a former Haugean layman and leader in the Eielsen Synod – had openly attacked the Conference and the "Public Declaration.." However, in an evident softening of his views, he began to call for self-examination within the Synod. By 1880 Rusmussen sent out a proposal to each of the Synod's district meetings. In his proposal he stressed the sin of continued disunity among Norwegian Lutherans. He pointed to sins on both sides, and called for each to confess his sins and recognize each other as true Lutherans.[5] A meeting was proposed for the summer of 1881 to be held between the Synod and the Conference, with theologians brought from Norway to arbitrate.

The reaction of the districts in the Synod was mixed. The Minnesota District rejected Rasmussen's proposal and decried the Conference as having a totally different faith than that found in Scripture and the Lutheran Confessions. The proposal met a two to one acceptance, but was nullified by lack of a unanimous acceptance. The Synod's leaders were not willing to admit that they were guilty of error, and were not willing to admit to Rasmussen's claim that the Conference was orthodox. They furthermore had reservations regarding the theologians from Norway, whether they had the true understanding of God's Word in the controverted issues. No doubt, the primary concern in the matter was: Do they agree with us in our doctrinal position? Rasmussen's proposal thus did not meet with the approval it needed, especially in official circles, but his voice continued to be heard throughout the decade as free conferences were held. Always the voice promoted church union. His voice was also heard in general mission meetings, which brought men together from the various Norwegian groups. Rasmussen ultimately helped to form the Anti-Missourian Brotherhood group.

Another voice toward union was that of Pastor B. J. Muus. While being a staunch Synod man, he nevertheless became a promoter of church union. Muus succeeded in turning the heads of the officials of the three Norwegian groups, as well as individual district presidents of the Synod, so that they were favourably inclined toward calling a free conference at St. Ansgar, Iowa, in the summer of 1881. A surprisingly large number turned out to this conference: delegates from the Synod, the Conference, the Hauge's Synod, and the Norwegian Augustana Synod, as well as the Swedish Augustana Synod. The spirit was friendly. At this meeting the Synod men stated their willingness to give up the expression "justification of the world," since it was so easily misunderstood.[6] It should be noted that both the Lutheran Church – Missouri Synod and the Wisconsin Evangelical Lutheran Synod, as well as the remnant of the old Norwegian Synod, the Evangelical Lutheran Synod, to this day cling to this very expression.

The men who became leaders of the anti-Missourian forces – Pastors Rasmussen and Schmidt – showed that their theological position in the matter of Justification was that of the Conference, and that the issues of Election and Justification were closely related. Their view can be summarized in this way: God elects in view of faith, and God justified not the whole world but only those who come to faith. This, of course, raises the question: Did Christ die to merit forgiveness of sins for the whole world of sinners, or did he die only for those who would come to faith? Does faith create justification (forgiveness, imputed righteousness) from God for the sinner or does faith simply apprehend a justification which God decreed for all sinners for the sake of Christ's suffering, death, and resurrection? The Baptist introduced Jesus as "the Lamb of God, who takes away the sin of the world!" (John 1:29). Refer also to 1 John 2:2 – a similar statement.

That there was so much friendliness at this first free conference resulted from the fact that doctrines on which there was already agreement, were mainly discussed. The joint devotions were participated in by all; certainly a departure from precedent for the "doctrinal unity" men of the Norwegian Synod.

UNION EFFORTS BORE FRUIT, BUT THE SYNOD DID NOT INCLUDE ITSELF IN THE MERGER

Professor Sverdrup, who taught theology at Augsburg Seminary of the Norwegian-Danish Conference, saw two main obstacles to union. One was the Synod's close affiliation with the Missouri Synod and the resultant assimilation of "Missourianism," that is, emphasis on doctrinal purity to be achieved by doctrinal essays. The other obstacle was the Hauge's Synod's liberal endowment with the old Norwegian "narrow mindedness" or "party spirit." Sverdrup called for the plain language of the Catechism and the confessions, rather than doctrinal theses, as the means to achieve union. He also emphasized that there should first come a cooperation among the congregations *before* church union is attempted, and that congregational freedom must be maintained.

The Norwegian Synod, however, stressed that church union had to be preceded by doctrinal unity, and therefore promoted free conferences as the best means to achieve such unity. Later, when Sverdrup saw that his opposition to the union efforts – insisting that union had to be preceded by cooperation – was not checking the advance toward merger, he changed his stand and threw his energies into the union effort, which continued and finally bore fruit. But the free conferences begun by the Norwegian Synod, which later brought about union of some of the Norwegians, did not include the very body which had proposed them. The Norwegian Synod held itself aloof from the Union of 1890, and allowed another generation to pass before including itself in a merger with other Norwegian Lutherans. The fact is that holding free conferences with fellow Norwegians was not the only interest of the Synod during the 1870s. The Synod found itself reaching out to the doctrinally conservative element of German Lutheranism. Note that a further discussion of the free conferences will be taken up in the chapter titled, "The United Norwegian Church."

THE SYNODICAL CONFERENCE: HERE THE NORWEGIAN SYNOD FINDS UNITY

The Synod tended toward conservative ties. Hence it accepted the Ohio Synod's invitation to meet with representatives of the Missouri and Wisconsin Synods very early in 1871 to see what could be done regarding a federation of synods. Out of this meeting came a proposed constitution for a Synodical Conference. While these synods had felt the need for closer union, it was quite evident to them that the situation in American Lutheranism had come to a sorry state of affairs, with deplorable disunity of spirit evident among the various Lutheran groups. Still these synods that met in 1871 claimed to be in complete accord, and so the aim of the Conference was stated:

WE ARE. . . ABOVE ALL IN COMPLETE AGREEMENT, THANKS TO GOD, THAT WE WILL KEEP THE TREASURE OF THE PURE DOCTRINE AS OUR HIGHEST GOOD AND DEAREST JEWEL. THIS PRICELESS TREASURE, TAKEN FROM THE WORD OF GOD AND SET DOWN IN THE DOCTRINAL WRITINGS OF OUR LUTHERAN CHURCH WE WILL KEEP AS A WHOLE AND IN EVERY DETAIL UNCHANGED AND UNCHANGE-ABLE. WITH GOD'S HELP WE WILL FAITHFULLY WITNESS AND FIGHT AGAINST ANY FALSIFICATION THEREOF. FURTHER . . . WE WILL MAKE A DETERMINED WIT-NESS AGAINST. . . RATIONALISM, UNIONISM, INDIFFERENCE AND EMOTIONALISM. WE WILL EQUALLY WITNESS AGAINST THE SPECIAL PLAGUES FROM WHICH LUTHERAN CHURCH POLITY SUFFERS IN MANY PLACES, E.G. ROMANISING TEN-DENCIES IN THE TEACHING ABOUT THE MINISTRY, ABOUT THE CHURCH AND THE MEANS OF GRACE, CHILIASM, THE FALSE FREEDOM OF THEOLOGICAL RESEARCH IN THE SCRIPTURES AND IN THE DEVELOPMENT OF CHURCH DOCTRINE. AND THIS UNITY OF SPIRIT IN REGARD TO STRICT ADHERENCE TO DOCTRINE AND . . . OPPOSITION TO ALL DEVIATIONS FROM IT REPRESENTS THE DISTINCTIVENESS OF OUR ECCLESIASTICAL POINT OF VIEW AND OF THE CONSEQUENT TASK TO WHICH, BY THE GRACE OF GOD, WE CONSIDER OURSELVES CALLED.[7]

In the 1871 Constitution of the Evangelical Lutheran Synodical Conference of North America, Article III, Aim and Purpose, states:

THE EXTERNAL EXPRESSION OF THE SPIRITUAL UNITY OF THE RESPECTIVE SYN-ODS; MUTUAL STRENGTHENING IN BELIEF AND CONFESSION; FURTHERANCE OF UNITY IN TEACHING AND PRACTICE, AND THE ELIMINATION OF POTENTIAL OR THREATENING DISTURBANCE THEREOF; COMMON ACTIVITY FOR MUTUAL AIMS; THE ENDEAVOUR TO FIX THE LIMITS OF THE SYNODS ACCORDING TO TERRITORIAL BOUNDARIES, PROVIDED THAT LANGUAGE DOES NOT SEPARATE THEM; THE CON-SOLIDATION OF ALL LUTHERAN SYNODS OF AMERICA INTO A SINGLE, FAITHFUL, DEVOUT AMERICAN LUTHERAN CHURCH.[8]

The constitution was accepted by the Norwegian Synod in 1872. But it also had an immediate question of doctrine for the Conference to work on. The question was, "the objective justification of the world by Christ." The men of the Norwegian Synod taught this doctrine, but they had been attacked for it by

241

their opponents. The Augustanians – the Scandinavian Augustana Synod (1860-'70), followed by the Norwegian Augustana Synod (1870-'90) – did not agree with the Norwegian Synod, which taught that in Christ God declared the world forgiven, that the gospel imparts forgiveness to all, but that not all accept it. The Augustanians taught that God offers forgiveness, but there is no forgiveness until it is accepted by faith. The Synod taught that what the unbeliever rejected was not just an offer on the part of God to forgive sins, but rather a universal forgiveness which Christ truly paid for with his own blood. Forgiveness is already a universal purchase made by Christ, something God declared to be so by raising up Christ from the dead. In the 1860s the controversy between the Synod and the Augustanians centered in the practice of absolution, which then led to the Synod's statement regarding Objective Justification and Augustana's denial of it. When the German Iowa Synod accused the Norwegian Synod of heresy regarding Objective Justification, the latter then asked the Constituting Convention of the Synodical Conference in 1872 to discuss it. Bitter theological infighting is something that characterized the Norwegian Lutheran Church in the years 1860 to 1890. Yet to come was the election controversy in the Synod ,with the anti-Missourians versus the Missourians, and the disruption of the new United Church (org. 1890) over the ownership of Augsburg Seminary.[9]

THE ELECTION CONTROVERSY

CIVIL WAR IN THE SYNOD

The controversy in the Norwegian Synod over the doctrine of Election was by far the most bitter. What a hurt it caused! None were so drastically effected by the election controversy as were the members of the Norwegian Synod. The controversy within this body has been described as civil war: pastor against pastor, congregation against congregation, family against family, brother against brother.[10]

Not only were its ranks sorely divided during the controversy, they ultimately thinned. Some, the anti-Missourians, siding with Prof. Schmidt in his attack against Dr. Walther of the Missouri Synod, finally seceded from the Synod. When the split finally came, a third of he pastors and membership were gone.

CAUSE OF THE CONTROVERSY
(Refer also to the chapter detailing the history of the Missouri Synod)

The controversy was begun by Professor Friedrich August Schmidt, a theologian of the Synod, who originally came out of the Missouri Synod and whose ethnic roots were in Germany. To the dismay of many in the Norwegian Synod, Prof. Schmidt began his attack against Walther in January 1880, accusing him of Calvinism. The attack was based on an essay which Dr. Walther delivered three years earlier to the Missouri Synod's Western District. The attack was open and vehement. It is amazing that Schmidt should accuse Walther of Calvinism, when Walther so clearly and forcefully took his stand against the Reformed doctrine of Election, referred to as "double predestination."

Dr. Walther contended that it is false doctrine to teach that "in us there is a cause for the election of God." He repudiated the saying, "Since man is now saved through faith, God must have decided in eternity to save man for the sake of his faith." Dr. Walther declared that the doctrine of Scripture is that "faith is not the cause of justification, but rather its means."

Prof. Schmidt's main point of contention with Dr. Walther was this statement by the latter: GOD HAS FROM ETERNITY CHOSEN A CERTAIN NUMBER OF PERSONS TO SALVATION; HE HAS DETERMINED THESE SHALL AND MUST BE SAVED; AND AS SURELY AS GOD IS GOD, SO SURELY THESE SHALL BE SAVED, AND NONE EXCEPT THEM.[11] Prof. Schmidt went the one step further and added a meaning to Walther's teaching which Walther claimed he never intended, namely, that while "the one part must be saved, the other excluded." The Calvinism of which Schmidt accused Walther is contained in the last three words of Schmidt's own addition to Walther's words: *the other excluded.* But they were Schmidt's words, not Walther's!

What is even more amazing is that Schmidt attacked Walther so openly and so vehemently, even organizing a new publication, *Altes und Neues* (Old and New), just for this purpose. Schmidt claimed that he held to the old Lutheran doctrine, while Walther and the Missouri Synod were inventing a new doctrine.

TWO SCHOOLS OF THOUGHT IN THE SYNOD:
MISSOURIANS AND ANTI-MISSOURIANS

Dr. Walther and the Missouri Synod, together with the pro-Walther and pro-Missouri faction of the Norwegian Synod, heartily condemned the teaching of synergism in any form. (Synergism is the teaching that man can and does co-operate in his conversion, thus working together with the Holy Spirit to bring about faith in his heart. This, in spite of the fact that man is by nature spiritually dead). The Missourians, together with Dr. Walther, taught that from beginning to end conversion is God's work not man's work. They saw in Prof. Schmidt's teaching regarding the doctrines of Conversion and Election, the tendency toward synergism that man is in some way responsible for his conversion. Prof. Schmidt taught election "in view of faith." The issue thus involved "natural powers" in man before and during conversion. There were finally two schools of thought in the Norwegian Synod which no amount of theological debate could overcome. Siding with the Missouri Synod, the Missourians within the Norwegian Synod taught the following:

GOD'S ELECTION OF THE PERSON IN NO WAY DEPENDED ON HIS FOREKNOWLEDGE WHEREBY HE SAW SOMETHING IN MAN THAT WOULD LEAD TO HIS ELECTING HIM, SUCH AS FOREKNOWLEDGE OF THE PERSON'S ACCEPTANCE OF OFFERED GRACE.

GOD'S GRACE IS UNIVERSAL. GOD INVITES AND WELCOMES ALL SINNERS. HIS

ARMS ARE THUS OPEN TO RECEIVE ALL. EVERY PART OF MAN'S SALVATION IS BY GRACE ALONE . . . A GIFT OF GOD. ON THE BASIS OF GOD'S GRACE IN CHRIST, GOD IN ETERNITY CHOSE CERTAIN INDIVIDUALS TO SALVATION. THOSE SO ELECTED SHALL BE BROUGHT TO FAITH IN CHRIST THROUGH THE MEANS OF GRACE. THIS DOCTRINE IS FOR THE COMFORT OF THE CHRISTIAN, FOR HIS SALVATION HAS BEEN DETERMINED AND PLANNED BY GOD ON THE BASIS OF GRACE ALONE, EVEN BEFORE HE WAS BORN. COMING TO FAITH IS A SURE SIGN OF ELECTION. THIS ELECTION IS UNTO FAITH AND SALVATION. CHRISTIAN CONVERSION OR TURNING FROM UNBELIEF TO FAITH IN CHRIST TAKES PLACE IN REGENERATION, AND THIS IS ACCOMPLISHED BY THE HOLY SPIRIT THROUGH THE GOSPEL IN BAPTISM AND THE WORD.

In clinging to these positive doctrines, the Norwegian Synod at the same time took issue with the question raised by human reason—a question which has been termed "the Cross of the Theologian"—Why some and not others? It is an unanswerable question. The Norwegian Synod repudiated the answer which Calvinism gives to this question, namely, that God not only had elected some to salvation, but that he elected others to damnation as well. The Norwegian Synod denied that God elected any to damnation. It claimed that no answer to this age old question should be given that falls short of, or goes beyond what Holy Scriptures say regarding the matters of Election, Conversion, and Grace. The Norwegian Synod, together with the Missouri Synod, the Wisconsin Synod, and the Minnesota Synod, rejected the theory of "*intuitu fidei*," namely, that God elected "in view of the faith he saw that the Christian would have. Election rather results in the individual being brought to faith and saved."[12]

In 1880, conflict came to light in the Norwegian Synod when President B.G. Muus in his presidential address to the Synod, made his anti-Missourian stand clearly evident. His views on election coincided with those of Prof. Schmidt. The side in the Synod which sympathized with Schmidt, and which came to be know as the anti-Missourians, entertained a school of thought that followed Pontoppidan's Catechism. The following is a quote from the English translation of this catechism: GOD HAS APPOINTED ALL THOSE TO ETERNAL LIFE WHOM HE FROM ETERNITY HAS FORSEEN WOULD ACCEPT THE OFFERED GRACE, BELIEVE IN CHRIST AND REMAIN CONSTANT IN THE FAITH UNTO THE END.

THE JOINT OHIO SYNOD SIDED
WITH PROFESSOR SCHMIDT

The Joint Ohio Synod the following year aligned itself with Prof. Schmidt. Its representatives walked out of the specially called meeting of the faculties of the Synodical Conference held in January 1881 in Milwaukee. Schmidt rejected a proposal for the group to meet again the same year and to refrain the meanwhile from public controversy. He made it crystal clear that he wanted to do battle with Dr. Walther. The latter took up the cudgel, stating in his reply; "Be it so! You want war; you shall have war!"

The Joint Ohio Synod contended that if election is taken in a narrow and particular sense, which was Missouri's teaching, then it must be said that election takes place "in view of faith" and is not the cause of faith. Joint Ohio drew up Four Theses stating its position in the doctrine of Election:

THESES 1: IF BY ELECTION WE UNDERSTAND, AS IS DONE IN THE FORMULA OF CONCORD, "THE ENTIRE PURPOSE, COUNSEL, WILL, AND ORDINATION OF GOD PERTAINING TO OUR REDEMPTION, VOCATION, JUSTIFICATION, AND SALVATION," WE BELIEVE TEACH AND CONFESS THAT ELECTION IS THE CAUSE OF OUR SALVATION AND EVERYTHING THAT IN ANY WAY PERTAINS TO IT.

THESES 2: BUT IF BY ELECTION, AS THE DOGMATICIANS GENERALLY DO, WE UNDERSTAND MERELY THIS, THAT FROM ETERNITY GOD ELECTED AND INFALLIBLY ORDAINED TO SALVATION CERTAIN INDIVIDUALS IN PREFERENCE TO OTHERS, AND THIS ACCORDING TO THE UNIVERSAL WAY OF SALVATION, WE BELIEVE, TEACH, AND CONFESS THAT ELECTION TOOK PLACE IN VIEW OF CHRIST'S MERIT APPREHENDED BY FAITH, OR, MORE BRIEFLY STATED BUT WITH THE SAME SENSE, IN VIEW OF FAITH. ACCORDING TO THIS UNDERSTANDING FAITH PRECEDES ELECTION IN THE MIND OF GOD . . . AND THUS ELECTION PROPERLY SPEAKING IS NOT THE CAUSE OF FAITH.[13]

To Dr. Walther, the two points at controversy were these: (1) whether God out of pure mercy and only for the sake of the most holy merit of Christ, elected and ordained the chosen children of God to salvation and whatever pertains to it, consequently also to faith, repentance, and conversion; or (2) whether, in His election God took into consideration anything good in man, namely the foreseen conduct of man, the foreseen non-resistance, and the foreseen persevering faith, and thus elected certain persons to salvation in consideration of, with respect to, on account of, or in consequence of their conduct, their non-resistance, and their faith. (Walther affirmed the first question while denying the second).[14]

We now quote Theses IX, X, XI from Missouri's *Thirteen Theses* of 1881, which were focal points in the controversy. Missouri's *Thirteen Theses* did much to augment the controversy and to cause the Joint Ohio Synod to draw up its own theses the same year.

THESES IX: WE BELIEVE . . . : 1ST, THAT THE ELECTION OF GRACE DOES NOT CONSIST IN A MERE DIVINE FOREKNOWING OF WHICH MEN ARE SAVED; 2ND, THAT ELECTION OF GRACE IS ALSO NOT THE MERE PURPOSE OF GOD TO REDEEM AND SAVE MEN, SO AS TO BE A UNIVERSAL ONE AND TO PERTAIN TO ALL MEN IN COMMON; 3RD, THAT ELECTION OF GRACE DOES NOT CONCERN THOSE BELIEVING FOR A TIME ONLY (LUKE 8:13) 4TH, THAT ELECTION OF GRACE IS NOT A MERE DECREE OF GOD TO SAVE ALL THOSE WHO WOULD BELIEVE UNTO THE END. WE, THEREFORE, REJECT AND CONDEMN THE CONTRARY ERRONEOUS DOCTRINES OF THE RATIONALIST, HUBERIANS, AND ARMINIANS.

THESES X: WE BELIEVE . . . THAT THE CAUSE WHICH MOVED GOD TO ELECT THE ELECT, IS ONLY HIS GRACE AND THE MERIT OF JESUS CHRIST, AND NOT ANYTHING GOOD FORESEEN BY GOD IN THE ELECT, NOT EVEN FAITH FORESEEN BY GOD IN THEM; AND WE, THEREFORE, REJECT AND CONDEMN THE CONTRARY ERRONEOUS DOCTRINES OF THE PELAGIANS, SEMIPELAGIANS, AND SYNERGISTS, AS ERRORS WHICH ARE BLASPHEMOUS AND HORRIBLE, AND WHICH SUBVERT THE GOSPEL AND, BY CONSEQUENCE, THE WHOLE CHRISTIAN RELIGION.

THESES XI: WE BELIEVE . . . THAT ELECTION OF GRACE IS NOT THE MERE DIVINE FORESIGHT OR FOREKNOWLEDGE OF THE SALVATION OF THE ELECT, BUT EVEN

A CAUSE OF THEIR SALVATION AND OF ALL THAT WHICH PERTAINS TO IT, AND WE, THEREFORE, REJECT AND CONDEMN THE CONTRARY DOCTRINES OF THE ARMINIANS, SOCINIANS, AND ALL SYNERGISTS.[15]

So, while the theses put forth by Missouri settled matters for that synod and for the Synodical Conference, they augmented the dispute for Joint Ohio and the anti-Missourians in the Norwegian Synod. The historian R.C. Wolf summarized the history leading to the withdrawal of Joint Ohio from the Synodical Conference thus: *As the controversy grew heated, the Missouri Synod took action forbidding its delegates to the Synodical Conference to meet with individuals who had accused the Synod of Calvinism or to regard as members of the [Synodical] Conference such synods as had charged Missouri with Calvinism. . . . The Joint Synod of Ohio saw this action as an ultimatum to agree with the Missouri Synod or to withdraw from the Synodical Conference. The Ohio Synod published its own set of theses on predestination, held a special convention, discussed all aspects of its relation to the Missouri Synod and the Synodical Conference, and then voted to withdraw from the Synodical Conference.* [16]

THE "ANTI-MISSOURIANS" IN THE NORWEGIAN SYNOD

In 1881, while the affair was for all practical purposes settled in the Synodical Conference—the following year it adopted Walther's Thirteen Theses—it was far from settled in the Norwegian Synod. Indeed, the controversy was just getting started. Schmidt, who had been a professor at Concordia Seminary, St. Louis, from 1872 to 1876, failed to impress the leadership of the Norwegian Synod (with the exception of B.J. Muus) by his attack on Walther. However, the man was not without his supporters, and these became known as the "anti-Missourians." In dealing with Schmidt and his supporters, the officialdom of the Synod tried to show that there really was no need for controversy, since the anti-Missourians also confessed that one's faith is entirely and wholly the gift of God. The official paper of the Synod in December 1881 summarized the situation as the editors saw it: WHEN IT IS INSISTED ON THAT FAITH IS WHOLLY AND ENTIRELY GOD'S GIFT, WHY THEN PONDER OVER AND STRIVE ABOUT HOW GOD IN ETERNITY SAW THIS HIS OWN GIFT IN THOSE HE CHOSE TO SALVATION? SO ALSO WITH OUR CERTAINTY OF SALVATION . . . . SINCE WE ALL INSIST ON THESE THINGS, WHAT IS THERE THEN TO STRIVE ABOUT?[17]

What then was there to strive about? Due to the course of events which occurred, the election controversy more and more led into the doctrines of the Call and Conversion, which in turn generated more strife.

When in 1881 Prof. Schmidt's charges were repudiated in a "Declaration" by six Norwegian pastors, Schmidt felt that the controversy had "broken in earnest." The result was that repudiation of charges brought on new charges. Schmidt accused the Missourians of Calvinism. On the basis of the Missouri Synod's teaching that faith is the *result* of the Christian's election, Schmidt felt that the conclusion could be drawn that those whom God did not elect to faith and salvation must have been chosen for eternal damnation. That, of course, is the teaching of John Calvin. However, Schmidt too agreed that faith is completely the work of God and not of men. But if faith is the work of God alone,

246

and not all are brought to faith, would that not urge the question: Then what of those who are not believers? Is it not then that God chose them to be without faith and without salvation . . . in other words, to be damned? It is a natural question. However, the Missourians felt that this question, resulting in such a conclusion, should not be voiced and that there remains an inscrutable mystery connected with God's election of grace.

So, while Schmidt and the Missouri Synod agreed that faith is completely the work of God and not of men, the Missouri Synod was willing to leave it at that, counting it an unsearchable mystery, while Schmidt sought the answer to the unanswerable: Why are some converted, and not others? Finally, Schmidt went so far as to say that those who are converted are converted because they offered less resistance. This brought a countercharge from Walther, that such a doctrine of lesser resistance finally made man his own savior. Neither Schmidt nor his controversy, which led the Joint Ohio Synod out of the Synodical Conference and brought a long and painful war to the Norwegian Synod resulting in a permanent split, have solved the question.

When the Synodical Conference met in Chicago in 1882, Schmidt came as a delegate. His being seated as a delegate, however, was disputed, and in the ensuing discussion Schmidt refused to answer the question whether he came as a friend or as a foe. Finally, the Synodical Conference adopted the resolution no longer recognizing Schmidt as a brother in Christ, and refused him a seat and voice in the meeting. Penitence over his sins and a public apology were demanded of him. But he was not given the opportunity to defend the charges he made against the Missouri Synod, accusing it of Calvinism and of bringing dissension into the congregations.

THE NORWEGIAN SYNOD LEAVES
THE SYNODICAL CONFERENCE

This action against Schmidt aroused the ire of the anti-Missourian forces, and the agitation they stirred up within the ranks no doubt contributed directly to the Synod's decision in 1883 to withdraw from the Synodical Conference for the sake of trying to avoid a split in its ranks. While membership in the Conference ended for the time being, the hand of fellowship was not, however, withdrawn.

AN ACCOUNTING

A few of the pro-Missouri pastors were deposed by their congregations. Things finally came to a head in 1884 at the General Convention in Minneapolis. Pastor Koren, who had opposed Schmidt from the outset, had carefully prepared a document consisting of sixty-three theses, titled "An Accounting." Pastor Koren wrote the theses with the man in the pew in view. While taking care to be fair to the opponents, and accepting their statements as far as he felt that truth would allow, Pastor Koren drew the line where he felt that espousing false doctrine was at stake. Prof. Schmidt did not subscribe to "An Accounting."

For example, he wrote: "I believe and teach now as before, that it is not synergistic error, but a clear teaching of God's Word and our Lutheran Confessions, that 'salvation in a certain sense does not depend on God alone.'"[18] And of the sixty-three theses, Schmidt wrote: "If I should want to confess the doctrine that conversion and salvation in every respect depends on God alone and that man's conduct here is entirely an indifferent matter, I would much rather subscribe to a Reformed Confession than to this 'Account.' I reject it therefore with my whole heart as 'containing false doctrine'"[19]

THE ANTI-MISSOURIANS DRAW TOGETHER

While calling for the deposing of all pastors who signed "An Accounting," the anti-Missourians went about to solidify their ranks, going so far as to establish their own seminary at St. Olaf School in Northfield, Minnesota in 1885. Two years later the Norwegian Synod called for the group to admit their error and to stop their seminary project. A private meeting was held by the anti-Missourians, whose numbers had swelled by more than fifty names. They had protested that the seminary was a conscience matter as long as the Missouri Synod's doctrine was being taught in the Synod's schools. They resolved to withdraw from the Synod. In the subsequent split about one-third of the Synod's membership was lost to the opposition. The point of debate in the closing arguments amounted to this: Is man saved by grace alone, or due in part to his own effort? Pastor Koren and others like him who remained in the Synod maintained that it is by grace alone. Professor Schmidt and the anti-Missourians had made it clear on the other hand that "in a certain sense (salvation) does not depend on God alone."

Later, the Anti-Missouri Brotherhood (not a synod) joined with the Norwegian Augustana Synod and the Norwegian-Danish Evangelical Lutheran Conference to form the United Norwegian Lutheran Church in America.

A REVIEW OF THE HIGHLIGHTS
OF THE ELECTION CONTROVERSY

(1)   In January 1880 Prof. Schmidt of the Norwegian Synod began a public attack against Dr. Walther of the Missouri Synod, accusing this synodical leader of Calvinism.

(2)   Discussion of the doctrine of Election in the Synod's Convention in 1881. The matter remained unsettled. Already in 1880, conflict came to light when President B.J. Muus made his anti-Missourian stand evident in his presidential address.

(3)   Battle lines were drawn up in the Synod. U.V. Koren was the recognized leader of the Norwegian pro-Missouri force. Supporting him were J.A. Ottesen, H.A. Preus, H.G. Stub, J. Ylvisaker, Lauritz Larsen, T.A. Torgerson and J.B. Frich. The anti-Missourian side was led by Prof. F.A. Schmidt with followers in B.J. Muus, P.A. Rusmussen, M.O. Bøckman, and J.N. Kildahl.

(4)   The religious press was brought into the controversy, two periodicals on the Missourian side and two on the anti-Missourian side.

(5)   There was confusion over what constituted the issues. It was evident that the doctrine of Conversion was the real issue.

(6)   The Missourians accused the anti-Missourians of teaching synergism (co-operation by man in his conversion) while the anti-Missourians accused the Missourians of Calvinism (i.e. of teaching irresistible grace, as well as double predestination—some elected to salvation, others elected to damnation).

(7)   P.A. Rasmussen circularized the congregations of the Synod with a letter asking for the Norwegian-Synod to withdraw from the Synodical Conference. His action came about after Schmidt was denied a seat at the Convention of the Synodical Conference.

(8)   In 1883 the Norwegian Synod took action, leaving the Synodical Conference for the purpose of setting its own house in order. This action lay the ground work for establishing closer ties among the Norwegians and lessening the influence of the German Lutheranism of the Missouri and Wisconsin Synods, and to some extent lay the first blocks in the foundation of the merger of 1917.

(9)   There arose disunity and contention in the ranks of the Norwegians. Three Missourian pastors in 1883 and 1885 were deposed by their congregations. Missourian forces succeeded in electing men from their ranks to district offices.

(10)   Pastor Muus, an anti-Missourian, came forth with a statement to the effect that unregenerate man with abilities God gives him through the Word is able to convert himself by putting to right use the powers given him. Missourians countered this, saying that man is spiritually dead, with no powers to turn to God. Conversion is wrought by God's grace alone.

(11)   In 1884 schism was seen as being inevitable. "An Accounting" was prepared by Koren, a Missourian, covering Grace, Conversion, Election, and Assurance. Eighty-seven men signed this document. The anti-Missourians did not sign but had their own private session, drawing up their own "Confession" which sixty-nine men then signed. Also, the anti-Missourians advertised an auxiliary treasury and encouraged contributions to it, instead of to the regular Synod treasury. And so, they sought a means to finance their cause and to provide support for professors and students. This constituted the breaking point which resulted in schism.

(12)   In October 1885, at Red Wing, Minnesota, in view of the fact that Missourian forces were in control of the Synod, the anti-Missourians met and lay the groundwork for secession (among other things) and demanded the removal of those who had signed "An Accounting" from office. Included were two district presidents (Minnesota and Iowa).

(13)   At the Iowa District Convention at Austin, Minnesota, in 1886, the anti-Missourians voted to establish their own seminary. Arrangements were made to use St. Olaf School at Northfield, Minnesota. Schmidt and Bøckman were to be the professors. In 1890 this seminary was assimilated by the United Church seminary, The Lutheran Seminary.

(14)   The 1887 Convention of the Norwegian Synod labeled anti-Missourians as schismatic, denouncing also their seminary. Anti-Missourians met and decided to withdraw, calling themselves the "Anti-Missourian Brotherhood." And so, a mass exodus from the Synod took place, which left it with two-thirds

of its former membership.

(15) Irreparable damage was done to the Synod, to congregations, and to individual friendships, to mission work, as well as to education.

(16) The Anti-Missourian Brotherhood quickly promoted interest in a merger of all Norwegian American Lutherans who were anti-Missourian in outlook, but also had other mutual interests.

LESSONS FOR THE CHURCH FROM
THE ELECTON CONTROVERSY

There are, no doubt, many lessons to be learned from the election controversy. It would seem to this writer that one of the most important ones has to do with the proper approach to controversy itself. There are peaceful means by which serious attempts can be made to settle differences among brethren. Unless pride and a taste for fame are involved, every attempt toward a peaceful and quiet settlement of the issues on the basis of God's Word and the Lutheran Confessions will be made. Before public attack (along with its attendant damaging, often confusing publicity) is launched, serious consultation should be held with the persons involved. The desire to preserve sound, scriptural doctrine must never degenerate into a fleshly lust for a "fight." Persons who raise controversy, and those who finally participate in it, must keep in mind that they bear a heavy responsibility not only to the Word of God but to the entire church. Souls are bound to be affected, often adversely. The collateral damage done to the membership of the church can be enormous.

The rest of the history of the Norwegian Synod will be told in the chapter, THE NORWEGIAN LUTHERAN CHURCH OF AMERICA, which deals with the union efforts which finally resulted in the merger of 1917.

Footnotes for Chapter Sixteen

1 E. Clifford Nelson-Eugene L. Fevold, *The Lutheran Church Among Norwegian-Americans*, Vol. 1, (Augsburg Publishing House, Minneapolis, MN, 55415, 1960), p. 155.

2 Nelson-Fevold, *The Lutheran Church Among Norwegian-Americans*, Vol. 1, p. 182.

3 Nelson-Fevold, *The Lutheran Church Among Norwegian-Americans*, Vol. 1, p. 291.

4 Nelson-Fevold, *The Lutheran Church Among Norwegian-Americans*, Vol. 1, p. 310.

5 Nelson-Fevold, *The Lutheran Church Among Norwegian-Americans*, Vol. 1, p. 312.

6 Nelson-Fevold, *The Lutheran Church Among Norwegian-Americans*, Vol. 1, p. 316.

7 Richard C. Wolf, *Documents of Lutheran Unity in America*, (Fortress Press, Philadelphia, PA, 1975), pp. 188, 189; Doc. #87.

8 Wolf, *Documents of Lutheran Unity in America*, p. 196; Doc. #88.

9 Nelson-Fevold, *The Lutheran Church Among Norwegian-Americans*, Vol. 1, p. 242.

10 Theodore A. Aaberg, *A City Set On A Hill*, (Published by Board of Publications, Ev. Lutheran Synod, Mankato, MN, 1968), p. 10.

11 Aaberg, *A City Set On A Hill*, p. 20.

12 Aaberg, *A City Set On A Hill*, pp. 12-17.

13 Wolf, *Documents of Lutheran Unity in America*, p. 203; Doc. #90.

14 Aaberg, *A City Set On A Hill*, p. 22.

15 Wolf, *Documents of Lutheran Unity in America*, pp. 201, 202; Doc. #89.

16 Wolf, *Documents of Lutheran Unity in America*, p. 199.

17 Aaberg, *A City Set On A Hill*, pp. 24, 25.

18 Aaberg, *A City Set On A Hill*, p. 36.

19 Aaberg, *A City Set On A Hill*, p. 36.

CHAPTER SEVENTEEN

THE NORWEGIANS
THE UNITED LUTHERAN
CHURCH
1880-1917

THE NORWEGIAN CHURCH:
A DIVIDED CHURCH

In the old country the State Church had been a strong factor in uniting the sons and daughters of Norway in one church body, although even under this system there was some unrest and dissatisfaction, resulting in various religious movements. There was the Haugean lay-movement which, however, was not apart from the State Church but was carried on within it. There arose theological leaders who held to a certain pattern of thinking and these had their followers. Grundtvig was a case in point. Nevertheless, the State Church, with its part in the old caste system, continued to dominate the scene.

However, when the Lutheran Church came to America in the steady flow of immigrants, the stream divided itself into several tributaries. The Haugean movement became dominated by the spirit and personality of a stormy lay preacher named Eielsen. This group, which resented the high church character of the Church of Norway, showed a very independent attitude, emphasizing congregational freedom, while suspicious of synodical organizations. It manifested the least desire for uniting the Norwegian Lutherans.

The Norwegian Synod (or, simply, the Synod) insisted on purity of doctrine and complete agreement as a prerequisite for union. And, of course, this attitude was highly influenced by the Missouri Synod, a German group. The election controversy was destined to cause a tremendous upheaval in its midst. In 1876 a division ocurred among the followers of Eielsen, resulting in the reforming of the Hauge's Synod. Eielsen, along with a small group of followers, went his own way and perpetuated the old Eielsen synod. There had also been a split up of the Norwegians in the Norwegian-Danish Augustana Synod, resulting in the formation of the Norwegian Lutheran Conference (or, simply the Conference).

ATTEMPTS TO PROMOTE UNION

All things considered, there was still an amount of interest in uniting the Norwegian churches. Not all shared the Norwegian Synod's rigid attitude toward doctrine, and some accused it of separatism and dogmatism – among other things. Mention has been made in a previous chapter about the call that went out in 1870 from the ranks of the Norwegian Synod to explore union possibilities. The first meeting had been attended only by men of the Synod. However, in 1871 a general conference was held between the Synod and the Norwegian Lutheran Conference. Though this was a friendly conference, the one following it the next year uncovered open hostilities. Between 1877 and 1878 meetings were held between the Synod and the Conference, with the Hauge's Synod also represented.

A free conference was held at St. Ansgar, Iowa, in 1881. Delegates attended from the Synod, the Conference, and the Hauge's Synod, as well as from the Norwegian Augustana Synod and the Swedish Augustana Synod. A friendly spirit prevailed, since the doctrines on which there was already agreement, were discussed.

One of the free conferences was held in the fall of 1882. The discussion centered in faith as the means of appropriating the fruits of Christ's redemption. Again, the discussions were quite amicable. This conference resolved that an official general committee of twenty-eight members confer on the obstacles to unity and make recommendations with closer union in mind. The last free conference was held in the summer of 1883 in Goodhue County, Minnesota, with study centered in the doctrine of Absolution. The Conference* subscribed to a set of theses on Absolution which raised almost no opposition. However, there was not a unanimous spirit even in the Norwegian Synod regarding certain aspects of this doctrine.

The free conferences gave way to "joint meetings" held under official sanction of the groups involved. These conferences were set up by a joint committee. The first joint meeting of these Norwegian Lutheran groups was held in Chicago early in 1885.

The conference was marked by little doctrinal progress on the doctrines of Redemption and Forgiveness, but rather forged a statement declaring what was necessary for the Norwegian Lutherans to be united in one synod and to acknowledge each other as Lutherans. The statement consisted of three points: (1) acceptance of the canonical books of Holy Scripture as God's revealed word, and therefore the only source and rule of faith, doctrine, and life; (2) acceptance without reservation, and the firm maintenance of the confessional writings of the Norwegian Lutheran Church (the three ancient creeds, the *Unaltered Augsburg Confession*, and *Luther's Small Catechism*); (3) the church bodies must not by any official act deny their acceptance of said Scripture and Confession.

A second joint meeting was held in Goodhue county, Minnesota, in spring of 1886. Practical problems were discussed (e.g. mission work). A doctrinal statement on Absolution was drawn up, and the Minnesota District of the Synod was requested to withdraw its "judgment" pronounced in 1880 on the Conference. (The judgment amounted to accusing the Conference of having a totally different faith from that found in Scripture and the Lutheran Confessions). The Minnesota District complied to the extent that only the New School in the Conference remained under the judgment.

A PUSH FOR UNION EXERTED BY THE ANTI-MISSOURIAN BROTHERHOOD

The third meeting was held at Willmar, Minnesota, in the fall of 1887. By the time of this meeting the Norwegian Synod had split in its ranks over the election controversy. The men of the Anti-Missourian Brotherhood, once a part of the Synod, were treated as having no synodical affiliation. This group, instead of establishing a new synod, pushed for union of the Norwegian churches.

At the Willmar meeting the doctrine of Justification was the subject of deliberation. A division in the ranks of the Synod over this doctrine became evident, for a few of its pastors still held to the once popular phrase "justification of the world." (At the joint conference in 1881 at St. Ansgar, Iowa, the Synod men had stated their willingness to give up the expression "justification of the world," since, as they said, it was so easily misunderstood.[1] Aligned against those who held out for the expression "justification of the world," were the delegates from the Anti-Missourian Brotherhood, the Conference, and the Augustana Synod. Prof. F. A. Schmidt, the leading protagonist in the election controversy, once believed in "world justification." Later, he changed his thinking and squarely opposed this expression. In the election controversy, he proposed that God elected men unto salvation in view of their faith (*intuitu fidei*). Consistency demanded that Schmidt and his followers hold also to the doctrine that God justifies only those who come to faith – Subjective Justification. God elected those he saw would believe in Christ and so, naturally, God justifies only those in whom he finally sees faith. That Schmidt had gained much support for his views became evident already when the majority of the synod stated their willingness to drop the phrase "justification of the world." In the election controversy it was indeed a case where the anti-Missourians pitted *Pontoppidan's Catechism against the Formula of Concord.*

253

IMPORTANT MEN IN THE UNION MOVEMENT

These names, especially, should be listed: Pastor Gjermund Hoyme (President of the Conference); Pastor J. N. Kildahl (an anti-Missourian); Prof. Georg Sverdrup (Norwegian-Danish Augustana); Pastor B.J. Muus (Norwegian Synod, President of the Minnesota District and founder of St. Olaf School); Pastor P.A. Rasmussen (Norwegian Synod); Prof. F. A. Schmidt (an anti-Missourian).

THE ANTI-MISSOURIANS CHOOSE UNION RATHER THAN FULL ORGANIZATION

The joint meeting at Willmar adopted the resolutions which stated that no church-dividing disunity existed concerning the doctrines of Justification and the Atonement. Actually, an agreement had been reached by the language of compromise. In effect, it was adopted that : (1) Justification or the forgiveness of sins has been acquired and made available to all – Objective Justification (the Synod), and that the individual is not justified before he believes – Subjective Justification (the Conference). Several of the Synod men did not vote for these statements since they felt they were incomplete.

In spite of some accord reached at Willmar, and in spite of the decision to meet again, there was a notable deterioration in the relationship of the Synod to the union venture. Already that summer the anti-Missourian force had left en masse from the Synod. The doctrinal unity men, sympathizers with the Missouri doctrine and the Missouri way, showed that they were not reconciled to the anti-Missourians. On the other hand, the anti-Missourians drew closer to the other synods. The Norwegian Synod dropped out of the joint meetings for the time being.

THE ANTI-MISSOURIANS CHOOSE UNION RATHER THAN FULL ORGANIZATION

The homeless anti-Missourians, faced with the question whether or not to start their own separate body ,but aware also that much agreement had been shown between their group and the others, eventually decided at Minneapolis in 1888 to strive for church union, asking the Conference, Hauge's Synod, and the Norwegian Augustana Synod to participate in another joint meeting. Also, willingness was shown to confer with the Norwegian Synod, should that body be willing. However, the feeling was that while merger ought to be sought with those Norwegian groups with whom they had much in common, they should not seek merger with the Synod with whom, at the time, union seemed beyond realization.

Instead of organizing itself into a synod, the "Brotherhood" appointed an interim administration committee to hold things together in prospect of future merger. An important step taken by the "Brotherhood" was though repudiation of the judgment passed against the Conference in 1880 by the Minnesota District of the Synod and a request to be forgiven their share of the responsibility for the judgment.

Members of the "Brotherhood" attended meetings of the other synods to promote interest in the merger. Favorable response was received from the Norwegian Augustana Synod. The Conference at first showed a coolness toward the proposal to merge, but after sharp debate, with the Old School men actually urging union, the tide was turned and resolutions were passed favoring the merger proposals.

The Hauge's Synod agreed to send representatives to the joint meeting proposed by the Anti-Missourian Brotherhood, after being assured that the "Brotherhood" did not espouse Missouri's doctrinal position in certain matters such as Sunday lay-activity, and "justification of the world" which the Synod held to.

When the score was tallied, it was evident that Eielsen's Synod was totally disinterested, Hauge's synod was not very enthusiastic, and the Synod, which had just suffered a schism by the very group now promoting merger, was not going to be involved this time around. If merger of any of the Norwegian Lutheran bodies came about, it had to involve the Anti-Missourian Brotherhood, the Conference and the Norwegian Augustana Synod – Lutheran bodies which for quite some time had shown that they were close to one another in their thinking.

THE MERGER PLAN

The Joint Committee on Church Union met at Eau Claire, Wisconsin, August 15 to 23, 1888. Three subcommittees were elected to handle the matters of framing a constitution and a doctrinal settlement, and of drawing up articles of union. Out of the Joint Committee came a complete plan for carrying out the merger.

The doctrinal settlement or *Opgjør* reflected the non-dogmatism of the participants, as compared to the dogmatism of the "Missourian" Norwegian Synod:

. . . WE REGARD OUR HARMONIOUS SUBSCRIPTION TO THE HOLY SCRIPTURES, THE CONFESSIONS OF THE NORWEGIAN LUTHERAN CHURCH AND THE CATECHISM NOW IN USE IN OUR SYNODS AND CONGREGATIONS AS COMPLETELY SUFFICIENT BASIS FOR CHURCH UNION, SINCE THERE IS EVIDENCE OF NO OFFICIAL ACT ON THE PART OF ANY OF THE SYNODS IN DENIAL OF THE SCRIPTURE AND THE CONFESSIONS.

Note the absence of presentation and discussion of theological theses as the basis for arriving at church union. So ostensibly "non-Missourian"!

In settling the doctrinal issues, the following points should be mentioned: the doctrine of the "redemption of the world by Christ," was rejected as being another way of saying "justification of the world." It was agreed that JUSTIFICATION be used only to designate God's judicial act when the individual sinner comes to faith. On the one hand, while it was stated that the content of the

255

gospel is not dependent upon man's relation to it, no person is saved without conversion and faith. In regards to the doctrine of Absolution, the objective aspect of absolution (e.g. the pastor's announcement of it to the assembled congregation) is always an *offer* of forgiveness, while the subjective aspect of the absolution (e.g. announcing forgiveness to the individual) is the actual *imparting* of forgiveness to that person who believes, and further, that there is an imparting of forgiveness by God only when there is faith. On the practical side, it was agreed that the churches would use their individual liturgical practices in administering absolution. In regards to the Sunday observance question, Luther's explanation of the Sabbath Commandment was considered an adequate settlement of this matter. Finally, the doctrine of Election, which had brought such a storm of controversy, was settled by the joint acceptance of Pontoppidan's answer to Question 548 in his explanation of the Catechism (which the Norwegian Synod said was an insufficient statement of doctrine).

The Joint Committee gave its blessing to Christian lay activity. The formulated Constitution proposed the name the Norwegian Lutheran Free Church in America and protected the rights and freedom of individual congregations. It made no provision for a Church Council to handle affairs between the synodical meetings. All synodical institutions were to be turned over, debt-free, to the new body.

From November 15 to 21, 1888, the congregational delegates of the proposed merger bodies met at Scandinavia, Wisconsin. Other voting members beside congregational delegates (one to each congregation) were: pastors, theological professors, members of the Joint Committee. The proposed Constitution was accepted and the name, the United Norwegian Lutheran Church in America, was adopted. To protect the congregations from becoming synodically controlled, and to promote a "free church," the Constitution was even changed to allow two delegates from each congregation. And, to satisfy the Haugeans, the church's objectives listed the promotion of Christian lay activity.

THE HAUGE'S SYNOD STANDS AGAINST UNION

A landmark in Norwegian Lutheran co-operation was reached at the end of the conference when Holy Communion was celebrated with inter- synodical participation by the pastors. There was no doubt that the foundation of a united Norwegian Church had been laid. Only the Hauge's Synod seemed to be dissatisfied with affairs, finally opposing union. All along, the Haugeans had expressed suspicion that sufficient unity of faith and practice did not in fact exist to warrant a merger of synods. There was also the question of whether genuine "living Christianity" or piety was present in the other bodies. Also, there was doubt on the part of the Haugeans that lay activity would not be suppressed in the merger body. Bear in mind also that the Haugeans had a dislike for liturgical worship and clergy vestments. Also questioned were the qualifications of the Augsburg Seminary as a proper training school for its workers.

At its annual summer convention in 1880, held in Chicago, Hauge's Synod took itself out of the merger movement in order to have more opportunity to consider these matters. The synod did not enter the movement again for another fifteen years, when "it took the initiative in the new union movement which culminated in the 1917 merger."[2]

SYNODICAL RATIFICATION OF THE CONSTITUTION

The Anti-Missourian Brotherhood approved the constitution for the merger body, appending its own interpretation of the synod's authority: ". . . that the synod in relation to the individual congregation is advisory, not legislative." Once again the alarm had been sounded regarding synodical dominance over congregations, an aversion to which was deeply ingrained in Norwegian Lutherans.

The Norwegian Augustana Synod in 1890 at its convention ran into no opposition to merger. The Conference for the Norwegian-Danish Evangelical Lutheran Church gave enthusiastic support and approval to the full union report. All that was lacking was the actual consummation of the merger.

THE MERGER FORMING THE UNITED NORWEGIAN LUTHERAN CHURCH

The three church bodies had all agreed to hold their final conventions on June 11, 1890, in Minneapolis. There were 788 congregations among the three conferring bodies, all of which unanimously favoured merger. By the time of the 1890 meetings, 688 congregations had accepted the Constitution and the Articles of Merger. The three church bodies each adopted the Constitution of the United Church and concluded their individual existences. Each body also elected professors for the joint seminary.

On June 13th, in the morning, all three delegations met at Trinity church, a congregation of the Conference. Altogether, more than 2,000 people packed themselves into this church. After singing and praying, the delegation adjourned to Augustana Church, "the mother church of the Swedish Augustana Synod in Minneapolis."[3] The Constitution, earlier adopted by each body, was in turn ratified by all present, and officers were elected. The results: President - Pastor G. Hoymes (the Conference): Vice-President - Pastor L. M. Biørn (Anti-Missourian Brotherhood); Secretary - Pastor J. N. Kildahl (Anti-Missourian Brotherhood); Treasurer - Mr. Lars Swenson (the Conference).

NUMERICAL STRENGTH

While 688 congregations had accepted the Constitution at the time of the merger, of these, 379 had been members of the Conference, 268 had been members of the Anti-Missourian Brotherhood, and 41 had been members of the Norwegian Augustana Synod. In addition, 31 independent congregations were

257

received, making a total of 719 congregations in the United Church. There were 260 pastors listed. However, the rolls were not complete for various reasons, with the result that the number was short of the actual total. There were possibly as many as 830 congregations, with approximately 83,500 confirmed members and 152,200 baptized souls.[4] By comparison, the Hauge's Synod numbered 65 pastors, 185 congregations, 12,741 confirmed members, and 22,279 baptized members. the Norwegian Synod numbered 187 pastors, 516 congregations, 51,534 confirmed members, and 94,166 baptized souls. In the merger forming the United Norwegian Lutheran Church, the Anti-Missourian Brotherhood contributed 55 pastors and 49,944 baptized souls; the Norwegian Augustana Synod contributed 32 pastors and 8,000 to 9,000 (?) souls; the Conference contributed 115 pastors and 70,632 baptized souls. These numbers, though not to be considered totally accurate, nevertheless afford us basis for comparisons.

ORGANIZATION

The new merger body was divided into nineteen geographical areas, with a pastor appointed as visitor over each non-administrative district. Two union committees, one to negotiate with the Norwegian Synod, and the other with the Haugeans, were elected. Some leaders honestly thought that speedy union would be accomplished now between the United Church and these two bodies. However, this was not to be achieved for another twenty-seven years!

CHURCH PAPER

The Luthersk Kirkeblad, a weekly paper, became the official organ of the United Church.

MISSIONS

An intensive home mission program was begun. A mission committee was provided to handle a sum of $10,000 for the first year's mission program.

CHARITABLE INSTITUTIONS

After the Norwegian Augustana Synod joined the United Church in 1890, its Beloit Seminary was turned into the Beloit Children's Home. After the founding of the United Church, interest in homes both for the aged and children increased and by 1914 it was reported that there were twelve Norwegian Lutheran Children's homes and seven Homes for the Aged. Norwegian deaconess homes and hospitals also came to be established along with numerous Lutheran hospitals. These latter institutions were usually private corporations. The United Church, after the turn of the century, carried on work among the handicapped: deaf, dumb, and blind persons. The Church also brought the Word to prisoners, and in some large cities extensive "inner mission" work was carried on.

COLLEGES

At its constituting convention, the United Church made St. Olaf College of Northfield, Minnesota, its college. No synodical body had claimed this school, but after the anti-Missourian forces split from the Norwegian Synod, they threw their support to it, generally claiming it as their school.

LOOKING AHEAD

The era of greatest strife and dissension among Norwegian Lutherans in America was over. Not until 1917, however, would almost all remaining Norwegian Lutherans be brought into the union of churches, and then only after a period of rehashing the old election strife, with all sides making concessions in the "Madison Agreement" or *Opgjør*. Even then, an element in the Synod would remain aloof from union, choosing instead to walk apart from their fellow Norwegians, while seeking a continuation of fellowship with the German Lutheran element so disdained by the anti-Missourians and by the "New School" men in the Conference. They chose as their close friends and associates the doctrinally orthodox Missouri and Wisconsin Synods. Thus the Evangelical Lutheran Synod (ELS) – see the separate chapter – would remain to the present day the embodiment of the old spirit of the Norwegian Synod. The Hauge's Synod remained plagued with the question of lay activity, while the Norwegian Synod was yet troubled by the United Church's settlement of the election controversy.

THE AUGSBURG CONTROVERSY IN THE UNITED NORWEGIAN LUTHERAN CHURCH

For seven years after the union of 1890, bitter controversy raged over the control of Augsburg Seminary in Minneapolis. In spite of the union of the three bodies, one should not conclude that there was a complete meeting of minds. Differences had been played down, but differences were there nonetheless. So were old distrusts and suspicions, as well as memories of old antagonisms.

IT WAS CLEAR, THEREFORE, THAT THE DYING EMBERS OF OLD FIRES COULD BE FANNED INTO FLAMES. ALL THAT THE SITUATION REQUIRED WAS AN INCIDENT. THIS INCIDENT WAS PROVIDED IN THE DECISION OF THE FIRST ASSEMBLY OF THE UNITED CHURCH IN 1890 TO MAKE ST. OLAF COLLEGE OF NORTHFIELD, MINNESOTA, AN INSTITUTION OF THE UNITED CHURCH.[5]

Recall that the anti-Missourians had established a seminary on the St. Olaf campus and had urged that the United Church accept the transfer of ownership offered by the St. Olaf College Corporation. This acceptance of the college

259

was approved by a large majority of the United Church. It was at this point that personalities came to the fore and set the stage for bitter controversy. Prof. Sverdrup looked to this action of the delegates as a blow to Augsburg Seminary, which was his pet project fostering his thinking concerning ministerial education. Sverdrup's bias was that all phases of education leading up to the ministerial training were to be under the control of one faculty.

Those who supported St. Olaf as a college in the United Church considered that a divinity school was a theological seminary, giving a three-year course of special theological training. The "Friends of Augsburg," however, considered a divinity school as comprising a nine-year course embracing not only direct theological study but the preparatory and college training as well. This was Sverdrup's pet which he worked so hard to achieve and he was not, together with the New School men, about to give it up. According to the thinking of Sverdrup and his followers, church schools were for training ministers, and the whole course from preparatory to seminary must fill this bill. The church should not feel any major responsibility for training people for non-theological professions – a far cry from the attitude expressed by the majority of Lutheran bodies in this country.

However, St. Olaf College was envisioned by its founders and supporters to be an institution where non-theological Norwegian students could also study, receiving a general Christian education which would help them take their places as Lutheran Christians in their communities. The college would be co-educational. Sverdrup did not want the college with its broad and liberal curriculum independent of the seminary. He looked upon the whole situation as dangerous, for the future pastors would receive humanistic training.

And so, Sverdrup and his colleague, Oftedal, together with the "Friends of Augsburg," set out to fight the transfer of Augsburg Seminary to the control of the United Church, which would in turn transfer the preparatory and college departments away from Minneapolis to Northfield (St. Olaf College).

In the course of time, incidents arose which added fuel to the fire of debate and the issue became more and more hotly contested. Personalities played an important part n this bitter, non-theological controversy, even as they had back in the days of doctrinal strife. There were charges and counter-charges. The defenders of the Augsburg School found it hard to be objective, for every word said in favour of the St. Olaf College was interpreted as a personal attack on Sverdrup and the "Friends of Augsburg," and an attack on their educational methods as well.

Meanwhile, the money contributed by members of the congregations toward the "professors' fund" was held in trust by the board of trustees of the incorporated Augsburg Seminary, since the United Church had not been able to become incorporated at its first meeting.

A threatening cloud of disunity hovered over the first annual convention of the United Church. In fact, President Hoyme's remarks spoke of the possibility of a disunited church, and he chided those who had been at odds for airing the issues in the public press, while the convention was the proper place to settle the issues. At this convention the United Church incorporated itself under the laws of the State of Minnesota. That accomplished, it was then prepared to receive the transfer of St. Olaf College and Augsburg Seminary.

Because of the explosive climate at the convention regarding the school issue, the delegates voted to keep the preparatory department temporarily at Augsburg. They did not mean to say that Augsburg should not be divided in the future, nor did they give tacit approval to the system of education stemming from Augsburg. Only the theological department at Augsburg was designated as the divinity school. While this procedure amounted to a delaying action, it also did not promote Sverdrup's educational system.

At the close of its first convention, the United Church still did not have under its control either the Augsburg Seminary, the St. Olaf College, or the fund of the Anti-Missourians, which had been held in trust by the trustees of Augsburg.

FORMATION OF THE "FRIENDS OF AUGSBURG"

Things did not get better over the next two years, even though a college committee had been appointed to look into the problem of educational institutions in the Church. In the 1893 Convention an impasse was acknowledged between the factions, with two results: (1) the United Church established a new seminary, thus circumventing Augsburg and its educational system, and (2) Professors Sverdrup and Oftedal formed their group known as the "Friends of Augsburg" and brought about a schism in the young merger synod. Both men resigned from the United Church, but not from their professorships at Augsburg.

It is of interest to note that Prof. Oftedal and another person forcibly occupied the Augsburg Publishing House for two days after the 1893 Convention. This matter of the seizure of the publishing house was taken to court and the following year judgment was made in favour of the United Church.

By the time of the 1894 Convention, the two sides were moving further apart instead of drawing together. The Friends of Augsburg tried their hand at fundraising to ensure the continued operation of the seminary. But their drive for funds also did much to advertise the breach that had occurred within the Church. The 1895 convention of the United Church refused to seat Professors Sverdrup and Oftedal as delegates from Trinity Church in Minneapolis (located near the seminary). The convention also expelled twelve congregations which supported the Augsburg board of trustees. In retaliation, steps were taken to dissociate the seminary from the United Church.

In 1896 the United Church elected trustees for Augsburg, and these then proceeded to make a formal demand that the Augsburg property be transferred to the United Church. Again, the Friends of Augsburg retaliated by ordering the Augsburg trustees to use every lawful means to keep the seminary from falling into the hands of the enemy.

Next, the United Church tried the help of the civil courts. The final outcome, handled in District Court, was a decision favourable to the United Church. Undaunted by this decision, the old Augsburg trustees appealed to the Supreme Court, which then reversed the District Court's decision, giving exclusive control to the original five incorporators of 1872. Since Augsburg Seminary was a corporation outside the church body, the trustees appointed by the United Church had no legal title to offices in the corporation's board of trustees.

THE ESTABLISHMENT OF
THE LUTHERAN FREE CHURCH

In the meantime, the Friends of Augsburg had organized themselves as the Lutheran Free Church. Both bodies while in convention heard the decision of the Supreme Court and also the added opinion that the matter of who should control Augsburg be decided in a court of equity. The United Church then named a committee to carry on the work of seeking justice.[6]

In 1898 a way of settling the controversy was found which gave the United Church the library as well as the professor's fund which had been collected to January 1876. The United Church, in return, surrendered all claims on the property so that the campus and buildings remained with the Friends of Augsburg.

The Lutheran Free Church came into being in 1896 with the drafting of a set of principles and rules for carrying on church work.[7] Never did this body adopt a constitution. Twelve principles and fifteen rules for church work which formed the basis of government in the body actually gives the local congregation the right of autonomy, with no higher body over it. While there was a conference or association of free congregations, such a meeting of congregations had no power other than to make requests or recommendations to the congregations. The work of the Free Church was carried on by boards which were elected at the annual meeting of the conference. Legal procedure was not performed by the Free Church as a corporate body, which it was not, but through its Board of Organization.

(For a thorough discussion of this portion of Norwegian Lutheran history, see the separate chapter giving the history of the Lutheran Free Church).

SUMMARY: UNION AS WELL AS DISUNION

While the last decade of the nineteenth century saw some solidifying of Norwegian Lutherans, it also once again witnessed the splintering that can occur in the church over non-theological matters, especially when men are willing to be led by overpowering personalities such as Sverdrup and Oftedal demonstrated. The two professor were quite capable of swaying men's emotions and allegiances with forceful, and at times, vehement rhetoric. In such times men's minds can become supersensitive to a common cause. Nothing else seems important compared to it. The cause becomes their rallying point, while their minds remain closed to other ideas and suggestion, and therefore are incapable of viewing alternatives. Personalities or groups who do not share the same conviction become "the enemy." Schism nearly always is the result.

The United Church, bereft of Augsburg Seminary, turned its attention to an

262

abandoned project, the asimiliation of St. Olaf as an official institution.

There can be no doubt that Norwegian Lutheranism in America in the closing decades of the nineteenth century was a battle ground and the scene of periods of bitter strife. The United Church kept up its interest in uniting Norwegian Lutherans, a goal that had to wait until 1917 to be achieved. At that time larger union was accomplished than perhaps many dared to hope for, although even this union could be brought about only by splintering the church.

Footnotes for Chapter Seventeen

*That is, the Norwegian Lutheran Church body by this title.

1 E. Clifford Nelson-Eugene L. Fevold. *The Lutheran Church Among Norwegian-Americans*, Vol. 1, (Augsburg Publishing House, Minneapolis, MN, 1960), p. 316.

2 Nelson-Fevold, *The Lutheran Church Among Norwegian-Americans*, Vol. 2, pp. 19, 20.

3 Nelson-Fevold, *The Lutheran Church Among Norwegian-Americans*, Vol. 2, p. 25.

4 Nelson-Fevold, *The Lutheran Church Among Norwegian-Americans*, Vol. 2, p. 35.

5 Nelson-Fevold, *The Lutheran Church Among Norwegian-Americans*, Vol. 2, p. 39.

6 Nelson-Fevold, *The Lutheran Church Among Norwegian-Americans*, Vol. 2, p. 79.

7 Nelson-Fevold, *The Lutheran Church Among Norwegian-Americans*, Vol. 2, p. 79.

CHAPTER EIGHTEEN

THE NORWEGIANS
THE LUTHERAN FREE CHURCH
1897-1963

THE HAUGEAN SPIRIT: SUPPORTERS OF THE
CHURCH REFORM MOVEMENT IN NORWAY

The Norwegians who formed the Lutheran Free Church (LFC) took particular pride in identifying themselves with Hans Nielsen Hauge and the lay-led revival in Norway which bears his name.

In the 1840's in Norway, the relation between Church and State came under discussion (refer to the chapter, LAND OF THE NORSEMEN). The movement which called for reform did not lead to unified action and only minor victories were won for its side. However, one of the eventual victories was that of granting to layman the right to speak in churches (1888) and the opening of church buildings to mission meetings (1889). The founders of the Lutheran Free Church were supporters of the Church Reform Movement in Norway, which had as its aim greater freedom for the church from state control, and freedom for the individual Christian –"a free church in a free state." These were things which Hauge did not live to experience.

ROOTS OF THE LUTHERAN FREE
CHURCH WERE IN THE NORWEGIAN-DANISH
EVANGELICAL LUTHERAN CONFERENCE
(1870 - 1890)

Some of the early Norwegians, Swedes, and Danes who migrated to America joined the Synod of Northern Illinois. Later, in 1860, they left this synod and formed their own Scandinavian Augustana Synod at Jefferson Prairie, Wisconsin. Here the Swedes outnumbered the Norwegians three to one. The Norwegians were Haugeans; the Swedes were pietists. Professor Weenaas of Augustana Seminary encouraged separating the two Scandinavian forces for language and nationalistic reasons. The first step the Norwegians took was to establish their own seminary at Marshall, Wisconsin, in 1869, calling it Augsburg Seminary (as a testimony to the *Augsburg Confession)*. The next step for them was to establish their own synod. At the June 1870 Convention of the Scandinavian Augustana Synod in Andover, Illinois, an amicable separation was reached. But practical differences among the Norwegians resulted in the formation of two bodies rather than one. Some – the newly arrived pastors – favored using the Dano-Norwegian liturgy, together with the customary rites and vestments, whereas older men, who had started out as lay preachers and had been ordained later, had reservations concerning traditional liturgies, rites, and vestments. They believed in Americanizing church form and customs. In separating themselves from the Swedes, the Norwegians called themselves the Norwegian-Danish Augustana Synod – at first, a loosely organized group. A division among these Norwegians came about when late in summer, 1870, a group met with Pastor Claus L. Clausen at St. Ansgar, Iowa, in order to woo him from the Norwegian Synod. This meeting turned out to be the constitution convention of the Norwegian-Danish Conference (or, simply the Conference), which then proceeded to dissolve the Norwegian-Danish Augustana Synod. However, a group of pastors and congregations took exception to the handling of affairs at St. Ansgar and, while meeting together, voted to continue the Norwegian-Danish Augustana Synod.

Thus, in 1870 two Norwegian Lutheran bodies were organized after the friendly separation from the Swedes: the Norwegian-Danish Augustana Synod (lay-oriented, Haugean, Americanizing) and the Norwegian-Danish Conference (traditional, more churchly, with Claus Clausen an important leader at the beginning). Let it be remembered that both groups were influenced by Haugeanism, but the Augustanans clung to the earlier type and were influenced by the environment in America, which was free of State Churchism. The Conference was influenced in its views by Gisle Johnson's modified approach to Haugeanism (Refer to the chapter: THE EARLY SMALL NORWEGIAN GROUPS).

After a year the congregations were included in the membership of the Conference, but decisions reached by the Conference were not binding on a congregation unless the congregation approved them. The Conference stood against centralization of authority. Thus member congregations kept their freedom.

A balance was sought between doctrine and Christian life. The Conference liked neither the rigid orthodoxy – and the polemics which went with it – of the Missouri Synod, with which the Norwegian Synod was allied, nor the weaknesses of Eielsen's Synod, with its lack of churchliness, its opposition to Norwegian Church practices, and its fears of an educated clergy.[1]

ENTER, TWO VERY INFLUENTIAL MEN: SVERDRUP AND OFTEDAL

George Sverdrup and Sven Oftedal became professors at Augsburg and had a profound influence on the shaping of the Lutheran Free Church. Sverdrup was the outgoing, dynamic leadership type of man, while Oftedal was more reserved. The latter was a scholar and theologian, a serious-minded professor, a writer, and a teacher. Both were committed to the ideal of the free church, emphasizing lay-witnessing, personal Christianity, spiritual awakening, evangelism, a democratic ministry and a New Testament type of church life.[2] Both the Conference and the Lutheran Free Church were strongly influenced by Augsburg Seminary.

The polemics of the Conference were carried on chiefly with the Norwegian Synod, which emphasized God's grace and Objective Justification, while the Conference emphasized faith, and justification by faith. To be fair, it must be stated that the Norwegian Synod also emphasized justification by faith (commonly called "subjective justification"), but also emphasized that this faith accepts personally and individually what God through the resurrection of Christ has declared for the world (commonly called "objective justification"). Like the Conference, the Norwegian Synod taught that only those who have faith in Jesus Christ are saved. Sverdrup denied that God justified the world. He taught that "forgiveness of sins must not be separated from the experience of individual justification."[3] The Norwegian Synod taught that what is offered in the gospel is forgiveness of sins, which Christ won for every sinner, and which the repentant sinner is urged to personally accept by faith. Without faith the individual sinner does not take personal possession of God's forgiveness and is therefore lost and damned.

Three months after his arrival in America, Oftedal published a brief "Public Declaration" (signed also by Prof. Weenaas). It was an attack on the Norwegian Synod. The Synod's stress on scholastic orthodoxy, and also its strong synodical or authoritarian organization, were labelled as dangerous threats to the Christian life and congregational freedom. Oftedal didn't like the Norwegian Synod's exclusive character whereby it required agreement in doctrine and practice prior to declaration of fellowship. There was violent reaction against the "Declaration" even within the Conference. Later, before returning to Norway, Weenaas withdrew his signature from the document.

The guns of the Augsburg professors were kept trained on the Norwegian Synod. Many unkind, harsh and unsubstantiated charges were made by the Conference. Sometimes the barrage met with return fire from the Synod, which was openly critical and judgmental of the Conference.

RIFF IN THE CONFERENCE: THE "OLD SCHOOL" VERSUS THE "NEW SCHOOL"

The "Old School" did not like the new and alien spirit introduced by the "New School" men, who were led by the two professors. Oftedal's "Public Declaration" was opposed by a group of men who signed the "Declaration of the Thirty," which then protested a new and alien emphasis that had been introduced by the "Declaration." They wanted the Conference to repudiate the "Declaration." While the New School men justified divisions in the Norwegian Church and disliked the holding of free conferences and discussion of doctrine, the Old School men deplored divisions and advocated union movements and were thus willing to have doctrinal theses, discussions, and conferences.

THE MERGER MOVEMENT OF THE 1880's PRODUCES THE UNITED NORWEGIAN LUTHERAN CHURCH

Pastor P. A. Rasmussen of the Norwegian Synod sent out a strong plea in 1880 for unity. He proposed a meeting of representatives of the Synod and the Conference with theologians from Norway. Though his proposal was rejected, it nevertheless started people thinking. There followed three free conferences: 1881 (St. Ansgar, Iowa), 1882 (Roland, Iowa), and 1883 (Holden, Minnesota). Official conferences were held by the Norwegian Synod, the Conference, the Hauge's synod, and the Norwegian Augustana Synod: 1885 (Chicago), 1886 (Gol, Minnesota), and 1887 (Willmar, Minnesota). For a more extensive coverage of this history, refer to the chapter, THE UNITED NORWEGIAN LUTHERAN CHURCH.

The predestination or election controversy in the Norwegian Synod "served as a catalyst in hastening the merger process."[4] Though the anti-Missourians withdrew from the Synod (1886-1887), they did not form a new synod. Instead they pushed hard for union of the various Norwegian Lutheran bodies.

Prof. Sverdrup at first was skeptical of union with others but later became a leading force behind the union movement. He had deplored the Missourian spirit, characterized by learned doctrinal deliberations, as seen in the Norwegian Synod. He was happy to see the formation of an anti-Missouri party in that synod, brought about by the election controversy. Sverdrup felt that the Norwegians were one in faith and spirit by virtue of their common heritage, and should strive for one "Norwegian Lutheran Free Church in America." The main problem, as he saw it, lay with the Norwegian synod. He was disappointed over the Hauge's Synod's decision to withdraw from the merger negotiations (1889). Sverdrup sounded the theme of co-operation in church work as the means to soften the attitude of each toward the other.

The Union Committee met in Eau Claire, Wisconsin, August 15-28, 1888, having full representation from all groups except the Hauge's Synod (only two men attended). Pastor Hoyme was chosen chairman. Two of the three officials of the committee were anti-Missourian. Sverdrup was a member of the subcommittee on Articles of Union, and helped to work out the doctrinal settlement.

Basis for the merger was the acceptance of Scripture and the Confessions of the Church of Norway (the three Ecumenical Creeds, the *Augsburg Confession*, Luther's *Small Catechism*, and the Catechism in common use – Pontoppidan's. Union was not based on doctrinal theses or new doctrinal statements. Past doctrinal differences were considered resolved to the point they were no longer a hindrance. The church body was composed of congregations, each having one or two delegates. The synodical districts had no administrative authority and no synodical council as provided for. The constitution, which was similar to that of the Conference, safeguarded against centralized authority. It was decided that Augsburg Seminary would be the theological school, with endowment to be made to the school by each participating synod.

The annual meetings of the Conference, the Norwegian Augustana Synod, and the Anti-Missourian Brotherhood were held in Minneapolis early in June 1890. Each adopted the proposed constitution and thus merged themselves into one body, which then proceded to hold its first convention (June 13, 1890). The name chosen: the United Norwegian Lutheran Church in America.

EVENTS LEADING TO THE FOUNDING OF THE LUTHERAN FREE CHURCH

THE AUGSBURG CONTROVERSY
DEVELOPS ALMOST IMMEDIATE IN THE UNITED CHURCH

THE LUTHERAN FREE CHURCH WAS BORN OUT OF A CONTROVERSY WHICH ENVELOPED THE UNITED NORWEGIAN LUTHERAN CHURCH ALMOST IMMEDIATELY AFTER ITS FORMATION IN 1890. THE CONTROVERSY REVOLVED AROUND AUGSBURG SEMINARY IN MINNEAPOLIS. AT ISSUE WAS THE QUESTION OF OWNERSHIP OF THE SCHOOL, BUT ALSO INVOLVED WERE DIVERGENT THEORIES OF THEOLOGICAL EDUCATION RIVALRY BETWEEN AUGSBURG AND ST. OLAF COLLEGE IN NORTHFIELD, MINNESOTA. A MINORITY IN THE UNITED CHURCH – ESSENTIALLY THE NEW SCHOOL GROUP OF THE ANTECEDENT CONFERENCE – RALLIED AROUND AUGSBURG WHEN IT BECAME CLEAR THAT DEVELOPMENTS IN THE UNITED CHURCH WERE TO THEIR WISHES AND EXPECTATIONS.[5]

Differences of opinion were held on the subject of what constitutes a seminary. The New School men (in the antecedent Conference), under the leadership of Professors Sverdrup and Oftdal, regarded the Academy, the College, and the theological departments as an indissoluble unit to prepare men for the ministry. It was especially the ideal of Prof. Sverdrup that all phases of education leading up to the ministerial training were to be under the control of one faculty. To Sverdrup and the Friends of Augsburg, a divinity school consisted not only of a seminary but of an entire nine year course, comprising the preparatory school and college department as well. To them, the Church's responsibility was mainly for training ministers and not for training people for non-theological professions. On the other hand, St. Olaf College was envisioned by its founders and supporters as an institution for training non-theological students as well as those who wished to prepare for the ministry. And St. Olaf

College – operated by anti-Missourian men – had been designated as the college of the United Norwegian Lutheran Church! Immediately, then, this action was regarded by the New School of the Conference as a threat to Augsburg's unified education program - Sverdrup's pet project. This then became the crux of the matter. Augsburg was to have a unified program and St. Olaf was not to become a substitute for the college department. At least this was the contention of the New School men.

Oftedal suspected collusion against Augsburg by the anti-Missourian, Norwegian Augustana, and Old School Conference men. The United Church, as a whole, did not share Sverdrup's and the New School's ideal of integrated departments at Augsburg as essential for ministerial education in a free church. The United Church, it became apparent, did not feel obligated to continue all three departments at Augsburg.

What is the authority of the church body over against a dissenting minority within it? This became a perplexing question. Furthermore, sharp debate evolved as criticism arose that the preparatory department at Augsburg was educationally inferior. This criticism then drew the rebuttal from the "Friends" (of Augsburg) that St. Olaf was a secular and humanistic school.

After 1891 the question of ownership of Augsburg Seminary and the transfer of the school to the United Church became primary. It was discovered that the board of trustees of the Conference could not legally turn over Augsburg to the United Church, since the old Conference had never been incorporated. The ownership resided in the Augsburg Corporation, and this corporation was composed of the five original incorporators. Thus the Conference really had no legal right to turn over Augsburg to the United Church (not an intentional oversight). The five-man Augsburg board was unwilling to transfer Augsburg Seminary to the United Church unless an essentially unchanged structure and program would be assured. This proposal was rejected; yet action was taken to serve as a temporary solution.

In 1891, at its first annual convention, storm clouds of disunity hung low over the United Church. Delaying tactics were employed, and this included incorporating the body, in order to pave the way to receiving the transfer of St. Olaf College and Augsburg Seminary. Furthermore, the synod essentially agreed to what the Augsburg Board had desired, for it voted to keep the preparatory department, at least temporarily, at Augsburg. It thus accepted a unified program of theological education at Augsburg. However, this was not done to give the stamp of approval to Sverdrup's philosophy of education, nor did the United Church mean to convey the impression that Augsburg should not be divided in the future. Only the theological department at Augsburg was designated as the divinity school. But an attempt had been made to cool an explosive situation.

In August of 1892 the original incorporators provided for enlarging the Augsburg corporation to at least thirty members, each of whom was required to be a member of the United Church. The new members were sympathetic with Oftedal and the majority of the board. By summer of 1892 the Friends of Augsburg decided that a transfer of the Augsburg property to the United Church was desirable. A congregational referendum revealed that the people wanted only one college and that the preference was for Augsburg, but many voted for Augsburg College on the condition that the United Church obtain control and ownership. In 1893 the United Church severed its ties with St. Olaf College, an action which seemed to throw the weight to Augsburg.

However, a climate unfavorable to Sverdrup and his followers was created when both President Hoyme and the United Church pushed for quick settlement of the Augsburg matter. Hoyme wanted the matter resolved in 1893, and the majority of the delegates were insistent that the matter be solved without further delay. The United Church could not support a school it did not own or control. Therefore, it asked that Augsburg and the endowment fund and all other property be turned over by July 15. (The "professors' fund" was held in trust by the board of trustees of the seminary, since the United Church had not been able to become legally incorporated at its first meeting). Oftedal wanted to provide for negotiations, but his request met with disapproval.

Should the Augsburg Board not transfer title to the Augsburg Seminary by the time stipulated, the United Church was to relocate its theological seminary as soon as possible. The Minority felt that the authorizing of a new seminary was in violation of the Articles of Union. Both Oftedal and Sverdrup resigned as theological professors of the United Church, but not of Augsburg, and this action subsequently set the stage for the formation later on of the Lutheran Free Church.

The Augsburg Board deemed the stipulation of the United Church unreasonable and refused to comply by the deadline that had been set. Immediate preparation was made by the United Church to begin operating a temporary seminary on Franklin Avenue in Minneapolis. New facilities for the preparatory department also had to be obtained, since all instructors remained with Augsburg. When the United Church seminary began operating in the fall of 1893, Augsburg Seminary continued its existence, having Sverdrup and Oftedal as the theological professors.

The explosive situation continued. Following the 1893 Convention, Professor Oftedal forcefully occupied the Augsburg Publishing House in Minneapolis for two days, and this action of seizure brought the issue to court. In June 1894 the court gave control of Augsburg Publishing House to the United Church. In the fall of the same year the Friends of Augsburg – the Minority – formed a permanent organization.

In 1896 a board of trustees for Augsburg Seminary was elected by the United Church, with instructions to obtain control of Augsburg Seminary and to take legal actions if necessary. The Augsburg Corporation's board refused to tender the school to the newly elected board of trustees, and litigation was then begun. The attorney general, however, did not agree with the United Church's claim to the school, and instead gave the opinion that it had no right to elect trustees to it. However, the District Court ruled in the United Church's favor. The old board then made an appeal to the Supreme Court of Minnesota, which in June 1898 reversed the decision of the District Court, designating the old board (Oftedal and company) as the legal board of trustees of the seminary. Final settlement of the Augsburg case was accomplished out of court, giving each of the parties half of the property. The United Church received the endowment fund, which had a paper value of $50,000 (not all the money had been collected), and a portion of the Augsburg Seminary library. The Augsburg

Seminary Corporation retained all other property, including the campus and buildings.

THE FRIENDS OF AUGSBURG

In the years 1893 to '97 the Friends of Augsburg amounted to the Lutheran Free Church in embryonic form. It was on June 14, 1893, when Sverdrup and Oftedal resigned from their professorships in the United Church and that an informal meeting was held at Augsburg Seminary resulting in the formation of the Friends of Augsburg. This group was made up of pastors and laymen who were attending the annual meeting of the United Church. They were worried about the continued existence of the school, and were opposed to the transfer either of the school or of the endowment fund to the United Church, unless certain guarantees were made. Furthermore, they pledged to keep the school open in the event the United Church withdrew its support of Augsburg. They also insisted on free negotiations between the United Church and the Augsburg Board, and asked that the Minority congregations remain in the United Church.

A bold step was taken in November 1893 by the Friends of Augsburg in the electing of an Ordination Committee. The Committee ordained candidates turned down by the United Church, without regard to the procedures followed by that body, while technically giving the impression that the "Friends" were yet members of it. Later, in November 1893, the group received its formal organization. The action to formally organize stemmed in part from a growing feeling among the Minority that they were being mistreated and even persecuted by the Majority. While obtaining students for the seminary did not present much of a problem, financing the school did. Already in 1893 the United Church passed a resolution cutting off funds for subsidised congregations and pastors where mission work was not being carried on in full loyalty to the church. As a result, funds were cut off from certain Minority home mission pastors and congregations. But a group within the Minority set about to collect funds to carry on these home missions and give what support was possible. This became the permanent Mission Committee of the "Friends."

As soon as it began to operate, the Mission Committee also received funds that were designated by their donors for foreign missions. In 1895 the "Friends" took over the financial support of the two missionaries in Madagascar, who were Augsburg graduates and had resigned from the United Church at the height of the controversy. Another missionary in Madagascar also received support from the "Friends." Thus began a trend by the Friends of Augsburg that was to continue throughout the history of the Lutheran Free Church: greater financial support of foreign missions than of home missions.

In 1894 the "Friends" adopted a statement of goals to guide them. In summary: these goals pledged support of Augsburg Seminary ("the rightful theological school of the United Church"), gave promotion and support to home mission work without partiality, considered foreign mission work a chief responsibility, and gave the congregations the right to call a pastor without interference from the church body or officials. It further promoted "powerful and spiritual lay activity," and utilization of "all of the spiritual gifts of a congrega-

272

tion." The "Friends" had the additional goal of settling the strife in the United Church by brotherly negotiations. The "Friends" stipulated that a church body is not to judge or bind consciences or require obedience on the part of the congregations, but rather be a means by which congregations may co-operate to carry out specific functions.[6]

The "Friends" were moving further and further in the directing of functioning as a church body. Finally, out of the Augsburg Seminary controversy, the Lutheran Free Church emerged.

THE FRIENDS OF AUGSBURG BECOME
THE LUTHERAN FREE CHURCH

The Lutheran Free Church actually became organized the year before final settlement was reached in the Augsburg case. The movement in the direction of functioning as a church body received additional thrust in 1895 when the United Church in convention refused to seat the two Augsburg Seminary professors as delegates, and in 1896 when the United Church expelled twelve congregations associated with the "Friends." These congregations had passed resolutions absolving themselves of giving support to the new seminary of the United church and refused to retract them. The feeling of President Hoyme was that the congregations had , in fact, severed ties with the United Church. The "Friends" regarded the body's action as schismatic. And so, by June 1896 the stage had been set for the transformation of the Friends of Augsburg into the Lutheran Free Church. A total of more than thirty congregations were involved in the transformation, with others contemplating action.

Within six days after the Untied Church's Convention had adjourned, the Friends of Augsburg assembled at Fargo, North Dakota, with Pontoppidan Congregation serving as host. Here the Minority gathered to lick their wounds inflicted by the Majority. A five-man committee was appointed "to work out rules for a Norwegian Lutheran Free Church." Others of similar views were invited to participate.

The 1897 meeting of the "Friends" was regarded as the constituting convention of the Lutheran Free Church, making separation from the United Church complete. No doctrinal issue had been at stake. The division had occurred in the area of church polity. With the adoption of "Rules For Work" on Jun 12, 1897, the Lutheran Free Church officially came into being.

Probably the number of congregations, most of them very small, was less than 125, involving about 6,250 souls. By 1903 it had grown to 270 congregations; by 1907, to 283 congregations, 81 preaching stations, 105 pastors, and 26,442 souls. By 1910 the LFC numbered 28,000 souls compared with 194,552 souls in the United Church, 145,203 souls in the Norwegian Synod, and 33,192 souls in the Hauge's Synod. By 1950 there were 70,000 souls in 355 congregations.

GOVERNMENT OF THE LUTHERAN FREE CHURCH: FREE CONGREGATIONS

The "Guiding Principles and Rules of the Lutheran Free Church," which the congregations adopted in 1897, thereby forming the Lutheran Free Church, were not considered a constitution. Nor did the "Rules" provide for the establishing of a church body or synod. The local congregation was emphasized, with no external authority wielded over it by the Annual Meeting (conference) of the Lutheran Free Church. The Free Church's stress on congregational freedom and a democratic form of government is clearly expressed in the "Guiding Principles and Rules:"

1. THE CONGREGATION IS, ACCORDING TO THE WORD OF GOD, THE RIGHT FORM OF THE KINGDOM OF GOD ON EARTH.

10. FREE CONGREGATIONS HAVE NO RIGHT TO DEMAND THAT OTHER CONGREGATIONS SHALL SUBJECT THEMSELVES TO THEIR OPINION, WILL, JUDGMENT OR DECISION; FOR WHICH REASON EVERY DOMINION OF A MAJORITY OF CONGREGATIONS OVER A MINORITY IS TO BE REJECTED.

11. THE JOINT-AGENCIES WHICH ARE FOUND DESIRABLE FOR THE CO-OPERATION OF CONGREGATIONS – SUCH AS LARGER OR SMALLER MEETINGS, COMMITTEES, OFFICERS, ETC. – MAY NOT, IN A LUTHERAN FREE CHURCH, IMPOSE ON THE INDIVIDUAL CONGREGATION ANY DUTY, OBLIGATION, RESTRICTION, OR BURDEN, BUT HAS THE RIGHT ONLY TO PRESENT MOTIONS AND REQUESTS OF CONGREGATIONS AND INDIVIDUALS.[7]

Thus the Lutheran Free Church taught that only the congregation is essential to Christianity, and looked upon synodical organization as an erosion of that authority God has bestowed on congregations. But some went so far as to regard even congregational organization as unnecessary. From such radicals, however, the Lutheran Free Church finally had to disassociate itself. These were called the "free-free." When, soon after the formation of the Lutheran Free Church, a group left the United Norwegian Lutheran Church to establish the Lutheran Brethren, claiming that the church could distinguish between believers and unbelievers and could rid themselves of the latter, the Lutheran Free Church found it necessary to deny such an extreme position. While the Lutheran Free Church was deeply skeptical of ecclesiastical organization, it nevertheless emphasized fellowship and working together as congregations ("common mind—common action"). While the congregations were expected to abide by the decisions of the Annual Conference, they were not obligated to do so.

The governmental structure was as follows: (1) The Annual Meeting (June). (2) All members had the right to vote (thus those in congregations near to the conference site had a disproportionate influence on the decisions made). (3) The Annual Meeting elected officers, committees, emissaries, and heard reports. (4) Elected officers: President (served as Moderator), Secretary, Ordinator. (5) Committees: Home Missions, Foreign Missions, and Organizations. (6) Freedom and autonomy of the congregation was guaranteed. (7) No real authority was granted either to officers or to the Annual Meeting. Rather, a fellowship of congregations was maintained. (8) The Annual Meeting served as "the great spiritual power house" (Oftedal). (9) Congregations were free to elect delegates if they wished. (10) Women had the right to vote in the Annual Meetings. (Several congregations also granted suffrage to women in congregational meetings.) (11) Other Lutherans could become voting members by signing acceptance of "Fundamental Principles and Rules For Work." (12) The LFC was divided into districts. By 1916 there were eighteen, including districts in Canada. They were not administrative but rather promoted inspirational and evangelistic meetings, disseminated information, and later became important especially in the area of stewardship. (13) Later, a vice-president and full-time Home Mission Superintendent were added. (14) An Ordinator was provided since individual congregations were not allowed to ordain. Though lay preaching was practiced, the LFC was very cautious about ordaining non-theologically trained men. (15) Committees and boards were very important. (16) Separate legal corporations were formed for the supervision of home and foreign missions. (17) The Organization Committee became very important, as the coordinator of activities of the various boards.

CHANGE

With the loss of the old leaders, the little ship foundered a bit in the second decade of the new century. The Lutheran Free Church body had to cope with the winds of change. In 1921 President Slettin observed that it served no good purpose to deny that the Free Church was a church body. He further observed that it was the congregations, rather than individuals, who held the Annual Meetings; therefore the congregations ought to have representation. He finally suggested a representative system which met with little enthusiasm, for it was felt that adoption of such a system would transform the Free Church into a synod, with authority over the congregations. On the other hand, some authority evidently was needed. The joint treasury was often short of funds; still, the Annual Meeting had no authority to require congregations to make payment into it for the various enterprises of the Free Church, including the funding of schools and missions.

In 1921 it was decided that the Free Church have full-time president. His duties included serving as an advisory member of three important committees (Organization, Home, Foreign Missions), and giving guidance and council to pastors and congregations desiring it. There was, however, opposition to having a fulltime president, for some felt that the office would then pose a threat to congregational freedom, the president being more an authority over, than a servant of, the congregations.

In 1929 a model constitution for congregations was adopted. Article 2 describes the nature of the congregation: THE CONGREGATION IS THE BODY OF CHRIST. IT CONSISTS OF BELIEVERS WHO SEEK THEIR SALVATION AND THAT OF THEIR FELLOWMEN USING THE MEANS OF GRACE AND THE SPIRITUAL GIFTS AS DIRECTED IN THE WORD OF GOD. Confessional Articles subscribed to the Holy Scripture as . . . THE WORD OF GOD . . . THE ONLY SOURCE AND RULE OF FAITH, DOCTRINE AND LIFE. The constitution declared acceptance of the three Ecumenical Creeds, the *Unaltered Augsburg Confession,* and Luther's *Small Catechism.* It also subscribed to the "Fundamental Principles and Rules of Work." Conditions for membership were broad: membership was open to baptized adults who BY CONFESSION

275

AND LIFE SHOW THAT THEY SEEK THE KINGDOM OF GOD AND HIS RIGHTEOUSNESS. Subscription to the Constitution was also required. In 1947 a significant change and addition to the Constitution was made: THIS CONGREGATION AFFILIATES WITH THE LUTHERAN FREE CHURCH, ENDORSES GUIDING PRINCIPLES AND RULES FOR WORK, AND SUPPORTS ITS BENEVOLENCES, THAT IS, MISSIONS AT HOME AND ABROAD, CHRISTIAN EDUCATION AND CHARITIES.

The Lutheran Free Church, while disavowing structure, nevertheless found itself functioning more and more like other Lutheran bodies. Beginning in he 1940s, the Lutheran Free Church became more and more knowledgeable of itself as being more than just a movement. More change was in store. In1946 the office of Ordinator was discontinued and the duties were given to the president. In 1959 the delegate system was introduced, the number of delegates from congregation to be determined on the basis of its baptized membership. Voting was limited to elected delegates; others were given the right to speak. In 1952 the office of Stewardship Director was established. In 1954 the Advisory Committee on Minimum Goals was established, but later changed, in 1959, to the Advisory Committee on Benevolences. In 1959 the office of Stewardship Counselor was established. It would be difficult to imagine the accomplishing of some of these changes during the lifetimes of Sverdrup and Oftedal.

THE LUTHERAN FREE CHURCH AT WORK

PUBLICATIONS

The People's Paper (private) was published by the People's Paper Publishing Company. In 1896 the Free Church Book Concern was formed. A hymn book of George Sverdrup's collected works was published. In 1922 the People's Paper Publishing Company and the Free Church Book Concern merged forming the Lutheran Free Church Publishing Company, which in 1946 became The Messenger Press. The *Lutheran Messenger* became the official paper. Translation of badly needed relegous literature into English from Norwegian was for a time accomplished by an English Conference formed in 1906 to promote systematic work in English in the Lutheran Free Church. Other agencies later took over the task. Later, when the Free Church merged into The American Lutheran Church (TALC) in 1963, publishing was assumed by the Augsburg Publishing House, which was owned and operated by the Evangelical Lutheran Church. (This publishing house was originally operated by the Conference and later by the United Church). The *Lutheran Standard* succeeded the *Lutheran Messenger*.

CHARITY WORK

An orphanage and Old Folks Home were maintained at Paulsbo, Washington. Bethesda Homes for children and the elderly were also established. A Lutheran Deaconess Home and Hospital was located in Minneapolis in 1888. This consisted in a school, hospital, and home to train deaconesses to care for the ill. It also served as home and headquarters for single women who were consecrated to the deaconate work.

HOME MISSIONS

The philosophy of the Lutheran Free Church in this department was simply this: HOME MISSIONARIES WERE PRIMARILY EVANGELISTS PREACHING "AWAKENING AND LIFE," AND ONLY SECONDARILY ORGANIZERS OF CONGREGATIONS, AFTER THE NEEDED PREPARATORY WORK HAD BEEN COMPLETED.[8]

The philosophy of evangelism in the Lutheran Free Church embraced the belief that every one who is a Christian is an evangelist. Traveling evangelists were provided for the purpose of holding special meetings in the congregations. The Free Church also perpetuated the Haugean tradition of lay activity by encouraging lay preaching. About the time of World War I, a decline in lay preaching set in, and in the 1930s it dropped off sharply.[9] What mainly caused the decline was the Free Church's transition to English, whereas most lay preachers were used to communicating in Norwegian.

The Free Church co-operated in inter-Lutheran evangelism programs, including conferences, and the congregations participated in the Preaching-Teaching-Reaching Missions involving the National Lutheran Council churches.

Areas of concentration for the Free Church were: Minnesota, North Dakota, Washington, and Canada. It was often felt that opportunities were not seized as they should have been, and the delay in starting congregations made it difficult to compete with other Lutherans. The point of emphasis in the Free Church was not to gain new church members or to start new congregations, but to confront the unsaved with the saving gospel.

For a number of years (1916 – 1943), the Siloah Seamen's Mission was located in downtown Seattle to minister to the physical and spiritual needs of seamen.

Before World War II, home missions often suffered from lack of funds. No doubt the Great Depression was partly to blame for this, and after the War this situation improved greatly. A new policy adopted in 1952 is worthy of note. The aim was to have fewer Home Mission Department aided churches and to give them more adequate support. Those congregations which had received mission aid for a considerable length of time were advised that they must make strenuous efforts to become self-sustaining. It was also felt that it would be well to consider limiting the years any one congregation could receive Home Mission aid where extraordinary circumstances did not prevail.

By 1959 $75,000 in loan funds alone were required for each new congregation. This was increased to $85,000 (building site $15,000, parsonage $15,000, first unit $55,000).[10]

In 1956 the first three California Home Mission congregations were begun. Looking in the opposite direction, we note that the Free Church up to that time had only one congregation in the Bronx of New York.

The Free Church helped organize at Minneapolis the Inter-Synodical Mission Council, representing home mission boards of several bodies operating in the upper Midwest.

277

FOREIGN MISSIONS

Early in its history the congregations of the Lutheran Free Church developed a deep and abiding love for foreign mission work and readily supported it. (Two foreign missionaries were supported by the "Friends" before the Free Church was organized). In fact, the chief emphasis in the Free Church came to be foreign missions. By 1950 the church had sixty missionaries in its own service and in the service of other mission boards. The Free Church continued the work in Madagascar undertaken by the Friends of Augsburg. The Board of Foreign Missions, which was established in 1897, became the Lutheran Board of Missions. Sadly, there was frequent illness and death among the missionary staff.

In 1913 work was begun in China. Later, the work became a part of the Lutheran Church in China (org. 1920). At times it became very difficult for the tiny Free Church to support two foreign missions – the other being Madagascar. The greatest source of gifts to missions came at times from societies rather than from congregations. Often the contributions for foreign missions were double the amount for home purposes. The outbreak of World War II necessitated abandoning the China field. There was a burst of mission activity after World War II, but the China field was finally lost to the Communists in 1948. At the time the Free Church left China, there were twenty-two congregations, thirty-two preaching places, and about 2500 baptized Christians.

In the 1950s work was begun in Hong Kong and Taiwan (which was cooperative work with others). Approval came in 1951 for cooperative work in Japan with the Evangelical Lutheran Church (ELC). The Madagascar missions of the Free Church and the Evangelical Lutheran Church were consolidated in 1960. In 1962, because of its approaching merger with The American Lutheran Church (TALC), the final report on world missions was given to the last Annual Conference. It showed the following statistics. Madagascar: 8,919 baptized souls, 127 congregations, 13 pastors, 16 missionaries. Hong Kong: (A joint mission) 11,119 baptized souls, 25 congregations, 17 pastors, 16 mission pastors (LFC=2), 5 lady missionaries (LFC=1). Taiwan: (A joint mission) 6,157 baptized souls, 25 congregations, 8 pastors, 28 evangelists, 14 Bible Women, and 61 missionaries including wives (LFC=5). Japan: (A joint mission) 845 baptized souls, 13 congregations, 4 pastors, 70 missionaries and wives (LFC=5).[11]

ORGANIZATIONS

WOMEN'S

The Women's Missionary Federation was formed at Willmar, Minnesota, in June 1916 to give support and encouragement to the work of missions. The WMF helped with the salaries of missionaries and initiated the Home Missions Church Extension Fund. The women tried to do the "extra thing," that otherwise might have been left undone. By 1962 the WMF was budgeting $8,000 annually for the Church Extension Fund. Dissemination of information about mission work, particularly in the Free Church's program, was a fundamental goal.

YOUTH WORK

Beginning in 1944 provision was made for a part-time youth director for the Free Church. A call was extended for such a director by the Luther League Federation. Beginning in 1955 it became a full-time office. In 1956 the Free Church established a Youth Board to give direction to "the total program of the youth activities in the church." The Free Church participated in the All-Lutheran Youth Leaders' Council (American Lutheran Conference). This also, in its own way, helped prepare the way for merger with The American Lutheran Church. Societies for youth were common by the early twentieth century. In November 1920, the Young People's Federation was organized in Minneapolis. In 1932 its name was changed to the Lutheran League Federation. Its goal was the "spiritual awakening of the young people of the congregation."

EDUCATION

Augsburg College and Seminary were, until the merger, the chief educational institutions of the Free Church. In 1921 the Annual Conference approved the admission of women to Augsburg College with final approval coming the following year. In1923 the academy was also designated as coeducational. In 1933 Augsburg Academy was discontinued. In 1920 the Annual Conference decided that the Free Church should establish a Bible School for training laymen. The school became located at Willmar, Minnesota, and began operations in the fall of 1921. After six years the school was transferred to Fargo, North Dakota, and eventually was phased out.

In the merger of the Lutheran Free Church with The American Lutheran Church (1963), the college and seminary were separated. The seminary became a unit of the unified theological seminary of TALC, merging thus with Luther Theological Seminary. The merged school was located on the St. Paul campus. Thus, what the United Norwegian Lutheran Church could not accomplish – the separation of the college and seminary – was accomplished three generations later by the merger.

In 1961-62, the enrollment at Augsburg reached 1402 students, of whom only thirty-one were seminary students. By 1961-62 synodical affiliation of the students leaned heavily outside the Free Church; in fact, non-LFC students comprised more than half the enrollment.

Augsburg was a central factor in the merger discussions which began in the early 1950s. Its president was outspoken in advocating merger, and the board members pretty much favored it also. Augsburg College is located in Minneapolis, adjoining the campus of the University of Minnesota. The Free Church also maintained Oak Grove Lutheran High School (a Ladies Seminary) at Fargo, North Dakota. It was established in 1906. In the merger this school came under control of a corporation of congregations in that general area, members of three districts. A high school established at Everett, Washington in 1904 had but a brief history.

WORSHIP FORMS

The Lutheran Free Church emphasized freedom and simplicity in worship. It also made allowance for informal fellowship (prayer, Bible study, and the sharing of Christian experience) and, of course, lay preaching. There was a deep-rooted fear of formalism. However, at times a desire for more uniformity and less diversity in worship forms made itself evident. In 1900 a Liturgical Committee was set up which made suggestions in worship forms to the congregations and also made changes in the forms for the Lord's Supper and Baptism. There remained in some a deep concern and skepticism regarding the forms for administering Baptism and the Lord's Super, as well as Confirmation, since these had been inherited from the State Church of Norway. However, many others in the Free Church did not share this extreme view, and a good share of the pastors used liturgical forms similar to those in the *Altar Book*. In many small rural churches, the order of service was very simple with no liturgical forms per se. The chief hymnal used was *Landstad's Hymnal*.

In 1920 a survey revealed that twenty-eight English hymnbooks were in use in the Lutheran Free Church congregations. In 1932 a revised edition of the *Concordia Hymnal* was used by the large majority of the Free Church congregations. In the 1950s most congregations switched to the *Service Book* and *Hymnal* published by the member bodies of the National Lutheran Council.

During much of the Free Church's history it was not the usual practice for the pastor to wear a pulpit gown. In the 1940s the gown had become quite common among the younger pastors. Also, by the forties, Sunday evening services and mid-week prayer services, especially in the cities, were becoming unpopular.

THE LUTHERAN FREE CHURCH
AND OTHERS

RELATIONS WITH THE HAUGE'S SYNOD
AND THE LUTHERAN BRETHREN

Closer relations were felt with the Haugeans at the turn of the century than with any other Norwegian American Lutheran body. While the Free Church and the Hauge's Synod had much in common, both being committed to Haugean pietism, they differed in the area of church polity. The Hauge's Synod used the congregation-synodical form of organization so prevalent in America among Lutherans. On the other hand, the Free Church – until much later in its history – was afraid of anything that even smacked of synodical authority. When in 1905 the Hauge's synod spoke of the possibility of merging the various Norwegian American Lutheran Church bodies, the Free Church was unwilling to consider it, but did support a committee to confer with the Hauge's Synod regarding cooperation. While both sides agreed that a broad range of cooperation was possible, only a limited amount was actually achieved.

The Free Church disassociated itself from the Brethren's teaching concerning pure congregations. An interest in possible union or merger with the

280

Lutheran Brethren became fruitless, for few in the one group shared the interest of the other group.

RELATIONS WITH THE UNITED CHURCH AND THE EVANGELICAL LUTHERAN CHURCH

Before its merger in 1963 with The American Lutheran Church, the Lutheran Free Church did not participate in mergers with other Lutherans. In 1912 and 1913 meetings were held with the United Church, with that body taking the initiative. But relations with the United Church were strained, for while that body was caught up in the fervor of the merger movement and wanted to let bygones be bygones, claiming there was not doctrinal difference to separate the two groups, the Free Church was not ready either to forget the past or to promote merger. Deep wounds had been inflicted which would require a great deal of time to heal. The old grievances were still much present. The Free Church was ready, however, to promote cooperation in practical church work and brotherly understanding. The discussions were ended.

In the big merger movement which culminated in 1917 in forming the Evangelical Lutheran Church (ELC), the congregations of the Lutheran Free Church clearly showed their disinterest. After the merger was accomplished, the Free Church was not enthusiastic regarding the finished product, for it did not feel spiritual unity with the new body which emerged. Cooperation in the practical work of the Church, but not merger, was the theory advanced by the Free Church.

The Evangelical Lutheran Church made overtures in 1923 to the Free Church but was turned down. In 1928 Dr. Lars Qualben, professor at Augsburg, promoted merger with the ELC. However, his move aroused much antagonism within the Free Church and he later resigned his teaching position. Still, much of what he wrote in favor of merger would influence thinking within the Free Church a generation later.

Interestingly enough, cooperating in church work – which the Free Church allowed – would eventually do much to lead to union. When the Free church at first became involved in the union movement, it was suspicious and cautious to the extreme, but later it directed a great deal of time and effort to the union cause. The Free Church overwhelmingly rejected merger with the ELC in 1928. Consideration of possible merger with other Lutheran bodies did not come until the later 1940s.

The Free Church did not want additional confessional statements. Nor did it desire doctrinal disputation that was too meticulous. There was a conviction that IT IS ALL TOO POSSIBLE FOR PASTORS AND PROFESSORS TO BECOME ENGROSSED IN THEORETICAL DEFINITIONS AND THEOLOGICAL CONTROVERSIES AND THEREBY BE LED TO PLACE LESS EMPHASIS UPON THE FUNDAMENTAL CALLING OF THE CHURCH OF CHRIST, NAMELY, THE PREACHING OF THE GOSPEL AND THE LEADING OF MEN TO PERSONAL EXPERIENCE OF ITS SAVING POWER.[12] On the basis of the three ancient symbols and *Luther's Small Catechism* and the *Augsburg Confession*, the Free Church was willing to cooperate with others. But it was not in favor of organic union of the various Lutheran synods into one Lutheran Church.

THE LUTHERAN FREE CHURCH AND
THE NATIONAL LUTHERAN COUNCIL

The Free Church participated in the NLC (formed September 6, 1918) from its beginning, thus manifesting its spirit of cooperation with other Lutherans. Between 1920 and 1924 the Free Church contributed $27,000 to the Council. The Free Church did not agree that the NLC needed additional doctrinal statements (e.g. the *Chicago Theses*, which had been drawn up by the ELC's H.G. Stub). The Free Church principle continued to be that doctrinal theses are unnecessary and that agreement on the Lutheran Confessions is an adequate basis for cooperation.[13]

The Free Church also participated in the early beginnings of the Lutheran World Federation (at the time, the Lutheran World Convention).

The early effort (1944) of the ELC to explore union was not ready for reciprocal action by the Free Church. In 1949 the Free Church accepted President P.O. Bersell's invitation (of the Augustana Lutheran Church) to participate in exploring the possibilities for closer organizational affiliation by the National Lutheran Council bodies. However, the Annual Conference took note of the fact that it "is not in favor of organic union and instructs its delegates accordingly." A two-fold choice lay before the Free Church: (1) organic union of the NLC churches, or (2) transformation of the NLC into a federation. The NLC found it had to continue its existence in unaltered form.

AMERICAN LUTHERAN CONFERENCE NEGOTIATIONS

By its membership in the National Lutheran Council and later, in the American Lutheran Conference* (org. 1930), the Free Church identified itself with middle-of-the road theology – between the liberal United Lutheran Church in America (ULCA) on the one side and the doctrinally conservative Synodical Conference synods on the other.

The American Lutheran Conference was based on the *Minneapolis Theses*, which included also the *Chicago Theses*. In a meeting held in Minneapolis in 1930 it was found that the representatives of the Free Church were in perfect agreement with the *Minneapolis Theses*. Therefore the Free Church declared pulpit and altar fellowship with the Joint Synod of Ohio, the Iowa Synod, and the Buffalo Synod (the three bodies that formed the American Lutheran Church in 1930). The Free Church approved the constitution of the American Lutheran Conference, and with its approval began to move away from its isolationist stand. The American Lutheran Conference was discontinued in 1954, since the practical functions of the Conference had been supplanted by the National Lutheran Council.

In April 1951 the Free Church had observers at the meeting held by American Lutheran Conference bodies to discuss possibility of organic union. The president of the Free Church was in favor of exploring organic union though the Free Church was against it. In 1951 a Committee on Relations was chosen, which committee played a crucial part in the remaining history of the Free Church, and laboriously guided this body along the road to merger.

When the Joint Union Committee formulated "The United Testimony on Faith and Life," the Free Church representatives considered it "an excellent statement and indicates its essential agreement in many areas." It was, however, recognized that considerable diversity of practice and emphasis was represented by the various groups. They felt that more restriction was placed on lay preaching than was desirable. The 1952 Free Church Annual Conference approved "The United Testimony" by a vote of 383 to 12, a rather surprising majority. However, the Free Church still was not committed to organic union, but remained open to merger discussion.

THE MERGER QUESTION

THE PRESIDENT LOOKS WITH FAVOR AT UNION

Beginning with the year 1949, the Lutheran Free Church was much occupied with the question of merger with other Lutherans. President Stensvaag became an ardent supporter of the merger movement and led the Free Church into union with The American Lutheran Church in 1963. The Free Church Policy Committee proposed that the Free Church be allowed to take part in the proposed merger as a non-geographical district, thus retaining its form and its educational institutions. However, the Joint Union Committee did not favor the proposal. In 1954 the Annual Conference voted to receive the Report on Polity and Organization of the Joint Union committee for consideration. During the following year, the merger issue was discussed extensively throughout the Free Church at its various meetings.

ANTI-MERGER FORCES

The goal of the anti-merger forces was to preserve the distinctive heritage of the Free Church. Their question was: Would prayer and testimony meetings, lay-witnessing and evangelistic preaching be preserved in the merger? They also questioned whether the low church liturgical practices of the Free Church would be jeopardized. Then too they were suspicious of centralized authority, a matter which was basic to the very existence of the Free Church as a separate body up to this time. In addition, the delegate system employed by the other bodies was not acceptable to some. For some of the anti-merger people it appeared to be difficult to part with the cozy, family-type-fellowship which characterized the Free Church. A small organization was to be preferred. Some reasons for opposing merger were simply not tangible.

It should be mentioned here that the Free Church was against seeking membership in the World Council of Churches, whereas the Augustana Synod, the American Lutheran Church (1930), and the United Evangelical Lutheran Church (Danish) had joined in 1948, the year of its organization. The merger documents provided for seeking membership in the World Council of Churches. This was a matter that some felt had to be considered.

PRO-MERGER FORCE

Those in favor of the merger felt that opportunity for sharing the Free Church's heritage with others would be broadened, and that there would be more opportunities for service. From their contacts with others, the pro-merger people had come to the conclusion that the opinion held by many, that the Free Church was more "spiritual" than the others, should be laid to rest. They were in favor of rapprochement with the Evangelical Lutheran Church in particular, for here were most of their fellow Norwegian American Lutherans. They also recognized the changes that had occurred in the Free Church's form of organization, causing it to become more like other Lutheran bodies.

The pro-merger force felt that basic Free Church emphasis could be preserved within the framework of the merger. The Free Church had found that others had an intense interest in evangelism and lay activity. Joint work of the congregations of the Free Church would be strengthened and opportunities for more effective service greatly increased. It also seemed to the pro-merger force that the practice of good stewardship indicated merger. Generally speaking, the Free Church missionaries were in favor of union. It was felt that uniting the Lutheran bodies would make possible participation in other mission fields, and that the small size of the Free Church would no longer be a disadvantage on the home mission front. "We need each other!" Pro-merger members of the Free Church felt that the World Council of Churches would provide a worldwide forum of Christian consultation, thus a greatly enhanced opportunity for Lutherans to bear more effective witness to their faith within the Christian family without compromising their faith. This, of course, was the very opposite opinion from that which had been expressed many times by the conservative Lutheran bodies of the Synodical conference, which refused to enter the fellowship of the World Council of Churches lest they jeopardize their confessional position. It should be noted that over the years the influence of the WCC has greatly weakened.

LEADING UP TO THE MERGER
SOME WERE LOST TO THE LFC

The issue of whether or not to enter the merger was to be decided by congregational referendums. The referendum of 1955 lacked the membership votes needed to continue in the merger talks. Yet two-thirds of the congregations favored continuing merger negotiations, whereas six years earlier the Annual conference had gone on record opposing organic union. The 1955 referendum had dammed the stream, "nevertheless water was spilling over the dam." The 1956 Annual Conference decided to continue the Committee on Relations as a permanent committee, even though it could not participate in union negotiations. Meanwhile, the congregations were to study the merger documents in light of Free Church principles. The 1957 Annual Conference voted to reopen negotiations.

A congregational referendum that same year again failed, and thus eliminated the possibility of the Free Church participation in the merger, which was

284

to be consummated in 1960.* Already in 1956 the Evangelical Lutheran Church, the American Lutheran Church, and the United Evangelical Lutheran Church had committed themselves to the merger. There ensued a period of self-evaluation for the Free Church. From 1958 to 1961 it was relatively quiet on the merger front, so far as official action was concerned. For the pro-merger forces, however, it was business as usual, a period of intense planning.

The third and last congregational referendum was conducted in the fall of 1961. The Annual Conference earlier that year had gone on record as favouring union negotiations with The American Lutheran Church. The referendum overwhelmingly favored merger. The minority – a little less than one-third – firmly held to their convictions, opposing merger. Therefore, congregations of the minority began to withdraw from the Free Church.

MERGER ACCOMPLISHED

A congregation had the right to withdraw from The American Lutheran Church during a three month period immediately following the merger. Articles of Agreement had been worked out and the delegates to the sixteenth Annual Conference adopted them, reaffirming the body's approval of "The United Testimony of Faith and Life," approving also the Constitution and Bylaws of The American Lutheran Church. The vote was 530 to 112 in favor of the merger. Under the section titled EDUCATION, we have already reviewed the course of action followed regarding Augsburg Seminary and College in the merger (their separation), and the placing of Oak Grove High School at Fargo, North Dakota, under local control (a corporation of area congregations). And under PUBLICATIONS, we learned of the arrangement whereby Augsburg Publishing House assumed all publishing responsibilities. The Free Church brought into the union a Merger and Mission Fund of $101,339. The official merger of the Lutheran Free Church joined the third largest unit of U.S. Lutheranism, numbering 2,365,000 members.

THE ANTI-MERGER MINORITY BECOMES THE
ASSOCIATION OF FREE LUTHERAN CONGREGATIONS

A small but vocal minority refused to take part in the merger. This group held a conference at Thief River Falls, Minnesota, October 25-28, 1962, to form an association of congregants which did not desire to enter the merger. It took the name The Lutheran Free Church (not merged), claiming to be the rightful continuation of the Lutheran Free Church. A court order caused the group to change the name to The Association of Free Lutheran Congregations. By January 31, 1963, forty-one congregations had requested to be omitted from the merger. Later, eleven more congregations withdrew, but one earlier withdrawal asked for re-admittance. By May 1, 1963, a total of fifty-one congregations had not participated in the merger, whereas two hundred seventy-seven had. The non-participating congregations had a total membership of 5,997 representing only 6.34% of the total 1962 Free Church membership.[14] Fifteen Free

285

Church pastors were not certified to The American Lutheran Church, while two hundred forty-four were. By the end of the year 1986, the Association of Free Lutheran Congregations (headquartered in Minneapolis, Minnesota) numbered 160 congregations and 19,508 members.

In 1987 The American Lutheran Church merged with the Lutheran Church in America, and the Association of Evangelical Lutheran Churches to form the Evangelical Lutheran Church in America (ELCA), with 5,316,522 baptized members and a total of 11,035 congregations.

ADDENDUM:

More about the Association of Free Lutheran Congregations: The forty congregations of the former Lutheran Free Church who declined to join the merger forming the new ALC (1960) gave five reasons for their action: (1) The ALC's membership in the World Council of Churches. (2) The trend of merging bodies towards liberal theological positions and practices. (3) Church polity which moved from the Free Church's historic congregational form of government to a more centralized government. (4) The high church worship tradition within the membership of the ALC. (5) The lack of emphasis on the historic Free Church's practice of Christian piety.

By 1985, 153 congregations were listed on the roster of the AFLC. In 1986, when the congregations of the American Lutheran Church (ALC) voted in the referendum favouring taking part in the merger to form the Evangelical Lutheran Church in America (ELCA), many of the dissidents who opposed the merger withdrew from the ALC and the merger. Some of the dissidents joined the new group, the American Association of Lutheran Churches (AALC), but the majority joined the Association of Free Lutheran Congregations.

A summary of AFLC beliefs: (1) Recognizes the Bible as being inerrant and the authority in all areas of life. (2) Recognizes that the teaching and preaching of God's word is the main task of the Church. The Word of God is to be taught and preached in such a way that the saints are built up in the faith and unbelievers see their need for salvation. (3) Believes that the congregation is the right form of the Kingdom of God on earth, with no authority over it but the Word and Spirit of God. (4) Believes that Christian unity is a spiritual concept and not a man-made organization or body such as the World Council of Churches, the National Council of Churches, etc. (5) Believes that Christians are to be different from unbelievers and are to be a salt in the world (pietism). This difference is to be reflected also in the work of the Christian congregations and the institutions of the church.

The AFLC seminary was founded in 1964. The Association's Bible school has a two year program. Foreign mission work is conducted in Brazil, Mexico, and India and an orphanage is maintained in India.[15]

Association of Free Lutheran Congregations
3110 East Medicine Lake Blvd.
Minneapolis, MN 55441

Footnotes for Chapter Eighteen

1 Eugene L. Fevold, *The Lutheran Free Church – A Fellowship of American Lutheran Congregations 1897 - 1963*, (Augsburg Publishing House, Minneapolis, MN, 1969), p. 30.

2 Fevold, *The Lutheran Free Church* . . . , p. 33.

3 Fevold, *The Lutheran Free Church* . . . , p. 38.

4 Fevold, *The Lutheran Free Church* . . . , p. 51.

5 Fevold, *The Lutheran Free Church* . . . , p. 60.

6 Fevold, *The Lutheran Free Church* . . . , p. 87.

7 Richard C. Wolf, *Documents of Lutheran Unity in America*, (Fortress Press, Philadelphia, PA, 1966), pp. 243, 244; Doc. #103.

8 Fevold, *The Lutheran Free Church* . . ., p. 126.

9 Fevold, *The Lutheran Free Church* . . . , p. 247.

10 Fevold, *The Lutheran Free Church* . . . , p. 243

11 Fevold, *The Lutheran Free Church.* . . . , p. 238.

12 Fevold, *The Lutheran Free Church* . . . , quoting Bernhard Christiansen, p. 321.

13 Fevold, *The Lutheran Free Church* . . . , p. 182.

*Lutheran bodies which were members of the American Lutheran Conference: Lutheran Free Church, Evangelical Lutheran Church, American Lutheran Church, United Evangelical Lutheran Church, Augustana Synod.

* The American Lutheran Church Constituting Convention took place at Minneapolis, April 22-24, 1960. The new church began official operations January 1, 1961.

14 Fevold, *The Lutheran Free Church* . . . , pp. 299, 300.

15 David B. Barnhart, *The Church's Desperate Need For Revival* (Eagan, MN: Abiding Word)

CHAPTER NINETEEN

THE NORWEGIANS
THE NORWEGIAN LUTHERAN
CHURCH OF AMERICA
(EVANGELICAL LUTHERAN
CHURCH)
1917-1960

ATTEMPTING FURTHER UNION OF
NORWEGIANS

MEETINGS BETWEEN THE UNITED CHURCH AND THE NOR-
WEGIAN CHURCHES

In the chapter concerned with the history of the United Norwegian Lutheran Church (org. 1890), we saw the first successful attempt to unite the various factions of Norwegian Lutheranism in America. Soon after this union of the Anti-Missourian Brotherhood, the Norwegian Augustana Synod, and the Norwegian Lutheran Conference, a schism occurred which brought about the formation of the Lutheran Free Church. The cause of this schism was not doctrinal disagreement but church polity, stemming especially from the Augsburg Seminary controversy. See again the history of the Lutheran Free Church and also the history of the United Norwegian Lutheran Church.

In 1900 the United Church endured a second schism, this one on a smaller scale. Led by Pastor K. O. Lundeberg, who had been filled with the "pure congregation" fervor, a group of eight pastors seceded and formed the Church of the Lutheran Brethren. (See the chapter, THE NORWEGIANS: THE SMALL EARLY GROUPS).

The Norwegian Synod (or, simply the Synod) and the Hauge's Synod, though not taking part in the 1890 union, nevertheless stated their interest in a union of Norwegian Lutherans. However, the Synod through its spokesman insisted that union of churches must come from unity of faith based on scriptural truth. The Synod took the same stand in the matter as did the Missouri and Wisconsin Synods. They shared similar stand in the matter of joint prayer and therefore requested that the union meetings not be opened with joint prayer, since the participants did not all teach the same things in regards to all doctrines.

At Willmar, Minnesota, a meeting was held between the Norwegian synods, with the Hauge's Synod abstaining. This meeting mainly served the purpose to point up the differences among the Norwegian Lutherans which had not been discussed at previous intersynodical conferences. Focus centered on two important doctrines: Prayer Fellowship and Inspiration of Scripture. The Synod did not believe in praying with those with whom it was not in doctrinal agreement. The Synod also felt that the doctrine of Verbal Inspiration must be clearly presented; at the same time offering the opinion that this doctrine was inadequately treated in paragraph one of the "Scandinavian Agreement." The United Church did not share the Synod's feelings. However, the Synod men were suspicious that many of the pastors on the Norwegian scene in America did not subscribe to the doctrine of Verbal Inspiration. Nevertheless, the United Church was not at all eager to take up the question of Verbal Inspiration. As a result, short shrift was made of the matter when a committee, appointed to the task, drew up the following statement, which finally met with unanimous approval: IN REGARD TO CHURCH UNION BETWEEN THE SYNOD AND THE UNITED CHURCH, WE CONSIDER THE UNANIMOUS ACCEPTANCE OF THE CANONICAL BOOKS OF THE HOLY SCRIPTURES AS GOD'S REVEALED, INFALLIBLE WORD ON THE PART OF BOTH CHURCH BODIES, AS FULLY SUFFICIENT BASIS FOR UNION. Reference was then made to Pontoppidan's Catechism for further clarification.

The two groups found themselves at odds regarding the question whether all congregations should be required to subscribe to the *Book of Concord*. The United Church expressed the opinion that it should not be required, since the congregations are not familiar with it. And so, the Willmar meeting pointed up the additional differences of viewpoints among Norwegian Lutherans.

THE OLD ELECTION CONTROVERSY FLARES UP

Conditions were not favorable again for several years for the calling of another free conference. Finally, in 1897 Pastor B.J. Muus, upon receiving 69 signatures from pastors, issued the invitation to hold a free conference at Lanesboro, Minnesota, in the fall of the same year. When the conference convened it soon found itself back in the election controversy. The controversy in brief: What part, if any, does man play in his conversion? The two sides were the pro-Missouri part, which assigned salvation alone to God, and the anti-Missouri part, which pointed out that man is a responsible personality, who must decide the matter of his conversion. Lines were drawn up. The two sides stood toe to toe on the issue for the next thirteen years. The next free conference, held in 1899 at Austin, Minnesota, had poor attendance. The result was but a further indication of a stalemate that already existed.

AT FIRST, A DREARY OUTLOOK FOR CHURCH UNION

By 1905 the union cause seemed doomed, but then the Hauge's Synod, meeting at Red Wing, Minnesota, made it known that it had elected a Union Committee to consider union with the other Norwegian Lutheran Synods. By telegram the Hauge's Synod requested the conventions of the United Church and the Norwegian Synod, which were in progress at the time, to follow their example and also appoint Union Committees. The spark ignited a small fire and both synods complied. Also invited to the union talks were the Church of the Brethren, the Eielsen Synod, and the Lutheran Free Church. The first two did not respond but the latter agreed to appoint a committee to look into cooperation, though it did not consider itself to be a synod.

DRAWING UP DOCTRINAL AGREEMENTS

Three meetings of the Union Committees were held in 1906. The Norwegian Synod, which before had balked at prayer fellowship with those with whom it was not in doctrinal agreement and fellowship, now participated in joint prayer. Agreement was reached on the doctrine of Absolution in the first two meetings, and on lay activity in the church at the third meeting. In the document of agreement, both the Universal Priesthood of all believers and the divine institution of the Ministerial Office were spelled out. In the Absolution document, absolution was defined as: GOD'S OWN ABSOLVING ACT THROUGH THE MINISTRY OF THE WORD . . . IN ABSOLUTION GOD DECLARES TO THE SINNER THE GRACIOUS FORGIVENESS OF ALL HIS SINS AS A BLESSING OF GRACE AND RECONCILIATION, WHICH HAS BEEN INSTITUTED AND ACQUIRED THROUGH THE MERIT OF THE BLOOD OF JESUS AND EMBODIES IN THE MERCIFUL PROMISE OF THE GOSPEL FOR APPROPRIATION BY THE SINNER. FAITH WAS DESCRIBED AS: THE INSTRUMENT BY WHICH THE SINNER RECEIVES, APPROPRIATES AND THUS BECOMES A PARTAKER OF THE GIFT AND TREASURE OF FORGIVENESS OF SINS.[1] . . . .The last sentence of the final theses in the document on Lay Ministries in the church, is significant: IT SHALL NOT BE CONSIDERED UNCHURCHLY PRACTICE OR RELIGIOUS FANATICISM FOR PEOPLE TO COME TOGETHER FOR PRAYER AND EARNEST PROMOTION OF SPIRITUAL AWAKENING AND SPIRITUAL LIFE.[2] As far as lay preaching was concerned, though it was allowable in the document, it was also to be supervised.

In the theses concerned with the doctrine of the Call and with the doctrine of Conversion, the element of cooperation is ruled out: BEFORE REGENERATION, MAN DOES NOT RECEIVE ANY INDWELLING POWER WHICH HE POSSESSES AS HIS OWN, AND WHEREBY HE THEN IS ABLE TO DECIDE TO ACCEPT GRACE.[3] In the doctrine of

Conversion, this statement forms the next to the last theses: WHEN A PER-
SON DOES NOT BECOME CONVERTED, HE ALONE BEARS THE RESPONSIBILITY AND
BLAME, BECAUSE HE WOULD NOT HEED THE CALL; THAT IS, IN SPITE OF THE FACT
THAT GOD THROUGH THE CALL MAKES IT POSSIBLE FOR MAN TO BE CONVERTED
OR CONVERT HIMSELF . . . HE RESISTS AND RENDERS INEFFECTIVE THE WORK OF
THE HOLY SPIRIT THROUGH BOTH LAW AND GOSPEL, SOMETHING IT IS POSSIBLE
FOR MAN TO DO AT ANY STAGE . . . The final point reads: WHEN A PERSON IS
CONVERTED, THE GLORY BELONGS TO GOD ALONE, BECAUSE IT IS HE THROUGH-
OUT, FROM BEGINNING TO END, WITHOUT ANY COOPERATION ON THE PART OF MAN
WHO WORKS CONVERSION IN THE PERSON WHO BECOMES CONVERTED; THAT IS, AC-
KNOWLEDGES HIS SIN AND BELIEVES IN CHRIST.[4] Note that both in the doctrine
of the Call and in Conversion, the point is made that God gives the sinner
the power to be converted, or "to convert himself."

The doctrine of Election, Article V, also referred to as the *Madison
Agreement*, speaks of the presentation of Election in two forms. The First
Form is set forth in Article XI of the *Formula of Concord*, and the Second
Form is set forth in Pontoppidan's *Truth Unto Godliness*. Under Section 3
the differences are brought out. On the one hand are those (the *Formula
of Concord* men) who INCLUDE UNDER THE DOCTRINE OF ELECTION THE WHOLE
ORDER OF SALVATION OF THE ELECT FROM THE CALL TO THE GLORIFICATION . . .
AND TEACH AN ELECTION UNTO SALVATION THROUGH THE SANCTIFICATION OF
THE SPIRIT AND BELIEF OF THE TRUTH.[5] On the other hand are those who with
Pontoppidan, DEFINE ELECTION MORE SPECIFICALLY AS THE DECREE CONCERN-
ING THE FINAL GLORIFICATION, WITH FAITH AND PERSEVERANCE WROUGHT BY
THE HOLY SPIRIT AS ITS NECESSARY PRESUPPOSITION, AND TEACH THAT GOD HAS
APPOINTED ALL THOSE TO ETERNAL LIFE <u>WHO HE FROM ETERNITY HAS FORESEEN</u>
<u>WOULD ACCEPT THE OFFERED GRACE, BELIEVE IN CHRIST AND REMAIN CONSTANT</u>
<u>IN THIS FAITH UNTO THE END.</u>[6] (emphasis added) In spite of reference in the
Call and Conversion to the power to convert oneself, the following state-
ment was made under Election: WE REJECT: . . . THE DOCTRINE . . . THAT
THIS FAITH IS THE RESULT OF AN ABILITY AND POWER IMPARTED BY THE CALL OF
GRACE, WHICH THEREFORE NOW DWELL WITHIN AND BELONG TO THE UNREGEN-
ERATE HEART ENABLING IT TO MAKE A DECISION OF GRACE.[7] Also rejected: . . .
THE DOCTRINE THAT GOD IN ELECTION ACTS ARBITRARILY AND UNMOTIVATED, SO
THAT HE POINTS OUT AND COUNTS A CERTAIN ARBITRARY NUMBER OF ANY INDI-
VIDUALS WHOMSOEVER AND APPOINTS THEM TO CONVERSION AND SALVATION
WHILE ALL OTHERS ARE EXCLUDED.[8]

The language of the doctrinal agreements seems fraught with unclarity
and double-talk.

The resolution at the end of the doctrinal agreements points out that
satisfactory agreement concerning the doctrine of Election has been
reached as the result of the deliberations of "our new committees" . . . and
that the deliberations have led TO AN UNRESERVED AND UNANIMOUS ACCEPT-
ANCE OF THAT DOCTRINE OF ELECTION WHICH IS SET FORTH IN ARTICLE XI, PART
II OF THE *FORMULA OF CONCORD* AND QUESTION 548 IN PONTOPPIDAN'S *TRUTH
UNTO GODLINESS* . . . . ,WE THEREFORE DECLARE HEREBY, THAT THE ESSENTIAL
AGREEMENT CONCERNING THESE DOCTRINES WHICH HAS BEEN ATTAINED IS SUF-

FICIENT FOR CHURCH UNION.[9]. .

What actually had been agreed upon, was to recognize the right of each side to adhere to their particular doctrine of Election.

OBSTACLES TO UNION

In spite of gains, union was not to come that easily. In 1908 the ship went aground again on the shoals of disunity in the doctrine of Election. That issues were still unresolved between pro-Missourian and anti-Missourian forces can be easily seen in the meeting of 1909. In 1910 the committees broke up their meetings. Between 1905--when it seemed agreement had been reached-and 1910, the joint committees had become deadlocked. However, the United Chruch decided to continue discussions. Furthermore, there were elements in the Norwegian Synod who felt that the doctrine of Election in two forms should not keep the synods apart.

Late in the fall of 1910 another joint meeting was held. However, the delegates from the Norwegian Synod withdrew from the negotiations over the queston of what basis was to be used for discussion. A sour note had already been introduced by Dr. Stub of the Norwegian Synod, who in epxressing the fact that the Synod did not consider the use of the Second Form devisive, nevertheless pointed out that President Dahl of the United Church had in his message to his synod accused the Norwegian Synod of being unbiblical and unLutheran in its stand. Dr. Stub demanded that the United Church furnish the proofs for such allegations and to let these points be the basis for further deliberation.

The next day, the delegates of the United Church and the Hauge's Synod adopted theses presented to the conference and declared themselves doctrinally prepared for merger, at the same time, deploring the Synod's withdrawal from negotiations.

THE BATTLE RESUMES

The year 1911 marks the return to theological warfare by the Norwegians. The very man who was to defend the Norwegian Synod's aloofness from doctrinal negotiations was destined, strangely enough, to have a great deal to do with bringing about the merger of 1917, and of becoming the first president of the merger body, and the following year, president also of the National Lutheran council. Dr. H. G. Stub, the new president of the Norwegian Synod, was the man.

Each side defended their stand and past actions in public print. The Norwegian Synod's position in brief: GOD IN DIVINE SOVEREIGNTY, ELECTED SOME TO ETERNAL SALVATION. FAITH IN THE INDIVIDUAL BELIEVERS IS THE OUTCOME OF ELECTION. THAT OTHERS WERE NOT ELECTED IS A DIVINE MYSTERY.

The United Church's position in brief: GOD ELECTS THOSE WHOM HE SAW WOULD COME TO FAITH. THUS THEY ACCUSED THE NORWEGIAN SYNOD AND THE MISSOURI SYNOD OF HARBOURING CALVINISM, WHICH TEACHES THAT GOD ORDAINS SOME TO ETERNAL DAMNATION. FOR IF GOD ELECTS TO FAITH, THEN HIS GRACE IS IRRESISTIBLE AND WHAT THEN OF THOSE NOT SO ELECTED? DID GOD DECREE THEM BY TO ELECTING THEM, TO ETERNAL DAMNATION? THE UNITED CHURCH AND ANTI-MIS-

SOURIANS SOUGHT TO RESOLVE THE ISSUE BY DECLARING THAT MAN IS A RESPONSIBLE AGENT, NOT AN AUTOMATON MOVED BY IRRESISTIBLE GRACE TO BELIEVE IN CHRIST. FAITH IS NOT THE CAUSE OF ELECTION, YET ELECTION IS NEVER APART FROM FAITH, AND EVERY MAN IS HELD RESPONSIBLE BY GOD TO BELIEVE IN CHRIST.

Involved in the theological debates in the second decade of the twentieth century were personalities who had played such important roles of shaping the controversy in the last part of the nineteenth century. F.A. Schmidt, the old protagonist for the anti-Missourian side in the election controversy, remained an outspoken critic of Walther's doctrine, which he continued to find in the Norwegian Synod and was quick to label as "Calvinism."

Dr. Stub, despite his adamant stand on Election, was nevertheless a "liberal" theologian in the sense that he was not willing to isolate the Synod by refusing to come to grips with the controversy. He was willing to try every possible means, including making room for differences, in order to keep the union negotiations going. Vice-president Stub (professor at Luther Seminary 1900-17) did not agree with the degree of strictness which the leadership of the Synod had shown. When standing in for President Koren in 1910 at the district conventions, he omitted an important paragraph from the president's message dealing with the union question. As a result, the delegates were deprived of important instruction. Dr. Lauritz Larsen (emeritus) shared Dr. Stub's views and backed his efforts to bring about union. These men, together with a third man, did much to keep the Synod in the forum of doctrinal negotiations. But other factors were also involved.

HELPS TOWARD UNIONS

A situation existed among the Norwegians that paralleled similar efforts among the German Lutherans. The Norwegians, like the Germans, were cooperating in the publishing of a hymnal. Bear in mind that the German synods finally succeeded in bringing about a union of forces, resulting in the United Lutheran Church in America in 1918. Some of the credit for accomplishing this federation goes to the joint work performed on the new hymnal.

The three Norwegian bodies which were jointly preparing an English hymnal, helped their merger cause also, for the work kept them in contact. This work kept on through the period of theological warfare and served as a constant reminder that someday there was to be a united Norwegian Lutheran Church. These revealing sentiments are contained in the Preface to The Lutheran Hymnary: THE DESIRABILITY OF A COMMON HYMNARY, ESPECIALLY IN THE EVENT OF A UNION OF THE CHURCH BODIES CONCERNED . . . THE PRAYER. . . THAT "THE LUTHERAN HYMNARY" MAY PROVE NO SMALL FACTOR IN THE EFFORTS MADE TO UNIFY THE VARIOUS NORWEGIAN LUTHERAN CHURCH BODIES OF OUR LAND.[10]

Another factor which kept the churches working toward union was the attitude of the laymen, many of whom clearly wanted to be united with their neighbors. They were growing weary of witnessing a division among their own kind.

The United Church took steps to see that the union movement did not die. These steps included the appointment of a new Union Committee composed of

294

parish pastors, and the sending of a delegation to the meeting of the Synod. The Synod followed the example of the United Church and also elected a new Union Committee.

In the ensuing deliberations, the Hauge's Synod decided to remain apart, since it felt itself already one with the United Church, and also considered the controversy a matter between that body and the Synod. The first meeting did little more than give the men friendly acquaintance with each other. A second meeting of the Joint Committees was set to be held in Madison, Wisconsin, in February 1912. A subcommittee was appointed to draft proposals and present them before the Madison meeting.

THE "MADISON AGREEMENT" (OPGJØR): HOW TO ACCEPT TWO OPPOSING VIEWPOINTS

In February 1912 the second meeting of the Joint Committees was held at Madison, Wisconsin. Several days were spent discussing the doctrine of Election as presented in the *Formula of Concord*, Article XI. This was followed by a study of Question 548 in Pontoppidan's Catechism. After this, the Joint Committees heard the report of the subcommittee. This report must have been a little startling at first for it began with these words: THE UNION COMMITTEES OF THE SYNOD AND THE UNITED CHURCH UNANIMOUSLY AND WITHOUT RESERVATION ACCEPT THAT DOCTRINE OF ELECTION WHICH IS SET FORTH IN THE *FORMULA OF CONCORD*, PART II, ARTICLE XI, AND IN PONTOPPIDAN'S *TRUTH UNTO GODLINESS*, QUESTION 548.

After this, came a statement of the relation between the two forms of doctrine. Here things were not so amicable; in fact, a deadlock again seemed pending. And so, a sub-subcommittee of two pastors was assigned the problem. The Joint Committee showed they meant business when they told the two pastors "to thrash this out." The two pastors were told, "We are going to lock you in a room, and will not open the door until you have found the right way of stating this matter."[11]

The two-man committee brought the following report, which was unanimously adopted by members of the Joint Committees:

Paragraph One: IT CONTAINS A DECLARATION OF UNANIMOUS ACCEPTANCE OF THE DOCTRINE OF ELECTION SET FORTH IN ARTICLE XI OF THE *FORMULA OF CONCORD* AND PONTOPPIDAN'S *TRUTH UNTO GODLINESS*.

Paragraph Two: SINCE BOTH THE CONFERRING BODIES ACKNOWLEDGED THAT ARTICLE XI OF THE *FORMULA OF CONCORD* PRESENTS THE PURE AND CORRECT DOCTRINE OF THE CHILDREN OF GOD UNTO SALVATION AS TAUGHT BY THE WORD OF GOD AND THE CONFESSIONS OF THE LUTHERAN CHURCH, IT IS DEEMED UNNECESSARY FOR CHURCH UNITY TO SET UP NEW AND MORE ELABORATE THESES ON THIS ARTICLE OF FAITH.

Paragraph Three: HOWEVER, SINCE IT IS WELL KNOWN THAT IN PRESENTING THE DOCTRINE OF ELECTION TWO FORMS OF DOCTRINE HAVE BEEN USED, BOTH OF WHICH HAVE WON ACCEPTANCE AND RECOGNITION WITHIN THE ORTHODOX LUTHERAN CHURCH:

SOME, IN ACCORDANCE WITH THE FORMULA OF CONCORD, INCLUDE UNDER THE

DOCTRINE OF ELECTION THE WHOLE ORDER OF SALVATION OF THE ELECT FROM THE CALL TO THE GLORIFICATION. . . AND TEACH AN ELECTION "UNTO SALVATION THROUGH THE SANCTIFICATION OF THE SPIRIT AND BELIEF OF THE TRUTH;

WHILE OTHERS, WITH PONTOPPIDAN, IN AGREEMENT WITH JOHN GERHARD, SCRIVER AND OTHER RECOGNIZED TEACHERS OF THE CHURCH, DEFINE ELECTION MORE SPECIFICALLY AS THE DECREE CONCERNING THE FINAL GLORIFICATION, WITH FAITH AND PERSEVERANCE WROUGHT BY THE HOLY SPIRIT AS ITS NECESSARY PRESUP-POSITION, AND TEACH THAT "GOD HAS APPOINTED ALL THOSE TO ETERNAL LIFE WHO HE FROM ETERNITY HAS FORESEEN WOULD ACCEPT THE OFFERED GRACE, BELIEVE IN CHRIST AND REMAIN CONSTANT IN THIS FAITH UNTO THE END:" AND SINCE NEITHER OF THESE TWO FORMS OF DOCTRINE, THUS PRESENTED, CONTRADICTS ANY DOCTRINE REVEALED IN THE WORD OF GOD, BUT DOES FULL JUSTICE TO THE ORDER OF SALVA-TION AS PRESENTED IN THE WORD OF GOD AND THE CONFESSIONS OF THE CHURCH;

WE FIND THAT THIS SHOULD NOT BE CAUSE FOR SCHISM WITHIN THE CHURCH OR DISTURB THAT UNITY OF THE SPIRIT IN THE BOND OF PEACE WHICH GOD'S WILL SHOULD PREVAIL AMONG US.

Thus the *Madison Agreement* or *Opgjør* draws the conclusion that the two forms should not be cause for schisms within the Church or disturb the unity of the spirit in the bond of peace. God's will should prevail.

Paragraph Four: It sets out to soothe ruffled feathers on either side, since charges had been leveled in the past by each against the other: WE HAVE AGREED TO REJECT ALL ERRORS WHICH SEEK TO EXPLAIN AWAY THE MYSTERY OF ELECTION. . . . EITHER IN A SYNERGIZING, OR A CALVINIZING MANNER . . . EVERY DOCTRINE WHICH WOULD DEPRIVE GOD OF HIS GLORY AS ONLY SAVIOR, OR . . . WOULD WEAKEN MAN'S SENSE OF RESPONSIBILITY IN REACTION TO THE ACCEPTANCE OR REJECTION OF GRACE.

Paragraph Five: It rejects the teaching that the cause of the Christian's elec-tion is not solely the mercy of God and the holy merit of Christ, and rejects the teaching that there is a cause in the Christian on account of which God elected him to eternal life. Rejected is the teaching that in electing us, God has taken into account, or has been influenced by, man's good attitude or anything else man is, does, or omits TO DO AS OF HIMSELF AND BY HIS OWN POWERS. Also rejected are the teachings that faith in Christ in connection with the doctrine of election is IN WHOLE OR PART A PRODUCT OF MAN'S CHOICE, POWER OR ABILITY. . .

OR THAT FAITH IS THE RESULT OF AN ABILITY AND POWER IMPARTED BY THE CALL OF GRACE, WHICH THEREFORE NOW DWELL WITHIN AND BELONG TO, THE UNREGEN-ERATE HEART, ENABLING IT TO MAKE A DECISION FOR GRACE.

Paragraph Six: It rejects further the doctrine that God in election acts in an arbitrary and unmotivated way appointing a certain arbitrary number of in-dividuals to conversion and salvation, while all others are excluded.. Also re-jected is the doctrine that there are two kinds of saving will in God, one revealed in Scripture in the general order of salvation, and one that is unknown to man concerning only the elect, treating them with a more cordial love or more powerful call from God and with greater grace than it treats those who remain unbelieving and therefore are lost. Rejected furthermore is the doctrine THAT WHEN THE RESISTANCE WHICH GOD REMOVES IN CONVERSION FROM THE SAVED IS NOT REMOVED FROM THOSE WHO ARE FINALLY LOST, THAT THE CAUSE FOR THIS DIFFERENT RESULT LIES IN GOD AND A DIFFERENT WILL TO SAVE IN HIS ELECTION.

Rejected is the doctrine that the believer can have an absolute assurance of his election and salvation instead of an assurance of faith . . With the possibility of falling away. Finally, rejected are any doctrines which conflict with the doctrine of salvation and would not give to all a full and equally great opportunity to be saved, and which would then conflict with the Word of God which says that God "would have all men to be saved, and to come to the knowledge of the truth," – IN WHICH GRACIOUS AND MERCIFUL WILL OF GOD ALL ELECTION TO ETERNAL LIFE HAS ITS SOURCE.[12]

BASIS FOR MERGER LAID

Following the Opgjør or "Agreement," is a set of resolutions declaring agreement in the doctrine of Salvation as a whole, confessing salvation by grace alone without man's cooperation, and concluding with: WHEREAS, THE DELIBERATIONS OF OUR NEW COMMITTEES HAVE LED TO A SATISFACTORY AGREEMENT OF THAT DOCTRINE OF ELECTION WHICH IS SET FORTH IN ARTICLE XI, PART II OF THE *FORMULA OF CONCORD* AND QUESTION 548 IN PONTOPPIDAN'S *TRUTH UNTO GODLINESS.* . . . ,WE THEREFORE DECLARE HEREBY, THAT THE ESSENTIAL AGREEMENT CONCERNING THESE DOCTRINES WHICH HAS BEEN ATTAINED IS SUFFICIENT FOR CHURCH UNION. . .

Thus the union committees had finally been able to cope with a vexing problem: How to express two opposing viewpoints and allow them to exist side by side, either one to be accepted or rejected by the sides in the controversy without either side in the process refusing the hand of fellowship to the other. To boil it all down: A way had been found to achieve union without complete doctrinal unity, merely by saying that historical usage of two doctrinal statements would presuppose tolerance to each.

Thus the basis for the merger of 1917 was laid, but also laid was the basis for further agonizing on the part of some, who felt that their position remained different from the anti-Missourians in the United Church, and that their position had been compromised by a settlement, which they felt was no settlement. To them, the matters which had divided the Norwegians in the past remained, in fact, unchanged.

CAUSE FOR JUBILATION FOR MANY, BUT CAUSE FOR SADNESS FOR SOME

Those who were in accord with the "Madison Agreement" *Opgjør* were jubilant and rang church bells. Those who were not in accord felt a deep sadness as they watched men who once stood staunchly against the doctrine of Election present in the United Church, now follow the main stream of opinion that the theological battles were finally over, that peace by compromise was better than to remain a divided Church. It appears that what actually happened in the general acceptance of the "Madison Agreement" was the acceptance of a document far from being theologically pure and profound, but a document nonetheless by which each side could save face by accepting it. Hadn't the document laid open to view and condemned teachings which each side had accused the other of harbouring (e.g. synergism on the part of man, and arbitrariness on the part of God)? Prof. E.C. Nelson, writing in 1969, has perhaps captured the mood of the whole matter of the "Agreement" when he states:

THE OPGJØR ITSELF CAN BEST BE DESCRIBED AS THE INSTRUMENT OF AN EC-CLESIASTICAL RAPPROCHEMENT RATHER THAN AS AN ASTUTE AND FLAWLESS DISPLAY OF THEOLOGICAL FINALITY WITH REGARD TO THE DOCTRINE OF ELEC-TION. BOTH SIDES, EAGER FOR UNION AND WEARY OF CONFLICT, SOUGHT DES-PERATELY TO FIND A WAY IN WHICH THEY COULD BE DELIVERED FROM THE CLUTCH OF BITTERNESS AND EACH COULD JOIN THE OTHER WITHOUT GIVING UP HIS OWN VIEWS. IT WAS A CASE OF THE VICTORY OF HEART OVER HEAD . . . MADI-SON WAS NOT A MEETING OF MINDS BUT OF HEARTS. [13]

Theodore Aaberg in *A City Set On a Hill*, points out that prior to the merger of 1917, "The Settlement" (Madison Agreement) was hailed as a document which settled the controversy between the Norwegian Synod and the United Church regarding the doctrine of Election, that it has since been publicly stated that it is instead a compromise. The author quotes from the May 18, 1949 issue of the *Lutheran Herald*: WHEN OUR UNION DOCUMENTS ARE TERMED 'COMPRO-MISES,' THE EXPRESSION IS APT; ONE WILL SEARCH IN VAIN TO FIND THAT ONE PARTY OR ANOTHER 'GAVE IN.' THE NEGOTIATORS SIMPLY LEARNED THAT THE DIFFERENCES WERE NOT BREACHES OF THE UNITY OF THE FAITH, THAT A UNITY OF FAITH HAD, IN FACT, BEEN PRESENT ALL THE TIME. [14]

THE UNION REPORT GOES TO THE SYNODS

On February 22 ,1912, the "Madison Agreement" (Settlement," *Opgjør*) was signed, thus paving the way for union of the Norwegians. There were still some practical problems to be worked out. There were adjustments to be made, in-cluding in the area of doctrine. The leaders of the union movement set the year 1917 as the year for merger as a means to celebrate the 400th anniversary of the Reformation. Only hard driving on their part made the meeting of this deadline possible.

First, the synods themselves had to ratify the action of their union commit-tees. The United Church, in its meeting at Fargo, North Dakota, June 6-12, unanimously accepted the whole union report. This was celebrated by the 6,000 people gathered together by singing, "Now Thank We All Our God." The United Church also accepted the previous union reports on Absolution, Lay Activity in the Church, the Call, and Christian Conversion. This was followed by the res-olution to negotiate for immediate union of the three Norwegian bodies and the election of a new union committee to work out practical problems. Also a committee was formed to negotiate with the Lutheran Free Church, the Eielsen Synod, and the Church of the Lutheran Brethren.

The Hauge's Synod, meeting at Red Wing, Minnesota, also approved the union documents and followed the example of the United Church in electing a new union committee.

Unlike the above mentioned synods, the Norwegian Synod did not have a regular convention in 1912; therefore, its five districts took independent action on the union report. While the districts each unanimously approved the previ-ous committee reports on Absolution, etc., they did not receive the "Madison

Agreement" so enthusiastically. The snag was the acceptance of the doctrine of Election in two forms. President Stub spoke in favor of the "Agreement," emphasizing that the Synod should not ask for more than this.

The five districts of the Synod accepted the "Agreement," but did so on the very emphatic statements by members of the doctrinal committee that the first paragraph of the "Agreement" does not compel the Synod to accept the so-called Second Form (Pontoppidan's) of the doctrine of Election, and that the Norwegian Synod's committee accepts without reservation the First Form of the doctrine as that of Scripture and the Confessions; but can nevertheless recognize as brethren those who hold the Second Form as seen in the light of the subsequent paragraphs of the "Agreement."

The three members of the committee assured the districts that acceptance of paragraph one in no way implied, nor was intended to imply, a yielding up on any point of doctrine at any time officially promulgated by the Synod.

The clarifications was offered, that . . . IN SPITE OF THE DIFFERENCES IN PRESENTATION, EVERYONE SHALL BE FREE TO USE THE FORM WHICH HIS OWN CONVICTION DICTATES WITHIN THE FRAME FIXED BY THE *OPGJØR* ITSELF, WITHOUT ANY STRICTURES ON FELLOWSHIP OR RECOGNITION AS A GOOD LUTHERAN.

It is worthy of note that as the result of discussions within the Norwegian Synod the actual meaning of various statements in the "Agreement" became ever more clear due to the explanations given. Key statements in the "Agreement" became ever more clear due to the explanations given. Key statements in the "Agreement" were purposely written in such a way as to let two sides disagree with one another without letting this disagreement prevent church union.

THE SYNOD COMMITTEE ACCEPTS WITHOUT RESERVATION THE FIRST FORM (*FORMULA OF CONCORD*) OF THE DOCTRINE AS THAT OF THE SCRIPTURES AND THE CONFESSIONS, BUT CAN NEVERTHELESS RECOGNIZE AS BRETHREN IN THE FAITH THOSE WHO HOLD THE SECOND FORM OF DOCTRINE AS SEEN IN THE LIGHT OF THE SUBSEQUENT PARAGRAPH OF *OPGJØR*.

While neither side, it was claimed, was required to accept the doctrinal form of Election of the other side, yet, neither was either side to consider the other side's form of doctrine schismatic.

In the Minnesota District of the Synod, the 209 delegates voted unanimously to accept the "Agreement." Minnesota's action was pretty much followed by the other districts, and the final tally of votes was as follows: 591 voting members and 67 advisory delegates favored the "Madison Agreement." Only 15 delegates opposed it, and a total of 20 abstained from voting. All districts also favored continuing union negotiations with the United Church and the Hauge's Synod.

BUMPS IN THE ROAD TO UNION

At this point the road ,which many thought was being graded smooth, began to show some bumps. The United church did not accept the explanation of matters by the Synod's Union Committee. The United Church's negative reaction was verbalized by Pastor S. Gunderson, who termed the questions whether faith may or may not be called a cause of election "hair-splitting," and declared that there was no man who could give the final word in this matter. This, of course, cut deeply and reopened old wounds. The Norwegian Synod had clearly accepted the "Agreement," determining that its old stand was not jeopardized. That stand had always been that faith is not the cause but the result of election in man. A movement was begun by a few professors of the Synod to delay action on the "Agreement" until this latest development could be cleared up.

However, President Stub–himself a member of the Union Committee–spoke out at the 1913 convention against the tactics of the Minority, saying in effect that it was in the hands of the doctrinal committee, not anyone else's hands, to clear up what difficulties remained. In spite of the fact that there was clear-cut evidence of disharmony between the committees of the two synods, he nevertheless tried to affect some kind of alliance between the two Norwegian bodies. Stub pressed for alliance even though the Synodical Conference, when approached in 1912 with the "Agreement" did not endorse the document, but rather elected a committee to meet with the Norwegian Synod in order to foster some changes. Criticism by the Synodical Conference closely matched those of the Minority in the Synod. For the next eight years, the Synodical Conference sought a hearing with the Synod but without success. President Stub was not interested in pursuing the matter, but instead had the attitude that the members of the Synod desired and needed peace and rest.

The Minority within the Synod became an organized force, whose goal was to defer union until the changes they felt where needed in the "Agreement" were indeed made. The recognized leaders of the Minority were Prof. C.K. Preus (Luther college) and Pastor I.B. Torrison (Decorah, Iowa).

In September 1912 the three new Union Committees met in joint session. There was, however, a difference of opinion as to what was to be accomplished. Both the United Church and the Hauge's Synod looked on the task as that of discussing organic union. The Norwegian Synod's committee was not empowered to enter union negotiations. In fact, the German theologians in the Synodical Conference had begun their attack on *Opgjør*, with the result that the Norwegian Synod was already facing a division of feelings within its ranks for the reason that many respected the Missouri Synod theologians and what they had to say on the matter. Dr. Stub felt he had to proceed with extreme caution in fostering the union movement, fearing that quick action might bring about a reaction in the Synod unfavourable to the union cause.

UNREST IN THE NORWEGIAN SYNOD OVER THE "MADISON AGREEMENT" (*OPGJØR*)

The unrest that had now risen in the Synod due to attacks upon its action of accepting the "Agreement" caused an extraordinary Convention to be called by the Church Council. The Synodical Conference had requested the following of the Synod: (1) to eliminate the coordination of the First and Second Forms in the "Agreement" (only the First Form was acceptable to the Synod); (2) to reject from paragraph five the following; "that the cessation of wilful resistance either through natural or imparted power, afforded an explanation of the mystery of predestination;" and (3) to begin a discussion with the Synodical Conference of Conversion and Election, the aim being to strengthen the ties of fellowship which had united the Norwegian Synod and the Synodical Conference.

Literary attacks against the "Agreement" came from both the Wisconsin and Missouri Synods' publications. Circulated in the Synod among those not in agreement with the "Agreement" was a document titled, "The Petition," which, though at first published anonymously, was later revealed to be the work of three of Stub's colleagues on the seminary faculty. The "Petition" was not aimed at destroying the union movement, but at cautioning that true union must be based on unity of faith. The authors proceeded to set down documentary evidence to show the disunity which yet remained between the Synod and the other side. Included was also what amounted to be a charge of "unionism" against the United Church, which fellowshiped with "opponents" of the Norwegian Synod. The document was presented at the 1913 meeting of the Synod. Dr. Stub, however, openly attacked it and its formulators.

The "Petition" did, however, manage to rally some supporters to the Minority cause. When the vote was finally taken, 394 favored adoption of the Majority report, which favored adoption of the suggestion of the joint committee to empower it to work for organic union of the three bodies. The Minority report reminded the delegates of the unsettled state of affairs in the Synod which must be clarified before the Union Committee could be given the task of negotiating a union.

The Synod's next step was to submit the Majority report to the congregations for approval. This was done, and overwhelming approval was forthcoming. But the Minority did not remain silent. Encouraged by the Wisconsin and Missouri Synods, they mounted a vigorous attack against the "Agreement."

WORKING OUT THE ARTICLES OF UNION

Before the joint meeting of the Union Committees, Dr. Stub met with Dr. Kildahl of the United Church and together they drafted a "Declaration" to overcome the objections which had been raised in the Synod against the "Agreement." This "Declaration" was unanimously accepted. The Joint Committee later went on to construct the framework for the union. A document consisting of nineteen articles of the union was drawn up and studied. These rules bound the participants to full acceptance of the Confessions of the Norwegian Church. Acceptance of the "Agreement" and earlier agreements was made mandatory for the union of the Norwegian Churches, while unionism with the Reformed Churches and others who did not accept the Norwegian Confessions was denied.

More practical issues having to do with church rites and ceremonies were also outlined. The Church was given the authority to choose the "most serviceable" ceremonies, but also authority was granted to use rites which conformed with Scripture and were honored by long usage. The liturgy of the Church of Norway was recommended. Public confession and absolution was to be administered according to congregational jurisdiction. Laying on of hands or general absolution was safeguarded. Lay activity (conducting prayer meetings and awakenings, use of individual spiritual gifts, proclaiming God's Word in public assembly) was safeguarded also.

The school question was settled by the stipulation that one seminary would be operated, two normal schools, and two senior colleges. Permission was granted for the individual synods to continue other schools, each bearing their own expenses unless the schools came under the supervision of the Church. Publishing houses would be consolidated into a single institution, which in fact became the Augsburg Publishing House. Pension funds and publications also were to be consolidated.

THE SYNODS' REACTION TO THE ARTICLES OF UNION

When the nineteen articles were studied by the three synods, they met with vigorous debate and questioning, especially the article having to do with unionism. It is evident that there was a feeling in the United Church not to let the article on unionism be too restrictive. In 1915 this body adopted the Constitution proposed for the merger, and when it met in June 1916 fervor for the merger resulted in the shortest meeting in its history. All that was left for the United Church to do was to approve the enabling acts—which it did unanimously—and to appoint a committee for implementing the practical matters involved in the union.

The Hauge's Synod, in 1915, referred the constitution, as well as the Articles of the Union, to its congregations, asking them to empower their delegates to act conclusively on both documents at the Annual Convention in 1916. When this synod met, its convention turned out to be more lively than that of the United Church. By then a Minority group opposing union had developed in the Hauge's Synod, as well as the Norwegian Synod. The thing that bothered the Minority was that the true "spirit" of Haugeanism would be quenched. Of the 117 congregations, only sixty-four—a little more than half—voted unconditionally in favor of the union. An "Interpretation," which presented the Haugean view on certain portions of the Articles of Union and the constitution, was given and this mollified a considerable number of delegates who had expressed reservations. Thus schism was avoided. The three enabling acts were then approved by large majorities, and a committee appointed to meet with the two other bodies to make final preparations for the union.

In 1914 the Norwegian Synod met in Convention at Sioux Falls, South Dakota. President Stub did what he could to refute the stand of the Minority and to prove the position expressed in the "Agreement" was the same which the Synod had expressed back in the 1880's. President Stub was clearly pushing for union with the Hauge's Synod and the United Church. The committee presented its Articles of Union, which were adopted 360 and 170. A peace committee was also formed to tackle the problem of division in the Synod's ranks. The laymen at this convention spoke overwhelmingly in favor of the union.

In 1915 the Norwegian Synod held a special convention in San Francisco. At this meeting an atmosphere of peace prevailed. The resolutions of the committee and the constitution for the new church body were read but not discussed.

Things were still stirring in the Norwegian Synod by the time of its 1916

Convention held in Minneapolis. A different atmosphere hovered over the assembly. The battle lines between the Majority and the Minority were clearly drawn. In the meanwhile President Stub circularized the Synod with a long pamphlet in which he attacked the critics of the "Agreement" and the proposed church union which was to be consummated on the basis of matters as they then stood. The Minority did not remain silent but offered their own pamphlet "An Answer to the Rebukes." Futhermore, at the convention one of the Minority leaders presented a substitute motion calling for several changes to be made in the "Agreement" and it also asked the United Church and the Hauge's Synod to make the same changes. These men asked that adoption of the new constitution be deferred until the requirements stated in the Minority motion were met. This substitute motion of the Minority was tabled and the motion was called which set forth the three-point proposal of the Convention Committee on Union Matters. When it was all over, the Minority had clearly lost in their bid to keep the merger from taking place without first bringing about a meeting of minds on the doctrine of Election.

The proposed constitution for the new merger body was adopted by this 1916 Convention. The proposal carried to enable the Synod to form a union with the United Church in the event the Hauge's Synod declined to participate in the merger. The proposal also carried to provide for the incorporation of the merging bodies and to turn over all of the Synod's property to the new organization. The Majority had spoken!

The Minority, however, made it clear in a statement at the convention that they could not with clear conscience enter the new church body before the required corrections were made in the document (the "Agreement") which served as the doctrinal basis. The Minority also served notice that they regarded the Synod as a body that would continue its existence if the difficulties could not be removed. There would be enough congregations which would remain in the Synod "so that it will be able to live and assert its great principle: 'The Word Alone and Grace Alone'." At an earlier convention, the Minority had already expressed the opinion that for them to accept the Articles of Union would infer the existence of unity of doctrine.

The Peace Committee which had been appointed never accomplished its aims. By the time it made its report, the union matter had already been disposed of: union of the Norwegian Synod with the other two had been assured by an overwhelming majority vote.

SMALL SYNODS WHICH CHOSE TO
BE LEFT OUT OF THE MERGER

Meanwhile, the United Church's meetings with the Lutheran Free Church were unsuccessful in the bid to reestablish old fellowships. The United Church proposed that both sides forgive and forget the past circumstances of the Augsburg controversy. The Free Church insisted, however, that the United Church admit that it acted in an unjust and unChristian manner in the controversy which centered in the Augsburg Seminary; and it listed five points of misconduct by the United Church.

In its approach to the Eielsen Synod and the Lutheran Brethren, the United Church met with refusals to negotiate a union. The Brethren even went so far as to point out that differences in congregational principles made a union impossible.

REVERSAL BY A MAJORITY OF THE MINORITY
IN THE NORWEGIAN SYNOD

Strange things were yet to happen in the Norwegian Synod by the time the merger took place. When 1917, the appointed year, came along, the Minority were not as consolidated as was thought. In fact, most of them were discovered assembling in St. Paul Auditorium alongside the Majority of the Synod and the delegates of the United Church and the Hauge's Synod. They were there in order to consummate the long awaited merger. Stranger still was the fact that this merger was affected without the merger synods giving in on any of the points requested by the Minority of the Synod. What caused this reversal by so many of the Minority of the Synod?

It was the Joint Union Committee which, after the 1916 Convention of the Synod, successfully negotiated with the Minority so that the opposition to the union greatly dwindled by the time set for the merger—a year hence. A series of meetings were held between the Minority and the Joint Committee of the three bodies. The Minority had hoped to move the Joint Committee to do what it had not been able to move the bodies to do, thereby securing the changes in the "Agreement" that must be changed if they were to join the merger, and that these were conscience matters. C.I. Preus and I.B. Torrison—the first a professor, and the latter a pastor—were leaders of the Minority. The Joint Committee appointed a new subcommittee to negotiate with these men, with the result that in a meeting held in Austin, Minnesota, in 1916, a new agreement called the "Austin Settlement" was drafted.

The events which transpired took a strange route. The "Austin Settlement" did not settle the issue raised by the Minority and this was due especially to a note appended by the Joint Committee to it. The note stated: IT IS SELF-EVIDENT THAT THE ABOVE STATED RESOLUTION MUST NOT BE INTERPRETED TO MEAN THAT "OPGJØR" AS THE BASIS FOR THE UNION BETWEEN THE THREE CONTRACTING CHURCHES, IS THEREBY ABBREVIATED OR CHANGED.[15] The synods passed a resolution recognizing the three reservations to the "Agreement" held by Preus and Torrison. This resolution declared that there was nothing in their request contrary to Scripture and that the position taken in their document constituted a sufficient expression of the unity of faith. Still, the "Agreement" was not to be considered abridged or altered! In effect, the "Austin Settlement" left matters the way they were! It seems that the Majority of the Synod together with the Joint Committee, were unwilling to back away in any degree from the "Agreement."

If merger was to be effected, it would be done on the basis of the proposal of the Joint Committee and not on the basis of any "concession" made to the Minority within the Synod. The issue that remained unresolved was that unregenerate man has a feeling of duty or "responsibility in relation to the acceptance or rejection of grace." The Minority had claimed all along that unregenerate man is suffering from spiritual deadness and therefore cannot experience such a sense of responsibility.

In order to seek counsel of the Missouri brethren, a trip was made to St. Louis regarding the "Austin Settlement." Later, in January 1917, a meeting of the Minority was held at the West Hotel in Minneapolis, and a letter from the Missouri brethren stated that they could not advise anyone to enter the new body, but advised the Minority to remain in the Synod for the present and testify.[16] An invitation had been extended to the Minority by the Joint Union Committee to join the merger. During the meeting at the West Hotel, most of the Minority members present decided to accept the invitation. Strangely enough, in accepting the invitation, no claim could be made of any ground gained by their recommendations to the Joint Committee. Rather, the invitation was accepted on the basis that the Joint Committee in its invitation to the Minority had acknowledged their attitude and found nothing therein to contradict Scripture. This, in spite of the fact that the Minority could not accept certain statements in either the "Madison Agreement" or the "Austin Settlement."

The whole history of the negotiations of the Minority of the Synod with the Joint Committee and the subcommittee is one fraught with confusion and shrouded in fog. It is the story of a group of men trying to be faithful to Scripture and attempting to keep peace with their own consciences, while determined, if at all possible, to be included in a merger that would bring together a large segment of Norwegian Lutherans. The overall feeling which was evident since 1912 in the United Church had become the feeling of the greater portion of the Norwegian Synod (and even most of the Minority of the Synod)— the feeling expressed in these words: "You have your position on the doctrines of the Election and Conversion, and I have mine. I'll recognize the true doctrine as being stated in your terms and you recognize the true doctrine as being stated also in my terms. Neither side shall accuse the other side of heresy." Strong doctrinal stands were replaced with a willingness to make concessions. Emotions finally gained the upper hand. In the long run, it was a matter of agreeing to disagree without being disagreeable, in order to unite the greater portion of the Norwegian Lutherans.

An important factor in the about-face of some of the opposition to merger on the basis of the "Madison Agreement" was this: Minority pastors found that the people in the pews did not necessarily back them in opposing the union. In fact enthusiasm for the union was running high among them. As a result of the pressure mounting in their parishes for union, and their own positions in their parishes becoming untenable, not a few Minority pastors found themselves actually on the side of the union when the merger came.

CONCESSION TO THE HAUGE'S SYNOD

Even as token concession was made to the Minority of the Synod, so token concession had to be made to a Minority group within the Hauge's Synod. The concession amounted to accepting the Haugean Minority's 1916 "Explanation" as a condition of their joining the body. The United Church unanimously allowed the "Explanation." The Norwegian Synod did so only with the understating that it was not committed to an approval of the "Explanation," and at the same time the Synod declared its right to witness against the practices enumerated in the Haugeans' "Explanation." (This "Explanation" or Interpretation presented the Haugean view on certain portions of the Articles of Union and the Constitution so as to assure the continuation of the "spirit" of Haugeanism.)

THE NORWEGIAN LUTHERAN CHURCH OF AMERICA AND THE NORWEGIAN SYNOD OF THE AMERICAN EVANGELICAL LUTHERAN CHURCH

MERGING THE NORWEGIAN SYNOD, THE UNITED NORWEGIAN LUTHERAN CHURCH, THE HAUGE'S SYNOD INTO THE NORWEGIAN LUTHERAN CHURCH OF AMERICA

On June 8, 1917 the three synods completed their separate affairs and voted themselves out of existence. The following day the three became the Norwegian Lutheran Church of America. The delegates from the three synods met early on Saturday morning at St. Paul Armory and marched together to St. Paul Auditorium. It was indeed a spectacular occasion as thousands of people crowded into the auditorium to celebrate the merger and begin the business of the new body. Dr. H. G. Stub was elected President, J.N. Kildahl, Vice-president, N.H. Lohre, Secretary, and Erick Waldeland, Treasurer. The following were the presidents of the Norwegian Lutheran Church in America until it became a part of the merger which created The American Lutheran Church in 1960: H.G. Stub 1917-25; J.A. Aasgaard 1925-54; F.A. Schiotz 1954-60 (In 1960 Dr. Schiotz was elected to his first six-year term as president of TALC.)

SOCIAL ORGANIZATION

The new synod was divided into districts, and districts into circuits. Conventions were to be held every three years. Officers: (listed above). The official board was the Church Council, consisting of the general president, the district presidents, and one layman from each district. Other boards were provided for supervision of various aspects of the church's work.

WHAT HAPPENED TO THE SMALL REMAINING MINORITY OF THE NORWEGIAN SYNOD?

The resolutions drafted by the Joint Committee dealing with the Minority in the Synod were adopted by all three bodies, thus paving the way for the Minority pastors to be a part of the merger. This, however, did not completely silence the opposition to union. A small group of the Minority chose to remain out of the merger and to continue the legal existence of the Norwegian Synod.

The group met at the Aberdeen Hotel in St. Paul in 1917 at the same time the union convention was being held. Upon learning that the Norwegian Synod could not be legally perpetuated, the forty pastors and laymen made the decision to begin a new synod, yet voicing the conviction that their organization is actually a continuation of the old Norwegian Synod. Moral support came from the Synodical Conference for their bold venture. The next year, on June 14, this small remnant of the once large and vocal Minority of the Synod organized the Norwegian Synod of the American Evangelical Lutheran Church. Later, the name was simplified to the Evangelical Lutheran Synod (ELS). See the separate chapter reviewing the history of this Lutheran body.

THE WORK OF THE NORWEGIAN
LUTHERAN CHURCH OF AMERICA

PUBLICATIONS

In the merger of 1917, three separate publishing houses owned by the merging bodies were combined to form a single operation, the Augsburg Publishing House, located in Minneapolis, Minnesota. At first most printing was done in Norwegian, but eventually the mother tongue gave way to English. By the time The American Lutheran Church (TALC) was established in 1960, the Augsburg Publishing House ranked sixth in volume of printing among thirty-six Protestant publishing concerns. The *Lutheran Herald* was the official publication. Augsburg has been a major publisher, not only of Sunday School materials, but also of music for churches. In 1958 Augsburg published the new *Lutheran Service Book* and *Hymnal*, a joint project of eight Lutheran bodies.

EDUCATION

"Parochial" schools were in the form of summer schools and weekend schools based on release time from public institutions. Emphasis in the Norwegian Lutheran Church of America was on college education. The church maintained the following list of colleges and seminary at the time of the 1960 merger creating The American Lutheran Church: Augustana College- Sioux Falls, South Dakota; Concordia College – Moorhead, Minnesota; Luther College – Decorah, Iowa; Pacific Lutheran University – Tacoma (Parkland), Washington; St. Olaf College – Northfield, Minnesota; Luther Theological Seminary – St. Paul, Minnesota.

HOME MISSIONS

In *The Lutheran Church Among Norwegian-Americans*, Volume 2, author E. Clifford Nelson lists distinct periods of home mission activity. It would be beneficial to summarize them. Before 1917, the main mission thrust was toward winning and holding the Norwegian immigrants for the American version

307

of the religion of Norway. In this respect it is of interest to note that a large number of Norwegian-Americans did not hold membership in a church. T.H. Dahl is reported to have advanced the figure of 1,000,000 such non-churched Norwegians. So the task of work within the "camp" was a formidable one. The home mission work was aimed at those Americans within the "Norwegian culture."

The mission period following the 1917 merger extended from 1917 to 1930 and is titled by Nelson, "Expansion Under a Cultural Pattern." This period closely resembled the pre-merger period. Congregations were built on a Norwegian cultural basis. The prospects for growth were determined from the Norwegian immigrants or their sons and daughters. Under "missions" were included quite a few various services. Home missions included the work ordinarily termed as such, but also included work in the slums, hospitals, prisons, as well as work among the seamen, the deaf and the immigrants. Many Norwegian immigrants arrived in the 1920's and these were the welcomed by the "Norway House" or Immigrant Mission in Brooklyn. Evangelistic services were conducted in the congregations for "saving" the church members. These employed traveling evangelists. This was, of course, reminiscent of Haugeanism. Also characteristic of the first period were large expenditures of money for home missions so that the church entered the depression years in debt.

The second period was from 1930 to 1944 and was termed "The Stern Years." Mission spending was drastically reduced and programs sharply curtailed. And what programs there were, were financed in a "pay as you go" manner. A new emphasis was laid on outreach to the unchurched Lutherans. The Norwegian Lutheran Church of America joined in 1932 with the American Lutheran Church, the Augustana Synod, the Lutheran Free Church, the Suomi Synod the United Danish Church and the United Lutheran Church in America in organizing the Lutheran Home Mission Council of America. The Council was organized especially for the purpose of bringing more orderliness into Lutheran home mission work and to aid in avoiding "needless competition and duplication of efforts." Here then was a break with strictly Norwegian culture, and a step toward a more Americanized Norwegian Church.

The third period was from 1944 to 1954 and is titled: "Operation New Church: Radical But..." Radical innovations in mission work were introduced into the Church. The rapid shift of population at the height of the War years called for more concerted efforts on the part of the Church. Resolutions were adopted calling for a full-time executive secretary and regional directors. When this new plan was expedited an increase in new congregations was felt the first year. Included in the new policy was a quick and complete financing of new projects in the way of loans. Under this plan, the field was surveyed and a successful parish pastor called. A parsonage was purchased, together with minimum equipment including bulletins, typewriter, and communion set. Visits were made in the area and church services were organized; hopefully leading to formal organization of a congregation. Nelson reports: "Under this plan almost phenomenal results occurred. Twenty new churches were organized in 1945, twenty-two the next (one in 17 days)." Backing the plan was a large Church Extension Fund. Later, the sponsoring of new congregations by established congregations was inaugurated. Also a plan for parish evangelism was introduced with concerted evangelism efforts being made at the congregational level and by multiple congregations (Preaching-Teaching-Reaching program).[17]

FOREIGN MISSIONS

The Norwegians' love for and interest in, foreign mission was deeply rooted in their history. This feeling was transplanted to America along with the Norwegian Lutheran Church. Foreign mission work of the individual merger synods became the general body's immediate concern, with fields in operation in China, Madagascar, and South Africa. Besides making China and Madagascar its responsibility, the new body supported the Union Lutheran Theological Seminary near Hankow, together with the Augustana Synod and the Norwegian and Finnish Societies (European). After World War II and the Communist takeover of 1949, the Norwegians, together with other participating bodies, were forced to leave the Lutheran Church of China in the hands of the Chinese themselves.

In Madagascar the Norwegians also entered upon a cooperative venture with other Lutherans in maintaining a seminary. Later, an independent church, the Malagasy Lutheran Church was formed in 1950. In 1957 it became a member of the Lutheran World Federation.

In 1917 the Norwegian Lutheran Church of America also took under its wing the Schrueder mission in Zululand, South Africa, providing it with missionaries and money. It took control of the mission ten years later.

In 1943 the Norwegians began a mission in South America and two years later took over an independent Lutheran mission (Celmosa Mission) in Columbia, South America. For many years—until 1945—the NCLA had been influenced by the Lutheran Church in Norway. But then came the beginning of the independent outreach. Missions were begun in Hong Kong (1949) and Formosa (1950). A Japan mission was begun in 1949.

FOREIGN MISSIONS – COOPERATION WITH OTHERS

In the South American Mission, the NLCA cooperated with the United (Danish) Evangelical Lutheran Church. In the Formosa Mission it cooperated with seven other American and European missionary groups. The Japan Mission was a cooperative venture with the Lutheran Free Church and later with the Japanese Evangelical Lutheran Church (ULCA and UELCA).

In the 1950's the NLCA also expanded into the French Camerouns and Equatorial Africa and Brazil (1958).

The emphasis in the NLCA's foreign mission program was toward the formation of indigenous (national) churches which are autonomous and self-supporting.

INNER MISSIONS - WORKS OF CHARITY

From the time of its founding in 1917, the NLCA carried on institutional social welfare. A Board of Charities was implemented. Chaplains were established in institutions for the mentaly ill and those in prisons. Work was carried on among the deaf, with the immigrants and the seamen, as has already been mentioned under Home Missions. Professional training of social workers was undertaken early in the history of the synod. In 1952 Luther Theological Seminary established a program to provide theoretical and clinical training for institutional chaplains. Providing aid for the aged became an integral part of the work of the Board of Charities, using also Federal Aid under the Hill-Burton legislation. By 1958 there were twenty-nine homes for the aged operating within the NLCA.

SPECIAL ORGANIZATIONS

For Women: The Women's Missionary Federation, Lutheran Daughters of the Reformation (for business and professional women).
For Men: The Brotherhood of the Evangelical Lutheran Church.
For Youth: The Young People's Luther League.

THE NAME IS CHANGED

An early move to drop the word "Norwegian" from the official name met defeat. Still, by 1930 the trend toward English was definitely established and by the end of the 1940's was about complete. At the Convention in 1946 the name of the synod was changed to the Evangelical Lutheran Church (ELC). A Norwegian Conference was begun two years later to soothe the small Minority who were resisting the change from Norwegian to English, and who also resented the action of dropping the word "Norwegian" from the official title.

THE NORWEGIAN LUTHERAN CHURCH OF AMERICA AND OTHER LUTHERANS

THE NATIONAL LUTHERAN COUNCIL
(Organized September 6, 1919)

The NLCA helped in the formation of the Council in 1918. Thus the newly merged Norwegian body found itself in a common agency which was formed to assist nine Lutheran Bodies. Participating were: the General Council*, the General Synod*, the Joint Synod of Ohio, the Synod of Iowa and Other States, the Augustana Synod, the Norwegian Lutheran Church of America, The Norwegian Free Church, the Danish Lutheran Church, and the United Synod

South*. This cooperative agency was formed for the following purposes: to give help in the field of Lutheran statistics, Lutheran Church publicity, awareness of areas needing attention and action, to organize activities to deal with problems arising out of war and other emergencies, to help solve problems affecting religious life and consciousness, to foster true Christian loyalty and to emphasize right relation between Church and State.

The first president and secretary of the Council were men of the NLCA: Dr. H.G. Stub and Dr. Lauritz Larsen, respectively. The Council brought the Norwegians into contact with other Lutheran Bodies and Lutheran culture. The member synods of the Synodical Conference did not participate in the Council. The Synodical Conference emphasized full agreement in doctrine and practice even for cooperation among Lutherans. The Council did not share this attitude, and finally accepted into membership the liberal United Lutheran Church in America (org. 1918). Thus the Norwegians found themselves in cooperation with a Lutheran body of whose theology and practice it was suspicious. This was a cause of uneasiness among the Norwegians.

Upon a request of Dr. Stub, a Joint Committee on Doctrine and Practice was formed, whose membership comprised the presidents of the National Lutheran Council bodies. This committee met in March 1919 in Chicago. Doctrinal papers were presented. Certain articles in Dr. Stub's paper subsequently came to be known as the "Chicago Theses." The papers by Dr. Stub and two other synod presidents (Knubel and Jacobs) did much to lay the ground work for things to come. Meanwhile, however, an element in the Norwegian Lutheran Church of America, were especially men of the former Norwegian Synod, were critical of that body's participation in the National Lutheran Council. The more liberal members of the Council wanted a declaration to come out of the Joint Committee that would define "a catholic spirit" which would allow for cooperation of the churches without the settlement of past doctrinal differences which Stub's "Chicago Theses" enumerated.

At the second meeting of the Joint Committee on Doctrine and Practice early in 1920, a paper bearing the signatures of C. M. Jacobs and Dr. F. H. Knubel, and having to do with the "essentials of catholic spirit," had been recast from an earlier paper by Knubel. The original paper had been read at the first meeting but not discussed for lack of time. This paper became known as the "Washington Declaration." While Stub's theses were found acceptable to the Missouri Synod, Stub himself voiced objections to the Knubel-Jacobs paper. For one thing, their paper went too far in pressing the matter of catholicity, for it went outside the boundaries of Lutheranism. (This catholicity, about which the Norwegians were apprehensive, ultimately became the very spirit of the Lutheran World Federation.) The Norwegian Lutheran Church of America was bound by its Articles of Union to refrain from churchly cooperation with non-Lutherans.

The Lutherans in the Midwest, including the Norwegians, were becoming more and more suspicious of the United Lutheran Church in America, fearing that this body was pressing for something contrary to their wishes. There was also a feeling that the ULC and the Midwestern Lutherans did not agree on the question of lodge membership (how lodge members should be dealt with), and the practice of unionism (churchly cooperation with non-Lutherans).

As a result, in 1920 there came about a theological division within the National Lutheran Council. One side rallied around Stub's "Chicago Theses," while the other side rallied around the "Washington Declaration." We want to bear in mind that when the National Lutheran Council was begun in 1918 the Norwegian Lutheran Church of America had not given its full sanction to membership in the organization (which membership had been the action of the synod presidents). And there was some apprehension on Dr. Stub's part that full acceptance of membership by the NLCA would not be forthcoming due to the liberal view held by the eastern Lutherans regarding cooperation among church bodies and the practice of unionism. Thus Dr. Stub had to convince the districts of the NLCA that the cooperation involved as a member of the National Lutheran Council would only be of an external sort, not involving cooperation in a churchly sense.

The NLCA finally did approve membership in the National Lutheran Council after much debate and without examining or accepting Dr. Stub's "Chicago Theses." Reservations were made, however, in that the NLCA's participation in the Council's activities would be under full control of the Church and that action would be taken between church meetings only by the advice of the Church Council. The NLCA also declared that its participation in the Council did not mean that it "has acknowledged the doctrinal position and practice of the church bodies with which it has been connected."

Out of the relief program to help overseas Lutherans, came the Lutheran World Convention in 1923, which the NLCA helped sponsor.

As the twenties wore on, the NLCA began to draw away from the United Lutheran Church in America and closer to the Joint Synod of Ohio and the Iowa Synod. Suspicions as to the ULCA's stand on the question of the Inerrancy of the Scriptures contributed a great deal to the Norwegians' negative feelings toward that body. The Midwest Lutherans felt that it wasn't sufficient to speak only of "the supreme importance of the Word of God" and of "the authority of Scripture... the only rule and standard by which all doctrines and teachers are to be judged." They felt that it was imperative that a statement be adopted putting forth the verbal Inspiration and Inerrancy of Scripture. And so the Midwest Norwegians were aligning themselves more and more with the Midwest Germans and withdrawing from eastern Lutheranism. Nelson speaks of both cooperation and a "cold war" being carried on in the Council.[18]

RELATIONS WITH THE LUTHERAN WORLD CONVENTION AND THE LUTHERAN WORLD FEDERATION

A SUMMARY

1919- Dr. John A. Moorhead, chairman of the European Commission of the National Lutheran Council urgently requests the Council to consider leading the way in forming a world federation of Lutheran Churches.

1920- Morehead, Stolie, and Larsen make formal recommendations that the holding of an international free Lutheran conference be arranged for.

1921- The National Lutheran Council appoints an American Committee. Dr. C. M. Jacobs (ULCA) is made the chairman. The purpose is to plan for a world congress of Lutherans and issue the call for such a meeting.

1923- The first meeting of the Lutheran World Convention is held at Eisenach, Germany. Several leaders of the NLCA (Stub, Larsen, Stolee, Boe) had done much to direct the work of the National Lutheran Council to help the suffering Lutherans of devastated Europe after World War I. Dr. Stub is sent by the NLCA to the World Convention, and preaches the opening sermon of the congress. There was no "membership" in the Lutheran World Convention. It remained a "free conference." Dr. Boe represented the NLCA until 1942.

1940- The outbreak of World War II prevents the Convention from meeting in Philadelphia.

1946- The Lutheran World Convention is revived and drafts a constitution for a new body to be known as the Lutheran World Federation.

1947- The Evangelical Lutheran Church (ELC)—until 1946 known as the Norwegian Lutheran Church of America—is represented at Lund, Sweden at the first meeting of the Convention, and through its delegates becomes affiliated with the newly organized Lutheran World Federation. The Evangelical Lutheran Church neither ratifies nor repudiates the membership. Actually, ELC men were strong supporters of the Federation by serving in official capacities. Nelson makes this observation: IN FACT, PERHAPS NO OTHER AMERICAN LUTHERAN GROUP HAS HAD PROPORTIONATELY SUCH A LARGE NUMBER OF ITS MEMBERS ACTIVELY ENGAGED IN THE PROGRAM OF THE LUTHERAN WORLD FEDERATION. UNQUESTIONABLY MUCH OF THIS INTEREST HAS BEEN A FRUIT OF THE FORTHRIGHT ADVOCACY OF LUTHERAN COOPERATION AND UNITY AT HOME AND ABROAD BY L.W. BOE.[19]

THE AMERICAN LUTHERAN CONFERENCE - 1930

The Norwegian Lutheran Church of America found in the German Lutherans of the Ohio and Iowa synods a people they could consider orthodox brothers, without going to what they considered to be the extreme orthodoxy of the Wisconsin and Missouri Synods. Ohio's president invited the NLCA's new president, J.A. Aasgaard in 1925 to participate in a joint conference to discuss a doctrinal basis for fellowship between the Joint Synod of Ohio, the Iowa Synod, the Buffalo Synod, and the NLCA. In Minneapolis on November 18, 1925, this historic meeting of synods was held. A set of theses which incorporated Stub's "Chicago Theses," and which became known as the "Minneapolis Theses," was formulated. An interesting feature was that it spelled out areas of concern regarding the United Lutheran Church in America on three points. These were: (1) Inspiration and Inerrancy of Scripture, (2) unionism, and (3) lodgism (stating that pastors who have affiliated themselves with any anti-Christian society should not be tolerated). These points were back of the hand slap at the ULCA.

The Minneapolis Colloquy, which resulted in accord among the conferees, resulted also in further outreach to the Augustana Synod, the United Danish Church, and the Lutheran Free Church. A constitution was drafted, and in Minneapolis, on October 29-31,1930, the American Lutheran Conference was organized, affording pulpit and altar fellowship among the following National Lutheran Church bodies: the American Lutheran Church (formed the same year, 1930, by a merger of the German synods of Ohio, Iowa, and Buffalo), The Augustana (Swedish) Synod, the Lutheran Free Church, the Norwegian Lutheran Church of America, and the United Danish Lutheran Church. There would be cooperation in the areas of home mission, inner missions, student service, foreign missions, publications, and exchange of theological professors. Nelson makes the observation that a step had been made toward ultimate Lutheran union, and on the other hand, the Missouri Synod had received persuasion that true Lutheranism was still alive outside of the Synodical conference.[20]

In the minds of the officialdom of the various synods, the formation of the American Lutheran Conference provided a protective league overagainst other Lutherans (for example, the liberal United Lutheran Church in America). Another interesting note is that anti-Missourianism that once was a force to reckon with, had by this time given way to the feeling that Missourianism was orthodox Lutheranism. Meanwhile, the ULCA felt miffed that it had been excluded, and exception was taken to the "Minneapolis Theses." The Theses bore witness that the United Lutheran Church in America was seriously deficient on the issues of Inspiration of Scriptures, the Lutheran Confessions, fellowship with other churches, and its attitude toward secret religious societies.[21]

FURTHER UNITY EFFORTS

In the decade that followed the formation of the American Lutheran Conference, the Norwegian Lutheran Church of America did not occupy itself as others did, in furthering Lutheran unity. It had too many problems of its own, for the 1930's were physically hard and difficult years, due to the country's unfavorable economic condition.

Together with other synods, including those outside the American Lutheran Conference (the Wisconsin Synod and the Norwegian Evangelical Synod) the NLCA declined the invitation by the United Lutheran Church to join in union discussions. The United Lutheran Church had hoped that such discussions could be held on the basis of its adoption of the "Savannah Declaration" by which it reaffirmed its adherence to Scripture and the Lutheran Confessions. The Missouri Synod and the American Lutheran Church did, however, respond to the invitation.

The ensuing discussions ended between the Missouri Synod and the United Lutheran Church when an impasse was reached over the old question which plagued that body, namely, Verbal Inspiration of Scripture. The "Baltimore Declaration" was found unacceptable to the Missouri Synod and discussions were ended. (The Baltimore Declaration, 1938, is a "Declaration of the Word

314

of God and the Scripture.") Missouri found it lacking as a clear presentation of the doctrine of the Verbal Inspiration of Scripture. The American Lutheran Church, however, continued negotiations with the United Lutheran Church in spite of the fact that the Norwegians could see evidence of liberalism in that body. Through a series of meetings, the American Lutheran Church became convinced that the United Lutheran Church accepted Verbal Inspiration, a conclusion not shared in the more orthodox quarters of Lutheranism. The United Lutheran Church's position that "… by virtue of a unique operation of the Holy Ghost… by which He supplied to the holy writers content and fitting word, the separate books of the Bible are related to one another, and taken together, constitute a complete errorless, unbreakable whole, of which Christ is the Center," was untenable to the Wisconsin and Missouri Synods as an acceptable statement of the true doctrine of Verbal Inspiration and Inerrancy of Scripture.

Neither union nor pulpit and altar fellowship resulted from the joint adoption of a document in 1940 by the American Lutheran Church and the United Lutheran Church, called the "Pittsburgh Agreement," whose doctrine of Scripture has been partly enumerated in the above paragraph.[22]

The National Lutheran Council, near death, received its shot of adrenalin by the events of World War II, and a new era of cooperation among Lutherans, including the Norwegian Lutheran Church of America, began. And with this new era of cooperation, came also a renewed spirit to unite Lutherans in organic union, not simply to be content with agencies of cooperation in external matters. While the American Lutheran Church volunteered fellowship with either the Missouri Synod or the United Lutheran Church, the American Lutheran Conference made its move toward drafting and sending out to all Lutheran bodies in America the "Overture on Lutheran Unity" (1944). The "Overture" subscribes to the "Minneapolis Theses" and names the "Brief Statement" (Missouri Synod), the "Pittsburgh Agreement" (ULCA, ALC) as sufficiently clear statements of the doctrinal positions of the three major groups within American Lutheranism. The "Overture," while subscribing to the "Minneapolis Theses" also states; "We as earnestly expect of those with whom we seek complete fellowship that their doctrine and practice shall conform to their respective declarations."

The "Overture" was not accepted by the United Lutheran Church or acted on by the Missouri Synod. The Norwegian Lutheran Church of America continued to oppose the movement within the American Lutheran Conference to include the United Lutheran Church.

In 1946, as was mentioned previously, the Norwegian Lutheran Church of America was changed and simplified to the Evangelical Lutheran Church (ELC). Under its new name, the Evangelical Lutheran Church declined to participate with the other synods in a venture proposed by the United Lutheran Church to compose a joint hymnal and service book. It was feared by the ELC that the ULCA "spirit" would pervade the new publication.

As the ELC moved out of the forties into the fifties, the lines became drawn in even sharper detail between those inclined toward fellowship with the ULCA and those not so inclined. Finally, two large mergers resulted at the beginning of the sixties from this polarization of theology. The liberal attitude toward church union and the doctrine of the Scriptures was shared finally by the ULCA, the Augustana Synod (Swedish), the Suomi Synod (Finnish), and the American Evangelical Lutheran Church (Danish). These formed the Lutheran Church in America (LCA). The more confessional theology of the ELC was shared by the United Evangelical Lutheran Church (Danish), the American Lutheran Church (German), and a little later, by the Lutheran Free Church (Norwegian). This resulted in the formation of The American Lutheran Church (TALC).

A brief outline of the events that led to the merger forming The American Lutheran Church: First, bear in mind that in connection with the history of the ELC (or formerly the NLCA), already in 1949 and 1950 a federation of the ELC, UELC, and the ALC was being pressed in some quarters by the opinion that the National Lutheran Council had outlived its usefulness. The ELC cautioned that "the time is not now at hand for complete organic union of the National Lutheran Council churches," and that the Council was the agency which could best serve the several Lutheran bodies. Of course, at the bottom of this caution against uniting all the Council Churches was the ELC's hesitance to participate in organic union with the ULCA. On the other hand, the ELC urged the organic union of itself and the ALC and the UELC. The ELC had thus committed itself to a course to seek union, a union that was finally accomplished ten years later in the formation of The American Lutheran Church in April 1960.

It should be noted that only until 1952 did the Augustana Synod participate in union negotiations. It withdrew, finally, because of its intentions that the ULCA be included in a union, should it come about. The ELC, of course, as we have pointed out, took the position exactly opposite of this, wanting neither federation nor merger, if this included the ULCA.

1949 – 1950 The ELC finds that merger of some National Lutheran Council churches is being pressed.

1952   Withdrawal of the Augustana Synod (Swedish) from union negotiations with the National Lutheran Council. The same year the ELC approves a statement on faith and life, "The United Testimony."

1954   American Lutheran Conference officially is dissolved because of mitigating circumstances in American Lutheranism, since there was a decided polarization of loyalties among the merger bodies. The same year the Joint Union Committee is authorized to prepare Articles of Incorporation, a Constitution and Bylaws, as well as Articles of Union.

1955 & 1956 Congregational referendums result in the Lutheran Free Church withdrawing from the projected union. The documents formulated by the Joint Union Committee are approved by the ELC for adoption by the Constituting Convention of The American Lutheran Church.

1959   The Missouri Synod invites the merging synods to unifying conversations.

1960   Formation of The American Lutheran Church (TALC).

THE EVANGELICAL LUTHERAN CHURCH AND
THE WORLD COUNCIL OF CHURCHES

From its founding in 1917, the Evangelical Lutheran Church (or, at that time known as the Norwegian Lutheran Church of America) had expressed caution in regards to relations with non-Lutherans. Hence its cold attitude toward the ULCA's "essentials of a catholic (universal) spirit." Still, the United Church and the Hauge's Synod did not share the same spirit as the Norwegian Synod (the three bodies that merged to form the Evangelical Lutheran Church – as it came to be known) in this matter. In 1948 the First Assembly of the World Council of Churches (WCC) was held in Amsterdam. Most of the world's Lutherans accepted membership in the Council. However, the Missouri Synod, and the Lutheran Free Church consistently declined to be members. The Evangelical Lutheran Church also declined the invitation extended to the 1948 organizational meeting. President Aasgaard had recommended membership in the council, for it did not imply pulpit and altar fellowship.

Debate in the ELC over membership continued between 1946 and 1948. The Church Council and leaders of the ELC in general were in favor of membership, but the majority of the pastors and lay people took an opposite stand. Both sides of the debate were represented in an official published pamphlet: "Should We Join The World Council of Churches?" The debate culminated at the 1948 Convention, with the decisive defeat of the Church Council's resolution to accept membership in the World Council of Churches.

The issue, however, was not dead, and in 1956, in its second vote on the invitation by the WCC, the convention voted decisively to become a member. A large factor in overturning the former decision was, of course, the approaching merger of the ELC with churches who were members of this large world ecumenical council. How could aloofness to the WCC be justified when union was already assured with those who were participants? There can be no doubt that a union of churches must also constitute a sharing in, and a commingling of, theology and practice. Besides, more and more pastors, especially the young graduate candidates, were imbued with the existing spirit of ecumenism.

That participating in the ecumenical movement is the best or even proper manner of testifying God's truth in the world, is a subject worthy of serious debate. Some feel that this step is inevitable for every church body. But there are others who are convinced that one does not strengthen his testimony to the truth by extending the hand of fellowship to those who deny or vitiate it. For some, St. Paul's words in Romans 16:17-18 still raises a very real and necessary warning against unionism: "I urge you, brothers, to watch out for those who cause divisions and put obstacles in your way that are contrary to the teaching you have learned. Keep away from them. For such people are not serving our Lord Christ, but their own appetites. By smooth talk and flattery they deceive the minds of naïve people." (NIV)

When a church body once commits itself to the modern ecumenical movement, and when the leaders, especially, become imbued with it, the outcome is almost assured. The ELC is a case in point. Observe how far it departed from the spirit of the old Norwegian Synod!

If one were to use a single word to describe the flow of history for the mainstream of Norwegian Lutheranism in America, perhaps the term "accommodate" would suite best. Norwegian Lutherans have come out of various backgrounds, deeply rooted in their distinguished religious culture and traditions, at times with strong emotional fervor asserting the correctness of their individual positions and the incorrectness of those on the other side, and yet these same people (with but few exceptions) have shown a remarkable capacity for accommodating their way of thinking, their religious ideals, their expressions of doctrine and practice, to those of other Lutherans. And the cause for which they are willing to do this? Church union. Yes, for this cause the Norwegian Lutherans have for the most part adjusted well to the spirit of ecumenicity that so pervades the modern Lutheran Church.

Footnotes for Chapter Nineteen

1 Richard C. Wolf, *Documents of Lutheran Unity in America,* (Fortress Press, Philadelphia, PA, 1966), p. 288; Doc. #100.

2 Wolf, *Documents of Lutheran Unity in America,* p. 230; Doc. #100.

3 Wolf, *Documents of Lutheran Unity in America,* p. 231; Doc. #100.

4 Wolf, *Documents of Lutheran Unity in America,* p. 232; Doc. #100.

5 Wolf, *Documents of Lutheran Unity in America,* p. 233; Doc. #100.

6 Wolf, *Documents of Lutheran Unity in America,* p. 233; Doc. #100.

7 Wolf, *Documents of Lutheran Unity in America,* p. 234; Doc. #100.

8 Wolf, *Documents of Lutheran Unity in America,* p. 234; Doc. #100.

9 Wolf, *Documents of Lutheran Unit in America,* p. 235; Doc. #100.

10 Theodore A. Aaberg, *A City Set On a Hill,* (Published by Board of Publications Ev. Lutheran Synod, Mankato, MN, 1968), p. 47.

11 E. Clifford Nelson-Eugene L. Fevold, *The Lutheran Church Among Norwegian Americans,* Vol. 2, (Augsburg Publishing House, Minneapolis, MN, 1960), p. 178.

12 Wolf, *Documents of Lutheran Unity in America,* pp. 232-235; Doc. #100.

13 Nelson-Fevold, *The Lutheran Church Among Norwegian-Americans,* Vol. 2, p. 181.

14 Aaberg, *A City Set On a Hill,* page____.

15 Aaberg, A City On a Hill, p.65

16 Aaberg, A City On a Hill, p. 65

17 Nelson-Fevold, *The Lutheran Church Among Norwegian-Americans,* Vol. 2, pp. 255-259.

*The General Synod (1821), the General Council (1867), the United Synod in the South (1864) merged the same year, on November 14th, to form the United Lutheran Church.

18 Nelson-Fevold, *The Lutheran Church Among Norwegian-Americans,* Vol. 2, p. 303.

19 Nelson-Fevold, *The Lutheran Church Among Norwegian-Americans,* Vol.2, pp. 327, 328.

20 Nelson-Fevold, *The Lutheran Church Among Norwegian-Americans,* Vol. 2, pp. 305, 306.

21 Wolf, *Documents of Lutheran Unity in America,* -- Quoting Fred W. Meuser, *The Formation of the American Lutheran Church* (Wartburg Press, Columbus, OH, 1958) pp. 247, 248. / Wolf, p. 339.

22 Wolf, *Documents of Lutheran Unity in America,* p. 379.

CHAPTER TWENTY

THE NORWEGIANS
THE NORWEGIAN SYNOD OF THE AMERICAN EVANGELICAL LUTHERAN CHURCH (EVANGELICAL LUTHERAN SYNOD) (1918-   )

THE NEW RISES FROM THE OLD

This body of Norwegian Lutherans regards itself as the successor (and even the continuation) of the old Norwegian Synod, the conservative body of Norse Lutheranism founded in 1853, and which officially terminated its existence when it entered the merger of Norwegian synods in 1917. We begin our review of this small but interesting Norwegian Lutheran body by recalling some important facts already presented in previous chapters.

The circumstance that mostly influenced the founding of the American Evangelical Lutheran Church as a continuation of the old Norwegian Synod after the merger, had its roots in the election controversy of the 1880's. This controversy has been thoroughly dealt with in the chapter detailing the history of the Norwegian Synod and will be presented again in the section that reviews the history of the Missouri Synod. Brief mention will be made of the election controversy as we proceed with our present review. When the movement to merge the Norwegian Synod with the United Church and the Hauge's Synod got up a full head of steam, there appeared two forces within the Synod: the Majority, who were willing to go along with stating the doctrine of Election under two forms, and the Minority dwindled in numbers until only a small portion of the original group was left. In the preceding chapter the events are presented which changed the minds of so many in the Minority. And now a glance at events that resulted in the formation of two new Norwegian Lutheran bodies: one that was large, and the other that was tiny.

UNION EFFORTS LEADING UP
TO THE 1917 MERGER

1890   A private meeting was held between professors from the Augsburg Seminary in Madison, Wisconsin, and professors of St. Olaf College, Northfield, Minnesota. A free conference was then initiated by the Norwegian Synod.

1892   A free conference was held by thirty representatives from the United Church and thirty from the Norwegian Synod. Two more free conferences were held but finally abandoned as a means to union.

1900   An invitation was extended by the Norwegian Synod resulting in several meetings between the presidents and theological faculties of the Norwegian Synod and the United Church. Prof. Schmidt's appearance as a delegate of the United Church caused resentment in the Norwegian Synod and the meetings finally ceased. (Prof. Schmidt is regarded as the single cause of the election controversy).

1905   The aloofness of the Hauge's Synod toward union changed, and it invited all Norwegian Lutheran Churches to hold joint doctrinal meetings. The invitation was accepted by the Norwegian Synod and the United Church.

1908   By this time some progress was achieved and agreement in some doctrines was reached.

1910   The Norwegian Synod's committee felt compelled to withdraw from the joint meetings. The committee felt the need for antitheses which lay out and rejected the errors of the anti-Missourians (e.g. that since natural man has power to choose to reject Christ, he therefore also has the power to choose to accept him). The representatives failed to agree on the doctrine of Conversion. The United Church charged the Norwegian Synod's theses on Election with not being Biblical or Lutheran. In spite of the charges and impasse, the Norwegian Synod decided to go on with negotiations, with a new committee acting. Meanwhile it was participating inter-synodically in the production of a new hymnbook. Dr. Stub, vice-president of the Norwegian Synod, leaned towards the "liberal" viewpoint and used his influence to keep the Norwegian Synod negotiating with the United Church.

1912   The "Madison Agreement" or *Opgjør*. This document worked out at Madison, Wisconsin, presents the two forms of the doctrine of Election commonly held by the negotiating parties. Paragraph three gives the two forms:
SOME, IN ACCORD WITH THE *FORMULA OF CONCORD*, INCLUDE UNDER THE DOCTRINE OF ELECTION THE WHOLE ORDER OF SALVATION OF THE ELECT FROM THE CALL [TO

FAITH] TO THE GLORIFICATION... AND TEACH AN ELECTION 'UNTO SALVATION THROUGH THE SANCTIFICATION OF THE SPIRIT AND BELIEF OF THE TRUTH' [POSITION OF THE MISSOURI AND WISCONSIN SYNODS];... WHILE OTHERS, WITH PONTOPPIDAN, IN AGREEMENT WITH JOHN GERHARD, SCRIVER AND OTHER RECOGNIZED TEACHERS OF THE CHURCH, DEFINE ELECTION MORE SPECIFICALLY AS THE DECREE CONCERNING THE FINAL GLORIFICATION, WITH FAITH AND PERSEVERANCE WROUGHT BY THE HOLY SPIRIT AS ITS NECESSARY PRESUPPOSITION, AND TEACH THAT "GOD HAS APPOINTED ALL THOSE TO ETERNAL LIFE WHO HE FROM ETERNITY HAS FORSEEN WOULD ACCEPT THE OFFERED GRACE, BELIEVE IN CHRIST AND REMAIN CONSTANT IN THIS FAITH UNTO THE END" AND SINCE NEITHER OF THESE TWO FORMS OF DOCTRINE, THUS PRESENTED, CONTRADICT ANY DOCTRINE REVEALED IN THE WORD OF GOD, BUT DOES FULL JUSTICE TO THE ORDER OF SALVATION AS PRESENTED IN THE WORD OF GOD AND THE CONFESSIONS OF THE CHURCH; WE FIND THAT THIS SHOULD NOT BE CAUSE FOR SCHISM WITHIN THE CHURCH OR DISTURB THAT UNITY OF THE SPIRIT IN THE BOND OF PEACE WHICH GOD WILLS SHOULD PREVAIL AMONG US.[1]

1912   The individual districts of the Norwegian Synod accepted the "Madison Agreement," 591 voting members and 67 advisory delegates favoring it; 15 opposing it; and 20 abstaining from voting. All districts favored continuing union negotiations. The highly favorable vote was the result of the Union Committee's explanation that acceptance of paragraph one in no way implies a yielding of any point of doctrine at any time officially promulgated by the Synod. The paragraph in question states that the Union Committees accepted unanimously and without reservation the doctrine of Election set forth in the *Formula of Concord* and in Pontoppidan's *Truth Unto Godliness*... the two forms of doctrine of Election expressed among Norwegian Lutherans. According to the "Madison Agreement" neither side (holding to one or the other of the two forms) was required to accept the doctrinal form of Election of the other side, yet neither side was to consider the other side's form of this doctrine schismatic.

1912   Pastor Gunderson (United Church) opened old wounds, claiming no one can give the final word in the matter of whether faith may or may not be called a cause of election. A movement was begun by a few professors of the Norwegian Synod to delay action on the "Agreement" until this development could be cleared up. Disharmony arose between the Union Committees of the Synod and the United Church. President Stub (Synod) spoke out against the Minority, who had become a force to defer union until changes in the "Agreement" were made. In September three new Union Committees met in joint session. Dr. Stub decided to proceed slowly toward union because of the danger of a split in the Synod. The German synods (Missouri and Wisconsin) in the Synodical Conference attacked the "Agreement." Unrest existed in the Synod over the "Agreement." An extraordinary convention of the Synod's Church Council was called.

1913   The "Petition" circulated by three professors of the Synod cautioned that true union must be based on unity of faith and charged the United Church with unionism. The "Petition" rallied supporters to the Minority cause. Bear in mind that the Minority men opposed stating the doctrine of Election in two forms. The Majority report favored giving the Union Committee the task of negotiating union. The Minority mounted a vigorous attack against the "Madison

Agreement."

1914 The Joint Union Committee's "Articles of Union" were presented to the Synod and were adopted. Laymen overwhelmingly spoke for union. A Peace Committee was appointed.

1915 The constitution for the merger body was read and discussed. No action was taken.

1916 Battle lines between the Minority and Majority were clearly drawn. Pastor Stub presented a pamphlet that defended the "Agreement" and the proposed union on the basis of matters as they then stood, and attacked the Minority position. The Minority countered with "An Answer to Rebukes." The Minority leaders called for several changes to be made in the "Agreement," but lost their bid to keep the merger from taking place without first bringing about a meeting of minds on the doctrine of Election. The proposed constitution was adopted by the Synod. The Majority succeeded with their proposal to form a union with the United Church (and hopefully also with the Hauge's Synod), and also provided for incorporating the new body and for turning over the Synod's property to the merger body. The Minority stated that their consciences required certain corrections to be made in the "Agreement" before they are able to enter the new church body. This group of men also served notice of their intention to continue the existence of the Norwegian Synod if difficulties were not removed. By this time, union of the three bodies was assured. Following the Synod's convention the Joint Committee held a series of meetings with the Minority (which had hoped to move the Committee to work their desired changes in the "Agreement"). A subcommittee was appointed by the Joint Committee of the three synods to deal with the leaders of the Minority. This resulted in a meeting held in Austin, Minnesota, and the drafting of the "Austin Settlement." Through this "Settlement" recognized the three reservations held by the Minority leaders, it in effect left matters as they were. The issue remained unresolved that unregenerate man has a feeling of duty or "responsibility in relation to the acceptance or rejection of grace." The Minority claimed that unregenerate man suffers spiritual deadness and therefore cannot experience this sense of responsibility. Again, this position of the Minority was, and still is, the position of the Missouri and Wisconsin Synods. It is also the position today of the Evangelical Lutheran Synod, the successor to the old Norwegian Synod, established by the tiny remnant of the Minority, who did not take part in the merger.

1917 In January a meeting was held by the Minority in Minneapolis, and a letter was read from the theologians of the Missouri Synod which counseled the Minority to remain apart from the merger. At the same meeting an invitation was extended to the Minority by the Joint Union Committee to join the merger, which invitation was accepted by most of the Minority members present. No concessions had been made to the Minority, only that the Committee acknowledged the attitude of these men and found nothing therein contrary to Scripture, even though, on the other hand, the Minority could not accept certain statements in either the "Madison Agreement" or the "Austin Settlement." A powerful determining force for many of the Minority men as far as which way they should finally go, was the strong sentiment in their congregations toward union.

1917 On June 8th the three synods voted themselves out of existence and the following day joined together to become the Norwegian Lutheran Church of America. Later the name was changed to the Evangelical Lutheran Church (ELC).

FORMING A NEW, BUT VERY SMALL NORWEGIAN SYNOD

1917: UNION AND DISUNION

June 8, 1917 was the day of hello's and goodbyes for the Norwegians. The Majority group of the old Norwegian Synod had been joined by most of the Minority. They met in final convention at St. Paul, Minnesota. This was the time of farewells to the tiny group left in the Minority, all that remained, really, of the old Norwegian Synod. The next day the delegates of the former Norwegian Synod walked over to St. Paul Auditorium to say their hello's to the delegates of the United Church and the Hauge's Synod, and together with them, organize the Norwegian Lutheran Church in America. The remaining Minority, a tiny group, met in the Hotel Aberdeen to unite, if they could, to form a Norwegian synod that would be true to the Scriptures in all matters, and faithful in all ways to the Lutheran Confessions.

FROM MINORITY STATUS TO SYNODICAL ORGANIZATION

While most of the old Norwegian Synod marched to the big auditorium, the remnant of the Minority united in declaring that they could not for conscience' sake join the new church body on the present basis, but that they continue to stand on the old confession and organization. Their declaration showed that they intended to defend and continue to work under that confession and organization. A temporary organization was then effected, with the election of officers. Bravely, they also even arranged to publish a church paper. The elections produced the following results: President, Pastor Bjug Harstad of Parkland, Washington; Vice-president, John A. Moldstad of Chicago; Secretary, Pastor C.N. Peterson; Treasurer, Pastor O.T. Lee of Northwood, Iowa.

Great were the festivities of union at St. Paul Auditorium, marking the organization of the Norwegian Lutheran Church of America (NCLA). However, the few, who for conscience reasons could not unite, joined with each other for services and for doctrinal discussions.

In an April 1918 issue of the church paper, pastors and members of congregations who desired to continue in the old doctrine and practice of the Norwegian Synod were called to their annual meeting, to be held in Lime Creek, Iowa, in June. An interesting aspect of this spirited meeting was that it was finally held in a tent across the Minnesota state line. Being wartime, the governor of

Iowa had decreed that all public gatherings use only the English language. No such restriction was imposed in Minnesota. On account of the scarcity of elected delegates from the participating congregations, certain resolutions were then referred to the congregations for their approval. The name chosen, to be acted upon by the congregations, was the Norwegian Synod of the American Evangelical Lutheran Church. The source of faith and doctrine was recognized to be the Word of God as revealed in the canonical books of the Old and New Testaments. The Lutheran Symbols contained in the *Book of Concord* of 1580, constituted the Confession. A committee of three was elected to work up the necessary changes in the old Constitution and propose them in as short a time as possible for consideration by the congregations.

And so, it came about that in the convention held in a tent in Minnesota, June 14-15, 1918, the Norwegian Synod of the American Evangelical Lutheran Church (later, simply the Evangelical Lutheran Synod) had its humble beginning, at which thirteen pastors were in attendance. (The simplified name "The Norwegian Synod" also came to be applied to this Norwegian body, and this is the name that shall mostly be used in the remainder of this chapter.)

WILLING TO STAND ALONE

The Synodical Conference through its Committee, which had never really been able to deal in the situation which had arisen in the old Synod, did much, nevertheless, to encourage the tiny Minority to remain faithful. It is a strange twist that thirty-eight years after its founding this small synod, for reasons of conscience, had to once again take a stand that would alienate itself from those who had for many years been its close allies. This time the delegates would find themselves declaring a state of suspended fellowship with their dearly loved fellow Lutherans in the Missouri Synod. The cause would again be unionism. The Missouri Synod would find itself drawn farther and farther into doctrinal discussions with the American Lutheran Church, even drawing up and adopting doctrinal statements which the brethren of both the Norwegian Synod and the Wisconsin Synod felt constrained to rigorously attack.

The stand against unionism, which caused the alienation of this Norwegian group from a large segment of its own ethnic element, would not be altered in the decades to come, but would cause the Norwegian Synod to continue to remain firm against the prevailing theory of the time, that church union can and should be effected between Lutheran bodies without first having arrived at full and complete unity of doctrine and practice. The Norwegian Synod has not gloried in size and power of organization. Like its close ally, the Wisconsin Synod, it has shown a willingness to stand alone and be a small but powerful voice of Lutheranism, declaring those truths which it feels for conscience sake must be declared. Staying on the side of Scripture and faithful to the historic Lutheran Confessions allows for no choice in the matter—this is the stand the Norwegian Synod has adhered to throughout its history. We will review the Synod's doctrinal dealings with the Missouri Synod later in this chapter.

THE WORK OF THE NORWEGIAN SYNOD

MISSION WORK: THE CHURCH MUST NOT ONLY DEFEND, BUT ALSO PUBLISH AND PROCLAIM THE WORD OF GOD

HOME MISSIONS

Over the years, mission work for the Norwegian Synod consisted to a great extent in beginning mission congregations to serve small groups of Lutherans who for confessional reasons found themselves outside the mainstream of Norwegian Lutheranism. Had the Norwegian Synod been able to preserve within its ranks a larger number of the Minority—many of whom finally went with the Majority into the merger—it could no doubt have become a much larger body than it is today. Because it lacked both the financial and manpower resources, due to its tiny size, the Norwegian Synod was not able to meet many of the mission challenges it faced and as a result lost many transient members to the Missouri and Wisconsin Synods.

Still, the Norwegian Synod has not been without growth. According to Theodore A. Aaberg, the few hundred souls represented at the Lime Creek meeting in 1918 had by 1968 grown to some fifteen thousand souls. A goodly number of the present congregations had their start as home missions. However, there have been bumps in the road along the way. An endeavor in California begun in the fifties, which flourished for a time, became a tremendous disappointment to the Norwegian Synod. The two congregations established with Christian day schools in the Los Angeles area, in 1960—together with their pastors—decided to leave the Synod for the Missouri Synod. Yes, there have been disappointments in the area of home missions, and as speakers within the Norwegian Synod have at times warned, there has not been the interest within the body for mission work that there should have been. All church bodies which feel called by the Lord into the field of polemics as defenders of the truth ought to consider "that it is also our God-given mission to make use of every opportunity to publish and spread the truth of the Word—to use the trowel as well as the sword."[2] Concerning work among minority ethnic groups, it should be mentioned that Missionary Bakke, though never a formal member of the Norwegian Synod, and yet a member by virtue of his confession, was a shining light in the missions which the Synodical Conference carried on among the Negroes in the South.*

FOREIGN MISSIONS

From its beginning, the Norwegian Synod has been interested in and zealous for, this broader kind of mission work. And from its beginning much of this mission work was done in association with the Missouri Synod. Pastor George O. Lillegard, with experience as a missionary in China under the old Synod, was sent in 1921 back to China under the Board for Foreign Missions of the Missouri Synod. Earlier in the year, the Norwegian Synod had placed a

325

representative on this board. Under the auspices of the Missouri Synod's Foreign Mission Board, the Norwegian Synod in 1926 sent Missionary Anena Christensen to India. Pastor Henry M. Tjernagel served the Saude-Jericho parish conducted by the Norwegian Synod in 1923. Later, in 1935 when the Synodical Conference entered the Nigeria, West Africa field, the Norwegian Synod supported it and later sent men from its own midst to help with this work. Norwegian Synod representatives worked in the Missouri Synod Mission in the Philippines, as well as China.

In 1950 the Norwegian Synod undertook its first independent foreign mission, sending Pastor Joseph N. Peterson to work in Cornwall, England. At first the field looked promising, but later turned out to be discouraging and finally, in 1959, the field was given over to the Evangelical Lutheran Church of England, an affiliate of the Missouri Synod. Men who were not affiliated with the Norwegian Synod, but who trained at the Synod's Bethany Seminary entered mission fields in Norway and Hong Kong.

In 1963 the Norwegians withdrew from the Synodical Conference. After that it lent some financial support to foreign missions of the Wisconsin Synod, seeking at the same time to establish its own independent foreign fields. With the calling of Pastor Theodore F. Kuster, the Norwegian Synod eventually entered the Latin American field in Lima, Peru. By 1972, this field had two workers.

When the world entered the twenty-first century, the Norwegian Synod could list the following foreign missions: Peru, South Africa; Chile; South America; Czech Republic; Latvia; and Ukraine.

PUBLICATIONS

The *Evangelisk Lutheresk Tidende* was published from 1917, and the *Lutheran Sentinel* from 1919. These were supplemented by the "Annual Synod Report." The Norwegian Synod organized the Lutheran Synod Book Company in 1920. The 1953 Convention voted to discontinue the publication of the Norwegian language paper. The Synod publishes a theological journal, the *Lutheran Synod Quarterly*. There is an elected Board for Publications. The synod's roster of pastors, teachers, and congregations, and schools is published in the "Yearbook" of the Wisconsin Evangelical Lutheran Synod.

EDUCATION

The very existence of a church body, to say nothing of its growth, depends in large part on its supply of pastors for its pulpits and teachers for its classrooms. Throughout its history, the Norwegian Lutheran Synod has shown its willingness to carry on Christian education, in spite of its small size. At first, the synod established a professorship at Missouri's Columbia College, with Dr. S.C. Ylvisaker looking after the pre-theological Norwegian students enrolled there. Responding to an invitation of the Wisconsin Synod, another professorship was established at Dr. Martin Luther College, New Ulm, Minnesota (now Martin Luther College). Thus arrangement was made to care for the special needs of Norwegian students who would enroll at this institution to prepare for the teaching ministry. Without establishing Norwegian professorships at Missouri's St. Louis Seminary, the Norwegians were able to use this school to train their pastors, until 1946 when their own Bethany Seminary in Mankato, Minnesota, was opened. The Norwegian students also made use of Wisconsin's Northwestern College in Watertown, Wisconsin, the seminary in Thiensville (now Mequon), Wisconsin, and the Missouri Synod's Concordia Seminary at Springfield, Illinois (now Fort Wayne, Indiana). (Wisconsin's Northwestern College at Watertown later merged with Dr. Martin Luther College at New Ulm, Minnesota, forming Martin Luther College. The Preparatory School remains in Watertown.)

While Christian day schools in congregations involved in the 1917 mergers which formed the Norwegian Lutheran Church of America, finally died out, schools were maintained in the tiny new synod. The number of day schools in the Norwegian Synod fluctuated over the years. In the past, the Synod has not always shown the deep interest vital to this institution that it might have. Nevertheless a number of the congregations maintain day schools today. Ultimately, with the acquisition of Bethany College, a normal school department was set up for the part-training of day school teachers.

In 1925 Bethany Lutheran College was offered to the Norwegian Synod meeting in convention at Nicollet, Minnesota. The prospect of taking over and managing this college was met with joy in many hearts. However, the practical side of the issue won out, and the convention felt it necessary to decline the offer. The Wisconsin Synod also declined to purchase the college, which at the time was in a tight financial bind, with foreclosure of the bonds imminent. Again the Norwegians were approached. This time a group of one hundred pastors and laymen formed an association, which purchased the college for a sum of $90,000. This action was taken before the Norwegian Synod could express itself on the convention floor, since a decision to purchase could not be deferred. When the Synod met, it voted not to assume responsibility at that time for the college; nevertheless it voted to express full confidence in the Bethany Lutheran College Association "that it will conduct the school on a true Lutheran, Christian spirit."

However, in 1927 the sentiment prevailed that the great need for a school of its own existed, and that ways could be found to maintain such as institution. It was also urged that the purchase of Bethany College presented such a bargain as could hardly be expected to come their way again. The majority of the delegates voted for the Norwegian Synod to assume the operation of the college. The National Lutheran Educational Association, whose continued concern was that Bethany be open to all the youth of the Synodical Conference, provided much help over the years in paying off the college's indebtedness. Finally, in 1944 the last bond of indebtedness was paid. After that, programs of remodeling and new construction, as well as purchasing houses in Mankato, increased the value of the college by more than 1.5 million—evidence of what even a small church body can do. When the members of a church body pull together, pool their resources, and most important of all, approach the throne of the Almighty with prayers that dare to ask great things of a truly great God, much can be accomplished through few. A thing may be either a burden or a blessing, depending upon the attitude and faith with which it is handled.[3]

It was the 1946 Convention of the Norwegian Synod that resolved to establish a full theological seminary course at Bethany. Doctrinal controversy within the Synodical Conference related to Missouri's discussions with the American Lutheran Church, more and more convinced the Norwegians that they would finally reach the point where they could no longer depend on the Missouri Synod to train their pastors. The seminary opened in the fall of 1946 with five students of theology. Six professors presented the courses. In the next twenty years, forty-eight men were graduated from the seminary. Eventually Bethany was pressed into service by the Wisconsin Synod to help with preparing older men who wished to enter the Wisconsin Synod Seminary at Mequon. Following the suspension of fellowship with the Missouri Synod in 1961, the Wisconsin Synod could no longer look to the practical seminary at Springfield, Illinois, to train men for the ministry who lacked the customary preparatory schooling.

THE NORWEGIAN SYNOD AND UNION NEGOTIATIONS

WATCHMEN STANDING ON ZION'S TOWERS

The role which the Norwegian Synod took in regards to doctrinal negotiations carried on by member synods of the Synodical Conference with Lutheran bodies outside the Conference, was that of watchmen standing on Zion's towers, ready to alert the Church to dangers both within and without the camp that threaten faith and doctrine. The Norwegian Synod, sometimes referred to as the "little Norwegian Synod," was received into the Synodical Conference in 1920. (It's predecessor, the "old Norwegian Synod" joined the Conference in 1872 at its inception, but in 1883 left the Conference to attempt to set its house in order because of threatening division due to the election controversy.) The Synodical Conference by resolution encouraged the "little Norwegian Synod" in its fight for the truth. At the same time, the Conference recognized with great sorrow that the "old Norwegian Synod," by holding fast to the *Opgjør* or "Madison Agreement" or "Settlement," and by its union with the other two Norwegian synods in the Norwegian Lutheran Church of America (later the Evangelical Lutheran Church), "has severed its bond of faith and church fellowship with the Synodical Conference."[4]

DOCTRINAL CONTROVERSY WITH THE MISSOURI SYNOD

However close the Missouri Synod and the "little Norwegian Synod" were in fellowship, there was destined to come a sorrowful parting of ways. Much of the history of the long controversy between the member synods of the Conference that finally brought about division is discussed in the histories of the American Lutheran Church and the Missouri and Wisconsin Synods. A brief history of the controversy will have to suffice here.

1935 Both the United Lutheran Church in America (ULCA) and the American Lutheran Church (ALC) invited the other Lutheran bodies to take part in discussions hopefully leading to closer relations. The Missouri Synod accepted the invitation and held out hope that conferring with one another on matters involving doctrine, internal unity, and church practice would result in establishing unity based in the Word of God and the Lutheran Confessions. The Norwegian Synod declined to confer with the ULCA for the reason that it did not think that these discussions offered an opportunity to reach the unity of doctrine and practice the Missouri Synod hoped for.

1936 The Norwegian Synod explained its position in a synodical essay, "Unity, Union, and Unionism." The old discussions of 1912-1917 still haunted the little synod, as can be seen in the following statements from that essay.

WE WHO HAVE OBSERVED AT CLOSE RANGE AND STUDIED THE HISTORY OF EFFORTS MADE TO BRING THE NORWEGIAN LUTHERANS INTO AGREEMENT BY MEANS OF COMMITTEES, ARE CONSTRAINED TO SAY, WHEN ASKED TO FOLLOW THIS METHOD AGAIN: VESTIGIA TERRENT (THE FOOTSTEPS TERRIFY). WE ARE AFRAID OF HISTORY REPEATING ITSELF, AND THEREFORE CONSIDER IT A GOD-GIVEN DUTY TO SOUND A WARNING TO ALL EARNEST DEFENDERS OF THE TRUTH AGAINST EXPOSING THE TRUE WELFARE OF THE CHURCH OF CHRIST TO THE DANGERS INVOLVED IN THE PROCEDURE. [5]

The attitude of the Norwegian Synod at this time is well summarized in this same essay (which was later approved by the 1938 Watertown Synodical Conference Convention).

WHEN WE ELECT A COMMITTEE TO BE CLOSETED IN CONFIDENTIAL NEGOTIATIONS WITH LIKE COMMITTEES FROM ERRORIST BODIES WHO WILL STRIVE TO GAIN ACCEPTANCE OF THEIR FALSE VIEWS, WE HAVE EVERY REASON TO FEAR THAT WE MUST RECKON WITH ALL THE WILY TACTICS OF THE ARCH-ENEMY OF TRUTH. IF 1 PETER 3:15 IS CITED TO JUSTIFY SUCH PROCEDURE, THE PASSAGE IS MISAPPLIED, AND THOUGH UNINTENTIONALLY, MADE TO NULLIFY ROMANS 16:17; TITUS 3:10, ETC. LET IT BE NOTED, TOO, THAT THE PROSPECTS OF CONVINCING BY OUR TESTIMONY TO THE TRUTH A COMMITTEE WHICH REPRESENTS A BODY CONFIRMED IN ERROR, AND THROUGH IT THE BODY ITSELF, ARE VERY, VERY POOR INDEED. BE IT REMEMBERED ALSO THAT THE CHAMPIONS OF FALSE DOCTRINE ARE USUALLY SATISFIED IF THEY GAIN FOR THEIR ERROR EQUAL STANDING WITH THE TRUTH; HENCE EVERY MANNER OF COMPROMISE IS RESORTED TO. THE DANGER IS MULTIPLIED WHEN, AS IS COMMON, THE ERRORISTS SHOWER PRAISES UPON THEIR OPPONENTS IN ORDER TO GAIN THEIR PERSONAL GOODWILL. WHEN THE CHAMPIONS OF TRUTH ARE BROUGHT TO ADMIRE THE ERRORISTS FOR THEIR GENTLEMANLY BEHAVIOR AND THEIR FAIR MINDEDNESS, AND BEGIN TO THINK OF THE MANY ABLE AND GOOD MEN AND WOMEN WHOM THEY REPRESENT, THEN "THE LUST OF THE FLESH" IS NEAR TO VICTORY.[6]

SCRIPTURE WARNS US CLEARLY AND EMPHATICALLY AGAINST ENTANGLEMENT WITH ERRORISTS (ROMANS 16:17; TITUS 3:10; 1 TIMOTHY 6:3-5). ANY RELUCTANCE TO HEED THESE WARNINGS AND COMMANDS OF SCRIPTURE IS UNIONISM ALREADY CONCEIVED IN THE HEART, WHICH IF ALLOWED TO DEVELOP, WILL RE-

What especially troubled the Norwegians—and this can be said also of the Wisconsin Synod—was the lack of evidence of an existing unity of spirit, a conclusion reached by observing published reports of conventions and various meetings, addressed by representative members, and review of constitutions and bylaws. Note was also taken of the practice carried on in individual congregations, which practice was public knowledge. Under the circumstances the Norwegian Synod was leery of setting up inter-synodical committees to deal in matters of doctrine and practice involved among the invited groups. What concerned the Norwegians was the past history of unionism practiced by the ALC and the ULCA, for they both showed a willingness to unite in fellowship without first having reached complete agreement in doctrine and practice.

1938   The ALC had asked the Missouri Synod to be tolerant toward certain of its teachings and interpretations of Scripture which had hitherto been rejected in Synodical Conference circles. In its 1938 Convention, the Missouri Synod resolved its belief... "that under the most favorable circumstances much time and effort may be required before any union may be reached." Still, the Missouri Synod called on its Committee on Lutheran Union to seek full agreement with the ALC in the doctrines at which they were at variance and also stated the need for church practice to conform to church doctrine—lodges and unions being specifically mentioned.

The Missouri Synod's "St. Louis Articles" joined its "Brief Statement" to become with the ALC's "Doctrinal Declaration" a joint settlement of past differences. The document that was thus formed was titled "Doctrinal Affirmation" (1944). But bear in mind that the ALC only qualifiedly endorsed the Missouri Synod's "Brief Statement." In its own "Sandusky (Ohio) Resolutions" the ALC stated: "That we believe the 'Brief Statement' viewed in the light of our 'Declaration' is not in contradiction to the 'Minneapolis Theses.'" The ALC's consistent philosophy in dealing with the Missouri Synod was: "... we are firmly convinced that it is neither necessary nor possible to agree in all non-fundamental doctrines. Nevertheless, we are willing to continue negotiations..." This was the ALC's answer to Missouri's call to work for full agreement in those doctrines for which the ALC had asked for toleration.

The "St. Louis Articles of Union," having been drawn up and accepted by the Missouri Synod as the doctrinal basis for union with the ALC were given to the Norwegians for their approval. However, the Norwegian Synod found it to contain what it recognized as "the old error of the Iowa and Ohio Synods on the central doctrine of justification (the claim that Scripture does not speak of "objective justification" or "justification of the world"). The Norwegians also found certain "unscriptural principles on church fellowship" by the ALC. Both the Wisconsin Synod and the Norwegians later petitioned the Missouri Synod to revoke its 1938 "St. Louis Articles," for neither synod could approve them. The Norwegians flatly charged that they contained false doctrine (e.g. the statement on Justification in the "Declaration" reads, "to this end He also purposes to justify those who have come to faith," thus omitting Objective Justification).

The Committee of the Norwegian Synod charged with studying the union movement, in 1938 sent a letter to President Dr. John W. Behnken of the Missouri Synod enumerating three points: (1) the need for remembering the unionistic spirit manifest in the ALC by its membership in the American Lutheran Conference; (2) the need for official documents (rather than relying on assurances and explanations which men give on their own); (3) the necessity of insisting on a church practice in conformity of doctrine.[8] The Norwegian Synod also embarked, as did the Wisconsin Synod, on a course of study within its own ranks of the issues involved.

1939   The Wisconsin Synod called the Missouri Synod to seek a single joint statement covering the contested doctrines, thetically and antithetically, and accepted by both parties of the controversy. Furthermore, such doctrinal statements were to be made in clear and unequivocal terms which do not require laborious additional explanations. Finally, the Wisconsin Synod in convention told Missouri:

> UNDER EXISTING CONDITIONS FURTHER NEGOTIATIONS FOR ESTABLISHING CHURCH FELLOWSHIP WOULD INVOLVE A DENIAL OF THE TRUTH AND WOULD CAUSE CONFUSION AND DISTURBANCE IN THE CHURCH AND OUGHT THEREFORE BE SUSPENDED FOR THE TIME BEING.[9]

In the same year, the ALC's "Pittsburg Agreement" conceded to the ULCA on the doctrine of Inspiration of Scripture. As an example, Part III: (1) THE BIBLE...IS PRIMARILY NOT A CODE OF DOCTRINES, STILL LESS A CODE OF MORALS, BUT THE HISTORY OF GOD'S REVELATION, FOR THE SALVATION OF MANKIND, AND OF MAN'S REACTION TO IT... IT IS ITSELF THE WORD OF GOD, HIS PERMANENT REVELATION, ASIDE FROM WHICH, UNTIL CHRIST'S RETURN IN GLORY, NO OTHER IS TO BE EXPECTED. (2)... BY VIRTUE OF A UNIQUE OPERATION OF THE HOLY SPIRIT...BY WHICH HE SUPPLIED TO THE HOLY WRITERS CONTENT AND FITTING WORD... .[10]

1940   The Synodical Conference, meeting in Chicago, appealed to the Missouri Synod not to enter into "fellowship (prayer-altar-pulpit fellowship) with the ALC" until the matters objected to by other member synods had been clarified and the whole matter presented once more to the Synodical Conference. Missouri was reminded to consider framing one document.

1941   The Missouri Synod at Fort Wayne instructed its Committee on Doctrinal Unity to prepare a single document of agreement with the ALC. It began joint work with the ALC in the areas of relief and missions, and also in the establishment of service centers (for the military). Missouri instructed its Commission that "the immediate objective be not organic union, but doctrinal unity and that the controverted doctrines be given careful study to establish full agreement. The Missouri Synod also concluded that no fellowship had been established and should not be practiced.

1943   The Wisconsin Synod memorialized the Missouri Synod to halt its negotiations with the ALC, because of the false basis underlying those negotiations. The Norwegians memorialized the Missouri Synod to revoke the "St. Louis Union Articles" of 1938 at its forthcoming 1944 Saginaw (Michigan) Convention. The reason: the "Articles" contain false doctrine (e.g. regarding Justification) and do not require full agreement in Eschatology (doctrine of End Times) and the Doctrine of Church Fellowship.

The Norwegians felt that their position against further negotiations by Missouri with the ALC was exonerated by historical development. While on the one hand the ALC accepted Missouri's "Brief Statement" in the light of its own

"Declaration," on the other hand, in 1940 the ALC together with the ULCA adopted the "Pittsburg Agreement" (referred above). The ALC and the ULCA had no trouble seeing eye to eye on the doctrine of the Inspiration of Scripture; still, the Missouri Synod, when dealing with the ULCA, got (in the late President John Behnken's words) "little farther than the opening paragraph of the 'Brief Statement': Of the Holy Scriptures."[11] The Missouri Synod found the "Pittsburg Agreement" unsatisfactory. Perhaps the reader can better understand the reasoning behind the request by the two sister synods that the Missouri Synod cease negotiations.

1944 Up to this time the Norwegians' pleas to the Missouri Synod "were not directly nor satisfactorily answered." Missouri and the ALC published a single document called the "Doctrinal Affirmation." Both the Norwegian and the Wisconsin Synods criticized the wording of the "Affirmation" as not being precise and definite enough in a number of instances. As a result, the Missouri Synod Committee submitted a set of "Clarifications" to the ALC Commissioners. Meanwhile the "Doctrinal Affirmation" was receiving cold reception from the rank and file of the ALC. Many felt that the "Affirmation" was unacceptable to the ALC because it canceled the position for which the ALC stood in the "Declaration", which advocated a certain attitude of freedom under God and His Word, as explained by the Fellowship Committee. The "Clarifications" were said to be even less acceptable, because they nullified what little had been brought into the "Doctrinal Affirmation" from the "Declaration" and because they contained statements that could not be approved. [12]

As far as the ALC was concerned, Missouri's Committee readily admitted what the representatives of the ALC stated: that Missouri's "Brief Statement" and the ALC's "Doctrinal Declaration" presented "two trends of thoughts, that they expressed differences in doctrine which do exist, but which in the opinion of the Fellowship Committee do not preclude fellowship."[13] Note that the doctrines involved were: Election, Conversion, the Church, and the Last Things. Missouri's Fellowship Committee flatly stated that in respect to their synod and the ALC, the phrase "doctrinal agreement" should not be used, because doctrinal agreement does not exist. In 1946 the ALC in Convention despaired "of attaining Lutheran Unity by way of additional doctrinal formulations and reformulations."[14]

The Missouri Synod's Saginaw Resolution of 1944 attempted to draw a distinction between "joint prayer" and "prayer fellowship", a distinction the synod previously had not made. The Saginaw Convention also abandoned Missouri's former position on Scouting, when it took no formal stand against the deistic religion of Scouting, but left it up to the individual congregation to either accept or reject the Scout movement. The Norwegian Synod Convention at Koshkonong, Wisconsin, expressed pessimism for the future of the Synodical Conference. In the meantime, Missouri reiterated its warning to congregations not to enter into acts of fellowship with the ALC. It should be noted that Missouri at its Saginaw Convention made the following statement concerning prayer: HOWEVER, JOINT PRAYER AT INTERSYNODICAL CONFERENCES, ASKING GOD FOR HIS GUIDANCE AND BLESSING UPON THE DELIBERATIONS AND DISCUSSIONS OF HIS WORD, DOES NOT MILITATE AGAINST THE RESOLUTION OF THE FORT WAYNE CONVENTION, PROVIDED SUCH PRAYER DOES NOT IMPLY DENIAL OF TRUTH OR SUPPORT OF

ERROR. LOCAL CONDITIONS WILL DETERMINE THE ADVISABILITY OF SUCH PRAYER. ABOVE ALL, THE CONSCIENCE OF A BROTHER MUST NOT BE VIOLATED NOR OFFENSE BE GIVEN.[15]

1945 Forty-four pastors and professors signed the "Chicago Statement" also called the "Statement of the Forty-Four". The Norwegians, and even many within the Missouri Synod felt that this document cracked the door to unionism and laid down unscriptural principles of church fellowship. Though the Norwegians repeatedly asked Missouri in committee meetings to either require the signers of the 'Statement" to retract, or to exercise discipline over against them, satisfactory doctrinal discipline—in the judgment of the Norwegians—was not exercised, nor did these signers retract their "Statement." In fact, their number grew quite rapidly. The Norwegians also protested the agreement which Missouri worked out with the National Lutheran Council to enter into joint welfare work and joint armed service work with Lutheran bodies of the Council, with whom Missouri was not in doctrinal agreement or fellowship.

1947 While the Norwegians had protested Missouri's newly made distinction regarding joint prayer and prayer fellowship, on the grounds that this distinction cannot be supported on the basis of Scripture and opens the door to further unionistic practices, the Missouri Synod answered by reaffirming its 1944 "Saginaw Resolution" (concerning joint prayer and prayer fellowship, and the Scouting movement). At the same time Missouri also renewed its allegiance to the "Brief Statement"—a document acceptable to both the Norwegian and Wisconsin Synods. Missouri also rescinded the 1938 "St. Louis Articles."

The Norwegians, of course, were overjoyed when the Missouri Synod reiterated its stand that the "Brief Statement" correctly expresses its doctrinal position. On the other hand, the Norwegian Synod had to call the Missouri brothers to task for individual cases of fellowship carried on with the ALC. What bothered the Norwegians was that some of the persons involved were men of high standing in the Missouri Synod, and that instead of being disciplined for their impetuous action, in certain cases they were elevated to positions of even higher responsibility. Once again the Norwegians called on Missouri to discontinue for the time being doctrinal discussions with those outside the Synodical Conference, in order that the member synods could imbibe the deep meaning of the "Brief Statement" and study the Lutheran Confessions together.

The ALC's commissioners issued a "Friendly Invitation" to renew negotiations, contending for an "allowable and wholesome latitude of theological opinion on the basis of the teachings of the Word of God." The Missouri Synod again called on its Committee on Doctrinal Unity to arrive at one document which is "clear, concise, and unequivocal."

1949 The Wisconsin Synod addressed six questions to the Missouri Synod concerning the following: Lutheran men of America, cooperation in Welfare Agencies, cooperation with the National Lutheran Council, first Bad Boll (conference held in Germany), the booklet *Scouting in the Lutheran Church*, and applicability of Romans 16:17 to all errorists, whether Lutheran or not. At the same time Wisconsin stated: "With deep concern we note that the ties which have united us particularly with the Synod of Missouri are being loosened."[16]

The Norwegians too in 1949 in Convention took the Missouri Synod to task

333

for a number of things, including its practice of "cooperation in externals"—citing it as unionism—and for tolerating doctrinal indifferences and error in its midst.

1950 The Missouri Synod and the ALC adopted the "Common Confession," which was hailed as a settlement of the past doctrinal differences between those two bodies and sufficient basis for union between them.[17] The Norwegians, after a thorough study of the document, once again had to state their disapproval, finding it to be "a document of compromise which does not in any way reject the errors of the ALC which, therefore, is inadequate as a settlement of past doctrinal differences and unsatisfactory as a basis for union." Specifically involved was the toleration by the ALC of the teaching that some parts of Scripture are not divinely inspired; also the open denial of Objective (world) Justification. The Norwegians also took exception to the section on Conversion since it failed to spell out the fact that the unconverted offer willful resistance and not just natural resistance, which then results in their failure to be converted. Exception was taken to the ALC's doctrine on Election, that it takes place "in view of faith." Exception was also taken to the statement that the Means of Grace belongs to the essence of the Holy Christian Church. (The saints in heaven are members of the Christian Church and do not need forgiveness, which is assured to the sinner in the Means of Grace, and the Gospel in Word and Sacraments.) The Norwegians also drew the conclusion that the "Common Confession" does not reject wholly, errors regarding the Last Things: namely that the papacy may not be the Antichrist, that a wholesale conversion of the Jews may be looked for, and that there will be some kind of millennial reign of Christ on earth.

Again the Norwegians petitioned Missouri to "reconsider its adoption of the 'Common Confession' and to reject it as a settlement of its doctrinal differences with the ALC."[18] Here the Norwegians gained a little ground, for their petition was met by resolutions in the Missouri Synod calling for postponement and delay. Of the "Common Confession" Missouri stated that it had found nothing in it that contradicts Scripture. But it did not on the other hand state that it settled past differences that existed between the two bodies.

1951 The Norwegians requested the Missouri Synod to cease negotiations except on the basis of full acceptance of the "Brief Statement."[19] The Wisconsin Synod, the same year, also rejected the "Common Confession" and went so far as to say that adoption of the "Common Confessing" by the Missouri Synod "involves an untruth and creates a basically untruthful situation, since this action has been officially interpreted as settlement of past differences which are in fact not settled," and asked the Missouri Synod to repudiate its stand.[20] The Wisconsin Synod furthermore resolved: "That we inform the President of the Lutheran Church-Missouri Synod through our President, that if the appropriate action in the matter treated in this report is not forthcoming, at least through the Praesidium of that body, we shall feel constrained to carry the issue to the Synodical Conference at its next regular convention."[21]

1952 When the Synodical Conference met at St. Paul, Minnesota, the delegates of the Wisconsin Synod declared themselves in a state of confession because they felt that the issues had not been met at all. Discussion on the

"Common Confession" was terminated by majority vote (thus actually by the vote of the Missouri Synod delegates) and the Convention was told that the Missouri Synod is preparing Part II of the "Common Confession" and that the bodies should wait for the document. The Norwegians were awe struck by the action of the majority, to throw out the committee's work and kill discussion.

1953 The Missouri Synod met in Convention at Houston. At this Convention no action was taken by that body favorable to the position of either the Norwegians or the Wisconsin Synod. Wisconsin, later the same year, listed examples of Missouri's adherence to unionistic practices. These included "negotiation for purposes of union with a church body whose official position it is that it is neither possible nor necessary to agree in all matters of doctrine, and which contends for an allowable and wholesome latitude of theological opinion on the basis of the teaching of the Word of God."[22] The Wisconsin Synod further stated that the Missouri Synod "has brought about the present break in relations that is now threatening the existence of the Synodical Conference and the continuance of our affiliation with the sister Synod."

Perhaps the feeling of the Norwegians toward the Missouri Synod in its role of helping to produce the "Common Confession" and its willingness to accept it as a viable union document (which it wanted the other synods in the Conference to also accept), can be summarized in an address by Pastor Robert Preus at the 1953 Norwegian Synod Convention.

> OUR SISTER SYNOD OF MISSOURI HANDS US A DOCUMENT CALLED THE "COMMON CONFESSION" WHICH IS SUPPOSED TO SETTLE ALL DIFFERENCES BETWEEN HER AND THE ALC, BUT WHICH IN REALITY SCARCELY MENTIONS THESE DIFFERENCES, AND THEN SHE SAYS TO US, PLEASE ACCEPT THIS. WE HAVE NO RECOURSE BUT TO REJECT THE CONFESSION AS SETTLING NOTHING, AND TESTIFY TO OUR DEAR SISTER SYNOD, GOD FORBID, REPENT! . . . OUR CONCERN AND ZEAL WILL BE MISTAKEN FOR PRIDE AND STUBBORNNESS. BUT WE HAVE NO CHOICE. WE MUST SPEAK OUT . . . IT IS NOT ONLY A MATTER OF DUTY, IT IS A MATTER OF OUR SALVATION . . .[23]

Neither the Wisconsin Synod nor the Norwegian Synod would accept the "Common Confession" Part I as a settlement of doctrinal differences between the two negotiating bodies. When in 1953 the Missouri Synod asked these sister synods to study Part II, which was supposed to add clarifications of the "Common Confession," neither synod would accede to the request. How could they consider Part II to be one document with Part I, when it had not even been accepted officially by either body whose committees produced it? Furthermore, it bothered these sister synods that while matters were supposed to have been settled regarding those doctrines covered by the "Common Confession," nevertheless statements coming out of the ALC, and also actions on its part, did not bear this out. Professor G.O. Lillegard of the Norwegian Synod, in commenting on the Missouri Synod's Houston Convention (1953) stated:

> REFERENCE COULD BE MADE TO ONE STATEMENT AFTER THE OTHER (MADE WITHIN THE LAST YEAR OR TWO BY PROMINENT ALC LEADERS) TO SHOW THAT THEY HAVE NOT CHANGED A PARTICLE IN THEIR ATTITUDE TOWARD CONSERVATIVE LUTHERANISM, AND THAT THEY REGARD THE "COMMON CONFESSION" PART I AS ANYTHING BUT A VICTORY FOR TRUE "MISSOURIANISM."[24]

And so, while the Missouri Synod looked to the "Common Confession" as a document promulgating the "Old Missouri theology," the ALC did not so interpret it. That body was not about to become Missourian in its theology! Was the "Common Confession" then really specific enough and clear enough in covering the controverted points? History itself bears out that it wasn't. For at the same time that the ALC was reaching toward Missouri through the "Common Confession," it was also reaching the hand of fellowship to other Lutheran bodies with whom Missouri could not at the time find itself in fellowship, because of doctrinal disagreements. The "Common Confession" was finally dropped by Missouri as a functioning union document, and especially so, because of historical developments!

1954 The controversy within the Synodical Conference accelerated. At this point both the Norwegian Synod and the Wisconsin Synod published pamphlets to bring the issues into sharp focus before the minds of their members. Things were indeed shaping up for the 1954 Synodical Conference Convention that met both in Detroit and in Chicago. Both the Missouri and Wisconsin Synods distributed printed testimony. Doctrinal discussions were held on the issues involved. At the second Convention of the Synodical Conference, the Norwegian Synod sent an urgent and prayerful plea to the Conference as a court of last appeal to petition the Missouri Synod to take some action to remedy the many offenses with which it had been charged. The Norwegians asked the Synodical Conference to vote on five resolutions which it put forth, dealing with the doctrines of objective Justification, Unionism, Prayer Fellowship, the "1938 Resolution," and the "Common Confession."

Regarding the "Common Confession," the Norwegians asked the Synodical Conference to pass a resolution stating that the "Confession" does not settle the doctrinal difference between the Synodical Conference and the ALC. The Norwegians furthermore wanted a resolution passed rejecting the "St. Louis Resolution of 1938" as well as the "Common Confession" as satisfactory doctrinal statements. The Norwegians hoped that if the Synodical Conference adopted these resolutions it would influence Missouri to make them its own at its forthcoming 1956 Convention, and thus avert the threatened break in fraternal relations. Only the first and second resolutions covering the historical position of the Synodical Conference on Objective Justification and Unionism were adopted. The last three resolutions covering the actual points of disagreement were not adopted but assigned to committees for further study. This greatly disappointed the Norwegians, who had come to the conclusion that there had been more than enough committee discussions and that the more things were discussed the farther apart the two sides had become. They were also saddened by what they characterized as the "unyielding spirit shown there (at East Detroit) by the Missouri Synod spokesman in defending every point covered in our Resolutions III, IV, and V."

And so, in neither the regular nor the recessed sessions was the Synodical Conference able to deal with the precarious situation that had developed in its midst. Neither side was convinced by arguments presented by the other side. Instead of rejecting the "Common Confession," the Synodical Conference merely resolved to ask the Missouri Synod "not to use the 'Common Confession' as a functioning union document." By this time, the ALC was preparing to merge with the other synods in the American Lutheran Conference, and as a result talks had been suspended with the Missouri Synod.

This was to be the Norwegians' final testimony to their sister synod within the bonds of fellowship. At its 1954 Convention the Norwegian Synod resolved that its Union Committee have no further dealings with the Unity Committee of the Missouri Synod. The Norwegians were becoming deeply concerned about taking care of their own spiritual welfare.

1955 This year witnessed the suspension of fellowship with the Missouri Synod. When the Norwegian Synod met in Convention, the Convention Doctrinal Committee was ready with a lengthy report covering the history of the Synod's fellowship with the Missouri Synod and also with an up-to-date summary of the union controversy. Since it was felt that an impasse had been reached in negotiations with the Missouri Synod and that further negotiations would result in indifferentism and in compromise of scriptural doctrine and practice, the Report concluded with a declaration of suspension of fellowship with the Missouri Synod on the basis of Romans 16: 17. It was to be a suspension in fellowship, not a final and complete break between the two bodies. Finally, by a rising vote of 65 to 10 the Doctrinal Committee's report was made the official policy of the Norwegian Synod. Here, then, is the Doctrinal Committee's report, adopted by the Norwegian Synod.

AS FOR OURSELVES, WE AFFIRM THAT WE WANT TO REMAIN TRUE TO THE WORD OF GOD AND THE LUTHERAN CONFESSIONS. WE WANT TO CONTINUE IN THE OLD PATHS IN WHICH OUR FATHERS WALKED, TOGETHER WITH THE FATHERS OF THE LUTHERAN CHURCH-MISSOURI SYNOD. BEFORE GOD, THEREFORE, WE FEEL THAT WE HAVE ONLY ONE CHOICE. SINCE THE LUTHERAN CHURCH-MISSOURI SYNOD HAS SHOWN US IN ITS OFFICIAL PROCEEDINGS THAT IT NO LONGER WALKS IN THE OLD WAYS WITH US, WE MUST DECLARE THAT THE LUTHERAN CHURCH-MISSOURI SYNOD HAS BROKEN THE BOND THAT HAS BOUND US TOGETHER FOR 100 YEARS. THE TIME HAS COME WHEN WE MUST TESTIFY BY ACTION AGAINST THE UNIONISM WHICH HAS BECOME SO COMMON IN THE LUTHERAN CHURCH-MISSOURI SYNOD IN RECENT YEARS. TO CONTINUE THE ARGUMENTS BY WORD AND PEN WILL BE MORE LIKELY TO FURTHER AGGRAVATE THAN TO RESOLVE OUR DIFFERENCES. THEREFORE WE HEREBY DECLARE WITH DEEPEST REGRET THAT FELLOWSHIP RELATIONS WITH THE LUTHERAN CHURCH-MISSOURI SYNOD ARE SUSPENDED ON THE BASIS OF ROMANS 16:17, AND THAT THE EXERCISE OF SUCH RELATIONS CANNOT BE RESUMED UNTIL THE OFFENSES CONTRARY TO THE DOCTRINE WHICH WE HAVE LEARNED HAVE BEEN REMOVED BY THEM IN PROPER MANNER. . . IT IS OUR FIRM CONVICTION THAT WE AND THOSE WHO STAND WITH US REPRESENT THE SCRIPTURAL PRINCIPLES AND SPIRIT OF THE SYNODICAL CONFERENCE AND THAT IT IS THE LUTHERAN CHURCH-MISSOURI SYNOD WHICH HAS DEPARTED FROM THEM.[25]

At the same time, the Norwegian Synod made it clear it had no intention of suspending fraternal relations in the Synodical Conference with those who agree with its stand (namely, the Wisconsin Synod) but to continue these relations and to labor for realignment of Lutherans faithful to the Lutheran Confessions "on more realistic lines than those which prevail under the present chaotic conditions in the Synodical Conference."[26]

THE MISSOURI SYNOD RESPONDS

In his answer to the action of the Norwegian Synod (as reported in the *Lutheran Witness*), Dr. Behnken was decisive: "We do not admit the charges. On the contrary, we emphatically deny them" (August 2, 1955, pp. 6ff.). In the following issues of the Lutheran Witness the venerable leader sought to answer the charges by the two sister synods with which she had found herself in disagreement. In his autobiography, the now sainted Dr. Behnken made this observation concerning the withdrawing of former sister synods from the Synodical Conference in 1963–which action, of course, was inevitable:

I FIND IT DIFFICULT TO EXPRESS IN WORDS THE DEEP SADNESS I FEEL THAT OUR SISTER CHURCHES FELT CONSTRAINED TO SEVER THE TIES WHICH FOR 90 YEARS HAD BOUND US TOGETHER IN A BLESSED AND FRUITFUL FELLOWSHIP. THEIR DECISION IS THE MORE REGRETTABLE SINCE THE DIFFERENCES BETWEEN US LIE ALMOST ENTIRELY IN THE AREA OF PRACTICE RATHER THAN THE PRINCIPLES THEMSELVES. THEIR ACTION IN WITHDRAWING FROM THE SYNODICAL CONFERENCE WAS CERTAINLY PREMATURE, FOR THE COURSE ADVOCATED BY OUR OVERSEAS BRETHREN THAT WE MUTUALLY APPROACH THE GOAL OF AGREEMENT "BY THE TRADITIONAL HIGHWAY OF THE DOCTRINE OF THE CHURCH" OFFERED A PROMISING OPPORTUNITY TO THE HOLY SPIRIT TO LEAD US INTO THE TRUE UNITY IN THE BOND OF PEACE, WHICH HE DESIRES AND FOR WHICH WE PRAY. [27]

Dr. Behnken laid his finger on a sore spot in synodical relationships within the Conference when he stressed that the difference was in practice, "rather than in the principles themselves." That a "different spirit" had developed over the years in the Missouri Synod in this respect, many, even within its own ranks testified. However, even if it were "only a matter of practice" the Norwegians would still have found it necessary to go their separate way from the Missouri Synod, for the reason that the practice of a church body ought to carry out its confessions. A church's practice pretty well states what it thinks of doctrine. And we can include under a church body's practice the action of placing under discipline those professors, teachers, and pastors whose practice and whose official statements and pronouncements do not agree with the doctrinal statements and the practice of the body itself. Both the Norwegians and the Wisconsin Synod noted a failure on the part of their much larger sister synod to carry out church discipline to the extent they deemed was necessary.

But doctrine too was the issue as far as both sister synods were concerned. And eventually cleavage over doctrine would become the burning issue within the Missouri Synod itself. The great controversy which began in 1972 as a struggle between the conservatives and the moderates was over doctrine, particularly the doctrine of Holy Scripture. Interestingly enough, it was kicked off by a report made public by the president of the Missouri Synod, Dr. J.A.O. Preus, in which he accused a majority of the faculty of Concordia Seminary, St. Louis, of holding a "view of Scriptures which in practice erodes authority" of the Bible.[28] He pointed out: "Within the faculty the doctrine of Holy Scripture is subverted to the point where, in effect, false doctrine is proclaimed regarding them." In the years that followed the action of suspending fellowship with the Missouri Synod by the Norwegians and the Wisconsin Synod, issues separating the two groups became clearly defined and at the same time, chances of recon-

338

ciliation grew even dimmer.

1956 In its convention of this year the Norwegian Synod restated its resolution in these words: "That for the present the exercise of our fellowship relations with the Lutheran Church-Missouri Synod remain in suspension. It is to be noted that the Wisconsin Synod in its 1956 Saginaw Convention voted to "hold the judgment of our Saginaw resolutions in abeyance until our next convention," and furthermore resolved, "That our fellowship with the Lutheran Church-Missouri Synod be one of vigorous protesting fellowship to be practiced where necessary in the light of 2 Thessalonians 3:14,15."

NOT A PLEASANT TASK FOR THE "LITTLE" NORWEGIAN SYNOD

The termination of fellowship was not a task that came easy for the Norwegians. Yet, what they finally felt they had to do, was done in the spirit of making partial payment on a debt of love owed the Christian brethren in the Missouri Synod. The Norwegian Synod had received many and rich blessings in the past by its association with Missouri. When Dr. S.C. Ylvisaker addressed the 1944 Saginaw Convention of the Missouri Synod in behalf of his own synod, his words were gentle but showed the concern which was already evident in many hearts:

WE ASK TO RECEIVE THIS OVERTURE AS PROOF OF MOST INTIMATE FELLOWSHIP IN CHRIST...AS YOUR SYNOD CAME TO US IN THE YEAR 1917 WITH YOUR HEART-FELT CONCERN FOR THE CAUSE OF SOUND LUTHERANISM AMONG YOUR NORWE-GIAN BRETHREN, SO WE CAME IN LIKE FRATERNAL SPIRIT TO ASK YOU TO LOOK AGAIN TO THE ROCK FROM WHICH YOU WERE HEWN, TO MAKE SURE AGAIN OF THE FOUNDATION OF TRUTH UPON WHICH THE CHRISTIAN CHURCH MUST BE BUILT IF IT WOULD KEEP THE SURE PROMISES OF GOD...GOD AND MANY MEN LOOK TO YOU TODAY TO CONTINUE YOUR NOBLE WORK, YOUR HONEST CONFESSION, YOUR VICTORIOUS COURSE IN THE DEFENSE OF PURE GOSPEL. OUR SYNOD ASKS FOR NO GREATER HONOR THAN TO STAND AT YOUR SIDE IN PREACHING, TEACHING, AND CONFESSING THE PURE GOSPEL OF AN UNMERITED GRACE, THAT HEALING BALM FOR THE WOES OF MEN. WILL YOU NOT LOOK WITH US AGAIN TO MAKE SURE THAT THIS PURE GOSPEL IS STILL THERE AS THE ONE SOL-ACE FOR SOULS IN DISTRESS? WILL YOU NOT GO WITH US AGAIN TO THE RAMPARTS TO MAKE SURE THAT THERE IS NO BREACH WHERE THE FOE MAY TAKE US UNAWARE AND THAT NO PART IS LEFT UNDEFENDED? FOR IF WE LOSE THE GOSPEL OF FREE GRACE, ALL IS GONE..." [29]

Already in 1928–about the time the first ominous clouds were building on the horizon–Rev. Justin A. Peterson addressed the Norwegian Synod Convention in commemoration of the Centennial of the Saxon Immigration. Speaking on the subject "Our Debt, Under God, to Our Brethren of the Missouri Synod," he went on to call upon the Norwegian Synod to pray for "our benefactors of the Missouri Synod, her congregations and pastors, her schools, higher and lower, and her teachers, and not least for her Theological Seminary..." The writer expressed the hope that such sincere prayer would naturally lead to a "...humble, sympathetic understanding of the position and problems of our brethren. We shall be quick to praise and slow to find fault. We shall not act like little dogs that constantly bark and rant at every shadow. We shall look for the bright and not the shady side. Our very position as members of the Synodical Conference and especially of the Norwegian Synod makes it so easy to develop the holier-than-thou attitude. We should shun suspicion and carping criticism as the devil himself and ever be mindful also in Synodical relations of the eighth commandment (e.g. concerning bearing false witness) which admonished us to excuse our neighbor, speak well of him, and put the best construction on everything. This does not mean, of course, that we must never criticize, admonish, and, if needs be, even rebuke. Such spirit is not evidence of true love. We must not regard the Missouri Synod as an aggregation of saints perfected in themselves...wherever you have the human equation, there you have sinners with depraved and deceitful hearts, the fountain-head of all evil, ready to flow over at any time...We must not, therefore, canonize the Missouri Synod...Not the hosts of the Lord, but the Lord of hosts will we worship. God bless the Missouri Synod!...May no strange fires ever burn her sacred altars." [30]

KEEPING THE UNITY OF THE SPIRIT

At their 1956 St. Paul Convention, the Norwegians, on the recommendation of their Doctrinal Committee, resolved: THAT OUR SYNOD EXPRESS ITS DESIRE TO TAKE PART IN THE PROPOSED INTERNATIONAL CONFERENCE OF CONSERVATIVE LUTHERAN THEOLOGY, AFFILIATED WITH THE SYNODICAL CONFERENCE. At the same time it was also resolved to meet with other synods of the Conference TO DETERMINE WHETHER OR NOT THE CONSTITUENT SYNODS OF THE SYNODICAL CONFERENCE ARE NOW IN DOCTRINAL AGREEMENT. [31] The Norwegian Synod's Union Committee was designated to serve as official representative to these meetings. Discussions of the Joint Committee began early in 1957 and agreement was reached on the areas of study. Some practical areas were to be covered, namely: Scouting (deistic religion), the Antichrist, Fellowship, Unionism, Separatism, Church Discipline, and the Military Chaplaincy. However, by the time the Norwegians held their Convention in 1957, its Doctrinal Committee was showing signs of edginess. With the approaching Synodical Conference Convention the following year, the Committee recommended bringing the Norwegians' case again to the Conference, and if no remedy to the situation be found there, that it would be time for the Synod to consider breaking ties that had bound it to the Conference.

Dissension set in at the 1957 Norwegian Synod Convention. One pastor, reviewing the situation, asked that the Synod withdraw from the Synodical Conference. His memorial was declined and the Doctrinal Committee's recommendations that the Synod continue to participate in the Joint Committee meetings was accepted.

ROUGH SEAS FOR THE LITTLE SHIP

A tense situation was now building in the Norwegian Synod. In 1958, when the Convention again voted to continue in the Joint Committee meetings, eight pastors and one layman recorded their negative votes. The following year, two more memorials opposing continuation in the Synodical Conference added to the tense situation in the Synod. These memorials hinted that the Synod was involving itself in unionism through continuation of joint mission work and prayer with those whom it found to be causing divisions and offenses, and requested the Synod to leave the Conference. However, the Synod again resolved to continue participation in the Joint Committee meetings, because its Committee testified that the discussions were bearing fruit and were held in a spirit of frankness and willingness to abide by the Scriptures.

But discouraged by the restlessness within its own ranks, the Convention urged the Committee to finish their work the following year and present a finished report to the next Convention. This action was not strong enough for two pastors and their congregations, and these withdrew from the Norwegian Synod. Furthermore, six pastors and four lay delegates registered their negative votes.

In order to help heal the breach that was beginning in their own ranks, the Norwegians called a special general pastoral conference, and the question whether or not the Synod was erring by continuing in the Synodical Conference under the circumstances was given a thorough airing. Throughout the conventions of the Norwegian Synod, whenever the question of continuation in the Synodical Conference was discussed, Professor Lillegard, as much as anyone, was instrumental in bringing a balance into the situation that was developing among the Norwegians. He cautioned against not only giving in on the truth, but also against separatism, the negative approach. He strove for the attitude that the Norwegian Synod had a duty to perform toward the erring brother, and that as long as the Wisconsin Synod was on the side of the Norwegian Synod, joining the testimony against errors of the Missouri Synod, it was not standing alone in the Conference and therefore should not give up the battle. His attitude was that the Wisconsin Synod should not be attacked for its continuation of fellowship (which was a protesting one) with Missouri.

OUT OF SYNODICAL CONFERENCE

By 1960, conditions in the Synodical Conference had deteriorated badly. The Committee found it could not go along with the Missouri Synod's announced intention of meeting with the National Lutheran Council. The meeting was for the stated purpose of setting up a new Lutheran inter-action agency to supersede the National Lutheran Council. (The meetings which were subsequently held resulted in the formation of the Lutheran Council in the U.S.A. [LCUSA], of which the Missouri Synod in 1965 voted to be a member.) The Norwegians could not go along with the Missouri Synod's stand on Church Fellowship as expressed in "The Theology of Fellowship." Therefore, the Committee brought its recommendation to the 1960 Convention that the Doctrinal Committee cease its work with the Joint Committees and that the Norwegians also present their reasons to the Synodical Conference later that year. The Norwegian Synod agreed with its Committee, calling for a special convention later to review the action of the Synodical Conference concerning the Synod's memorial, and to determine whether or not the Synod could continue in the Conference.

This Convention, however, lost two more pastors. The recessed Convention was not able to grapple with the problem, because the Synodical Conference itself had been recessed and did not give answer to the Norwegian Synod's memorial. It also reiterated its suspension of fellowship with the Missouri Synod. Four more pastors left.

The situation did not improve in the Synodical Conference and finally in 1963 the Evangelical Lutheran Synod–as it now called itself–withdrew. By this time the Wisconsin Synod had also suspended fellowship with the Missouri Synod, which suspension was declared in August 1961.

A CHURCH BODY NOT SHAMED BY SMALL
SIZE AND LACK OF INFLUENCE

If one were looking for a sentence to describe the Evangelical Lutheran Synod (the former "little" Norwegian Synod) in regards to its doctrinal stand, one could consider the following statement by author Theodore A. Aaberg in his history of the Synod, A CITY ON A HILL: THE ELS DOES NOT SAY THAT IT IS THE ONLY ONE IN THE WORLD TEACHING AND CONFESSING LUTHERAN DOCTRINE TODAY, BUT IT DOES SAY THAT THE DOCTRINE WHICH IT TEACHES AND CONFESSES IS THE DOCTRINE RESTORED BY LUTHER 450 YEARS AGO. Commenting on an attack made on the Evangelical Lutheran Synod by the Evangelical Lutheran Church at the time (1955) that the Norwegians suspended fellowship with the Missouri Synod, and was thus labeled by *the Lutheran Herald* (July 26, 1955 Issue) "the most reactionary splinter group of Lutherans in America," and that by its action it had taken itself "completely out of the stream of Lutheran Life, the author comments: IF 'THE STREAM OF LUTHERAN LIFE' MEANS WORSHIPING AND WORKING WITH OTHER CHURCHES IN SPITE OF THEIR DENIAL OF SCRIPTURAL DOCTRINE, AS IS DONE BY LUTHERAN CHURCH BODIES HOLDING MEMBERSHIP IN SUCH UNIONISTIC ORGANIZATIONS AS THE LUTHERAN COUNCIL UNITED STATES OF AMERICA; THE LUTHERAN WORLD FEDERATION; THE NATIONAL COUNCIL OF CHURCHES; AND THE WORLD COUNCIL OF CHURCHES; THE ELS HAS INDEED TAKEN ITSELF OUT OF 'THE STREAM OF LUTHERAN LIFE." [32]

A WORD ABOUT THE NAME CHANGE

The name, the Norwegian Synod of the American Evangelical Lutheran Church, or briefly, the Norwegian Synod or "little" Norwegian Synod, was retained until as late as 1957. A widespread movement to simplify church names had its effect on this body too, and finally the name was shortened to the Evangelical Lutheran Synod (ELS).

ADDENDUM:
2010 STATISTICS
169 pastors and professors (including two from the WELS and those who are

emeriti).

92 elementary and preschool teachers.

25 elementary and preschool schools.

8 area high schools.

1 college (Bethany, Mankato, MN).

1 theological seminary (Bethany, Mankato, MN).

John F. Brug, author of *The WELS And Other Lutherans—Second Edition*, informs us: "In recent decades the ELS has had extended internal discussion over the doctrine of the Lord's Supper and the doctrine of the Ministry." A number (8) of congregations and pastors did not approve the doctrinal statement on the Public Ministry of the Word, adopted by the ELS in 2005 and these left the ELS. These recently founded a cooperative association called the Association of Confessional Lutheran Churches (ACLC). Three conferences have been held with the Orthodox Lutheran Confessional Conference of Independent Churches with the Evangelical Lutheran Diocese of North America. [John F. Brug, *The WELS And Other Lutherans—Second Edition* (Northwestern Publishing House, Milwaukee, WI, 2009), p. 179]

Growth in the ELS: In May 1977 a brochure was sent out to pastors by the ELS. In it was this statement regarding home missions: "Many home mission congregations have been and are being established across the land. From the mountains of Colorado to the sandy beaches of Florida, from the plains of the Midwest to the towering fir trees of Washington, from the inner city of Chicago to the stately mansions of New England the greatest story ever told is being proclaimed by our missionaries."

Footnotes for Chapter Twenty

1 Richard C. Wolf, *Documents of Lutheran Unity in America*, (Fortress Press, Philadelphia, PA, 1966), p. 233; Doc. #100

2 Evangelical Lutheran Synod *Report*, 1952, p. 18

* In May 1977 a brochure was sent out to pastors by the ELS. In it was this statement regarding home missions: "Many home mission congregations have been and are being established across the land. From the mountains of Colorado to the sandy beaches of Florida, from the plains of the Midwest to the towering fir trees of Washington, from the inner city of Chicago to the stately mansions of New England the greatest story ever told is being proclaimed by our missionaries."

3 Theodore A. Aaberg, *A City Set On A Hill*, (Published by Board of Publications, Evangelical Lutheran Synod, Mankato, MN, 1968), p.99

4 Synodical Conference *Proceedings 1920*, p. 23.

5 Norwegian Synod Convention, *Report 1936*, p. 47 Quoted in Aaberg, *A City...*, p. 137.

6 Norwegian Synod Convention, *Report 1936*, pp. 42,43

7 Norwegian Synod Convention, *Report 1936*, p. 47

8 Aaberg, *A City Set On A Hill*, p. 145

9 Synodical Conference *Proceedings 1939,* p. 61

10 Wolf, *Documents of Lutheran Unity in America*, pp. 378, 379; Doc. #157.

11 John W. Behnken, *This I Recall*, (Concordia Publishing House, St. Louis, MO, 1964), p. 167.

12 Missouri Committee *Report 1947*, in Chicago, p. 495.

13 Missouri Committee *Report 1947*, in Chicago, p. 495.

14 Missouri Committee *Report 1947*, in Chicago, p. 495.

15 Missouri Synod Saginaw Convention *Report 1944,*pp. 251, 252

16 Wisconsin Synod Synodical *Proceedings 1949*, p. 117

17 Wisconsin Synod *Synodical Proceedings 1949*, p. 117.

18 Norwegian Synod *Convention Report 1951*, pp.54,55

19 Norwegian Synod *Convention Report* 1951, pp. 54, 55.

20 Wisconsin Synod *Synodical Proceedings* 1951, pp. 147, 148.

21 Wisconsin Synod *Synodical Proceedings* 1951, p. 148.

22 Wisconsin Synod *Synodical Proceedings* 1953, p. 104.

23 Aaberg, A City Set On a Hill, p. 182. A quote from "Clergy Bulletin,' May-June 1953.

24 Aaberg, A City Set On a Hill, p. 183. A quote from "Our Relations," pp.12, 13.

25 Wolf, *Documents of Lutheran Unity in America*, p. 434.

26 The information for the above chronology of events was taken to a great extent from "Suspension of Relations with the Lutheran Church-Missouri Synod" by the 38th Regular Convention of the Norwegian Synod June 1955, p. 5, and from the Wisconsin Synod Proceedings 1955, Saginaw, Michigan, pp. 82ff.

27 John W. Behnken, *This I Recall*, pp. 178, 179.

28 For a quick review of the Missouri Synod's battle for the Bible, and the attacks from within it against the Bible, read Harold Lindsell's *The Battle For the Bible*, Zondervan, 1976, pp. 72-88, 207.

29 Aaberg, *A City on A Hill*, pp. 154, 155. Quoted from the Lutheran Sentinel, (27;14)-July 27, 1944, pp. 210-212.

30 Norwegian Synod Convention *Report 1938*, pp. 47-57

31 Aaberg, *A City on a Hill*, pp. 207, 208.

32 Aaberg, *A City on a Hill*, pp. 4,5.

CHAPTER TWENTY-ONE

THE SWEDES
LAND OF THE SWEDES

HISTORICAL BACKGROUND
OF THE SWEDISH IMMIGRATION

THE CHURCH OF SWEDEN

The official title "The Church of Sweden" does not carry the name Lutheran, although it professes the faith stated in the *Augsburg Confession*. In its doctrine, the Church of Sweden is a departure from Roman Catholicism. However, in its organization the Church has been only slightly affected by the introduction of the Lutheran Reformation. Though apostolic succession is claimed, it is not stressed, so for practical purposes one could say that there is no apostolic succession in the Church of Sweden. The Bishop is a superintendent. While the Church of Sweden is marked by a centralized power, the Swedish Church in America strived for the opposite, and decentralization of power became the form not only for the Augustana Synod itself, but for its mission program and even its school organization.

The church, bishops, and pastors retained most of the privileges which had been held under the medieval system. The Lutheran pastor of Sweden is both an ecclesiastical person as well as a servant of the state, and this was especially true in the 1800's. Thus the pastor was a highly respected and influential man, and not a little feared in his dual role. Up to 1866 the clergy as an estate were represented in a separate chamber in parliament.

It is sad but true that there are not a few instances of impiety found among the clergy.

Up into the nineteen century, every child had to be baptized within eight days of birth. As a teenager he was sent to the pastor for catechetical instructions. As late as the middle of the 1880's every confirmed person was required to commune once a year in order to retain the rights of citizenship, even to marry or find work. It can be truthfully said that the church was the community center.

Church services sometimes lasted three hours and were held in unheated churches. The pastors changed the liturgy and retained the ornamental gown. The peasants regularly attended church, which was formal. Informal Bible and prayer groups were disdained. THE CHURCH BECAME A BODY OF FRIGID, MECHANICAL FORMS AND CEREMONIES, WHICH QUENCHED THE SPIRIT AND GAVE TO THE PEOPLE ONLY THE DRY HUSKS OF FORMALISM. PERSONS WITH SCARCELY A SPARK OF SPIRITUALITY REGARDED WITH HORROR THE OMISSION OF ANY PART OF THE LITURGY.[1]

At the time that emigration to America began, the religious/political climate was changing. Old ideas, both political and religious, were assailed. Religious movements were happening, including Pietism and Revivalism. There was much protest against the worldliness of the pastors by the various sects. Among the sects in Sweden were the Methodists, Baptists, Eric-Jansonists, and Mormons. Irrationalism characterized some of the revivalistic groups, such as the Eric-Jansonists. Before 1840, sectarianism was almost unknown in Sweden. While the State Church frowned heavily on pietistic movements, the pietists themselves were nevertheless attached to the Church of Sweden. Persons who led conventicles were liable to fines under the Conventicle Act of 1726, and until 1860 banishment could even result from holding private religious gatherings. Though the Constitution in 1809 granted religious liberty, the State Church made as few concessions as possible. As a result, many immigrants arrived in America with bitter memories of injustices done to Swedes who dared to depart from "the true faith." Reports brought back to Sweden of religious freedom in America helped to hasten the day when the Conventicle Law was softened and then finally repealed altogether.

GEORGE SCOTT AND THE FREE MOVEMENT

George Scott came to Sweden in 1830 as a chaplain to English workmen. He was a Wesleyan missionary and a disciple of John Wesley—in other words, a Methodist revivalistic preacher. Within a year he was preaching to Swedes in their own language and attracting a large following. He became the promoter of the free church movement in Sweden. However, Scott won disfavor with a statement he made regarding certain conditions in Sweden, and finally his career there was brought to an end because of adverse propaganda from his enemies. He did not favor separating from the State

Church. His attitude, rather, was to breathe new life into it. Disliked by many leaders in the State Church, he nevertheless contributed toward a moral renaissance in Sweden.

Scott painted the following picture of church life: CHRISTIAN EXPERIENCE SEEMS UTTERLY DISREGARDED IN THIS COUNTRY; AN EMPTY UNINFLUENTIAL FORM IS THE HIGHEST OBJECT AT WHICH THEY AIM.... THE LUTHERAN CHURCH, BY ALL THE ACCOUNTS I CAN GET, IS FAST ASLEEP, IF NOT DEAD; THE PRIESTHOOD HAS BECOME WORLDLY, SENSUAL AND MERCENARY; THE ORDINANCES ARE NEGLECTED AND EXPERIMENTAL RELIGION IS UNKNOWN...THERE IS SUCH AN UTTER WANT OF SPIRITUALITY–SUCH A MISERABLE IGNORANCE OF EXPERIMENTAL RELIGION–SUCH A DISPOSITION TO WORLDLY MINDEDNESS AND THE PURSUIT OF SEVERAL PLEASURES....[2]

Others agreed with Scott in his severe criticism of the spiritual state of Sweden. A pastor of the State of the Church wrote in 1854: THE SPIRITUAL LEVEL IN CHURCH AND STATE IS SO LOW THAT CONDITIONS COULD HARDLY BE WORSE IF WE WERE UNDER THE DOMINION OF THE PAPACY.

The preaching of the State Church had little in it to appeal to souls and draw them to a childlike faith, or to arouse consciences to an awareness of sin and to awaken sinners to a more Christian life. Furthermore, the lives of many of the clergy did not conform to their teachings. Drunkenness was a severe problem in Sweden in the early 1830's. It was such a widespread plague upon the land that it was partly responsible for the economic depression, poverty, and crime of that era. Whiskey stills were common place in Sweden, and the potion was drunk morning, noon, and night. The per capita consumption of alcohol in Sweden exceeded that of every other country in Europe. All landowners could operate stills. Even clergy did so. It was no wonder that temperance was an important feature in the message of the pietistic and revivalistic preachers.

THE NATIONAL EVANGELICAL FOUNDATION

There were Swedes who wanted a Church totally separated from the Church of Sweden. In 1855 Fjellstedt proposed the establishing of a free Lutheran Church. However, this was too revolutionary at the time for many to swallow. Instead, a young man, Hans Jacob Lunborg, proposed a plan–later called the National Evangelical Foundation. This society distributed devotional literature and provided speakers within the bosom of the State Church, thus intending to be a leaven in it. But it actually tended toward separatism. It infused lay preaching into the Church; however, the lay preachers were found to come in conflict with the parish pastors.

RELIGIOUS REVIVAL, INCLUDING PIETISM

THE RELIGIOUS LIFE IN SWEDEN IN THE MIDDLE OF THE 19TH CENTURY WAS CHARACTERIZED BY A SPIRITUAL AWAKENING. WHILE THE ESTABLISHED CHURCH WAS NOT WITHOUT EARNEST SPIRITUAL LEADERS AND PASTORS, IT IS TRUE THAT IN MANY PARTS, RATIONALISM AND WORLDLINESS

HAD INVADED THE CHURCH. THE SHEEP WERE NOT PROPERLY FED. HERE AND THERE THE LORD RAISED UP GREAT PREACHERS WHOSE POWERFUL SERMONS REACHED THE CONSCIENCES OF MANY. THE RESULT WAS REPENTANCE, A FEAR OF DIVINE JUDGMENT AND A LEGALISTIC OUTLOOK, BUT THAT GAVE NO PEACE. THERE CAME THE PIETISTIC MOVEMENT INTO SWEDEN.[3]

Revivalism was something understood best of all by the Swedish lower-middle class. While some leaders wanted total separation from the State Church, others tried to maintain a middle-of-the-road policy. They remained loyal to the established church while endeavoring a spiritual renewal in both church and nation. Such men were Peter Fjellstedt, P. Wieselgren, and C.O. Rosenius.

Many of the pastors—both conservative and otherwise—championed the cause for temperance. The religious revival took deep root especially in the poorer class of Swedes, who gave the greatest number of their people to the Swedish emigration.

The Lutheran pietists met to read the Bible, to sing and pray, and simply to have spiritual enjoyment. The Swedish term for pietist, "läsare," means "readers." Historian Conrad Bergendoff points out that Luther, Nohrborg, Pontoppidan, as well as the Bible were authoritative for the 'readers,' as they were called in Norrland [North Sweden].[4] In Norrland the pietists had some who delved into Pentecostal experiences, including speaking in tongues. "A strange phenomenon called 'preaching sickness' also took over strongly in Småland. A large number of people all ages went into trances, saw visions, jerked, contorted, shouted, and groaned. That part of Sweden, which produced the most spectacular religious phenomena, also had the greatest number of emigrants to America, especially in the early years. These were eventually provoked into leaving by their less enthusiastic neighbors!"[5]

Lars Laestadius, who worked among the Lapps, and Per Brandell in Norrland, were leaders of Pietism in Northern Sweden. Since the pietists were often provoked by their fellow countrymen to emigrate, it was the pietistic pastors and laymen of the Swedish Church who then laid the foundation for the Swedish Lutheran Church in America. "The pietistic strain of the members was so strong that no pastor would be tolerated who did not share their views, which were essentially those of the New England Puritans."[6]

CARL OLOF ROSENIUS (1826-1868)

Rosenius was born and raised in upper Norrland. Thoroughly grounded in Luther, he accepted Scott's pietistic ideas. He had a great love for the Bible. Rosenius felt that the Lutheran faith in the State Church was too spiritually cold; however, he did not separate from the established Church. Though working for revival in the Church, Rosenius did not enter the ministry but remained a layman all his life. While emphasizing revival of sound Christian living, Rosenius made justification by faith and the atonement accomplished by Jesus Christ the central theme of this revival movement.

PAUL PETER WALDENSTROEM (1838-1917)

Waldenstroem, theologian and educator, was the greatest free church leader for almost fifty years. Mostly conservative in his theology, he promoted the administration of the Lord's Supper at conventicles. He also promoted lay preaching. Later, however, he veered from the truth of Christ's atonement for he could not accept the teaching that Christ's death could propitiate God. He concluded that the world was not justified by the death of the Savior, because God is love and his nature is unchangeable. Christ was God's messenger to tell the world this in order that the people might return to him. Briefly, Waldenstroem's idea of reconciliation through Christ is not the reconciling of God to sinners, but the reconciling of sinners to God. Thus he denies the wrath of God. Waldenstroem was attacked by both the State Church and the free churches. He had little faith in the Church of Sweden and was not enthusiastic about America. He did much writing, some of which was published in America. The Augustana Synod bitterly attacked him. Nevertheless, his doctrine won a large number of followers.

HYPER-EVANGELICALISM

This was a movement which went to the extreme in preaching release from the bondage under the law.

SWEDISH MISSION CONVENT

This group, founded August 2, 1878, at a free church meeting in Stockholm, was composed of delegates from mission societies. It became the largest free church movement. It also existed as something of a phenomenon, since its members retained membership in the State Church, though it functioned as a church body.

CAUSES OF THE SWEDISH EMIGRATION

There were various causes of the migration of great numbers of Swedes to America. Economics, politics, and religion were once again major factors in mass movement of Scandinavians from the old lands to the new land that seemed to offer everything.

SWEDEN WAS SADDLED WITH AN ARCHAIC POLITICAL AND ECCLESIASTICAL SYSTEM WHICH BRED SEPARATISM, DISSENSION, STRIFE, TUMULT, MASS MEETINGS, PIETISM AND AGNOSTICISM AND MAGNIFIED AMERICA IN THE MINDS OF THOUSANDS OF HER SONS AND DAUGHTERS AS THE LAND OF CANAAN WHERE THERE WERE NOT ONLY MATERIAL BLESSINGS, BUT WHERE CHURCH, SOCIETY, LAWS, AND CUSTOMS WERE INCENTIVES TO A CLOSER WALK WITH GOD.[7]

Class distinctions—as in Norway—were an insufferable burden for many Swedes. America was looked upon as a land of equality, of freedom, of unlimited opportunity to get ahead and make a place for one's self in the world, and even acquire a degree of wealth. America was looked upon especially as the place where one could enjoy freedom from political, social, and religious restrictions. The poor people in Sweden were kept out of voting because of a property qualification. But in America any man of good character could finally qualify to vote and could even qualify to be elected to office.[8] "American Fever" burned in many a Swedish mind and heart.

Economics played a large part in the decision of many Swedes to leave the motherland. For one thing there were years of high employment. When one did find work the wages paid in Sweden were lower than those paid in America. For example, in Sweden a good farm hand 200 miles north of Stockholm could earn 100 Kroner a season-A Kroner was 27 cents. A Swedish farm hand working on a farm in Minnesota was paid 64 Kroner and board each month.[9]

The years 1867 to 1869 were times of very bad famine in Småland. In fact, in much of Sweden there were crop failures. This resulted in a heavy migration from the country. The years 1865 to 1895 constituted the period of greatest emigration from Sweden. A POLICY OF FREE TRADE IN THE 80'S THREATENED RUIN TO THE SMALL FARMERS; A LATER POLICY OF HIGH TARIFFS AND A RISING COST OF LIVING BORE HEAVILY ON WAGE EARNERS. INDUSTRIALISM WAS RAPIDLY CHANGING THE OLD SOCIAL AND ECONOMIC ORDER, LOCAL CRAFTS AND HOME INDUSTRIES WERE DISAPPEARING.[10] This, of course, did much to add to the unemployment rate. There was also compulsory military service in Sweden, which many young men wanted to avoid.

Religion too was an important factor in the decision of many Swedes to leave their native land. Abdel Wentz in a *Basic History of Lutheranism in America* points out:

IN THE CHURCH OF SWEDEN ALSO THERE WAS UNREST. THE EVANGELICAL MOVEMENTS AGITATING THE RELIGIOUS CIRCLES OF OTHER COUNTRIES FOUND FERTILE SOIL IN SWEDEN. PIETISTS FROM GERMANY, METHODISTS FROM ENGLAND, ADVOCATES OF 'LAY ACTIVITY' FROM NORWAY, TEMPERANCE REFORMERS FROM AMERICA, ALL COMBINED TO FOSTER SENTIMENT OF SEPARATISM FROM THE CHURCH AND EMIGRATION FROM THE COUNTRY. THE EVANGELICAL FERMENT LED NOT ONLY TO MOVEMENTS FOR MORAL REFORM BUT ALSO TO THE WIDE DISTRIBUTION OF BIBLES AND TRACTS, ACTIVE INTEREST IN FOREIGN MISSION, CONVENTICLES OF LAY PEOPLE FOR CULTIVATING THEIR SPIRITUAL LIFE, AND MOVEMENTS FOR SOCIAL REFORM.... THE EFFORTS OF POLITICAL AND ECCLESIASTICAL AUTHORITIES TO STEM THE TIDE OF THE EVANGELICAL MOVEMENTS BY REPRESSIVE MEASURES WAS ONE OF THE REASONS FOR THE EXODUS TO AMERICA IN THE MIDDLE OF THE 19TH CENTURY.[11]

The period between 1865 and 1895, which saw the greatest emigration from Sweden, also witnessed the greatest change in religion in the motherland. Many cherished the thought of going to wonderful America, where the religious liberty they cherished in their hearts could be obtained. In Sweden, during the 1880's, the free church movement really came into its own. Free religious meetings became popular, not only for the reason that they furnished the people something to do and a place to meet their friends, they were reminders of America to which they hoped to go.

Very few Swedes who emigrated returned to their native land. There was little inducement to do so. Sweden was a country of "poor journeymen, scanty wages, tyrannical and brutal masters, gloomy future, and high titles."[12] Many Swedes could only look forward to living out their declining years in the "poor house." A far different picture is painted in the eulogy written by one pastor about his new country: "In America, every working man can, if he will, become a nobleman, baron, and count."[13] Whereas there was a scarcity of land in Sweden, the Homestead Law in America fulfilled the dreams of many Swedes and brought them to these shores and helped to keep them here.

The number of Swedish immigrants speaks for itself. Between the years 1850 and 1880, 299,616 Swedes emigrated from their homeland. In just one year, 1881, a total of 64,607 Swedes came to these shores. From 1880 to 1890, 376,401 immigrants arrived in America from Sweden. And so, the Swedes constituted their fair share of the more than two million Scandinavian immigrants who came to this country between 1820 and 1920. And what became of the Lutheranism of the many transplanted Swedes? That is an issue that will be discussed in the next chapter.

Footnotes for Chapter Twenty-One

1 George M. Stephenson, *The American Immigration Collection*, (Arno Pussan, The New York Times, 1969. Copyright originally, 1932, University of Minnesota Press, Minneapolis, MN), p. 5.

2 Stephenson, *The American Immigration Collection*, p. 8.

3 Oscar N. Olson and George W. Wickstrom (Editors), *A Century of Life and Growth-1848 to 1948 Lutheran Augustana Synod*, (Augustana Book Concern, Rock Island, IL, 1948), page reference lost.

4 Conrad Bergendoff, *The Church of the Lutheran Reformation-A Historical Survey of Lutheranism*, (Concordia Publishing House, Saint Louis, MO 63118-3968, 1967), p. 216.

5 Arthur J. Clement, *Pentecost or Pretense?-An Examination of the Pentecostal and Charismatic Movements*, (Northwestern Publishing House, Milwaukee, WI, 1981), pp. 40, 41..

6 Stephenson, *The American Immigration Collection*, p. 386.

7 Stephenson, *The American Immigration Collection*, p. 58.

8 Ben Maddow, *A Sunday Between Wars-The Course of American Life from 1865-1917*, (W.W. Norton & Company, New York, NY, 1979), pp. 180,181.

9 Ben Maddow, *A Sunday Between Wars*, pp. 180, 181.

10 Oscar N. Olson, *The Augustana Lutheran Church in America 1860-1910*, Lutherans in U.S.A., 1956, p. 15.

11 Abdel Ross Wents, *A Basic History of Lutheranism in America* (Philadelphia, PA: Muhlenberg Press, 1955), pp. 127,128.

12 Stephenson, *The American Immigration Collection*, p. 400.

13 Stephenson, *The American Immigration Collection*, p.401

CHAPTER TWENTY-TWO

THE SWEDES
THE SCANDINAVIAN
EVANGELICAL LUTHERAN
AUGUSTANA SYNOD IN NORTH
AMERICA
THE AUGUSTANA
EVANGELICAL LUTHERAN CHURCH
1860 - 1962

THE COMING OF THE SWEDES

WHERE THEY SETTLED

The earliest settlements of Swedes in America consisted of people transplanted from the same neighborhoods and communities in the old country. Later, group immigration was not so common. There were Swedish settlements in Illinois, Indiana, Iowa, Minnesota, New York, and Pennsylvania. The Swedes did not settle in the South except in Texas. During the American Civil War the Swedish pastors were vehemently pro-Lincoln and many Swedes fought on the side of the North. Chicago was early the distribution center for the immigrants. Galesburg, Illinois, became very "Swedish" with a portion of the city called "Swedetown." The Civil War had its effect on the Swedish migration, but when victory for the North seemed certain, immigration from Sweden increased.

Nebraska had several important Swedish settlements. S.G. Larson was the most prominent of the earliest pastors here, but life was at first very hard for him and his family. His first winter in Nebraska, the family had scarcely enough food and only a scanty supply of fuel.[1] Pastor Larson helped to found a colony at Saunders County.

An important settlement at Stanton, Iowa, was founded through efforts of Bent Magnus Halland, a Swedish Lutheran Pastor. His community became one of the most prosperous in Swedish-America.

The gold fever in California attracted Swedes there, and as early as 1860, efforts were made to organize a Swedish Lutheran congregation in San Francisco. This congregation ultimately joined the Norwegian Synod. It was not until 1874 that the Augustana Synod began its work in California. Pastors who tried to serve Swedes in logging camps or in railway construction had a difficult time of it, partly due to the people's mobility.

Except in Texas, efforts to colonize the Swedes in Southern states failed.[2] Swedish efforts in Texas began already in the 1840's. The names of Swen M. Swenson and Svante Palm stand out. The greatest influx of Swedes to Texas occurred between 1878 and 1895. The Gulf Coast and Rio Grande Valley attracted quite a few in the later period of migration. Austin is the center of the Texas Swedish Community.

In the sixties and seventies a considerable number of Swedes settled in New England. In Massachusetts the chief settlement was at Worchester— by 1893, 10,000 Swedes lived here. But there were several other cities, including Hartford, Providence, Boston, and Brockton, with a considerable Swedish population. The Swedes who settled in these places were the new type of immigrant, having arrived later. They were more faithful to the State Church, and were more "high church," since they left Sweden after the pietistic movement had run its course.[3] Among the eastern states, New York, New Jersey, and Pennsylvania have the highest number of Swedes.

Before 1880 very few Swedes settled in Canada. Some of those who worked on railroads stayed on when work was completed. After 1887 Canada began to attract Swedish immigrants, mainly from the Northern provinces. Winnipeg is the most important center of Swedish population but there are settlements in Manitoba, Saskatchewan, Alberta, and western Ontario.[4]

Minnesota attracted many of the Swedes. It was a land fit for northern immigrants. The first Swedish settlers to Minnesota came in the fall of 1850 to what is now called Marine. The first permanent settlement was at Chicago Lake (Center City). With the ever-expanding westward frontier, settlers eventually crossed over into South Dakota. The Red River Valley area in Minnesota came to attract many Swedish settlers. Glowing letters from Peter Cassel, published in Sweden, caused many immigrants to head for Iowa. New Sweden thus came to be established. Towns with names like Swedenburg, Swedepoint, Swede Bend, Winterville, Bergholm, speak for the Swedish influence in Iowa.

Mention has already been made of the Swedes responding to the gold rush in California. But the discovery of gold in Colorado brought a number of Swedes in the 1870's to this state too. The Mormons in the 1850's carried on propaganda programs in Scandinavia inducing people to emigrate. A very large number of Swedish Lutherans became Mormon, and more will be said of this later on. Montana attracted Swedes already in the 1880's. Life here was primitive and the work of the missionary was especially rugged. When the great gold rush to Alaska occurred, many Swedes were attracted to this far north territory.

In 1880, states with the highest Swedish-born population were: Illinois, Minnesota, Iowa, Kansas, New York, Nebraska, Michigan, Wisconsin, Pennsylvania, Massachusetts, and Utah—in that order. By 1910 Minnesota was already ahead of Illinois, New York was third, Massachusetts fourth, Michigan fifth, California sixth, Washington seventh, and Iowa eighth. Then followed Wisconsin, Nebraska, Pennsylvania, and Connecticut—in that order. By 1920 Oregon, New Jersey, and North Dakota had entered the competition for Swedish population. Later, the Swedish-born population was concentrated in the northern Mississippi Valley, which contained half of the entire number. In 1930 this population was somewhat over 230,000. [5]

THE FOUNDING OF THE SWEDISH LUTHERAN CHURCH IN AMERICA

THE SWEDES HAD TO BE SELF-RELIANT

The founders of the Swedish Lutheran Church in America did not feel a close bond with the State Church. In fact, the Swedes in America received little or no assistance from the Church of Sweden (and only meager help from other Lutheran bodies). Thus it was necessary for the Swedish Church to immediately be self-reliant, adapting readily to American conditions.

There were many difficulties which the pastors and churches faced in America. A great share of the immigrants who arrived in America felt completely freed from the State Church. As a result, they raised objections against the use of anything that smacked of the old church system. That included clerical garb, the church handbook, and the liturgy. High churchism and clerical hierarchy were bad tastes in the mouths of the first immigrants. However, on the other hand there was an inherited respect for the ministerial office and for authority, and thus the congregational spirit was kept from going to the extreme. The early founders of the Swedish Church in America were pastors Esbjourn, Hasselquist, Carlsson, and Swensson. These men-most of whom were free church—were greatly dissatisfied with the State Church and, as a result, established a church in the Mississippi Valley that bore as little resemblance to the Church of Sweden as possible.

When the Swedish Church in America became organized, it patterned its policy on the American model, but followed the Church of Sweden in its form of worship. At first, the worship was very simple and contained a great deal of freedom, for that sort of thing fit the rough sod or log church. It is of interest that the first sermon which Esbjourn preached in America was delivered in a log cabin without a ceiling, and it was dark, the room lit only by a few candles held in the hands of worshipers.

With the introduction of liturgical worship, which was considered dead formalism by the revivalistic elements in the church, considerable controversy arose both among the Swedish immigrants and among the Norwegians. Eventually clerical garb was allowed, although it met with no little opposition from some; and the liturgy of the Swedish Church was followed, with minor changes to accommodate time and circumstance. In fact, the Swedes through most of their history showed overwhelming preference for the liturgical patterns set by the mother Church in Sweden. It is of interest that the Luther gown was not introduced in the Augustana Synod until 1924 to take the place of the Swedish Church clerical garb (*praestrock*).

Only a relatively few pastors came from Sweden. The attitude of the Church of Sweden toward sending pastors to America was that the need in Sweden was as great as in America, and the Swedes who emigrated had a Bible they could read. Furthermore, they left the old country of their own free will and for personal gain.[6] And so, the home Church and country were simply not responsive to the American Swedes' request for pastors. They felt that the Swedes who emigrated were little more than deserters. Furthermore, the conclusion was drawn that the church in America could not set up an episcopate because the President of the United States was not the head of the Swedish Church or any other church. The need was immediate for the American training of Swedish pastors.

Many of the pastors in the early period of immigration were influenced for the ministry by the pietistic movement in Sweden. A number of Swedish pastors in America were former students for Peter Fjellstedt, who was a man of untiring vigor and sharp intellect. Having been a traveling missionary in Asia and Europe, he pressed the cause of missions and gave advice and financial aid to the Church in America. He trained colporteurs (to sell Bibles and to witness) and lay preachers. He also induced young men to prepare for the work of the Lutheran ministry in America. The first Swedish-American Lutheran pastor was Lars P. Esbjourn, whose history we shall touch upon shortly.

THE SWEDISH IMMIGRANTS AND THE SECTS

Many of the Swedes had departed widely from the *Augsburg Confession* by the time they migrated, having adopted other religious beliefs. THE RELIGIOUS REVIVAL IN SWEDEN TOOK DEEP ROOT ESPECIALLY IN THE POORER CLASS OF SWEDES, WHO GAVE THE GREATEST NUMBER OF THEIR PEOPLE TO THE SWEDISH MIGRATIONS. THESE PEOPLE HAD WITNESSED SE-

RIOUS CLEAVAGES IN THEIR HOME COUNTRY OVER THE SUBJECT OF RELI-
GION, AND THEY BROUGHT WITH THEM TO AMERICA MUCH CONFUSION IN
THEIR MINDS. AS A RESULT NOT A FEW SWEDES WERE EASY PREY TO SEC-
TARIAN PROSELETIZING, WHICH WAS CARRIED ON IN FORCE IN THE NEW
LAND.[7]

The Swedish settlements became the scenes of bitter religious controversies.

In the early immigrations of Swedes, the Methodists were more successful than the Episcopalians in gaining converts. Two brothers, Olaf and
Jonas Hestrom, were quite energetic in bringing Swedes into the
Methodist Church. Both had strategic positions. Olaf worked in New York
harbor and gave much assistance to the Swedish immigrants and sought
to turn them to Methodism. Brother Jonas served as a Methodist pastor
in Victoria, Illinois. Many of the immigrant parties were directed by the
brother in New York to the brother in Victoria. As a result the struggle for
souls began in earnest.[8]

The experience was the same in other settlements: various religious denominations vied for the souls of the immigrants. Included among these
proseletizers were the Baptists. A sailor, O. Nison, who had been converted to the Baptist faith in America, returned to Sweden and there
started a Baptist movement. Expelled from Sweden, he started to seek re-
cruits for the Baptist beliefs among the Swedes in America. Gustav
Palmquist, who had previously moved among the Lutherans as a friend of
two of the earliest Swedish Lutheran pastors, joined the Baptists. He created considerable excitement and won enough followers to help in organizing at Rock Island, Illinois, the first Swedish Baptist Church in America,
in 1852.

In the 1870's the Waldenstroemian controversy came along. As you recall, this concerned the doctrine of Christ's Atonement. Peter Paul
Waldenstroem was a Swedish theologian and educator and one of the primary leaders of the free church movement in Sweden. In 1872 he promoted his idea of Christ's atonement or reconciliation, that it did not
reconcile a wrathful God to sinful man (it did not pay for sinful mankind's
transgressions and thereby satisfy a just and angry God). Rather Waldenstroem believed that Christ's atoning work reconciled sinful man to God
(thus changing sinful man's attitude toward God). His influence was extensive both in Sweden and America.[9] The Waldenstroemian controversy
caused a split in the evangelical ranks. When the controversy reached
these shores the result was the establishing of the Swedish Mission
Covenant in America.

Men such as those aforementioned, as well as some from the Episcopal
Church, did much proseletizing among the Swedish immigrants, resulting
in not a few Lutherans being won over to other churches. Naturally, these
proseletizers were a cause of much trouble to the early Swedish Lutheran
pastors. For example, Esbjourn, the earliest of the Swedish Lutheran immigrant pastors, found when he reached Andover, Illinois, in 1849 that
many of his party had been influenced by the Methodist pastor, the Rev.
Jonas Hedstrom, who moved to Victoria. This greatly discouraged Esb-

357

journ, whose journey to Andover had been fraught with tragedy and heartache, with even more to come.

EARLY TRACES OF SWEDES

In 1638 the Swedes succeeded in establishing a colony in Delaware, calling it New Sweden. However, as we have already discovered in an earlier chapter, Swedish Lutheranism did not succeed in America from this early venture, but was lost in the Episcopal Church. It was not until 1848 that the first Swedish Lutheran Church was organized from the new venture of the Swedish movement to this country. Strangely enough, this occurred in a community once again bearing the name New Sweden, but this time, located in Iowa. The following year, the first ordained Swedish Lutheran pastor arrived, whose name was Lars Paul Esbjourn. The Swedish Missionary Society had granted both permission and authorization for Esbjourn to emigrate, as well as the money to do so. In 1850 Esbjourn organized a church at Andover, Illinois.

LARS PAUL ESBJOURN, FOUNDING FATHER (1808-1870)

Already in 1841 a small community of Swedes was organized at Pine Lake, near Milwaukee, Wisconsin. It was the scene of constant bitter rivalry among the various denominations. Four years later five families emigrated from Sweden to Jefferson County in eastern Iowa, and there founded Little Sweden. Their first Pastor was M.F. Hokanson, a layman. Hokanson became the first preacher of what later became the Augustana Lutheran Church.

Lars Esbjourn was ordained a minister in the Swedish State Church on June 11, 1832. He leaned toward Pietism and promoted the temperance cause, and, in fact, was well known as a temperance agitator. Esbjourn had close ties to men like George Scott and Peter Wieselgren, which connection caused Esbjourn many problems with the people. Being sympathetic toward the Methodists, he accepted invitations to preach in their churches and was even asked to join. The simple fact was that while he labored in Sweden, Esbjourn longed for religious freedom, which the Lutheran State Church did not provide.

On June 29, 1848, Esbjourn led an emigrant party of 146 Swedes. He was accompanied by his wife and six children. As they were rounding southern Sweden, before they were even out of sight of the mainland, Esbjourn lost an infant son. On the way to Chicago another of his children died, and he buried it on the bank of Lake St. Clair. Death also took its toll on other families of the party as it headed west through Illinois. Cholera was an ever-present danger, and Esbjourn himself contracted the deadly disease in Chicago but recovered. Still more sorrow was to tear at the heart of this pioneer pastor. His wife died only three years after leaving Sweden. Esbjourn married again, but his second wife and little babe

358

passed away in September 1853. Just how hard the times were for the immigrants can be seen in Esbjourn's own report of the fact that the church the Swedes were building could not be finished because some of the boards had to be used to build coffins for members of the group who had died from the cholera. At one time he wrote: "We have in all buried at least forty persons." They had, of course, died of the cholera. Esbjourn's own wife was one of those for whom the boards had to be taken from the church to provide a coffin. Ten years later Esbjourn would return to his native land.

One of the most powerful reasons for Esbjourn's emigration was the thought of religious freedom to gain a firsthand acquaintance with the practical working of a free church system.[10] But this man who came to be known as the "Prairie Shepherd" also came to America in order to serve the Swedish immigrants. Frustrations with his position in Sweden no doubt also had an influence on his decision to come to America. The truth is that Esbjourn, Hasselquist, and Carlsson—the first three pastors to arrive in America and lay the foundation of the Swedish Church – had jeopardized their chance for advancement in the Swedish Church by their association with the pietistic and liberal element in Sweden. A note of interest is that Esbjourn later became disillusioned and even bitter concerning the free church system in this country. He was a man of very strong will, and no doubt his personality had much to do with forming his negative opinion in this matter. Esbjourn found it difficult to get along with even his fellow pastors.

Most of Esbjourn's immigrant party settled at Victoria, Illinois, but some settled at Andover. Immediately, religious forces set to work on the people. A case in point was the Baptists, who made inroads into the Lutheran camp. Swedish Baptist preachers began leaving the old country and, upon arriving in America made life even more difficult for Esbjourn. The people's training in Pietism made them easy prey for the sects and any new kind of religion.

In order to fight fire with fire, Esbjourn adapted himself to the Reformed American churches, laying aside his robe and setting aside the Lutheran liturgy.[11] He admitted into membership only those who had "experienced" conversion (consciousness of sin, living hunger for salvation in Christ). Esbjourn professed to be different from, and apart from, the old Church. Nevertheless, he exhorted his followers to be faithful to the *Augsburg Confession* and *Luther's Small Catechism*.

On March 18, 1850, only ten charter members organized the church at Andover, Illinois – startling evidence of the great loss to other churches that had been encountered. Esbjourn was on leave from the Church of Sweden and emigrated as an emissary of the Swedish Mission Society. On arrival at Andover, he was almost penniless. His life at first was terribly hard, which caused him to accept financial support from the non-Lutheran Central Association of Illinois. This Calvinistic organization required of him only that none but believers should be accepted into membership.

In 1851 Esbjourn visited Ohio, Pennsylvania, New York, and Massachusetts to enlist the support of Lutherans and non-Lutherans. Esbjourn wrote letters asking for more Swedish pastors to be sent, organized congregations, built churches, made preaching tours, and assisted his fellow countrymen in many other ways. But his life was full of heartbreak and physical hardships. The early Swedish missionaries – and this was also true of other missionary pastors – had to cope with making long, hard journeys to serve widely scattered people, all the while enduring the heat of summer, the cold of winter, and living conditions that were often meager and primitive. And the pay for all of this? A tiny salary that had to be stretched and stretched to try to make ends meet.

The difficulties of preaching were often compounded by stony hearts in which the seed of the Gospel was sown. The missionary often found an antagonistic spirit toward religion, since religion itself reminded the Swedish immigrant of his old country. The memories were often bitter ones. Esbjourn and the other missionary pastors also had to cope with the cleavage among Lutherans which was begun in Sweden and carried over to America. One element wanted to do away with every thing reminiscent of Sweden. Still others wanted the old church ways transplanted intact to America. To top it off, Esbjourn had to contend with competition from the Episcopalians and the sects.

WITH ERIC-JANSONISTS, EPISCOPALIANS, METHODISTS, BAPTISTS, MORMONS, AND LUTHERANS CONTENDING FOR THE FAITH [AMONG THE SWEDES], THE FIRST TWO DECADES OF THE HISTORY OF SWEDISH AMERICA WERE RICH IN CONTROVERSY. THE LUTHERANS REAPED THE GREATEST HARVEST, BUT ALL OF THEM FOUND MORE TARES THAN WHEAT. IN PROPORTION TO THE TOTAL SWEDISH POPULATION, CHURCH MEMBERS WERE GREATLY IN THE MINORITY. THE LUTHERAN PASTORS PLEADED IN VAIN WITH MANY OF THEIR COUNTRYMEN THAT THEIR CHURCH WAS VERY DIFFERENT FROM THE INSTITUTIONS THEY WERE COMPELLED TO SUPPORT IN THE OLD COUNTRY.[12]

Finally, it can be reported that fewer than one-fourth of the immigrants from Sweden found their way into the Lutheran Church here in America.

SYNODICAL AFFILIATION:
THE SYNOD OF NORTHERN ILLINOIS

Esbjourn recognized from the beginning the need of uniting with other Lutherans. As a beneficiary of the American Home Mission Society he was obligated to find synodical affiliation. One of the reasons for uniting the Swedish churches with other Lutherans was, of course, a matter of dire economic necessity – there was much poverty in the Swedish congregations. As early as 1850 he wrote a letter in which he stated his desire to have a synod established in Illinois with which he would unite, with the provision that it would stand firmly on the *Augsburg Confession*. As the number of Swedish Lutheran congregations grew, the need for synodical affiliation became more apparent. We note that in the Chicago area, where Esbjourn labored, Swedish Lutheranism got an early start so that by 1848 there were thirty-eight Swedish congregations here.

In looking for synodical affiliations, Esbjourn beheld the conflict between orthodox, confessional Lutheranism and the New School. As the years passed during his stay in America, Esbjourn tightened his theology. He saw the inroads other church bodies and the sects were making and it hardened him against their unLutheran theology. He also became very disenchanted with Methodism because of their intense proselytizing efforts among the Swedes.

After viewing the Lutheran situation, Esbjourn decided that he and his congregations could not affiliate with any of the synods. However, when Paul Anderson, a Norwegian Lutheran Minster in Chicago, suggested that his Norwegians and Esbjourn's Swedes unite with Americans in organizing a synod in the west to help solve problems common to all frontier churches, Esbjourn reacted favorably. Anderson, however, was an ultraliberal, ordained by the unLutheran Franckean Synod. Anderson succeeded in negotiating with some liberal brethren, who then helped him organize the Evangelical Lutheran Synod of Northern Illinois, at Cedarville, September 18, 1851. This new synod became one of the district synods of the General Synod (org. 1820). The Swedish and Norwegian pastors, while enjoying the spirit portrayed by the men of the General Synod, found that they could not agree with its doctrinal position because of its qualified acceptance of the *Augsburg Confession*. Esbjourn was somewhat dissatisfied with the new synod's approach to this primary document of the Lutheran Church, for it designated the *Augsburg Confession* as "mainly correct." Thereupon he insisted that the confessional basis of his congregation and himself be inserted into the synod's minutes. This basis stated that the symbolic books of the Lutheran Church contain "a correct summary of our faith and doctrine, next to the Holy Scriptures." Thus Esbjourn became a defender of Lutheranism in the midst of an unLutheran body.

As other pastors came to America from Sweden, they too joined the Northern Illinois Synod. Eventually, in 1855, the Swedish and Norwegian pastors organized the United Scandinavian Conference within the Northern Illinois Synod. This afforded them opportunity to discuss and expedite matters distinctive to Scandinavian interest. The Norwegian members formed the Chicago Conference, and the Swedes, the Mississippi Conference. After a time, the Swedes greatly outnumbered the Norwegians in the synod.

Eventually the Norwegians and Swedes became aware of serious differences between the Scandinavian Conference and the rest of the Synod of Northern Illinois. Furthermore they did not feel at home in the General Synod. Dissatisfaction with the "Definite Platform" and opposition to the admission of the unLutheran Melanchthon Synod into the General Synod in 1859 finally necessitated a break in relations between the Scandinavian Conference and the General Synod. Later, a break would also be made from the Synod of Northern Illinois, and a new synod composed of the pastors and congregations of the Scandinavian Conference would be formed. More of this later.

ESBJOURN AS A PROFESSOR

The Synod of Northern Illinois established Illinois State University at Springfield – a bold name for a tiny venture! Esbjourn was elected to the Board of Trustees of Illinois State University at the first meeting of the Synod of Northern Illinois in 1851. Though Swedish students enrolled at the Springfield institution, it was a poor choice of location, for there was not a single Lutheran Church, nor even a Swedish settlement here. The institution soon became racked with doctrinal strife. Later, it was hit with lack of finances due to the depression of 1857. Esbjourn was selected to solicit funds and this action finally caused much dissension.

It was decided to establish a Scandinavian professorship at the University. Esbjourn was elected to this position and in 1858 settled at Springfield. He came to regret his move, calling it his "Babylonian Captivity." Soon the synod found itself engulfed in a theological storm. Almost from the time Esbjourn took over his duties there was misunderstanding and friction among the members of the faculty, and especially between Esbjourn and others. For the moment, the more orthodox Scandinavians in the synod seemed to have their way. However, an attack against the *Augsburg Confession* from the American side, called "the new measure" faction almost brought about a breech. A mealy-mouthed "settlement" of the differences only spurred Esbjourn to take up his pen and urge his Swedish brothers to establish an independent Scandinavian synod or a district synod in the Joint Synod of Ohio. He was actually working for seccession from the Northern Illinois Synod. The split came in 1860 as Neo-Lutheranism assumed more and more control of the school. It should be noted that the Swedes often found themselves rebuffed by the orthodox branch of Lutheranism – the Missouri Synod, Norwegian Synod, and Joint Synod of Ohio – for their affiliation with the liberal side of Lutheranism. To the orthodox side, unionism to any degree was to be condemned. Nor did the orthodox side countenance affiliation with liberal General Synod.

Esbjourn's unhappiness was growing at Springfield and finally, after heated arguments with President Reynolds, he wrote out and presented his resignation. He also advised the Scandinavian students to withdraw, and these then followed Esbjourn's advice. While his departure from Springfield helped to feed the fires of discontent and bring about a more hasty separation from the Northern Illinois Synod, the fact remained that the Swedes were ready for separation.

SPURRED BY ESBJOURN'S RETREAT FROM SPRINGFIELD, A NEW SCANDINAVIAN SYNOD BEGUN

In considering Esbjourn's actions, the Scandinavian Conference in 1860 voted unanimously to withdraw peacefully from the Synod of Northern Illinois (April 23-27, 1860), and to hold a convention of delegates from Scandinavian congregations in order to organize a separate synod. The delegates convened later in the Norwegian Lutheran Church at Jefferson

362

Prairie (near Clinton), Rock County, Wisconsin, from June 5 to 11, 1860, and organized the Scandinavian Evangelical Lutheran Augustana Synod in North America. The choice of Jefferson Prairie was a gesture of courtesy to the Norwegians, especially Pastor Ole Andrewsen, who, as secretary of the Chicago Convention, had issued the call to the Scandinavians.

The organizational meeting for the Augustana Synod was attended by 11 Swedish and 7 Norwegian pastors, representing 36 Swedish and 13 Norwegian congregations, with a combined membership of about 4,947 communicants. (Swedes: 3,747 communicants; 25 pastors. Norwegians: 1200 communicants; 8 pastors.) The Swedish congregations were scattered in Illinois (15), Minnesota (13), Iowa (3), Indiana (3), New York (1), and Pennsylvania (1).[13] There were also in attendance at this meeting 9 Swedish and 5 Norwegian lay delegates. Pastor T.N. Hasselquist was chosen president, Ole J. Harlestad, secretary, and Mr. A.A. Klove, treasurer. The Constitution was formulated by Esbjourn in co-operation with Pastor Erland Carlsson. It followed that of the Synod of Northern Illinois.

The following doctrinal statement was incorporated in the new synod's constitution: IT IS GROUNDED ON THE WORD OF GOD, THE OLD AND NEW TESTAMENT PROPHETIC AND APOSTOLIC WRITINGS AND COMPRISED IN THE THREE CHIEF CONFESSIONS: THE *APOSTOLIC*, THE *NICENE* AND *ATHANASIAN*, AND IN THE *UNALTERED AUGSBURG CONFESSION* OF 1530, AND BY THE COUNCIL OF UPPSALA 1593 AND AS EXPLAINED IN THE ENTIRE SO-CALLED *BOOK OF CONCORD*.[14]

The name "Augustana" is the Latin form of the *Augsburg Confession* (*Confession Augustana*) and constituted a declaration of the Synod's adherence to Lutheran symbolism.

OTHER EARLY SWEDISH PASTORS WHO HELPED TO FOUND THE AUGUSTANA SYNOD

T.N. HASSELQUIST (1816 - 1891):

Esbjourn's letters to Sweden resulted in the coming of Tuve Nilson Hasselquist in 1852, and Erland Carlsson in 1853. It has been said of Hasselquist that he was "the most versatile and ablest leader in the annals of Swedish-American Lutheranism, and Carlsson was a man of affairs and a business manager."[15] These men led the church after Esbjourn's return to Sweden.

Having been granted leave by the State Church, Hasselquist arrived at Galesburg, Illinois, October 28, 1852, "the man for the place." He was known as a good preacher who soothed his hearers. He was, however, puritanical in his objection to things worldly. On the other hand, he became imbued with the free church spirit. Among the contenders in Sweden for the free church movement were the colporteurs. Ultimately Hasselquist came to look upon these men with a different view. He saw the harm which a fanatical spirit could do, for the colporteurs taught what came close to being hatred against ministers.

Hasselquist was at first a unionist, cooperating with other denominations, but pressures later caused him to modify his views and he became more conservative and uncompromising. He conducted his church services in low church form. Among Hasselquist's accomplishments was the founding of the first Swedish paper in America. He was also president of the Augustana Synod (1860) and professor at Augustana College and Seminary, Paxton, Illinois. While laboring at Galesburg he soon extended his work to the area around the town.

ERLAND CARLSSON (1822 - 1893)

Carlsson was ordained in 1849 and arrived in Chicago in 1853 to take up his work. Like Esbjourn and Hasselquist he had been granted a leave of absence from the State Church. Failure of advancement in the Church of Sweden, due to his activity in the temperance movement, no doubt did much to further his ambition to go to America. Carlsson was a highly energetic man, a man of earnest piety and of no little organizing ability. He was a great influence to many of the Swedes. His home in Chicago became a clearing house through which many Swedish immigrants passed, carrying Carlsson's influence with them where they went. His Emanuel Church became a sort of mother church to many, not only in and around Chicago but elsewhere as well.

Carlsson's Chicago field was a very difficult one, for it was the settling place of many different types of persons. Among his accomplishments: he was business manager of Augustana College and one of its directors from its founding, and he was president of the Augustana Synod from 1881 to 1889. Carlsson also served for many years as an editor of *Missionaeren*. A church constitution drawn up by him became a model for others who followed.

STILL OTHER EARLY SWEDISH PASTORS

Two more pastors arrived in 1856: Olaf Andren (to Moline, Illinois, for four years) and Jonas Swenson. Strong Pietism was rooted in both men. Swenson ultimately succeeded Esbjourn at Andover in 1858 after serving congregations in the East. These early pastors were aided by a few men who were ordained by the Synod of Northern Illinois.

ERIK NORELIUS (1833 - 1916, died in Sweden)

This Swedish pastor came to America in 1850 with a party of Hedbergians from Hälsugland with hopes of founding a "true" Lutheran congregation. Norelius was a voluminous writer, but also a pastor, teacher, editor, and synodical president. He studied at Capital University, Columbus, Ohio. Thus he became imbued with the emphasis on the Lutheran Symbols which was held by the Joint Synod of Ohio. Norelius was repelled by the unionistic, free spirit which he at first saw in Hasselquist.

Employing the leaven of Pietism, this little band of pietists listed above had come to America to serve Swedish immigrants who were only nominal Lutherans. It was this little group of pastors who founded the Augustana Synod and gave it its distinctive character.

AUGUSTANA, SWEDEN, AND THE SWEDISH IMMIGRANT

After the Scandinavians separated from the Synod of Northern Illinois, it was necessary for the Swedes to turn to Sweden for support. The future looked dark. A great challenge lay before them: to establish their own institution for training pastors, while having no money to do so. Andren, pastor in Moline, Illinois, was sent to Sweden to collect money. He pledged the cordiality of the congregations in America with the "Mother Church in the Old Fatherland." He was allowed the selection of some 5,000 volumes from the private library of King Charles XV, and these became the nucleus for the library of Augustana Seminary. More than $10,000 was collected in Sweden.

Of the great flow of Swedish immigrants following the Civil War, only a small proportion were won by the Augustana Synod. The synod appealed neither to the Swedes who had been affected by religious revival which had swept Sweden, nor to those who were hostile or indifferent toward organized religion. The pietistic pastor, who was often "strait-laced and crude (uneducated)," did not appeal to the religiously invigorated Swedes arriving from the old country.

By 1870 there were about 200,000 Swedes in America, but the Augustana Synod had only about 16,000 communicant members, with a total baptized membership of 30,000. The arrival in America of the Swedish immigrant was the great moment of truth for the Swedish State Church. By refusing to join a Swedish Lutheran congregation under a free church system, many Swedes showed that their hearts really were not in the Lutheran Church. They had been born, baptized, confirmed, and perhaps married in the Lutheran Church system, but a large number were only nominally Lutheran – "paper" members. Freedom from the State Church gave them the opportunity to assert what they really felt themselves to be. For the church, it was a jolting revelation.

By 1870 the State Church had furnished only six pastors, two of whom had returned. By 1890 there were 291 pastors, of whom only eight had been ordained in Sweden. The men from whom pastors were recruited were mainly colporteurs, school teachers, and students in missionary training.[16]

AUGUSTANA SEMINARY

At first there was such a great need for Swedish pastors in America that it was necessary to license suitable laymen to perform ministerial functions and to ordain men with a minimum of education. Yet the church continued to desire a well-educated ministry.

In 1850 the Swedes contacted the Capital University, Columbus, Ohio, which was operated by the Synod of Ohio, and made arrangements for theological students to be educated there. The first student was Eric Norelius, who was enrolled from 1851 to 1855. The Swedes' first venture into higher education was, of course, the establishing of a Scandinavian professorship at Illinois State University at Springfield. This ill-fated venture, with Esbjourn as professor, lasted just two years (1858-1859).

When Esbjourn left Springfield with the Scandinavian students, he went on to Chicago, where instructions were continued in a school house of Emanuel Lutheran Church. The Conference of the Scandinavian churches held in April 1860 in Chicago upheld the action of Esbjourn and at the same time voted to withdraw from the Synod of Northern Illinois. Later in the summer, when the Scandinavians met and organized their own Augustana Synod at Jefferson Prairie, Wisconsin, it was decided that while the Scandinavian professor had relinquished his position at Springfield, the professorship itself was to continue. So Esbjourn was simply transferred to the Chicago Institution.

Augustana Seminary was not placed in Chicago permanently. Men were charged with the task of finding a suitable location and the choice finally fell upon Paxton, Ford County, Illinois. The seminary began its first academic year here in 1863. Esbjourn, unhappy with the move to Paxton, resigned and in 1863 returned to Sweden where he reentered the State Church. T.N. Hasselquist succeeded him. The last academic year at Paxton was 1874-75, for the school here never flourished. As a result of national upheaval due to the Civil War, the seminary failed to attract a goodly number of students. (It is of interest, that while Swedish immigration dropped off sharply during the war years, it began to increase when victory for the North seemed assured. The Swedes fought on the side of the North, and a number of officers from the Swedish army took part in the war and rose to high rank.)

In 1873 construction began on a hill located between Rock Island and Moline, Illinois. The seminary has been located on "Zion's Hill" ever since and here Augustana College is also located.

The missionary schools in Sweden – the Fjellstedt School (Upsala), the Ahlberg School (Hvetlanda), and the Johannelund School (near Stockholm) – sent men to America to serve the Swedish immigrants. Men from these institutions were given a brief and hurried course at Augustana Seminary before they were sent out into the field. The students recruited in Sweden were often given free board and tuition, and their expenses paid, by the Gustavus Adolphus Foundation at Gothenburg.

THE MINNESOTA CONFERENCE
AND ITS OWN SCHOOLS

The Minnesota Conference (org. 1858) established its own St. Ansgar's Academy (East Union) to better serve its students. The synod had to treat the Minnesota Conference diplomatically, fearing it would secede. In 1876 Gustavus Adolphus College opened its doors in St. Peter as successor to St. Ansgar. The school question was often an acrimonious one in Minnesota, since there was a disagreement as to where the school should be located.

EDUCATION IN THE SYNOD

For a time there was a parochial school fever in the synod. Finally, these schools came to be brief summer sessions taught by the pastor or a student. The Swedes also made use of the vacation Bible school in order to enhance the children's religious education. At the Augustana Church's 100th Annual Convention, the delegates recorded opposition to establishing parochial schools for secondary education, preferring instead public, tax-supported schools. The Swedes simply did not have the fear of public schools that the Norwegians had. On the other hand, the Swedes have demonstrated that they consider it important to provide institutions of higher learning through the Church.

UPSALA, which was started as an institution of higher learning by the New York Conference in 1893 as a commemoration of the 400th year of Luther's birth, became a full-fledged college in 1902. Begun in Brooklyn, it finally found its way to East Orange, New Jersey. For a time it was the largest college in point of enrollment in the Augustana Synod.

BETHANY ACADEMY was begun in 1881 at Lindsborg Kansas. The founder of Bethany was Carl Aaron Swensson, who graduated from Augustana Seminary in 1877 and was ordained two years later. Swensson was pastor at Lindsborg, Kansas, until his sudden death in 1904. Besides founding Bethany College and serving as its president, he was also an editor, lecturer and politician. He has been called "the most striking personality among the Swedish church men in America." [17]

In 1947 AUGUSTANA SEMINARY and AUGUSTANA COLLEGE became separate institutions, each with its own administrative officers and board of directors. It is of interest to note that Augustana has ranked in the top ten percent of all private colleges and universities in the number of alumni listed in *Who's Who in America.*

Not until 1885 did a woman enroll in the college department at Augustana. Many years later, in 1957, the Augustana Synod passed this resolution: "That women who meet the qualifications for entrance and who agree to the resolutions of the administration be allowed to study at Augustana Theological Seminary.

Augustana College had a rough go of it financially for a number of years. There was no endowment fund, but every communicant in Synod was levied 25 cents to support it. There were also other sources of income, including that generated by tuitions and by earnings on real estate in and around Paxton. Later, part of the earnings of Augustana Book Concern, as well as certain royalties, went to the school. Generally speaking, the schools of the Augustana Synod had a hard go of it for many years. An appalling teaching load and too little pay were some of the burdens borne by the faculty members. It can be mentioned too that the list of educational institutions of the Augustana Synod that have passed into nonexistence is long. At times more zeal than wisdom was shown in beginning schools.

In 1894 the combined debt of all the institutions in the synod was $125,000, and the debt was growing at a rate of $25,000 a year. Augustana College, as late as 1905, was in arrears with salaries of its professors. While individual conferences and sections of the synod have promoted the cause of owning their own colleges – the Swedes emphasized decentralization of education in the synod – these have not always worked out. Some did. LUTHER ACADEMY opened its doors at Wahoo, Nebraska in 1883. It finally became the institution of the Nebraska Conference. After 1909 it became LUTHER COLLEGE, and still later it came to function as a Junior College. HOPE ACADEMY was opened at Moorhead, Minnesota, and EMANUEL ACADEMY, at Minneapolis. While academies remained strong institutions in the Missouri* and Wisconsin Synods, they outlived their usefulness in the Augustana Synod and dropped away, one after the other. Only a few in the synod remained in favor of academies, regarding them as the best feeders for colleges and seminary.

THE NORWEGIANS PART COMPANY WITH THE SWEDES

The Swedes were constantly criticized by the Norwegian Synod for staying as long as they did in the Synod of Northern Illinois, which body the Norwegian Synod regarded as heretical. H.A. Preus listed the chief points of difference between the Norwegian and the Augustana Synods as: the conception of the ministry (the Swedish pastors were poorly trained), laymen's activities, the Sabbath question, the "new birth", absolution (in the communion service), and chiliasm (the supposed 1,000 year reign of Christ on earth). The Swedes and Norwegians had little in common. While the Swedes had little trouble "Americanizing" themselves, a spirit of nationalism ran deep in the Norwegian mind and heart. Furthermore, the Norwegians were more conservative in their practice than were the Swedes, who were somewhat inclined toward unionism.

In the Augustana Synod, the Norwegians – as the minority group – felt that the Swedish interests received preference. Appeals to nationalism also helped to draw away the Norwegians from Augustana. Furthermore, the Norwegians had misgivings about the use of "altar-bog" or ministerial garb, and the laying on of hands in administering the absolution. Plainly, within the Augustana Synod much of the controversy that arose regarding ministerial gowns and use of the liturgy was felt among the Norwegians also. Then there was the feeling that the Norwegians had that they were neglected. In this spirit they also found the Augustana Synod unsatisfactory. It was just too Swedish.

Provision was made that neither synod should accept pastors and congregations of the sister synod without mutual agreement, and that small minorities of either nationality should join existing local congregations of either synod. This rule met with opposition among the Norwegians. One of the things which rankled the Norsemen was the fact that the Augustana Synod leadership was seen gravitating toward the General Council (which the Swedes joined in 1870). This inspired strong separatistic propagandizing among the Norwegians. After nineteen years of fellowship, the formal parting of the Swedes and the Norwegians occurred at Andover, Illinois, in June 1870. The friction among the Norwegians continued and resulted in their splitting into two groups" the Norwegian-Danish Augustana Synod and the Norwegian-Danish Conference.

In 1930 the Swedes and Norwegians got together again in a spirit of cooperation in the American Lutheran Conference. When the Augustana Synod pushed for the admission of the United Lutheran Church (org. 1918) into the Conference, it found itself once again pulling in an opposite direction from the Norwegians.

ORGANIZATION IN AUGUSTANA

The Augustana Synod, from its beginning, opposed centralization of power. Even faculty members of the educational institutions were elected on the floor of the synod conferences. The strongest feeling against centralization of power in the synod was expressed in the Minnesota Conference. Nevertheless, the decentralization that had characterized the synod – even in the manner of establishing educational institutions – finally gave way to a more and more centralized from of government. Rock Island, Illinois, became more and more the capital of Swedish Lutheranism. In 1889 the synod published its official organ, *Augustana*, a consolidation of two existing church papers.

In 1922 the term of president was extended from one to four years, and he received a large enough salary to enable him to give full time to his office. The power and authority of the office were practically Episcopal. As time went on, the layman's movement in the synod became more and more powerful, resulting in the election of laymen to synodical positions (e.g. secretary of stewardship, in 1929). Women received the right of suffrage. At the 1930 Synodical Convention a resolution was passed entitling women to election as delegates to the conventions. However, they were not accorded the right of election to offices of trustee and deacon.

The first native born president was Larence A. Johnston of St. Paul (1911-1918). Synod headquarters was maintained at Minneapolis, Minnesota.

NAME CHANGES

The Augustana Synod in its history underwent the following name changes:

1860 Organized as the Scandinavian Ev. Lutheran Augustana Synod in North America. After separating peacefully from the Norwegians (1870) the name became the Swedish Ev. Lutheran Augustana Synod.

1894 The name was changed to Evangelical Lutheran Augustana Synod in North America. (The nationalistic part of the name was dropped, marking the Americanization of the synod.)

1948 The name changed to the Augustana Ev. Lutheran Church. It was known simply as the Augustana Lutheran Church.

GROWTH OF AUGUSTANA

When the Augustana Synod was organized in 1860 (joint Norwegian-Swedish venture), it numbered 49 congregations and 4,967 members. (The Swedish contingent of the synod numbered 36 congregations and 3,747 communicant members.) In a few years – during the Augustana Synod's first decade – the Swedes completely cut off any dependence they had upon the Church of Sweden. The synod commissioned pastors to bring the word to Swedish Lutherans in Kansas, northern Minnesota, western Iowa, New York State, Massachusetts, Vermont, Michigan, and Nebraska. In short order a large geographical area was included within the synod's boundaries.[18]

At the end of the first fifty years, the Augustana Synod numbered 888 congregations, with 119,149 communicants. By 1948, one hundred years after the first Swedish congregation was organized with ten communicants, the synod numbered 1,175 congregations and 306,786 confirmed members. By that year Augustana had located itself in thirty-five states, plus the District of Columbia and Canada. Augustana then had 933 ordained pastors, 124 foreign missionaries, 12 children's homes, 11 hospitals, 21 old folk's homes, and 10 hospices. In addition there was the deaconess mother house at Omaha, and also the Lutheran Seaman's Center in New York City. The total number of institutions numbered 54.[19] There were also five colleges, a theological seminary, and a publishing house. Around the time that the Augustana Lutheran Church merged with other synods to form the Lutheran Church in America, it numbered around 600,000 baptized members. After 1900 the Augustana Synod profited little from the Swedish immigrations. The immigrants were by then either irreligious or members of the sects.

AUGUSTANA AND THE GENERAL COUNCIL
(ORG. 1867)

While Augustana delegates were sent to meetings of the General Council from the time the Council was organized, this synod did not commit itself to an unconditional affiliation with the Council until 1870, which was the year that separation from the Norwegians took place. Augustana's cooperation in foreign mission work with the General Council continued until

1918, when the Council, together with the General Synod and the United Synod in the South, formed the United Lutheran Church in America (ULCA). The Swedes held themselves aloof from participation in the merger, though many in the synod were favorably inclined. Augustana maintained friendly relations with the ULCA and even after the merger was established, continued participating in missionary work with this body in India and Puerto Rico, which had been a project of the General Council before the merger.

Not all of the pastors and presidents of the Augustana Synod felt kinship with the General Council. Larence A. Johnston of St. Paul, who was the first native-born president of the synod, held himself aloof from the Council and was an uncompromising foe of unionism. This spirit was shared commonly by the older pastors, with some exceptions. In 1878 the synod came forth with this statement:

IF OUR UNION WITH THE GENERAL COUNCIL IMPLIED ASSENT INTO UNIONISM [IN THIS CASE, FELLOWSHIP WITH NON-LUTHERANS], WE ARE READY TO PROPOSE THAT OUR SYNOD SEVER ITS RELATIONS WITH THE COUNCIL. IT IS RECOGNIZED THAT OUR SYNOD IS OPPOSED TO ALL UNIONISM AND WILL NOT HESITATE TO DISCIPLINE PASTORS AND CONGREGATIONS WHO ARE GUILTY OF UNIONISTIC PRACTICES.

Thus while some Lutherans who affiliated with the General Council exchanged pulpits with other denominations, the Augustana Synod opposed this practice. There were those in the synod who agitated for "close" communion even before the Galesburg rule was adopted be the General Council. (The rule: Lutheran pulpits for Lutheran pastors and Lutheran altars for Lutheran communicants.) However, individual pastors and congregations insisted on exception to the rule at their own discretion. The presidents of the synod were not one-minded as far as promoting the cause of purity of doctrine. While some were known for their orthodoxy and their stand against unionism, others pressed cooperation with other Lutherans and dealt lightly with doctrine.

AUGUSTANA ECUMENICAL RELATIONSHIPS

The fact of the matter is that the Augustana Synod was from the very beginning ecumenical in spirit, which spirit at times involved contact with non-Lutheran groups. The first Swedish Lutheran pastors in America were glad – out of dire economic necessity – to accept aid from the American Home Mission Society, a Reformed organization. As has already been pointed out, the Swedes were for a time members of the Synod of Northern Illinois, which was a member of the liberal General Synod. While the Swedes finally withdrew from the Synod of Northern Illinois and from the General Synod, they somewhat later joined the General Council after participating in the Council from the time it was organized in 1867.

Pastor William A. Passavant, a member of the Pittsburgh Synod in the East, had a great interest in mission work and was a close friend of the Swedes. He was willing to use the Augustana Synod to foster the cause of

Lutheranism in the Northwest.

During the First World War Augustana provided chaplains and camp pastors for the armed services. Fifty-two Augustana pastors served as military chaplains during the Second World War. Fourteen others served as Lutheran Center pastors under the auspices of the National Lutheran Council.

When the National Lutheran Council was formed, the Augustana Synod had a great deal to do with its formation, and some of Augustana's pastors served as officers in the Council, including president. When the American Lutheran Conference was organized in 1930, Augustana became one of its member synods. In 1947 the Lutheran World Federation came into being. Augustana proved loyal in its support of this world organization of Lutheranism. It participated officially both in the formation of the World Council of Churches and the National Council of Churches of Christ in the U.S.A., and worked together with other church bodies (i.e. non-Lutheran bodies) in these Councils. Augustana sent representatives to the meetings of the Lutheran World Convention, and some of its members were active in the commissions of the World Council and served on its Central Committee.

In the words of one of Augustana's own authors: OUR SYNOD HAS CONSISTENTLY LABORED FOR CLOSER UNITY AMONG THE LUTHERANS IN AMERICA AS EXPRESSED IN PULPIT AND ALTAR FELLOWSHIP. THERE ARE OTHER WAYS TOO IN WHICH THE AUGUSTANA SYNOD HAS CROSSED PATHS ALSO WITH THE FEDERAL COUNCIL OF CHURCHES, OF THE CHURCHES OF CHRIST IN AMERICA, HOME MISSION COUNCIL, FOREIGN MISSION CONFERENCE, INTERNATIONAL RELIGIOUS COUNCIL, AND UNITED STEWARDSHIP COUNCIL. IT IS ALSO A MEMBER OF THE WORLD COUNCIL OF CHURCHES.[20]

Later, in 1962, the Augustana Synod decided to merge its corporate identity with those of the United Lutheran Church in America, the American Evangelical Lutheran Church (Danish), and the Suomi Synod (Finnish) to form the Lutheran Church in America (LCA), which began functioning January 1, 1963. (See the separate chapter of the LCA.) In this merger the Suomi Synod phased out its seminary at Hancock, Michigan, and merged with the Augustana Synod seminary.

AUGUSTANA AND THE ENGLISH LANGUAGE

The first English Lutheran Church of the Augustana Synod was organized in 1883. The first English hymnal was published in 1901, and a second English hymnal was published in 1925. The first English-Swedish paper was published in 1882. English rapidly became the language of the people in Augustana's congregations. Unlike the Norwegians, Danes, and Finns, the Swedes were willing to give up their language and Americanize themselves, and expected their children – if not themselves – to speak English. From 1900 to 1914 the Augustana Synod remained Swedish. Very few congregations had gone exclusively to English, but the World War, of course, did much to speed the transition to English, both in the church services of the congregations and in the publications of the synod.[21]

THE LODGE ISSUE

The Swedes wrote into their constitution that no member of a secret society could become or remain a member of the church. At first, the Synod through church discipline strictly enforced its stand against secret societies, but this enforcement caused many controversies, and in many places the prohibition against lodge membership remained a dead letter. Modified definitions were adopted by the Augustana Synod in 1894, 1907, 1939.[22] As time went on many congregations outlawed the synodical rule excluding lodge members. It is of interest that at least one king of Sweden was head of the Church of Sweden and of the Masonic Order at the same time.

THE AUGUSTANA SYNOD AND
THE CHURCH OF SWEDEN

At the end of the nineteenth century Augustana could criticize the Church of Sweden for slighting the Swedish Lutheran Church in America. Over the decades since its founding the Augustana Synod felt the desire for recognition by the Swedish Church. At various times the mother Church had sent bishops over to visit the American Swedes; however, the Augustana Synod was concerned about the friendly atmosphere that existed between the Church of Sweden and the Episcopal Church. The tendency seemed to be to recognize both the Augustana Synod and the Episcopal Church among the Swedes as "daughter" churches. A side note: There was some question among the high church Episcopalians whether the Church of Sweden had apostolic succession. The Church of Sweden does in fact lay claim to apostolic succession, without placing any specific importance on it. In 1920 altar fellowship between the Episcopal Church and the Church of Sweden was established.

Early in 1930 the archbishop in the Church of Sweden extended the right hand of fellowship to the Augustana Synod by presenting a bishop's cross to the president as a recognition of the apostolic character of his office. This has been termed "the most significant gesture made by the Church of Sweden since the organization of the Augustana Synod."[23] However, there was opposition to accepting the cross, since the synod had no bishop and it is not an Episcopal arm of the diocese of Scandinavia, nor an appendix to the Church of Sweden.[24] This gesture was regarded as setting up a barrier with other Lutheran synods in America, as well as a barrier to mission work.

The action which the Augustana Synod took in 1930 was to state the synod's appreciation for the noble motives of the archbishop and bishops of Sweden in bestowing the cross upon the president of the synod, at the same time stating "always though we do not hereby adopt an episcopal insignia for the incumbent of the presidents office, we acknowledge the pronounced desire for stronger fellowship of our churches and join heartily therein; the Synod accepts the gift as a symbol of unity in purpose between independent

Lutheran churches."[25] (Note the use of the word "independent.") Thus the Augustana Synod rejected the office of bishop.

AUGUSTANA'S COMPETITION
FROM OTHER GROUPS

Augustana had to cope with the following Swedish church bodies in America: Episcopal, Baptist, Methodist, and elements in the synod influenced by the Mission Friends movement in Sweden. The Mission Friends were a revival-oriented group that formed within the Augustana Synod and were a part of it for a time. Finally, this faction left the synod over the issue of polity rather than theology and in 1873 organized the Swedish Evangelical Mission Synod of America. Some Mission Friends did not join in organizing the Mission Synod but rather organized their own synod, the Swedish Ansgarius, a year later. They decided to join the General Synod. Later, in 1885, the two rival synods got together and formed a merger calling themselves the Swedish Evangelical Mission Covenant of America, with C.A. Bjork as the first President.

After the two groups of Mission Friends got together in the merger of 1885 they ceased to be Lutheran. Indeed, they did not consider themselves Lutheran. The Mission Covenant adopted no formal creed – not even the *Augsburg Confession* – thus eliminating from the constitution all references to Lutheranism. (Some Mission Friends, who did not join the merger, organized the Mission Free Church under the leadership of J.G. Princell.) The Mission Covenant accepts the Word of God, Old Testament and New Testament, as the only rule of faith, doctrine and conduct. It accepts the Waldenstromian doctrine of the atonement, which emphasizes the effect Christ's atonement has on the individual, and therefore is not recognized as Lutherans by Lutheran bodies. It has no Galesburg rule governing altar and pulpit fellowship and practices open communion. "The Mission Covenant represents a compromise between congregationalism and Presbyterianism, whereas the Free Church is Congregational."[26] (The Swedish Evangelical Free Church [incorporated in Minnesota in 1908] was consecutively known as the: Work of the Christians in Common," the "Swedish-American Missionary Society," and the "Free Mission." In 1929 the membership was about 6,000 persons in 100 congregations.)[27] As an American Swedish church body, the Mission Covenant reached the point where it was second only to the Augustana Synod in size. In 1930 the membership numbered about 33,000, with 485 preachers and 402 congregations.[28]

The Augustana Synod also had to cope with the Mormons. According to the report of the Mission Board in 1887, "nearly half of the Mormons in Utah had formerly been Lutherans," many of them being Swedes. "Upon their arrival they soon found themselves deluded, but there was little turning back after they were once within the embraces of the Mormon organization."[29]

It has been said that the Swedes Americanized more quickly and thor-

374

oughly than any other immigrant stock. A great proportion of the immigrants were not affiliated with church of any kind, much less the Lutheran Church. It has already been pointed out that fewer than one-fourth of the Swedish immigrants took up membership in the Lutheran Church here in America. No doubt the variety of church bodies competing for the opportunity to provide spiritual nurturing to the Swedish immigrants, along with a long-felt desire for freedom from the Swedish Lutheran Church, was both a cause for confusion and a turn-off for many a Swedish immigrant.

The Swedish Episcopal Church found its followers among those Swedes who preferred the formal ritual of the Episcopal service to the freer evangelical worship found in the pietistic groups. The Swedish Episcopal Church was subsidized and governed by the American Episcopal Church.

PUBLICATIONS

In 1884 it was decided to organize a stock company under the name Augustana Book Concern at Rock Island, Illinois. In 1889 the Augustana Synod made provision to purchase the publication house. Reference has already been made to the publication of an official synodical paper, as well as to the publication of hymnals.

HOME MISSION WORK

When Augustana was organized in 1860, a Mission Committee was appointed. One full-time missionary, Eric Norelius, was chosen. Other missionaries were also called for longer or shorter terms. The process of reaching out to form new congregations – gathering people together and visiting the ever-increasing number of settlements – was preformed by pastors in the synod who were requested to spend a month or more in new fields. Laymen who were endowed with special gifts from the Lord were licensed to preach, thereby helping with the outreach efforts.

The constant problem of the Augustana Synod was the same problem which plagued other Lutheran synods: where to find laborers. Not enough candidates came from Sweden to carry on the work over an ever-expanding Lutheran territory and a rapidly moving western frontier. In 1870 the Augustana Synod decided to organize itself more strongly and more deliberately for mission work, providing for a central Home Mission Board, whose duty it was to make possible the preaching of the Word and administration of the sacraments to the synod's widely-scattered countrymen. The Home Mission Board was given the right to call and commission itinerant preachers, catechists, and colporteurs. Each conference (or district) of the synod constituted a mission district. A Conference Mission Board elected by the conference consisted of a president, together with two elected pastors and two elected laymen. This method of organizing home mission work tended to decentralize the overseeing, financing, and promotion of missions. With the conference presidents serving as mission superintendents, aided by field secretaries, not much remained from the Central Mission Board to do except care for those fields which were outside of conference boundaries.

Missionary interest began to lag after immigration more or less came to a stand still, and congregations became more self-centered. With the transition from Swedish to English, the whole mission thrust of the synod took on a difference character, for then it had to include neighbors who were of other than Swedish extraction. As a result the Swedish Church took on a more international flavor and character. So then, the work of establishing English home missions began, and in 1908 an association of English churches of the synod was organized with its own field secretary. By 1936 the process of Americanization of the Swedish church was, for all practical purposes, completed. By 1920 memberships in the Augustana had become almost static. Because of a shift of population from the rural to the city, rural congregations began to dwindle and some were even dissolved. Few new congregations were organized or new fields occupied.

An interesting side note is that in its history the Augustana Synod showed some inclination, especially through a Dr. Gene Olsson, for work among the liberated Negroes. Furthermore, the synod for a number of years in the 1870's showed an interest in taking up missionary work among the American Indians. However, not much resulted from these plans.

Mention has already been made of the concentration of Swedes in Illinois – to the south, the northeast and northwest. Swedes also poured across the border into Iowa. These had to be served. Congregations were formed and eventually those located west of the Mississippi were organized into the West Mississippi Conference (1868). Two years later the conference was divided into the Iowa and Kansas Conferences.

The synod missionaries followed the immigrants into Minnesota and the Dakotas, and even into Montana and Utah. In 1854 Erland Carlsson went to Minnesota and organized a congregation in Center City, which congregation is considered the mother church of the Minnesota Conference. Another interesting side note is that Pastor Peter Carlsson labored fifty years as an Augustana pastor in Minnesota, and formed thirty-two congregations. His pastorate or parish was sometimes 620 miles long. The Red River Valley Conference grew out of his labors.

Montana attracted Swedes already in the 1880's but securing and keeping pastors in this field proved a difficult task. In 1900 the synod had only one pastor in the entire state, and he served his congregation without the amenity of a church building. Sadly, most of the 20,000 Swedes who established themselves in Montana were not won for the Lutheran Church.

In an attempt to win Swedish Mormons back to the Lutheran Church, a missionary was sent to Utah, who then organized a congregation in Salt Lake City. However, the field was most difficult and progress was slow. Work was also carried on in other places in Utah.

Between 1868 and 1886 twenty congregations were organized in the Nebraska Territory. (In 1854 what is now the present State of Nebraska, along with much of what is now the Dakotas, Wyoming, Montana, and Colorado, was organized into Nebraska Territory – a huge area of land, sparsely settled and little explored.) In 1886 these congregations were given permission to organize their own separate conference.

With the opening of mining and logging in Michigan, Swedish immigrants were attracted here in the 1870's. The first church organized in Michigan was at Sparta in Kent County. The church organized in 1870 at Ishpeming, in Michigan's Upper Peninsula, became the mother church of a number of congregations. Congregations were also established in Michigan's Lower Peninsula, especially along the shore of Lake Michigan. This brought about the Superior Conference.

After the Civil War Swedes came in large numbers to Texas on "labor contracts," which meant that they had to work off the debt incurred for their passage to America. The first Augustana congregation was organized in Texas in 1876, although the beginnings of the Swedish Church in Texas reach all the way back to 1830.

When gold was discovered in Colorado, many Swedes followed their dreams here. The first Swedish church in Colorado was organized in 1873 at Golden. The Swedes also migrated to the West Coast, but it was not until 1882 that a congregation of Swedes was organized at San Francisco. This was followed by the organizing of several other churches in California in the 1880's, including congregations as far south as Los Angeles and Riverside. Thus the California Conference had its beginning.

The first congregation of the Columbia Conference was located in Portland, Oregon. Begun in Portland in 1873, the West Coast Mission District later became divided north and south. In 1888 the district (which then had two divisions) became a conference which, five years later, was divided into two conferences, the California and the Columbia. The Columbia Conference consisted of congregations in Washington, Oregon, British Columbia, Idaho, Utah, and Montana.

Work was begun in Florida to serve the Swedes in and around Usala. A congregation was organized in 1884, and work was later carried to other places. The field came under the supervision of the New York Conference.

A missionary was commissioned to investigate missionary possibilities far north, in Alaska. While work was begun in a few places, progress was slow, and the work was later abandoned.

Congregations were, of course, established on the East Coast. The New York Conference was organized in 1870. The New England Conference was organized in 1912 from a part of the New York Conference. One of the pastors established thirty-two congregations and directed the building of twenty-one churches in the New York Conference over a period of thirty-one years.

After 1880 an increasing number of Swedes emigrated to Canada, some from Sweden, others directly from the United States – especially from the northern states. These Swedes scattered over the provinces of Manitoba, Saskatchewan, Alberta, and British Columbia. In 1885 the Augustana Synod decided to take up mission work in Canada and called its first missionary. Later, this field was relinquished to the Minnesota Conference, which carried on the work until 1913, when the congregations there con-

377

stituted their own independent conference. The Canadian Conference was organized in New Stockholm, Saskatchewan. The congregation there was considered the mother church of the synod in Canada. The Minnesota Conference underwrote the venture with an annual contribution of $5,000. The work in Canada proved very difficult, because of the climate, the travel conditions, and the small, poor congregations. The pastors for the field were few and their stay brief. Progress was slow and discouraging. The need was long felt to establish a school in Canada to train a native-born ministry. In 1947 the Augustana Synod endorsed a plan to establish a Lutheran theological seminary on the campus of the University of Saskatchewan, Saskatoon. The seminary was a cooperative venture by the Augustana Synod, the United Lutheran Church in America, and the American Lutheran Church.

The home mission program of the Augustana Synod was reorganized in 1938 under the leadership of Dr. P.O. Bersell, who took office in 1935. In the reorganization the new Board of Home Missions was created. Also, the thirteen conferences, the Women's Missionary Society, and special mission projects were all coordinated in one unit to make one united approach in America. The Swedish Church had become Americanized. Through its newly organized mission program it was to reach out to the great unchurched multitudes in America, using its synod-wide program of activity. In spite of all this effort to evangelize the unchurched in general, the outreach effort to the unchurched among Swedish-speaking peoples would have had to treble in order to equal Norwegian-American Lutheranism.

FOREIGN MISSION WORK

By the time of Augustana's organization in 1860, the Swedish immigrants already showed an interest in foreign missions and were supporting them with offerings from their meager earnings. At the very first annual meeting of the Augustana Synod it was resolved to appoint a Foreign Mission Committee. Having become a part of the General Council in 1870, the synod took part in the mission work of that body in India and Puerto Rico. Rev. A.B. Carlson was the Augustana Synod's first foreign missionary. He served India for many years and died there.

Lacking finances to carry on its own foreign mission programs, Augustana for a long time supported the programs of other Lutheran bodies. But it took the initiative to work independently in China and Africa. The Minnesota Conference had begun the China Mission, but the synod took it over in 1908. The same year, the synod acted favorably on the suggestion to establish a Foreign Mission Board of its own, independent from the General Council.

In spite of many difficulties, including political upheavals, the Chinese mission bore fruit. After forty years of labor, the China Church had twenty Chinese pastors, about 280 workers, eighty organized congregations, thirty-six outstations and about one hundred preaching places. There were also a number of parochial and Sunday Schools, besides more advanced

378

schools. In the medical field there was also a theological seminary. The work, of course, suffered greatly from the Second World War. After the war the missionaries returned and the work resumed, but then came the Communist takeover in China, and the work suffered again.

Work was begun in East Africa, in the Tanganyika Territory from which the German missionaries had been expelled in the First World War. After 1926 the work was returned to the Germans. After fewer than twenty years the mission had nine congregations, of which six had more than 1,000 members each. Enrollment in primary schools totaled 883 children, while 2,831 children were enrolled in chapel or bush schools. The mission also maintained hospitals and dispensaries, and maintained training schools, secondary schools, and a theological seminary.

Augustana went into Puerto Rico after the Spanish-American War. Though actually begun by an Augustana College student, the work there was carried on during its first years by members of the Augustana Synod. This mission venture was officially under the auspices of the General Council. When the United Lutheran Church in America was organized in 1918, the mission was transferred to the West Indies Mission Board of that Body.

MISSION SOCIETIES

AUGUSTANA FOREIGN MISSION SOCIETY

On April 10, 1886, students at Augustana College organized the Augustana Foreign Mission Society. This student enterprise eventually grew into a synod-wide organization, whose primary goals were to stimulate interest in foreign missions, to gather funds for the cause, and to urge independent mission work by the synod among non-Christian nations. In 1897 the synod gave warm endorsement to the society. Through the years the society continued to promote missionary education and interest and gave considerable financial support for the cause. The society was centered among the students at Augustana College and Theological Seminary in Rock Island, Illinois. Active missionary societies came to be organized on the campuses of other colleges in the Synod as well.

WOMEN'S MISSIONARY SOCIETY

At the synodical meeting at Lindsberg, Kansas, in 1892 a group of fifty women petitioned Augustana for the privilege of organizing a Women's Missionary Society. Their request was heartily granted. After fifty years the Women's Missionary Society, in 1942, numbered 1,334 local societies, which included those organized for adults, for young women, and for juniors...with a total membership of 57,495.[30]

In 1924 the Foreign Mission Board of the Church invited the Board of the Women's Missionary Society to sent two advisory members to its meet-

379

ings. In 1941 the Board of Foreign Missions amended its constitution, granting two voting memberships to the board of the Women's Missionary Society. And in 1955 the constitution of the Board of Foreign Missions was amended again, providing that the Board shall include two women nominated by the Women's Missionary Society and elected by the synod.

A Golden Jubilee gift of $50,000 for foreign missions was given on the society's anniversary in 1942. The society has also supported inner mission work, targeted to the youth. The Women's Missionary Society has had extensive impact in the synod in the area of raising funds and stimulating interest for missions.

ORGANIZATIONS WITHIN THE AUGUSTANA SYNOD

Mention has just been made of the Women's Missionary Society in connection with the synod's foreign mission program. There were other organizations as well. A constitution for the Luther League was approved in 1910 and the League was formally organized on December 3, 1910, at Chicago. With the synod's sanction the league was reorganized in 1924 into the Synodical Luther League Council. And in 1926 the Council was officially organized as representing the Young People's work.

The first Men's Group organized throughout the Synod was formed in 1915 for the purpose of gathering $500,000 for the ministerial pension fund. After the First World War, this movement was transformed into a Lutheran Brotherhood Insurance Company. In 1922 another Layman's group was formed, since the Lutheran Brotherhood could no longer function strictly as a church organization; thus was formed the Augustana Lutheran Brotherhood. One of the Brotherhood's activities has been to support boys' work. Later, the Augustana Brotherhood became a unit of the American Federation of Lutheran Brotherhoods.

CHARITABLE WORK AND INSTITUTIONS

At first, children's homes were established because so many parents died of cholera. These were hospices or temporary homes.

In establishing colleges in the individual conferences and sections of the synod, ambition sometimes got ahead of wisdom, with the result that the schools did not always work out. However, Augustana did better in the area of charitable institutions. In every conference of the synod one or more institutions of mercy were established. According to historian Abdel R. Wentz, in 1955 – just a few years before Augustana entered the merger forming the Lutheran Church in America (1962)-the following institutions were carried on by Augustana: twelve children's homes, eleven hospitals, twenty – one old folks homes, and ten hospices. There was also the Lutheran Seaman's Center in New York City. The large list of institutions enabled Wentz to draw this conclusion: "Both in number and in the quality of its institutions of charity, the Augustana Synod, in proportion to its size, leads the Lutheran bodies in America and stands among the first of all American Protestant bodies."[31]

In 1903 Augustana entered into Lutheran Deaconess work, assuming ownership and control of Immanuel Deaconess Institute in Omaha. After twenty-five years, the venture was discontinued, since very few women were attracted to the work.

AUGUSTANA ENTERS THE MERGER FORMING THE LUTHERAN CHURCH IN AMERICA (LCA)

When the General Council, General Synod, and the United Synod in the South made plans to merge into the United Lutheran Church in America (ULCA) in 1917, the Augustana Synod, wishing to continue its own separate identity, did not take part in the merger preparation. However, this spirit of retaining its separate identity did not keep Augustana from courting the friendship of the ULCA, even from the time that the merger commenced. And then, in 1962 in Detroit, Michigan, Augustana merged with the ULCA (1918-1962), the American Evangelical Lutheran Church [Danish] (1872-1962), and the Suomi Synod [Finnish] (1890-1962). Thus Augustana took its stand with the liberal branch of American Lutheranism.

Augustana's cooperation and fellowship with other Lutheran bodies certainly did much to prepare it to merge with the three other Lutheran bodies mentioned above. In fact, Augustana had a rather vigorous spirit of joining in with other Lutherans. In 1930 the Swedes joined the American Lutheran Conference – an association of five Lutheran bodies. Since World War I days, Augustana cooperated in the National Lutheran Council. But it was chiefly through its membership in the American Lutheran Conference that the Swedes "had gained considerable experience in inter-church matters."[32] Joining the merger of 1962 was a logical and no doubt inevitable undertaking. In doing so, Augustana – as has been pointed out – chose to be a part of liberal American Lutheranism. No doubt Augustana's contact with modern Swedish theology helped to point it in this direction.

Footnotes for Chapter Twenty-Two

1 George M. Stephenson, *The American Immigration Collection*, (Arno Pussan, The New York Times, 1969. Copyright originally, 1932, University of Minnesota Press, Minneapolis, MN), p.302.

2 Stephenson, *The American Immigration Collection*, p. 304.

3 Stephenson, *The American Immigration Collection*, p. 306.

4 Stephenson, *The American Immigration Collection*, p. 306, 307.

5 Stephenson, *The American Immigration Collection*, p. 307, 308.

6 Stephenson, *The American Immigration Collection* pp. 179,180.

7 Oscar N. Olson & George W. Wickstrom (Editors), *A Century of Life and Growth- 1848 to 1948 Lutheran Augustana Synod,* (Augustana Book Concern, Rock Island, IL, 1948), p. 41.

8 Olson-Wickstrom, *A Century of Life and Growth...*, p. 42.

9 Erwin L Lueker, Editor-in-Chief, *Lutheran Cyclopedia*, (Concordia Publishing House, St.

Louis, MO, 1954), p. 1116.

10 Stephenson, *The American Immigration Collection*, p. 155.

11 Stephenson, *The American Immigration Collection*, p. 158.

12 Stephenson, *The American Immigration Collection*, p. 209.

13 Abdel Ross Wentz, *A Basic History of Lutheranism in America*, (Muhlenberg Press, Philadelphia, PA, 1955), p. 19.

14 Oscar N. Olson, *The Augustana Lutheran Church in America 1860-1910*, Lutherans in U.S.A., 1956, p. 3.

15 Stephenson, *The American Immigration Collection*, p. 167.

16 Stephenson, *The American Immigration Collection*, pp. 225, 226

17 Stephenson, *The American Immigration Collection*, p. 338

* It is to be noted that in later years academies serving as preparatory schools in the Missouri Synod ceased operations.

18 Wentz, *A Basic History of Lutheranism in America*, p. 199.

19 Wentz, *A Basic History of Lutheranism in America*, p. 204

20 Olson-Wickstrom, *A Century of Life and Growth...*, pp. 157, 158.

21 Wentz, *A Basic History of Lutheranism in America*, p. 204, 205.

22 Oscar N. Olson, *The Augustana Lutheran Church in America 1860-1910*, p. 42.

23 Stephenson, *The American Immigration Collection,* p. 240.

24 Stephenson, *The American Immigration Collection,* p. 241.

25 Stephenson, The American Immigration Collection, p. 242.

26 Stephenson, *The American Immigration Collection*, p. 288.

27 Stephenson, *The American Immigration Collection*, p. 288.

28 Stephenson, *The American Immigration Collection*, p. 292.

29 Olson-Wickstrom (editors), *A Century of Life and Growth...*, pp.72-73.

30 Olson-Wickstrom (editors), *A Century of Life and Growth...*,p. 129.

31 Wentz, *A basic History of Lutheranism in America*, p. 204.

32 Johannes Knudsen, *The Formation of the Lutheran Church in America* (Philadelphia, PA: Fortress Press, 1978), p. 16.

CHAPTER TWENTY-THREE

THE DANES
DENMARK AND THE
DANISH IMMIGRATION

DENMARK CHRISTIANIZED

Christianity first came to Denmark six centuries before the discovery of America. The gospel took over Denmark slowly. It was not forced on the people by the sword as in some countries, but rather the gentle persuasion of the gospel little by little Christianized the country.

LUTHERANISM COMES TO DENMARK

The coming of Lutheranism to Denmark has already been told in a brief way in Chapter Three of this volume. Under King Frederick I (1523-33) Lutheranism was allowed free course in Denmark, and equal toleration with Catholicism. Finally, the Catholic religion was abolished by law and the Lutheran Church became established under royal patronage – and under control of the king. The first Lutheran pastor to come to America was a Dane by the name of Rasmus Jensen, who served as the chaplain of an expedition in 1619 led by the explorer Jens Munk. The party entered Hudson Bay and wintered at the mouth of Churchill River. Munk called the harbor and surrounding country Nova Dania or New Denmark. A severe winter accompanied by scurvy and other diseases killed most of the exploration party, including Pastor Jensen. Only the captain and two others survived, finally making it safely back to Denmark on Christmas Day 1617.

THE CHURCH IN DENMARK: ITS LEADERS

Arthur Paul C. Nyholm divides the history of the Church of Denmark from 1810 to 1930 into four periods.[1]

(1)   THE FIRST PERIOD, 1810-40. This was the age of Bishop I.P. Mynster, the father of the so-called high churchly party that emphasized beauty and dignity in the Sunday morning services and stressed the value of the sacraments. Rationalism had become strongly established in the State Church of Denmark and robbed it of its evangelical spirit. The work of both Peter Mynster (1775-1854) and N.S. F. Grundtvig (1783-1872) brought a renewal of evangelicalism to the Church. Mynster came to the realization that the New Testament is historically true, and once he had accepted this fact, he began to preach in an eloquent manner the message of conversion, justification, and sanctification. He was an advocate of the established Church and is considered the father of the high church trend in Danish life. In modern times, his followers are the "middle of the road" group in the Church.[2]

(2)   THE SECOND PERIOD, 1840-72. The great hymn writer, Bishop N.F.S. Grundtvig, was the most influential leader in the Church. He discarded the concept of the primacy of the Bible and replaced it with the primacy of the Church, and taught that Christ himself is "the Word," who lives in his Church and nourishes it through his "living Word", the *Apostles Creed*, the Lord's Prayer, and the Sacraments. According to Nyholm, Grundtvig's position was: "The Bible is a sacred source-book of the Christian faith but may not be identified with the true 'Word of God.'"

Grundtvig at first found no essential difference between Christianity and Scandinavian mythology. But later, after years of spiritual unrest and after he had become a theological candidate, Grundtvig experienced Christian conversion. Still later, after entering the ministry, Grundtvig found himself at odds with orthodox Lutheranism, and it was at that time that he no longer was able to accept the New Testament as the inspired word of God. And so, while searching for the true and original Christianity, he came to the conclusion that true Christianity is given by the Church, which is older than the Scriptures. It was in 1825 that Grundtvig produced his "matchless discovery", that the true "living Word" of God is the *Apostles Creed* and that through this Word of God comes to the Christian, reborn through Baptism. He believed that the renunciation of sins, together with the *Apostles Creed*, had been the Church's confession, given it from the Lord's own mouth after his resurrection. Through the person's Baptism, the confession becomes the true "Word of life" for the believer. Grundtvig maintained that the Lord's Supper was also an act of Christ and that "only at the washing and at the table do we hear God's Word to us." As far as the Bible is concerned, Grundtvig considered it a glorious book of in-

384

struction, indispensable for the Church but it is not the giver of spiritual life. But while Grundtvig accused the more orthodox Lutherans of making a fetish of the written word in the Bible, he seemed to do the same thing with the words of the *Apostles Creed.*[3]

There can be no doubt about the powerful and far-reaching influence of Grundtvig on the Danish Church. This, in spite of the fact that he had embarked on a course deviating from the old accepted truths of Christianity. He even came to regard conversion as unnecessary – Baptism itself is the supplier of all necessary spiritual strength. He regarded the Ten Commandments as only Jewish civil laws, and therefore to be left out of the Catechism. He came to reject also the doctrine of man's natural, total corruption, and accepted the possibility of conversion after death (based on the episode of Christ's descent into hell). In spite of Grundtvig's deviations from Scripture he nevertheless was a prolific hymn writer and many of his hymns are still sung today – even in very conservative Lutheran circles. Examples are: "God's Word is Our Great Heritage," and "Built on the Rock the Church Doth Stand." The folk high school movement, which was begun among the peasants, was supported by Grundtvig. Grundtvig also wrote many patriotic songs and was deeply respected, especially in rural areas, for his intense nationalism. He was a man who influenced Danish society and culture and is considered the father of the Danish Folk High School. Furthermore, Grundtvig greatly stressed the value of national characteristics and the mother tongue and actually claimed that Denmark was the modern Palestine: "God's favored country". These views had great and far-reaching influence in America in the minds of many immigrants.

(3)   THE THIRD PERIOD, 1872-1901. Bishop Grundtvig died in 1872. Vilhelm Beck, Denmark's greatest revivalist preacher and leader of the pietistic Inner Mission Movement became the new spiritual leader in Denmark. An existing organization was reorganized as the Church Society for Inner Mission, with Pastor Beck and Pastor Johannes Clausen as members. The group, begun earlier by laymen, sought to bring new spiritual life into the existing church. The emphasis was on the work of laymen in spreading the Word of God. Laymen who had been sent out to distribute Christian literature were later commissioned as lay preachers who then conducted meetings in private homes as well as in public places. Vilhelm Beck remained the leader of the movement until his death in 1901. It should be noted that this movement continued, and by 1961 there were more than three hundred men working full time as lay preachers. As Beck and Clausen went around holding meetings there was a large response from the people, and mission halls were frequently built where informal meetings and social gatherings could be held.

The preachers of the Inner Mission emphasized repentance and personal faith, and a decisive break with the world. Some of their prohibitions smack of those promoted by Pentecostal groups today. Revivals were an important tool of the movement and were well attended. We could say that there was a strong element of Methodism in the group. There was also strong emphasis on the difference between unbelief and faith. Grundtvigianism and the Inner Mission movement were at opposite ends of the spectrum, with no love lost between the two groups. Dr. Nyholm points out these differences:

GRUNDTVIG STRESSED THE VALUE OF GENERAL CULTURE AND THE NATIONAL

385

SPIRIT, AND EMPHASIZED MAINLY THE OBJECTIVE ELEMENT IN CHRISTIANITY, PARTICULARLY THROUGH BAPTISM INTO "THE LIVING WORD." HE IS THE FATHER OF THE DANISH EVANGELICAL LUTHERAN CHURCH IN AMERICA. BECK, ON THE OTHER HAND, STRESSED ALSO THE SUBJECTIVE ELEMENTS IN CHRISTIANITY, [SUCH] AS CONVERSION AND SANCTIFICATION, AND TOOK A MORE NARROW CULTURAL VIEW, CONCENTRATING ON 'THE ONE THING NEEDFUL,' ALTHOUGH HE HIMSELF WAS MORE BROADMINDED AND MORE INTERESTED IN NATIONAL QUESTIONS THAN WERE HIS FOLLOWERS. BECK IS THE SPIRITUAL FATHER OF THE UNITED EVANGELICAL LUTHERAN CHURCH.

(4)   THE FOURTH PERIOD, 1901-31. Pastor Olfert Richard (died in 1929) was the most prominent leader. He was the father of the "Fourth Party" in the church of Denmark. His party insisted on a clear individual Christian conviction, combining with it a broad cultural and social interest. Pastor Richard was born at the time that Marxian Socialism was introduced into Denmark from Germany. This movement estranged great numbers in the laboring class from the Church. Another movement, Realism and Rationalism, introduced by a Jew, Georg Brandes, went on to separate many of the educated class from the Christian faith. Later, Pastor Richard led a counter-attack on these two movements which had had such an adverse effect on the influence of Christianity in Denmark – an effect from which the Church in Denmark never fully recovered and which also had a great effect on the emigrants who had started to leave in large numbers for America.[4]

Nyholm points out that only a minority of the 98% of the population of Denmark who are labeled Lutherans can be classified fully as belonging to any of these four movements. He points out that the majority of the Danes are either "outside the parties" or are quite indifferent of the church.

DANISH EMIGRATION AND CHURCH LIFE IN DENMARK

THE GREATER PART OF THE DANISH SETTLEMENTS IN AMERICA WERE FOUNDED AT A TIME WHEN LIFE IN THE CHURCH OF DENMARK WAS AT A LOW EBB. NOT ONLY WAS THERE A GOOD DEAL OF DIVISION AND STRIFE, ESPECIALLY BETWEEN THE INNER MISSION PEOPLE AND THE GRUNDTVIGIANS, BUT THERE WAS ALSO MUCH OPPOSITION TO CHRISTIANITY ITSELF, BOTH FOR HER DOCTRINES AND HER MORAL STANDARDS, FROM MANY OF THE BEST EDUCATED PEOPLE AS WELL AS FROM THE MEMBERS OF THE LABORING CLASSES, BOTH IN THE CITIES AND IN THE RURAL COMMUNITIES.[5]

The majority of Danish immigrants were the poorer class of people, who had very little contact with the State Church. About 30,000 Danes had come to America before the first Danish Lutheran pastors came, and these were scattered, it is reported, in every state and territory of the United States. It is further reported that twenty-five years separated the first Danish settlement (at Harland Wisconsin, 1846) and the first mission efforts of the Danish mother Church.[6] The Danes had a newspaper twenty-five years before they had a

386

Danish Lutheran synod. This history reflects not only an apathy towards the Lutheran Church, but a disdain also for the Lutheran clergy. This negative attitude was experienced already in hearts in the mother country and later brought to America by many of the immigrants, people who belonged mainly to the laboring class.

AGNOSTICISM IN DENMARK

Georg Brandes (1842-1927) began in 1870 to attack the Church through a series of lectures. Brandes, who received a large following from young intellectuals, was an agnostic who advocated freethinking and freedom from the restrictions of sexual morality. He also denied the truth of the Christian faith. Another movement was begun about the same time in Denmark, the labor movement, which formally began in 1871 and served as the basis of the Socialist party. It was basically hostile to the Church. What effect did these two movements have on the Danish immigrants who entered this country? THE MAJORITY OF THE IMMIGRANTS CAME FROM THOSE CLASSES, WHICH HAD BEEN MOST RECEPTIVE TO BRANDESIAN AND SOCIALISTIC IDEAS.[7]

The result of this was that the agnostic spirit of many of the Danish immigrants was a major obstacle to evangelism among them. Another proven obstacle to making a good church member of a Dane who immigrated here was the feeling of light-heartedness and an easy-going spirit (those "happy Danes") inherent in the Danish mind. Putting it simply: The Danish people like "the good life."

CAUSES OF THE DANISH EMIGRATION

CLASS INFLUENCE ON THE MIGRATION

The following observation was made by the historian John M. Jensen: UNFORTUNATELY, DANISH SOCIETY RETAINED ITS DISTINCT SOCIAL STRATA, EVEN AFTER THE ABOLITION OF THE FEUDAL SYSTEM. THE UPPER CLASSES WERE THOSE WHO, BECAUSE OF BIRTH, WEALTH, OR POSITION, WERE CONSIDERED OUTSTANDING. THEY INCLUDED THE NOBILITY, LARGE LANDOWNERS, AND HIGHER ADMINISTRATIVE OFFICIALS. IN RURAL AREAS THE PROFESSIONAL MEN AND THE PASTORS WERE ALSO CONSIDERED AS BELONGING TO THE UPPER CLASS; IN THE CITIES THEY WERE OF THE UPPER MIDDLE CLASS, WHILE SKILLED LABORERS WERE OF THE LOWER MIDDLE CLASS AND UNSKILLED LABORERS OF THE LOWEST CLASS. THESE CLASS DISTINCTIONS WERE VERY PRONOUNCED IN THE ENTIRE 19TH CENTURY. IT WAS CONSIDERED A MISFORTUNE TO MARRY OUTSIDE ONE'S CLASS. AND A PEASANT'S SON MUST NOT MARRY A HIRED GIRL EVEN IF SHE WAS EVER SO ABLE AND BEAUTIFUL. THERE WAS THEREFORE A CERTAIN AMOUNT OF HOSTILITY BETWEEN THE CLASSES. SINCE THE PASTORS WERE OF THE UPPER OR MIDDLE CLASS THE CHURCH SELDOM HELD ANY APPEAL FOR LABORERS. WHEN EMIGRATION TO AMERICA BEGAN IN EARNEST, IT WAS NOT FROM

THE MIDDLE CLASS. THEIR POSITIONS IN SOCIETY WERE RELATIVELY SECURE, AND THEY WERE MAKING GAINS BOTH ECONOMICALLY AND CULTURALLY. BUT MEMBERS OF THE LABORING CLASSES, PARTICULARLY IN THE RURAL AREAS, STRONGLY DESIRED THE INDEPENDENCE AND IMPROVED STATUS THAT THEY HOPED COULD BE FOUND IN THE NEW WORLD. THE MERE POSSIBILITY OF OWNING AN AMERICAN FARM, WHICH WOULD BE LARGER THAN THAT OF HIS DANISH EMPLOYER, PROVED AN ALMOST IRRESISTIBLE LURE TO MANY A DANISH HIRED FARM HAND.[8]

POLITICAL CAUSES OF THE DANISH MIGRATION

In 1864 Prussia and Austria combined forces to bring the southern most part of Jutland under German control. Rather than live under German rule many of the Danes in the south migrated either north into Denmark or to America. It was at this point in Danish history that the migration to America began in earnest.

THE IMMIGRATION OF DANES

The total Danish immigration from 1820-30 was 189, and from 1820-40, only 1,252. In the 1840's the greater share of Danish immigrants came to Wisconsin, and as immigration increased in subsequent years, Wisconsin continued to be more important to the Danes than any other state.
Danish Immigration by decades:

    1820-1829...189
    1830-1840...1,063
    1841-1850...539
    1851-1860...3,749
    1861-1870...17,094
    1871-1880...31,771
    1881-1890...88,132
    1891-1900...50,231
    1901-1910...65,285
    1911-1920...41,983
    1921-1930...32,430
    1931-1940...2,661
    1941-1950...4,602
    1951-   ...8,828
In 140 years a total of 345,936 immigrants came from Denmark.

From 1820-70 about 250,000 immigrants arrived in this country from Norway and Sweden, but only about 30,000 from Denmark. By 1900 the number of Danish immigrants was less than half the number of those who migrated from Norway. Like the Swedes, many Danes fell prey to Mormonism (about 23,000) from 1850 to 1900.[9] Most of the Danes settled in the Middle West.

DANISH COLONIES

The Danish migration took place later than the migration of the Norwegians and the Swedes. It consisted in fewer numbers and there was a tendency for the Danes to scatter, while the other Scandinavians tended to form settlements. Enok Mortensen points out that as late as 1870 there were in the United States only five cities and six counties with a population of more than 500 Danes.[10] But during the 1870's the rate of Danish migration sharply increased, with settlements established throughout the Middle West. The Danes chose to make their homes in Michigan, Wisconsin, Minnesota, Iowa, Nebraska, and South Dakota. In 1884 the Danish Ev. Lutheran church in America set about to form colonies for its people. One such colony was established in southern Lincoln County, Minnesota. (Pastor Hans Pederson, 1851-1905, became the first resident pastor of the Danebod Colony, established in 1888). A second colony was formed at Withee, Wisconsin, in 1893 by the Synod. (Pastor A.S. Nielsen from Chicago was the first resident pastor.)

Mortensen lists other colonies of Danes, which were established later; however, not under sponsorship of the Danish Church. There were colonies at Danevang, Texas, Askov, Minnesota and Dalum, Alberta in Canada. These were sponsored by the Danish Folk Society. The guiding light of this society was Pastor Frederik Lange Grundtvig (1854-1903), a son of Bishop N.F.S. Grundtvig. Grundtvig's idea was that America was "a union of independent nationalities, each one retaining its ancestral language and culture in addition to the common English language."[11] The first colony established by the Society was seventy-two odd miles southwest of Houston, Texas (Danevang). The second Colony, Askov, was established in Pine County, Minnesota. Pastor H.C. Strankov, a disciple of Grundtvig, became the first resident pastor of the colony.

In 1906 a colony was started out of Clinton, Iowa, at Dagmar, Montana, and was headed by E.F. Madsen. Another colony was established at Solvang, California, in 1911 by three men, two of whom were pastors (B. Nordentoft and J. Gregersen) together with Mr. P. Hornsyld. Gregersen became pastor in the colony. The colony in Canada at Dalum, Alberta, was founded by the Danish Folk Society in 1917, and was shepherded by Pastor P. Rasmussen. By then immigration had switched from the United States to our neighbor in the north.

The last Danish colony, Granly, was founded in 1931 in the State of Mississippi, very near the Gulf of Mexico. Pastor K. Knudsen became its first pastor. As time went on, the Danish Church became Americanized and people lost their incentive for isolating themselves with their own language and cultural group. At first, the attitude was to establish "little Denmarks" in America. But this lost out to Americanization.

Footnotes for Chapter Twenty-Three

1 Paul C. Nyholm, *The Americanization of the Danish Lutheran Churches in America – An Interpretation,* (Augsburg Publishing House, Minneapolis, MN,), pp. 62-64.

2 John M. Jensen, *The United Ev. Lutheran Church-An Interpretation,* (Augsburg Publishing

House, Minneapolis, MN.), p. 6.

3 Jensen, *The United Ev. Lutheran Church-An Interpretation*, p. 7.

4 Nyholm, T*he Americanization of the Danish Lutheran Churches in America,* p. 64.

5 Nyholm, *The Americanization of the Danish Lutheran Churches in America*, p. 64.

6 Nyholm, *The Americanization of the Danish Lutheran Churches in America*, p. 65.

7 Jensen, *The United Ev. Lutheran Church-An Interpretation*, p. 15.

8 Jensen, *The United Ev. Lutheran Church-An Interpretation*, p. 4.

9 Nyholm, *The Americanization of the Danish Lutheran Churches in America*, p. 67.

10 Enok Mortensen, *Stories of Our Church*, (Blair, NE: Lutheran Publishing House, 1952), p. 50.

11 Mortensen, *Stories of Our Church*, p. 76.

CHAPTER TWENTY-FOUR

THE DANES
THE DANISH LUTHERAN
CHURCH COMES TO AMERICA:
EARLY BEGINNINGS

THE DANES WERE CLOSELY TIED TO THE
NORWEGIANS

SCARCITY OF DANISH PASTORS

While the sects were quick to show an interest in winning over the Danish immigrants, the mother Church in Denmark was slow to respond to the needs of her transplanted people. Much of the Lutheran work among the immigrants was carried on by Norwegian pastors, with help from only a few scattered pastors of Danish background. Lutheran work among Danes was first carried on in Wisconsin at Hartland and at Denmark. The oldest congregation of the United Evangelical Lutheran Church was Emmaus Lutheran Church, organized in 1851 at Racine, Wisconsin.

The Norwegian Lutherans were actually the ones who at first kept the sects from making more of an inroad into the Danish community than they did. Over the years many Danish pastors were instructed and ordained by the Norwegian Synod, and these pastors then served Danish congregations. (Because of their strict orthodoxy, these pastors did not join the Danish Church when finally it was established.) Many early Danes joined Norwegian Lutheran churches. However, it is also true that many of the early Danes did not respond very readily to the work of the Lutheran missionaries. The early Danish missionaries did not possess an easy life, for they often received a cold reception from their own countrymen, who treated them with suspicion. One of the reasons for the cold reception was the immigrants' situation during the first years following their arrival in America. They were mainly interested in establishing themselves in the new land. They did not want their time and attention taken up with religion. On the other hand, there were also many stories told of deep devotion afforded the pastor, and of a sincere longing in the immigrants' hearts for a church to be established in their area.

During the 1870's immigration of Danes increased; still, there was only a handful of missionaries and pastors to serve the widely scattered settlers. Michigan, which had huge tracts of virgin forests, attracted Danes. While they farmed, they also worked in logging camps. The missionaries traveled through the forests and along the shore of Lake Michigan in order to serve these Danes. They also served people farther east in Michigan toward what is now Lansing, the State Capital. Mention has already been made in the previous chapter of pastors serving various Danish colonies scattered over the country, particularly in the Midwest.

At the beginning of the 1870's there were only two Danish pastors (Dan and Thomsen) in America. There were two congregations "in active contact with the Danish mother Church."[1] Before the decade was over there were a few congregations on the East Coast (New York and New Jersey), and one west of the Missouri River. Most Danish congregations were located in the states bordering Lake Michigan, with a few in Minnesota and Iowa.

Most Danish pastors were also part-time traveling pastors, who, besides their home congregations, served scattered groups, sometimes at considerable distances. At first, Danish Lutheran congregations were very widely scattered. Several states had only one such congregation apiece.

THE NORWEGIAN-DANISH LUTHERAN CONFERENCE

The Norwegians did considerable work among the Danes during the first quarter century of the Danish immigration. However, the Danes often hoped for their own pastors and for services held in their own language. The cooperation between Danes and Norwegians resulted in the Norwegian-Danish Lutheran Conference, organized in 1870 with Pastor C.L. Clausen as president. Though further mention will be made in the next two chapters of the Conference, it might prove helpful to the reader to offer a brief summary of its history here.

1870 The Conference was organized when the Scandinavians left the liberal Northern Illinois Synod. While some banded together to form the Norwegian-Augustana Synod, others formed the Norwegian-Danish Evangelical Lutheran Conference.

1872 There were four pastors who did not join the Conference and were referred to as the "Danish Brethren." They organized the Church Mission Society to do mission work among the Danish immigrants in America.

1874 The name of the Church Mission Society was changed informally to the Danish Evangelical Lutheran Church in America. It was now a church body.

1875 A separate Danish Mission Board was created by the Danes in the Conference.

1877 A Danish paper, *Dansk Luthersk Kirkebald,* was begun.

1878 The name the Danish Evangelical Lutheran Church in America was officially adopted by the group that had informally taken this name in 1874. Commonly called the Danish Church.

1882 The first plans for organizing a Danish synod separate from the Norwegians in the Conference were made at Munson Creek, Nebraska.

1883 A committee was named to consider the question of organizing a separate Danish synod. With increasing Danish immigration it was felt that Danish pastors within the Conference could serve more effectively with a separate Danish organization.

1884 A friendly separation took place. On September 11-14, at Argo, Nebraska, nine pastors, serving nineteen congregations and fifteen preaching places, organized the Danish Evangelical Lutheran Association in America. All but one of the pastors were born in Denmark, and most had their roots in the Inner Mission Movement in the old Country. The new synod was usually referred to as the "Blair Church" (its headquarters was located in Blair, Nebraska). The same year Trinity Seminary was begun at Blair. (In 1956 it was moved to Dubuque, Iowa, and in 1961 was merged with Wartburg Seminary.)

1887 A theological seminary was begun at West Denmark, Wisconsin, by the Danish Church.

1894-1895 Grundtvigianism and the Inner Mission – two movements within the Church of Denmark – were present in the Danish Church (org. 1872 and 1874). These two forces clashed in Denmark and were destined to clash in America. A quarrel arose at the seminary between Th. Helveg (a Grundtvigian) and P.S. Vig (Inner Mission Movement). Thirty-six pastors, chiefly Grundtvigians, remained within the Danish Church, while twenty-two pastors, mostly of the Inner Mission persuasion, organized in 1895 the Danish Evangelical Lutheran Church in North America. Commonly referred to as the North Church.

1896 The two Inner Mission focused Danish churches – the North Church and the Blair Church – merged, organizing in Minneapolis the United Danish Evangelical Lutheran Church in America. Both were pietistic, with their roots in the Inner Mission Movement in the old country. In 1896 the United Church had sixty-four pastors and ninety-seven congregations, while the Danish Church had thirty-six pastors and forty congregations. (The Americanization process had been slower with the Danish Church than with the United Church because of the Grundtvigian philosophy of the use of the Danish language and culture.)

MINISTERIAL EDUCATION FOR DANISH PASTORS

A man intent on studying for the Danish Lutheran ministry was able to receive theological training at the University of Copenhagen, and some did. As in Germany and elsewhere, so in Denmark, a man could also find theological and practical training at mission schools. Some Danish pastors took the young men under their wing to give them private theological training. But most of the pioneer Danish pastors were trained at one of the Danish folk schools, especially at the Askov school in Denmark. This is important to note because the founder of the folk school movement was Bishop N.F.S. Grundtvig.

The need for pastors in the pioneer Danish Church in America was great; still, the Danish State Church did not show much interest in the immigration church. Furthermore, the pastors who came from Denmark often found it difficult to adjust to the work here. Some of the pastors for the Danish Church were trained in the seminary of the Norwegian-Danish Conference. Some were trained at Augsburg Seminary operated by the Norwegian Lutheran Synod. Finally, in 1884 the Blair Church opened its own Trinity Seminary in Blair, Nebraska, and three years later the Danish Church opened its seminary at West Denmark, Wisconsin – the location of a short-lived folk school.

Before 1900 all but three of the pastors who served in the Danish-American congregations were born in Denmark. With few exceptions the pastors of the United Church were, from the beginning, trained in America. Within the Danish Church, before 1899, almost twice as many pastors were trained in Denmark as in America, but in the next fifty years the trend was reversed; twice as many were trained in America as had their training in Denmark.

EARLY DANISH PASTORS

CLAUS LAURITZ CLAUSEN (1820-92)

The coming of the Danish Lutheran Church to America is closely allied with the immigration of C.L. Clausen who, as you no doubt recall, figured strongly in the history of Norwegian Lutheranism in America. Clausen was a teacher in Denmark who for a long time was inclined to become a missionary in a foreign land. But instead, he was led to Muskego, Wisconsin, to serve as a teacher in a Norwegian settlement there. Not only did Clausen teach school, he also filled in as a lay preacher. Accepted in this capacity by the Norwegian immigrants, he was soon urged by them to become their pastor and on October 18, 1843, C.L. Clausen was ordained.

Clausen was closely involved with the immigrants, even helping them to find free land. On an exploratory trip to Iowa, he held the first Danish Lutheran services in that state. Clausen was an indefatigable worker, using his many talents in various capacities, and was recognized as a leader of people, not only by the church but by the community as well. Together with three other pastors he founded the Evangelical Norwegian Lutheran Church in America. He also became the first president of the Norwegian-Danish

Lutheran Conference (1870).

While most of Clausen's work was with the Norwegian Lutherans, neverthe-less with increasing Danish immigration he lent his talents and energies to assist in organizing Danish Lutheran churches. On a lecture tour of Denmark, Clausen inspired the formation of The Commission to Further the Preaching of the Gospel among the Danes in North America. Later, Clausen was instru-mental in founding Danish settlements in Wisconsin and Iowa.

M.F. WIESE

Considered to be the first Danish minister ordained to serve a congregation of Danish Lutherans in America.

NIELS THOMSEN (1842-92)

Became the pastor of a Danish congregation at Indianapolis. He was the first of the pastors of the Danish Ev. Lutheran Church. However, about 1883 he left that synod and in 1892 he died while serving a congregation near Greenville, Michigan. Little is known of the man. While Thomsen was pastor in Wisconsin he served also as a part-time traveling pastor.

ADAM DAN (1848-1931)

Ordained and installed at Emmaus Congregation at Racine, Wisconsin, in 1871, Dan became the second pastor of the Danish Ev. Lutheran Church. Dan was teaching in a Syrian orphanage in Jerusalem at the time he received the call to the Danish congregation in Racine. Enok Mortensen describes Adam Dan, the second of the four "church fathers" of the Danish Ev. Lutheran Church in America, as probably the most gifted, certainly the most eloquent of the four. (The four "church fathers" were: Niels Thomsen, Adam Dan, Anders Nielsen, and Rasmus Anderson.) Adam Dan had been greatly influenced by Bishop Grundtvig. Because of his bright and cheerful manner he came under suspi-cion and was opposed by Norwegian ministers imbued with the stern and solemn orthodoxy of so many Norwegians of that time.[2] Dan did extensive traveling, organizing congregations in California, and serving congregations in the Midwest and even on the East Coast in Boston. Dan was a writer, poet, and a hymnist.

The same year that Adam Dan was ordained, three men were sent to the Danish ministry in America by the Commission in Denmark. Pastor Grove-Rasmussen was one of these. After a short time, however, due mainly to illness and disappointment over the attitude of his fellow countrymen, he returned to Denmark. The other two men, who had come to America with him, remained and helped to build the Danish Church in this country.

ANDERS SIXTUS NIELSEN (1832-1909)

Began work at Cedar Falls and Fredsville, Iowa, in 1871. He was installed by C.L. Clausen at St. Ansgar, Iowa, that year. Nielsen has been characterized as "the practical leader and wise counselor, both for individuals and congregations."[3] He had served for a year as a missionary to India but had to leave the ministry for a time because of ill health. He served congregations in Iowa, Chicago, and finally in Wisconsin. Nielsen was the first ordained and three-time president of the Danish Ev. Church in America.

RASMUS ANDERSEN (1847-1930)

He was a student at the time he arrived in America and finished his studies at Augsburg Seminary in Marshall, Wisconsin. He was ordained at Waupaca, Wisconsin, in 1872. His ordination marked the first time a Danish pastor was ordained by another Danish pastor in America. Pastor Dan and Thomsen took part. The original four pastors of the Danish Lutheran Church met at Anderson's ordination. Three months later Anderson and Dan met at Neenah, Wisconsin, and organized a Church Mission Society, whose purpose it was to gather Danish Lutherans into congregations. The tiny group put out a paper called *Church Gatherer*. From this meager beginning grew the Danish Ev. Lutheran Church in America. Rasmus Anderson ultimately left Waupaca and spent most of the remainder of his life in Brooklyn, New York. He became a pastor to the seamen as well as to the immigrants. Andersen was an author and historian.

OTHER PIONEER DANISH PASTORS

P.C. TRANDBERG (1832-96)

He was a revivalistic preacher who, while never joining the Blair Church, wielded a great deal of influence on the pastors and the outlook of that body. He emphasized revival preaching and free congregations. His was a tolerant viewpoint in matters of doctrine. Trandberg emphasized the holy life and was responsible for the viewpoint expressed in the congregational constitution regarding discipline. He was a rugged individualist. While rejecting the call as a professor at Trinity Seminary of the Blair Church, he began to lecture at the Congregational Seminary in Chicago, and conducted meetings for Scandinavians in the Congregational Tabernacle in Chicago, which later became Siloam Free Church. Trandberg did much traveling, especially in the summer, preaching at Danish settlements. Dismissed from the Congregational Seminary in 1900, he began his own seminary, which he conducted for three years. He then until his death worked as a traveling preacher. Trandberg was a premillenialist, who believed in and eagerly awaited the coming of Christ to establish a thousand year messianic reign on earth. He educated a large number of pastors who finally became members of the United Church. It is said that he preached in almost every Danish congregation in the Middle West.[4]

I.A. HEIBERG (1848-1936)

He trained in theology at the University of Copenhagen. His first charge was in Chicago. Though he became a leader in the Danish Church he did not remain in America but chose instead to return to Denmark in 1879.

SØREN HAMBORG MADSEN (1842-1911)

Having received his training in a mission school at Copenhagen, he came to America in 1869 and taught school. Ill health sent him back to Denmark, but in 1876 he returned as a pastor. Madsen held pastorates in Indianapolis and Wisconsin, and did pioneer work in Nebraska, helping to establish Nysted, Nebraska. Later, ill health caused him to move west. He built the first Danish Lutheran Church on the Pacific Coast. He later came to Danevang, Texas, where he died.

PEDER KJØLHEDE (1844-1937)

He was a native of Jutland. He came to be concerned about the spiritual welfare of Danish emigrants to America. After studying at the Askov Folk School, he left for America at the age of thirty-six. Up to that time Kjølhede had been a farmer. For fifty-seven years he labored as a pastor to the Danes, beginning at Muskegon, Michigan. Kjølhede served as the Danish Church's president from 1895 to 1903. From 1901 to 1936 he served his synod as ordainer. From 1901 to 1936 he served his synod as ordainer. Kjølhede was a builder, author and historian.

KNUD CLAUSEN BODHOLDT (1855-1931)

Having immigrated in 1870, he later desired to be a pastor. First, he studied under Pastor A.S. Nielsen and later, at the Askov Folk School in Denmark. His first pastorate was in Marquette, Nebraska (1882). Bodholdt served as president of the Danish Church at various times. He died at Racine, Wisconsin, while serving a congregation there.

In the next two chapters we shall examine the histories of the Lutheran synods, which were formed by the Danish Immigrants and their pastors.

Footnotes for Chapter Twenty-Four

1 Enok Mortensen, *Stories From Our Church* (Blair, NE: Lutheran Publishing House, 1952),

p. 50.

2 Mortensen, *Stories From Our Church*, p. 35.

3 Mortensen, *Stories From Our Church*, p. 33.

4 John M. Jensen, *The United Ev. Lutheran Church: An Interpretation*, (Minneapolis, MN: Augsburg Publishing House, 1964), p. 104.

CHAPTER TWENTY-FIVE

THE DANES
THE AMERICAN EVANGELICAL
LUTHERAN CHURCH
Formerly:
The Danish Evangelical Lutheran
Church in America
(1872 - 1962)

FIRST CAME THE CHURCH MISSION SOCIETY

The Church Mission Society was the forerunner of the Danish Ev. Lutheran Church in America. In the previous chapter a brief accounting was given of the four early Danish pastors who were responsible for forming the Society. They were: Adam Dan, who arrived from Syria to serve the Emmaus Congregation at Racine, Wisconsin, in 1871; N. Thomsen, who arrived in 1871 from India to become pastor of a congregation in Indianapolis, Indiana; A.S. Nielsen, who began his work at Cedar Falls and Fredsville, Iowa, in 1871; and Rasmus Andersen, who came as a student, finishing his studies at Augsburg Seminary (then at Marshall, Wisconsin) in 1872.

There four pastors met at Waupaca at Andersen's ordination, which was performed by A.S. Nielsen. Up to that time, these Danish pastors and their congregations had operated independently from others. But the desire to form a Danish Lutheran church body was present in the minds of these men; therefore the four met later that fall at Neenah, Wisconsin, and together with some laymen organized a Church Mission Society. At the same time they undertook the bold venture of publishing a bimonthly church paper. The society's purpose was stated as follows: THE SOCIETY SHALL CONDUCT MEETINGS, SEND OUT LAY PREACHERS, AND INVITE PEOPLE TO THE CHURCH SO THAT THE HOUSE OF GOD MAY BE FILLED WITH SAVED PEOPLE. The Society did not profess to be another synod, and made only a superficial, generalized doctrinal statement. (However, the date 1872, when the Society was organized, is recognized as the starting date of what later became a synod.)

Other Danes were at the same time expressing the desire to get together and form a Danish Lutheran Church apart from the Norwegians and Swedes. In fact, the Norwegians in the Norwegian-Danish Conference understood the feelings of their Danish brethren and encouraged them to form an independent church body so that they might carry on their Danish work. In the meeting of the Norwegian-Danish Conference at Rock Prairie, Wisconsin, June 18, 1872, the matter of how a Danish Lutheran Church could best be established was brought up for discussion. An invitation to attend the meeting had been sent out by the Conference to the "four pastors," who at that time were without synodical affiliation. However, these men declined to attend since they intended to negotiate with the mother Church in Denmark, and went on to organize their Church Mission Society.

FORMING A TIGHTER ORGANIZATION

With the coming of more pastors and the establishing of many new congregations, the Church Society began to change from the loosely-knit organization it had been, to attaining more the character of asynod. Two days after the Chicago Convention of the Church Society in 1874, the pastors gathered again at Racine, Wisconsin, and informally decided to change the name of the organization to The Danish Evangelical Lutheran Church in America. The date was June 27, 1874. At this time the organization did not bother about having official delegates from the congregations, and there was no constitution to guide them. The church board or council through which the affairs of the church were conducted consisted of both pastors and laymen. In 1874 the first pastor ordained in Denmark to serve this synod also became its president. He was Pastor I.A. Heiberg.

By 1878 the need was felt for a more thorough organization of the synod. An invitation was extended that year to hold a convention, consisting not only of pastors but also of delegates elected from all the congregations. At the same time the congregation at Neenah, Wisconsin, where the Convention was held, asked that the following agenda be considered: (1) A common constitution; (2) Election of a bishop; (3) Establishment of a seminary; (4) Appointment of committees to: work for building a seminary, examine candidates for ordination, work for mission projects, work for publications.[1]

The meeting began May 22, 1878, with fifteen pastors and fifteen lay delegates. There was considerable debate on the subject of electing a bishop. The majority favored, not the creation of an autocratic bishopry, but pastoral and congregational autonomy. The convention tabled the matter of electing a bishop. Finally, fearing that the president or bishop might have too much power, his office was made an annually elective one. The power to ordain pastors was turned over to an ordainer, who was elected to office for life.

The convention in 1878 cut the apron strings that had held the infant church to the mother Church in Denmark. No longer did it consider itself a branch of the State Church. It was now a church by itself. Plans were made for a constitution to be formulated, with adoption to come later in the year. Finally, the delegates officially declared themselves to be The Danish Evangelical Lutheran Church in America. (In 1945 the preposition was changed to "of.")

GRUNDTVIGIANISM AND THE "DANISH CHURCH"

Grundtvigianism, as you recall, was a movement begun by Danish Bishop N.F.S. Grundtvig, the most influential leader in the Church of Denmark. His "matchless discovery" was that the Apostles Creed must be a "living word" from Christ himself, who is "the Word", and hence is the real basis of the Christian Faith, not the Bible. Grundtvig's belief was that the Christian Church produced the Bible, the Bible did not produce the Church. Thus the Bible is not the only source and norm of Christian faith and life, which, of course, is the very opposite teaching from that of true Lutheranism. But then, according to Grundtvig, the primacy of the Church replaces the primacy of the Bible. Christ lives in his Church and nourishes it through his "living word", the Apostles Creed, the Lord's Prayer, and the sacraments. Thus Grundtvig emphasized the living faith of the living Church, a faith expressed in the Apostolic Creed.[2]

Grundtvig was opposed in his doctrine by Vilhelm Beck, a pastor of the Inner Mission, a pietistic movement. Thus there arose in Denmark a division among the Lutherans. There were the followers of Grundtvig, and the followers of Beck. The Danish immigrants brought this controversy to America with them. Adam Dan, one of the first of the pastors and a founder of the Danish Church, was attacked for his Grundtvigian views right from the start. He was opposed especially by the confessional Norwegian pastors. Dan's own congregation split as a result of charges of heresy brought against him.

The pastors of the Danish Ev. Lutheran Church in America were Grundtvigian by and large, but not wholly so. Some were pietists who were followers of the Inner Mission movement. (The term "Inner" describes the Church's work as being focused inside the nation, rather then constituting a foreign mission work.) There would finally come bitter controversy between the two forces, resulting in schism.

401

DANISH FOLK SCHOOLS

Before entering upon the controversy between the followers of Bishop Grundtvig and the followers of the pietistic Inner Mission Movement within the Danish Ev. Lutheran Church in America, mention should be made of the folk school, which came to figure in the controversy. It was pointed out in the previous chapter that most of the pioneer Danish pastors were trained at one of the Danish folk schools, especially at the Askov School. Grundtvig emphasized the training of young people, and the folk schools were to accomplish this, aiming at laying a foundation for the student's richer and fuller life – the opposite of the pietistic ideal. These folk schools in the old country were a pattern copied in America by the Danes. The need for the folk school was felt as the children grew out of the congregational schools and there were no other Danish schools for them to attend. The idea at the time was to keep alive the Danish language and culture. And so it was that in 1876 Pastor H. Rosenstand made the motion to begin what would amount to the first Danish folk school in America. The result was that a school was opened at Elk Horn, Iowa, built there in1878. However, the school did not flourish and ultimately had to be given up. Other folk schools were built, some of which succeeded fairly well up until World War II.

CONTROVERSY BETWEEN THE GRUNDTVIGIANS AND THE INNER MISSION FOLLOWERS

By the time the controversy got started in the Danish Ev. Lutheran Church in America, another Danish Lutheran synod had appeared on the American scenes. In 1884 the Danes in the Norwegian-Danish Conference separated from the Norwegians in a friendly fashion and established their own church body, the Danish Evangelical Lutheran Church Association, commonly called the "Blair Church." By 1894, through a split in the Danish Evangelical Lutheran Church in America, there would be three Danish synods in America.

There were several causes of controversy in the Danish Ev. Lutheran Church in America. One of them was the question of the lodge. This was not only a matter that troubled the German synods but one that came to be an issue among the members of the Danish Church as well. F.L. Grundtvig, a son of Bishop Grundtvig, and a leader in the synod, staunchly opposed all secret societies. However, not a few Danes belonged to The Danish Brotherhood, and some were even Free Masons. Thus the question of whether or not to tolerate membership in secret societies became a source of bitter debate in the Danish Church. (For the sake of brevity, we will henceforth speak of the synod formed in 1872, the Danish Ev. Lutheran Church in America, simply as the Danish Church.) Grundtvig, while opposing secret societies, was a leader of a program called the Danish Folk Society, dedicated to preserving and enriching Danish culture. It was open to all Danes, Lutheran or not. To the opponents of Grundtvigianism in the Inner Mission faction, this sounded too much like Bishop Grundtvig's feelings for living a rich and full human life on earth. And so, the pietists attacked the "cultural society" for not renouncing the world. A very bitter debate on the matter of the continuation of the Folk Society was carried on in the 1887 Convention. The Society was continued. Enok Mortensen quotes from *A History of the Danes in America* (1896), which states: FROM THAT TIME THERE WAS NOT A SEMBLANCE OF HARMONY IN THE DANISH CHURCH IN AMERICA. THE MEMBERS OF THE INNER MISSION SOCIETY NOW BEGAN AN ACTIVE CRUSADE AGAINST ALL THE PLANS OF THE GRUNDTVIGIANS. DOCTRINAL DIFFERENCES WERE EMPHASIZED MORE AND MORE, AND THE GENERAL INDIFFERENCE TO THE GRUNDTVIGIAN SCHEME OF EDUCATION WAS CHANGED TO ACTIVE OPPOSITION.[3]

THE SEMINARY AT WEST DENMARK FIGURES IN THE STRIFE

The controversy between the followers of Bishop Grundtvig and the followers of the pietistic Inner Mission Movement within the Danish Church surfaced also in the seminary at West Denmark, Wisconsin (founded in 1887). The president of the seminary, Pastor Thorvald Helveg, leaned to the views of Grundtvig. He had as his assistant, Pastor Peter L. Vig, who became the leader of the Inner Mission faction of the Danish Church. The two clashed repeatedly. When one of the students, taking Helveg's side, wrote an article, which contained the remark "the Bible is not the Word of God," the matter came up for discussion in 1890 at the Manistee (Michigan) Convention when Pastor Vig demanded to know what the synod's view toward the Bible was. The convention disavowed the remark, "the Bible is not the Word of God." However, dissatisfaction and debate continued in the synod, and at the next Convention, held in Clinton, Iowa, in 1891, the issue came up again. There were by then two factions: the Grundtvigians on the side of Helveg, and the Inner Mission faction on the side of Vig. Both men finally resigned their duties.

Attempts to reconcile the two men were futile. Finally, a motion was made and passed to discontinue the seminary at the end of the school year and to dispose of the buildings. The synod was divided and the crack between the two sides continued to widen. The controversy raged in the church papers, and bitter charges were made. This portion of the controversy was waged especially by Pastor J. N. Jersild of the Inner Mission faction.

The convention at Waupaca, Wisconsin, took up the task of trying to restore harmony in the synod. The seminary, which had previously been voted closed, was voted open again. Pastors Helveg and Vig were asked to continue their teaching duties, with one man added to the faculty to serve as a buffer between the protagonists. The seminary was moved to the former folk school at Elk Horn, Iowa, by vote of the convention. However, this could not be carried out, for the dissension, which was thought to have dissipated, flared up anew. A majority of the committee charged with moving the school would not recognize Helveg as the president and were dissident regarding Helveg's proposals for the school. Helveg and Vig once more resigned. The gloom that spread over the synod due to this development is described in the *Kirkelig Samler*, as quoted by Enok Mortensen: OUR SEMINARY IS DISCONTINUED; PEOPLE WHO HAVE ASKED

403

FOR PASTORAL SERVICES ARE FORCED TO WAIT; OUR MISSION IN UTAH REMAINS UN-
TOUCHED; OUR HOME MISSIONS, CHILDREN'S HOMES AND FOREIGN MISSIONS CRY FOR
HELP FROM THE CONGREGATIONS; BUT STRIFE AND DISSENSION WITH ITS RESULTANT
DESPONDENCY HAVE MADE OUR HEARTS COLD.[4]

THE NEW CONSTITUTION: A SOURCE OF STRIFE

There was a small movement directed toward dissolving the synod, but in
the end the proponents did not even support their own motion, which was made
at a specially called convention in Chicago in February 1893. The convention
voted to continue the synod and at the same time adopted a new constitution,
which latter action simply added fuel to the flame of dissension burning in Pastor Vig. He even went so far as to claim that "he alone constituted the old synod
since he alone had refrained from voting for the new constitution." The matter
of the new constitution was an issue before the regular convention at Racine,
Wisconsin, in September 1893. Once more the synod revised and adopted a
constitution, which was based on the Grundtvigian view of Scripture and thus
did not consider the Scripture to be the Word of God. It was also resolved that
"no pastors or congregations who will not sign the synod's constitution within
three months can belong to the synod." Soon there were attempts to discourage
pastors and congregations from signing. The matter of signing or not signing
the new constitution became a new point of controversy in the already trouble-
ridden synod. This new controversy was also the straw that broke the camel's
back. As never before, congregations, pastors, and homes were divided over the
constitutional issue. A number of pastors refused to sign the new constitution
(36 to 57 signed), and an even larger number (more than half) of the congregations refused to sign. Only 40 out of 120 congregations signed. This led to
schism at the Racine Convention in 1894, the leading voice being that of the dissident professor, P.S. Vig.

A THIRD DANISH SYNOD IS FORMED

During the convention, twelve pastors and twelve laymen organized The
Society for Danish Evangelical Lutheran Church Mission Among Danes in
America, hoping thus to carry on mission work "in the spirit of the Inner Mission Society of Denmark."[5] More than half the members had refused to sign the
new constitution of the Danish Church. Out of the Society, which was rapidly
formed at the Racine Convention, emerged in a meeting held at Elkhorn, Iowa,
in September of that same year (1894), The Danish Evangelical Lutheran
Church of North America. This synod, which had nineteen pastors and two
missionaries, brought the total number of Danish synods in America to three.
They were:
(1)   The Danish Evangelical Lutheran Church in America (org. 1872 as
the Church Mission Society and more tightly organized in 1874 with its new
name). It was commonly known as the Danish Church.
(2)   The Danish Evangelical Lutheran Church Society in America (org.
1884 as a split-off from the Norwegian-Danish Conference). It was com-

404

monly known as the Blair Church.

(3)   The Danish Evangelical Lutheran Church in North America (org. 1894 as a split-off from the Danish Church). It was commonly called the North Church.

THE UNITED EVANGELICAL
LUTHERAN CHURCH – 1896
(See the separate chapter for its history.)

The ambitious new synod immediately undertook the task of establishing a seminary in Elk Horn. Pastor P.S. Vig, who had figured so strongly in the original controversy that split the Danish Church, became president for the seminary. Two years later, on October 1, 1896, the newly formed synod, called North Church, merged with the Blair Church and took the name the United Danish Evangelical Lutheran Church in America. In 1946 the word "Danish" was dropped from the official title. The merging bodies agreed on the seminary in Blair, Nebraska, as the seminary for the new synod.

THE AMERICAN
EVANGELICAL LUTHERAN CHURCH

THE DANISH CHURCH: GREATLY REDUCED IN SIZE

After the schism, the Danish Church numbered only thirty-six pastors and forty congregations. It had been dealt a staggering blow by the withdrawal of so many pastors and congregations and never recovered. The United Ev. Lutheran Church was destined to become much larger than the Danish Church. Growth for the Danish Church over the following decades was painfully slow. Though the Danish Church never grew to a large synod, over the years it did gain background it lost and was able to expand its area of work. Mortensen reports that there were congregations of the synod from Maine to California, from Wisconsin to Texas by 1895. In 1889 the synod organized itself into eight districts. Later, another district was added to cover the Northwest. But most of the congregations of the synod are still found in the Midwest. Mortensen gives this account of the growth:

FOLLOWING THE SCHISM THERE WERE ONLY FORTY CONGREGATIONS IN THE SYNOD. THIS NUMBER GREW GRADUALLY AND EVENLY. THE PEAK WAS REACHED IN THE PERIOD BETWEEN 1914 AND 1924, WITH THE NUMBER OF CONGREGATIONS AMOUNTING TO 104. THEN SLOWLY THE NUMBER WAS DIMINISHED WITH THE LOW EBB COMING IN THE PERIOD AROUND 1945. COUNTING BAPTIZED MEMBERS THE LOW POINT WAS REACHED IN 1934 WITH 17,437. THEN THE NUMBER ROSE AGAIN WITH A TOTAL BAPTIZED MEMBERSHIP IN 1951 OF 19,899. LATE REPORTS INDICATE A BAPTIZED MEMBERSHIP OF 19,912.[6]

SLOW, EVEN LACK OF GROWTH

The Danish language was used up to World War I as the means of communication. After the war this changed sharply. Of course, until the language question was settled in favor of using English, especially in church services, an approach could hardly be made to the non-Danish element. It was not until 1924 that a congregation began to use English regularly in its church services. And it was not until 1934 that the synod decided to publish an English church paper, the *Lutheran Tidings*.

Many of the pastors of the synod migrated back to the old country to fill pulpits there, leaving a shortage of pastors in the American congregations. The shortage of pastors that resulted greatly hampered the outward thrust of the small synod. There was also a definite lack of organizational unity and direction in the synod due to the suspicion held by many of the Danes of centralized authority – an authority such as was evident in the State Church in Denmark. Thus, while the congregations fought for their autonomy, they failed to set up proper avenues of leadership to carry on the synod's work to the extent and with the success that might have been.

Unlike the Norwegians, the Danes did not have the mission mindedness to go forth and conquer with the Gospel. THE VERY NATURE AND MENTAL MAKEUP OF A MAJORITY PREFERRED A CHURCH WITHOUT TOO MUCH MISSIONARY AND EVANGELISTIC ZEAL. THIS WAS ESPECIALLY TRUE AS TO CONTACTS WITH NON-DANISH PEOPLE. MANY OF OUR EARLIER PASTORS WERE MISSIONARY-MINDED AND TRAVELED CEASELESSLY IN AN EFFORT TO GATHER THEIR COUNTRYMEN INTO CHURCHES; THEY OFTEN FAILED, OR WERE UNABLE TO CONSIDER THEMSELVES CALLED, TO EVANGELIZE AMONG PEOPLE WHO WERE NOT DANISH.[7]

GRAND VIEW SEMINARY

Because of the clash between the two professors, the synod closed the seminary at West Denmark in 1892, and in 1893 decided to establish a seminary at Des Moines, Iowa. Overcoming insurmountable obstacles, Grand View Seminary was finally finished, staffed, and opened for business in September 1896. There was only one problem. There were as yet no students! Eventually thirty-four students made up the first class. Pastor R.R. Vestergaard from Denmark became the school's first president. Grand View Seminary grew and eventually enjoyed an accredited academy department. Later, a Junior College was added. There was also an accredited teachers' training course. Most of the pastors of the Danish Church were trained at Grand View Seminary. Des Moines became the headquarters of the Danish Church.

PUBLISHING

The publishing house of the Danish Church was really not owned by the Danish Church, nor did this body ever own its own publishing house, The Danish Book Concern. The Danish Book Concern in Cedar Falls and the C. Rasmussen Publishing Company in Minneapolis were operated by two men who were members of the Danish Church, and arrangements were made with these firms to take care of the publishing needs of the synod.

It is interesting to note the dearth of English literature in the two Danish bodies, even though the Church was becoming Americanized. AS A WHOLE IT MUST BE SAID THAT ALTHOUGH THE DANISH LANGUAGE GRADUALLY DISAPPEARED FROM THE PRINTED PAGE, THE PRODUCTION OF BOOKS IN ENGLISH WAS NEGLIGIBLE. THE FULL AMERICANIZATION PROCESS OF THE DANISH-AMERICAN CHURCHES HAD IN THIS RESPECT BARELY HAD A START BY 1950. THE MAJORITY OF BOOKS PUBLISHED WITHIN THE TWO CHURCHES WERE IN DANISH. BY MID-CENTURY MORE THAN TWO-THIRDS OF THE PASTORS IN THE TWO SYNODS WERE NATIVE AMERICANS, AND FOUR-FIFTHS HAD BEEN TRAINED IN AMERICA; YET THERE WERE MORE THAN SIX TIMES AS MANY DANISH AS ENGLISH BOOKS WRITTEN BY THE PASTORS.[8]

In 1934 the *Kirkelig Samler* (1872), which was the official paper of the Danish Church, was discontinued as a separate paper and an official English paper appeared under the name *Lutheran Tidings*. By 1948 it was "the voice of the synod." There were also a few other publications, including those oriented to the youth.

THE DANISH CHURCH IS
AMERICANIZED AND RECEIVES A NEW NAME

Mention has been made of the tardiness of English publications in the Danish Church. This body was slower to Americanize than its counterpart, the United Church. Even well into the 1940's, how far and how fast to proceed with the work in English to non-Danish people was a question enjoying serous debates. But in 1939 Pastor C.A. Stub wrote: I SOMETIMES THINK THAT WE IN OUR CHURCH HAVE BEEN GUILTY OF LIVING TOO MUCH IN THE MEMORY OF WHAT OUR FATHERS DID AND NOT ENOUGH WITH OUR IDEALS IN THE FUTURE. WE HAVE HOARDED OUR HERITAGE INSTEAD OF INVESTING IT WISELY IN THE BUSINESS OF LIFE. Furthermore, Dr. Paul Nyholm has concluded: FOR MANY YEARS THE CHURCH MAY HAVE BEEN TOO EXCLUSIVE, SELF-CONTAINED AND SELF-SATISFIED. SHE IS NOW BEGINNING TO SEE MORE CLEARLY THAT THE ONLY WAY TO KEEP A SPIRITUAL HERITAGE IS BY GIVING IT AWAY, PASSING IT ON TO ALL THOSE WHO ARE WILLING TO RECEIVE.[9]

In 1953 the word "Danish" was omitted from the name of the synod in order to indicate that all nationalities are welcome. In 1955 the Danish Church changed its name to the American Evangelical Lutheran Church. However, even with the Americanization of the two Danish churches, by far the greatest proportion of the membership remained Danish. By 1960 most of the Danish members were third generation Danes.

More recently, the greatest concentration of congregations both in the Danish Church and in the United Church were to be found in Wisconsin, Iowa, Minnesota, and Nebraska. Even in California.

MISSIONS IN THE AMERICAN EVANGELICAL LUTHERAN CHURCH (THE DANISH CHURCH)

HOME MISSION

Danish churches in America were from the first, missions of the mother Church in Denmark. Mission work was conducted among the Danish people in America by the pioneer pastors from Denmark. To help bear the workload, laymen were employed and licensed to preach the Gospel. In later years, a Home Mission Council composed of all the district presidents and the synodical board was set up to direct mission work. A Church Extension Fund was also set up from which infant congregations were permitted to borrow for the construction of their buildings. A Women's Mission Society was founded in 1908 "to strengthen and support the mission work of the Danish Lutheran Church wherever needed."[10]

FOREIGN MISSIONS

Most of the foreign mission work of the Danish Church was carried on in Northern Indiana, work which had been established in 1867. This mission later became larger than the synod itself. In subsequent years the missionaries came from Norway and Denmark, as well as from America.

WORKS OF CHARITY

In 1905 the Danish Church built a children's home in Chicago to care for orphans and for children from broken homes. A second home was established at Tyler, Minnesota, with new facilities dedicated in 1910. Later, in 1950, it ceased operating as a children's home for the simple fact there was a lack of children to care for. Another children's home was established at Perth Amboy, New Jersey, but this home too long since ceased to operate for lack of need. An old people's home was built opposite Grand View College in Des Moines, Iowa, in 1914. In 1906 a sanitarium was built near Brush, Colorado, an institution that later came to include a hospital, an old people's home, a training school for deaconesses and a church. The United (Danish) Evangelical Lutheran Church helped to support this institution. The Danish Church also established a Danish Seamen's Mission in Brooklyn, New York. A synodical Board of Welfare came to be organized in 1947 to synchronize the synod's welfare activities.

REACHING OUT TO OTHERS

The Danish Church (AELC) and the United Church (UELC) failed to get together. The Danish Church clearly showed an ecumenical spirit. But though the synod looked around for fellowship on the broader spectrum, the bitterness

408

of the conflict which led to the schism back in 1894 induced the synod to remain aloof from the United (Danish) Church. Attempts had been made to bring the two Danish bodies together but without success. A joint meeting on November 15, 1921, resulted in the recommendation that an English hymnbook be published jointly. Approved by the conventions of the two bodies, the *Hymnal For Church and Home* came from the press in 1927. Cooperative endeavors were carried out, but in the years that followed there was no real desire for union among the rank and file members of the two bodies. The desire for union was not felt nearly as strongly in the Danish Church (AELC) as within the united Church (UELC). From 1949-1950 the two synods cooperated in the program of United Evangelism, which linked them with seven Lutheran synods and with a great share of the Protestants.

What was the relationship of the Danish Church to the national and world bodies? When the National Lutheran Council was organized on September 6, 1918, in Chicago, the Danish Church was on hand to become a member. After some years, it became disinterested toward the work of the Council and severed its connection. However, in 1936 the Danish Church again made application to become a member of the Council. When the first Lutheran World Convention met on August 19, 1923, at Eisenach, Germany, the two Danish-American churches were represented. In 1947 the Danish Church took part in the Lutheran World Federation Conference at Lund, Sweden, and the World Council of Churches at Amsterdam, Holland, in 1948. The Danish Church became an official member of the Lutheran World Federation, the National Council of Churches, as well as the World Council of Churches. Already in 1939 the decision had been made to join the Word Council, which decision was reaffirmed in 1946. The decision to join the National Council of Churches of Christ in the United States of America was made in 1950.

By 1948 the American Evangelical Lutheran Church (Danish Church) found itself interested in knowing more about the United Lutheran Church in America (ULCA), a large body of American Lutheranism formed in 1918. And so the Danes decided to "explore points of cooperation with the ULCA," with the result that conferences were held between the two bodies. First an informal conference was held with Dr. Franklin Fry, of whom questions were asked. The outcome of the conferences proved to be favorable and both bodies began to think positively about merger. Meetings were also held jointly with the Augustana Evangelical Lutheran Church and the Finnish Evangelical Lutheran Church in America through the Joint Commission of Lutheran Unity. In 1957 the Danish Church (AELC) adopted a constitution in which its doctrinal statement was worded in such a fashion as to permit its entry into the merger forming the Lutheran Church of America (LCA) in 1962. In 1957 the Joint Commission on Lutheran Unity laid before the negotiating bodies a statement covering the points of agreement reached both in doctrine and polity, as well as in the possible organizational structure of the merger body. It also scheduled the representation of a constitution and bylaws in 1960. The statement of the Joint Commission was adopted by all, including the American Evangelical Lutheran Church, and later, when the proposed constitutions (not only for the merger body but also for the constituents synods and member congregations) were laid before the bodies, adoption followed. The forming convention was held in June

409

1962, with official operation of the new body beginning January 1, 1963. And so ended the separate existence of this Danish Lutheran body. While it did not achieve union at this time with the other Danish body, it did find a home with the bodies that constituted the liberal branch of Lutheranism in America.

Footnotes for Chapter Twenty-Five

1 Enok Mortensen, *Stories From Our Church*, (Blair, NE: Lutheran Publishing House, 1952), p. 53.

2 Mortensen, *Stories From Our Church,* pp. 95,96.

3 Mortensen, *Stories From Our Church*, p.___.

4 Mortensen, *Stories From Our Church*, p. 106.

5 Mortensen, *Stories From Our Church*, p. 108ff.

6 Mortensen, *Stories From Our Church*, p. 123.

7 Mortensen, *Stories From Our Church*, p. 125, 126.

8 Paul C. Nyholm, *The Americanization of the Danish Lutheran Churches in America*, (Minneapolis, MN: Augsburg Publishing House,___), p. 371.

9 Nyholm, *The Americanization of the Danish Lutheran Churches...*, p. 138.

10 Morensen, *Stories From Our Church,* p. 152.

CHAPTER TWENTY-SIX

THE DANES
THE UNITED EVANGELICAL
LUTHERAN CHURCH
(1896 - 1960)

Includes:
THE 'BLAIR CHURCH'
THE 'NORTH CHURCH'

ROOTS IN THE
NORWEGIAN-DANISH CONFERENCE

THE QUESTION: HOW TO TAKE THE STEP OF
INDEPENDENCE?

The Norwegians did considerable work among the Danes during the first quarter century of the Danish immigration. However, the Danes often hoped for their own pastors, who would then conduct services in the mother tongue.

411

There was of course the Norwegian-Danish Conference, which body ordained young Danish ministerial candidates. As students, these young men had formed their own special fellowship group, and later continued their circle of fellowship with the Conference.

The Norwegians in the Conference had themselves parted company with the Swedes, with whom they had worked and fellowshipped a number of years. (Augsburg Seminary had been started at Marshall, Wisconsin, near Madison, by the Norwegians, which enterprise then led to a peaceful separation from the Swedes.) The Norwegians could easily relate to the feelings of their Danish brethren, and encouraged them to form an independent church body to make possible the Danish work their hearts were set on doing. Already in June 1872 the meeting of the Conference afforded time for a discussion of how to proceed with the establishing of a Danish Lutheran Church. The three independent Danish pastors-Adam Dan, A.S. Nielsen, and N. Thomsen-declined the invitation to the meeting and went on to organize their own Church Mission Society, as noted in the preceding chapter.

It was through the Danish theological students who were to be a graduated from Augsburg Seminary that the new Danish synod would have to be formed, and Danish work – free from the Grundtvigian influence –carried on. The 1873 meeting of the Conference again called attention to the need to organize an independent Danish church "as soon as possible." There was a strong feeling among the Norwegians that such action was needed to counteract the work of the Grundtvigians – i.e. Adam Dan and company – who were closely connected to the other Church in Denmark, and to serve Danish congregations with Danish pastors "who have a clear Lutheran confession."

In 1876 the Conference suggested that the Danish pastors establish their own church paper. While it is true that the establishing of such a paper made the Danes feel more independent, it is also true that it was especially the Danish students and their own fellowship group who, as time went on, brought the Danes closer to establishing an independent synod.

In the fall of 1882 a formal discussion on the subject of independence was held by the Danish pastors in a sod house at Munson, Nebraska. The three pastors who met realized that there was a definite need for the Danes to be a separate group from the Norwegians, but at the same time they were well aware of the doctrinal differences between themselves and the Danish Lutheran Church in America, which differences made it impossible for them to join that group.

And so, it was decided that the only solution was to organize a Danish Evangelical Lutheran Free Church. A year later a small group of Danish pastors and laymen (Omaha District) met in Hampton, Nebraska, to again consider the issue of independence from the Norwegians. They agreed that the best way seemed to be to organize a new church and seek cooperation with the Inner Mission in Denmark. A committee was selected to write a constitution, to correspond with the Inner Mission, and even to send a man to Denmark for negotiations with Vilhelm Beck.

In the early part of 1884 the Omaha District of the Conference again met and passed some important resolutions: (1) THAT WE DANISH PASTORS AND CONGREGATIONS WITHDRAW IN A FRATERNAL MANNER FROM THE NORWEGIAN-DANISH

CONFERENCE; (2) THAT WE ELECT A MAN TO CORRESPOND WITH THE OFFICIALS OF THE DANISH CHURCH IN AMERICA REGARDING A POSSIBLE MERGER WITH THAT BODY; (3) THAT WE SEEK TO BECOME AFFILIATED WITH INDRE (INNER) MISSION IN DENMARK AND THAT WE SEND A REPRESENTATIVE TO DENMARK THIS COMING SUMMER TO BRING THIS ABOUT; (4) THAT WE ESTABLISH A PUBLISHING BUSINESS; (5) THAT THE PROVISIONAL CONSTITUTION, SIGNED BY 24 LAYMEN AND 5 PASTORS, BE ADOPTED; (6) THAT THE OLD DANISH HOME MISSION COMMITTEE OF THE CONFERENCE CONTINUE ITS WORK FOR THE TIME BEING; (7) THAT PASTOR A.M. ANDERSEN BE SENT TO DENMARK TO NEGOTIATE WITH THE INDRE MISSION AND INFLUENTIAL CHURCHES THERE.

The Danes withdrew from the Conference in an amicable way at the annual Convention of the Conference (Westbrook, Minnesota, June 11-19, 1884). The new synod was not officially organized until September 11 of that year and received the name: the Danish Evangelical Lutheran Church Association in America. The meeting was held at St. John's Church, Argo, Nebraska.

THE "BLAIR CHURCH"

ORGANIZED SEPARATELY FROM THE INNER MISSION

Pastor A.M. Anderson was the representative sent to attend the Indre (Inner) Mission convention in Denmark. Nothing earth-shaking was accomplished through the trip, though ties of relationship between the two groups were cemented through the talks that were had. The mother Church, however, gave little encouragement to the pastors as they went about to form the new Danish body. While Indre Mission encouraged the struggling pastors to affiliate with the Danish Church (in America), Anderson had made it clear that unity between the two groups would have to be on the basis of the confession of the mother Church and the acceptance of the Holy Scriptures as the Word of God. The Indre (Inner) Mission agreed to this proposal, while a bishop of the State Church made his feelings known to Andersen, that requirement of the acceptance of the Holy Scriptures as the Word of God would wreck an attempt at cooperation.[1] Historian and author, John M. Jensen asserts: ...THERE WAS NEVER ANY SERIOUS ATTEMPT TO JOIN THE DANISH CHURCH, AND THE IDEAS ABOUT COOPERATION WITH THAT BODY NEVER TOOK CONCRETE FORM.[2]

At the organizing convention held September 11-14, 1884, at Argo, two decisions had to be made almost immediately. One was to organize separately from Indre Mission (Denmark). This decision was forced upon the delegates on the basis of A.M. Andersen's report. The other decision was to turn down the invitations extended to it by the Danish Church to attend the annual convention of that body, since discussion of conditions for unity was not on the agenda. All the Danish pastors who had withdrawn from the Conference were present (9 pastors, representing 19 congregations and 15 preaching places). The name, which was chosen, contained the word "association" to emphasize that this was a fellowship of congregations. Because the seminary and headquarters were located at Blair, Nebraska, the synod became generally known as the "Blair Church." Pastor H. Hansen was elected the first president, Pastor A. Ras-

413

mussen, vice-president, and Pastor A.N. Andersen, secretary. A layman, Mr. Peter Clausen, was elected treasurer.

THE CONSTITUTION

Under Chapter I CONFESSIONS AND CHURCH ORDINANCES, the following statement is made: "This Church association believes, teaches, and confesses that in the Holy Scriptures we have an authentic and complete statement of the revealed Word of God for the salvation of men." It proclaims the Holy Scriptures "the highest authority." Subscription is declared to "the confessional writings of our mother church, i.e. (1) the old symbols (the ancient creeds) and (2) the *Unaltered Augsburg Confession* and *Luther's Small Catechism.*"

In Chapter II under MEMBERSHIP AND AIM, while the goal of furthering "the kingdom of God and its establishment in general," is listed, nevertheless the special goal was given to work "among our fellow Danes in America" to gather them in Christian congregations. As far as government of the group was concerned, the Constitution called for annual meetings, with each congregation represented by one delegate. Pastors and theological professors of the church were also voting members. Officers of a Church Council consisted of five members: three pastors and two laymen, with the president of the body a member ex officio on the Council. Decisions were ordinarily in the hands of the Council with the president able to make decisions in special cases "based on the Word of God and bound by conscience."

MEMBERSHIP OF THE BLAIR CHURCH

The new Danish body had an inauspicious beginning. For membership it counted nine pastors, nineteen congregations and fifteen preaching places, totaling an overall membership of fewer than 2,000 baptized individuals. The congregations were mainly located in Nebraska, but Iowa and Kansas each had one congregation, and Minnesota had two congregations.

THE BLAIR CHURCH AND THE OTHER DANES

Immediately, no love was lost between the Danish Church (AELC) and the Blair Church. The Danish Church feared that it would lose members to the Blair Church, and that these members would be attracted by the statements of the Blair group claiming to be true followers of Indre Mission. The Danish Church also feared division within its own congregations because of the new group, a division such as had already taken place at Waupaca, Wisconsin. The Danish Church openly attacked the name of the new group as being dishonest "claiming that it had only added the word 'Association' to the name of the Danish Church."[3] The Danish Church maintained that its honest offers of fellowship had been rejected by the other group of Danes, and the members of the Blair Church were even given the nickname "seceders". Recall that at the time that the Blair Church was established, the Danish Church did not yet have a constitution, nor did it succeed in getting one passed for a long time to come. It remained a loosely knit organization. The establishing of the Blair Seminary showed a different kind of philosophy from that of the Danish Church. Flames of discord between the two Danish groups were also fanned but the Grundtvigian tendencies in the men of the Danish Church, which were then opposed by the men in the Blair Church. The old group stressed the spoken word (i.e. the Apostles Creed) while the new group emphasized, as did the Conference from which it separated, the principle that the Bible is the Word of God and the basis of Christianity. The animosity between the two synods over the doctrine of Holy Scripture continued into the 1940's, when a theological thaw finally began.

EDUCATION IN THE BLAIR CHURCH

Trinity Seminary opened its doors the year the synod was formed. A.M. Andersen (1847-1941) accepted the call to be the first professor of the seminary, conducting classes at the beginning in his own home. The aim of the school was to turn out pastors as quickly as possible to fill the great need experienced by the new body. In two years the synod was able to build the first seminary building on a lot, which the town donated. Andersen was planner for this first building. Nelsen, in his *"An Interpretation"*, makes the following interesting point regarding the seminary in its early history:

THE EMPHASIS AT THE SCHOOL WAS ON TRAINING GOOD REVIVAL PREACHERS. SCHOLARSHIP TOOK SECOND PLACE...THE FOUNDATION FOR THE THEOLOGICAL THINKING AND THE CHURCH CONCEPT OF THE UNITED EV. LUTHERAN CHURCH WAS LAID DURING THESE YEARS [THE 12 YEARS OF THE BLAIR CHURCH'S EXISTENCE]. THE ELEMENTS WERE THOSE OF THE REVIVALISTIC INDRE MISSION, OF P.C. TRANDBERG [REVIVALISTIC PREACHER WHO, WHILE NEVER JOINING THE BLAIR CHURCH, WIELDED A GREAT INFLUENCE ON IT], AND OF THE AUGSBURG SEMINARY (THE CONFERENCE). P.S. VIG THEN CAME AND HELD THE CHURCH TO SOBER THINKING WHEN IT MIGHT HAVE BECOME TOO EMOTIONAL.[4]

The Blair Church was in constant financial difficulties with its seminary. The institution survived as Dana College, a four-year, fully accredited, coeducational, liberal arts college. The 230 acre campus is located just west of the city of Blair. Dana is the only college in America of Danish background.

PUBLISHING IN THE BLAIR CHURCH

When the synod was formed in 1884 an already existing paper, *Dansk Luthersk Kirkeblad* (Danish Lutheran Church Paper), begun in 1877, was continued under the new name *Kirkebladet* (The Church Paper). In 1892 *Danskeren* was started. In January 1921 these two papers merged to form the *Luthersk Ugeblad*, which remained the official Danish organ of the United Church until the paper was discontinued at the end of 1960. In 1961 the United Church became a part of The American Lutheran Church (TALC). (In

1896 the Blair Church merged with the North Church to form the United Church.)

In 1885 a small mail order business was formed. In 1893 Danish Lutheran Publishing House was established at Blair. This concern was actually begun in 1890 as a private venture in the home of Pastor H.P. Bertelsen. In 1898 it received its own building. Much later, in 1953, a new building had to be erected to replace the one that burned. On January 1, 1961, it became a part of the Augsburg Publishing House in the merger that formed The American Lutheran Church. Blair, Nebraska, became and remained the true hub of the synod wheel.

THEOLOGY AND MISSIONS OF THE BLAIR CHURCH

As adherents to the Indre (Inner) Mission in Denmark, which constituted a revival movement within the mother Church, the Blair Church through its pastors preached repentance and conversion, and the pastors did this in the halls and homes and in meetings held in the open. The emphasis was on revival, and revivals might last nearly a week. While pastors were on the revival circuit, laymen conducted the services at the home congregation. The Blair Church depended upon such revivals for their mission beginnings. "When a little group had been converted, they were organized into a congregation."[5] The order of things was: preaching, conversion, organization. In affecting the organization of a congregation, the converts were asked to confess the *Apostolic Creed*. In the process of their revival campaigns, the pastors aimed at organizing new congregations, and if they were not successful in doing this, they left the area. While the larger cities did not care for this revivalistic approach, it was the approach that nevertheless did work in the smaller towns and rural areas.

In his *An Interpretation*, Jensen calls our attention to the fact that two groups would become evident in connection with newly formed congregations:

WHEREVER A CONGREGATION WAS FORMED, THERE AROSE A SHARP DISTINCTION BETWEEN MEMBERS AND NON-MEMBERS. ON THE ONE HAND THERE WAS THE SMALL GROUP OF CONVERTED PEOPLE UNITED INTO A SMALL CONGREGATION, LIVING A PIOUS LIFE AND ABSTAINING FROM ALL WORLDLY PLEASURES. THE OTHER GROUP, ALTHOUGH NOT NECESSARILY IRRELIGIOUS, WOULD GENERALLY JOIN A SECULAR SOCIETY, THE DANISH BROTHERHOOD. THE MEMBERS OF THAT SOCIETY MIGHT CALL UPON THE DANISH PASTORS FOR BAPTISMS, WEDDINGS, AND FUNERALS, BUT THEY WERE NOT INTERESTED IN BECOMING MEMBERS OF THE CHURCH, FOR IN ORDER TO DO SO THEY HAD TO BE ABLE TO TELL OF A DEFINITE CONVERSION EXPERIENCE. THE SECULAR SOCIETIES WERE OFTEN COMPOSED OF THE SO-CALLED UPPER CLASS DANES. THUS IT WAS OFTEN THE POORER PEOPLE WHO RESPONDED TO THE GOSPEL, ESPECIALLY IN THE TOWNS AND CITIES.[6]

Growth of the Blair Church through the years was slow. Nor was the great increase in Danish immigration reflected as it might have been, or should have been, in the increase in membership in this Danish church body. There are various answers that might be given. No doubt, the revival method of doing mission work was a hindrance in the larger cities, where it did not have great appeal. Then too the emphasis was on "holy congregations" (each member had to have a conversion experience that he could testify to). The so-called puritanical outlook on pleasures turned many people off toward the church. Also the fact that there were two groups claiming to be the Danish Church in America was confusing and upsetting to many, who had been lulled into a type of security by dependence on the State Church system. We must remember too that about the time of the great thrust of Danish immigration, Socialism and agnosticism were taking over in the lower portion of Denmark from which the immigrants came. Large numbers of the population were simply not in the mood for a religious experience of any kind, to say nothing of taking up membership in a church. Even the lack of training in the Danish pastors has been cited as a reason for the slow growth of the church. Add to it the lack of mission organization within the synod and the lack of mission funding, both of which conditions impaired the outreach to Danish immigrants, where more work might well have been done.

More will be stated on the subject of missions when we cover the actual history of the United Church, which later came about and which had a more zealous spirit toward mission work than did the Danish Church. The spirit in the United Church toward a more international mission program began about 1927.

CHURCH GOVERNMENT IN THE BLAIR CHURCH

As the church grew and expanded its area of work it was divided into districts, but the districts had no official authority.

In the revised congregational constitution the following statement regarding church discipline is of special interest:

JUST AS THE PEOPLE OF GOD ARE TO USE CHRISTIAN WISDOM, CAUTION, AND PRUDENCE IN ORGANIZING CONGREGATIONS, SO IT IS NECESSARY THAT GREAT CARE BE USED TO KEEP THE ORGANIZED CONGREGATIONS ON THE PURE PATHS OF TRUTH AND LIFE. THEREFORE ALL OPEN AND COURSE VIOLATIONS BY THE MEMBERS OF THE CHURCH IN MATTERS OF FAITH, DOCTRINE, LIFE, AND CONDUCT MUST BE PREVENTED AS MUCH AS POSSIBLE WITH HOLY ZEAL, AND BE SUPPRESSED AND PUNISHED AND ELIMINATED (HEBREWS 12:15-16; MATTHEW 7:6), ALL ACCORDING TO THE CLEAR AND UNCHANGEABLE BASIC RULE OF THE LORD WITH RESPECT TO CHURCH DISCIPLINE (MATTHEW 18:15-18).

THE "NORTH CHURCH"

ROOTS IN THE DANISH CHURCH

A brief history of the forming of the "North Church" as a dissident group breaking from the Danish Church has already been given in the chapter titled: American Evangelical Lutheran Church. A summary of this history is neces-

417

sary also here.

The Danish Church was established in 1872, twelve years before the founding of the so-called Blair Church. The "First Four" – A.S. Nielsen, Adam Dan, Niels Thomsen, and R. Andersen – represented divergent theological views. Two were supporters of Grundtvig's views and one leaned to the old Lutheran doctrine. One was moderate in his views. That these four could hope to get together in an organization we can understand better if we recall that they considered themselves under the mother Church in Denmark. Opposing theological views coexisted in the old country. At the time, the Commission in Denmark sent men of varying theological views to work in America. The Norwegians in America opposed the view of Grundtvig and attacked the Danish Church as being unLutheran. The Blair Church, after it came into existence, also trained its guns on the Danish Church. These attacks helped to force into the open the issue of theology within the Danish Church. As it did, two opposing forces emerged within that group. A factor was added with the establishing of the Danish Church's own seminary in 1887 at West Denmark, Wisconsin. An open conflict emerged between the first professor, Theodore Helveg, and his assistant, P.S. Vig. The former followed the principles of Grundtvig, the latter the principles of the Indre Mission. The one believed the Apostles Creed is the word of God and the other gave this distinction to the Holy Scriptures. The conflict between Helveg and Vig affected not only the students at the seminary, but the whole synod as well.

Still another factor entered the synodical scene to increase tensions and cause dissension. The son of N.F.S. Grundtvig had come to America and was ordained. True to Grundtvigianism, he promoted the cause of Danish culture, helping to organize the Danish Folk Society. At the same time he waged war on the Masonic Lodge and the Danish Brotherhood. But this Folk Society caused dissension within the Danish Church, since pastors who were advocates of Indre (Inner) Mission came to look upon the Society as a source of competition to the Church. Of course, as is usual in matters such as these, personalities came into conflict and there were accusations and counter accusations over the years, with the result that much bitterness was engendered in the ranks of the clergy, while many of the lay people shrank back in bewilderment over the confusion and noise of battle.

Finally, in 1892 the seminary of the Danish Church was closed at West Denmark. In agonizing over the situation, a group of pastors of the Indre Mission persuasion proposed dissolving the synod. However, on the advice of the Commission in Denmark, a convention was called for February 20, 1893, at Chicago. At the convention the Indre Mission pastors gave a report stating that the synod was already in a state of dissolution and that it was hopeless to think that fruitful work could be done. However, the feeling ran high against dissolving the synod, and the vote that was taken defeated the proposition.

The convention tentatively adopted a constitution, which, it was hoped, would settle the issues between the two sides. However, the passage in the constitution concerning the Scriptures was weak and vague, failing to give a clear presentation of the doctrine of Scripture:

THE HOLY SCRIPTURES ARE IN THE CLOSEST HARMONY WITH THE CHRISTIAN FAITH, THAT IS, BOTH THE CANONICAL WRITINGS OF THE OLD AND NEW TESTA-

418

MENTS. WE ACCEPT AND RECOGNIZE THEM AS THE WORD OF GOD TO THE CON-
GREGATION, CONTAINING WISDOM UNTO SALVATION FOR THOSE OF THE HOUSE-
HOLD FAITH; IT IS A BOOK OF ENLIGHTENMENT AND EDIFICATION ON THE
FOUNDATION OF FAITH.

The freedom of the congregations was always an issue at stake in the Danish
Church, and the following paragraph was inserted in the Constitution to pro-
tect it: ... OUR SYNOD WILL PROTECT AND MAINTAIN THE SAME CHRISTIAN LIBERTY
AND FREEDOM OF EXPRESSION WHICH PREVAIL IN THE FOLK CHURCH OF DENMARK.
HE WHO DEMANDS A MORE NARROW OR A MORE BROAD BASIS CANNOT REMAIN A MEM-
BER.

Dissension arose already before the convention adjourned, and later the
flames of discord were fanned higher and higher. The convention had adopted
the motion that the pastors and congregations who would not subscribe to the
constitution could not belong to the synod. Sides were clearly drawn again.
Professor Vig, for example, accused the synod of having fallen away from
Lutheran doctrine, for it had confessed that it did not recognize the Bible as the
Word of God and it had departed from the mother Church of Denmark. By
the time of the next convention the mood was one of impatience toward those
who failed to sign (a large group). It was resolved that these no longer had
membership in the synod.

THE MISSION SOCIETY –
THE BEGINNING OF A NEW CHURCH

The deadline for signing the constitution was February 15, 1894. P.S. Vig
and J.N. Jersild, who had been asked to leave the synod if they could not consider the "churchly" view of Scripture Christian (the view that the Scriptures
came from the church, instead of the other way around), began to carry on a
printed attack against the constitution and the "unscriptural views" of the Danish Church. When finally the vote was counted, forty-one of fifty-six pastors
had signed the constitution, and only forty out of one hundred nineteen congregations signed. P.S. Vig joined the newly formed Mission Society, established
by a group, which hoped to work out peace between the two sides, and was
striving for a revival of spirituality within the Danish Church. With their failure to sign the constitution, the Mission Society members had been excluded
from membership in the Danish Church.

The Mission Society went on to function as a church body while claiming
not to be one. It acquired the Elk Horn Folk High School with the intention of
conducting a theological seminary. In September 1894 a meeting of all interested parties was called at Elk Horn, Iowa, with one of the stated purposes
being to discuss how their common cause could best be accomplished. The following statement was adopted by those present:

WE BELONG AND WANT TO BELONG TO THE DANISH EV. LUTHERAN CHURCH,
AND WE ARE IN FULL HARMONY WITH ITS TEACHING AND CONFESSION. WE OB-
JECT TO ALL FALSE TEACHINGS, BECAUSE WE ACCEPT THE REVEALED WORD OF
GOD, THE HOLY SCRIPTURES, AS OUR RULE AND GUIDE FOR OUR FAITH, TEACH-
ING AND LIFE. ON THE BASIS OF THIS WE SEEK FELLOWSHIP WITH ALL DANISH

Ev. Lutheran Christians, and we will by the help of God work toward one Danish Ev. Lutheran Church in America. We are sure that this aim is well-pleasing to God, and that it will be a blessing to our people.[7]

From what little has been preserved for posterity from this meeting it seems to be a self-understood matter that the group had formed themselves into a church body. The masthead of the paper published by the Mission Society was changed from listing "the Society for Evangelical Lutheran Mission Among the Danes in America," to "the Danish Ev. Lutheran Church of North America." The membership claimed to be the real Danish Lutherans within the Danish Lutheran Church in America. To avoid confusion they added the word "North" in their official name to distinguish themselves from the other group which went on calling themselves the Danish Lutheran Church in America. The new group felt that they were in reality the continuation of the old church. The strange part of the whole situation was that when the constitution was first put forth for adoption in the Danish Church, it had been adopted without dissenting vote, and these men who formed the North Church had been present at the time. What had happened to their voices?

THE NORTH CHURCH WITH
HEADQUARTERS AT ELK HORN, IOWA

The exact date of the founding of the North Church is shrouded in mystery, but by the first of the year 1895 it had been incorporated. Headquarters for the new Danish synod were at Elk Horn. The group's stated purpose was given to be that of...UPHOLDING THE FAITH AND DOCTRINE OF THE MOTHER CHURCH, THE EVANGELICAL LUTHERAN CHURCH OF DENMARK, TO ORGANIZE AND BUILD CHURCHES, SCHOOLS, AND COLLEGES FOR THE YOUNG, THEOLOGICAL SEMINARIES, ORPHANS ASYLUMS, AND OTHER CHARITABLE INSTITUTIONS, AND TO PUBLISH AND PRINT BOOKS, TRACTS, AND PAPERS. This was a rather formidable goal for such an inauspicious beginning. The original church officers were: Rev. P.L.C. Hansen, president, Rev, H.J. Dahlstrom, secretary, Rev. A.L.J. Soholm, treasurer.

THE DANES FURTHER DIVIDED

The establishing of this new church body resulted in prolonging the verbal battle which had already been going on for some time and which now intensified as the Danish Church attempted to exonerate itself of the charges that had been leveled. Congregations split and new congregations formed. The result was that in many a community, two different forces were pulling at the people. One force – the Indre (Inner) Mission people, who now constituted the North Church – decried innocent pleasures, prohibiting them as a sin. The Grundtvigians – those who remained in the Danish Lutheran Church in America – gave the stamp of approval to living a life of more freedom, in which many things the Danes had long enjoyed-for example, folk dancing-could be participated in without sin.

420

MEMBERSHIP AND ORGANIZATION
IN THE NORTH CHURCH

The membership of the North Church in 1895 was given as twenty-three pastors and fifty-four congregations, with some seven thousand baptized members, although a majority of the congregations had not joined the synod officially. The synod was divided into the following districts: Michigan, Eastern, Iowa, Wisconsin, and Nebraska. The states of Kansas and Illinois were represented in the district divisions. The district had a district president and one of his duties was to see to it that evangelistic services were held in the congregations.

MISSION WORK IN THE NORTH CHURCH

Mission work was chiefly carried on, as in the Danish Church, through the revivalistic type services. Each pastor was responsible to a great extent for the mission work performed in the North Church. Much sought after was the type of conversion where a man could point to the occasion, time and place when he first became a believer.

FORMING THE UNITED CHURCH

MERGING THE BLAIR CHURCH
(THE DANISH EV. LUTHERAN CHURCH ASSOCIATION IN AMERICA) AND THE NORTH CHURCH (THE DANISH EV. LUTHERAN CHURCH OF NORTH AMERICA)

From the beginning it did not seem likely that the North Church would continue its separate existence for any great length of time. There was common ground between the Blair Church and the North Church where minds and hearts could meet. And the day for such meeting was not far away. Already in 1895 a Joint Committee also worked up a constitution to govern the merging bodies. At the Blair Church's convention the following year, the synod president suggested among other things that the Convention decide to merge and help choose the time and place of the Merger Convention. In conferring with each other the two merger groups found that they both emphasized the sanctified life of the Christian as following justification. Their's was a more stern outlook on life then that of the Grundtvigians (Danish Church). The proposed constitution of the merger body emphasized life and practice as the important considerations. Taken for granted were the Lutheran Confessions.

421

THE COMPLETED MERGER – 1896

Once the Committee had brought forth their proposed constitution, merger of the two churches became an urgent matter. The Blair Church held its final convention in June 1896, while the North Church convened separately for the last time in September of the same year. The Merger Convention was held September 30 to October 2, 1896, at Minneapolis, with twenty-three Blair Church pastors and thirteen North Church pastors in attendance. There were in addition twenty-three lay delegates. On October 1st, the convention by vote merged the two Danish church bodies into the United Danish Evangelical Lutheran Church in America.

The first officers were: G.B. Christiansen, president; A.L.J. Soholm, vice-president; A.S. Nielsen, secretary. Other pastors, as well as laymen helped to form the Church Council or governing body. The United Church at its organization had sixty-three ordained pastors, one hundred twenty-seven congregations, and almost 14,000 baptized members.

TIES WITH THE MOTHER CHURCH

From the beginning, the United Church felt strong ties with the mother Church in Denmark and especially with Indre (Inner) Mission. But it was with Indre Mission that ties were established, and it was Indre Mission, not with the mother Church as such, that lines of communication were established and kept open. Until much later, the mother Church had no dealings with the United Church. Even the relationship which the synod had with Denmark through the Indre Mission, was of little significance.

ORGANIZATION OF THE UNITED CHURCH

When the Blair Church merged with the North Church, the newly formed synod was divided into districts, containing no more than twelve pastors. However, the districts were not given any real function. Seven districts were formed and each district was to meet annually. In 1904 the synod was divided into eight districts: Atlantic, Illinois, Wisconsin, Iowa, Minnesota, North Dakota, Nebraska, and Pacific. Ultimately there came to be nine districts, with the laymen having a vote in the choice of district chairman, who also served as visitator. (The ninth district was the West Canada District: Alberta, Saskatchewan and Manitoba). By 1905 the districts were made responsible for home missions within their own boundaries. But even with this arrangement, the carrying on and supervising of the work was often times left in the hands of the Church Council of the United Church, since so often the districts were too weak to shoulder the work themselves.

It never was the work of the district presidents to ordain men to the ministry or to dedicate new churches. These were duties of the synodical president, who generally ordained the candidates as a group at the annual convention.[8]

As the slow and painful transition from Danish to English occurred, requests came in for a change in the synod's name. Many different names were suggested, but in 1945 the synod officially voted to change its name by dropping out the word "Danish" so that it read instead, the United Evangelical Lutheran Church.

DOCTRINE OF THE UNITED CHURCH

Jensen informs us:

THE THEOLOGY OF THE BLAIR AND NORTH CHURCHES AND LATER OF THE UNITED DANISH EVANGELICAL LUTHERAN CHURCH WAS NOT VERY INVOLVED. THE MEMBERS SIMPLY REFERRED TO THE FAITH OF THE MOTHER CHURCH AND TOOK THE LUTHERAN CONFESSION FOR GRANTED. THE CONFESSIONAL STATEMENTS OF THE CHURCHES WERE SIMPLE AND BRIEF. THE BIBLE WAS ACCEPTED AS THE INSPIRED WORD OF GOD, AND NO QUESTIONS WERE ASKED AS TO THE MODE OF INSPIRATION. THE EARLY PIONEERS SIMPLY TOOK VERBAL INSPIRATION FOR GRANTED.[9]

The *Book of Concord* was never mentioned by the churches in their confessional statements. Through men like P.S. Vig, the synod was introduced against Grundtvigianism. Some preachers emphasized revival and de-emphasized doctrine. Vig expressed the fear, as did others, that the synod was becoming too Methodistic. Except for essays on the Sacraments, doctrinal papers were not presented at annual conventions. The pastors of the UELC at times presented a diverse background in theological training, yet there was little occasion for doctrinal discipline in the synod. There was little doctrinal conflict in the synod. The synod did not have an officially pronounced and accepted theology beyond the confessional writings of Lutheranism, and of those only the *Augsburg Confession* and *Luther's Small Catechism* were specifically mentioned in the constitution. Because of lack of doctrinal conflict in the United Church there were few proponents of "pure doctrine." "The confessional position of the UELC was characterized by freedom."[10]

Much emphasis was placed on the sacraments. In this freedom of confessional position, and emphasis on the sacraments, the ULEC did have something in common with at least part of the spirit of Grundtvigianism, although the members may not have realized it, and no doubt would not have admitted it. At times the pietistic spirit engendered such legalism in the preaching of the pastors that congregational growth was made impossible. Until about 1945 the sermons were characterized by the pastors calling on the hearers to make a decision for Christ. Later, the emphasis shifted to a call to Christian service.

MISSION WORK IN THE UNITED CHURCH

HOME MISSIONS

Slow growth and limited outreach are terms that describe the work in home missions carried on by the United Church. Still, in a few years after its founding the synod had congregations in seventeen states, with its strength contin-

423

uing to be concentrated in Wisconsin, Iowa, Minnesota, and Nebraska. Revival meetings were still the thing, and pastors for many years left their pulpits at home for a period to go on a revival circuit. The overall responsibility for promoting mission work in the synod and overseeing it was in the hands of the synodical Church Council, the only administrative body in the synod. (As noted earlier, by 1905 the individual districts were made responsible for mission outreach within their boundaries.)

The fact remains that the establishing of new congregations after 1897 became a slow process and eventually came more-or-less to a standstill. Of course, the lack of ability among the pastors to speak English, and the reticence on the part of the Danes to Englishize their work was a large factor in the lack of outreach and growth in some areas. Often the congregations established in the cities did not last. So often the story was repeated that the Danish Church simply could not make an impact even on its own people. Pastors were often met with coldness and even open hostility on the part of the Danish people. A factor to be considered regarding the slow growth of Danish churches was this attitude found in many Danish immigrants: Since the Norwegian and Swedish immigrants had gotten well underway before the Danish immigration had begun, and as a result had established Scandinavian settlements and Lutheran churches, there was no need to establish separate Danish communities and churches.

North Dakota was one area where work for the United Church went well, and the settlements gave good reception to the Danish pastors. Laymen were used in some areas to help with home mission work and this was especially true in North Dakota.

The church remained Danish until 1925. For a long time the pastors could not think of the work of the church as applying to anyone but Danes. However, the First World War did more than anything to open the eyes of the people to the need for preaching and teaching in English. The church eventually discovered that its success as a mission agency was in direct proportion to the efforts expended to deliver the gospel in English and to acclimate to the American environment.

The United Evangelical Lutheran Church had a more zealous spirit toward missionary work than did the American Evangelical Lutheran Church (Danish Church). This spirit toward a more international mission program began about 1927. It began to dawn upon the Danish minds that the salvation of souls is more important than language. One editorial put it this way: OUR CHRISTIANITY CANNOT BE VERY CHRISTIAN IF WE WILL NOT HELP OUR NEIGHBOR GO TO HEAVEN IRRESPECTIVE OF HIS NATIONAL BACKGROUND...IT WILL MORE AND MORE BE THE TASK OF OUR CHURCH TO FIND HER PLACE IN THE AMERICAN SOCIETY.[11] But it was not until the decade between 1930 and 1940 that the church went from the Danish language to English. Even then there were those who hung on to the Danish language and who felt that evangelism meant witnessing the gospel to fellow Danes.

REASONS FOR LACK OF GROWTH – A SUMMARY

WHEN ONE TAKES NOTE OF THE SLOW PROGRESS OF HOME MISSION WORK, ONE

SHOULD NOT OVERLOOK THE FACT THAT THE PASTORS HAD TO SOW THEIR SEED MOSTLY ON HARD GROUND AND IN WEEDY SOIL.[12]

MOST OF THE NEWCOMERS HAD HAD NO INTEREST IN THE CHURCH IN DENMARK, AND THE TRIP ACROSS THE ATLANTIC DID NOT SUDDENLY AROUSE SUCH AN INTEREST. THE PASTORS IN DENMARK HAD NOT, AS A RULE, TAKEN MUCH INTEREST IN THE LOWER CLASSES. THE ONLY PREVIOUS CONTACT THAT THE IMMIGRANTS HAD HAD WITH PASTORS WAS USUALLY CONFINED TO BAPTISMS, CONFIRMATIONS, WEDDINGS, AND FUNERALS. IT WAS THE CUSTOM, TOO, TO BRING AN OFFERING TO THE PASTOR THREE TIMES A YEAR, AND THIS DID NOT ENHANCE THE LOVE AND RESPECT OF THE POORER PEOPLE FOR THE CHURCH. THE PASTORS IN AMERICA OFTEN HEARD THE REMARK, "WE HAD NOTHING TO DO WITH THE CHURCH IN DENMARK, SO WHY SHOULD WE BOTHER WITH IT HERE?" THE FACT THAT THE MEMBERS HAD TO SUPPORT THEIR CHURCH MADE MATTERS WORSE. THE IMMIGRANTS FORGOT THAT THEY HAD SUPPORTED THE CHURCH IN DENMARK THROUGH TAXES. THUS THE IMMIGRANT WAS PREJUDICED AGAINST THE CHURCH AND ALL IT STOOD FOR FROM THE VERY BEGINNING.[13]

Most of the immigrants were poor, having been farm laborers, working for others. In Denmark they had a bare existence. In America, they had the chance to work for themselves and to own their own farm. And this they wished to do, and to this venture they applied themselves with great zeal. They had as a goal to become more wealthy than the farmers they worked for in the old country. Thus many had no time for the church. They were bound up in purely worldly pursuits and goals.

The widely read Danish newspaper *The Danish Pioneer*, published at Omaha, Nebraska, no doubt did much damage to the church through its very negative attitude in matters spiritual, and through its open and vicious attacks against both the Church and the pastors, and religion in general. The immigrants, suspicious always that people were going to take advantage of them, often accepted as fact such articles appearing in papers like the *Pioneer*, and as a result were turned off toward the Church. The *Pioneer* was no doubt the cause of Danish pastors being turned away from many a Danish home.

Recall that Socialism and Marxism were gaining in strength in Denmark, and that a good number of immigrants leaned toward this kind of philosophy, and that the *Pioneer* promoted the ideals of Georg Brandes, himself an antiChristian, socialistic writer back in Denmark.

By the time of the Twenty-fifth Anniversary of the synod in 1919 the synod had 176 congregations, 42 preaching stations, and 25,000 baptized members. The synod grew but very slowly in the twenties. Two problems incessantly plagued the small group: (1) financing their educational institutions and ridding them of internal friction, and (2) the lack of an aggressive and well-organized mission program. Another problem was of course the language, as has already been mentioned. Continued emphasis on the Danish language risked losing the youth, while a transition to English risked offending the oldsters. By the early 1930's another question was gnawing at the very heart of the synod: justification for its continued existence as a small and independent body. Nor did the synod always have the kind of leadership that it needed, especially in the sphere of home missions.

425

In one fifteen year period (1920-1935) only seven congregations were added. Until the late thirties, there was not much of an attempt made by congregations to reach their own communities. This outreach came about more and more with a lessening of the emphasis on the Danish language, Danish customs, and "holy people in holy congregations."

Growth of the synod by way of adding new congregations increased considerably after the Second World War, so that in the mid 1950's there were 175 pastors serving 184 congregations with about 57,000 members. By 1960 the baptized membership doubled over what it had been in 1940 (from 34,626 to 70,149). After the war there was a pronounced increase also in the building of new churches. The outnumbered Danes began to build self-confidence. By 1950 both Danish church bodies were aggressively pursuing home mission work, and the Danish members were becoming increasingly cosmopolitan in their attitudes toward outreach. Still, looking back a few years to 1946, only 14% of the members in the United Church and 3% of the members in the Danish Church were non-Danish people.[14]

A SPIRITUAL MAN OF INFLUENCE

Jens Dixon (1885-1931) headed Brorson Folk High School in North Dakota for about ten years and influenced many young men toward the ministry and missionary work. He himself served as a traveling missionary and has been called a "spiritual giant."

COUNTERING MORMONISM

Danes were moving to Utah, and as they did so, many fell prey, like the Swedes, to Mormonism. Eventually a mission was successful at Salt Lake City, although under great difficulties and personal frustrations to the missionary. Over the years converts have been won over from Mormonism.

CANADA

From 1925-35 mission work among the Danish immigrants in Canada increased sharply, largely due to the fact that while immigration to the United States was pretty much a closed chapter, immigration to Canada was occurring at a rapid pace, and this development was reflected in the intensity of Danish mission work there. Nyholm points out that the United Church in its Home Mission budget was supporting a greater number of pastors in Canada than in the United States. This went on for some time, and even in the year 1950 the money budgeted for mission work in the United States had not yet equaled the money going to Canada.[15]

In the later years of its independent existence (before taking part in the merger that formed The American Lutheran Church) the United Church concentrated much of its home mission program in California, and with good success.

426

FOREIGN MISSIONS

The first foreign mission work of the United Church was among the Cherokee Indians in Oklahoma. (It is of interest to note that the first "foreign" mission work of the Wisconsin Synod was also among American Indians, the Apache tribes on reservations in Arizona.) For many years this enterprise in Oklahoma remained the Danes' only "foreign" mission work. Other Lutherans also, of course, became involved in Indian Mission work, much of it frustrating and disappointing in results – work carried on to a great extent by individual pastors under their own initiative. In 1892 N.L. Nielsen visited the Oklahoma Territory with the consent of the synod to find a place to start a mission among the "Red Men" – an undertaking, which had been his dream for many years. He was successful in starting a school among the Indians. The work progressed slowly over the years as the mission became firmly established.

Dr. J.M.T. Winther was one of the most distinguished missionaries of the United Church. His work in Japan was officially taken over by the synod in 1903. Sent to Japan in 1898, he was still in that field in 1964, although almost ninety years old at the time. The emperor of Japan bestowed upon him the order of "The Rising Sun," one of the highest decorations ever given to a foreigner in Japan. Although the Japanese Mission was taken over by the ULCA in 1919 the United Church continued to support it.

In 1934 the Sudan Mission in Nigeria, West Africa, under the supervision of the Danish Board, became an official extra-synodical mission. Before this time, the Lebanon Society at Brorson High School in North Dakota had helped to support it. In 1934 the Society was dissolved and a committee of three was elected to govern the affairs of the Sudan work and to represent the Danish Sudan Mission in this country. The greater share of the workers came from Denmark.

Interest among the members of the United Church in the Santal Mission in India had been aroused very early in the synod's history. While support had come from within the United Church, there was no official connection of the synod to the mission. In 1925 three members of the United Church were sent out as missionaries to the Santals and were supported chiefly by the synod. A woman doctor joined the mission from the synod in 1931 and finally in 1945 the United Church adopted the Santal Mission officially. An important part of the work centered in colonies for persons suffering from leprosy.

A woman missionary of the United Church was sent to work in Colombia, South America, in 1942 and was joined in 1943 by a pastor of the synod. The mission in which they labored was conducted by the Colombia Evangelical Lutheran Mission of South America. In 1947 the Evangelical Lutheran Church (ELC-Norwegian) took over the field and the United Church started officially to cooperate with the Norwegians in the mission. When in 1958 the ELC began work in Brazil, the United Church sponsored a missionary to work in that field. Rather than sponsor independent foreign missions, the United Church after 1919 chose instead to cooperate in carrying out the foreign mission work of the larger Lutheran bodies.[16]

Groups were organized within the United Church to promote foreign mis-

427

sion work of the synod. Such was the North Dakota District Evangelical Lutheran Foreign Mission Society. There was also the Lebanon Society, which promoted the Sudan Untied Mission of Denmark.

ORGANIZATIONS WITHIN THE UNITED CHURCH

The women, it appears, had voting rights in the congregations of the United Church from beginning, although it is doubtful that they exercised this right during the early years of the synod. Ladies' groups in the congregations were often strong organizations, and in 1932 a national Women's Missionary Society was begun, which showed special interest in the support of foreign missions.

A group for the men was begun in 1932 and later became known as Church Men of the United Ev. Lutheran Church. Early in the history of the Blair Church, special work among the Danish youth was commenced. The congregational groups became known as Luther Leagues. In 1935 the Young People's Lutheran League of the United Ev. Lutheran Church was organized, and twenty years later a full-time youth directorship was inaugurated. After 1925 Youth Bible Camps became an integral part of the youth work in the synod.

CHARITY WORK

Several orphanages and Old People Homes were begun and supported by independent groups within the United Church, sometimes in cooperation with other churches.

PUBLICATIONS

The United Church maintained the Danish Lutheran Publishing House, Blair, Nebraska. Publishing was confined mostly to the church papers, of which there were several. Danish hymnals and editions of *Luther's Small Catechism* were also on the list of publications.

EDUCATION

Recall that the Blair Church had established Trinity Seminary and Dana College at Blair Nebraska. The North Church had purchased Elk Horn College and Folk School at Elk Horn, Iowa, and used the high school as its seminary in the short term of its existence as a separate synod (1894-1896). When the two synods merged, the seminary was moved to Elk Horn for a year but then returned to Blair together with the college department of the Elk Horn School. Elk Horn kept the folk high school. Indre (Inner) Mission Pietism and seventeenth century theology were predominate in the school lectures, with school life and instruction influenced by the pietistic life that was so emphasized in the synod.[17]

In 1884 the Blair school was named Trinity Seminary. In 1899 it became Blair College and Theological Seminary. In 1903 the name finally became Dana College and Trinity Seminary. Dana College was established as a four-year, fully accredited, coeducational, liberal arts college, attracting students from all parts of the United States and from several foreign countries as well. It is the only college in America of Danish background.

THE DANES AND OTHER LUTHERANS

During its first twenty-five years, the United Church more or less isolated itself. Its first presidents were strong Indre (Inner) Mission men who had a deep sense of Danish nationalism. When N.C. Carlsen became president in 1925, the synod began to look more toward other Lutherans, and with the coming of C.B. Larsen to the theological staff in 1926 the synod began to develop a broader theological outlook. By then a spirit of cooperation was evident on the American scene between Lutheran Church bodies, especially those in the National Lutheran Council.

Both the United Church and the Danish Church joined the National Lutheran Council, which was organized September 6, 1918, in Chicago. The United Church, which joined the Council in 1919, remained a member and was active, while its counterpart, the Danish Church, after some years became disinterested and severed its connection for a time, rejoining in 1936. Before joining the Council the United Church had helped support the National Lutheran Commission for Soldiers' and Sailors' Welfare, which had been organized in 1917.

When the first Lutheran World Convention met on August 19, 1923, in Eisenach, Germany, the two Danish-American churches were represented. At the second Lutheran World Convention, June 26 to July 4, 1929, in Copenhagen, Denmark, many members of the United Church took part in the public meetings.

On October 29-31, 1930, the United Church joined with four other Lutheran bodies in the American Lutheran Conference. The association of the United Church with other Lutheran groups in the Conference helped to beg the question of its need for continued existence as a separate body. With the transition from Danish to English, coupled with continued problems financial and otherwise in its schools, some Danes really wondered whether or not the synod had a special mission to perform to justify its continuance. As the United Church approached its Fiftieth Anniversary, more and more pastors spoke of union with other Lutheran bodies, for at that time growth of the synod had been slow, and while existing as an independent synod it had not accomplished a great deal. At least, so it seemed to some.

When the question of joining the World Council of Churches came up, there was but a minimum of opposition to this organization, and in 1947 the United Church officially joined. (In the Danish Church there never was any publicly expressed opposition against the World Council, and already at its 1939 Convention it was dedicated to join the Council.)

429

THE UNITED CHURCH AND THE DANISH CHURCH

In 1921 the United Church met with the Danish Church for the first time. The result was the decision to translate the Danish Sunday morning service into English along with the rituals for baptism, confirmation, communion, marriage, and funerals. The translation was published in 1924. The first English hymnbook for use in the two churches (*Hymnal for Church and Home*) – another joint endeavor – was published in 1927. A larger edition of the same was published jointly in 1938.

Though voices were heard expressing desire for union of the two churches, and though initial negotiations were set up, nevertheless the two synods remained apart. A final effort to get together was made in 1946 by a Joint Committee meeting in Blair, Nebraska. Joint doctrinal resolutions were passed regarding the synods' stand on Scripture, but when these were brought to the individual synods – even though they were more-or-less accepted – no further action toward union was taken. The two synods were actually at this time drifting in different directions, toward other fellowships. The United Church was voting to work for the union of the American Lutheran Conferences churches (eventually resulting in The American Lutheran Church), while the Danish Church was instructing its committee on Lutheran church relations to study the possibility of merger of that group with the United Lutheran Church in America (ULCA). The courses of the two Danish churches appeared to be set, and hopes to unite them were abandoned.

One thing had changed for them. They no longer participated in the bitter feud of the past and were now able to talk to one another. Still, there were areas of deep lack of understanding between the two bodies. The emphasis from the pulpit in the United Church was repentance and conversion. That from the Danish Church pulpit was baptismal regeneration. Also in church life they differed, the United Church being pietistically inclined, while the Danish Church was much more tolerant toward the list of pleasures it allowed its members to participate in.

THE UNITED CHURCH AND THE MERGER TO FORM THE AMERICAN LUTHERAN CHURCH (TALC)

On January 1, 1961, the United Evangelical Lutheran Church (Danish), the American Lutheran Church (German), and the Evangelical Lutheran Church (Norwegian) merged to form The American Lutheran Church (TALC). Only three of the eight National Lutheran Council churches participated in the merger.

The interest in uniting with other Lutherans had been present in the membership of the United Church for many years. It can be stated that when finally The American Lutheran Church was formed of the merger of the three synods just mentioned, it was the United Church, which set the wheels of merger in motion. A group of United Church pastors in northwest Iowa drew up a resolution which was accepted by the Church Council and presented to the 1948 Convention, which called for the Council to be instructed to contact the appropriate officials of the other bodies of the American Lutheran Conference to invite them "to initiate discussions collectively by representatives of the five bodies with a view of bringing about greater cooperation and a merger of some form with the five bodies of the American Lutheran Conference."

Two of the Conference synods could not be counted on to begin discussions. The Augustana Lutheran Church had already stated its unwillingness to meet unless the United Lutheran Church in America (ULCA) was included. The Lutheran Free Church was not prepared to take up the matter at that time. President Carlsen of the United Church felt the possibility was there that the American Lutheran Church and the Evangelical Lutheran Church (ELC) might be willing to meet with his synod, and let his synod know that he was for a merger of some kind, even if it were only with the Evangelical Lutheran Church. The resolution drawn up by the group of Iowa pastors passed on June 17, 1948, at Fresno, California, and as a result a commission was appointed to contact the officials of the other bodies of the Conference to invite them "to initiate discussions collectively by representatives of the bodies with the view of bringing about a greater cooperation and an eventual merger of the bodies of the American Lutheran Conference and the other Lutheran Churches in our land."[18] Already a week prior to the United Church Convention at Fresno, California, the Evangelical Lutheran Church had adopted a resolution instructing its Church Council to appoint a Union Committee with the authority to initiate negotiations with the United Church and other bodies of the American Lutheran Conference as might be officially interested.

Meanwhile, the Augustana Church had adopted a resolution that its Executive Council invite all National Lutheran Council churches to discuss organic merger of the member churches. Such a merger would of course include the United Lutheran Church in America, whose fellowship the Augustana Church coveted. Two meetings were held in January 1949 in Minneapolis, just a day apart. On January 4, 1949, the NLC representatives (Committee of Thirty-four) met and passed the following resolution: "That it is the sense of this group that a closer organizational affiliation of the participating bodies in the National Lutheran Council is desirable and should be sought by all proper means."[19] A committee was appointed to study the facts and report back in the fall. On January 5th Dr. Carlsen's meeting was held to take up the issue of merger of American Lutheran Conference churches. (President Carlsen very much favored uniting with the ALC and the ELC.) The following proposal for "Lesser Approaches" was adopted: "Resolved…that in view of the action proposing closer organizational affiliation of the churches participating in the National Lutheran Council which was voted in January 4, 1949, it is the sense of this meeting that every effort should be made to lesser approaches to unity within the framework of the American Lutheran Conference."[20]

Later, upon contacting the presidents of the Evangelical Lutheran Church and the American Lutheran Church, Dr. Carlsen found that both presidents were willing to attend a meeting for consideration of a merger of the three churches.

The United Church Convention the following year resolved the appointment of a seven man committee: "...to continue discussions with interested bodies of the American Lutheran Conference with a view to possible merger. The committee shall also be authorized to discuss Lutheran unity with any other Lutheran body in America." It is of interest to note here the ecumenical spirit shown by the United Church in its willingness to meet with any Lutheran body in America. The United Church no longer considered itself Danish, but American. On the other hand, the United Church leaned away from the United Lutheran Church in America, feeling that merger on such a broad plain would consume too much time – there were too many obstacles in the way – while merger with other synods seemed much closer at hand and easier to achieve. There was also a feeling that the Missouri Synod should be included in the merger, and of course the American Lutheran Church had been conducting talks with the Missouri Synod for a number of years. Thus it was the feeling of some that the Missouri Synod should be given a little more time to come into the union picture.

The Joint Union Committee of the three participating synods was drawn up and set to work bringing a preliminary report to the Conventions in 1952 after studying the doctrine and practice of the three churches. Dr. Carlsen, who had pushed to get the merger talks underway, died just as the work began (February 6, 1950). Pastor Hans C. Jersild, as Carlsen's successor also pushed for the merger.

The United Church accepted the Joint Union Committee's report given in 1952 and titled, "The United Testimony of Faith and Life." In 1954 a polity report was adopted, and in 1956 the final documents necessary for merger were adopted. Trouble then arose regarding Trinity Seminary at Blair. As the merger became assured several of the faculty members held back in the matter of merging Blair with another seminary, and suggested that it be moved to California or Texas, which suggestion received no support. The Board of Education of the synod proposed that the seminary be moved to another seminary campus but remain independent until the merger. The Board later changed its mind and began promoting the idea that the seminary be preserved and relocated (West Coast, Texas, or Nebraska). There was, as a result, confusion within the Joint Committee and within the synods themselves as to what policy should be taken regarding Dana College and Trinity Seminary. In 1956 the synod voted to move the seminary to the campus of Wartburg Seminary at Dubuque, Iowa, and the move was accomplished in the fall of 1956. Dana College soon began to expand as the American Lutheran Church congregations in Nebraska and Colorado looked on it as their college.

Dr. William Larsen became president of the United Church the last four years of its independent existence and also became chairman of the Joint Union Committee. For this reason he was also the presiding officer at the Constitutional Convention of The American Lutheran Church (TALC), held April 22-24, 1960, at Minneapolis, Minnesota.

And so, both segments of Danish Lutheranism in America had found what they had been searching for: sanctuary in a greater fellowship, not a fellowship in which they gravitated toward the other but toward those who more nearly carried out the policy and doctrine of each.

We will now take up a brief history of the final segment of Scandinavian

Footnotes or Chapter Twenty-Six

1 John M. Jensen, *The United Evangelical Lutheran Church-An Interpretation*, (Minneapolis, MN: Augsburg Publishing House, 1964), pp. 74,75.

2 Jensen, *The United Evangelical Lutheran Church...*, p. 76.

3 Jensen, *The United Evangelical Lutheran Church...*, p. 82.

4 Jensen, *The United Evangelical Lutheran Church...*, p. 86.

5 Jensen, *The United Evangelical Lutheran Church...*, p. 89.

6 Jensen, *The United Evangelical Lutheran Church...*, p. 90.

7 Jensen, *The United Evangelical Lutheran Church...*, p. 118.

8 Jensen, *The United Evangelical Lutheran Church...*, p. 213.

9 Jensen, *The United Evangelical Lutheran Church...*, p. 227.

10 Jensen, *The United Evangelical Lutheran Church...*, p. 233.

11 Paul C. Nyholm, T*he Americanization of the Danish Lutheran Churches in America*, (Minneapolis, MN: Augsburg Publishing House,___), p. 131.

12 Jensen, *The United Evangelical Lutheran Church...*, p. 155.

13 Jensen, *The United Evangelical Lutheran Church...*, p. 156.

14 Paul C. Nyholm, *The Americanization...*, p. 152.

15 Nyholm, *The Americanization...*, p. 152.

16 Jensen, *The United Evangelical Lutheran Church...*, p. 206.

17 Jensen, *The United Evangelical Lutheran Church...*, p. 131.

18 Richard G. Wolf, *Documents of Lutheran Unity in America*, (Philadelphia, PA: Fortress Press, 1966), pp. 496, 497; Doc. #210.

19 Wolf, *Documents...*, p. 478; Doc. #195.

20 Wolf, *Documents...*, p. 484; Doc. #200.

CHAPTER TWENTY-SEVEN

THE FINNS
LAND AND RELIGION OF THE FINNS

THE REFORMATION COMES TO FINLAND

In 1523 the Lutheran Reformation came from Sweden to Finland under the rule of King Gustavus I.* Finland's exposure to the Reformation came about through Martin Skytte ("Bishop of the Reformation"). Skytte sent young men to Germany to receive theological training, and these men upon their return as pastors and teachers urged the people to accept Luther's evangelical doctrine of justification by faith.

A Finnish student of Dr. Luther, Michael Agricola, carried the reformer's recommendations back to his people. He was the first man to write books in the Finnish language and in 1548 completed a translation of the Bible into that tongue.[1]

FINLAND – THE COUNTRY

The area of Finland makes it one of the largest countries in Europe, with 130,559 square miles. However, the population of Finland does not match its area and is one of the smallest in Europe. The 1997 *World Almanac* lists a population of 5,105,230 inhabitants.[2] At one time, in 1721, there remained only about 200,000 inhabitants in Finland, mostly old people, women and children. This was due to a series of calamities, including wars (in which Finnish men had to fight for the Swedish Crown), famine, and loss of territory to the Russians. Finland is a country known for its strong-willed, industrious and vigorous people. Yet it is a land that has witnessed terrible suffering and what would seem to be intolerable setbacks.

Swedish rule over Finland brought great hardships. Through a series of wars Sweden bled the country of its manpower, which it pressed into military service. When the armies of the Czar advanced on Finland, they were met with little resistance from the Swedes, who at the time were deeply concerned about a possible French invasion during the Napoleonic Wars. Finnish peasantry, fearing that the Czar would make them full serfs, offered resistance to the Russians, but finally were driven across the Torneo River into Sweden. The Finnish fears, however, were ungrounded, for the Czar treated the country with generosity.

In 1809 Finland was proclaimed an autonomous state after the Russian conquest. The Russian Czar became Grand Duke of Finland, and the powers which the Swedish king had held in the affairs of the Lutheran Church became the right of the Czar. The rights of the Finnish Lutheran Church went pretty well unrestricted. While the Czar did not write church laws, he did however, have to assent to them, and he had absolute right of decision in important internal ecclesiastical matters. Surprisingly enough, the Russian domination of Finland did not work undue hardship on the Church.

FINLAND – THE CHURCH AND THE PEOPLE

Already before the year 1,000 Christianity had been brought to Finland, perhaps even by organized mission endeavors. Finland has always been a sparsely settled land, with the result that the old pagan religions continued undisturbed for a long time in many parts of the country.

Through the Church Law of 1686, the Church became a state establishment, with all members of the state required to be members of the Lutheran Church. To a great extent, then, the Church was ruled by the state, with the king choosing the bishops, who then administered the dioceses into which the Finnish Church was divided. The Church had the power to sentence its members to ecclesiastical punishments and to require public repentance.

Finland went through a period of Enlightenment, when nontheological men could very well be called to fill offices of bishops and chairs of theology. But eventually the pietistic movement succeeded in separating those who strove for orthodoxy from the Enlightenment.

Before 1869 the chief authority in the church was the monarch and his government. After the passage of the New Church Law of 1869 decisions concerning the church's internal life became the responsibility of the Church Assembly, which is the highest organ of the church. However, in matters involving a church law, the decision of the Assembly must be passed on to the parliament and the president for action. Much later (1908) a Bishops' Conference was implemented to hold meetings at least once a year and was given advisory powers.

The New Church Law of 1869 was important. The attitude of the committee that formulated it can best be seen in their own words: THE COMMITTEE IS AGAINST RELIGIOUS COERCION, SINCE THERE IS NO REAL PIETY WITHOUT FREEDOM, JUST AS THERE CAN BE NO FREEDOM, IN THE HIGHEST SENSE OF THE WORD, WITHOUT RELIGION. Czar Alexander II confirmed the New Church Law after it had been accepted by the Church Assembly in 1869. As a result of the new law, the nineteenth century laymen were given the authority to preach the gospel, and conventicles were allowed. No longer did the Czar have the final decision in matters of church policy, for this was placed in the hands of the Church Assembly, in which body the laity were to be in the majority.

A law known as the "Dissenters" Law, passed in 1889, made possible the establishing of other church organizations. The "Religious-Freedom-Law" (1923) guaranteed complete religious freedom. This law enabled a person to change his religion without the consent of a guardian. At the age of fifteen the child could not be forced to join in the conversion of a parent or guardian. If there were a sufficient number of applicants (20), a new denomination could be formed. And so, the Lutheran Free Church and several non-Lutherans churches, including the Roman Catholic Church, were granted status as legalized denominations in Finland.

The New Church Law of 1869 suppressed to some extent the relationship of Church and State. For example, the schools were made independent of the church. Already in 1865 the church parishes had been separated from the municipalities.

FINLAND – UNDER RUSSIAN DOMINATION

Finland was under Russian domination from 1809 to 1917, but the Finnish people who at one time did not even write their own history, nevertheless resisted Russification. During the Russian domination, the Finnish people came to the decision that they wanted to be just that, Finnish people: neither Swedes nor Russians. However, prior to Russian domination, Sweden had absorbed the main territory of the Finnish people and had wielded great influence on them. As a result, the Finns remained close to the Swedes even after the Czar's rule began. Eventually strong anti-Russian feelings were aroused among the Finnish people. The writings of certain authors were a powerful influence in this direction. Men came to the fore who attempted to regenerate Finnish nationalism as well as the Finnish language, which had lain dormant since the days of Agricola.

After 1881 came stormy years for Finland, when Russia's attitude in respect to its leniency toward Finland changed. Through the ensuing years Russia refused to honor any requests for Finland's independence. However, in 1909 the medieval Diocese of Turku did become the autonomous State of Finland. Finally came the March Revolution (the Bolshevik Revolution) in 1917, which overthrew the Czar and his government. Kerensky's Provisional Russian government gave back to Finland all the rights it ever had, but the Finnish Parliament passed a bill proclaiming Finland independent, thus severing all ties with Russia. Still, Finland desired to maintain a common foreign policy and national defense. On December 6, 1917, the modern Finnish Republic was formed when Finland's independence became complete.

THE AWAKENING MOVEMENTS

Early in the eighteenth century, pietist movements began to have a firm grip – even the radical forms – on the hearts of the Finnish people. However, later in the century they were all but extinguished except for small circles of activity. Then, in the nineteenth century, the awakening movements took hold of Finland once again, characterized by vigor and vitality.

One of the features of the nineteenth century movements was that the new Pietism came from within Finland and was promoted by the Finnish people themselves. Laymen were the leaders and remained so. Another feature was that the members of the movements kept close to the established church; they continued to attend the worship services and to participate in the Lord's Supper. Still another feature was that pastors, gripped by the movement, made special efforts to serve those involved in it.

PERSONALITIES IN FINNISH PIETISM

PAAVO RUOTSALAINEN

A simple farmer from the wilderness of Savo in Central Finland. To experience Christ within one's self was an important aspect of his movement. Faithful to this cause to a fault, Ruotsalainen did a great deal of traveling, possibly a distance equal to a trip around the world, much of it on foot. He taught that communion with Christ is a reality to those who recognize their own wretchedness. He emphasized looking to Christ in faith, trusting Christ to act in one's life. This Pietism emphasized that a person has an "inner feeling" of grace; hence there was a lack of assurance of salvation.[3] Ruotsalainen and others who promoted Pietism in Finland found themselves in trouble with authorities for holding illegal meetings and for collecting money. There were subtle ways to punish pietistic preachers, namely, by denying them advancement or by transferring them to a prison chaplaincy.

HENRIK RENQVIST

An awakening preacher from Karelia, who emphasized among other things, prayer in the kneeling position. Since drunkenness was long a problem in Finland, he promoted complete abstinence from alcohol, a thing that Ruotsalainen on the other hand did not teach. (Ruotsalainen differed from Renqvist in other matters too, and regarded the latter's form of devotional exercise hypocrisy and lip-service.)

WILHELM MALMINVAARA

A layman who became leader of the awakening movement in 1880.

Even after Rutsalainen's death, laymen kept the movement alive, especially with the help of farmer-preachers. Since 1892 the pietists held annual Summer Meetings in various places, sometimes with great numbers attending. These meetings proved very useful to the movement.

All of the awakening movements displayed a friendly attitude toward the church, which attitude has not always been reciprocated by the church. Often the people involved in these movements are the hard workers in the parish church. The pietists in Finland have translated Luther, stressed sermons that people can understand, emphasized responsibility toward the suffering, have written hymns, placed men into the ministry, and have supported the Outer Mission. (In 1862 a mission institute for training missionaries was built and missionaries were sent out, for example, to South West Africa.) The pietists have also stressed patriotism. The message of the pietist is mainly the salvation of the immortal, blood-bought soul.

While pietists are faithful to the church, they are yet inclined to lead independent spiritual lives. They meet together in extra meetings and hold their own pietistic devotions, at times with the leadership of the parish pastor, if he is a pietist. These meetings are not held in the church building but in a farmyard or house. Singing interspersed with sermon reading or informal talks are characteristics. The pietists founded Folk Schools, institutions of "popular cultural training."

THE PRAYING MOVEMENT IN FINNISH PIETISM

One of the oldest and smallest of the awakening movements is identified by its teachings and practices regarding prayer. Among its proponents were Abraham Achrenius (d. 1769), a preacher; his son Anders (d. 1810); Matti Pukanhaava (d. 1833); and Matti Paavola (d. 1859). Henrik Renqvist (1789-1866), as was mentioned earlier, deemed praying in the kneeling position of great importance, and his followers were thus called the "Praying Ones." Frequent and long prayers characterized the followers of his movement. Members prayed the Lord's Prayer often. As was stated previously, Ruotsalainen did not accept Renqvist's views. Renqvist taught: "Pray that you may grow and God will give you his Spirit and you will pray again."[4] Ruotsalainen, on the other hand, preached, "Repent, believe in Christ and then you may pray." Repentance, faith and new life were the trilogy propounded by these old-time pietists. Being members of the "Praying Ones" is an extra-curricular affair, for the members attend church faithfully and partake of the Lord's Supper with the other parish people. It is not a growing movement, being unattractive to the young people.

THE LAESTADIANS

This movement is located in northern Finland. The followers stress conversion, the new life, and the assembly of believers. The guiding light was a Swedish pastor, Lars Levi Laestadius (1800-1861), who served parishes in northern Sweden near the Finnish frontier. He worked among the Lapps as well as among the Finns, whose lives were very disorderly. He spoke in no uncertain terms against the prevailing moral abuses. He trained and sent out lay preachers and catechists. The movement, begun in the nineteenth century, continues and has two main branches: the conservative, and the newly awakened Laestadians. Private confession is stressed, but this confession of sin may be made before a fellow Christian or before the entire congregation. "The spoken word is the proper medium of the Holy Spirit and absolution by a believing Christian is necessary for conversion."[5] Usually, confession is made to an individual who proclaims absolution, followed by a brief confession before the congregation. Ecstatic visions have an important part in all groups. First the individual may be overcome with remorse for sins at hearing the law preached, marked by weeping and wailing, and then when absolution is tendered, he or she experiences outbursts of joy. Modest living is also a characteristic of the group. Fellowship in small, closely-knit groups is emphasized, rather than attendance at the parish church; nevertheless, they receive the Lord's Supper and baptism in the church.

Regarding all the awakening movements it may be said that though the members remain with the organized church, yet their attitudes toward the establishment causes problems. The fact is that their presence in the church services is possibly more of body than of spirit. It has been said that many inwardly do not belong to the local church – it simply is not their spiritual home. Some regard the church as no more than a mission field where they can try to promote the program of their own movement.

THE EVANGELICAL MOVEMENT (NOT PIETIST)

In 1844 the Evangelical Movement came into being through Pastor Frederik G. Hedberg (1811-1893). Hedberg, who broke away from the pietists, was concerned that Christians base their faith on Christ, not on their own personal feelings or experiences. He had tremendous respect for the writings of Luther and his doctrine of reconciliation and justification. Baptism and baptismal regeneration were stressed, especially for children. He also stressed the certainty of salvation. He taught that through faith the whole man is hallowed, even his flesh and body – thus a kind of perfectionism. That being the case, what use did the preaching of the law to Christians serve? The movement is still popular in southern Finland. Hedberg's movement was more firmly organized in 1873 and given the name Lutheran Evangelical Association in Finland. The movement employs lay preachers as well as parish pastors.

SOCIALISM

At the turn of the century, the Social Democrat party was organized (1903). This was a workers' movement and stressed materialism, and at the same time it demanded separation of Church and State and the removal of religious instructions from the school curriculum. This movement had no little influence on some of the Finnish people who emigrated to America, and served as a cause for the immigrants' failure to identify with the Finnish Church in their new country.[6]

Footnotes for Chapter Twenty-Seven

* Finland at the time was a province of Sweden.

1 Erwin L. Lueker, Editor-in-Chief, *Lutheran Cyclopedia*, (St. Louis, MO: Concordia Publishing House, 1954), p. 376.

2 Robert Famighetti, Editor, *The World Almanac and Book of Facts,* (Mahwah, NJ: K-III Reference Corporation, 1996), p. 764.

3 Lueker, Editor-in-Chief, *Lutheran Cyclopedia*, p. 376.

4 Geert Sentzke, *Finland-Its Church and Its People*, (Helsinki, Finland: printed by Kirjapaino Oy Lause, 1963), p. 89.

5 Lueker, Editor-in-Chief, *Lutheran Cyclopedia*, p. 376.

6 Much of the information for the historical background of Finland in this chapter was gleaned from: Geert Sentzke, *Finland-Its Church and Its People.* (See footnote #4)

CHAPTER TWENTY-EIGHT

THE FINNS
THE FINNISH EVANGELICAL
LUTHERAN CHURCH OF
AMERICA
(THE SUOMI SYNOD)
1890 – 1962

Also:
THE FINNISH NATIONAL LUTHERAN CHURCH
(NATIONAL EVANGELICAL LUTHERAN CHURCH)
1998 – 1964

MANY FINNS IMMIGRATED TO THIS COUNTRY
AND TO CANADA

Alfred Haapanen in *Our Church. The Suomi Synod...*, points out: A REMARK-
ABLY LARGE PART OF THE FINNISH PEOPLE, PERHAPS ONE NINTH, HAVE MIGRATED
ACROSS THE SEAS TO THE NORTH AMERICAN CONTINENT – TO THE UNITED STATES
AND CANADA. IT IS ESTIMATED THAT AT THE HEIGHT OF THE IMMIGRATION THERE
WERE APPROXIMATELY 500,000 FINNS [IN NORTH AMERICAN], INCLUDING THE AMER-

ICAN BORN. OF THESE OVER 400,000 WERE IN THE UNITED STATES AND ABOUT 60,000 TO 70,000 IN CANADA.[1]

Between 1865 and 1901, 231,000 Finnish immigrants came to the United States.[2] Some Finns arrived very early in America, having come here in the mid 1600's as part of the Swedish Colonization Party, and thus helped to establish the first Lutheran Church in this land. General migration, however, did not begin until the 1860's, with 1870 marking the beginning of the mainstream of immigrants. But the greater part of the Finnish migration occurred later, between 1880 and 1914. When World War I cut off the flow of immigrants to the United States, the Finnish migration was deflected to Canada. Finns came to the mines of Michigan, Minnesota, and the mountain states, as well as to the steel mills and docks of Ohio and Pennsylvania, and to the factories of Massachusetts and New York.[3] When we count the Finns together with the Swedes, Danes, and Norwegians who immigrated here between 1820 and 1920 the total amounts to a little over two million. The Finns were mainly interested in mining, logging and farming and settled areas where these industries were strong. Michigan's Upper Peninsula became the Finnish Center of America. Often times spiritual pursuits were abandoned as the immigrants labored to establish themselves in a largely wilderness area, and make enough money to return to the homeland for which there was a great deal of homesickness. The first years of the Finnish migration can be characterized by gross worldliness in many of those who came.[4]

Among the large numbers of Finnish immigrants who settled in the mining districts of the Michigan's Upper Peninsula, the Copper Country, were people who not only came from the northern part of Finland (Oulu Province), but also from Sweden and Norway. It was in this Copper Country that the largest number of immigrants became established and that the Finnish Church in America had its beginning. The Finnish American Evangelical Lutheran Church, or Suomi Synod, thus had its birth here.

FEW FINNISH PASTORS

At first there were no Finnish Lutheran pastors in America. The first services for Finns were carried on jointly with the Swedes and Norwegians, and often the pastors worked through interpreters. The Church of Finland did little to help its fellow countrymen abroad, and many Finns were lost to the Church. THE BETRAYAL OF THESE PEOPLE BY THE LUTHERANS OF FINLAND REMAINS ONE OF THE BLACKEST MARKS IN THE HISTORY OF THAT CHURCH.[5]

The first Finnish Lutheran pastor in America was the Rev. Alfred Elieser Backman, who arrived in Calumet, Michigan, on September 10, 1876. He had been called through the Finnish Missionary Society. Backman helped to organize the Calmut Bethlehem congregation and the Hancock-Quincy congregation. He also made trips into Minnesota and Ohio. Backman remained in America about seven years. After a year and a half, another pastor, the Rev. John Kustaa Nikander came from Finland, arriving in Hancock, Michigan, on January 3, 1885. Pastor Kikander is called the "father of the Suomi Synod." He geared himself to the work of a missionary, always on the move, visiting one group of

Finns and then another, going from logging camp to mining towns. His work was not without blessing. People came to the services he conducted and responded to his ministry. New congregations were organized in the Copper Country and the surrounding territory.

THE FIRST FINNISH LUTHERAN SYNOD

As the number of congregations grew, so did the desire to organize a Finnish Lutheran Synod. Ultimately the organization of a synod was worked out, the constitution drafted, and the first church convention called. This was held on March 25, 1890, in Calmut Michigan. All four of the Finnish pastors attended, and nine congregations were represented by seventeen delegates. The result of the convention was the establishment of a Finnish Synod. The constitution which had been drafted was approved. J.K. Kikander was elected as president. Also elected were a secretary, a treasurer, and a notary.

The Preamble of the original constitution of the synod reads:

WE, THE PEOPLE OF FINNISH STOCK IN AMERICA, CONFESSING THE EVANGEL-ICAL LUTHERAN FAITH, IN ORDER TO FORM A MORE PERFECT CHURCH UNION; TO STABILIZE THE GOVERNMENT OF THE CHURCH; TO PRESERVE THE PURE EVAN-GELICAL FAITH; TO SPREAD THE LIGHT OF THE GOSPEL; TO REVIVE TRUE CHRIS-TIANITY; TO INSURE FOR OURSELVES AS WELL AS FOR OUR POSTERITY THE COMMUNION OF UNION IN THE HOLY SAINTS; AND TO PROTECT THE PROPERTY OF OUR CONGREGATIONS, DO HEREBY ORDAIN AND ESTABLISH THE FOLLOWING CONSTITUTION, AS REQUIRED...[6]

The name chosen for the synod was the Finnish Evangelical Lutheran Church of America, the shorter from of which is simply the Suomi Synod. The following are a few of the items covered in the synod's constitution:

THE FINNISH EVANGELICAL LUTHERAN CHURCH OF AMERICA CONFESSES THE CHRISTIAN FAITH THAT IS BASED UPON THE WORD OF GOD, THE PROPHETIC AND APOSTOLIC BOOKS OF THE OLD AND NEW TESTAMENTS AND PUBLISHED IN THE THREE ECUMENICAL CREEDS OF THE EARLY CHURCH, IN THE *AUGSBURG CONFESSION*, AND IN THE OTHER SYMBOLIC BOOKS OF THE EV. LUTHERAN CHURCH AND MAINTAINS AS THE HIGHEST PRINCIPLE OF CONFESSION THAT THE HOLY WORD OF GOD IS THE ONLY RULE AND STANDARD BY WHICH ALL DOC-TRINES OF THE CHURCH ARE TO BE TRIED AND JUDGED.

Then follows Articles lll through X in which the following matters are pointed out:

...THAT THE SYNOD'S ACTIVITIES SHALL COVER THE UNITED STATES AND CANADA, THE OBJECT OF THE SYNOD IS TO PROVIDE MINISTERS AND TEACHERS; TO ORGANIZE AND ADMIT CONGREGATIONS INTO MEMBERSHIPS, TO ESTABLISH MISSIONS AND LIBRARIES, TO BUILD CHURCHES, ACADEMIES, SCHOOLS, MEETING-HOUSES, CHURCH HOMES AND HOSPITALS....THE PROPERTY OF THE SYNOD AT THE TIME OF ITS FOUNDING WAS DETERMINED TO BE $1,832....THE SYNOD'S GOVERNMENT AS FOLLOWS: A CONSISTORY, COMPOSED OF FOUR MINISTERS, WHO WERE THE PRESIDENT, VICE PRESIDENT, SECRETARY, AND NOTARY, ELECTED BY THE CHURCH CONVENTION; SECOND, AN ANNUAL SYNODICAL CON-VENTION ELECTS ANNUALLY A TREASURER (EITHER LAYMAN OR PASTOR)....THE

SYNODICAL HEADQUARTERS TO BE WHERE THE PRESIDENT HAS HIS HOME.

The highest governmental power was vested in the annual Church Convention. Thus the congregations governed the synod through the representatives they sent to the annual meeting. The government was administered by the Consistory. Among the duties of the Consistory:

TO SUPERVISE THE CARRYING OUT OF DECISIONS OF THE CHURCH CONVENTION,... TO MAINTAIN LAW AND ORDER IN THE SYNOD...TO EXAMINE CANDIDATES FOR THE MINISTRY AND TO ORDAIN THEM....TO INVESTIGATE AND ARBITRATE DISSENSIONS AND DISTURBANCES... TO SEE THAT PURITY OF DOCTRINE IS PRESERVED,...TO SUPERVISE THE DIGNIFIED ADMINISTRATION OF THE SACRAMENTS... TO ATTEND TO THE CHRISTIAN TRAINING OF THE CHILDREN AND YOUTH OF THE SYNOD... TO SUPERVISE IN GENERAL THE WORK OF THE CHURCH.

Congregations were to send one representative for every one hundred members or fraction thereof. Either men or women could serve as delegates to the Church Convention and all pastors were delegates ex officio.

The synod was divided into a number of regional conferences or districts. At the time of the writing of *Our Church...* the author listed the following conferences: Eastern, Ohio-Pennsylvania, Michigan, Minnesota, Columbia, and California. Each conference had its own rules of administration, boards and annual conferences.

In matters of doctrine it might be noted that the Suomi Synod was not divided on the question of public confession of sins as was the Norwegian Lutheran Church. General Confession of sins in the church service, followed by a declaration of forgiveness of sins by the pastor as God's servant, was always a part of both the regular and communion services.[7] (In the Finnish Apostolic Church "great emphasis is laid on the 'power of the Keys.' Forgiveness must be orally proclaimed to the burdened sinner by another Christian." [8]) Furthermore, private confession, followed by absolution (from either a lay person or the pastor) must accompany conversion.

THE WORK OF THE SUOMI SYNOD

EDUCATION

A Board of Education was created to direct the Sunday school work of congregations. Summer schools were held from the beginning. The main subjects were religion and Finnish, and also Finnish history and geography. In later years Vacation Bible Schools to a great extent took the place of the summer schools.

The most important institution of the synod was Suomi College at Hancock, Michigan. As time went on, the prospects for receiving permanent pastors from Finland did not appear bright, and the need for an institution to train Finnish pastors in America were deeply felt. As the author of *Our Church...* put it: "Circumstances, however, were hardly favorably for such a great attempt." Still, the hopes and prayers of the people were eventually realized, and on September 8, 1896, Suomi College opened its doors with twenty-two students and four teachers. Dr. J.K. Kikander was the president, and also one of the instructors.

Seven years were required to complete the work of both the Academy and College. There was also a two-year course in the theological seminary. The first candidates to graduate from the synod's theological seminary were ordained in Hancock, Michigan, June 5, 1906. There were five candidates altogether. Later, in the merger of Lutheran bodies that formed the Lutheran Church in American (1962), Grand View Seminary of the American Ev. Lutheran Church (Danish Church) and Suomi Theological Seminary united with Chicago Lutheran Theological Seminary (United Lutheran Church in America), and moved to Maywood, Illinois.[9]

In 1930 the Academy was discontinued and more emphasis was placed on the Junior College, which had been organized a few years before. The Church Convention in 1957 decided to unite the Theological Seminary of Suomi College with the Chicago Lutheran Theological Seminary in Maywood, Illinois, because of the limitations of the Suomi Seminary faculty and library facilities.

Suomi College, the only college founded by Finnish people in America, became a two-year coeducational college of the Lutheran Church in America (LCA) and served students coming from foreign countries as well as from the States and from the United States Trust Territories of the Pacific Islands.

PUBLICATIONS

"The printed word has had a particularly important place in (the) Synod. In early times a church paper was the only preacher that visited our people in distant sections for months and even years."[10]   The oldest Finnish Church paper, *The Shepherd's Message*, was begun in 1889 and published once a week. A children's paper was begun in 1892 and published for more than fifty years in Finnish, and after that it was published in English. A youth paper was begun in 1915 and later became an English paper. There were also special holiday publications as in other Scandinavian circles.

The oldest publishing house of the Suomi Synod was established in Hancock, Michigan in 1889. A small bookstore established by Pastors Nikander and Tolonen in the home of Mr. J.H. Jasberg, plus the small printing (hand) press owned by Dr. Nikander on which was printed the *Shepherds Tidings* became the nucleus for the Finnish Lutheran Book Concern. In 1900 the Synod purchased the press and bookstore from their owners for $10,241.22. However, at the time of the sale the synod had no funds for publishing and the deal amounted to a credit arrangement. The Book Concern undertook the publishing of a Finnish newspaper three times a week. It also published textbooks for summer and Sunday schools as well as hymnals and songbooks in English.

The other publishing house of Suomi was established in 1921 in Astoria, Oregon, which then undertook to publish a Finnish language newspaper for the West Coast area. In 1930, after eight years of financial struggle, as well as a devastating fire, the Book Concern in Astoria was rented out and five years later it was sold. The Book Concern at Hancock fell into deep financial trouble in the 1950's. Later, after the merger forming the LCA, the Book Concern be-

447

came a part of the Board of Publication of the LCA Consistory. A year later (after 1962) it was sold and the business moved off the Suomi College Campus.

HOME MISSION WORK

Migrating to America from the old country brought a whole new experience to the Finnish people, church-wise. In Finland, under the State Church system, each citizen was born and reared in the routine of the Church. Each citizen was obliged to take part. In America the scene was different. Democracy meant also freedom to attend or not attend church services. Since church life was a voluntary matter, many of the Finnish Lutherans upon arriving in America chose not to join a Lutheran congregation. This presented a challenging situation for the home mission work of the Suomi Synod. The fact that the immigrants were scattered over a wide area, many of then in tiny settlements, added to the mission pastor's burdens, who then had to travel far and conduct many devotional services in order to include as many of the immigrants as possible in the ministry of the Word and administration of the sacraments.

From the beginning of its history, the Finnish Church in America did home mission work, which work proceeded as long as funds were available. When funds ran out mission work ceased, temporarily. After 1916 a special Home Mission Board was created, with the result that home mission work was carried on more efficiently and with greater effectiveness.

In 1921 the Suomi Synod made an agreement with the United Lutheran Church in America to carry on joint work for the development of home mission activity, which included all of the United Stats and Canada. The United Lutheran Church in America (ULCA) gave 50% of the financial support, also financially aiding Finnish seminary students. This joint work continued for fifteen years. In 1931 the Suomi Synod's Canadian congregations and their mission work were taken over by the ULCA, since it was not financially feasible for the synod to care for these churches. The cooperation begun with the ULCA in 1921 ceased in 1935 for the reason that certain leaders in the ULCA made it imperative that the Suomi Synod join the ULCA. However, the Finns were not ready for such a step and in a friendly manner terminated the cooperation. Under the cooperative plan the seminarians of the Suomi Synod had been receiving $200 a year each for their education.

At first, support of the church's work came largely from church suppers and other social activities. The Finnish people, imbued with the life of the State Church were not used to giving regular offerings to the support of their pastor and church properties. In Finland the government paid the account; in America the people had to learn the values and ways of proper Christian stewardship. Eventually the synod came to adopt the budget system in which the yearly expenses were computed and the individual offerings set accordingly.[11]

In 1950 a Church Advancement Program was inaugurated to collect $100,000 for repairs and improvements at Suomi College and for home missions, foreign missions, as well as for synod administration. $93,000 was collected. Some missions were started as a result of the Church Advancement Program. Since a large number of Finns were living in Florida, the Home Mission Board succeeded in developing a congregation at Lake Word, and another at Newport Richey. A congregation was also begun at North Madison, Ohio, and Northwestern Immanuel Lutheran Church was established in Detroit. The Fund also made it possible to send five missionaries to the mission fields in Japan.

FOREIGN MISSION WORK

K.L. Tolonen, an early pastor of Suomi Synod had been a missionary in Africa, as was true of several of the synod's early pastors. The Finnish Missionary Society had looked on America as a field and called these missionaries into it. But interest in foreign missions was kept alive in Suomi, especially by such men as Dr. Nikander. Finally, in 1916 the church convention in Superior, Wisconsin, established a Foreign Mission Board. Rev. Niilo Korhonen was sent as the Suomi Synod's missionary to Finland's mission field in China.

With their donations, congregations of the synod also supported foreign missions in the Finland Church. Until World War II Suomi cooperated with the Foreign Mission Society in Finland, sending $1,000 annually for the support of one missionary in China. After the beginning of the war, the Synod cooperated in the support of foreign mission work with the National Lutheran Council, and participated in the Lutheran World Action. Suomi also conducted missions in Japan, as was pointed out under "Home Mission Work."

INNER MISSION WORK

Although interested at an early stage in its history in establishing charitable institutions, the Suomi Synod did not find it feasible to venture forth in this area.

YOUTH WORK AND ADULT ORGANIZATIONS

Early in Suomi's history, there was a tendency on the part pf the pastors to organize youth work in the congregations. And so, there came into being the Young People's Christian Association (YPCA). This name, inherited from the mother Church in Finland was later succeeded by the name Luther League. The use of the Finnish language held on tenaciously over the years in the Luther League societies. Mature Finnish people who once held membership in the Luther League societies organized other groups for themselves, including Women's Guilds, Mission Circles, and Brotherhoods. In 1944 the first Luther League Field Secretary was appointed. The same year, delegates from congregational Luther Leagues voted to establish a Synodical League (which had been tried before, but failed to endure).

In the field of youth work, the Bible Camp came to be an important institution. The first Bible Camp for Finnish Lutheran Youth was held in Minnesota in 1931. Later, every conference established Bible Camps, not only for children, but even for older members as well, which camps were held separately. *The Lutheran Counselor* came to be the official publication of the youth groups of Suomi.

THE SUOMI SYNOD AND OTHER LUTHERANS

RELATIONS WITH THE STATE CHURCH OF FINLAND

The Suomi Synod maintained close contacts with the State Church in the old country. It has already been pointed out how the synod helped to maintain foreign missions of the Finland Church. The close relationship which the mother Church had with her daughter in America was evidenced in the stipend granted to Suomi pastors to study in the Theological Department of the University of Helsinki.

RELATIONS WITH OTHER FINNS

Discussions were held with the Finnish National Synod (National Evangelical Lutheran Church) 1915-1916. This synod had been organized in Rock Springs, Wyoming, in 1868, but its headquarters were located in Ironwood, Michigan. The National Synod at the time had no theological seminary, and many of its pastors had been colporteurs or lay preachers before their ordination. The chief question in the union discussions revolved around the standards to be set for future ministerial candidates. Under the proposed merger plan the current ministers of the National Church would be required to take some courses in theological subjects in order that the congregations might accept them as qualified ministers. A new synod was to be formed of the merging bodies. A few National Church ministers were willing to go ahead with the plan, but the leaders of the church were reluctant, and the merger fell through. At first the National Church did not represent any particular type of Lutheranism. For example, its first president, the Rev. W.A. Mandelof, had leanings toward Laestadianism, and a later president, the Rev. Wm. Williamson, represented the congregationalist type of Lutheranism. Later, the National Church came to stand for ultra-evangelical Lutheranism.[12] (In the matter of Laestadianism, refer to the previous chapter.)

Discussions between the two Finnish Lutheran bodies were later resumed during the years 1935 to 1938. Two more discussions were held after that, the last one taking place in 1952. Doctrinal discussions became the chief issue, since the National Church had established friendly relations with the Missouri Synod and was influenced in its doctrinal stand by that conservative body. What finally brought an end to the merger discussions was the question put to the Suomi Synod by the National Church representatives: Would you be willing to have a colloquy with the Missouri Synod? The Suomi Synod, at that time independent, felt that it needed no approval from any other Lutheran body. Later, the National Church officially united with the Lutheran Church-Missouri Synod (1964). A brief summary of the National Church is given at the

450

close of this chapter.

Relations of the Suomi Synod with the Laestadians or Apostolic Lutherans – as they are called in America – have been meager, almost non-existent. It should be noted, however, that some overtures to them succeeded, and in a few places joint churches were conducted. The majority of the Apostolic Lutherans are found in Michigan, Minnesota, and the Dakotas. They are followers of Lauri Levi Laestadius, a minister of the Church of Sweden in the diocese of Lulea. The Laestadians were the first of the modern Finnish migration to America, coming from the northern part of Norway and Sweden. They are divided into at least five separate groups, each with its own doctrinal practices. They do not have spiritual fellowship with each other. They are unorganized and have no theological seminary, relying mainly on lay preachers.

The Suomi Synod cooperated in the National Lutheran Commission for Soldiers' and Sailors' Welfare from the beginning (1917). However, it did not join the National Lutheran Council, but did cooperate with it, finally joining in 1941. Meanwhile, Suomi also carried on friendly relations with the Augustana Synod and the Norwegian Lutheran Church of America, both members of Council.

Starting in 1921 joint work was carried on for fifteen years with the United Lutheran Church in America. In 1930 the question was even raised whether or not Suomi should become a part of the ULCA, but a proposal of merger at that time was premature.

In the 1950's the Suomi Synod accepted the joint invitation extended to it by the Augustana Lutheran Church and the United Lutheran Church to discuss and take steps toward the creation of a comprehensive merger of Lutheran bodies. The Suomi Synod, together with the American Evangelical Lutheran Church (Danish) and the two bodies extending the invitation, formed the Joint Commission on Lutheran Unity. By 1958 Suomi, together with the others, had adopted a statement covering the points of agreement in doctrine, polity, and possible organizational structure. In 1960 Suomi, along with the others, accepted the proposed constitution and bylaws. The Forming Convention for the Lutheran Church in America was held in June 1962, and the LCA began operating as a new merger body, January 1, 1963. At the time of the merger, Suomi numbered slightly more than 36,000 members.

MANY OF THE YOUNGER SUOMI SYNOD PASTORS HAD ALREADY MOVED INTO OTHER LUTHERAN SYNODS TO SERVE AS PASTORS OF CONGREGATIONS OR AS PROFESSORS IN THE THEOLOGICAL SEMINARIES. THE YOUNGER LAITY WAS ALSO READY FOR THE MOVE. FOR THE OLDER ELEMENT THE MERGER DID NOT COME SO NATURALLY. THEY COULD NOT ADJUST THEMSELVES TO THE THOUGHT THAT THEY WOULD NO LONGER BE A SUOMI SYNOD. "WHAT WILL BECOME OF US?" THEY ASKED.[13]

A few pastors and congregations, particularly in Minnesota, had strong leanings toward the former Evangelical Lutheran Church (Norwegian) – later, a part of The American Lutheran church (TALC) – and wished the Suomi Synod to merge with that group. At the time of merger talks the synod was growing very slowly and the number of subscribers to church publications was decreasing.

451

"In order that the former Suomi Synod congregations and the ones in Canada might have spiritual fellowship with one another, a free conference of these congregations was organized at the time of the merger. This was done with the approval of the Constituting Convention of the Lutheran Church in America. This organization took the name of Suomi Free Conference. An international festival is held annually, where church people from Canada and the United States can come together. Regional festivals are held oftener."[14]

THE FINNISH NATIONAL LUTHERAN CHURCH

(NATIONAL EVANGELICAL LUTHERAN)

The reader would no doubt be interested in at least a brief historical sketch of this Finnish body, which remained very small. This group was organized in 1898 in the Midwest under the leadership of W.A. Mandellöf. Its roots were in the Evangelical Society of Finland (founded by F.G. Hedberg) and in the Gospel Society of Finland. During the first twenty years most of the pastors began their ministries as lay preachers. Hedberg, having broken away from the pietists, emphasized full and free salvation to all, and since he stressed that the Christian's whole man became hallowed, even his flesh, the preaching of the law to Christians could be omitted.

The Finnish American National Evangelical Lutheran Church was organized as an alternative to the Suomi Synod. The reasons for its existence go back to the controversy regarding centralization in the Suomi Synod. Suomi's constitution provided for a centralized polity limiting congregational rights and placing much authority in the hands of the president and the Consistory or Executive Board. This aroused bitter disagreement, for a clergy-dominated church body was not what the Finnish people desired. The number of delegates to the Annual Convention became the governing authority in the synod, rather than the Consistory.[15]

In early years there was some cooperation between the National Church and the Suomi Synod, but when strife arose the National Finns began leaning toward the Missouri Synod. Since the National Church never succeeded in establishing its own seminary, its students were sent to Missouri Synod schools to prepare them for the ministry (Concordia College and Seminary, Springfield, Illinois – now Fort Wayne, Indiana).

Over the years, the spirit and doctrine of the National Church changed from that of the Evangelical Society in Finland to the spirit and doctrine of the Missouri Synod. In 1923 it related itself to that synod and later, in 1964, merged with it. The National Church was a small body, about a third the size of Suomi at the time of the LCA merger.[16]

During the time it existed as an independent body, the National Church carried on limited home mission work, while also sending a missionary to serve the widely scattered Finns in Australia.[17] It also associated with the Finnish

Lutheran Gospel Association, whose mission outreach was to Japan.

Footnotes for Chapter 28

1 Alfred Haapanen, *Our Church. The Suomi Synod, the Finnish Ev. Lutheran Church of America*, (Hancock, MI: Finnish Lutheran Book Concern, 1945), p.7.

2 E. Clifford Nelsen, T*he Lutherans in North America*, (Philadelphia, PA: Fortress Press, 1975), p. 272.

3 Nelsen, *The Lutherans in North America*, p. 272.

4 Ben Maddow, *A Sunday Between Wars-The Course of American Life from 1865 to 1917*, (New York, NY: W.W. Norton & Company, 1979), p. 179.

5 Robert P. Hetico, *America's Lutherans* (The Orphans are Three), edited by Omar Bonderud and Charles Lutz. Reprinted from One Magazine, (Columbes, OH: Warburg Press), p. 44.

6 Haapanen, *Our Church...*, p. 21.

7 Haapanen, *Our Church...*, p. 34.

8 Haapanen, *Our Church...*, p. 34.

9 Johannes Knudsen, *The Foundation of the Lutheran Church in America*, (Philadelphia, PA: Fortress Press, 1978), p. 67.

10 Haapanen, *Our Church...*,p.____

11 Haapanen, *Our Church...*,p. 75, 76.

12 Haapanen, *Our Church...*,p. 128.

13 Haapanen, *Our Church...*,p. 119

14 Haapanen, *Our Church...*,p. 120.

15 Nelsen, *The Lutherans in North America*, p. 274.

16 Nelsen, *The Lutherans in North America*, p. 275, 276.

17 Hetico, *America's Lutherans*, p. 46.

CHAPTER TWENTY-NINE

THE SLOVAKS
THE SLOVAK EVANGELICAL
LUTHERAN CHURCH (SELC)
1902 - 1971

Brief Mention:
THE SLOVAK ZION SYNOD
1919 - 1962

NATIONAL BACKGROUND

TROUBLE IN THE OLD COUNTRY

A dual monarchy of Austria-Hungary, established in 1867, made the Germans the legal masters of Austria, and the Hungarians the masters of Hungary. The Hungarians were in the minority of Hungary, nevertheless they wanted to achieve a "rigid" supremacy over the various Slavic groups living in Hungary.[1] The Slovaks living in the twenty-four northwest counties of Hungary before World War I comprised one of these groups.

The Magyars (i.e. the dominant people of Hungary) became the unquestioned masters over Hungary in the mid 1800's and seized the opportunity to enforce their principles, one of which was to force all ethnic groups in Hungary into one nation and culture. The policy enforced was denationalization of all non-Hungarian racial groups.

"In Hungary there can be only Hungarian Culture." Hungary was in effect forbidden to be a melting pot of nationalities and races. It rather became a mold by which all were forced to change to fit what was deemed best for all, namely, Hungarian culture and language. By 1848 Hungarian had become the language of officialdom. It was the language to be taught in the schools. After a time non-Hungarian languages were driven out of the courts and other official institutions. Repressive measures were adopted, such as closing Slovak schools and taking away voting privileges. In practice, it became impossible to elect Slovak representatives to the Hungarian parliament. Even some Slovak children (orphans and the poor) were deported to what later became Yugoslavia. Slovak libraries were destroyed; charters were refused to Slovak banks and licenses to Slovak businesses. Slovak self-expression was discouraged, even to the point of forbidding the singing of Slovak songs.

The persecution, plus economic hardships, induced many Slovaks to leave their homeland. (Slovakia is mountainous and quite barren.) Most of the existing fertile land was in the hands of rich landowners. Very little land was in the hands of the peasants, who were not only grossly disadvantaged economically, they were also overburdened with taxes. One Slovak leader maintained that the position of the Slovak in Hungary was worse than that of the Christian in Turkey.

The Slovaks were virtual slaves in an economic system that sorely exploited them, and as though this were not bad enough, had World War I not intervened, the Hungarians would probably have exterminated the Slovak nation. The oppressed Slovaks had no legal protection in their own homeland.[2]

The Slovaks were members of the Lutheran Church of Hungary, in which institution the policy of denationalization also applied. The church was forced to cooperate with the enforcement of the policy of Magyarization where all ethnic groups were forced to accept Hungarian language and culture and dominance. A Slovak church man might, for example, be persecuted and intimidated for the most trivial reasons. Slovak became outlawed even as a language of Christian instruction.

Hungarianization of the church was enforced at sword point. Furthermore, the government interfered in the seminary and in the calling of pastors.

THE POLICY OF THE HUNGARIAN GOVERNMENT AS APPLIED TO NON-HUNGARIANS IN VARIOUS AREAS OF LIFE WAS RESPONSIBLE TO A GREAT EXTENT FOR THE MASS EMIGRATION OF NON-MAGYAR NATIONALITIES, WHICH TOOK PLACE IN THE LAST DECADES OF THE 19TH CENTURY.[3]

This, coupled with the low economic life of the Slovak peasant caused many to emigrate in the last decade of the 19th and the first decades of the 20th centuries. And for the average man it was the economic conditions more than anything else, plus his being persecuted and exploited, that persuaded him to leave his homeland. Of course, adventurism also played a part. But bear in mind that the Hungarian peasants also had a terrible time of it, eeking out a living under intolerable conditions. He was poor, and at the mercy of the wealthy. Ben Maddow concludes: "The wonder is not why some peasants left for America, but why all of them did not go." [4]

MIGRATION TO AMERICA

The Revolution of 1848 produced some migration already then, and a Slovak colony was quite early established at Streator, Illinois. Slovaks settled around New York in 1879, the anthracite region of Pennsylvania in 1885, and in Minnesota in 1880. Some Slovaks were also settling as far west as California. Most immigrants at the time were from eastern Slovakia. Between 1880 and 1890 a total of 470,089 Hungarian subjects emigrated. In 1899 between 160,000 and 200,000 Slovaks were settled in the United States. In 1902 about 431,000 came.

The founders of the Slovak Evangelical Lutheran Church (SELC) came from Slovakia, the eastern part of what later came to be the Czechoslovakian Republic. The emigration began in 1875, but its greatest intensity was 1890-95.

Three-fourths of the immigrants found work in the coal mines of Pennsylvania, others, in factories. It was a far cry from the rural background and training the immigrant had come to know in the old country. Most were from the peasant class. However, some were skilled tradesmen. Many went into business for themselves. About one-fourth of the immigrants finally found their way back to the homeland.

Because of poverty and petty persecution, the Slovaks tended to be clannish and to live in urban communities with numbers of their fellow countrymen. In the early years it was often only the head of the family who emigrated.

THE SLOVAK CHURCH IN AMERICA

ESTABLISHING CONGREGATIONS

To meet the need for fellowship among the immigrants, a number of Slovak fraternal organizations were established. By 1893 there were at least eight Slovak Lutheran independent societies in existence.[5]

Though fraternal societies flourished among the immigrants, the Slovaks were not usually eager to start congregations in America. Nor did the Lutheran Church of Hungary help take care of the spiritual needs of those who emigrated. In fact, the General Evangelical Church of the *Augsburg Confession* in Hungary did nothing for the spiritual welfare of its former members. Sad to say, it was filled with the spirit of Magyarization. And so, without their own Slovak pastors many immigrants backslid. But strong, religiously conscious Slovak laymen kept the Church together. They took upon themselves the organizing of congregations and the calling of pastors from Slovakia. Homes were often used for worship services.

When the mass of immigration began in about 1880 there were no Slovak pastors to greet the newcomers, and for many years the Church suffered a

457

scarcity of men of the cloth. The first Slovak pastor ordained in the United States was the Rev. Karol Hor'ak, a native of Bohemia. He ministered in the cities in Pennsylvania. When he came to America he was a Lutheran teacher, but he continued his studies and was finally ordained to the holy ministry. He moved to Streator, Illinois, where he served Holy Trinity Church. The Rev. Cyril Droppa had begun services at Streator on March 30, 1884.

By 1895 there were a least nine Slovak Lutheran pastors in the country.[6] The Slovak ministerial students used the seminaries of the Missouri Synod at St. Louis and at Springfield, Illinois. The Slovak Synod never owned a theological seminary, nor any institution of higher learning, but rather continued to use the institutions of the Missouri Synod. Pastors of other Lutheran bodies, including the General Council, the Iowa Synod, the Synod of the Northwest, and the Missouri Synod, often gave help where they could to the Slovak Lutheran immigrants, even loaning church buildings for service use.

Strict confessional lines were not always followed. In case there was no Lutheran pastor to help out, the immigrant might turn to pastors and pulpits of the Reformed Church. At times Slovak Lutherans joined with Slovak Reformed people to found joint parishes, such as the First Slovak and Hungarian Lutheran and Reformed Parish of St. Paul, located in Pittsburgh, Pennsylvania.[7] A willingness was shown to cross denominational lines to participate in the ceremonies of others.

Because of the existing unsettled circumstances, many Slovak immigrants were lost from the Lutheran Church. Many times there was a long delay between the time of the arrival of the Lutheran immigrants and the establishing of congregations. For example, in Yonkers, New York, twenty-five years lapsed before a congregation was formed.[8] Often the mission pastor heard the excuse, "I am a member of the Lutheran Church in the Old Country."

In the 1880's, congregations existed in Illinois, Minnesota, and Pennsylvania. Sometimes Slovak Lutheran Religious Societies filled the gap where no congregations were organized, and congregations finally resulted from their labors. The Slovak Evangelical Union, founded in Freeland, Pennsylvania, in 1893 played a large part in establishing congregations. It even collected money and purchased lots for congregations and aided them in acquiring and equipping their property. The Union also provided for worship services and even helped in calling pastors.[9]

DIFFICULTIES ENCOUNTERED IN
ESTABLISHING CONGREGATIONS

(1) Lack of enthusiasm on the part of the immigrant to start congregations in America... (2) Finding places to worship...(3) Finding a permanent pastor or even one to fill the pulpit on a Sunday or to visit the sick and dying, to take care of funerals, etc...(4) The distance involved for the circuit riding pastors...(5) Short pastorates and difficulty in finding replacements...(6) Factions in the congregations, often arising over trivial matters...(7) Proselytizing activities of the sectarian churches and the activities of the Socialists...(8) Willing-

ness of the Lutherans to fraternize with the sects, to cross denominational lines; thus a lack pf allegiance to strict, confessional Lutheranism... (9) Finding the resources to purchase property and build churches...(10) Unscrupulous men who ingratiated themselves as pastors but did not live up to their high calling.

FOUNDING THE SLOVAK
EVANGELICAL LUTHERAN SYNOD

A series of events led to the founding of the Slovak Evangelical Lutheran Church (SELC or commonly called simply Slovak Synod). First there was the formation of the Seniorate in 1894. The idea originated in the Slovak Evangelical Union at its second convention. One of the stated purposes of the Union was: "That by its entire activity it works thereto that when the number of congregations increases, a Slovak Lutheran Seniorate be formed." The lay members urged the pastors to form such a Seniorate. This was done June 4 or 5, 1894. The Rev. Karol Hauser was elected Senior. The *Church Letters* was to be the official organ. By this time the Slovaks had been in America for years.

It seems that the Seniorate was from the start without much life and finally died a natural death. This was due mainly to the negative attitude of the pastors, who came from different backgrounds and offered varying points of view regarding the new body and its operation. The difference in theological background made itself evident in regards to the question of the affiliation with other Lutheran bodies. Some expressed the desire to affiliate with the Missouri Synod. Others felt that the new body should hold itself aloof from American Lutheran synods. Of course, the question could be asked whether the pastors really desired the formation of a union of congregations. Organizing the Seniorate only amplified attitudes that were already present, thus resulting in controversy.

As more immigrants came, the need for organizing Slovak churches naturally became more apparent. The disorganization of the churches begged for the establishing of order through a union of congregations. A series of three meetings was held (1899-1902) for the purpose of attempting another union of Slovak Lutherans. Here again the Slovak Evangelical Union was present, exerting its influence. It had sent out an invitation prior to its 1899 Convention at Wilkes-Barre, Pennsylvania, to all Slovak pastors, with the stated purpose of organizing a pastoral conference. Six pastors from an area that extended from Pittsburgh to New York City attended the conference. The four Wilkes-Barre Points were drafted. In brief they declared: (1) The doctrinal stand is to be the foundation of the Gospel of Christ and all the Symbolic Books of the Lutheran Church. (2) The purpose of the organization is to spread the Gospel of Christ by pure evangelical teaching and an exemplary blameless life, and to foster brotherly love, harmony and unanimity. (3) The Lord's Supper is not to knowingly be administered to adherents of the Helvetic Confession (Reformed Confession adopted in Switzerland, Scotland, Hungary, France, and Poland; adopted 1566 and has 30 articles covering the Christian faith). (4) The holding of picnics and balls for the benefit of the Slovak Evangelical Lutheran Church is condemned.

The field of labor was divided up by this first conference and a system for handling cases of misunderstanding and pastoral discipline was provided for.

At the second meeting, held in January 1900, eight pastors attended, three of whom were at the time members of the Missouri Synod. These recommended that the congregations consider themselves missions of that synod. However, the majority of the Slovaks desired to remain a separate body. The three Missouri Synod pastors left the meeting in dissatisfaction. In spite of its small number, the remaining group decided to organize an independent Slovak Lutheran Church. The five remaining pastors then resolved to form The Brotherhood of American Slovak Churches of the Evangelical *Augsburg Confession* in the United States of America. The term "synod" was used interchangeably with the term "brotherhood." Some of the pastors were yet members of other synods.

A division occurred between those who were pro-Missouri Synod and those who wanted an independent Slovak Church. The pro-Missouri Synod pastors held a meeting in Cleveland, Ohio, April 16, 1901. Steps were taken to lay the foundation for a General Slovak Evangelical Synod to be affiliated with the Synodical Conference. An invitation was sent out to other Slovak pastors regardless of synodical affiliation. These attempts were not successful, and so the body, which the pro-Missouri men attempted to found never came into being. No doubt the strict practice of the Missouri Synod turned the pastors of the Brotherhood off regarding the proposition.

When the third preparatory meeting was held on June 4, 1902, the pro-Missouri Synod men were in attendance. Nine pastors in all met together. The Four Wilkes-Barre Points were accepted together with the following four points: (1) The Slovak American Evangelical Church of the *Augsburg Confession* in the United States of America confesses the divinity of the Holy Scriptures (canonical books). Its denial has served and (still) serves merely the cause of political oppression. (2) Individual churches (local congregations) are completely independent with regard to their internal affairs. However, in matters pertaining to salvation they are united by the Four Wilkes-Barre Points fixed in the minutes of the Braddock Meeting. (3) The administration (the administrative service and not the officials) of the Slovak American Church of the *Augsburg Confession* in the United States of America is conducted by the pastors who alternate for the purpose according to alphabetical order. (4) As we take over the administration we do not hereby separate ourselves from anyone; on the contrary, just by using it for the spreading of the Gospel of God and its tasks (love to the new country and our people) we thereby unite ourselves with all true believers and the elect of God.[10]

The name "Brotherhood" was changed to "Church," and the draft was signed by all the pastors present. These then had to go home and sell their congregations on the idea. In order to save on expenses, congregations up to this time had not been invited to the preparatory meetings. However, they were to be represented at the meeting to be held on September 2, 1902, in Connelsville, Pennsylvania. Technically, then, the Slovak Evangelical Church of the *Augsburg Confession* existed from the time of the Connelsville meeting, when the lay delegates were present and participated. This is the official date and place of organization recognized later by a group of officials.

Ten pastors helped to found the synod. These served congregations in Ohio, Illinois, New York, Pennsylvania, Minnesota. Four laymen participated, most of whom were from Pennsylvania.

GOVERNMENT IN THE SYNOD

Pastors Laucek and Kvacala prepared a constitution for the group. An interesting aspect of the amended constitution was that it required the clergy to earn their living by the Gospel. The synod was chartered in Pennsylvania. In the original charter granted to it, the name the Slovak Evangelical Synod of the *Augsburg Confession* in Pennsylvania appears. On January 24, 1945, this charter was amended to correspond to the new constitution and the name Slovak Evangelical Lutheran Church (SELC).

The doctrinal stand of the Slovak Synod was conservative and bound to the Holy Scriptures and to the Lutheran Confessions. Thus: THE SLOVAK EVANGELICAL LUTHERAN CHURCH, AND EVERY MEMBER THEREOF, ACCEPTS WITHOUT RESERVATION: (1) THE SCRIPTURES OF THE OLD AND NEW TESTAMENT AS THE REVEALED AND INSPIRED WORD OF GOD AND THE ONLY RULE AND NORM OF FAITH AND PRACTICE. (2) ALL THE SYMBOLICAL BOOKS AS A TRUE PRESENTATION AND EXPOSITION OF THE WORD OF GOD, TO WIT: THE THREE ECUMENICAL CREEDS; *THE UNALTERED AUGSBURG CONFESSION OF 1530; THE APOLOGY OF THE AUGSBURG CONFESSION; THE SMALCALD ARTICLES; THE LARGE AND THE SMALL CATECHISM OF LUTHER; AND THE FORMULA OF CONCORD.*[11]

The Constituting Convention proclaimed the new synod to be one mind with the "orthodox Missouri Synod." Fellowship with the sects was forbidden. The Slovak Synod declined the offer of membership made by the General Council (org. 1867), for it didn't want to have the status of a mission of that body. In fact, the Slovak Synod threatened to discharge any pastor proven to be in the service of the General Council and subsidized by it.

Government of the synod was in the hands of the duly elected officers and a Board of Directors. It held conventions every two years. Screening applicants for the ministry was placed in the hands of the pastoral conference. The Slovak Synod had six visitors and was divided up into three districts, the Eastern, Central, and Western. In some cases, in deciding territorial jurisdiction, the convention ordered duplicate churches in the same areas to close. The first president of the Slovak Evangelical Lutheran Church was Rev. Daniel Laucek. Other offices were: vice-president, treasurer, secretary, and English secretary.

PASTORAL SUPPLY

Appeals were made to the homeland for pastors to alleviate the shortage that was growing more and more acute as the flow of immigrants increased. Pleas were coming in from various groups for pastoral services. The synod published appeals for pastors in the *Church Letters*, the semi-official organ of

461

the Lutheran Church in Hungary. As time went on, growth came to the tiny synod. Helping this growth was the step taken by Slovak pastors in other synods to seek their release in order to affiliate with the Slovak Synod. There were also congregations which joined.

GROWTH OF THE SLOVAK EVANGELICAL LUTHERAN CHURCH (SLOVAK SYNOD)

1909   24 congregations, plus 13 additional congregations. Smaller preaching stations were also served.

1913   27 congregations, plus 14 other affiliates, including mission stations. 8,270 baptized members, and 20 pastors.

1927   39 congregations, plus 18 other affiliates and mission stations. 14,238 baptized members, 32 pastors, 1 professor, 2 Christian day schools with 4 teachers.

1951   63 organized congregations and 4 preaching places, 15,250 communicate members, 20,808 baptized members, 59 ordained pastors, and 6 teachers.

1954   A total of 21,187 baptized members compared to nearly 2,000,000 members in the Missouri Synod. Membership of the Slovak Synod (as it was commonly referred to) was scattered over the eastern half of the UnitedStates.

THE SLOVAK SYNOD AND THE SYNODICAL CONFERENCE

Since its policies and doctrine paralleled that of the Missouri Synod the Slovak Synod had no difficulty convincing itself to join the Synodical Conference, which it did in 1908. In 1935 the Slovaks, together with the Norwegian members of the Conference, gave their opinion that the language condition that then prevailed did not permit organic union on their part with other synods in the Conference. There had been a movement in the early thirties to unite all the synods of the Conference.

THE SLOVAK SYNOD AT WORK

PUBLICATIONS

At first the Slovak Synod had no publications of its own, but used the *Slovak Herald*, the official organ of the Slovak Evangelical Union. Eventually, the official organ of the Slovaks became *The Lutheran*, published in Cleveland, Ohio, by John Pankuch. This was followed in 1906 by *The Witness* published in the Slovak language, and the *Lutheran Beacon*, which the synod published in English. The official publication later became *Svedok*. The Slovak Synod purchased the Svedok Publishing House in Streator, Illinois, in 1910 from the Rev.

Andrew Chovan. Finally, because of increasing indebtedness on the printery, a synodical printing company which offered shares for sale was formed. The Svedok Publishing House was founded in 1915. At times, due to lack of financing, *Svedok* was not published. However, as finances permitted, religious books, including *Luther's Catechism*, were published in Streator. The articles appearing in *Svedok* were strongly confessional and for that reason often came under attack from liberal publications. After a time a publication for youth, the *Young Lutheran,* appeared and was popular.

Later, the Svedok Publishing House was dissolved, again due to money problems. Another attempt also ended in failure, and in 1924 the Slovaks gave up the idea of acquiring their own printery. In spite of its failure, the synod had ambitiously published, among other things, a hymnal and the *Book of Concord.* The synod had maintained a Publication Department in close business association with the Missouri Synod's Concordia Publishing House in St. Louis. The Lutheran Hymnal, introduced in the beginning of the 1940's by the Synodical Conference, came to be introduced in all the congregations of the Slovak Synod.

MISSIONS

An acute shortage of pastors plagued the synod for many years, and most pastors, of necessity, had to serve numerous parishes. The Slovak Synod was appreciative of the work done by the Missouri Synod among the Slovak people and volunteered to supply a Slovak pastor to help the Missouri Synod's work among the Slovaks in Detroit.

In 1913 the Slovak Synod elected its own Mission Board. The synod subsidized mission stations at home and collected money for foreign missions. In 1919 it provided a traveling missionary to serve widely scattered Slovaks. Two years later he reported that his field consisted of eighteen settlements in seven states, with a total of seven hundred souls. These mission stations were located mainly in Indiana, Illinois, Minnesota, Wisconsin, and Iowa. By the early 1920's the synod's mission field extended from Colorado to Virginia and from Texas to Minnesota.

Between 1926 and 1928 the Slovak Synod gave $2,000 to foreign mission work and also helped support the Synodical Conference mission in the South. In 1927 Canada beckoned, for there had been an influx of immigrants there.

During World War I the Slovaks Synod served its members in the Armed Forces mainly through Christian literature.

EDUCATION

Since the Slovak students used the Missouri Synod's Springfield Seminary for their ministerial training, it was the wish of the Slovak Synod to place a professor at Springfield and support him financially. Finally, in 1909 the synod was able to place its professor at the seminary with half of his salary paid by the Missouri Synod. Pastor Stephen Tuhy became the first Slovak instructor to be installed in a Lutheran Seminary anywhere. As it turned out, the professor stayed only one year, accepting a call back into the parish ministry. For more than a decade there was not another Slovak instructor at Springfield.

Some of the pastors organized Christian day schools. However, most of the Christian instruction in the congregations was given, not in day schools, but in classes held after school hours or on Saturday's. It was in the synod's second decade that marked progress was made in establishing church schools.

WORKS OF CHARITY

The Slovak Synod accepted an offer of forty acres of land and $90,000 to establish and maintain the Luther Haven in Oviedo, Florida. This institution of mercy directed its care to orphans, the aged, and superannuated pastors and teachers.

TROUBLED WATER

COMMUNION PROCEDURE DIFFICULTY

Some members of the Slovak congregations felt constrained to sever their connection with the synod over the issue of having to announce for communion. However, by 1926 the issue seemed to be resolved and people accepted the procedure as correct practice.

THE LANGUAGE QUESTION

The member churches of the Slovak Synod clung tenaciously to the Slovak language while, of course, using also the English. The language transition did produce difficulties. To serve the older people in the Slovak language while building a bridge of understanding between them and their Americanized children, and to teach the young pastors to speak Slovak, presented a long-standing problem.

THE SLOVAK SYNOD AND
THE UNION COME TO BAD TERMS

By 1902 the Slovak Evangelical Union had ninety-two chapters with 2,668 members, which number also included pastors. During the first years of the Slovak Synod's existence, it was on friendly terms with the Union, and even accepted financial aid from it. Incidents arose however, to disturb the tranquility. Already in 1895 an opinion was expressed by the Union in convention favoring admission of Reformed Church members. The Union also arranged dances on Saturday nights, which practice was upsetting to the pastors. But the synod also took exception to burial prayers printed in the Ritual Book used by the National Slovak Society and the Slovak Evangelical Union – prayers characterized by the synod as "modern paganism."

The Slovak Synod and the Union came to very bad terms. The synod's charges against the Union can be summed up as follows: It fostered a worldly spirit... tolerated unbelievers and socialists in its midst... treated the pastors of the Slovak Synod with contempt and denounced them in an undignified manner... was unionistic in spirit, fostering union of all Slovak Lutherans regardless of their doctrinal platforms. It also published error in its paper, the *Slovak Herald.*[12] In the past many of the synod pastors had been active in the Union, so active that one of the presidents (John Pelikan) at one time stated that some pastors were more active in the life of organizations than in the service of the church.

In 1905 Pastor Laucek, one of the founders of the Slovak Synod, and its first president, broke all connections with the body because he failed to win support for his contention that the confessional prayer was incorrect, stating it denied the Son of God since it did not expressly say that Christ is the Son of God. The synod's position in this controversy was that both his prayers and the confessional were correct. Laucek was followed by the secretary, Pastor Kvacala, who felt that the Slovak Synod by affiliating with the Synodical Conference was sacrificing its independence. He was upset also by the friendly relations of the synod with the Missouri Synod. Not content with being separatistic, both men became bitter opponents of the synod.

By 1908 there was open hostility between the Slovak Union and the Slovak Synod. The Union took up the cause of Pastor Laucek, accusing the synod – among other things – of denying the Son of God and of being a mission of other synods and even of invalidation the Symbolic Books of the Lutheran Church.

The Slovak Synod responded at its 1908 Convention testifying against "the unionism, syncretism, and various disorders prevailing" in the Union.[13] Time had surely arrived for divorcing church matters completely from the Union. In 1909 the president of the Slovak Synod had to admit that the relations were still not improved. Indeed, it was noted that the Union was still publishing false doctrines, encouraging a spirit of worldliness and was existing as a church within a church. The Union had even established a mission fund of its own in opposition to the Slovak Synod's fund. Accusations continued to bounce back and forth between the two groups.

Things came to a head after the 1911 Convention of the Slovak Synod. Two pastors, in defense of the Union, left the synod and soon a new opposition was formed. The two pastors who separated from the synod over the confessional prayer issue also took part in founding a new synod, which was comprised of only five pastors and two congregations. Three other congregations also severed their connection with the Slovak Synod. The attempt that was made in 1912 to unite the parties who were opposed to the Slovak Synod, into a new synod, came to be called the Slovak Evangelical Church of the *Augsburg Confession* in the United States. The men of this group had not been educated in the Missouri Synod but in bodies that became members of the United Lutheran Church in America. As the strained relations continued between the Slovak Synod and the Union, a new fraternal organization was founded, the Evangelical Slovak Union. However, there arose ill feelings among synod pastors toward the new Union, for some felt that this fraternal organization was not making a clear distinction between secular and religious matters.[14]

THE SLOVAKS SYNOD AND OTHERS

THE SLOVAK SYNOD AND THE GENERAL COUNCIL
(ORG. 1867)

At first, most of the Slovak pastors were affiliated with other Lutheran bodies, including the Missouri Synod. After the organization of their own synod the Slovaks continued strong ties with this orthodox German body, including the use of Concordia Seminary at Springfield, Illinois, for the training of its ministerial students. The Generations Council had its own Slav Mission Board, which was very active, carrying on work among the Slovaks through about a dozen Slovak Lutheran pastors who were members of the Council. No love was lost between the Slovak Synod and these pastors. The synod was highly critical of the work performed by the Council and felt that it was intruding into the synod's territory. It accused the Council of false doctrine and practice and of trying to establish good terms with the Lutheran Church in Hungary. At times charges were lodged against the Slovak Synod, accusing it of teaching false doctrine, which charges the synod denied. The General Council wanted to merge the activities of its Slav Board with those of the Slovak Synod, even offering financial support, but the offer was refused.

THE SLOVAK SYNOD AND
THE LUTHERAN CHURCH IN HUNGARY

Though there were strained feelings between the Slovak Synod and the Lutheran Church in Hungary, especially due to published attacks by the latter against the former, nevertheless the Lutheran Church in Hungary wanted the members of the Slovak Church in the United States to be under its jurisdiction voluntarily. In turn the Church in Hungary was willing to promise some kind of benefits.[15]

The leaders of the Slovak Synod expended much energy defending the synod against published charges made against its doctrines and practices. Finally, in 1911 it resolved to publish a brochure, which both set forth its position and outlined the aberrations of the Lutheran Church in Hungary. The synod reached the conclusion that orthodox Christians could not remain in the Lutheran Church in Hungary, and accused it of tolerating error and unionism and of having hierarchical tendencies. The Slovak Synod did not consider the leaders in that Lutheran body to be true Lutherans.

The First World War brought an end to the Austro-Hungarian Empire. Nationalities which had been clamoring for independence received it. The result was the formation of several new states besides Hungary: Finland, Estonia, Latvia, Lithuania, Poland, Yugoslavia, and Czechoslovakia. Thee new nation of Czechoslovakia contained both German and Slovak Lutherans. These were organized in two bodies: the German Evangelical Church in Bohemia, Moravia, and Silesia (the smaller church) and the Evangelical Lutheran Church of the *Augsburg Confession* in Slovakia (some 400,000 members). The Hungarian Lutheran Church of the *Augsburg Confession* (about 500,000 members) became scattered over the entire country.

Yugoslavia was home to the southern Slavs and consisted of parts of the former Austro-Hungarian Empire. The Lutherans in Yugoslavia, as in Czechoslovakia, were divided into a German as well as a Slovak body. Germans from the Lutheran Church of Hungary formed the German Evangelical Lutheran Church of the *Augsburg Confession*. The Slovak body was made up of people belonging to the former countries of Serbia, Croatia, and Slovenia.

It took three years following the end of Word War II and the formation of the Republic of Czechoslovakia for the Slovak Lutherans in Slovakia to effect the permanent organization of the Lutheran Church of Slovakia. However, in America the Slovak Synod promoted the founding of a free Slovak Lutheran Church – a church not encumbered by ties to the government. It should be noted that Slovak Lutherans in the United States- including some from the Slovak Synod – participated in the liberating of Czechoslovakia, having volunteered for service with the Czech Army of Liberation. The Slovak Synod even provided a chaplain. (After World War I the Slovaks disassociated themselves from Hungary and instead allied themselves with the Czechs of Bohemia, thus forming the Republic of Czechoslovakia [October 28, 1918]. Two decades later (1939) Germany invaded Czechoslovakia and declared Slovakia independent. However, later, after World War II, Slovakia rejoined Czechoslovakia (1945). Toward the end of the twentieth century [January 1, 1993] Czechoslovakia divided into two separate states – the Czech Republic and Slovakia. Slovakia lies to the east of the Czech Republic.)[16]

It was though the Rev. John Pelikan that the Slovak Synod in America tried to help the Slovakia Lutheran Church reorganize itself independent of the state. This venture failed, but two independent (free) congregations were organized, which then the Slovak Synod subsidized. The synod even opened a seminary in Val'ká. At the same time it founded a synod in Czechoslovakia. (The Wisconsin and Missouri Synods were both asked to provide professors for the seminary). Classes began at the seminary in January 1922, but within six months the school had to close. The new synod in Slovakia did not receive state recognition. By the end of 1927 the Slovak Synod's work in Slovakia had gained three free congregations, numbering 450 souls, served by one pastor. It owned property upon which it owed over $9,000.

THE SLOVAK SYNOD AND THE SLOVAK CONGRESS –
THE FOUNDING OF THE ZION SYNOD

A congress of Slovak Lutherans was held in Pittsburgh in 1919. Up to this time many voices were heard for uniting all Slovak Lutherans in the organization. To the calls for union, the Slovak Synod answered that true unity of spirit is necessary before there can be any organic union.[17] The union which some desired would be a union apart from fellowship with the Missouri Synod, and a union which would embrace various teachings of doctrine rather than the strict orthodoxy of that body, which some felt was leaving too deep an impression on the Slovak Synod. However, the Slovak Synod felt that the spirit of true unity forbade entering into a union with false teachers – such as were found

467

outside its own ranks. While desiring true union of all Slovak Lutherans, the synod maintained the position that union would have to be based on God's Word and the Symbolic Books of the Lutheran Church. Just how deep did the desire for union go among the Slovaks? The Slovak Synod reasoned that if this desire was great enough the Slovaks would attempt to establish a union on the above-mentioned basis.

To the main proponents of union, the dividing issues were of little consequence. To the Slovak Synod, however, they were not mere formalities, which divided the Slovaks but truly important issues, issues of doctrine.

A preliminary meeting in the spirit of 1919 was attended by twenty pastors and twenty-three laymen. The question discussed was whether or not the proposed alliance of Slovak Lutherans should be a nationalistic or a religious union. A number of points were adopted including the favoring of forming an alliance, the purpose of which would be to achieve harmonious cooperation of Slovak Lutherans in social, national, and religious affairs...to achieve cooperation among Slovak Lutherans in charitable work...to promote mutual respect for each other's interests by the church and fraternal organizations...to serve as a joint preparation for religious union of Slovak Lutherans in America. Congregations, organizations, choirs, and individuals could become members of the alliance. Temporary officers were elected.

A Committee on Religious Affairs was elected. However, in its second meeting it became apparent that there were difficulties to be surmounted. Present were representatives of the Slovak Synod and of the United Lutheran Church in America (ULCA). The platform of the Slovak Synod was used to discuss the teachings and practice of the Lutheran Church. When asked whether they agreed with this document, the ULCA men replied that they came not as individuals but as members of their church body and that it was their desire to have the position of the ULCA discussed. A statement which was not complete was read, but the Slovaks could not understand what it embraced. Admitting that the statement was not complete, the ULCA pastors nevertheless wanted the Slovak Synod pastors to accept it in good faith, which they felt they could not do.

While the ULCA Slovaks found no fault with the Slovak Synod's platform, they nevertheless stated that they could not subscribe to it. The Slovaks in the ULCA stated that they could not separate from that body and furthermore, the Slovaks were too weak to maintain separate synods. They felt that the Slovak Lutherans would find better support and protection from the more powerful synods; therefore they invited the Slovak Synod to join the ULCA.[18]

Here is the significant reply made by the members of the Slovak Synod to this invitation: BY THE GRACE OF GOD OUR SYNOD HAS THE PURE TEACHING AND THE CORRECT PRACTICE. MOREOVER, OUR SYNOD IS A SLOVAK BODY. WHY SHOULD WE JOIN A BODY, WHICH DOES NOT HAVE THE PURE TEACHING AND A CORRECT PRACTICE AND WHICH IN ADDITION TO THIS, IS FOREIGN TO US IN SPIRIT AND LANGUAGE?[19]

The ULCA men, of course, did not like being called the apostate party, but they nevertheless continued to extend the invitation to unite. Before the fall meeting of the congress in Pittsburgh the Slovak pastors in both bodies met separately. The Slovak pastors of the ULCA met in Braddock, Pennsylvania, on June 10-12, 1919, and organized the Slovak Zion Synod with nineteen pastors and thirty-two congregations. This new synod was received into the ULCA the year following its organization. The Slovak Zion Synod existed as a bilingual nongeographical synod within the ULCA, and remained such upon entering the merger (as member of the ULCA) forming the Lutheran Church in America (LCA) in 1962. It was the only nongeographical synod in the LCA. Most of the new synod's congregations were located in Pennsylvania, New Jersey, and New York. By 1953 the synod had forty-two pastors and forty-eight congregations, with a baptized membership of about 21,000.

THE SLOVAK CONGRESS CONTINUES AND PRODUCES THE ALLIANCE OF SLOVAK LUTHERANS IN THE UNITED STATES

When the pastors of the Slovak Synod met they decided to demand that religious union be discussed first at the Congress and that a method of procedure for the Slovak Synod be drawn up. Later, when the meeting of the Congress proceeded with the first speaker (from the Slovak Synod) without opening with prayer, a protest was heard from the ULCA side. Pastor Pelikan answered: SINCE THERE ARE AMONG THOSE HERE PRESENT BASIC DIFFERENCES IN DOCTRINE AND PRACTICE, WE OUGHT FIRST OF ALL COME TO AN AGREEMENT AND THEN JOIN IN PRAYER. Debate followed and when a resolution was agreed upon that joint prayer be made after agreement was reached, some left the meeting.

Forty-four congregations and seventeen organizations were represented at the Congress. There were fifteen pastors, thirty-seven lay delegates representing the congregations, and twenty-three lay delegates representing the societies. Both sides were heard from. The Slovak Synod also accused the ULCA of not having a doctrine of plenary (full or total) inspiration of the Scriptures, but the ULCA maintained that it did. The Slovak Synod also accused the ULCA of placing other Lutheran confessional writings on a lower level than the *Augsburg Confession* and of teaching election "in view of faith." (Refer to the discussions on the subject of the election controversy in the chapters concerning the histories of the Norwegian Synod, the Norwegian Lutheran Church in America, the Norwegian Synod of the American Ev. Lutheran Church, the Missouri Synod.) The Slovak Synod accused the ULCA of not having real church discipline and of being lax in its treatment of the problem of secret societies. The ULCA answered these objections by stating that it was impossible to introduce church discipline everywhere, and that it in fact condemned societies whose principles are in opposition to religion. The Slovak Synod maintained its position of purity of doctrine and of putting it into practice. The synod also reiterated its unwillingness to tolerate those not in agreement with all its doctrines, and who refuse to be instructed. The ULCA gave its position as not admitting to altar and pulpit fellowship those who were not one with it in faith.

The doctrinal platform accepted by the entire Congress covered the following doctrines and produced the Alliance of Slovak Lutherans in the United States: (1) HOLY SCRIPTURES: Full inspiration. (2) THE HOLY TRINITY: One God but in three equal persons. Acceptance of the three Ecumenical Creeds and of the *Book of*

Concord as pure exposition of the truth. (3) THE WAY OF SALVATION: Purely by God's grace through faith in Christ; synergism (cooperation in conversion) is condemned. (4) SIN: The cause is in the perverted will of man, not God. Man has original sin and all are born spiritually dead and are inclined to evil. Inherited sin is damnable. (5) FREE WILL: No free will in man in spiritual matters before conversion, not even passive inclination to God's grace. (6) CONVERSION: Not dependent on man in any way, but is totally the Spirit's work. Conversion is not a correction of the old man nor an awakening of dormant powers in man but a divinely wrought rebirth, new spiritual life. (7) JUSTIFICATION: Salvation is solely by God's grace for Christ's sake by faith without man's worthiness or merit. (8) ELECTION: God's grace is universal; God desires all to be converted and saved. Calvinism (predestination to damnation) is rejected. While God does harden hearts, this hardening is not an eternal decree but a punishment brought by God on those who stubbornly resist his grace. There is an election to eternal life. (9) THE CHURCH: Comprised of the total number of the elect. It is the communion of believers, who believe through the Gospel. The Ministry of the Keys belongs to the Christians. The ministers exercise the power of the Church entrusted to all believers. The Church of Christ in every community has the Keys. The Church is invisible due to faith. Every Christian is to affiliate with a visible church organization. The true one teaches the Word of God purely and sincerely in all articles of faith and administers the sacraments strictly according to Christ's institution. A translation of faith into life. The Alliance stands against dead orthodoxy or formalism. Christians should not join larger church bodies or synods whose teachings are not pure and who tolerate pulpit fellowship with the heterodox and errorists, and tolerate in their churches individual members of secret societies. (10) CHILIASM: This doctrine is not founded on the Holy Scriptures and therefore it is to be rejected. (11) THE ANTICHRIST: The teaching of the Alliance accords with the *Smalcald Articles*, Article IV, par. 10. (12) RELATION TO FRATERNAL ORGANIZATIONS: All societies, which foster a false worship and carry on a false religious mission activity are condemned. Benevolent societies such as the following are allowed to stand: SEJ-Slovak Ev. Union; ESJ-Ev. Slovak Union; ZEJ-Women's Ev. Union; SES-Slovak Ev. Society; NSS-National Slovak Society. There is no objection to them as long as they do not assume some secret or aforementioned character.[20]

THE ALLIANCE FAILS

The Alliance was formally confirmed and officers elected. However: IN SPITE OF THE FACT THAT THE ALLIANCE WAS FORMALLY DECLARED TO BE IN EXISTENCE, THERE IS LITTLE EVIDENCE OF ANY LIFE ON ITS PART.[21] This attempt to unite all Slovak Lutherans in the United States was a failure. The mistake, acknowledged by the Slovak Synod's official periodical, was to think that an alliance of Slovak Lutherans could be formed regardless of religious differences. It was a mistake, furthermore, to have secular organizations represented at a meeting or church union and placed on level with Christian churches. Finally, it was a mistake to make such haste in the discussion on religion. Thus it was only a "paper" success. Some wanted to make of the Alliance a new religious body, with all Slovaks leaving their respective synods to become members. But *Sve-*

dok, the official publication, stated that it was opposed to everything, which would be harmful to the Slovak Synod. (It amounted to building a new structure on the ruins of the Slovak Synod.) To some minds, the Alliance, in reality, served to circumvent the Slovak Synod's call to perfect unanimity in doctrine.

THE SLOVAK SYNOD BOWS OUT OF THE ALLIANCE

At its convention in September 1919, the Slovak Synod voted not to aid the founding of an Alliance of Slovak Lutherans in the United States. It argued that it already had a true union based on God's Word and the Lutheran Symbolical Books and did not need a new union. But it declared its willingness to unite with every individual and every true church body, which stood on the foundation of God's Word and the Confessions of the Lutheran Church, but wanted no union with those who didn't. And since the ULCA did not stand on such pure and true foundation, the Slovak Synod could not unite with it as long as it remained unchanged in its position. The Slovak Synod declared the Alliance thus far "infeasible."[22]

Some blamed the Slovak Synod's pastors' refusal to unite in prayer with the others as the reason for the failure of the Alliance. Still, as was mentioned, the other side, though not being able to refute the Slovak Synod's platform, nevertheless could not accept it either. Furthermore, the Slovak Synod pointed out that almost one half of those present at the Congress had scoffed at the Word of God. Also that non-Lutherans and even Socialists had taken part in the Congress. The synod men maintained that joint prayer under such conditions was out of the question.[23]

The Slovak Synod went so far as to declare in 1921 that Rev. Karlovsky, without consulting the officers of the Slovak Synod, had drawn the synod into dangerous negotiations with those who had fallen away from the Lutheran Church, and that he was carelessly engaged as a busy body in attempts to unite outwardly true Lutherans with false Lutherans. Strong words indeed!

THE SLOVAK SYNOD AND THE SLOVAK ZION SYNOD

In 1920 the Slovak Synod and the Slovak Zion Synod carried on polemics regarding union, as well as doctrine and practice, with the result that much bitterness was created. In 1920 the young Zion Synod affiliated with the United Lutheran Church in America. Since the Lutherans in the Zion Synod had received much help from the General Council, and since the General Council was then a part of the ULCA merger, it was an easy matter for that group of Slovaks to rationalize their union with the ULCA. Zion accused the Slovak Synod of tolerating error. Zion's dislike for the Missouri Synod can be seen in the label which it had applied to that synod's doctrine of Absolution, calling it the "Prusso-Missourian Absolution." Many differences separated the two bodies of Slovak Lutherans and feelings ran high between them.

471

THE SLOVAK SYNOD AND A THIRD SLOVAK GROUP

A movement later got under way to form a third body of Slovak Lutherans. The Slovak Synod could only ask, "Why? Why not unite with us? Where are we wrong?" An alliance was formed at a meeting in Cleveland, Ohio, September 26, 1926. The Slovak Synod did not send representatives. However, the appeal for this meeting had not been addressed to the synod officials.

A month after the Cleveland meeting a third party came into existence, which then found itself in agreement with neither the Slovak Synod nor the Slovak Zion Synod. A group of pastors organized the Conference of Slovak Lutheran Pastors in Youngstown, Ohio, in October 1926. This group did not constitute a synod. Its purpose was to study the idea of uniting Slovak Lutherans in the United States. The members of the Conference were independent of synodical affiliation. They felt that personal prejudices, false doctrine, and anarchy were forces keeping the Slovak Church divided.[24] Meanwhile, the Slovak Synod defended both its Platform and its existence. It also recommended free conferences as a means to further the goal of uniting the Slovak Lutherans.

THE SLOVAK SYNOD AND THE
LUTHERAN COUNCIL IN THE U.S.A.

In 1963 the Slovak Synod joined the Inter-Lutheran Consultation, which had been formed the year before, comprising the Lutheran Church-Missouri Synod, the Lutheran Church in America, and The American Lutheran Church. A condition stipulated "that at no time shall the Doctrinal Unity Committee or the representatives of the Slovak Synod violate or compromise the scriptural position of the Slovak Synod."

In 1964 the Slovak Synod and the Missouri Synod were the only members left in the Synodical Conference. When the two synods met at Ann Arbor, Michigan, July 28-30, 1964, the delegates asked the Wisconsin Synod and the Evangelical Lutheran Synod (Norwegian) to reevaluate their actions in withdrawing from the Synodical Conference, as well as the basis for doing so, considering the opportunities and challenges the Conference presented.

The following year found the Slovak Synod approving membership in the Lutheran Council in the U.S.A., the same year that its affiliate did.

After the 1965 Slovak Convention, at which it voted to join the Council (LCUSA), the Doctrinal Commission of the Wisconsin Synod asked President Oscar J. Naumann to address a letter to the Slovak Synod in which was expressed...

...OUR DEEP REGRET WITH RESPECT TO THE DOCTRINAL POSITION WHICH THE SLOVAK SYNOD HAS TAKEN IN RECENT YEARS IN THE MATTER OF CHURCH FELLOWSHIP...AS YOU WILL RECALL, IT WAS PRIMARILY THE DOCTRINE OF CHURCH FELLOWSHIP WHICH OVER THE PAST TWO DECADES WAS THE SUBJECT OF INTENSE STUDY AND DISCUSSION INVOLVING BOTH YOUR SYNOD AND OURS. WE REFER TO THE VARIOUS FORUMS SET UP BY THE SYNODICAL CONFERENCE, THE SEVERAL THEOLOGIANS' CONCLAVES, AND, MORE RECENTLY, THE TWO MEET-

INGS OF OUR RESPECTIVE DOCTRINAL COMMITTEES. DURING THE EARLY YEARS OF THESE DISCUSSIONS WE HAD FELT THAT YOUR SYNOD STILL SHARED THE POSITION OF THE WISCONSIN SYNOD.

AT THE LAST TWO MEETINGS, HOWEVER, BETWEEN YOUR DOCTRINAL UNITY COMMITTEE AND OUR COMMISSION (FEB. 1964 AND MAY 1965) YOUR REPRESENTATIVES GAVE EVIDENCE OF HOLDING A DIVERGENT POSITION. AS YOU MAY RECALL, WE CONTENDED ON THE BASIS OF GOD'S WORD THAT PULPIT FELLOWSHIP, ALTAR FELLOWSHIP, PRAYER FELLOWSHIP, FELLOWSHIP IN WORSHIP, FELLOWSHIP IN CHURCH WORK, IN MISSIONS, IN CHRISTIAN EDUCATION, IN CHRISTIAN CHARITY, IN SO FAR AS THEY ARE JOINT EXPRESSIONS OF FAITH, ARE ALL ESSENTIALLY ONE AND THE SAME THING, AND ARE ALL PROPERLY COVERED BY A COMMON DESIGNATION, NAMELY, CHURCH FELLOWSHIP. WE FURTHERMORE HELD THAT SUCH CHURCH FELLOWSHIP, IN ORDER TO BE GOD-PLEASING, IS POSSIBLE ONLY FOR SUCH AS SHARE A COMMON DOCTRINAL POSITION IN AGREEMENT WITH THE HOLY SCRIPTURES. YOUR REPRESENTATIVES NOT ONLY FELT CONSTRAINED TO TAKE ISSUE WITH THE FELLOWSHIP POSITION HELD BY OUR SYNOD, BUT ALSO DEFENDED THE PARTICIPATION OF OFFICIAL SLOVAK SYNOD REPRESENTATIVES IN THE JOINT DEVOTIONS HELD IN CONJUNCTION WITH THE INTER-LUTHERAN CONSULTATION OF RECENT YEARS, INVOLVING REPRESENTATIVES OF CONFLICTING CONFESSIONAL POSITIONS.

SUBSEQUENT TO THESE DISCUSSIONS YOUR SYNOD HAS NOW DECIDED TO JOIN THE PROPOSED LUTHERAN COUNCIL IN THE U.S.A. IN THIS CONNECTION WE NOTE THE VARIOUS AREAS OF JOINT CHURCH WORK WHICH WILL BE CARRIED ON IN THE NAME AND UNDER THE AUSPICES OF THE PROPOSED LCUSA. WE HOLD THAT ALL MEMBERS OF THE LCUSA MUST ASSUME RESPONSIBILITY FOR ITS ENTIRE PROGRAM, EVEN THOUGH INDIVIDUALLY MEMBERS MAY EXERCISE THE OPTION OF REFRAINING FROM THIS OR THAT PARTICULAR SPHERE OF ACTIVITY. IN VIEW OF THE FOREGOING IT HAS BECOME APPARENT TO US THAT THE SLOVAK SYNOD NO LONGER SHARES THE POSITION WE ONCE HELD IN COMMON...WE DEEM IT NECESSARY REGRETFULLY TO REPORT TO THE MEMBERSHIP OF OUR SYNOD THE CHANGE IN FELLOWSHIP PRINCIPLES, WHICH WE NOW OBSERVE IN YOUR SYNOD'S COURSE...[25]

Vice president Kucera of the Slovak Synod responded for the president, who was in Argentina at the time:

YOU VOICE YOUR "DEEP REGRET WITH RESPECT TO THE DOCTRINAL POSITION WHICH THE SLOVAK SYNOD HAS TAKEN IN RECENT YEARS IN THE MATTER OF CHURCH FELLOWSHIP," AND YOU STATE THAT AT THE LAST TWO MEETINGS BETWEEN OUR DOCTRINAL UNITY COMMITTEE AND YOUR COMMISSION...OUR REPRESENTATIVES "GAVE EVIDENCE OF HOLDING A DIVERGENT POSITION."

BROTHER NAUMANN—I AM FIRMLY CONVINCED IN MY OWN HEART THAT OUR SLOVAK SYNOD IS STILL A FAITHFUL FOLLOWER OF THE LORD JESUS CHRIST AND, IMPERFECT THOUGH WE MAY BE, UNDER THE GUIDANCE OF THE HOLY SPIRIT AND TO THE BEST OF OUR SINCERE CHRISTIAN ABILITY WE ARE ALWAYS STRIVING TO DO THE WILL OF OUR LORD...WHEREVER WE CAN AND HOWEVER WE CAN, TO HIS GLORY AND FOR THE BEST POSSIBLE WELFARE OF OUR NEIGHBOR. THE FACT THAT OUR SYNOD HAS DECIDED TO JOIN THE PROPOSED LUTHERAN COUNCIL IN THE U.S.A. IS NO INDICATION WHATSOEVER THAT WE HAVE GONE ASTRAY OR EVEN COMPROMISED OUR POSITION. WE SIMPLY FEEL, AFTER MUCH

PRAYERFUL CONSIDERATION, THAT THIS IS THE THING TO DO FOR SUCH A TIME AS THIS. SHOULD GOD IN THE FUTURE REVEAL TO US EVIDENCE THAT WE HAVE NO RIGHT TO PARTICIPATE IN THE COUNCIL, WE WILL NATURALLY OBEY HIS WILL — GLADLY AND WILLING.[26]

The 1967 Convention of the Wisconsin Ev. Lutheran Synod resolved to suspend fellowship with the Slovak Synod on the basis of Romans 16:17-18, in an action similar to that preformed toward the Missouri Synod six years earlier. Among the reasons given for this action were:

...THAT THE SLOVAK SYNOD HAS JOINED THE LUTHERAN COUNCIL IN THE UNITED STATES OF AMERICA, A NEWLY CONSTITUTED ORGANIZATION OF SYNODS OF CONFLICTING CONFESSIONAL POSITIONS, AND IT HAS BECOME EVIDENT FROM A RECENT OFFICIAL COMMUNICATION THAT THE SYNOD OF EV. LUTHERAN CHURCHES NO LONGER HOLDS ITS FORMER SCRIPTURAL PRINCIPLES ON CHURCH FELLOWSHIP.[27]

THE SLOVAK SYNOD MERGES WITH
THE LUTHERAN CHURCH-MISSOURI SYNOD

The Slovak Synod had been close to the Missouri Synod from the beginning. From its infancy the Slovak Synod declared its position in doctrine and practice to be in full agreement with that of the Missouri Synod. The Slovak Synod's closeness to the much larger synod, whose founders were German, was exemplified in its use of that synod's educational institutions, and by standing faithfully by Missouri's side when the other members of the Synodical Conference (ELS and WELS) suspended fellowship with her. The Slovak Synod even accompanied the Missouri Synod into membership in the LCUSA. Finally, the Slovak Synod merged with its much larger sister synod in January 1971. When 20,000 member Slovak Synod merged with the 2.5 million member Missouri Synod, it became known as the Slovak Evangelical Lutheran Church District of that synod.

Footnotes for Chapter Twenty-Nine

1 George Dolak, *A History of the Slovak Evangelical Lutheran Church*, 1902-1927, (St. Louis, MO: 1955), p. 3.

2 Dolak, *A History...*, pp. 4-7.

3 Dolak, *A History...*, pp. 9.

4 Ben Maddow, *A Sunday Between Wars- The Course of American Life From 1865-1917*, (New York, NY: W.W. Norton & Company, 1979), p. 169.

5 Dolak, *A History...*, pp. 15.

6 Dolak, *A History...*, pp. 17.

7 Dolak, *A History...*, pp. 19.

8 Dolak, *A History...*, pp. 23.

9 Dolak, *A History...*, pp. 25.

10 Dolak, *A History...*, pp. 40.

11 Edwin L. Lueker, Editor-in-Chief, *Lutheran Cyclopedia*, (St. Louis, MO: Concordia Publish-

ing House, 1954), p. 984.

12 Dolak, *A History*..., pp. 132, 133.

13 Dolak, *A History*..., pp. 64.

14 Dolak, *A History*..., pp. 67.

15 Dolak, *A History*..., pp. 71.

16 Robert Famighetti, Editor, *The World Almanac and Book of Facts* 1987, (Mahwah, NJ: K-III Reference Corporation, 1996), p.817.

17 Dolak, *A History*..., pp. 88.

18 Dolak, *A History*..., pp. 91.

19 Dolak, *A History*..., pp. 91.

20 Dolak, *A History*..., pp. 95-98.

21 Dolak, *A History*..., pp. 99.

22 Dolak, *A History*..., pp. 99.

23 Dolak, *A History*..., pp. 99.

24 Dolak, *A History*..., pp. 104.

25 *Proceedings 1967*, Wisconsin Evangelical Lutheran Synod, pp. 275-277.

26 *Proceedings 1967*, Wisconsin Evangelical Lutheran Synod, pp. 275-277.

27 *Proceedings 1967*, Wisconsin Evangelical Lutheran Synod, pp. 297.

CHAPTER THIRTY

THE AMERICAN LUTHERAN CHURCH
1920 - 1960
MEMBER SYNODS

1

THE EVANGELICAL LUTHERAN JOINT SYNOD OF OHIO
1818 - 1930

The American Lutheran Church (ALC) was organized on August 11, 1930, at Toledo, Ohio. It was formed by a merger of the Evangelical Lutheran Joint Synod of Ohio and Other States (1818), the Evangelical Lutheran Synod of Iowa and Other States (1854), and the Evangelical Lutheran Synod of Buffalo (1845).

This body continued through 1960, in which year it took part in the constitution convention with the Evangelical Lutheran Church (Norwegian) and the United Evangelical Lutheran Church (Danish) to form the American Lutheran Church (TALC). TALC began to function as a Lutheran body on January 1,

1961.

The histories of the three synods which formed the American Lutheran Church (ALC) are especially interesting. In this chapter a summary of these histories awaits you.

EARLY HISTORY OF THE OHIO SYNOD

INFLUENCE OF THE ALLEGHENY MOUNTAINS

At the close of the eighteenth century many Lutherans settlers left the old settlements east of the mountains and crossed over into the Northwest Territory. The Allegheny Mountains formed a natural boundary separating the new frontier from the old civilization. When Ohio was made a state in 1803 many more Lutheran settlers crossed over and made their home within its borders. The wonderfully fertile land in the river valleys served as a powerful attraction to many who were willing to move on to the west. Crops far exceeded expectations in their abundance. Rivers and Lake Erie afforded transportation routes. Lutheran pastors soon followed the pioneers into Ohio.

PIONEER PREACHERS IN OHIO

Lutheran historian Abdel Wentz explains early Lutheran mission work thus:

FOR A LONG TIME IT HAD BEEN THE CUSTOM OF MINISTERS WHO LIVED NEAREST TO THE FRONTIER TO UNDERTAKE MISSIONARY TOURS ON THEIR OWN INITIATIVE, TRAVELING INTO REMOTE DISTRICTS, PREACHING THE WORD AND ADMINISTERING THE SACRAMENTS. THE PIONEER WORK IN THE LUTHERAN CHURCH WEST OF THE ALLEGHENIES WAS DONE BY MEN WHO ENTERED THE FIELD AS "INDEPENDENT PREACHERS," WITHOUT SYNODICAL CONNECTION, TO ANSWER THE CALL OF LUTHERAN FRONTIERSMEN...THE WORK OF HOME MISSIONS, AS WE CALL IT TODAY, WAS OFFICIALLY UNDERTAKEN BY THE MINISTERIUM OF PENNSYLVANIA IN 1804. THE PLAN OF THE SYNOD, AS IT WENT INTO EFFECT IN 1806, PROVIDED FOR THE SENDING OUT OF TWO OR THREE MEN EACH YEAR DURING THE SUMMER MONTHS.[1]

The first of the pioneer preachers to follow the people across the Alleghenies was John Stauch. Licensed by the Pennsylvania Ministerium in 1793, Stauch was ordained in 1804. In 1806 he moved to Columbia County, Ohio. In his own words: ...THE FIRST LUTHERAN SETTLEMENT IN OHIO WAS MADE IN 1800 IN JEFFERSON COUNTY. THE FIRST YEAR I ORGANIZED TWELVE CONGREGATIONS IN THE COUNTIES OF COLUMBIA, JEFFERSON, WARREN, STARK, BEAVER, AND MERCER. (The last two counties listed were in Pennsylvania.) That Stauch was a missionary at heart is shown by the astounding record he left by his travels, for it is said that he journeyed 100,000 miles on horse back and on foot in the wilderness of Ohio. Bear in mind that 95 percent of Ohio was covered by forest when the pioneers first started to settle in the state.

The second pastor in Ohio was William Foerster, who came from Shenandoah, Virginia, and settled in Fairfield County in 1806. In 1807 he brought his

478

family of fifteen children from Virginia and settled them on a tract of 1920 acres north of Lancaster.

In 1807 Paul Henkel, who had pastorates in the Valley of Virginia (including New Market) made his first missionary trip to Ohio. His son Charles also worked there. Paul Henkel was very energetic. Not only did he engage himself with extensive missionary travels, he was also several times an author, as well as a publisher. Furthermore, he was also an organizer of the North Carolina Synod (1803), the Ohio Synod (1818), and the Tennessee Synod (1820).

John Reinhard occupied a unique position among the pioneers. It was he who asked the Pennsylvania Ministerium for pastors in Ohio. After Stauch arrived, Reinhard became his catechist, as well as his student. After being trained by Stauch, he was admitted by the Pennsylvania Ministerium in 1812. In 1819, as a pioneer missionary, he forged westward, almost to Fort Wayne, Indiana.

Other pioneers in Ohio included G.H. Weygandt, Jacob Leist and Henry Huet. Weygandt was instructed by Stauch in his parent's home, was licensed in 1810, and ordained in 1815. (The gavel used at the conventions of the Ohio Synod was made from wood taken from the old Weygandt parsonage in which the first conference of Ohio pastors was held.) Leist served in Ohio from 1812 to 1871. During 1818 he served as principal of the academy at Tarlton, Picaway County. Henry Huet was also prepared by Stauch, licensed in 1812 and served fourteen congregations. He is buried at Youngstown, Ohio.

THE FIRST CONFERENCE WEST OF THE ALLEGHENIES

In October of 1812 the first conference of Lutheran ministers west of the Allegheny Mountains was convened in Westmorland County, Pennsylvania, at Stecher's church. Eight pastors were present, including Weygandt and Heim as guests. Four pastors were absent.

In 1814 the Pennsylvania Ministerium informed this Ohio Special Conference that it would be satisfactory if the conference sent but one pastor as delegate to the annual meeting of the synod. The conference was also given the right to examine sermons, journals of candidates for the ministry, and was also given the right to transfer candidates from place to place, indicating this on the candidate's license. In 1816 the conference asked the Pennsylvania Ministerium for permission to organize a separate ministerium. Permission was granted, and on September 14, 1818, the ministers in Ohio met together for the first General Conference of Evangelical Lutheran Preachers in the State of Ohio and Adjacent States. The ministerium met at Somerset, Perry County, Ohio. Its first president was John Stauch. Paul Henkel was secretary, and G.H. Weygandt was the treasurer. Fifteen pastors and two catechists were placed on the roll. Later, the designation "synod" was substituted for "ministerium" in the title. The young synod faithfully maintained contact with its parent body, the Pennsylvania Ministerium.

The number of synods being formed about this time gave renewed interest to the establishment of closer relations among the Lutherans. Pastor Gottlieb Shober's "Proposed Plan" for a new central body, the General Synod, was presented to the Pennsylvania Ministerium in June 1819 and adopted. Copies of the Proposed Plan were printed and distributed over a wide area to facilitate congregational discussion and reaction, a process that took about a year. When the Proposed Plan was presented to the Ohioans it was adopted by them. However, a little latter, in 1820, they changed their minds and declined to join the General Synod due to this body's noncommittal attitude regarding Chiliasm, pulpit and altar fellowship, and lodge affiliation. When the Pennsylvania Ministerium withdrew in 1823 from the General Synod, the Ministerium advised the Ohioans not to affiliate with it. Patterned after the constitution of the General Assembly of the Presbyterian Church, the Proposed Plan established what some feared to be too much centralized authority in the General Synod, resulting in infringement on the liberties of individual congregations.

ESTABLISHING OHIO'S OWN SEMINARY

In 1827 Pastor Andrew Henkel and Pastor Heinicke were commissioned, each to spend a month as traveling missionaries in the State of Indiana. The following year, plans for a Theological Seminary were discussed. At this meeting, William Schmidt presented himself, with testimonials from the University of Halle in Germany. In 1830 the first seminary was established in Canton, Ohio, with Schmidt as its first professor. In 1831 this school was moved to Columbus. A note of interest: In 1826 Gettysburg Seminary was opened at Gettysburg, Pennsylvania, by the General Synod. Prior to this, Hartwick Seminary, had been opened at Hartwick, New York, in 1815. In 1830 Hazelius, of Hartwick Seminary, sent letters out advertising this school as an alternative to Gettysburg Seminary, and it was this invitation which helped to prod the Ohioans to act toward founding their own seminary. When the Ohio Synod had arrived at this decision, candidate Schmidt offered to take charge of the institution without remuneration. The school was named the Theological Seminary of the Evangelical Lutheran Synod of Ohio. When it opened it had a grand enrollment of two students.

In 1831, fourteen acres of land were purchased at Columbus, Ohio, for the transferral of the seminary from Canton. Among the first students at Columbus were C. Spielmann and W. Lehmann. After Professor Schmidt's death in 1829, Charles E. Schaeffer of Hagerstown, Maryland, and F. Winckler of Newark, New Jersey, were called as professors.

Language trouble began. Evidently Schaffer believed that all classes should be taught in German, while Winckler promoted the use of English. Schaeffer finally resigned and Winckler remained. At the Synod of Zanesville, 1844, it was resolved that German should be the only medium of instruction at the seminary, while English should be taught as a subject. The ensuing dissatisfaction caused Winckler to resign in 1845. The seminary was closed until 1847 when Professor Lehman began to teach. The seminary came to be known as Capital University.

FRIENDS WITH EVERYONE

The Ohio Synod was friendly with all Lutheran synods – also with the Reformed Church. At the fifth meeting of the Ohio Synod, two Reformed pastors were recognized as "advisory brethren." In the meeting of 1826 a Methodist preacher by the name of Plimpton had preached at one of the services. Such unionistic practice in Lutheran synods was widely promoted mid-century by a movement called "American Lutheranism," sponsored by leaders of the General Synod. Its aim was to accommodate Lutheranism to American life, thus causing it to blend in with prevailing religious movements and practices. The result was a faux Lutheranism.

DIVISION INTO DISTRICTS- A NEW NAME

In 1831 the Ohio Synod was divided into an Eastern and a Western District, with other districts to be added later. Among these was the first English District (1836). Language difficulty caused the first English District to leave Ohio and to join the General Synod in 1841. It became known as the East Ohio Synod. Still later, it withdrew and joined the General Council, taking the name English Synod of Ohio. Yet a third English District was organized in 1857 and later, in 1867, without the consent of the mother synod, joined the General Council in 1867. It took the name English District Synod of Ohio. Then a fourth English District was added in 1869.

Other districts were also added: Southern (later merged into the Western), Northwestern (largely due to a group seceding from the Missouri Synod during the predestination controversy, when many accused Missouri of preaching a "new doctrine"), Northern (1851), Concordia (1876), Wisconsin (1890), Minnesota (1890), Kansas-Nebraska (1890), Texas (1890), Canada (1908), and Australia (1908).[2]

Several attempts were made to publish a German paper but proved unsuccessful. A German language church paper published 1840-45 by the Pennsylvania Ministerium, and *Der Lutheraner*, published by the Missouri Synod, were read by the Ohio Synod's members. In 1842 *The Lutheran Standard* appeared, followed later, in 1860, by a German language paper.

THE COMING OF THE LOEHE MEN – A HEART FOR AMERICAN MISSIONS

In Neuendettelsau, Bavaria, lived and labored a Lutheran pastor by the name of Johann Konrad Wilhelm Loehe. About the middle of the nineteenth century his name became synonymous with foreign mission work in America. Missionary F.C. Wyneken – who himself had come to American in 1838 to bring spiritual aid to the many scattered Lutherans here—later returned to Germany in 1841 to report on the spiritual needs of the Lutherans and the terrible shortage of missionary manpower as he had personally viewed it in Indiana, Ohio, and Southern Michigan. While Wyneken toured Germany,

481

lecturing on the deplorable conditions of Lutheranism in the "western" settlements of America, he met Loehe, who immediately felt the challenge of supplying Lutheran—that is truly Lutheran—missionaries for frontier America.

Loehe published a plea for the people to give preachers for America. A fund of 600 gulden (a gulden was worth about 40 cents at the time) was donated by the churches. Besides this, two men, Adam Ernst and George Burger, responded to the appeal and revealed their desire to be trained for the Lutheran ministry and to be sent to America. Loehe, with the help of Pastor Wucherer, set up a course of training for these two students, the objective being to qualify Ernst and Burger as teachers. These men arrived in America in 1842. Ernst taught in a German school in Columbus, and Burger attended the seminary at Columbus in order to finish his training.

Another man, Wilhelm Sihler, who later played on important role in organizing the Missouri Synod, came to America with Ernst and Burger. Wyneken's "Appeal" had impressed itself on his heart and so, after giving up his job of private tutor, and armed with recommendations from Dr. Rudelbach and Pastor Loehe, Sihler came to America and began a preaching ministry in Pomeroy, Ohio, January 1, 1844. These men were called *Sendlings* or emissaries, and also *Nothelfer* or emergency men. By 1847 Loehe had prepared and sent to America twenty-three such emergency men. By 1853 his efforts placed eighty-two theological candidates in America.

When Loehe sent his emissaries to American he instructed them to pledge allegiance to the Lutheran Confessional Writings and also advised them to join a truly Lutheran synod. Walter A. Baepler points out:

> AFTER SURVEYING THE LUTHERAN CHURCH IN AMERICA, LOEHE REACHED THE CONCLUSION THAT THE MICHIGAN AND THE OHIO SYNOD WERE THE ONLY ORTHODOX LUTHERAN GROUPS IN THE UNITED STATES. HE SUGGESTED TO HIS MISSIONERS, THEREFORE, THAT THEY ASSOCIATE THEMSELVES WITH EITHER OF THESE SYNODS. UNTIL THE TIME OF THE ORGANIZATION OF THE MISSOURI SYNOD ALL OF LOEHE'S MEN HAD BEEN MEMBERS OF THE OHIO SYNOD WITH THE EXCEPTION OF CRAEMER, HATTSTAEDT, LOCHNER, AND TRAUTMANN, WHO HAD JOINED THE MICHIGAN SYNOD. LOEHE WAS INTERESTED ESPECIALLY IN THE THEOLOGICAL SEMINARY OF THE OHIO SYNOD AT COLUMBUS, OHIO, AND HOPED THAT IN SOME MANNER HE COULD USE THIS INSTITUTION IN THE DEVELOPMENT OF HIS AMERICAN MISSION PROJECTS.[3]

ATTEMPTS AT FORMING A NEW CONSERVATIVE SYNOD—LOEHE'S MEN LEFT THEIR MARK

The influx of German candidates for the ministry strengthened the conservative party of the synod. However, they did not remain long in Ohio. Disappointed by its use of the unionistic formula for the Lord's Supper ("Christ says this is my Body, etc."—wording accepted by the Reformed Church) and disappointed by other liberal tendencies (e.g. allowance of lodge membership among the clergy), and on the other hand, encouraged by the sound confessional stand of Dr. Walther in *Der Lutheraner*, of which Walther was the editor, Loehe's men finally, on September 18, 1845, severed their connection with the Ohio Synod. These men, together with Wyneken, agreed to call a meeting at Cleveland to organize a confessional Lutheran synod. Pastor Ernst informed C.F.W. Walther, who ministered to the newly immigrated Saxons in Missouri, of the contemplated meeting. Since the Saxons had held aloof from joining any synodical body, neither Walther nor other representatives of that group attended the meeting, but in a letter to them, Walther praised and blessed their efforts. At the Cleveland meeting it was decided not to form a new synod at that time; instead, they would send delegates to Missouri to meet with the Saxons and endeavor to include them.

Though the conservatives withdrew from the Ohio Synod, nevertheless the synod under the leadership of Lehman and Loy declared its unconditional acceptance of the Lutheran Confessions in 1848. Loehe's men had indeed left their mark on the synod.

OHIO'S CONTACT WITH OTHER SYNODS

OHIO AND THE MISSOURI SYNOD

Efforts to form a new, truly Lutheran synod did succeed and in 1847 the Missouri Synod was founded. Ohio's contact with this young synod in the free conferences of 1856-59 deepened the confessionalism of the Ohio Synod and caused it to take a determined stand against anti-Christian secret societies. And it was finally the failure of the General Council to define its position of the "four points"—one of which concerned lodge membership—that caused the Ohio Synod to withdraw from the Council, although it was present at the preliminary meetings in 1866 and 1867.

In 1868 fraternal relations were established with the Missouri Synod (org. 1847). This was the outcome of a resolution passed by the Ohio Synod at Woodville, Ohio, in 1866 to appoint a committee to confer with a similar Missouri Synod committee, to promote friendly relations. A colloquy was then held at Columbus, March 4-6, 1868. This was followed by a colloquy between the Missouri and Wisconsin Synods on August 4-5, 1869.

At first the Missouri and Ohio Synods disagreed on the Office of the Ministry. But in its convention at Dayton, Ohio, October 1870, the Ohio Synod declared its acceptance of Missouri's doctrine. At this convention the Ohio Synod also set the stage for cooperation between the two synods, which saw eye to eye doctrinally.

A meeting of representatives of the Ohio, Norwegian, Missouri, and Wisconsin Synods took place in Chicago, January 11-13, 1871. On July 20, 1872 the Synodical Conference was organized, the following synods taking part: Ohio (1818), Missouri (1847), Wisconsin (1850), Norwegian Lutheran Synod (1853), Minnesota (1860), Illinois (or, Synod of Illinois and Adjacent States, 1846).

At this time the Ohio Synod was prepared to accept Walther's plan of state synods. According to the plan, the boundary lines of synods using the same language would be fixed along geographical boundaries lines. For the synods this meant surrendering their present identity and amalgamating congregations of various synods into new geographical bodies. The Wisconsin Synod was also ready to adopt the state synod proposal, if the state synods would actually remain as synods and not merely become districts of a larger synod, for example, the Missouri Synod.

The intimate friendship which existed between Ohio and Missouri is shown by the action of Ohio's Capital University conferring the degree of Doctor of Divinity upon Walther in 1878. This friendship was also evidenced in the calling of Professor Frank from the Missouri Synod as successor to Professor Lehman as President of Capital University. However, the friendship and fellowship existing between the two synods was destined to change...dramatically ...because of the predestinarian controversy.

In 1877 and 1879 Dr. Walther of the Missouri Synod read from an essay before the Western District of that synod, which caused a deep reaction in the Ohio Synod. The essay was read in connection with the general theme of the two conventions: ALSO WITH ITS DOCTRINE CONCERNING THE ELECTION OF GRACE THE EVANGELICAL LUTHERAN CHURCH GIVES ALL GLORY TO GOD ALONE. In 1877, at the Convention held at Altenburg, Missouri, Walther discussed Predestination on the basis of the *Formula of Concord*. The Third Theses reads: THE LUTHERAN CHURCH TEACHES THAT IT IS FALSE AND WRONG TO TEACH THAT NOT THE MERCY OF GOD AND THE MOST HOLY MERIT OF CHRIST ALONE, BUT THAT ALSO IN US THERE IS A CAUSE OF THE ELECTION OF GOD, FOR THE SAKE OF WHICH GOD HAS ELECTED US UNTO ETERNAL LIFE. In explanation, Dr. Walther declared: GOD FORESAW NOTHING, ABSOLUTELY NOTHING, IN THOSE WHOM HE RESOLVED TO SAVE WHICH MIGHT BE WORTHY OF SALVATION, AND EVEN IF IT BE ADMITTED THAT HE FORESAW SOME GOOD IN THEM, THIS, NEVERTHELESS, COULD NOT HAVE DETERMINED HIM TO ELECT THEM FOR THAT REASON, FOR, AS THE SCRIPTURES TEACH, ALL GOOD IN MAN ORIGINATES IN HIM. Thus Dr. Walther rejected a terminology used earlier in the Church, namely, that God elected people to salvation "in view of faith."

Professor F.A. Schmidt of the Norwegian Seminary at Madison, Wisconsin, presented Walther on January 2, 1879, with his objections to Walther's statements, saying, "I can no longer go with you." In January 1880 Schmidt, in a monthly periodical *Altes Und Neus (Old and New)*, vehemently attacked Dr. Walther, and the predestination controversy was on. A special pastoral conference of the Missouri Synod was held at Chicago for a week, September 29 to October 5, 1880, to discuss the controversy.

Later, when a meeting of the faculties of the Synodical Conference failed to produce an agreement on Predestination, the Ohio representatives left. Schmidt had declared war with Walther on the issue and the latter agreed to give him battle. The Ohio Synod backed Schmidt in a publication.

At the 1881 Fort Wayne Delegate Convention of the Missouri Synod, thirteen theses prepared by Walther on the doctrine in question were accepted by the synod. After the meeting, the pastors resolved that they could no longer recognize Walther's opponents as co-workers. An opposition party left the Missouri Synod and joined the Ohio Synod in 1882 as the Northwestern District. Professor Stellhorn of Fort Wayne had proved to be an opponent of Walther and of Missouri in the controversy and finally accepted a call to the Columbus Seminary of the Ohio Synod.

484

OHIO LEAVES THE SYNODICAL CONFERENCE

In September 1881 the Ohio Synod resolved to sever its fellowship with the Synodical Conference. Professor Frank withdrew as professor from Columbus. He organized the Concordia Synod of Pennsylvania and the Other States (1882), which later became a part of the Missouri Synod. During the controversy, which raged for four years, Professor F. Pieper and Pastor G. Stoeckhardt were leading defenders of Walther's position. Those who opposed Walther and supported Ohio's position, as put forth by Professors Schmidt and Stellhorn, were Dr. Loy of Capital University and Pastors Allwardt, Eirich, and Ernst.

The Iowa Synod and an element of the Norwegians sided with Ohio. (For a thorough discussion of the predestinarian controversy refer to the chapters dealing with the history of the Norwegian Lutheran Church and the Missouri Synod.) The position of the anti-Missourians may be summarized very briefly, namely, that God elects people to salvation "in view of faith" in the merits of Christ. The Norwegian Synod left the Synodical Conference in 1882 mainly to seek agreement among its own members regarding the issues in controversy.

OHIO AND IOWA

Approachments between the Ohio and Iowa Synods came about soon after the Ohio Synod withdrew from the Synodical Conference in 1881. In 1883, at Richmond, Indiana, an informal conference was held. Ten years later, in July 1893 the representatives of Ohio—M. Loy, F.W. Stellhorn, H. Ernst, H.A. Allwardt—met with representatives of the Iowa Synod, among whom were S. Fritschel and W. Proehl, and held a colloquy. As a result six theses were drawn up. However, the theses were not adopted by the synods until another colloquy was held at Toledo in 1909. The Michigan Theses were revised and adopted and became known as the Toledo Theses.

Still, fellowship was not declared between the two synods until Iowa separated from the General Council, of which it had been a quasi-member. This action was taken in 1917, thus paving the way for a declaration of fellowship between the two synods the following year.

OHIO AND THE BUFFALO, IOWA, MISSOURI, AND WISCONSIN SYNODS

From 1903 to 1906 five Intersynodical Conferences were held at Watertown, Wisconsin; Detroit; and Fort Wayne by these five synods. The purpose was to attempt to solve the issues which had arisen concerning the doctrines of Predestination and Conversion. These conferences failed. Some progress was made about a decade later. After 1917 an Intersynodical Committee made up of representatives appointed by their respective synods conferred again on the issues. The theses proposed by the Committee declared that ...CONVERSION IS DUE SOLELY TO GOD'S GRACE AND IN NO

485

RESPECT TO MAN'S CONDUCT, AND THAT THE UNCONVERTED MAN CAN IN NO WAY, NEITHER BY HIS NATURAL POWERS, NOR BY HIS NEW POWERS GRANTED BY GRACE, SUPPRESS OR DIMINISH THIS RESISTANCE.

On April 15, 1925, the Chicago Theses on Conversion, Predestination, and Other Doctrines was accepted by all synods participating—the above mentioned five. Later that same year, representatives of Ohio, Iowa, and Buffalo met with representatives of the Norwegian Lutheran Church (November 18) and adopted the Minneapolis Theses.

A revision was made in the Chicago Theses, which the Missouri Synod rejected at its meeting at River Forest in 1929 upon the recommendation of the examining committee. Missouri saw the revision as not settling the differences, especially in the doctrines of Conversion and Election.

THE MISSOURI SYNOD THEN DREW UP A CONFESSION OF ITS OWN, SETTING FORTH IN CLEAR AND UNMISTAKABLE LANGUAGE ITS DOCTRINAL POSITION. THIS DOCTRINAL STATEMENT, ADOPTED BY THE MISSOURI SYNOD IN 1932 AND KNOWN AS THE BRIEF STATEMENT, WAS ALSO TO SERVE AS THE BASIS FOR ANY FURTHER DELIBERATION WITH THOSE DIFFERING FROM THE MISSOURI SYNOD IN DOCTRINE.[4]

The Minneapolis Theses, adopted at Minneapolis on November 18, 1925, were of great importance to the Ohio, Iowa, and Buffalo Synods. Not only did they become the basis for pulpit and altar fellowship with each other in 1928, they served as the basis for their fellowship with the Norwegian Lutheran Church (later known as the Evangelical Lutheran Church). Two years later, on August 11, 1930 the Ohio, Iowa, and Buffalo Synods merged to form the American Lutheran Church. And on October 29-31, 1930 the Minneapolis Theses also served as the basis for forming the American Lutheran Conference. This was a federation formed by the newly formed American Lutheran Church, the Augustana Synod, The United Evangelical Lutheran Church in America, the Lutheran Free Church, and the Norwegian Lutheran Church.

Briefly, the Minneapolis These stood for the following; (1) Accept...all the canonical books of the Old and New Testaments... as the divinely inspired...Word of God. (2) Accept the "symbolical books" of the Evangelical Lutheran Church...because, they are the presentation of the pure doctrine of the Word of God. (3) Church fellowship presupposes unanimity in the pure doctrine of the Gospel and the confession of the same in word and deed. "Lutheran pulpits for Lutheran pastors only, and Lutheran altars for Lutheran communicants only." (Galesburg Rule). (4) In points of doctrine...endorse the Chicago Theses (1919). (5) No fellowship with lodges.

OHIO ENTERS THE MERGER FORMING
THE AMERICAN LUTHERAN CHURCH (ALC)

At Toledo, Ohio, August 11, 1930, the Ohio Synod merged with the Iowa and Buffalo Synods to form the American Lutheran Church (ALC). The Evangelical Joint Synod of Ohio contributed more than 55% of the constituent element of the merger body, while the Evangelical Lutheran

Synod of Iowa and Other States supplied about 40%, and the tiny Buffalo Synod supplied less than 3%. An Ohio man, C.C. Hein of Columbus, Ohio, was elected first president of the American Lutheran Church. More will be said of the actual merger process in the section dealing with the Iowa Synod.

SUMMARY FACTS ABOUT THE OHIO SYNOD

PROMINENT MEN

W.F. LEHMAN (1820-1880, b. in Wuerttemberg, Germany): He came to America in 1824 and studied under William Schmidt (the first seminary professor) at Columbus. His board was 46 cents a week. He also studied under Pastor Demme of Philadelphia. Lehmann was pastor from 1840-46 in Fairfield County and in Sommerset, Ohio. In 1846 he became professor and later served as president of Capital University. He served as an editor and also was a president of the Synodical Conference.

F.W. STELLHORN (1841-1919, b. in Hanover): He was preeminently the scholar of the Ohio Synod. Educated at Fort Wayne and St. Louis, he was pastor at St. Louis (1865-67) and in Indiana (1867-69). From 1869 to 1874 he served as professor at the Wisconsin Synod's Northwestern College in Watertown, Wisconsin. He taught at Fort Wayne from 1874 to 1881, in which year he severed his connection with the Missouri Synod and accepted a call to Columbus, Ohio. He was president of Columbus Seminary in 1894. Besides authoring commentaries on Romans and the Pastoral Epistles, and Greek Lexicon for the New Testament, he served as editor of two German-language church publications.

M. LOY (1825-1915): He was the most influential man in the Ohio Synod. He studied at Columbus and afterward was pastor at Delaware, Ohio. He became professor at Columbus in 1866. He served as the president of the Ohio Synod and was an editor of the *Standard*, 1864-91. He published *Sermons on the Gospels*, *Sermons on the Epistles*, and other works, including *Story of My Life*.

H.A. ALLWARDT (1840-1910, b. Mecklenberg, Germany): He was educated at Ft. Wayne and St. Louis. He served as pastor at Crystal Lake, Wisconsin, 1874-1910. He became a bitter opponent of his own Missouri Synod. In 1882 he was suspended by his synod, whereupon he organized the Northwestern District of the Ohio Synod. He was particularly outspoken against the Missouri Synod at the Intersynodical Conference of the 20th century.

B.H. SCHUETTE (1843-1926, b. Hanover): He was educated at Capital University and later taught mathematics there. Since 1881 he was professor of theology. He became president of the National Lutheran Council in 1923.

H. ERNST (1842-1928, b. in Hesse-Nassua): He received his education at Wartburg Seminary of the Iowa Synod and at Missouri's St. Louis Seminary. In 1884 he was made professor and president of the Lutheran seminary in St. Paul.

R.C.H. LENSKI (1864-1936): He received his education at Columbus and later was pastor at Baltimore, Trenton, Springfield, and Anna—all in Ohio—

1887-1911. He became a professor at Capital University in 1911 and was the outstanding exegete and homiletician of the Ohio Synod. His exhaustive Commentary on the New Testament and Outlines on the Periscopes are still in wide use.

C.C. HEIN (1869-1937): He was active as the president of the Western District of the synod. He served as president of the Ohio Synod 1925-30 and of the American Lutheran Church 1930-37. He served as delegate to the Eisenach Lutheran World Convention in 1923.

E. POPPEN: Served as president of the American Lutheran Church 1937-1950.

EDUCATIONAL INSTITUTE

Theological Seminary – Columbus, Ohio; Capital University – Columbus, Ohio; Lutheran College – Regina, Saskatchewan; Luther Seminary – St. Paul, Minnesota; Hebron Academy – Hebron, Nebraska; St. John's Academy – Petersburg, W. Virginia.

PUBLICATION HOUSE

The Lutheran Book Concern, Columbus, Ohio.

MEMBERSHIP OF THE SYNOD

At the time of the merger in 1930, the Ohio Synod had 830 pastors, 176,880 communicants, and 275,859 baptized members.

MEMBER SYNODS

2

THE EVANGELICAL
LUTHERAN SYNOD OF IOWA AND OTHER STATES
1854-1930

EARLY HISTORY OF THE IOWA SYNOD

LOEHE'S INFLUENCE

We have already learned about the zealous mission work conducted by Wilhelm Loehe of Neuendettelsau. The Iowa Synod owes its existence in no small way to this man. Not only did Loehe furnish the American mission scene with some of the men who later helped to found the Iowa Synod, he also did much to influence their attitude concerning the doctrine of Church and Ministry, which finally led to their separating from the Missouri Synod. The founding of the Iowa Synod was a direct outcome of the split, which finally occurred between Loehe and his emissaries, and the Missouri Synod.

Between 1842 and the time of his death in 1872, Loehe sent a continuous stream of missionaries to promote the work of the Lutheran Church here in America. Most of these workers ultimately joined the Missouri Synod, for it was Loehe's wish that they seek out and join a truly confessional Lutheran synod. The Ohio and Michigan Synods, to which he directed his first emissaries, ultimately caused him disappointment, for they proved themselves to be synods which did not faithfully adhere to the Lutheran Confessions.

Loehe and his close friend, Wyneken—the pioneer missionary to America who had greatly influenced Loehe toward sending missionaries to America—recognized in the Saxons who had emigrated to Perry County, Missouri, and St. Louis, true sons of the Lutheran Church. Thus it was that Loehe advised his missioners to get in touch with the Saxons. Loehe's emissaries, Sihler and Ernst, communicated with C.F.W. Walther in 1844, asking in a letter whether or not the establishment of a joint synod would be possible. At the time, Sihler and Ernst were members of the Joint Ohio Synod. The next year they withdrew from Ohio in protest of that synod's use of the unionistic formula (i.e. "Christ *says* this is my body, etc...") in the distribution of the Lord's Supper.

In September 1845, at Cleveland, Ohio, Loehe's men met to explore the possibilities of forming a new synod. It was decided to establish personal contact with the Saxons through Sihler and Ernst. These men then journeyed to St. Louis, where they conferred with Walther and his companions. At this meeting Loehe's men were surprised to learn that the various Saxon congregations were presented with a constitution for the purpose of discussing it and even passing on it.

Then, in July 1846 a final preliminary meeting was held at Fort Wayne, Indiana, by the organizers of the Missouri Synod in order to once again go over the proposed constitution of the new synod. Several of Loehe's men were present at this meeting and even signed the draft of the constitution. Formal organization of the Missouri Synod was scheduled for the following year at Chicago.

LOEHE'S RELATIONSHIP WITH
THE MISSOURI SYNOD BEGINS TO COOL

While the reaction of the Loehe men was favorable to the proposed constitution, Loehe's own reaction was somewhat cool. Upon receiving the report from his missionaries, Loehe remarked: THE ENTIRE REPORT GIVES THE IMPRESSION OF SOMETHING THAT IS COMPACT AND COMPLETE... IT IS TOO BAD THAT THE SYNOD HAS NOT YET GROWN MORE MATURE IN ITS ATTITUDES ON CONSTITUTIONAL MATTERS. HOWEVER, IT CANNOT BE DENIED THAT THIS CONSTITUTION, COMPARED WITH ALL OTHER CONSTITUTIONS OF PROTESTANT ORGANIZATIONS IN NORTH AMERICA THAT HAVE COME TO MY ATTENTION, IS BY FAR THE MOST SERVICEABLE AND THE BEST.[5]

When Loehe wrote to the officials of the Missouri Synod in September 1847, transferring the title of the Fort Wayne Seminary to the Saxons—Missouri had asked him to relinquished all rights to the institution, while continuing to support it financially—he stated: WE NOTICE WITH GROWING CONCERN THAT YOUR SYNODICAL CONSTITUTION AS IT HAS NOW BEEN ADAPTED, DOES NOT FOLLOW THE EXAMPLE OF THE FIRST CHRISTIAN CONGREGATION. WE HAVE GOOD REASON TO FEAR

THAT THE STRONG ADMIXTURE OF DEMOCRATIC, INDEPENDENT AND CONGREGATIONAL PRINCIPLES IN YOUR CONSTITUTION WILL DO GREATER DAMAGE THAN THE INTERFERENCE OF PRINCES AND GOVERNMENTAL AGENCIES IN THE CHURCH OF OUR HOMELAND.[6]

In Loehe's remark we see the old European background of the Lutheran Church showing through: a church that is clergy-managed and clergy-controlled. The laymen had little or nothing to say about things. On the other hand, the founders of the Missouri Synod had broken off European ties and had suffered their trial by fire in the Martin Stephan case, which shall be covered in detail in the history of the Missouri Synod. Suffice it to say here that Pastor Stephan, the leader of the Saxons who emigrated from Europe, proved to be a rogue, who tried to establish a clergy-dominated hierarchy, imposing himself at the center as a Lutheran pope. While the people were asked to contribute money, they had little voice in the affairs of the church. His case probably did more than anything else to turn the founding fathers of the Missouri Synod against a clergy-controlled church, for before their very eyes such a church had turned into a pitiful spectacle of popery.

But Loehe, on the other hand, reasoned that the congregations were not competent judges of the ability and worthiness of candidates for the holy ministry, and therefore the choosing of pastors was to be left in the hands of the clergy. Furthermore, he was afraid it would finally come to a display of politics in the church, similar to those involved in choosing representatives for the legislature. Loehe also had his doubts that laymen were advanced far enough in their knowledge of the Scriptures and the Lutheran Confessions to pass their judgment on doctrine.

LOEHE'S BREAK WITH THE MISSOURI SYNOD FINALLY COMES

In spite of the fact that Loehe did not approve constitutions that granted such a degree of power to the congregations, he nevertheless allowed his men to work for a time under the Missouri Synod Constitution. In fact, it seems that Loehe's men did not even seek his advice and opinion regarding the adoption of this important document.

Twice Loehe was invited to attend synodical meetings (1848 and 1850). When he failed to come, the synod appointed President Wyneken and Professor Walther to undertake a journey to Neuendettlesau to meet with Loehe in person to see if the differences could be resolved. A number of meetings took place, which while not settling the matter, did seem to remove some of the difficulties.

However, when the Missourians in the Michigan colonies insisted that their doctrine was that of the Bible, the break with Loehe could no longer be averted. This break finally came about in 1855. Walter A. Baepler, writing in *A Century of Grace*, remarks: LIKE GRABAU [BUFFALO SYNOD], LOEHE DID NOT BELIEVE THAT EVERY CHRISTIAN HAS ALL THE RIGHTS AND PRIVILEGES OF THE OFFICE OF THE KEYS, NOR THAT THE OFFICE OF THE MINISTRY IS DERIVED FROM THE SPIRITUAL PRIESTHOOD OF THE BELIEVERS. ONLY IN EXCEPTION INSTANCES MAY A CONGREGATION CALL A PASTOR WITHOUT THE PRESENCE OF AN ADVISING PASTOR, FOR NOT THROUGH

THE LOCAL CONGREGATIONS, BUT THROUGH THE CHURCH, THAT IS, THE CONGREGA-
TION AND THE CLERGY, THE LORD CALLS AND ORDAINS MEN FOR THE MINISTRY.[7]

The errors which Missouri claimed to find in Loehe's writings and the teachings of his followers were the same that they had been debating so long with the men of the Buffalo Synod. Consider, for example, the letter written in December 1840 by Pastor Grabau of the Buffalo Synod of Pastor G. Loeber of the Saxons in Missouri. The *Hirtenbrief* or pastoral letter warned the churches against receiving any pastor not ordained according to the old church customs, claiming that ordination was a divine and necessary institution. Going even further, Grabau claimed that only properly called pastors could administer the sacraments, and only they could give valid absolution of sins. The congregation, he said, must follow their pastor in all things not forbidden by God's Word. Loehe, on this point, did not go as far as Grabau.

Grabau taught that only the Church has the right to say what is forbidden in the Scriptures. The long and short of it was that Grabau and the Buffalo Synod took the Office of the Keys away from the communion of saints and placed it alone in the hands of the clergy in the congregations. Later, when we review the history of the Missouri Synod we shall see how that synod opposed Grabau and engaged him and the Buffalo Synod in a controversy regarding the Office of the Ministry that spanned some twenty-two years.

TROUBLE IN THE SAGINAW VALLEY OF MICHIGAN

After Wyneken and Walther had visited Loehe in Bavaria, the latter consented to establish a teacher-training institution. The school was begun at Saginaw, Michigan, in 1852. However, G.M. Grossman, its first director, came into trouble with the Missouri congregation at Saginaw when he insisted upon adhering to Loehe's doctrine of the Ministry. He finally withdrew from the congregation. Another of Loehe's missioners, Pastor Deindoerfer, who was stationed at Frankenhilf, Michigan, sided with Pastor Grossman. Feelings ran high between these two missioners and the Missouri men, and finally Pastor Closter of Saginaw faced them with an "either-or"—either join the Missouri Synod or remain with Loehe. They chose the latter. Wyneken suggested that they go to Iowa. Grossman accepted Wyneken's advice and subsequently requested Loehe's permission to relocate the seminary to Iowa. By choosing to remain with Loehe, the two men had placed the seminary in Saginaw, together with Deindoerfer at Frankenhilf, beyond the government of the Missouri Synod, even while they actually existed within the territorial confines of that body.

LOEHE BREAKS WITH MISSOURI—THE MOVE TO IOWA

On August 4, 1853, Loehe wrote a letter of farewell on black-bordered paper to the pastors and congregations in the Saginaw Valley. A month later, Grossman and Deindoerfer migrated with about twenty souls to Dubuque, Iowa. Grossman, together with five students from Saginaw, remained at Dubuque,

491

while Deindoerfer and others went sixty miles farther northwest, where they founded St. Sebald. It was at St. Sebald, on August 24, 1854, that the Iowa Synod was organized by Pastors G.M. Grossman, John Deindoerfer, Candidates S. Fritschel and M. Schuller (who was ordained at this convention), and a layman. S. Fritschel had been sent over in 1854 from Neuendettlesau with some immigrants. A brother, Gottfried, arrived for Germany in 1857. Maximilian, a son of Sigmund, later became a noted theologian (even the leading theologian) of the Iowa Synod. These and the other Fritschels, John and George J., became some of the leading men of the Iowa Synod.

THE FORMATION OF THE IOWA SYNOD

A constitution was not adopted at the organization of the Iowa Synod since the meetings were devoted to a discussion of principles according to which the new synod was to operate. Iowa's relaxed position regarding doctrine was evident from the beginning. For example, the following was among the guiding paragraphs that were adopted:

SYNOD ACCEPTS ALL THE SYMBOLICAL BOOKS OF THE EV. LUTHERAN CHURCH, BECAUSE IT BELIEVES THAT ALL THEIR SYMBOLICAL DECISIONS OF DISPUTABLE QUESTIONS WHICH HAD ARISEN BEFORE OR DURING THE TIME OF THE REFORMATION WERE MADE IN ACCORDANCE WITH THE WORD OF GOD. BUT BECAUSE WITHIN THE LUTHERAN CHURCH THERE ARE DIFFERENT TENDENCIES, SYNOD DECLARES ITSELF IN FAVOR OF THE TENDENCY, WHICH, BY MEANS OF THE CONFESSIONS AND ON THE BASIS OF THE WORD OF GOD, STRIVES TOWARD A GREATER COMPLETION.[8]

Hence, they were giving room to Loehe's doctrine that Luther's Reformation did not result in defining all Scripture doctrines, but that it was only a progressive movement. Doctrinal completeness should be sought after, yet no one can claim he has arrived at the full truth. Absolute unity can never be attained and so full doctrinal unity should not be a condition of church fellowship.

This attitude had father-reaching effects. In 1879 Iowa officials declared in regards to the doctrine of Church Fellowship:

OUR SYNOD WAS FROM THE VERY BEGINNING PERSUADED TO MAKE A DISTINCTION BETWEEN SUCH IN THE CONFESSIONS OF THE EV. LUTHERAN CHURCH AS ARE NECESSARY ARTICLES OF FAITH AND SUCH OTHER DOCTRINES AS ARE NOT DOCTRINES NECESSARY FOR SALVATION; AND OUR SYNOD HAS CONSIDERED IT ONE OF HER DUTIES VERY EARNESTLY AND EMPHATICALLY TO TEACH AS AN IMPORTANT TRUTH THAT THERE ARE DOCTRINES, EVEN DOCTRINES OF THE SCRIPTURE, CONCERNING WHICH MEMBERS OF OUR CHURCH MAY HOLD DIFFERENT VIEWS AND CONVICTIONS WITHOUT THEREBY BEING COMPELLED TO REFUSE EACH OTHER CHURCH FELLOWSHIP; AND THAT THESE ARE THE VERY DOCTRINES FOR THE SAKE OF WHICH THE MISSOURIANS ADJUDGED US TO BE HERETICAL. IN SUCH MATTERS UNITY SHOULD, INDEED, BE SOUGHT, BUT IT IS NOT ABSOLUTELY REQUIRED AS IN THE DOCTRINES OF FAITH.[9]

The uncertain and indefinite position manifested in this basic principle is characteristic of Loehe and the Iowa Synod and explains their peculiar doctrinal attitude in the past. This attitude permitted them to consider as "open questions" what the Scriptures teach concerning the doctrine of Sunday, the Antichrist, the Millennism (or Chiliasm), the Conversion of the Jews, and the Resurrection of the Martyrs (the question whether or not there is more than one resurrection of the dead). These were referred to as teachings or opinions, which are not clearly stated in the Scriptures.

The Missouri Synod pointedly condemned Iowa's position on open questions and its position that there is "an allowable latitude of doctrine," as "unionistic poison that drives congregations into the arms of skepticism and infidelity." In their place the Missouri Synod insisted upon only one correct interpretation for each Bible doctrine.

Dr. Walther and company taught that the Roman pope is the Antichrist in person, and that this only is truly Lutheran doctrine, being taught in Scripture prophecy and finding precedence in Luther's writings and in the *Smalcald Articles*. However, while Iowa agreed that the papacy contained anti-Christian elements, it could not agree that the pope is the very Antichrist spoken of in the New Testament. The synod relegated this matter to the category of open questions—mere human conviction—which should not determine fellowship among Lutherans. Furthermore, while agreeing that Sunday observance is not commanded in the Scriptures, Iowa disagreed with the treatment those Lutherans should receive who insisted that Sunday observance is an ordinance of God. Missouri would deny them fellowship; Iowa would accept them.

In regards to the lodge membership question, Iowa stood on common ground with the Missouri, Wisconsin, and Ohio Synods, denying membership to those affiliated with secret societies.

WARTBURG SEMINARY AND GOTTFRIED FRITSCHEL

In 1857 the Wartburg Seminary was transferred to St. Sebald from Dubuque. (In 1874 it was moved to Mendota, Illinois, and then back again to Dubuque in 1889.) At Dubuque, the seminary for a time became the center of missionary activities. Being in a strategic position to serve pioneer America, which was pushing on into the vast West, Iowa established missionaries all the way from the Alleghenies to the West Coast. Through Pastor Grabau, Iowa was able to take over sections of the mission territory in southwest Wisconsin (Madison), Detroit, and Toledo.

1857 was also the year that brought Gottfried Fritschel to America. A scholarly theologian, a prolific writer, and a strong controversialist, he was a leader for many years in the synod. He was also professor of Exegesis and Dogmatics in Wartburg Seminary—first at St. Sebald and later at Mendota, Illinois, when the seminary moved there.

FOR A TIME, CLOSE TIES WITH THE BUFFALO SYNOD

In 1855 Grabau of the Buffalo Synod asked the young, tiny Iowa Synod to take charge of the Buffalo congregations around Toledo, Detroit, and Madison—a gesture that displayed the affinity between the two bodies. Soon, how-

493

ever, this relationship was broken when Iowa's statement regarding the Lutheran Confessions came up. The Buffalo Synod was unequivocally committed to the Lutheran Confessions. In 1858 Buffalo disagreed with Iowa regarding that synod's doctrine of Chiliasm.

THERE WERE OVERTURES TO THE MISSOURI SYNOD, BUT A FAILURE TO REACH ACCORD

In 1867 the Iowa Synod held its convention at Toledo, Ohio. At this convention it was declared: There never has been absolute doctrinal unity in the church, and it should not be made a condition of church fellowship. At this same convention, Iowa cast its eyes upon the Missouri Synod and resolved to request a colloquy—no doubt for the reason that some of its pastors were favorably impressed by that synod. The Missourians consented, and the colloquy was held later in the same year in Milwaukee (November 13-18). The points of discussion were the attitudes of the two synods in regards to the Lutheran Confessions, open questions, and some points of Eschatology (associated with the events of the last time).

It is interesting to note that the doctrines of the Church and of the Office of the Ministry—doctrine upon which the two synods had originally parted—were not discussed, as time did not permit. Except in some minor points, agreement was not reached between the two synods. Iowa would not join Missouri in the belief that the doctrine of Sunday, the doctrine of the First Resurrection (Missouri holds that there is only one resurrection—a general resurrection of all the dead, and that the martyrs shall be raised up at the same time with all the others), and the doctrine of the Antichrist, are symbolically fixed by the Lutheran Church.

Though Iowa was not ready to substitute the word "problems" for open questions, the synod could not agree with Missouri on what things were to be called "problems." Finally, in 1873 Iowa defined open questions as "doctrines not divisive of church fellowship." Iowa reiterated its stand on Open Questions and church fellowship by declaring in 1879: ...OUR SYNOD HAS CONSIDERED IT ONE OF HER DUTIES VERY EARNESTLY AND EMPHATICALLY TO TEACH AS AN IMPORTANT TRUTH THAT THERE ARE DOCTRINES, EVEN DOCTRINES OF THE SCRIPTURE, CONCERNING WHICH MEMBERS OF OUR CHURCH MAY HOLD DIFFERENT VIEWS AND CONVICTIONS WITHOUT THEREBY BEING COMPELLED TO REFUSE EACH OTHER CHURCH FELLOWSHIP....[10]

IOWA AND THE GENERAL SYNOD— THE WANING INFLUENCE OF THE LIBERALS

Wyneken, as one of Loehe's emissaries, had attacked the General Synod (org. 1820) in his "Distress of the German Lutherans in North America," a pamphlet which he published with Loehe's help. Finally, when the General Synod refused to defend itself against his charges, Wyneken and his congregation severed their connection with this body. He wrote to Loehe: SINCE THE GENERAL

494

SYNOD REJECTED BOTH PROPOSALS; I AGAIN HAD TO REPEAT PUBLICLY THAT SHE IS HARBORING AND NURTURING FALSE DOCTRINE. AS AN HONEST MAN AND A CHRISTIAN, I WISHED TO DECLARE WAR AGAINST HER...I DESIRED TO TELL HER IN ADVANCE THAT I WOULD DO ALL IN MY POWER TO OPPOSE HER INFLUENCE, ESPECIALLY THAT I WOULD WARN AGAINST HER, SO THAT THE FEW IN GERMANY WHO ARE ON THE SIDE OF THE TRUTH DO NOT BOTHER WITH HER.[11]

In return, Loehe showed that he sided with Wyneken against the General Synod by remarking: WYNEKEN IS HEREWITH BEGINNING A WAR WHICH HE MAY CARRY ON WITH THE DEEPEST PEACE OF SOUL, A WAR IN WHICH ALL TRUE CHILDREN OF THE LUTHERAN CHURCH WILL HAVE TO JOIN HIM.[12] Wyneken was later joined by the Missouri, Iowa, and Buffalo Synods in his battle against the unLutheran "American Lutheranism" of the General Synod and carried on sharp polemics against it. The liberals in the General Synod made a last-ditch stand to repel the tide of conservatism, but their cause was doomed. Dr. Schmucker's "Definite Platform," which appeared in 1855, was one of these attempts to repel the conservative tendency of the General Synod at that time. The "Definite Platform" actually proposed a revision of the *Augsburg Confession*, in which the "Platform" claimed to have found "errors." However, the district synods gave their unqualified disapproval of this attempt to revise the basic creed of Lutheranism. After the rejection of the "Definite Synodical Platform," the influence of the liberals continually waned.

IOWA AND THE GENERAL COUNCIL (ORG. 1867)

The disruption of the General Synod finally came in 1866 when the convention at Fort Wayne refused to seat the Pennsylvania delegates. This body then withdrew from the General Synod and issued a call "to all synods which confess the *Unaltered Augsburg Confession (UAC)*, for the purpose of organizing a new general body upon distinctively Lutheran principles." As a result of this call, a convention was held at Reading, Pennsylvania, December 12-14, 1866. Among the thirteen synods present were the Iowa, Ohio, Wisconsin, and Missouri Synods. Krauth's "Fundamental Principles of Faith and Church Polity" were unanimously adopted, and were referred to the respective synods for adoption. Later, at the Fort Wayne meeting in November 1867 it was found that the Iowa Synod, together with the following synods, had adopted the confessional basis: Pennsylvania, New York, Pittsburgh, English Ohio, Michigan, Swedish Augustana, Minnesota, Illinois, and Canada. However, Iowa did not join the General Council, since it deemed its answer to the Four Points (Pulpit Fellowship, Altar Fellowship, Lodge Membership, and Chiliasm) unsatisfactory. The question of the Four Points initiated by Iowa and Ohio was not cleared up by the Council at this time but was simply referred to the individual synods for consideration until—one might say—the unity of the synods in the Council became more mature.

The Joint Synod of Ohio also sent delegates, but, like the Iowa Synod, it did not join the Council. Iowa continued its friendly relations with the Council and sent delegates to its conventions in "an advisory capacity."

Regarding lodge membership: Iowa, like Ohio, demanded immediate and

495

drastic surgery within the General Council—the discipline of all lodge members. In 1868 the Council did warn all its laymen and pastors against membership in lodges and threatened discipline should they join or remain in membership. However, discipline proved lax, and at the instigation of Iowa and Ohio the subject was subsequently debated for many years to come.

THE IOWA SYNOD AND THE PREDESTINARIAN CONTROVERSY

In the controversy over Predestination, Iowa sided with the Ohio Synod, particularly with reference to the *Intuitu Fidei* theory (that God elects people to salvation "in view of the faith which he foresees in them"). The Iowa Synod stated its position as follows:

THE LUTHERAN CHURCH HAS EVER CONSIDERED IT CALVINISTIC ERROR...TO SPEAK OF ELECTIONS HAVING BEEN MADE WITHOUT REFERENCE TO THE CONDUCT OF MAN, MERELY IN ACCORDANCE WITH THE PLEASURE OF THE DIVINE WILL, AND TO DENOUNCE AS AN ERROR THAT GOD MADE HIS ELECTION IN RESPECT TO THE FAITH WHICH HE FORESAW, BECAUSE, ACCORDING TO THE DOCTRINE OF THE LUTHERAN CHURCH, GOD, IN HIS ETERNAL DIVINE COUNSEL, HAS DECREED THAT HE WOULD SAVE NO ONE EXCEPT THOSE WHO WOULD KNOW CHRIST, HIS SON, AND TRULY BELIEVE IN HIM.

The Missouri Synod (and also the Wisconsin Synod), on the other hand, taught that God elects to faith. The individual's faith in Christ comes to him through the operation of the Holy Spirit as a result of God's gracious election, which election took place before the world was created, thus making the individual's faith and salvation completely the work of God.

In 1882 the Iowa Synod charged the Missouri Synod with fundamental error in the predestinarian controversy. Whereas Iowa felt that nothing in the past stood in the way of fellowship between the two synods, it declared that now there can no longer be any church fellowship!

THE IOWA SYNOD AND THE TEXAS SYNOD

In 1849 a request was received by Christian Spittler near Basel, Switzerland, for missionaries to be sent to Texas to serve the many Germans who were settling there. Spittler was a layman who had founded a training school for missionaries and within a year Texas became a target for his mission endeavors. At first, only two men were sent to this vast foreign field, but soon these were joined by others. On November 10, 1851, five of the Chrischona missionaries, together with C. Braun (who had been sent to Texas by the Pittsburgh Synod), organized the First Evangelical Lutheran Synod of Texas. From 1868 to 1895 this synod was affiliated with the General Synod, but finally, in 1895, due to the influence of G. Fritschel, the larger portion of the Texas Synod voted to join the Iowa Synod. (The remaining portion ultimately found their way into the General Council, and still later, into the United Lutheran Church in America.) The Texas group, first as a synod and later as a district of the Iowa Synod, enjoyed rapid growth—with its influence deeply felt in that part of the country. More Lutherans belonged to this district of Iowa than to any other Lutheran body located in Texas.

THE IOWA SYNOD PRIOR TO THE FORMATION OF THE AMERICAN LUTHERAN CHURCH (ALC)

The Iowa Synod was divided into the following districts: Iowa, Northern and Southern and West Wisconsin, South and North Dakota, and Texas.

The foreign mission work of the Iowa Synod was carried on in connection with the General Council and also in connection with the Neuendettlesau, Hermannsburg, and Leipzig Mission Societies. After the First World War, Iowa conducted the mission in former German New Guinea in conjunction with the United Evangelical Lutheran Church in Australia. It also had a mission in East Africa.

Before joining the merger forming the American Lutheran Church, the Iowa Synod maintained Wartburg Seminary at Dubuque; Wartburg Normal School in Waverly; Wartburg College at Clinton (all in Iowa); an Academy at Eureka, South Dakota; Martin Luther Academy at Sterling, Nebraska; and a Junior College at Seguin, Texas.

The Iowa Synod maintained the Wartburg Printing House at Chicago.

IOWA TAKES PART IN DISCUSSIONS BETWEEN THE MIDWESTERN GERMAN LUTHERAN SYNODS

Between 1903 and 1906 a total of five Intersynodical Conferences were held involving the Midwestern German Lutheran synods. These meetings were held at Watertown and Milwaukee in 1903; at Detroit in 1904; and at Fort Wayne, Indiana, in 1905 and 1906. Involved were theologians of the four synods: Wisconsin, Missouri, Iowa, and Ohio. Wisconsin and Missouri were willing to accept the seemingly conflicting Bible passages concerning man's conversion and election—God wants all to be saved, and yet he elected only a certain number to salvation. What about the others? This conflict was a problem for the other side. Missouri and Wisconsin taught that human responsibility was in no way involved in God's election of individuals. The other side wanted "to keep the reality of human responsibility from being stripped of all meaning."[13]

A dry period, as far as holding further Intersynodical Conferences was concerned, followed the meeting in 1906 and lasted almost ten years. Reaching agreement among the theologians appeared hopeless. Then, in 1915, a small group of Synodical Conferences pastors began meeting with pastors of the Ohio and Iowa Synods in Minnesota. Their meetings were carried out without polemics. Professors were prohibited from taking part in the discussions—in a way, a rebuke for failing to reach accord over the years. Remarkably, agreement was reached on the doctrines of Election and Conversion in the St. Paul Theses of 1916. Upon being circulated in all the synods involved, these unofficial Theses were signed by 550 pastors. However, as Nelson points out, the Theses were later judged by the "experts" to be somewhat inadequate. This, of course, struck a blow to a quick recognition of doctrinal unity among the Midwestern German synods. There would be many years of discussion among the German Lutherans on the controverted doctrines.[14]

Nevertheless, the favorable response of the pastors of the Midwestern German synods to the unofficial St. Paul Theses of 1916, coupled with the prevalent hope for the settlement of the doctrinal disputes and the establishment of pulpit and altar fellowship, resulted in the Ohio, Iowa, Wisconsin, and Missouri Synods appointing official Intersynodical Committees. These Committees then formed a joint Intersynodical Committee, whose goal it was to seek official agreement on the controverted doctrines (Conversion and Election or Predestination), which would then open the door to church fellowship and cooperation. The Iowa Synod was a key force in bringing about the discussions that resulted, for it had extended an invitation to the Lutheran bodies to have open and general conferences for discussing the points at issue. Since the unofficial St. Paul Theses were considered inadequate, the need was felt for new theses and antitheses to be formulated by the Intersynodical Committee. It was agreed that no theologian who lived after the compilation of the *Book of Concord of 1580* would be cited in the discussions. Furthermore, more pastors than theological professors were placed on the Committee of the various synods.

The Intersynodical Committee met for several days two or three times a year. It was the aim of the Committee to achieve a precise formulation of the issues involved, there would not be compromise. Nelson informs us: "Agreement was attained early on election, conversion, the Confessions, church fellowship, the church, the ministry, the Antichrist, the last things, the days and forms for worship, and 'open questions.' On all of these Missouri had had a long-standing conflict with Iowa and to a lesser degree with Ohio."[15] A thesis on Verbal Inspiration was also added. This proposed agreement came about at Chicago on April 15, 1925.

The Intersynodical (Chicago) Theses (not to be confused with the 1919 Chicago Theses) were presented to the respective participating bodies. Agreement was reached on the doctrine of Election. Thus, Ohio and Iowa's doctrine was renounced and Missouri's teaching was validated. In order to come to a more complete agreement, the Theses underwent further discussion and revision until a final form was drafted in 1928. However, there was still disagreement and ill feelings concerning the Theses. As we shall later discover, Iowa was not satisfied with the Theses' statement on the Inspiration and Inerrancy of Scripture. The Ohio Synod, for several reasons, did not act on the Theses. There was, for example, friction that had built up with the Missouri Synod on the one hand, and favorable negotiations with the Norwegian Lutheran Church (which body the Missouri Synod did not approve of) on the other hand. The Buffalo Synod had come on the scene in 1925 by making possible a committee to investigate merger with Iowa and Ohio. Later, in 1929, the Buffalo Synod approved the Chicago Theses.[16]

In spite of the progress made by the Intersynodical Committee, hopes for uniting the four synods in fellowship waned as time wore on. Various factors accounted for this: Ohio's fellowship with the Norwegians, who had accepted the Madison Agreement on the doctrine of Election—which was actually a compromise; tensions over the National Lutheran Council, the Lutheran World Convention, and the Lutheran Brotherhood; the question of how to deal with lodge members; and participation by Ohio in various unionistic conferences. What about the Missouri Synod? In 1929, faculty members of Missouri's Springfield Seminary called the Intersynodical Committee's Chicago Theses "unclear, ambiguous and inadequate." The revised Chicago Theses were presented to the Missouri Synod River Forest (Illinois) Convention in 1929. Missouri's Intersynodical Committee and also an examining committee (composed of two professors and a pastor), concurred in the recommendation that the Missouri Synod not adopt the Theses. Acting upon their recommendation, the synod then rejected the Chicago Theses and at the same time elected a new committee to draw up the doctrinal statement of the Missouri Synod, which became known as the "Brief Statement" (1932).

It remained, then, for the three German Synods—Ohio, Iowa, and Buffalo—to finally come together in fellowship as one Lutheran body. By 1929 the merger of these three synods was imminent, and all synods then rejected the Chicago Theses.

THE IOWA SYNOD TAKES PART IN MERGER NEGOTIATIONS WITH THE OHIO AND BUFFALO SYNODS

Since the Ohio and Iowa Synods were of the same spirit (in regards to Open Questions, the Four Points, and Predestination) steps were initiated by certain of the Iowa Districts toward union with the Ohio Synod. In June 1919 the Eastern District asked the Executive Board of Iowa to approach Ohio on the matter of union. This was followed later in the same year by other districts and conferences, who made the same request. This request was the result of a movement toward union, which had begun years before. When the Ohio Synod withdrew from the Synodical Conference in 1881, a private conference was called between the leaders of the two synods. Later, in 1887, arrangements were made for an official committee of the two synods, which then met together in the 1890's for talks aiming at tearing down the barriers to fellowship. They again met together for talks in 1907 and 1912. When the representatives of the two synods met in 1893 at Michigan City, Indiana, the long discussion resulted in the Michigan City Theses. However, the Theses failed to receive official acceptance, but they did stimulate further discussions, which finally resulted in the "Toledo Theses" in 1907. These theses serve as the basis on which the synods later declared themselves in fellowship.

A barrier to fellowship between the Ohio and Iowa Synods was Iowa's limited membership in the General Council, which Ohio distained. However, in 1917, when the merger of the General Synod, the General Council, and the United Synod in the South (to form the United Lutheran Church in America) appeared imminent, the Iowa Synod renounced the merger and withdrew from the Council. In 1918 Ohio agreed to pulpit and altar fellowship with Iowa. The following year Iowa's Eastern District urged that a plan for "organic union" of the two synods be prepared. Then, in 1920, the two synods appionted committees for the purpose of conferring "on questions looking to a closer union."[18] As historian R.C. Wolf points out, the two synods were envisioning a "middle way" between the positions of the ULCA on the one hand, and the Synodical Conference on the other.[19] In 1924 the two negotiating committees recommended "organic union." All of the districts of the Ohio Synod approved the proposed merger, as did a great majority of pastors and laymen in the Iowa Synod. In the same year the Buffalo Synod requested to be included in the merger.[20] In 1926 it was agreed that 1928 should be the target date for the merger (date proposed by the Ohio Synod).[21]

In 1925 a Joint Merger Commission began to put together plans for organizing the new Lutheran body. But a serious disagreement occurred later over the article on Scripture in the constitution. The proposed merger of the two synods was stalled—even threatened—by the "inspiration controversy." As a testimony against modern theology so prevalent in America in the 1920's, the Intersynodical Committee (Iowa, Ohio, Missouri, Wisconsin) produced, in 1925, the Intersynodical (Chicago) Theses, and included an article on the Scriptures. The article stated: "We believe and confess that Scripture not only contains God's Word, but is God's Word, and hence no errors or contradictions of any sort are found therein." In the same year, representatives of the Iowa, Ohio, and Buffalo Synods—as well as the Norwegian Lutheran Church of America—drew up an agreement known as the "Minneapolis Theses" which also included an article stating a very conservative view of Scriptures: "The synods signatory to these Articles of Agreement accept without exception all the canonical books of the Old and New Testament as a whole, and in all their parts, as the divinely inspired, revealed, and inerrant Word of God..."[23] And so the Joint Commission of the three bodies suggested that the proposed constitution for the new body accept Scripture " as the inspired and inerrant Word of God."

This wording unexpectedly created quite a stir. Professor J.M. Reu of Iowa's Wartburg Seminary led the opposition to the wording, which made total inerrancy a doctrine in the Church. His point: The Bible proclaims its reliability only in matters pertaining to salvation, faith, and Christian living. A four-year debate on the issue of Inerrancy resulted. Iowa at first favored Professor Reu's position but later, when Ohio (which wanted strict interpretation of the statement that Scripture is the inerrant Word of God) pressed the issue of total inerrancy as a condition for the proposed merger, Iowa joined Ohio's view, that the original manuscripts of the Bible were without error of any kind. (The ULCA did not accept narrowing the doctrine of Inspiration to "a particular theory of inspiration.")[25]

Finally, formal adoption of the constitution and ratification of merger by all three synods took place on August 11, 1930, at Toledo, Ohio, thus forming the American Lutheran Church (ALC).

At the time of the merger, the Iowa Synod had 610 pastors, 217,000 communicants, and 1,046 congregations.

LENDING MEN OF THE IOWA SYNOD

THE FRITSCHELS

SIGMUND FRITSCHEL (1833-1900): He was born at Nurenberg, studied under Loehe, and was sent to America in 1853. He helped to organize the Iowa Synod. He assisted Grossman at the seminary and was also in temporary charge of a congregation in Wisconsin, serving also a congregation of the Buffalo Synod in Detroit. Sigmund returned to the seminary in 1858, working there with his brother, Gottfried, for more than thirty years. He taught practical theology and contributed to two church publications. Sigmund died at Dubuque. Sigmund's sons: John F. Fritschel: Professor and president of Wartburg College, Clinton, Iowa; Maximilian F. Fritschel: Professor and president of Wartburg Seminary, Dubuque.

GOTTFRIED FRITSCHEL (1836-1889): He was born Nurenberg, studied under Loehe and also at Erlangen, and came to America in 1857. He was professor of Exegesis and Dogmatics in the Wartburg Seminary. He was an author and prolific writer, contributing to many theological periodicals. He died at Mendota, Illinois. Gottfried's son, George J. Fritschel, pastor at Galveston, Texas and professor at Wartburg Seminary, beginning there in 1906. He was the author of several German works.

GEORGE M. GROSSMAN (1823-1897): He studied at Erlangen and came to America in 1852. George was inspector of the Teacher's Seminary at Saginaw, Michigan, and in 1853 moved to Iowa. He was president of the Iowa Synod (1854-93) and president of the Seminary until 1875. He was also the founder of the Teachers' Seminary at Waverly, Iowa, in 1879.

JOHANNES DEINDOERFER (1829-1907): He studied at Neuendettlesau and Nurenberg and came to America—to Frankenhilf, Michigan—in 1851. In 1854 Johannes went with George Grossman to Iowa. He was vice-president of the Iowa Synod 1854-92; president 1892-1904. He authored a book on the history of his synod.

F. RICHTER (1852-1934): He was born in Saxony and educated at Erlangen and Leipzig. He came to America in 1870 and studied at St. Sebald (1870-74), after which he studied at Leipzig and Erlangen. He was professor at Mendota (1876-94), and was president of Clinton College (1894-1902). He served as president of the Iowa Synod (1904-26).

JOHN MICHAEL REU (1869-1943): He was born in Bavaria and educated at Goettingen and Neuendettelsau. He came to America in 1889. He was pastor at Rock Falls, Illinois 1890-99 and professor at Dubuque since 1899. Reu was a prolific author and editor. He is credited with writing many books.

3

THE BUFFALO SYNOD
1845-1930

THE PRUSSIAN UNION—
TROUBLE IN THE OLD COUNTRY (PRUSSIA)

On September 27, 1817, Friedrich William III of Prussia proclaimed his intention of celebrating the 300th Anniversary of the Reformation by uniting the Reformed and Lutheran Churches of Potsdam. Other Lutheran and Reformed churches in the land were urged to follow the example. At first, this was a voluntary endeavor, but soon the "Prussian Union" became the law of the land. In 1821 candidates for the ministry were required to pledge loyalty to the Union, and by 1830 it was forbidden to use the names "Lutheran" and "Reformed" any longer. A new Agenda was published, whose worship formulas were supposed to cover both Lutheran and Reformed needs. By 1834 the use of the *Union Agenda* became compulsory. Thus the state, by decree, endeavored to involve the Lutheran Church in blatant unionism (union without unity) with the Reformed Church.

JOHN ANDREW AUGUSTUS GRABAU (1804-79):
PRESECUTED FOR NONCONFORMITY

GRABAU STANDS IN OPPOSITION TO THE UNION

The name of John Grabau especially comes to the fore in this setting of compulsory church unionism. Grabau had become pastor of St. Andrew's Church at Erfurt in 1834. Grabau opposed the Prussian Union, for he felt that such a union was false, since it paid no heed to the doctrinal differences which, in fact, still existed between the Lutherans and the Reformed. Conscience and Scripture-bound, Grabau stressed the differences between the two denominations rather than the similarities. By 1836 he realized that he could not function under such unionistic conditions and declared war on the Union. He informed the church government that he would use the *Union Agenda* no longer, and would instead go back to using the old Lutheran form. He immediately forfeited his office, for he was suspended by the Consistory and forbidden to enter or to preach in his church. His congregation, however, requested him to function as a Lutheran pastor and met for worship in the parsonage. Further services were held in a mill outside the city gate.

GRABAU ENDURES PERSECUTION AND IMPRISONMENT

When Grabau continued to function as a Lutheran pastor, he was impris-

502

oned—a fate suffered by many other Lutheran pastors of his time. Here, briefly, is how the tragedy unfolded: After the divine services in Storch's mill were prohibited, Grabau preached at night at various homes of the members, in spite of police activities. His congregation at Erfurt numbered between seventy and eighty families, but he also ministered to another group of Lutherans in Magdeburg, who also had separated from the Union and assembled in the house of Lieutenant von Rohr for divine worship. (An interesting note is that his son, Philip, later became a president and very influential man in the Wisconsin Synod, in America.) It was at von Rohr's suggestion that these Lutheran Christians publicly withdrew from the established church with which they could not agree to worship.

Throughout Thuringia new church life became apparent. And so, in this change of climate, Grabau's congregation appealed to the king himself to reinstate Grabau. It was as the result of this appeal that their pastor was called before the mayor of Erfurt. He was then legally detained and later sent to prison at Heiligenstadt. Grabau's congregation was also penalized for attending Lutheran services and for failing to send their children to the Union school.

From prison, Grabau wrote to the royal *Kommissionsrat*, Heiligenstadt. He complained: (1) that he now sits 6 ½ months in prison and no one has taken the pains to investigate in which respect this situation is pressing upon him or not; (2) that he does not receive adequate nourishment, but rather food which is unfit to eat and not digestible; (3) that the prison is filled with unhealthful stenches, and he pleads that his release from this unjust confinement be expedited.

Grabau's wife, having appealed at the same time to the Minister of Justice in Berlin, received the information that Grabau would be exiled to Muenster, whither she might follow and live with him. By this time there were some twenty pastors imprisoned in Pomerania. Grabau was advised by his friends that he should effect an escape from prison. About this time, Lieutenant von Rohr was deposed from his office in the Prussian army because he had his child baptized by a Lutheran pastor and refused to attend services in a Union Church. Thereupon he was invited to live in Pomerania. The hautboy (oboe) player, Fr. Mueller, was also deposed for his religious stand. Von Rohr and Mueller met Grabau one day while he was exercising with a guard and spirited him away in a covered wagon, escaping north through Wittenberg to Berlin. Here Grabau preached at a conventicle (secret religious meeting, unlawfully held). After weeks of travel, they finally escaped their pursuers, arriving at Seehof. This, then, was the area of Grabau's religious activities, which he carried on chiefly at night. But he also ministered to his flock in Erfurt.

GRABAU IS IMPRISONED AGAIN
BUT FINALLY IS ALLOWED TO EMIGRATE

In 1838 Grabau was again imprisoned at Heiligenstadt. While imprisoned he took ill and lay for weeks in his cell with practically no care.

When Grabau suffered his first imprisonment, his congregation already at that time urged emigration to America in order that they might seek religious freedom there. At first, Grabau resisted the movement to America because he had hopes of gaining freedom for the Lutheran Church in Prussia. However, King Frederick William III answered a petition by the Lutherans by declaring that he would tolerate the Lutheran Church only as a part of the United Church. The king's refusal to grant freedom of worship to the Lutheran Church more or less settled the score for Grabau. And so, in October 1838 he appealed to the king for permission to leave the country, since it was apparent to him that the Lutheran Church had no future possibilities in the kingdom. No answer arrived from the king.

On November 9, 1838, Grabau's congregation at Magdeburg asked him to accompany them as pastor in America. Then on November 25th Grabau was informed by Berlin that he might emigrate under the following conditions: (1) that he neither at Erfurt nor at Magdeburg could travel in regard to family nor other matters; (2) that he should be exported from Heiligenstadt direct to Hamburg by a police official; (3) that he should state where he would be able to raise the cost of travel; (4) that the police official who was sending him away, place him in the custody of the police department at Hamburg until such a moment as he could be sent on his way.

Grabau replied that he would consider the matter and advised his members not to emigrate for the sake of having to bear a cross, but only if life were no longer safe. He informed his congregations at Magdeburg and Erfurt that they ought to demand that he accompany his congregations in an honorable manner. However, the congregations replied that he should accept the stipulations of the government for Christ's sake.

In the meantime Grabau again became seriously ill. Convinced that he was about to die, he appealed to the government for permission to spend his last days with his family. At a hearing he was asked if he would desist from functioning as a pastor, and if he recovered from his illness, would he emigrate? Grabau replied in the affirmative. Two months later he was permitted to leave prison and live with his family under the condition that he must emigrate immediately upon the recovery of his health.

When Grabau's wife asked the king if the Lutheran Church would be tolerated in Prussia, the answer was: "The Lutheran Church is within the Union and outside the same, would no Lutheran Church in the land be tolerated."

On April 26, 1839, Grabau received official notice that he could emigrate, although he was not to be permitted to visit his relatives or travel with his family. About 1,000 souls assembled in Hamburg to emigrate under Grabau's leadership. The group sailed in five ships for New York, landing there September 18, 1839.

THE IMMIGRANTS—
ORGANIZING CONGREGATIONS IN AMERICA

Upon arriving in America a small group of the immigrant party remained in New York, and there they formed a parish, calling Candidate M. Oertel as their pastor. Soon, however, Oertel defected to the Roman Catholic Church. P. Brohm became their second pastor. The other immigrants went by steamer to Albany, and thence by canal boats to Buffalo. Most of them stayed on here, but a small group went on to Wisconsin, some settling in Milwaukee. The greatest number of the immigrants went further on settling as pioneers northwest of Milwaukee. They established the town of Freistadt (Free City). Those who came to Wisconsin were under the leadership of Lieutenant von Rohr.

One of the most gifted pioneer pastors of that time was a man named Leberecht Friedrich Ehregott Krause. He had been sent to Militsch, near Breslau, in order to find a suitable place for a settlement. He proceeded to Buffalo where he then met the immigrants from Silesia, Pomerania, Erfurt, Magdeburg, and Berlin, who had come to America in five ships under the leadership of Lieutenant von Rohr and Pastor Grabau. Pastor Krause organized a congregation with a group of Silesians at Buffalo, dedicating their church on Pentecost 1840. This day was memorable for another reason also: On this day Frederick William III of Prussia, who had caused them so much grief and made their emigration necessary, died.

In 1841 the congregation called Pastor Buerger, one of the Saxon clergymen who had emigrated from Saxony, but who, along with Dr. Marbach, was enroute back to Germany. After the fall of "Stephanism" (a matter taken up in the history of the Missouri Synod), Buerger and Marbach became convinced that it had been wrong for them to leave Saxony with the Stephanites. They then sold their household goods in order to buy passage back to Germany and began to make the trip together. Enroute to Germany, the men stopped off at Buffalo, and it was at this time that Buerger was prevailed upon to remain in America and become pastor at Buffalo.

MORE EMIGRATIONS TO AMERICA

After King Frederick William III of Prussia died in 1840, his son, Frederick William IV came to the throne. He did not persecute the Lutherans as his father had done, and so the general emigrations to America ceased. Still, there was some dissatisfaction among the Lutherans, for they were compelled to send their children to state schools, which were controlled by the United Church of Prussia. Adherents of Pastors Kindermann and Ehrenstroem opposed this rule. They also opposed the way the Breslau Synod allowed laymen to participate in the administration of the Office of the Keys. Finally, it was decided to emigrate. The two groups—the Pomeranians, led by Pastor Kindermann, and the Ukermarkers, without their pastor—immigrated to America toward the end of 1843. Their pastor, the Reverend Ehrenstroem, had been arrested by the Prussian authorities for inciting the people against the Prussian State Church through his sermons. A year later he was allowed to emigrate and thus follow his people to America. The Pomeranians settled near Freistadt in Wisconsin, while the Ukermarkers settled near Buffalo. Bergholz, Wallmore, and Martinsville were cities founded by them.

GRABAU WARNS THE CHURCH THROUGH HIS
HIRTENBRIEF OR PASTORAL LETTER

The freedom enjoyed by the Lutheran Church in America was a wonderful tonic to a man of Grabau's initiative. He became an active missionary in the Buffalo territory. In 1840 he even personally opened a seminary at Buffalo to help supply the urgent need for pastors in this young nation with such intense growing pains. The first graduates, interesting enough, were Lieutenant Henry von Rohr and Hautboyist Fr. Mueller.

Still, there were not enough pastors. Furthermore, some of the congregations, unable to secure a pastor, began to make use of the services of laymen. But this was very distasteful to Grabau, who considered it a violation of the doctrine of the Holy Ministry. He therefore took upon himself, through a Pastoral Letter, to warn the churches against making use of preachers who were not ordained according to the old church ordinances. To Grabau, ordination was essential. Private confession was the rule and absolution, he felt, could only be pronounced by rightfully called pastors, and only they could administer the sacraments.

COMMUNICATING WITH THE SAXONS

On December 1, 1840, Grabau wrote the afore-mentioned Pastoral Letter, which he then sent on to the Saxons in Missouri through Pastor G.H. Loeber. Grabau entertained high hopes that the Saxons, together with Loehe's emissaries, could be united together with the Buffalo group, since all three groups—in the face of liberal "American Lutheranism"—were pledged to strict adherence to the old Lutheran Confessions. The Pastoral Letter was sent to the Saxons for their criticism. When the Saxons examined Grabau's letter, they immediately noted tendencies in his doctrines of Church Government and Public Ministry that were identical to those of Martin Stephan, who had shortly before fallen from power.

The Saxons, however, were reluctant to come right out and tell Grabau about their findings, for they recognized in him one who was standing on the conservative side of Lutheranism on the American scene. Therefore they delayed their answer to his Pastoral Letter for over two-and-a-half years. In the meantime, both Grabau and Krause corresponded with the Saxons, emphasizing church union and urging a critical opinion of the letter.

The Saxons finally replied with a letter formulated in July of 1843. According to Walter A. Baepler, writing in his history of the Missouri Synod, the letter told Grabau in effect:

...THAT WITH RESPECT TO THE SO-MUCH-EMPHASIZED CHURCH ORDINANCES, ESSENTIALS AND NON-ESSENTIALS HAVE BEEN CONFUSED AND THEREBY CHRISTIAN LIBERTY HAS BEEN CURTAILED; MORE HAS BEEN ASCRIBED TO THE MINISTERIAL OFFICE THAN BELONGS TO IT, AND THUS THE SPIRITUAL PRIESTHOOD OF THE BELIEVERS HAS BEEN FORCED INTO THE BACKGROUND. THE OLD CHURCH ORDERS DO NOT EXIST BY DIVINE RIGHT; ORDINATION IS A WHOLESOME CEREMONY, BUT HAS NOT BEEN ORDERED BY GOD AND IS THEREFORE NOT ESSENTIAL

506

TO THE MINISTRY. TO SAY THAT A CONGREGATION MUST OBEY ITS PASTOR IN ALL THINGS NOT CONTRARY TO GOD'S WORD GOES BEYOND THE WORD OF THE SAVIOR: "WHOEVER HEARETH YOU, HEARETH ME." ONLY WHEN AND INASMUCH AS THE PASTOR PROCLAIMS THE WORD OF GOD, CAN HE DEMAND OBEDIENCE, AND THE DECISION WHETHER OR NOT HE IS PROCLAIMING GOD'S COMMAND RESTS WITH THE INDIVIDUAL CHRISTIAN. THE EFFICACY OF THE MEANS OF GRACE DOES NOT DEPEND ON THE OFFICE OF THE MINISTRY BUT ON CHRIST'S WORD. THUS, ACCORDING TO BAEPLER, THE "SAXONS RECOGNIZED IN GRABAU'S POSITION THE SAME ERRORS USED BY STEPHAN TO GAIN CONTROL OVER HIS CONGREGATION."[26]

Instead of helping to unite the Prussians and the Saxons in America as it was hoped, Grabau's Pastoral Letter only aroused suspicions in the Saxons toward Grabau, for they were greatly opposed to any and all hierarchical tendencies, which they had too long endured under Stephanism, much to their sorrow. Grabau retaliated against the Saxons' reply by accusing the Missouri Synod of seventeen errors. A bitter controversy resulted, which led to the establishing of Missouri Synod congregations among the Prussians. Though Missouri tried to bring about a reconciliation, Grabau refused to submit his orthodoxy to the test.

Grabau's manner of lording it over others in the church caused several fine congregations to withdraw from the Buffalo Synod and enter Missouri's fellowship. A further cause of aggravation was the fact that the Missouri Synod (org. 1847) ministered to those people whom it felt had been unjustly excommunicated by Grabau. A final appeal by the Missouri Synod for reconciliation in 1859 was answered by Grabau with formal excommunication of the entire Missouri Synod—numbering at the time some 200 congregations. Once again, we are reminded of the adage: "Power corrupts, and absolute power corrupts absolutely." And here again we find an example of something recorded many times in history, that the persecuted becomes the persecutor.

FOUNDING THE BUFFALO SYNOD

In the year 1845, between June 3rd and the 25th, four pastors and eighteen lay delegates met to organize the Buffalo Synod. The pastors were: J.A.A. Grabau of Buffalo, New York; H. von Rohr of Huberston, Canada; Lebrecht Krause of Freistadt, Wisconsin, and G.A. Kindermann of Kirchhayn, (state?). Ten congregations were represented. Actually, two meetings were held. The first one took place June 3 to 19 at Freistadt, and the second meting was held June 23 to 25 in Milwaukee. Grabau was the leading spirit of the new synod from its formation until his death in 1879. He held the office of the Senior Ministerii, which later—after 1866—was simply titled, the Office of President.

Until 1886 the synod was officially called the Synod of the Lutheran Church Emigrated from Prussia. But, with headquarters located at Buffalo, the body came to be called simply the Buffalo Synod. The synod was very strict in requiring private confession, in administering church discipline, and in opposing secret societies. It should be added that beginning with 1891, public absolution was allowed, and lodge membership came to be tolerated after 1918.

BUFFALO'S ALLIANCE WITH THE IOWA SYNOD

For a short time Buffalo had an alliance with the Iowa Synod and even placed some congregations around Madison, Wisconsin, in Iowa's care. A couple of congregations even called Iowa pastors. But when the controversy between the Iowa and the Missouri Synods arose in 1857 over the doctrines of Chiliasm and the Antichrist, Buffalo sided with Missouri and thus lost her alliance with Iowa. Iowa's attitude toward the Confessions and Open Questions was another reason for Grabau to sever connections.

SCHISM PRODUCES THREE BUFFALO SYNODS

A dissension arose between Grabau and Pastor C. Hochstetter. Pastor von Rohr sided with Hochstetter and promoted his cause. Many of the pastors and congregations were becoming weary of Grabau's hierarchy, which his controversy with the Missouri Synod naturally helped to bring into sharp focus. Hochsetter and von Rohr's group took a colloquy from the Missouri Synod in November 1866. They at first formed as the Missourian Buffalo Synod, which declared itself to be the true Buffalo Synod (February 1867). Soon after, however, this group dissolved as a synod and joined the Missouri Synod. Henry von Rohr and his party remained as a separate group until 1877, when some returned to Grabau and the others joined the Wisconsin Synod and became very influential in the entire Synodical Conference (org. 1872).

And so, at least for a time, there were three Buffalo Synods: the new Missourian Buffalo Synod under the direction of Hochstetter; and old synod under von Rohr (by far the greater part of the old Buffalo Synod sided with him), and then there was the new Buffalo Synod headed by Grabau.

THE BUFFALO SYNOD'S DEFINING DOCTRINES

In 1886 Grabau's synod drew up its first constitution. At this time many old peculiarities were dropped. But Buffalo stressed that ordination was essential to the rite vocatus of the *Augsburg Confession*. In regards to the Office of the Ministry, Baepler points out that Buffalo taught...THAT IT IS NOT THE CONGREGATION WHICH GIVES OR CONVEYS THE HOLY MINISTRY, BUT THE SON OF GOD, TOGETHER WITH THE FATHER AND THE HOLY GHOST; THAT A CONGREGATION HAS NO RIGHT TO CALL A PASTOR WITHOUT THE ASSISTANCE AND PRESENCE OF A REPRESENTATIVE OF THE MINISTRY; THAT THE MINISTRY FORMS A DISTINCT RANK, OR CLASS; THAT A CONGREGATION HAS NO RIGHT TO CALL A PASTOR WITHOUT THE ASSISTANCE AND PRESENCE OF A REPRESENTATIVE OF THE MINISTRY; THAT THE MINISTRY FORMS A DISTINCT RANK OR CLASS; THAT A CONGREGATION MUST OBEY ITS PASTOR IN ALL THINGS NOT CONTRARY TO GOD'S WORD; THAT NOT THE CONGREGATION, BUT ONLY THE MINISTRY HAS THE RIGHT TO JUDGE DOCTRINE, THAT ORDINATION IS A DIVINE ORDER AND GIVES VALIDITY AND EFFICACY TO THE WORK OF THE PASTOR.[27]

Baepler furthermore reminds us that Grabau taught...THAT THE ONE HOLY CHRISTIAN CHURCH IS A VISIBLE CHURCH, THAT BY IT IS NOT MEANT SCATTERED BELIEVERS BUT THOSE WHO GATHER ABOUT THE WORD AND THE SACRAMENT, THAT

MEMBERS OF THE TRUE CHURCH ARE NOT FOUND IN COMMUNIONS THAT TEACH ERROR, THAT COMMUNION WITH THE INVISIBLE CHURCH IS NOT SUFFICIENT TO OBTAIN SALVATION. Regarding the terms "visible" and "invisible"—pertaining to the Church—Buffalo stated...THAT THE CHURCH AS THE BODY OF CHRIST IS INVISIBLE, ACCORDING TO ITS INNER GLORY, BUT THAT THE CHURCH IS VISIBLE AS THE BELIEVERS IN A CONGREGATION GATHER AROUND THE PURE WORD AND SACRAMENTS.[28]

Regarding the Office of the Keys, Baepler points out that...BUFFALO TAUGHT THAT CHRIST DID NOT GIVE THE KEYS OF THE KINGDOM OF HEAVEN TO THE CHURCH AND TO EVERY TRUE BELIEVER, BUT SOLELY AND EXCLUSIVELY TO THE PASTORS; THAT A CONGREGATION DARE NOT JUDGE AND DECLARE THAT THE SINNER IS TO BE HELD AS A HEATHEN AND A PUBLICATION, FOR THE PASTOR ALONE HAS THE POWER TO EXCOMMUNICATE SINNERS.[28]

These doctrines, of course, stood in the way of achieving a union with the Missouri Synod. In fact, in 1866 Grabau excommunicated a number of his own synod "For entertaining Missouri principles." He even excommunicated an entire congregation for the same cause.

But under the new constitution the Office of Senior Ministerii was dropped, and in its place provisions were made simply for the Office of President. Before that time, the Senior Ministerii had been elected by the pastors of the synod, but under the new constitution the president was to be elected by the synod.

SCHOOLS AND PUBLICATIONS

SCHOOL

From 1840 to 1929 a seminary (which developed into Martin Luther Seminary, 1954) was maintained. Parochial schools were considered absolutely essential.

PUBLICATIONS

There were two publications for a time, but both were discontinued in 1929 in lieu of the three-way merger forming the American Lutheran Church. Grabau even published a hymnal.

THE BUFFALO SYNOD ENTERS THE MERGER FORMING THE AMERICAN LUTHERAN CHURCH (ALC)

In 1924 Buffalo made overtures for inclusion in the proposed merger of the Ohio and Iowa Synods. Buffalo's action has been noted already in the individual histories of these two synods. Buffalo resolved: THAT DEFINITE STEPS BE TAKEN AT OUR SYNODICAL CONVENTION IN JUNE (1925) TO EFFECT A MERGER OR UNION WITH THE IOWA SYNOD AND POSSIBLY ALSO WITH OHIO, PROVIDING SATISFACTORY ARRANGEMENTS CAN BE MADE; ALSO THAT A COMMITTEE BE APPOINTED TO NE-

By 1928 the matter of Iowa's doctrine of Scripture (concerning inerrancy) had been taken care of to the satisfaction of Ohio and Buffalo and by 1930 the three synods agreed on the final form of the constitution. The merger was officially formed on August 11, 1930. At the time of the merger Buffalo numbered 38 pastors, 1 foreign missionary, 2 professors, 48 congregations, 11,000 baptized members and 7-8,000 communicants. Buffalo furnished but 3% of the total membership of the new body.

Footnotes for Chapter Thirty

1 Abdel Ross Wentz, *A Basic History of Lutheranism in America*, (Philadelphia, PA: Muhlenberg Press, 1955), p. 68.

2 Erwin L. Lueker, Editor in Chief, *Lutheran Cyclopedia*, (St. Louis, MO: Concordia Publishing House, 1954), p. 757.

3 Walter A. Baepler, *A Century of Grace—A History of the Missouri Synod 1847-1947*, (St. Louis, MO: Concordia Publishing House, 1954), p. 70.

4 Tract #1 of a series titled: Continuing in His Word; "Lutheran Bodies in the U.S.A.", published by the Wisconsin Ev. Lutheran Synod, p. 5.

5 Carl S. Mundinger, *Government in the Missouri Synod*, Concordia Historical Series Vol. IV, (St. Louis, MO: Concordia Publishing House, 1947), p. 193.

6 Mundinger, *Government...*, p. 199.

7 Baepler, *A Century of Grace...*, p. 44.

8 Baepler, *A Century of Grace...*, p. 146.

9 Baepler, *A Century of Grace...*, p. 147.

10 Baepler, *A Century of Grace...*, p. 147.

11 Baepler, *A Century of Grace...*, p. 63, 64.

12 Baepler, *A Century of Grace...*, p. 64.

13 E. Clifford Nelson, The Lutheran Church in North America, (Philadelphia, PA: Fortress Press, 1975), p. 379.

14 Nelson, *The Lutheran Church...*, pp. 378, 379.

15 Nelson, *The Lutheran Church...*, pp. 445, 446.

16 R.C. Wolf, *Documents of Lutheran Unity in America*, (Philadelphia, PA: Fortress Press, 1966), pp. 360, 361.

17 Nelson, *The Lutheran Church...*, pp.

18 Wolf, *Documents...*, p. 328.

19 Wolf, *Documents...*, p. 328.

20 Wolf, *Documents...*, p. 328.

21 Wolf, *Documents...*, p. 328.

22 Wolf, *Documents...*, p. 364, Doc. #151.

23 Wolf, *Documents...*, p. 342, Doc. #146.

24 Nelson, *The Lutheran Church...*, p. 449.

25 Nelson, *The Lutheran Church...*, p. 449.

26 Baepler, *A Century of Grace...*, p. 139.

27 Baepler, *A Century of Grace...*, pp. 140, 141.

28 Baepler, *A Century of Grace...*, pp. 140.

29 Baepler, *A Century of Grace...*, pp. 141.

30 Wolf, *Documents...*, p. 330, Doc. #138, Item 6.

CHAPTER THIRTY-ONE

AMERICAN LUTHERAN CHURCH (ALC)
1930 - 1960

HISTORY SUMMARY

We have already touched upon much of the history of forming the American Lutheran Church (ALC) by examining the history of the three merger synods: the Joint Ohio Synod, the Iowa Synod, and the Buffalo Synod. This chapter will serve as a historical summary of the event.

EARLY NEGOTIATIONS
AMONG THE MERGER SYNODS

THE OHIO SYNOD FURNISHES THE INITIATIVE

Richard C. Wolf points out that for over thirty years after its formation in 1854, the Iowa Synod lived a lonely existence among German bodies in the west because of its stand on Open Questions and its limited membership in the somewhat liberal General Council. Joint Ohio gravitated to the Synodical Conference (1872), thus choosing the Conference over Iowa. After the Ohio Synod withdrew from the Synodical Conference over the predestinarian controversy in 1881, a private conference was held between leaders of the Ohio and Iowa Synods at the urging of Professor Gottfried Fritschel. In 1887 Ohio proposed to Iowa that an official conference of representatives be held. Six years later a colloquy was held in Michigan City, Indiana, at which time theses were formulated, but were not accepted officially by the two synods.

THE TOLEDO THESES

Not until fifteen years had passed were negotiations renewed. As a result, a meeting was held in 1907 in Toledo. Here the Toledo Theses were formulated, which actually amounted to a revision of the Michigan City Theses, and were later accepted by both synods: Iowa in 1908, and Ohio in 1910. In the Toledo Theses it is of interest to note the following in regards to the Office of the Ministry: THE CALL (TO A PASTORATE) IS A RIGHT OF THE CONGREGATION WITHIN WHOSE BOUNDS THE MINISTER IS TO DISCHARGE HIS OFFICE. ORDINATION IS A PUBLIC AND SOLEMN CONFIRMATION OF THE CALL AND IS BUT AN APOSTOLIC CHURCHLY CUSTOM OR ORDER.[1] Compare this with the teaching of Pastor Grabau and the Buffalo Synod, that ordination is a divine institution and as such, must always be adhered to.

Also of special interest is Theses IV, Open Questions. It is stated: COMPLETE AGREEMENT IN ALL ARTICLES OF FAITH IS THE INDISPENSABLE CONDITION OF CHURCH FELLOWSHIP. PERSISTENT ERROR IN AN ARTICLE OF FAITH ALWAYS CAUSES DIVISION. COMPLETE AGREEMENT IN ALL NON-FUNDAMENTAL DOCTRINES CANNOT BE ATTAINED ON EARTH, BUT IS NEVERTHELESS THE GOAL AFTER WHICH TO STRIVE.[2]

In regards to Predestination, Theses VI reads: WE FIND THAT THE CHURCH-DIVIDING FACTOR IN THE MISSOURI DOCTRINE OF PREDESTINATION IS THE SEVERANCE OF THE UNIVERSAL GRACIOUS WILL OF GOD AND THE SPECIAL COUNSEL OF ELECTION INTO TWO *CONTRADICTORIAE VOLUNTATES* [CONTRADICTORY WILLS] FORMED APART FROM AND BESIDES EACH OTHER, WHEREBY THE BASIS ON WHICH OUR SALVATION RESTS IS MADE UNSURE, AND THE DIFFERENT DEPARTURES FROM THE LUTHERAN DOCTRINE, WHICH UNDER OTHER CIRCUMSTANCES COULD BE FAVORABLY INTERPRETED, BECOME FUNDAMENTAL ERRORS.[3]

In regards to Conversion, These VI proclaims against synergism (the teaching that sinful man can cooperate in his conversion), and yet goes on to say: WE DENY THAT THE HOLY GHOST WORKS CONVERSION ACCORDING TO THE MERE PLEASURE OF HIS ELECTIVE WILL OR ACCOMPLISHES IT IN THE ELECT IN SPITE OF THE MOST WILLFUL RESISTANCE; BUT WE HOLD THAT BY SUCH STUBBORN RESISTANCE BOTH CONVERSION IN TIME AND ELECTION IN ETERNITY ARE HINDERED.[4]

The acceptance of the Toledo Theses by Iowa and Ohio established some degree of cooperation between the two synods. In the National Lutheran Council, Ohio and Iowa cooperated with other Lutheran bodies—and thus with each other—in ministering to servicemen in the Great War. The NLC was organized on September 6, 1918.

FELLOWSHIP BETWEEN OHIO AND IOWA

IOWA WITHDRAWS FROM THE GENERAL COUNCIL

In 1917 the one thing, which had kept Ohio from declaring full fellowship with Iowa, was removed by Iowa when it withdrew from the General Council. Iowa took this action when it became apparent that the Council would merge with the General Synod and the United Synod in the South to form the United Lutheran Church in America (ULCA), a church body to the left of center as far as doctrine and church practice were concerned. The following year, the Joint Ohio Synod agreed to enter into pulpit and altar fellowship with the Iowa Synod.

EXPLORATION OF POSSIBLE MERGER OF OHIO AND IOWA

In 1919, at a convention of the Eastern District of the Iowa Synod, possible merger with Ohio was discussed. As a result, a resolution was adopted asking the synod to get together with Joint Ohio in formulating a plan for organic union of the two bodies. The Northern Illinois Conference and the Texas District Synod of Iowa also adopted the resolution. Thus it was that Iowa contacted the Ohio Synod, which responded in 1920 by authorizing representatives to work in a Joint Committee with Iowa to consider a possible merger.

Two years later, the Joint Committee recommended that a Committee of Inquiry be set up in each synod. Though approved by the Ohio Synod, the recommendation met with inaction on the part of Iowa. Things were at a standstill until petitions were sent out in 1923 by a joint pastoral conference, inquiring of all pastors of the two synods their attitude toward a merger. Ninety percent were found to be in favor of such a move. This then caused the Joint Committee to resume work, with the result that they proposed a union of the two synods to be brought about in 1924. The districts of the Ohio Synod approved the union by an almost unanimous vote.

ENTER, THE BUFFALO SYNOD AND THE NORWEGIANS

In 1925 the Buffalo Synod entered into the negotiations by making possible a committee to investigate merger with the other two bodies. Also in 1925, the Iowa Synod, following the lead of Ohio's districts, voted in favor of the union. Before the year was up, on November 18, representatives of the three synods, meeting in Minneapolis, adopted the Minneapolis Theses. Recall that in 1919 a set of Theses had been formulated by the representatives of the nine Lutheran bodies, which brought about the National Lutheran Council in Chicago in September 1918. These Theses, known as the 1919 Chicago Theses, were later reexamined at the Minneapolis meeting in 1925 and were included as Section IV (Statement of Doctrine) of the Minneapolis Theses.

At the time that the three synods were negotiating with one another, hoping

513

to form a merger, they were also carrying on talks with the Norwegian Lutheran Church (later known as the Evangelical Lutheran Church), thus hoping to come to doctrinal agreement with that segment of Scandinavian Lutheranism. So it was that the Norwegian Lutheran Church of America was also represented at the meeting in Minneapolis, whose representatives then adopted the Minneapolis Theses. The Norwegians concurred with the other representatives to each submit the Theses to his own synod for action.

THE MINNEAPOLIS THESES – 1925

Among the pertinent points of the Minneapolis Theses are the following: THESE SYNODS...ACCEPT WITHOUT EXCEPTION ALL THE CANONICAL BOOKS OF THE OLD AND NEW TESTAMENTS AS A WHOLE, AND IN ALL THEIR PARTS, AS THE DIVINELY INSPIRED, REVEALED, AND INERRANT WORD OF GOD,... THESE SYNODS ALSO, WITHOUT RESERVATION, ACCEPT THE SYMBOLICAL BOOKS OF THE EVAN-GELICAL LUTHERAN CHURCH, NOT INSOFAR AS, BUT BECAUSE THEY ARE THE PRESENTATION AND EXPLANATION OF THE PURE DOCTRINE OF THE WORD OF GOD AND A SUMMARY OF THE FAITH OF THE LUTHERAN CHURCH... (THE NORWEGIAN LUTHERAN CHURCH OF AMERICA...HAS OFFICIALLY ACCEPTED ONLY THE THREE ECUMENICAL CREEDS, THE *UNALTERED AUGSBURG CONFESSION*, AND *LUTHER'S SMALL CATECHISM*. THIS POSITION DOES NOT IMPLY THAT THE NORWEGIAN LUTHERAN CHURCH OF AMERICA IN ANY WAY REJECTS THE REMAINING SYMBOL-ICAL BOOKS OF THE LUTHERAN CHURCH...BUT...IT HAS NOT BEEN DEEMED NEC-ESSARY TO REQUIRE FORMAL SUBSCRIPTION TO THE ENTIRE *BOOK OF CONCORD*.)...WHERE THE ESTABLISHMENT AND MAINTENANCE OF CHURCH FEL-LOWSHIP IGNORES PRESENT DOCTRINAL DIFFERENCES OR DECLARES THEM A MAT-TER OF INDIFFERENCE, THERE IS UNIONISM, PRETENSE OF UNION WHICH DOES NOT EXIST... (THE GALESBURG RULE), IMPLYING THE REJECTION OF ALL UNION-ISM AND SYNCRETISM, MUST BE OBSERVED AS SETTING FORTH A PRINCIPLE ELE-MENTARY TO SOUND AND CONSERVATIVE LUTHERANISM.[5]

In summary of other important points: In regards to doctrine, the doc-trinal section of the Chicago Theses of 1919 was used. It is to be noted that in the point on Justification, no mention is made of Objective Justifi-cation, but of only that which comes by faith...justified...on account of the imputation of the righteousness of Christ by faith. Regarding faith: FAITH IS NOT IN ANY MEASURE A HUMAN EFFORT...THE POWER TO BELIEVE AND THE ACT OF BELIEVING ARE GOD'S WORK AND GIFT IN THE HUMAN SOUL OR HEART. Re-garding Conversion: IF MAN IS NOT CONVERTED, THE RESPONSIBILITY AND GUILT FALL ON HIM...IF MAN IS CONVERTED, THE GLORY BELONGS TO GOD ALONE, WHOSE WORK OF GRACE IT IS THROUGHOUT. BEFORE CONVERSION OR IN CONVERSION, THERE IS NOT COOPERATION OF MEN, BUT AT THE VERY MOMENT MAN IS CONVERTED, COOPERATION BEGINS THROUGH THE NEW POWER GIVEN IN CONVERSION... Regarding Election: THE CAUSES OF ELECTION TO SALVATION ARE THE MERCY OF GOD AND MOST HOLY MERIT OF CHRIST; NOTHING IN US ON ACCOUNT OF WHICH GOD HAS ELECTED US TO ETERNAL LIFE... WE REJECT ALL FORMS OF SYNERGISM...WE REJECT ALL FORMS OF CALVINISM...[6] Regarding the Lodge Question: The Church of Christ and its congregations can have no fellowship with them (as defined),

514

and should not tolerate pastors who have affiliated with any antiChristian society. Pastors are to testify against the sin of lodgery and persuade lodge members to sever their connection with the lodge.[7]

THE MINNEAPOLIS THESES—A DISCOURAGEMENT TO THE SYNODICAL CONFERENCE:

While the Minneapolis Theses, adopted late in 1925, was to serve as the basis of the merger of Ohio, Iowa, and Buffalo in 1930 and also served as the basis of the new federation the same year of five Lutheran synods, forming the American Lutheran Conference, nonetheless it also became a divisive document.

From 1918 to 1920, committees of the Ohio and Iowa Synods met with similar committees of the Wisconsin and Missouri Synods. These discussions produced a document called the Intersynodical Chicago Theses, which discussed Conversion, Predestination, and other doctrines. The representatives of all four synods, plus the representatives of the Buffalo Synod, unanimously adopted the Theses on April 25 at Chicago. However, the possibility of the Intersynodical Theses becoming the basic document for union, or even for further union talks among the five bodies, was brought to naught when Iowa, Ohio, and Buffalo adopted the Minneapolis Theses later the same year along with the Norwegian Lutheran Church. (Since the Synodical Conference was not in fellowship with this Norwegian group, the Missouri Synod came to the conclusion that fraternal relations with the Iowa, Buffalo, and Ohio Synods were excluded. More will be said on this matter a little later.) The Minneapolis Theses naturally served not only as the basis of pulpit and altar fellowship between the Iowa, Ohio, and Buffalo Synods (1928), it also became the basis in 1929 for fellowship with the Norwegian Lutheran Church.

FINALLY, MERGER IN 1930

THE PROPOSED CONSTITUTION

A constitution with bylaws was prepared by the Joint Commission. Among the most interesting points in the proposed constitution were the following: (1) Full subscription to the Confession of the Lutheran Church. (2) Unity in doctrine and practices are the necessary prerequisite for church fellowship, and there must be adherence to the Galesburg Rule (Lutheran altars for Lutheran communicants, Lutheran pulpits for Lutheran pastors). (3) Rejection of all fellowship with societies, secret or open, that are avowedly religious and do not teach the Triune God, and teach salvation by works. (4) The object of the synod: to promote and disseminate the Christian religion as expressed in the doctrine and practice of the Evangelical Lutheran Church. (5) The synod is given power

515

to supervise its pastors, teachers, congregations, and institutions in regard to doctrine and practice. (6) The synod is an advisory body; any local church connected with the synod remains its own highest authority in all matters subject to the Word of God, and does not in any degree surrender ownership or control of its property. But in joining the synod the local congregation obligates itself to cooperate in the work of the synod and maintenance of synod's regulations. (7) Pastors and congregations may be subject to disciplinary actions and excluded from the membership of the synod. (8) The Canonical Books of the Old and New Testaments in their original texts are, as a whole and in all their parts, the inspired and inerrant Word of God, and accepts these Books in the now generally recognized texts as substantially identical with the original texts and as the only inspired and inerrant authority, source, guide and norm, in all matters of faith and life.

TROUBLE FOR A WHILE WITH THE IOWA SYNOD

In 1926 Iowa approved the proposed constitution and also authorized union. However, Iowa made a small change in the confessional article, which it adopted, and which then led to consternation on the part of Ohio. Iowa seemed to have a different doctrine regarding Inspiration of Scripture. Ohio wanted strict interpretation of the statement that Scripture is the inerrant Word of God, while some in Iowa opposed this strict confessionalism. Buffalo sided with Ohio is this matter. After long discussion, Iowa, in 1928, approved the doctrine of Inspiration and Inerrancy of Scripture in the strict sense that Ohio understood.

Since no further obstacles stood in the way of merger, on August 10, 1930, the three German synods met in St. Paul's Lutheran Church in Toledo, Ohio, and formally organized the American Lutheran Church (ALC) on the basis of the Minneapolis Theses. Rev. C.C. Hein, D.D. was the first elected President.

THE AMERICAN LUTHERAN CONFERENCE

Two months after the American Lutheran Church was formed, it entered into a fellowship agreement with four other Lutheran bodies, who through a number of colloquies came to accept the Minneapolis Theses. They were: the Augustana Lutheran Church (Swedish), the Lutheran Free Church (Norwegian), the United Evangelical Lutheran Church (Danish), and the Norwegian Lutheran Church (later known as the Evangelical Lutheran Church). The American Lutheran Conference, like the Synodical Conference, was a federation, not a merger. Each synod remained autonomous. As has already been mentioned, the basis that served to unite the synods in the fellowship of the American Lutheran Conference was the Minneapolis Theses. The American Lutheran Conference was formally organized on October 29-31, 1930, at Minneapolis.

The Conference embodied the same middle-of-the-road policy as that of the American Lutheran Church. Neither group could find themselves in fellowship with the liberal United Lutheran Church in America (ULCA) on the one hand, nor the ultra-conservative Synodical Conference on the other. Fred W. Meuser in *The Formation of the American Lutheran Church,* as quoted by Wolf, writes:

AGAINST THE SUSPICIOUS AND ISOLATIONIST SPIRIT OF THE SYNODICAL CONFERENCE, THE AMERICAN LUTHERAN CONFERENCE AFFIRMED A SUFFICIENT UNITY OF FAITH, IN SPITE OF SOME DIFFERENCES, FOR CLOSER COOPERATION IN WORSHIP AND WORK. AGAINST THE UNITED LUTHERAN CHURCH IN AMERICA, THE CONFERENCE'S MINNEAPOLIS THESES BORE WITNESS THAT ON THE ISSUES OF INSPIRATION OF THE SCRIPTURES, THE LUTHERAN CONFESSIONS, FELLOWSHIP WITH OTHER CHURCHES, AND ATTITUDE TOWARD SECRET RELIGIOUS SOCIETIES THE UNITED LUTHERAN CHURCH IN AMERICA WAS SERIOUSLY DEFICIENT.[8]

The five constituting bodies in the American Lutheran Conference had (in 1930) 1,384,000 members, compared with 1,520,000 members in the United Lutheran Church.[9]

ORGANIZATION OF THE AMERICAN LUTHERAN CHURCH (ALC)

A UNION OF THIRTEEN DISTRICTS:

The American Lutheran Church, unlike the American Lutheran Conference, was not a federation but rather an organic union, a completely new body. Old district and synod boundaries were torn up, and the new body was organized into the following synodical districts: California, Texas, Northwest, Minnesota, Iowa, Canada, Eastern, Michigan, Wisconsin, Dakota, Illinois, Central, and Ohio. At the time of the merger, the American Lutheran Church numbered about 322,000 communicants. By 1953 it had become the fourth largest general Lutheran body in the United States. In the American Lutheran Church there were 1,890 pastors, 2,017 congregations, and over 790,000 baptized members. By the time of the formation of The American Lutheran Church (TALC) in 1960, the American Lutheran Church (ALC) numbered 1,034,377 baptized members.

ORGANIZATIONS

At Lakeside, Ohio, August 13, 1930, the General Luther League of the Ohio Synod, the Wartburg League of Iowa, and the Young Peoples Society of Buffalo, merged into the Luther League of the American Lutheran Church.

At Toledo, May 29, 1930, the Women's Missionary Conference of Ohio, the General Federation of Lutheran Women's Organizations of Iowa, together with representatives of the Buffalo Synod, organized the Women's Missionary Federation of the Lutheran Church with a full-time president.

The Brotherhood of the American Lutheran Church was organized in 1942 to stimulate lay participation in the programs of the church and to promote lay contacts across synodical lines.

EDUCATION

Educational Institutions, missions, charitable institutions, as well as publications—all became matters to be handled by the ALC and not by individual districts. There were three colleges in the ALC, one university, and two seminaries (Capital at Columbus, Ohio, and Wartburg at Dubuque, Iowa).

MISSIONS

The ALC became well organized for home missions, using the "Mission Package Plan." A sum of about $50,000 was set aside for each new mission that was planned. This money was later paid back by the mission. The ALC did mission work among the Mexicans in the United States and Mexico. It conducted thriving missions in India and New Guinea though it never itself began foreign missions.

PERIODICALS

The *Lutheran Standard* was the weekly English magazine, and the Kirchenblatt, the German biweekly publication. The *American Lutheran Hymnal* was published, which came to be used by other Lutheran bodies also. The publishing house of the ALC was the Lutheran Book Concern, Columbus, Ohio.

INSTITUTIONS

There were five charitable institutions, including one in Canada, owned by the church; there were three church-related institutions, and also other institutions recognized by the ALC. A deaconess motherhouse was located in Milwaukee. [10]

EARLY EFFORTS TOWARD FELLOWSHIP WITH THE SYNODICAL CONFERENCE

At the same time that doctrinal agreement was being hammered out by representatives of the merger synods with the independents synods, which finally resulted late in 1930 with the formation of the American Lutheran Conference, negotiations were being carried on with the Synodical Conference. The committees of the Ohio and Iowa Synods had met six times between 1918 and 1920 with similar committees of the Missouri and Wisconsin Synods to discuss the doctrines of Conversion and Election.

The Intersynodical Committee of the synods continued to meet, taking up doctrines that were in controversy before 1880: Universal Priesthood of Believers, Office of the Ministry, Antichrist, Chiliasm, Sunday, and Open Questions. Finally, on April 15, 1925, the representatives reached unanimous agreement on these doctrines, in what is known as the Chicago (or Intersynodical) Thesis.

However, by 1926, when Missouri met in convention, something had taken place with the three merger synods, which caused Missouri to suspect that the Chicago Theses were, in fact, inadequate. Iowa, Ohio, and Buffalo were negotiating fellowship the Norwegian Lutheran Church of America on the basis of the Minneapolis Theses. The Synodical Conference had objected to the formation of this Norwegian body (formed in 1917 by a union of the Hauge Synod, the United Lutheran Church, and the Norwegian Synod majority—all Norwegian bodies). The reason for the Conference's stand against the Norwegian Lutheran Church was this body's stand on the doctrine of Election. In fact, the Norwegian Lutheran Church had been formed on the basis of a compromise on this doctrine (the Madison Agreement). Thus, when the merger synods, on the one hand, claimed to agree with the Missouri and Wisconsin Synods regarding Election and Conversion, but, on the other hand, agreed to fellowship with the Norwegian Lutheran Church in America, with which the Synodical Conference had not come to agreement, the Missouri Synod questioned whether the Chicago Theses were adequate to serve as the basis for fellowship.

Upon hearing the recommendations of its committee, the 1926 Missouri Synod Convention decided that it could not accept the Chicago Theses in the present form and requested its committee to work for changes. The Theses were placed into the hands of a special Examining Committee. At its 1929 River Forest Convention, the Missouri Synod was faced with a decision on the Chicago Theses as modified during the previous three years. By this time, the three merger synods had taken important steps toward establishing a confederation of synods with others with whom the Synodical Conference was not in doctrinal agreement and fellowship.

The Examining Committee recommended separate action on the Chicago Theses and on the question of entering fraternal relations with the synods with which they had been conferring. The committee then recommended that the Chicago Theses be rejected as a basis for union, declaring them to be inadequate and ambiguous, yes, even declaring it "a hopeless undertaking to make these Theses unobjectionable from the view of pure doctrine. It would be better to discard them as a failure."[11]

The Examining Committee cited the fact that the three merger synods had entered into a closer relationship with "the adherents of the Norwegian *Opgjoer* (the Madison Agreement)" as proof that they do not hold Missouri's position in the doctrine of Conversion and Election. The Committee also concluded: "IT OUGHT NOW ALSO TO BE APPARENT THAT THE MATTER OF CONDUCTING THESE CONFERENCES, TO WIT, THE EXCLUSION OF ALL HISTORICAL MATTERS, IS WRONG. AS A RESULT THE OPPONENTS HARDLY UNDERSTAND EACH OTHER."[12]

The Missouri Synod then decided to discontinue further dealings with the other side, pending the outcome of their relations with the Norwegians. It was at this time that Missouri appointed a committee to formulate the synod's own doctrinal theses, and this resulted in 1932 with the adoption of the "Brief Statement." The Chicago or Intersynodical Theses, written with hopes of uniting the Lutheran synods, when finally laid alongside the Minneapolis Theses, became a complete failure to itself as a comprehensive union document.

HISTORICAL DEVELOPMENTS BETWEEN THE ALC AND THE MISSOURI SYNOD

NEW OVERTURES

At the Missouri Synod's Cleveland Convention in 1935, a communication from the American Lutheran Church was placed before the delegates. It was an endeavor by the ALC to establish pulpit and altar fellowship with Missouri. Missouri's reply, in effect, was that it was willing to confer with other Lutheran bodies on problems of Lutheran union, with a view towards effecting true unity on the basis of the Word of God and the Lutheran Confessions. At the same time, Missouri resolved to appoint a committee of five—designated the Committee on Lutheran Church Union—to meet with representatives of the American Lutheran Church.

It was also stipulated that this committee confer with the other members of the Synodical Conference and keep them informed on matters.

CAN TWO WALK UNLESS THEY ARE AGREED?

By the time that the 1938 Convention of the Missouri Synod convened, the two bodies had met a total of six times. Missouri's committee reported to its St. Louis Convention that agreement had been reached on such past disputed doctrines as Inspiration, Predestination, and Conversion, as well as Sunday and the Office of the Public Administration of the Means of Grace. On the other hand, they reported that the American Lutheran Church had asked for tolerance for certain teachings and interpretations concerning the doctrine of the Last Things, which Missouri had previously rejected.

The Missouri Synod then adopted recommendations which covered several aspects: (1) That the Brief Statement, together with the Declaration, which the American Lutheran Commission had written in answer to the Brief Statement, as well as the provision which Missouri's committee had presented at St. Louis, be regarded as the doctrinal basis for future fellowship between the two bodies. (2) That regarding nonfundamental doctrines (Last Things and Antichrist), Missouri should endeavor to reach full agreement. (3) That in regards to the "visible" side of the church, Missouri's committee was to work to attain uniform and scripturally acceptable terminology and teaching. (The Declaration states that to speak of a visible side of the church when defining its essence "is not false doctrine if by this visible side nothing else is meant than the use of the means of grace.")

Thus Missouri issued a call to the ALC for self-discipline to correct what it felt were variations from sound Bible practices based on sound doctrine. Missouri referred specifically to antiChristian lodges and to antiscriptural pulpit and altar fellowship. Missouri condemned also all unionism. The Missouri Synod in convention also made recommendations regarding fellowship to the effect that: (a) it will depend on individual synodical action on the Brief Statement, the Declaration, and the Missouri committee's report; (b) it will depend on the ALC's establishing doctrinal agreement with all church bodies with which it fellowships (that is, bodies in the American Lutheran Conference); (c) the whole matter of fellowship must be taken to the other synods of the Synodical Conference for approval; (d) pastors of both bodies are encouraged to meet and discuss doctrinal basis for union, and questions of church practice; (e) until fellowship is officially announced, no fellowship is to be practiced by pastors or congregations.

FUTURE UNION OF THE TWO
SYNODS PLAGUED WITH DOUBT

The ALC, meeting the same year at Sandusky, Ohio, formed resolutions of its own regarding the union matter, and these caused Missouri's committee to be apprehensive. Among other things, the ALC resolved: (a) that it is neither possible nor necessary to agree in all nonfundamental doctrines; (b) that the ALC believes that the Brief Statement reviewed in the light of the ALC's Declaration is not in contradiction to the Minneapolis Theses. (Note: The ALC merger was based on the Minneapolis Theses.)

A sentence in the ALC's Declaration caused many in the Missouri Synod consternation: "God purposes to justify those who have come to faith." This statement troubled the Missourians even though the Declaration states: "That which Scripture and the Confessions call eternal election, or predestination unto the adoption of children did not take place *intuitu fidei* (in view of the person's coming to faith)." Statements by the American Lutheran Commissioners regarding the Brief Statement left the Missouri Synod with the impression that the ALC's stand regarding Prayer fellowship, Objective and Subjective Justification, and also regarding fundamental and nonfundamental doctrines, needed to be clarified.

Missouri's committee became even more disturbed when in 1939 it was informed that the Fellowship Commission of the American Lutheran Church and the United Lutheran Church in America had adopted the Pittsburgh Agreement. The article on Inspiration in this new document was not regarded as acceptable by Missouri. The article in question read: THE BIBLE...IS PRIMARILY NOT A CODE OF DOCTRINES, STILL LESS A CODE OF MORALS, BUT THE HISTORY OF GOD'S REVELATION...BY VIRTUE OF A UNIQUE OPERATION OF THE HOLY GHOST, (2 TIMOTHY 3:16; 2 PETER 1:21) BY WHICH HE SUPPLIED TO THE HOLY WRITERS CONTENT AND FITTING WORD...[13] The Missouri Synod strictly taught Verbal (word by word) Inspiration of the Scriptures, and claimed that the Scriptures contain no errors or contradictions, but in all parts and words are infallible truth. Naturally, then, this synod was suspicious of the generalizing, which it found in the Pittsburgh document.

THE ALC HOLDS OUT HANDS BOTH
TO THE RIGHT AND TO THE LEFT

This statement is an apt description of the kind of negotiating which became a characteristic of the American Lutheran Church and of the American Lutheran Conference, of which it formed a major part. They both showed a willingness to sit down with liberals on the one hand and with conservatives on the other hand and then state their agreement with both sides. In a tract titled, "Lutheran Bodies in the U.S.A." issued by the Conference of Presidents of the conservative Wisconsin Synod, the attitude of the American Lutheran Conference is summarized thus: THE SYNODS OF THE AMERICAN LUTHERAN CONFERENCE WANT TO ASSUME A MIDDLE-OF-THE ROAD POSITION IN AMERICAN LUTHERANISM AND IN THEIR DESIRE FOR UNITING ALL OF LUTHERANISM IN AMERICA, HOLD OUT THEIR HANDS TO THE RIGHT AND TO THE LEFT. THEY DO NOT DEMAND COMPLETE AGREEMENT IN DOCTRINE AS THE BASIS FOR CHURCH FELLOWSHIP, AND SOME OF THEM HAVE DIFFERED ALL THESE YEARS FROM THE SYNODICAL CONFERENCE IN THE DOCTRINES OF ELECTION, OBJECTIVE JUSTIFICATION, CONVERSION, THE CHURCH, OPEN QUESTIONS, SUNDAY, AND THE LAST THINGS. A further characterization of the union efforts on the part of the American Lutheran Church and of the other bodies in the American Lutheran Conference is made in this tract: THE HISTORY OF ONE OF ITS MEMBERS, THE IOWA SYNOD, REVEALS A REGRETTABLE LACK OF ZEAL FOR PURE SCRIPTURE DOCTRINE. IN THE CIVIL WAR DAYS, WE COULD NOT IDENTIFY OURSELVES WITH IOWA'S STAND ON OPEN QUESTIONS. TODAY THE AMERICAN LUTHERAN CHURCH, THE MERGER GROUP TO WHICH THE FORMER IOWA SYNOD BELONGS, STILL MAINTAINS: "WE ARE FIRMLY CONVINCED THAT IT IS NEITHER NECESSARY NOR POSSIBLE TO AGREE ON ALL NON-FUNDAMENTAL DOCTRINES."[15]

It is little wonder, then, that the Wisconsin Synod—as well as the small Norwegian Synod (Norwegian Synod of the American Evangelical Lutheran Church, later simply the Evangelical Lutheran Synod)—even want so far as to ask the Missouri synod after 1940 to cease negotiating with the American Lutheran Church.

UNION EVENTS OF THE 1940's

In March 1940, at a joint meeting, the American Lutheran Church Commissioners asked for a statement from the Missouri Synod listing all obstacles yet in the way of fellowship. Missouri then listed the following; (1) The ALC membership in the American Lutheran Conference. The ALC's sister synods in the Conference must occupy Missouri's position. (2) Missouri's membership in the Synodical Conference. No fellowship would be established with the ALC if Missouri's sister synods could not share the fellowship. (3) The points of the Sandusky resolutions aforementioned, plus the Declaration's statements, viz., that God "purposes to justify those who have come to faith." Missouri felt that this militated against the doctrine of Objective Justification, viz., that God pronounced the world justified through Christ, and it is this justification won for the world that the individual sinner accepts through faith, resulting in subjective justification. (4) The ALC's approach to the United Lutheran Church in America, which body does not share Missouri's doctrinal position. (5) Church practice: lack of uniformity of practice with doctrine.

The American Lutheran Church Convention in Detroit in 1940 failed to produce satisfaction on all Missouri's points. Later in the same year, the American Lutheran Church in the Convention of the American Lutheran Conference at

Minneapolis made no attempt to bring that body to the same doctrinal position held by the American Lutheran Church, but rather assured the Conference that it had no intention of leaving it.

In 1941 Missouri's committee reported: THE QUESTION ARISES WHETHER THERE IS NOT A FUNDAMENTAL DIFFERENCE BETWEEN THE AMERICAN LUTHERAN CHURCH AND OUR SYNOD ON THE MEANING OF CONFESSIONAL LOYALTY."[16]

In spite of discouragements and in spite of overtures from both the Wisconsin Synod and the small Norwegian group—made early in 1941—Missouri voted later in the same year to continue striving for unity with the ALC. Missouri also took note of the fact that the Synodical Conference itself, meeting in 1940, had taken no such action as the Wisconsin and Norwegian Synods had called for, but had earnestly asked the Missouri Synod to consider framing only one document between the Joint Committees. At this convention, Missouri also reaffirmed its St. Louis Declaration regarding "agreement in practice."

In its own Convention at Mendota, Illinois, in 1942, the American Lutheran Church declared its readiness to establish pulpit and altar fellowship with either the Missouri Synod or the United Lutheran Church in America, or with both, on the basis of the Pittsburgh agreement, the Brief Statement in the light of the Declaration, and its own Declaration.

This new development was distressing to the Missouri Synod, whose representatives had not found doctrinal agreement with the ULCA on the doctrine of the Inspiration of Scripture. Did the American Lutheran Church's declaration of agreement with the ULCA mean that Missouri and the ALC were really not united on this very basic doctrine?

In 1943, the Wisconsin Synod, disturbed over what it felt was a clearly defined liberal movement in the ALC—while at the same time striving to maintain fellowship with conservative Missouri—addressed the following memorial to that synod: IN VIEW OF THE UNIONISTIC ATTITUDE OF THE AMERICAN LUTHERAN CHURCH, WHICH HAS BECOME INCREASINGLY EVIDENT, WILL YOU NOT AGREE THAT FURTHER NEGOTIATIONS FOR ESTABLISHING CHURCH FELLOWSHIP COULD ONLY UNDERMINE THE TESTIMONY THAT HAS PREVIOUSLY BEEN GIVEN, AND SHOULD THEREFORE BE DISCONTINUED FOR THE TIME BEING? [14]

The Missouri Synod did not reply to this question. Instead, it reported to its 1944 Convention that the first steps in preparing a single document were completed and that this document, called "Doctrinal Affirmation," had been presented in a preliminary way to the American Lutheran Church Commissioners, with the promise by them that the Affirmation would be placed before their own 1944 Convention. This document was to a great extent a combination of the Brief Statement and phraseology added from the Declaration. Missouri members were instructed to be prepared to vote on the Doctrinal Affirmation at its 1947 Convention. If accepted by both bodies, it would supersede all previous doctrinal documents and resolutions accepted by the Missouri Synod in 1938 and 1941. However, nothing came of these high hopes.

In 1946 the American Lutheran Church, meeting at Appleton, Wisconsin, rejected the Doctrinal Affirmation as "not generally acceptable." The American Lutheran Church also declared that it "despaired of attaining Lutheran unity by way of additional formulations and reformulations."

In the year that followed, the ALC Commissioners issued "A Friendly Invitation," repeating its 1938 resolution and declaring the Brief Statement along with its Declaration as sufficient doctrinal basis for fellowship. While the ALC felt that discussion had not turned up any fundamental doctrinal differences to prohibit fellowship between the two bodies, it also expressed the belief that "there is an area where there exists an allowable and wholesome latitude of theological opinion on the basis of the teachings of the Word of God." The ALC regarded the demand for a unified statement as a basis for fellowship a "threat to evangelical liberty of conscience."

In its 1947 Convention, Missouri heard this report by its Committee on Doctrinal Unity, listing three impediments to union with the American Lutheran Church: (1) The manifest lack of doctrinal unity. (2) The difference in conviction regarding the degree of doctrinal unity required for fellowship. (3) The membership of the American Lutheran Church in the American Lutheran Conference.

THE COMMON CONFESSION

Missouri set aside its 1938 Union Document and Resolutions, not retracting them but rather considering them as no longer adequate. At the same time the delegates decided to go ahead with negotiations with the American Lutheran Church. Quite evidently this body no longer despaired of attaining Lutheran unity by way of "additional formulations and reformulations." The ALC's Committee on Fellowship went ahead with its counterpart in the Missouri Synod, and by 1950 had succeeded in drawing up a new document, "The Common Confession." This document was adopted by both bodies the same year. The ALC adopted the Common Confession after only a few minutes study and without debate. Missouri's resolution reads: WHEREAS, BY THE GRACE OF GOD THE COMMITTEE ON DOCTRINAL UNITY OF THE SYNOD AND THE COMMITTEE ON FELLOWSHIP OF THE AMERICAN LUTHERAN CHURCH HAVE JOINTLY PRODUCED THE DOCUMENT KNOWN AS THE COMMON CONFESSION...RESOLVED, THAT WE REJOICE AND THANK GOD THAT THE COMMON CONFESSION SHOWS THAT AGREEMENT HAS BEEN ACHIEVED IN THE DOCTRINES TREATED BY THE TWO COMMITTEES.[18]

The 1950 Missouri Synod Convention had instructed its Unity Committee to continue negotiations with the American Lutheran Church Commissioners on matters not covered by the Common Confession: unionism, lodgery, and "practical matters." The result was a Common Confession Part II, longer than Part I.

In Missouri's 1953 Houston Convention it adopted the following resolution: Whereas, Part II of the Common Confession is intended as a supplement to Part I; therefore, be it resolved that for purposes of study, Parts I and II of the Common Confession hereafter be treated as one document, with the understanding that Part I has not been adopted. Missouri's Houston Convention voted to take no action on the overtures received regarding the Common Confession Part I, but urged all to study the Common Confession in its present form (Part I and II). It also asked the Wisconsin and Norwegian Synods, as well as its own protesting members, to wait until the Missouri Synod's action on the matter at its 1956 Convention, before taking any (disciplinary) action themselves.

The Common Confession Part II did not solve the problems that existed, as far as the Wisconsin and Norwegian Synods were concerned, and relationships between Missouri and the protesting sister synods became more strained. In fact, in 1953 the Wisconsin Synod adopted a resolution which listed, among other things, Missouri's reaffirmation of its acceptance of the Common Confession as "a settlement of past differences which in fact are not settled," as being responsible for bringing about the break in relations which at that time was threatening the Synodical Conference and the continuation of Wisconsin's fellowship with Missouri.

The Norwegians took exception especially to the fact that the Common Confession did not cover the doctrine of Objective Justification or the doctrine of Sunday.

A NEW MERGER IN THE WORKS

Twenty years of intensive efforts by both bodies to arrive at a basic document for church union came to nothing when in the mid-fifties the ALC found itself on the verge of merger with other synods in the American Lutheran Conference. The bodies with which the ALC had been carrying on discussions were: the Evangelical Lutheran Church (Norwegian), the United Evangelical Lutheran Church (Danish), and the Lutheran Free Church (Norwegian). The Augustana Synod (Swedish), meanwhile, was working out plans to unite with the United Lutheran Church in America.

Work on the merger had been underway since the 1950 Convention of the ALC, at which time the delegates had voted in favor of such a merger. In the 1954 Convention at Beatrice, Nebraska, the ALC committed itself to vote on the merger question at its 1956 Convention. The merger of the four out of five bodies of the American Lutheran Conference seemed a strong possibility. Enthusiasm ran high at Beatrice. Dr. Edw. Schram, reporting in the November 13th Issue of the *Lutheran Standard* described it thus: THE CONVENTION MOOD WAS THE ECCLESIASTICAL COUNTERPART OF THE FOOTBALL CROWD MOOD THAT SHOUTS: "WE WANT A TOUCHDOWN!" "WE WANT A MERGER!" As to the possible merger date, Dr. Schram could say with certainty only that "We are on the way...and gathering speed as we go."

The Fellowship Committee was instructed to "continue to work constructively toward full unity and ultimate pulpit and altar fellowship." The constructive work of this committee finally came to naught. The ALC was not able at the time to work out a merger with the United Evangelical Church (Danish). And hopes of working out agreement with the Missouri Synod were also dashed at that body's St. Paul Convention in 1956. Further attempts by the Missouri Synod to unite with the American Lutheran Church were pointless. Missouri's resolutions pertaining to the Common Confession directly reflected its reaction to the ALC's proposed merger with three of the other bodies of the American Lutheran Conference. While Missouri's action did not rescind the Common Confession, it simply set it aside from use as a "functioning union document." Regarding the Common Confession, Missouri passed the following

525

resolutions: (1) ...THAT HEREAFTER THE COMMON CONFESSION PART I AND II BE NOT REGARDED OR EMPLOYED AS A FUNCTIONING BASIC DOCUMENT TOWARD THE ESTABLISHMENT OF ALTAR AND PULPIT FELLOWSHIP WITH OTHER CHURCH BODIES...(2) THAT THE COMMON CONFESSION, ONE DOCUMENT COMPOSED OF PARTS I AND II, BE RECOGNIZED AS A STATEMENT IN HARMONY WITH THE SACRED SCRIPTURE AND THE LUTHERAN CONFESSIONS.

But Missouri also passed the following resolution:...THAT WE AGREE NOT TO ENTER DISCUSSIONS OR NEGOTIATIONS WITH OTHER LUTHERAN SYNODS WITHOUT HAVING INFORMED THE SISTER SYNODS OF THE SYNODICAL CONFERENCE OF OUR INTENTIONS AND WITHOUT HAVING INVITED AND URGED THEM TO JOIN WITH US IN THESE DISCUSSIONS.[2]

THE FORMATION OF THE AMERICAN LUTHERAN CHURCH (TALC)

On April 22, 1960, The American Lutheran Church (TALC) was created by the merger of the American Lutheran Church (ALC) with the Evangelical Lutheran Church, and the United Evangelical Lutheran Church—a union of German, Norwegian, and Danish Lutherans. The Constituting Convention of the new church was held on April 22-24, 1960. The American Lutheran Church (TALC) officially began to function on January 1, 1961.

The American Lutheran Church (TALC) contributed 1,034,377 members to TALC; the Evangelical Lutheran Church contributed 1,153,566 members, while the United Evangelical Lutheran Church—the smallest of the three—contributed 70,149 members. It had been hoped that the small Lutheran Free Church would also join the merger, but it twice voted against it. However, when the Free Church later took a third referendum, two-thirds of the membership voted to join The American Lutheran Church. Almost three years late, the Free Church, on February 1, 1963, joined the merger. By May 1, 1963, fifty-one congregations of the Free Church had not participated in the merger, whereas 277 congregations had. A total of almost 6,000 members of the Free Church refused to join with the three other congregations in TALC. On October 25-28, 1962 The Association of Free Lutheran Congregations was formed by the dissidents.

The Augustana Evangelical Lutheran Church, formerly a member of the American Lutheran Conference, voted early in 1960 to adopt merger plans with the United Lutheran Church in America (ULCA), the Finnish Evangelical Lutheran Church (Suomi Synod), and the American Evangelical Lutheran Church (Danish).

A brief overview of The American Lutheran Church (TALC) is given in another chapter.

Footnotes for Chapter Thirty-One

1 Richard C. Wolf, *Documents of Lutheran Unity in America*, (Philadelphia, PA: Fortress Press, 1966), p. 217; Doc. #96.

2 Wolf, *Documents*, p. 217; Doc. #96.

3 Wolf, *Documents*, p. 218; Doc. #96.

4 Wolf, *Documents*, p. 218, 219; Doc. #96.

5 Wolf, *Documents*, p. 340-342; Doc. #146.

6 Wolf, *Documents*, p. 299, 399; Doc. #133.

7 Wolf, *Documents*, p. 342; Doc. #146.

8 Wolf, *Documents...*, p. 339; quoting Fred W. Meuser, *The Formation of the American Lutheran Conference*, pp. 247, 248.

9 Wolf, *Documents*, p. 339.

10 Erwin L. Lueker, Editor-in-Chief, *Lutheran Cyclopedia*, (St. Louis MO: Concordia Publishing House, 1954), p. 26.

11 Wolf, *Documents*, p. 370; Doc. #152.

12 Wolf, *Documents*, p. 370; Doc. #152.

13 Wolf, *Documents*, p. 378, 379; Doc. #157.

14 Tract #1: Continuing in His Word—a series. The tract is titled "Lutheran Bodies in the U.S.A."—issued by the Joint Synod of Wisconsin, pp. 2,3,5,6.

15 Tract #1: Continuing in His Word—a series. The tract is titled "Lutheran Bodies in the U.S.A."—issued by the Joint Synod of Wisconsin, pp. 2,3,5,6.

16 Walter A. Baepler, *A Century of Grace—A History of the Missouri Synod 1847 – 1947*, (St. Louis, MO: Concordia Publishing House, 1947), p. 325.

17 Proceedings 1943, Joint Synod of Wisconsin Convention, p. 69.

18 Proceedings 1950, Joint Synod of Wisconsin Convention, p. 585.

19 Proceedings 1953, Joint Synod of Wisconsin Convention, p. 520.

20 Wolf, *Documents*, p. 439, 440; Doc. #173.

CHAPTER THIRTY-TWO

THE AMERICAN LUTHERAN CHURCH (TALC) (THE "NEW" AMERICAN LUTHERAN CHURCH) 1960 - 1988

The American Lutheran Church (TALC), which began to function officially in 1961, was formally organized on April 22, 1960, at Minneapolis, Minnesota. It took ten years of negotiations to finally bring this about. TALC, or simply the ALC (the "new" one) as it was later generally referred to, was the result of a merger in 1960 of Lutheran bodies that had been members of the federation known as the American Lutheran Conference (1930). These were the American Lutheran Church (the "old" ALC—1930), the Evangelical Lutheran Church (ELC—1917), and the United Evangelical Lutheran Church (UELC—1896). The Lutheran Free Church (LFC—1897(later joined the merger in 1963. The Augustana Lutheran Church (1860), though a member of the American Lutheran Conference, withdrew from negotiations, because it felt that negotiations ought not be confined to member synods of the Conference, thus excluding the United Lutheran Church in America (ULCA—1918). Augustana finally consolidated in 1962 with the United Lutheran Church, the American Evangelical Lutheran Church (AELC—1872), and the Finnish Evangelical Lutheran Church of America (Suomi Synod—1890), to form the Lutheran

Church in America (LCA).

The "new" American Lutheran Church proclaimed itself to be the first United States Lutheran merger to cross national lines. The American Lutheran Church was of German origin, the Evangelical Lutheran Church was itself a merger of three Norwegian bodies, and the United Evangelical Lutheran church was of Danish origin. The Lutheran Free Church, which joined in 1963, was also Norwegian. And so, with the formation of the new American Lutheran Church, the lines of national origin began fading away in earnest.

The new American Lutheran Church was at the time the third largest Lutheran body in the United States, surpassed in size by the Lutheran Church in America and the Lutheran Church-Missouri Synod—in that order. It also had the distinction of being the tenth largest Protestant body in America.

The old American Lutheran Church contributed 51% of the membership to the new American Lutheran Church, the Evangelical Lutheran Church contributed 46% of the membership, the United Evangelical Lutheran Church contributed 3%, and the Lutheran Free Church contributed only 1%. The new American Lutheran Church had (in round numbers): 1,200,000 communicant members; 2,300,000 baptized members; 5,300 pastors and about 5,300 congregations.

HOW THE MERGER CAME ABOUT

The United Evangelical Lutheran Church (UELCA) in Convention in 1948 invited the American Lutheran Church and the Evangelical Lutheran Church to consider working toward union of the three bodies. At the same time, another proposal for merger or federation was being made by conventions of the United Lutheran Church in America (ULCA) and the Augustana Lutheran Church. Such a union would bring together Lutherans on a much broader scale, including all member bodies of the National Lutheran Council (NLC), which at that time included about 95% of the Lutheran Churches in this country. But reaction to this call to unite was mixed. The question whose answers provided by the large Lutheran bodies proved vexation to union was: Does confessional unity require theological uniformity? The ULCA and subsequently the LCA said no, while the Missouri Synod and the ALC said yes.[1]

As it turned out, two separate merger movements were formed. At the American Lutheran Conference meeting in Detroit in November 1948, resolutions were passed calling for "an all-Lutheran free conference" under NLC auspices. On January 4-5, 1949, separate meetings of representatives of the NLC and representatives of the American Lutheran Conference were held to discuss organic merger of the NLC bodies, or at least a federation of these bodies.

When the representatives of the NLC bodies met on January 4, a resolution was passed without dissenting vote to seek "by all proper means a closer organization-affiliation of the participating bodies."[2] It was then voted to appoint a committee of fifteen, whose duty it would be to prepare a structural plan for closer organizational affiliation of the NLC participating bodies, and report back to the full committee, consisting of thirty-four representatives.[3] A negative note was voiced by the president of the UELC, warning that his body would hesitate to take the step toward closer affiliation of the NLC bodies because of certain lax practices by the United Lutheran Church (including lodge membership by pastors).

The next day the American Lutheran Conference representatives met. Finally, a resolution was passed pressing for enactment of the plans of the NLC meeting held the day before. Again, criticism of the ULCA was heard, this time regarding its doctrinal stand on Verbal Inspiration.

As time passed, the two groups—Augustana and the ULCA on the one hand, and the AELC, ALC, UELC, and Lutheran Free Church on the other hand— grew farther apart, thus nullifying the movement to unite all the NLC bodies. What remained of the union movement was the thrust to unite the member bodies of the American Lutheran Conference. The ULCA was purposely excluded from these union efforts. The Augustana Church leaned toward the ULCA and therefore withdrew from the Conference union movement. Three of the bodies forming the American Lutheran Conference (ELC, ALC, UELC) formed a Joint Union Committee, which ultimately drafted a "United Testimony of Faith and Life" to serve as a basis for future union. Other Lutheran bodies that were members of the NLC entered into merger negotiations with the result that in June 1962 a constitution was drawn up for the Lutheran Church in America (LCA). The merger bodies were: the ULCA, the Augustana Church, the AELC, and the Finnish Evangelical Lutheran Church of American (Suomi Synod).

When the United Testimony received approval from the ELC, ALC, UELC and the LFC, the Committee went on with its work of drafting plans for a merger. After a congregational referendum in 1955 failed to obtain enough votes in favor of a merger, the Lutheran Free Church withdrew from union negotiations. A second referendum in 1957 again failed to produce enough favorable votes. But while not participating in the original merger forming the new American Lutheran Church, the Lutheran Free Church finally gave approval of the merger in a third congregational referendum in the fall of 1961. And then, in the fall of 1962, the Free Church, while meeting in Milwaukee, voted to apply for membership in the new ALC.

The actual forming of the ALC suffered some delay due to questions that arose, which caused problems. Can the Augustana Church be included? Shall we join the World Council of Churches? Perhaps we can include the United Lutheran Church? But then, after more than ten years of negotiations, formal organization of the new American Lutheran Church was finally achieved on April 22, 1960, at Minneapolis. The first elected president was Dr. Fredrick A. Schiotz, the president of the ELC.

ORGANIATION OF THE NEW ALC

Supreme authority was posited in the Biennial General Convention. Between conventions, the authority was held by a forty-six member Church Council.

THE NEW AMERICAN LUTHERAN CHURCH IMMEDIATELY SHOWED AN ECUMENICAL SPIRIT

In 1961 the Constitution Convention of the ALC adopted a budget of $18,000,000 for the first year. At the same time the new body voted to seek membership in the Lutheran World Federation, the National Lutheran Council, the World Council of Churches, and the Canadian Lutheran Council. This became subject to mandatory review the following year. Because of opposition, membership was not sought in the National Council of Churches in the U.S.A. The American Lutheran Church maintained a standing committee on relations with other Lutheran bodies, and declared its willingness "to enter into discussions looking toward altar and pulpit fellowship with any and all Lutheran Churches which confess their adherence to the Holy Scriptures as the Word of God in all matters of faith and life, and subscribe to the Confession of the Lutheran Church."

A its 1964 Convention, which has been dubbed "the Positive Convention," the delegates heard a memorial introduced by the Southeastern Minnesota District, which requested that the ALC declare immediate fellowship with the Lutheran Church in America. In making this request, the memorial took into consideration that this declaration of fellowship by the body would only be a public acknowledgment of what the ALC had been practicing right along. Dr. Schiotz then explained to the delegates the delicate position that the American Lutheran Church found itself in at the time. While he agreed in principle with the desire to declare full fellowship with the LCA, he felt that to do so might jeopardize the proposed Lutheran Council in the U.S.A. (LCUSA), which would include the Missouri Synod as well. He pointed out that the historical tradition in the Lutheran Church in this country of discussing each other's doctrinal stand before declaring altar and pulpit fellowship was especially strong in the Missouri Synod. On the other hand he pointed out that the LCA had declined on several occasions to join in discussions of church fellowship with the ALC and the Missouri Synod on grounds that there is already sufficient agreement on the basis of the Lutheran Confessions, and that no more doctrinal statements are necessary as a prelude to altar and pulpit fellowship. Furthermore, Dr. Schiotz pointed out that inasmuch as doctrinal discussion had been going on between the ALC and the Missouri Synod it would be "administratively intolerable," at this time, to declare pulpit and altar fellowship with the LCA. Pointing out that progress in ALC-Missouri relationships was excellent, Dr. Schiotz expressed the hope that with the completion of negotiations between these two bodies, altar and pulpit fellowship might be declared among all three bodies. It was hoped that the LCA would not construe the ALC's action of not declaring fellowship at this time with the LCA, as being unfriendly toward them.

The memorial of the Southeastern Minnesota District, together with other memorials on the subject of fellowship with the LCA, was referred to the Standing Committee on Relations to Lutheran Churches. The *Lutheran Standard* in its November 17, 1964 edition, summarized the matter this way: THE CHOICE BEFORE THE CONVENTION WAS EITHER TO DECLARE FELLOWSHIP WITH ONE LARGE

Lutheran body immediately or to withhold official declaration of that fellowship at this time in the hopes that in the near future all three major Lutheran groups might be in fellowship. The decision of the convention was that holding out for total Lutheran unity was the more positive action.

FOREIGN MISSIONS

The following missions were brought into the "new" ALC merger by the "old" ALC: India, New Guinea, and Ethiopia. Foreign missions of the ELC brought into the merger: Nationalist China and Hong Kong; Madagascar; Zululand; the Cameroon, Africa; South American fields: Columbia and Brazil; Japan; Mexico—a total of eight fields.

HOME MISSIONS

The goal was set early in the new ALC's existence to open 100 new missions per year. This goal was not achieved. The greatest mission expansion was during the 1960's, but then the '70's witnessed a tapering off process.

A SMILING GALESBURG RULE

The Akron-Galesburg Rule of the old American Lutheran Church (org. 1930) came up for new interpretation at the 1964 Convention of the new ALC. This interpretation gave a pastor the right to give a visitor communion if the visitor accepts the words of institution as explained by *Luther's Small Catechism*. The new interpretation also pointed out that the rule is not a doctrine, but a principle of action for the church:

To apply it rigidly will be to destroy its original intent, and in our day, to hinder our witness to the world which must be a witness to both truth and love.

Also, an interpretation of the rule reads:

A pastor and a congregation are not irresponsible stewards of the Gospel if they participate in interdenominational pastoral conferences, city and state councils, doctrinal dialogue with other Christian churches, and in occasional evangelical services where a community-wide testimony is made to the Saviorhood and Lordship of Christ. On the other hand, the evangelical paradox in our documents also requires continuing and alert concern that the faith be not denied, and that genuine doctrinal differences be not ignored. The world must see that we love one another, but it must also know that we hold our message and ministry as a mandate for out Lord.

533

FELLOWSHIP DECLARED WITH THE LUTHERAN CHURCH IN AMERICAN AND WITH MISSOURI SYNOD

At its October 18, 1968 Omaha, Nebraska, Convention, the American Lutheran Church declared pulpit and altar fellowship with its three partners in the Lutheran Council in the U.S.A. (LCUSA): the Lutheran Church in America, the Lutheran Church-Missouri Synod, and the Synod of Evangelical Lutheran Churches (Slovak). This action, in view of the recent formation of the general cooperative Council came as no surprise to the Lutheran world. The action was taken by a unanimous standing vote of nearly 1,000 delegates. The fellowship declaration had to be approved by a two-thirds majority of the total votes in the eighteen ALC district conventions the following year. But in the meantime, in 1968, the individual district conventions of the Missouri Synod gave the matter of fellowship with the American Lutheran Church their attention in preparation for the Denver Convention in 1969. This approval came at Denver after much stormy debate.[4]

THE NEW AMERICAN LUTHERAN CHURCH AND THE LUTHERAN COUNCIL IN THE U.S.A.

Movements toward formation of a new Lutheran Council began in 1958 when the National Lutheran Council (NLC) invited all nonmembers to participate in a discussion to determine what is necessary to bring about cooperation between Lutheran bodies in America. The NLC itself was headed toward its own demise, for with the mergers taking place at that time only two bodies would finally make up the Council. The seeking of broader fellowship through joint cooperative efforts seemed to be indicated. The major Lutheran bodies had, of course, kept an eye on the Missouri Synod over the years, coveting to have its fellowship. The NLC proposed that a new agency be formed to bring about cooperative efforts among Lutherans, to include especially the Missouri Synod.

The Missouri Synod accepted the NLC's invitations. The result was a series of three meetings held over the next few years between NLC representatives (which included men from the ALC) and representatives of the Missouri Synod. At each of these meetings the representatives agreed that some cooperation among the various participating bodies was possible.

And so, it came about that at the conventions in 1962 of the new ALC, the newly formed LCA, and the Missouri Synod, the Lutherans found themselves acting on the reports of their representatives to the joint NLC-Missouri Synod discussions. All three conventions decided to accept the recommendations of their representatives and further pursue the matter of a new joint cooperative agency. Hence, each body appointed seven representatives to work together in drafting a constitution. This group of representatives, soon joined by representatives of the Synod of Evangelical Lutheran Churches (Slovak), labeled itself the Inter-Lutheran Consultation.

The common Council for Lutheran cooperation was not based upon doctrinal

534

union, or oneness in practice. The differences remained between them. The ALC could still find in the newly merged ULCA (forming the LCA) cause for criticizing deviations from sound Lutheran practices. The basis of cooperation is stated in the Preamble:

WHEREAS, IN THEIR RESPECTIVE CONSTITUTIONS, THE PARTICIPATING LUTHERAN CHURCH BODIES ACKNOWLEDGE THE HOLY SCRIPTURES OF THE OLD AND NEW TESTAMENTS AS THE ONLY SOURCE AND THE INFALLIBLE NORM OF ALL CHURCH DOCTRINE AND PRACTICE, AND SEE IN THE THREE ECUMENICAL CREEDS AND IN THE CONFESSIONS OF THE LUTHERAN CHURCH, ESPECIALLY IN THE *UNALTERED AUGSBURG CONFESSION* AND *LUTHER'S SMALL CATECHISM*, A PURE EXPOSITION OF THE WORD OF GOD; AND WHEREAS, THE PARTICIPATING BODIES ARE OF THE CONVICTION THAT THEY SHOULD AND CAN MORE EFFEC-TIVELY CARRY ON THEIR WORK AND FURTHER A LUTHERAN WITNESS BY COOP-ERATING IN MATTERS OF COMMON INTEREST AND RESPONSIBILITY, COOPERATION IN WHICH IS NOT AT VARIANCE WITH THEIR DOCTRINE AND PRACTICE; THERE-FORE, THE PARTICIPATING BODIES DO HEREBY ESTABLISH AND WILL MAINTAIN A COMMON AGENCY TO BE GOVERNED BY THE FOLLOWING CONSTITUTION.[5]

The December 1964 issue of the *American Lutheran* reported the follow-ing: BY A UNANIMOUS VOTE THE AMERICAN LUTHERAN CHURCH IN CONVEN-TION AT COLUMBUS OHIO, OCTOBER 21 TO 27, BECAME THE FIRST OF THE MAJOR LUTHERAN BODIES TO APPROVE THE PROPOSED CONSTITUTION FOR THE NEW LUTHERAN COUNCIL IN THE U.S.A. THE VOTE CAME IMMEDIATELY AFTER THE PRESENTATION OF THE RESOLUTION BY DR. FREDERICK A. SCHIOTZ, PRES-IDENT OF THE AMERICAN LUTHERAN CHURCH. IN PRESENTING THE RESOLU-TION DR. SCHIOTZ EMPHASIZED THAT THE CONSTITUTION MADE IT MANDATORY FOR ALL PARTICIPATING BODIES TO TAKE PART IN THE DIVISION OF THEOLOGI-CAL STUDIES. THIS, HE INDICATED, WAS A DEPARTURE FROM THE PRACTICE OF THE FORMER NATIONAL LUTHERAN COUNCIL. HE ALSO INDICATED THAT THERE WERE SOME AREAS, E.G., THE CAMPUS MINISTRY AND VARIOUS PHASES OF THE HOME MISSION PROGRAM, IN WHICH NOT ALL LUTHERAN BODIES WOULD BE PAR-TICIPATING AT THE FIRST. HE EXPRESSED HOPE, HOWEVER, THAT THE NEW LUTHERAN COUNCIL WOULD PROVIDE THE OPPORTUNITY FOR A "GROWING RE-LATIONSHIP."

After Dr. Schoitz' presentation he asked for discussion. None followed and the question was immediately called. Following the unanimous standing vote Dr. Schiotz then expressed joy in being the first of the Lutheran bodies "to have the privilege of approving the proposed constitution for the new Council." Fol-lowing acceptance of the constitution of the LCUSA by the other two bodies, the new agency came into being on January 1, 1967, replacing the NLC.

THE AMERICAN LUTHERAN CHURCH AND THE MISSOURI SYNOD

The 1949 proposal for a merger or a federation of the National Lutheran Council churches failed to accomplish its goal, especially for the reason that the Missouri Synod, whose fellowship was highly desired, would find it impos-sible to participate, for it could not accept the theology and practice of the ULCA and the Augustana Church. There were those, then, who preferred forming a church whose fellowship would be less difficult for the Missouri Synod to accept.

And so, in line with this way of thinking, contacts between the Missouri Synod and the synods of the projected new American Lutheran Church were made in the late 1950's. These synods, through their Joint Union Committee, informed Missouri that they would welcome an invitation to "conduct doctrinal discussions looking to pulpit and altar fellowship." Missouri accommodated them with a favorable reply in 1959, issuing the requested invitation, which was then accepted by the new ALC at its Constituting Convention in April 1960.[6]

Since it was felt that a Missouri-ALC alliance would not set well with the new Lutheran Church in America, this body was subsequently invited to join the fellowship negotiations, but the LCA declined to participate. Imbued with the philosophy of the former ULCA, the LCA was already committed to inter-Lutheran fellowship and therefore viewed additional discussions as unnecessary. The LCA felt that there was already confessional unity, if not theological unity. Theological differences could be discussed in an environment of fellowship based on confessional unity (acceptance of Article VII of the *Augsburg Confession*). The theological differences that existed need not hinder fellowship but be discussed within the confessional unity that exists between Lutherans.

The Missouri Synod and the ALC were not satisfied with this position taken by the LCA and went a head with negotiations.[7]

While some in the ALC wanted this body to declare itself in fellowship with all Lutherans (thus also with the LCA), the ALC—not wanting to jeopardize negotiations with the Missouri Synod—did not bow to pressure to declare itself in fellowship with every other Lutheran body. ALC-Missouri negotiations were conducted for more than a year beginning in November 1964. A "Joint Statement and Declaration" was adopted by both bodies, thus announcing to the world that there existed doctrinal agreement between the two. The Missouri Synod went on to invite the LCA to join fellowship discussions in order to arrive at a clear and formal statement regarding issues not treated explicitly in the Lutheran Confessions of the sixteenth century. Missouri clearly went further than the ALC in defining what was needed in order for doctrinal unity to be declared and fellowship to be established among Lutherans. Subsequently, the ALC voted in 1968 to approve President Schiotz' suggestion made in 1966 to declare fellowship with both the LCA and the Missouri Synod.

It was Oliver Harms, the successor to retiring long-time President John W. Behnken, who led the Missouri Synod into closer relations with the ALC and set the stage for the momentous decision of the 1969 Denver Convention. While voting in a new, conservative president (Jacob Preus) the Convention made the decision to reciprocate the action of the ALC and thus declare fellowship with this body, a move most unwelcome to the conservative side in the synod. The battle lines between conservatives and moderates in the Missouri Synod were being drawn. The decision to declare fellowship with the ALC was made over the objections voiced by the new synod president, a conservative. The issues involved would ultimately tear the Missouri Synod apart. The Missouri Synod's dealing with the ALC is presented in the chapter detailing Missouri's history. Furthermore, the change in Missouri's theological climate, which divided it into two theological groups, is also documented in that chapter.

An additional note: Neither the ALC nor the Missouri Synod joined the National Council of Churches. Yet they were given the privilege—one they accepted—to be represented on committees and commissions of their choice.[8]

THE AMERICAN LUTHERAN
CHURCH'S THEOLOGY

Patsy A. Leppien and J. Kincaid Smith, in their book *What's Going On Among the Lutherans?* draw the following conclusion:

THE ALC MERGER WAS A FURTHER BLENDING OF VARYING DEGREES OF CONFESSIONAL LOYALTY. IT WAS NOT A VICTORY FOR THE CONSERVATIVE MEMBERS BUT A CONCESSION TO THE MORE LIBERAL ELEMENTS...HISTORICAL CRITICISM HAD ENTERED THE NORWEGIAN SEMINARY IN 1947. THUS, INERRANCY AND THE AUTHORITY OF SCRIPTURE WAS AN IMPORTANT ISSUE BOTH BEFORE AND AFTER THE MERGER. HOWEVER, A COMPROMISE WAS REACHED IN MUCH THE SAME MANNER AS IN THE "OLD" ALC MERGER OF 1930, AND THE DOOR WAS THROWN OPEN FOR THE USE OF THE HISTORICAL-CRITICAL METHOD.

The writers point out that the new ALC's first president, Dr. Fredrik A. Schiotz—president of the merging Norwegian Synod or Evangelical Lutheran Church—was a strong supporter of historical criticism.[9]

In summary: the historical-critical method of Bible interpretation was widely used in the ALC. This action, of course, did much to help tear down the barrier that had kept the LCA and the ALC apart. When later the great merger of Lutherans took place establishing the Evangelical Lutheran Church in America (ELCA), the words inerrant and infallible were left out of the proposed constitution for the new Lutheran body (in its Statement of Faith). And when the ELCA came into being it forbid congregations to have a statement in their constitutions declaring the Bible to be the inspired and inerrant Word of God.

The point had been well made that each merger that a church participates in weakens the confessional position of the new body. The cause is not only compromise but the withdrawing of the most confessional members and pastors.

THE ALC AND THE ABORTION ISSUE

On January 22, 1973, the Supreme Court of the United States made a ruling that has since divided the nation and also brought about division in the church. A woman's legal right to have an abortion was assured. As a result of the High Court's decision church bodies felt constrained to take their stand on the issue of abortion. What stand did the ALC take? At its October 14, 1974 General Convention, the ALC declared that it accepts the possibility that an induced abortion may be a necessary option in individual human situations. It further declared that each person needs to be free to make this choice in light of each

537

individual situation. [11]

The ALC claimed to reject induced abortion as a ready solution for problem pregnancies, for it recognized that an induced abortion deliberately ends a developing human life. On the other hand the ALC accepted the possibility that an induced abortion may be necessary as an option that each is free to make. Those who choose this option are obligated to do so after they first weigh the various options and are also obligated to bear the consequences of their decision. The ALC claimed to take a pro-life position. Preventing a possible problem pregnancy is a much preferable action to abortion.[12] There were, of course, those in the ALC who felt that the stand taken on abortion was too liberal.

THE AMERICAN LUTHERAN CHURCH AND THE CHARISMATIC RENEWAL (MOVEMENT)

The charismatic explosion was set off by Father Dennis Bennett, an Episcopal priest serving a parish in Van Nuys, California. Through the charismatic renewal or movement "modern Pentecostalism, which was born in Topeka, Kansas, at the beginning of the twentieth century, and came of age in Los Angeles some five years later, after about fifty years began to spill over into Protestantism's historic churches. In less than a decade the spill grew into a tidal wave as once-cautious tongue-speakers came out in the open to tell of their experiences." All main-line denominations have been effected, including Roman Catholicism.

THERE IS GOOD REASON TO BELIEVE THAT WITHIN THE PROTESTANT FOLD THE LUTHERANS, NEXT TO THE EPISCOPALIANS, HAVE BEEN MOST RECEPTIVE TO CHARISMATIC RENEWAL.[14]

About the same time that the late Father Bennett experienced his personal "Pentecost" a pastor of the American Lutheran Church in San Pedro, California, Larry Christenson, after attending a service in a Four Square Gospel Church, awoke that night to hear himself speaking in tongues. Later, Pastor Christenson became a recognized leader of the charismatic renewal, and wrote a book titled *The Charismatic Renewal Among Lutherans.* Helped by such men as the ALC's Larry Christenson, practically every segment of the worldwide Lutheran Church has been touched by the charismatic renewal.[15]

In 1963 the ALC ordered a special committee to study the renewal and pointed out that "there is a danger of over-emphasis on glossolalia (speaking in tongues) on the part of some, with a distorted Christian perspective as the outcome."[16]

An important feature of the charismatic renewal is that it is both ecumenical and unionistic. "Charismatic assemblies and conferences (both intra-denominational and inter-denominational), local, but also international in scope, "soon became a way of life with the charismatics.[17] " Many of the charismatic activities openly conflict with long-established denominational teachings and traditions, as well as with church polity...For many, old hostilities toward other denominations have all but disappeared via ecumenical, charismatic involvement."[18] The question to ask each other is not "What doctrine do you have?" but "Have you experienced Baptism in the Spirit; do you speak in tongues?"

Larry Christenson not only emphasized speaking in tongues, he also emphasized involvement in a healing ministry, going so far as to claim that the matter of the church today conducting a ministry of healing is a question of obedience. Lack of a ministry of healing is disobedience to the Lord.[19] What is meant, of course, is involvement in miraculous cures of sickness and disease. Faith healing, if you will.

The charismatic renewal in its ecumenical, unionistic spirit does not come to grips with the important issues, which divide churches and keep denominations apart. It simply bypasses them, overlooks differences, and pretends they are not there.

CHURCH FELLOWSHIP WITHOUT DOCTRINAL UNITY BASED UPON GOD'S WORD IS UNIONISM, AND THE MODERN CHARISMATIC MOVEMENT IS FULL OF IT. THE GREATEST OFFENSE IS THE UNIONISM PRACTICED BY PROTESTANT EVANGELICAL CHARISMATICS WITH ROMAN CATHOLICISM TO FORM A UNITED THRUST FOR EVANGELIZING THE WORLD. MISSION WORK IN LEAGUE WITH ROMAN CATHOLICISM CAN ONLY SPREAD A TEACHING OF WORKS RIGHTEOUSNESS—WHICH IS NOT THE WORK OF GOD'S HOLY SPIRIT.

THE HOLY SPIRIT IS…THE "SPIRIT OF TRUTH" (JOHN 14:17; 15:16; 16:3). HOLY SCRIPTURE IS HIS BOOK. THE DOCTRINES IN IT ARE HIS DOCTRINES. IT WOULD BE LOGICAL TO CONCLUDE THAT ANY BELIEVER FILLED WITH THE HOLY SPIRIT WOULD, FIRST OF ALL, HAVE A LOVE FOR THE WORD AND A LOVE AND REVERENCE FOR EVERY TEACHING CONTAINED IN IT. SIMPLY PUT, THIS IS LOVE FOR THE TRUTH. HOW CAN A PERSON WHO LOVES GOD'S TRUTH COMPROMISE WITH FALSE DOCTRINE BY JOINING HANDS WITH IT IN THE CHARISMATIC RENEWAL? HOW CAN TRUE LOVE FOR GOD'S GOSPEL OF FORGIVENESS LEAD OTHERS TO JOIN HANDS WITH THOSE WHO DENY THAT VERY GOSPEL? THE TRUE SPIRIT OF CHRIST IS NOT THE SOURCE OF THIS KIND OF LOVE.[20]

This is an important and valid point, which conservative Lutheranism understands and readily accepts. What, then, is conservative Lutheranism's conclusion regarding Pentecostalism and the charismatic movement or renewal? Consider the following points presented in *The Pentecostals and Charismatics*:

- PENTECOSTAL/CHARISMATIC SPIRIT BAPTISM WITH ALL THAT ACCOMPANIES IT DOES NOT MATCH THE SCRIPTURAL EXPERIENCE IN WHICH THE SPIRIT BRINGS A PERSON TO FAITH IN CHRIST. WHAT THE PENTECOSTAL/CHARISMATIC MOVEMENT EXPERIENCES FINDS NO PARALLEL WITHIN THE EARLY CHURCH.

- MODERN TONGUES-SPEAKING CANNOT BE EQUATED WITH THE TONGUES OF PENTECOST DAY OR WITH THE TONGUES GOD GAVE THE CHURCH IN THE YEARS FOLLOWING PENTECOST DAY.

- THE PHENOMENON OF MODERN "HEALINGS" DOES NOT MATCH THE HEALINGS OF JESUS AND THE APOSTLES.

- THE PERSONAL REVELATIONS MANY IN THE MOVEMENT CLAIM TO HAVE DO NOT FIT THE PATTERN OF SUCH REVELATIONS AS THEY ARE DESCRIBED IN THE EARLY CHURCH.

- THE UNIONISTIC ACTIVITIES OF CHARISMATICS UNDERMINE THE TEACHINGS OF JUSTIFICATION BY FAITH.

- THE PENTECOSTAL/CHARISMATIC MOVEMENT STATES OR IMPLIES THAT ALL WHO ARE TRULY BORN OF THE SPIRIT CAN EXPECT TO RECEIVE BOTH FORGIVENESS OF SINS AND THE VARIOUS GIFTS OF THE SPIRIT. THIS UNDERMINES JUSTIFICATION BY

FINALLY THE GREAT LUTHERAN MERGER

The many years of inter-Lutheran talks finally brought about the largest Lutheran merger in United States history. In 1988 the Lutheran Church in America (LCA, 1962,); the American Lutheran Church (ALC, 1960); and the Association of Evangelical Lutheran Churches (AELC, 1974) united to form the Evangelical Lutheran Church in America (ELCA). This history will be covered later in a separate chapter.

Footnotes for Chapter Thirty-Two

1 E. Clifford Nelson, *The Lutherans In North America* (Fortress Press, Philadelphia, PA, 1975), p. 471.

2 Nelson, *The Lutherans...*, p. 504.

3 Nelson, *The Lutherans...*, p. 504.

4 *The Northwestern Lutheran*, November 24, 1968, Milwaukee, WI.

5 R.C. Wolf, *Documents of Lutheran Unity in America* (Philadelphia, PA: Fortress Press, 1975), p. 630; Doc. #250.

6 Nelson, *The Lutherans...*, p. 529.

7 Nelson, *The Lutherans...*, p. 529.

8 Nelson, *The Lutherans...*, p. 536.

9 Patsy A. Leppien and J. Kincaid Smith, *What's Going on Among the Lutherans?—A Comparison of Beliefs* (Milwaukee, WI: Northwestern Publishing House 1992), p. 330.

10 Leppien and Smith, *What's Going On...*, p. 337.

11 *The Christian News Encyclopedia*, Vol. I (New Haven, MO), p. 13.

12 *The Christian News Encyclopedia*, Vol. I, p. 23.

13 Arthur J. Clement, *Pentecost or Pretense?—An Examination of the Pentecostal and Charismatic Movements* (Milwaukee, WI: Northwestern Publishing House, 1981), p. 63.

14 Clement, *Pentecost or...*, p. 72.

15 Clement, *Pentecost or...*, pp. 72-74.

16 Clement, *Pentecost or...*, (a quote) p. 75.

17 Clement, *Pentecost or...*, pp. 85.

18 Clement, *Pentecost or...*, pp. 85.

19 Clement, *Pentecost or...*, pp. 126.

20 Arthur J. Clement, *The Pentecostals and Charismatics—A Confessional Lutheran Evaluation* (Milwaukee, WI: Northwestern Publishing House, 2000), pp. 209, 210.

21 Clement, *The Pentecostals and Charismatics...*, pp. 212, 213.

CHAPTER THIRTY-THREE

THE LUTHERAN CHURCH IN AMERICA (LCA) (1962-1988)

FOUR BECAME ONE

Cobo Hall, Detroit, Michigan, was the scene from June 28 to July 1, 1962, of the Constituting Convention of the Lutheran Church in America (LCA). This new body, which began its corporate existence on June 1st of that year, was a consolidation or merger—thus a joint continuation—of four church bodies. This new church corporation did not call itself a synod, preferring instead the term "church" in its official title. However, the new body, under its constitution, was to be divided up into synods.

The Lutheran bodies which were brought together in organic union were the following: (1) THE UNITED LUTHERAN CHURCH IN AMERICA (ULCA): This Lutheran body was itself a merger in 1918 of: The General Synod (1821), The General Council (1867), The United Synod in the South (1863). (2) THE AUGUSTANA EVANGELICAL LUTHERAN CHURCH: This body, formed in 1860, was a union of Swedish, Norwegian, and Danish Lutherans. The latter two groups withdrew in 1870. Augustana was strongly influenced by the Swedish Pietism of Rosenius. (3) THE AMERICAN EVANGELICAL LUTHERAN CHURCH: This body, established in 1871, was of Danish background. It represented the Grundtvigian element of Danish Lutheranism. (4) THE FINNISH EVANGELICAL LUTHERAN CHURCH OF AMERICA (SUOMI SYNOD): Established in 1890, this was the newest of the Scandinavian Lutheran churches, with its congregations concentrated mainly in Northern Michigan, Minnesota, and Wisconsin.

Together, the four Lutheran bodies formed the largest Lutheran merger consummated in America up to that time. Each of the four was represented at the Constituting Convention by its president, who read the following announcement for his church: THE _____ IN ACCORDANCE WITH ITS OWN REGULATIONS AND WITH THE PROVISION OF THE AGREEMENT OF CONSOLIDATION HAS ADOPTED SAID AGREEMENT TO FORM THE LUTHERAN CHURCH IN AMERICA, AND I AM PRIVILEGED TO ANNOUNCE IN ITS BEHALF THIS AFFIRMATIVE ACTION.

Each of the four bodies met prior to the Constituting Convention for the purpose of conducting its final closing out of business.

THE AUGUSTANA LUTHERAN CHURCH (630,000) ORDAINED 46 THEOLOGICAL GRADUATES TO THE MINISTRY AND BROUGHT ITS 102 YEARS OF EXISTENCE TO A DRAMATIC END BY SINGING THE HYMN, RISE, YE CHILDREN OF SALVATION. THE AMERICAN EVANGELICAL LUTHERAN CHURCH (25,000) PAID TRIBUTE TO ITS PIONEER DANISH PASTORS AS IT TERMINATED ITS 84 YEARS. THE FINNISH LUTHERAN CHURCH IN AMERICA (SUOMI SYNOD) (36,000) CONCLUDED ITS SEPARATE HISTORY AND IN ITS FINAL CONVENTION DECIDED THAT THE PECTORAL CROSS WORN BY ITS PRESIDENTS SHOULD BE PLACED IN THE ARCHIVES OF SUOMI COLLEGE. THE UNITED LUTHERAN CHURCH IN AMERICA (2,500,000), THE LARGEST OF THE FOUR, WHOSE ORIGINS GOES BACK TO COLONIAL TIMES, IN A CONCLUDING ACTION PRESENTED ITS PRESIDENT, DR. FRANKLIN CLARK FRY, WITH A NEW AUTOMOBILE IN RECOGNITION OF HIS 18 YEARS OF SERVICE AS PRESIDENT. (From a report in *Christianity Today*, July 20, 1962.)

STEPS LEADING UP TO MERGER

Since its inception in 1918 the United Lutheran Church in America (ULCA) had called for and worked toward the union of all Lutheran churches in America. Article VI of its constitution stated the following objectives:

TO EXPRESS OUTWARDLY THE SPIRITUAL UNITY OF LUTHERAN CONGREGATIONS AND SYNODS, TO CULTIVATE COOPERATION AMONG ALL LUTHERANS IN THE PROMOTION OF THE GENERAL INTERESTS OF THE CHURCH, TO SEEK THE UNIFICATION OF ALL LUTHERANS IN ONE ORTHODOX FAITH, AND THUS TO DEVELOP AND UNFOLD THE SPECIFIC LUTHERAN PRINCIPLE AND PRACTICE AND MAKE THEIR STRENGTH EFFECTIVE...TO ENTER INTO RELATIONS WITH OTHER BODIES IN THE UNITY OF THE FAITH AND TO EXCHANGE OFFICIAL DELEGATES WITH THEM.[1]

In carrying out this objective, the ULCA again and again called for the immediate merger of all Lutheran bodies in America. However, such a union of all Lutherans was not forthcoming. Instead, history records that efforts during the 1950's to unite the Lutherans were directed toward forming two separate mergers instead of only one (the LCA and the "new" ALC). And even these two mergers failed to include all Lutheran bodies. Actually, both of these merger movements had their beginnings in 1948, one involving the member Lutheran bodies in the American Lutheran Conference; the other involving member bodies of the National Lutheran Council (NLC). (Refer to Chapter Thirty-four: LUTHERAN COOPERATIVE AGENCIES FORMED IN THE

542

In 1948 an invitation was extended by the United Evangelical Lutherans Church (UELC, Danish) to the American Lutheran Church (ALC, German) and the Evangelical Lutheran Church (ELC, Norwegian) to consider taking steps that would unite the three bodies. Since the Lutheran bodies that were members of the American Lutheran Conference were already in a state of fellowship, the American Lutheran Church (ALC) proposed that all of these bodies merge. This proposal appealed to the ELC instead of attempting to forge a union of the NLC churches that naturally would include the liberal ULCA. The Augustana Church (Swedish) desired the opposite course—merger talks that would include the ULCA. The result was that the ELC and the Augustana Church—both fair-sized bodies—finally went their separate ways.

From a meeting held by the above-mentioned members of the American Lutheran Conference came the proposal to form a Joint Union Committee. In 1950 such a Committee received the approval of the three respective synod conventions. Once set up, the Joint Union Committee (JUC) then extended invitations to the two other groups of the Conference—the Augustana Lutheran Church and the Lutheran Free Church—to take part in the negotiations. From this Committee came a document, "United Testimony on Faith and Life." This somewhat lengthy document, produced in 1952, was to serve as the basis for future union. It contains this statement:

AS AN EXPRESSION OF THEIR COMMON CHRISTIAN FAITH AND A WITNESS TO THEIR UNDERSTANDING OF THE HISTORIC LUTHERAN CONFESSIONS AND TO THE THEOLOGICAL AGREEMENT WHICH HAS BEEN FOUND TO EXIST AMONG THEM, THEY JOIN THIS UNITED TESTIMONY TO OUR TIME AND SITUATION...[2]

As could be expected, the Augustana Church remained aloof to the negotiations and did not approve the United Testimony. Not that Augustana disagreed with this document, it simply felt that the negotiations should be open to all Lutheran general bodies (with the ULCA specifically in mind) and furthermore, that the discussions should include "the consideration of the subject of ecumenical relations."

In 1958 the constitution was drawn up for the "new" American Lutheran Church (TALC), and even a timetable was established for the actual merger to take place. From April 24-27, 1960, the Constituting Convention was held at Minneapolis, at which time Articles of Incorporation, together with the constitution and bylaws, were adopted. The "Articles of Union" were also affirmed and officers were elected. January 1, 1961, was the date set for The American Lutheran Church (TALC) to function as a new body. The Lutheran Free Church was added as a member two years later. And so, the first of the two merger bodies whose union efforts began in 1948 and took shape in the 1950's was in operation.

In 1948 the National Lutheran Editor's Association asked the National Lutheran Council to take steps " to further, by frank and open discussion, the union of all Lutheran Churches in America." Also, in 1948, there came a request from the Kansas Conference of the Augustana Synod to declare in favor of the "organic union of the constituent bodies of the NLC." Augustana concurred with the request and declared in favor of such an organic union. Augustana instructed its Executive Council to "initiate action on behalf of the church looking toward such union...with federation as an intermediate step if necessary."[3]

Six of the eight bodies comprising the NLC—the American Lutheran Church, the Augustana Lutheran Church, the Evangelical Lutheran Church, the Lutheran Free Church, the United Evangelical Lutheran Church, the United Lutheran Church in America—provided representatives comprising the "Committee of Thirty-four on Lutheran Unity." On January 4, 1949, the Committee had its first meeting. The outcome was that the Committee agreed that a "closer affiliation" of the bodies compromising the NLC was desirable. A fifteen member subcommittee was appointed to prepare a plan to accomplish this goal. The subcommittee posed certain questions to be laid before the NLC bodies: (1) Were the bodies willing to approve organic union in principle and to join in forming the necessary Ways and Means Committee? (2) Would the NLC bodies approve in principle the transformation of the NCL "from a common agency to a federation?" However, when the poll of the NLC bodies was conducted, both organic union and the intermediate step of federation were rejected.[4]

There were Lutheran bodies in the NLC that were also members of the American Lutheran Conference. Among them were those who doubted the doctrinal soundness of the ULCA. They would therefore shun entering an organic union which included the ULCA. Furthermore, there was the hope within the American Lutheran Conference of internal merging of the member bodies. When it was proposed that a conference of representatives of all major Lutheran bodies in American be held, the proposal did not go over well. The UCLA through its Special Commission Relations to American Lutheran Church Bodies rejected the proposal for such a general conference. For one thing it saw no need for further doctrinal discussions as "a fruitful approach to union." What the ULCA desired were conferences called specifically to discuss the uniting of Lutheran bodies in America.

When the Augustana Church failed to open the Joint Union Committee of the American Lutheran Conference to include the ULCA in merger negotiations, Augustana withdrew from the work of the Committee and aligned itself with the ULCA in 1955 to jointly issue a general invitation to Lutheran leaders to a meeting in order to consider "such organic union as will give real evidence of our unity in the faith." Augustana and the ULCA even went so far as to propose drafting a constitution and devising organizational procedures "to effect union" as agenda items for this proposed meetings. The overture was rejected by the Missouri Synod and, of course, by the Joint Union Committee of the three bodies of the American Lutheran Conference, since they were already committed to forming a merger (TALC).

The invitation extended by Augustana and the ULCA was accepted by the American Evangelical Lutheran Church (small Danish) and the Finnish Evangelical Lutheran Church of America (Suomi Synod). The four churches then formed the Joint Commission on Lutheran Unity (JCLU), to work toward a complete merger of the four bodies.

It was only natural that the wide range of cooperation—including mission work—among the bodies comprising the NLC would eventually soften their approach to one another and bring about a desire for closer ties—union of some sort. In considering the union of the aforementioned NLC bodies, Augustana and the ULCA desired a more inclusive merged church body than that being worked out by the American Lutheran Conference bodies. They also desired a fellowship in which they could retain their memberships in the World Council of Churches (WCC) and the National Council of Churches of Christ in the U.S.A.

When the 46 representatives of the four churches of the NLC met for the first time in Chicago in December 1956, they at that time chose the designation "Joint Commission on Lutheran Unity" or JCLU. The doctrinal statements of the four churches were read, and then the resolution of agreement was read and adopted. Progress was swift and the newly seated JCLU rejoiced in noting that there was...

> ...SUFFICIENT GROUND OF AGREEMENT IN THE COMMON CONFESSION OF OUR FAITH, AS WITNESSED BY THE LUTHERAN CONFESSIONS, TO JUSTIFY FURTHER PROCEDURE IN SEEKING FOR A BASIS FOR THE ORGANIC UNION OF THE CHURCHES, INCLUDING THE FORMULATION OF A PROPOSED CONSTITUTION FOR A UNITED CHURCH, HAVING IN IT ARTICLES ON DOCTRINE AND PRACTICAL MATTERS OF ORGANIZATION.[5]

Dr. Franklin Clark Fry of the ULCA carried the most weight on the Commission and...CAME TO THE TASK OF ORGANIZING A NEW CHURCH WITH MORE INSIGHT AND EXPERIENCE THAN ANYONE ELSE; HIS COMPETENCE RANGED FROM MATTERS OF DOCTRINE TO CORRECT PUNCTUATION.[6]

It took a series of plenary sessions and committee meetings covering six years to complete the task of bringing about the merger of the four bodies. A time schedule was adopted and followed: THE TARGET DATE WAS SET FOR A COMPREHENSIVE REPORT [BY THE JCLU] TO THE CHURCHES, AND A FIRST VOTE BY CHURCH CONVENTIONS WAS TO BE IN 1960. THIS MEANT THAT A FINAL VOTE COULD BE TAKEN AND THAT MERGER COULD TO BE CONSUMMATED IN 1962.[7] And so, a constitution had to be readied by the spring of 1960; and it was, along with a report to the churches. The report also included an official "Agreement of Consolidation." The final details were taken care of in plenary sessions of the Commission in 1961 and 1962, with the merger and Founding Convention taking place at Cobo Hall in Detroit, Michigan, June 25 to July 1, 1962. The Lutheran Church in America began its corporate functions on January 1, 1963.

When the congregations of the four bodies voted to form the merger, they did so with the knowledge that there were many "practical problems yet to be settled," which problems were not constitutional in nature.[8] Among the problems which remained to be solved was that involving lodge membership. It should be noted that when this problem came up for discussion in the JCLU, the Augustana leaders questioned the lax attitudes of the ULCA.

Because of the much greater size of the ULCA, the Joint Commission extended this caution:

> THIS IS A NEW CHURCH, NOT THE CONTINUANCE OF ANY ONE OF THE FOUR BODIES. ACTUALLY THIS IS NOT A MERGER IN THE LEGALLY EXACT MEANING OF THE WORD. THAT WOULD IMPLY THE ABSORPTION OF THREE OF THE BODIES BY THE FOURTH. RATHER IS IT A CONSOLIDATION OF FOUR BODIES TO FORM AN ENTIRELY NEW CHURCH ENTITY. THIS MEANS THAT ALL OF US WILL HAVE ADJUST-

MENTS TO MAKE AS WE ACCUSTOM OURSELVES TO THE NEW.

Johannes Knudsen, who reports the above words in his history of the LCA's formation, points out that the new church would be more church and less federation than what the members of the ULCA were used to over the past forty years.

Whereas the new Lutheran body did not refer to itself as a synod, preferring the title "church" instead, it nevertheless wrote into its constitution:

THIS CHURCH SHALL BE DIVIDED INTO SYNODS, WHOSE NUMBER AND BOUNDARIES ARE TO BE DETERMINED BY THIS CHURCH IN ITS BY-LAWS. SYNODS HAVING DISTINCTIVE LINGUISTIC OR NATIONAL CHARACTERISTICS AT THE TIME OF THE ORGANIZATION...MAY AT THEIR OPTION ENTER THIS CHURCH ON A NON-GEOGRAPHIC BASIS. (Article VIII Synods: Section 1)[11]

The 32 synods of the ULCA, the 13 conferences of the Augustana Synod, the 7 conferences of the Suomi Synod, and the 9 districts of the AELC were merged into one and then rearranged into 31 synods. All except the Slovak Zion Synod were sited geographically. The synods of the LCA, listed alphabetically:

CARIBBEAN, CENTRAL CANADA, CENTRAL PENNSYLVANIA, CENTRAL STATES, EASTERN CANADA, EASTERN PENNSYLVANIA, FLORIDA, ILLINOIS, INDIANA-KENTUCKY, IOWA, MARYLAND, MICHIGAN, MINNESOTA, NEBRASKA, NEW ENGLAND, NEW JERSEY, NEW YORK, NORTH CAROLINA, OHIO, PACIFIC NORTHWEST, PACIFIC SOUTHWEST, RED RIVER VALLEY, ROCKY MOUNTAIN, SLOVAK ZION, SOUTH CAROLINA, SOUTHEASTERN, TEXAS-LOUISIANA, VIRGINIA, WESTERN CANADA, WESTERN PENNSYLVANIA-WEST VIRGINIA, WISCONSIN-UPPER MICHIGAN.

Authority in the LCA was divided among the church, the synods, and the congregations. While the individual synod within the LCA were to shepherd their constituent congregations and pastors, the president of the body was the spiritual and temporal head of the church.

LUTHERAN CHURCH IN AMERICA

When the LCA began its corporate functions on January 1, 1963, it did so as the largest Lutheran group, and the fourth largest Protestant body in America. The following statistics given in round numbers shows the picture as it was at the time of the merger

MEMBERSHIP   Combined Assets: $1,000,000,000 plus
Baptized souls....................3,200,000
Pastors............................   7,000
Congregations.....................   6,000
Confirmed souls..................2,200,000

PERCENTAGE OF MEMBERS CONTRIBUTED BY EACH BODY
United Lutheran Church in America......................79%
Augustana Lutheran Church...............................19%
Suomi Synod............a little more than..................1+%
American Ev. Lutheran Church...A little less than.......-1%

BUDGET (Requests for the first 2 years of the LCA's existence)
1963........$26,057,128
1964...........$28,393,708

ELECTED OFFICIALS (1962-1964)
President: Rev. Franklin Clark Fry, D.D.
Secretary: Rev. Malvin H. Lundeen, D.D.
Treasurer: E.F. Wagner, L.L.D.

CHURCH HEADQUARTERS: 231 Madison Avenue, New York, NY 10016

THE LUTHERAN CHURCH IN AMERICA CONSTITUTION

At the end of the Preamble there is a prayer asking for successful Lutheran union endeavors:...THAT HE WHO IS THE LORD OF THE CHURCH MAY THEREBY LEAD US TOWARD A MORE CONCLUSIVE UNION OF ALL LUTHERANS ON THIS CONTINENT.

Under Article II Confession of Faith. Section 1:
THIS CHURCH CONFESSES JESUS CHRIST AS LORD OF THE CHURCH. THE HOLY SPIRIT CREATES AND SUSTAINS THE CHURCH THROUGH THE GOSPEL...SECTION 2: THIS CHURCH HOLDS THAT THE GOSPEL IS THE REVELATION OF GOD'S SOVEREIGN WILL AND SAVING GRACE IN JESUS CHRIST. IN HIM, THE WORD INCARNATE, GOD IMPARTS HIMSELF TO MEN. SECTION 3: THIS CHURCH ACKNOWLEDGES THE HOLY SCRIPTURES AS THE NORM FOR THE FAITH AND LIFE OF THE CHURCH. THE HOLY SCRIPTURES ARE THE DIVINELY INSPIRED RECORD OF GOD'S REDEMPTIVE ACT IN CHRIST, FOR WHICH THE OLD TESTAMENT PREPARED THE WAY AND WHICH THE NEW TESTAMENT PROCLAIMS...SECTION 4,5,6 DECLARE THE LCA'S ACCEPTANCE OF THE ECUMENICAL CREEDS...AS TRUE DECLARATIONS OF THE FAITH OF THE CHURCH...*THE UNALTERED AUGSBURG CONFESSION*, AND *LUTHER'S SMALL CATECHISM* AS TRUE WITNESSES TO THE GOSPEL, AND ACKNOWLEDGES AS ONE WITH IT IN FAITH AND DOCTRINE ALL CHURCHES THAT LIKEWISE ACCEPT THE TEACHINGS OF THESE SYMBOLS...AND...ACCEPTS THE OTHER SYMBOLICAL BOOKS OF THE EVANGELICAL LUTHERAN CHURCH, *THE APOLOGY OF THE AUGSBURG CONFESSION, THE SMALCALD ARTICLES, LUTHER'S LARGE CATECHISM*, AND *THE FORMULA OF CONCORD* AS FURTHER VALID INTERPRETATIONS OF THE CONFESSION OF THE CHURCH. SECTION 7 DECLARES: THIS CHURCH AFFIRMS THAT THE GOSPEL TRANSMITTED BY THE HOLY SCRIPTURES, TO WHICH THE CREEDS AND CONFESSIONS BEAR WITNESS, IS THE TRUE TREASURE OF THE CHURCH, THE SUBSTANCE OF ITS PROCLAMATION, AND THE BASIS OF ITS UNITY AND CONTINUITY. THE HOLY SPIRIT USES THE PROCLAMATION OF THE GOSPEL AND THE ADMINISTRATION OF THE SACRAMENTS TO CREATE AND SUSTAIN CHRISTIAN FAITH AND FELLOWSHIP.[12]

It is to be noted that the Confession of Faith does not begin with a statement of biblical authority, which is the usual course that is followed. Rather than confess the Inerrancy of the Scriptures, the Confession of Faith begins with a

547

statement regarding Christ. And in what follows it is primarily Christ, rather than Holy Scriptures, who is designated the Word of God. In reading the Confession of Faith one can receive the impression that the Inspiration of Scripture is reduced to the act of the Holy Spirit giving the church the Gospel. We note that the Confession of Faith makes only mild, general statements regarding acceptance of the Lutheran Confessions. The wording appears weak compared with the wording used by the conservative element of Lutheranism. The LCA wording—a generalized description of the value of the Lutheran Confessions— is an umbrella under which just about any liberal Lutheran theology can take its place.

Under Article V, Objects and Powers, Section 1: A strong ecumenical spirit is shown:

THIS CHURCH LIVES TO BE AN INSTRUMENT OF THE HOLY SPIRIT...SPECIFI-
CALLY E) TO STRIVE FOR THE UNIFICATION OF ALL LUTHERANS WITHIN ITS
BOUNDARIES IN ONE CHURCH AND TO TAKE CONSTRUCTIVE MEASURES LEADING
THERETO. F) TO PARTICIPATE IN ECUMENICAL CHRISTIAN ACTIVITIES, CON-
TRIBUTING ITS WITNESS AND WORK AND COOPERATING WITH OTHER CHURCHES
WHICH CONFESS GOD AND FATHER, SON AND HOLY GHOST....

Section 2 provides that all questions of doctrine and life are to be decided on the basis of the Holy Scriptures in accordance to the Church's Confessions of Faith.[13] Take note that as fine as this sounds, in actual practice, however, the LCA clearly showed that it did not always use the guidance of Holy Scripture— its clear wording that spells out God's holy will—but instead was strongly influenced by the historical-critical method of interpreting Scripture, to which method the LCA had strongly attached itself. As a result, long-held beliefs based on Holy Scripture were called into question, or set aside, and at times were even denied. More of this later.

Article VII Ministers, Section 4, is especially noteworthy for in effect it prohibits those in the ministry of the church to have membership in religious lodges.[14] We note that lay members were not subject (in the LCA congregational constitution) to any rule prohibiting lodge membership—no doubt an accommodation to the many laypersons who held lodge memberships.

THE LCA: AN ECUMENICAL CHURCH
REACHING OUT TO THE LEFT AND TO THE RIGHT

The Lutheran Church in America was from its inception—like the ULCA before it—deeply, organically, constitutionally, unashamedly and habitually ecumenical. It desired to be an inclusive church that enjoyed the fellowship of *all* Lutherans, and of *non-Lutheran* churches as well. The LCA pledged itself to fellowship with other churches on the basis of the barest agreement of faith. This Lutheran body very clearly testified in its constitution that it did not require doctrinal agreement based on Scripture as a prerequisite for church fellowship or church union. The fact is that in its history the LCA even considered itself one with those Lutheran bodies which did not reach out the hand of fellowship to it. Historically, the LCA tried to court the hand of the conservatives while boldly practicing fellowship with the most apostate bodies, including the World Council of Churches (WCC). The LCA also was a member of the Lutheran World Federation (LWF), as well as the apostate National Council of Churches of Christ in the U.S.A. Regarding the loose theology of the LWF we furnish this example: At a meeting of the LWF in 1963 in Helsinki, Finland, a long discussion failed to produce a united statement on the doctrine of Justification, the core teaching of Scripture. Some Lutherans at the meeting even spoke of this doctrine as being "an embarrassment" for the church of today. (A note of reminder: The name Lutheran contains the name Luther, which reformer made the doctrine of Justification by God's Grace through Faith in Christ the central thrust of his Reformation movement. Clearly, there are Lutherans in the world who in no way deserve to bear the reformer's name.)

It is important that we note how dedicated the LCA was to reaching out to non-Lutheran churches. Beginning in 1962 several consultations were held (until 1965) between representatives of the LCA and the Presbyterian (Reformed) tradition. The outcome was a published report that contended that "no insuperable obstacles to pulpit and altar fellowship" existed. The Catholic-Lutheran dialogue, which began in 1965, witnessed 17 meetings by the end of 1973. These meetings produced four volumes of reports on a number of doctrinal questions. "These reports indicated that surprising progress in mutual understanding had been achieved."[15]

It has already been mentioned that the LCA entered the fellowships of the Lutheran World Federation and the World Council of Churches. And, of course, the antecedent ULCA had been a member of the National Lutheran Council (NLC), which cooperative body had been formed the same year (1918) as the ULCA. The other three Lutheran bodies which merged with the ULCA to form the LCA were also members of the NLC. Because of the two mergers forming the LCA and the new ALC, there remained only two Lutheran bodies in the NLC, which therefore did not warrant its continuation.

And so, the time was ripe to replace the NLC with a new cooperative body, one that would enjoy more extensive cooperative activities. The Constituting Convention of the LCA went on record as being in favor of a successor organization to the NLC. The delegates voted unanimously to authorize negotiations with The American Lutheran Church (1960) and the Missouri Synod for the formation of such a new cooperative agency. The LCA favored an agency whose purpose is to provide opportunities for cooperation among the Lutherans, which then can lead to fellowship for the participating bodies and, finally, to union. An interesting side note to consider is this: One of the reasons put forth in the LCA for uniting all Lutherans in one church was to make ecumenical participation with the other church bodies more effective. First unite the Lutherans, and then it will be easier to unite the Lutherans with other churches.

Because of the upcoming mergers forming the new ALC and the LCA, the National Lutheran Council in 1958 extended invitations to all Lutheran bodies in America to participate in consultations, with the view to more extensive cooperative activities. An approach was especially made to the members of the Synodical Conference. The Missouri Synod accepted the invitation and participated in the first general consultation in July of 1960. Both the Wisconsin Synod (WELS) and the small Norwegian Synod (Evangelical Lutheran Synod of ELS) rejected the invitation. Six small independent groups also did not accept the invitation.

The results of the first general consultation encouraged the calling of a second one, to be held soon afterwards in November of 1961. The progress was subtly reflected in the question discussed at that time: WHAT KIND OF COOPERATION IS POSSIBLE IN VIEW OF DISCUSSIONS TO DATE? As a result it was declared that ...SUFFICIENT CONSENSUS HAS BEEN REVEALED TO WARRANT THE EXPLORATION OF THE FEASIBILITY OF A NEW ASSOCIATION TO SUCCEED THE NATIONAL LUTHERAN COUNCIL IN WHICH DOCTRINAL STUDIES AND COOPERATIVE ACTIVITIES WOULD BE UNDERTAKEN SIMULTANEOUSLY.

The LCA, together with TALC and the Missouri Synod, approved the proposal at hand to form a new association to replace the NLC. In January 1963 the representatives of the three major bodies of Lutheranism who came to the consultation constituted themselves under the name "Inter-Lutheran Consultation." Thus, at that time 95% of the Lutherans in North America were consulting together with the aim to establish areas of cooperation. Out of this group ultimately came the arrangements for a new agency, to be called The Lutheran Council in the U.S.A. (LCUSA). Upon ratification by the general bodies, the new Council would begin to function in 1967. The LCA was the last of the participating bodies to give its approval to the new organization. Unanimous approval was given at its June 1966 Convention. Headquarters for the LCUSA were to be located in New York, which was also home to the LCA.

In speaking of the LCUSA, which would have its Constituting Convention in Cleveland, Ohio, November 16-18, 1967, Dr. Fry in the President's Report to his own body's 1966 Convention spoke glowingly of the new Council. Here are some of his words:

THE BOONS THAT WILL COME FROM THE LUTHERAN COUNCIL IN THE U.S.A. ARE MANY. FIRST AND FOREMOST, OF COURSE, SO GREATLY SO AS TO COME CLOSE TO ECLIPSING ALL ELSE, IN ITS COMPREHENSIVENESS OF MEMBERSHIP. NINETY-FIVE PERCENT OR THEREABOUTS OF ALL LUTHERANS IN THE UNITED STATES...99% IN THE LUTHERAN COUNCIL IN CANADA WILL BE IN IT. OPPORTUNITIES FOR ACQUAINTANCE WILL BE AFFORDED THAT CAN RIPEN INTO FRIENDSHIP. MUTUAL, REVERENT LISTENING TO GOD'S WORD AND OCCASIONALLY ACTING IN CONCERT ON IT...WILL DRAW US TOGETHER. WE SHALL NOT FOREVER BE DISPUTANTS, OR IN THE CRITIC'S SEAT AS IN THE PAST, BUT COLLEAGUES....

....IN CONTRAST TO THE EXPIRING NATIONAL LUTHERAN COUNCIL, WHICH CONSISTS MAINLY OF PRECISELY DEFINED ACTION PROGRAMS AND HAS BEEN LARGELY LIMITED TO THEM, THE LCUSA WILL SPREAD ACROSS NEARLY THE WHOLE SPECTRUM OF CHURCH ACTIVITY. IT WILL EMBRACE PARISH EDUCATION AND WORLD MISSIONS, FOR EXAMPLE, AS HAS NEVER BEEN THE CASE IN THE PAST...THE COMMON AGENCY OF THE FUTURE IS DESIGNED MAINLY TO BE A TALK-SHOP, A PLACE FOR EXCHANGING IDEAS AND TAKING COUNSEL WITH ONE ANOTHER, NOT PRIMARILY AN INSTRUMENT FOR ACTION...LCUSA WILL HAVE THE DUTY "TO ESTABLISH PROCEDURES AND PROVIDE RESOURCES" BY WHICH "TO SEEK TO ACHIEVE THEOLOGICAL CONSENSUS IN A SYSTEMATIC AND CONTINUING WAY ON THE BASIS OF THE SCRIPTURES AND THE WITNESS OF THE LUTHERAN CONFESSIONS"...ONLY A MINOR FRACTION OF THE TIME OF THE DIVISION WILL BE DEVOTED, WE WOULD HOPE, TO CATECHIZING ONE ANOTHER,

AND EVEN WHEN THAT HAPPENS THE SETTING WILL BE ONE THAT DOES NOT CALL FOR EITHER AGRESSIVENESS OR DEFENSIVENESS. NO PART OF LCUSA'S FUNCTION WILL BE TO COMPOSE NEW DOCTRINAL STATEMENTS OF A QUASI-CONFESSIONAL TYPE.

....

....LCUSA MAY WELL MEET ITS MOST DECISIVE TEST IN THE SECTOR OF AMERICAN MISSIONS...ASSIGNMENT OF A SPECIFIC FIELD TO A SPECIFIC CHURCH BODY, WITH THE ASSURANCE THAT IT WILL NOT BE ENCROACHED ON, WILL BE A THING OF THE PAST. NOBODY WILL HAVE "EXCLUSIVE" RIGHTS ANYWHERE ANY LONGER....

ALL THAT REMAINS IS A CLOSING WORD ON PULPIT AND ALTAR FELLOWSHIP. SUFFICE IT TO SAY THAT I EARNESTLY HOPE THAT THE RECOMMENDATION OF THE STANDING COMMITTEE ON APPROACHES TO UNITY WILL COMMEND ITSELF TO THE DELEGATES TO THIS CONVENTION AND THAT IT WILL BE ADOPTED WITHOUT EXTENDED DEBATE. AS ONE OF OUR MOST DISCERNING AND IRENIC LCA THEOLOGIANS HAS RECENTLY WRITTEN, THE BASIC NEED IN AMERICAN LUTHERANISM RIGHT NOW IS TO TRUST ONE ANOTHER'S INTEGRITY, TO RESPECT THE HONESTY OF EACH OTHER'S CONFESSIONAL SUBSCRIPTION, AND TO STRIVE EACH WITHIN HIS OWN CIRCLE TO CONFORM ALL PREACHING AND PRACTICE TO OUR COMMON DECLARATION OF FAITH. BLESS THE LCUSA, IT PROMISES TO BE AN ADMIRABLE INSTRUMENT FOR AWAKENING SUCH TRUST AND A MATCHING RESOLVE TO BE TRUSTWORTHY.[16]

REACHING OUT TO THE MISSOURI SYNOD

Nothing would have pleased the liberal bodies of American Lutheranism more than to enjoy fellowship with the Missouri Synod. And it was the hope of these groups that Missouri's participation in the LCUSA would evolve into actual church fellowship and finally into church union. We can imagine the joy which the newly elected president of the LCA, Dr. Fry, as well as the delegates to the convention, felt over the visit paid to their convention by Dr. John W. Behnken, retiring president of the Missouri Synod, whose own church body was now being superceded in size by this newest of the Lutheran mergers. The words with which Dr. Behnken greeted the LCA Convention, and the response presented by Dr. Fry, are worthy of note.

After extending THE CORDIAL GREETINGS AND HEARTY FELICITATIONS OF THE LUTHERAN CHURCH-MISSOURI SYNOD, Dr. Behnken spoke of the Bible as the infallible Word of God and the Lutheran Confessions as a faithful and correct exposition of God's Holy Word. In the closing paragraph of his greeting, Dr. Behnken stated: WE LOOK FORWARD WITH GREAT ANTICIPATION TO THE FIRM RESOLVE AND WHOLE HEARTED DETERMINATION OF YOUR NEW CHURCH BODY, THE LUTHERAN CHURCH IN AMERICA, TO STAND SOLIDLY ON HOLY WRIT AS THE TRUE FOUNDATION. WE PRAY THAT GOD MAY GRANT YOU EVER-DEEPER CONVICTIONS ABOUT THE LUTHERAN CONFESSIONS AS GOD'S WONDERFUL GIFT TO THE LUTHERAN CHURCH. WHAT THE FUTURE MAY BRING WE CANNOT FORETELL, BUT SURELY PRAY FERVENTLY THAT ULTIMATELY IT MAY PLEASE GOD TO BRING ABOUT UNION ON THE SOLID BASIS OF TRUE UNITY. WE PLEAD WITH GOD TO EQUIP AND STRENGTHEN ALL

OF US FOR THE CONFLICT RAGING TODAY AGAINST SCRIPTURE WHETHER IT BE NEO-ORTHODOXY, NATIONALISM, ATHEISTIC COMMUNISM, OR ANY OTHER "ISMS." I KNOW THAT YOU WILL JOIN ME IN THE PRAYER THAT GOD MAY MAKE US EVER MORE FAITH-FUL AND LOYAL TO HOLY WRIT. MAY WE EVER BEAR IN MIND THAT THE VERY HEART AND CORE OF ALL THIS IS "JESUS CHRIST AND HIM CRUCIFIED." TO THAT GOD-PLEAS-ING END THE LUTHERAN CHURCH-MISSOURI SYNOD GREETS YOU AND CONGRATU-LATES YOU. MAY GOD GRACIOUSLY BLESS YOU.

Dr. Fry then responded to Dr. Behnken:

YOUR PRESENCE IN THE CONVENTION TODAY IS AN ACT OF GRACE AND FELLOWSHIP. THERE IS SOMETHING SYMBOLIC ABOUT THE FACT THAT, AT THIS POINT OF HISTORY, WHICH IS FULL OF CHANGE FOR US AND ALSO FOR THE LUTHERAN CHURCH-MISSOURI SYNOD, YOU HAVE COME TO US ON THE LAST DAY OF YOUR PRESIDENCY DURING THE FIRST CONVENTION OF THE LUTHERAN CHURCH IN AMERICA AND HAVE SPREAD YOUR ARMS IN AN EMBRACE OF FELLOWSHIP. YOU FEEL THE WARM RESPONSE, I AM SURE, OF YOUR BRETHREN IN THE FAITH WHO ARE ASSEMBLED HERE. WE HAVE GREETED WITH A SALVO OF JOY THE ANNOUNCEMENT, WHICH I HOPE IS CORRECT, THAT THE LUTHERAN CHURCH-MISSOURI SYNOD HAS AUTHORIZED FURTHER CONVERSATIONS AND NEGOTIATIONS MOVING TOWARD THE POSSIBLE FORMATION OF A NEW ASSOCIA-TION [I.E. LCUSA]. WE LOOK FORWARD WITH KEEN ANTICIPATION TO EARNEST AND DEVOUT DISCUSSIONS OF OUR COMMON CHRISTIAN FAITH WITH THE LUTHERAN CHURCH-MISSOURI SYNOD IN THAT ASSOCIATION, AND WE STRONGLY HOPE ALSO THAT THE NEW ASSOCIATION WILL INCLUDE MANY FACETS OF ACTIVE CHRISTIAN COOPERA-TION, ABOVE ALL IN A DAY LIKE THIS WHOSE PRESSURES ARE SO GREAT THAT WE CAN HARDLY WAIT TO BEGIN TO ACT UNTIL WE HAVE COME TO FINAL AGREEMENT. [17]

THE LCA SEMINARIES

One of the problems encountered in merging the four churches was the over-abundance of theological seminaries. The ULCA owned ten seminaries, in-cluding two in Canada, while the other three bodies owned one seminary apiece. Concurrently with the merger forming the LCA, Grand View Seminary (AELC) and Suomi Seminary moved to Maywood, Illinois, to join Chicago Lutheran Theological Seminary (ULCA). The three seminaries negotiated with Augustana Seminary, Rock Island, Illinois, merging the four seminaries into one on two campuses—for the time being. The sacrifices made by the three church bodies engendered the strong feeling that the ULCA should reciprocate and merge seminaries, which it operated.[18] As far as ownership and control of the seminaries was concerned, it was finally decided that the synods should own and administer the seminaries but that the general church body should de-termine their location. Eventually a plan for alignment of synods and seminar-ies was adopted. The seminary problem had not been settled by the JCLU prior to the merger but was passed on to the new body where it was finally set-tled.

THE LCA COLLEGES

There were eighteen four-year colleges and four two-year colleges that were brought to the merger. In the LCA bylaws to the constitution, the following rule is stated:

THE RELATIONS OF THIS CHURCH [THE LCA ITSELF] TO COLLEGES SHALL BE SUSTAINED ENTIRELY THROUGH THE SYNODS, EXCEPT AS SPECIFIED HERE-INAFTER AND IN OTHER WAYS PROPOSED BY THE CONVENTION OR BY THE BOARD OF COLLEGE EDUCATION AND CHURCH VOCATIONS TO WHICH THE SYNODS CONCERNED HAVE IN EACH CASE AGREED.[19]

THE LCA BOARD OF AMERICAN MISSIONS

The functions of this board:

....FINDING FIELDS, SURVEYING FIELDS, APPROVING FIELDS FOR OCCUPANCY, DEVELOPMENT FIELDS, PROVIDING PARSONAGES, SELECTING CHURCH SITES, SELECTING TEMPORARY PLACES OF WORSHIP, SUPPLYING INITIAL EQUIPMENT, ORGANIZING CONGREGATIONS, CALLING PASTORS, SUPPORTING PASTORS, AND ASSISTING ESTABLISHED CONGREGATIONS CONFRONTING SPECIAL PROBLEMS.[20]

THE LCA BOARD OF WORLD MISSIONS— THE LCA WOLRD MISSION ENDEAVORS

THE BOARD OF WORLD MISSIONS

The objects of the board: a) The proclamation of the Gospel in word and deed and the administration of the sacraments in behalf of the LCA outside the Dominion of Canada and the United States of America. b) Assistance and support of sister churches in areas that are named, where evangelical Christians are a small minority. c) Establishment of indigenous churches where they do not exist.[21]

THE WORLD MISSIONS OF THE MERGING BODIES

All four churches that merged to form the LCA had world mission programs. Of course, the ULCA and the Augustana Church had more extensive endeavors. It was found that there was no overlapping of efforts on the world scene by the four merging bodies. Here is the list of mission fields of the four merging bodies:

ULCA: Argentina, British Guiana, Hong Kong, India, Japan, Liberia, Malaya, Uruguay

Augustana: India, Taiwan, and Hong Kong, Tanganyika, North Borneo,

Japan, Uruguay
   American Evangelical Lutheran Church: India (Santal)
   Suomi: Japan
   By 1972 the following overseas churches of the LCA were listed:
   ARGENTINA (1948), CHILE (1962), ETHIOPIA (1963), FIJI, GUYANA & JAMAICA
   (1943), HONG KONG (1956), INDIA/ANDHRA (1928), INDIA/SANTAL (1952),
   INDIA/SURGUJA (1952), INDONESIA (1930), JAPAN (1927), LIBERIA (1947),
   MALAYIA & SINGAPORE (1963), MIDDLE EAST, PERU (1966), TAIWAN (1954),
   TANZANIA (1963), TRINIDAD (1966), URUGUAY (1957)

THE LCA BOARD OF SOCIAL MINISTRY

The constitution and bylaws of the LCA established a Board of Social Min-
istry with two departments: Department of Social Mission and Department of
Social Action. In regards to social action the following provision is stated:
....THE BOARD OF SOCIAL MINISTRY SHALL CONDUCT RESEARCH RELATING TO
MORAL ISSUES IN THE LIFE OF SOCIETY FOR THE GUIDANCE OF THE CHURCH IN EX-
PRESSING ITS SOCIAL CONCERN...THE BOARD SHALL, AT ITS DISCRETION, FORMULATE
STATEMENTS ON MORAL AND SOCIAL QUESTIONS FOR CONSIDERATION BY CONVEN-
TIONS.[22]
As we shall see, the LCA proved to have a very liberal outlook on some key
moral issues: e.g. abortion, homosexuality, sex outside of marriage, the use of
pornographic films in counseling sessions. Note: we shall not list the numerous
other boards and commissions.

THE LCA PUBLICATIONS

The ULCA, Augustana Church, and the Suomi Synod had publishing
houses: Muhlenberg Press, Augustana Book Concern, the Finnish Book Concern. The ULCA church paper, *The Lutheran*, was designated the official paper
of the new body. It was proposed that the printing plants at Philadelphia
(ULCA) and Rock Island, Illinois (Augustana) be equipped for specialization in
certain types of work. Suomi's plant in Hancock, Michigan was to continue to
operate as it was then operating.[23]

THE LCA DEPARTED FROM
SOME OF THE OLD WAYS

In the decade following the Constituting Convention in Detroit, the LCA
made some rather tradition-shattering decisions. For example, at Minneapolis
it was decided that children of ten years of age or younger could partake of the
elements in the Lord's Supper, instead of waiting to age 13 or 14, when most
children in the Lutheran Church become communicant members by confirmation, after thorough indoctrination in the Christian faith.
   On the subject of abortion it was decided that a woman or couple may decide

responsibly on such an operation with respect for the laws of the land. Those contemplating abortion were urged to seek the advice of their pastors as well as their physicians.

There was also a softening of the church's stand on homosexuality. Thus the convention decided that homosexuals are sinners only as are other persons alienated from God and neighbor. Often the victims of prejudice and discrimination, it was, according to the Convention, essential that homosexuals be treated with understanding and justice. More on this subject later.

At San Antonio, Texas, in a close vote of 560 to 414, the LCA consented to the ordination of women to the ministry. In doing so it joined other major Protestant bodies that already were permitting this practice (e.g. United Presbyterian Church, United Methodist Church, United Church of Christ, Disciples of Christ, American Baptist Convention). In allowing this change of policy the LCA pointed out that the New Testament does not confront the question of ordination of women and therefore does not speak directly to it. And that on the other hand nothing in the New Testament speaks positively against it. However, conservative Lutheran bodies have consistently ruled against the ordination of women to the ministry, for the reason that Scripture teaches that women are to remain silent in the churches, and that they are not to have authority over the man (1 Corinthians 14:34, 1 Timothy 2:12-14).

APOSTASY IN THE LCA

The United Lutheran Church in America (ULCA) had long taken its stand on the liberal side in matters of doctrine and church polity. This, then, was the approach to doctrine and practice brought by the ULCA into the merger forming the Lutheran Church in America. Under the leadership of its liberal officials and theologians the new church very quickly distinguished itself by standing far to the left in regards to its doctrine and practice, and pronouncements on moral and sociological issues. The theology of this Lutheran body could hardly be regarded either as soundly scriptural or as confessionally sound Lutheranism. Many statements are found in the published writings of LCA leaders and theologians that not only attack the validity of what Lutherans (and not only Lutherans but other church bodies as well) have long held to be God's Truth. These attacks became so numerous and so bold as to warrant a fairly extensive review of them here. We shall treat them as examples of apostasy.

Without doubt this is a serious and highly consequential matter. Millions of souls have been and still are affected by the theology once taught in the LCA and now being taught in its successor body, the Evangelical Lutheran Church in America (ELCA), the largest Lutheran body ever formed in the USA. When we examine the history and doctrine of this latest Lutheran merger body we will once again see an example of extreme liberal Lutheranism steeped in heterodox treatment of Scripture and the Lutheran Confessions. The point, then, is that what is stated in this chapter regarding the LCA can later be applied to the ELCA. Bear this in mind as we lay out some matters that are of extreme importance and consequence. We are dealing with two very large Lutheran bodies (LCA and ELCA) that give ample evidence of having lost their way.

Two books, especially, stand out as valuable reference works in examining the doctrinal statements of LCA theologians and examples of published works that are used in teaching the Bible and Bible doctrines to seminary students, to adult lay persons and also to the youth. The first is titled *The Church's Desperate Need For Revival.* Its author is David R. Barnhart, who once pastured a fairly large congregation in the LCA in Minnesota, but then was forced by his conscience to resign his post and leave the LCA. He then joined a small orthodox Lutheran body. The second book is titled *What's Going On Among the Lutherans—A Comparison of Beliefs.* This book has two authors. First, there is Patsy A. Leppien, described as a "wife, mother, grandmother, and registered nurse." She was a member of the ALC (1956-1985), and taught both Sunday school and the *Bethel Series* adult Bible studies. She struggled as a laywoman to understand the "great theological changes taking place in most of Christendom." In the PREFACE of her book Leppien gives her explanation leaving the ALC and her reason for writing this book:

THE STRUGGLE THAT LED TO THIS VOLUME BEGAN IN 1984 WHEN A SMALL GROUP OF LAY PEOPLE IN AN AMERICAN LUTHERAN CHURCH (ALC) CONGREGATION ENGAGED IN EXTENSIVE RESEARCH ON THE COMING MERGER THAT WOULD MAKE THEIR CHURCH BODY A PART OF THE EVANGELICAL LUTHERAN CHURCH IN AMERICA (ELCA) IN 1988. WHEN THEY BECAME AWARE OF THE RADICAL NATURE OF THE THEOLOGICAL CHANGES TAKING PLACE IN MOST CHRISTIAN DENOMINATIONS, AND HOW DEEPLY THESE CHANGES HAD INFILTRATED LUTHERANISM, THEY FELT CALLED TO LEAVE THE ALC. CONVINCED THESE CHANGES COULD ULTIMATELY DESTROY THEIR FAITH, AS WELL AS THE FAITH OF THEIR CHILDREN AND GRANDCHILDREN, THEY FELT AN OBLIGATION TO SHARE THE RESULT OF THEIR RESEARCH WITH THEIR BROTHERS AND SISTERS IN CHRIST. THUS, IN 1986, THEY JOINED WITH OTHER CONCERNED LUTHERANS AND ORGANIZED LUTHERANS INFORMED FOR TRUTH (L.I.F.T.) THIS BOOK IS THE CULMINATION OF LIFT'S ONGOING EFFORTS TO INFORM LUTHERANS IN ALL SYNODS OF THE REAL DOCTRINAL DIFFERENCES DIVIDING TODAY'S LUTHERANS.[24]

The author found spiritual refuge in the much smaller but conservative Evangelical Lutheran Synod (ELS), which is in fellowship with the Wisconsin Evangelical Lutheran Synod (WELS), the publisher of the book.

Pastor J. Kincaid Smith is the other author of *What's Going On Among the Lutherans?* He is introduced to us in a blurb on the back cover of the book, which describes him to us as a man who has journeyed from the liberal side of theology to the orthodox side:

WHEN J. KINCAID SMITH GRADUATED FROM THE LUTHERAN CHURCH IN AMERICA HAMMA SCHOOL OF THEOLOGY, SPRINGFIELD, OHIO, IN 1973, HE WAS FIRMLY ESTABLISHED IN THE LIBERAL POSITION HELD BY HIS SEMINARY. WHILE SERVING IN HIS FIRST CALL, HE BEGAN A PILGRIMAGE TOWARD THE ORTHODOX LUTHERAN POSITION HE NOW CONFESSES. HE HOLDS A DOCTOR OF MINISTRY DEGREE FROM CONCORDIA THEOLOGICAL SEMINARY, FORT WAYNE, INDIANA.[25]

Smith also joined the Evangelical Lutheran Synod, where he served in the parish ministry until his retirement. We will have more to report on his journey to faith and orthodoxy later.

Much of what now follows is information contained in both of the above-

556

mentioned volumes. In all examples that are given of the LCA's departure from sound scriptural and Lutheran theology and practice, the information is readily available in various publications to anyone desiring to search it out. Much of the material comes to us in official publications of the LCA. Space permits us to give only a limited overview of the problem areas in the LCA's theology, practice, and moral (and sociological) pronouncements.

THE LCA'S HETERODOX VIEW OF THE HOLY SCRIPTURES—THE HISTORICAL-CRITICAL METHOD OF INTERPRETATION:

Confessional, conservative Lutheranism has historically regarded the Holy Scriptures as the infallible and inerrant Word of God, while affirming its absolute authority. Even the old ALC championed Verbal Inspiration and Inerrancy. In its Minneapolis Theses (1925) the ALC stated its acceptance of the canonical Scriptures...AS A WHOLE AND IN ALL PARTS, AS THE DIVINELY INSPIRED, REVEALED, AND INERRANT WORD OF GOD. However, the ULCA theologians denied Verbal Inspiration and Inerrancy as man-made theories, and as a result denied also the absolute authority of the Scriptures. Officially, the ULCA in 1920 it its Washington Declaration...REFUSED TO SPEAK OF VERBAL INSPIRATION AND INERRANCY OF THE SCRIPTURES. And in the 1930's the ULCA commissioners declared their inability to...ACCEPT THE STATEMENT OF THE MISSOURI SYNOD THAT THE SCRIPTURES ARE THE INFALLIBLE TRUTH "ALSO IN THOSE PARTS WHICH TREAT OF HISTORICAL, GEOGRAPHICAL, AND OTHER SECULAR MATTERS, JOHN 10:35."[27]

What was causing such a "low" view of the Scriptures? The ULCA, along with other church bodies, was employing the historical-critical method in its approach to the Scriptures. By 1930 the historical-critical method was entering some Lutheran churches in the USA and was widely accepted in the ULCA. In that same year it was introduced in the Augustana Church Seminary in Rock Island, Illinois, by new faculty members. Already in the 1920's this rationalistic approach to the Scriptures, which began in Europe, was a point of controversy as Lutheran bodies began working out mergers. As the mergers took place, the historical-critical method of approach was finding its way into seminaries and churches.

In the early 1960's two large Lutheran mergers resulted in the "new" ALC and the LCA. Why were two mergers formed instead of one very large one? The answer lies in the different approach to the Scriptures used by the Lutheran bodies forming the two mergers. At that time, the "old" ALC had leaders who insisted that the Scriptures are "the divinely inspired, revealed, and inerrant Word of God." However, the leaders of the Lutheran bodies which merged to form the LCA were steeped in the historical-critical approach to the Scriptures. And so, in 1962 the new merger body—which included the ULCA—in its constitution avoided the use of the words "inerrant" and "infallible" in describing the Scriptures, and instead used terminology which was a testimony to the widespread use of the historical-critical method of approach: THE HOLY SCRIPTURES ARE THE DIVINELY INSPIRED RECORD OF GOD'S REDEMPTIVE ACT IN CHRIST FOR WHICH THE OLD TESTAMENT PREPARED THE WAY AND WHICH THE NEW

TESTAMENT PROCLAIMS.[28]

Later, the new ALC entered rough waters because of a document incorporated into its Articles of Union. Titled, the "United Testimony on Faith and Life," the document was framed by theologians of the American Lutheran Conferences and left the door open to the use of historical criticism. This document was in deference to those who did not advocate the doctrine of Inerrancy. However, the document did not sell well with those who did hold to Inerrancy. Sad to say, the leadership of the ALC was now in the liberal camp, and the president, Dr. Fred Schiotz, with the help of the publication, *The Bible: Book of Faith,* promoted the historical-critical method of interpreting Scripture. Having received official approval and favor, historical criticism was widely, though not universally accepted. Naturally, this development helped to prepare the way for the merger in 1988, which created the Evangelical Lutheran Church in America (ELCA).[29]

So then, what is the historical-critical method of approach to the Scriptures? Kurt E. Marquart, a professor of theology in the Missouri Synod gives this explanation:

IT IS CLEAR....THAT THE HISTORICAL-CRITICAL METHOD AROSE OUT OF THE RATIONALISTIC ENLIGHTENMENT AND DIFFERS FROM TRADITIONAL BIBLICAL SCHOLARSHIP IN THAT IT INSISTS ON TREATING THE BIBLE NOT AS AN UNQUESTIONED AUTHORITY, BUT AS ONE ANCIENT BOOK AMONG OTHERS. ALL BIBLICAL STATEMENTS ARE THEREFORE OPEN TO CHALLENGE BEFORE THE COURT OF SOVEREIGN HUMAN REASON. HISTORICAL CRITICISM UNDERSTANDS ITSELF SIMPLY AS THE GENERAL SCIENTIFIC METHOD APPLIED TO PAST EVENTS, NAMELY HISTORY. THIS MEANS THAT THE CRITIC AND HIS REASON ARE JUDGE AND JURY, WHILE THE BIBLE, LIKE ALL OTHER ANCIENT DOCUMENTS, IS ON TRIAL, WHETHER AS DEFENDANT OR AS WITNESS; FOR EVEN AS A WITNESS ITS CREDIBILITY DEPENDS ENTIRELY ON THE FINDINGS OF THE CRITICAL "COURT." THIS SITUATION, OF COURSE, REPRESENTS A COMPLETE REVERSAL OF THE CLASSIC ROLES OF REASON AND SCRIPTURE IN LUTHERAN THEOLOGY. UNDER THE NEW CRITICAL REGIME, REASON IS MASTER AND SCRIPTURE IS SERVANT, WHEREAS FORMERLY IT WAS THE OTHER WAY ROUND.[30]

The late Dr. Siegbert W. Becker, conservative theologian of the Wisconsin Evangelical Lutheran Synod (WELS) had this to say about the historical-critical method:

IT MUST BE EMPHATICALLY STATED THAT THE METHOD IS NOT NEUTRAL. IT CLEARLY REJECTS THE CLAIM OF SCRIPTURE TO BE A BOOK WHICH IS DIFFERENT FROM EVERY OTHER BOOK IN THE WORLD...[WITH THIS METHOD] EACH INDIVIDUAL ACCOUNT OF A HISTORICAL NATURE IN THE BIBLE IS SIMPLY STUDIED WITHOUT ANY PRECONCEIVED NOTION OF WHETHER IT IS RIGHT OR WRONG, FACTUAL OR NON-FACTUAL...WE ARE TOLD UNENDINGLY THAT THE HOLY MEN WHO WROTE THE BIBLE WERE CHILDREN OF THEIR TIME WHO WERE LIMITED IN THEIR KNOWLEDGE AND UNDERSTANDING OF SCIENCE AND HISTORY BY THE UNDEVELOPED STATE OF THE CULTURE IN WHICH THEY DID THEIR WORK.

IT IS OBVIOUS FROM WHAT HAS BEEN SAID THAT THE METHOD CERTAINLY CANNOT BE NEUTRAL ON THE QUESTION OF BIBLICAL INERRANCY. IT IS A FOREGONE, FIXED CONCLUSION, PRESUPPOSED IN THE PRACTICE OF THIS KIND OF INTERPRETATION, THAT THE BIBLE CAN BE WRONG AT ALMOST ANY POINT. THE MORE

CONSERVATIVE PRACTITIONERS OF THE METHOD TRY TO SAFEGUARD WHAT THEY CALL THE THEOLOGICAL SIDE OF SCRIPTURE, BUT EVEN THEY HOLD THAT THE BIBLE COULD BE WRONG ON ALMOST EVERY POINT AT WHICH IT TREATS EITHER HISTORY OR NATURAL SCIENCE.

WHENEVER MEN HAVE GIVEN UP THE DOCTRINE OF BIBLICAL INERRANCY THEY HAVE EVENTUALLY COME TO REALIZE AND ADMIT THAT IF THAT PREMISE IS ONCE ACCEPTED, THE DOCTRINE OF VERBAL INSPIRATION SIMPLY CANNOT BE MAINTAINED FOR LONG.

WHEN THE VERBAL INSPIRATION AND INERRANCY OF THE HOLY SCRIPTURE ARE DENIED, THE DOCTRINE THAT THE BIBLE IS THE WORD OF GOD CAN NO LONGER BE MAINTAINED. IF THE WORDS OF THE BIBLE ARE NOT GIVEN BY GOD TO THE HOLY WRITERS AND IF, AS IS UNIVERSALLY ASSERTED BY THOSE WHO HOLD TO THE HISTORICAL-CRITICAL METHOD, THE STATEMENTS OF THE BIBLE ARE IN NUMEROUS PLACES CONTRARY TO FACT, THEN IT MUST BE CLEAR THAT NOT ALL OF THIS BOOK, AND PERHAPS NONE OF THIS BOOK, CAN REALLY, IN A LITERAL WAY, BE CALLED GOD'S WORD.

ONCE THE CRITIC HAS DISPOSED OF THE DOCTRINE OF VERBAL INSPIRATION AND INERRANCY AND HAS GIVEN UP THE IDENTIFICATION OF THE BIBLE AS THE WORD OF GOD, THE CONCEPT OF BIBLICAL AUTHORITY HAS ALSO BEEN UNDERMINED. IF THE WORDS OF THE BIBLE ARE NOT THE WORDS OF GOD AND IF THOSE WORDS ARE NOT TRUE JUST BECAUSE THEY ARE NOT THE WORDS OF GOD, THEN OBVIOUSLY IT IS NO LONGER POSSIBLE TO BELIEVE WHAT THE BIBLE SAYS JUST BECAUSE IT IS WRITTEN IN THE BIBLE. "IT IS WRITTEN" BECOMES NOT A FINAL ARGUMENT, AS IT IS IN THE NEW TESTAMENT AND ON THE LIPS OF JESUS, BUT JUST THE PROPOSAL OF A HUMAN OPINION, WHICH MAY OR MAY NOT BE TRUE.[31]

Dr. Becker makes the following observation about the historical-critical method:

THOSE WHO ADOPTED THE HISTORICAL-CRITICAL METHOD ARE CONVINCED THAT THEY HAVE MADE SPIRITUAL PROGRESS. LIKE THE PERSECUTORS OF THE APOSTLES AGAINST WHOM THE SAVIOR WARNED HIS FOLLOWERS, THEY ARE CONVINCED THAT BY THIS ADOPTION THEY HAVE DONE GOD AND THEIR CHURCH A SERVICE...PROPONENTS OF THIS METHODOLOGY BELIEVE THAT THE HISTORICAL-CRITICAL METHOD HAS MADE IT POSSIBLE FOR US TO UNDERSTAND THE BIBLE BETTER...ON THE OTHER HAND, OTHER CHRISTIAN SCHOLARS ARE JUST AS FIRMLY CONVINCED THAT THE HISTORICAL-CRITICAL-METHOD DOES NOT BENEFIT THE CHURCH...THE HISTORICAL-CRITICAL METHOD IS A DAMNABLE HERESY AGAINST WHICH ALL CHRISTIANS OUGHT TO BE ON THEIR GUARD...MAY GOD HELP US TO SEE THE DANGERS INTO WHICH IT PLUNGES THE CHURCH.[32]

The *Wisconsin Lutheran Quarterly*, the theological journal of the WELS—and publisher of the article quoted above—has over time included various articles attacking the historical-critical method. Here is another sample:

CHRISTIANITY BASES ITS BELIEF ON THE PREMISE OF A GOD WHO HAS SAID AND DONE DECISIVE THINGS IN THE PAST. THE HISTORICAL-CRITICAL METHOD IS PREDICATED ON THE IMPOSSIBILITY OF ISOLATING AND IDENTIFYING CONCRETE ACTS AND WORDS OF GOD AMONG PAST EVENTS...THE RESULT...IS NOT MERELY A LOSS OF BIBLICAL AUTHORITY, BUT ALSO THE DEVASTATION OF CHRISTOLOGY AND OF ALL CHRISTIAN SUBSTANCE...THE CHRISTOLOGY ON WHICH THE ECU-

MENICAL CREEDS BASE THEIR CONFESSIONS RESTS ON AND FINDS TOTAL CON-
FIDENCE IN THE FACT THAT EVERYTHING WRITTEN ABOUT JESUS IN THE HOLY
SCRIPTURES IS TRUE. IF THIS CONFIDENCE COLLAPSES, THE DOCTRINE OF
CHRIST DECAYS INTO A QUAGMIRE OF DOUBTFUL SPECULATIONS AND OPINIONS.[33]

Leppien and Smith, authors of *What's Going On Among the Lutherans?* give
this astute observation:

REMEMBER THAT THE REAL UNDERLYING PRESUPPOSITION OF THE WHOLE HIS-
TORICAL-CRITICAL METHOD IS THE ASSUMPTION OR CONVICTION THAT THE SU-
PERNATURAL IS NOT POSSIBLE. IF THE READER GRASPS THAT POINT, HE WILL BE
ABLE TO UNDERSTAND WHY THE LIBERAL SCHOLARS MUST DENY ALL THE UN-
DERLYING ESSENTIALS OF THE FAITH.[34]

Here are additional comments by Leppien and Smith, both of whom came
out of Lutheran bodies steeped in the historical-critical approach to the Scriptures:

...THE HISTORICAL CRITICISM SCHOLARS APPROACH THE BIBLE AS IF IT WERE
JUST ANOTHER MAN-MADE DOCUMENT, NOT AS A BOOK OF SPECIAL REVELATION,
DIFFERENT FROM ALL OTHER BOOKS. IT IS ASSUMED THAT THE BIBLE, LIKE
MANY ANCIENT DOCUMENTS FROM THE PAST, CONTAINS LEGENDS, MYTHS, STO-
RIES, FABLES, AND FOLKLORE THAT MUST BE STUDIED AND SORTED OUT USING
THE BEST "SCIENTIFIC" TOOLS AVAILABLE. THESE SCHOLARS REASON THAT
THERE IS NO WAY TO BE SURE OF WHAT IS ACTUAL HISTORY AND WHAT IS
MERELY "TRADITION." TRADITION IS DEFINED AS THE HANDING DOWN OF STO-
RIES, OPINIONS, BELIEFS, AND CUSTOMS FROM PARENTS TO CHILDREN OVER SUC-
CEEDING GENERATIONS. THINGS CONSIDERED "TRADITION" WERE SEEN AS
ORIGINATING FROM MAN...MIRACLES...ARE MERELY ADDED BY THE WRITERS OF
SCRIPTURE TO ADD "EMPHASIS" AND TO IMPRESS PRIMITIVE READERS WITH THE
AUTHORITY AND VALIDITY OF THEIR MESSAGE...THOSE WHO USE THE HISTORI-
CAL-CRITICAL METHOD CONCLUDE THAT THE BIBLICAL WRITERS SAW THE WORLD
IN VERY PRIMITIVE AND UNSCIENTIFIC TERMS AND MERELY RECORDED WHAT
THEY BELIEVED WAS HAPPENING OR WHAT THEY HEARD FROM SOME ONE ELSE.[35]

Again, quoting Leppien and Smith:

THE HISTORICAL-CRITICAL METHOD IS A RADICAL CHANGE IN THINKING. IT IS A
CHANGE OF THINKING THAT, WHEN CARRIED TO ITS EXTREME BY THEOLOGIANS,
LEADS TO THE DENIAL OF EVERY BASIC DOCTRINE OF CHRISTIANITY. USED IN
A LESSER DEGREE, IT LEADS AT BEST TO A PARTIAL DENIAL AND THE CASTING OF
DOUBT UPON THE REMAINDER. IT IS IMPORTANT TO REMEMBER THAT THE TEN-
DENCY WITH THIS KIND OF THINKING IS NOT TO REMAIN AT SOME POINT OF MOD-
ERATION BUT TO MOVE INTO THE EXTREME.[36]

Historical-critical interpretation of Scripture is, in the words of Joe E.
Schruhl, a conservative LCMS Pastor...AN ATTEMPT TO SYNTHESIZE SCRIPTURE
WITH SILENCE. IT HOLDS THAT THE MIRACULOUS, THAT IS, THE DIRECT INTERVENTION
BY GOD INTO HUMAN HISTORY, IS UNACCEPTABLE.[37]

The bottom line in this whole discussion is that those who practice the historical-critical method abandon the absolute authority of Scripture. What then
is God's truth? In the minds of those who use this rationalistic heterodox
method of interpreting Scripture, God's truth is relevant. Or in the words of a
WELS theologian, it is the belief...THAT THROUGH ANALYSIS AND CRITICISM WE
MUST COME TO DOCTRINAL FORMULATIONS, WHICH ARE APPROPRIATE FOR TODAY.

(*Wisconsin Lutheran Quarterly,* vol. 89, #4, 1992, p. 256.) And so, whatever the truth is, it must accommodate the day and age we now live in. It must pass the scrutiny of modern science as man sits in judgment over Scripture. The result of such theology is, of course, such practices as ordaining women to the pastoral ministry, the acceptance of homosexuality as an approved and blessed life-style, the denial that miracles actually happen (demythologizing the Scripture), employing the Social Gospel (dedicated to improving the lives of the less fortunate and relieving the suffering and in general working to make this world a more perfect world in which to live—liberation theology), non-gender references to God, ecumenism (in which doctrinal absolutes are not insisted upon and agreement in scriptural doctrine and practice is not a requirement—i.e. union-ism), the presenting of an altogether different picture of Jesus Christ from that portrayed in the Gospels. (What did Jesus *really* say? What did Jesus really do?—Thus promoting the constant search outside of Scripture for the real, the *historical* Jesus.)

The natural result of employing the historical-critical method is that doubt takes the place of certainty in one's religion. Confusion as to what really is the truth reigns, for the scholars who hold to the historical-critical method furnish the world with a large array of interpretations of God's Book. The contradictions and inconsistencies they present are indeed considerable. In the final analysis we would have to conclude that the historical-critical method of biblical interpretation is diametrically opposed to the confessional Lutheran teaching of the Verbal Inspiration, Inerrancy, and Absolute Authority of Scripture.

The Lutheran Church in America (LCA) was deeply rooted in the historical-critical method, and its successor (as we shall see in a later chapter), the Evangelical Lutheran Church in America (ELCA), is deeply rooted in this method to the present. And now just a few words from LCA theologians who hold to the historical-critical method.

> IF THE STORIES OF THE BIBLE ARE TO HAVE MEANING TODAY IT MUST BE SOUGHT ON A DIFFERENT PLANE OF REALITY. FOR MIRACLES CANNOT BE RETAINED ON THE LEVEL OF HISTORICAL FACT...IT MAKES A DIFFERENCE TO THE WAY ONE THINKS OF JESUS...THE [HISTORICAL-CRITICAL] METHOD RELEASES US FROM THE NECESSITY OF BELIEVING THE INCOMPREHENSIBLE AND THE IMPROBABLE [I.E. MIRACLES] OUT OF DEVOTION TO THE CHURCH; FOR IT MAKES PROPER UNDERSTANDING POSSIBLE.[38]

Christian Dogmatics is a work produced only a few years before the merger forming the Evangelical Lutheran Church in America (ELCA). Published by the LCA's Fortress Press in 1984, it is the primary theology textbook used in the seminaries of the ELCA to train students studying for the ministry. It presents many outright examples of the denial of doctrines clearly taught in Scripture, doctrines which are fundamental to the Christian faith.

> TODAY IT IS IMPOSSIBLE TO ASSUME THE LITERAL HISTORICITY OF ALL THINGS RECORDED [IN SCRIPTURE]. WHAT THE BIBLICAL AUTHORS REPORT IS NOT ACCEPTED AS A LITERAL TRANSCRIPT OF THE FACTUAL COURSE OF EVENTS. THEREFORE, CRITICAL SCHOLARS INQUIRE BEHIND THE TEXT AND ATTEMPT TO RECONSTRUCT THE REAL HISTORY THAT TOOK PLACE.[39]

In future quotations from LCA sources we shall see how the historical-critical method employed in this Lutheran body has adversely affected its stand on a variety of basic Christian doctrines, as well as its stand on certain moral/social issues. In closing this section dealing with the LCA and the use of the historical-critical method we will let Pastor J. Kincaid Smith, who once accepted and defended this heterodox approach to the Scriptures but later turned to the orthodox side, inform us as to how destructive this approach is to saving faith in Christ.

IN 1973 WHEN I GRADUATED FROM AN LCA SEMINARY IN OHIO, I DID NOT BE-LIEVE IN THE VIRGIN BIRTH NOR, FOR THAT MATTER, IN THE BODILY RESUR-RECTION OF CHRIST, AND NEITHER DID ANY OF MY FELLOW GRADUATES, AND CERTAINLY NONE OF OUR PROFESSORS. WE HAD BEEN SYSTEMATICALLY LED TO REJECT ANY ELEMENT IN SCRIPTURE WHICH COULD NOT BE EXPLAINED BY NAT-URAL SCIENCE. WHAT AN EMPTY CHRISTMAS I KNEW IN THOSE DAYS, WHAT AN EMPTY FAITH! WE DID NOT REALIZE, OR COULD NOT FACE, THAT IN LETTING GO OF ALL THE MIRACULOUS THINGS IN THE SCRIPTURES, THE VERY FAITH ITSELF HAD SLIPPED AWAY.

Smith further writes:

AS A FORMER LIBERAL WHO HELD AND DEFENDED THE HISTORICAL-CRITICAL METHOD (THE NON-INSPIRED VIEW OF THE BIBLE), I CAN TELL YOU THIS: THAT THE DIFFERENCE BETWEEN HISTORIC LUTHERANISM AND THE "NEW THINKING" IS NOT SOME MINOR INSIGNIFICANT DIFFERENCE. THEY ARE 180 DEGREES APART—TOTALLY OPPOSED. IN THE LIBERAL POSITION I LOST MY FAITH IN CHRIST. THE KNOWLEDGE THAT THE BIBLE IS TRUE, AS HISTORIC LUTHERANISM TEACHES, RESTORED MY FAITH AND CONTINUES TO SUPPORT IT. A REAL PUZZLE TO ME NOW IS TO UNDERSTAND, HOW BACK THEN, I ACTUALLY CONSIDERED MYSELF A CHRISTIAN.[40]

And where did the average member of the LCA stand in regards to the historical-critical method? Many lay members were in the dark regarding this Bible study method. The church leaders were, however, determined to introduce the lay members to historical criticism and win them over. They recognized such adult Bible study courses as *Search* to be the ways and means to bring this about. Comprehensive Bible studies had become very popular with the lay people in the various churches in America. The popularity of the *Bethel Bible Series*, introduced in 1961 by Bethel Lutheran Church (ALC) in Madison, Wisconsin, attests the people's interest in Bible study. In book, *The Death of the Lutheran Reformation*, Craig Sanford relates his experience with the *Search* Bible study program:

THE LEADERSHIP OF THE ALC AND LCA SAW THIS RENEWED INTEREST [IN BIBLE STUDY] AS A GREAT OPPORTUNITY TO ADVANCE THEIR AGENDA AND IN-TRODUCE HISTORICAL CRITICISM INTO THE LOCAL CONGREGATION. THE *SEARCH* BIBLE STUDIES SERIES WOULD PROVE TO BE THE REAL WORKHORSE FOR THIS TASK AND IT HAS EXCEEDED EVERYONE'S EXPECTATIONS. DISGUISED AS THE MOST COMPREHENSIVE BIBLE STUDY PRODUCED BY AUGSBURG, IT HAS BEEN THE ELCA'S SINGLE MOST EFFECTIVE TOOL IN ALTERING THE WAY LUTHERAN LAY PEOPLE THINK ABOUT THE BIBLE. THIS FIVE-YEAR PROGRAM, WITH AN ES-TIMATED 90,000 PARTICIPANTS HAS TURNED TENS OF THOUSANDS OF LUTHERAN LAY PEOPLE INTO HIGHER CRITICAL THINKERS WITHOUT THEIR KNOWING IT.

(Bear in mind that many of ELCA's lay members were originally members of LCA.)

The author of the above words later makes this additional comment:

THE LCA'S *WORD AND WITNESS* PROGRAM [OF BIBLE STUDY] MADE ITS AP-
PEARANCE IN 1977...A REVIEW OF *WORD AND WITNESS* REVEALS THE INFLU-
ENCE OF THE HISTORICAL-CRITICAL METHOD.

From what the above quoted author has reported, we learn that the leaders of the LCA targeted especially lay persons who were leaders of Bible study classes. Some of these persons were naturally also congregational leaders. Recommended resource books for these leaders boldly reveal the conclusions about Scriptures drawn by the historical-critical method of interpretation. The aim of course was that these leaders could and would "encourage other church members to accept the 'new thinking.'"[41]

We shall now proceed to review some of the devastating effects, which the historical-critical method, adopted by so many pastors, church leaders and theologians, had on the theology and church polity and even some of the moral standards of the LCA. We let the LCA's printed word speak for itself. The reader should compare what he or she finds in the following statements to what was learned from studying the catechism and the Bible.

HISTORICAL CRITICISM AND THE
LCA'S DOCTRINE OF CREATION

WE HAVE DEALT WITH THE ISSUES OF THE PICTURE OF CREATION AND THE DI-
VISION INTO SEVEN DAYS. WE KNOW THAT THE PICTURE OF CREATION IS ONE
WE CANNOT ACCEPT IN A STARKLY LITERAL SENSE. WE HAVE CONCLUDED THAT
THE SEVEN DAY PHENOMENON IS A LITERARY DEVICE. WHAT THEN IS LEFT FOR
US OF VALUE IN GENESIS 1?[42]

On September 24, 1964, the LCA put into use a totally new curriculum for religious training, which required nine years and $5 million to prepare. Part of the curriculum, titled "The Mighty Acts of God," accounts for the origin of certain verses in Genesis chapter one with the explanation that some priest in Babylonia, hearing the Babylonian myths, wrote these verses to have the God of the Jews replace the Babylonian gods. Furthermore, the explanation is offered that the story of Adam and Eve was invented by someone in southern Palestine where sheep herding was prominent. The curriculum furthermore allows the view that God used evolution to create the world. It also points out that the Bible contains errors. While the conservative Lutherans accept the literalness of the creation story, the LCA very openly suggested in some of its publications that the very opposite is true. *Resource*, which was the official publication of the Board of Parish Education of the LCA suggested in its March 1963 issue:

WE SHOULD APPROACH THESE CREATION STORIES AS RELIGIOUS TRUTH...AT
THE SAME TIME WE SHOULD REALIZE THAT THE STORIES ARE PARABLES AND NOT
SCIENTIFIC ACCOUNTS. THEY ARE CONVEYING TRUTH TO US IN A POETIC FORM,
USING FIGURES AND SYMBOLS WHICH ARE NOT TO BE LITERALIZED....WHEN WE
ARE ATTACKED BY THOSE WHO WOULD CHALLENGE THE "TRUTHFULNESS" OF
THESE CREATION STORIES, WE SHOULD BE QUICK TO AGREE THAT THESE ARE

NOT FACTUAL SCIENTIFIC ACCOUNTS. AS CHRISTIANS WHO ARE INTELLECTU-
ALLY HONEST WE ARE QUITE WILLING TO LISTEN TO THE CONTRIBUTIONS OF THE
WORLD OF SCIENCE. AND WE SHOULD NEVER HAVE TO FEEL THAT WE MUST DE-
FEND GENESIS 1 AND 2 ON SCIENTIFIC GROUNDS. THE BASIC THEME OF THESE
STORIES IS NOT THE HOW AND THE WHAT OF CREATION BUT THE WHO AND THE
WHY. AS CHRISTIANS, THEREFORE, WE HAVE NO QUARREL WITH THE INSIGHTS
ARRIVED AT BY THE HONEST NATURAL SCIENTISTS. TO US IT DOES NOT REALLY
MATTER HOW THE WORLD WAS MADE. IT MAY HAVE BEEN INSTANTANEOUSLY,
OR IN SIX DAYS. OR IN MILLIONS OF YEARS. OUT OF OUR FAITH AND COMMIT-
MENT WE ARE SURE THAT THE GOD WE KNOW AS LORD IN JESUS CHRIST IS
ALSO THE CREATOR AND LORD OF THE WORLD...HOW SHALL WE HANDLE THE
CREATION STORIES IN THE TEACHING SITUATION? FIRST, WE MUST INSIST THAT
THESE CREATION STORIES ARE A PART OF GOD'S WORD. SECONDLY, WE MUST
POINT OUT AS EARLY AS POSSIBLE THE DIFFERENCE BETWEEN SCIENTIFIC TRUTH
AND POETIC TRUTH. IN THE THIRD PLACE, WE SHOULD NEVER TEACH THESE
STORIES, EVEN TO KINDERGARTENERS OR PRIMARY CHILDREN, AS LITERALLY
TRUE...WE OUGHT TO ENCOURAGE OUR YOUNG PEOPLE TO TURN TO THE BEST
ENCYCLOPEDIAS TO LEARN WHAT HONEST MEN OF SCIENCE ARE SAYING IN THIS
FIELD.[43]

HISTORICAL CRITICISM AND THE
LCA'S DOCTRINE OF ADAM AND EVE

IF THE STORY OF ADAM AND EVE IS REALLY A STORY ABOUT ALL OF HUMANKIND,
THE STORY OF CAIN AND ABEL IS THE SAME. WE HAVE SAID THAT, LIKE OTHER
MATERIAL IN GENESIS 1-11, THESE CHAPTERS ARE NOT CONCERNED ONLY WITH
GOD'S PEOPLE, BUT WITH ALL PEOPLE. AND THEY ARE NOT HISTORICAL REPORTS
BUT RATHER STORIES OR NARRATIVES, WHICH SAY SOMETHING ABOUT ALL
MANKIND.[44]

HISTORICAL CRITICISM AND THE LCA'S
DOCTRINE OF JESUS CHRIST—HIS LIFE

THE PICTURE WE HAVE OF JESUS' LIFE IS MADE OF BITS AND PIECES TAKEN
FROM VARIOUS GOSPELS, WITH GENEROUS PORTIONS OF IMAGINATION ADDED.[45]
...MANY OF THE STORIES ABOUT JESUS PRESENTED BY THE EVANGELISTS MUST
BE RECOGNIZED AS NARRATIVES AND NOT AS REPORTS. THEY WERE WRITTEN
WITH THE INTENTION OF SHOWING HOW IMPORTANT AND SIGNIFICANT JESUS IS.
THEY ARE NOT NEUTRAL AND UNBIASED FACTUAL REPORTS.[46]
THIS [BOOK] IS OFFERED IN ORDER TO SUGGEST WHY IT SHOULD NO LONGER BE
POSSIBLE TO PRESENT AS SERIOUS HISTORY THE TRADITIONAL "LIVES" OF THE
SORT WHICH DEAL WITH JESUS "FROM THE CRADLE TO THE GRAVE"—AND TO IN-
DICATE WHY EVEN THE TEACHINGS ATTRIBUTED TO JESUS NEED TO BE SIFTED
CRITICALLY SO AS TO SEPARATE WHAT MIGHT ACTUALLY HAVE BEEN SPOKEN BY
JESUS FROM THAT WHICH STEMS FROM THE EARLY CHURCH.[47]

HISTORICAL CRITICISM AND THE LCA'S
DOCTRINE OF JESUS CHRIST—HIS MIRACLES

YET TODAY EVEN THE SEVEREST CRITICS OF THE NEW TESTAMENT SOURCES ADMIT THAT JESUS DID INDEED PERFORM ACTS THAT HIS CONTEMPORARIES REGARDED AS MIRACULOUS AND THAT WE STILL CONSIDER HIGHLY UNUSUAL...WE MUST CONCEDE THE POSSIBILITY THAT MIRACLES MUST HAVE BEEN ATTRIBUTED TO PEOPLE SIMPLY TO ENHANCE THEIR STATUS, THAT IS, THEIR SPECIAL RELATIONSHIP TO THE GODS. EACH CLAIM TO THE TRUTH MUST BE CAREFULLY ANALYZED, AND IT SHOULD NOT BE EXCLUDED A PRIORI THAT SOME OF THE MIRACLES ATTRIBUTED TO JESUS MAY HAVE NO HISTORICAL BASIS AND SERVE ONLY TO EMPHASIZE HIS EXCEPTIONAL STATUS.[48]

THE NEED TO DEMYTHOLOGIZE THE STORY SHOULD NOT, HOWEVER WEAKEN OUR SENSES FOR THE MESSAGE IT CONTAINS...THE END OF JESUS' TIME ON EARTH [WHEN HE ASCENDED INTO HEAVEN, PICTURED IN PAINTINGS DEPICTING JESUS BODY' MOVING THROUGH THE CLOUDS] IS LIKE THE BEGINNING. IT IS A MYSTERY CLOTHED IN LANGUAGE OF MYTH AND SYMBOL. HISTORY DOES NOT GIVE US A KEY TO UNLOCK IT.[49]

HISTORICAL CRITICISM AND THE LCA'S
DOCTRINE OF JESUS CHRIST—HIS VIRGIN BIRTH

....THE STORY OF THE DESCENT OF THE SON OF GOD TO EARTH AND HIS ASCENT INTO HEAVEN CANNOT BE TAKEN LITERALLY. THE QUESTION IS WHETHER THE MEANING OF THE MYTH OF THE INCARNATION CAN BE SAVED WITHOUT TAKING IT LITERALLY YET WITHOUT GETTING RID OF ITS MYTHIC STRUCTURE.

....FINALLY, THE HISTORY AND PHENOMENOLOGY OF RELIGIONS HAVE CALLED OUR ATTENTION TO THE MYTHIC CHARACTER OF THE INCARNATION. THE NOTION OF THE PRE-EXISTING SON OF GOD BECOMING A HUMAN BEING IN THE WOMB OF A VIRGIN AND THEN RETURNING TO HIS HEAVENLY HOME IS BOUND UP WITH A MYTHOLOGICAL PICTURE OF THE WORLD THAT CLASHES WITH OUR MODERN SCIENTIFIC WORLD VIEW.

THE PRIMARY INTEREST OF DOGMATICS IS TO INTERPRET THE VIRGIN BIRTH AS A SYMBOL AND NOT AS A FREAKISH INTERVENTION IN THE COURSE OF NATURE. THE MAIN STATEMENTS OF THE APOSTLES CREED ARE SO BOUND UP WITH ITS MYTHOLOGICAL FORM THAT TO GET RID OF THE MYTH WOULD DESTROY THE CREED IN TOTO. CAN MODERN PEOPLE STILL BE EXPECTED TO ACCEPT THE CREED WITH ITS MYTHOLOGICAL ELEMENTS?[50]

HISTORICAL CRITICISM AND THE LCA'S
DOCTRINE OF JESUS CHRIST—HIS DEITY

...THE STARTLING DISCOVERY WAS THAT THE ECCLESIASTICAL DOGMAS ARE NOT TO BE FOUND IN THE BIBLE, BUT ARE PRODUCTS OF A LATER TIME. IN THE AGE OF CHRISTENDOM, THE DOGMAS OF THE TRINITY AND OF CHRIST, AS FORMULATED IN THE NICENE AND ATHANASIAN CREEDS, WERE NECESSARY TO BELIEVE FOR SAL-

VATION. NOW THE BIBLICAL CRITICS COULD APPLY THE SCRIPTURE PRINCIPLE OF PROTESTANTISM TO SHOW THAT THESE DOGMAS CANNOT BE REQUIRED FOR FAITH, SINCE THEY LACK SOLID BIBLICAL SUPPORT.[51]

BUT WHAT DOES IT MEAN TO SPEAK OF JESUS AS "DIVINE"? DOES NOT THIS WORD ALSO CALL FOR SOME INTERPRETATION? THEOLOGIANS TODAY ARE CONCERNED TO INTERPRET THE DIVINITY OF JESUS IN THE MANNER WHICH AVOIDS TURNING HIM INTO A BIZARRE, MYTHOLOGICAL CREATURE WHO CONTAINS BOTH A DIVINE AND A HUMAN NATURE."[52]

HISTORICAL CRITICISM AND THE LCA'S DOCTRINE OF JESUS CHRIST—THE TRINITY

TRULY, THE HOLY TRINITY IS SIMPLY THE FATHER AND THE MAN JESUS AND THEIR SPIRIT AS THE SPIRIT OF THE BELIEVING COMMUNITY.[53]
THE FORMULATION OF THE TRINITY AS A DOCTRINE IS NOT FOUND IN THE NEW TESTAMENT. IT WAS HAMMERED OUT DURING THE FOURTH CENTURY IN WHAT IS CALLED THE TRINITARIAN CONTROVERSY...NOR IS THE LANGUAGE OF THE FOURTH CENTURY DOGMA TO BE REGARDED AS SACRED AND ABSOLUTE.[54]

HISTORICAL CRITICISM AND THE LCA'S DOCTRINE OF JESUS CHRIST—THE ATONEMENT

BUT WHAT IS THE MOST IMPORTANT OF THIS TRADITION [I.E. CHRIST'S ATONING WORK]? PUT IN ITS MOST CRASS FORM, THIS VIEW WOULD HOLD THAT JESUS' DEATH IS A SACRIFICE IN WHICH HE IS A SUBSTITUTE FOR US WHO PAYS THE DIVINE JUSTICE THAT IS DUE FOR HUMAN SIN AND/OR APPEASES THE DIVINE WRATH. AS WE SHALL SEE, THERE IS A LONG TRADITION, ESPECIALLY AMONG WESTERN CONSERVATIVE CHRISTIANS, WHICH HAS TAKEN THIS LINE. THERE SEEMS TO BE A VIRTUAL CONSENSUS AMONG CONTEMPORARY BIBLICAL SCHOLARS, HOWEVER, THAT THIS TRADITION FINDS LITTLE SUPPORT IN THE SCRIPTURES, EITHER IN THE OLD OR NEW TESTAMENTS. SCRIPTURE NEVER SPEAKS OF GOD AS ONE WHO HAS TO BE SATISFIED OR PROPITIATED BEFORE BEING MERCIFUL OR FORGIVING.[55]
JESUS DIES FOR US AND NOT FOR GOD. THERE IS NOT JUST A LITTLE PERVERSITY [CONTRARY TO THE EVIDENCE] IN THE TENDENCY TO SAY THAT THE SACRIFICE WAS DEMANDED BY GOD TO PLACATE THE DIVINE WRATH. WE ATTEMPT TO EXONERATE OURSELVES FROM THE TERRIBLE NATURE OF THE DEED BY BLAMING IT ON GOD. THE THEOLOGY OF SACRIFICES BECOMES PART OF OUR DEFENSE MECHANISM. THIS MUST NOW CEASE. NOTHING IN THE SCRIPTURES WARRANTS IT. JESUS' SACRIFICE FOR US CANNOT BE EXPLAINED IN THAT FASHION. A NEW UNDERSTANDING OF THE NATURE OF THAT SACRIFICE IS DEMANDED. THIS NEW UNDERSTANDING MUST ARISE FROM THE EVENT ITSELF AND NOT IMPOSE PREVIOUSLY CONSTRUCTED THEORIES ON IT.[56]
GOD HAS SOMETIMES BEEN SEEN...AS REQUIRING THE BLOODY SACRIFICE OF HIS SON IN ORDER TO SATISFY HIS WRATH. WHEN SUCH LANGUAGE IS USED

566

IT OFTEN CONTRADICTS OTHER THINGS WE KNOW ABOUT GOD FROM THE SCRIPTURES, INCLUDING HIS POWER OVER EVIL AND HIS STEADFAST LOVE AND FORGIVENESS.[57]

"SATISFACTION" THEORY—THIS WAS THE DOMINANT VIEW OF THE MIDDLE AGES. ACCORDING TO THIS VIEW, HUMAN SIN IS AN INFINITE OFFENSE AGAINST GOD; THIS INFINITE OFFENSE REQUIRES INFINITE SATISFACTION. IT WAS NECESSARY FOR GOD TO BECOME HUMAN. THUS JESUS, WHO WAS PERFECT, DIED TO SATISFY THE OFFENSE CREATED BY HUMAN SIN.58

In regards to the historical-critical method's view of the atoning death of Jesus Christ and how this view mitigates against the well-established view of confessional Lutheranism that Jesus' death propitiated God in regards to mankind's sins, J. Kincaid Smith's confession as a former liberal LCA pastor is informative:

I WAS TRAINED IN THE "NEW THINKING" AT HAMMA SCHOOL OF THEOLOGY, NOW MERGED WITH CAPITAL AND CALLED TRINITY....WE DENIED TRUE BLOOD ATONEMENT, IN THE VERY CLEAR SENSE OF PROPITIATION. THAT CENTRAL CONCEPT IS THE CHIEF DOCTRINE OF THE CHURCH, THAT GOD TOOK HIS HORRIBLE WRATH AGAINST OUR SINS OUT ON HIS ONLY BEGOTTEN SON. WE PREACHED ABOUT JESUS "DYING FOR US" BUT THIS WAS HIM DYING FOR HIS FRIENDS, NOT PROPITIATION, JUST KIND OF A VERY SPECIAL GOOD GUY.[59]

HISTORICAL CRITICISM AND THE LCA'S DOCTRINE OF JESUS CHRIST—HIS RESURRECTION AND THE RESURRECTION OF BELIEVERS

MYTHOLOGICAL SYMBOLISM CONTRIBUTED TO THE INTERPRETATION OF THE EVENT OF THE RESURRECTION. THE QUESTION HAS BECOME ACUTE IN MODERN THEOLOGY WHETHER IN THE RESURRECTION WE ARE DEALING ONLY WITH A MYTH OR WITH A TRULY HISTORICAL EVENT.[60]

SINCE WE ARE ENDOWED NEITHER WITH DIVINE QUALITIES NOR WITH AN IMMORTAL SOUL IN THE PLATONIC OR GNOSTIC SENSE, MEANINGFUL EXISTENCE BEYOND DEATH MUST BE A RESURRECTION OF THE DEAD. THIS HOPE IS EXPRESSED IN THE APOSTLES CREED, WHERE WE SAY THAT WE BELIEVE "IN THE RESURRECTION OF THE BODY." THIS DOES NOT MEAN A BIOLOGICAL REVIVIFICATION, SUCH AS IS FOUND IN THE CASE OF THE YOUNG MAN IN THE VILLAGE OF NAIN LUKE 7:15 OR LAZARUS (JOHN 11:44).

And:

CONTRARY TO OTHER "RESURRECTION" STORIES IN THE BIBLE, JESUS IS NOT PERCEIVED AS HAVING RETURNED TO THIS LIFE. HIS RESURRECTION WAS NOT A RESUSCITATION INDICATING THAT IN CERTAIN EXCEPTIONAL INSTANCES PEOPLE CAN BE RETURNED TO THEIR FORMER STATE OF LIFE.[61]

WHAT IS INVOLVED IN BELIEVING IN THE RESURRECTION OF THE BODY IS SIMPLY THAT WE ARE SAVED AS INDIVIDUALS AND DO NOT LOSE OUR INDIVIDUALITY IN THE NEXT LIFE.[62]

RESURRECTION IS NOT A CASE OF A RETURN OF LIFE TO THE PHYSICAL BODY. IT IS DESTINED TO RETURN TO THE EARTH. THE RESURRECTED BODY IS A NEW,

SPIRITUAL, GLORIFIED BODY, WHICH MAY HAVE CHARACTERISTICS OF THE PHYS-
ICAL BODY, BUT IT IS NOT THE SAME, FOR FLESH AND BLOOD DO NOT INHERIT
THE KINGDOM OF HEAVEN.[63]

We again quote from J. Kincaid Smith, a former LCA pastor, now a conservative Lutheran:

...WHEN I GOT OUT OF THE SEM WE USED THE SAME WORDS AS OUR CONSER-
VATIVE COUNTER PARTS, BUT WE MEANT SOMETHING QUITE DIFFERENTLY BY
THEM. THUS I MIGHT SPEAK OF THE "EMPTY TOMB" ON EASTER BUT I WOULD
NOT HAVE MEANT THAT I BELIEVED THAT JESUS ACTUALLY, PHYSICALLY ROSE
FROM THE DEAD. IF YOU HAD SPECIFICALLY ASKED ME SOMETHING LAY-PEOPLE
ARE EXTREMELY RETICENT TO DO, WHAT I MEANT BY "EMPTY TOMB" I WOULD
HAVE SQUIRMED.[64]

HISTORICAL CRITICISM AND THE LCA'S
DOCTRINE OF THE IMMORALITY OF THE SOUL
AND THE EXISTENCE OF THE SOUL

THESE THEORIES SUGGEST THAT SOME PORTION OR ESSENCE OF THE PERSON IS
NOT MORTAL AND WILL SURVIVE DEATH. CHRISTIANS HAVE SOMETIMES TALKED
ABOUT THE IMMORALITY OF THE SOUL IN THIS WAY, BUT TO DO SO IS INAPPRO-
PRIATE.[65]

DEATH PUTS AN END TO OUR TOTAL EXISTENCE, BODY, SOUL, AND EVERYTHING.[66]

INDIVIDUAL DESTINY—CONCERNING THE INDIVIDUAL, WE HAVE REJECTED THE
NOTION OF AN IMMORTAL SOUL AND HAVE SPOKEN INSTEAD OF THE RESURREC-
TION OF THE BODY...THIS RESURRECTION OF THE BODY DOES NOT MEAN A RE-
ASSEMBLING OF THE CHEMICAL PARTICLES THAT HAVE CONSTITUTED OUR
BODIES HERE.[67]

HISTORICAL CRITICISM AND THE LCA'S
DOCTRINE CONCERNING HOMOSEXUALITY

In 1979 Hebert W. Chilstrom, Bishop of the Minnesota Synod of the LCA
sent out a 14 page pastoral letter concerning homosexuality. Here are a few
brief quotes from this letter.

WHAT I PROPOSE IS THAT AT THIS POINT IN TIME IN THE DEBATE OVER HOMO-
SEXUALITY WE MAY HAVE LITTLE CHOICE IN THE CHURCH EXCEPT TO SAY THAT
WE ACCEPT THE PERSON, BUT QUESTION THE BEHAVIOR. NOTE THAT I AVOID
USING THE TERMS "SINNER" AND "SIN." THE LCA STATEMENT ON "SEX, MAR-
RIAGE, AND THE FAMILY" STATES THAT "PERSONS WHO ENGAGE IN HOMOSEXUAL
BEHAVIOR ARE SINNERS ONLY AS ARE ALL OTHER PERSONS...ALIENATED FROM
GOD AND NEIGHBOR." I AM COMPLETELY AT EASE WITH OUR LCA POSITION (P.
9).

The bishop further states in his letter:

...THE SEXUAL ORIENTATION OF A HOMOSEXUAL PERSON SHOULD BE AS INCI-

DENTAL FOR HIS OR HER MEMBERSHIP AS THAT OF A HETEROSEXUAL PERSON.[68]

David R. Barnhart, like J. Kincaid Smith, was an LCA pastor. As he witnessed the doctrinal slide of his church body, he became more and more deeply troubled. In his book *The Church's Desperate Need For Revival*, he writes at length of the LCA's treatment of the homosexuality issue. The congregation he pastored is in Minnesota, thus a member of the Minnesota Synod over which Herbert W. Chilstrom was bishop.

SHORTLY AFTER ASSUMING MY PASTORATE [TRINITY, IN MINNEHAHA FALLS, MINNESOTA], OUR SYNODICAL DISTRICT MEETING WAS HELD AT TRINITY. ON THE AGENDA WAS A PRO-HOMOSEXUAL RESOLUTION, WHICH THE DISTRICT INTENDED TO PRESENT TO THE SYNOD CONVENTION THE FOLLOWING SUMMER. AS I READ THE RESOLUTION, I COULD NOT BELIEVE MY EYES; THEN AS IT SANK IN, I COULD NOT BELIEVE THEIR AUDACITY... "HOW IS IT POSSIBLE," I ASKED, "THAT YOU WOULD SEEK TO PROMOTE AN EVIL WHICH THE BIBLE CLEARLY CONDEMNS?" LITTLE DID I REALIZE THAT IN MINNESOTA SOME CLERGY ACTUALLY HAVE A CHURCH ANSWER TO THAT QUESTION. THAT ANSWER IN ESSENCE STATES–"THE BIBLE DOES NOT MEAN WHAT IT SAYS; THE WRITERS OF SCRIPTURE WERE SPEAKING ONLY FOR THEMSELVES IN THEIR DAY, BUT WE NOW HAVE NEW INFORMATION ON THIS SUBJECT." I CONTINUED, 'IT IS IMPOSSIBLE FOR ME TO BELIEVE THAT YOU WOULD COME INTO THIS PARISH WHICH HAS STOOD SO FIRMLY FOR SCRIPTURAL AUTHORITY AND SEEK TO PASS THIS UNGODLY RESOLUTION.[69]

Minnesota Bishop, Herbert W. Chilstrom—later, president of the ELCA—informed Pastor Barnhart that he had been "ordaining homosexuals for several years," and that he knew "other bishops in the church who have ordained them also." However, he advised against ordaining practicing homosexuals. They had to agree to refrain from homosexual activities.

As members of the Minnesota Council of Churches, the LCA leaders were largely responsible for the preparation of the following statement on homosexuals and lesbians issued by the Council and printed in the public press:

THERE MAY BE CREATIVE AND WHOLESOME EXPRESSIONS OF SEXUALITY AT VARIOUS LEVELS IN RELATIONSHIPS BETWEEN MEN AND WOMEN, BETWEEN MEN AND OTHER MEN, AND BETWEEN WOMEN AND OTHER WOMEN (OCTOBER 1982).[70]

Farther on in his book, Pastor Barnhart makes this evaluation of the homosexual issue in the LCA:

THE HOMOSEXUAL MOVEMENT HAS INVADED OUR CHURCH. PROPONENTS OF THIS EVIL PERVERSION ARE ENCOURAGED AND ENABLED THROUGH OFFICIAL CHURCH STRUCTURES. THEOLOGIANS HAVE GONE TO THEIR AID TO REINTERPRET SCRIPTURE AND REEDUCATE THE LAITY INTO BELIEVING THAT THE HOMOSEXUAL LIFESTYLE IS NORMAL AND VIRTUOUS AND SHOULD BE FULLY ACCEPTED BY THE CHURCH. THESE TEACHINGS NOT ONLY VIOLATE SCRIPTURE; THEY ENSLAVE HOMOSEXUALS IN A SIN AND LIFE-STYLE, WHICH THROUGH REPENTANCE CHRIST CAN FORGIVE AND HEAL.[71]

Barnhart reported that homosexual materials were freely handed out at the Minnesota Synod Convention. Here is a list of Bible passages that were especially under fire by those in the LCA (and, presently, in the ELCA) who defend homosexuality as acceptable conduct: Genesis 1:27; 2:24; ch. 19; Leviticus 20:13; Roman 1:18-27; 1 John 1:9; 1 Corinthians 6:9,10. These passages are commonly used by the conservative side of Lutheranism to show that God condemns this lifestyle.

Finally, we include an audacious statement by Robin Scroggs, in defense of homosexuality:

THE CONCLUSION I HAVE DRAWN SEEMS INEVITABLE: BIBLICAL JUDGMENTS AGAINST HOMOSEXUALITY ARE NOT RELEVANT TO TODAY'S DEBATE. THEY SHOULD NO LONGER BE USED IN DENOMINATIONAL DISCUSSIONS ABOUT HOMOSEXUALITY, SHOULD IN NO WAY BE A WEAPON TO JUSTIFY REFUSAL OF ORDINATION, NOT BECAUSE THE BIBLE IS NOT AUTHORITATIVE BUT SIMPLY BECAUSE IT DOES NOT ADDRESS THE ISSUES INVOLVED.[72]

Note: For a thorough, scripturally accurate treatment of the subject of homosexuality, the following book, authored by a pastor of the conservative, confessional Wisconsin Evangelical Lutheran Synod (WELS) is recommended: Richard Starr, *Speaking the Unspeakable! Homosexuality—A Biblical and Modern Perspective* (Milwaukee, WI: Northwestern Publishing House, 1987)—Order Services: 1-800-662-6022.

While we are considering the matter of the LCA's liberal attitude toward homosexuality, we ought to consider another—quite bazaar—sexual issue that stirred up much controversy within and without the LCA. The controversy reverberated across this country with thorough coverage by the news media. We refer to the use of pornographic films in family counseling by the Minnesota Lutheran Social Services to—in Pastor David Barnhart's words—"treat ill and hurting children." Pastor Barnhart lays out the situation in his book, *The Church's Desperate Need for Revival*. It was also covered by *Christian News*, edited by Herman Otten.

Pastor Barnhart informs us that Lutheran Social Services of Minnesota, in which the LCA was deeply involved, operated a counseling program in which entire families, including the young children, were required to view pornographic films portraying explicit, sexual scenes. Some of the viewers were so upset that they were unable to talk about their experience without crying. These films were acquired from "regular commercial pornographic sources" (a quote from the president of the LSS of Minnesota). The University of Minnesota had a similar program (as did other universities across the nation) of using explicit sex films in counseling. Barnhart referred to the films as "unadulterated slime from the pits of hell." In spite of the controversy, which the use of such films caused, the Minnesota Synod (LCA) Convention in 1983 affirmed the continuation of this practice. The decision to continue the use of pornographic films by the LSS represented the view of the LCA's church leadership at the highest levels, "since all the bishops and presidents of the involved church bodies are part of the LSS Board."[73]

HISTORICAL CRITICISM AND THE LCA'S SOCIAL GOSPEL, INCLUDING LIBERATION THEOLOGY

First, we need to answer the questions: What is liberation theology? and What is the Social Gospel? First, the Social Gospel.

THE TEACHING OF A SOCIAL SALVATION, WHICH HAS AS ITS OBJECTIVE THE RE-

BIRTH OF SOCIETY THROUGH THE CHANGE OF THE SOCIAL ORDER BY MASS OR GROUP ACTION. ALTHOUGH DIRECTED MAINLY TOWARD SOCIAL CLASSES, IT IS SUBJECTIVISTIC IN ITS ATTEMPT TO PERSUADE INDIVIDUALS TO ADOPT AND PRACTICE THE SOCIAL ETHICS OF CHRIST. THUS THE CONCEPTION HAS APPLICABILITY OF THE TEACHINGS OF CHRIST TO SOCIAL AND INDIVIDUAL MORALITY. AMONG EXTREME EXPONENTS OF THE SOCIAL GOSPEL THERE IS NO PREREQUISITE OF RECONCILIATION OF THE INDIVIDUAL TO GOD THROUGH GRACE, BY FAITH IN CHRIST JESUS, THE DIVINE REDEEMER, AND LITTLE REFERENCE TO THE REGENERATIVE WORK OF THE HOLY SPIRIT IN THE INDIVIDUAL. FOR MANY ADHERENTS THE SOCIAL GOSPEL IS ESSENTIALLY A THIS-WORLDLY GOSPEL OF WORKS AND NOT A GOSPEL OF GRACE FOR THIS LIFE AND HEAVEN.

Furthermore,

CRITICS OF THE SOCIAL GOSPEL HAVE SEEN IN IT AN IDEALISTIC, PURELY HUMANITARIAN, FALSELY OPTIMISTIC, UTOPIAN AND PACIFISTIC, SOCIAL REFORMIST MOVEMENT NOT ESSENTIALLY CHRISTIAN, BECAUSE IT BYPASSED THE ESSENTIAL ELEMENTS OF CHRISTIAN DOCTRINE AND LIFE, OR BECAUSE IT HAS NOT FULFILLED THE EXPECTATIONS OF ITS ADVOCATES.[74]

Thus, when the Social Gospel is preached in the church, the Gospel of Grace and salvation from sin through Jesus Christ is either slighted or omitted altogether. And what is liberation theology? Authors Leppien and Smith, as well as David Barnhart, have provided us with a fairly comprehensive view of this more recent version of the Social Gospel. First Leppien and Smith.

ONE CANNOT WRITE ABOUT THE SOCIAL GOSPEL WITHOUT SOME MENTION AND EXPLANATION OF THE MOVEMENT'S MOST DANGEROUS DEVELOPMENT—LIBERATION THEOLOGY. LIBERATION THEOLOGY IS ANOTHER RESULT OF THE HISTORICAL-CRITICAL METHOD OF BIBLICAL INTERPRETATION, WHICH ATTACKS AND DENIES THE DEITY OF CHRIST. JESUS IS NOW SEEN AS THE "MAN" FOR OTHERS, ESPECIALLY THE POOR AND DOWNTRODDEN, WHOSE CHIEF CONCERN WAS THE ELIMINATION OF POVERTY AND OPPRESSION. THIS NEW VIEW OF JESUS AND HIS MESSAGE IS THE FOUNDATION OF LIBERATION THEOLOGY.

THE DANGER OF LIBERATION THEOLOGY CANNOT BE OVERESTIMATED. IT DENIES THE TRUE IDENTITY AND MESSAGE OF JESUS AND CONSEQUENTLY PERVERTS THE TRUE MISSION OF THE CHURCH—THAT OF PROCLAIMING THE SAVING GOSPEL OF JESUS CHRIST FOR ALL THE WORLD TO HEAR. INSTEAD, ANOTHER GOSPEL IS PREACHED—THAT OF THE KINGDOM OF GOD ON EARTH. THE ULTIMATE MISSION OF LIBERATION THEOLOGY GOES BEYOND PERSONAL RELIGIOUS BELIEFS. ITS REAL GOAL IS TO CHANGE THE POLITICAL-ECONOMIC STRUCTURE OF THE ENTIRE WORLD. THIS GOAL MAY BE MORE EASILY UNDERSTOOD IF WE TAKE A LOOK AT THE REAL MESSAGE OF LIBERATION THEOLOGY AS DESCRIBED BY DR. WILLIAM R. LEROY, WHO SERVED AS A MISSIONARY IN BRAZIL FOR MORE THAT 25 YEARS: *THE MESSAGE OF LIBERATION THEOLOGY IS VERY SIMPLE. SALVATION MEANS POLITICAL LIBERATION FROM EVERY FORM OF OPPRESSION (DEFINED BY THEM) THAT COULD PREVENT MAN FROM TRUE AND FULL HUMANIZATION. SIN AND GUILT ARE BASICALLY SOCIAL IN THEIR DEFINITION AND ORIGIN. IF THEIR DEFINITION OF SIN IS SYNONYMOUS WITH SOCIAL OPPRESSION AND "INJUSTICE" OF ANY KIND, THEN IT ONLY FOLLOWS THAT LIBERATION FROM "SIN" BECOMES POSSIBLE ONLY BY THE OVERTHROW OF THOSE OPPRESSIVE SOCIAL STRUCTURES. SIN BECOMES EXTERNALIZED AND FINDS ITS*

ORIGIN ONLY IN A SOCIAL CONTEXTUAL FRAMEWORK. THE POINT OF REFERENCE FOR CONVERSATION IS NO LONGER THE SINFUL HEART OF MAN, WHICH IS IN A STATE OF REBELLION AGAINST A HOLY GOD, BUT NOW THE POINT OF REFERENCE FOR CONVERSION REFERS TO THAT WHICH IS EXTERNAL, SUCH AS SOCIAL STRUCTURES. THE THEOLOGIANS OF LIBERATION ARE CONVINCED THAT SOCIALISM IS THE NECESSARY PRE-CONDITION FOR THE CONSTRUCTION OF A JUST AND HUMAN SOCIETY. ONLY THE SOCIAL APPROPRIATION OF THE MEANS OF PRODUCTION WILL PAVE THE WAY TO A NEW ORDER IN WHICH THE NEEDS OF ALL THE PEOPLE CAN BE MET.

Leppien and Smith also quote Humberto Belli, a "native Nicaraguan, lawyer, and sociologist" who was once a Marxist. He describes the teaching of liberation theology thus:

IF WE LOVE JESUS, WE HAVE TO LOVE THE POOR. BUT TO BE EFFECTIVE IN OUR LOVE FOR THE POOR, WE HAVE TO DESTROY THE STRUCTURE, WHICH OPPRESSES THE POOR. THIS IS DONE THROUGH SOCIAL-POLITICAL ACTION AND IT CALLS FOR REVOLUTION TO CHANGE THE SYSTEM AND CREATE A NEW WORLD...

THE THEOLOGIANS NO LONGER TALK OR PREACH ABOUT PERSONAL SIN, BELLI EXPLAINS; INSTEAD, THEY TALK ABOUT "SOCIAL SIN," MEANING CAPITALISM, WHICH, THEY SAY, OPPRESSES THE POOR. CHRISTIANS MUST FIGHT AGAINST CAPITALISM, ACCORDING TO THESE THEOLOGIANS. THE REVOLUTIONARY PARTY BECOMES THE MESSIAH, THE NEW CHRIST, FREEING THE PEOPLE FROM SOCIAL SIN, AND THE KINGDOM OF GOD IS SOCIALISM IN THIS IDEOLOGY. CONVERSION IS GETTING CONNECTED WITH "THE PEOPLE" AND WORKING FOR REVOLUTION. CHRIST IS NOT DENIED, BUT CHRIST IS TRANSFORMED INTO A GUERILLA FIGHTER, BELLI NOTES. THE REVOLUTION IS GOD[75].

So then, what about the LCA and liberation theology? Pastor J. Kincaid Smith tells his readers that he was trained in this theology in the LCA seminary that he attended, and that he assimilated this theology into his ministry before he moved to the conservative side of Lutheranism:

LOOKING BACK NOW, I WOULD HAVE TO SAY THAT GIVEN WHAT I WAS TAUGHT AND HAD COME TO BELIEVE AS A STUDENT IN A LIBERAL LUTHERAN SEMINARY, I WAS LITTLE MORE THAN A HUMANIST DRESSED UP IN THE GARB OF CHRISTIAN LANGUAGE. POLITICALLY I WAS VIRTUALLY A MARXIST, ALTHOUGH I WOULD NOT HAVE CALLED MYSELF THAT AT THE TIME—I DON'T THINK THAT I COULD HAVE ADMITTED THAT EVEN TO MYSELF.

IN THE BIG SHIFT THAT OUR THEOLOGY HAD TAKEN, THE FOUNDATION FOR OUR BELIEFS HAD COMPLETELY CHANGED WITHOUT OUR WANTING TO RECOGNIZE IT. INSTEAD OF BEING BASED ON GOD'S WORD, OUR BELIEFS HAD SHIFTED AROUND UNTIL THEY FINALLY LEANED ENTIRELY ON THE SAME PHILOSOPHIES UPON WHICH KARL MARX HAD BUILT HIS "HOUSE."

THERE WERE CONSEQUENTLY SOME VERY CRITICAL BLIND SPOTS THAT WERE BUILT INTO OUR WAY OF UNDERSTANDING THE NATURE OF MAN, THE WORLD, AND SOCIETY.

CONSIDERING MY OWN FORMER POSITION IN RETROSPECT, IT WAS BECAUSE CERTAIN VITAL ELEMENTS WERE MISSING IN OUR SCHEME OF THINGS THAT WE WERE COMPLETELY OBSTRUCTED FROM BEING ABLE TO RECOGNIZE THE REAL PROBLEM IN SOCIETY. AS A RESULT, OUR PROPOSALS OF WHAT THE CHURCH'S MISSION TO THE WORLD SHOULD BE WERE UTTERLY ILL CONCEIVED AND MISGUIDED. WE

WERE CRIPPLED IN OUR CAPACITY TO ACCESS THE NATURE OF THE REAL ROOT
PROBLEM, BECAUSE VITAL TRUTHS THAT ARE FOUND ONLY IN THE BIBLE HAD
GOTTEN LOST IN THE HISTORICAL-CRITICAL SHUFFLE.

Smith continues:

IN THE BIBLE, WE FIND OUT WHAT MAN IS REALLY LIKE—THAT HE IS NOT A
PRODUCT OF MERE CHANCE AND EVOLUTION BUT A CREATURE OF GOD, CREATED
PERFECT BUT THEN FALLEN INTO SIN.

THE WORLD TODAY IS CONSEQUENTLY A FALLEN WORLD AND AS SUCH IS NOT
PERFECTIBLE. IN HIS FALL INTO SIN, MAN TURNED AWAY FROM HIS CREATOR.
HE TURNED TO HIMSELF AND TO HIS OWN WAY. THE NATURE OF MAN SINCE THE
FALL IS SINFUL AND SELF-CENTERED AND BECAUSE OF THIS, MAN IS NOT CAPA-
BLE OF BRINGING ABOUT THE PERFECT PEACEFUL UTOPIAN SOCIETY THAT WE AS
LIBERATION THEOLOGIANS SO HOPEFULLY PROPOSED. WE WERE LIKE MEN TRY-
ING TO PLAN AND CONSTRUCT A BUILDING WHILE HAVING A TOTALLY WRONG
UNDERSTANDING OF THE NATURE AND STRENGTH OF THE BUILDING MATERIALS
AND OF THE PURPOSE OF THE BUILDING ITSELF.

Smith concludes with this very important observation:

ONLY IN GOD'S WORD CAN WE FIND THE TRUE NATURE OF THE PROBLEM, SIN
AS DISOBEDIENCE TO GOD. HERE ALSO WE FIND GOD'S SOLUTION TO THE FATAL
ILLNESS OF SIN. HE SENT HIS VIRGIN-BORN SON, JESUS CHRIST, TO REDEEM
THE WORLD THROUGH THE SHEDDING OF HIS BLOOD. ONLY HERE CAN WE DIS-
COVER WHAT THE TRUE MISSION OF THE CHURCH SHOULD BE—SPREADING THE
GOOD NEWS OF THIS REDEMPTION IN A FALLEN WORLD UNTIL THE DAY OF HIS
COMING.[76]

We will conclude our discussion of liberation theology in the LCA with these
remarks by David R. Barnhart, who, like J. Kincaid Smith, left the LCA to become a member of a small conservative Lutheran body.

IN OUR TWENTIETH CENTURY CHURCH, A CARBON COPY OF THE LAODICEAN
CHURCH OF REVELATION, THE SOCIAL GOSPEL IS BEING SUBSTITUTED FOR THE
AUTHENTIC PREACHING OF BIBLICAL LAW AND GOSPEL. IN THESE LIFE-ROBBING
PULPITS, IT IS SAID THAT CHRIST'S FIRST COMING WAS FOR NO OTHER PURPOSE
THAN TO VANGUARD SOCIAL REFORM. LIBERATION THEOLOGY, WHICH SEEKS
TO BRING SOCIAL REDEMPTION TO MANKIND, IS THE GREAT APOSTASY OF MOD-
ERN MISSION.

....TO PREACH THE DIVINE, SUBSTITUTIONARY ATONEMENT OF CHRIST FOR THE
SINS OF MANKIND IS CONSIDERED BY THESE LIBERATION THEOLOGIANS AS AN
OUTMODED CONCEPT OF A "BLOODY RELIGION."...TODAY'S LIBERAL EMPHASIS
ON "UNIVERSALISM" [EVERY ONE WILL BE SAVED AND THUS NO NEED TO PREACH
A GOSPEL OF GRACE AND SALVATION] RENDERS CHURCH MISSIONS OBSOLETE.[77]

In his book Pastor Barnhart pretty well sums up the unorthodox, unscriptural course that the LCA was following due to the employment of the historical-critical method by this body's theologians and many of its pastors. He asks:

....HOW COULD I ASK MY PEOPLE TO CONTRIBUTE MONEY AND SUPPORT THE
SHOWING OF PORNOGRAPHIC FILMS TO YOUTH? HOW COULD I ASK THEM TO FI-
NANCIALLY SUPPORT THE SYNOD'S ACTIVE PROMOTION OF HOMOSEXUALITY, OR
TO PAY THE SALARIES OF PROFESSORS AND TEACHERS WHO TAUGHT FALSE DOC-
TRINES IN OUR COLLEGES AND SEMINARIES? HOW COULD I ENCOURAGE MY
YOUNG PEOPLE TO ATTEND OUR CHURCH COLLEGES WHERE THEIR FAITH WOULD

BE UNDER ATTACK, OR WHERE THEY WOULD BE TOLD THAT WHAT THEY LEARNED BACK HOME WAS NOT TRUE...HOW COULD ANY ORTHODOX, BIBLE-BELIEVING PASTOR ENCOURAGE YOUNG MEN PREPARING FOR THE MINISTRY TO ATTEND A SEMINARY WHERE MANY HISTORIC-SCRIPTURAL ACCOUNTS ARE QUESTIONED AND WHERE THE TEACHING OF UNIVERSALISM AND LIBERATION THEOLOGY ARE BOTH PROMOTED AND TOLERATED? A GROUP OF YOUNG SEMINARIANS FROM TRINITY WHO SAT IN MY LIVING ROOM ONE EVENING HAD TOLD ME OF A PROFESSOR AT OUR LUTHERAN SEMINARY WHO DENIED THE BODILY RESURRECTION OF CHRIST.[78]

Of his eventual withdrawal from the LCA, Pastor Barnhart stated the following, in summary of his reason for doing so:

I MUST MAKE MY WITHDRAWAL FROM THE LUTHERAN CHURCH IN AMERICA BECAUSE THE LCA'S ABUSES OF THE WORD OF GOD ARE SO MANY AND SO SERIOUS THAT THEY HAVE TAKEN MY CONSCIENCE TO THE BREAKING POINT.[79]

It would be very natural at this point, after having considered the widespread liberal theology and practice of the LCA to ask: How could...how did this happen? Where were the conservatives in all this? We will allow Pastor Barnhart to enlighten us once more:

...MOST EVANGELICAL, CONSERVATIVE PASTORS LACKED THE COURAGE TO STAND AGAINST THOSE CHURCH LEADERS WHO CONTROLLED THEIR FUTURES. IN ADDITION, EVERY COLLEGE, SEMINARY, PUBLISHING HOUSE, AND CHURCH HEADQUARTERS IN OUR TWO LUTHERAN BODIES [LCA AND ALC] WERE FIRMLY IN THE UNRELENTING CONTROL OF LIBERALS. TO ADD INSULT TO INJURY, THEY HAD THE SUPPORT OF THE VAST MAJORITY OF THE PASTORS. THE LIBERAL SEMINARIES HAVE EFFECTIVELY PRODUCED SEVERAL GENERATIONS OF LIBERAL CLERGY, WHOSE INFLUENCE IN THE CONGREGATIONS IS BEYOND CALCULATION. HOW OFTEN AT CHURCH CONVENTIONS WE HAVE WITNESSED LAY-DELEGATES, IGNORANT OF ISSUES AND INEPT IN THEOLOGICAL MATTERS, VOTE ON ISSUES ACCORDING TO THE COUNSEL OF THEIR PASTORS.[80]

Pastor Barnhart also makes this observation:

LIBERAL CHURCH LEADERS KNOW ALL TOO WELL WHAT THE WORDS INERRANT AND INFALLIBLE MEAN. IT IS FOR THAT REASON THEY REJECT THEM IN REFERENCE TO SCRIPTURAL AUTHORITY. THESE THEOLOGIANS AND CHURCH LEADERS KNOW THAT THE ACCEPTANCE OF A STRONG AFFIRMATION OF SCRIPTURES ON THE PART OF THEIR CHURCH BODIES WOULD REQUIRE THEM TO BANISH THEIR OWN FALSE TEACHINGS AND PRACTICES OR FACE THE CONSEQUENCES. ONE CANNOT ORDAIN HOMOSEXUALS, AFFIRM THE HOMOSEXUAL LIFESTYLE, ADVOCATE ABORTION ON DEMAND, PROMOTE UNIVERSALISM [ALL ARE SAVED] AND LIBERATION THEOLOGY, OR SHOW PORNOGRAPHIC FILMS TO YOUTH IN A CHURCH TREATMENT PROGRAM, IF THE CHURCH MAINTAINS THAT THE BIBLE IS THE ABSOLUTE AND FINAL AUTHORITY CONCERNING THE TRUTH OF THESE MATTERS. NO! CHURCH LEADERS MUST FIRST SET ASIDE THE ABSOLUTE AUTHORITY OF THE WORD FROM THE OFFICIAL CONFESSIONS OF THEIR CHURCH BODIES IF THEY ARE GOING TO BE FREE TO ESTABLISH THEIR OWN OPINIONS AS EQUAL OR HIGHER THAN THE TEACHINGS OF HOLY SCRIPTURE.[81]

One might wonder why we would spend so much time reviewing the history and theology of a church body that no longer exists. However, the LCA really has not gone out of existence. It is very much alive as a part of the three-body

574

merger that formed the Evangelical Lutheran Church in America (ELCA) in 1988. The ELCA, which we will examine in a separate chapter is a sum total of its parts. What the LCA and the ALC and the AELC were in their separate existences, the ELCA is now as a merger—and in a way, even more so. The things we learned about the LCA in this chapter are matters that are perpetuated in the new body. In the words of Pastor Barnhart:

THE NEW LUTHERAN CHURCH [I.E. ELCA] WILL BE NO DIFFERENT THAN THE SUM OF THE THREE BODIES, WHICH ARE UNITING. THE PRESENT LIBERAL THEOLOGIES AND PRACTICES, THE PRESENT LIBERAL PUBLICATIONS AND INSTITUTIONS—SEX FILMS AND ALL—WILL BE TRANSFERRED "LOCK, STOCK, AND BARREL." THE LEFT-WING POLITICAL EMPHASIS [I.E. AS A PART OF LIBERATION THEOLOGY] WHICH NOW HOLDS SWAY IN SO MUCH OF THE CHURCH IS A MIRROR IMAGE OF WHAT THE NEW LUTHERAN CHURCH WILL BE.

THE NEW LUTHERAN CHURCH DOCUMENTS BEING DRAFTED WITH A DELIBERATE AMBIGUITY WILL MAKE THE NEW LUTHERAN CHURCH TOTALLY INCLUSIVE. NOT INCLUSIVE IN THE SCRIPTURAL SENSE OF RECEIVING ALL REPENTING SINNERS TO THE FOUNTAIN OF GOD'S GRACE, BUT INCLUSIVE IN RECEIVING ALL FORMS OF THEOLOGY AND PRACTICE, INCLUDING UNREPENTANT SINFUL LIFESTYLES.

ONE DOES NOT HAVE TO BE A PROPHET OR THE SON OF A PROPHET TO KNOW THAT THE NEW LUTHERAN CHURCH WILL BE ALIGNED WITH THE APOSTATE NATIONAL COUNCIL OF CHURCHES AND THE WORLD COUNCIL OF CHURCHES. THE MERGING BODIES ARE A PART OF THOSE ORGANIZATIONS NOW.

What is stated in the chapter covering the Evangelical Lutheran Church in America (ELCA), demonstrates the accuracy of Pastor Barnhart's words.

Footnotes for Chapter Thirty-Three

1 Richard C. Wolf, *Documents of Lutheran Unity in America* (Philadelphia, PA: Fortress Press, 1966), pp. 275, 276; Doc. #119.

2 Wolf, *Documents...,* p. 499; Doc. #213.

3 Wolf, *Documents...,* p. 472; Doc. #192, #193.

4 Wolf, *Documents.,* pp. 472, 473; Doc. #195, #197.

5 Johannes Knudsen, *The Formation of the Lutheran Church in America* (Philadelphia, PA: Fortress Press, 1978), p. 23. Quoting from Dr. Fry, *Desk Book Letter.*

6 Knudsen, *The Formation.,* p. 26.

7 Knudsen, *The Formation...,* p. 27.

8 Knudsen,*The Formation.,* p. 28.

9 E. Clifford Nelson, ed., *The Lutherans in North America* (Philadelphia, PA: Fortress Press, 1975), p. 507.

10 Knudsen,*The Formation,* p. 39.

11 Wolf, *Documents...,* p. 571; Doc. #227.

12 Wolf, *Documents...,* pp. 565,566,567; Doc. #277.

13 Wolf, *Documents...,* pp. 568, 569; Doc. #227.

14 Wolf, *Documents,* pp. 570, 571; Doc. #227.

15 Nelson, *The Lutherans...,* p. 535. See *Marburg Revisited,* ed., Paul C. Empie and James I. McCord (Minneapolis, MN: Augsburg Publishing House, 1966), p. 191

16 Minutes of the Biennial Convention of the Lutheran Church in America, 1966.

17 Minutes of the Constituting Convention, Lutheran Church in America, 1963.

18 Knudsen, *The Formation...*, p. 67.

19 Knudsen, *The Formation*, p. 83.

20 Knudsen, *The Formation...*, p. 83.

21 Knudsen, *The Formation.*, p. 86.

22 Knudsen, *The Formation*, p. 91.

23 Knudsen, *The Formation...*, p. 109.

24 Patsy A. Leppien and J. Kincaid Smith, *What's Going On Among the Lutherans—A Comparison of Beliefs* (Milwaukee, WI: Northwestern Publishing House, 1992), p. 7.

25 Leppien-Smith, *What's Going On...?*, Biography of author on back cover.

26 Kurt E. Marquart, *Anatomy Of An Explosion* (Fort Wayne, IN: Concordia Theological Seminary Press, 1977), pp. 101, 102. Quoting E. Clifford Nelson, *Lutheranism in North America 1914-1970* (Minneapolis, MN: Augsburg Press, 1977), pp. 72, 73 (note 71), 37 (note 87).

27 Leppien-Smith, *What's Going On...?* p. 46.

28 Leppien-Smith,*What's Going On...?*, pp. 47, 48. Quoting Todd W. Nichol, "How Will ELCA View the Bible? The Lutheran Standard, October 15, 1986, pp. 12, 13.

29 Leppien-SAmith, *What's Going On...?*., pp. 47. 48. Quoting Nichol, Ibid., pp.12, 13.

30 Marquart, *Anatomy...*, pp. 113, 114.

31 Leppien-Smith, *What's Going On...?* Quoting Siegbert W. Becker, "The Historical-Critical Method of Bible Interpretation, *Wisconsin Lutheran Quarterly*, vol. 74, 1977, pp. 133-148.

32 Leppien-Smith, *What's Going On...?*, p. 42. Quoting Becker, Ibid., pp. 13-15.

33 *Wisconsin Lutheran Quarterly,* vol. 89, #4, 1992, p. 263.

34 Leppien-Smith, *What's Going On...?*, p. 120.

35 Leppien-Smith, *What's Going On...?* pp. 35,36.

36 Leppien-Smith,*What's Going On...?*, p. 52.

37 Leppien-Smith,*What's Going On...?*, p. 34. Quoting Joe E. Schruhl, "Historical-Critical Method of Bible Interpretation," *Christian News Encyclopedia*, 4 vols., ed. Herman Otten (Washington, MO: Missourian Publishing Co., 1983), 1:237.

38 Marquart, *Anatomy...*, pp. 121,122. Quoting E. and M.L. Keller, *Miracles in Dispute*, pp. 176, 177, 215, 217, 224 (for reference reading).

39 Leppien-Smith, *What's Going On...?* p. 56. Quoting Carl E. Braaten, *Christian Dogmatics*, 2 vols., eds. Carl E. Braaten and Robert W. Jenson (Philadelphia, PA: Fortress Press, 1984), 1:76,77.

40 Leppien-Smith, *What's Going On...?*, pp. 42,43. Quoting from J. Kincaid Smith, "The Real Virgin Birth of Our Lord Jesus Christ," *The Lutheran Sentinel*, December 1987, p. 4 and (the second paragraph) "The Dismantling of the Christian Faith or the Historical-Critical Method,"*Christian News*, April 29, 1985, p. 11.

41 Leppien-Smith, *What's Going On...?* pp. 50,51. Quoting from Craig Stanford, *The Death of the Lutheran Reformation* (Fort Wayne, IN: Stanford Publishing, 1988), pp.271-274.

42 Leppien-Smith, *What's Going On...?* p. 62. Quoting Foster R. McCurley, Jr. and John Reumann, *Word and Witness* (Philadelphia, PA: Fortress Press, 1977), pp. 186, 187. (A Bible study program for adults.)

43 Harold E. Wicke, *A Catechism of Differences* (Milwaukee, WI: Northwestern Publishing House, 1964). Quoting Resources, March 1963, pp.

44 Leppien-Smith, *What's Going On...?* p. 67. Quoting James Limburg, Search, Unit 3, Genesis 1-17, Leadership Guide (Minneapolis, MN: Augsburg Publishing House, 1983), p. 49.

45 Leppien-Smith, *What's Going On...?*, p. 79. Quoting Donald H. Juel, *Search*, Unit 5, Matthew 1-16, Leader's Guide, Ibid., p. 17.

46 Leppien-Smith, *What's Going On...?* p. 80. Quoting Hans Schwartz, *What Christians Believe*

(Philadelphia, PA: Fortress Press, 1987), p. 40.

47 Leppien-Smith,*What's Going On...?*, p. 80. Quoting John Reumann, *Jesus in the Church's Gospels* (Philadelphia, PA: Fortress Press, 1968), p. vii.

48 Leppien-Smith, *What's Going On...?*., p. 84. Quoting from Hans Schwarz, *Christian Dogmatics*, 2 vols., ed., Carl E. Braaten and Robert W. Jenson (Philadelphia, PA: Fortress Press, 1984) 2:282, 283.

49 Leppien-Smith, *What's Going On...?*, p. 85. Quoting Carl E. Braaten, *Christian Dogmatics*, Ibid., 1:552,553./528, 529.

50 Leppien-Smith, *What's Going On...?*, p. 90. Quoting Carl E. Braaten, *Christian Dogmatics*, 1:529, 527, 546.

51 Leppien-Smith, *What's Going On..?* pp. 97,98. Quoting from Carl E. Braaten, *Christian Dogmatics*, 2 vols., eds., Carl E. Braaten and Robert W. Jenson (Philadelphia, PA: Fortress Press, 1984), 1:71.

52 Leppeien-Smith, *What's Going On...?*, p. 99. Quoting from Paul Jersild, *Invitation to Faith*, (Minneapolis, MN: Augsburg Publishing House, 1978), pp. 99, 100.

53 Leppien-Smith, *What's Going On...?*, p. 102. Quoting from Robert W. Jenson, *Christian Dogmatics*, Ibid., 1:155.

54 Leppien-Smith,*What's Going On...?* , pp. 102, 103. Quoting from Paul Jersild, *Invitation to Faith*, (Minneapolis, MN: Augsburg Publishing House, 1978), pp. 130, 131.

55 Leppien-Smith, *What's Going On...?*, p. 107. Quoting Gerald O. Forde, *Christian Dogmatics*, Ibid., 2:14,15.

56 Leppien-Smith, *What's Going On...?*, pp. 107, 108. Quoting Carl E. Braaten, *Christian Dogmatics*, 2 vols., eds., Carl E. Braaten and Robert W. Jenson (Philadelphia, PA: Fortress Press, 1984), 2:82.

57 Leppien-Smith, *What's Going On...?*, p. 108. Quoting *The Evangelical Catechism*, American Edition, trans. Lawrence W. Denef (Minneapolis, MN: Augsburg Publishing House, 1982), pp. 209, 210, 211.

58 Leppien-Smith, *What's Going On...?*, p. 117. Quoting Marshall D. Johnson, *Affirm, The Apostles Creed*, Teacher's Guide, eds. Irene Getz, Susan Niemi Tellie, and Gretchen L. Weidenback (Minneapolis, MN: Augsburg Publishing House, 1984), pp. 22, 23.

59 Leppein-Smith, *What's Going On...?*, p. 109. Quoting J. Kincaid Smith, "The Confession of a former Liberal LCA Pastor," *Christian News Encyclopedia*, 4 vols., ed. Herman Otten (Washington, MO: Missourian Publishing Co, 1988), 3:21, 65.

60 Leppien-Smith, *What's Going On...?*, pp. 114, 115. Quoting Carl E. Braaten, *Christian Dogmatics,* 1:549.

61 Leppien-Smith, *What's Going On...?* p. 115. Quoting from Hans Schwarz, *Christian Dogmatics,* 2 vols., eds., Carl E. Braaten and Robert W. Jensen (Philadelphia, PA: Fortress Press, 1984), 2:2:566-568.

62 Leppien-Smith, *What's Going On...?*, p. 117. Quoting Marshall D. Johnson, Affirm Series, *The Apostles Creed*, Teacher's Guide (Minneapolis, MN: Augsburg Publishing House, 1984), p. 43.

63 Leppien-Smith, *What's Going On...?*, p. 117. Quoting John R. Brokoff, "Morning Has Broken," *The Lutheran*, April 18, 1984, p. 4.

64 Leppien-Smith, *What's Going On...?*, p. 119. Quoting J. Kincaid Smith, "The Confession of a former Liberal LCA Pastor," *Christian News Encyclopedia*, 4 vols., ed. Herman Otten (Washington, MO: Missourian Publishing Co, 1988), 3:21, 65.

65 Leppien-Smith, *What's Going On...?*, p. 123. Quoting Stanley N. Olson, *Search*, Unit 11.1 Corinthians, Leader's Guide (Minneapolis, Augsburg Publishing House, 1985), pp. 85, 88.

66 Leppien-Smith, *What's Going On...?*, p. 124. Quoting Hans Schwarz, *Beyond the Gates of*

Death: A Biblical Examination of Evidence for Life After Death (Minneapolis, MN: Augsburg Publishing House, 1981), p. 20.

67 Leppien-Smith, *What's Going On...?* p. 125. Quoting Martin J. Heinecken, *We Believe and Teach* (Philadelphia, PA: Fortress Press, 1980), p. 119.

68 Herbert W. Chilstrom, "A Pastoral Letter: The Church and Homosexual Person, 1979. (Bishop, Minnesota Synod, Lutheran Church in America.)

69 David R. Barnhart, *The Church's Desperate Need For Revival* (Eagan, MN: Abiding Word Publications, copyright 1986 by Abiding Word Ministries, Inc.), p. 8.

70 Barnhart, *The Church's Desperate Need...*, pp. 9, 10.

71 Barnhart, *The Church's Desperate Need...*, p. 53.

72 Leppien-Smith, *What's Going On...?* p. 135. Quoting Robin Scroggs, *Homosexuality in the New Testament* (Philadelphia, PA: Fortress Press, 1983), p. 127.

73 Barnhart, *The Church's Desperate Need...*, pp. 18, 21, 26, 41.

74 Erwin L. Lueker, ed. in chief, *The Lutheran Cyclopedia*, (St. Louis, MO: Concordia Publishing House, 1954), pp. 987,988.

75 Leppien-Smith, *What's Going On...?* pp. 177, 178, 179. Too, the authors quote from William R. LeRoy, "Liberation Theology," *Christian News Encyclopedia, Ibid.*, 2:1133. They also quote from Frank Teskey, "Belli Denounces Liberation Theology in Nicaragua," *Christian News Encyclopedia, Ibid.*, 4:2554.

77 Barnhart, *The Church's...*, p. 4,

78 Barnhart, *The Church's...*, pp. 8,9.

79 Barnhart, *The Church's...*, p. 60.

80 Barnhart, *The Church's...*, p. 27.

81 Barnhart, *The Church's...*, pp. 32,33.

82 Barnhart, *The Church's...*, pp. 56, 57.

CHAPTER THIRTY-FOUR

LUTHERAN COOPERATIVE AGENCIES FORMED IN THE TWENTIETH CENTURY

NATIONAL LUTHERAN COUNCIL 1918-1966
AMERICAN LUTHERAN CONFERENCE 1930-1954
LUTHERAN COUNCIL U.S.A. 1966-1987

NATIONAL LUTHERAN COUNCIL
1918-1966

THE FORMATION OF THE
NATIONAL LUTHERAN COUNCIL

Among American Lutheran churches the need was felt for cooperative efforts to celebrate in 1917 the 400th Anniversary of the Reformation. A Lutheran publicity agency, the Lutheran Bureau, was subsequently quickly organized in 1917. Furthermore, World War I brought about a need to serve Lutheran military personnel. This resulted in the formation of the National Lutheran Commission for Soldiers' and Sailors' Welfare in the same year. Most of the Lutherans in America joined this enterprise of cooperative work. The Synodical Conference, however, did not join but carried on "an external cooperation with this Commission." When the war ended the Lutheran bodies, having grown used to cooperative enterprises, desired to carry on the spirit of cooperation that they enjoyed in the Commission. The feeling was aired that there ought to be a permanent organization to represent common interests among the Lutherans. Subsequently, a committee was appointed by a meeting of Lutheran bodies in 1918 to formulate plans for a national council of Lutheran churches. On September 6, 1918, the group of nine Lutheran bodies meeting in Chicago heard the report of this committee and then organized the National Lutheran Council (NLC).

The following Lutheran bodies were represented at the Chicago meeting: General Council, United Synod in the South, General Synod, Norwegian Lutheran Church, Augustana Evangelical Lutheran Church, American Evangelical Lutheran Church, Iowa Synod, Ohio Synod, Lutheran Free Church. Later, before the year's end, the United Evangelical Lutheran Church, the Buffalo Synod, and the Icelandic Synod gave their support to the venture.[1] In November of the same year three of the bodies—General Synod, General Council, United Synod in the South—merged to form the United Lutheran Church in America (ULCA). Most of the members of the NLC remained through its history. However, for eleven years (1920-1930) the Iowa Synod withdrew from the Council, later returning as a member of the American Lutheran Church. The Buffalo Synod and the American Evangelical Lutheran Church (the Danish Church) both withdrew in 1925. The Buffalo Synod returned in 1930 as a member of the American Lutheran Church, and Danish Church returned in 1937.

From 1918 to 1945, the NLC operated under the "code of regulations." In 1945 it adopted a formal constitution. Headquarters were set up in New York City at the time of the Council's founding. An office was also opened immediately in Washington, D.C., in order to facilitate contact with government agencies. The NLC was the first organization to bring about a joint participation of nearly all Lutherans in America.

The NLC listed the following Divisions and Departments: Division of Public Relations: Publicity, Statistics and Radio; Division of Welfare (included service to hospitalized veterans); Division of American Missions; Division of Student Service; Commission on Younger Churches and Orphaned Missions (i.e. resulting from wars' devastations); Bureau of Service to Military Personnel; Lutheran Service Commission; European Desk; Lutheran Resettlement Service.

FINALLY, A CONSTITUTION

Excerpts from the constitution: Article III, lists the following Purposes and Objectives: A. TO WITNESS FOR THE LUTHERAN CHURCH ON MATERS WHICH REQUIRE AN EXPRESSION OF COMMON FAITH, IDEALS, AND PROGRAM. B. TO BRING TO THE ATTENTION OF THE PARTICIPATING BODIES MATTERS WHICH IN ITS JUDGMENT MAY REQUIRE UTTERANCE OR ACTION ON THEIR PART. C. TO REPRESENT LUTHERAN INTEREST

IN AMERICA IN MATTERS, WHICH REQUIRE COMMON ACTION, BEFORE (1) NATIONAL AND STATE GOVERNMENTS, (2) ORGANIZED BODIES AND MOVEMENTS OUTSIDE THE LUTHERAN CHURCH. D. TO EMPHASIZE THE CONTINUING IMPORTANCE OF A RIGHT RELATION BETWEEN CHURCH AND STATE. E. TO FURTHER THE INTERESTS AND THE WORK OF THE LUTHERAN CHURCHES IN AMERICA. F. TO UNDERTAKE AND CARRY ON SUCH WORK AS MAY BE AUTHORIZED BY THE PARTICIPATING BODIES IN FIELDS WHERE COORDINATION OR JOINT ACTIVITY MAY BE DESIRABLE AND FEASIBLE, SUCH AS PUBLICITY, STATISTICS, WELFARE WORK, MISSIONS, EDUCATION, STUDENT WORK, AND OTHER FIELDS. G. TO TAKE THE NECESSARY STEPS TO MEET EMERGENCIES REQUIRING COMMON ACTION, EACH PARTICIPATING BODY TO DETERMINE THE EXTENT OF ITS COOPERATION IN EMERGENCY WORK. H. TO UNDERTAKE ADDITIONAL WORK WITH THE SPECIFIC CONSENT OF THE PARTICIPATING BODIES.[2] Membership in 1945: American Lutheran Church, United Lutheran Church in America, Evangelical Lutheran Church, American Evangelical Lutheran Church, United Evangelical Lutheran Church, Augustana Evangelical Church, Finnish or Suomi Synod, Lutheran Free Church.

THE NATIONAL LUTHERAN COUNCIL AT WORK

"The NLC was organized as an agency for service to the churches and to the world." In carrying out this work of service the relationships of the participating bodies was harmonious. The formation of the NLC occurred near the end of World War I, but this in no way subtracted from the challenge that lay before the new Council. Historian Conrad Bergendoff points out: "The council's most dramatic program was the part it played in relief work and service to the cause of foreign missions in years following World War I." He goes on to state: "…in every possible way assistance was given to suffering brethren [in Germany, Poland, France, and Russia]. In the first decade of its existence the council raised around $8 million for relief of congregations, pastors, and institutions." He also reports: "Soon after the war the council was instrumental in setting up the Lutheran Foreign Missions Conference to consider the needs of Lutheran fields throughout the world, many of which had been deprived of German leaders and funds." In a ten year period close to three-quarters of a million dollars was collected for this program.[3]

Part of the work of the NLC was keeping tabs on a moving Lutheran population and integrating them into congregations, conducting religious surveys among racial groups to facilitate reaching out to them, and turning mission fields over to participating bodies. As the result of a mandate from the Federal Council's General Committee on Army and Navy Chaplains, the NLC was charged with recruiting chaplains, processing applicants, and maintaining contacts between chaplains and their churches.[4]

The NLC's Division of Welfare and its Student Service were very active and far-reaching in their work. Of course, World War II presented a huge multifaceted challenge to the Council's Division of Welfare. The Council also represented American Lutherans in the Lutheran World Federation. According to historian Abdel Wentz, the first emphasis was on material relief, with quick infusion of large-scale provision of food, clothing and medicine, in order to save lives. After that, institutions of mercy were restored, Christian literature was distributed, and measures were taken to recruit pastors for the depleted ranks. Further work included providing shelter and spiritual assistance for thousands of displaced and homeless people, as well as guidance for uprooted youth and aid for oppressed minorities. By the beginning of the 1950's long-range plans were being made for the reconstruction of church buildings, support for church bodies, and the moral and spiritual rehabilitation of the people. Wentz adds that more than $3,000,000 were spent for repairs of damaged churches and to build new ones. Several times that amount was spent feeding and clothing children, caring for the aged and sick, providing salaries to impoverished pastors, caring for the needs of penniless students, and publishing Bibles, catechisms, theological and other books and devotional materials. Wentz also informs us that "...there were only a few countries in all Europe that did not see one or more of the agents of the NLC of America extending the hand of love in the name of Christ and building bridges of understanding and co-operation on the solid ground of charity, brotherly affection, and a common faith."[5] Lutherans here at home in America felt a deep sense of responsibility toward serving not only the needs of military personnel but the needs of also an enormous number of people suffering from the ravages of war.

THE NLC: DIVIDED IN THEOLOGY

The Lutheran bodies compromising the NLC were divided in their theology. Those compromising the United Lutheran Church in America contended for a "dynamic" principle—the modern principle—of interpreting the Lutheran Symbols, and the others stood for a repristination interpretation (the old Lutheran way).[6] The two forms of interpretation would later influence the outcome and the speed of Lutheran union: the one resulted in the formation of the Lutheran Church in America (LCA), which was liberal in theology and polity, the other form of interpretation resulted in the formation of the "new" American Lutheran Church, which embraced an approach to theology that was not as liberal as that of the United Lutheran Church, but not as conservative as that embraced by the Synodical Conference.

The NLC was not formed with theological studies and discussions between participating bodies as one of its objectives. Rather, it was organized as a cooperative agency for service both to the Lutheran Church and to the needy of the world. The NLC did not regard itself as a promoter of theological unity, nor as the means to achieve such unity. This was to be an enterprise whose purpose was service, not fellowship.

The United Lutheran Church, along with taking a liberal attitude toward the Scriptures, endorsed an ecumenical approach to non-Lutheran church bodies. On the other hand, the member bodies in the NLC that formed the American Lutheran Conference (org. 1930) took a conservative approach to other non-Lutheran bodies, considering fellowship with them to be unionism. To the United Lutheran Church full agreement in doctrine and practice was not an issue as far as establishing fellowship with other Lutherans. The Midwestern synods (represented in the American Lutheran Conference) took a more conservative and cautious approach regarding the practice of fellowship between Lutheran bodies not in agreement in doctrine and polity. The United Lutheran Church shunned a legalistic approach to lodge membership (a person would not be threatened with loss of church membership if he would not relinquish his membership in the lodge). In regards to the Midwestern Lutheran synods' approach to theology and polity, bear in mind that they desired to have the fellowship of the Missouri Synod, a fellowship they had coveted for some time. And this was the reason for a series of doctrinal discussion, which came about between the Midwestern bodies and the Missouri Synod. (The Midwestern bodies even viewed themselves as a sort of connecting force between the United Lutheran Church on the left and the Missouri Synod on the right.) More will be reported on these discussions later.

At this point it would be helpful to refer to the 1926 Doctrinal Preamble of the NLC, which states that the participating bodies accept the Holy Scriptures as the Word of God and only source, norm, and guide of Christian faith and life, and that the bodies in their respective constitutions accept the *Unaltered Augsburg Confession* and *Luther's Catechism* as the true exposition and presentation of the doctrines of the Holy Scriptures. This rather general statement served to encompass and protect the various degrees of theological allegiance to both the Scriptures and the Lutheran Confessions given by the participating bodies. The individual theologies of the participating bodies were further protected by the Preamble, which stated that the cooperation involved between the Lutheran bodies is "in matters of common interest and responsibility, cooperation in which does not affect their distinctive principles nor presupposes nor involve church fellowship."[7]

THE NLC: A STIMULANT TO SEEKING UNITY AND UNION

The NLC, which was organized for cooperation in external matters in order to render service to fellow Lutherans in need, rather than carry on fellowship among the participating bodies, nevertheless through the years stimulated interest among these bodies to bring about Lutheran unity and union. Thus, as history records, the NLC helped to pave the way for the formation of the first American Lutheran Church (ALC) in 1930, the second American Lutheran Church (at first designated with a capital T on the article; thus, The American Lutheran Church [TALC]) in 1960. This was a merger of the bodies in the American Lutheran Conference. The NLC also helped bring about the Lutheran Church in American (LCA) in 1962. This was a merger of: the ULCA, the American Evangelical Lutheran Church (AELC), the Augustana Evangelical Lutheran Church, and the Finnish Evangelical Lutheran Church of America. Finally, the NLC, followed by its successor, the Lutheran Council U.S.A., was the catalyst that brought about not only these Lutheran unions, but the most encompassing union of them all, the Evangelical Lutheran Church in America (ELCA). This union included both the American Lutheran Church and the Lutheran Church in America.

There was a movement during the late 1940's to bring about either an organic merger of the eight bodies in the NLC or to bring about a federation of

583

these churches as an intermediate step.[8] This movement did not succeed. One of the factors discouraging to the merger movement was the issue of the United Lutheran Church's different view of the doctrine of the Inspiration of Scripture, a view which—as presented in a published book, *The Doctrine of the Word*—criticized the old Lutheran view of Verbal Inspiration.[9] Note that the United Lutheran Church was a member of the NLC but not of the American Lutheran Conferences—a deliberate omission. In both the NLC and the Conference there appeared an intense interest in promoting Lutheran unity. But eventually, the synods in the NLC—representing the two different theologies regarding the Scriptures—drifted farther apart, and it remained for the member synods banded together in the American Lutheran Conferences to carry on merger negotiations among themselves.

In 1955 the United Lutheran Church and the Augustana Lutheran Church sent out an invitation to all Lutherans to…CONSIDER SUCH AN ORGANIC UNION AS WILL GIVE REAL EVIDENCE OF OUR UNITY IN FAITH, AND TO PROCEED TO DRAFT A CONSTITUTION AND DEVISE ORGANIZATIONAL PROCEDURES TO EFFECT UNION. The Missouri Synod declined the invitation because of doctrinal differences. The Joint Union Committee of the American Lutheran Conference synods also declined because of the impending union of the Evangelical Lutheran Church (ELC), the United Evangelical Lutheran Church (UELC), and the American Lutheran Church (ALC) to form the "new" American Lutheran Church. (Later, the Lutheran Free Church, in 1963, joined the merger.)[10]

The invitation extended by the United Lutheran Church and the Augustana Lutheran Church was accepted by the American Evangelical Lutheran Church and by the Finnish Evangelical Lutheran Church of America (Suomi Synod). The four church bodies formed the Joint Commission on Lutheran Unity to prepare the way for organic union. With the approval of union documents by the four churches, and a favorable vote on the constitution, the merger was approved. The Constituting Convention was held in Detroit, June 28 to July 1, 1962, with the actual operation of the Lutheran Church in America (LCA) set to begin January 1, 1963.

Should these two mergers that took place with participating bodies of the NLC surprise us? Hardly. The authors of *What's Going on Among the Lutherans*—a critical evaluation of what is being believed, taught, and practiced in the modern Lutheran churches here in America—have made this astute observation: COOPERATION IN "EXTERNALS," PRACTICAL WORK NOT INVOLVING DOCTRINE, OFTEN LEADS TO COOPERATION IN "INTERNALS," ALTAR AND PULPIT FELLOWSHIP AND ORGANIC UNION.[11] The question is naturally raised in the minds of those who are involved in cooperative enterprises, working together to achieve common goals: If we work so well together in these areas of Christian service, why can't we worship and commune together and our pastors preach in each others' pulpits? What must we do to break down the barriers that divide us?

In a tract issued in the 1950's by the Joint Synod of Wisconsin, we have the following observation offered by this ultra conservative Lutheran body, which at the time was strongly opposed to the Missouri Synod's involvement in doctrinal talks with the American Lutheran Church, fearing that Missouri was compromising its doctrinal stand:

NO ONE HAD TO BE A PROPHET OR THE SON OF A PROPHET TO PREDICT THE

SORRY OUTCOME OF THESE VENTURES IN PRACTICAL COOPERATION. WHEN LUTHERANS OF VARIOUS STRIPES ARE ENCOURAGED TO ASSOCIATE WITH EACH OTHER AND INCREASINGLY CLOSER CONTACTS ARE BEING CULTIVATED AMONG THEM, IT COMES AS NO SURPRISE IF THEY BEGIN TO FELLOWSHIP ON A MORE INTIMATE SPIRITUAL LEVEL. TO TRUST THAT IT WILL BE OTHERWISE IS TO BE…BLISSFULLY UNAWARE OF REALITY.

IN 1917, WHEN THE NLC WAS ORGANIZED BY THE SYNODS OF THE PRESENT AMERICAN LUTHERAN CONFERENCE AND THE PRESENT UNITED LUTHERAN CHURCH, ITS PURPOSE WAS INTENDED TO BE PURELY EXTERNAL. THEY JUDGED THAT THEY SHOULD BE ABLE TO WORK TOGETHER IN "EXTERNALS" IN SPITE OF DIFFERENCES IN DOCTRINE AND PRACTICE. THIRTY YEARS LATER THE *LUTHERAN OUTLOOK* ARGUES: "IT IS EVIDENT FROM THE AGGRESSIVENESS WITH WHICH THE COUNCIL IS EXPANDING ITS COOPERATIVE ACTIVITIES IN VARIOUS DIRECTIONS THAT IT IS LAYING THE FRAMEWORK FOR A LARGER LUTHERAN UNITY." FIRST, COOPERATION WITH "SAFEGUARDS"; THEN THE CALL FOR COMPLETE CONSOLIDATION, THUS BRINGING THE MOVEMENT TO ITS INEVITABLE CLIMAX.[12]

Leppien and Smith, who jointly authored *What's Going On Among the Lutherans?* draw the following conclusions:

THE INEVITABLE CLIMAX WAS THE ORGANIC UNION OF THE BODIES OF THE NLC INTO THE [NEW] ALC AND THE LCA. SINCE THE NLC WAS NOT STRUCTURED TO SERVE TWO BODIES, IT WAS SUCCEEDED IN 1966 BY THE LUTHERAN COUNCIL U.S.A. ITS MEMBERSHIP INCLUDED THE ALC, LCA, LCMS, AND THE SLOVAK SYNOD (SELC—SOON TO MERGE WITH THE LCMS). THE PRESENCE OF THE LCMS NEEDS FURTHER COMMENT.

WHILE THE LCMS HAD DECLINED MEMBERSHIP IN THE NLC, IT HAD COOPERATED IN THE NLC'S WORLD WAR II EFFORTS, PARTICULARLY IN THE CHAPLAINCY PROGRAM, THE JOINT OPERATION OF SERVICE CENTERS, AND OTHER WAR RELIEF EFFORTS. THIS WAS SEEN BY SOME OBSERVERS AS "A MINOR BREACH IN THE WALL OF MISSOURI THAT WAS ULTIMATELY TO SHATTER THE SYNODICAL CONFERENCE AND TO BRING THE MISSOURI SYNOD INTO A CLOSER RELATIONSHIP WITH THE CHURCHES OF THE NATIONAL LUTHERAN COUNCIL.[13, 14]

There will be more to report concerning the Missouri Synod (LCMS) in its connection with the cooperative agencies of American Lutheranism when we discuss the Lutheran Council in the United States of America (LCUSA).

An added postscript to the above stated observations regarding the tendency for close cooperation in externals to lead to fellowship and even to church union, is an observation made by Dr. L. W. Boe, the president of St. Olaf College, and a representative of the Norwegian Lutheran Church on the National Lutheran Council. Looking back on President H.G. Stub's assurance to the synod that the Council was but an organ of services and would not assume the character or the functions of a church, Dr. Boe recalled years later that while they had attempted to respect this restriction, "…the Holy Ghost kept pushing us across the line again and again."[15]

The NLC was also a stimulant to fellowship on an international scale. In 1921 the Council recommended an International Lutheran Conference and authorized preparation of plans and a program for such a Conference, to be known as "An International Lutheran Convention." This led to the first meeting of the Lutheran World Convention of Lutherans at Eisenach, near Wartburg in Germany, in 1923, and the establishment of a permanent organization.[16]   This took place after World War II in an assembly convened in Lund, Sweden, in the summer of 1947. A constitution was adopted and the name changed to read "Lutheran World Federation." This federation committed itself to, among other things, "cultivate unity of faith and confession among the Lutheran churches of the world;...to promote fellowship and co-operation and study among Lutherans;...to achieve a united Lutheran approach to ecumenical Christian movements and groups in need of spiritual or material aid."[17] Meetings were to be held every five years.

SUCCESSOR TO THE NLC: LUTHERAN COUNCIL IN THE UNITED STATES OF AMERICA

The NLC in 1958 proposed "an exploratory meeting" with representatives of the Missouri Synod and other Lutheran bodies to examine the existing co-operation between them and "the possibility of extension of such activities." In October of the same year an invitation was sent to the Missouri Synod to take part in such an exploratory meeting. After conferring with the sister synods, Missouri declined the invitation due to current conditions in the Synodical Conference and to the "state of flux" of the doctrinal positions of the two Lutheran bodies that were in the process of being formed from current mergers of bodies in the NLC (e.g. the "new" American Lutheran Church, and the Lutheran Church in America). Later, to avoid any further confusion that the expression "state of flux" could cause, President Behnken withdrew it.

There later occurred a series of discussions between the representatives of the Missouri Synod and of the NLC concerning the doctrinal agreement necessary to engage in cooperative work. This series of discussions occurred in 1960 when NLC leaders invited the Missouri Synod to discuss the possibility of forming a future inter-Lutheran agency to succeed the NLC. Missouri's Committee on Doctrinal Unity suggested that the theological and confessional aspects of such an alliance be given priority, and the NLC officials showed a willingness to follow this suggestion. From July 1960 to November 1961 a series of exploratory discussions were held involving theologians from the three large Lutheran bodies: the "new" ALC; the LCA; which was in the process of being formed; and the Missouri Synod.[18] A summary Report stated that there was "a far greater extent of consensus on the subjects discussed than had been generally realized." The exploratory talks between the three large Lutheran bodies concerning the possibility of future cooperation produced an Inter-Lutheran Consultation, compromising seven members of each of the three bodies. Some who had been opposed to doctrinal discussions changed their minds and became convinced of their great and timely importance.

The exploratory discussions resulted in 1961 in the decision to form a new cooperative agency "to replace the National Lutheran Council as presently constituted." [19] Pulpit and altar fellowship were not implied. The area of operation for the new agency would be: common theological study and Christian service.

In February 1962 the presidents of the Missouri Synod, the new American Lutheran Church, and the Lutheran Church in America (in process of formation), drew up an empowering resolution for the Inter-Lutheran Consultation to draw up the documents necessary for the establishing of the proposed new Lutheran cooperative agency. By October 1962 the three bodies had approved the resolution of the Consultation. A year later SELC (Slovak Synod) passed an enabling resolution to participate fully in the Consultation.[32]

By early 1964 the Consultation had completed the provisional constitution for the new agency, given the tentative name the Lutheran Council in the United States of America (LCUSA). In 1966 LCUSA succeeded the NLC as the cooperative agency of American Lutheranism. An important note: "All the Participating Bodies shall take part in the Division of Theological Studies." Was this a portend of later unity talks which would then lead to the great merger forming the Evangelical Lutheran Church in America—a large Lutheran body that would include both the ALC and the LCA? Time would reveal this answer.[21] The Lutheran Council U.S.A. will be discussed to a greater extent after we first consider a brief history of the American Lutheran Conference.

AMERICAN LUTHERAN CONFERENCE
1930-1954

FORMING THE AMERICAN LUTHERAN CONFERENCE

The American Lutheran Conference was organized in October 1930, only two months after the formation of the American Lutheran Church (ALC), a merger of three Midwestern Lutheran synods. It was formed as a cooperative agency and eventually included all the bodies, which were members of the National Lutheran Council (NLC), except the United Lutheran Church in America (ULCA). While the American Lutheran Conference bodies cooperated heartily with the ULCA in NLC projects, they nevertheless intentionally excluded the ULCA from Conference membership and worked toward organic union among themselves as well as a closer cooperation.

The Lutheran bodies in the American Lutheran Conference were similarly inclined regarding doctrine and polity and toward the Lutheran Confessions, occupying a theological position between the ultra-conservative, dogmatical Synodical Conference and the liberal branch of Lutheranism that was represented in the ULCA. Thus, in practice, as historian Abdel Wentz points out, they were more exclusive and aloof than the ULCA toward non-Lutheran church bodies, but not as much as so the Synodical Conference.[22] They were of the same geographical area, the Upper Mississippi Valley, and this is where a greater number of Norwegian, German, Swedish, Danish, and Finnish immigrants settled. It has been pointed out that the American Lutheran Conference brought together in fellowship second and third generations of descendants of these immigrants.[23]

The representatives of the Ohio, Iowa, and Buffalo Synods and the Norwegian Lutheran Church held a colloquium in Minneapolis in 1925 and drew up an agreement known as the Minneapolis Theses. The Theses became the basis of pulpit and altar fellowship between the three Midwestern German synods in 1928, and in the same year became the basis for fellowship with the Norwe-

587

gian Lutheran Church. (The latter body in time changed its name to the Evangelical Lutheran Church.) On August 11, 1930, the Theses also became the basis for the merger of the three Midwestern German synods, forming the American Lutheran Church (ALC). Furthermore, the Theses were used as the basis for the federation of the American Lutheran Church, the Norwegian Lutheran Church, the Augustana Evangelical Lutheran Church, the United Evangelical Lutheran Church (United Danish Lutheran Church), and the Lutheran Free Church, to form the American Lutheran Conference.

The Minneapolis Theses incorporated eight points of doctrine quoted from the 1919 Chicago Theses, summarized as follows: (1) Christ's redemption and reconciliation: Christ paid the penalty for the whole world, and brought about the reconciliation of the Triune God, whose justice required satisfaction. (2) The Gospel offers forgiveness of sins and gives the power to accept what it offers. (3) Absolution is the direct application of forgiveness of sins to the individual desiring the consolation of the Gospel. (4) Holy Baptism and the Gospel are both justly called means of regeneration, since the Holy Spirit works regeneration through both. (5) Justification is God's act, not man's. God declares the repentant and believing person just...on account of the imputation of the righteousness of Christ by faith. (6) Faith is not at all a human effort. Man believes, but both the power to believe and the act of believing are God's work and gift in the human soul or heart. (7) Conversion is made up of contrition and faith produced by the Law and the Gospel. Man's failure to be converted is his fault, not God's. If man is converted, the glory is God's alone, for it was his work of grace throughout. No cooperation in man before or in conversion. At the moment of conversion, cooperation begins through new powers given in conversion in connection with the Holy Spirit and never independent from him. (8) Election: The cause of election to salvation is the mercy of God and the most holy merit of Christ; nothing in man on account of which God has elected him to eternal life.

There follows an article in the Theses calling for avoidance of fellowship with non-Lutheran pastors and people, and another article calling for avoidance of membership in antichristian or antiTrinitarian religious associations and societies.[24] On this basis the Lutheran bodies involved voted to establish fellowship.

Because of the favorable attitude of the conferring bodies toward the Minneapolis Theses their respective presidents were encouraged to draft a constitution and bylaws for the proposed new cooperative agency. The preamble of the constitution states the purpose for the organization: IN THE PROVIDENCE OF GOD, THE TIME APPEARS TO HAVE COME WHEN LUTHERAN CHURCH BODIES IN AMERICA THAT ARE ONE IN FAITH AND THAT HAVE DECLARED PULPIT AND ALTAR FELLOWSHIP WITH ONE ANOTHER, SHOULD MANIFEST THEIR ONENESS BY SEEKING TO FOSTER FRATERNAL RELATIONS AND BY COOPERATING IN THE EXTENSION OF THE KINGDOM OF CHRIST. [25]

THE WORK OF THE AMERICAN LUTHERAN CONFERENCE

In the constitution the *Object* of the Conference is stated thus: [IT IS]

FOUNDED FOR THE PURPOSE OF GIVING TESTIMONY TO THE UNITY IN THE FAITH OF PARTICIPATING BODIES...AND...HAS AS ITS OBJECT: (1) MUTUAL COUNSEL CONCERNING THE FAITH, LIFE AND WORK OF THE CHURCH. (2) COOPERATION IN MATTERS OF COMMON INTEREST AND RESPONSIBILITY, SUCH AS: A. ALLOCATION OF WORK IN HOME MISSION FIELDS; B. ELEMENTARY AND HIGHER EDUCATION; C. INNER MISSION WORK (CHRISTIAN SOCIAL SERVICE); D. STUDENT SERVICE IN STATE SCHOOLS AND UNIVERSITIES; E. FOREIGN MISSIONS AND OTHER MISSIONARY ACTIVITIES; F. JOINT PUBLICATION OF CHRISTIAN LITERATURE; G. PERIODIC EXCHANGE OF THEOLOGICAL PROFESSORS AT THE THEOLOGICAL SEMINARIES; H. SUCH OTHER INTERESTS AS FROM TIME TO TIME MAY CALL FOR CONSULTATION. [26]

The Conference put into action a Commission on Lutheran Unity to study Intersynodical relations. The Commission worked toward helping to strengthen internal ties and toward bringing about closer relationships with other Lutheran bodies.

The Conference sponsored biennial all-Lutheran seminars (general attendance of Lutheran pastors) held in selected key cities. Uniformity was sought in public worship forms and in the publication of a common hymnal. The *Lutheran Outlook* was the official publication, geared to promoting Lutheran unity.

The area of operation of the Conference was limited to counsel and advice in matters of common interest, and those in which its advice might be sought. Its powers were limited to those specifically delegated to it by the participating bodies. As time went on many of the Conference objectives were taken over by the rapidly expanding work of the National Lutheran Council. Wentz states that the Conference thereafter devoted its major efforts to the improvement of relations among all Lutheran bodies in America. And, of course, toward establishing organic union.[27]

Wentz makes the observation that the distinctive mission of the American Lutheran Conference is not easy to find. He quotes the secretary of the Conference as once saying that the Conference was "Conceived as largely a defensive alliance, created for the purpose of protecting its members against possible aggression by the ULCA and the Synodical Conference."[28]

THE AMERICAN CONFERENCE PASSES OUT OF EXITENCE

In 1954 the American Lutheran Conference was dissolved, since its membership felt it had achieved the purposes for which it had been formed. At the same time, the aim for creation of a larger Lutheran fellowship was expressed: THEREFORE, IN AN ATTEMPT TO CREATE A LARGER LUTHERAN FELLOWSHIP...THE AMERICAN LUTHERAN CONFERENCE AUTHORIZED THE EXPENSES NECESSARY AND THE PROMOTION NEEDED TO CALL TOGETHER...A "FREE CONFERENCE." FURTHERMORE, IT WAS STATED: WHAT THIS "FREE CONFERENCE" MAY LEAD TO, WE CANNOT NOW PREDICT, BUT WE DO PRAY THAT IT MAY LEAD TO A GREATER LUTHERAN FELLOWSHIP, THAT OUT OF IT MAY COME A DEEPER UNITY OF LOVE AND FELLOWSHIP AMONG ALL THE LUTHERANS OF AMERICA.[29]

Of course, what this finally led to was the organizing of the Lutheran Coun-

589

cil in the United States of America (LCUSA), with the Lutheran Church-Missouri Synod as a member body, a reality long coveted by the American Lutheran Church. Two years before the Conference was dissolved it claimed 2,153,350 baptized members. The membership of the American Lutheran Conference compared favorably with that of the ULCA and of the Synodical Conference.

LUTHERAN COUNCIL U.S.A.
1966-1987

The National Lutheran Council (NLC) was succeeded in 1966 by the Lutheran Council in the United States of America (LCUSA). How this new and final cooperative agency came about has to some extent already been discussed. However, a brief review here should prove helpful.

THE FORMING OF THE LUTHERAN COUNCIL U.S.A.

When the National Lutheran Council was reduced in size to just two bodies as a result of the merger movements that involved the participating churches—thus forming the new American Lutheran Church (for a while referred to as The American Lutheran Church or TALC) and the Lutheran Church in America, it was plain to see that the Council's continued existence was very much in doubt. Between 1958 and 1966 a successor organization, the Lutheran Council U.S.A., which embraced the Lutheran Church-Missouri Synod (LCMS) and the Synod of Evangelical Lutheran Churches (SELC), as well as the ALC and the LCA, was established.[30] As previously reported, it should come as no surprise when working in close proximity to each other in an agency geared to cooperative enterprise leads finally to organic union of participating bodies.

The NLC in 1958 requested the participating bodies to approve an exploratory meeting of the Executive Committee of the Council with representatives of the Lutheran Church-Missouri Synod and other bodies in the United States "...in order to examine present cooperative activities in American Lutheranism and the possibilities for extension of such activities." It was proposed that upon approval of this proposal by the participating bodies, the NLC would then authorize its Executive Committee to invite all other Lutheran bodies in the United States to appoint representatives for such a meeting and at its discretion to proceed to convene this meeting.[31]

A formal invitation was extended to the Missouri Synod on October 6, 1958, to attend such as exploratory meeting. However, the Missouri Synod declined the invitation after conferring with her sister synods (Wisconsin Synod and the Evangelical Lutheran Synod). Nevertheless, there followed a series of discussions between the Missouri Synod and the NLC concerning the doctrinal agreement necessary for cooperative work, and from these discussions came the decision in 1961 to establish a new cooperative agency "to replace the NLC as presently constituted."[32]

In February 1962 an empowering resolution was drawn up by the presidents of the three Lutheran bodies involved—the American Lutheran Church, the Lutheran Church in America, and the Lutheran Church-Missouri Synod—permitting the Inter-Lutheran Consultation to draw up the documents necessary to establish a new cooperative agency to replace the NLC. All three bodies approved the resolution by October 1962. The Synod of Evangelical Lutheran Churches (SELC) sent observers to the meeting held by the Consultation, January 22-23, 1963. In the fall of the same year, SELC resolved to fully participate in the Inter-Lutheran Consultation.[33]

By January 1964 the Consultation was ready to form a Constitution Committee consisting of the presidents or their representatives and proposed the name, the Lutheran Council in the United States of America. In October 1964 the new American Lutheran Church became the first of the three participating bodies to adopt the proposed constitution (by unanimous vote). In June the following year the Missouri Synod approved the constitution, and the Slovak Synod or SELC later followed Missouri's example. The Lutheran Church in America adopted the constitution in June 1966. The new agency was set to be formed by January 1, 1967. Involved were more than eight million Lutherans.

THE WORK OF THE LUTHERAN COUNCIL U.S.A.

The *Preamble* of the LCUSA Constitution reads as follows:
WHEREAS, IN THEIR RESPECTIVE CONSTITUTIONS, HE PARTICIPATING LUTHERAN CHURCH BODIES ACKNOWLEDGE THE HOLY SCRIPTURES OF THE OLD AND NEW TESTAMENT AS THE ONLY SOURCE AND THE INFALLIBLE NORM OF ALL CHURCH DOCTRINE AND PRACTICE, AND SEE IN THE THREE ECUMENICAL CREEDS AND IN THE CONFESSIONS OF THE LUTHERAN CHURCH, ESPECIALLY IN THE *UNALTERED AUGSBURG CONFESSION* AND *LUTHER'S SMALL CATECHISM*, A PURE EXPOSITION OF THE WORD OF GOD; AND WHEREAS, THE PARTICIPATING BODIES ARE OF THE CONVICTION THAT THEY SHOULD AND CAN MORE EFFECTIVELY CARRY ON THEIR WORK AND FURTHER A LUTHERAN WITNESS BY COOPERATING IN MATTERS OF COMMON INTEREST AND RESPONSIBILITY, COOPERATION IN WHICH IS NOT A VARIANCE WITH THEIR DOCTRINE AND PRACTICE; THEREFORE, THE PARTICIPATING BODIES DO HEREBY ESTABLISH AND WILL MAINTAIN A COMMON AGENCY TO BE GOVERNED BY THE FOLLOWING CONSTITUTION.[35]

ARTICLE IV *PURPOSES AND OBJECTIVES*: A. TO FURTHER THE WITNESS, THE WORK, AND THE INTERESTS OF THE PARTICIPATING BODIES. B. TO SEEK TO ACHIEVE THEOLOGICAL CONSENSUS IN A SYSTEMATIC AND CONTINUING WAY ON THE BASIS OF THE SCRIPTURES AND THE WITNESS OF THE LUTHERAN CONFESSIONS. C. TO PROVIDE AN INSTRUMENTALITY THROUGH WHICH THE PARTICIPATING BODIES MAY WORK TOGETHER IN FULFILLING THEIR RESPONSIBILITY OF CHRISTIAN SERVICE WHERE COORDINATION OR JOINT ACTIVITY IS DEEMED BY THEM TO BE DESIRABLE AND FEASIBLE. [36]

ARTICLE V *FUNCTIONS* (THE FOLLOWING POINTS ARE OF SPECIAL INTEREST) A: TO PROVIDE A FORUM IN WHICH THE PARTICIPATING BODIES WILL DISCUSS THEIR MUTUAL CONCERNS AND MAY PLAN COMMON ACTION. B. TO ESTABLISH PROCEDURES AND PROVIDE RESOURCES FOR THEOLOGICAL STUDY AND DISCUS-

SION. C. To PROMOTE UNDERSTANDING, AMITY, AND HELPFUL RELATIONSHIPS WITH OTHER LUTHERAN CHURCHES IN THE UNITED STATES OF AMERICA. E. TO REPRESENT THE INTERESTS OF THE COUNCIL, AND THE INTERESTS OF A PARTICIPATING BODY SO REQUESTING, IN MATTERS WHICH REQUIRE COMMON ACTION BEFORE (1) THE AMERICA PUBLIC, (2) THE NATIONAL GOVERNMENT AND STATE GOVERNMENTS, (3) ORGANIZED BODIES AND AGENCIES OUTSIDE THE LUTHERAN CHURCH. F. To MAKE STUDIES AND SURVEYS REGARDING PRESENT OR PROPOSED FIELDS OF WORK AND TO SUBMIT RECOMMENDATIONS TO THE PARTICIPATING BODIES BASED THEREON. I. To TAKE NECESSARY STEPS TO MEET EMERGENCIES REQUIRING COMMON ACTION...[37]

In 1967 the Missouri Synod voted to join the Lutheran Council U.S.A. This was an about-face for the synod, which officially had not been involved in the National Lutheran Council. Through its boards or agencies the Missouri Synod had participated in certain aspects of the NLC's work, but now this body was willing to be counted a member of the NLC's successor, the LCUSA. It is of interest to further note that two years later, in Convention at Denver, the Missouri Synod not only elected an outspoken conservative to the presidency (Jacob A.O. Preus, Jr.), but also voted to declare fellowship with the American Lutheran Church, a victory for the moderate faction of the synod. The walls separating the Missouri Synod from the main stream of Lutheranism were indeed crumbling! But this also signaled an inner turmoil and struggle that would tear at the very heart of this synod, which down through its history had been known for its unwavering conservatism.

The LCUSA officially began to function on January 1, 1967. Membership at the time (in round numbers): The American Lutheran Church = 2,544,000; Lutheran Church in America = 3,227,000; Lutheran Church-Missouri Synod = 2,700,000.

THE MEMBERSHIP OF THE LUTHERAN COUNCIL U.S.A. PRESENTED A DIVIDED THEOLOGY

Two of the LCUSA bodies generally favored the historical-critical approach to Scripture whereas—according to the Report titled "The Function of Doctrine and Theology in Light of the Unity of the Church" (FODT for short)—the Missouri Synod representatives rejected the legitimacy of the historical-critical method. They argued that any effort to read the Scriptures precisely like other ancient literature not only diminishes their revelatory character as the Word of God but frequently results in conclusions that challenge the authority, truthfulness, and unity of the Scriptures. This report was issued by the LCUSA's Theological Studies Division, and reported on official inter-synodical discussions held between 1972 and 1977.[38]

The FODT reported the following: "The LCMS representatives agree that a less-than-complete commitment to the Scripture, an uncertainty about their truthfulness, a hesitancy or disagreement in regard to some of their contents, will endanger the proclamation of the gospel. The question is not simply how far the Scriptures can be trusted in what they say about Christ, but really whether the Christ we confess is the Christ of the Scripture or a Christ constructed according to some human standard."[39]

The FODT Report also stated: "The ALC and LCA representatives also affirm the reliability and truthfulness of the Scriptures, but they link these characteristics with the purpose of the Scriptures—their gospel-bearing function. This view sees the Scriptures as completely reliable in communicating all the promises of God to humankind, not to the exclusion of history but through it. The concern is that this central message of the Scriptures not be clouded, called into question, or confused in its application by creating false tests of faith."[40] We note that this statement really describes and assents to what is referred to as "Gospel Reductionism"—the reliability of Scripture is reduced to its gospel content, and does not include historical, geographical or scientific statements that are found in Scripture. This amount, of course, to a less than total commitment to the Scriptures.

Christian News reported in December 1977: "A recent news release from LCUSA says that a five-year study of the function of doctrine and theology in light of the unity of the church 'has concluded that representatives of the three major U.S. Lutheran bodies tend to be in two theological camps on certain questions related to their common confession of faith.'"[41]

By the late 1970's the Council's stability had already weakened considerably. It had become clear that the Council would not be the tool for uniting Lutherans.

The LCUSA took a left-wing stand on many political and social issues. Legalized abortion was one of them. Both the LCA and the ALC took a pro-abortion stand. The Division of Theological Studies of the LCUSA was faulted for presenting and promoting material that did not present correct doctrinal statements. It's a matter of record that not all of the Lutheran theologians who participated in the LCUSA discussions would even affirm the doctrine of Justification by Faith Alone. The Deity of Christ and even the doctrine of the Vicarious Satisfaction of Christ were attacked by individuals within the LCUSA. And, as already emphasized, the bodies comprising the LCUSA were not of one accord regarding the doctrine of Inspiration, the doctrine of Holy Scripture. It would become increasingly clear that the Missouri Synod was not united in doctrine and in practice with the other bodies of the LCUSA.

THE LUTHERAN CHURCH-MISSOURI SYNOD
AND THE LUTHERAN COUNCIL U.S.A.

Many on the conservative side in the Missouri Synod wanted neither fellowship with the American Lutheran Church nor membership in the LCUSA. Nevertheless, in 1967 the Missouri Synod voted to join the LCUSA, and in 1969 voted to declare fellowship with the American Lutheran Church. Richard E. Koenig, writing in the *Lutheran Forum*, an independent journal published by the American Lutheran Publicity Bureau, observed that Missouri's administration continued with plans for the synod to cooperate in the new LCUSA in the face of mounting opposition (in 1965). He pointed out that Missouri's action was the culmination of a process of greater openness toward other Lutherans and Christians and a more flexible and relaxed attitude on Biblical authority that began in 1938. Koenig described the atmosphere that prevailed at the Missouri Synod 1965 Detroit Convention, and the measures that were adopted there, as leading most observers to believe that Missouri had "finally broken free of the strict confines imposed upon it by its older Tradition and was ready to take its place in the mainstream of American Christianity."[42]

In the mid-1970's the Missouri Synod began "to cut back financial support of the Council's work and to withdraw from some programs."[43] When the Association of Evangelical Lutheran Churches (AELC)—the so-called moderate group that left the Missouri Synod—was admitted to the Council, Missouri's relationship to this cooperative agency was further strained. Doctrinally, a wedge had already been driven between the liberal ALC and LCA, and the more conservative Missouri Synod.

Some conservatives within the Missouri Synod sent the following petition to the 1977 Synod Convention: TO WITHDRAW FROM MEMBERSHIP IN LCUSA: WHEREAS, THE LUTHERAN COUNCIL USA HAS LOBBIED FOR VARIOUS POLITICAL CAUSES IN WASHINGTON, D.C. AND WHEREAS, A LCUSA DIVISION HAS PUBLISHED A WIDELY DISTRIBUTED "WHO CAN THIS BE?", A STUDY DOCUMENT WHICH ATTACKS THE VICARIOUS SATISFACTION AND DEITY OF CHRIST; AND WHEREAS, NO TOP OFFICIAL OF LCUSA HAS PUBLICLY DECLARED THAT "WHO CAN THIS BE" CONTAINS FALSE DOCTRINE AND MUST BE RETRACTED; AND WHEREAS, LCUSA HAS LEFT THE DOOR WIDE OPEN FOR THE ORDINATION OF WOMEN TO THE HOLY MINISTRY; AND WHEREAS, CONFERENCES SPONSORED BY LCUSA HAVE ATTACKED THE INSPIRATION AND INERRANCY OF HOLY SCRIPTURE (SEE "THE LUTHERAN COUNCIL U.S.A. TODAY," A CHRISTIAN HANDBOOK ON VITAL ISSUES, PP. 675-682), AND WHEREAS, LCUSA HAS REMAINED SILENT IN AREAS WHERE THE LUTHERAN CHURCH DOES HAVE A RIGHT TO SPEAK (E.G. LCUSA HAS REFUSED TO CONDEMN THE KILLING OF UNBORN INFANTS AND THE PERSECUTION AND MURDER OF MILLIONS BY THE COMMUNISTS AND WHEREAS, LCUSA INVITED GUNNER MRYDAL, A SIGNER OF HUMANIST MANIFESTO II, A DOCUMENT WHICH REPUDIATES THE ENTIRE HISTORIC CHRISTIAN FAITH AND CALLS FOR THE LEGALIZATION OF "THE RIGHT TO DIE WITH DIGNITY, INCLUDING EUTHANASIA AND THE RIGHT OF SUICIDE," TO BE THE CHIEF SPEAKER AT THE 1976 ANNUAL MEETING OF LCUSA, AND WHEREAS, FOCUS ON GOVERNMENT AFFAIRS, A PUBLICATION OF THE OFFICE FOR GOV'NT AFFAIRS, LCUSA, REGULARLY SUPPORTS LEFT-WING POLITICAL CAUSES, THEREFORE BE IT RESOLVED, THAT WE RESPECTFULLY ASK THE LCMS TO WITHDRAW FROM LCUSA.[44]

By this time the fellowship, which the Missouri Synod had declared with the ALC in 1969 at Denver, was severely strained. Missouri had requested multi-level discussions with the ALC, but received a negative response. The August 15, 1977, issue of the *Reporter* noted that the ALC Church Council expressed "no interest in participating in the multi-level discussions requested by the LCMS." Rather, the ALC officials were willing only to discuss "the nature and basis of fellowship."[45]

IN 1977 AND 1979 THE LUTHERAN CHURCH-MISSOURI SYNOD DECLARED FELLOWSHIP IN PROTEST WITH THE ALC AFTER CITING DISAGREEMENTS ON THE ORDINATION OF WOMEN, MEMBERSHIP IN ECUMENICAL BODIES, AND DOCTRINE. IN 1981 THE LCMS BROKE OFF FELLOWSHIP WITH THE ALC AND BEGAN A

MASSIVE WITHDRAWAL FROM THE LCUSA CAMPUS MINISTRY PROGRAMS. IT ALSO ELECTED A NEW PRESIDENT, DR. RALPH BOHLMANN, WHO CALLED FOR THE FORMATION OF A NEW INTER-LUTHERAN ASSOCIATION. [46]

THE DEMISE OF THE LUTHERAN COUNCIL U.S.A.

Late in 1987 LCUSA was disbanded in view of the forth-coming union of three of the Lutheran bodies to form the Evangelical Lutheran Church in America (ELCA). The merging bodies were the ALC, LCA, and AELC. What hastened the demise of the LCUSA was the small Association of Evangelical Lutheran Churches (AELC), the dissident group which departed the Missouri Synod. Upon joining the LCUSA, this group quickly issued "A Call to Lutheran Union." This call to union "called for a commitment to organic union without prior consideration of the process through which this would be accomplished— that could be worked out later. There was no mention of doctrinal discussion."[47] This, of course, met with approval by the LCA, whose long time philosophy had been: church union does not require doctrinal discussions; indeed, room must be made for theological diversity within an organic union. While the ALC gave a negative response to the AELC proposal, it nevertheless agreed to a four-year study. At their annual meeting in January 1981, the seminary presidents and deans of the ALC, LCA, and AELC issued a "Call to Lutheran Union Now," considering union not to be an option, but an action to be taken.[48] The following year, the union of the three bodies was assured, and the seventy-member Commission for a New Lutheran Church (CNLC) was formed. The Missouri Synod disallowed participation in the union.

The new body came into being in January 1988. The Evangelical Lutheran Church in America (ELCA) became at its inception the largest Lutheran body in American history. LCA= 3 million members; ALC = 2.3 million members; AELC = 110,000 members. Total: close to 5½ million members.

Both this new body and the Missouri Synod supported the LCUSA's successor, the Department of Immigration and Refugee Services. The Evangelical Lutheran Church in America (ELCA) is a body committed to ecumenism, not only seeking relations with other Lutherans, but with non-Lutherans as well. The ELCA's practice and theology and its stand on Scripture are the modern-liberal approach, which welcomes the historical-critical view of Scripture and recognizes and cordially tolerates diversity in theology. (See the separate chapter which reviews the history of the ELCA.)

Footnotes for Chapter Thirty-Four

1 E. Clifford Nelson, Editor, *The Lutherans in North America* (Philadelphia, PA: Fortress Press, 1975), pp. 403, 404.

2 R.C. Wolf, *Documents of Lutheran Unity in America* (Philadelphia, PA: Fortress Press, 1966), pp. 464, 465, Doc. #185.

3 Conrad Bergendoff, *The Church of the Lutheran Reformation, A Historical Survey of Lutheranism* (St. Louis, MO: Concordia Publishing House, 1967), pp. 260, 261.

4 Abdel Ross Wentz, *A Basic History of Lutheranism in America* (Philadelphia, PA: Muhlenberg Press, 1955), p. 309.

5 Wentz, *A Basic History...*, p. 317.

6 Wolf, *Documents...*, p. 116.

7 Wolf, *Documents...*, p. 462; Doc. #184.

8 Nelson, *The Lutherans...*, p. 504.

9 Nelson, *The Lutherans...*, p. 506.

10 Nelson, *The Lutherans...*, p. 506.

11 Patsy A. Leppien and J. Kincaid Smith, *What's Going on Among the Lutherans?—A Comparison of Beliefs,* (Milwaukee, WI: Northwestern Publishing House, 1992), p. 333.

12 *Cooperation in Externals,* a tract issued by the Conference of Presidents of the Evangelical Lutheran Joint Synod of Wisconsin and Other States, 1954, p. 6.

13 Leppien-Smith, *What's Going On...?*, p. 333.

14 See also Nelson, *The Lutherans in North America*, pp. 478, 495, 496. See also Wentz, *A Basic History of Lutheranism in America*, pp. 348-365.

15 From a booklet titled *Toward Cooperation Among American Lutherans*, see an essay titled "What Kind of Cooperation is Possible in View of the Discussions to Date?" By Alvin N. Rogness (Published jointly by the NLC and the Missouri Synod), p. 12.

16 Wolf, *Documents...*, p. 596.

17 Erwin L. Lueker, Editor in Chief, *Lutheran Cyclopedia* (St. Louis, MO: Concordia Publishing House, 1954) p. 642.

18 These discussions produced the two booklets containing doctrinal essays delivered by theologians of the conferring bodies: *Essays on the Lutheran Confessions Basic to Lutheran Cooperation* and *Toward Cooperation Among American Lutherans*. Published jointly by the NLC and the Lutheran Church-Missouri Synod, 1961.

19 Wolf, *Documents...*, p. 615.

20 Wolf, *Documents...*, pp. 615, 161, 629, 630; Doc. #249.

21 See Missouri Synod's former President John W. Behnken's personal recollections concerning meeting with representatives of the NLC to discuss doctrinal accord, and his impressions regarding the formation of the LCUSA: *This I Recall* (St. Louis, MO: Concordia Publishing House, 1964), pp. 183-185.

22 Wentz, *A Basic History...*, p. 322.

23 Lueker, *Lutheran Cyclopedia*, p. 26.

24 Wolf, *Documents...*, pp. 298-300; Doc. #133.

25 Wolf, *Documents...*, p. 343; Doc. #147.

26 Wolf, *Documents...*, pp. 343, 344; Doc. #147.

27 Wentz, *A Basic History...*, pp. 323, 354.

28 Wentz, *A Basic History...*, p. 321.

29 Wolf, *Documents...*, pp. 526, 527; Doc. #217.

30 Nelson, *The Lutherans...*, p. 527.

31 Wolf, *Documents...*, pp. 616, 617; Doc. #245.

32 Wolf, *Documents...*, p. 615.

33 Wolf, *Documents...*, pp. 629, 630.

34 Wolf, *Documents...*, p. 616.

35 Wolf, *Documents...*, p. 630; Doc. #250.

36 Wolf, *Documents...*, p. 632; Doc. # 250.

37 Wolf, *Documents...*, pp. 632, 633; Doc. #250.

38 The FODT Report is quoted in *The Christian News Encyclopedia*, Vol. II (New Haven, MO), pp. 1266, 1267. The original source is the *Theological Observer*, December 11, 1978. The FODT Report, pp. 7,8.

39 The FODT Report, p. 5, quoted in *The Christian News Encyclopedia*, Vol. II, pp. 1266, 1267.

40 The FODT Report, p. 6. Quoted in the *Christian News Encyclopedia*, Vol. II, pp. 1266, 1267.

41 *Christian News Encyclopedia*, Vol. II, p. 1267.

42 "What's Behind the Showdown in the Lutheran Church-Missouri Synod,"—Three articles by Richard E. Koenig published in the *Lutheran Forum*, an independent journal published by the American Lutheran Publicity Bureau. Printed in the November 1972 and the February and May 1973 issues.

43 Leppien and Smith, *What's Going On...*, p. 334.

44 Herman Otten, Editor, *Christian News Encyclopedia,* Vol II, p. 1262.

45 *The Michigan Lutheran*, September 1977, p. 8.

46 Leppien and Smith, *What's Going On...*, pp. 334, 335.

47 Leppien and Smith, *What's Going On...*, p. 335.

48 Leppien and Smith, *What's Going On...*, p. 335.

CHAPTER THIRTY-FIVE

LUTHERAN CHURCH - MISSOURI SYNOD (1847 -)

BRIEF SUMMARY: ASSOCIATION OF EVANGELICAL LUTHERAN CHURCHES

The Lutheran Church-Missouri Synod was formally organized on April 26, 1847 in Chicago. After a little more than a century and a quarter, its membership accounted for roughly one-third of the Lutherans in North America. A study of the Missouri Synod is a particularly interesting one, for several reasons. In its history this large and influential body of Lutherans (of German heritage) has been the hallmark of conservative Lutheran confessionalism. And yet, more recently, it has undergone an intense struggle over matters of doctrine and practice, and this struggle has resulted, as could be expected, in a degree of fracturing. The history of the synod and its component parts and of the individuals that helped form and shape such a remarkable body of Lutheranism has often been a fascinating and intriguing story. Add to this the fact that the Missouri Synod has enjoyed a high rate of growth and has implemented and consistently carried out a mission program felt throughout the world. In addition the Missouri Synod has been a pioneer in Radio and Television ministry and has led the way in religious publications.

In order to understand how such a body came to be organized we must first study the component parts which came together to form a Lutheran synod which from its beginning served as the counterforce to the liberal, unionistic, Methodistic, and rationalistic "American Lutheranism" that had invaded the American scene. The component parts of the Missouri Synod were the Saxon group (at the time headed by C.F.W. Walther in Missouri) and the missionaries who had been sent to this country by Pastor Wilhelm Loehe, the Bavarian promoter of American missions. Both groups had their origin in Germany, thus making the Missouri Synod at its founding a truly "German" synod—a heritage closely guarded for a long time.

THE SAXONS

THE GERMAN MIGRATION (WITH SPECIAL ATTENTION GIVEN TO THAT COMING FROM SAXONY)

The nineteenth century witnessed a huge number of German immigrants reaching these shores. Germans constituted 24.98% of the total number of immigrants to arrive in this country between 1820 and 1903. Their number finally reached 5,098,005. The reasons for this remarkable migration from Germany to America were mainly religious—especially at the beginning—and also economic.

The State of Saxony, from which the founders of the Missouri Synod came, had been hit hard by industrial and agrarian troubles. Competition in the market by other countries was creating a formidable crisis for the backward industries of Saxony. People were not able to pay their debts. Often they lacked the means to buy sufficient food, and frequently food was not available even to those with the means to purchase it. A strong feeling lay in the hearts of a large number of Germans to emigrate to America. The Stephanite emigration of Saxon Lutherans no doubt served as a powerful stimulus to others, so that its effects were felt not only in Saxony but in many other parts of Germany as well. The Saxon emigration was highly publicized in the newspapers of the time.

THE PROTESTANT CHURCH IN SAXONY: PIETISM AND RATIONALISM

In the later part of the seventeenth century a movement was felt within the Church to unite all Protestantdom. Pietism and later, rationalism, were the champions of this movement. One of the characteristics of Pietism was that it emphasized the Christian life at the expense of Christian doctrine. In his book, *Zion on the Mississippi,* Walter Forster lists Pietism's primary effects as:...A RE-NEWED EMPHASIS UPON THE STUDY OF THE BIBLE, A REVIVAL OF DYNAMIC PREACH-ING, A HIGH DEGREE OF EMOTIONALISM IN RELIGION, A RENEWAL OF LAY ACTIVITY IN THE CHURCH, THE ABANDONMENT OF THE DOCTRINAL FORMS OF THE OLD LUTHERAN

598

THEOLOGY, THE STRESSING OF A MORAL LIFE AND PRACTICAL PHILANTHROPY, AND A SEPARATISTIC TENDENCY WITHIN THE CHURCH.[1]

A counteraction to Pietism came along in the form of rationalism. Science was more and more coming to the forefront. The "light of reason" (*Aufklaerung*) was beginning to take over. The attitude on the part of the proponents of this movement was to *prove* theological truths. What could not be proven according to reason came to be regarded as unworthy of belief. Rationalism held that "natural laws" ruled the world, and therefore Bible miracles were excluded—they never happened! It taught that while God began nature and its laws, the laws once begun, work independently of God. Thus sermons—whose basis were not established in the Bible, in God, or in the doctrine of Christ and his atonement—were commonly preached. There was little or no room for even the doctrine of God's providence. Christ was regarded simply as a great religious philosopher, not the Redeemer of sinners. Rationalistic sermons were preached on the "value of early rising," "the value of vaccination against small pox," etc.[2] Sound "common sense" was more highly valued than Bible revelation.

Saxony felt the impact of rationalism about the least. The greatest inroads were in the universities and among the church leaders, and consequently also among the candidates of theology who graduated from the schools. Books, hymnals, and catechisms became rationalistic also. In its effort to counteract rationalism, the antirationalistic movement in Saxony took on several aspects and embraced many shades of religious opinion. There were Lutheran elements and there were definitely unLutheran elements. The movement as a whole came under the name "Enlightenment" (*Erweckungsbewegung*) and was promoted by various Bible and mission societies.

A movement back to the Lutheran Confessions was also afoot. This included the group which was compromised of men like Claus Harms, Martin Stephan and his associates, and others, together with barons, princes, and other influential men who urged Bible preaching and took a firm stand on the old Lutheran Confessions. The very fact that staunch confessional preachers such as Harms and Stephan attracted large followings among the laymen showed grass roots yearning for the Bible and the Confessions.

THE CHURCH AND THE GOVERNMENT

The conclusion is not warranted that the Germans enjoyed complete religious liberty or that complete freedom of expression existed in the pulpit. The Church was controlled by the government. The children were educated in Christian principles in *public* schools. The future pastor received his studies at a state-controlled university. A state agency, the Consistory, examined the candidates for the ministry. Kings and princes had the right of appointing ministers over parishes in their territory. Author Carl Mundinger points out that in the District of Dresden there were 173 parishes under private appointment of some baron or prince, and 107 under appointment of the king through the Consistorium. The congregations had little or no control over the calling of a pastor. Pastoral salaries were paid in part by the state and in part by taxes and fees levied by the state on the populace (e.g. tithes of produce).

Nationalism, a product of the Napoleonic wars, emphasized faithfulness to the state. In order for the church to be faithful to the state and to be controlled by it, a religious unity between all Protestants was thought to be a necessity. Such a union originated in Prussia in 1817 (refer to the history of the Buffalo Synod) and was enforced in 1830. The Prussian Union emphasized doctrines wherein there was agreement between the Lutheran and Reformed Churches. On the other hand, the Union downplayed all doctrinal disagreements. Thus unionism was actually forced upon the various churches.

Many of the smaller German states were influenced by the Prussian examples, with the result that similar Reformed/Lutheran unions were affected within their borders. In Saxony many of the pastors adopted the liturgy of the Union, and there were other effects as well.

Among the pastors who did not subscribe to the Prussian Union was Klaus Harms, archdeacon at Keil, who led an attack against rationalism and unionism as early as 1817. He became somewhat of an influence on pastors who later took part in the Saxon emigration (e.g. Pastor Loeber).

The "Enlightenment" movement, which opposed rationalism and urged the return of the Lutheran Church to the Bible and the Lutheran Confessions, had a far-reaching effect upon the upper and lower classes of people. In many localities people flocked to hear a preacher of the old Lutheran doctrines. Rationalism was late in arriving in Saxony and late in leaving, so that at the time of the Saxon emigration rationalism had a strong influence over the preaching, while conservative preachers were few and far between.

In Saxony the pastors were pledged to the Lutheran Symbols, but for many this amounted to a sham. Hiding under this pledge, the pastors preached rationalism and in some cases openly defied the Confessions. Thus the battle waged by conservatives like Stephan and others was mostly with the rationalists of their day. In spite of the inroads of rationalism a movement in favor of good, sound Lutheran preaching was definitely afoot. This is pointed up, for example, in the fact that by the 1830's, when the Saxon emigration occurred, a candidate who pledged himself to the Bible could usually find a charge more easily than the rationalist. He could seek and usually received an appointment from a Bible-loving baron. Thus both C.F.W. Walther and his friend, Buerger, received appointments at a notably young age.

From this political and religious setting came the emigration of the Saxons in 1839. The instigator and leader of this migration was the pastor and "bishop" of the group, Martin Stephan. He was aided by pastoral associates, who gave him unfledging devotion and obedience.

We next take a look at the man who planned and directed the first mass exodus from Saxony in the nineteenth century. We shall also want to conduct a brief study of some of the pastors who by their association with Stephan and their willing obedience to his self-styled ecclesiastical regime were an invaluable aid to the man in obtaining such a large backing from Lutherans scattered in several parishes.

MARTIN STEPHAN: PASTOR AND "BISHOP"

Martin Stephan was born in Stramberg, Moravia, August 13, 1777. Born and reared in poverty, Martin became an orphan at a young age. He had received strict Bible training at home and had been taught the trade of linen weaving. He received very little elementary education. In 1797 Stephan came as a journeyman linen weaver to Breslau. With the help of some pietists he was able, around 1803, to enroll in the Gymnasium. Having also free access to the church library, Stephan read a great deal, supplementing not only his formal education but also laying the ground work for a conservative theology. In 1804 he entered the University of Halle, and two years later the University of Leipzig. His studies continued there until 1809. Stephan cared little for the rationalistic studies of these institutions, and studied pietistic works instead.

Stephan was able to obtain a pastorate at Haber, Bohemia, in 1809 without taking the usual examination. When the Bohemian congregation of St. John's in Dresden became vacant, Stephan took over the work there the following year. This was a congregation of the descendents of Bohemians who had fled there in 1639 during the Thirty Years War. This congregation received special dispensation from the government to carry on worship customs not allowed in Saxony (regarding holding meetings and calling their own pastor). German services were conducted at seven o'clock in the morning, with Bohemian services following at ten o'clock. Thus Stephan actually ministered to two congregations. There were three classes of members: Anfaenger (beginners), Fortschreitende (making progress), and Volkommene (regular members). Stephan, like his predecessors, conducted private meetings in his parsonage to review his sermons.

After a time people began to establish themselves with Stephan, many of them crossing congregational lines. In an age of rationalism, Stephan held up the lighted beacon of Holy Scripture, and to it folks of many stations of life soon gathered. They did not respond to his oratory (for he was a very plain, even monotonous speaker), but to the manner in which he appealed to the conscience, his knowledge of the human heart, and to the simple and easy-to-understand words that he used. Above all, his strict confessionalism served as a powerful attraction.

But there was something else Stephan used to attract people, and that was his recognized ability as a counselor. People came to him with troubled souls and went away with the burdens lifted, their hearts directed to Christ the Redeemer. C.F.W. Walther tells of his own experience. While in great spiritual distress, Walther was directed to write to Stephan for advice. He later recalled: WHEN I READ THIS REPLY (OF STEPHAN) I FELT AS THOUGH I HAD BEEN TRANSLATED FROM HELL TO HEAVEN...HE DIRECTED ME TO THE GOOD SAMARITAN AND SHOWED ME WHAT FAITH IN CHRIST MEANS. PEACE AND JOY ENTERED MY HEART...HE APPLIED THE GOSPEL TO MY OWN SOUL.[4] As a result of Stephan's ability, people forsook their own pastors' advice and sought instead counsel with the pastor of the Bohemian congregation. Over a period of a few years St. John's Church increased from a tiny congregation of some thirty souls to a thousand or more!

OPPOSITION TO STEPHAN AND STEPHANISM

Stephan's popularity, his strict doctrine, and his ministering to sheep not his own, did nothing to endear him in the hearts of other pastors, who then complained about him to the Consistory.

The meetings, which Stephan held, first in his parsonage and then in the school, were meetings in which he afforded hungry souls additional opportunity to receive the Word. These meetings attracted more and more people to them, until finally opposition was aroused not only among the clergy, but also from the government and the public press. In Saxony there was an ever-present fear of political conspiracy, resulting in laws, which regulated private meetings and prohibited conventicles (secret meetings). But taking advantage of the special rights granted to the Bohemian congregation in years past, Stephan spent much energy promoting these meetings. His opponents, however, felt that St. John's had lost its original Bohemian character—so much so that the Bohemian language service was no longer really necessary—and should be governed by the general laws.

In August 1821 a newspaper article attacked Stephan as a separatist and a mystic and even accused him of causing several cases of criminal insanity through his extreme teaching. Finally, in the following November Stephan published his defense in the *Nationalzeitung der Deutschen* in which he denied all charges.[5] Stephan followed this defense in 1823 by publishing two sermons so that people might know what he preached. These in turn were followed in 1825 by the publishing of a volume of sermons. One must be careful not to underestimate the influence which the publications had upon people and their high regard for Stephan.

STEPHAN'S FOLLOWERS

People who were drawn to him included two prominent lawyers, Dr. A. Marbach and Dr. C. Vehse. Among the clergymen attracted to him were: E.G. Keyl of Niederfrohna, G.H. Loeber of Eichenberg, O.F. Gruber of Reust, E.M. Buerger of Lunzenau and also O.H. Walther of Langenshursdorf and his brother C.F.W. Walther of Braeunsdorf. The list included also several candidates of theology.[6] One of the mysteries of the time was the hold which Stephan had upon such intelligent people as these. Their unqualified obedience to him bordered on idolatry and contributed to the establishment of Stephan's office of bishop—a position of authority over the emigrants that Stephan sought for himself.

OPPOSITION MOUNTS

In the 1830's public assaults upon Stephan multiplied. There were several reasons for these assaults. Of course one reason they occurred was Stephan's well-known proselytizing activities. Another reason was the change that gradually came over the man and which finally gave rise to "Stephanism." More and more, Stephan exerted an unwholesome influence on the hearts of people who came to him. While they came to hear the Word, he adroitly succeeded in turning them to be followers of his person. He promoted the high position and the power of the ministerial office, and his followers championed his efforts. There developed a reverence and fear for Stephan's office that was evident among the emigrants even when they later had to depose their "Bishop." Stephan had succeeded in completely casting his spell upon his followers. However, there were those outside of the circle of Stephan's admirers who recognized the unwholesomeness of his relationship to his followers. These detractors became a strong opposing force against "Stephanism." During this time political upheavals were taking place. (In 1830 and 1831 university students, for example, led mild opposition to the government.) These upheavals were a threat to Stephan's safety, for he was regarded with suspicion by those in authority, who kept a watchful eye on his activities (e.g. holding forbidden conventicles).

But how did such a thing as "Stephanism" come about? How could this man gain so much power over people? People like C.F.W. Walther, who had been lifted "from hell to heaven" through Stephan's words of comfort, felt they owed the man much and were willing to give him obedience and promote his name as payment on their debt. What their pastor and bishop did for them and meant to them seemed to blot out from their minds all his strange idiosyncrasies.

Nor did Stephan resist his followers' veneration. Originally Stephan was a man with an inferiority complex, but then he literally became sold on himself. He became bolder in his claims for his office. He also became bolder in holding meetings. During the second decade of his ministry the meetings took on a new appearance of social ramblings or clubs. Stephan would appear quite late at these meetings. Furthermore, he dared to go on nightly walking excursions, accompanied sometimes by a man, sometimes by a woman. He even had a lodge in a vineyard to which he and his "associates" resorted, sometimes for the entire night. After 1830 Stephan's social ramblings became more and more the object of criticism, and rumors flew about. Common knowledge that he and his wife did not get along only made the situation worse.

Eventually, rumors regarding his private life aroused suspicions in the authorities. When they received reports of abuses of conventicles in other parts of Germany (with political implications) they also looked to Stephan with a suspicious eye.

THE GOVERNMENT CLOSES IN

Finally, in 1835 Stephan was forbidden to conduct religious meetings past ten o'clock at night. But the pastor of St. John's continued the conventicles and, upon being caught, was suspended from office on November 8, 1837. This marked the end of his preaching in Dresden. The charge levied against him: immoral conduct, misappropriation of congregational funds, and neglect of pastoral duties.

PLANS TO EMIGRATE

It was strange that Stephan did not come to his defense in the early 1830's; instead, he remained silent. In 1883 his own congregation prepared and published a defense for him. About the same time that this defense appeared Stephan was considering migrating to America. He had contacted Pastor Benjamin Kurtz of Baltimore, whom he had met in Dresden in 1827, and sought his advise as to the best place to settle. The State of Missouri seemed most favorable. For a while the matter of emigrating to America lay dormant. But then, in 1835 Stephan's troubles began in earnest when he was arrested at a conventicle and restricted in his movements.

In May 1836 Stephan met with a number of friends, pastors, laymen, and candidates to discuss the matter of emigration. The following resolution was adopted: EMIGRATION TO A COUNTRY WHERE THE CHURCH MAY ENJOY PERFECT RELIGIOUS LIBERTY HAS BECOME AN URGENT NECESSITY.

Plans were initiated for such an undertaking, and a common treasury was established to which everyone would be expected to make payments. After his arrest in 1837, Stephen called on his followers to emigrate with him. In the following year, Stephan's followers in Dresden, Leipzig, and Niederfrohna held meetings under the leadership of Dr. Marbach (a lawyer) and resolved to leave Germany even if Stephan were detained by the authorities.

On May 17, 1838, the emigration committee adopted regulations for emigrants in which the cause, end, and aim of the emigration was stated:

AFTER THE CALMEST AND PUREST REFLECTION THEY SEE THE HUMAN IMPOSSIBILITY BEFORE THEM TO RETAIN, CONFESS, AND TRANSMIT TO THEIR DESCENDANTS THIS FAITH IN THEIR PRESENT HOMELAND. THEY ARE THEREFORE CONSTRAINED BY THEIR CONSCIENCE TO EMIGRATE AND SEARCH FOR A LAND WHERE THE LUTHERAN FAITH IS NOT ENDANGERED AND WHERE THEY CAN SERVE GOD UNHINDERED ACCORDING TO THE WORD OF GRACE AND WHERE THEY CAN ENJOY THE USE OF THE MEANS OF GRACE, ORDAINED BY GOD FOR THE SALVATION OF ALL MEN, IN THEIR COMPLETENESS AND PURITY AND PRESERVE THEM FOR THEMSELVES, AND THEIR DESCENDANTS.[7]

FLEEING BABEL

The time to flee Babel had come. On September 4, 1838, seven hundred and seven persons had joined the emigrating group. As to the destination, Stephan had the most say. Having considered Australia and Virginia, as well as Maryland, he finally settled on the State of Missouri. The following is a list of the emigrant groups and their points of origin, together with the names of the pastoral leaders:

Dresden and vicinity	240 (Stephan)	Eichenberg, Halle	108 (Loeber)
Leipzig	31	Paitzdorf	48 (Gruber)
Frohna and vicinity	109 (Keyl)	Langenchursdorf	16* (O.H. Walther)
Lunzenau	84 (Buerger)	Braeundsdorf	19*(C.F.W. Walther)
			*brothers

Besides the seven pastors, there were pastoral candidates, ten in number. The emigrants included several schoolmasters and normal school graduates, three physicians, two lawyers (Vehse and Marbach), two medical students, a number of state officials, two artists, merchants, and farmers.

The common treasury would be used for defraying expenses, purchasing land, establishing a church and school, and for advancing credit to the needy. The emigrants purchased a large theological library, pipe organ, collection of church music, instruments for a band, four church bells, sacred vessels and the like (including material for elaborate gowns for Stephan). The amount in the treasury amounted to about $80,000.

Five vessels were chartered for the exclusive use of the emigrants: Olbers, Johann Georg, Kopernikus, Republik, and Amalia. The emigrant party agreed to sail to New Orleans and thence via the Mississippi to St. Louis. In his zealous adherence to Stephan, C.F.W. Walther had removed his orphaned nephew and niece from the home where they were staying. Having the consent of their grandparents but not of their guardian, Walther took the two orphans as far as a Saxon border city, where he turned them over to widow Buenger, who then brought them to Bremen, the port. But in the meantime the guardian swore out a warrant for both Walther brothers and Mrs. Buenger. Walther hurried on ahead and boarded the Johann Georg on November 3, 1838, and escaped to the high seas before the warrant arrived. His brother, O.H. Walther, managed to sail on the Olbers on November 18 and thus also escaped. Mrs. Buenger was not so fortunate. Accused of kidnapping, she was detained until December 11th, when she, her daughter, and her ministerial candidate son were also allowed to leave.

The manner in which the emigration was carried out certainly was a blot on the whole affair. Not only do we have the episode with Walther and the two orphans, we have evidence showing that married people left their spouses, and parents even left their children in order to take part in the emigration. Stephan himself left behind not only his wife but also seven of his eight children, whom then the government had to partially support. There were also cases where children left their parents.[8] A number of girls whose parents refused to grant them permission to emigrate were encouraged to do so on the sly.

DEPARTURE

Stephan sailed on the S.S. Olbers together with Pastor O.H. Walther, candidate Brohm, and the leading laymen. Enroute he persuaded the passengers to confer upon him the dignity of bishop, and this was done on January 14, 1839, just after entering the Gulf of Mexico.[9] Stephan's lust for power had been coming more and more to the surface. While urging the necessity of establishing a central authority to direct all temporal and spiritual affairs of the emigrants, and while giving the impression that he only wished to be advisor to the bishop, Stephan nevertheless assured his followers that he was the only one suited for the office and therefore it was best to confer it on him.

The first ship reached New Orleans on December 31, 1838; the last arrived on January 20, 1839. The Amalia never reached port but went down with all

605

hands and passengers in one of the fierce storms the ships encountered.

From New Orleans the group proceeded up the Mississippi on four river steamboats, the last one reaching St. Louis on February 19, 1839. Enroute to St. Louis, Stephan had a "Declaration of Submission" drawn up, which was later ratified by the immigrants. This "hellish decretal" as Beurger later termed it, pledged the pastors and laymen to submit entirely to Stephan's authority—in temporal, as well as in spiritual matters. Stephan was beginning to fear revolt.

IN ST. LOUIS

The Saxons remained in St. Louis until April 26, 1839, living in rented quarters. After a time, services were held in the basement of Christ Protestant Episcopal Church. Shunning a good offer of a large tract of land near St. Louis, Stephan insisted upon purchasing 4,400 acres in Perry County, about 100 miles south of St. Louis, spending $10,234.25 for it. This included a landing at Wittenberg. Pastor Keyl and Pastor Loeber did the preaching. In St. Louis, Stephan was busy planning his ecclesiastical establishment. After removal to Perry County, the people had to build roads, bridges, etc., to make the wilderness look like the villages in Germany. To top it off, Stephan planned an espiscopal palace with a seventy-foot frontage. In the meantime the German newspaper, *Anzeiger des Westens*, attacked the Saxons, especially Stephan's priest-ruled hierarchy.

THE BISHOP DEPOSED

On Rogate Sunday, 1839, following a sermon preached by Pastor Loeber, two ladies confessed to him they had been guilty of misconduct with Pastor Stephan. Loeber then informed C.F.W. Walther at St. Louis about the matter, who was promptly dispatched to Perry County to confront Stephan with the written statements of the ladies (the ladies' actions were independent of each other), and at the same time to secure the support of the association's trustees, whose names appeared on the deed of transfer. The immigrants in St. Louis arrived in Perry County on two steamboats. The following day the Council, consisting of five laymen, together with the pastors, deposed Stephan, although he consistently denied his guilt and the charges advanced against him. They not only deposed him from office, they also eliminated him from the settlement. A week later he was rowed across the Mississippi to the Devil's Bakeoven on the Illinois side. Stephan died on February 26, 1846, after serving as pastor of a congregation at Horse Prairie.

On May 27, 1839, a statement was drawn up renouncing all association with Stephan, and this statement was subsequently published in the *Anzeiger des Westens*.

CHAOS!

The Saxons divided themselves up into five congregations under the lead-

606

ership of five pastors. C.F.W. Walther was in charge of the congregation, which remained in St. Louis.

During all the trouble and turmoil, candidates Brohm, Fuerbringer, and Buenger, erected a small log cabin in Perry County, which was to serve as an institution of learning. An announcement appeared in the *Anzeiger des Westens* advertising such subjects to be taught as religion, Latin, Greek, Hebrew, and also the German, French, and English languages. Also to be taught were history, geography, mathematics, physics, natural history, elementary philosophy, music, and drawing. The aim was to qualify students for university studies. This spirit of the Saxons was truly amazing in the face of the poverty to which they had been reduced. Furthermore, much of the population was afflicted by sickness. The buildings in which they lived became hospitals filled with the sick and the dying. Often there were scarcely enough healthy persons to take care of the ones who were ill. Many of the houses that had been hastily erected were no more than shacks and so the lack of proper shelter also plagued the immigrants. It was indeed a time that tried men's souls. Koestering remarked: All this had to come, that they might be weaned away from putting their trust in man, and cast themselves into the arms of God's gracious protection.[10]

SPIRITUAL CONFLICT

In November 1839 Dr. Vehse, H.E. Fischer, and Gustav Jaeckel addressed a *"Protestations Schrift"* to the Saxon pastors, in which they protested against "the false, medieval, papistic, and sectarian Stephanistic church government." Among the things emphasized by the lay party's document—as principles upon which they wanted the government of the church to be based—were these: "All Christians are priests through baptism by faith and must exercise the priestly office not only as a matter of right but as a matter of command...As spiritual priests, laymen have the right to judge all doctrine and to supervise all the activities of the clergy...The final decision in all disputes rests with the local congregation...The local congregation has the power and the duty to establish all rules regarding liturgy, ceremonies, and church constitutions...The true church is invisible...It is dangerous to judge people as to doctrine and as to their faithfulness over against established teachers. Equally dangerous is the habit of extolling clergymen as a class because such a habit engenders servility and hypocrisy...The association of individual congregations is not necessary and may be harmful...The concept...that the Church is represented in the clergy, leads to the Papacy and to a lack of interest in church matters on the part of the laity...All pastors should be placed on the same level and exercise the same power. The episcopacy develops love of personal glory and leads to the Papacy...In case of an emergency a congregation may engage a man who has not studied...Men who have not studied, yea, ordinary laymen, may administer the sacraments...In judging clergymen the chief stress, it is true, should be placed upon doctrine; but life, the fruits of doctrine, should not be overlooked." Forster concludes from this list (not totally complete) that the principles stood for "an extreme congregationalism with heavy emphasis on the individual."

He also concludes that had the laymen prevailed the church polity of the Missouri Synod "would have been a highly individualistic congregationalism somewhat akin to the polity of the Baptist Church in America."[11]

And while this document tore into the concept that the church is represented in the clergy and placed all pastors on the same level, exercising the same power, the principles involved were invoked by a group of laymen who had been severely burned by an overbearing, papistically inclined pastor. The principles were a caution against being burned a second time. Still, in an extreme manner this side of the conflict demanded rights for the individual layman and for the individual congregation. Was it a matter of placing laymen where Stephan had been?

On the other side were men like Marbach (a lawyer), Barthel, Sproede, candidate Luegel and others. Marbach's position was that the immigrants, by separating themselves from the church in Germany, had ceased to form a Christian congregation and lacked all power and authority to perform any ecclesiastical functions. This too went to the extreme, only in another direction.

The debates and discussions on the issues were endless. Good did come from it, however, for it drove talented men like C.F.W. Walther back to the Scripture and to Luther's writings to find out the truth.

On the one hand were those who questioned the validity of any and every ministerial act, were once they had been willing to make Stephan their "bishop" and to make the validity of administering the Sacraments depend on ordination by Stephan. On the other hand, adding to the confusion were those who had come to doubt and even to deny that the immigrants were Christians and that the emigration from Saxony was legitimate. Yes, they even considered the Saxon emigration the work of the devil. This was a remarkable turn around for a group who once thought they were the only visible Church on earth. THE DISILLUSIONMENT AND BITTERNESS OF SOUL AMONG THE COLONISTS WAS COMMENSURATE WITH THE SPIRITUAL BLESSINGS, WHICH THEY FORMERLY BELIEVED WERE WRAPPED UP IN THE PERSON OF MARTIN STEPHAN. [12]

While C.F.W. Walther came out of the conflict a powerful leader of confessional Lutheranism, his brother, Otto Herman Walther, died of a broken heart (a claim made by his widow) caused by the sad state of affairs that was unveiled when the hypocrisy and deceit of Stephan became public.

THE GREAT DEBATE

For two years the questions aroused by the two sides—clergy/laity—disturb the minds and hearts of the people. Finally, to settle the questions, which so deeply divided the people, a debate was arranged between Walther and Dr. Marbach at the college in Altenburg in April 1841. Walther presented his arguments on the basis of eight theses which were later developed and published in two books. Walther was assisted by Pastors Loeber and Keyl. In an address Walther recognized that the Saxons had been wrong in following Stephan, whom Walther labeled "a great oppressor." He also recognized God's great mercy and compassion in awakening men who gave public testimony of what they recognized as a remaining corruption. Walther further acknowledged how at first he was ungrateful for the document of Dr. Vehse and the other two laymen, but how without it, he and the people might have for a long time pursued their way of error.

So well and convincing did Walther demonstrate the scriptural doctrine of the Church and the Ministry that Dr. Marbach, after the first debate declared himself in full agreement with the five paragraphs discussed. After additional instruction from Walther, Marbach found that he could take part in the Christian Church that was present there among the Saxons. And so, the Altenburg Debate gave the pastors and most of the immigrants peace of mind and heart.

ORGANIZING THE CONGREGATIONS

In Perry County, parishes were organized under Pastors Loeber, Walther, Buerger, Gruber and Keyl. The immigrants in St. Louis called Pastor O.H. Walther to serve them. He was a noble pastor, who served his congregation faithfully and well. After preaching three sermons on "Heaven and Earth" during the Christmas season in 1840, he died shortly thereafter on January 21, 1841, at the age of thirty-one, having served as a pastor for only about 2½ years. Following the Altenburg Debate, C.F.W. Walther left for St. Louis to succeed his deceased brother as pastor. He preached his first sermon in his new charge on Jubilate Sunday in the basement of Christ Episcopal Church. Henceforth Walther's place of labor was St. Louis. St. Louis, not Perry County, became the center of Lutheran orthodoxy, mainly through the efforts of Walther. In addition to the district comprising Trinity congregation, three districts made up of Immanuel, Zion, and Holy Cross were established in later years. Each district had its own resident pastor. However, the four districts, with Walther as senior pastor, actually continued as one congregation until his death in 1887.

THE VOICE OF LUTHERAN ORTHODOXY

At a time when "American Lutheranism" was being paraded in the East, a clear voice sounded forth on the side of Lutheran orthodoxy in the West. On September 7, 1844, Walther published in the first issue of *Der Lutheraner* (The Lutheran). Some years later Walther commented on the reasons which compelled him and a handful of other pastors to publish this journal of orthodox Lutheranism:

THESE CONDITIONS, NAMELY, THE CONDITION OF THE LUTHERAN CHURCH IN AMERICA, CAUSED US TO RESOLVE TOGETHER WITH SEVERAL OTHER LUTHERAN PASTORS WHO HAD EMIGRATED WITH US TO PUBLISH A LITTLE PAPER WHICH UNDER THE FRANK AND HONEST NAME OF DER LUTHERANER WAS TO SERVE OUR BELOVED CHURCH ACCORDING TO LOCAL NEEDS, AS GOD WOULD GIVE US GRACE…OUR EXPECTATIONS OR, AT LEAST, OUR PRETENSIONS DID NOT EXTEND ANY FURTHER THAN TO CARRY ABOUT AS MANY PAPERS INTO WIDER CIRCLES AS WERE NECESSARY TO PRESENT AN UNMISTAKABLE PUBLIC TESTIMONY AS TO

Der Lutheraner proved to be a beacon which drew the attention of other Lutherans who were seeking a genuine voice of Lutheranism at a time when many no longer knew what Lutheranism was; and of those who once did, there were many who no longer cared. Friedrich Wyneken, who was destined to play an important role in the founding of the Missouri Synod, was overjoyed when he examined a copy of the first issue sent to him. His hearty comment was: "Thank God, there are still Lutherans in America." Because of the poverty of the Saxons, Walther dared send copies of *Der Lutheraner* to only two men, both of whom headed "so-called Saxon congregations." Dr. Sihler of Pomeroy, Ohio, received the other copy. In his biography he wrote: IT WAS A GREAT JOY TO RECEIVE THE FIRST NUMBER OF *DER LUTHERANER*, AND AFTER I HAD READ THE SUCCEEDING ISSUES, I DID NOT HESITATE TO RECOMMEND THE PAPER TO ANY CONGREGATION, SINCE THE LUTHERANS NEEDED SUCH A PERIODICAL, FOR MANY OF THEM DID NOT KNOW WHAT LUTHERANISM WAS AND WHY THEY CALLED THEMSELVES LUTHERANS. NATURALLY, I SOON ENTERED INTO EXTENDED CORRESPONDENCE WITH THE EDITOR.[14]

THE LOEHE MEN

F.C.D. Wyneken: Friedrich Conrad Dietrich Wyneken was an important figure in Loehe's missionary activities in America. Not a Loehe missionary himself, Wyneken none-the-less was responsible for Loehe's activities in America. He was a well-educated man, who served first as a private tutor in a wealthy German family, and later as head of a Latin School. His keen interest in finding sound Christian literature caused him to discover some missionary journals, which described the miserable spiritual conditions of the German settlers in America. His conscience became burdened with this picture and finally drove him to volunteer for duty in America. He passed his final examination for the ministry just in time to sail for these shores.

Wyneken's first assignment was from the Mission Committee of the Pennsylvania Ministerium, which sent him to work in Indiana to gather the Protestants into congregations. His missionary journeys took him not only through Indiana, but into Ohio and Michigan as well. In the meantime the congregation at Fort Wayne wanted Wyneken to take charge. Permission was granted him to do this, and he was released by the Ministerium from his missionary call, provided he would minister to the neighboring country and settlements. Fort Wayne became Wyneken's center for missionary activity.

Wyneken was greatly distressed by what he saw on the frontier. Living conditions for the German settlers were meager indeed, and the work was long and hard. To a large extent the people had become disinterested in church and religion. Bibles and hymnbooks were scarce. The people suffered from both material and spiritual poverty. And there were very few Lutheran pastors to guide the settlers back to God and his Word. Few of the Lutheran pastors and synods located in the same area where the Missouri Synod came to be organized could be recognized as true to the Lutheran Confessions and totally committed to the Word of God. There was the Ohio Synod, but orthodox Lutherans found it to be, in the words of one observer (Dr. Loy), "a unionistic corporation." The Ohio Synod ministered to both Lutherans and Reformed within the same congregation. A tolerance toward such religious unionism was well entrenched among the members.

While some of the Loehe men tried out the Michigan Synod, they were compelled in short while to leave it for conscience reasons. It too had "union congregations" (ministering to both Lutherans and Reformed), and did not always require full subscription to the Lutheran Confessions. There was also the Buffalo Synod. While it had the goal of being a truly Lutheran body, it also followed the hierarchical doctrines of Pastor Grabau, which all too well reminded the Saxons of the sad experience they had endured in connection with Martin Stephan and his popish theology. The Synod of the West, of which Wyneken was at one time a member, joined the unLutheran General Synod in 1841, thus making itself unacceptable to confessional Lutherans. The General Synod was ridden from the start with "American Lutheranism," whose advocates were avowed enemies of the Lutheran Confessions, and at the same time it reached out to the Reformed sects. Wyneken was a member of the General Synod for a time, but finally severed his connections with it, having failed to influence it in the direction of sound Lutheranism.

The oldest synod—the Pennsylvania Ministerium—was also represented in the Midwest, for it had a few pastors who traveled about investigating spiritual conditions of the settlers. But the ministerium swung back and forth between sound and liberal Lutheranism. It was friendly for some time with the General Synod, and finally joined that body in 1853.

The Tennessee Synod vainly tried to promote the cause of sound Lutheranism. However, due to its small size it simply could not carry out the work it was challenged to do in the Midwest. Furthermore, the fact that the Tennessee Synod was moving toward adopting the English language lessened its impact on such groups as the Saxons in Missouri, who were thoroughly involved with the German language.

Various obstacles stood in the way of existing Lutheran bodies providing effective service to the large numbers of newcomers pouring into the Midwest. These obstacles became the basis finally for a new German Lutheran synod. Walter A Baepler observes:

…THE LUTHERAN CHURCH AS IT WAS ORGANIZED IN AMERICA IN 1846 WAS UNABLE TO MEET THE CHALLENGE OF THE LUTHERAN IMMIGRATION. IT WAS NOT MERELY THE GEOGRAPHICAL REMOTENESS, WHICH PREVENTED THE EASTERN LUTHERANS FROM MAKING AN IMPACT UPON THE WEST, NOR WAS IT ONLY THE DEARTH OF MINISTERS THAT HANDICAPPED THE WESTERN LUTHERANS IN THEIR EFFORTS TO PROVIDE FOR THE NEWCOMERS IN THEIR TERRITORY. THE TROUBLE LAY DEEPER. IT WAS THE LACK OF CONFESSIONAL LUTHERANISM WITHIN THESE BODIES THAT UNFITTED THEM FOR THE TASK OF GIVING SPIRITUAL CARE TO THE THOUSANDS OF FELLOW LUTHERANS ARRIVING IN AMERICA. AND, ON THE OTHER HAND, IT WAS THE DESIRE TO PROMOTE CONFESSIONAL LUTHERANISM IN AMERICA THAT BROUGHT THE LOEHE MEN AND THE SAXONS TOGETHER IN THE MISSOURI SYNOD AND WHICH STIMULATED THE NEW BODY TO GATHER THE LUTHERAN IMMIGRANTS INTO CONGREGATIONS, WHICH WERE TRULY

LUTHERAN.[15]

To Wyneken the solution to having sufficient manpower to serve the large number of unchurched Lutherans lay in Germany. Thus he wrote constantly to the mother country—both to individuals and to German Mission Societies— trying to interest them in coming to the aid of the immigrants. The meager results were disappointing to Wyneken. It is interesting that at this time Wyneken was himself a unionist, who was willing to go along with the prevailing custom of ministering to both Reformed and Lutheran members in the same congregation, and even to welcome Reformed preachers to his pulpit and Reformed members to his altar. He was also at the time a member of the General Synod. Wyneken prevailed upon the Mission Committee of that body to send him to Germany in 1841 for the purpose of securing more manpower for America. In Germany Wyneken wrote and lectured, stirring up the hearts of the people to the plight of their fellow Germans in America. And it was while he was doing this that his own mind was turning to a more truly Lutheran position. He had contacts with conservative Lutheran leaders and especially with Pastor Wilhelm Loehe of Neuendettelsau, Bavaria, of whom we learned earlier in our discussion of the Ohio and Iowa synods. Wyneken persuaded Loehe to send missionaries to America.

When Wyneken arrived back in America and resumed his work in Fort Wayne, after being gone twenty-one months, the change in his attitude was at once noticeable. The Reformed element of his congregation had left in order to organize a separate congregation. Wyneken surprised the people by taking a firm stand for sound Lutheranism based on the Confessions, at the same time opposing Methodism. It was following his return to America, during his effort to make his Lutheran stand known and felt by his flock, that he received his first copy of *Der Lutheraner* from Walther and the Saxons in Missouri.

While in Germany Wyneken attacked the General Synod in a church paper, even accusing it of attempting to destroy the church and of promoting a union in America of the Lutheran and Reformed Churches. After returning to America Wyneken finally severed connections with the General Synod when that body failed to answer his charges. Wyneken not only severed connections with the General Synod, he went so far as to declare war upon it. His action brought this response from Loehe: WYNEKEN IS HEREWITH BEGINNING A WAR WHICH HE MAY CARRY ON WITH THE DEEPEST PEACE OF SOUL, A WAR IN WHICH ALL TRUE CHILDREN OF THE LUTHERAN CHURCH WILL HAVE TO JOIN HIM.[17] By this time Wyneken had followed a call to Baltimore. He and his new charge found themselves in 1845 unaffiliated with any Lutheran synod.

Other Loehe Men: The reports that came out of Fort Wayne from Wyneken concerning the spiritual condition of Germans in the American wilderness did not go unheeded. They were promoted by the church press. Loehe wrote an especially appealing article. After telling of the cries of their brethren in America for help, he laid it heavily on the consciences of the Lutherans in Germany to come to their aid. He closed with the appeal: SHALL OUR BRETHREN NO LONGER WORSHIP IN THE CHURCH OF THEIR FATHERS, FILLED WITH THE BREATH OF THE LORD, BUT INSTEAD RECLINE IN THE MISERABLE SHACKS OF SECTARIANISM? SHALL GERMAN PIETY DECAY IN THE NEW WORLD UNDER THE INFLUENCE OF HUMAN PROPAGANDA? I BEG OF YOU, FOR JESUS' SAKE, TAKE HOLD, ORGANIZE

SPEEDILY, DO NOT WASTE TIME IN CONSULTATIONS. HASTE, HASTE, IMMORTAL SOULS ARE AT STAKE.[17]

Help soon came in the form of contributions from the readers. Among those who read Loehe's stirring appeal was Adam Ernst of Asch, Bohemia. He volunteered for work in America, and was finally turned over to Loehe, who began to instruct him together with Ernst's friend George Burger. These men came to America in the fall of 1842 as Loehe's first emissaries.

Others followed. The Meckelenburgers transported and equipped August Craemer and Fr. Lochner in 1845. Baepler reports: AT THE TIME OF THE ORGANIZATION OF THE MISSOURI SYNOD (1847), LOEHE HAD PREPARED AND SENT TO AMERICA TWENTY-THREE EMERGENCY MEN. BY 1853, THE YEAR IN WHICH LOEHE AND THE MISSOURIANS PARTED, EIGHTY-TWO CANDIDATES OF THEOLOGY, EMERGENCY MEN, AND STUDENTS FOR THE FORT WAYNE SEMINARY HAD COME TO AMERICA THROUGH HIS EFFORTS. MOST OF THEM JOINED THE MISSOURI SYNOD AFTER ITS ORGANIZATION.[18]

Loehe's missioners at first became members of either the Ohio Synod or the Michigan Synod, the greatest number holding membership in the Ohio Synod. Loehe regarded these two synods as the only two truly Lutheran bodies in America. However, in September 1845 the Loehe men who were affiliated with the Ohio Synod seceded from this body because of its unLutheran position regarding unionism. The Loehe men in Michigan left the Michigan Synod for the same reason in 1846. Meanwhile, in 1845 Wyneken removed himself from the General Synod.

The removal of Loehe's missioners from the Ohio Synod stopped Loehe's plans to use the Columbus Theological Seminary for the further training of his men. After Dr. Sihler broke with the Ohio Synod he volunteered to head an orthodox Lutheran seminary so that Loehe's missionaries and teachers could get part of their training in America. In October 1846 such a school was opened in Fort Wayne, Indiana, with an enrollment of eleven men. The small school, which Wyneken had begun in 1844, and the work which Loehe had undertaken in 1841, were merged in the practical seminary at Fort Wayne in 1846.[19] This school became Concordia Theological Seminary, operated as the practical seminary of the Missouri Synod. It was later moved to Springfield, Illinois (this writer's alma mater) and still later, in the 1970's, was moved back to Fort Wayne.

It is of interest to note that Loehe was concerned not only with the plight of German Lutherans who had migrated to America but also with bringing the gospel to the North American Indians. Pastor W. Hattstaedt, one of his missioners living at Monroe, Michigan, was asked to investigate the possibilities of work among the Indians. The best course seemed to be to carry on missionary work among the Indians in conjunction with work among the Lutherans living Michigan. Loehe determined to establish Lutheran congregations near Indian villages, with the pastors serving as missionaries to the Indians living there. Seven young men and five young women volunteered to come to America to form the nucleus of such a congregation.

This brought to America a very able teacher and pastor, who was destined to become president of the practical seminary at Fort Wayne, and later when it was reestablished at Springfield, Illinois, to labor there for many years as

613

president and professor. August Friedrich Craemer has been described as "an indefatigable worker." While teaching at Oxford University, Craemer read the "Appeal" of Wyneken. Learning of Loehe's missionary plan he offered his services. He was chosen pastor of the small mission congregation, which was organized at Neuendettlesau and due to emigrate to America. Craemer was ordained to the ministry the day before the departure.

The destination of Craemer and his group was a new colony to be found in Michigan about fifteen miles from Saginaw. There, in July of 1845, the settlement known as Frankenlust was founded in the dense, virgin forest.[20] With the sound of axes ringing through the air, Craemer began his work among the Indians, baptizing his first converts, a boy and his two sisters, on Christmas Day 1846.

The Frankenmuth venture was a success and an encouragement to Loehe to try others. Thus followed Frankenmuth and Frankenhilf.

Craemer played a very important part in bringing about the meeting between Loehe's missioners and the Saxons in Missouri to help organize the orthodox, confessional Lutherans synod that was so much needed in America at the time.

Another remarkable man was Pastor (Dr.) Wilhelm Sihler. He was born near Breslau, Silesia. A very intelligent person, Sihler graduated from the Gymnasium at the young age of fifteen and then embarked on what he thought at the time would be a military career. However, after a few years he changed his mind and entered the University of Berlin. Later, the University of Jena awarded him the degree of Doctor of Philosophy.

During his student years Sihler had attended church services, but had not been brought to Christ. Pharisaical self-righteousness has been described as his religion. But while living in Dresden, Sihler underwent a Damascus-type conversion, which he compared to that experienced by the apostle Paul. An episode occurred that caused Sihler to become suddenly aware of his sinfulness, and just as suddenly, he became aware of Christ with all his saving grace. Sihler became a different person. He became a constant student of Scripture.

Ultimately, Sihler was brought into contact with the Dresden Mission Society, whose president was one of the patrons of the Saxon fathers. Another man, Dr. Rudelbach, who was a recognized leader of confessional Lutheranism, interested Sihler in the study of the Lutheran Confessions. After his study of the *Lutheran Book of Concord* Sihler's mind was made up. He became an avowed Lutheran. At the same time he had only contempt for the Reformed Church. At a time when many in Germany and America were championing union of the Lutheran and Reformed Churches, Sihler took an absolute stand against doctrinal compromise and religious unionism. In the next few years, he served as a tutor, and while thus occupied he began to feel drawn to the Christian ministry. He too came across Wyneken's "Appeal" and his soul was gripped by it. Sihler felt himself torn by two forces. On the one hand he felt God urging him to go to America, but on the other hand, since he at the time did not agree with American politics, the very thought of living in America was revolting to him. He kept this controversy in his soul as a secret. Ultimately the urging of friends and the prompting of the Dresden Mission Society left Sihler with no further resistance. In November 1843 Sihler arrived in New

York. The following year he was installed in his first pastorate at Pomeroy, Ohio.

Sihler took a firm stand for true Lutheranism, which in his view, had the pure Gospel and unadulterated sacraments. At the same time he gave no quarter to Methodism and Reformed theology. Sihler applied for membership in the Western District of the Ohio Synod and ultimately was ordained and received into membership of that body. However, his membership in the Ohio Synod lasted only for somewhat over a year. When the Ohio Synod rescinded an earlier resolution by the German faction, headed by Sihler, to have all theological instruction given in the seminary only through the German language, with English taught only as a literary study, and when Ohio also rejected the memorial by Sihler and others to abolish the unionistic formula for the Lord's Supper ("Christ says this is my body," etc.), Sihler, together with Loehe's other emissaries, felt constrained to sever his connections with that body. About the same time (1845), Sihler became the pastor of Wyneken's former church in Fort Wayne. He and his friends, including Wyneken, contemplated the possibilities of founding a truly Lutheran synod in the Untied States. By this time Sihler had become acquainted with *Der Lutheraner*, published by the Saxons. He rejoiced in its wonderful Lutheran stance and promoted its reading among his own parishioners.

ORGANIZING A NEW LUTHERAN SYNOD

THE LOEHE MEN AND THE SAXONS KEEP CONTACT

In 1845 there were eleven Saxon pastors and one teacher. Loehe was represented in America by twelve pastors and two teachers. Wyneken kept in close touch with the Loehe men, who, together with Loehe himself, were interested in the Saxons. Before leaving Germany for America, Pastor W.G.C. Hattstaedt was handed a set of instructions by Loehe advising him to travel to the West and visit the Saxons in Missouri before permanently establishing himself. On behalf of Loehe, Hattstaedt was to request the Saxons to help the brethren in Ohio spread Christ's kingdom. A number of questions were addressed by Loehe to the Saxons for use as points of discussion during Hattstaedt's visit.

However, Hattstaedt could not make the journey to the West, having been detained at Monroe, Michigan. He then asked Sihler and Ernst to make the contact for him. They in turn contacted Walther, writing to him and sending the questions with their letter. Question number six proposed in writing a matter that had been circulating in not a few minds at the time: "Would it not be possible to establish a synod with our brethren in the East?" Walther's answer was very encouraging, for he stated that he not only thought it possible but also desirable and good for the welfare of all. He also stated that it was for the cause of affecting a church union that he dared, in God's name, to send forth a periodical such as *Der Lutheraner*, to do what he could to call the orthodox together. Walther was overjoyed when later he was informed in a letter that the Loehe men were disassociating themselves from the Ohio Synod. The

Saxons, at first very cool and cautious regarding synodical affiliations, were gradually coming out of their isolationism.

It was Walther's desire that if there were to be a new synod...(1) that in addition to the Word of God, the synod should be founded on all the Confessions of "our church", including, if possible, the Saxon Articles of Visitation; (2) that all syncretistic activities of members of the synod be eliminated and excluded by a special paragraph in the constitution; (3) that the synod be mainly concerned about the preservation, nourishing, and supervision of the unity and purity of Lutheran doctrine; (4) that the synod be an advisory body, to which a congregation can go for recourse, and not a powerful court; the synod must not encroach on the congregation's right to call; (5) everyone who belongs to the synod should be entitled to suffrage—the lay delegates as well as the pastors have the right to vote. Walther also desired that every individual should have the right to appeal to the synod in all matters not decided by the synod.[21]

After attending the Cleveland Convention of the Ohio Synod, the Loehe men, by a signed document, severed their connections with that body. These men subsequently felt that a new body should be formed, with an attempt made to include the Saxons. Thus a conference was held and delegates were appointed to go to Missouri to meet with them. Sihler and Ernst were assigned this task, with Lochner of the Michigan Synod invited to accompany them.

PRELIMINARY MEETINGS BETWEEN THE LOEHE MEN AND THE SAXONS

The three pastors from the East arrived in St. Louis early in the spring of 1846. They were warmly greeted by the Saxon pastors. Several points in their "instructions" were taken up and ironed out and referred back to Loehe. Work was begun at once on the draft of a synodical constitution. After a week at this task copies were made and sent out to the other men who had left the Ohio Synod and to other friends for their study. Invitations were included to attend a conference at Fort Wayne, beginning July 2, where it was proposed to discuss the plan more carefully. The plan was presented at this time to the congregation in St. Louis, which sharply disputed certain points. The visiting pastors were asked to preach as a testimony of the unity of faith, which existed between the two groups.

Shortly before the Fort Wayne meeting, on June 25, 1846, pastors Hattstaedt, Trautmann, Craemer, and Lochner withdrew from the Michigan Synod for the reason that it promoted religious unionism with the Reformed churches and accepted into membership a missionary who steadfastly refused to subscribe to the Lutheran Confessions.

When the July meeting took place at Fort Wayne to consider further the draft of a synodical constitution, sixteen pastors were present. Six others who could not attend sent word that they heartily approved the plan to organize an orthodox synod. It was, of course, the Saxons who had to lead the way in the difficult work of writing a constitution to which all could agree, and which would serve then as the basis for governing the new, orthodox synod, should it finally materialize. With cheerful confidence the men present resolved to meet at Chicago in the spring of 1847, and to bring delegates with them from the congregations for the purpose of forming "a small orthodox synod." (Sihler's report) It was Loehe's plan to invest the president of the new synod with greater powers than those actually granted by the proposed constitution. At the same time, he would have allowed less governing power to the congregations.

In his report to Loehe, Hattstaedt pointed out the following governing principles, which appertained in formulating a constitution for the new synod:

ACCORDING TO THE EXPERIENCE OF ALL BRETHREN WHO ARE ASSEMBLED HERE AND WHO HAVE BEEN IN OFFICE FOR SOME LENGTH OF TIME, A DEMOCRATIC FORM OF SYNODICAL GOVERNMENT IS THE ONLY FEASIBLE ONE FOR THE LUTHERAN CHURCH IN AMERICA. THE WORD OF GOD IS THE ONLY POWER WITH WHICH TO RULE THE PEOPLE, AND IF THIS POWER DOES NOT ACCOMPLISH THE DESIRED END, NOTHING ELSE WILL. YOUR PLAN OF GRANTING GREATER POWERS TO THE PRESIDENT WAS REJECTED BY ALL PRESENT. THE CONGREGATIONS WERE GIVEN ALL RIGHTS IN SETTLING THEIR OWN AFFAIRS. THEY MAY CALL THEIR PREACHERS, AND THEY MAY DISMISS THEM, PROVIDED THAT THE PASTOR PROVES TO BE A WOLF AND PREACHES FALSE DOCTRINE OR LEADS AN UNGODLY LIFE. IF THE CONGREGATIONS DISMISS THEIR PASTORS FOR OTHER REASONS, THEY CANNOT BE MEMBERS OF SYNOD AND MUST BE REGARDED AS NON-CHRISTIANS AND AS UNORTHODOX.[22]

All the men present signed the constitution. The six not present indicated their approval by letter. A meeting was called, to be held in Chicago in April 1847 for the purpose of formally organizing the synod. The latest draft of the constitution was printed in *Der Lutheraner* for the congregations to study. They were invited, if they found themselves in agreement with it, to assist in establishing the new synod.

THE GERMAN EVANGELICAL LUTHERAN SYNOD OF MISSOURI, OHIO, AND OTHER STATES

At Chicago—then a city of only some 20,000 people—the pastors and lay delegates met in the church of Pastor C. August T. Selle, who only a year before had preached the first Lutheran sermon in Chicago. He had been installed as pastor of the Lutheran-Reformed congregation, whose church had been built three years earlier by the German Protestants living in Chicago. Incidentally, this congregation split a year after the synod was organized, leaving Pastor Selle with only four members.

On Monday morning, April 26, 1847, the Convention was opened with devotions, which included an address, by Pastor Selle. Following the devotions, the men who had been present at Fort Wayne signed the constitution, thus establishing the synod. C.F.W. Walther was temporarily elected president. Acting upon Walther's offer of *Der Lutheraner*, the new synod took over the publishing of this voice of Lutheran orthodoxy, retaining Walther as the editor.

At the close of the Convention the officials of the synod were elected to serve the three-year period between conventions: C.F.W. Walther, president; Dr. W. Sihler, vice-president; Pastor F.W. Husmann, secretary; Mr. F.W. Barthel, treasurer. A Mission Board was appointed, with Missionary A. Craemer a member.

The tiny synod was immediately divided into six conference circuits: St. Louis, Missouri; Chicago, Illinois; Fort Wayne, Indiana; Monroe, Michigan; Fairfield, Ohio; and New York, New York. The charter members of the Missouri Synod numbered twenty-two pastors and two ministerial candidates. Pastor C.D. Wyneken of Baltimore joined the Missouri Synod in 1848.

RAPID GROWTH FOR THE INFANT SYNOD

The Midwest, in which the new synod was mainly located, was enjoying a rapid growth in population. The greater part of the people who came over in the "old immigration" were people from Scandinavia, Germany, Ireland, and Great Britain. The immigration from Germany became particularly strong about the time the Missouri Synod was founded, and remained so until a short time after the Franco-Prussian War. A large portion of the immigrants from Scandinavia and Germany settled in the Midwest, and most of these turned to farming. Of course, many Lutheran families were among the immigrants, and while the Lutheran pastors and missionaries considered it their primary task at the moment to gather these Lutherans into congregations, the shortage of pastors left many Lutherans out of touch with the church, and eventually not a few of these were absorbed by various Protestant sects.

Nevertheless, the growth of the Midwest was reflected also in the growth of the Missouri Synod. In 1850 there were seventy-five pastors and ten teachers. By 1872 the Synod numbered 428 pastors, 251 teachers, and 72,120 baptized members. The rapid growth and great distances over which the synod extended itself—not to mention the difficulties of travel in those days—made it imperative for the synod to be divided into districts. Already suggested to the 1849 Convention, it was finally carried out in 1855, when four districts (Western, Central, Northern, and Eastern) met for the first time as separate groups, with the entire synod meeting in convention every third year. In 1874 the "delegate synod" was introduced. In the course of time, districts were divided into small groups. At the time of this writing the Missouri Synod is divided into a total of 35 districts.

In its early period of expansion we can note certain important steps that the synod took, besides district division. In 1852 the synod officially moved to fill the manpower gap by use of the colporteur. The colporteur, a layman, was to go into settlements having no Lutheran pastor and sell books of a devotional nature. At the same time, he was to use the opportunity to show the Lutherans the need for establishing the office of the ministry in their midst, and he was even to assist them in calling a pastor. The colporteur was to encourage and help the people to organize home devotions and instruct their children in the catechism. He was also to perform emergency baptisms.

In 1860 the synod resolved to call men to be missionaries at large, and this was implemented finally in 1865. Those were the days when a missionary had to be a "giant" of a man, a man with selfless determination to spread the gospel in spite of overwhelming difficulties: the heat, the cold, the trackless forests, the great distances to be traveled with no greater convenience then riding for long hours and days on horseback or enduring the jolting ride of a buggy or wagon or balancing in a canoe paddled by Indians. Often enough, the missionaries' journeys were accomplished by plodding along on foot. Every day was a forthright challenge to the love for souls that burned in the hearts of these men. And the God-loving, God-fearing women these men married shared their sufferings, as well as their dreams of establishing the church on the American frontiers.

Beginning in 1843 Lutherans in Washington, D.C. were cared for by a man who was later to be associated with the Missouri Synod. In 1848 the first congregation of the synod was organized in Pennsylvania at Philadelphia. The oldest Missouri Synod congregation in Virginia was organized in 1852. In 1853 the first synod pastor was sent to New Orleans to serve an already established congregation of Lutherans. In 1854 the first congregation of the synod was organized in Canada at Middleton, Ontario. In 1858 Texas was added to the field of labor when Pastor Ilian, who had brought a colony of Wends from Germany to Serbin, joined the synod. In 1860 a single congregation was established in California, where the missionary worked all alone for eighteen years, until a second pastor was finally sent to join him in that vast territory. The same year a congregation in Memphis, Tennessee, became a member of the synod. Massachusetts was entered by way of Boston in 1862. In 1866 the synod entered Connecticut and Rhode Island through the pastor at Boston. In the same year the pastor and congregation at Egg Harbor, New Jersey, joined the synod. In 1868 the synod moved into Nebraska, and by the next year, after a year's labor, there were two congregations established in Arkansas. In 1870 the first Missouri Synod pastor was installed in a congregation in Mobile, Alabama. Thus came to a close the first quarter century for the Missouri Synod. Its congregations were scattered from the Atlantic to the Pacific, from Canada to the Gulf of Mexico.

By the close of the year 1961, the Missouri Synod had grown to a size that outranked all other Lutheran bodies on the American Continent. Since 1918 the distinction of being the largest Lutheran body in America had gone to the United Lutheran Church in America (ULCA). By 1962 the United Lutheran Church had merged with three other bodies producing the Lutheran Church in America (LCA), which then won from the Missouri Synod its short-lived distinction of being largest of the Lutheran bodies. In 1963, after two large Lutheran bodies had been formed from mergers, the Missouri Synod ranked second of the top three. (LCA=3,227,157 members; LC-MS=2,683,876 members; ALC=2,544,617 members.) Added note: The Wisconsin Synod numbered fourth with a total membership of 354,840. At the beginning of the twenty-first century the membership statistics were as follows:

THE MISSOURI SYNOD'S
EDUCATIONAL INSTITUTIONS

THE SEMINARIES: ST. LOUIS
AND SPRINGFIELD, ILLINOIS (NOW, FORT WAYNE)

Shortly after their arrival in Perry County, Missouri, the Saxons began to provide for higher education. Three candidates: Brohm, Fuerbringer, and Buenger, together with some lay members, erected "The Old Log Cabin" in 1839 in what is now Brazeau Twp. Buenger was the chief leader. On August 13, 1839, a notice appeared in the *Anzeiger des Westens* at St. Louis, announcing the plan and scope of the new school. This was indeed a bold venture of faith, considering the poverty and extreme hardships with which the Saxons at the time were being tested. Dedicated in October, the school opened for business on December 9, 1839. As announced in the St. Louis newspaper, the school included "all college sciences necessary to a true Christian and scientific education," qualifying students for entry into university studies. Buenger soon left to take over the congregation school in St. Louis. Walther followed him to St. Louis in 1841, and Fuerbringer shortly thereafter followed a call to Illinois. Finally, the last of the original instructors, Brohm, left for New York. Meanwhile, a new log cabin had been built near the parsonage at Altenburg, and it fell to Pastor Loeber to be in charge of the school, assisted to some extent by Pastor Keyl of Frohna. In 1843 the congregation in St. Louis called out of its membership Candidate J. Goehner, whom they salaried as professor at the college. The congregation in Altenburg provided him with support by way of food and the like. The theological training was in the hands of Pastors Loeber, Mueller, and Blitz.

When the Missouri Synod organized, the congregation in Altenburg offered its college to the synod, but asked that it remain in the present location. The synod accepted the offer but requested that the academy (preparatory school) remain in Altenburg, while the seminary department should be moved to St. Louis. In 1849 Trinity congregation in St. Louis offered two acres of land and $2,000 in cash to have the entire institution moved to St. Louis. The 1849 Synod Convention resolved that this be done. Meanwhile Pastor Loeber died, and Pastor Walther was elected president of the St. Louis Seminary on November 8, 1849. In the same year Pastor Goehner came from Altenburg with nine students, thus accomplishing the transfer of the academy department to St. Louis. In June 1850 a new building was dedicated for the school, and in the same year A. Biewand came to St. Louis as the third professor. He died in 1858, shortly before the dedication of the second wing of the college building. In 1861 the college section was moved to Fort Wayne, Indiana, while the so-called "practical" seminary department at Fort Wayne came to St. Louis. A new and larger building was erected in 1883, to which an annex was attached in 1907. However, overcrowded conditions, street noises and other inconveniences made it necessary to relocate the seminary to Clayton, a suburb of St. Louis, where a whole new educational plant was built. The present imposing structure was dedicated in 1926.

The practical seminary founded at Fort Wayne by Pastor Loehe in 1846—a merger of Wyneken's small school begun in 1845 and Loehe's endeavor begun in 1841—was deeded to the Missouri Synod in 1847 upon the request of this new body. The practical seminary was headed by Dr. Wm. Sihler. Additional professors were F. Wolter and August "Uncle" Craemer. In 1861 the school was transferred to St. Louis with the Fort Wayne Concordia College serving as a preschool for the St. Louis Seminary. However, by 1874 the preparatory department was moved to Springfield, Illinois, with the "practical" seminary department following it the next year. Here it remained until it was moved in the 1970's to Fort Wayne. Outstanding men connected with this school: Craemer, Wyneken, R. Pieper, Herzer, Streckfuss, and Wessell.

A note of interest is that the Springfield Seminary was actually voted closed in 1935. For a few days its official existence was terminated, but then another vote was taken, the outcome being favorable for the seminary's continued existence. Many improvements were made beginning in the early 1950's, including the addition of several fine new buildings and professorages. The author is himself a graduate of this seminary and cherishes many fond memories of a dedicated faculty, who were thoroughly committed to a thoroughly scriptural, truly orthodox Lutheran training for the students. When a "more liberal" view began to enter the thinking and teaching of the St. Louis Seminary faculty, the Springfield faculty for years successfully resisted the trend, setting a proper example for the sister seminary. In 1975 the Anaheim Convention resolved that the seminary at Springfield be transferred to the campus at Fort Wayne by June 1, 1977. The vacated Springfield campus was sold to the State of Illinois to serve as a training school for State Troopers.

TEACHER TRAINING SCHOOLS
AND PREPARATORY SCHOOLS

In 1855 a teacher training school was founded as a private venture in Milwaukee. Two years later this normal school was transferred to Fort Wayne and combined with the practical seminary. In 1864 it was moved again, this time to Addison, Illinois. Outstanding men who taught in this school: Fleishman, Lindemann, Krauss, Brohm, Kohn, and Kaeppel. By 1913 a completely new plant had been erected at River Forest, Illinois, where it remains.

The great need of pastors induced men of the synod to open more preparatory schools. In 1881 Pastor Loeber, with the assistance of Pastor Wunder of Chicago, opened the Milwaukee Concordia. This institution passed under the control of the synod in 1887. Outstanding men were Huth, Ross, Mueller, Hattstaedt, and Albrecht.

On June 7, 1881, the New York Local Pastoral Conference asked St. Matthew's Church to organize a gymnasium class in its academy. In 1894 this school was transferred to Hawthorne, and accepted by the Missouri Synod in 1896. In 1910 it came to Bronxville, New York. Outstanding men: Feth, Stein, and Heintze.

In January 1884 the Progymnasium was opened at Concordia, Missouri, by Professor A. Baepler. It was accepted by the synod in 1896. Outstanding men: Kaeppel, Schoede, Schaller. In 1893 a college was opened at St. Paul, Minnesota, at the suggestion of Dr. Franz Pieper. The leading men of this institution were:

Buenger, Wollaeger, Abbetmeyer, and E.L. Arndt.

Concordia College, Connover, North Carolina, was founded and controlled for more than twenty years by a private educational society. From 1877 to 1881 it was known as Concordia High, when it was incorporated as a college under the auspices of the Tennessee Synod. Early in the 1890's the school was offered to, and accepted by, the Missouri Synod. It was closed in 1935. Outstanding men: Dau, Romoser, and Hemmeter.

In 1893 J.P. Baden of Winfield, Kansas, erected and donated the college at Winfield, later giving it to the English Synod. Outstanding men were: A.W. Meyer, Scaer, Stoeppelwerth, and Steiner. In 1908 the Missouri Synod accepted the school.

The school at Oakland, California, was opened in 1906 with Theodore Brohm as president. The school at Portland, Oregon, was opened in 1905 with J. Sylwester as first professor and president. In 1911 it was offered to the synod, which offer was declined, for the synod deemed it wiser to pay the salaries of the teachers and leave the upkeep of the school in the hands of the Oregon and Washington District. In 1920 the Missouri Synod voted to open a school in Western Canada. Edmonton, Alberta, was settled upon, with the institution having its opening in rented quarters on October 31, 1921. A.H. Schwermann was called as president. Another school, at Austin, Texas, was opened in 1926 with Studtmann as president. A second normal school was begun at Seward, Nebraska, in 1893.

THE CURRENT EDUCATION PICTURE IN THE LCMS— EARLY TWENTY-FIRST CENTURY

The LCMS has ten colleges and universities in the Concordia Universities System. They are:

Ann Arbor, MI: Austin, TX; Bronxville, N.Y.; Irvine, CA; Mequon, WI; Portland, OR; River Forest, IL; St. Paul, MN; Selma, AL; Seward, NE.

The LCMS has two theological seminaries: Fort Wayne, IN; St. Louis, MO.

In the year 2004 there was a total enrollment in the colleges, universities and seminaries of 17,568 students, with a teaching staff of 1,556.

According to the 2004 Report, there were at that time in the LCMS the following:

2,481 Lutheran schools, including 1,361 early-childhood centers, 1,028 elementary schools, 92 high schools, with a total enrollment of 287,395 students. In addition there were 5,229 Sunday Schools (469,003 students); 4,280 weekday religion schools (195,198 students); 3,968 VBS schools.

President Jerry Kieschnick reported in 2004 that the number of Sunday schools and their enrollment have been decreasing for more than a decade, with the number of weekday religion schools and their enrollment increasing during that same time. In his 2004 report in the February 2004 issue of the *Lutheran Witness*, President Kieschnick also reported a total of about 16,000 professional teachers and 65,000 volunteer teachers of the educational ministers of The Lutheran Church-Missouri Synod. (page 28)

The 1964 Lutheran Annual of the LCMS reported that in 1964 82,604 children were baptized in the LCMS. LCMS Department of Statistics reported 23,464 children baptized for 2010. A Handbook for Christian Matrimony published by Christian News maintains that birth control is a major cause for the tremendous decrease of child baptisms.

THE LCMS's "LUTHERAN HOUR"—
BRINGING CHRIST TO THE NATIONS THROUGH RADIO

The St. Louis Seminary is blessed with its own radio station, KFUO, which went on the air for the first time on October 26, 1924. It has served, and still serves, as a "Gospel Voice" for the Missouri Synod, especially through the part it has played for so many years in producing the ever-popular program, "The Lutheran Hour."

On October 2, 1930, the "Lutheran Hour" was launched by the Lutheran Laymen's League of the Missouri Synod. It began as a religious program conducted over a coast-to-coast network of thirty-eight stations. On June 11, 1931, the last "Lutheran Hour" broadcast was made. Then, early in 1935 the "Lutheran Hour" was resumed over WXYZ in Detroit and WLW in Cincinnati. It has remained on the air as a regular weekly broadcast since that time.

In 1939 the number of stations carrying the broadcast was increased to 99 and the broadcast also was extended into areas outside the United States. From the first "Lutheran Hour" broadcast until 1950, when he died at age 58 of a heart attack, Dr. Walter A. Maier—a professor at the St. Louis Seminary— was the speaker. Dr. Maier was known for his urgent speaking style that quickly caught the listener's attention and held it. He was uncompromising in his messages, which clearly and forcefully presented "old fashioned" Law and Gospel, sin and grace—not the modern social gospel that was the message (and still is) of so many speakers. Dr. Maier's Law-Gospel sermons, far from being an impediment to gaining listeners and holding them, were directly a cause of the "remarkable" growth of "The Lutheran Hour." Dr. Maier faithfully called the nation to turn to Christ, and the Holy Spirit of God used his messages to bring souls to the Savior.

An intriguing account of Maier's radio ministry has been written by his son, Dr. Paul L. Maier. His book, titled *A Man Spoke, A World Listened: The Story Of Walter A. Maier*, was published in New York by McGraw Hill in 1963, and has been reprinted by Concordia Publishing House, St. Louis, MO. *Christian News*, in 2008, published *Walter Maier Still Speaks – Missouri and the World Should Listen*. In 1957 the editor of *Christian News* wrote his M.Div. thesis on Maier with the help of Mrs. Maier.

By 1988 it could be reported that the "Lutheran Hour" was being heard on almost 2,000 radio stations around the world. The broadcast became one of the most popular—if not the most popular—programs on radio. Dr. Maier was succeeded eventually by Dr. Oswald C.J. Hoffman, who served as the main "Lutheran Hour" speaker for many years, until his retirement.

The LCMS also ventured into television. Many will recall the popular series produced by the synod, titled "This Is The Life."

THE MISSIONS OF THE MISSOURI SYNOD—
EARLY HISTORY

MISSIONARY WORK TO FELLOW
GERMANS AND TO INDIANS

Many of the founders of the Missouri Synod were sent to America to do mission work, which included preaching the Gospel to the Indians. There were the Loehe men: Sihler, Craemer, Ernst, Lochner, and Wyneken. The Saxons were also interested in mission work. In September 1839 Loeber confirmed sixteen adults in his church at Altenburg—former members of Reformed and Catholic churches.

German colonies were established in Michigan near Saginaw, where several plots had been selected by Pastor Schmidt of Ann Arbor, president of the Michigan Synod. On a site on the Cass River, Frankenmuth was founded. While settlers were getting established, August F. Craemer undertook work among the Indians. He gathered their children in the school at Frankenmuth and on Christmas Day 1846 the first three Indians were baptized. On Pentecost in 1848 Craemer baptized his nineteenth Indian child. A year earlier he had received a co-worker, Missionary Baierlein, who, aided by the colonists, built a house at a place called Bethanien, the center of mission activity. Craemer was later called as professor to Fort Wayne, then to St. Louis, and finally to Springfield. He was an untiring worker, also caring for parishes even as a professor. He was affectionately referred to as "Uncle" Craemer—a dearly loved and respected man of God. August Craemer died May 3, 1891. His funeral was the largest held in Springfield, after that of Abraham Lincoln.

Loehe continued to send immigrants to Michigan so that in 1851 Frankenmuth boasted eighty cabins and farmhouses, as well as a post office. In 1847 the colony of Frankentrost was begun under John Henry Philip Graebner, and a year later Frankenlust was begun under Ferdinand Severs. In 1850 Frankenhilf was established under the leadership of John Deindoerfer.

At its first Convention in 1847 the Missouri Synod commissioned Candidate Frincke as missionary at large. However, this office was soon canceled due to lack of funds. Even so, pastors continued to plow and seed their individual territories. Pastor F. Severs in 1856 traveled through Minnesota. J.M. Buehler in 1860 was sent to the western coast. J. Hilgendorf in 1872 explored Colorado, and in 1880 the great Northwest was opened, in part due to the efforts of Dr. F. Pfotenhauer. From the beginning the Missouri Synod had a Board for Home Missions, and each district had its own home Missions Board. After 1932 the synod maintained a Secretary or Director of Missions. The arrangement was made whereby districts too weak financially to support their local mission endeavors could receive subsidies from the General Board For Home Missions. In 1902 a General Church Extension Fund was established. The individual districts also established District Church Extension Boards.

To a large extent the mission thrust of the Missouri Synod, even into the twentieth century, lay in reaching out to German-speaking people, and in gathering into congregations the Lutherans who were among the German immigrants pouring into America. Dr. John W. Behnken, former president of the synod, made the following observation in his autobiography:

ALREADY WHEN THE SYNOD OBSERVED ITS GOLDEN JUBILEE (1897), DR. A.L. GRAEBNER IN A SERIES OF ARTICLES IN SYNOD'S OFFICIAL ORGAN (*DER LUTHERANER*)...CALLED ATTENTION TO THE FACT THAT WHILE THE USE OF GERMAN BY OUR CHURCH HAD BEEN A GREAT BLESSING, ESPECIALLY TO THE GREAT FLOOD OF IMMIGRANTS, OUR CHURCH MUST NOW REALIZE THAT "THE YEARS OF THE GREAT IMMIGRATION OF GERMANS ARE PAST." IF OUR CHURCH HOPES TO CONTINUE TO GROW, HE EMPHASIZED, WE MUST THINK IN TERMS OF A TYPE OF MISSION WORK DIFFERENT FROM GATHERING SCATTERED GERMAN LUTHERANS INTO CONGREGATIONS. POINTING TO THE MANY LOSSES IN MEMBERSHIP DUE TO "MIXED" (GERMAN-ENGLISH) MARRIAGES, HE TRUMPETED THE URGENT NEED FOR CONGREGATIONS TO INTRODUCE ENGLISH SERVICES AND TO CONCENTRATE THEIR EFFORTS ON AMERICA'S VAST NUMBERS OF UNCHURCHED PEOPLE. HE QUOTED THE WORDS OF A LEADER OF ANOTHER LUTHERAN BODY: "YOU MISSOURIANS OUGHT TO LET YOUR LIGHT SHINE AMONG THE ENGLISH-SPEAKING PEOPLE OF THIS COUNTRY; YOU WOULD FIND AMONG THEM A FIELD EQUALLY AS LARGE AS YOU FIND AMONG THE GERMANS."[23]

As Dr. Behnken reported, Graebner's call went mostly unheeded. However, the fast growth of the English Synod Missouri was a lesson to the German Synod as to what could be done in English with the Gospel!

Rapid expansion of the Missouri Synod began early in the second decade of he twentieth century, but not without problems. Expansion in the mission fields required expansion in the educational institutions, which supplied the workers, so that the synod was, as a result, plunged deeply into debt. Special collections had to be used at times to liquidate these debts. The Lutheran Laymen's League (LLL) was organized mainly to help the synod out of debt, and had the stated objective: "To aid Synod by word and deed in business and financial matters." It later set up a large endowment fund to be used in supporting the "veterans of the cross" and their dependants.

WORK AMONG THE NEGROES

The work among Negroes in the South was actually undertaken through the Synodical Conference. Still, because the ratio of support among the member synods fell so heavily to the much larger Missouri Synod, it could almost be said that the work was Missouri's endeavor. It was in 1877, at a meeting of the Synodical Conference, that a motion made by Pastor H.A. Preuss of the Norwegian Synod resulted in a resolution by the Conference to work among the neglected Negroes in the United States, numbering then about 6,000,000. A Board for Negro Missions was appointed. The first missionary sent out was J.F. Doescher, who visited Memphis, Tennessee. He organized a Sunday school in Little Rock, Arkansas, and in New Orleans and explored several states in the South. In 1878 Rev. F. Berg organized the first Negro congregation in Little Rock. In 1880 Rev. Niles J. Bakke, who got around by walking on crutches—a Norwegian graduate of St. Louis—took up work in New Orleans.

In 1915, following an appeal by Miss Rosa Young of Rosebud, Alabama, work was taken up in the so-called Black Belt of Alabama. In 1903 two institutions were founded for training Negro pastors and teachers, the Springfield Seminary having served up to this time for this purpose. Thus Immanuel Lutheran College was founded at Greensboro, North Carolina, and Lutheran College at New Orleans. The latter school closed in 1925. Alabama Teachers College, Selma, was opened in 1922.

EARLY MISSIONS OF THE MISSOURI SYNOD IN OTHER COUNTRIES

ORGANIZING ORTHODOX LUTHERAN BODIES OUTSIDE AMERICA

The Missouri Synod had connections in Europe with Germany from the very beginning. There were of course the connections with Loehe, which have already been described. Beginning in 1860 a preparatory school, founded by F. Brunn of Steeden, was operated. From this school nearly 300 men were sent to America. Brunn published a mission paper in the interest of this work. Meanwhile church conditions were bad in Saxony. In 1865 a group of devout laymen in Dresden banded together for their own edification and to further the cause of true Lutheranism. They organized in 1867 the *Lutheranerverein*. They established connections with Brunn and organized similar societies in Zwickau and Planitz. Having appealed in vain to the State Church to discontinue unionistic practices, some members left the state church and organized the Independent Evangelical Lutheran Church in Saxony in 1871. An appeal was made to Walther of the Missouri Synod for a pastor, who then suggested Pastor H. Ruhland. Soon several other pastors joined him. In 1876 the group organized the Evangelical Lutheran Synod of Saxony and Other States. Their official church paper was *The Evangelical Lutheran Free Church*. Prominent men were: Ruhland, Stoeckhardt, Willkomm, and Stallman.

The work in Europe flowed over into Denmark and Finland. Tiny conservative Lutheran bodies were organized in these countries. Besides the small German Free Church, the Alsatian Free Church was started, as was the Finnish Free Church.

A large number of Germans had for years migrated to South America, especially to Brazil. They organized themselves into school districts, which at the same time constituted church parishes. Church conditions were extremely poor. When Pastor F. Brutschin, a German Lutheran pastor in Brazil (who had been receiving the church papers of the Missouri Synod) was forced to retire because of old age, the Missouri Synod in 1899, acting upon his request for a successor, resolved to take up the work in Brazil. A friend of this work donated $2,000 to enable the Board to make a beginning, and Pastor F. Broders was asked to reconnoiter the field. In twenty-five parishes that Broders visited he did not find a single ordained pastor.

Churches were served by vagabond preachers. Broders established the first congregation of the Missouri Synod at Sao Pedro, Rio Grande de Sul. News spread rapidly, and people came from far and near to hear the new preacher. However, the work was made difficult because of much opposition from spiritual vagabonds. In February 1901 Pastor W. Mahler went to Sao Pedro, leaving Broders to continue explorations. The same year three candidates went to Brazil, and in 1902 four more were called. The year 1904 saw the first institution opened by the Synod, which even occurred at Bom Jesus in Sao Lourence. The same year also witnessed the organizing of the Brazil District. At that time there were fourteen pastors and one teacher in the field. Later, the college and seminary were moved to Porto Alegro (Alegre), where also a publishing house was established.

In 1905 the Missouri Synod was called to Argentina. There the work developed rapidly. A college was established at Crespo. As time passed, the synod's thrust widened on the great continent of South America.

MISSION WORK IN INDIA AND CHINA

In the earlier days of the Missouri Synod the fathers supported European Lutheran Missionary Societies. Soon the synod was urged to take in foreign fields. (The work carried on in Germany and among the Germans in South America was, in a sense "home missions in other countries.") In 1893 the first board was appointed for work in Japan. However, conditions in Japan were unfavorable at the time, so interest shifted to India. Their missionaries Theodore and J. Mohn had severed their connections with the Leipzig Mission Society because of its stand in regards to the doctrine of the Verbal Inspiration of Scripture. Recommended to the Missouri Synod by the brethren in Europe, they were subsequently called by the synod's Board of Missions and commissioned on October 14, 1894. Missionary Naether began his work at Krishnagiri in 1895, and soon stations at Ambur (where Mohn came to labor), Bargur, and Vaniyambadi were added. This comprised the Northern Field. A third missionary, formerly of the Leipzig Society, was soon added in the person of O. Kellerbauer. In 1907, through G. Jesudason, secretary to a British resident at Triviandrum, the Missouri Synod was called into the Southern Field. Work was begun at Nagercoil, 500 miles south of the Northern Field. In 1913, to help allay the suspicions of the natives, medical work was begun under the direction of Miss Lulu Ellerman, R.N. A beautiful mountain retreat, called Bergheim, was provided for the missionaries and their families at Kodaikanai by the Ladies Aid Societies of the Synod. The work progressed with many more congregations and outstations being established. Hundreds of native missionary helpers were acquired. A theological seminary was established at Nagercoil.

The Father of the China Missions was Professor E.L. Arndt. His glowing appeals aroused many hearts within the Synodical Conference to take a Christian interest in China and its 400,000,000 inhabitants. Thus, in 1912 the China Mission Society was organized. It sent out Rev. Arndt as the first missionary in 1913. Arndt chose Hankow as the center of his field of labor and after one-half year began to preach in the Chinese language. He baptized his first convert in September 1914. E. Riedel was sent as his associate in 1915. In 1917 the synod took over the mission work in China. In order to train indigent pastors, Concordia Seminary was established in Hankow.

A BRIEF GLIMPSE OF THE MISSION PICTURE IN THE LCMS—EARLY TWENTY-FIRST CENTURY

The rapidity of LCMS mission expansion among immigrant peoples is, in the word of one observer, "remarkable." The increase in missions to Muslims seems particularly noteworthy.

	1994	2000
African	0	64
Vietnamese	3	10
Asian Indian	0	15
Chinese	16	30
Hispanic	90	112
Hmong	3	20
Japanese	0	3
Korean	18	50
Muslim	2	15

According to a 12/12/00 news release, the LCMS "planted 65 new congregations" in the last year and only 24 had English as their primary language.

In 2003 the number of congregations in the LCMS increased by 94, the largest increase for this body in 15 years and over half of these new congregations consist of ethnic minorities, and the majority of the new congregations were started as daughters by existing congregations—not by synodical mission boards. One congregation, Christ Assembly Lutheran Church, an African immigrant congregation in Staten Island, New York, started ten new congregations in the last eight years. The multicultural and ethnic congregations in the LCMS have been particularly active in starting missions.* Like other church bodies, the LCMS in recent years had to do some serious financial belt-tightening due to the economic downturn that has affected much of the nation.

SYNOD OF MISSOURI AND OTHER STATES (ENGLISH)—THE ENGLISH DISTRICT OF THE MISSOURI SYNOD

AT FIRST, AN ENGLISH CONFERENCE WITHIN THE MISSOURI SYNOD

The eighteenth century saw Lutherans settling in the Smoky Mountain region of western North Carolina and eastern Tennessee. Some of these Lutherans later moved westward, on into Arkansas and Missouri. In 1872 several orthodox, English-preaching Lutheran pastors who served these

Lutherans, contacted the seminary faculty (Missouri Synod) at St. Louis. As a result a free Lutheran conference was held at Gravelton, Missouri. With Walther's blessing, the group organized The English Evangelical Lutheran Conference of Missouri. The three original pastors were: Andrew Rader, J.R. Moser, and Polycarp Henkel. Later, Pastors A.W. Meyer and William Dallmann were added to the roster. The Missouri Synod itself used German almost exclusively for about half a century. Professor F. Schmidt, however, spoke English and he then helped to bring about the English Conference.

In 1886 the English Conference, invigorated by the calling of Pastors Meyer and Dallmann, began to establish English parochial schools and also conducted missions in the English language. In 1887 the English Conference requested the German Synod to receive it as a separate English Mission District. Instead of granting this request, the German Synod advised the Conference to organize an independent English Synod (1887).

The following year a constitution containing the word "Conference" in the official name was adopted by eleven pastors and eight congregations. It was resolved to join the Synodical Conference. At their next Convention, which met in St. Louis in 1891, the designation "Conference" was changed to "Synod." The English Synod grew rapidly. Already in 1888 a "city" mission had been started in Baltimore. Others followed. Younger generations of Germans were learning English as they grew up. To meet the changing language climate, English-speaking pastors were trained and more and more English-speaking missionaries were sent out. An agreement was reached with the German Synod that as English-speaking congregations were organized in its districts through home missionary operations, these congregations in whatever district or state they might be, would not affiliate with the German Missouri Synod but with the English Synod of Missouri. With its rapid growth the English Synod soon covered the same area as the German Synod. The official paper of the English Synod was the *Lutheran Witness*, founded in 1882 at Cleveland, Ohio. Later it became the official church paper of the Missouri Synod when this body turned from German to English. The English Synod founded its own publishing house. It also accepted as a gift, St. John's College, Winfield, Kansas, a school founded by Mr. John P. Baden.

THE ENGLISH SYNOD FINALLY BECOMES
THE ENGLISH DISTRICT OF THE MISSOURI SYNOD

At first the German Synod was suspicious of the use of the English language—not an isolated experience among the Lutheran bodies in America, which at first stressed their ethnic heritage. There was a tendency to associate liberal doctrine and practice with teaching and preaching in English. It was thought that true Lutheranism could best be preserved through the medium of Luther's German. However, as years passed it became more and more evident that sound Lutherans were also to be found among those who spoke English. In fact, the German Synod found a strange thing happening in its very midst—the rapid growth of not only bilingual services but even of all-English services. By 1911 it was discovered that more English services were being conducted in the German Synod than in the English Synod.

In the meantime, the English Synod had been negotiating with the Missouri Synod, asking why the barriers, which had kept that body from becoming an English District of the German Synod, could not be removed. Finally, by 1911 the merger was accomplished and the English Synod became officially an English District of the Missouri Synod. The next year the first convention of the English District was held at Baltimore. At the time of its founding this district numbered sixty congregations, fifty-eight voting pastors, fourteen professors and advisory pastors, and two teachers.[24]

The English Synod's *Lutheran Witness* became the official English paper of the German Synod, and the publishing house operated by the English Synod was transferred to Concordia Publishing House in St. Louis. By 1917 the designation "German" was dropped from the official name of the synod. The use of the German language persisted to a large extent in the rural and small town congregations. The outbreak of the First World War, with the suspicions and antagonisms, which it aroused in the minds of the populace against the use of the German language in public meetings, certainly helped hasten the transition to English in the Missouri Synod, and in other German Lutheran bodies as well.

THE ENGLISH DISTRICT

A More Liberal Attitude: Historically, the English District has tended toward liberal doctrine and practice. In the controversy, which later occurred in the Missouri Synod between the moderates (liberals) and the conservatives, the English District sided with the moderates. In its 1975 Convention this non-geographical district, numbering 130,000 of the synod's 2.8 million members, took a definite stand supporting the Evangelical Lutherans in Mission (ELIM)—the moderate group within the Missouri Synod—and recognized Seminex (Seminary in Exile) as a synodical institution. Seminex was formed when a large part of the St. Louis Seminary faculty and student body left in order to form their own Seminary in Exile in protest of the suspension of Dr. Tietjen as president of the seminary. The English District at the same time affirmed that congregations of the Missouri Synod have the right to call and ordain candidates to the ministry—thus, the right to call and ordain graduates from the maverick Seminex. The English District's position paper stated:

AS WE NOW AFFIRM OUR DESIRE TO REMAIN IN THE LCMS, WE DO SO BECAUSE WE BELIEVE THAT WE ARE THE SYNOD IN THE BEST OF HER DOCTRINE, CONFESSION AND PROCLAMATION. WE ARE, NEVERTHELESS, WITH GREAT SADNESS PREPARED TO ASK OUR CONGREGATIONS TO REVERT TO OUR STATUS AS AN INDEPENDENT SYNOD OR TO SEEK OTHER INSTITUTIONAL AFFILIATION IF IT BECOMES CLEAR THAT THE LCMS DOES NOT INTEND TO RETURN TO ITS FORMER CONFESSIONAL POSITION, AND TO ITS FORMER EVANGELICAL PRACTICE WHICH RESPECTS DIVERSITY WITHIN THE UNITY OF THE CHURCH.

The position paper also went on to deny the Missouri Synod the right to discipline the district or its members because of "this confessional stance," which action would lead to the district's considering "the alternatives in mission and ministry." A minority of "conservatives" disagreed with the position paper and even called on President Harold Hecht to cease authorizing ordination and installation of uncertified Seminex graduates and urged uncertified pastors to become certified.

Dr. Martin Marty, professor of history and member at that time of the English District, has long been a spokesman for the liberal side. Regarding the doctrine of the Inerrancy of Holy Scripture, which became the main point of controversy within the Missouri Synod in the seventies, Dr. Marty said: REASONING BASED ON CERTAIN PHILOSOPHIES HAVE BEEN SATISFYING TO MANY, INCLUDING MANY FATHERS OF THE ENGLISH DISTRICT. BUT EVEN ITS SERIOUS ADVOCATES REGULARLY HAVE TO ADMIT THAT INERRANCY IS AN IDEA THAT NOWHERE, NOT ONCE, IS EXPLICITLY TAUGHT IN SCRIPTURE.

At its June 1976 Convention the English District voted 296 to 75 for an "orderly and peaceful separation" from the Missouri Synod. The district at that time numbered 227 congregations. Earlier in the year (April 2), District President Harold Hecht had been ousted from office by Missouri Synod President Dr. J.A.O. Preus for ordaining ineligible Seminex graduates. President Hecht then resigned his office. His action was followed by a majority of the vice presidents, together with the district's Board of Directors. Those congregations of the district which voted to leave the synod formed a new body, which filed incorporation papers in Illinois under the name English Synod of the Evangelical Lutheran Church. Dr. Hecht was asked to serve as head of the new synod until a constituting convention could be held.

The Minority group which chose to remain with the Missouri Synod elected Rev. George Bornemann of Elmhurst, Illinois, as the new English District president. Like his predecessor, Bornemann had ordained graduates of Seminex. More will be noted later on in this chapter concerning internal problems that eventually confronted the Missouri Synod and caused much hardship and heartache.

CONTROVERSY WITH OTHER LUTHERANS BODIES

While the orthodoxy of the Missouri Synod soon won it the respect and admiration of those who stood for confessional Lutheranism, both on the American continent and in Europe, on the other hand the stand the synod took in matters relating to the Church and to the Office of the Ministry, as well as its stand on the doctrine of Predestination or Election, eventually resulted in the alienation of several influential leaders in the Lutheran Church, and ultimately in the alienation of entire synods.

CONTROVERSY WITH THE BUFFALO SYNOD AND PASTOR GRABAU

John Grabau had fled Prussia in 1839 with about 1,000 other emigrants

631

under his leadership. Having arrived in America, he established himself in Buffalo, New York (see: ALC, the Buffalo Synod). Other emigrations followed. A group of Pomeranians settled near Freistadt, Wisconsin, and another group, the Ukermarkers, settled near Buffalo. There was an immediate lack of pastors to fill the needs of these Lutheran immigrants. In 1840, due to the lack of pastors among the Prussian Lutherans, some congregations began to enlist the services of laymen to perform ministerial acts. Grabau was in disagreement with this practice, for he felt it constituted a violation of the Holy Ministry. And so, the practice prompted the Prussian leader to address a "Pastoral Letter" to the brethren in Buffalo, Milwaukee, and other areas. He also sent a copy of this *Hirtenbrief* to the Saxons in Missouri, requesting their opinion (December 1, 1840). The Saxons, however, were in a crisis of their own, having renounced all association with their leader, Martin Stephan, the year before. Their action had raised some important questions, as yet unsettled, in their own midst regarding the Office of the Ministry, the Pastoral Call, and other doctrinal issues. In examining Grabau's Pastoral Letter, the Saxons noted some similarities between Grabau's stand on the ministry and that of their own deposed leader. And yet, respect for Grabau as one who was trying to uphold conservative Lutheranism in America, together with the turmoil in their own midst, kept the Saxons from responding to Grabau's letter for two-and-a-half years (December 1, 1840 and July 3, 1843). In the meantime, two Saxons pastors were serving in Prussian congregations in the East.

The Saxons were finally forced into answering Grabau's repeated requests for criticism of his Pastoral Letter. When he suggested that a seminary be conducted by himself and the Saxons, and through Pastor Krause requested a formal opinion of his letter, the Saxons could no longer delay their response. Their answer was in the form of dissent, covering sixteen closely printed pages. The Saxons criticized Grabau for ascribing more to the ministerial office then belongs to it, forcing the spiritual priesthood of the believers into the background. They also concluded that ordination—contrary to Grabau's teaching—is not essential to the ministry and that it is claiming too much to say that a congregation must obey its pastor in all things not contrary to the Word of God. The Saxons left it to the individual Christian to decide whether or not the pastor proclaims the Word of God. Furthermore, they concluded that the efficacy of the Means of Grace does not depend on the Office of the Ministry, but on Christ's Word. The Saxons were opposed to all hierarchical tendencies in the Church. They had been badly burned by Stephan. They were not about to endure such pain a second time. Upon studying the Saxon reply, Grabau and his associates accused the Saxons of seventeen errors and declared that they could no longer consider them Lutheran pastors. It was at this time that the sobriquet "Missourians" was coined by Grabau in referring to the Saxons, and the designation stuck.

After the organization of the Missouri Synod the controversy was transferred to that body. The doctrines in dispute were: The Church, The Ministry, and the Office of the Keys. Grabau taught that the one holy Christian Church is visible, and that it consists not in scattered believers, but in believers gathered around Word and Sacrament, and that communion with the visible Church is necessary to salvation. He even went so far as to say that true believers are not found in communions which teach error. Missouri countered that the Church in its true sense is invisible and that believers are to be found in churches that teach error, even as they were in St. Paul's time, citing the congregations in Corinth and Galatia.

With reference to the Ministry, the Buffalo Synod maintained that the congregation does not confer the Holy Ministry upon a man, but the Son of God, together with the Father and the Holy Ghost. Also, that the congregation does not have a right to call a pastor except with the assistance and presence of a ministerial representative. The Ministry forms a distinct rank or class. Only the clergy, not the congregation, has the right to judge doctrine. Ordination is a divine order. It gives validity and efficacy to the pastor's work. The Missouri Synod maintained against the Buffalo Synod that all Christians, as a royal priesthood, have the power to elect ministers, and its call is valid even without assistance and presence of clergymen. Furthermore, the clergy are not a distinct class, since all Christians are called priests, and the minister is not a ruler whom all members must obey. Finally, the Missouri Synod claimed that it cannot be proved from Scripture that ordination is a divine institution.

Regarding the Office of the Keys, the Buffalo Synod taught that Christ did not give the Keys of the kingdom of heaven to the Church, to every believer, but solely and alone to pastors; nor does the congregation have the right to judge who is to be regarded as a heathen and a publican, for only the pastor has the right to excommunicate. The Missouri Synod, taking its stand on Matthew 18: 17-20, maintained that the Office of the Keys has been given by Christ to the whole Church, and that this authority was not given through the ministers to the congregation.

Repeated efforts were made to bring the opposing parties together in the form of a conference. Already in 1846 the Saxons invited Grabau to come to Fort Wayne to confer on the matter. St. Matthew's in Detroit asked Grabau to confer with Craemer in its church. Both the Leipzig Conference and the Breslau Synod urged Grabau to meet the Missouri Synod in colloquium, but Grabau refused this and all overtures. As late as 1856 the Missouri Synod, upon the urging of the Ohio Synod, made it known that it stood ready to establish closer relations with the Buffalo Synod, but to no avail. In 1859 Grabau prevailed upon his synod to renounce all fraternal relations with the Missouri Synod. And he himself excommunicated the entire Missouri Synod, which by that time consisted of more than 200 congregations. In 1866 he excommunicated many of his own synod for "entertaining Missouri principles," and in one instance, even an entire congregation!

Pastor Grabau's papistic rule finally became more than some in his synod could tolerate, and a split occurred resulting in the withdrawal of Grabau and a few adherents. In 1866 a colloquium was held at Buffalo. Von Rohr, Hochsetter, and P. Brandt of the Buffalo Synod met with Walther, Schwan, and Sihler of the Missouri Synod. Only von Rohr disagreed with Missouri, and the following year a formal recognition of fraternal unity was sealed at a meeting between twelve pastors and five lay delegates of the Buffalo Synod, and five pastors of the Missouri Synod. Grabau, however, maintained his position until his death, after which his adherents modified their views regarding the questions of doctrine involved.[25, 26]

633

Until 1853 most of the men whom Pastor Loehe sent over to America became members of the Missouri Synod. Loehe, however, was not pleased with the constitution of this body. The issue involved was the Church and the Ministry. Loehe took an intermediate position between the Missouri Synod and Grabau of the Buffalo Synod. Much of the impetus for forming the Missouri Synod had come from Loehe's men, and when the constitution was adopted his workers took part in signing it. The strange thing is that they did not seek the opinion and advice of the one who had sent them.

Loehe maintained that, not through the local congregation but through the church, that is, the congregation and clergy, the Lord calls and ordains men for the ministry. To Loehe, ordination is not a mere church ordinance. He did not believe that every Christian has the Office of the Keys, and therefore did not believe that the ministerial office is derived from the spiritual priesthood of the believers. Thus, except for rare cases a minister must be present when a congregation calls a pastor. However, Loehe did not go to the extremes to which Grabau went. He neither approved Grabau's practice of arbitrary excommunication nor did he agree that members of the congregation must obey their pastors in all things not contrary to the Scriptures.

The Missouri Synod attempted to bring the two sides together. After two invitations to Loehe to attend Missouri Synod conventions brought no results, the synod sent Walther and Wyneken as delegates to Germany in 1851. While in conference with Loehe, the two men discussed the problem of the shortage of teachers for the parish schools. Loehe agreed with their suggestion that a teacher-training institution be opened in America. Loehe opened such a school at Saginaw, Michigan, in July 1852. Loehe's break with the Missouri Synod was precipitated by the refusal of Inspector G.M. Grossman of the Saginaw school to disavow Loehe's doctrine of the Church and Ministry, and adopt instead the Missouri Synod's stand. In Saginaw Pastor Cloeter, whose congregation afforded membership to the professor and his students, threatened to discipline Grossman if he continued to abide by Loehe's doctrine. One other pastor of the Missouri Synod sided with Grossmann, while the other Missourians in Michigan insisted that their doctrine was that of the Bible.

Finally, tensions became unbearable between the faction and the Missouri Synod, resulting in a request by Grossmann and Deindoerfer for permission to migrate to Iowa, to establish a school there. This permission was granted, and the move was made. However, only two of the original five students continued on with Professor Grossmann. On August 24, 1854, the Iowa Synod was organized at St. Sebald, Iowa, by Professor G.M. Grossmann, J. Deindoerfer, Siegmund Fritschel, and M. Schueller. This event, of course, helped to bring on the alienation of Loehe's affection for the Missouri Synod.

Grabau of the Buffalo Synod had a hand in this alienation. When he and von Rohr visited Loehe in 1853, Loehe became even more convinced that the time had come that he could no longer work together with the Missouri Synod. And so, in a letter dated August 4, 1853, and written on black-bordered paper, Loehe bid his farewell to the Missourians, to both pastors and congregations in the Saginaw Valley of Michigan.

When the Iowa Synod was formed, no official constitution was adopted, only certain guiding principles. The first of these uncertain principles reads:

SYNOD ACCEPTS ALL THE SYMBOLICAL BOOKS OF THE EVANGELICAL LUTHERAN CHURCH BECAUSE IT BELIEVES THAT ALL THEIR SYMBOLICAL DECISIONS OF DISPUTABLE QUESTIONS, WHICH HAD ARISEN BEFORE OR DURING THE TIME OF THE REFORMATION, WERE MADE IN ACCORDANCE WITH THE WORD OF GOD. BUT BECAUSE WITHIN THE LUTHERAN CHURCH THERE ARE DIFFERENT TENDENCIES, SYNOD DECLARES ITSELF IN FAVOR OF THAT TENDENCY WHICH, BY MEANS OF THE CONFESSIONS, AND ON THE BASIS OF THE WORD OF GOD, STRIVES TOWARD GREATER COMPLETENESS.[27]

The uncertain principles adopted by the Iowa Synod led to the so-called "open questions" for which the Missouri Synod took the Iowa Synod to task. A colloquium was held at Milwaukee, November 13-18, 1867, between the two synods. In the same year Iowa drew up a list of nine theses to answer the question: What is Essential to Church Unity? In this list, Iowa quite clearly shows that agreement is necessary only in fundamental doctrines (doctrines essential to salvation). Theses VI states: COMPLETE UNITY OF DOCTRINE HAS NEVER EXISTED IN THE CHURCH AND MUST NOT BE MADE THE CONDITION OF FELLOWSHIP. Theses VIII and IX state: ACCORDINGLY, THE SYMBOLS (OF THE LUTHERAN CHURCH) CONTAIN THE SUM OF DOCTRINES ON WHICH DOCTRINAL AGREEMENT IS NECESSARY...HOWEVER, THIS DOES NOT REFER TO ALL THE UNESSENTIAL OR INCIDENTALLY MENTIONED DOCTRINES IN THE CONFESSIONS, BUT TO ALL ARTICLES OF FAITH; THESE MUST BE RECOGNIZED AS DEFINITELY DEFINED BY THE CHURCH.[28]

Finally, in the "Davenport Theses," 1873, the Iowa Synod published twenty-one paragraphs stating its relation to the Missouri Synod. Among other things, Iowa stated that it did not agree with the Missouri Synod that the Church in its nature is invisible, but rather taught that the Church is also the communion of the Word and the Sacraments, and that in this sense it is at once visible and invisible. Iowa did not agree with Missouri that the Office of the Ministry originates through the transfer of the rights of the spiritual priesthood possessed by the individual Christian, but that the public office is transmitted by God through the congregation of believers in its entirely and essence by the means of the regular call. Regarding the Antichrist, Iowa maintained that it did not agree with Missouri's stand that the pope alone and exclusively is the Antichrist, but would only acknowledge that all the marks of Antichrist which the Symbolical Books enumerated agree with the pope's kingdom and members. In effect, Iowa left it up to the individual to believe what he would regard identifying the Antichrist in a particular individual or system.

On the matter of Chiliasm (a Greek term denoting the supposed 1,000 year reign of Christ on earth, a doctrine promoted especially by some of the sects), Iowa agreed with Missouri that every doctrine of the Millennium (Latin form of the Greek term) which would at any time rob the spiritual kingdom of grace and the cross and convert it into an outward, earthly and worldly kingdom, must be rejected. But Iowa also stated its belief that the idea could be tolerated that the reign of Christ with his saints for 1,000 years is still a matter of fulfillment in the future, thus not an error which necessitated exclusion from Iowa's church fellowship. Iowa also pointed out that the fundamental difference between Missouri and Iowa was a matter of "open question." Iowa recognized their existence, Missouri denied them. According to Iowa's definition, open questions are not doctrines which are necessary to salvation or to the existence of the church, but are such as are not touched upon in God's Word at all, or at least are not taught in perfectly clear passages of Scripture. Involved, therefore, are doctrines on which no consensus has been reached in the church, but with respect to which varieties of opinion have always been found among orthodox teachers. Iowa included the interpretation of Sunday as an open question. The Missouri Synod was willing to regard only those matters not discussed by Scripture as points upon which there could be differences of opinion, at the same time pointing out that there must be agreement in all doctrines drawn from Scripture, whether or not they bear on faith or life. There dare be only one interpretation.[29]

When the Missouri Synod was drawn into the controversy on Election and Conversion, Iowa made an official statement accusing Missouri of a fundamental error and heresy, which then constituted sufficient cause for separation.

To summarize the matters of controversy as they existed between the Missouri and Iowa Synod: The two synods differed as to doctrinal purity and doctrinal unity in the Church. Iowa taught that no church body can claim to be in possession of the whole truth, that doctrinal completeness should be desired and sought, but that it has not yet been attained; therefore, within certain limits doctrinal differences and various theological tendencies should not abolish church fellowship. And so, conforming to its peculiar position, the Iowa Synod had its open questions or problems on such doctrines as Sunday (does it take the place of the Old Testament Sabbath?), Antichrist, and Chiliasm (Millennialism). While the Missouri Synod maintained that Scripture speaks clearly and sufficiently on such matters, so that the Church can and ought to be in agreement—with all teaching the same thing—the Iowa Synod took the opposite position. Regarding the doctrines of Election and Conversion as taught by the Missouri Synod, the Iowa Synod saw in it the error of Calvinism (e.g. irresistible grace, double predestination, limited atonement).

Controversial matters between the Iowa and Missouri Synods were, of course, later transferred to the American Lutheran Church when that body was formed in 1930 through a merger of the Buffalo, Iowa, and Ohio Synods. The early issues that separated Iowa and Missouri could not be overlooked by Missouri when it dealt with the American Lutheran Church's proposal that fellowship be declared between the two bodies.

CONTROVERSY WITH THE OHIO SYNOD

In 1872 the Synods of Missouri, Ohio, Wisconsin, Minnesota, Illinois, and the Norwegian Synod, organized the Synodical Conference (see the separate chapter dealing with the history of the Conference). On January 25, 1878, the Ohio Synod through its Capital University at Columbus, Ohio, conferred on Walther the degree of Doctor of Divinity. In the same year the delegate synod of Missouri called Professor Loy of Columbus to St. Louis to fill the chair of English Theology. However, he chose not to accept the position. Two years later the Ohio Synod declared Dr. Walther a heretic. The bone of contention

636

between them was the related doctrines of Election and Conversion. Already in 1872 Dr. G. Fritschel of the Iowa Synod had insisted on "dissimilar conduct in the matter of conversion." Dr. Fritschel taught that God "earnestly endeavors to take away the resistance from some as well as from others, but that by some persons his gracious purpose is frustrated because they stubbornly and willfully resist the grace offered to them, whereas in the others God's work is accomplished because they do not willfully resist, but let God's work be done on themselves." Walther and Professor F.A. Schmidt (at the time a member of the faculty of the St. Louis Seminary) refuted Dr. Fritschel. Professor Schmidt, by the way, was German by birth and had been confirmed by Walther. He mastered the Norwegian language and taught for a time at the Norwegian College, Halfway Creek, Wisconsin. Later, he accepted the position of teaching in Norwegian at St. Louis, and in 1876 transferred to the Norwegian Seminary at Madison, Wisconsin. This information regarding Professor Schmidt is given here for the reason that he came to figure so strongly in the Predestination Controversy that raged for so many years, and which finally wrecked all hopes of uniting the Ohio Synod permanently with the Synodical Conference.

In 1877 Dr. Walther discussed the doctrine of Predestination before the Western Districts of the Missouri Synod on the basis of theses taken verbatim from the *Formula of Concord*. Theses III reads: THE LUTHERAN CHURCH TEACHES THAT IT IS FALSE AND WRONG TO TEACH THAT NOT THE MERCY OF GOD AND THE MOST HOLY MERIT OF CHRIST ALONE, BUT THAT ALSO IN US THERE IS A CAUSE OF THE ELECTION OF GOD FOR THE SAKE OF WHICH GOD HAS ELECTED US TO ETERNAL LIFE. DR. WALTHER DECLARED: GOD FORESAW NOTHING, ABSOLUTELY NOTHING, IN THOSE WHOM HE RESOLVED TO SAVE, WHICH MIGHT BE WORTHY OF SALVATION, AND EVEN IF IT BE ADMITTED THAT HE FORESAW SOME GOOD IN THEM, THIS, NEVERTHELESS, COULD NOT HAVE DETERMINED HIM TO ELECT THEM FOR THAT REASON, FOR AS THE SCRIPTURES TEACH, ALL GOOD IN MAN ORIGINATES IN HIM.[30] Walther also rejected the "unfortunate terminology of the dogmaticians of the seventeenth century" that God elected *intuitu fidei* (in view of faith), a term invented by Aegidius Hunnius. The meaning is that God chose a person to be saved because he foresaw that he would have persevering faith. Thus faith is made the cause of the election and not the *result*.

It was this discussion that led to the Predestination Controversy. Soon Walther's essay was on the market through the *Proceedings* of the Western District. The following year witnessed official approval granted by the Synodical Conference to the doctrinal contents of the district report, including Walther's essay. At the very beginning of the year 1879 Professor Schmidt presented Walther with his personal objections to the district report of 1877 and concluded: "I can no longer go with you...I dare no longer keep silence." Walther waited over a month to reply. Schmidt's next step was to inform District President Schwan that he would dissent publicly with the report of the Altenburg Convention if things did not change. Later in the year, at the Convention of the Northwestern District, Professor Schmidt began public agitation against the 1877 Altenburg Report. In spite of being admonished by Schwan to abide by the agreement of the Synodical Conference not to attack each other until every means of adjusting doctrinal differences had been exhausted, and in spite of being invited to meet with Pastor Fuerbringer of

Frankenmuth, Michigan, president of the Northern District, Schmidt went ahead with his public, printed attack.

In January 1880 he published a paper, *Altes und Neues* (Old and New), which continued for four years and had the purpose of combating the "Crypto-Calvinism" (Hidden-Calvinism) of Missouri. In his paper Schmidt violently assailed the statements of his former teacher. This action on the part of Schmidt was rather strange considering that in February 1878 he advocated at the Pastoral Conference of the Norwegians at Milwaukee, that the Norwegians withdraw from those who were opposing the Missouri Synod. Also bear in mind that again on May 7, 1878, some months after the Western District Report was published containing Walther's essay, Schmidt again wrote to President Wunder of his willingness to serve on the St. Louis faculty.

Schmidt was not elected to the St. Louis Seminary faculty. Elected in his place was Franz Pieper, who became the leading dogmatician of the Missouri Synod. In the fall of 1878 Schmidt's colleagues at Madison heard him complain of the "terrorism" of Walther. It was not long after that Schmidt corresponded his objections to the District Report directly to Walther. On September 29, 1880, a pastoral conference was held at Chicago, attended by 500 pastors of the Missouri Synod. The opposition against the synod was led by Schmidt; his brother-in-law, Allward; and Professor Stellhorn of Fort Wayne, together with Pastors Doermann and Ernst. The Missouri Synod appealed to Professor Lehmann of the Synodical Conference to call an extra meeting to prevent the controversy from becoming general. Lehmann refused. But after his death on December 1, 1880, Vice-President L. Larson (a professor) arranged a meeting of the theological faculties of the Synodical Conference at Milwaukee, January 5, 1881. After five days of fruitless debate, the members of the Ohio Synod withdrew, declaring that they were unable to stay. A motion to meet again during the year, and in the meantime to refrain from public polemics, failed to pass. Schmidt maintained that he was commanded of God to wage this war.

At the Fort Wayne Delegate Convention, held May 11-12, 1881, the Thirteen Theses of Walther were adopted as the official statement of the Missouri Synod on the doctrine involved. Walther and his co-workers felt that they should strengthen and fortify the minsterium of the synod; hence another meeting of the pastors was held at Fort Wayne, May 23-24. The dissenting voters thereupon left the Convention, and at Blue Island, Illinois, organized themselves as a conference and seceded from the synod. At a later Convention, held in September 1881 the Ohio Synod, which had aligned itself in February of that year with Schmidt, resolved to withdraw from the Synodical Conference. Two years later the Norwegian Synod withdrew in order to preserve peace within its own ranks. The Norwegians were divided in their attitudes toward Schmidt, who was their professor, against whom some fairly strong action had been taken. At the Synodical Conference meeting at Chicago, October 4, 1881, the delegates of the Missouri, Wisconsin, and Minnesota Synods had protested the seating of Schmidt as a lay delegate, as long as he would not admit that he caused divisions and offenses by his action of personally and without prenegotiations accusing the Synodical Conference of Calvinism. And when he refused to answer whether he came as friend or foe, Schmidt was denied recognition as a delegate.

From 1880 through 1884 the conflict raged bitterly, with its effects being felt for decades afterwards. The Thirteen Theses adopted by the Missouri Synod can be summarized as follows: (1) God's love is all-inclusive from eternity...and he created all men to salvation, not damnation. (2) Christ is everyone's Savior, redeeming all men from their sins. (3) God earnestly calls all men through the Means of Grace, having full intention of bringing them to faith, preserving and saving them. (4) Men are lost because they are unbelievers and resist the Word and grace of God. Damnation is man's fault, not God's. (5) Only those who believe unto the end, or at the end of their lives are brought to faith, are the elect. Election is particular not universal. (6) Divine election is immutable; every one of the elect will be saved. None can be lost. (7) It is highly dangerous for men to search out the eternal mysterious decree of God (of election). (8) Man should try from the revealed Word of God to become sure of his election and not (as Catholicism teaches) to seek it through a new and immediate revelation. (9) Election is not the mere foreknowledge of God as to which will be saved; is not the mere purpose of God to redeem and save mankind (thus not universal); does not concern temporary believers, is not the mere decree of God to save all those who believe to the end, (10) The cause of election is God's grace and the merit of Christ alone, not any good God foresaw in the elect, or the faith God foresaw in them. (11) Election is not the mere foresight or foreknowledge of the salvation of the elect, but also a cause of their salvation and what pertains to it. (12) God has kept secret and concealed much concerning this mystery for his own wisdom and knowledge alone, which no man should or can search out. Man should not try to search out the unrevealed or try to harmonize this doctrine with human reason. (13) This doctrine should not be kept secret from the people, but should be taught to Christians, it being wholesome and not dangerous to do so.[31]

To the Missouri Synod it was a matter of Professor Schmidt piling error upon error, and of the Ohio Synod taking part with him. The Missouri Synod accused Schmidt of teaching synergistic doctrines, for his teachings led to this end that man cooperates in his conversion. In 1887 the Ohio Synod expressed the following thought in its *Zeitblaetter*: IT IS UNDENIABLE THAT IN A CERTAIN RESPECT CONVERSION AND FINAL SALVATION ARE DEPENDENT UPON MAN AND NOT UPON GOD ALONE.[32]

Intersynodical conferences between the two synods were held at Watertown, Wisconsin, 1903; Detroit, 1904 and 1905; and Fort Wayne, 1906. In a tract produced in 1954 by the Wisconsin Synod Conference of Presidents, and titled, *Not By My Own Reason or Strength,* the following observation concerning theses conferences is made:

IN THESE DISCUSSIONS THE SYNODS WHICH WERE LATER TO FORM THE AMERICAN LUTHERAN CHURCH, CONTINUALLY SPOKE OF TWO KINDS OF RESISTANCE IN MAN: NATURAL RESISTANCE, WHICH WILL BE OVERCOME BY THE HOLY SPIRIT WITH THE RESULT THAT MAN IS CONVERTED; AND WILLFUL RESISTANCE, WHICH CANNOT BE OVERCOME BY THE HOLY SPIRIT, WITH THE RESULT THAT HE IS NOT CONVERTED. ALTHOUGH THEY TOO SPOKE OF MAN'S CONVERSION AS THE WORK OF GOD, THEY ALWAYS TRIED TO SOLVE THE PROBLEM, WHY SOME ARE CONVERTED AND OTHERS NOT, BY REASONING THAT IT MUST BE BECAUSE OF A DIF-

FERENCE IN MAN'S CONDUCT, SOME RESISTING ONLY NATURALLY, OTHERS WILL-
FULLY. THEY SPOKE OF A PRELIMINARY KIND OF GRACE, WHICH GOD GIVES TO
NATURAL MAN, ENABLING HIM TO AVOID WILLFUL RESISTANCE.[33]

The Synodical Conference representatives showed from Scripture and the
Lutheran Confessions that it is right to speak of only one kind of resistance,
namely, willful resistance; and that man's conduct, accordingly, in no way con-
tributes toward his conversion. The representatives of the Conference conceded
that through his natural powers man can decide to read and hear the Word of
Scripture, but he cannot dispose his heart to accept and believe it; he cannot
by his own reason or strength believe in Jesus Christ or come to him. For natural man is completely corrupt, an enemy of God, who resists his Holy Spirit.
Moreover, it was stressed by the Synodical Conference representatives that if
man's conversion is in any way dependent upon his conduct, it is no longer by
grace alone.

The year 1915 found the two sides again discussing the issues, with the
meetings continuing until 1928. At that time the Chicago Theses were proposed by the other side as a statement of agreement. However, when the Missouri Synod's examining committee studied the theses, which dealt particularly
with Conversion and Election, it found them unsatisfactory. The Reports and
Memorials, 1929, p. 132 reports: "...the distinction between natural and willful
resistance (was not) ruled out, so now as before our opponents can still say:
Converted is only he who resists 'naturally;' he who resists 'willfully' makes it
impossible for the Holy Spirit to convert him."

At the 1929 Missouri Synod Convention a new committee was elected and
assigned the task of drawing up the doctrinal statement of the synod. Events
had shown that the time had come for a definite statement to be formulated by
the synod, which would unequivocally rule out the distinction between natural
and willful resistance. The Report of the committee was adopted by the synod
in 1932 and is known as the Brief Statement. A statement concerning Election
and Conversion was included.

This brings us to yet another facet of the Missouri Synod's intriguing history:
union efforts between that synod and the American Lutheran Church (ALC).
But before we explore this history further, which we have already touched on
in our study of the ALC, we would do well to run through a brief review of the
part played by the Missouri Synod in the formation of the Synodical Conference. The union negotiations between the Missouri Synod and the ALC would
finally play an important role in the eventual demise of the Conference.

FORMING A NEW FEDERATION,
THE SYNODICAL CONFERENCE

Things were going well for the Missouri Synod as it entered the 1870's. The
atmosphere among the conservative Lutheran synods in the Midwest was a
cordial one, and the hand of the Missouri Synod was being sought in fellowship.
Already in 1866 the Joint Ohio Synod decided it wanted to promote friendly relations with Missouri. A colloquy followed two years later between the two
synods. In 1868 representatives of the Wisconsin and Missouri Synods met in

Milwaukee in the fall at the request of the Wisconsin Synod for the purpose of establishing doctrinal agreement. The following year a colloquy was held with the Illinois Synod in late summer, conducted at the request of its president. The 1869 Missouri Synod Convention recognized the existence of fellowship between it and the Wisconsin Synod, and the two bodies exchanged professors. However, the Missouri Synod declined at the same time to enter fellowship with the Ohio and the Illinois Synods. But then in the fall of 1870 the Ohio Synod declared its acceptance of Missouri's doctrine of the Office of the Ministry and announced its appointment of a committee to meet with similar committees of other synods with which it was in doctrinal agreement to confer on the possibility of cooperating in maintaining institutions of learning. President Walther was thus asked to appoint such a committee. A meeting held at Chicago in January 1871 between representatives of the Ohio, Norwegian, Missouri, and Wisconsin Synods resulted. The president of the Illinois Synod was present but did not take part, since his synod was still a member of the General Council. At this meeting, and in a subsequent meeting held later in the year, a constitution for a synodical conference was drafted. In the latter meeting the president of the Minnesota Synod, as well as delegates of the Illinois Synod, were present upon the invitation of Dr. Walther. Professor F.A. Schmidt pushed for the organization of a synodical conference. Hopes were high as the representatives resolved that the participating synods meet in order to organize and convene the first convention of the Synodical Conference, this meeting to be held in St. John's Church, Milwaukee, June 10-16, 1872. Before this fateful week came about, the Missouri Synod, having ratified its committee's action, recognized itself in fellowship with the Illinois Synod, which by then had severed its connections with the General Council. Missouri also held a colloquy with representatives of the Minnesota Synod, which produced favorable results. This synod had already the year before entered fellowship with the Wisconsin Synod.

When these doctrinally-agreed synods came together at Milwaukee in July, a new federation of synods was formed and adopted the official name, the Evangelical Lutheran Synodical Conference of North America. Professor C.F.W. Walther was elected the first president. For further information regarding the Missouri Synod's role in this federation of conservative Lutheran bodies, refer to the separate chapter dealing with the Synodical Conference. The doctrinal dispute, which finally led to the demise of the Conference, is outlined there.

THE MISSOURI SYNOD AND
THE AMERICAN LUTHERAN CHURCH

STRIDES TOWARD LUTHERAN UNITY

While the doctrines of Election and Conversion had remained divisive issues in a segment of the Lutheran Church, with the two sides trying to reach agreement through the discussion of theses and antitheses, other efforts toward achieving union between Lutheran bodies were meeting with success. A stride toward unity with the Scandinavian synods had been achieved by the Buffalo,

Ohio, and Iowa Synods when they accepted the Minneapolis Theses in 1925, which incorporated the doctrinal section of the Chicago Theses of 1919. This Theses had been adopted on March 11, 1919 by representatives of the Augustana Synod, the Iowa Synod, the Joint Synod of Ohio, the Lutheran Free Church, the Norwegian Church of America, the United Danish Church, and the United Lutheran Church. In 1930 the Buffalo, Iowa, and Ohio Synods merged to form the American Lutheran Church (ALC). And in the very year of its inception, the ALC entered a federation with the Augustana Evangelical Lutheran Church (Swedish), the Evangelical Lutheran Church (Norwegian), the Lutheran Free Church (Norwegian), and the United Evangelical Lutheran Church in America (Danish). This federation was called the American Lutheran Conference.

At the same time that doctrinal agreement by representatives of the Buffalo, Iowa, and Ohio Synods was being hammered out with the independent synods, resulting finally in the American Lutheran Conference, negotiations were also begun with the United Lutheran Church in America (org. 1918) on the left and with the Missouri Synod on the right, with hopes of reaching doctrinal agreement and of forming a union of almost all Lutherans in North America. Representatives of the Buffalo, Iowa, and Ohio Synods had met three or four times a year between 1920 and 1923 with Wisconsin Synod representatives and with the Missouri Synod's Committee on Lutheran Union. However, in 1923 the Missouri Synod resolved to discontinue doctrinal discussions. Intersynodical Theses drawn up during the years of discussion were rejected by Missouri in 1929 as insufficient and incomplete for the purpose of serving as a basis for doctrinal agreement. As was stated previously, the Missouri Synod appointed a new committee, gave it the task of writing a new doctrinal statement of the synod, and then adopted its work in 1932. The Brief Statement still stands as an official statement of doctrine in the Missouri Synod, and has been accepted by other synods as well.

AN OVERTURE BY THE AMERICAN LUTHERAN CHURCH

At the Missouri Synod's Cleveland Convention in 1935 a communication from the American Lutheran Church was placed before the delegates. It had become the endeavor of that body to seek to establish pulpit and altar fellowship with the Missouri Synod. Missouri's reply, in effect, was that it was willing to confer with other Lutheran bodies on problems of Lutheran union, with a view towards effecting true unity on the basis of the Word of God and the Lutheran Confessions. At the same time the delegates resolved to appoint a committee of five—to be known as the Committee on Lutheran Church Union—to meet with representatives of the American Lutheran Church. It was also stipulated that this group confer with the other members of the Synodical Conference and keep them informed on matters.

By the 1938 Convention the two bodies had met six times. The Missouri Synod's committee reported to its St. Louis Convention that agreement had been reached on such past disputed doctrines as Inspiration, Predestination and Conversion, Sunday, and the Office of the Public Administration of the

Means of Grace. On the other hand, it was reported that the American Lutheran Church asked for tolerance for certain teachings and interpretations concerning the doctrine of the Last Things, which the Missouri Synod had previously rejected.

MISSOURI'S RECOMMENDATIONS AND RESOLUTIONS REGARDING FELLOWSHIP

The Missouri Synod adopted recommendations which covered several aspects of fellowship negotiations: (a) That the Brief Statement, together with the Declaration (which the ALC Commission had written in answer to the Brief Statement) and the provisions of Missouri's committee presented at St. Louis, be regarded as the doctrinal basis for future fellowship between the two bodies. (b) That regarding nonfundamental doctrines (e.g. of the Last Things and Antichrist) the Missouri Synod endeavor to reach full agreement. (c) That in regards to the visible side of the church, the Missouri Synod's committee should work to attain uniform and scripturally acceptable terminology and teaching. It should be noted that the ALC's Declaration states that to speak of a visible side of the church when defining its essence "is not a false doctrine if by this visible side nothing else is meant than the use of the means of grace." (d) That true unity includes not only doctrinal agreement, but also agreement in practice. Thus the synod issued a call to the ALC for discipline to correct deviations from sound Biblical practice. The Missouri Synod referred specifically to antichristian lodges and antiscriptural pulpit and altar fellowship. All unionism was condemned.

Missouri also made recommendations regarding fellowship to the effect that (a) It will depend on the action taken by the individual synods as to the Brief Statement, the Declaration, and the Missouri Synod Committee's report. (b) It will depend on the ALC's success in establishing doctrinal agreement with all church bodies with whom it fellowshipped (members of the American Lutheran Conference). (c) The whole matter of fellowship must be taken to the other synods of the Synodical Conference for approval. (d) Pastors of both bodies are encouraged to meet and discuss doctrinal basis for union and questions of church practices. (e) Until fellowship is officially announced, no fellowship is to be practiced by pastors or congregations.[34]

The following statement recommended by the synod fairly well summarizes the 1938 St. Louis Resolution (which later fell out of favor): THAT SYNOD DECLARE THAT THE BRIEF STATEMENT OF THE MISSOURI SYNOD, TOGETHER WITH THE DECLARATION OF THE REPRESENTATIVES OF THE AMERICAN LUTHERAN CHURCH AND THE PROVISIONS OF THIS ENTIRE REPORT OF COMMITTEE 16 NOW BEING READ AND WITH SYNOD'S ACTIONS THEREUPON, BE REGARDED AS A DOCTRINAL BASIS FOR FUTURE CHURCH FELLOWSHIP BETWEEN THE MISSOURI SYNOD AND THE AMERICAN LUTHERAN CHURCH.

As shown above, there were issues that Missouri's Committee 16 needed to discuss with the ALC's Committee. Differences still existed, at least between some members of the ALC and the Missouri Synod. But then came the resolutions passed by the ALC at its 1938 Sandusky Convention (held in October).

There were items that caused apprehension to Missouri's Committee 16:
(1) THAT IT IS NEITHER POSSIBLE NOR NECESSARY TO AGREE IN ALL NONFUN-
DAMENTAL DOCTRINES. (2) THAT THE AMERICAN LUTHERAN CHURCH WILL
NOT GIVE UP ITS MEMBERSHIP IN THE AMERICAN LUTHERAN CONFERENCE. (3)
THE PHRASE "IN THE LIGHT OF," OCCURRING IN THE SENTENCE: "WE BELIEVE
THAT THE BRIEF STATEMENT VIEWED IN THE LIGHT OF OUR DECLARATION IS
NOT IN CONTRADICTION TO THE MINNEAPOLIS THESES." [ALSO, THE STATEMENT
THAT GOD "PURPOSES TO JUSTIFY THOSE WHO HAVE COME TO FAITH," DIS-
TURBED MANY IN THE SYNOD. WAS IT A WAY OF DENYING UNIVERSAL JUSTIFI-
CATION TAUGHT BY THE MEMBERS OF THE SYNODICAL CONFERENCE?][35]

Missouri's Committee on Lutheran Union became even more disturbed
when in 1939 it was informed that the Fellowship Commission of the ALC and
the ULCA had adopted the Pittsburgh Agreement. Especially disturbing was
the fact that the ULCA had never endorsed what Missouri's Brief Statement
declares on the subject of the Verbal Inspiration of Scripture. Nevertheless, the
ALC and ULCA were now in agreement regarding the doctrine of Inspiration—
in spite of the fact that Missouri was under the impression that it had reached
agreement with the ALC regarding this doctrine.[36] Article III of the Pittsburgh
Agreement (1940) contains this statement: THE BIBLE...IS PRIMARILY NOT A CODE
OF DOCTRINES, STILL LESS A CODE OF MORALS, BUT THE HISTORY OF GOD'S REVELA-
TION, FOR THE SALVATION OF MANKIND, AND OF MAN'S REACTION TO IT....[B]Y VIRTUE
OF A UNIQUE OPERATION OF THE HOLY SPIRIT...BY WHICH HE SUPPLIED TO THE HOLY
WRITERS CONTENT AND FITTING WORD...THE SEPARATE BOOKS OF THE BIBLE ARE
RELATED TO ONE ANOTHER, AND, TAKEN TOGETHER, CONSTITUTE A COMPLETE, ERROR-
LESS, UNBREAKABLE WHOLE OF WHICH CHRIST IS THE CENTER...THEY ARE RIGHTLY
CALLED THE WORD OF GOD. THIS UNIQUE OPERATION OF THE HOLY SPIRIT UPON THE
WRITERS IS NAMED INSPIRATION....[37]

The Missouri Synod was suspicious of the generalizing which it found in the
Pittsburgh document, which in declaring belief in the verbal inspiration of the
Scriptures, claimed that the Scriptures contain no errors or contradictions, but
are in all parts and words infallible truth. Missouri regarded this statement
as not being explicit enough in regards to what constitutes the verbal inspiration of Scripture.

OBSTACLES IN THE WAY OF
FELLOWSHIP WITH THE ALC

In March 1940, at a joint meeting, the ALC Church Commissioners asked
for a statement from the Missouri Synod listing all obstacles yet in the way of
fellowship. Missouri listed the following obstacles: (1) The ALC's membership
in the American Lutheran Conference. The ALC's sister synods must occupy
Missouri's position. (2) Missouri's membership in the Synodical Conference.
There would be no fellowship if the other synods could not share the fellowship.
(3) The points of the Sandusky Resolutions aforementioned, plus the Declaration's statement, viz., that God "purposes to justify those who have come to
faith." (4) The ALC's approach to the ULCA, which body did not share Missouri's doctrinal position. (5) Church practices...lack of uniformity of practice

with doctrine.[38]

The ALC's Detroit Convention in 1940 failed to produce satisfaction regarding all the obstacles to fellowship that Missouri had outlined. In the Minneapolis Convention of the American Lutheran Conference later in the same year, the ALC made no attempt to bring that body to the same doctrinal position that it held. Instead, the ALC assured the Conference that it had no intention of leaving it.

In 1941 the Committee of the Missouri Synod reported: "The question arises whether there is not a fundamental difference between the American Lutheran Church and our Synod on the meaning of Confessional loyalty." The Wisconsin Synod and the small Norwegian Synod (the Evangelical Lutheran Synod) requested the Missouri Synod to cease negotiating with the ALC. Still, in spite of the discouragement, Missouri voted in 1941 to continue its search for unity with the ALC. Missouri also took note of the fact that the Synodical Conference had earnestly asked them to consider framing only one document between the Joint Committees. At this convention the synod also reaffirmed its St. Louis Declaration regarding "agreement in practice."

CONTINUING NEGOTIATIONS WITH THE ALC IN SPITE OF OBSTACLES

In its 1942 Convention at Mendota, Illinois, the ALC declared its readiness to establish pulpit and altar fellowship with either the Missouri Synod or the ULCA, or with both, on the basis of the Pittsburgh Agreement, the Brief Statement in the light of the Declaration, and its own Declaration. In 1943 the Wisconsin Synod, disturbed over what it felt was a clearly defined liberal movement in the ALC, while at the same time striving to maintain fellowship with the Missouri Synod, addressed to it the following memorial: IN VIEW OF THE UNIONISTIC ATTITUDE OF THE AMERICAN LUTHERAN CHURCH, WHICH HAS BECOME INCREASINGLY EVIDENT, WILL YOU NOT AGREE THAT FURTHER NEGOTIATIONS FOR ESTABLISHING CHURCH FELLOWSHIP COULD ONLY UNDERMINE THE TESTIMONY THAT HAS PREVIOUSLY BEEN GIVEN, AND SHOULD THEREFORE BE DISCONTINUED FOR THE TIME BEING?[40]

The Missouri Synod did not reply to this question. Instead it reported to its 1944 Convention that the first steps in preparing a single document were completed and that this document called "Doctrinal Affirmation" had been presented in a preliminary way to the ALC Commissioners with the promise by them that they Affirmation would be placed before their 1944 Convention. This document was, to a great extent, a combination of the Brief Statement and phraseology added from the Declaration. The members of the Missouri Synod were instructed to be prepared to vote on the Doctrinal Affirmation at its 1947 Convention. If accepted by both bodies, it would supercede all previous doctrinal documents and resolutions accepted by the Missouri Synod in 1938 and 1941. However, nothing came of these great hopes.

In 1946 the ALC, meeting at Appleton, Wisconsin, rejected the Doctrinal Affirmation as "not generally acceptable." The ALC also declared that it "despaired of attaining Lutheran unity by way of additional doctrinal formulations and reformulations."

However, in 1947 the ALC Commissioners issued "A Friendly Invitation," repeating its 1938 resolution, which declared the Brief Statement along with its Declaration as sufficient doctrinal basis for fellowship. While they felt that discussions had not turned up any fundamental doctrinal differences to prohibit fellowship between the two bodies, they also expressed the belief that "there is an area where there exists an allowable and wholesome latitude of theological opinion on the basis of the teachings of the Word of God." The demand for a unified statement of doctrine as a basis for fellowship was branded as a "threat to evangelical liberty of conscience."

In its 1947 Convention the Missouri Synod heard the report by its Committee on Doctrinal Unity, listing three impediments to union with the ALC: (1) The manifest lack of doctrinal unity. (2) The difference in conviction regarding the degree of doctrinal unity required for fellowship. (3) The membership of the ALC in the American Lutheran Conference.

THE "COMMON CONFESSION"—
ADVERSE REACTION TO IT

The Missouri Synod set aside its 1938 union document and resolutions, not retracting them but rather considering them as no longer adequate. (The St. Louis Resolution recognized Missouri's Brief Statement and the ALC's Declaration as a doctrinal basis for future fellowship between the two bodies.) At the same time the synod decided to go ahead with negotiations with the ALC. Quite evidently the ALC no longer despaired of attaining Lutheran unity by way of "additional formulations and reformulations." For its committee went ahead with Missouri's committee and by 1950 had succeeded in drawing up a new document, which bore the name "Common Confession." This document was adopted by both bodies the same year. The ALC adopted the Common Confession after only a few minutes of study and without debate. The Missouri Synod resolution reads:

WHEREAS, BY THE GRACE OF GOD THE COMMITTEE ON DOCTRINAL UNITY OF THE SYNOD AND COMMITTEE ON FELLOWSHIP OF THE AMERICAN LUTHERAN CHURCH HAVE JOINTLY PRODUCED THE DOCUMENT KNOWN AS THE "COMMON CONFESSION,"...RESOLVED, THAT WE REJOICE AND THANK GOD THAT THE "COMMON CONFESSION" SHOWS THAT AGREEMENT HAS BEEN ACHIEVED IN THE DOCTRINES TREATED BY THE TWO COMMITTEES.[41]

The 1950 Convention of the Missouri Synod had instructed its Unity Committee to continue negotiations with the ALC Commissioners on matters not covered by the Common Confession (e.g. union, lodgery, and practical matters). The result was Common Confession Part II, a longer document than Part I. In Missouri's 1953 Houston Convention the following resolution was adopted:

WHEREAS, PART II OF THE "COMMON CONFESSION" IS INTENDED AS A SUPPLE-MENT TO PART I; THEREFORE BE IT RESOLVED, THAT FOR PURPOSES OF STUDY PARTS I AND II OF THE "COMMON CONFESSION" HEREAFTER BE TREATED AS ONE DOCUMENT, WITH THE UNDERSTANDING THAT PART II HAS NOT BEEN

ADOPTED.[42]

This convention voted to take no action on the overtures received regarding the Common Confession, Part I, but urged all to study the Confession in its present form. It also asked the Wisconsin and Norwegian Synods, and its own protesting members to wait until the synod took action at its 1956 Convention, before taking any disciplinary action.

But the Common Confession, Part II, did not solve the problems as far as the two protesting sister synods were concerned, and relationships became more strained. In 1953 the Wisconsin Synod adopted a resolution which listed among other things the Missouri Synod's act of reaffirming its acceptance of the Common Confession as a "settlement of past differences which in fact are not settled," as threatening the continuation of fellowship and even of the continued existence of the Synodical Conference."[43] The Norwegians took exception especially to the fact that the Common Confession did not cover the doctrine of Objective Justification or the doctrine of Sunday.

PROSPECTS OF FELLOWSHIP
(MISSOURI/ALC) COME TO NAUGHT:

In the meantime the ALC found itself on the verge of merging with the Evangelical Lutheran Church (ELC), the United Evangelical Lutheran Church (UELC), and the Lutheran Free Church (LFC). Much work had been in progress since the 1950 Convention of the ALC when that body voted in favor of such a merger. In its 1954 Beatrice, Nebraska Convention, the ALC committed itself to vote on the merger question in its 1956 Convention. The merger of the four out of five bodies of the American Lutheran Conference seemed a strong possibility. (Note: The Augustana Synod leaned toward fellowship with the ULCA. The Lutheran Free Church, while not joining the merger at first, did so later.) Enthusiasm ran high at Beatrice. Dr. Edward Schram reported it thus in the November 13, 1954 issue of the *Lutheran Standard*: THE CONVENTION MOOD WAS THE ECCLESIASTICAL COUNTERPART OF THE FOOTBALL CROWD MOOD THAT SHOUTS, "WE WANT A TOUCHDOWN!" "WE WANT A MERGER!" AS TO THE POSSIBLE MERGER DATE, DR. SCHRAM STATED: "ABOUT ALL ONE CAN SAY WITH CERTAINTY IS, 'WE ARE ON THE WAY...AND GATHERING SPEED AS WE GO.'" THE FELLOWSHIP COMMITTEE WAS INSTRUCTED TO "CONTINUE TO WORK CONSTRUCTIVELY TOWARD FULL UNITY AND ULTIMATE PULPIT AND ALTAR FELLOWSHIP.

On a larger scale this "constructive" work finally came to naught. The ALC was not able at the time to work out a merger with the ULCA. Hopes of working out agreement with the Missouri Synod were also dashed at that body's 1956 St. Paul Convention. The synod's resolutions pertaining to the Common Confession directly reflected its reaction to the ALC's proposed merger with three of the other bodies of the American Lutheran Conference. However, the synod's action did not rescind the Common Confession but simply set it aside from use as a "functioning union document."[44] Regarding the Common Confession, the synod passed these resolutions: (1) THAT HEREAFTER THE COMMON CONFESSION PART I AND II BE NOT REGARDED OR EMPLOYED AS A FUNCTIONING BASIC DOCUMENT TOWARD THE ESTABLISHMENT OF ALTAR AND PULPIT FELLOWSHIPS WITH OTHER CHURCH BODIES, AND BE IT FURTHER RESOLVED, (2) THAT THE COMMON CON-

FESSION; ONE DOCUMENT COMPOSED OF PARTS I AND II, BE RECOGNIZED AS A STATE-
MENT IN HARMONY WITH THE SACRED SCRIPTURES AND THE LUTHERAN CONFES-
SIONS.* The Missouri Synod also passed the following resolutions: THAT WE
AGREE NOT TO ENTER DISCUSSIONS OR NEGOTIATIONS WITH OTHER LUTHERAN SYN-
ODS WITHOUT HAVING INFORMED THE SISTER SYNODS OF THE SYNODICAL CONFER-
ENCE OF OUR INTENTIONS AND WITHOUT HAVING INVITED AND URGED THEM TO JOIN
WITH US IN THESE DISCUSSIONS.**

On April 22, 1960, The American Lutheran Church (TALC, which later be-
came simply the American Lutheran Church was created by the merger of the
American Lutheran Church (the "old" one) with the Evangelical Lutheran
Church (ELC), and with the United Evangelical Lutheran Church (UELC).
The Constituting Convention of the new church was held April 22-24, 1960.
The American Lutheran Church (the "new" one) officially began to function on
January 1, 1961. The Missouri Synod would later declare itself in fellowship
with this body, and still later, undo this action.

THE MISSOURI SYNOD AND
THE LUTHERAN COUNCIL U.S.A

In its June 1965 Detroit Convention at Cobo Hall, the Missouri Synod took
a step which only a few years earlier would have been considered out of the
question: it voted (about 10-1) to join the new Lutheran cooperative agency
which brought together in formal organization 95% of the Lutherans in the
United States and Canada. The Lutheran Council in the U.S.A. (LCUSA)
began operations on January 1, 1967 (refer to the separate chapter:
LUTHERAN COOPERATIVE AGENCIES). A Missouri Synod clergyman, Dr.
C. Thomas Spitz, Jr., was nominated for election as the first general secretary
of the Council by the Inter-Lutheran Consultation.

The movement to form such a Council began in 1958 with an invitation from
the National Lutheran Council (NLC) membership extended to Lutheran bodies not in the NLC. The invitation proposed a meeting for the purpose of discussing just what was necessary to arrive at cooperation between all Lutherans
in America. In the works were the mergers that would form the Lutheran
Church in America (LCA), and The American Lutheran Church (commonly referred to as the "new" ALC), with the result that the NLC would be composed
of just two bodies, which many felt hardly warranted the continuation of this
special Council. Could a new cooperative agency be structured that would
bring other Lutheran bodies together in organization with the LCA and the
ALC? Eyes were cast especially in the direction of the Missouri Synod. This
synod accepted the extended invitation, and over the next few years its representatives joined with the Council in three meetings. The Wisconsin Synod
also received an invitation to the NLC meetings to discuss cooperation between
all Lutheran bodies in America. The Wisconsin Synod declined the invitation
and faulted the Missouri Synod for accepting the invitation extended to it, and
cited that synod's participation in the NLC meetings as evidence of having a
new position on church fellowship. In a booklet titled: *Entrenched Unionistic
Practices*, authorized by The Commission on Doctrinal Matters of the Wiscon-

sin Evangelical Lutheran Synod, Oscar Siegler points out: IT IS ONE THING TO JOIN SOMEONE IN WORSHIP OR PRAYER WHO HAS FALLEN INTO AN ERROR OR FALSE DOCTRINE BUT DOES NO YET DEFEND AND SPREAD HIS ERROR IN SPITE OF ALL ADMONITION. BUT THE OFFICIALS AND THEOLOGIANS OF THE NATIONAL LUTHERAN COUNCIL KNOW WHERE THEY STAND. THEY MAKE NO SECRET OF IT. THEIR SYNODS HAVE DEFENDED THEIR POSITION FOR THE LAST SEVERAL GENERATIONS. PART OF THEIR POSITION IS TO INSIST ON JOINT PRAYER, JOINT DEVOTION, IN ANY JOINT MEETING TO WHICH WE HAVE BEEN INVITED IN RECENT YEARS. THAT IS IN HARMONY WITH THEIR POSITION. IT IS NOT NECESSARY, THEY HOLD, TO BE IN FULL DOCTRINAL AGREEMENT TO EXERCISE THAT KIND OF FELLOWSHIP. SAD TO SAY THAT HAS ALSO NOW BECOME THE POSITION OF SOME OF THE SYNODS IN THE NLC: THE GENERAL POSITION OF SOME OF THESE SYNODS HAD BEEN ONE OF TOLERANCE TOWARD FALSE AND CONTRADICTORY TEACHINGS. WHILE ALL OF THEM HAVE SOUGHT IN THEIR WAY, TO PROCLAIM AND SPREAD THE SAVING GOSPEL OF CHRIST, THE EARLY LEADERS OF OUR SYNOD, AS WELL AS THE MISSOURI SYNOD, FOUND IT NECESSARY TO CHARGE PARTICULARLY THE UNITED LUTHERAN CHURCH AND THE AUGUSTANA LUTHERAN CHURCH WITH A DANGEROUS INDIFFERENCE TOWARD CHRIST'S WORD. THE INEVITABLE OUTCOME OF SUCH INDIFFERENCE IS ALL TOO OBVIOUS TODAY. GROSS FORMS OF FALSE DOCTRINE ARE NOW TOLERATED IN THE PERIODICALS, PULPITS, AND SEMINARIES OF THESE LUTHERAN SYNODS. IT IS NOT UNCOMMON TO HEAR PASTORS AND THEOLOGIANS OF ONE OR THE OTHER OF THESE SYNODS DENYING THAT THE BIBLE IS GOD'S WORD IN ALL ITS PARTS. AS MIGHT BE EXPECTED, ALL OF THE NATIONAL LUTHERAN COUNCIL SYNODS HAVE BEEN MOVING CLOSER INTO SUCH GENERAL PROTESTANT GROUPINGS AS THE WORLD COUNCIL OF CHURCHES, REPRESENTING ALL SHADES AND DEGREES OF HERESY AND FALSE DOCTRINE, INCLUDING THE DENIAL OF CHRIST'S VIRGIN BIRTH, CHRIST'S DEITY, CHRIST'S RESURRECTION, TO MENTION BUT A FEW. AT ITS LAST CONVENTION THE UNITED LUTHERAN CHURCH RESOLVED TO STUDY THE MATTER OF INTER-COMMUNION WITH OTHER PROTESTANT CHURCHES.[45]

The purpose of the exploratory meeting called by the NLC was stated thus: "...in order to examine present cooperative activities in American Lutheranism and the possibility for extension of such activities..."[46] The Missouri Synod's acceptance of this invitation was also destined to have a direct bearing on the demise of the Synodical Conference. Not only did the Wisconsin Synod decline the invitation, the Evangelical Lutheran Synod also chose to not participate in the meetings with the NLC and the Missouri Synod. In declining, the president of the ELS stated the following:

...WE FIND IT IMPOSSIBLE TO BE A LONG IN THE PLANNING AND ERECTION OF THIS PROPOSED NEW LUTHERAN STRUCTURE, AND ONCE IT IS BUILT, WE WOULD FIND IT IMPOSSIBLE TO DWELL IN IT, ON THE BASIS PROPOSED IN THE SIX ESSAYS AND OTHER MATERIAL SENT WITH YOUR INVITATION...I HAVE CAREFULLY STUDIED THE SIX ESSAYS PRESENTED AT YOUR PREVIOUS MEETINGS, AND I FIND NO REAL AGREEMENT BETWEEN THE MISSOURI AND THE NLC REPRESENTATIVES ON THE QUESTION OF WHAT CONSTITUTES "THE DOCTRINE OF THE GOSPEL." AND WHEN I NOTE THE CAREFUL MODIFICATIONS ATTACHED TO THE WORD "CONSENSUS," ESPECIALLY IN YOUR "REPORT TO THE CHURCHES...," I REALIZE THAT YOU ARE MAKING NO CLAIM TO HAVING ACHIEVED DOCTRINAL UNITY. IN THIS PROPOSED NEW ASSOCIATION THERE IS TO BE A RECOGNITION OF ONE ANOTHER AS BRETHREN IN THE FAITH, FIRST, THROUGH MEMBERSHIP AS A STATUS

649

OF FELLOWSHIP, AND THEN THROUGH WORSHIP AND CHURCH WORK AS AN AC-
TIVITY OF FELLOWSHIP. WHILE DOCTRINAL TALKS ARE TO BE MANDATORY, THE
FORMATION OF THE ORGANIZATION ITSELF IS A PRE-JUDGING OF THE OUTCOME,
ESPECIALLY ON THE DOCTRINE OF CHURCH FELLOWSHIP, A PRACTICAL APPLI-
CATION OF THE PRINCIPLE THAT FIRST ONE MAY PRACTICE FELLOWSHIP, AT
LEAST IN SOME AREAS, AND THEN WORK FOR A POSSIBLE EVENTUAL DOCTRINAL
UNITY...AS NOTED ABOVE, YOUR INVITATION IS TO WORK FOR THE ESTABLISH-
MENT OF AN ORGANIZATION COMMITTED TO THE RECOGNITION OF ONE ANOTHER
AS BRETHREN IN THE FAITH, EVEN THOUGH DOCTRINAL UNITY DOES NOT EXIST.
THIS IS THE SAME UNIONISTIC BASIS ON WHICH THE NATIONAL LUTHERAN
COUNCIL WAS FOUNDED, AND TO WHICH WE OF THE SYNODICAL CONFERENCE
HAVE CONSISTENTLY OBJECTED. WE CANNOT, AND WILL NOT, TAKE WHAT GOD
HAS NOT GIVEN. I COR. 1:10; ROM. 16:17; MATT. 7:15; 2 JO. 9,10.[47]

The ELS 1963 Convention approved the action of its president. The Wisconsin Synod, as was pointed out, for the same doctrinal reasons declined the invitation. The Slovak Synod (SELC) accepted the invitation, first as observers,
and then later as full-fledged participants. It joined with Missouri in 1967
when the Council was formed, and later became the Slovak non-geographic
District of the Missouri Synod.

The Missouri Synod met with the representatives of the NLC in three exploratory meetings before an invitation was extended to other Lutheran bodies,
including the Wisconsin and Evangelical Lutheran Synods, to take part in
meetings designated to look into the possibilities of forming a new council. Two
such meetings were held between Missouri and the NLC in 1960, and one was
held in 1961. The first two meetings discussed the questions of the unity of the
Church and subscription to the Lutheran Confessions, while the third meeting
considered the question: What kind of cooperation is possible in view of discussions to date? The NLC rejected Missouri's stand that doctrinal unity is a prerequisite for fellowship. It also rejected the idea of joining hands in Christian
service while going separate ways as far as church fellowship was concerned.
Instead, the NLC essayist called for church fellowship, and then within that
framework of things work to iron out doctrinal differences. The NLC's attitude
was that Lutheranism in the United States could best meet the needs of the
hour if the Lutherans strove for doctrinal unity "as pledged brothers and not
as uneasy strangers."

The discussions led to an agreement among the participating representatives that a sufficient degree of unity existed between the participating
churches to make possible some form of cooperation. An agency was then proposed that would have as its purposes: (1) to carry on theological discussions,
and (2) to carry on cooperation in specified areas of Christian services. It was
the first point, especially, that seemed to win the hearts of many in the Missouri Synod toward this new cooperative agency. Many felt that by joining this
new agency a forum for doctrinal discussions with the other Lutheran bodies
would be opened. Others, however, felt that such doctrinal discussions could
be carried on outside the framework of a cooperative agency, which might actually involve a compromise of Missouri's doctrinal stand.

When all was said and done, he Missouri Synod was willing enough to strive
for doctrinal unity as "pledged brothers and not as uneasy stranger." But par-

ticipating in the formation of the new Lutheran Council, and finally joining it as a member, meant that the Missouri Synod had abandoned, at least partially, very old principles regarding church fellowship and unionism. It was no over-statement of facts when Dr. John H. Tietjen (at the time, president of the St. Louis Seminary) wrote in his book *Which Way to Lutheran Unity?* that Missouri's discussions with the NLC were important for the reason that they gave evidence of a change from Missouri's traditional approach, and that the principle which made it possible for the synod to enter the cooperative agency could "have far-reaching consequences for Missouri's relations not only with Lutheran groups but with other denominations."

There was the fear that the Missouri Synod's participation in the LCUSA could very well be the beginning of a domino effect in its relation to such groups as the Lutheran World Federation and the World Council of Churches, as well as the National Council of Churches U.S.A. And yet, the resurgence of conservatism in Missouri, which had been in evidence since the beginning of the second half of the 1970's forestalled such a domino effect.

At any rate, the discussions between the representatives of the Missouri Synod and the NLC revealed that "there are still points of doctrine which require further systematic study." Still, as Dr. Tietjen pointed out, the representatives found that "there is far greater extent of consensus on the subjects discussed than had been generally realized." And for that reason Missouri's representatives too thought further investigation of establishing a new agency was warranted.

In 1962 all three bodies—two of them brand new (LCA, TALC)—had conventions, heard the reports of their representatives, and approved the appointment of seven representatives to consider further the formation of a cooperative agency and to draw up a constitution. It was at this juncture that the Slovaks joined the effort with their representatives. The group of representatives called themselves the Inter-Lutheran Consultation.

The LCUSA Constitution made theological discussions mandatory for all participating bodies. One of the aims was to continue the discussions which had taken place previously between the Missouri Synod and the NLC churches, which then had met with some degree of success. The Constitution proposed five areas of cooperation besides the mandatory theological discussions: welfare services, public relations, education services, mission services, and services to military personal.

Note carefully the above list of services and bear in mind that the participating bodies would be associating in this agency and carrying out these services, not because they had declared themselves in doctrinal agreement, but on the basis of their common subscription to the Scriptures and the Lutheran Confessions. Participating in the LCUSA did indeed mark a change in the attitude of the Missouri Synod. It has often been cited that Missouri has from its inception aimed at uniting the Lutheran bodies in America. *Der Lutheraner* was published for this very purpose. But even the most causal student of the synod's history will have to acknowledge that from its beginning the Missouri Synod, under the direction of its conservative leaders, was a foremost promoter of what can be termed true Lutheran unity. Missouri's conservative leaders ever demanded that union between churches must be based on unity in doctrine and practice that is in full accord with Scripture. Dr. F. Pfotenhauer in 1936 pointed out that unionism is:...FELLOWSHIP BETWEEN CHURCHES WITHOUT CORRESPONDING HARMONY AND UNITY OF CONFESSIONS AND FAITH. IT IS TOLERATION OF FALSE DOCTRINE, MUTUAL RECOGNITION AS BRETHREN OF THE FAITH BY THOSE WHO PUSH ASIDE AND IGNORE DIFFERENCES IN DOCTRINE. THIS MUTUAL RECOGNITION AS BRETHREN OF THE FAITH IS THEN GIVEN EXPRESSION WHEN MEMBERS OF DIFFERENT CONFESSIONS BAND THEMSELVES TOGETHER IN ONE CONGREGATION, UNITE IN CHURCH FEDERATIONS, OR AT LEAST PRACTICE PULPIT, ALTAR, OR PRAYER-FELLOWSHIP, AND UNDERTAKE UNITED EFFORTS IN CHURCH WORK. THE ESSENTIAL THING IN UNIONISM IS THAT DIFFERENCES IN DOCTRINE ARE MINIMIZED AND IGNORED AND AS A MATTER OF PRINCIPLE THE SHARP DISTINCTION BETWEEN TRUTH AND ERROR IS REMOVED.[48]

Related to the question of what constitutes unionism as defined by the Missouri Synod is also the question of dangers which an orthodoxy body such as Missouri subjects itself to by cooperating with others who are not of the same doctrinal and polity persuasion. The same publication quoted above refers to a statement made by then Synod President, Dr. John W. Behnken, at Rockford, Illinois, on November 14, 1946: TODAY EFFORTS ARE BEING PUT FORTH TOWARD FELLOWSHIP VIA COOPERATION. COOPERATIVE EFFORTS HAVE BEEN PROCLAIMED AND HERALDED AS HARBINGERS OF LUTHERAN FELLOWSHIP AND LUTHERAN UNION. LET ME SPEAK FRANKLY. IF SUCH COOPERATION INVOLVES JOINT WORK IN MISSIONS, IN CHRISTIAN EDUCATION, IN STUDENT WELFARE WORK, IN JOINT SERVICES CELEBRATING GREAT EVENTS, <u>THEN COOPERATION IS JUST ANOTHER NAME FOR PULPIT, ALTAR, AND PRAYER FELLOWSHIP. WITHOUT DOCTRINAL AGREEMENT THIS SPELLS COMPROMISE.</u>[49] (*emphasis added*)

It is surprising that the good Doctor later seemed to favor Missouri's participation in the LCUSA, a viewpoint that he held mainly for the reason that mandatory theological discussions were required. In the chapter outlining the Lutheran Cooperative Agencies, we have already seen how cooperating with one another in rendering Christian services also carries implications for joint worship.

At its 1965 Detroit Convention, held at Cobo Hall, the Missouri Synod voted to become a member of the LCUSA, which began its official functioning on January 1, 1967. Four church bodies were in its membership: The American Lutheran Church, the Lutheran Church in America, the Lutheran Church-Missouri Synod, and the Synod of Evangelical Lutheran Churches. There was, of course, backlash toward Missouri's participation in the new Council. It began at the Detroit Convention and continued through the years that followed. Loudly voiced demands were heard that the synod not continued in the cooperative agency. The demands were defeated and the synod chose to remain a member.

The Missouri Synod entered the LCUSA with the purpose that doctrinal talks aimed at church unity be given top priority. However, two years after Missouri voted to enter the Council, Dr. C. Thomas Spitz, Jr.—a member of the synod, and general Secretary of the Council—reported the following to the synod's New York Convention: WE DARE NOT MAKE MORE OF THE COUNCIL THAN IT IS. IT DOES NOT ANSWER ANY OF THE PRESSING QUESTIONS REGARDING OTHER RELATIONSHIPS WITHIN CHRISTENDOM. NOR DOES IT EVEN WITHIN LUTHERANISM PRO-

VIDE FOR OR ACKNOWLEDGE THAT UNITY WHICH IS OUR LORD'S PRAYER FOR HIS CHURCH AND GIFT TO HIS CHURCH.

MISSOURI'S FELLOWSHIP WITH THE AMERICAN LUTHERAN CHURCH

THAT WHICH WOULDN'T COME ABOUT, FINALLY CAME ABOUT

Prior to the LCUSA joint cooperative ventures had resulted in strides toward more complete fellowship. The merger of the three Lutheran bodies in 1918 producing the United Lutheran Church in American (ULCA) was stimulated to a great extent by the joint work that was done among the three bodies in producing liturgical works and a hymnal. When the Missouri Synod broke off doctrinal discussions with the American Lutheran Church in 1956 it resolved not to continue the discussions until after the proposed merger forming the "new" American Lutheran Church had been completed. Responding, however, to an overture by the ALC's Joint Union Committee, the synod at its 1959 Convention authorized discussions. The Lutheran Church in America (LCA) was also invited to participate in the talks, but declined to do so, citing the danger involved to the formation of the new Lutheran Council by engaging in negotiations for establishing altar and pulpit fellowship. The LCA felt that first the new Council should be formed. So then, discussions went ahead between the Missouri Synod and the ALC. However, they did invite the Synod of Evangelical Lutheran Churches (SELC, a Slovak body) to participate. It should be noted that this body was welcomed into the Lutheran Church-Missouri Synod at its 1971 Convention (see the separate chapter on SELC). Merger of the 20,000 member SELC with the 2.5 million member LCMS took place officially on January 1st of that year, with SELC becoming the non-geographical Slovak District of the Missouri Synod.

The 1969 Denver Convention of the Missouri Synod was a tradition-shattering Convention in more than one way. First, by a fairly close vote (522 or 54.4% to 438 or 45.6%) the synod resolved to accept the ALC's offer of fellowship. "With joy and praise to God" for "creating this unity among us" the delegates declared their church body to be in altar and pulpit fellowship with the ALC. The expressions of fellowship were listed as follows: (1) Preachers may be invited to preach in churches of the other body. (2) Congregations of the two bodies may hold joint worship services. (3) Inter-Communion as long as this does not violate principles regulating Communion practices in the host congregation is allowed. (4) Transfers of membership from one body to the other are allowed.

Dr. Jacob A.O. Preus, who was elected at the Denver Convention to succeed Dr. Oliver Harms as president of the synod, opposed fellowship with the ALC. The irony of the whole situation was that Dr. Harms laid his presidency on the line for backing the fellowship move and was defeated for reelection, while Dr. Preus, who vigorously opposed the move to establish fellowship with the ALC was chosen as his successor...and then...the Convention followed the counsel of Dr. Harms and others by voting to declare itself in fellowship with the ALC.

A right wing element in the synod, which was evident already prior to the

653

Cleveland Convention in 1962 was becoming a political force that would influence future decisions of the synod. Conservatives were being placed on important boards and committees, which facilitated bringing the traditional conservative views to bear in shaping synod policy. In the process, the leadership of President Harms was seriously challenged, with the result that he lost out to the more conservative J.A.O. Preus.[50]

In the 1971 Milwaukee Convention the Missouri Synod voted to continue its altar, pulpit ties with the ALC. This, in spite of the fact that the ALC in the meantime had voted to ordain women to the ministry, something the Missouri Synod strongly, officially opposed in convention. Demands were also made that the synod withdraw from the Lutheran Council in the U.S.A. (Refer to the history of the LCUSA in the chapter: LUTHERAN COOPERATIVE AGENCIES.) But while these demands were rejected, the synod did order in-depth studies to be made of the Council's operations and its theological stance. The 1975 Milwaukee Convention resolved: THAT THE LCMS CONTINUE MEMBERSHIP IN THE LUTHERAN COUNCIL IN THE U.S.A. ON A SELECTED PROGRAM BASIS IN AN EFFORT TO ACHIEVE ITS ORIGINAL OBJECTIVES OF MEMBERSHIP...THAT THE SYNOD REQUEST THE COUNCIL TO INTENSIFY EFFORTS TO "SEEK TO ACHIEVE THEOLOGICAL CONSENSUS IN A SYSTEMATIC AND CONTINUING WAY ON THE BASIS OF SCRIPTURE AND THE WITNESS OF THE LUTHERAN CONFESSIONS."

The synod in 1971 also voted to cooperate in the production of a common service book and hymnal that proposed to unify the worship of most of the Lutherans in North America, if accepted by the participating bodies. However, Missouri ultimately turned down official adoption of the new hymnal and set itself on the course of compiling its own version.

The delegates to the 1971 Synod Convention expressed their readiness to meet officially with the Lutheran Church in America to find doctrinal agreement that could lead to fellowship with that body. On the other hand, the synod, as before, rejected membership in the Lutheran World Federation and also membership in the National and the World Council of Churches, ordering a continuing study of the matter. Later, doctrinal discussions were held with the Lutheran Church in America, engaging the services of the Division of Theological Studies of the Lutheran Council in the U.S.A.

FELLOWSHIP WITH THE ALC
MOVES TO SHAKY GROUND

A strong backlash was felt in the Missouri Synod protesting continued fellowship with the American Lutheran Church. Because of the number of overtures to the 1971 Convention urging the synod to withdraw, suspend, rescind, reconsider, etc., fellowship with the ALC, while expressing regret over that body's ordination of women to the pastoral ministry, and at the same time requesting further consultation with the leadership of the ALC, it was resolved: THAT THE LC-MS ADVISES ITS PASTORS, CONGREGATIONS, BOARDS, AND COMMISSIONS, BECAUSE OF DOCTRINAL CONCERNS STILL REMAINING BETWEEN THE TWO BODIES, TO DEFER NEW IMPLEMENTATION OF FELLOWSHIP WITH THE ALC UNTIL THE ALC HAS HAD THE OPPORTUNITY TO RESPOND TO OUR

Many voices were heard over the years, protesting the fact that the fellowship with the ALC had been established. The 1975 Convention Workbook found many memorials asking for termination of the fellowship. Others, however, requested that it be continued. Thus the LCMS-ALC fellowship had become, and was to remain, a dividing issue in the synod. At the 1975 Milwaukee Convention, Dr. Jacob Preus recommended continuation of fellowship with the ALC:...IN ORDER THAT ALL OF THE ISSUES MAY BE THOROUGHLY DISCUSSED AND ALL PARTIES PROPERLY INFORMED, BEFORE TAKING ACTION ON THIS MATTER [I.E. REGARDING ENDING THE FELLOWSHIP]. In the 1975 Workbook, the CTCR* recommended: THAT THE SYNOD... (B) STATE ITS DEEP REGRET THAT SIX YEARS OF DISCUSSIONS IN THE COMMISSION ON FELLOWSHIP HAVE NOT PRODUCED EVIDENCE THAT "SERIOUS DIFFERENCES" IN THE DOCTRINE OF THE AUTHORITY OF SCRIPTURE (1971 RESOLUTION 3-21, FOURTH WHEREAS...) HAVE BEEN RESOLVED OR THAT OUR TWO CHURCH BODIES HAVE ACHIEVED A COMMON UNDERSTANDING ON WHAT FELLOWSHIP INVOLVES... (C) CONSIDER THE RECOMMENDATION SUGGESTED IN THE 1973 RESOLUTION 2-40 TO DECLARE THE DENOMINATIONAL FELLOWSHIP TO BE IN A STATE OF SUSPENSION. (Page 43 of Workbook)

The Missouri Synod in convention admitted that disagreements in doctrine and practice existed between the ALC and itself...WHEREAS, DOCTRINAL DIFFERENCES CONTINUE TO AGITATE AND ARE THE CONTINUING CONCERN OF THE ALC AND THE LUTHERAN CHURCH-MISSOURI SYNOD COMMISSION ON FELLOWSHIP;...RESOLVED, THAT THE SYNOD'S REPRESENTATIVES ON THE ALC-LCMS COMMISSION ON FELLOWSHIP INTENSIFY THEIR EFFORTS TO RESOLVE THE DOCTRINAL DIFFERENCES WITH THE ALC.

The South Wisconsin District of the synod, meeting in Milwaukee in 1976, adopted memorials to the 1977 Synod Convention calling for termination of fellowship with the American Lutheran Church. Given as reasons for this action were: the ALC's stand on Scripture, the ordination of women, and unionistic practices by the ALC clergymen. The same convention passed resolutions calling for a curtailment of Missouri's involvement in the LCUSA for reasons similar to those listed above. Still another action called on the synod's Board of Directors to halt synodical participation in the preparation of a new hymnal for synods belonging to the Lutheran Council. In the spring of 1977 the continuing dispute over conservative vs. moderate doctrine resulted in the Commission on Theology and Church Relations recommending all but complete severance of the synod's eight-year-old ties with the ALC.

A CHANGING DOCTRINAL
CLIMATE—A REVIEW

The year 1938 marked an important turning point in the history of the Missouri Synod. Eight years earlier it had received an invitation from the newly formed American Lutheran Church to continue the fellowship discussions, which had broken down in 1929 with Missouri's rejection of the Chicago The-

655

ses. The new body hoped that Missouri would catch the fever for Lutheran union that was taking hold of the churches. It was five years before Missouri accepted the invitation and appointed a Committee on Lutheran Union to carry on discussions with representatives of the ALC. At the same time, the synod accepted the invitation of the ULCA to carry on talks in quest of closer fellowship. It took only three years for Missouri's Union Committee to bring a favorable report to the Synod convention. When the committee reported to the 1938 St. Louis Convention. It revealed that a number of differences did remain between Missouri and the ALC, especially in the area of Chiliasm or Millennialism. However, the convention seemed ready to gloss over these differences for the time being as "non-fundamental doctrines," doctrines upon which the two churches should try to come to full agreement. The St. Louis Articles were adopted as a safeguard that the divergent points would be settled. It was felt that the old issues, which had once been a deterrent to fellowship had been resolved. The ALC stated that it was "ready to officially declare itself in doctrinal agreement with the Honorable Synod of Missouri," and, of course, to enter into fellowship. Was Missouri ready? It seemed to be saying that it was.

This was indeed a strange turn to Missouri's history. Here was a definite liberalizing trend, a departure from a doctrinal tradition that had become a theological way of life for this synod. Under the old Franz Pieper tradition (Pieper was the leading dogmatician in the synod) full agreement on all doctrinal issues had to preclude any declaration of fellowship. Not that all within the Missouri Synod were willing to break with that tradition. Many were not, and were quick to raise their voices in sharp disagreement with the synod's action. The dissidents became a powerful and vocal force within Missouri, and yet it was clear that the synod had acquired a strong "moderate" force that would work with great fervor to bring Missouri out of its long-standing isolationism to at least meet and, hopefully, establish fellowship with other Lutherans.

By 1944 the Missouri Synod showed its willingness to change its stand on the matter of joint prayer at Intersynodical Conferences—"provided such prayer does not imply denial of truth or support of error." This was not the only indication that a moderate wind, calling for change, was blowing over the synod. A liberal trend was detected by the conservatives in some of the faculty members of the St. Louis Seminary. In 1945 "A Statement" was issued by forty-four prominent pastors and theological professors at Chicago (hence: the "Statement of the Forty-four"). It was a tradition-shattering document and aroused a storm of protest from the conservative side of the synod. There was held a series of meetings of ten representatives of the signers and ten representatives of the synod. No satisfactory solution was found. After members of the Synod Praesidium met with representatives of the signers, an agreement was reached that the signers withdraw "A Statement" as a basis for further discussion. The Praesidium agreed that a series of special study document be prepared by men chosen by President Behnken. Over the next few years five studies were authored and sent out to the pastors. Over time the "Forty-Four" ceased to exist as an organized group.[52]

These matters, of course, affected the relations which Missouri had with the Wisconsin Synod and the Norwegians. Both churches used the Synodical Conference meetings as the forum in which to protest the doctrinal laxity and false practice being observed in the Missouri Synod. In his autobiography, the now sainted Dr. John W. Behnken described the stresses and strains going on in the Synodical Conference during this time.

AT PRACTICALLY EVERY MEETING WE HAD TO LISTEN TO CHARGE AFTER CHARGE LEVELED AGAINST THE MISSOURI SYNOD...ON THE ONE HAND, THERE WERE CHARGES OF DOCTRINAL LAXITY OR CONFESSIONAL COMPROMISE RAISED PARTIC-ULARLY IN CONNECTION WITH THE DOCTRINAL STATEMENTS OF SYNOD ADOPTED IN SEEKING AGREEMENT WITH THE ALC. AT SUCH TIMES THE ATMOSPHERE OF OUR FRATERNAL CONSULTATIONS WAS RATHER HEAVILY CHARGED. ON THE OTHER HAND, I CAN VIVIDLY RECALL THAT OFTEN MEETINGS WERE SCARCELY OPENED WHEN THOSE REPRESENTING SOME OF OUR SISTER SYNODS WOULD START IN LISTING COMPLAINTS AND INDICTMENTS OF "UNIONISTIC PRACTICE," INTERSPERSED WITH THE INSISTENT DEMANDS OF WHAT WE WERE GOING TO DO ABOUT IT. THESE WERE, TO SAY THE LEAST, UNHAPPY OCCASIONS. THE SAD PART OF IT WAS THAT IN MANY INSTANCES WE HAD TO ADMIT THAT THE COM-PLAINT WAS WARRANTED. THIS OR THAT MEMBER OF SYNOD HAD SIMPLY DIS-REGARDED SYNOD'S PRACTICE OR HAD ACTED UNTHINKINGLY OR IRRESPONSIBLY WITHOUT CONFERRING WITH HIS BRETHREN AND WITHOUT DULY CONSIDERING THE EFFECT HIS ACTION WOULD HAVE ON THE CHURCH. SUCH ECCLESIASTICAL FREEWHEELERS ALL TOO OFTEN PLACED ME AND ALSO THEIR DISTRICT OFFI-CIALS ON SOME VERY PAINFUL AND EMBARRASSING SPOTS...THEY ONLY ADDED FUEL TO THE FIRE.

Dr. Behnken went on to admit:

ANOTHER DEEPLY DISTURBING AND DISHEARTENING EXPERIENCE THAT FELL TO MY LOT WAS THE CONTROVERSY WITHIN SYNOD CONCERNING THE INERRANCY OF THE SCRIPTURES. THIS DISPUTE, AS SO MANY OTHERS, HAD ITS ROOTS IN EU-ROPEAN THEOLOGICAL CIRCLES, WHERE A MOVEMENT KNOWN AS NEO-ORTHO-DOXY HAD DEVELOPED IN RECENT DECADES AS A REACTION TO THE RATIONALISTIC AND LIBERALISTIC ATTITUDE TOWARD THE BIBLE WHICH HAD LONG HELD SWAY...NEO-ORTHODOXY...STOPS A GOOD WAY SHORT OF ACCEPT-ING THE BIBLE IN ALL ITS PARTS AS THE INERRANT WORD OF GOD...UNFORTU-NATELY, SOME WHO HAD MADE THE PROBLEMS CONNECTED WITH BIBLICAL INTERPRETATION THEIR SPECIAL CONCERN, IN CONSIDERATION OF THE NEWER VIEWS REGARDING THE NATURE OF GOD'S REVELATION AND ALSO BECAUSE OF CERTAIN DIFFICULTIES AND VARIATIONS IN THE BIBLE RECORDS, ADVANCED THE OPINION THAT PERHAPS THE TERM "INERRANCY" OUGHT NO LONGER BE USED. THIS SET OFF A SHARP CONTROVERSY, WHICH LED TO SOME UGLY NAME CALL-ING, ACCUSATIONS, AND RECRIMINATIONS. NOTHING DURING MY TWENTY-SEVEN YEARS IN OFFICE CAUSED ME MORE HEARTACHE. [53]

As we can gather from Dr. Behnken's own observation, there were several sources of contention. One of the most burning issues was that of the doctrine of Holy Scripture. Another, the doctrine of Church Fellowship. Without a doubt, an issue that served to arouse fears and doubts in the minds of many—both inside and outside the synod—was Missouri's consultations with the American Lutheran Church, the goal of which was to arrive at a doctrinal con-sensus that could serve as the basis for fellowship with that body. Very early in the talks there were anxious moments. There were some who felt that Mis-souri was leaning toward a unionistic stand whereby it would be willing to overlook some of the past differences which existed between Missouri and the synods that came together to form the ALC. Thus, it seemed to some that Missouri was willing to engage in a convenient compromise instead of requiring full accord in all matters on the basis of Scripture. Involved were the doctrines of Inspiration, Church and Ministry, Election and Conversion, Chiliasm, and practical questions—especially membership in lodges and also unionism. There were those who expressed the belief that Missouri under the circumstances as they then existed, should not have even been involved in doctrinal talks with the ALC. One reason that was expressed was this: Points of controversy which were supposed to have been settled between the two bodies, were later found not to be settled; and while the ALC was reaching out the right hand of fellowship to the conservatives (Missouri), it was at the same time also reaching out the left hand to the liberals (ULCA).

Another sore spot uncovered by Dr. Behnken's personal observations was the practice by individuals of arbitrarily making statements either orally or in print, or committing acts of church practice which were contrary to the synod's official stand, thereby giving offence to others. There were many instances in which the conservative element in Missouri, and the representatives of synods in the Synodical Conference, asked for official explanations of affairs. Demands were made that disciplinary action be taken against the individuals or groups involved. By means of the feisty *Confessional Lutheran*, a group of conservatives continuously and vehemently attacked the aberrations in doctrine and practice of those in the synod who broke with synod's traditions. Sometimes newspaper and magazine articles (occasionally reinforced with pictures) were introduced as evidence that joint worship services were held between Missouri Synod clergymen and Catholic priests, as well as with others.

Among the most serious charges made against Missouri were those which accused professors in synodical schools of teaching and circulating false doctrines, even of attacking the Inerrancy of Holy Scripture.

Though more will be said of this a little later, brief mention of it here might prove helpful. The clash between the conservatives and the moderates (liberals) came to a head in late summer of 1972 when President J.A.O. Preus, an avowed conservative transplanted from the Evangelical Lutheran Synod (the little Norwegian Synod) in the 1950's, and head of the Synod since 1969, published his long-awaited report on the result of doctrinal discussions with members of the faculty of the St. Louis Seminary. In his report, President Preus charged the undermining of scriptural authority at the seminary. The report, covering more than 150 pages, was answered by Dr. John Tietjen's thirty-five page report in which the seminary head accused the handpicked investigating committee of being prejudiced from the start. He further accused the committee of using "grossly unfair" procedures, which operated on non-Biblical, non-Lutheran premises and its prejudgment's "predetermined results." Dr. Tietjen called the report "a strange blend of half-truths, misunderstandings and distortions which makes the profile it presents untrue." In hopes of bridging this doctrinal controversy, which flared into the open between the head of synod and the head of one of the largest seminaries in the world, the Council of Presidents stated among other things:

THAT WE ENCOURAGE EACH OF THE PROFESSORS OF CONCORDIA SEMINARY,

St. Louis, to assure the church of his biblical and confessional stance by setting forth (in writing) for use in discussion forms, what is believed, taught and confessed, giving special attention to the theological issues in controversy among us today such as Law and Gospel; Holy Scripture: its purpose, authority, infallibility, unity, and its interpretation; the relationship of the Gospel and Holy Scripture: the canonical text; Old Testament prophecy, and original sin; that we encourage these professors and the church to regard this exercise as an opportunity to edify the church.[54]

It was no overstatement that "controversy raged in the Missouri Synod." A synod once united in its theology and doctrinal practices became "torn with strife." As the synod continued along in the 1970's the moderates and conservatives were faced with the unavoidable issue: how long can two opposing doctrinal views, and two opposing views on church practice coexist in a group pledged to unity. The parting of ways began. This was marked by the formation of the Association of Evangelical Lutheran Churches (AELC) by moderates leaving the Missouri Synod, preceded by the departure of the greater part of the English District. To some, the tragedy lay in the occurrence of a schism which they hoped to avoid by exercising a more tolerant approach to those who questioned the old values of the synod. They breathed a word of caution against cracking the whip too often and too hard at those accused of error. In the judgment of others, the real tragedy would occur if the forces in synod would superficially unite at the expense of doctrinal purity and practice based on Scripture and the Lutheran Confession. To them it seemed incongruous to promote union without real unity.

One area, outstanding by way of showing a change in the doctrinal climate of the Missouri Synod, was the decision to grant the right of suffrage to women. The 1969 Denver Convention reversed a traditional stand on this issue that had lasted for more than a century. It approved the limited voting rights for women in congregations.

It is also evident from the definition of the franchise that it does not give those who have the right of suffrage the power to lord it over others [referring to 1 Tim. 2:11-15 and its prohibition concerning the woman usurping authority over the man]. On the contrary, the right of suffrage is given in order to prevent individuals or small groups from usurping authority over others.

In the matter of suffrage, then, we must conclude that there is nothing in Scripture to prohibit women from exercising the franchise in the voters' meetings of the congregations to which they belong. In such assemblies they are in no stronger position than anyone else to turn the franchise into an instrument of usurpation.[55]

The issue of franchise for women in the church had been under debate since 1953. The decision naturally opened the way for appointment of women to positions on boards and committees of congregations, as well as of districts and the synod itself. While the synodical declarations state "that Scripture does not prohibit women from exercising the franchise in congregational or synodical assemblies," on the other hand the declarations also state that according to Scripture "women ought not to hold the pastoral office or serve in any other capacity

659

involving the distinctive functions of this office." Furthermore congregational policy is to conform to the general scriptural principles that women "neither hold the pastoral office nor 'exercise authority over men.'"

It is of interest to note that while the 1969 Denver Convention declared the Missouri Synod to be in fellowship with the American Lutheran Church, the latter body the following year, in a close vote, formally approved the ordination of women to the ministry. Shortly before that, the Lutheran Church in America, meeting in Minneapolis, approved the ordination of women. Thus, of the three major Lutheran bodies in America, only the Missouri Synod denied the office of the ministry to women. Dr. Preus acknowledged that the ALC's act of approving the ordination of women could cause hardship in the relationship between Missouri and the ALC. On the other side of the coin, Missouri's overtures to the Wisconsin Synod for doctrinal discussions aimed at reestablishing fellowship would be hampered by its action of allowing the franchise to women. The Wisconsin Synod would remain adamant in its position against granting the franchise to women in the church, as well as to the ordination of women.

In spite of the controversy that had come to the fore, the Missouri Synod at the end of 1969 held its place as the fastest growing of all major Lutheran bodies in the United States. It had the highest numerical increase for twenty-four consecutive years.

THE BATTLE BETWEEN THE CONSERVATIVES AND THE MODERATES

THE "MILITANT" CONSERVATIVES FIGHT BACK— THE ELECTION OF J.A.O. PREUS

It was in July 1965 at Cobo Hall in Detroit that the Missouri Synod voted to enter the Lutheran Council in the U.S.A. (LCUSA). No doubt this was a victory for the moderate or liberal forces in the synod, who had been trying to steer Missouri away from its course of "isolationism" and place it in the "mainstream" of Lutheranism, thus preventing it from becoming a sect. Nevertheless, it was at this very convention that the conservatives came out publicly in their attempts to gain control of the synodical administration. A large number of nominations from the floor made by the conservatives from among their own number eventually were elected to office. Subsequent conventions of the synod swelled the ranks of the conservatives through the election process. A publication titled *Balance*, which subsequently was replaced by *Affirm*, and which was first organized in the Springfield home of Dr. J.A.O Preus, did much to propagandize for the "militant" conservatives and the candidates they espoused. The *Christian News* (formerly, *Lutheran News*) published in New Haven, Missouri, by Rev. Herman Otten also did much to publicize the conservative cause. In fact, *Christian News* has probably done more to keep people informed on the issues than any other publication, official or otherwise.

In 1969 the Denver Convention elected Dr. J.A.O. Preus to succeed Dr. Oliver Harms as president of the synod. Jacob Preus was elected by the conservatives of the synod to stem the floodwaters of the moderate movement.

For a quarter of a century and more the moderate position had been building strength throughout the synod with its impact felt the most at the St. Louis Concordia Seminary, where the great majority of the faculty were moderates. It should be pointed out that there were several professors at the Springfield Concordia Seminary who also espoused the moderate cause.

President Jacob Preus, together with his brother Robert, had grown up in the Norwegian element of Lutheranism, not in the German-Missourian tradition. They left the Evangelical Lutheran Church (the large Norwegian merger group of 1917) and joined the small Norwegian Evangelical Lutheran Synod (as it finally came to be called)—the tiny minority of the Norwegian Synod that had refused to go along with the 1917 merger and had refused to accept the "Madison Agreement," which was actually a doctrinal compromise concerning the Doctrines of Election and Conversion. At the time of the controversy between the Wisconsin Synod and the Norwegians on the one side and the Missouri Synod on the other side (in the 1950's), Jacob Preus, affiliated with the Norwegians, was both an officer and a member of their Union Committee, which then dealt with representatives of the Missouri Synod on the controverted issues. At the Norwegians' Convention in 1955 Jacob moved and Robert seconded the following motion:…THAT WE HEREBY DECLARE WITH DEEPEST REGRET THAT FELLOWSHIP RELATIONS WITH THE LUTHERAN CHURCH-MISSOURI SYNOD ARE SUSPENDED ON THE BASIS OF ROMANS 16:17, AND THAT THE EXERCISE OF SUCH RELATIONS CANNOT BE RESUMED UNTIL THE OFFENSES CONTRARY TO THE DOCTRINE WHICH WE HAVE LEARNED HAVE BEEN REMOVED BY THEM IN THE PROPER MANNER.

This motion was adopted, and fellowship with the Missouri Synod was suspended. Suddenly and dramatically, the very men who were so instrumental in bringing about the break between the Norwegians and the Missouri Synod took positions of responsibility and leadership in this body. In 1957 and 1958 both men accepted professorships in Missouri Synod schools, Robert at Concordia Seminary in St. Louis, and Jacob at Concordia Seminary in Springfield, Illinois.[56, 57]

In 1973 the moderate group tried to run Dr. Oswald C.J. Hoffmann, the Lutheran Hour speaker, against Preus. However, he declined to have his name placed in nomination due to his call as speaker on the Lutheran Hour broadcast. It had been the hopes of the moderates that such a name as Hoffmann could win the confidence of the majority, and yet allow the possibility of the synod turning toward the neo-Lutheranism being advocated by the majority of the faculty at the St. Louis Seminary.

By the time of the New Orleans 1973 Convention Preus succeeded in obtaining sufficient backing, so that the conservative swept into office all but five of their candidates for 150 positions on key church boards, agencies and commissions. The conservatives finally came together to make their impact felt on the synod. The battle between the "militant" conservatives and the moderates had begun in earnest with the rise of Jacob Preus to power as the synod president in 1969.

At first the moderates were not organized:

FROM 1969 TO 1971, THE EFFORT [I.E. TO ORGANIZE IN PURSUIT OF THEIR COMMON INTERESTS] WAS LIMITED TO OCCASIONAL CONFERENCES, SEVERAL PUBLIC POSITION STATEMENTS AND OPEN LETTERS, AND AN ATTEMPT TO ESTABLISH A

COMMUNICATIONS NETWORK FOR INTERESTED DELEGATES TO THE MILWAUKEE CONVENTION 1971. FROM 1971 TO 1973, THE "MODERATES" BECAME IDENTIFIED AS THE FREY-LUEKING COALITION, FUNDS WERE RAISED, ISSUE PAPERS WERE PRODUCED AND DISTRIBUTED TO INTERESTED PARTIES, MEMORIALS WERE PREPARED FOR PRESENTATION TO THE NEW ORLEANS CONVENTION, PERSONS WERE IDENTIFIED FOR NOMINATION AT THE CONVENTION, AND AN ATTEMPT WAS MADE TO ACQUIRE PERSONS SYMPATHETIC TO THE "MODERATE" CAUSE TO SERVE AS DELEGATES TO THE CONVENTION.

...FOLLOWING THE NEW ORLEANS CONVENTION, MODERATES MET IN CHICAGO TO ORGANIZE EVANGELICAL LUTHERANS IN MISSION (ELIM).[58]

ELIM became vocal in its disagreement with the position taken by the synodical administration and the manner in which it was implementing the program of the synod. And to help its cause, it published a newspaper, *Missouri in Perspective.*

At issue was doctrine, especially the doctrine of the Word of God. There had been attacks made on the Authority of Scripture and the Inerrancy of Scripture. In latter years the traditional method of Bible interpretation was questioned by those favoring the historical-critical method. Should the Missouri Synod be an island of Lutheran Confessionalism in the sea of historical-critical Scripture interpretation that has become so much a part of modern Lutheran theology? Or, should Missouri join forces with most of the Lutheran world and adopt the historical-critical method? To the minds of the moderates the question was: Will Missouri "join" the Lutheran Church or be a "sect" apart from the mainstream of Lutheranism? Writer James E. Adams gives his view that "the principal theological issue (is) whether 95% of all biblical passages must be interpreted literally."[59] At issue then: Does the Bible speak literally in the Creation Account, the Flood Account, the Account of the Fall of Man into Sin, the Miracles of Christ? —as examples. Or, are these parables, mere linguistic means to convey a divine truth?

The issue of ecumenicity also played an important role in the moderates versus conservative's drama being played out in the Missouri Synod. The moderates took position toward ecumenism that "we're quite open to finding church life in the larger Lutheran community." These words were spoken by F. Dean Lueking, a Chicago-area pastor and a leader of the moderate coalition. The moderates had won a victory for their stand when earlier, in 1969 at Denver, the synod declared fellowship with the American Lutheran Church. Already in the 1950's moderates on the St. Louis faculty showed a favorable attitude toward cooperation with the ALC, which attitude provoked fierce attacks from the conservative side. When a schism was finally affected, with a portion of the moderates leaving the synod, an immediate ecumenical gesture was made. These moderates, who then formed the Association of Evangelical Churches (AELC) declared themselves in fellowship with all Lutherans. They furthermore followed in the footsteps of the liberal Lutheran bodies with which they declared themselves to be in fellowship, and approved the ordination of women, a practice the Missouri Synod continues to flatly oppose.

On January 31, 1970, at St. Louis, a liberal document was adopted by a group of Missouri Synod moderates. "A Call To Openness and Trust" asked the synod not to insist upon such doctrines as the Inerrancy of the Bible and the

Real Presence (of Christ's body and blood in the Lord's Supper). President Jacob Preus took issue with the document's liberal tone and wrote the following in a letter to the pastors of the synods:

BUT NOW ANOTHER GROUP, WHICH INCLUDES IN ITS NUMBER PROMINENT AND RESPONSIBLE PROFESSORS AND SYNODICAL OFFICIALS HAS ARISEN. THESE BROTHERS ARE NOT CONTENT WITH MEETING, ORGANIZING, AND SOLICITING FUNDS, BUT ALSO BRING IN THE SECULAR PRESS TO HELP CARRY OUT THEIR PROGRAM. THEY HAVE IGNORED EXISTING SYNODICAL CHANNELS AND PROCEDURES FOR VOICING THEIR CONCERNS AND HAVE ISSUED INSTEAD A STATEMENT IN WHICH THEY ESTABLISH FOR THEMSELVES A HIGH DUBIOUS CONFESSIONAL STANCE, CALL FOR A NEW DEFINITION OF THE DOCTRINE OF THE REAL PRESENCE OF THE BODY AND BLOOD OF OUR LORD IN THE SACRAMENT OF THE ALTAR, WITH A CONCURRENT PRACTICE OF OPEN COMMUNION, AND ATTACK OUR SYNODICAL STAND REGARDING THE INERRANCY OF HOLY SCRIPTURE, A SUBJECT UPON WHICH OUR SYNOD HAS SPOKEN CLEARLY AND REPEATEDLY.

MAKE NO MISTAKE ABOUT THIS, BROTHERS. WHAT IS AT STAKE IS NOT ONLY INERRANCY BUT THE GOSPEL OF JESUS CHRIST ITSELF, THE AUTHORITY OF HOLY SCRIPTURE, THE "QUIA" SUBSCRIPTION TO THE LUTHERAN CONFESSION [I.E. THE CHURCH ACCEPTS THE CONFESSIONS *BECAUSE* THEY ARE A TRUE EXPOSITION OF SCRIPTURE, NOT INSOFAR AS THEY ARE...] AND PERHAPS THE VERY CONTINUED EXISTENCE OF LUTHERANISM AS A CONFESSIONAL AND CONFESSION MOVEMENT IN THE CHRISTIAN WORLD. THE SITUATION CANNOT BE IGNORED OR ENDURED.

Preus called for such people to leave our fellowship stating that it would be far better than for these people to work from within to torment and ultimately destroy the Synod. The Commission on Theology and Church Relations (CTCR) attacked the document, and the 1971 Convention repudiated it by a 390 to 384 vote.[60]

In *The Lutherans in North America*, we find the following observation regarding the crucial position which the Doctrine of Verbal Inspiration and Inerrancy held in the controversy between the conservative and moderate groups in the Missouri Synod:

CENTRAL TO THE CONFLICT WAS THE CONTINUING QUESTION OF BIBLICAL AUTHORITY COUCHED IN THE NOW FAMILIAR OLD LUTHERAN TERMINOLOGY OF VERBAL INSPIRATION AND INERRANCY. THE CONSERVATIVES INSISTED THAT DOCTRINAL PURITY WAS IMPERILED BY THE NEO-LUTHERAN VIEW THAT THE BIBLE'S AUTHORITY RESTED ON ITS CHARACTER AS THE BEARER OF THE PRIMARY WITNESS TO THE GOSPEL, THE DIVINE MESSAGE OF THE GRACIOUS FORGIVENESS OF SINS AND OF THE GIFT OF NEW LIFE IN THE SPIRIT BY THE USE OF THE HISTORICAL-CRITICAL METHOD OF BIBLICAL STUDY [THE MODERATE VIEW]. PREUS AND THE CONSERVATIVES CHARGED TIETJEN [PRESIDENT OF THE ST. LOUIS CONCORDIA SEMINARY] AND THE FACULTY MAJORITY WITH "GOSPEL REDUCTIONISM," THAT IS, RESTRICTING SCRIPTURAL AUTHORITY TO THE GOSPEL BUT NOT TO SCIENTIFIC, GEOGRAPHIC, OR HISTORICAL MATTERS FOUND IN THE BIBLE. THE SCRIPTURES MUST BE FACTUALLY INERRANT IF THEY ARE TO BE THE NORM FOR THE FAITH AND LIFE OF THE CHURCH. EACH OF THE OTHER MAJOR LUTHERAN BODIES HAD IN GREATER OR LESSER DEGREE FACED THE PROBLEM OF THE BIBLE; HENCE, MUCH OF THE GROUND THAT THE MISSOURI

SYNOD WAS COVERING HAD BEEN TRAVELED BEFORE. BUT OF THE THREE MAJOR BODIES MISSOURI ALONE WAS DRIVEN TO A POSITION THAT FORCED A VOTE ON THE ISSUE AT ITS BIENNIAL CONVENTION.[61]

THE ISSUES
(OUTLINED IN THE PRESIDENT'S REPORT—
1971 CONVENTION)

President Jacob Preus was sharp in his reaction to the document "A Call To Openness and Trust." Nor was he in a mood to mince words when he addressed the 1971 Convention. The following is taken from that report:

SOME IN OUR CHURCH WHO CLAIM TO ACCEPT THE DOCTRINAL CONTENT OF THE LUTHERAN CONFESSIONS OPERATE WITH A VERY RESTRICTIVE UNDERSTANDING OF WHAT CONSTITUTES "DOCTRINE." FOR EXAMPLE, THEY APPARENTLY DO NOT REGARD THE GENESIS ACCOUNT OF THE CREATION OF ADAM AND EVE AND OF THE FALL AS A "DOCTRINAL" ITEM BUT RATHER AS AN EXEGETICAL QUESTION OR A THEOLOGICAL CONSTRUCT, WHERE THERE CAN LEGITIMATELY BE A VARIETY OF INTERPRETATIONS WITHOUT EFFECTING WHAT THEY CONSIDER TO BE "DOCTRINE."

SOME HOLD THAT OUR CONFESSIONAL SUBSCRIPTION IS LIMITED TO THE DOCTRINAL POINTS AT ISSUE, AND THAT IT DOES NOT EMBRACE DOCTRINAL POSITIONS EXPRESSED IN THE CONFESSIONS SOMEWHAT INCIDENTALLY. FOR EXAMPLE, IN THE CONFESSIONAL STATEMENT REGARDING ORIGINAL SIN, SOME SAY THAT THE CONFESSIONS' REFERENCES TO THE HISTORICITY OF ADAM AND EVE DO NOT BIND US, SINCE THE CONFESSIONS MERELY INTENDED TO TALK ABOUT THE FALLEN STATE OF MAN.

REGARDING THE INSPIRATION OF SCRIPTURE, SOME IN OUR SYNOD HOLD THAT THERE IS NO PRECISE AND UNIFORM CONFESSIONAL POSITION. SOME BELIEVE THAT THE INSPIRATION OF THE SCRIPTURES IS NOT QUALITATIVELY DIFFERENT FROM THE ACTIVITY OF THE HOLY SPIRIT IN THE TRADITION OF THE CHURCH AND IN OUR PREACHING AND WITNESS TODAY. OTHERS HOLD THAT THE CONFESSIONS CLEARLY TEACH THAT THE SCRIPTURES ARE UNIQUE AND DIFFERENT FROM ALL OTHER LITERATURE IN THAT THEY ARE VERBALLY INSPIRED BY GOD SO THAT IN ALL THEIR WORDS THEY ARE THE WORD OF GOD. IN THIS VIEW, BOTH THE AUTHORS AND THE WORDS OF SCRIPTURE ARE INSPIRED, FOR MEN OF GOD WROTE THE WORDS THAT THE HOLY SPIRIT WANTED THEM TO WRITE...WE HAVE A WELL-KNOWN DIFFERENCE AMONG US ON THE DOCTRINE OF THE INERRANCY OF SCRIPTURE. SOME HOLD THAT THE SCRIPTURES ARE INERRANT ONLY IN THEIR FUNCTION, THAT IS, THAT THEY FAITHFULLY ACCOMPLISH THEIR PURPOSE OF CREATING FAITH IN MAN.

WE ALSO HAVE PROBLEMS WITH REGARD TO THE RELATIONSHIP BETWEEN THE MATERIAL AND THE FORMAL PRINCIPLES OF THEOLOGY. THE "FORMAL PRINCIPLE" IS THAT THE BIBLE IS THE INSPIRED WORD OF GOD AND THE SOURCE AND NORM OF ALL DOCTRINE; THE "MATERIAL PRINCIPLE" IS THAT CHRIST AND HIS GRACIOUS JUSTIFICATION OF THE SINNER IS THE HEART AND CENTER OF THE ENTIRE SCRIPTURE. IN KEEPING WITH OUR LUTHERAN CONFESSIONS, WE HAVE TRADITIONALLY HELD TO A VERY CAREFUL DISTINCTION BETWEEN THESE PRINCIPLES. THUS WE HAVE HELD THAT SCRIPTURE IS THE SOURCE AND NORM OF

ALL DOCTRINE, WHILE THE GOSPEL IS THE CHIEF DOCTRINE AND A BASIC PRE-
SUPPOSITION FOR THE INTERPRETATION OF SCRIPTURE. BUT TODAY THERE IS
A FREQUENT CONFUSIONS OF THESE PRINCIPLES, WITH THE RESULT THAT THE
GOSPEL, RATHER THAN THE BIBLE, IS EMPLOYED AS THE NORM OF OUR THEOL-
OGY. THIS IS SOMETIMES CALLED "GOSPEL REDUCTIONISM."
THOSE WHO CONFUSE THESE PRINCIPLES SOMETIMES REJECT THE FACTUAL
CLAIMS OF A GIVEN TEXT ON THE GROUNDS THAT IT DOES NOT INVOLVE THE
GOSPEL. THEY ASSERT THAT THE INTERPRETATIONS OF A SCRIPTURE PASSAGE
NEED NOT BE REJECTED IF THEY DO NOT HARM THE GOSPEL. FOR EXAMPLE, IT
IS SAID BY SOME THAT ALTHOUGH THE BIBLE SPECIFICALLY COMMANDS WOMEN
TO KEEP SILENCE IN THE CHURCH, YET SINCE THIS DOES NOT IMPINGE ON THE
GOSPEL, THE MATTER OF ORDINATION OF WOMEN TO THE PASTORAL MINISTRY
IS A MATTER OF INDIFFERENCE AND MAY BE PRACTICED OR NOT ACCORDING TO
HUMAN CONVENIENCE. BY THE SAME METHOD OF INTERPRETATIONS, THE FALL
OF ADAM AND EVE, THE UNIVERSAL FLOOD, AND OTHER HISTORICAL TEACHINGS
OF SCRIPTURE ARE NOT ACCEPTED BY SOME AS FACTUAL BECAUSE THEY ARE
CONSIDERED TO BE NONESSENTIAL TO THE DOCTRINAL LESSON OF SIN AND
GRACE...
WITH REGARD TO MIRACLES, SOME MEMBERS OF OUR CHURCH, WHILE AC-
KNOWLEDGING THAT CHRIST COULD HAVE PERFORMED ALL MIRACLES THAT ARE
ATTRIBUTED TO HIM IN THE GOSPELS, CLAIM THAT IT IS PERMISSIBLE FOR EX-
EGETICAL REASONS TO REINTERPRET BIBLICAL MIRACLE-STORIES SO AS TO ELIM-
INATE THEIR REALITY BY REGARDING THEM AS PARABLE OR ANOTHER TYPE OF
LITERARY DEVICE. ACCORDING TO THIS VIEW, IT IS PERMISSIBLE, FOR EXAMPLE,
TO DENY THAT CHRIST WALKED ON WATER OR CHANGED WATER INTO WINE.
SUCH STORIES, IT IS HELD, WERE INTENDED TO TEACH SOMETHING QUITE DIF-
FERENT FROM THE PERFORMANCE OF A MIRACLE.
FOR SIMILAR REASONS, SOME ARE EVIDENTLY HAVING DIFFICULTY IN AFFIRMING
THAT THERE REALLY ARE ANGELS OR A PERSONAL DEVIL.[62]

In his 1971 President's Report, Jacob Preus continued to lay bare the synodical wound that wouldn't heal. He reported:

...ENTIRE DISTRICT PASTORAL CONFERENCES AND DISTRICT CONVENTIONS, AS
WELL AS OTHER RESPONSIBLE GROUPS AND INDIVIDUALS, HAD EXPRESSED GREAT
CONCERN ABOUT THE THEOLOGICAL STANCE OF VARIOUS MEMBERS OF THE FAC-
ULTY. ALTHOUGH SUCH CRITICISMS HAVE BEEN EXPRESSED FOR SEVERAL
YEARS, A SERIES OF EVENTS WHICH INVOLVED MEMBERS OF THE FACULTY THEM-
SELVES OCCURRED IN THE LAST MONTHS OF 1969 AND EARLY IN 1970 WHICH
MADE IT IMPERATIVE FOR ME TO DETERMINE WHAT THE DOCTRINAL SITUATION
AT OUR SEMINARY WAS. AMONG THESE EVENTS WERE THE FOLLOWING: (1) AT
A JOINT MEETING OF BOTH SEMINARY FACULTIES TOGETHER WITH THE COUNCIL
OF PRESIDENTS IN LATE 1969, IT BECAME OBVIOUS THAT THERE WERE SERIOUS
DISAGREEMENTS IN THE WAY IN WHICH MEMBERS OF THE FACULTIES UNDER-
STAND THE AUTHORITY OF THE SACRED SCRIPTURES AND ITS IMPLICATION FOR
BIBLICAL INTERPRETATION. IN ADDITION, A MEMBER OF THE ST. LOUIS FAC-
ULTY STATED THAT THE PRESUPPOSITIONS WITH WHICH CERTAIN MEMBERS OF
THE FACULTY WERE APPROACHING THE SCRIPTURES WERE NOT LUTHERAN.
(2) IN JANUARY 1970 SEVERAL MEMBERS OF THE FACULTY IN ST. LOUIS WERE
INVOLVED IN THE ISSUING OF "A CALL TO OPENNESS AND TRUST," A DOCUMENT

WHICH THE COMMISSION ON THEOLOGY AND CHURCH RELATIONS LATER EVAL-
UATED AS BEING CONTRARY TO THE CONFESSIONAL POSITION OF THE SYNOD.
(3) IN FEBRUARY 1970, THE FACULTIES OF BOTH SEMINARIES MET JOINTLY AND
DISCUSSED AN ESSAY BY A MEMBER OF THE ST. LOUIS FACULTY. IN THIS MEET-
ING A SHARP THEOLOGICAL DIVISION WAS EVIDENT. THE SYSTEMATICS DEPART-
MENTS OF BOTH SEMINARIES ADOPTED A RESOLUTION STATING THAT THE ESSAY
UNDERMINED THE AUTHOR OF THE SCRIPTURE AND CONFUSED THE LAW AND
GOSPEL.
(4) IN APRIL, I RECEIVED A LETTER FROM A SENIOR MEMBER OF THE ST. LOUIS
FACULTY [DR. SCHARLEMANN] WHICH POINTED OUT THEOLOGICAL PROBLEMS
OF SUCH A MAGNITUDE AS TO REQUIRE THE RESOURCES OF THE SYNODICAL
PRESIDENT'S OFFICE TO A SOLUTION.
THEREFORE I DID NOT UNDERTAKE THE INVESTIGATION ON THE ASSUMPTION
THAT ANYONE WAS GUILTY OF FALSE DOCTRINE, BUT RATHER TO FIND OUT WHAT
THE SITUATION ACTUALLY WAS. IF THE PRESIDENT OF THE SYNOD COULD BE
PREVENTED FROM ASKING QUESTIONS OF OUR PROFESSORS, WHO COULD EVER
ASK THEM?[63]

It is noteworthy that early in 1967 honorary President, Dr. John W.
Behnken had addressed questions to the faculty of the St. Louis Seminary
through Dr. A.O. Fuerbringer. These questions had to do especially with the
faculty stand on the doctrine of Creation as put forth in Genesis, the Fall, Adam
and Eve, portions of Israelite history, and biblical miracles. These questions
were prompted by a deep concern which Dr. Behnken felt after attending two
meetings of the Council of Presidents and the Theological faculties. In his own
words: "I was troubled very much."[64]

HISTORY OF THE SEMINARY
FACULTY CONTROVERSY

The election of Jacob Preus to the presidency in 1969 was a mandate to the
synod to return to the old conservative ways, yes, to the long standing Franz
Pieper theology, and to straighten out matters at the St. Louis Seminary, which
many felt had gotten out of hand. It was soon after this, that Dr. Martin
Scharlemann—himself a highly controversial figure, who had been defended
by his colleagues against charges of false doctrine—made allegations to Dr.
Preus that false doctrine was being taught at the seminary and that the problem was serious. Dr. Scharlemann, as well as others, urged that an investigation be conducted.

In April 1970 President Preus announced that he would appoint a Fact
Finding Committee to investigate charges of false doctrine in the teaching of
St. Louis Seminary faculty members. He proposed that he and the synodical
vice-presidents handle the investigation, using Article II of the Synodical Con-
stitution. The St. Louis Seminary was at the time the largest assembly of
Lutheran scholars and students in the world.

In September 1970 the Seminary Board of Control proposed that it handle the investigation of the charges against the faculty as mandated by the Bylaws. Preus declined. Instead, he named a five-member Fact Finding Committee. In October this Committee began its work. From December 1970 to March 1971 faculty interviews were conducted, the faculty members having pledged their cooperation, although they questioned whether the procedure to be used would provide an accurate picture of the teachings conduced on campus.

On June 15, 1971, the Report of the Fact Finding Committee was delivered to President Preus. This very detailed and complete report was referred by the 1971 Synod Convention to the Seminary Board of Control for study. The Convention directed the Board to take appropriation action on the basis of the report, commending or correcting faculty members where necessary. The Board was to report to the synod president and to the Board of Higher Education. The president was requested to issue a report to the synod within one year.

During 1971 and 1972 the Board reviewed the report issued by the Fact Finding Committee and interviewed faculty members during the academic year. In March of 1972 President Preus issued his "A Statement of Scriptural and Confessional Principles." The stated purpose of the document was not to be "a new standard of orthodoxy" but to serve as a "tool" to "facilitate the task of the Board of Control." It was shared with the synod for purposes of "information" and "guidance." During the same month, Doctor Ehlen's renewal of appointment was refused by the Board of Higher Education and his professorship was terminated. This action resulted from lecture notes given anonymously to Dr. Preus. When Dr. Ehlen convinced the Board that the notes falsified his position, the Board offered him a one-year contract to continue discussions with him. Dr. Preus instructed President Tietjen not to permit Ehlen to teach certain courses. The impasse that resulted was overcome through a compromise between Preus and Tietjen. Ehlen would teach some courses, not others. Within one month Preus informed the synod's Board for Higher Education (appointed by Preus) that apparently no progress was being made, and the Board voided Ehlen's contract.

In June 1972 the Board of Control gave its report after studying the Fact Finding Committee report and after interviewing faculty members regarding it. The announced conclusion of the Board of Control was: "The board to this date has found no false doctrine among the members of the seminary faculty."[65] However, a minority report of the St. Louis Seminary Board charged, "We cannot report in good conscience that there is no false doctrine."

In his prefatory letter to his 160 page "Blue Book" report (a response with material from the Fact Finding Committee's report, personal observations, and such things as correspondence with the Board of Control) Dr. Preus stated: WE DO HAVE PROBLEMS AT THE SEMINARY, WHICH HAVE INCREASINGLY THREATENED THE UNITY OF OUR SYNOD...WE HAVE BEEN DIVIDED TOO LONG...WHILE THE ISSUES ARE MANY AND COMPLEX, THE BASIC ISSUE IS THE RELATIONSHIP BETWEEN THE SCRIPTURES AND THE GOSPEL. TO PUT THE MATTER IN OTHER WORDS, THE QUESTION IS WHETHER THE SCRIPTURES ARE THE NORM OF OUR FAITH AND LIFE OR WHETHER THE GOSPEL ALONE IS THAT NORM.[66]

President Preus felt that evidence gathered by the Fact Finding Committee substantiated the following, if not with reference to all, then at least with ref-

667

erence to individual faculty members: (a) A false doctrine of the nature of the Holy Scriptures coupled with methods of interpretation which effectually erode the authority of the Scriptures. (b) A substantial undermining of the confessional Doctrine of Original Sin by a *de facto* denial of the historical events on which it is based. (c) A permissiveness toward certain false doctrines. (d) A tendency to deny that the Law is a normative guide for Christian behavior. (e) A conditional acceptance of the Lutheran Confessions. (f) A strong claim that the seminary faculty need not teach in accord with the Synod's official doctrinal statements and resolutions.[67]

Summarizing his feelings, Dr. Preus pointed out: IT IS EVIDENT THAT THE USE OF THE HISTORICAL-CRITICAL METHOD HAS BROUGHT ABOUT CHANGES BOTH IN OUR DOCTRINAL STANCE, OUR CERTAINTY, AND OUR ATTITUDES TOWARD DOCTRINE...WE HAVE TWO THEOLOGIES. WITH THE INFLUENTIAL POSITION THE SEMINARY HOLDS IN THE CHURCH, ITS VIEWS WILL PREVAIL UNLESS THE SYNOD DIRECTS OTHERWISE AND SEES TO IT THAT ITS DIRECTIVES ARE IMPLEMENTED.[68]

It was evident of course that a disagreement existed between the Seminary Board of Control, as it was constituted at that time, and Dr. Preus. This especially involved the question whether the issues existing between the synod and the St. Louis faculty were theological or doctrinal in nature. The Board of Control held to the former, President Preus to the latter position. The Commission on Theology and Church Relations (CTCR) stood with President Preus in this matter. Simply put, "The President's report holds that in the report of the Fact Finding Committee there is evidence of 'false doctrine' pertaining to the nature of the Holy Scriptures."[69] Furthermore, while the Blue Book of the president (quoted in the above report) stated that there was no false doctrine concerning the great, central doctrines of Christianity, much of the material, however, conveyed the opposite impression.

In regards to the doctrine of Scripture, the basic difference that existed between Dr. Preus and the synod on the one hand, and the St. Louis Seminary faculty majority on the other, can be summarized by listing three points from Preus' "Statement of Scriptural and Confessional Principles," followed by the same three points in the faculty document "Faithful to Our Calling—Faithful to Our Lord," Part I.

(1) INSPIRATION PERTAINS TO THE HOLY SPIRIT'S AUTHORSHIP OF EVERY WORD OF THE SCRIPTURES (IV, A);

(2) INERRANCY PERTAINS TO THE TRUTHFULNESS OF THE SCRIPTURES IN ALL THEIR PARTS AND WORDS. THE VIEW IS REJECTED THAT THE SCRIPTURES ARE INERRANT ONLY IN MATTERS THAT PERTAIN DIRECTLY TO THE GOSPEL (IV, F);

(3) THE SOTERIOLOGICAL PURPOSE OF SCRIPTURE [I.E. PERTAINING TO SALVATION] IN NO SENSE PERMITS US TO CALL INTO QUESTION OR DENY THE HISTORICITY OR FACTUALITY OF MATTERS RECORDED IN THE BIBLE (IV,B)

Relative to the above points, the seminary faculty document expresses itself thus:

(1) THE INSPIRATION OF THE WRITTEN WORD PERTAINS TO THE EFFECTIVE POWER OF THE SCRIPTURES TO BRING MEN AND WOMEN TO SALVATION (P. 36);

(2) INERRANCY OF THE SCRIPTURES PERTAINS ONLY TO THE DISCLOSURE OF THE TRUTH ABOUT WHAT GOD WAS DOING IN CHRIST [I.E. THE GOSPEL OF SAL-

(3)   SINCE FAITH RESTS IN THE PROMISES OF A FAITHFUL GOD AND NOT IN THE ACCURACY OF ANCIENT HISTORIANS (P. 26), IT IS NOT NECESSARY TO INSIST ON THE HISTORICITY OF EVERY DETAIL OF THE LIFE OF JESUS AS RECORDED BY THE EVANGELISTS (P. 25).[70]

The following conclusion was reached on the basis of he comparison:

A COMPARISON OF THE TWO POSITIONS RELATIVE TO THE ABOVE THREE POINTS SUBSTANTIATES THE JUDGMENT THAT WITH RESPECT TO THE DOCTRINE OF HOLY SCRIPTURES THE ALTERNATIVES ARE SHARP AND MUTUALLY EXCLUSIVE, AND THAT THE SYNOD MUST FACE THE GRAVE ISSUE OF FUNDAMENTAL DISAGREE-MENT WHICH HAS FAR-REACHING IMPLICATIONS FOR ALL OF THEOLOGY.

...THE PRESENT DISAGREEMENT IN OUR SYNOD, THEN, MUST STEM FROM THOSE WHO CANNOT ACCEPT THE PRESIDENT'S "STATEMENT" AND WHO ARE THERE-FORE IN DISAGREEMENT WITH THE POSITION OF THE SYNOD ITSELF.[71]

Dr. Tietjen's response to the report of the Fact Finding Committee came within a week (September 8, 1972). His "Fact Finding or Fault Finding?" was a double-column, thirty-five page document which rejected the validity of the report, calling it "unfair," "unreliable," "untrue," "less than Scriptural," and "unLutheran,"—even though in his accompanying letter Dr. Tietjen admitted that "there are indeed genuine doctrinal issues that must be confronted and re-solved," and that the "issue is a doctrinal issue." Dr. Tietjen spoke of President Preus and the member of the Fact Finding Committee as "our adversaries."

On September 9, 1972, the faculty majority stated: "We agree with President Tietjen's letter in response to the Report and with his analysis of the fact find-ing process." Dr. Tietjen had dismissed the procedural method of the FFC as "garbage in, garbage out."

Later, at a meeting of the Council of Presidents, the seminary president characterized the theology of the synodical president and of the Fact Finding Committee as "sub-Biblical" and "unLutheran."[72]

The New Orleans Convention in 1973 heard the following report concerning the faculty's position:

THE FACULTY OF THE ST. LOUIS SEMINARY INDICATED HOW SERIOUSLY IT DIS-AGREES WITH THE DOCTRINAL POSITION OF THE SYNOD'S PRESIDENT WHEN IT CALLED HIS "STATEMENT OF SCRIPTURAL AND CONFESSIONAL PRINCIPLES" "DI-VISIVE," THEREBY DECLARING THAT IN THE FACULTY'S OPINION THE SYNODICAL PRESIDENT'S POSITION IS SO RADICALLY OPPOSED TO THE FACULTY'S POSITION THAT THE SYNODICAL PRESIDENT'S POSITION MUST BE REGARDED AS INJURIOUS TO THE UNITY OF THE SYNOD.

THE FUNDAMENTAL DISAGREEMENT IN OUR CHURCH, POSING ALTERNATIVES THAT ARE SHARP AND MUTUALLY EXCLUSIVE, HAS TO DO PRINCIPALLY WITH A DOCTRINE OF BASIC IMPORTANCE FOR LUTHERAN THEOLOGY, NAMELY THE DOC-TRINE OF THE AUTHORITY OF THE HOLY SCRIPTURES AS CONFESSED IN ARTICLE II OF THE SYNOD'S CONSTITUTION.[73]

In his document, "Fact Finding or Fault Finding?" the president of the St. Louis Seminary accused the theology of the Fact Finding Committee and of the synod's president as constituting "an incipient distortion of the Biblical Gospel of our Lord and Savior Jesus Christ" and that it "threatens our Synod with grave danger." Furthermore, that it "needs to be exposed and corrected lest it worsen, and in worsening, destroy the faith by which we live."[74]

In December 1972, acting in response to a request by the Council of Presidents, the seminary faculty issued two documents called "Faithful to Our Calling—Faithful to Our Lord." The faculty's stated purpose was to assure the church...THAT WE DO INDEED TEACH IN ACCORD WITH THE DOCTRINAL POSITION OF THE LC-MS AS SET FORTH IN ARTICLE II OF THE CONSTITUTION, AND THAT WE CONTINUE TO STAND UNDER THE NORMS OF THAT ARTICLE. Dr. Robert Preus sent a letter with this request: ... "list my name as opposing the joint confession."

Part I of the document represents the joint stance of the faculty except for "the minority five." Part II constitutes a more extensive project on the part of the faculty and provides individual statements by the members. The following paragraphs are excerpts from especially pertinent portions of the document, "Faithful...," Part I:

GOD's CREATION AND THE BEGINNINGS: REGARDING THE SCRIPTURAL ACCOUNTS OF CREATION: THROUGH EACH OF THESE DESCRIPTIONS GOD'S SPOKESMEN CONFRONT US WITH A MESSAGE OF GOD, NOT A TEXTBOOK ON SCIENCE. THEY SPEAK PRIMARILY TO OUR FAITH RATHER THAN OUR INTELLECT...ANY EFFORT, THEREFORE, TO EQUATE THESE DESCRIPTIONS OF CREATION WITH GIVEN SCIENTIFIC THEORY ABOUT THE ORIGIN OF THE WORLD IS TO BE REJECTED. LIKEWISE, ANY SUGGESTION THAT A GIVEN SCIENTIFIC THEORY ABOUT THE ORIGIN OF LIFE OR THE STRUCTURE OF THE UNIVERSE IS BINDING ON BELIEVERS MERELY BECAUSE IT IS WIDELY ACCEPTED IS ALSO TO BE REJECTED...THE BIBLE ACCOUNTS OF GOD CREATING THE WORLD, HOWEVER, CALL FOR A RESPONSE OF PRAISE AND WONDER, NOT BIOLOGICAL OR GEOLOGICAL INVESTIGATION.

GOD's CREATION AND HUMAN BEGINNINGS: ANY CONSIDERATION OF GENESIS 2-3 IN THIS CONNECTION MUST TAKE INTO ACCOUNT THE KIND OF LITERATURE EMPLOYED HERE AND THE INTENTION OF THE BIBLICAL WRITER. WE DISTINGUISH TODAY BETWEEN NEWS REPORTS, EDITORIALS, SHORT STORIES, POEMS, DRAMAS, AND OTHER TYPES OF LITERATURE AND THE VARIOUS WAYS IN WHICH THEY COMMUNICATE A MESSAGE. THE HOLY SCRIPTURES ALSO INCLUDE MANY DIFFERENT KINDS OF LITERATURE INCLUDING POEMS, HISTORICAL NARRATIVES, PARABLES, AND SERMONS. REGARDLESS OF WHAT FORM OF LITERATURE A GIVEN BIBLICAL WRITER MAY EMPLOY, HIS ULTIMATE PURPOSE IS ALWAYS TO CONVEY THE WORD OF GOD TO HIS PEOPLE. A LEGITIMATE DIFFERENCE OF OPINION OFTEN EXISTS AMONG STUDENTS OF THE SCRIPTURES ABOUT THE PRECISE TYPE OF LITERATURE BEING EMPLOYED OR THE EXTENT TO WHICH A NARRATIVE IS HISTORICAL, POETIC, OR PARABOLIC.

...THE DISCUSSION IN OUR CHURCH ABOUT GENESIS 2-3 IS A DEBATE ABOUT THE KIND OF LITERATURE FOUND IN THIS TEXT RATHER THAN ABOUT ITS DOCTRINAL CONTENT. MANY WITHIN OUR SYNOD HOLD THAT THESE CHAPTERS ARE A LITERAL HISTORICAL ACCOUNT OF THE LIVES OF TWO SPECIFIC INDIVIDUALS KNOWN AS ADAM AND EVE. THOSE WHO HOLD THIS POSITION RECOGNIZE THAT THE MESSAGE OF THE TEXT DEALS WITH OUR NATIVE SINFULNESS. OUR CORRUPTION IS A REALITY THAT IS AS TRUE FOR US AS IT WAS FOR OUR FIRST PARENTS.

OTHERS IN OUR SYNOD MAINTAIN THAT GENESIS 2-3 IS NOT AN EYEWITNESS REPORT OR A HISTORICAL ACCOUNT SIMILAR TO MODERN HISTORICAL ANNALS.

THEY CONTEND THAT THE EVIDENCE WITHIN THE TEXT ITSELF INDICATES THAT IT IS AN ANCIENT THEOLOGICAL DOCUMENT, WHICH USES THE NARRATIVE FORM. THIS TEXT IS MORE LIKE A SERMON THAN A NEWS REPORT...ANY EFFORT TO PRESS THE DETAILS OF THIS NARRATIVE ACCORDING TO THE YARDSTICK OF MODERN HISTORIES IS NOT CONSISTENT WITH THE INTENT OF THE PASSAGE.

REGARDING THE PROMISE AND THE SCRIPTURES: ANY TENDENCY TO MAKE THE DOCTRINE OF THE INSPIRATION OR THE INERRANCY OF THE SCRIPTURES A PRIOR TRUTH, WHICH GUARANTEES THE TRUTH OF THE GOSPEL OR GIVES SUPPORT TO OUR FAITH IS SECTARIAN. THE GOSPEL GIVES THE SCRIPTURES THEIR NORMATIVE CHARACTER, NOT VICE VERSA. WE ARE SAVED BY GRACE THROUGH FAITH IN CHRIST ALONE, NOT THROUGH FAITH IN CHRIST AND SOMETHING ELSE, EVEN IF THAT SOMETHING ELSE BE THE BIBLE ITSELF.

...ANY TEACHING WHICH DOES NOT MAINTAIN THE ABSOLUTE CENTRALITY OF THE GOSPEL IN THE INTERPRETATION OF THE SCRIPTURES OR THE SOLE SUFFICIENCY OF THE PROMISE FOR OUR REDEMPTION IS UNBIBLICAL AND LESS THAN LUTHERAN.

...ANY APPROACH TO THE SCRIPTURES WHICH FOCUSES ON THE NEED FOR HISTORICAL FACTUALITY RATHER THAN ON THE PRIMARY NEED FOR CHRIST LEADS US AWAY FROM CHRIST RATHER THAN TO HIM. FOR JESUS CHRIST IS THE PROMISE WHICH GOD KEPT FOR US. AND THAT PROMISE IS OURS BY FAITH ALONE, NOT BY THE VERIFICATION OF HISTORICAL DETAILS.

THE FACT THAT A GIVEN BIBLICAL EPISODE IS HISTORICAL IS NOT IMPORTANT IN AND OF ITSELF. THE IMPORTANCE OF SUCH HISTORICAL EVENTS LIES IN WHAT GOD WAS DOING IN AND THROUGH THEM. WE SEARCH THEM FOR THE PROMISE; WE LOOK FOR WHAT DRIVES US TO CHRIST...BY THAT PROMISE WE LIVE, IN ITS LIGHT WE CARRY OUT OUR THEOLOGICAL TASK, AND FROM ITS ORBIT WE INTERPRET THE SCRIPTURES.

EVEN THOUGH WE MAY NOT BE ABLE TO HARMONIZE HISTORICAL DISCREPANCIES WHICH APPEAR IN THE NEW TESTAMENT GOSPEL ACCOUNTS, THAT FACT DOES NOT SHAKE OUR FAITH OR INVALIDATE THESE ACCOUNTS AS WORD OF GOD. OUR FAITH RESTS IN THE PROMISE OF A FAITHFUL GOD, NOT IN THE ACCURACY OF ANCIENT HISTORIANS.

REGARDING THE HOLY SPIRIT AND THE COMMUNITY OF GOD: FOR THE SPIRIT IS THE LIVING, ACTIVE POWER OF GOD WORKING THROUGH THE WORD TO LEAD HUMAN BEINGS TO JESUS CHRIST, WHETHER THAT WORD BE WRITTEN OR ORAL, IN THE OLD TESTAMENT PROMISE OR THE NEW TESTAMENT GOSPEL. ACCORDINGLY, THE INSPIRATION OF THE WRITTEN WORD PERTAINS TO THE EFFECTIVE POWER OF THE SCRIPTURES TO BRING MEN AND WOMEN TO SALVATION THROUGH THE GOSPEL. WE AFFIRM, THEREFORE, THAT THE SCRIPTURES ARE THE INSPIRED WORD OF GOD. (NOTE: THIS LAST STATEMENT ON INSPIRATION WAS A KEY STATEMENT IN THE CONTROVERSY, AS HAS ALREADY BEEN POINTED OUT.)

THE BREATH OF GOD WORKING IN AND THROUGH THE SCRIPTURES EXPRESSES THE SAME IDEA [I.E. THAT GOD'S POWER ACTIVELY ACCOMPLISHES HIS PURPOSES]. FOR, AS A RESULT OF THIS DIVINE IN-BREATHING, THE SCRIPTURES HAVE THE CAPACITY TO TEACH, REPROVE, AND EDIFY THE COMMUNITY OF GOD. ALL OF THIS IS TRUE BECAUSE FIRST OF ALL, THE SCRIPTURES ARE ABLE THROUGH THE SPIRIT "TO INSTRUCT YOU FOR SALVATION THROUGH FAITH IN

CHRIST JESUS" (2 TIM. 3:15).
THROUGHOUT THE SCRIPTURES LITTLE IS SAID ABOUT PRECISELY HOW THE
PROPHETS OR APOSTLES WERE INSPIRED. THE SPIRIT IS SEEN AS THE LIVING
POWER OF GOD ACCOMPLISHING HIS PURPOSES THROUGH THEM; AND HIS UL-
TIMATE PURPOSE IS THE SALVATION OF ALL MEN THROUGH JESUS CHRIST. TO
FOCUS ON THE HOW OF INSPIRATION, THEREFORE, IS TO DIVERT OUR ATTENTION
FROM THE CHRIST TO WHOM THE SPIRIT DIRECTS US. IN ACHIEVING GOD'S PUR-
POSE, THE SPIRIT OPERATES WITH MEN AND WOMEN WHO ARE LIMITED AND
CONDITIONED BY THE CULTURE AND LANGUAGE OF THEIR TIMES. THE WORD OF
PROMISE WAS SPOKEN AMID THE AMBIGUITIES OF HUMAN LIVES AND WITHIN
THE LIMITATIONS OF HUMAN LANGUAGES. YET THE WORD ALWAYS GETS
THROUGH TO GOD'S COMMUNITY, AND HIS PROMISE IS TRUE FOR ALL WHO BE-
LIEVE IT. THEY CAN RELY ON THAT WORD THROUGH WHICH THE SPIRIT WORKS.
BECAUSE OF THE GOSPEL WE AFFIRM THE RELIABILITY OF THE SCRIPTURES,
NOT VICE VERSA. WE BELIEVE THE SCRIPTURES BECAUSE WE BELIEVE IN JESUS
CHRIST. HE IS THE ONE WHO INTERPRETS THE FATHER TO US; HE IS THE KEY
TO UNDERSTANDING THE SCRIPTURES.
REGARDING THE HOLY SPIRIT AND THE TEACHING ACTIVITY
OF THE CHURCH: THE SACRED SCRIPTURES LAY DOWN NO RULES FOR IN-
TERPRETATION AND PRESCRIBE NO METHOD FOR COMMUNICATING THE MESSAGE
OF THE SCRIPTURES TO SUCCESSIVE GENERATIONS OF CHRISTIANS. THE SCRIP-
TURES ARE IN A UNIQUE SENSE THE WRITTEN WORD OF GOD AND DESERVE DUE
REVERENCE. BUT THE FUNDAMENTAL PRINCIPLES OF INTERPRETATION, SUCH
AS "A TEXT MUST BE STUDIED IN THE LIGHT OF ITS LITERARY CONTEXT," "SCRIP-
TURE INTERPRETS SCRIPTURE," "EACH PASSAGE HAS ONE LITERAL SENSE," "ALL
FEATURES OF THE TEXT MUST BE INTERPRETED IN THEIR HISTORICAL MILIEU,"
ARE NOT LAID DOWN IN THE SCRIPTURES.
BASICALLY ALL THE TECHNIQUES ASSOCIATED WITH "HISTORICAL-CRITICAL"
METHODOLOGY, SUCH AS SOURCE ANALYSIS, FORM HISTORY AND REDACTION
HISTORY ARE LEGITIMATED BY THE FACT THAT GOD CHOSE TO USE AS HIS WRIT-
TEN WORD HUMAN DOCUMENTS WRITTEN BY HUMAN BEINGS IN HUMAN LAN-
GUAGE...BECAUSE OF THE WEALTH OF INFORMATION ABOUT THE BIBLICAL
MILIEU THAT WE ARE PRIVILEGED TO POSSESS, "HISTORICAL-CRITICAL" METHOD-
OLOGY PROVIDES US WITH VALUABLE INSIGHTS INTO THE INTENDED MEANING OF
THE WRITTEN WORD OF GOD AS WE HAVE IT. NEITHER THE SACRED SCRIP-
TURES NOR THE BOOK OF CONCORD ENJOINS A PARTICULAR METHOD AS THE
ONLY WAY OF INTERPRETING SCRIPTURES.[75]

In March 1973 the Board of Control of the seminary voted to commend Pres-
ident John Tietjen and all faculty members, noting with gratitude that no false
doctrine had been found. This, of course, did not agree with the findings of
President Preus or of the Commission on Theology and Church Relations. The
CTCR adopted an evaluation of the faculty majority's document "Faithful To
Our Calling..." which concludes that the document is not suitable for use in discussion forums in the synod unless its serious inadequacies are pointed out.
Later, the commission asked the synod to reject any historical-critical method
of Biblical interpretation that deprives the Scriptures of their divine authority.
   On May 22, 1973, the faculty majority adopted the "Response of the Faculty
of Concordia Seminary, St. Louis, to the 'Report of the Synodical President.'"

As reported by the 1973 Convention Proceedings: THIS DOCUMENT SERVES TO REITERATE THE FACULTY'S VIEWS AS EXPRESSED IN THE "FAITHFUL" DOCUMENTS, AND, IN ADDITION, REFUSES TO RECOGNIZE THE VALIDITY OF ANY OF THE CHARGES OF FALSE TEACHING.[76]

Three areas of concern were outlined and expressed to the 1973 New Orleans Convention:

(1) REGARDING THE AUTHORITY OF THE SCRIPTURAL WORD: THE FACULTY WOULD MAKE THE GOSPEL THE "GOVERNING PRINCIPLE" INSTEAD OF THE SCRIPTURAL WORD: "IT IS OUR CONVICTION THAT ANY EFFORT, HOWEVER SUBTLE, TO SUPPLEMENT THE GOSPEL SO THAT IT IS NO LONGER THE SOLE GROUND OF OUR FAITH OR THE GOVERNING PRINCIPLE FOR OUR THEOLOGY IS TO BE REJECTED AS UNLUTHERAN, CONTRARY TO OUR CONFESSION, AND INJURIOUS TO THE MISSION OF THE CHURCH. ("FAITHFUL..., PART I," P. 3)

(2) REGARDING THE THREAT TO THE GOSPEL THROUGH "GOSPEL REDUCTIONISM" ("A SUBORDINATION OR LIMITATION OF THE NORMATIVE AUTHORITY OF SCRIPTURE TO ITS GOSPEL CONTENT OR FUNCTION...A REDUCING OF ALL DOCTRINE TO THE ONE DOCTRINE OF THE GOSPEL AND MAKING THE GOSPEL [OFTEN UNDEFINED] THE ONLY NORM FOR ALL DOCTRINE AND LIFE, (PREUS, QUOTED IN THE 1973 PROCEEDINGS, P. 136): AS PRESIDENT PREUS CORRECTLY POINTS OUT, THIS OFTEN LEADS TO AN EROSION OF THE SCRIPTURE'S AUTHORITY, ESPECIALLY AS REGARDS MATTERS LIKE HISTORY, GEOGRAPHY, AND NATURE BUT ALSO OF SUCH IMPORTANT MATTERS AS THE ORDERS OF CREATION AND OTHER EXPRESSIONS OF GOD'S WILL FOR WHAT WE ARE TO BELIEVE AND DO.

The report also pointed out:

SUCH "GOSPELISM" CORRESPONDS TO "FIDEISM," A CHIEF FAULT IN CONTEMPORARY THEOLOGY. IT SEPARATES MATTERS OF BELIEF FROM FACT, FROM MIRACULOUS EVENTS OR DETAILS AND QUESTIONS SCRIPTURE'S ACCURACY AND HISTORICITY IN A RUTHLESS MANNER...IT MUST BE POINTED OUT THAT THROUGHOUT "FAITHFUL...,I," IN SPITE OF THE EMPHASIS ON "GOSPEL," THERE IS ONLY A SUBDUED REFERENCE TO THE GOSPEL EXPRESSED IN TERMS OF THE FORGIVENESS OF SINS, IN FACT, TOTAL AVOIDANCE, IN TERM AND CONCEPT, OF VICARIOUS SATISFACTION, SUBSTITUTIONARY ATONEMENT, IMPUTATION OF CHRIST'S RIGHTEOUSNESS...AND THE HOPE OF ETERNAL LIFE IN HEAVEN. IN ITS PLACE THERE APPEARS RATHER A STRONG EMPHASIS UPON WHAT AT BEST CAN BE DESCRIBED AS A LATERAL-MOVING SORT OF "GOSPEL" THAT SEEKS FOR "THE LIBERATION OF HUMAN BEINGS FROM ALL EVILS" AND WAITS TO BE INSTRUCTED BY "THE THOUGHT PATTERNS OF EVERY CULTURE."[77] (CF. "FAITHFUL..., PART I," PP. 32,20,24)

REGARDING THE "THIRD USE" OF THE LAW, AS A GUIDE TO CHRISTIAN BEHAVIOR: IT IS THIS LATTER STRESS WHICH IS CONSPICUOUSLY SIDETRACKED IN THE FACULTY'S MOST RECENT DOCUMENT, "RESPONSE." THE ASSURANCE IS GIVEN THAT "NO ONE ON THE FACULTY REJECTS THE THIRD USE OF THE LAW AS OUTLINED IN THE FORMULA OF CONCORD." YET THE EXPLICATION WHICH FOLLOWS UPON THIS IS A STUDIED EFFORT AT EMPHASIZING "THE CONTINUING SIGNIFICANCE OF THE TEN COMMANDMENTS AS GOD'S LAW EXPOSING HUMAN SIN"— A THING WHICH NO LUTHERAN DENIES BUT WHICH IS THE "SECOND USE" OF THE LAW! THE FACULTY THEN ADDS THE AMBIVALENT ASSERTION THAT "THE CHRISTIAN IS LED BY THE SPIRIT OF CHRIST TO BE FREE AND TO FACE UP TO THE

CRITICISM OF THE LAW AND MOVE BEYOND THAT CRITICISM TO DEAL IN LOVE WITH PEOPLE," AND THAT "THE SCRIPTURES DO OFFER GUIDANCE IN WHAT IT MEANS TO LOVE ONE'S NEIGHBOR AS ONESELF." THE SAME KIND OF "CONFUSION AND AMBIGUITY," IN FACT "REJECTION OF THE THIRD USE OF THE LAW," WAS NOTED IN THE FACT FINDING COMMITTEE'S REPORT, (P. 120FF.). (Note: This material is taken from a resolution passed by the Convention, titled: "To Declare Faculty Majority Position in Violation of Article II of the Constitution.)[78]

Up to this time, President Preus was not able to make much progress in his work of stemming the tide of moderate theology sweeping through the synod. But in the summer of 1973 his hand was strengthened by his own reelection to office and by the election of a pro-Preus majority to the Seminary Board of Control. Furthermore, the New Orleans Convention in July adopted Preus' "A Statement" as scriptural and in accord with the Lutheran Confessions and "binding" on the membership of the synod. The vote was 562 to 455. Of course this action did not set well with the moderates, who were reluctant to add to the historic Lutheran Confessions, and who had responded on April 4, 1973, to "A Statement" with harsh criticism, which we have already noted: "unnecessary," "improper," "inadequate theologically," of "a spirit alien to Lutheran Confessional theology," "divisive and "invalid both as an assessment and as a solution of presumed problems at our seminary."

At the New Orleans Convention the Seminary Issues Committee drafted two resolutions that were strongly antiseminary. One condemned the faculty majority position in the discussion of issues in "Faithful to Our Calling..." as "not to be tolerated in the Church of God." The vote to condemn the faculty majority position which called for legitimizing the historical-critical method of biblical interpretation was adopted 574-451.

The second resolution contained ten charges against Dr. Tietjen and called for his removal from office, if he failed to resign. Dr. Tietjen dismissed the charges against him as trumped up, without supportive evidence. The moderates felt that Bylaw 1.27 had been violated, which called for the synodical president to screen out resolutions that contain defamatory allegations, that involve suspension or expulsion, or that call for actions for which there are other procedures. When it became evident to the Convention that the Bylaw had been violated, a substitute resolution was passed turning the case back to the Board of Control of the Seminary. The Board was now made up of conservatives.

James E. Adams in his book, *Preus of Missouri*, reports that John Tietjen was summoned to the presidential suite on the fourth day of the New Orleans Convention, which was July 10th, and handed the offer for him to resign within seventy-two hours as president of the seminary, under the agreement that no charges would be pressed publicly, but in their place a resolution would be offered for the delegates to act upon, praising Tietjen's "God-pleasing" and selfless churchmanship. Tietjen was given till three o'clock that afternoon to arrive at his decision. The seminary head refused, and the controversy was on in earnest.

In a speech delivered by Dr. Tietjen at the Convention he stated:

ON TUESDAY MORNING THE CHAIRMAN OF COMMITTEE #3, SPEAKING FOR COMMITTEE #3, TOGETHER WITH PRESIDENT PREUS, GAVE ME THE OPPORTU-

NITY OF RESIGNING FROM MY OFFICE SO THAT IT MIGHT NOT BE NECESSARY FOR RESOLUTION 3-12 TO COME TO THE FLOOR, AND SO THAT I MIGHT BE SPARED THE EMBARRASSMENT OF THAT RESOLUTION. BRETHREN, I DECLINED THAT OPPORTUNITY ON THE GROUNDS OF CONSCIENCE BECAUSE THE CALL THAT I HAVE TO MY POSITION AS PRESIDENT OF CONCORDIA SEMINARY, I BELIEVE, IS FROM GOD. COMMITTEE #3 PRESENTED RESOLUTION 3-12 WITH ITS GRIEVOUS ACCUSATIONS TO THE MEMBERS OF THIS CONVENTION, TO THE DELEGATES. IT HAS BEEN WITHDRAWN OR IT WAS NEVER BEFORE YOU, ONE OF THE TWO. YOU KNOW WHAT IT SAYS. I HAVE A COPY IN MY HAND, AND IT HAS BEEN REPORTED ON ALL OVER THE NATION. IN ADDITION TO THAT, GOOD BROTHERS, INSTEAD OF REPRIMANDING COMMITTEE #3 FOR PRESENTING THAT MATERIAL TO YOU, RATHER THAN RECOGNIZING, AS THEY NOW DO, THAT ADEQUATE PROCEDURES ARE AVAILABLE IN THE *HANDBOOK OF SYNOD* TO DEAL WITH THE MATTER, YOU DECLINED TO APOLOGIZE TO ME FOR ALL OF THOSE MATTERS THAT HAVE BEEN PUBLICLY PRESENTED. I REPEAT, LADIES AND GENTLEMEN OF THE CONVENTION, THAT I HAVE BEEN GRIEVOUSLY WRONGED. DR. TIETJEN THEN WENT ON TO TELL THE DELEGATES THAT HE FORGAVE THEM.

Mr. Adams in his book raises the question of ethics concerning Preus' actions. He, as others, noted a tendency in the administration to solve Missouri's problems by political maneuvering. His question constitutes a harsh indictment of Preus' methods:

IF IRREDUCIBLE DOCTRINAL GAPS EXIST, THEN A "MORAL" CHURCHMAN CANNOT EXPLOIT THOSE GAPS FOR PARTISAN GAINS. HE CANNOT PRETEND, AS PREUS SEEMED TO DO FROM THE BEGINNING, THAT A LITTLE MANEUVERING HERE AND A LITTLE PHYSIOLOGICAL PRESSURE THERE WILL SOLVE THE PROBLEM. AN ETHICAL CHURCHMAN COULD ONLY PRESIDE OVER A PEACEFUL AND DIGNIFIED SEPARATION OF THE PARTIES RATHER THAN TRYING TO SOOTHE THE FAITHFUL WITH TALK THAT PEACE WAS POSSIBLE IF ONLY THE RIGHT PARTY HELD POWER...IF, AS PREUS CONTENDED, NO COMPROMISE WAS POSSIBLE ON THE DOCTRINE OF THE INERRANT BIBLE, THEN HOW COULD PREUS HAVE ACTED ETHICALLY, BY ENGAGING IN ANY POLITICS, MUCH LESS PARTISAN POLITICS?[79]

In August 1973 the newly constituted Board of Control of the St. Louis Seminary in its first meeting voted to suspend Dr. Tietjen, since it was eager to have him out of office before the fall term began. However, legal aspects of the case surfaced and the following month the Commission of Constitutional Matters instructed the Board of Control to follow more orderly procedures. The Board then vacated its suspension decision of August.

In October 1973 two pastors who had accused Dr. Tietjen of false doctrine were granted interview by the seminary head. The following month they refiled their charges, adding two more which they had not discussed with him.

In November 1973 the Seminary Board of Control declined to renew the appointment of Professor Paul Goetting, who was not interviewed by the board nor given reasons for the board's action. Seven professors were notified of their impending retirement. One of those, Dr. Arthur Carl Piepkorn, died the following month of a heart attack. Five members of the board protested the manner in which the matter had been handled.

On December 8, 1973, Dr. Tietjen was offered a "deal." In return for his resignation, the administration would find him another post, drop all charges, rehire Professor Goetting, and allow the seven professors to come out of retirement. Tietjen declined the overture and ended the discussion. On March 1, 1974, after repeated denials , Jacob Preus admitted his involvement in the "deal" offered to Dr. Tietjen. To the Atlantic District Convention he stated, "I'm sorry that I did it."

On January 20, 1974, Dr. Tietjen was suspended as president of Concordia Seminary, St. Louis, on the grounds of malfeasance in office and dissemination of false doctrine. Three more professors, including Dr. Fuerbringer, were notified of their retirement effective the following month. Doctor Scharlemann was named acting president and all department heads were changed. Calling the proceedings against him a charade, Dr. Tietjen declined to participated in further discussions, claiming it was futile to continue when no one was listening.

By noon the next day, the majority of 680 students at the seminary suddenly propelled themselves into the theological fracas at Concordia. Some 300 of the 500 resident students called a class moratorium. Weary of the manner in which their education was being interrupted, and confused, they demanded that the heretics among the professors be named and fired, otherwise the board should cease and desist from making accusations. No answer was forthcoming to the students.

On January 22nd the faculty majority (40 professors and 9 executive staff members) called their own boycott and demanded that President Preus intervene with the Board of Control. A demand was made that the professors either be charged or cleared. The faculty majority reasoned that in suspending Dr. Tietjen the board had also suspended them since they held the very positions held by Tietjen. They dismissed the malfeasance charges as absurd and expressed the opinion that the "charge of false doctrine" was "trumped up, because President Tietjen accepts without reservation as we do, the Scriptures of the Old and New Testaments as the written Word of God and the only rule and norm of teaching and practice, and the Lutheran Confessions as a correct exposition of the Word of God." Their letter decried the fact that no heresy trial had been held. If Tietjen was in error then they shared his error. And so they demanded that President Preus either carry through with a proper heresy trial or else clear Tietjen and the faculty so they could get back to their classes. The letter was signed by forty-six faculty members who joined the boycott.[80]

During January and February 1974 there was exchange of correspondence between the faculty and President Preus. Preus was asked to exercise his pastoral and constitutional responsibility to "protect pastors, teachers and congregations in the performance of their duties and maintenance of their rights." Preus refused to intervene. According to Preus: "What is at stake is the Word of God in all its authority, clarity, and inerrancy" (January 29, 1974) Preus came forth with a "Message to the Church" (January 30th) which contained serious allegations against the faculty majority by "conservative" students who refused to identify themselves. Strangely enough this action was repudiated by "conservative" students on campus. For a month Preus and the seminary faculty and student body endured a standoff.

Efforts to solve the matter through a forum of involved parties on February 15 and 16 failed of success. At the same time, acting President Scharlemann announced that faculty paychecks would be withheld. On February 17, in the evening, the Board of Control notified all professors that they must declare their willingness by noon on February 18 to return to classes on Tuesday, the following day, or their appointments would be terminated. On February 18, the Board of Control voted to terminate all appointments of the faculty majority, issuing instructions for the vacating of offices and homes. Furthermore, the Board issued the order that all students who failed to register for the spring quarter were to vacate student dormitories and apartments by March 4.

Instead of returning to their classrooms the dissident professors (except for one, who was about to retire) announced that they would continue their teaching duties at a "Concordia Seminary in Exile" (which became known as "Seminex). Previous to their self-imposed exile, the students organized outreach teams to visit churches all over the country. It was during one of the rallies, organized by the students at Christ Church Cathedral in downtown St. Louis, that the idea of a "Seminary in Exile" was born. Here the faculty pledged to complete the students' education and also place the candidates come spring.

On February 19, all but about 50 students voted to leave Concordia. They marched across the campus and entered the quadrangle where they planted white crosses and then read a resolution which further protested and denounced the Board's action, declaring the action to be unchristian and immoral. The students draped the Martin Luther statue in black and then symbolically boarded up the main archway of the seminary. In their protest the students declared that they had "exiled" themselves from Concordia's campus. Dr. Scharlemann, the acting president, dismissed the student exodus as "mass madness." Marching, singing, weeping, the students and faculty marched away. In the words of writer James E. Adams: "By Tuesday, Concordia as it had long existed was dead." Only fourteen students continued to study under the few remaining faculty members.

What was especially irksome to the professors who left Concordia was the fact that Preus, a relatively new name in the synod, had succeeded in clearing out the moderate faction, which had gained such a powerful grip on the world's largest Lutheran seminary. Perhaps the words of Myron and Shirley Marty capture the prevailing mood of the faculty majority as they marched away in self-imposed exile:

THE FACULTY FAMILIES WOULD NOT BE HUMAN IF THEY DID NOT FEEL SOME ANGER AND RESENTMENT THAT, IN THE SIXTEEN YEARS SINCE THEY CAME INTO THE MISSOURI SYNOD, JACOB AND ROBERT PREUS, RESPECTIVELY SYNOD PRESIDENT AND SEMINARY VICE-PRESIDENT, SUCCEEDED SO WELL IN HARNESSING THE FEARS AND HOSTILITIES OF A SUBSTANTIAL NUMBER OF MEMBERS THAT THEY COULD DRIVE INTO EXILE MEN WITH DEEP ROOTS IN THE MISSOURI SYNOD—A FUERBRINGER, A CAEMERER, A HOYER, A BERTRAM, A MAYER....REGRET, SHAME, GRATITUDE, PUZZLEMENT, RESENTMENT—SUCH A MIXED BAG OF EMOTIONS.[81]

On February 20, 1974, the Seminary in Exile ("Seminex") opened classes at St. Louis University and Eden Seminary with 385 students. Seminex was at first a seminary conducted within the Missouri Synod. The hope was that their action would force "serious dialogue in the synod calling for all parties to recognize their errors in deeds and words."

On March 22, 1974, the Council of Presidents voted to place 124 Seminex vicarage candidates with supervision by the Board for Higher Education. The following day the Constitution Commission (appointed by Preus) ruled that Seminex graduates could not receive pastorates without obtaining finishing credits from St. Louis Seminary. Congregations calling them were told they risked forfeiting synodical membership.

In April 1974 Dr. Scharlemann resigned as acting president of the seminary due to nervous exhaustion. Robert Preus was appointed to fill his place.

In May 1974 the Council of Presidents, by a one vote margin, refused to place Seminex grads unless they agreed to an interview and were approved. The Seminex candidates declined interviews as constituting tacit approval of the "unjust and unloving way" the seminary administration had dealt with the former faculty majority. Many district presidents decided not to abide by the administration's views regarding the placing of candidates. However, in September 1974 the Constitution Commission declared "null and void" ordinations, investitures, commissionings and other rites, which committed ministries of Word and Sacrament to Seminex pastoral candidates.

In October the Board of Control of the Seminary convicted Dr. Tietjen of all charges at a special meeting. Dr. Tietjen himself was not able to be present. In January 1975 Professor Edgar Kretz resigned his position at Concordia since he had been barred from teaching. In February Dr. Tietjen was elected to the presidency of Seminex and was installed in a service held at Christ Church Cathedral (the same church which in 1838 had offered its facilities to the Saxon exiles). The following month the seminary was accredited by the Association of Theological Schools and granted associate membership.

ELIM: THE DISSENTING MOVEMENT

By the time the New Orleans 1973 Convention was over, there could be little doubt in any mind that the conservatives were on the march in the Missouri Synod and had become a force to be reckoned with. And the moderate faction? Up to this time, though vocal in their dissent, the moderates were nevertheless not an organized movement within the synod. However, this was soon to change, for following the Convention the moderates met in Chicago to organize themselves. The result was: Evangelical Lutherans in Mission (ELIM). The moderates became an organized voice of disagreement, not only with administration policy in handling the internal conflict raging in the synod, but also with the administration's philosophy toward the synod's program of outreach in missions. They feared that the synod was not concerned enough with ministering to the total man, that is, the synod lacked a social ministry. They also feared that the synod was too unbending toward ecumenical involvement in the mission field, and regarded this attitude as a departure from the spirit of the "Mission Affirmation" of the 1960's. Many interpreted the "Affirmation" as a movement toward a more social-conscious ministry and a more ecumenical approach to missions.

ELIM took two steps which brought it much criticism in the Missouri Synod.

In 1974 the organized group of moderates adopted as part of the ELIM mission program the launching of an independent mission society, "Partners in Mission." This agency began sending missionaries abroad, giving them financial support. The second step was to adopt the "Concordia-in-Exile" or Seminex as part of the ELIM program "for continued theological education." Furthermore ELIM established its own newspaper, *Missouri in Perspective*, and openly solicited funds from congregations, requesting that ELIM be included in congregational budgets.

ELIM leaders continued to assure the synod that their dissident group was not seeking division of the synod. The claim was made: "Our objectives are positive and helpful..." Nevertheless, ELIM went on to ordain graduates of Seminex, knowing that it would cause a disturbance, since placement of graduates is the sole responsibility of the Council of Presidents of the Missouri Synod. Furthermore, on October 17, 1974, an "Urgent Notice" to all pastors and congregational chairmen of the synod was sent out in which was contained this statement by ELIM's Director of Development: YOU AND YOUR CONGREGATION CAN BE A PART OF A GROWING MOVEMENT OF PEOPLE WHO SAY, "WE WILL NOT SUPPORT ANY INSTITUTION WHICH MAKES A MOCKERY OF JUSTICE, BYPASSES DUE PROCESSES, AND TOLERATES INHUMAN AND GODLESS ACTS...THE SITUATION IN OUR SYNOD IS NOW OF SUCH NATURE THAT WE MUST QUESTION WHETHER IT IS DESERVING OF OUR CONTINUED SUPPORT." This statement was made in reference to the dismissal of Dr. Tietjen from the presidency of the St. Louis Seminary. A letter sent with this notice appealed for financial support for ELIM in the congregation's budget and/or by individual donations.

To the practical person, ELIM constituted a church within a church and for that reason tended to be divisive and schismatic.

On August 13-15, 1975, ELIM, meeting in assembly in the Chicago area, passed a resolution...(1) To encourage study, consultation, worship and mission activities which intensify and celebrate Lutheran unity. (2) To recognize and celebrate complete pulpit and altar fellowship with all Lutherans. And so, ELIM espoused complete fellowship with all Lutherans. The dissident Missouri group had plainly spoken in favor of a state of unionism with all those Lutheran bodies with which the Missouri Synod was not in fellowship because of lack of agreement in doctrine and polity. What could be more indicative of ELIM's potential move out of the Missouri Synod to the status of an independent body?

What to do with ELIM? The 1975 Anaheim Convention faced this perplexing problem. It was the old problem of how to solve the conflict between the moderate and conservative positions. President Preus laid the matter out before the delegates:

IT IS EVIDENT THAT FOR THE PAST TWO DECADES AT LEAST WE HAVE HAD TWO OPPOSING THEOLOGIES, PARTICULARLY WITH REFERENCE TO THE DOCTRINE OF HOLY SCRIPTURE. NO CHURCH BODY CAN LONG SUPPORT TWO THEOLOGIES WHICH ARE IN CONFLICT. WE HAVE SPOKEN AND SET FORTH CLEARLY OUR DOCTRINAL POSITION BOTH AT NEW ORLEANS AND THROUGHOUT THE ENTIRE HISTORY OF OUR SYNOD. THE PEOPLE OF OUR CONGREGATIONS HAVE A RIGHT TO BE ASSURED AND TO KNOW THAT THE MEN AND WOMEN WHO ARE CALLED TO SERVE AS WORKERS IN THEIR MIDST ARE FIRMLY DEDICATED TO THE SCRIPTURES

AND THE LUTHERAN CONFESSIONS AND THAT THEY WILL TEACH AND CARRY
OUT THE DUTIES OF THEIR OFFICE IN CONFORMITY WITH OUR FAITH AND PRAC-
TICE.
...WE HAVE THE PROBLEMS OF SEMINEX AND UNCERTIFIED GRADUATES WHO
ARE ENTERING THE PARISHES OF THE SYNOD...WE ALSO HAVE A SAD AND DIF-
FICULT PROBLEM IN THAT A SMALL NUMBER OF DISTRICT PRESIDENTS, FOR REA-
SONS WHICH ARE WELL UNDERSTOOD AND WITH WHICH ONE CAN CERTAINLY
SYMPATHIZE, HAVE FOUND THEMSELVES AT ODDS WITH THE CONSTITUTION AND
BYLAWS OF THE SYNOD. THE COUNCIL OF PRESIDENTS HAS DISCUSSED THIS
MATTER AT VERY GREAT LENGTH, AND EFFORTS HAVE BEEN MADE IN THE COUN-
CIL TO HAVE ALL OF THE MEMBERS TAKE A UNITED STAND IN REGARD TO OUR
COMMITMENT TO THE CONSTITUTION AND BYLAWS OF THE SYNOD.....THE
SYNOD SPEAKS, AND HER SERVANTS EITHER AGREE TO PERFORM THEIR DUTIES
IN KEEPING WITH THE WILL OF THE SYNOD OR REMOVE THEMSELVES FROM OF-
FICE.
....WE HAVE ALSO HAD THE PROBLEM OF THE DISSENTING MOVEMENT KNOWN
AS ELIM....THE CHURCH CANNOT LONG ENDURE AN ORGANIZATION IN HER
MIDST WHICH ESTABLISHES ALTERNATE OR COMPETING PROGRAMS FOR SUCH
VITAL MATTERS AS THE EDUCATION OF CHURCH WORKERS AND THE MISSION
PROGRAM OF THE SYNOD AND EVEN GOES SO FAR AS TO PLACE UNCERTIFIED
CANDIDATES IN CONGREGATIONS OF THE SYNOD AND THE MISSION FIELD OF
THE SYNOD. THE DIVISIVENESS AND CONFUSION CAUSED BY THIS ORGANIZA-
TION, AS WELL AS THE DRAINING OFF OF FUNDS, CONTRIBUTE TO POLARIZATION
AND LACK OF TRUST AND LOVE AMONG US. ELIM HAS ANNOUNCED A BUDGET
OF $1,800,000. THINK OF WHAT THIS COULD DO FOR MISSION EXPANSION IF WE
COULD GET TOGETHER AS A SYNOD AND SETTLE OUR DIFFICULTIES. I WOULD,
ON BEHALF OF THE SYNOD, BESEECH THE PEOPLE INVOLVED IN ELIM TO USE
THE CHANNELS OF DISSENT WHICH THE SYNOD HAS CREATED FOR THIS PURPOSE.
THE SYNOD WELCOMES DISSENT. WE NEED PROPER CRITICISM. WE ALL ERR
AND NEED CORRECTION...BY THE SAME TOKEN I WOULD BESEECH THOSE WHO
HAVE BEEN INVOLVED IN DIVISIVE MOVEMENTS THAT THEY COME TO TERMS
WITH THEIR CHURCH AND TRY TO LIVE AT PEACE WITH THEIR BRETHREN. IF
THERE ARE THOSE WHO ARE DOCTRINALLY AT SUCH ODDS WITH THE CHURCH
THAT THEY CANNOT LIVE AT PEACE WITH THEIR CHURCH OR TEACH IN CONFORM-
ITY WITH OUR DOCTRINAL POSITION, THEN FOR THEIR OWN GOOD, AS WELL AS
THAT OF THE SYNOD, IT WOULD SEEM THAT WISDOM WOULD DICTATE THAT THEY
TRY TO FIND A CHURCH HOME IN WHICH THEY COULD LIVE WITH GREATER HAP-
PINESS.[83]

And the Missouri Synod's official reaction to ELIM? While the Anaheim
Convention declared 175 members of ELIM and Seminex instructors eligible
to be seated as delegates, it nevertheless went on record as being opposed to the
continued existence of either institution. First consider the position of the
Board of Directors of the Synod, June 3, 1975 (reported in the *Proceedings*):

WHEREAS, ELIM HAS BEGUN INGATHERING OF FUNDS, THE PURPOSES OF
WHICH ARE TO OPERATE A SEMINARY-IN-EXILE, TO FUND AN INDEPENDENT MIS-
SION SOCIETY, TO ISSUE PUBLICATIONS SUCH AS "MISSOURI IN PERSPECTIVE,"
AND TO FUND AN ORGANIZATIONAL STRUCTURE TO SUPPORT THESE PURPOSES;
AND WHEREAS, THESE OBJECTS DEFINE IN PART A VISIBLE CHURCH HERE ON

EARTH AND ELIM THEREFORE BECOMES SUBSTANTIALLY A CHURCH WITHIN THE CHURCH; THEREFORE BE IT RESOLVED, THAT THE BOARD ENCOURAGE ALL WITHIN THE SYNOD WHO ARE INVOLVED IN THE ACTIVITIES OF ELIM TO RE-FRAIN FROM ANY DISTURBANCE OF THE CHURCH OR ANY IMPROPER ATTEMPT TO TAKE UPON THEMSELVES THE OBJECTS OF THE SYNOD.[84]

In its resolution concerning ELIM, the 1975 Anaheim Convention in July declared:

(1) THAT THE WAY IN WHICH ELIM FUNCTIONS IS "SCHISMATIC AND THERE-FORE IN VIOLATION OF THE FIRST OBJECT OF THE SYNOD: 'THE CONSERVATION AND PROMOTION OF THE UNITY OF THE TRUE FAITH.'"

(2) THAT PARTICIPANTS IN ELIM ARE "ACTING INCONSISTENTLY WITH THEIR MEMBERSHIP IN THE SYNOD, ARE FAILING TO COOPERATE WITH THE SYNOD, AND ARE GIVING OFFENSE IN THEIR CONDUCT."

(3) THAT PARTICIPANTS IN ELIM WHO ARE HOLDING OFFICE IN THE SYNOD, DISTRICT, ETC., ARE "GIVING OFFENCE IN THEIR CONDUCT."

(4) THAT MEMBERS OF THE SYNOD SHOULD DISASSOCIATE FROM ELIM "SO LONG AS IT CONTINUES THOSE SCHISMATIC FUNCTIONS, OR…IN CONSCIENCE TERMINATE THEIR MEMBERSHIP IN THE SYNOD RATHER THAN TO CONTINUE TO ACT SO AS TO DIVIDE AND WEAKEN IT."

(5) THAT WHERE ADMONITION IN THE CASE OF OFFICERS AND MEMBERS OF FACULTIES AND SYNODICAL INSTITUTIONS HAS PROVEN FUTILE, "APPROPRIATE ACTION BE TAKEN ON THE BASIS OF THE SYNOD *HANDBOOK*."

(6) THAT SYNOD PLEDGES ITSELF WILLING TO LISTEN AND DISCUSS ISSUES AND GRIEVANCES AT ALL APPROPRIATE LEVELS.[85]

The Convention also had something to say about Seminex graduates and those district officials who arbitrarily place them, as well as about Seminex itself: RESOLVED, THAT THE SYNOD ENCOURAGE GRADUATES OF THE JOINT PROJECT (SEMINEX) WHICH HAVE NOT BEEN ENDORSED BY THE FACULTY OF A SYNODICAL SEM-INARY TO REQUEST ADMISSION TO THE PASTORAL MINISTRY OF THE SYNOD BY MAKING THEIR DESIRE KNOWN TO THE COLLOQUY BOARD FOR THE PASTORAL OFFICE.[86]

The synod asked those conducting Seminex to close it, and if the school was not closed, then the synod was to treat it as any other theological school not affiliated with the synod.

As far as dealing with district presidents who ordained or authorized ordination of persons not properly endorsed, the following were resolved:

(1) THAT SUCH DISTRICT PRESIDENTS SHALL PROMPTLY DO WHAT IS NECES-SARY TO ENCOURAGE AND DIRECT ALL OF THOSE PERSONS WHO HAVE BEEN SO ORDAINED TO BECOME ENDORSED.

(2) THAT IF A DISTRICT PRESIDENT CANNOT IN GOOD CONSCIENCE UPHOLD THE CONSTITUTION AND BYLAWS OF THE SYNOD, WHICH HE HAS SWORN TO DO AT THE TIME OF HIS INSTALLATION, AND THAT IF HE CANNOT REFRAIN FROM OR-DAINING OR AUTHORIZING THE ORDINATION OF CANDIDATES FOR THE HOLY MIN-ISTRY WHO HAVE NOT RECEIVED ENDORSEMENT FOR ORDINATION THROUGH THE DULY AUTHORIZED SYNODICAL PROCESS, THEN THE SAID DISTRICT PRESIDENT FOR THE PEACE AND THE GOOD ORDER OF THE SYNOD, SHALL RESIGN FROM THE OFFICE OF DISTRICT PRESIDENT.

(3) THAT IF ANY OF SAID DISTRICT PRESIDENTS DOES NOT RESIGN, HE SHALL BE COMMENDED TO THE PASTORAL CARE AND DISCIPLINE OF THE SYNODICAL

PRESIDENT, ASSISTED BY THE COUNCIL OF PRESIDENTS, FOR THE RESOLUTION OF THIS MATTER.[87]

MEMBERSHIP LOSSES

The controversy in the Missouri Synod was not without its statistical effect: Backdoor losses of the Synod for 1972 and 1973 were equivalent each year to 156 congregations with an average communicant membership of 334.

FORMING THE ASSOCIATION OF EVANGELICAL LUTHERAN CHURCHES (ALEC)

The following news item was issued from the Communications Staff of the AELC:

"MODERATE" LUTHERANS HAVE LAUNCHED A NEW NORTH AMERICAN CHURCH BODY, CONCLUDING THEIR CONVENTION IN CHICAGO, DECEMBER 3-4 (1976). THE NEW BODY, THE ASSOCIATION OF EVANGELICAL LUTHERAN CHURCHES (AELC), BEGAN WITH A REPORTED 75,000 BAPTIZED MEMBERS IN 150 CONGREGATIONS FROM COAST TO COAST.

MOST OF THE MEMBERS ARE CUTTING OR HAVE CUT THEIR FORMAL TIES—IF NOT THEIR EMOTIONAL TIES—TO THE 2.7 MILLION MEMBER LUTHERAN CHURCH-MISSOURI SYNOD, WHICH "MODERATES" BELIEVE HAS BECOME TOO "CONSERVATIVE," "SEPARATISTIC," "OPPRESSIVE," AND "UNJUST."

THE 172 DELEGATES ADOPTED A CONSTITUTION AND A SET OF BYLAWS AND THEN ELECTED THE REV. DR. WILLIAM KOHN OF MILWAUKEE, WISCONSIN, AS PRESIDENT.

THE DELEGATES GAVE OVERWHELMING SUPPORT:—TO FULL FELLOWSHIP AND COOPERATION WITH THE 3.1 MILLION MEMBER LUTHERAN CHURCH OF AMERICA AND THE 2.5 MILLION-MEMBER AMERICAN LUTHERAN CHURCH;—TO MEMBERSHIP IN THE LUTHERAN COUNCIL U.S.A.;—TO MEMBERSHIP IN THE LUTHERAN WORLD FEDERATION;—TO CONTINUING FELLOWSHIP WITH THE MISSOURI SYNOD ["OUR BROTHERS AND SISTERS"].

RESOLUTIONS WERE ALSO ADOPTED CALLING:—ON MEMBERS TO SUPPORT TWO "MODERATE" PROGRAMS, CONCORDIA SEMINARY-IN-EXILE AND PARTNERS IN MISSION, WHICH "MODERATES" HAD FIRST SUPPORTED THROUGH EVANGELICAL LUTHERANS IN MISSION (ELIM), THEIR PROTEST MOVEMENT IN THE MISSOURI SYNOD;—FOR SUPPORT OF $140,000 ANNUAL WORK PROGRAM WHICH WILL COORDINATE THE WORK OF THE FIVE REGIONAL AELC SYNODS WHICH WILL BE THE NEW CHURCH BODY'S PRINCIPAL AGENCIES IN MISSION;—FOR ITS SYNODS TO ENCOURAGE THE ORDINATION OF WOMEN TO THE PASTORAL MINISTRY.[89]

The AELC's Convention was held at the Holiday Inn—O'Hare Kennedy in suburban Chicago. The moderate faction of the Missouri Synod had divided itself into five regional synods across the country: (1) Pacific Synod, (2) East Coast Synod, (3) English Synod, (4) Southwest Synod, (5) Great Rivers Synod. The regional synods met in convention separately in November, prior to the AELC's initial Convention in December.

At first, a number of pastors and teachers who joined the AELC still held

682

membership in the Missouri Synod. *Christian News* pointed out that the 1980 Directory of the AELC listed some 100 clergymen and 35 parochial school teachers who were members both of the AELC and of the LCMS. Presidents Preus favored bearing with the situation for a time, since there was a need to minister and reach out to those who joined the AELC. By April 10, 1977, 75 congregations (of LCMS's 6,200 congregations) had voted to leave the LCMS. However, 37 of the pastors serving these congregations were still on the clergy roster of the LCMS.

THE CONSTITUTION'S PREAMBLE
SETS THE COURSE

The Preamble of the AELC's Constitution speaks in general terms regarding the Holy Scripture, thus allowing a latitude of expression regarding this doctrine which is quite different from the strict, narrow, unyielding presentation made by the Missouri Synod, which holds to the Inerrancy of Scriptures. The AELC's statement:

WE BELIEVE THAT THE SCRIPTURES ARE GOD'S WRITTEN WORD RECORDED BY PEOPLE OF FAITH AND INSPIRED BY THE HOLY SPIRIT, TO GIVE US THE WISDOM THAT LEADS TO SALVATION THROUGH FAITH IN CHRIST JESUS...THE SCRIPTURES ARE ALSO HISTORICAL DOCUMENTS: THE OLD TESTAMENT IS OUR HERITAGE FROM GOD'S PEOPLE ISRAEL, AND THE NEW TESTAMENT WAS WRITTEN AND COLLECTED IN THE EARLY CHRISTIAN COMMUNITY...OUR TRUST IN CHRIST DOES NOT FLOW OUT OF SOME PRIOR FAITH IN THE BOOK WHICH TELLS US OF HIM; IT IS THE GIFT OF GOD THROUGH THE GOSPEL...OUR FAITH IS NOT DEPENDENT UPON RATIONAL THEORIES ABOUT THE BIBLE, IT IS DEPENDENT SOLELY ON THE GRACE OF GOD, WHO CALLS US BY THE GOSPEL.[90]

Regarding the Missouri Synod's action of accusing the moderates of false doctrine regarding the Scriptures (in their use of the historical-critical interpretation of the Scripture and their failure thus to subscribe to the doctrine of the Inerrancy of Scripture):

THOSE WHO HAVE DISAGREED WITH OUR WITNESS HAVE BY MAJORITY VOTE ELEVATED THEIR UNDERSTANDINGS OF SCRIPTURE TO THE STATUS OF DOCTRINE NORMATIVE FOR THE WHOLE SYNOD, THUS GOING BEYOND THOSE CONFESSIONAL WRITINGS TO WHICH WE HAVE ALL VOLUNTARILY SUBSCRIBED. THEY HAVE CONDEMNED AS HERETICAL AND SCHISMATIC THOSE WHO TAKE ISSUE WITH THEIR UNDERSTANDINGS, THUS CREATING SUSPICION AND FEAR THROUGHOUT THE SYNOD AND FOSTERING HEARTBREAKING DISSENSION.

The ALEC immediately showed itself to be ecumenical and unionistic. That ecumenism and unionism were birthrights claimed by the AELC can be seen immediately in the Preamble of its Constitution. But not only birthrights, they were duties that the AELC felt duty-bound to carry out. *The Concordia Theological Quarterly* (Missouri's Fort Wayne Concordia Seminary) had this to say regarding certain statements in the Preamble:

[THE PREAMBLE] IS, IN EFFECT, A NEW CONFESSION, WHICH SUPERCEDES ALL THE SIXTEENTH CENTURY LUTHERAN CONFESSIONS BECAUSE IT PROVIDES AN OFFICIAL INTERPRETATION FOR THEM...IN ITS NEW CONFESSION THE AELC HAS

ADOPTED A VIEW OF THE CHURCH COMMON AMONG THE EPISCOPALIANS WHEREBY DENOMINATIONS ARE CONSIDERED MEMBERS OF CHRIST'S BODY. YET [THE APOSTLE] PAUL SPEAKS OF THE BODY OF CHRIST AS CONSISTING IN INDIVIDUAL BELIEVERS AND NOT DENOMINATIONS. THE AELC'S VIEW OF THE BODY OF CHRIST IS INTENDED, OF COURSE, TO PERMIT FELLOWSHIP AND ESPECIALLY INTERCOMMUNION ON ALL LEVELS. THE ECUMENICAL EXPRESSION OF THE NEW GROUP WILL UNDOUBTEDLY BE BOUNDLESS.[91]

The AELC went on to adopt resolutions clearly showing its enthusiasm for union with other Lutheran bodies, while ignoring differences of doctrine and church polity. The following resolutions were unanimously adopted by the AELC:

Resolved

(1) THAT THE ASSOCIATION OF EVANGELICAL LUTHERAN CHURCHES (AELC) PUBLICLY DECLARE ITS COMMITMENT TO THE ACTIVE EXPRESSION OF CHRISTIAN UNITY, TOWARD THAT END WE WILL PROVIDE FOR AND ENCOURAGE PARTICIPATION IN ACTIVITIES BY WHICH THE UNITY OF THE FAITH MAY BE ADVANCED, COOPERATING WITH OTHER CHRISTIAN COMMUNITIES AND FELLOWSHIP WHERE DESIRABLE AND FEASIBLE IN CARRYING ON THE MISSION OF CHRIST'S CHURCH.

(2) THAT THE AELC RECOGNIZE AND CELEBRATE FULL ALTAR AND PULPIT FELLOWSHIP WITH ALL WHOM WE SHARE SUBSCRIPTION TO THE SCRIPTURE AND THE CONFESSION OF THE EVANGELICAL LUTHERAN CHURCH AND

A. DECLARE OURSELVES IN CONTINUING FELLOWSHIP WITH THE LUTHERAN CHURCH-MISSOURI SYNOD AND EXPRESS THE HOPE THAT OUR BROTHERS AND SISTERS IN THAT BODY CONTINUING TO FELLOWSHIP WITH US.

B. SPECIFICALLY BY THIS RESOLUTION OFFER HAND IN FELLOWSHIP TO THE AMERICA LUTHERAN CHURCH AND THE LUTHERAN CHURCH IN AMERICA, IN WHICH CHURCH BODIES SISTERS AND BROTHERS HAVE EXPRESSLY VOICED THEIR DESIRE FOR ALTAR AND PULPIT FELLOWSHIP WITH THE AELC AND ITS MEMBERS.

C. EXTEND OUR OFFER OF FELLOWSHIP TO OTHER LUTHERAN CHURCH BODIES IN THIS CONTINENT AND THROUGHOUT THE WORLD.

(3) THAT THE AELC COMMIT ITSELF TO PARTICIPATION IN ALL EFFORTS TOWARD CONSOLIDATION OF THE LUTHERAN FAMILY

(4) THAT THE AELC COMMIT ITSELF TO PARTICIPATION IN ALL EFFORTS TOWARD CONSOLIDATION OF THE LUTHERAN FAMILY.

A. APPLYING FOR MEMBERSHIP IN THE LUTHERAN COUNCIL U.S.A.

B. APPLYING FOR MEMBERSHIP IN THE LUTHERAN WORLD FEDERATION.

C. APPLYING FOR PARTICIPATION IN THE NATIONAL LUTHERAN CAMPUS MINISTRY.

D. UTILIZING THE SERVICES OF LUTHERAN WORLD RELIEF IN OUR EFFORTS TO RELIEVE SUFFERING THROUGHOUT THE WORLD.

Also: The AELC was… "TO STUDY THE MATTER OF MEMBERSHIP IN THE NATIONAL COUNCIL OF CHURCHES OF CHRIST IN THE USA AND THE WORLD COUNCIL OF CHURCHES."[92]

The AELC Board of Directors, meeting in St. Louis March 3-4, 1978, adopted a document entitled "A Call to Lutheran Union," which spells out both the invitation and the process to bring it about. This document was recommended to the April 14-15, 1978, Convention of the AELC, "... to extend a call to Lutheran union to the other Lutheran Church bodies in North America." The document contended: "Only differences in understanding the nature and essence of the Gospel can be adequate reason for division of any nature within the Body of Christ."[93]

The AELC joined the Lutheran Council U.S.A. (LCUSA) in 1978. It immediately issued "A Call to Lutheran Organic Union." The Lutheran Church in America (LCA) responded favorably, while the American Lutheran Church (ALC) responded negatively. Nevertheless, the three bodies agreed on a four-year study plan. In 1981 the seminary presidents and deans convened for their annual meeting (set up by the Lutheran Council's Division of Campus Ministry and Educational Services) issued a "Call to Lutheran Union Now." By 1982, the union was a forth-coming reality, and the Commission for a New Lutheran Church took the place of the Committee on Lutheran Unity. The three bodies: LCA, ALC, and AELC formed the Evangelical Lutheran Church in America, which officially began its operations on January 1, 1988. The synod's headquarters are in Chicago, Illinois.

ORDINATION OF WOMEN

The AELC quickly set about to promote the ordination of women. Thus the following resolution was passed by the body: That we commend to the other Synods of the AELC the action of the Pacific Regional Synod in approving the ordination of women to the ministry of Word and Sacrament and urge them to take action of the issue.[95]

THE AELC: IN CONCLUSION

In concluding the Preamble of the Constitution for the AELC, the following statement is made:

IT IS OUR DESIRE TO BE CONSERVATIVE IN OUR FIDELITY TO THE FAITH ONCE DELIVERED AND PROCLAIMED IN APOSTOLIC TIMES TO THE PRESENT. WE WISH TO BE MODERATE IN OUR BEHAVIOR TOWARD THOSE WHOSE VIEWS ARE NOT PRECISELY THE SAME AS OURS. WE WISH TO BE LIBERAL IN OUR EAGERNESS TO APPLY OUR FAITH TO EVERY CIRCUMSTANCE OF HUMAN NEED. AND WE WISH FINALLY TO BE RADICAL IN OUR UNQUALIFIED OBEDIENCE TO THE TRUTH AS GOD HAS GIVEN US TO SEE THE TRUTH.[96]

THE MISSOURI SYNOD POST-SEMINEX

THE MISSOURI SYNOD IN SOME WAYS REMAINS A DIVIDED SYNOD

DIVIDED REGARDING THE DOCTRINES OF THE CHURCH AND MINISTRY

The WELS theologians who authored the book, *WELS AND OTHER*

685

LUTHERANS point out:

THE PRESENT LCMS POSITION ON THE DOCTRINE OF THE CHURCH AND THE
MINISTRY IS UNCLEAR AND UNCERTAIN. THERE ARE SOME WHO HOLD A MODI-
FIED LCMS VIEW, RECOGNIZING, FOR EXAMPLE, THAT CERTAIN PROFESSORS
MAY HAVE A DIVINE CALL. THE OFFICIAL POSITION DOES SEEM TO HOLD, HOW-
EVER, TO WHAT WAS DESCRIBED ABOVE THAT THERE IS A SPECIAL DIVINE INSTI-
TUTION FOR THE LOCAL CONGREGATION AND THE PASTORATE IN THE
CONGREGATION. THIS HAS AT TIMES CAUSED SOME PROBLEMS IN PRACTICING
DOCTRINAL DISCIPLINE ON THE SYNODICAL LEVEL.[97]

In the LCMS the teaching ministry is subordinated to the pastoral ministry.
However, the LCMS view that forms of ministry, such as teaching, are auxiliary branches of the pastorates is under dispute within the synod. There are
those who hold that these various ministries are branches of the church's ministry. There appear to be many within the LCMS who agree with the WELS
position on Ministry "that Scripture sets up no particular form of the church or
of public ministry as specifically instituted by God. God has not given his New
Testament church such ecclesiastical, ceremonial directives."

For legal purposes, the LCMS in 1981 established a distinction between
ministers of religion, ordained," "ministers of religion, commissioned," and certified professional church workers, lay." But keep in mind that in the Missouri
Synod, the public ministry is equated with the pastoral office.

Under the LCMS position, only pastors have a divine call. Professors and
teachers and synodical officials do not have a divine call. Furthermore, only the
congregation is a divinely instituted form of the church; the synod and its officials can practice discipline only according to the regulations established by
the synod. Consequently, church discipline per se can be carried out only on
the congregational level.[98]

DIVIDED ON THE ISSUE OF ALLOWING WOMEN
TO HOLD THE PASTORAL OFFICE

The Wisconsin Evangelical Lutheran Synod (WELS) and the Evangelical
Lutheran Synod (ELS)—once in fellowship with the Missouri Synod in the Synodical Conference—stand by such prescriptive Bible passages as 1 Corinthians
14:34 and 1 Timothy 2:11, 12. The LCMS no longer holds to the practice laid
out in these passages of not giving women positions of authority in the church
over men—men are to have the leadership roles in the church. In 1969 the
LCMS gave the right to vote to women and also allowed them to be placed in
positions of authority, including serving on the synod's board of directors.[99]
Only the office of pastor is considered prohibited to women by the above listed
passages.

A WELS theologian, writing in the *Wisconsin Lutheran Quarterly* (1998),
makes the following observation:

THE DENVER CONVENTION ENDED ONE STRUGGLE AND BEGAN ANOTHER. IT
BROUGHT TO AN END THE LCMS'S VALIANT ATTEMPT TO RESIST THE DEMAND
FOR WOMAN SUFFRAGE WHICH SWEPT ACROSS OTHER LUTHERAN CHURCHES IN
THE UNITED STATES AND BEYOND. IT OPENED THE DOOR TO ANOTHER: RESIST-

ING THE GROWING DEMAND FOR THE ORDINATION OF WOMEN IN THE LCMS. The WELS writer draws this conclusion:

PRESIDENT BARRY'S DEFENSE OF HIS SYNOD'S POSITION AGAINST THE ORDINATION OF WOMEN REFLECTS THE WELL-INTENDED THOUGHT OF OTHERS WITHIN THE LCMS IN RECENT YEARS. ONCE HIS SYNOD "DECIDED" THAT THE *SEDES DOCTRINAE* PASSAGES NO LONGER APPLY TO THE MATTER OF WOMEN SUFFRAGE, IT LOST THE ONLY FIRM GROUND TO SPEAK OUT AGAINST THE ORDINATION OF WOMEN. AS A RESULT PRESIDENT BARRY RELIES MAINLY UPON THE ARGUMENT OF PASTORAL OFFICE FOR MEN ONLY. THIS IS DERIVED FROM DESCRIPTIVE PASSAGES, WHICH SPEAK OF MEN SERVING OF MEN SERVING AS ELDERS AND OVERSEERS AND THE MALENESS OF THE TWELVE APOSTLES.

DOCTRINE AND PRACTICES BASED UPON DESCRIPTIVE PASSAGES FROM SCRIPTURES WILL NOT CARRY THE DAY. ONLY A RETURN TO THE PRESCRIPTIVE PASSAGES CAN. SCRIPTURE STILL ADDRESSES THE ROLES OF MEN AND WOMEN, IN THE HOME, IN THE CHURCH, AND IN SOCIETY. IT PRECLUDES NOT ONLY THE ORDINATION OF WOMEN, BUT WOMAN SUFFRAGE IN AUTHORITATIVE ASSEMBLIES OF THE CHURCH AS WELL.[100]

Voices are being heard more and more in the Missouri Synod, calling for the synod to take the next step, which is to allow women to hold the pastoral office. As could be expected: to many, the position of the synod allowing women to vote and hold important offices in the church but not to be ordained to the public ministry is untenable. And so, it is not farfetched to reason that this inconsistency is destined to be a cause of continual deeply felt irritation within the LCMS and could finally result in a tragic division. In fact, a survey taken back in the early 1990s showed that about 1,000 LCMS clergymen at the time no longer believed that the Bible opposes the ordination of women.[101] In the 2001 LCMS Synod Convention Workbook there were numerous overtures urging the ordination of women.[102]

DIVIDED REGARDING THE ISSUE
OF CLOSE (CLOSED) COMMUNION

The LCMS officially holds to the practice of close (closed) communion and has throughout its history considered the practice of close communion as an identifying factor of a church body's theological integrity, and its integrity in the practice of its theology.

Following a request of the 1998 LCMS Convention, the synod's Commission on Theology and Church Relations published "The Lutheran Understanding of Church Fellowship," which maintains that complete unity of doctrine is necessary for altar and pulpit fellowship. (It also stated that church fellowship, which requires unity of doctrine is limited to altar and pulpit fellowship. Prayer fellowship is specifically excluded.)[103]

In spite of the official stand of the LCMS on close communion, many voices have been heard in more recent times to discard this practice, certainly an indicator on the part of some members of the LCMS of a liberal theological attitude toward heterodox churches. Over the many years that *Christian News* (New Haven, MO) has been published, the editor has provided many examples of pastors and congregations (LCMS) who were involved in unionistic endeavors, including open communion. In the 2001 LCMS Convention *Workbook* there were numerous overtures to the synod urging that congregations be allowed to chart their own courses as far as doctrine and practice are concerned. Entire districts petitioned the LCMS to rethink its position on fellowship and communion practices.[104]

DIVIDED ON THE ISSUE OF SEMINEX AND ELIM AND ON THE DEGREE OF ORTHODOXY THE LCMS SHOULD PURSUE

When the moderate group under the leadership of Dr. John Tietjen left the LCMS back in the 1970s to form the Association of Evangelical Lutheran Churches (AELC) not every one or every congregation in sympathy with this moderate group left with them. Quite to the contrary. *Christian News* claims that many supporters of Seminex and Dr. John Tietjen remained with the LCMS.[105] Tietjen himself wrote: "I am convinced that 40% of those in the Missouri Synod compromised their integrity rather than pay the price of following through on principles to which they were committed. Only 250 out of an expected 1,200 congregations left the Missouri Synod in 1976 to form the AELC."[106] It is of interest to note that the LCMS vote in 2001 that classified the ELCA as "not an orthodox Lutheran Church" was passed by a 706-343 vote. About one-third of the votes cast declined to recognize ELCA as a heterodox church. Two different standards for true Lutheranism were evidently in use by the delegates. In other words, a fairly high percentage of the voting delegates were sympathetic toward the ELCA's brand of Lutheranism. Is there a correlation with the number of LCMS members who stayed with Missouri but remained sympathetic toward the moderate cause, a cause that resulted in Seminex and ELIM (within the LCMS), followed by the AELC (apart from the LCMS), and finally membership in the ELCA?

Even after the moderate group under the leadership of Dr. John Tietjen were repudiated by the LCMS, many voices have been raised in the LCMS and outside the LCMS concerning laxity in disciplining those in the synod who do not agree with or do not carry out Missouri's doctrinal stands and its established polity. There have been numerous cases of those who have committed unionism in one way or another. Plainly, the LCMS is divided as to the degree of orthodoxy practiced by its members. To say it another way: Within the LCMS you will find evidence of the presence of both the conservative and the moderate approaches to theology and practice. The very fact that there "were numerous overtures" to the 2001 LCMS Convention "urging the synod to let congregations chart their own course when it comes to doctrine and practice," says a lot.

In the March 2004 issue of the Lutheran Witness, a message from President Jerry Kieschnick issues "A Call To Prayer, Repentance and Spiritual Renewal." The president states: "A matter of importance among us is our recognition of the depth of sin in the world, in the church and in our own personal lives. Sin manifests itself in many ways. Sin is a necessary ingredient in separation, sectarianism and schism, as well as in a widespread lack of faithfulness to God's Word as revealed in Holy Scripture. To say the least, we are a church body experiencing significant tensions regarding numerous doctrinal issues, and regarding ways of carrying out the mission and ministry of the church. Left unresolved, these differences will continue to provide a foothold for Satan. His influence and subtle manipulations catalyze our individual and corporate sinful thoughts, words and deeds. Divisiveness and a spirit of contention are the result."[107]

THE LCMS AND THE EVANGELICAL LUTHERAN CHURCH IN AMERICA (ELCA)

In 2003 the LCMS renewed talks with the ELCA to discuss issues that divide the two bodies. "The Committee on Lutheran Cooperation (CLC), which consists of six members from each of the two church bodies agreed in November (2002) that they would...meet twice a year instead of once." (LCMS news, Dec. 6, 2002) The LCMS showed both a desire and a willingness to be back in the Lutheran dialogues with not only the ELCA but also with the Roman Catholic and Orthodox churches. But as a theologian of the WELS opined: "It would seem they would be embarrassed to be a part of a process that consistently produces statements that are an embarrassment to Lutheranism. How can the LCMS have cooperative pastoral arrangements with a church it has branded as heterodox?"

The writer then adds: "Unfortunately, it seems that the LCMS more and more places a greater priority on dialogue and some sort of loose cooperation with non-confessional churches like the ELCA and the national and territorial churches of Europe than on building and encouraging free, independent confessional churches of the kind Walther and Pieper promoted...[Some] seem to fear that the LCMS will be ecumenically irrelevant unless it has dialogues and some level of fellowship with many churches (preferably big churches)."[108]

It is of interest to note that President Gerald Kieschnick of the LCMS in August 2003 issued a statement of concern over the confirmation by the Episcopal Church, USA of its first openly gay bishop. Later he addressed the same issue during greetings to the ELCA Church wide Assembly, appealing to the ELCA to resist the trend toward acceptance and approval of homosexual behavior.

A further note of interest is the decline in membership in both the LCMS and the ELCA. This phenomenon, of course, is not limited to Lutheranism. In 2002 the ELCA lost 61,871 members, leaving it with a total membership of 5,038,006. Fewer new members, people taken off membership rolls, and congregations that were disbanded or left the denomination caused the decrease. The LCMS reported a total baptized membership of 2,512,714 in 2002, which is 27,331 fewer than in 2001. According to the WELS 2002 *Statistical Report*, the WELS has 403,345 baptized members, down 879 from 2001. (*Forward in Christ*, December 2003)

THE LCMS AND THE WISCONSIN
EVANGELICAL LUTHERAN SYNOD (WELS)

At this point in time there seems to be little hope that the LCMS and the WELS and the ELS will get together again as they once were in the Synodical Conference. Missouri is, in a way, not united within itself. There are opposing forces and voices constantly at work in this once staunchly orthodox body. Furthermore, the LCMS at times shows a tendency to handle disturbing issues and also differences that exist between individuals or groups, by political maneuvering.

The orthodox character of the LCMS has a tendency to change, depending on the political situation and who is in authority. Under President Ralph Bohlmann, the synod's orthodoxy suffered, and on the other hand it received a much-needed shot in the arm—so to speak—from the presidency of Dr. Al Barry. In commenting on the LCMS Convention at Wichita, Kansas, in July 1989, the WELS observers concluded that there is one overriding impression that was carried away from the 57th regular Convention of the LCMS: The LCMS is a house divided. The observers from the WELS who attended the Convention were members of their synod's Commission on Inter-Church Relations. In their report, the following conclusion:

> IN RETROSPECT, IT CAN HARDLY BE SAID THAT ANY ACTION TAKEN BY THE CONVENTION OFFERED ANY HOPE FOR A RESOLUTION OF THE DEEP-RUNNING DIFFERENCES SEPARATING THE WELS AND ELS FROM THE LCMS. IN FACT, BECAUSE OF THE FORCES THAT WERE OBVIOUSLY AT WORK TO SUPPRESS "CONSERVATIVE" VOICES IN THE SYNOD, IT WAS THE DISTINCT IMPRESSION OF THE UNDERSIGNED WELS OBSERVERS THAT MISSOURI TODAY IS IN SOME RESPECT PERHAPS CLOSER IN ITS THEOLOGY AND PRACTICE TO THE ELCA THAN TO ITS FORMER SISTER IN THE SYNODICAL CONFERENCE, [WHICH CONFERENCE] PASSED OUT OF EXISTENCE A QUARTER OF A CENTURY AGO. THE ELCA IS A PLURALISTIC CHURCH BODY, AND IT BECAME RATHER OBVIOUS AT WICHITA THAT MISSOURI— A HOUSE DIVIDED—IS PLURALISTIC TOO.[109] It does not appear that this picture has changed much over the ensuing years.

Much has been stated earlier in this chapter, and in Chapter Twenty and Chapter Thirty-Six in regards to the relationship of these two synods with the LCMS, and the issues that made it necessary for the two synods (WELS/ELS) to withdraw fellowship from the Missouri Synod. Therefore we will not belabor the issue by repeating what is elsewhere sufficiently reported.

THE LCMS AND THE
CHARISMATIC MOVEMENT

The charismatic movement, arising in the 1960s, was quickly assimilated by the liberal Lutheran bodies, gaining strong footholds there. However, a fairly large group of pastors in the Missouri Synod also became involved in the movement. In the early 1990s it was reported that 486 LCMS pastors were supportive of the charismatic movement. Formerly, charismatic pastors in the LCMS were removed from the clergy roster. Under President Ralph Bohlmann charismatic pastors were allowed to remain on the roster. RIM, which stands

690

for "Renewal in Missouri," is the charismatic movement within the Missouri Synod. Today its main aim is to help promote spiritual growth in the LCMS congregations. Pastor Herman Otten (who serves a Missouri Synod congregation) has extensively informed his readers in *Christian News* concerning the unbiblical teachings and practices of the charismatic movement and of the spiritual dangers that it poses. The *Pentecostals And Charismatics*, published by the Northwestern Publishing House, Milwaukee, WI, authored by Arthur J. Clement, clearly and thoroughly lays out for the reader the errors of this movement, and informs concerning the participation of LCMS pastors.

ALTAR AND PULPIT FELLOWSHIP WITH OTHER CHURCH BODIES

The LCMS has official "altar and pulpit" fellowship with 28 other national Lutheran Church bodies: Argentina, Brazil, Canada, Chile, Denmark, England, France (and Belgium), Germany, Ghana, Guatemala, Haiti, Hong Kong, India, Japan, Korea, Latvia, Lithuania, Mexico, Nigeria, Papua New Guinea, Paraguay, Philippines, Russia, South Africa (two bodies), Sri Lanka, Taiwan, and Venezuela. Many of these partner churches consist of congregations initiated and developed by LCMS missionaries.

THE LAST WORD

No one in the Missouri Synod has been more outspoken over the years regarding the faults and failures of the Missouri Synod than Pastor Herman Otten, pastor of Trinity Lutheran Church (LCMS), New Haven, MO, and editor of *Christian News*, and *The Christian News Encyclopedia*. Still, in 1992 Pastor Herman Otten presented a conference paper titled, "What Does the LCMS Have to Offer Today?" His paper was in response to a report in the *Minneapolis Star Tribune*, which began with this statement: CONSERVATIVES WITHIN THE LUTHERAN CHURCH-MISSOURI SYNOD CHARGE THAT THEIR DENOMINATION IS ROTTEN AT ITS CORE AND SAY THEY'RE WAGING A WAR TO WIN BACK ITS SOUL. In his paper Otten outlines why he thinks that the LCMS still has more to offer our nation and the world than any other church body. Otten points out: THERE ARE, OF COURSE, SOME SMALLER CONFESSIONAL CHURCH BODIES, SUCH AS THE WISCONSIN EVANGELICAL LUTHERAN SYNOD [WELS] AND THE EVANGELICAL LUTHERAN SYNOD [ELS], WHO TAKE A SOLID SCRIPTURAL STAND AND HAVE MUCH TO OFFER. UNFORTUNATELY, THEY ARE RATHER SMALL AND IN MANY SECTIONS OF THE NATION ONE WOULD HAVE TO DRIVE MANY MILES TO ATTEND AN ELS OR WELS CHURCH.

Here, then, is a summary of most of the things that Otten feels the Missouri Synod has to offer, things of course that set this synod apart from most of the other Lutheran church bodies, as well as churches of other denominations.

THE BLESSED GOSPEL OF JESUS CHRIST OF FREE AND FULL FORGIVENESS OF ALL SINS. THE SCRIPTURAL TEACHING OF JUSTIFICATION BY FAITH ALONE. SIN AND GRACE. LAW AND GOSPEL...THE LCMS MORE THAN WHAT ANY OTHER MAJOR DENOMINATION EMPHASIZES, SAYS THAT CHRISTIANITY ALONE IS A RE-

691

LIGION OF GRACE AND BASED ON SOLID HISTORIC FACT, WHILE ALL OTHER RE-
LIGIONS ARE RELIGION OF LAW AND FOUNDED ON MYTHS. / THE MEANS OF
GRACE, WORD AND SACRAMENTS. HOLY BAPTISM AND THE LORD'S
SUPPER...THE REAL PRESENCE OF CHRIST'S BODY AND BLOOD IN THE LORD'S
SUPPER. BAPTISM INVOLVES FORGIVENESS OF SIN. / THE TRUTH ABOUT CRE-
ATION...LONG BEFORE THE MODERN CREATIONIST MOVEMENT BEGAN IN THE
EARLY 1960S THE LCMS, MORE THAN ANY OTHER DENOMINATION, WAS DE-
FENDING THE HISTORICITY OF THE GENESIS CREATION ACCOUNT AND REFUTING
EVOLUTION. / THE TRUTH ABOUT THE END TIMES, MILLENNIALISM AND ISRAEL:
THE LCMS'S BRIEF STATEMENT REJECTS ALL MILLENNIALISM AND SOME [SORT
OF] GENERAL CONVERSION OF THE JEWISH NATION. 1.THE LCMS, ALONG WITH
II THESSALONIANS 2 AND THE LUTHERAN CONFESSIONS RIGHTLY TEACH THAT
THE PAPACY IS THE ANTI-CHRIST./ A PROVEN MISSION PROGRAM...LONG BEFORE
ALL THIS TALK ABOUT EVANGELISM PROGRAMS, CHURCH GROWTH, CRUSADES,
ETC., THE LCMS HAD A SOUND AND PROVEN MISSION AND EVANGELISM PRO-
GRAM. / A CONGREGATIONAL TYPE OF CHURCH GOVERNMENT AND AN EXCEL-
LENT CONSTITUTION WHICH HAS STOOD THE TEST OF TIME. UNLIKE SOME
DENOMINATIONS, THE LCMS IS NOT A BUREAUCRATIC HIERARCHY, WHICH DIC-
TATES TO ITS CONGREGATIONS. / THE BEST EDUCATIONAL SYSTEM FOR THE
TRAINING OF FUTURE PASTORS AND TEACHERS. / THE FINEST THEOLOGICAL AND
LITERARY HERITAGE IN THE U.S. / A REFUSAL TO MIX CHURCH AND STATE...THE
LCMS DOES NOT DICTATE TO THE GOVERNMENT AND DOES NOT WANT THE CIVIL
GOVERNMENT TELLING THE CHURCH WHAT TO PREACH...THE LCMS FOLLOWS
LUTHER AND DOES NOT RESORT TO THE POWER OF THE GOVERNMENT AS IT
PREACHES THE GOSPEL. / TAKES A SCRIPTURAL STAND ON CAPITAL PUNISH-
MENT...SUPPORTS CAPITAL PUNISHMENT...BECAUSE IT IS IN ACCORD WITH HOLY
SCRIPTURES AND THE LUTHERAN CONFESSIONS. / THE LCMS HAS ALWAYS
CONDEMNED ABORTION AS SINFUL KILLING...BECAUSE THE BIBLE REGARDS UN-
BORN INFANTS AS REAL HUMAN BEINGS, WHICH SHOULD NOT BE KILLED. / THE
LCMS CONDEMNS HOMOSEXUALITY. / THE LCMS HAS ALWAYS TAKEN A FORTH
RIGHT STAND AGAINST ADULTERY AND IMMORALITY OF EVERY KIND. / ...THE
LCMS IS NOW ONE OF THE FEW REMAINING MAJOR DENOMINATIONS WHICH
DOES NOT ORDAIN WOMEN IN THE HOLY MINISTRY. / THE LCMS TAKES A
SCRIPTURAL STAND ON THE LODGE AND CULTS...FIRMLY OPPOSED TO ALL SOCI-
ETIES, LODGES, AND ORGANIZATIONS OF AN UNCHRISTIAN OR ANTICHRISTIAN
CHARACTER. / THE LCMS APPRECIATES THE VALUE OF TRUE SCIENTIFIC AND
ARCHEOLOGICAL RESEARCH. ITS SCHOLARS DO NOT FEAR THE LATEST FINDINGS.
/ THE LCMS IS TRULY MISSION MINDED...STILL INSISTS THAT JESUS CHRIST IS
THE ONLY WAY TO HEAVEN AND THAT THOSE WHO DIE WITHOUT A SAVING
KNOWLEDGE OF CHRIST ARE LOST AS JESUS SAYS IN JOHN 14:6 AND AS ALL OF
CHRISTENDOM CONFESSES IN THE ATHANASIAN CREED. / THE LCMS WITH
LUTHER EMPHASIZES THE POWER AND EFFICACY OF GOD'S WORD...THE WORD
ITSELF CONVERTS AND SANCTIFIES. / THE LCMS RECOGNIZES THE REAL SIG-
NIFICANCE OF MESSIANIC PROPHECY AND THE TRUE UNITY AND CHRISTOCEN-
TRICITY OF BOTH THE OLD AND NEW TESTAMENTS. / THE LCMS PASTORS
OFFER SOLID SCRIPTURAL COMFORT IN THE HOUR OF DEATH AND AT FUNER-
ALS...THE LCMS PASTOR DIRECTS HIS DYING MEMBER TO THE CROSS OF JESUS
WHERE JESUS SAID, "IT IS FINISHED," AND NOT TO THE MEMBER'S OWN WORKS

692

OF LIFE.[110]

Considering these matters—and others as well—which the Missouri Synod has in its favor, those in such conservative, confessional bodies as the Wisconsin Synod and the Evangelical Lutheran Synod find even more reasons to plead with the Missouri Synod to come back fully to the theology and practice advocated by Walther, Pieper and other staunch scriptural, Lutheran leaders of former times, who helped to make the Missouri Synod the hallmark of orthodoxy. Thus to be a guiding light to the Lutheran world—and to others—leading God's people to God's truth, to correct doctrinal discipline, and to trustworthy, unswerving examples of scriptural practice.

Footnotes for Chapter Thirty-Five

1 Walter O Forster, *Zion on the Mississippi* (St. Louis, MO: Concordia Publishing House, 1953), p. 10.

2 Carl S. Mundinger, *Government in the Missouri Synod* (St. Louis, MO: Concordia Publishing House, 1947), p. 19.

3 Mundinger, *Government...*, p. 29, footnote #41.

4 Mundinger, *Government...*, p. 54, footnote #38.

5 Forester, *Zion...*, p.35.

6 Walter Baepler, *A Century of Grace—A History of the Missouri Synod* 1847-1947 St. Louis, MO: Concordia Publishing House, 1947), p. 20.

7 Baepler, *A Century...*, p. 24.

8 Baepler, *A Century...*, p. 25.

9 Forester, *Zion...*, p. 215.

10 Baepler, *A Century...*, p. 36.

11 Mundinger, *Government...*, pp. 99-101.

12 Mundinger, *Government...*, p. 95.

13 Baepler, *A Century...*, p. 52.

14 Baepler, *A Century...*, p. 52.

15 Baepler, *A Century...*, pp. 6.7.

16 Baepler, *A Century...*, p. 64.

17 Baepler, *A Century...*, p. 66.

18 Baepler, *A Century...*, p. 69.

19 For additional reading, *A Century of Blessing, A History of Concordia Theological Seminary, Springfield, Illinois*, by Dr. Walter A. Baepler.

20 For interesting and informative reading regarding this colony and pioneer life in Saginaw Valley of Michigan: *Church Bells In The Forest*, by Dr. Theodore Graebner. (Both books were published by Concordia Publishing House, St. Louis).

21 Baepler, *A Century...*, p. 86.

22 Baepler, *A Century...*, p. 94.

23 John W. Behnken, *This I Recall* (St. Louis, MO: Concordia Publishing House, 1964), p. 53.

* *Wisconsin Lutheran Quarterly*, Vol. 101, No. 4, 2004, p. 303.

24 Erwin L. Lueker, Editor-in-Chief, *Lutheran Cyclopedia* (St. Louis, MO: Concordia Publishing House, 1954), p. 706.

25 Baepler, *A Century...*, pp. 138-142.

26 Mundinger, *Government...*, pp. 165ff.

27 Baepler, *A Century...*, p. 146.

28 R.C. Wolf, *Documents of Lutheran Unity in America* (Philadelphia, PA: Fortress Press,

1966), p. 209; Doc. #92.

29 Wolf, *Documents...*, pp. 209-212; Davenport Theses, 1873; Doc. #93.

30 Baepler, *A Century...*, p. 200.

31 Wolf, *Documents...*, pp. 199-203; Doc. #89.

32 Baepler, *A Century...*, p. 206.

33 *Not By My Own Reason or Strength*, a Tract issued by the Conference of Presidents of the Ev. Lutheran Joint Synod of Wis. And Other States, 1954, p. 3.

34 Baepler, *A Century...*, pp. 321-323.

35 Baepler, *A Century...*, p. 323.

36 Lueker, *Lutheran Cyclopedia*, p. 820. See also: Wolf, *Documents...*, pp. 399, 400; Doc. #161; pp. 395, 396; Doc. #160.

37 Wolf, *Documents...*, pp. 378, 379; Doc. #157.

38 Wolf, *Documents...*, pp. 403-406; Doc. #164.

39 Baepler, *A Century...*, p. 325.

40 *Proceedings, 1943* Wisconsin Evangelical Lutheran Synod Convention, p. 69.

41 *Proceedings*, 1950 Lutheran Church-Missouri Synod Convention, p. 585.

42 *Proceedings*, 1953 Lutheran Church-Missouri Synod Convention, p. 520.

43 *Proceedings*, 1953 Wisconsin Evangelical Lutheran Synod Convention, p. 104.

44 Wolf, *Documents...*, p. 437; Doc. #172.

* "Report of the Standing Committee on Matters of Church Union to the Nine Districts of the Joint Synod of Wisconsin and Other States," (1956), p. 2.

** Ibid., pp. 4, 5.

45 *Entrenched Unionistic Practices—A Record of Unionistic Practice in the Lutheran Church-Missouri Synod*, Article II: Meetings With the National Lutheran Council. Authorized by the Commission on Doctrinal Matters, the WELS, pp. 5,6. Published in the early 1960's.

46 Wolf, *Documents...*, p. 616; Doc. #245.

47 Theodore A. Aaberg, *A City Set on a Hill* (Published by the Board of Publications of the Evangelical Lutheran Synod, Mankato, MN: 1968), pp. 252, 253.

48 Herbert O. Lussky, *The Missouri Synod Laymen and Lutheran Union*, Second Edition (Evanston, IL: 1950), p. 33.

49 Lussky, *The Missouri Synod Laymen...*, p. 34.

50 E. Clifford Nelson, *The Lutherans in North America* (Philadelphia, PA: Fortress Press, 1975), p. 528.

51 *Proceeding, 1971* Lutheran Church-Missouri Synod Convention, p. 137.

* CTCR=Commission on Theology and Church Relations.

52 Behnken, *This I Recall*, pp. 191-193.

53 Behnken, *This I Recall*, pp. 193-195.

54 Reference information not available. For an appraisal of the findings of the president's Fact Finding Committee, read Kurt E. Marquart's account in Anatomy of an Explosion, (Fort Wayne, IN: Concordia Theological Seminary Press, 1977), pp. 95-99.

55 Report of the Commission on Theology and Church Relations of the Lutheran Church-Missouri Synod, concerning "Women Suffrage in the Church." A study mandated by the New York Convention 1967 and presented to the Denver Convention 1969, p. 10.

56 Nelson, *The Lutherans...*, p. 532.

57 Richard E. Koenig, "What's Behind the Showdown in the Lutheran Church-Missouri Synod?" Three Articles from *Lutheran Forum*. See especially Articles II, III.

58 From: "Chronological Account of the Assumption and Use of Power During the Synodical Administration of J.A.O. Preus: "Conservatives" versus "Moderats."", p. 1.

59 James E. Adams, "The Seed of Schism: A Seminary in Exile," an article in a reprint of *The Christian Century* article: "From Concordia to Seminex: A Seminary in Exile," March 6, 1974.

60 Herman Otten, Editor, *A Christian Handbook on Vital Issues* (New Haven, MO: by Christian News, 1963-1973; Leader Publishing Co.).

61 Nelson, *The Lutherans...*, p. 531.

62 *Proceedings, 1971* Lutheran Church-Missouri Synod Convention, pp. 54, 55.

63 *Proceedings, 1971* Lutheran Church-Missouri Synod Convention, p. 56.

64 Otten, *Christian Handbook...*, p. 729.

65 *Proceedings, 1973* Lutheran Church Missouri Synod Convention, p. 3.

66 *Proceedings, 1973* Lutheran Church Missouri Synod Convention, p. 3.

67 *Proceedings, 1973...*, p. 25.

68 *Proceedings, 1973...*, p. 148.

69 *Proceedings, 1973...*, p. 140; quoting the "Blue Book," p. 25.

70 *Proceedings, 1973...*, p. 141.

71 *Proceedings, 1973...*, p. 141.

72 Minutes of the Council of Presidents of the LCMS, September 18-21, 1972, p. 15.

73 *Proceedings, 1973...*, p. 141.

74 John Tietjen, "Fact Finding or Fault Finding?" September 8, 1972, p. 12.

75 "Faithful to Our Calling—Faithful to Our Lord" Document #1 of the St. Louis Concordia Seminary faculty majority, pp. 13-41.

76 *Proceedings, 1973...*, p. 135.

77 *Proceedings, 1973...*, p. 136, 137.

78 *Proceedings, 1973...*, p. 136, 137.

79 James E. Adams, *Preus of Missouri* (San Francisco, CA: Harper and Row, 1977), p.__.

80 Robert Jewett, "The Gospel As Heresy: Concordia Seminary in Exile," an article appearing in "From Concordia to Seminex: A Seminary in Exile," *A Christian Century* Reprint. Material appeared in: May 23, 1973, August 1, 1973, March 6, 1974, March 27, 1974, April 17, 1974; pp. 336, 337 reference for above-named article.

81 *Christian Century*, "Moving Out and Moving In," April 17, 1974.

82 *Affirm*, November 28, 1975.

83 *Proceedings*, 1975 Lutheran Church-Missouri Synod Convention, pp. 58, 59.

84 *Proceedings, 1975...*, p. 97.

85 *Proceedings, 1975...*, p. 98.

86 *Proceedings, 1975...*, p. 144.

87 *Proceedings, 1975...*, p. 123.

88 *Proceedings, 1975...*, p. 81.

89 Association of Evangelical Lutheran Church's Communication Staff news item; quoted in *Christian News Encyclopedia, Vol. 1*. p. 131.

90 Quoted in the *Christian News Encyclopedia, Vol. 1*. p. 135.

91 *Concordia Theological Quarterly*, Concordia Seminary, Fort Wayne, IN, April 1977. Quoted in *Christian News Encyclopedia, Vol. 1*, p. 134.

92 Reported in *Christian News Encyclopedia, Vol. 1*, p. 135.

93 A news item from the AELC, March 7, 1978. Quoted in *Christian News Encyclopedia, Vol. 1*, p. 134.

94 Patsy A. Leppien and J. Kincaid, W*hat's Going on Among the Lutherans?—A Comparison of Beliefs* (Milwaukee, WI: Northwestern Publishing House, 1992), p. 325; quoting *The Lutherans in North America—Supplement*, p. 561.

95 Reported in *Christian News Encyclopedia*, p. 135, (Vol. 1).

96 *Christian News Encyclopedia*, Vol. 1, p. 135.

97 John F. Brug, Edward C. Fredrich II, Armin W. Schuetze, *WELS And Other Lutherans* (Milwaukee, WI: Northwestern Publishing House, 1995), p. 23.

98 Brug, Fredrich, Schuetze, *WELS...*, p. 20.

99 Brug, Fredrich, Schuetze, *WELS...*, p. 24.

100 *Wisconsin Lutheran Quarterly*, Vol. 95, No. 4, 1998, pp. 296, 297.

101 Herman Otten, editor, *Christian News Encyclopedia*, Vol. V, (Washington, MO: Missourian Publishing Co.), p. 3806.

102 *Wisconsin Lutheran Quarterly*, Vol. 99, No. 1, 2002 (Milwaukee, WI: Northwestern Publishing House), p. 63.

103 *Wisconsin Lutheran Quarterly*, Vol. 97, No. 1, 2000, p. 302.

104 *Wisconsin Lutheran Quarterly*, Vol. 99, No. 1, 2002, p. 63.

105 *Christian News Encyclopedia*, Vol. V. p. 3814.

106 John Tietjen, *Memoirs in Exile–Confessional Hope and Institutional Conflict* (Minneapolis, MN: Augsburg Fortress Press), pp. 283, 284

107 *The Lutheran Witness*, "A Call To Prayer, Repentance and Renewal," by President Jerry Kieschnick, March 2004 (Saint Louis, MO: Concordia Publishing House), p. 28.

108 *Wisconsin Lutheran Quarterly*, Vol. 97, No. 1, 2000, pp. 56, 58.

109 *Wisconsin Lutheran Quarterly*, Vol. 87, No. 1, 1990.

110 *Christian News Encyclopedia*, Vol. V, pp. 3799-3801.

CHAPTER THIRTY-SIX

WISCONSIN EVANGELICAL LUTHERAN SYNOD (1850 -   )

FROM THE OLD COUNTRY TO THE NEW

The State of Wisconsin is bounded on the west by the Mississippi River and on the east by Lake Michigan, which itself is a part of the Great Lakes—the largest fresh water system in the world. It is no wonder that this area, known for its beauty and variety, was called Wees-Konsan (the place of the gathering of the waters) by the Indians.¹ The year 1820 witnessed the first wave of white settlers moving into Wisconsin.² At first, settlement was chiefly by people who moved into the territory from other northern states. Some came from the South. 1850—the year the Wisconsin Synod was organized—was a census year, and the population survey revealed that 96% of the population of Wisconsin listed as native born were of Yankee origin. The population of Wisconsin that year was listed at 305,391 of whom 110,477 had been born in Europe. By 1870 the picture had changed drastically, for by then the native-born of American-born parentage constituted only one-third of the entire population of the state.

The great migration from Europe that began in the 1840's and brought one and three-fourths million people to American shores in ten years increased considerably after that so that in the following three decades an average of two and one-half million immigrants arrived in each decade. Remaining for the most part out of the old Confederate States, the immigrants settled in the North, the Middle West, and the West. Thus many of these newcomers arrived in Wisconsin, the bulk of whom were of German origin, with Milwaukee long remaining the center of German culture in America.

Adverse conditions in Europe—political, economic and religious—caused the steady stream of emigrants to leave their homeland to migrate to America. Michigan, Wisconsin, and Minnesota were at that time a vast wilderness region containing huge tracts of dense forests. One settler described Wisconsin as "woods, woods, woods, as far as the world extends." By the time of the great immigrations the Indians were no longer a menace to settlers in Wisconsin, a land that was named by many "the golden land." We are reminded, however, of the great Sioux uprisings in 1862 and the resultant massacres that occurred in Minnesota, in such places as New Ulm.

STOUT HEARTS AND STONG CONSTITUTIONS

To leave the homeland and travel the wide expanse of ocean in wooden ships, devoid often times of even meager comforts, certainly required stout hearts and strong constitutions. But it was not only the ocean voyage itself that tried people's spirits and taxed their physical endurance. After arriving at an American port there followed for many the long and tedious journey of hundreds of miles inland, with their destination a strange and primitive—often wilderness—home. The immigrant arrived with only a little food, a few articles of clothing, some household goods, and a heart that ached for friends and family left behind in the old country. For the religious, the whole affair turned out to be a venture of faith that tried his or her soul.

The author's own ancestors—some of them—made such a journey to the wilderness of Wisconsin from Norway in the 1860's, and one of the family has since compiled a brief but interesting history of that adventure. To quote from it will give a little insight to the traveling conditions encountered by those early brave souls:

To travel in those early days really took courage. For the voyage across the ocean, food and bedding had to be furnished by the travelers. There were several families who decided to leave their homeland at the time of our grandparents' emigration, and grandfather seems to have been the leader and shepherd of the company—over thirty in number. He and a few other men made the trip to Stavanger and contacted Captain Olson of the sailing vessel *Hebe* and made arrangements to sail with him to America. Captain Olson advised them what to prepare in the way of food, and they must take much food because they never knew how long the voyage might take. It meant baking much *flat brot*, putting down salt fish and salt pork. Thy must also provide dried peas, cheese, primost, potatoes, dried mutton, and other food that could be kept. Some of the farm owners tried to discourage these folks from going to America because they knew it would mean that hired help would be harder to get and wages

WOULD GO UP. HOWEVER, THESE BRAVE SOULS WERE NOT TO BE DETERRED FROM THEIR PLANS.

EACH FAMILY HAD AN AUCTION AND DISPOSED OF WHAT THEY COULD NOT TAKE WITH THEM. MOTHER HAD A PET HEN, WHICH BROUGHT HER A FEW PENNIES, THE FIRST MONEY SHE HAD EVER HAD. MOTHER ALSO REMEMBERED WELL THE PARTING WITH THEIR MANY FRIENDS; THERE WERE MANY TEARS SHED AMONG THE GROWNUPS, BUT THE CHILDREN, THEN AS NOW, WERE HAPPY TO BE FACING ADVENTURE. THE EMIGRANTS ARRIVED IN STAVANGER ON SUNDAY MORNING. ON MONDAY THE FREIGHT AND BAGGAGE WERE LOADED ON SHIP AND BUNKS ASSIGNED. BY EVENING THE PEOPLE WERE ON THEIR WAY TO AMERICA—THE LAND OF OPPORTUNITY! CAPTAIN OLSON HAD ADVISED THEM TO BUY TIN PLATES AND CUPS, AND IT WASN'T LONG BEFORE THEY LEARNED WHY. THE SHIP ROLLED; THE CUPS, PLATES, TRUNKS, AND BOXES STARTED THEIR MERRY CHASE BACK AND FORTH. THE SAILORS HELPED THE SITUATION BY NAILING SOME OF THE THINGS DOWN. MOTHER OFTEN TOLD ABOUT HOW FRIGHTENED SHE WAS WHEN HER BROTHER AND ANOTHER BOY CLIMBED UPON THE RAILING; BUT LUCKILY, AT SUCH TIMES, THE WATER WAS QUIET. THEY SAW MANY HUGE ICEBERGS, BUT ESCAPED THEM BY SAILING 70 MILES SOUTH OF THE REGULAR SEA LANE. THEY HAD RAPID PASSAGE FOR THOSE DAYS. AFTER ENTERING THE ST. LAWRENCE RIVER, THERE WAS REAL SCENERY; AND THEY FINALLY LANDED IN QUEBEC. CAPTAIN OLSON HELPED HIS PASSENGERS ON BOARD THE STEAMSHIP ENROUTE TO MONTREAL AND PUT THEM IN THE CARE OF A NORSEMAN WHO "KNEW THE ROPES." FROM MONTREAL THE TRIP WAS MADE BY TRAIN. AT DETROIT THEY CROSSED BY FERRY. THE TRAIN TRIP WAS RATHER TIRING; ON THE WAY, MOTHER RECALLED, THEY SPENT ONE NIGHT AT A PLACE WHERE THEY WERE HERDED INTO A WAREHOUSE. THE NEXT DAY THEY BOARDED ANOTHER TRAIN, AND THEIR BOXES AND BARRELS WERE LOADED INTO A FREIGHT CAR ATTACHED TO THE TRAIN. BEFORE LONG THE CHILDREN WERE CRYING FOR FOOD. WHEN THE TRAIN STOPPED, GRANDFATHER WENT OUT TO FIND SOMEONE WHO COULD UNLOCK THE FREIGHT CAR DOOR AND LET THEM ENTER TO GET AT A BARREL OF *FLAT BRØD*. WHEN HE FINALLY FOUND THE FOOD, HE WAS SURROUNDED BY HUNGRY PEOPLE WHO EXCLAIMED, "WHERE IS THE MAN WHO HAS BREAD?" FINALLY ARRIVING AT THEIR DESTINATION IN WISCONSIN, THE OLDER FOLKS AND MOTHERS WAITED FOR OX CARTS AND HORSE-DRAWN WAGONS TO TRANSPORT THEM THE REMAINING MILES FROM THE DEPOT TO THE FARM HOMES OF FRIENDS AND RELATIVES WHO HAD ALREADY ESTABLISHED THEMSELVES. OTHERS MADE THE LAST MILES ON FOOT.

Whether the people were Scandinavian or German, it was natural that people from the same community in the old country settle together in the same area of this land. To this day in Wisconsin there are areas that are predominately German, or Danish, or Norwegian or Swedish. Not a few areas were populated by German settlers, with communities abounding in that culture. Where these Germans came to settle determined for a long time to come where, for example, the Wisconsin Synod would have its congregations. The Wisconsin Synod, like the Missouri Synod, was almost wholly German in character from the beginning, ministering to German people in their mother tongue. Mission work would long remain the work of gathering into congregations German-speaking Lutherans who had been transplanted to the Wisconsin Territory.

MISSION SOCIETIES PLAYED AN IMPORTANT ROLE IN THE EARLY HISTORY OF THE SYNOD

Certain mission societies in Germany had an important part in providing Lutheran missionaries to work in America. The influence which some of these missionaries had in founding Lutheran synods in America has already been discussed to some extent in connection with the histories of such bodies as the American Lutheran Church and the Missouri Synod. But German mission societies also played a part in the early history of the Wisconsin Synod. Therefore we will consider a brief account of the German mission societies of that era. There are several interesting things that can be said about them. They had their beginning already in 1702 when A.H. Francke opened his Oriental Seminary at Halle for the purpose of training workers for the Orient. In the 19th century there was a proliferation of mission societies in Germany. The mission movement "coincided with the era of colonization by the new maritime powers of Europe."[3] Many Christians tend to think of foreign missionary work as a new, even twentieth century American phenomenon. The fact is that Lutherans have been genuinely interested in such work for a long time and have put out great effort to carry it out.

In the nineteenth century German missionaries were trained in various cities in Germany and also in Basel, Switzerland. Many of these workers were sent to labor in such far off places as India and China, Southeast Africa, Borneo, Sumatra, New Guinea, Madang, New Zealand, Western Africa, Persia, the Ukraine, and Brazil. The Scandinavian mission societies, as well as the English societies, also labored in the foreign fields. When Germans began to migrate in large numbers to America, many of their fellow Germans who were left behind were deeply conscious of their need for evangelical pastors. As a result, concerted effort was made to train and send over as many men as possible through the mission societies. When Lutheranism came to America, it was a long time before the first seminary was established. American training of Lutheran clergy came very slowly. In fact, by 1827 only ten pastors had been produced by Lutheran seminaries in this country!

The mission societies represented a genuine zeal on the part of some Christians to preach the gospel of Christ in the world at a time when rationalism was exerting a powerful influence on the churches in Germany. The societies showed an intense interest in the Bible at the very time that the Bible was being set aside as the basis of religion, and its divine character was being questioned and even openly assailed.

But while some societies—for example the Leipzig (Dresden) Society, the Hermannsburg Society, and the Neuendettelsau Society—were confessionally Lutheran, many others were greatly influenced by the Pietism of that age. Pietism, as you will recall, emphasized religious subjectivism—Christian experience and Christian life—while doctrine was deemphasized. The mission societies in their zeal crossed over confessional boundaries so that while the preaching of the gospel itself was emphasized, doctrine and Lutheran confessionalism were neglected. We should not forget in this connection that a union of the Reformed and Lutheran churches had been enforced in Germany by government decree. This had no little effect upon Lutheran congregations, resulting in a further breakdown of Lutheran confessionalism. The missionaries sent to America therefore brought unLutheran ideas with them. In some cases Pietism prevailed. Recall that C.D. Wynekan, an early missionary who later became a guiding light of the Missouri Synod, was at first deeply imbued with the pietistic spirit. Many of the Scandinavian missionaries were also steeped in Pietism. Some Lutheran missionaries upon arriving in America showed that they were not interested in identifying themselves with strict, confessional Lutheranism such as was found in the Missouri Synod. In many instances pastors not only served Lutheran congregations but those of other denominations as well. This practice was learned from the mission society which had instructed them.

An attitude quite prevalent in mission societies of Germany is found in this statement of purpose of the German Christendom Society, founded in 1788: "Our purpose is that in days when men seek to weaken the foundations of Christianity, the Christians of all confessions must be kept together.[4]

The German Christendom Society grew into the Basel Mission in 1815, which established branch societies in other cities. The mission society in Barmen, for example, was a Basel branch, which later—in combination with other societies in western Germany—became the Rhenish Missionary Society. Within this group special interest was created for missions in North America. The result was that by 1837 the mission societies in the three cities of Langenberg, Elberfeld, and Barmen consolidated to form the Evangelical Society for North America. Later it became known simply as the Langenberg Association. It received its patent of incorporation in 1841 and played an important role in furnishing pastors to the young Wisconsin Synod.

JOHN MUEHLHAEUSER—SYNOD FOUNDER

Muehlhaeuser, who was to become the key figure in beginning the tiny Wisconsin Synod, had been educated in the mission school of the Rhenish Society in Barmen. Muehlhaeuser had been a baker. He came into Switzerland from Wuerttemberg, Germany, and while at Basel he was influenced toward mission work. As a result this young man went on a missionary journey into Austria in 1829, remaining there about three years while he ministered to the scattered evangelical Christians. In 1835 he entered the Barmen mission school.

In 1837 Muehlhaeuser finished his studies and was ready to be sent out, together with Candidate Oertel. The Rhenish Missionary Society had already discussed the project of doing mission work in North America among the German Protestants, so it decided to send the two men as emissaries. Oertel was sent to New York City to pastor a church, while John Muehlhaeuser was sent over as a teacher in Oertel's church, arriving at his charge in October 1837. Later he left New York City because of the lack of progress in the work there and accepted a call to Rochester to a Lutheran congregation of the liberal General Synod. Here he was ordained and here he remained for about ten years, moving finally to Milwaukee. Of course, the reason for Muehlhaeuser's move to Wisconsin was his love for mission work.

WREDE AND WEINMANN
COME ON THE SCENE

While Muehlhaeuser was still in New York, two other missionaries who had been trained by the Langenberg Mission Society applied to be sent to America. The Langenberg Mission Society at the time decided to send a detachment of three more workers to America. Johann Weinmann was doing postgraduate work at Barmen, and Candidate of Theology W. Wrede—having completed his training—was serving a congregation in Pomerania. John Weinmann, like Muehlhaeuser himself, was a Swabain. Candidate Wrede came from Magdeburg in Germany. Both men were assigned to the work in America, and in July 1846 they sailed, together with a Pastor Rauchenback, from Bremen. From Bremen a dispatch reached Muehlhaeuser—a considerably older and more experienced worker—to expect the arrival of the two younger men. And so, upon their arrival to these shores they were met and cared for by Muehlhaeuser.

However, the three men were not together for long. Wrede accepted a call to Callicoon, New York, while Weinmann, who had accompanied Muehlhaeuser to Rochester, followed a pleading letter to the Territory of Wisconsin. At Oakwood, located on the Kilbourn road near Milwaukee, a congregation of 300 souls had been left without a shepherd when its pastor had disgraced his office with a shameful life. Weinemann, recognized by these people as a gift of God, became the shepherd of the flock, which later held the distinction of being the oldest congregation of the Wisconsin Synod.

MUEHLHAEUSER IN WISCONSIN

It was through Weinmann that Muehlhaeuser ultimately gave up his work in New York State and came to Milwaukee. His friend wrote to him encouraging him to come to Wisconsin and resume his calling as a traveling missionary in Milwaukee. And so, beginning in the summer of 1848 Muehlhaeuser started his work as a colporteur selling Bibles and tracts in the Milwaukee area for the New York Society, while doing mission work among the scattered German Lutherans. However, after a time Muehlhaeuser had to curtail his strenuous work of travel due to ill health.

Still, this factor in his life actually helped lead to the founding of Grace Church in Milwaukee—one of the three original congregations of the Wisconsin Synod. When Muehlhaeuser's health prohibited his travels, he decided to form a congregation in a section of Milwaukee instead of trying to serve so many scattered Germans. In this endeavor he was encouraged by two English sectarian clergymen: a Presbyterian and a Congregationalist.

At first the congregation was merely an evangelical church, but Muehlhaeuser wanted to be a Lutheran and to serve a Lutheran congregation, even though at the time he had certain dislikes for the old Lutherans and their insistence on Lutheran doctrine. He disdained doctrinal controversy as "a strife of words." Nevertheless, he contacted two Lutherans back in the East who stood for confessional Lutheranism. These were Dr. C.W. Schaeffer, pastor of a church in Germantown, Pennsylvania, and Dr. C.F. Schaeffer, professor at Gettysburg Seminary. These two men disparaged the lax doctrinal attitude of the General Synod (org. 1820) and later helped to found the more orthodox General Council in 1867. As a result, Muehlhaeuser reorganized his congregation under the name, German Evangelical Lutheran Trinity Congregation, changing the name later to Grace Congregation, since a Missouri Synod congregation in Milwaukee already had the name Trinity. The third of the three Langenberg emissaries followed the first two to Milwaukee the year after Grace congregation was established.

ORGANIZING THE WISCONSIN SYNOD—1850

In 1849 Pastor Wrede accepted the call of the United Congregation at Granville, five miles northwest of Milwaukee. And so, the three who had met and become friends in New York now found themselves neighbors in the Milwaukee area. In the *Northwestern Lutheran* Centennial Issue of May 21, 1950, Professor E. Schaller reported concerning this crucial point of the history of the Wisconsin Synod:

THE THREE FRIENDS WERE NEIGHBORS, DRAWN TOGETHER BY THEIR COMMON ORIGIN AND THE NEEDS OF MEN LABORING WITH THE GOSPEL IN A PIONEER AGE AND AREA. WHAT WAS MORE NATURAL THAN THAT THEY SHOULD WORK TOGETHER, CONSOLIDATE THEIR STRENGTH, AND SEEK TO RIVET THEIR CONGREGATIONS IN THE SAME BOND, WHICH UNITED THEM? THE MEETING WHICH THEY FINALLY ARRANGED AT GRACE CHURCH ON DECEMBER 8, 1849, WAS CERTAINLY AN EVENT THAT SEEMED OF VERY LITTLE IMPORTANCE EITHER TO THE WORLD OR THE CHURCH; YET IT WAS ON THAT DAY, IN THAT PLACE, THAT THE WISCONSIN SYNOD WAS BORN. IN ITS ORGANIZATION THE MANPOWER SUPPLY BECAME TOTALLY EXHAUSTED: MUEHLHAEUSER WAS ELECTED PRESIDENT, WEINMANN SECRETARY, WREDE TREASURER. THIS LITTLE SYNOD PLANNED FOR ITS FULL AND FORMAL ORGANIZATION BY ARRANGING A CONVENTION FOR MAY 27 OF THE COMING YEAR AT GRANVILLE. IN THE ENSUING FIVE MONTHS, PASTOR PAUL MEISS OF SCHLESINGERVILLE, WITH SEVEN CONGREGATIONS IN HIS PARISH, AND KASPER PLUESS OF SHEBOYGAN WITH FOUR CONGREGATIONS SOUGHT ADMISSIONS TO THE SYNOD. MEANWHILE, MUEHLHAEUSER WAS SERVING A SECOND SMALL CONGREGATION, WEINMANN ALSO, AND WREDE HAD THREE. SO THAT WHEN THE BRETHREN CAME TO GRANVILLE, FIVE PASTORS AND EIGHTEEN CONGREGATIONS WERE REPRESENTED IN THE ADOPTION OF THE CONSTITUTION, WHICH PASTOR MUEHLHAEUSER HAD PREPARED.

An interesting historical note is also observed by Professor Schaller:

"None of them remained here very long after they had founded the Wisconsin Synod. The first perished at sea in 1858 (Weinmann); the second died at Milwaukee in 1867 (Muehlhaeuser); and the third shortly returned to his native Germany (Wrede)."

INTERNAL ORGANIZATION OF THE SYNOD

At the time of its inception, the Wisconsin Synod, while giving to lay delegates the right to vote, nevertheless gave certain privileges to the clergy, such as the licensing and ordaining of ministers. The first paragraph of the synod's original Constitution, written by Muehlhaeuser, stated: "We call this our gathering: The German Evangelical Ministerium of Wisconsin and our meeting a ministerial assembly and our gathering with the delegates of the congregations assembled with us a synodical assembly."

The ordination and acceptance of pastors was something which the ministerial assembly, not the delegate assembly, decided. Furthermore, only the ministerial assembly voted in the matter of excluding a pastor from the synod. But those characteristics, which were common to a ministerium long ago, disappeared from this body. It can be pointed out that in this matter of special prerogatives granted the clergy is shown the influence which the Lutheran Church in the East had upon Muehlhaeuser's way of thinking, and this influence extended also to his doctrinal stand. He had spent ten years among the Lutherans in New York and naturally came to them to seek their advice at the time of the founding of the Wisconsin Synod. He also established connections with the Pennsylvania Ministerium and with individual pastors in the East. Naturally, their uncertain confessional attitude could be seen in Muehlhaeuser's own original stand.

LABORERS FOR THE HARVEST

One of the main reasons expressed at the time for grouping congregations into synods was to make possible the support of seminaries for training pastors. There seemed to be a chronic, critical shortage of pastors and missionaries for the vast fields to be served. The Lutheran Church here in America depended very heavily on the mission societies in Germany to provide the much-needed workers. However, not only were these societies unable to fulfill the demands, the men trained in them carried to America doctrinal beliefs and practice at variance with sound, orthodox Lutheranism. It was imperative for the growth and the orthodoxy of the church that seminaries be built here in America, and that they not be connected with the Union Church (Lutheran-Reformed) in Germany.

Furthermore, there were men in America who showed definite interest for the ministry, men who had to be provided the proper training. There was, for example, a layman by the name of Jacob Conrad who had been working as a colporteur. At the time of the founding of the Wisconsin Synod he made his interest in the ministry known. Since there was no seminary at the time, he then had to be placed in the home of one of the pastors—in this case Pastor Wrede—to be privately instructed and prepared. Such procedure was common practice in those days.

Still another reason for establishing seminaries in America was the presence of many religious free-booters and vagabonds who traveled about preying on unsuspecting congregations. Many an early congregation, desperate for a pas-

704

tor, installed a man who later was found unworthy of the office and thus had to be removed.

The Saxons in Missouri went about establishing a school for training workers almost immediately. The Saxons, having early passed through their period of trial and tribulation, had found themselves and determined to train their own pastors. As a result, their pastors were imbued with sound orthodoxy, which then came to characterize the young and vigorous Missouri Synod. The fact that the Saxons had a large concentration of their people in a small area—in Perry County and Saint Louis, Missouri—was of course favorable to their school adventure. With the Wisconsin Synod things were different.

In the Wisconsin Synod the orthodox spirit was much less prominent than in Missouri among the Saxons. For a while it was not clear to the Wisconsin Synod what it wanted or expected of its clergy. Furthermore, this synod began in an inauspicious manner, having but a very small group of pastors and congregations; and even then, its humble birth was followed by a slow and painful growth. As the cries came in from various parts of Wisconsin for spiritual help, the founders of this young German church body turned to Germany for workers. It was not unusual to do so, as we have repeatedly been shown. Recall that Wyneken addressed stirring appeals to the Lutherans back home, describing the desperate and often tragic spiritual conditions in this new land. These appeals moved many a heart to be zealous for American missions. In a similar way, Pastors Muehlhaeuser turned to writing letters to the folks back home, letters describing the critical need for men to preach God's Word to their fellow Germans scattered about Wisconsin. His pleas did not fall on deaf ears but made deep impressions in the hearts of Christians in his native land.

Three schools in particular supplied pastors and missionaries for the young, struggling synod. The institutions at Barmen and Berlin, together with the Langenberg Society, sent men by two's and three's—but sometimes one at a time—to labor in Wisconsin. Finally, after the synod had passed its first decade, a committee was appointed to consider the question of opening a seminary in Wisconsin.

This committee reported to the 1863 Convention, held at Grace Church in Milwaukee. As a result, despite the uncertainty that prevailed in the nation due to the Civil War, the synod decided to open its own seminary at Watertown, Wisconsin. It opened for business in a modest new building that very fall. If the building that housed the new school seemed small and modest, it can be said that it had a faculty and student body to match. Pastor Moldehnke, who had served as a traveling missionary, became the first theological professor, instructing the two students who enrolled. The following year eleven students had enrolled in the seminary. One year after that, at the 1865 Synod Convention, it was reported to the delegates that the new college building would soon be ready. This imposing structure with a coffee mill shape, which characterized so many buildings in that era, had three stories and was built at a cost just under $17,000.

But even in the area of building a physical plant for the training of future pastors for America, the Wisconsin Synod was not without help from across the ocean. Pastor Bading had traveled to Europe, visiting the Christians both in Germany and Russia, stirring up interest in the church planted in America, pleading at the same time for funds to help with the work. Not without success, Pastor Bading returned to Wisconsin with $10, 215, which then made the erection of the college building possible. The school started out under the imposing name, Northwestern University. While housing the theological seminary, the school also taught secular subjects as well. A few years later it was closed for nine years, during which time students attended the Missouri Synod seminary. The establishing of its own seminary worked a dramatic change in the Wisconsin Synod both numerically and confessionally.

THE WISCONSIN SYNOD:
AT FIRST, THEOLOGICALLY UNCERTAIN
AND COMPROMISING

A hundred years after its founding, the Wisconsin Synod, though still a small body compared with the Missouri Synod and the mergers that formed large Lutheran bodies, nevertheless made a significant contribution to Lutheranism in America. In a booklet printed in 1955 titled *America's Lutherans*, author James P. Schaefer wrote a brief sketch of the Wisconsin Synod under the heading, "Uncompromising" and made this observation:

THE WISCONSIN SYNOD IS PERHAPS BEST KNOWN FOR ITS UNCOMPROMISING AND ZEALOUS DEDICATION TO CONFESSIONAL LUTHERANISM.

With a view to its resultant relationship with other Lutherans, the author went on to point out:

THIS SAME ACUTE SENSE OF CONFESSIONALISM HAS KEPT IT FROM JOINING EVEN OTHER LUTHERANS, WITH WHOM IT IS NOT ONE IN CONFESSION, IN SPIRITUAL PROGRAMS AS CARRIED ON BY THE NATIONAL LUTHERAN COUNCIL AND LUTHERAN WORLD FEDERATION.

THE WISCONSIN SYNOD SAYS IT IS NOT "ISOLATIONIST;" IT IS AWARE THAT THERE ARE MANY FINE CHRISTIANS IN OTHER CHURCH BODIES DEVOTED TO THE GOSPEL. BUT THE WORD IS: NO UNION WITHOUT UNITY. IT IS CONVINCED THAT GOD'S WORD IS ALL OF A PIECE—THERE IS NO WARRANT FROM GOD TO PASS OVER EVEN ONE OF HIS JOTS AND TITTLES.

THE WISCONSIN SYNOD IS WILLING TO MEET WITH ANY CHURCH BODY, ANY TIME, ANY PLACE. 'WE ARE WILLING TO MEET," RESOLVED SYNOD, "FOR A DIS-CUSSION OF DOCTRINE AND PRACTICE, THE REPRESENTATIVES OF ANY CHURCH BODY, PROVIDING THAT IT FRANKLY ADMITS THAT DIFFERENCES EXIST, AND IN-SISTS THAT THEY MUST BY REMOVED BEFORE WE CAN ENTER INTO FELLOWSHIP WITH EACH OTHER." THAT, THE WISCONSIN SYNOD HOLDS, IS NOT ONLY LUTHERAN BUT SCRIPTURAL.[5]

The Reverend Schaeffer, the writer of these words, was for many years the pastor of a large Wisconsin Synod congregation in Milwaukee and later served for several years as editor of the synod's official publication, *Northwestern Lutheran* (now, *Forward in Christ*). At one time, years ago, he addressed the Greater Milwaukee Association regarding the Wisconsin Synod's orthodoxy. His presentation drew the following comments from an observer who was an editor for a Milwaukee Catholic Newspaper:

IN THE BATTLES BETWEEN LIBERAL AND CONSERVATIVE THEOLOGIES IN RECENT

YEARS WE HAVE TO STAY NEUTRAL. THE PROBLEMS, THE LANGUAGE, THE WORDS AND THE NUANCES ARE PUZZLING ENOUGH WITHOUT ONE-SIDED RECORDING OF THE DEBATES.

THIS DOES NOT MEAN, HOWEVER, THAT WE CANNOT APPLAUD THE PRESENTATION OF REV. JAMES P. SCHAEFFER, THE WISCONSIN EVANGELICAL LUTHERAN SYNOD SPOKESMAN, BEFORE THE GREATER MILWAUKEE MINISTERIAL ASSOCIATION THIS WEEK. IN THIS WE HAVE THE COMPANY OF MANY OF HIS AUDIENCE, THOUGH IT'S SAFE TO SAY THAT NONE WOULD GO FAR WITH HIM DOWN THE ROAD TO WISCONSIN SYNOD ORTHODOX THEOLOGY.

SCHAEFFER'S PRESENTATION WAS FORTHRIGHT, UNAPOLOGETIC, AND WITHOUT THE SLIGHTEST CONCERN ABOUT HOW "OLD FASHIONED" HIS DOCTRINE MAY BE. HE WAS SPEAKING FOR WHAT HE DEEMED TO BE "THE WORD OF GOD" AND THAT WAS THAT. IN THIS YEAR OF POLITICAL SPEECHES BY THE THOUSANDS, THERE IS SOMETHING REFRESHING ABOUT SOLIDLY HONEST DOCTRINAL TALK.

ASIDE FROM THIS IS THE FACT THAT THE WISCONSIN EVANGELICAL LUTHERAN SYNOD—LIBERAL OR CONSERVATIVE, BROAD OR NARROW, LOVABLE OR UNLOVABLE—IS A FACT OF ECCLESIASTICAL LIFE IN MILWAUKEE. IT IS A SOLID CHUNK OF LUTHERANISM WHOSE PASTORS AND TEACHERS, YOUNG AND OLD, DO NOT VARY IN THEIR BIBLICAL POSITIONS AND NOTHING BUT THEIR OWN CONSCIENCES CAN BUDGE THEM. THEY HAVE BEEN RIDICULED AND OPPOSED. MORE THAN A SCORE OF YEARS AGO IT WAS PREDICTED THAT THE SYNOD WOULD DIE OUT, BUT IT IS MORE NUMEROUS THAN EVER TODAY. FURTHERMORE, THOUGH THEY DO NOT, AS CHURCHMEN, SEEK ANY KIND OF TEMPORAL POWER, THEIR MEMBERSHIP EXERTS NO LITTLE INFLUENCE ON THE CONSERVATISM OF OTHER LUTHERANS, OTHER PROTESTANTS AND EVEN, PERHAPS, PART OF THE ROMAN CATHOLIC COMMUNITY.

SCHAEFFER'S TALK LEFT MANY OF HIS LIBERAL PROTESTANT HEARERS GOGGLING IN AMAZEMENT. IT IS WELL THAT THEY HEARD HIM, FOR MUCH OF THE RELIGIOUS COMMUNITY IN MILWAUKEE AND WISCONSIN IS BEYOND UNDERSTANDING UNTIL THEY UNDERSTAND THE WISCONSIN SYNOD.[6]

The astonishing thing is that the early history of the Wisconsin Synod did not show this later uncompromising confessionalism. At first the synod was uncertain of its confessional direction, and basically unionistic and compromising. Where to get the manpower to work fields white unto harvest, was not the only problem facing this tiny group. There was a far more basic problem of identification. Just what were the founding fathers and early pastors of the Wisconsin Synod? What, indeed, was the synod? Were the pastors and the synod Lutheran—were they perhaps Evangelical, or were they even a combination of Lutheran and Reformed? Perhaps they were simply Protestant?

We have already mentioned the fact that Muehlhaeuser wanted to be known as a Lutheran and so did the others. And yet, close ties with the mission societies back in Europe, which were strongly influenced by the Prussian Union—the enforced union of Lutheran and Reformed congregations—made it impossible to travel the road of strict Lutheran confessionalism and orthodoxy which at the time was clearly the goal of the Missouri Synod. The missionaries sent over from Germany had been thoroughly trained to minister to both Lutherans and Reformed on the American frontier.

SLOWLY, ORTHODOX
LUTHERANISM EMERGES

In the Centennial volume prepared by the Centennial Committee of the Joint Synod an interesting insight into prevailing unionism within the congregations during the synod's early history is given. At that time it was not unusual to find members of either Lutheran or Reformed backgrounds in the congregations. The theological and practical problems this caused at times is illustrated by the minutes of the Granville meeting of 1854:

IN ONE SUCH CONGREGATION A CONTROVERSY HAD ARISEN CONCERNING THE CEREMONIES IN THE SERVICES. THE LUTHERANS DESIRED THE PASTOR TO PRONOUNCE THE BENEDICTION AND TO USE THE LUTHERAN LITURGY, AND THE REFORMED PART OBJECTED. THERE WAS ALSO DISAGREEMENT OVER THE USE OF THE HOST [THE THIN BREAD WAFER USED BY THE LUTHERANS] OR THE USE OF BREAD IN THE SACRAMENT. THE PASTOR SEEMED INCLINED TO FOLLOW LUTHERAN PRACTICE, BUT HE WAS CRITICIZED IN THE MINISTERIAL ASSEMBLY, WHERE IT WAS POINTED OUT THAT THIS CONGREGATION HAD JOINED THE SYNOD WITH THE UNDERSTANDING THAT IT WOULD BE SERVED BY MEN OF AN EVANGELICAL SPIRIT. IT WAS DECIDED TO SEND A COMMITTEE TO THE CONGREGATION ADVISING THE USE OF BREAD IN THE DISTRIBUTION OF THE SACRAMENT AND THE DISCONTINUANCE OF THE OTHER LUTHERAN CEREMONIES. IF HARMONY WOULD NOT BE ESTABLISHED IN ANY OTHER WAY, THE USE OF BREAD AND OF HOSTS WAS TO BE ADVISED. PASTOR GOLDAMMER PROTESTED VIGOROUSLY AGAINST THIS ADVICE AS BEING CONTRARY TO THE VERY INTENTION OF THE SACRAMENT, WHICH WAS TO REPRESENT THE MOST INTIMATE COMMUNION BETWEEN ALL THOSE WHO PARTOOK OF IT. HE POINTED OUT PARTICULARLY THE EVIL EFFECTS IT WOULD HAVE IN PERPETUATING THE DISHARMONY IN THE CONGREGATION AMONG THE RISING GENERATION. THE MINUTES, HOWEVER, CLOSE WITH THE REMARK, "BUT NO FURTHER ATTENTION WAS PAID TO THAT."[7]

Slowly, there was a turn from unionism of this form to a more clear-cut testimony on the part of the synod and the individual pastors within the synod, calling for pure Lutheran confessionalism. An example of this is also given in the Centennial volume. Reference is made to a significant letter addressed to President Muehlhaeuser in 1857 by members of the Northwest Conference of the synod. It answered the statement a certain pastor had made in a letter sent to the synod: "I cannot as yet bid farewell to unionism, because since I came to know Jesus, I dearly loved it and felt happy in it."[8] The members of the Conference sent him a sharp protest and reported the wording of their reprimand to President Muehlhaeuser: "Whoever clings to unionism should belong to a unionistic synod...Are you of the opinion that one can be a member of a Lutheran synod with a heart bound to unionism? We do not think so. The Church Society of the West is United, and the Lutheran Synod of Wisconsin is Lutheran and desires to become more Lutheran. We desire to depart from the unrighteousness of appearing to be something we are not."[9]

This report was the opinion of the Conference, and was signed by three of the more recent arrivals from the mission schools in Germany: Reim, Bading, and Koehler.

AFFILATION WITH THE
MISSION SOCIETIES IS ENDED

In establishing its own seminary, the Wisconsin Synod had arrived at a turning point in its early history, for it meant that the synod could eventually conclude its dependence on the Union in Germany for pastors and teachers, aided by the mediation of the mission societies. But there were other occurrences that were also speeding on the day of a break with the Union Church and the mission societies in Germany. Things were happening and things were being said on the scene here which were causing consternation in the ranks of those who had been supporting the Wisconsin Synod with workers.

At the 1863 Convention of the synod it was reported that two pastors were still using the Union Catechism. The men were given six months to introduce the Lutheran Catechism, and if the congregations refused to introduce it, the pastors who were involved were then given no choice but to resign their pastorates. When apprised of this stand by the Wisconsin Synod, the mission society at Berlin sent a letter reminding the synod of the fact that it was desired that her pastors should be willing to serve a United Church in case of need. The reply that came out of Wisconsin in December 1863 stood firm on the position it held in the case of the two pastors, and also explained that the aggressiveness of the Reformed churches in America made it necessary to define one's doctrinal position unequivocally.

The Langenberg Mission Society, in a communication sent in June 1864, informed the synod that it did not approve the treatment accorded the two pastors in the case involving the use of the Union Catechism. It also expressed itself against the synod's refusal to grant honorable dismissals to the pastors joining Reformed churches, and at the same time the society boldly asserted that the traveling missionaries of the synod should be willing to serve Reformed churches where the need arose.

For a time the difference with the mission societies seemed to be smoothed over. The collection in Germany and Russia for the new college at Watertown went on, and the school building was erected. But in 1867—with a report by a committee headed by Professor Adolf Hoenecke—the synod tackled the question of its relations with the United Church. The majority report clearly and decisively rejected union, both in doctrine and administration. It cited how consciences and church properties of Lutherans in Germany had been violated by this enforced union of Lutherans and Reformed. The much milder minority report, however, was adopted by the synod, in which it was argued that the Berlin Society knew very well that the Wisconsin Synod rejected every form of unionism on the grounds that it hindered the free exercise of the Lutheran Confession. This report also justified the synod's action of using the mediation of the United mission societies in obtaining workers from the United Church in Germany. The argument was that this course of action was proper as long as there were Lutherans within these state churches who had purity of doctrine and the right administration of the sacraments, and who protested against this enforced union of Lutheran and Reformed by the government.

When, almost at the end of 1867, the mission societies received their copies of the resolutions their reactions were not long in coming, nor did they mince words: "We have the impression that the Synod did not deal with us according to truth and righteousness. You knew how we stood to the union and that we expected our emissaries to work in that spirit over there. Under the circumstances we can send no more workers."[10]

That letter came from a representative of the Langenberg Society. The Berlin Society also pledged to send no more workers and termed the Wisconsin Synod's action a slap in the face. Still another letter accused the Wisconsin Synod of setting aside old friends (in Germany) for new friends (the Missouri Synod). In answer to the harsh statements by the mission societies, Pastor Bading pointed out that the Lutheran Church in America was feeling a strong urge toward confessionalism and committed the Wisconsin Synod to it, saying that it could not lag behind.

A CALL TO CONFESSIONAL STABILITY

Nowhere do we find a more frank admission by the Wisconsin Synod as to its past history of confessional uncertainty, compromise and unionism than in President Bading's historical address to the synod in 1868. These were serious words, words that confessed past misdeeds, and words that issued the trumpet-like call to the synod to rally to the true doctrine and practice of the Lutheran Confessions.

FOR YEARS WE SUFFERED THE ACCUSATIONS OF STRICT CONFESSIONAL LUTHERANS, WHO, BECAUSE OF OUR CONNECTION WITH FRIENDS OF THE UNION, CHARGED US WITH HARBORING A UNIONISTIC ATTITUDE. OUR CONFESSIONAL FAITHFULNESS WAS QUESTIONED, OUR SYNOD WAS DESIGNATED AS UNLUTHERAN, AND EVERYTHING WAS DONE TO CHALLENGE OUR RIGHT OF EXISTENCE AS A LUTHERAN BODY.

LET US OPENLY AND FRANKLY CONFESS, THAT, WHILE MANY OF THE REPROACHES HEAPED UPON US WERE EXTREME, UNJUST, HATEFUL, AND NOT ACCORDING TO THE LOVE, WHICH EDIFIES, SOME WERE UNDENIABLY JUSTIFIED. IT IS TRUE THAT FOR SOME TIME OUR POSITION WAS A VACILLATING ONE. ON THE ONE HAND THERE WAS OUR DECLARATION OF UNQUALIFIED ADHERENCE TO ALL THE CONFESSIONAL WRITINGS OF THE LUTHERAN CHURCH, AS EXPRESSED BY SYNOD ALMOST ANNUALLY; ON THE OTHER HAND THERE WAS OUR CONNECTION WITH ASSOCIATIONS WHICH OPERATED WITHIN THE UNITED CHURCH (IN GERMANY) AND WHICH REGARDED THAT BODY AS A GOOD THING.... ESPECIALLY DID THE SENSE OF OBLIGATION FOR HELP RECEIVED (FROM EUROPED) PREVENT THE SYNOD FROM GIVING ADEQUATE PUBLIC EXPRESSION OF HER INNER CONFESSIONAL FIDELITY AND FROM REFUTING CHARGES OF UNIONISTIC INCLINATIONS BY UNEQUIVOCAL TESTIMONY AGAINST ALL UNIONISM IN DOCTRINE AND PRACTICE. THESE INCONSISTENCIES, WORTHY BRETHREN OF THE MINISTRY AND OF FAITH, MUST COME TO AN END.

Professor E. Schaller, writing in the Centennial issue of the *Northwestern Lutheran*, gave a frank and open reappraisal of attitudes and happenings in those early years of the Wisconsin Synod before the break with the United Church and its mission societies came about:

THIS CALL TO CONFESSIONAL STABILITY SUGGESTS THE INNER STRUGGLES, WHICH GRIPPED THE YOUNG SYNOD IN ITS INFANT YEARS. THE FOUNDERS HAD

BEEN MEN TRAINED IN GERMANY, WHERE IN THOSE DAYS LUTHERANISM SUF-
FERED UNDER BLIGHT OF THE UNION BY WHICH PEOPLE OF REFORMED AND
LUTHERAN CONVICTIONS WERE COMPELLED TO WORSHIP TOGETHER AND TO
TOLERATE ONE ANOTHER'S DOCTRINES.

TAUGHT TO REGARD THE RATIONALISTIC UNBELIEF AND THE EVER MILITANT
ROMAN CATHOLICISM AS THE DANGEROUS ENEMIES OF THE TRUTH, MEN LIKE
MUEHLHAEUSER AND HIS COMPANIONS FAILED TO RECOGNIZE THE SERIOUSNESS
OF THE ERRORS OF THE REFORMED CHURCHES AND DID NOT HESITATE TO CO-
OPERATE WITH METHODISTS, CONGREGATIONALISTS, AND OTHERS IN CHURCH
WORK OR TO RECOGNIZE THEM AS BRETHREN. THIS WEAKNESS IN CONFESSION-
ALISM, THEN, NATURALLY BECAME THE WEAKNESS ALSO OF THE SYNOD, WHICH
THEY FOUNDED. THOUGH IT PROFESSED ADHERENCE TO THE WORD OF GOD
AND THE LUTHERAN CONFESSIONS, IN PRACTICE IT DEPARTED FROM THEM AND
TOLERATED FELLOWSHIP WITH ERRORISTS. AS A RESULT, THE SOUND ORTHODOX
LUTHERANS OF THAT DAY, CHIEFLY THOSE OF THE MISSOURI SYNOD, REFUSED
TO ACCEPT OUR SYNOD AS A TRUE LUTHERAN BODY.

BUT BY GOD'S GRACIOUS GUIDANCE AND INTERVENTION THE TESTIMONY OF
SOUND DOCTRINE AND PRACTICE BECAME EVER MORE LOUD AND INSISTENT
WITHIN THE GROWING SYNOD. WHEN PASTOR WEINMANN, WHO HAD MEAN-
WHILE BEEN CALLED TO BALTIMORE, ADDRESSED THE SYNOD BY LETTER IN
1854, HE ASKED SOME POINTED QUESTIONS AND REQUESTED THE BODY TO DE-
CIDE THEM. MAY A LUTHERAN PASTOR, IN CHARGE OF A CONGREGATION OF HIS
OWN, ADMINISTER THE LORD'S SUPPER TO A METHODIST CONGREGATION? IS IT
RIGHT FOR HIM TO LECTURE OCCASIONALLY TO SUCH A CONGREGATION AND
THUS TO IDENTIFY HIMSELF DOCTRINALLY WITH IT?

THESE QUESTIONS INDICATE IN SOME MEASURE HOW SERIOUSLY THE SIN OF
UNIONISM WAS IMPAIRING THE SPIRITUAL HEALTH AND UNDERMINING THE CON-
FESSIONAL PURITY. AND WHILE IN 1854 THE SYNOD COULD STILL NOT AGREE
ON THE PROPER ANSWERS TO WEINMANN'S QUESTIONS, WHILE INDEED THE MA-
JORITY STILL HELD TO A UNIONISTIC POSITION, A FERMENT WAS IN PROCESS
WHICH DROVE MEN TO REAPPRAISAL OF THEIR POSITION IN THE LIGHT OF SCRIP-
TURE AND THE CONFESSIONS. AS THE SYNOD GREW NUMERICALLY, IT GAINED
INTO MEMBERSHIP A GROUP OF MEN WHO LABORED WITH EVER INCREASING DE-
TERMINATION FOR THE CAUSE OF SOUND LUTHERANISM; AND THEIR INFLU-
ENCES THROUGH THE WORD OF GOD GRADUALLY BECAME DOMINANT. IT WAS
NOT AN EASY OR A PAINLESS ADVANCE. THERE WERE BITTER CONTROVERSIES
AND SAD SEPARATIONS. BUT IT IS ONLY SO, BY THE SURGERY OF DISCIPLINE
AND THE CONVICTION OF GAINSAYERS, THAT THE CANCER OF UNIONISM CAN BE
ROOTED OUT AND THE CHURCH ENJOY A HEALTHY GROWTH.

"Those inconsistencies" came to an end. The Wisconsin Synod by that time
had its own seminary for the training of its pastors. And even though for a
time it felt constrained to close its seminary, the Synod was placed into even
closer contact with the confessionally sound and orthodox Missouri Synod. For
a period of nine years the clergy of the Wisconsin Synod received their training
at that synod's seminary.

Among the pioneer pastors who had been sent over by the mission societies
were: C.F. Goldammer, J. Bading, Ph. Sprengling, G. Facthmann, Dr. E. Moldehnke, and Dr. Th. Meumann.

THE WISCONSIN SYNOD
AND THE GENERAL COUNCIL (1867)

The Wisconsin Synod soon had a chance to prove that its days of vacillating were over. In 1866 Dr. Charles Porterfield Krauth issued a call in behalf of the Pennsylvania Ministerium "to all synods which confess the *Unaltered Augsburg Confession*, for the purpose of organizing a new general body upon distinctively Lutheran principles." This was a call to all orthodox Lutherans who were not members of the liberal General Synod (org. 1820) to form a new federation. Numerous Lutheran synods responded, and a convention was held at Reading, Pennsylvania, December 12-14, 1866. Among the synods, which sent delegates, was the Wisconsin Synod, as well as the Missouri Synod.

When the organizational meeting was held at Fort Wayne, Indiana, in November of the following year, the Wisconsin Synod was among twelve synods who had adopted the confessional basis of the Reading Convention. Immediately the organizing synods had to pass through a crisis. Ohio and Iowa raised the issue of the Four Points, which had been a cause of separation for a long time among Lutherans in America. These two synods asked that the Reading Convention declare itself on them. The Four Points, you will remember, involved questions mainly having to do with church practice. The first point had to do with chiliasm, for some Lutherans were teaching the false doctrine of an earthly reign of Christ. The second and third points had to do with altar and pulpit fellowship and struck at unionism, while the fourth point took a stand against secret societies (religious lodges)—an issue on which the Lutheran bodies in America were not united. There were even Lutheran pastors who held membership in such lodges.

The answers provided on the Four Points proved unsatisfactory to the delegates of the Ohio and Iowa Synods, who then declared themselves in the matter, refusing to unite in full measure with the new general body— the General Council. The Missouri Synod, unlike the Wisconsin Synod, did not join the Council. Both the Missouri Synod and the Iowa Synod criticized the Wisconsin Synod for its compromising and inconsistent ways as evidenced in its decision to join the General Council.

How would the Wisconsin Synod react to the refusal of the General Council to take a firm stand on the Four Points? The question of altar and pulpit fellowship was subsequently taken up by the Wisconsin Synod, and after a long debate it was resolved that to declare fellowship with those who were not agreed with the Wisconsin Synod in doctrine was contrary to the teaching and practice of the Lutheran Church. Therefore, fellowship with such Lutheran bodies had to be rejected by the synod. This was a stand, of course, that went contrary to the stand of the United Church in Germany. Things were coming to a head between the synod and that Church.

And so, it was resolved that the Wisconsin Synod's connection with the General Council be brought to an end if at the following meeting of the general body it did not adopt a position agreeable to the position of the

712

Wisconsin Synod. The General Council did not, of course, accede to the requests of the protesting synods, with the result that the Wisconsin Synod's connection with the Council was severed. Wisconsin had made good its intentions to have "those inconsistencies" brought to an end.

THE MISSION ZEAL OF THE FATHERS

So reads the title of an article in the Centennial Issue of the Northwestern Lutheran, and it tells of the efforts of the early pastors of the Wisconsin Synod to reach out to people living on the frontier of Wisconsin. The article is especially interesting because it anticipates a comparison which people are often inclined to make: the slow growth of the Wisconsin Synod compared with the fast growth of the Missouri Synod. We quote the article almost in its entirety.

THERE IS NO DENYING THAT OUR SYNOD, THE JOINT SYNOD OF WISCONSIN, DID NOT GROW NUMERICALLY AND PROSPER IN NUMBERS AS DID THE MISSOURI SYNOD, WHICH WAS BUT ONE YEAR OLDER THAN OUR OWN, RECKONED FROM THE TIME OF ITS FORMAL ORGANIZATION. LOOKING AT THE GROWTH OF OUR SYNOD FROM THIS POINT OF VIEW THE MISSION ZEAL OF THE FATHERS IS NOT OBVIOUS. IN FACT, IT WOULD SEEM TO THOSE WHO KNOW LITTLE ABOUT THE HISTORICAL DEVELOPMENT OF BOTH SYNODS THAT OUR FATHERS WERE DERELICT IN MISSION EFFORTS.

TO BE FAIR IN OUR JUDGMENT OF THE WORK OF THE FOUNDERS OF OUR SYNOD WE MUST REMEMBER THAT THE MISSOURI SYNOD HAD AN ENTIRELY DIFFERENT BEGINNING THAN DID OUR SYNOD. WHEN THE MISSOURI SYNOD FINALLY ORGANIZED IN 1848, MUCH PRELIMINARY WORK HAD ALREADY BEEN DONE; MANY MINISTERS IN FIVE DIFFERENT STATES HAD HAD CORRESPONDENCE WITH ONE ANOTHER OR HAD READ *DER LUTHERANER*, EDITED BY DR. C.F.W. WALTHER, THEN MINISTER IN ST. LOUIS, AND THE LEADING SPIRIT IN THE MOVEMENT FOR ORGANIZATION. THESE MINISTERS IN THE VARIOUS STATES WERE ALREADY SERVING MANY CONGREGATIONS AND BROUGHT THEM WITH THEM INTO THE NEW ORGANIZATION. SO THAT IN 1850, THE YEAR OF THE ORGANIZATION OF OUR WISCONSIN SYNOD, THE MISSOURI SYNOD ALREADY HAD A MEMBERSHIP OF 42 VOTING PASTORS, 33 ADVISORY PASTORS, AND ABOUT 60 CONGREGATIONS LOCATED IN MANY STATES OF THE UNION.

IN THAT SAME YEAR THE WISCONSIN SYNOD CAME TO LIFE WITH THREE PASTORS, AND FEW MORE CONGREGATIONS. THE PROPORTION THEN WAS 14 TO 1 IN FAVOR OF THE MISSOURI SYNOD; TODAY [1950] THE PROPORTION IS 6 TO 1. THEN, TOO, IT MUST BE REMEMBERED THAT OUR FATHERS CONFINED THEMSELVES TO WORK IN THE STATE OF WISCONSIN, WHILE THE FATHERS OF THE MISSOURI SYNOD HAD ALREADY LOCATED IN FIVE DIFFERENT STATES. FROM THIS IT MUST BE EVIDENT THAT OUR FATHERS AND OUR SYNOD WORKED WITH ZEAL AND DEVOTION TO REDUCE THE PROPORTION FROM 14 TO 1, TO 6 TO 1, UNDER MORE ADVERSE CIRCUMSTANCES THAN THOSE ENCOUNTERED BY THE SISTER SYNOD OF MISSOURI.

THE THREE PASTORS THAT ORGANIZED OUR SYNOD IMMEDIATELY SET OUT ON LONG MISSIONARY JOURNEYS. THE FIRST MISSION EFFORT TOOK THEM SOUTH TO RACINE AND KENOSHA, NORTH ALONG THE SHORES OF LAKE MICHIGAN TO

Manitowoc, Sheboygan and westward toward Watertown and Fond du Lac.

We must not underestimate these efforts. In our day of the automobile and fast trains and other conveniences the territories they covered would mean little. But our fathers had no such conveniences, and fast moving conveyances. They had to accommodate themselves to the means of travel at that time. They traveled either by water, on horseback, or, and as was mostly the case, on foot. Only this knowledge will help us to appreciate the great strides in growth made by our Synod early in its history.

From a history written by Professor A. Sitz in 1940 we cull the following: "The need of a traveling missionary was now (1857) felt more and more. (Pastors) Bading and Koehler had made an exploration trip on foot northward from West Bend through Manitowoc, Two Rivers, Kewaunee—as far north as Ahnappe (Algoma). As an immediate result Pastor Goldammer of Manitowoc extended his labors to Two Rivers. In 1857 Princeton and Montello asked to be served. In the person of Pastor Fachtmann the Synod now found a capable man able to size up men and situations, who undertook the arduous task of traveling missionary.... He had already explored the territory about Columbus and Beaver Dam and now [October 1857], he was sent on a more extended tour through the Fox and Wolf River Valleys...He...visited Fond du Lac, Neenah, Menasha, Hortonville and New London.

By the year 1875 we find the Wisconsin Synod active in other states. South Dakota had been invaded by Pastor Hillemann, who organized a congregation in Watertown and Tindal. A group of pioneers from Ixonia, Wisconsin, had settled near Norfolk, Nebraska, prior to this and had established a church for our Synod there. In Michigan, work had been begun. So that at the end of the nineteenth century, after but 50 years, our Synod had spread to many states and had made phenomenal growth considering its very inauspicious beginning.

OTHER SYNODS BECOME MEMBERS OF THE JOINT SYNOD

THE MICHIGAN SYNOD

EARLY HISTORY

The Synods of Wisconsin, Michigan, and Minnesota each developed on their own but maintained frequent contact with each other, until in 1892 they came together to form the Joint Synod of Wisconsin, Minnesota, Michigan and Other States. At first a loosely constructed federation, which granted each synod its independence, in 1917 it, established a closer union of the synods. The history of the Michigan Synod goes back to the year 1833, when Pastor Frederick Schmid was sent over from the Mission House at Basel to Washtenaw County

714

in Michigan (the Ann Arbor area). Schmid held the distinction of being the first Lutheran pastor in the State. In Scio Township, just west of Ann Arbor, Pastor Schmidt established Salem congregation.

Teeming with energy, Schmid's missionary travels extended far, ranging over the lower half of the state, resulting in the founding of more than twenty congregations.

In a few short years, two additional pastors were sent to Michigan. Joining forces with Schmid, they organized the first Michigan Synod, also designated the "Mission Synod," for it was Schmid's and his congregations' intention to do mission work among the Indians. Mission work among the Indians in the Saginaw Valley was placed by Loehe in Germany into the hands of the Michigan Synod—men like Lochner, Hattstaedt, Craemer, and Trautmann. But soon these men for confessional reasons felt compelled to withdraw from the Michigan Synod, which tolerated false church practice. And so, the first Michigan Synod expired.

However, when Stephen Klingmann and Christopher L. Eberhardt arrived from Basel, their appearance gave Schmid new hope for a Michigan Synod. Thereupon an organizing meeting was held at Pastor Mueller's home in Detroit on December 10 and 11, 1860, at which time eight pastors and three laymen brought into being the Evangelical Lutheran Synod of Michigan and Other States. The emphasis in the revived synod was mission work. Pastor Eberhardt, who had much influence on the character of the synod, was chosen to be the iterant missionary.

A great problem that pestered the tiny synod was the lack of manpower, for the synod did not establish its own school for training pastors. As a result, like the Wisconsin Synod, it had to depend on the mission societies back in Germany, or take a chance on men who volunteered their services, many of whom were not confessionally sound, or even fit for their high office. They often served as a genuine hindrance to the growth of the synod rather than a help.

In an essay written by Pastor Karl Krauss, which appeared in the Michigan District History (1972), mention is made of the fact that in the first ten or twelve years about one-third of the synod's pastors defected to the United Evangelicals (the name given to the Union of Lutheran and Reformed church bodies). The writer also mentions that the Lutheran congregations diverted a part of their mission offerings to other church bodies, particularly the United Evangelicals.

When Klingmann was elected to the presidency in 1867, a new impetus was given to Lutheran Confessionalism. While it is true that the Michigan Synod entered the General Council—hoping thus to relieve its manpower shortage—it also committed itself to some serious study of the Lutheran Confessions, which study was made necessary by questions arising in the general body. The Michigan Synod studied the Four Points raised by the Ohio Synod and in 1868 resolved the following: "...that we reject altar fellowship with those not in agreement with us...that we reject pulpit fellowship with the sectarians...that we reject lodgery as being opposed in spirit to Christianity."

But while the Wisconsin Synod severed connections with the General Council in 1868, the Michigan Synod stayed on, hoping that the Council would yet take a firm stand, although the Akron Resolutions and the Galesburg Resolutions were inadequate.

However, over the years that followed, the lack of clearly defined confessionalism on the part of the General Council asserted itself in "loose" practice by some of its pastoral members. Things came to a head at the 1884 Monroe Convention of the General Council. Several Council pastors preached in a local Presbyterian Church, thus giving offense to the Michigan Synod congregation hosting the Convention, and to the delegates of the Michigan Synod. In the following three years the protests of the Michigan Synod went largely unheeded, and this caused the synod to withdraw from the Council in 1888.

Isolationism was never the policy of the Michigan Synod, which had its eye on establishing fellowship with the Synodical Conference (org. 1872). In 1892 Michigan became a member of the Conference, and later the same year it united in a federation with the Wisconsin and Minnesota Synods to form the Joint Synod.

Meanwhile the Michigan Synod finally managed to establish its own seminary. Opened at Manchester, Michigan, (located southwest of Ann Arbor) in 1885, it was moved three years later to Saginaw. Dedication was held August 28, 1887. The first two candidates were sent out the following year.

THE MICHIGAN SYNOD AS A DISTRICT OF THE JOINT SYNOD—HOW IT ONCE WITHDREW

In the spring of 1892, representatives of the Michigan Synod met with those of the Wisconsin and Minnesota Synods to adopt a prospectus for the upcoming conventions. At its own convention the Michigan Synod adopted the following resolution regarding membership in the Synodical Conference:

INASMUCH AS WE ARE ONE IN DOCTRINE WITH THE HONORABLE EVANGELICAL LUTHERAN SYNODICAL CONFERENCE, AND ARE EARNESTLY ENGAGED IN ERADICATING ALL UNSOUND PRACTICE AMONG US, WE HEREWITH ADDRESS AN APPLICATION FOR MEMBERSHIP TO THE SYNODICAL CONFERENCE, WHICH MEETS IN NEW YORK LATER THIS SUMMER.

At its 1892 Convention the Conference accepted Michigan's application. This hurdle passed, the three Synods met in October of the same year in Milwaukee. Merger was completed. At the time of the merger the Michigan Synod agreed to support the activities of the Joint Synod and to abolish the theological department at Saginaw, revising the institution into a preparatory school—which it remains to this day.

It was at this juncture that trouble entered the scene. The seminary faculty was dissatisfied with the agreement made by the Michigan Synod to convert the Saginaw institution from a theological seminary into a preparatory school and petitioned for a temporary continuation of the theological department at Saginaw. The Michigan Synod failed to take a firm stand in the matter and thus did not demand fulfillment of the agreement. The Joint Synod also failed to take a firm stand in the matter and left it to the Michigan Synod to come up with a solution. The procedure of the Michigan Synod, in effect, extended the life of the theological school at Saginaw.

People in the Michigan Synod took sides thus causing a breach, which then grew wider as time passed. A minority of pastors, who declared themselves against the procedure of the Michigan Synod, brought charges against the administration of the synod and also the administration of the seminary before the Joint Synod meeting in St. Paul in 1895. The Joint Synod upheld the charges and rejected the petition of the Michigan Synod for retention of the theological seminary at Saginaw. A very bad feeling then swept through the Michigan Synod as the pastors and members of the faculty formed sides. The minority, who had challenged both the administration of the synod and of the seminary, withheld contributions to the Michigan Synod's treasury. The ten pastors involved were suspended. These men subsequently met at Sebewaing and organized themselves, resolving to send delegates to the 1896 Convention of the Synodical Conference for the purpose of filing charges against President Boehner of the Michigan Synod, and those supporting him. While the synod itself was not represented at the Conference meeting a committee was set up to look into the matter of the charges and report back.

Feelings ran high as the Michigan Synod met in convention at Sturgis in the fall of 1896. There it resolved to sever relations with the Joint Synod and also leave the Synodical Conference. The committee from the Conference was not even granted a hearing. The ten suspended pastors were excluded.*

Having severed connection with the Joint Synod, the Michigan Synod later took another step it would learn to regret. Seeking fellowship, the Michigan Synod affiliated with the Augsburg Synod, thus creating a General Synod with two districts. However, it became apparent that Augsburg tolerated false doctrine and practice in its midst, a fact that did not set well with the members of the Michigan Synod. Eventually things would take place in the synod that would change its course and bring it back into the Joint Synod. For example, there came about a change in the leadership of the Michigan Synod, and some of those who had been leaders in the agitation to leave the Joint Synod, resigned. Furthermore, events were occurring at the seminary in Saginaw that contributed to a whole new appraisal of the controversy that centered in this school. Things came to a terrible state of affairs at the seminary. Student after student left, evidently dissatisfied with the treatment they received. Finally, on August 10, 1907, the board declared the seminary closed and the office of director to be nonexistent. This sad state of affairs, which resulted in an empty campus, continued for three years.

In the meanwhile steps were taken to again be a part of the Joint Synod, and to be received once more as a member synod of the Synodical Conference. The Michigan Synod in 1904 gave this view of its withdrawal from the Conference:

WE MUST NOW DECLARE THAT STEP TO HAVE BEEN UNJUSTIFIED AND HASTY, BECAUSE WE MUST NOW SAY TO OURSELVES THAT NEITHER CONSCIENCE NOR NEED COMPELLED US TO TAKE SUCH A STEP, AND THEREFORE, WE HAD NO REAL REASON FOR OUR ACTION. WE CAN ONLY EXPRESS OUR DEEPEST REGRET THAT WE DENIED THE COMMISSION OF THE SYNODICAL CONFERENCE A HEARING AND SPURNED THEIR EFFORTS TO SERVE US; WE MUST DEEPLY DEPLORE THE PEREMPTORY MANNER IN WHICH WE DISMISSED THE COMMISSION.

Furthermore, in 1906 a meeting of the Michigan Synod with the Michigan District succeeded in composing the differences which had arisen between the two groups. Mutual acknowledgment of wrong and an attitude of willingness to forgive was the ointment, which healed old wounds.

And so, in August 1909 the Michigan Synod again found itself in the Joint Synod, but also with the problem of what to do with the empty school at Saginaw. The dilemma was resolved by reopening the seminary as a preparatory school. However, upon the suggestion of Dr. Ernst the school would retain in its name the word "seminary." And so, the official name became and remains, Michigan Lutheran Seminary—in spite of efforts over the years to change it.

When the amalgamation of the district synods occurred in 1917, the Michigan Synod—at the time numbering 52 pastors and 65 congregations—became then a district of the Joint Synod.[11]

"MICHIGAN SPIRIT"

Karl F. Krauss, writing in *Michigan District History*, makes an interesting observation regarding the so-called "Michigan Spirit." Since this mindset has been so commonly attributed to the Michigan District we will include Pastor Krauss' observation concerning it:

THE HISTORY OF THE DISTRICT IS INTIMATELY BOUND UP WITH THE SEMINARY AT SAGINAW. THIS IMPARTED TO THE DISTRICT A UNIQUE CHARACTER, WHICH HAS ALWAYS BEEN REFERRED TO AS THE "MICHIGAN SPIRIT." IT IS NOT EASY TO DEFINE; IT IS SOMETHING THAT NEEDS TO BE EXPERIENCED. FOR THOSE OF US WHO GREW UP IN THE DISTRICT IT IS EVEN MORE THAN AN EXPERIENCE; IT IS A "FLESH AND BLOOD" THING. WE ARE PART OF IT, AND IT IS PART OF US. IT WAS STAMPED INDELIBLY UPON OUR LIFE AND BEING. AS I SEE IT, THE "MICHIGAN SPIRIT" WAS CHARACTERIZED BY AN ALMOST FIERCE LOYALTY, A BURNING ZEAL, AND A CONGENIAL CAMARADERIE.

THIS SPIRIT MAY BE TRACED BACK TO EBERHARDT AND THE EARLY STUDENTS OF THE SEMINARY...IT IS MY CONSIDERED OPINION—AND I CHALLENGED CONTRADICTION—THAT IT WAS THE "MICHIGAN SPIRIT" WHICH MADE OUR DISTRICT UNIQUE IN MANY WAYS. I BELIEVE ALSO THAT IT WAS THE "MICHIGAN SPIRIT" THAT PRODUCED THE AGGRESSIVENESS AND PROGRESSIVENESS, WHICH HAS CHARACTERIZED OUR DISTRICT THROUGH THE YEARS. I BELIEVE ALSO THAT THE SEMINARY AT SAGINAW WAS THE RALLYING POINT OF THE DISTRICT.

There can be no doubt that the Michigan District served as a prod to the entire Joint Synod "to get things done." The expansion of the synod into the area of the East Coast and into Florida and other places in the South was carried on from the first through the Michigan District. Furthermore, there was continual mission expansion within the State of Michigan. But even the movement toward world missions by the Wisconsin Synod received much of its impetus from the Michigan District, which finally succeeded in getting the synod to pass the following resolution: "...That the Synod authorize the expansion of our mission work in foreign fields; and that the General Mission Board be instructed to continue its investigation and explore the most promising heathen fields and report to the General Synodical Committee for further instructions."

Just one hundred years after the founding of the Wisconsin Synod, a concentrated move began by this body, upon the promptings of the Michigan District, to carry the gospel into foreign fields. The first fields chosen were Northern Rhodesia (now called Zambia), Africa, and Japan. Up to that time, "foreign" mission work by the synod had been among the Apache Indians in Arizona.

Once again we allow Pastor Karl F. Krauss, writing in the *Michigan District History*, to inform us concerning the nature of the "Michigan Spirit":

THE FACT OF THE MATTER IS, THAT PRACTICALLY EVERY PROGRESSIVE PROGRAM OF OUR SYNOD DURING THESE 50 YEARS [SINCE THE AMALGAMATION] RECEIVED ITS START IN THE MICHIGAN DISTRICT. THIS IS NOT SAID IN A SPIRIT OF BOAST-ING BUT AS A STATEMENT OF FACT, WELL DOCUMENTED, AND ALSO READILY AC-KNOWLEDGED BY LEADERS IN OUR SYNOD. I AM CONVINCED THAT THIS IS DUE TO THE SO-CALLED "MICHIGAN SPIRIT" TO WHICH I ALLUDED EARLIER. IT WAS BORN OF THE INTENSE LOYALTY TO OUR SYNODICAL BODY, AN EARNEST ZEAL FOR OUR SYNODICAL WORK, AN EXERCISE OF VISION, A DETERMINATION TO GO FOR-WARD FOR CHRIST, A PROFOUND DESIRE TO CARRY OUT OUR SAVIOR'S COMMIS-SION TO GO INTO ALL THE WORLD AND PREACH THE GOSPEL TO EVERY CREATURE. WE REGARD THIS AS OUR FOREMOST RESPONSIBILITY AND OUR PRI-MARY PURPOSE, AS INDIVIDUALS, AS CONGREGATIONS, AS A DISTRICT, AND AS A SYNOD. IT SADDENS US TO SEE SO MANY OPEN DOORS THAT STAND UNENTERED BECAUSE OF THE SO-CALLED LACK OF MONEY AND MANPOWER. THIS IS NOT QUITE TRUE! WE LACK NEITHER OF THESE; WE JUST HAVEN'T LEARNED TO GIVE THEM TO THE LORD! TOO OFTEN OUR OWN CONGREGATIONAL NEEDS AND WANTS BLACK OUT OUR HIGHER VISION, THAT OF LOOKING AWAY FROM SELF FOR A WHILE AND SETTING OUR SIGHTS ON THE WORLD OF MEN OUT THERE WHO ARE DYING MEANWHILE!

THE OLD, TIME-HONORED "MICHIGAN SPIRIT" INCULCATED IN US THE LOVE OF MISSIONS AND THE PROMOTION OF MISSION WORK AT HOME AND AT LARGE. IT IS MY HUMBLE CONVICTION THAT THIS HAS BEEN OUR CONTRIBUTION TO THE LIFE OF OUR SYNOD. EVERYTHING PROGRESSIVELY, CONSTRUCTIVE, AND FOR-WARD-MOVING WHICH WE HAVE INITIATED AND PROMOTED HAS HAD BUT ONE MOVING THOUGHT AND PURPOSE: THE PROCLAMATION, PRESERVATION, AND PROPAGATION OF THE GOSPEL OF SALVATION.[12]

THE MINNESOTA SYNOD

IN THE BEGINNING, A TIME OF TESTING, TRIAL AND PURIFICATION

The founder of the Minnesota Synod was Pastor Johann Christian Friedrich Heyer. He was a most extraordinary man, who by the time of his arrival in Minnesota had served for a total of fourteen years in the foreign mission field of India, and twenty years as home missionary of the Pennsylvania Minis-terium. He arrived in Minnesota in the summer of 1857 as an emissary of the East Pennsylvania Synod, which had sent him to St. Paul for the purpose of es-tablishing a Lutheran mission there. Two years earlier the first German Lutheran service in St. Paul had been conducted by Pastor F.W. Walther, who then also started a congregation in that city. By the time of Heyer's arrival Wier had left, and the congregation had all but disintegrated. Heyer preached in German and also began English services. Through his work Trinity congregation was reestablished and legally incorporated. Heyer, for his age—he was in his sixties—was an untiring worker. He traveled to various parts of the state answering appeals, sometimes journeying 60 miles on foot or in an ox cart. On these journeys Heyer met numerous Lutheran clergymen, pioneer missionaries like himself. Under his persuasion a group of these men met with him at St. Paul in the summer of 1860 and founded the German Evangelical Lutheran Synod of Minnesota. Founders and charter members were: Pastors Heyer, Blumer, Brandt, Wier, Mallison, and Thompson. Hardly started, the new synod nearly ended:

THE MEMBERS WERE NEITHER DOCTRINALLY NOR IDEOLOGICALLY IN FULL HAR-
MONY. PASTOR WIER, WHO HELD A WEIRD AND ERRORISTIC CONCEPTION OF
THE DOCTRINE OF THE CHURCH AND MINISTRY, SOON SEVERED HIS CONNEC-
TION WITH THE GROUP. MALLISON AND THOMPSON, UNABLE TO SPEAK GERMAN
AND THUS NOT A NATURAL PART OF THE BODY WHOSE WORK WAS THOUGHT OF
AS HIGHLY SPECIALIZED FOR SERVICE TO SCATTERED GERMAN LUTHERANS,
WITHDREW. THAT LEFT HEYER, BLUMER, AND BRANDT. IT WAS A CREAKY AND
UNPROMISING VENTURE.[13]

Things changed for the Minnesota Synod when Pastor Heyer in 1863 resigned due to age, and a replacement in the person of Pastor G. Fachtmann arrived, who also became head of the synod. Through his efforts new workers were brought to the state, the majority coming from the Pilger Missionary Institute of Basel (St. Chrischona). Twelve years after its beginning the pastoral roster had grown to twenty-five active pastors serving twenty-six parishes.

Times of testing, trial, and purification were ahead for the Minnesota Synod. The confessional foundations of the small synod were uncertain at first, because the confessional standing of her early pastors was itself shaky and uncertain. How this could be possible, we believe has been sufficiently illustrated earlier in this chapter, where we have described the confessional instability of Lutheranism on the East Coast, of which the General Synod of 1820 is but one example. Furthermore, we need to consider the fact that the mission schools in Europe from which many of the pastors came at this time—with only few exceptions—did not stress a high degree of training in Lutheran confessionalism, but rather prepared workers for a United Church of Lutheran and Reformed persuasion. The attitude of not a few Lutheran pastors was that they wanted to bear the name Lutheran, but would tolerate being bound to Lutheran doctrine and practice only to a point. Otherwise, they were quite content to carry on friendly relations—which often included pulpit and altar fellowship—with the sectarians.

The General Synod was indeed a tree in which birds of many different colored feathers could perch together: The lax Lutheran confessionalism of the early pastors of the Minnesota Synod was shown by the entry of that synod into the General Synod in 1864. While the Minnesota Synod subscribed to the *Augsburg Confession* as its doctrinal basis, nevertheless unLutheran doctrine and practice, including unionism, was not only tolerated, but allowed to go unrebuked. Fachtmann has been described as the leading unionist in the synod, and he was the synod's president! Eventually, however, Fachtmann was forced from his office. Later, he was taken under discipline by the synod, suspended, and ultimately excommunicated. In having thus to deal with its former president in such a manner, the Minnesota Synod began to change its character. IN THE STRUGGLE, DOCTRINAL CONVICTION GREW, CLARIFIED, CRYSTALLIZED. NOTHING COULD HAVE SERVED SO WELL AS A CLEANSING AGENT. SCRIPTURE AND THE CONFESSIONS HAD THEIR DAY, AND THE MINNESOTA SYNOD MOVED TOWARD STRICT CONFESSIONAL PURITY. IN 1866 IT FOUGHT A VICTORIOUS FIGHT AGAINST AN ATTACK ON THE LODGE PARAGRAPH OF ITS CONSTITUTION, AND ELIMINATED PASTOR BLEEKER OF RED WING, A FREE MASON, FROM ITS FELLOWSHIP. THE DAY WAS DAWNING.[14] Where Fachtmann had been a quivering mass of doctrinal uncertainty, his successor, Pastor J.H. Sieker, was a bulwark of strong, confessional Lutheranism. Under his leadership the synod withdrew in 1866 from the General Synod, because of its acceptance of the unLutheran Frankean Synod, and then joined the General Council when it was organized in 1867. Founded on the principal of Lutheranism loyal to the Confessions, Sieker and his group later exposed the unsoundness and weakness inherent in the General Council, so that after 1871 the Minnesota Synod once more found itself without affiliation with other Lutherans. In the meanwhile, however, there were contacts with the Wisconsin Synod.

WHICH WAY WOULD THE MINNESOTA SYNOD GO— TO THE WISCONSIN SYNOD OR THE MISSOURI SYNOD?

The two synods were becoming more and more aware of each other, and then in 1866 the Wisconsin Synod took the initiative and in a friendly move sent a representative to the Minnesota Synod Convention, at the same time inviting that synod to reciprocate. The Minnesota Synod did just that, and two years later, President Sieker, speaking officially for his synod expressed the wish for a merger with the Wisconsin Synod. Instead of merger, Wisconsin's President Bading the following year recommended federation in which each synod would keep its own identity, schools and church government. The final proposal had to do with doctrine, and in it the Wisconsin Synod insisted on full doctrinal unity as a prerequisite for federation, therefore recommending doctrinal discussions between appointed representatives of the two bodies.

While the Minnesota Synod was found to be in doctrinal agreement with the Wisconsin Synod, the latter body hesitated to enter a federation at that time for the reason that while the Wisconsin Synod had left the General Council in 1869, the Minnesota Synod had not. It had decided to remain awhile longer, with the hopes of turning the Council to a more confessional Lutheranism by its own clear, scriptural testimony. In 1871 the Wisconsin Synod, having received assurance that Minnesota's severance with the Council was imminent, formally recognized the full orthodoxy of its sister on the other side of the Mississippi. The Wisconsin Synod representatives to the 1871 Minnesota Synod Convention brought a plan for joint work of the two bodies. Minnesota was given the privilege of training its pastors at Northwestern College,

721

and of calling one of its own men to the staff, and of helping with his support. Furthermore, the Minnesota Synod was to have a part in the production of the *Gemeindebiatt**, sharing also in its profits. (**Congregation News*)

The Minnesota Synod was represented in 1872 at the organizing meeting of the Synodical Conference in Milwaukee and became a charter member of that body. The Missouri Synod, having sent representatives earlier that year to the Minnesota Synod Convention, and having satisfied itself as to Minnesota's doctrinal orthodoxy, was happy to reach out the hand of fellowship.

For a while the Minnesota Synod actually moved more in the direction of the Missouri Synod and even withdrew its support from Wisconsin's Northwestern College and placed it with Missouri's Springfield Seminary. But something which Missouri proposed to the members of the Synodical Conference caused Minnesota to become somewhat disenchanted with establishing closer relations with Missouri. This synod had proposed a plan, which, if carried out, would have sounded the death knell of both smaller bodies as independent synods. Missouri proposed that all Lutherans of Synodical Conference congregations living in a state become members of the same district body. Those living in Wisconsin would be members of the District of Wisconsin; those living in Minnesota would be members of the District of Minnesota. These in turn would be districts or "sub-synods" of the Missouri Synod.

However, to cease to exist as a separate synod, and to be absorbed by the much larger Missouri Synod did not appeal to a majority of the Minnesota Synod membership. Therefore, President A. Kuhn, on his own, met with Wisconsin Synod representatives and by the time of the next convention had a plan worked out which would bring about federation with Wisconsin, but which would allow each synod to remain an independent unit and retain its schools. Furthermore, contact between the two synods was guaranteed by the sending of representatives to each other's conventions, and by holding joint conventions. Both synods agreed to the proposed plan and close federation was achieved.

To celebrate the 400th anniversary of the birth of Luther, the new president of the synod, Pastor C.J. Albrecht of New Ulm, in 1883 proposed that a school be built at New Ulm to train workers. The idea caught on, and Dr. Martin Luther College was built on property in New Ulm donated by Pastor Albrecht's congregation. Starting with a high school department, it soon added a theological department.

CLOSER FEDERATION OF MINNESOTA WITH WISCONSIN AND MICHIGAN—THE JOINT SYNOD

Recognizing that affiliation of the Michigan Synod with the Synodical Conference was imminent, the three synods began to make plans for a closer union than existed under the current federation. Plans were worked out for an organic union of the three bodies. Instead of protecting to such a high degree the independence of each synod, the plan limited the amount of independence of each when it came to joint work, so that for the purpose of carrying on tasks of the church together, each was to count itself a district of the larger body.

At first, the schools belonging to the more closely federated synods would remain in the possession of the respective districts, with the synod itself supervising them. These schools would be transferred to the general body if and when the district of its own volition chose to do so.

It was on October 11-13, 1892, that the Evangelical Lutheran Joint Synod of Wisconsin, Minnesota, Michigan, and Other States was formally organized. However, at the first the merger really fell short of being one, with Minnesota still retaining its own sovereignty and ownership of its school at New Ulm. The federated synods had merely moved a little closer together.

Over the ensuing years there were those who pushed for total merger of the three synods, and finally, in 1917, a complete reorganization of the federated synods was completed. At the time when closer union of all the synods was achieved, the Wisconsin Synod, largest of the three, was divided into three synodical districts, while Minnesota and Michigan gave their names to territorial districts of the body. And so, in 1917 the last convention of the Minnesota Synod was held, and the following year when the Minnesota congregations met, they did so under the new name, the Minnesota District of the Evangelical Lutheran Joint Synod of Wisconsin, Minnesota, Michigan, and Other States.

Already, in 1904, the Nebraska Synod had become a district of the Joint Synod. And by the time the synod in 1920 apprised the Synodical Conference of its 1917 merger, Wisconsin Synod congregations in Tacoma, Yakima, Leavenworth, Mansfield and other cities in the State of Washington had joined together to form the Pacific Northwest District of the Joint Synod. In the same year scattered congregations in the Dakotas and Montana became the eighth district (Dakota-Montana).

THE NEBRASKA DISTRICT

FROM IXONIA, WISCONSIN, TO NORFOLK, NEBRASKA

In 1866 a group of pioneers comprising an entire Lutheran congregation moved from the vicinity of Lebanon and Ixonia, Wisconsin, to Nebraska. These were the children of men and women who had fled the Prussian Union in the old country to seek religius freedom in Wisconsin. It is possible that the constant bickering which the Lutherans witnessed at Lebanon between the pastors of the Buffalo and Missouri Synods in their neighborhood helped them to decide to migrate. They had received reports of very good farmland available near West Point, Nebraska. After the return of an exploration committee, a train of fifty-three schooners, drawn by oxen, began the trek west on May 23, 1866. They arrived two months later at what is now Norfolk (pronounced "Norfork"), the home of the oldest congregation of the Wisconsin Synod in Nebraska.

The migrants were already a congregation when they arrived in Nebraska, but having witnessed the long and often vehement controversy between the Buffalo and Missouri Synods back in Wisconsin, they decided to remain independent and held themselves aloof from any synodical ties. They felt that their liberty would be encroached upon by a synodical body. When later their pastor died, they were in a quandary as to how and where to obtain a replacement.

Since the people had a profound trust and respect for Professor A. F. Ernst, the president of the Wisconsin Synod College at Watertown, Wisconsin, they appealed finally to him to come to their aid. Professor Ernst paid them a visit in Nebraska. He completely won their confidence, and upon his suggestion called a graduate from the Missouri Synod's Springfield Seminary. The members of the congregation at Norfolk continued to hold themselves aloof from synodical membership, but permitted their pastor to affiliate with the Wisconsins Synod. This led to the establishing of a Nebraska Conference of the Wisconsin Synod, which enabled the pastors to get together for Bible study and mutual edification. Finally, in 1901 the congregations tentatively organized as the Nebraska District of the Wisconsin Synod. However, they chose to exist as an independent synod in the federation forming the Joint Synod. In 1917, however, Nebraska became a district of the new Joint Synod, which constituted a merger of the once independent synods.

MISSION WORK PROGRESSED SLOWLY

At first, mission work by the Nebraska District pastors was confined to the use of the German language. Mission openings were slow in coming. After the First World War, English became much more the language in use, and the district branched out in its missions. However, for many years the opening of new churches was confined to rural areas. Later the mission thrust was redirected, aiming at the centers of population. Work also extended into the southern part of South Dakota, and with the calling of Im. P. Frey as missionary-at-large to Colorado, the Wisconsin Synod and the Nebraska District came to that state.

All in all, the growth of the Nebraska District has not been rapid. Nor are its congregations concentrated. They are scattered across the map, in many cases separated by great distances. By 1971 there were 29 congregations in the State of Nebraska. By the beginning of the twenty-first century, 36 congregations were located in the state. At this time the Nebraska District includes a small area in Iowa, together with these states: Nebraska, So. Dakota, Colorado, Kansas, Missouri, Wyoming, New Mexico, and Utah. Altogether, 89 organized congregations are located in the above-mentioned states, plus 6 preaching stations.

THE THREE WISCONSIN DISTRICTS

SOUTHWEST WISCONSIN DISTRICT

All of the early history of the Wisconsin Synod took place in the State of Wisconsin and especially in what is now known as the Southeastern Wisconsin District. The district takes in several cities of notable size, including: Milwaukee, Chicago, Kenosha, Racine. The three Wisconsin Districts were designated as such in the agreement, which formed the Joint Synod in 1917.

724

WESTERN WISCONSIN DISTRICT

The Western District of the Synod extends from southern Illinois to Lake Superior in northern Wisconsin. Thus it covers almost all of the State of Illinois, except for the area around Chicago and Gary, and covers also the western half of the State of Wisconsin.

NORTHERN WISCONSIN DISTRICT

This district includes the Upper Peninsula of Michigan and extends southward through the eastern side of Wisconsin, almost to Mequon—the Milwaukee area—home of the Synod's Seminary.

DISTRICTS WAY OUT WEST

PACIFIC NORTHWEST

ROOTED IN THE STATE OF WASHINGTON

The history of this district begins at Tacoma, Washington, in 1884, when in March of that year the first German Evangelical Lutheran Congregation in Tacoma was organized in a private home under the leadership of Pastor F.A. Wolf, formerly of Ohio. In 1898 Pastor Wolf and his congregation joined the Evangelical Joint Synod of Wisconsin and Other States. Over the years the ranks were swelled by other congregations established at such places as North Yakima, Leavenworth, Mansfield, Okanogan and Ellensberg. In 1907 the Synod's Mission Board saw the wisdom of sending a missionary into North-Central Washington. Wisconsin Synod members had moved there and requested services. Numerous preaching stations were set up by the few pastors called to work in this immense area. In November 1910 the first pastoral conference of the Pacific Northwest was held with four pastors in attendance.

EXPANSION OF THE WORK IN A HUGE TERRITORY

By 1912 the work had branched out into Lewiston, Idaho, and the congregation established there also joined the Wisconsin Synod. By that year there were eight missionaries is the district, who also the same year founded the Pacific Northwest Pastoral Conference.

As the members of the synod moved so did the synod. Members of the synod moved into Oregon, and soon the synod began work there. But frequent vacancies in the mission stations in Washington, shortage of manpower, and an altogether too-demanding workload on the few missionaries stationed there, hindered the synod from branching out more than it did.

In July 1918, pastors and lay delegates were present at Grace Church, North Yakima, for the purpose of organizing the congregations as a district of the Joint Synod.

725

MANPOWER SHORTAGE

Already at that time, the newly elected district president, Pastor Soll, called the Convention's attention to the critical need for additional manpower. His remarks are of particular interest, for they show the hardships of the time:

OUR DISTRICT IS IN GREAT DISTRESS. THOUGH CALLS HAVE BEEN SENT OUT, THERE HAS BEEN NO RELIEF. THERE IS A SCARCITY OF PASTORS AND STUDENTS, AND OUR PACIFIC NORTHWEST DISTRICT HAS THE DRAWBACK OF GREAT DISTANCE. FIRST OF ALL, YOU REMEMBER, HELP US PRAY TO THE LORD OF THE HARVEST THAT HE SEND LABORERS INTO HIS HARVEST, FOR THE HARVEST TRULY IS GREAT AND THE LABORERS ARE FEW—ONLY FOUR WORKER! HAVE PATIENCE IF SERVICES ARE FEW AND FAR BETWEEN. NO FIELD SHALL BE GIVEN UP; WE ARE NEITHER AUTHORIZED NOR INCLINED TO DO SO, BUT BE PATIENT AND DO NOT FORGET THAT THE INFLUENZA EPIDEMIC PREVENTS PROPER ARRANGEMENTS TO BE MADE. MEANWHILE, YOU MEMBERS DO NOT REMAIN IDLE, BEMOANING YOUR SAD SITUATION. IF YOUR PUBLIC SERVICES BY A MINISTER CANNOT BE CONDUCTED OFTEN ENOUGH, ARRANGE READING SERVICES. ALSO READ YOUR BIBLE AT HOME, ALONE AND IN THE FAMILY CIRCLE; IF YOU DID NOT DO SO, START NOW; YOU MAY NEVER HAVE A BETTER OPPORTUNITY; THE GOOD SHEPHERD OFFERS FOOD, TAKE IT. KEEP UP THE SUNDAY SCHOOL AND FEED THE LITTLE LAMBS OF CHRIST; HE DIED FOR THEM, AND WILL SHOW YOU THE WAY TO TELL THEM THE GOSPEL.

President Soll also promised a pastor for emergencies, and recommended that offerings continue to be taken during the vacancy. "Workers did come into this mission field. However, the rapid turnover of pastors continued to create problems. Through the years the ministration of the pastors serving in the Pacific Northwest, with few exceptions, was of short duration."[15]

FURTHER EXPANSION IN WASHINGTON AND OREGON

In 1935 the Joint Synod inherited from the Ohio Synod, the congregation at Rainer, Washington. In 1941 the two largest cities in Washington—Seattle and Spokane—were added to the growing list of preaching places for the Joint Synod.

An up-to-date account (for that time) of the Wisconsin Synod in Oregon was given in the September 24, 1972, issues of the *Northwestern Lutheran*:

AT THE END OF THE 1950'S, THERE WAS ONE SELF-SUPPORTING CONGREGATION AND TWO STRUGGLING MISSIONS FIGHTING FOR SURVIVAL IN THE WHOLE STATE. THE SELF-SUPPORTING CONGREGATION AND ONE MISSION WERE IN PORTLAND, AND THE OTHER MISSION WAS IN EUGENE SOME 100 MILES TO THE SOUTH. SINCE 1960, HOWEVER, THIS SITUATION HAS CHANGED GREATLY AS MISSION WORK IN OREGON HAS MOVED FORWARD WITH FIRM, STEADY STRIDES. IN THE 1960'S AND EARLY 1970'S THE TWO STRUGGLING MISSIONS HAVE BECOME WELL ESTABLISHED AND ARE MOVING STEADILY TOWARD SELF-SUPPORT; TWO MISSIONS WERE OPENED IN TIGARD AND BEND AND ARE ALREADY SELF-SUPPORTING CONGREGATIONS; AND TWO OTHER NEW MISSIONS HAVE BEEN OPENED AND ARE IN VARIOUS STAGES OF DEVELOPMENT. IN ADDITION, PRELIMINARY SURVEYS HAVE BEEN MADE IN OTHER PARTS OF OREGON WITH THE HOPE OF OPENING

MISSIONS IN ONE OR MORE OF THOSE AREAS IN THE FUTURE. WE HAVE TWO (WELL-ESTABLISHED) MISSIONS IN OREGON—BETHESDA OF PORTLAND AND TRINITY OF EUGENE.

In 1966 the Wisconsin Synod also began work in Salem, the capital. Later, the work branched out to Corvallis. The missionaries in Oregon found a field opening up in southern Oregon as the population spilled over from California. The Wisconsin Synod also had its sights on eastern Oregon and western Idaho. And so, the synod's mission work in the Pacific Northwest, which for so many decades remained in the toddling stage because of lack of manpower, and because of other serious setbacks, and hampered by the vast distances to be covered, was finally able to stretch its limbs and show its strength.

It should be mentioned here that the intense struggle that the synod experienced in the 1950's over the issue of continued fellowship with the Missouri Synod, which had been marked by the synod as causing divisions and offenses contrary to God's Word (Romans 16:17, 18), cost the district five pastors and congregations by December 1957. An additional pastor and part of his congregation also left the synod the following year. These pastors and congregations later helped to organize the Church of the Lutheran Confession (CLC).

Upon entering the twenty-first century, the Pacific Northwest District numbered 57 congregations scattered through a vast territory, comprising Alaska (9 congregations), Idaho, Oregon, and Washington. We need to bear in mind that the Northwest area of our country has historically posted the lowest rate of church attendance in the nation.

DAKOTA-MONTANA DISTRICT

ONCE AGAIN, SCATTERED CHURCHES IN A VAST REGION

One does not use large figures to describe the number of Wisconsin Synod congregations, or the rate of their growth in this northern part of the Great Plains, where the cold Canadian air in winter sends temperatures zooming downward, far below the zero mark. In fact, nothing outstanding occurred to bring about the establishing of this district. Furthermore, the most upsetting thing occurring during the district's relatively short period of existence was the controversy between the Wisconsin Synod and the Missouri Synod during the 1950's, which caused the loss of some pastors and the splitting of a few congregations. This occurred when some pastors—as in other districts of the synod—felt constrained to leave the synod in protest of its failure to suspend fellowship with the Missouri Synod. In some cases congregations, or portions of congregations, left with the pastors. While this was a fairly widespread occurrence in the Wisconsin Synod, it was no doubt felt more keenly in districts like this because of the small number of pastors and congregations scattered over a large area.

ORGANIZATION

The organization of the district took place in June 1920, and was a logical step for the congregations and pastors in the region to take. The territory involved is indeed a vast one, and the feeling was that the work of the Lord's kingdom can best be carried out if directed by men living in it. Further more, it was a long trip for the delegates and pastors to travel to Minnesota for the conferences and conventions. It was felt that the congregations and pastors could take a more active part in the affair of the church if they could meet within their own territory. Twenty-five pastors and six lay delegates undertook the step of forming their own district. At the time of its organization many of the congregations were quite old.

The rolling prairies and treeless plains of this great northern area became the home of people emigrating from Germany and South Russia. But a devastated economy of the country following the Civil War also impacted the populating of this region. Economics sent many settlers westward from Wisconsin and Minnesota. Additionally, government grants of homesteads to soldiers who had fought in the war also brought families westward to the plains.

A MISSION TERRITORY FOR THE WISCONSIN SYNOD

So then, what contributed to making this territory a vast mission field for the Joint Synod? Many settlers on the move were of Lutheran background. Not a few of theses settlers came to places where there were no Lutheran churches. The sad fact is that moving away from the established church does not necessarily contribute to a keen and abiding loyalty to the church. Even in modern times, when so many Americans are on the move, it often takes months and sometimes years for migrants to seek out and join a church and to attend worship services with any degree of regularity. To their dismay, many pastors have discovered, in making a call on a new Lutheran family that has moved into the neighborhood or community, that while they have already become involved in social activities, thus indicating that they are "here to stay," nevertheless these same persons may show a reluctance to establish themselves in a local Lutheran church. The excuse for delaying such an important step may be legitimate: they may not be able to find a church of their synodical affiliation, or a church that they can feel "comfortable" in. Still, all too often the excuse that is offered—that they want to take their time and shop around to find the church that is just right for them—is just that, an excuse.

Also back in the days of settling the plains, the people were often slow to connect with the church and attend worship services. However, their reasons for not getting settled in a church right away were often quite compelling. The rigors of making a home and a living in the new territory were, in a word, overwhelming. In fact, it is impossible for us today to fully appreciate what hardships those early settlers endured. Churches, like towns and cities, were few and far between. And the main reason for this was that there just weren't that many people who were settled in the region. In the 1960's North Dakota ranked 17th in area, yet it ranked only 44th in population. It is said that in

1870 the population of the area, which became North Dakota had only 500 inhabitants at the most.[16] The weather in North Dakota can represent the extreme. Hot summers, sometimes punctuated with periods of drought; and cold in the winter that turns fuel oil to gel. As someone once put it: Blizzards come from the North Pole across the plains with nothing to slow them down but barbed wire fences.[17] Still there were hardy souls that dared to come and stay and farm here. If there was adequate rain and the grasshoppers and locusts didn't intrude, there were bumper crops of grain, especially wheat, to harvest. North Dakota contains one of the continent's finest regions of rich black loam. As a result more than 90% of the state's land is in farms and ranches. Which, of course, makes for a scattered population.

Of the eleven nations from which the immigrants came who settled in the Dakotas, six were heavily invested with Lutheranism—Germany and the Scandinavian lands. These immigrants then provided special mission opportunities for the Wisconsin Synod, as well as for other Lutheran bodies.

Much of what is said concerning North Dakota, can be said also of Montana, and even more so. Montana is a region of mountains in the western third and vast plains in the eastern two-thirds. Here too is to be found weather in the extreme. Winter can provide bitter cold, icy winds that chill to the bone and summer can produce stifling heat—117 degrees above zero has been recorded.[18] And there simply is not the population density that is to be found in other states. Those who migrated to Montana came to mine, and to ranch and farm, which again produced a limited, scattered population.

1917, the year that the Joint Synod organized itself into a closer federation, was also the year that a great drought began in Montana. There was as a result bad farming in the 1920's, and this was followed by the Great Depression of the 30's. Many farmers and ranchers were forced into bankruptcy. At times there were plagues of grasshoppers, and also prairie fires, that destroyed crops and grasses. Over the years farms and ranches increased greatly in size in order to make them more profitable. But this too was a cause of low density in population.

But in spite of all the negatives connected with this vast region, it was nevertheless a mission field that beckoned to the Wisconsin Synod. There were new congregations to be formed, new churches to be built, and a great many Lutherans and other former church members who needed to be rewon. Early missionaries drove terribly long and monotonous distances to conduct services in private homes to which the faithful would gather from miles around. The arrival of large numbers of immigrants from South Russia and the Balkans to western South and North Dakota made it necessary for the pioneer missionaries to schedule visits to the West. An interesting account of the difficulties encountered by the missionaries of the Joint Synod in those days is given in the synod's Centennial volume:

MUCH HARM WAS DONE IN THIS VAST FIELD BY CHURCH BODIES AND SYNODS WHO WERE NOT ONE WITH US IN SPIRIT. THE REVIVALIST GROUPS AMONG THE AMERICAN CHURCHES FOUND FERTILE SOIL IN THE PIETISTIC SENTIMENTALISM OF MANY OF THE SETTLERS. (TAKE NOTE THAT PIETISM WAS QUITE STRONG AMONG CERTAIN SCANDINAVIANS. REFER TO THE HISTORIES OF THE DANISH AND NORWEGIAN LUTHERAN SYNODS.) OTHER SYNODS TRIED TO ENTICE AWAY

FROM THE SYNOD SUCH CONGREGATIONS AS THEY COULD. SOMETIMES THEY SUC-
CEEDED. IN OTHER PLACES THEY FOUNDED OPPOSITION ALTARS. IN THIS WAY THE
SYNOD LOST SEVERAL PARISHES IN WALWORTH COUNTY ON THE BANKS OF THE
"BIG MUDDY"...THE GREATEST DIFFICULTY OF ALL SEEMS TO HAVE BEEN THE UN-
WILLINGNESS OF MANY OF THE MISSIONARIES TO REMAIN IN THIS FIELD, FAR FROM
HOME, FOR A CONSIDERABLE PERIOD OF TIME. AGAIN AND AGAIN THE RECORD
READS, "AFTER ONLY A FEW MONTHS PASTORS_____ LEFT THIS FIELD, HAVING
ACCEPTED A CALL TO _____(SOME EASTERN CONGREGATION).[19]

A not unusual aspect of mission work for the Joint Synod of Wisconsin was
also found in the Dakotas. Up to the end of the First World War, mission work
concentrated on gathering German-speaking Russians and German Lutherans
together into German congregations, to preach the Gospel in German to them.
This rapidly changed after the War. Of course, as usual, there was an element
that resisted this change, preferring their religion *auf Deutsch*. But it came to
be realized and put into practice that God wants the Gospel preached to the
English-speaking community too, and by experience the Germans found that
even Luther could be made to speak English. Intermarriage of the young Germans with the English-speaking people helped to speed that day.

THE DISTRICT OPENS ITS OWN SCHOOL

In 1928 the Dakota-Montana District opened its own academy at Mobridge,
South Dakota. Both in the Joint Synod and in the district the feelings had
been voiced that the youth must be provided with the opportunity to attend a
high school maintained by the church. In a history of the school published in
1940, the following report was given as a reason for the establishment of the
small school, Northwestern Lutheran Academy:

IT SEEMED FAIR THAT CHRISTIANS WHO CONTRIBUTED SO CHEERFULLY TO THE
SYNOD'S WORK SHOULD ALSO BE GIVEN SOME OF ITS EDUCATIONAL ADVAN-
TAGES; AN ACADEMY WOULD MAKE IT POSSIBLY THAT AT LEAST A FEW IN EVERY
CONGREGATION COULD BE GIVEN A THOROUGH CHRISTIAN TRAINING; MORE
BOYS AND GIRLS FROM THE DISTRICT COULD BE PERSUADED TO ENTER THE
WORK OF THE CHURCH; AN ACADEMY WOULD SERVE THE PURPOSE OF KEEPING
THE CHRISTIAN SCHOOL IDEAL ALIVE AMONG THE CONSTITUENTS OF THE DIS-
TRICT; AN ACADEMY, IN BRIEF, WOULD SERVE AS A MISSION CENTER IN A MISSION
DISTRICT.[20]

The staff of the Academy was comparatively small; nevertheless the school
drew students from many communities. From its beginning, the Academy was
coeducational. In 1979 the synod resolved to "discontinue the operation of
Northwestern Lutheran Academy as a synodical institution." Instead the new
Martin Luther Preparatory School in Prairie du Chien, Wisconsin began operating in the fall of the same year. (This school was later closed, in 1993, and
combined with Northwestern Preparatory School in Watertown, Wisconsin.)

THE ARIZONA–CALIFORNIA DISTRICT

A LONG JUMP

Mission work among the Apache Indians brought the Wisconsin Synod to this Southwestern region of the country. Eventually, churches were established in various cities such as Phoenix, Flagstaff, Tucson and others, to serve the white people as well as the Indians. While the Indian mission work was carried out under the direction of the synod's World Mission Board, the Arizona Mission District was organized to administer the other mission affairs. The Second World War brought industry and people to Arizona. The Wisconsin Synod geared up to make the gospel available to these people. Over the years the Southwest has more and more become a resort area and wintering place for people from the North. This, too, has been a factor in the growth of the Wisconsin Synod in Arizona.

And What Of California? People had long been moving at an overwhelming rate into Arizona's neighbor to the west. About the time that the Wisconsin Synod celebrated its centennial it made its entry into California (the direct result of receiving persistent requests from a layman, Mr. Carl Loeper). The fact that the synod's workers in Arizona had experienced itching feet for quite some time to carry the gospel into California can be gathered from the Arizona Mission District report to the Joint Synod in 1951:

AFTER LONG AND MUCH URGING FROM OUR CIRCLES A BEGINNING HAS BEEN MADE BY OUR SYNOD FOR MISSION WORK IN [CALIFORNIA] UNDER THE SUPERVISION OF OUR DISTRICT. AFTER SPENDING MUCH TIME ON SURVEYS, ACQUISITION OF PROPERTY AND BUILDINGS FOR WORSHIP, TWO MISSIONARIES WERE SENT TO TARZANA AND MAR VISTA, LOCATED IN GREATER LOS ANGELES.

Two years later the Mission District Board reported:

THE ARIZONA MISSION BOARD BELIEVES THAT THE TIME HAS COME TO ESTABLISH MORE MISSIONS IN SOUTHERN CALIFORNIA.

In yet another two years, in 1954, the Arizona-California District was formed, becoming the Synod's ninth district. In 1959 the chairman of the Arizona-California District reported on the prodigious growth in the Los Angeles and San Francisco areas of California, and of the Phoenix and Tucson areas of Arizona, which made them outstanding mission fields. By 1972 the Wisconsin Synod listed 46 congregations and missions in Arizona and 32 in California.

THE FINAL DISTRICTS—TEN, ELEVEN AND TWELVE—ARE FORMED

The South Atlantic District—comprising Tennessee, Mississippi, Alabama, Georgia, South Carolina, and Florida—was formed in 1973 and numbered ten on the list.

The North Atlantic District—comprising the states from North Carolina to Maine—was formed in 1983 and numbered eleven on the list.

The South Central District—comprising Texas, Oklahoma, Arkansas, and Louisiana—was also formed in 1983. This was the twelfth and final district.

THE WISCONSIN SYNOD'S
HOME MISSIONS EXPANISION

It would be helpful at this point for the reader to have a survey of the synod's rapidly accelerating Home Missions Program that brought about these final three districts—districts that covered the entire Eastern section of the United States as well as the Southern states (except Kentucky).

In the 1950's the synod underwent a great change in the pace of its Home Missions development. For the ten-year period prior to 1958 the synod averaged ten new mission openings a year. Then, threats of serious cutbacks in mission openings due to lack of manpower and shortage of funds became evident. The manpower situation was later greatly alleviated by larger graduating classes from the seminary. In June 1973 a total of fifty-five men graduated from the Seminary at Mequon, Wisconsin. This constituted the largest class ever to graduate in the history of the institution, which at the time ranked as the fourth largest Lutheran seminary in the country (out of 18).

But the Wisconsin Synod, suddenly on the march with the gospel, reaching out to states and regions which only a short time before it had not anticipated entering, not only found itself woefully unprepared with insufficient manpower, but also woefully unprepared to fund the great mission opportunities now afforded it.

The mission work of the Wisconsin Synod expanded at such a fast rate that in 1972 it could be reported that some seventy mission churches had been recently opened. It was also reported that "in some sixty cities, a backing of concerned groups waits for the action that will bring them a [Wisconsin Synod] mission."

The Church Extension Fund (CEF) of the synod, from which money is loaned to mission congregations to build chapels, though increasing in assets each year, simply could not keep pace with the accelerated mission expansion. By 1972 it was reported: "To maintain its pace the CEF needs a minimum of $3,000,000 annually—an increase of $1,000,000 over present resources." By this time the Wisconsin Synod had set a goal of twenty new missions to be established each year.

To provide more manpower for the expanding field, the synod decided it had best expand its worker-training facilities. The 1965 Synod Convention authorized the Missio Dei (Mission of God) offering, the largest capital fund collection ever undertaken by the synod. The estimate was that during the following ten years, $10-$15 million would be needed to expand the schools which educate the synod's pastors and teachers. As the pledges came in from the people toward this special offering, the synod began to make plans for adding much needed buildings to its campuses.

To alleviate the shortage in the Church Extension Fund, the synod in 1971 authorized a whole new concept for helping to finance the fund. A loan program given the title, Lending To The Lord, was inaugurated, which receives loans at good interest rates from the members of the synod. The program became so successful the first year of its existence that in the spring of 1973 it could be reported that the synod could program eighteen new mission plants per year instead of twelve—an increase of fifty percent. In the first year 4,500 investors from all over the synod loaned a total of $2.8 million of their money to the CEF. By 2005 it could be reported that loans to congregations amounted to $59,418,125. Besides providing low-interest loans, outright matching grants (4:1) to qualifying congregations are also provided (July 1, 2003, through December 2004: $6.3 million). The Loan program is now ministered through the Loan Fund. By December 31, 2003, assets in the Loan Fund amounted to $109,069,717 of which $54,496,161 were in debt securities due to investors. The grant program is administered through the Assistance Fund, established in 1993. This Fund receives gifts and bequests from Wisconsin Synod congregations and members.[21]

There is certainly a uniqueness in the manner in which the Wisconsin Synod grew in later years—both in the number of congregations and the fields of mission endeavor. The later years of the Wisconsin Synod proved to be crucial, challenging, and invigorating for a church body that had been mostly Midwestern in the time that it had existed. In fact, there were large voids even in the Midwest where the Wisconsin Synod was not represented by established congregations. No mission thrust had been made to serve the population centers of the East Coast, literally teeming with millions of people. Except for joint work among the Negroes in the Bible Belt—a work carried on through the Synodical Conference—the South, including Florida, was wholly untapped by the Wisconsin Synod. The Negro missions in the South were carried on chiefly through big sister, the Missouri Synod.

But beginning in the 1950's this smaller, conservative, somewhat isolated Lutheran body that began in, and was confined mostly to, the State of Wisconsin at the first, began to expand its boundaries and widen its horizons in earnest. Expansion was not only westward but also—and especially—to the South, Southeast, and Northwest. The third quarter of the twentieth century was an especially decisive one for the Wisconsin Synod. It had already proved to the Lutheran world that it could be a leaven of sound, confessional Lutheranism in this country. Through its doctrinal controversies with the Missouri Synod in the 1940's and 50's the synod had held firm to its position against inroads of modernism, liberalism and unionism, which infected even the Missouri Synod. In the 1950's, doctrinal discussion and controversy, and also discussions regarding church practice, were matters of high priority at synod and district conventions, as well as at meetings of the various conferences. Finally, it became an intense struggle within the synod, which resulted in the loss of a number of pastors and congregations and portions of congregations.

And yet, when all has been said and done, it needs to be recognized that the Wisconsin Synod embarked upon an historical course of expanding its gospel outreach in this country and even in the world during those long and difficult years of doctrinal controversy. This Lutheran body, which has shown a propensity toward preserving the gospel, has also been expending much effort to preach it in this country and out in the world. A staunch confessionalism and strict adherence to biblical principles need not be a hindrance to an active and successful evangelism program. Many of the cities which the Wisconsin Synod entered in order to establish preaching stations and exploratory congregations had groups of Christians who recognized the synod's conservative doctrinal stand, who then sent pleas to the synod asking that services be conducted for them. On the one hand not a few individuals and families living in various parts of the country became disenchanted with the liberal tendencies of their pastors, congregations, and synods. On the other hand they were heartened by the Lutheran and scriptural confessionalism of bodies like the Wisconsin Synod. This then accounted in part for the period of rapid mission expansion by the synod.

Another reason for the Wisconsin Synod's interest in areas away from the Midwest is the fact that so many of its constituents have been on the move—something experienced by other church bodies as well. Much of this migration has been away from the Midwest. Florida, for example, has more and more become a way of life for families in retirement. The synod's mission thrust into Florida was directed at the first by the Michigan District Mission Board. Actually, people have been on the move ever since the Second World War, and the Wisconsin Synod, not wanting to lose its people, has had to move with them. In the second half of the twentieth century, the synod found itself on the move as never before in its entire history. By the twenty-first century the Wisconsin Synod could report that it has done mission work in every state of the union. "The 1998 Statistical Report indicates that the WELS has congregations in 48 states. Only Rhode Island and West Virginia have no established congregations."[22]

The Wisconsin Synod which, to a great extent, had directed its labors to the rural and small town and small city scene, has turned with its message to the huge cities and suburbs, thus to areas of dense population such as are found in California and on the East Coast, but also in Texas, Florida, and other Southern states.

People have responded to this mission thrust of the Wisconsin Synod. Many have shown that they like the doctrinal stand and the message from God's Word, which the synod's pastors and missionaries bring. Some are willing to put forth a great deal of effort, and even make sacrifices, in order to attend worship services. These services may be held at first in a private home or garage, a store front, a funeral chapel, or a school—a temporary home until a loan for a chapel can be secured from the synod's Church Extension Fund. This may take several years to accomplish.

By 1973 the Wisconsin Synod could report the following numbers of congregations being served in those states, which had been entered in the years that followed the synod's centennial in 1950. The numbers include both exploratory congregations and preaching stations, as well as established congregations. Under "Added" a separate grouping lists some additional states that have since been entered. The underlined numbers are from the *2004 Yearbook* and show the growth or lack of growth over the past 31 years.

Alabama -2 3
Alaska-1 9
California-32 50
Connecticut-2 2
Florida-14 39
Georgia-1 8

Hawaii-1 <u>1</u>
Kansas-7 <u>9</u>
Louisiana-2 <u>4</u>
Maryland-2 <u>4</u>
Massachusetts-3 <u>2</u>
Missouri-7 <u>10</u>
New Jersey-3 <u>3</u>

A NOTE CONCERNING THE DISTRICTS

The 12 districts are divided into 48 conferences, which are divided into 129 circuits. (A circuit can be comprised of up to 15 congregations.) Each district has a president, two vice-presidents, and a secretary. Each circuit is headed by a circuit pastor who also serves as the pastors' pastor. The 12 geographical districts comprise 14 mission districts—Arizona and Colorado comprise separate mission districts within their own geographical districts.

THE APACHE INDIAN "FOREIGN" MISSION-ARIZONA

We have already pointed out in connection with the history of the Arizona-California District that the Wisconsin Synod came originally to the Southwest to work among the Apache Indians. And this is in itself an intriguing story. In the later part of the 1800's the Wisconsin Synod felt compelled to do more than home missions, which up to that time had concentrated mostly on gathering German Lutherans into congregations to give them the gospel in Word and Sacraments. It was felt that in order to comply with Christ's command to preach the gospel to every creature, the synod should attempt work among the heathen. Japan was considered a possible field, but finally the synod settled on Arizona.

An exploration committee was sent out to find a tribe of Indians among whom no mission work was being done. The scouts were assured that no mission work was being attempted among the once fierce Apaches. The choice was made: Apache land would be the field of endeavor, and already there were men who could be sent there. This was a daring endeavor, for the last band of Apaches was not subdued until 1886, only six years before the choice was made to bring them the gospel of our Lord. During the Civil War the Apaches drove out every white person from Arizona, except for a few who found refuge in Tucson.[23]

Over the many years that have passed since the beginning of the bold venture of faith, work among the once fierce, ever proud Apaches progressed slowly. Eventually about one-third of the Apache Indians living on reservations in Arizona were counted as members of the Wisconsin Synod. Pastor Edgar Guenther had the distinction of being the only white man to be adopted by the Apaches as a member of the tribe. Thus a white man became legally an Indian, and an Apache at that. The gospel works strange changes in human hearts! It is noteworthy that the man the tribe adopted was an *Inashood*, a

735

preacher of the gospel to the Apaches. Another missionary of the Wisconsin Synod, Dr. Francis Uplegger, distinguished himself as the only man who ever reduced the Apache language to writing. Dr. Uplegger wrote a grammar of the Apache language, compiled a dictionary, and did numerous works of translation. Several other missionaries of the synod in addition to these two men have distinguished themselves by their deep and abiding love for the Apache and by their many years of dedication to a truly hard and challenging kind of gospel outreach. For many years the synod maintained a nursery for Apache infants at East Fork, Arizona. Many tiny lives were saved through this endeavor. Today there is a Youth and Family Center at East Fork, providing a needed fellowship and counseling haven for Apache young people. The Wisconsin Synod conducts elementary schools for Apache children, and conducts a high school at East Fork.

As the Apache mission endeavor entered the twenty-first century the emphasis of the Wisconsin Synod centered on native leadership in this Native American Mission. To this end the synod established the Apache Christian Training School (ACTS), which trains the Apache leaders "to lead worship, preach, teach, visit, and offer spiritual guidance" to their fellow Apaches.[24] The objective is to partner more traditional Wisconsin Synod ministries and outreach ministries. The need for Native Apaches to enter the service of the church is great. The report of the Native American Administrative Committee in 2002 bears this out:

YET THE WORK STILL HAS ITS CHALLENGES. WHERE THE LUTHERAN CHURCH ONCE STOOD TALL AMONG FOUR OR FIVE OTHER CHURCHES, NOW 60 CHURCHES ARE SOWING THE SEEDS OF CONFUSION WITH DIFFERENT GOSPELS. AT A TIME WHEN MANY ARE ADVOCATING A RETURN TO NATIVE BELIEFS AND RELIGIONS AS A SOLUTION TO SOCIAL PROBLEMS, THE TRUTH OF SCRIPTURE NEEDS TO STAND OUT. WHEN SO MANY MEMBERS NEED INDIVIDUAL SUPPORT AND GUIDANCE THE MOST, THERE ARE SIMPLY NOT ENOUGH PASTORS TO GO AROUND. THE PROSPECT LIST IN THE APACHE COMMUNITIES INCLUDES THOUSANDS OF NAMES, YET MORE WORKERS ARE NEEDED TO BRING IN THE HARVEST. WITH SO MANY FAMILIES IN CRISIS, APACHE PEERS NEED TRAINING TO BE COUNSELORS. WITH SO MANY DOORS OPEN TO THE GOSPEL AND SO MANY HEARTS CRYING FOR IT, APACHE CHRISTIANS ARE NEEDED TO BRING THE WORD.

IN FULFILLING THAT NEED, THE APACHE CHRISTIAN TRAINING SCHOOL (ACTS) CONTINUES TO BE A BLESSING TO THE OVERALL OUTREACH PROGRAM BY TRAINING FUTURE APACHE CALLED WORKERS FOR SERVICES…REGULARLY SCHEDULED CLASSES ARE NOW BEING OFFERED AT THE EAST FORK ACTS CENTER ON THE WHITE MOUNTAIN APACHE RESERVATION…A FULLY INDIGENOUS APACHE BOARD OF CONTROL GOVERNS THE ACTS PROGRAM AND MAKES ALL SUBSTANTIAL DECISIONS REGARDING ITS MANAGEMENT… IN AUGUST 2001 THE ADMINISTRATIVE COMMITTEE BEGAN THE IMPLEMENTATION OF A NATIVE AMERICAN MINISTRY PLAN. THIS MINISTRY PLAN IS AN EXCITING INITIATIVE TO USE PLANNING, ORGANIZATION, AND ACTION TO ACCOMPLISH SOME MAJOR STEPS TOWARD INDIGENIZATION FOR THE APACHE FIELD, NOW 109 YEARS OLD.

MISSION ENDEAVORS TO THE LAKOTA
AND NAVAJO NATIVE AMERICANS

The following information was reported to the 12 districts in June of 2002:
LAKOTA OUTREACH: THE EXPLORATORY OUTREACH WORK AMONG THE
LAKOTA IN SOUTH DAKOTA IS PROVIDING AN EXCELLENT EXAMPLE OF USING IN-
DIGENOUS PRINCIPLES FROM THE START. INSTEAD OF HAVING THE LAKOTA CON-
FORM TO TRADITIONAL WELS WAYS, THE MISSIONARY HELPS THE LAKOTA TO
SERVE ONE ANOTHER IN MISSION OUTREACH. THE PROGRESS MAY BE SLOW,
BUT GOD'S PROMISE IS SURE...(ISAIAH 55:10,11)
NAVAJO OUTREACH: AFTER THREE YEARS OF WORK AND STUDY, THE MIS-
SIONARY TO THE NAVAJO FEELS MUCH MORE COMFORTABLE IN THAT CULTURE.
HE CONTINUES NAVAJO LANGUAGE STUDY AND PRACTICE. THE LORD HAS LED
SOME TO SEEK OUT THE GOSPEL AS TAUGHT AT THREE SITES IN UTAH, ARIZONA,
AND NEW MEXICO. THERE ARE ONGOING BIBLE STUDIES AND THERE IS ASSUR-
ANCE THAT, IN TIME, SOME WILL BECOME COMMUNICANT MEMBERS. SEVERAL
OF THE PEOPLE HAVE HELPED WITH VACATION BIBLE SCHOOL AND VISITS AMONG
RELATIVES. THE MISSIONARY MEETS WITH THE TWO WELS PASTORS IN FARM-
INGTON FOR BIBLE STUDY AND COOPERATIVE PLANNING. BLESSINGS ON THE
WORK ARE EVIDENT.[26]

THE GLOBAL FOREIGN MISSION
WORK OF THE WISCONSIN SYNOD

Latin Missions
BRAZIL-The Lutheran Church of Brazil
CARIBBEAN
COLUMBIA-Confessional Evangelical Lutheran Church
CUBA-The Lutheran Church of Cuba
DOMINICAN REPUBLIC-The Confessional Evangelical Lutheran Church
MEXICO-The Confessional Evangelical Lutheran Church

Europe and Japan
ALBANIA-The Confessional Evangelical Lutheran Church of Albania
BULGARIA- Bulgarian Lutheran Church
JAPAN- The Lutheran Evangelical Christian Church (LECC)
RUSSIA (SIBERIA)- The Christian Evangelical Lutheran Church of Russia
SCANDINAVIA- The Lutheran Confessional Church of Sweden and Norway
The Evangelical Lutheran Confessional Church of Finland

Southeast Asia
INDIA- The Christ Evangelical Lutheran Ministries/Wisconsin Synod
INDONESIA- The Confessional Lutheran Church of Indonesia
HONG KONG- The Southeast Asia Lutheran Evangelical Mission
TAIWAN- Christian Lutheran Evangelical Church (CLEC)
THAILAND- Gereja Lutheran Indonesia=Lutheran Church body of Indonesia

Africa
CAMEROON- Lutheran Church of Cameroon (LCC)
CENTRAL AFRICA MEDICAL MISSION (CAMM)- Serves in Malawi and
Zambia
MALAWI- The Lutheran Church of Central Africa-Malawi Conference
NIGERIA- Christ the King Lutheran Church of Nigeria (CKLCN)
All Saints Lutheran Church of Nigeria (ASLCN)
ZAMBIA- The Lutheran Church of Central Africa-Zambia Conference

CONCERNING THE WISCONSIN
SYNOD'S GLOBAL MINISTRIES

There have been marvelous successes as well as serious—sometimes
heartrending setbacks—in the gospel outreach efforts carried on by the synod
in foreign lands and places. In some areas the lives of the missionaries and
their families have been imperiled by political unrest and other troubles—in
Columbia, Albania, Indonesia, Haiti. Sometimes government laws and red
tape have been, still are, or are threatening to be, obstacles to the synod's evangelism efforts. For example, for many years the Wisconsin Synod went up
against Mexican law, which didn't allow residency to foreign missionaries and
prohibited them from serving national churches. All church property in Mexico
is nationalized by the government. When the law changed in 1993 the Wisconsin Synod's missionaries moved into Mexico. The synod had been conducting
a seminary in El Paso, Texas, to train Mexican nationals for the ministry. Elsewhere the synod has had to deal with government law that grants visas for
only a short time, for example, three months, making it necessary for the missionary to keep reapplying for permission to enter the country (Cuba and perhaps Russia). Where the American dollar has been devalued the cost of mission
work in a nation rises substantially, at times dramatically.

In Scandinavia and the Baltic countries much has been accomplished by
the work done by the Wisconsin Synod's friendly counselor. Through his travels he has provided vital training to men who are serving as pastors of
Lutheran congregations not affiliated with the State Church and to those who
are interested in the gospel ministry. Pastors and professors of the Wisconsin
Synod serve as guest teachers to seminary students.

One of the main objectives of the synod's global mission work is to train men
for the ministry and provide additional training in doctrine and ministry to
nationals who are already serving as pastors. Behind the scenes in every Latin
American field is the newly established team of synod missionaries, the Latin
American Traveling Theological Educators (LATTE). The Latin American missions have been described as "fluid", due to plans being in constant flux and personnel being in continual transit.

Sometimes the synod's budget concerns—as occurred early in the twenty-
first century—and other difficulties, necessitate the removal of some or even all
of the synod's missionaries from a foreign mission field. Still, the field is not
abandoned, for the synod continues to provide help and guidance. Bulgaria is
an example of this. It needs to be emphasized here that the Wisconsin Synod

738

does not enter a foreign field intending a permanent stay. Rather, the goals of the synod in every mission field is to help the church there to be truly confessional; to teach the nationals how to do gospel outreach work; to train men for the ministry; to train men and women for the work of caring for the church, including supporting it financially, thus helping the church to be completely indigenous as soon as possible. And so, a great emphasis is placed on the thorough training of nationals. Eventually, the mission advances to the point where the synod missionaries' main work is to provide training and guidance to the nationals, who then carry on the actual work of evangelism. In addition to missionaries, the synod's foreign mission endeavors also utilize expatriate lay workers in various capacities.

The Wisconsin Synod has established seminaries and other training schools in foreign fields wherever feasible. For example, already by 1970 the Lutheran Church of Central Africa had opened a Bible Institute and Lutheran Seminary in Lusaka, Zambia. The newest such endeavor is the Asia Lutheran Seminary, opened in May 2005 in Kowloon, Hong Kong, to train Asians to be evangelists and pastors. In India a theological training program is supplied for both future pastors and for those serving congregations who need to continue their studies. In August 2005 a seminary was dedicated in Torreon, Mexico.

The African fields provide their own challenge to mission work with such things as poverty; AIDS; health problems of many kinds, including various diseases; malnutrition; shortage of pastors; apathy; and dependency on humanitarian aid. Still, there have been tremendous blessings, including the fact that the Lutheran Church of Central Africa-Zambia Synod, holds to the truths of God's Word and numbers 10,000 souls (year 2004). The Lutheran Church of Central Africa-Malawi Synod continues to grow and now numbers almost 40,000 souls (year 2004). The role of the missionaries there is mainly advisory. In Cameroon a training program for lay workers is led by the mission staff. The goal is to train native pastors to become trainers of future church workers. The Wisconsin Synod has worked in Nigeria for about 70 years (counting the Synodical Conference era). Here the synod counsels and assists existing church bodies, especially by helping to train new pastors, but does not maintain a missionary presence. The Wisconsin Synod provides medical aid to God's people in Zambia and Malawi through the Central Africa Medical Mission (CAMM), which is funded by the synod's laity. This mission has been in existence for over 40 years (year 2005). Tens of thousands of people have been helped, and countless lives have been saved by the medical mission, which also ministers to the people's souls.

There have been many instances when the Lord has suddenly thrown open the door to evangelism in unexpected places, or in places where the synod wanted to work, but was kept from doing so by the government or by other circumstances. Mexico is one example, Russia is another. There have been occasion when desperate pleas have suddenly come to the synod requesting the preaching of the gospel. In 1990 the Iron Curtain parted in Europe and two years later, in 1992, a team of Wisconsin Synod missionaries took up residence in Novosibirsk, the capital of Siberia. By 2005 there were five legally registered congregations established in Siberia, with a total membership of 621 baptized souls, 5 congregations, and 2 mission stations. This group of Lutheran congregations goes by the name, Christian Evangelical Lutheran Church of Russia. The Wisconsin Synod has had as many as six missionaries working in Siberia.

Handing out Christian literature has been as important evangelism tool for the synod's missionaries in the various foreign fields, including Siberia. And so, the synod has also been actively involved in providing translations of parts of the Bible and other religious works into the various languages of the people involved in gospel outreach. The synod maintains a Multi-Language Publications Committee.

A fascinating, newer mission of the Wisconsin Synod is that which it is privileged to operate in India. As reported in the September 2003 issue of *Forward In Christ* magazine, the synod at this date serves over 5,000 souls in 90 congregations and preaching stations. Forty-five men are enrolled in the theological training programs and 75 other men, most of whom serve congregations, continued their studies of God's Word in monthly seminars. Orphans are supported and support is given to students in two Christian day schools.

In conclusion, we repeat that much of the Wisconsin Synod's foreign mission work is advisory at this point of time. Thus it helps the church that has been planted to grow in numbers by reaching out to others with the gospel, and to gain strength spiritually through Word and sacrament. Therefore, while the church is still being planted, it is also being nurtured so that in every foreign field the goal of a truly indigenous church can someday be realized.

THE LUTHERAN WOMEN'S MISSIONARY SOCIETY

The Society's mission statement: "To increase interest in and to support mission endeavors which are part of, or in the interest of, our Wisconsin Evangelical Lutheran Synod." The first convention of the LWMS was held on June 27, 1964. Among the Society's projects: Support of the Central Africa Medical Mission, support of publications projects, support of the Taped Ministry program (videotaped worship services, for example furnished to armed forces personnel), production of Braille materials. Home mission projects are also chosen to receive financial support from the membership through donations.

SISTER CHURCHES OF THE WISCONSIN SYNOD ABROAD

EVANGELICAL LUTHERAN FREE CHURCH, GERMANY

This Lutheran body is more than 125 years old. Confessional Lutherans broke from the State Church, which allowed unLutheran, unscriptural teachings and practices. The church has 1,500 members in 37 congregations and preaching stations, served by 15 German pastors. In 2001 the

ELFK opened Martin Luther School, an elementary school, in Zwickau, Germany. The school, operated as a mission arm as well as a means to nurture the children with the gospel, has had significant support from members of the Wisconsin Synod. The German government is expected to finance a large portion of the school's budget.

CONFESSIONAL LUTHERAN CHURCH IN LATVIA

This Lutheran body was founded in 1999 by two congregations that left the Lutheran Church of Latvia, a liberal body. Six years after its founding, the Confessional Lutheran Church had grown from two to eleven congregations, with a baptized membership of more than 600 persons. Worship is conducted at this time mainly in rented quarters, but churches are being built. The Confessional Church has eleven pastors.

LUTHERAN CONFESSIONAL CHURCH (LBK) OF SWEDEN, NORWAY, AND FINLAND

The Wisconsin Synod furnishes a Friendly Counselor to the Scandinavian churches in fellowship with it, members of the Lutheran Confessional Church. Furthermore, gifts are sent to help fund this body, the LBK, in Scandinavia, and Wisconsin Synod pastors and professors serve as guest teachers to seminary students. The Evangelical Lutheran Confessional Church of Finland has been in existence about twenty years (year 2005) and is finally large enough to register with the government as a church body.

UKRAINE LUTHERAN CHURCH (ULC)

The Wisconsin Synod has been in formal fellowship with the ULC since 2001. A synod professor has been serving as a mentor to this church body. Twenty-six congregations (year 2005) are served by seventeen pastors.

CONFESSIONAL EVANGELICAL LUTHERAN CONFERENCE

This Conference has been called the successor to the Synodical Conference of North America (1872-1966). The CELC is international in scope. Twenty Confessional Lutheran Church bodies from around the world constitute the CELC. We have listed these bodies in our report of the Wisconsin Synod's global evangelism efforts. The CELC was formed in 1993 for the purpose of providing a worldwide forum for confessional Lutherans. Recently (year 2005) the Confessional Lutheran Church of Indonesia was taken into full membership of the Confessional Lutheran Conference. The Wisconsin Synod joined the CELC in 2001. The churches comprising the CELC meet every three years for fellowship, encouragement, and mutual strengthening in God's Word.[27]

MEMBERSHIP IN THE NATIONAL CHURCHES OF THE WORLDWIDE MISSION FIELDS OF THE WISCONSIN SYNOD

The following statistics were compiled for the year 2005: Baptized souls: 72,953; Communicant members: 35,272; National pastors: 122; Trained evangelists: 184; Bible Institute students: 229; Seminary students: 65.[28]

ADDITIONAL MINISTRIES OF THE WISCONSIN SYNOD

MILITARY SERVICES COMMITTEE (MSC)

This committee serves men and women in the military both at home and abroad through mailings of devotional material; through contact pastors, synod missionaries (in Japan and Okinawa), and chaplains (who serve synod members in the military in Europe [Germany, Switzerland, England]). The chaplains also provide a full range of pastoral services to non-military persons in Germany, Switzerland, England, and Italy.[29]

SPECIAL EDUCATION SERVICES COMMITTEE

Provides special religious training for developmentally disabled synod members.

INSTITUTIONAL MINISTRY COMMITTEE

Promotes gospel ministry to people residing in nursing homes, hospitals, group homes, centers for the disabled, and sheltered living arrangement. An important part of the work of this committee is to provide Bibles and Christian literature (including correspondence courses) for prisoners in jails and penitentiaries across the United States and Canada. The Wisconsin Synod is a leader among church bodies in providing this important service.

THE AGING COMMITTEE

"This Committee encourages and assists (synod) members and their congregations as they offer spiritual and other services to aging members in their parishes and communities, also through published materials."

MISSION FOR THE DEAF AND HARD OF HEARING

This mission provides materials to assist congregations in serving the hard of hearing as well as the deaf. It encourages outreach to unchurched people who are deaf (85% of deaf persons in the U.S. are unchurched).

MISSION FOR THE VISUALLY IMPAIRED

This mission serves such persons, and also the blind, by producing and distributing (synod) periodicals and books in Braille, large print, and on audiocassette. The mission reaches out to members and non-members of the synod. A group of about 65 people from the synod churches in the Twin Cities area volunteer to produce the various books and periodicals from Northwestern Publishing House in formats suited for the blind and visually impaired. This is not budgeted by the synod. Contributions from individuals, congregations, the Lutheran Women's Missionary Society, and church organizations fund the mission.

COMMITTEE ON MENTAL HEALTH NEEDS

The Committee's purpose "is to help (synod) congregations, institutions, called workers, and lay members as they minister to one another in love, especially to those who are experiencing mental health needs." The committee promotes the mental health of the student body at Martin Lutheran College in New Ulm. It provides guidance literature for therapists. It plans to provide a database of Bible-based therapists throughout the United States and Canada.[30]

AN ORGANIZATION THAT HELPS CONGREGATIONS REDUCE BUILDING EXPENSES

Builders For Christ is a division of the WELS Kingdom Workers, providing workers to aid congregations, schools and organizations build facilities at an affordable price. Over 350 men and women have volunteered to build more than 60 worship facilities and other structures.[31]

CHARITABLE ORGANIZATIONS OF THE WISCONSIN SYNOD

Central Africa Medical Mission: Supported by the Women's Organizations of the synod churches. The missions: The Mwembezhi Lutheran Rural Health Center in Zambia and The Lutheran Mobile Clinic out of Lilongwe, Malawi.

Calvary Academy, Inc.: Located in South Milwaukee...A "Home for Children in Crises."

Christian Life Resources (CLR): The CLR was established in 1983 "to better direct the broadened pro-life and family ministry of WELS Lutherans for Life." Also: Life Resources International. Subsidiaries: New Beginning—a home for mothers (for new single mothers and their children), and Christians Concerned for Life.

Committee On Relief: A Wisconsin Synod agency responsible for disaster relief and humanitarian aid (regardless of religious beliefs). Relief funds are generated through the generosity of the members of the synod. Worldwide.

Jesus Cares Ministries, Inc.: An outreach ministry of the Lutheran Home Association in Belle Plaine, Minnesota. Its purpose is to aid people with developmental disabilities and their families.

The Lutheran Home Association (Belle Plaine, Caledonia, Mankato, MN): Since 1898 the Association has been an outreach ministry to give physical, mental, emotional help to those entrusted to its care. An Association of more than 200 Wisconsin Synod and Evangelical Lutheran Synod congregations nation-wide.

Institutional Chaplaincy Program: Provides pastoral care especially to persons who are institutionalized at a distance from their home church. Also provides spiritual care to non-members as opportunities allow.

Wisconsin Lutheran Special Needs Resource Center (Milwaukee)

FINANCES: SPECIAL FUNDS

The CHURCH EXTENSION FUND (CEF) provides both low-interest loans and outright grants (4:1 matching) to qualifying newly established congregations. The Loan Program: the original fund of the CEF is a revolving fund. By December 31, 2003, assets were $109,069,717. There were $54,496,161 in debt securities due to investors. Administered through the LOAN FUND. The Grant Program is administered through the ASSISTANCE FUND, established in January 1992. The sources of the funds administered are in the form of gifts and bequests from Wisconsin Synod congregations and individual members of the synod.

In 1975 the synod set up the WELS Investment Board (later, Investment Commission). This board managed gifts given to the synod for long-term purposes. In 1997 the WELS INVESTMENT FUNDS was given the responsibility for investing various synod funds. "Today, WELS groups (e.g. Home and World Missions, Ministerial Education, WELS Church Extension Fund, WELS Foundation), the four synodical schools, several area Lutheran high schools, and almost 50 congregations invest in WELS Funds." Total market value for WELS Funds (as of May 31, 2004), nearly $100 million.

The Wisconsin Evangelical Lutheran Synod has four separately incorporated subsidiaries that report to the Synodical Council and the synod president: WELS Investment Funds, Inc., WELS Church Extension Fund, Inc., Northwestern Publishing House, Inc., WELS Foundation, Inc.

The synod has a PENSION COMMISSION that manages a portfolio worth more than $80 million to provide pensions for its employees in retirement.

The synod also operates a group medical plan, called the VOLUNTARY EMPLOYEE'S BENEFICIARY ASSOCIATION (VEBA).

THE COMMISSION ON INTER-CHURCH RELATIONS (CICR)

This Commission meets every two years with the Evangelical Lutheran Synod (ELS), the small Norwegian Synod with which it is in fellowship. The purpose of these meetings is to discuss mutual doctrinal concerns. The Wisconsin Synod's attitude toward doctrinal talks with the Missouri Synod has been that this synod must first set its own house in order before Wisconsin can meet with it.

EDUCATION IN THE WISCONSIN SYNOD
(As of June 2004)

ELEMENTARY SCHOOLS – 357...STUDENTS ENROLLED – 27,297
EARLY CHILDHOOD MINISTRIES – 364*...STUDENTS ENROLLED – 8,103
AREA LUTHERAN HIGH SCHOOLS – 24...STUDENTS ENROLLED- 5,671 (2002-2003)
PRIVATE COLLEGE – 1 (OPENED IN 1973 IN MILWAUKEE ON AN EXISTING CAMPUS)
SYNODICAL SCHOOLS:
WISCONSIN LUTHERAN SEMINARY (MEQUON, WI)
MARTIN LUTHERAN COLLEGE (NEW ULM, MN)
LUTHERAN PREPARATORY SCHOOL (WATERTOWN, WI)
MICHIGAN LUTHERAN SEMINARY (A PREPARATORY SCHOOL, SAGINAW MICHIGAN)[34]
*252 of early childhood ministries are extensions of Lutheran elementary school; 112 are self-standing.

EDUCATION IN THE WISCONSIN SYNOD— ADDITIONAL INFORMATION

The following breakdown of students who attend Lutheran elementary schools was reported for the school year 2002-2003: Mission prospects children (4%). Children from other Christian churches (7%). Children from other WELS/ELS churches (9%). Children from the congregation (80%).

At this reporting time, the synod recognized with dismay that Lutheran elementary school enrollments have been dropping, and the following observation was recorded in *Forward In Christ* magazine, May 2003: WE ARE VERY CONCERNED ABOUT THE DECLINING, COLLAPSING SYSTEM OF OUR LUTHERAN ELEMENTARY SCHOOLS BECAUSE THEY HAVE BEEN A BACKBONE FOR SO MANY THINGS IN OUR SYNOD, INCLUDING FUTURE CALLED WORKERS. WE ARE ENCOURAGING CHURCHES TO PREPARE AND TURN SCHOOLS TO OUTREACH IN ORDER TO CARRY OUT THE GREAT COMMISSION. (Statement by Commission on Parish Schools administrator Jason Nelson.)[35]

The seminary of the Wisconsin Synod was founded in 1863, and is the only theological seminary of the synod. Since 1929 the seminary has occupied a beautiful hilltop site in Mequon (formerly Thiensville), Wisconsin. The build-

745

ings were designed to reflect the architecture of the Wartburg Castle in Germany where Luther translated the New Testament from the Greek into German. The seminary is located about 15 miles north of Milwaukee, the synod's center.

While the Missouri Synod has lost its preparatory schools, the Wisconsin Synod has determined to continue its preparatory schools system. However, maintaining this "feeder" school system (for the college and seminary) is a difficult endeavor in tough economic times.

In 1959 a new Junior College was authorized in Milwaukee, which began operations the following year. In 1969 the synod resolved to merge the Junior College with Dr. Martin Luther College, New Ulm, Minnesota. However, in 1973 Wisconsin Lutheran College was opened in Milwaukee as a private venture. In 1979 the synod resolved to buy an existing campus at Prairie du Chien, Wisconsin, to house the preparatory school transferred from New Ulm. The same year the synod resolved to "discontinue the operation of Northwestern Lutheran Academy at Mobridge, South Dakota, as a synodical institutions." Instead, the new Martin Luther Preparatory School in Prairie du Chien began operations in the fall of the same year. In 1993 this school was voted closed and combined with Northwestern Preparatory School in Watertown, Wisconsin— on the same campus with Northwestern College. Later, when the college department was moved to New Ulm and combined with Dr. Martin Luther College, the combined college was given the new name, Martin Luther College, and the preparatory school at Watertown was renamed Luther Preparatory School.

WISCONSIN SYNOD PASTORS SERVING MEMBERS IN SPECIAL CIRCUMSTANCES (2004)

ON CAMPUSES

The synod has a network of pastors serving full-time, part-time, or as contact persons in educational institutions in 46 states plus five cities in Alberta and Ontario, Canada. Free copies of synod's periodicals.

IN HOSPITALS AND OTHER INSTITUTIONS

The synod has contact pastors serving institutionalized members in 22 states. Literature program for prisoners.

IN MILITARY INSTALLATIONS

The synod maintains contact pastors in military installations in 42 states, plus Puerto Rico. There are contact pastors in Japan (the Mainland and Okinawa) and in Europe.[36] Free copies of synod's periodicals, plus worship aids. The Wisconsin Synod does not, for reasons of conscience and confession participate in the United States Chaplaincy program. Still, it is eager to serve its

746

members in the Armed Forces through personal ministration in the camps and on the battlefields.[37]   Prior to the Vietnam War the synod used camp pastors to serve the synod's armed forces personnel at home bases and training camps. Contacts with men and women a way from the United States were made through an extensive mailing program.   When the Vietnam Conflict came along, the synod once again petitioned the United States government for permission to serve its members on foreign soil.   Finally, a civilian chaplaincy service was set up with the approval not only of our nation's government but also of the Vietnam government.   This allowed Wisconsin Synod civilian chaplains—financially supported by the synod—to travel freely in Vietnam in search of members to minister to them.   And so, while the chaplains did make use of military transportation, the actual expenses of keeping them in the theater of war operations was borne by the synod.   This civilian chaplaincy program has attracted inquiries from other church groups, who also have been disheartened by the government-regulated chaplaincy program.   The synod maintains a civilian chaplain(s) in Europe.

PUBLISHING

Northwestern Publishing House, Milwaukee, Wisconsin, was founded on October 8, 1891. Among the publications produced by Northwestern are the daily devotional booklet, *Meditations*; *Forward in Christ* (formerly *Northwestern Lutheran*), the official magazine of the synod. The most extensive publishing project undertaken by Northwestern is the *People's Bible* series, which targets the average layman. "The series includes the entire text of the Bible and is accompanied by commentary, maps, archaeological information, histories, and illustrations. Northwestern... published the first book in the People's Bible series in 1983 and brought the last to the shelves in January 2003...All of the series' authors were pastors..."[38]

Northwestern maintains a catalog department and bookstore at its location in Milwaukee. Many of the books that are offered for sale are authored by members of the Wisconsin Synod. All books and periodicals and religious instruction materials reflect the conservative scriptural and confessional position of the synod. Another extensive publishing endeavor is the *Christ-Light Curriculum for the School and Home*. This curriculum contains (according to the NPH Catalog) the resources a congregation needs to coordinate the curriculum for all its youth education agencies. *Christian Worship: A Lutheran Hymnal*, was published by Northwestern in 1993 as an alternative to the old standby, *The Lutheran Hymnal*, published by Concordia Publishing House in 1941.

THE SYNOD'S NAME IS CHANGED

In 1959 a new Constitution was adopted for the synod and at that time the name became officially the Wisconsin Evangelical Lutheran Synod (WELS). More than one sigh of relief was heard when the resolution passed to adopt this crisp new name. To many pastors and delegates it was a welcome change from "Joint" and "Other States" which for almost seventy years had occupied prominent places in the official title. More often than not, in this book we refer to the synod simply as the Wisconsin Synod.

THE DOCTRINAL CONTROVERY WITH THE MISSOURI SYNOD AND SUSPENSION OF FELLOWSHIP

THE CONTROVERSY IS ROOTED IN EVENTS IN THE THIRTIES

In 1872 the Wisconsin Synod and the Missouri Synod, along with others, joined hands to form the Synodical Conference. In 1955 the Evangelical Lutheran Synod (ELS-Norwegian), which had also become a member of the Conference, suspended fellowship with the Missouri Synod on the basis of Romans 16:17, and in this synod's own words, this fellowship is "not to be resumed until the offenses contrary to the doctrine which we have learned have been removed by them in a proper manner."[39] Six years later, in 1961, the Wisconsin Synod—after years of admonition marked by bitter controversy, also within its own ranks—repeated the action of the Evangelical Lutheran Synod by likewise suspending fellowship with the Missouri Synod on the basis of Romans 16:17. This action by the Wisconsin Synod for all practical purposes ended in 1961 that which had been established in 1872.

We will now considered from the perspective of the Wisconsin Synod the doctrinal controversy which finally split three sister synods apart (four, considering also the Slovak Synod) and ended a fellowship which had been held so dear for a very long time. As far as the Wisconsin Synod is concerned, what caused this controversy and the ultimate breakup of the Synodical Conference? When did the controversy actually begin? For certain, the breakup was not sudden, nor did it come without distinct warning signs. Even the casual observer as far back as the 1930's could tell that there was a strain in relations in the Synodical Conference. The Missouri Synod had been acting for some time in a manner which to some—both within and without the synod—appeared to be out of character for it, and certainly, also unwholesome.

There was already a difference of opinion in regards to participation in the government's military chaplaincy program. The Wisconsin Synod concluded that it could not participate by allowing its pastors to serve as government-sponsored and government-supported chaplains. The Missouri Synod concluded that it could allow its pastors to become military chaplains. The event that began the process of alienating the synods of the Synodical Conference was the Missouri Synod's negotiations in 1935 with the American Lutheran Church (ALC). In 1928 a document known as the Chicago Theses was drawn up. It had been hoped that the Theses could serve as the basis for uniting the Lutheran churches in America. The Missouri Synod, however, rejected the Theses as not settling the past differences, which lay between the Synodical Conference, and the three synods (Buffalo, Iowa, and Ohio) which merged in 1930 to form the American Lutheran Church. In fact, the Missouri Synod went

748

on to draw up its own confession of doctrine, the Brief Statement, which it adopted in 1932. This document meets the approval of both the Wisconsin Synod and the Evangelical Synod, which bodies regard it as both clear and scriptural and true to the Lutheran Confessions.

However, three years after the Brief Statement was adopted officially by the Missouri Synod, that body began to negotiate with the three synods of the American Lutheran Church, even though they did not accept the Brief Statement. It was these negotiations and their results which caused much of the contention that arose in the Synodical Conference. In 1938 the ALC through its committee found it necessary to supplement the Brief Statement in order to emphasize the points of doctrine it felt were essential. And so, the ALC Committee added its own Declaration to the negotiations, which were in progress. Covered in this document were the doctrines of Holy Scriptures and Inspiration, Universal Plan of Salvation, Predestination and Conversion, the Church, Office of the Public Administration of the Means of Grace, Sunday, and the Last Things.

The Missouri Synod then proceeded to take a step that amazed the theologians in the two sister synods. While not entering into fellowship at that time with the ALC, the Missouri Synod nevertheless declared its own Brief Statement together with the Declaration of the ALC to be an acceptable doctrinal basis for future fellowship. The Missouri Synod then went on to seek approval of the other synods in the Conference in respect to the conclusion it had drawn.

The Wisconsin Synod's response to the Declaration is summarized for us briefly in tract number two of the series *Continuing in His Word*. The tract is titled "1938-1953":

AT ITS 1939 CONVENTION THE WISCONSIN SYNOD MADE A THOROUGH STUDY OF THE PROPOSED DOCTRINAL AGREEMENTS. THE TERMS OF THE AMERICAN LUTHERAN CHURCH'S DECLARATION WERE CONSIDERED "AS NOT STATING THE TRUTH CLEARLY, NOR EXCLUDING ERROR, IN THE CONTROVERTED DOCTRINES." EVIDENCE OF THE AMERICAN LUTHERAN CHURCH'S COMPROMISING POSITION ON DOCTRINE WAS FURTHER FOUND IN THE FACT THAT EARLIER THAT VERY YEAR ITS REPRESENTATIVES HAD REACHED AN "AGREEMENT" AT PITTSBURGH WITH REPRESENTATIVES OF THE UNITED LUTHERAN CHURCH ON THE DOCTRINE OF INSPIRATION, "THE WORDING OF WHICH IS SUCH THAT A CLEAR CONFESSION TO THE INERRANCY OF THE SCRIPTURES IS LACKING." THE WISCONSIN SYNOD THEREFORE..."DECLARED THE PROPOSED DOCTRINAL BASIS FOR FELLOWSHIP BETWEEN MISSOURI AND THE AMERICAN LUTHERAN CHURCH TO BE UNACCEPTABLE, SINCE THE LATTER INSISTED ON READING THE BRIEF STATEMENT ONLY IN THE LIGHT OF ITS OWN INADEQUATE DECLARATION. IN VIEW OF THESE FACTS...(THE WISCONSIN SYNOD) DECLARED THAT "NOT TWO STATEMENTS SHOULD BE ISSUED AS A BASIS FOR AGREEMENT; [BUT] A SINGLE JOINT STATEMENT, COVERING THE CONTESTED DOCTRINES THETICALLY AND ANTITHETICALLY AND ACCEPTED BY BOTH PARTIES TO THE CONTROVERSY, IS IMPERATIVE; AND...THAT UNDER EXISTING CONDITIONS FURTHER NEGOTIATIONS FOR ESTABLISHING CHURCH FELLOWSHIP WOULD INVOLVE A DENIAL OF THE TRUTH AND WOULD CAUSE CONFUSION AND DISTURBANCE IN THE CHURCH, AND OUGHT THEREFORE TO BE SUSPENDED FOR THE TIME BEING."[40]

THE MISSOURI SYNOD ESTABLISHES
CLOSER TIES WITH THE ALC

In the Missouri Synod's 1941 Convention, resolutions were passed which to the eye of the Wisconsin Synod observer must have represented both ground gained and ground lost. The Missouri Synod did recognize by that time the necessity of a single document of agreement with the ALC. That was ground gained. It failed, however, to repudiate the confessional arrangement adopted in 1938, and despite the plea of the Wisconsin Synod, went on to establish closer ties with the ALC. That was ground lost. Missouri on the one hand resolved: THAT WE EXPRESS OUR WILLINGNESS TO CONTINUE OUR EFFORTS TOWARD BRINGING ABOUT TRUE UNITY IN THE LUTHERAN CHURCH OF THIS COUNTRY BOTH IN DOCTRINE AND PRACTICE, BUT THAT WE ARE DETERMINED TO DO SO ONLY ON THE BASIS OF THE WORD OF GOD AND THE LUTHERAN CONFESSIONS. ON THE OTHER HAND THE MISSOURI SYNOD RESOLVED: AND SINCE IT HAS BECOME QUITE EVIDENT THAT IT IS NOT ONLY DESIRABLE BUT NECESSARY TO HAVE ONE DOCUMENT, OUR COMMITTEE BE INSTRUCTED TO MAKE EVERY EFFORT THAT SUCH ONE DOCUMENT BE PREPARED. Missouri again reiterated its stand on the Brief Statement.

THE STRAW THAT BROKE THE CAMEL'S BACK

The Doctrinal Unity Committees went to work on this single document, which had been proposed by the 1941 Missouri Synod Convention. The result was actually the Brief Statement of the Missouri Synod interspersed with statements from the American Lutheran Church's Declaration. This document, titled the Doctrinal Affirmation, was to supplant the two former documents of the two negotiating churches.

Presented to the 1944 Convention of the Missouri Synod, the Doctrinal Affirmation was not accepted but rather referred to the members for study, with a final vote on the document forthcoming at the 1947 Synod Convention. The resolution stated: THIS DOCUMENT WILL, THEREFORE, AFTER ACCEPTANCE BY THE RESPECTIVE BODIES, CLEARLY SUPERCEDE ALL PREVIOUS DOCTRINAL DOCUMENTS AND RESOLUTIONS AS ACCEPTED BY SYNOD IN 1938 AND 1941. However, the issue was not that easily or quickly decided. When the ALC met in Appleton, Wisconsin, in 1946 it rejected the Doctrinal Affirmation as "not generally acceptable." It also made the provocative statement that it despaired OF ATTAINING LUTHERAN UNITY BY WAY OF ADDITIONAL DOCTRINAL FORMULATIONS AND REFORMULATIONS.

The issue between the Missouri Synod and the ALC was by no means dead. In 1947 the Fellowship Committee of the ALC issued "A Friendly Invitation." In this invitation it went back almost ten years, to 1938, and reiterated its resolution made at that time which declared the Brief Statement together with the Declaration to be a sufficient doctrinal basis for church fellowship, and at the same time it made the following observation: NO INTERVENING DISCUSSIONS HAVE REVEALED ANY FUNDAMENTAL DOCTRINAL DIFFERENCES...THAT FORBID ENTRY INTO PULPIT AND ALTAR FELLOWSHIP WITH THE MISSOURI SYNOD. And then the Fellowship Committee went on to make a statement which in the eyes of the Wisconsin Synod simply could not be harmonized with the position which all of the synods in the Synodical Conference held regarding the doctrine of Scripture: that there is...AN AREA WHERE THERE EXISTS AN ALLOWABLE AND WHOLESOME LATITUDE OF THEOLOGICAL OPINION ON THE BASIS OF THE TEACHINGS OF THE WORD OF GOD. This statement was, in the eyes of the Wisconsin Synod, the proverbial straw that broke the camel's back, for it could not be harmonized with Scripture. In fact, it raised the question in the mind of the Wisconsin Synod: What does the ALC really teach concerning the doctrine of Scripture? And there was another statement made by the ALC committee that caused the Wisconsin Synod consternation. The committee termed the demand for a unified statement of doctrine as an absolute condition of fellowship, "...a threat to evangelical liberty of conscience."

IN SPITE OF WARNINGS, MISSOURI'S NEGOTIATIONS WITH THE ALC CONTINUED

When the Missouri Synod met in Convention in 1947 it had to consider these latest developments: The ALC had rejected the Doctrinal Affirmation during the past triennium. What should that mean to the Missouri Synod? Furthermore, the ALC had issued its "Friendly Invitation" in which it went back to teaming up the Brief Statement with the Declaration as a sufficient doctrinal basis. What should the Missouri Synod do with the "Friendly Invitation"? Missouri's Committee On Doctrinal Unity set forth a rather gloomy picture for the 1947 Convention to consider. There was a manifest lack of doctrinal unity between Missouri and the ALC. There was even a difference between the two churches as to the degree of doctrinal unity that is required for fellowship. In addition, attention was called to the ALC's continued membership in the American Lutheran Conference.

At its 1947 Convention the Missouri Synod, while not retracting the 1938 union document and resolutions, nevertheless did set them aside, considering them no longer adequate. Still, the negotiations, which the Wisconsin Synod had warned against, were destined to go on. The Wisconsin Synod had also pleaded with the Missouri Synod to curb instances of unionistic practice, but the pleas were mostly not heeded.

By this time another bone of contention had surfaced between the Wisconsin and Missouri Synods. This had to do, strangely enough, with the Boy Scout program. While the Wisconsin Synod does not question the value of the practical aspects of the Scout program, and while it acknowledges that there is even much about Scouting that is wholesome, it nevertheless cannot accept the religious and moralistic principles set forth in the official Boy Scout program. The Wisconsin Synod's official stand regarding Scouting is a negative one. Back in 1938 the Missouri Synod had reviewed the Boy Scout program and at that time agreed with the Wisconsin Synod, passing resolutions, which spoke of "the naturalistic and unionistic tendencies still prevalent in the Boy Scout movement." But the attitude of the Missouri Synod had been changing and it no longer looked officially at Scouting with disfavor. The 1947 Convention of the Wisconsin Synod made a thorough study of Scouting through the theses, "A Study of Boy Scoutism." The Theses, which denounced Scouting's religious element and moral training program as utterly inconsistent with the Gospel of Christ, was adopted by the Convention. (Refer to Tract Number 7 of the series, "Continuing in His Word.")

THE SIX QUESTIONS

The rest of the history of doctrinal dispute between the Wisconsin and the Missouri Synods can to a great extent be shown in the ensuing reports to the synod by the Standing Committee on Church Union. To the 1949 Milwaukee Convention it was reported:

> YOUR COMMITTEE HAS WITH DEEP CONCERN OBSERVED AN EVER-INCREASING NUMBER OF INCIDENTS OF JOINT WORSHIP AND WORK UNDER CONDITIONS, WHICH ARE CONTRARY TO SCRIPTURE. WE ARE IMPRESSED BY THE GROWING FREQUENCY AND BOLDNESS OF THESE INCIDENTS. UNFORTUNATELY THEY OFTEN INVOLVE MEMBERS AND SOMETIMES OFFICIAL REPRESENTATIVES AND ORGANIZATIONS OF OUR SISTER SYNOD, MISSOURI. EFFORTS HAVE BEEN MADE TO DEAL WITH THESE SITUATIONS PRIVATELY OR THROUGH OFFICIAL CHANNELS. THEY HAVE MET WITH LITTLE SUCCESS.

The Church Union Committee suggested a series of questions be put forth to the Missouri Synod. It was felt that the answers to the questions, "should go far to determine our future Intersynodical relations." The questions themselves do much to show the causes of the rift that was developing in the Synodical Conference. There were six questions.

(1)   DOES THE MISSOURI SYNOD APPROVE OF THE PARTICIPATION OF ITS PASTORS IN THE PROGRAMS AND IN THE JOINT WORSHIP OF INTERSYNODICAL LAYMEN'S ORGANIZATIONS, SPECIFICALLY LUTHERAN MEN IN AMERICA? IF NOT, ONLY A PUBLIC DISAVOWAL OF THE OFFENSE WILL REMOVE IT.

(2)   DOES THE MISSOURI SYNOD APPROVE OF THE COOPERATION OF SOME OF ITS WELFARE AGENCIES WITH LUTHERANS WITH WHOM IT IS OTHERWISE NOT IN FELLOWSHIP, IN VIEW OF THE FACT THAT SUCH WELFARE WORK IS INSEPARABLY ASSOCIATED WITH SPIRITUAL IMPLICATIONS? IF THE SYNOD DOES NOT APPROVE, WHAT WILL YOU DO TO CLEAR YOURSELVES OF THE RESPONSIBILITY FOR THE OFFENSE THAT HAS BEEN GIVEN?

(3)   DOES THE MISSOURI SYNOD APPROVE THE COOPERATION OF ITS REPRESENTATIVES WITH THE NATIONAL LUTHERAN COUNCIL IN MATTERS, WHICH ARE ADMITTEDLY NO LONGER IN THE FIELD OF EXTERNALS? (E.G. "BUILDING A NEW LUTHERANISM IN GREAT BRITAIN," *LUTHERAN WITNESS*, 3-8-49, P. 76). IF NOT, WHAT WILL BE DONE TO CORRECT THE IMPRESSION THAT HAS BEEN GIVEN?

(4)   DOES THE MISSOURI SYNOD APPROVE THE POSITION TAKEN BY ITS REPRESENTATIVES AT THE FIRST BAD BOLL [A CONFERENCE HELD IN GERMANY] WITH REGARD TO THE PROGRAM FOR DEVOTIONS AND WORSHIP? IF NOT, WHAT WILL BE DONE TO REMOVE THE OFFENSE?

(5)   DOES THE MISSOURI SYNOD APPROVE OF THE ARRANGEMENT WHEREBY PROMINENT MEMBERS OF ITS OFFICIAL COMMITTEES ARE SERVING WITH REPRESENTATIVES OF OTHER LUTHERAN BODIES AS SPONSORS OF THE BOOK, *SCOUTING IN THE LUTHERAN CHURCH,* PUBLISHED BY THE NATIONAL SCOUT ORGANIZATION? IF NOT, WHAT WILL YOU DO ABOUT THE OFFENSE THAT WAS

THUS GIVEN?

(6) DOES THE MISSOURI SYNOD STILL HOLD TO ITS FORMER POSITION THAT ROMANS 16:17 APPLIES TO ALL ERRORISTS, WHETHER LUTHERAN OR NOT? (SEE STOECKHARDT, ROMERBRIEF, PP. 641 AND 642; ALSO PIEPER, DOGMATICK III, P. 474, SEC. 5; BRIEF STATEMENT, ART. 28.) IF SO, WHAT WILL BE DONE TO CORRECT THE GROWING IMPRESSION THAT THIS IS NO LONGER THE CASE?[41]

The Committee's report was unanimously adopted. The questions were sent out to President John W. Behnken of the Missouri Synod. At the same convention, the synod concurred with the reply sent to Dr. Behnken in regard to his invitations to participate in the "creation of a national inter-Lutheran committee for the purpose of arranging the proposed free conferences of Lutheran pastors and laymen" with the aim of "bringing about unity of Christian faith and fellowship." President John Brenner of the Wisconsin Synod had written in his reply: "...we are not ready to consent to the creation of a 'national inter-Lutheran committee.'" President Brenner further replied that the Wisconsin Synod is not convinced "that there is today a compelling need of an all-out effort to bring all Lutheran bodies together and that we are divinely called to support such a movement." He further stated: "...negotiations between synods should be carried on by representatives who are chosen for this work and that the proposed local free conferences are 'ill-advised,' since all too frequently the activities of self-appointed men do not unite the church, but will divide it eventually. They offer occasion for propaganda and for the formation of pressure groups that do not serve the interests of the truth."[42]

President Brenner then turned to the troubles at home in the Conference, which beg first consideration. He wrote to the effect that before the synods of the Synodical Conference undertake to correct and direct other Lutheran bodies they must first take care of the sharp divisions affecting matters of doctrine and practice in the Conference:...IT IS OUR FIRST DUTY, AND THIS IS A HOLY DUTY, TO SET OUR OWN HOUSE IN ORDER, AND THAT IN DOING THIS IN THE TRUE SPIRIT OF THE GOSPEL WE ARE MAKING THE MOST EFFECTIVE CONTRIBUTION TOWARD THE UNITY OF THE LUTHERAN CHURCH IN OUR LAND AND IN OTHER COUNTRIES.[43]

The last point of President Brenner's reply was in the form of a reprimand of Missouri's course of action in the matter of the National Inter-Lutheran Committee. The point was made that the constituent synods of the Synodical Conference should have been consulted before the plan for the free conference was proposed to the presidents of Lutheran bodies not in fellowship with the Conference. That course of action placed the Wisconsin Synod...IN THE UNENVIABLE POSITION OF FACING AN ACCOMPLISHED FACT WHICH LEAVES US NO CHOICE BUT OF EITHER FOLLOWING YOU [MISSOURI] UNQUESTIONINGLY INTO A SITUATION WHICH WE CONSIDER PRECARIOUS, OR OF EXPRESSING OUR DISSENT BY WORD AND DEED, AND SO BRINGING DOWN ON OUR SYNOD ANEW THE CONDEMNATION OF THE FERVID ADVOCATES OF A LUTHERAN CHURCH UNION.[44]

In closing its report, the Floor Committee on Church Union stated: WITH DEEP CONCERN WE NOTE THAT THE TIES WHICH HAVE UNITED US PARTICULARLY WITH THE SYNOD OF MISSOURI ARE BEING LOOSENED. IN ORDER THAT CERTAIN DISTURBING FACTORS MAY BE CLARIFIED, AND WITH THE HOPE THAT THE BOND OF UNITY MAY BE STRENGTHENED, WE MOVE THAT A LETTER BE ADDRESSED TO THE SYNOD OF MIS-

SOURI.[45]

By the time the 1951 Wisconsin Synod Convention met in New Ulm, Minnesota, the synod had received a reply from Dr. Behnken of the Missouri Synod to the questions put forth by Wisconsin. In this letter he passed on to the Wisconsin Synod the responses of his own body given in Convention in 1950. In reply to Wisconsin's first question, Dr. Behnken stated:

IN GENERAL, BE IT STATED THAT OUR SYNOD ADHERES EMPHATICALLY TO ITS DECLARED POSITION THAT CHURCH FELLOWSHIP CAN BE HAD "ONLY WITH ORTHODOX BODIES"; THAT "CHURCH FELLOWSHIP WITH ADHERENTS OF FALSE DOCTRINE" MUST BE AVOIDED "AS DISOBEDIENCE TO GOD'S COMMAND,"... "THAT IT IS DISPLEASING TO GOD WHEN PASTORS AND PEOPLE FORM ORGANIZATIONS AND INSTITUTE JOINT WORSHIP WHICH SHOWS THE MARKS AND CHARACTERISTICS OF UNIONISM, NAMELY, A SACRIFICING AND DENYING OF TRUTH AND DISREGARDING AND CONDONING OF ERROR. IF A VIOLATION OF THIS PRINCIPLE IS COMMITTED, WE MOST ASSUREDLY DISAVOW IT.

Dr. Behnken then followed with the synod's resolution which recognized that... "Many situations arise which plainly involve unionism and many others which obviously do not. Both unionism and separatism must be avoided." He then made mention of situations...

...WHICH CAN BE JUDGED ONLY ON THE BASIS OF AN ACCURATE KNOWLEDGE OF THE CONDITIONS PRESENT...WE THEREFORE HOLD THAT THE PRINCIPLE OF THE DENIAL OF CHURCH FELLOWSHIP IS NOT TO BE APPLIED MECHANICALLY OR LEGALISTICALLY NOR IS IT TO BE WEAKENED OR MADE RELATIVELY MEANINGLESS BY A FAILURE TO APPLY IT PROPERLY. THE PROCEDURE MUST BE BOTH CHARITABLE AND DEFINITE...CHARITY EXTENDS TOWARD ALL THE BRETHREN THAT ARE IN CHURCH FELLOWSHIP WITH US AS WELL AS TO OTHERS.

The Wisconsin Synod's second question having to do with cooperation of the Missouri Synod's welfare agencies with those not in fellowship with the synod was termed misleading, by the Missouri Synod. This synod then replied to the Wisconsin Synod, claiming...IT DOES NOT FOLLOW THAT, WHERE COOPERATION IN EXTERNALS EXISTS, THERE IS AUTOMATICALLY ALSO COOPERATION WITH RESPECT TO THE "SPIRITUAL IMPLICATIONS." The claim was made then by the Missouri Synod that cooperation of the welfare agencies extends only to some external features...while the "spiritual implications" are strictly taken care of by the several church bodies. Where this observation...IS NOT HEEDED, SCRIPTURAL PRINCIPLES OF CHURCH FELLOWSHIP ARE INDEED VIOLATED AND SUCH VIOLATION IS REPUDIATED BY OUR SYNOD...

In answer to the third question put to it, the Missouri Synod claimed that in its cooperative work in England, it was granting physical relief to displaced Lutherans...SO THAT THESE MAY BE ENABLED TO REESTABLISH THE OFFICE OF THE MINISTRY ON A FULL TIME BASIS AMONG THEMSELVES...HOWEVER, WE ARE HELPING THEM IN ANOTHER WAY, AND THAT INDEPENDENT OF ANY COOPERATION WITH THE NATIONAL LUTHERAN COUNCIL. WE ARE STRIVING TO ASSIST THESE UNFORTUNATE PEOPLE IN THE ESTABLISHMENT OF A SOUND LUTHERAN CHURCH IN GREAT BRITAIN.

The fourth question received a rather brief answer. The Missouri Synod flatly denied any scriptural or confessional improprieties regarding the devotions which its representatives entered into at the Bad Boll (Germany) meet-

754

ings: ...WE ARE SORRY THAT YOU SHOULD RAISE THIS ACCUSATION AGAINST US.

The fifth question—having to do with the book, *Scouting In The Lutheran Church*—was given a rather lengthy answer. First, the Missouri Synod denied the charge that members of the synod served as sponsors for the book: THEY MERELY JOINED WITH OTHER LUTHERAN SYNODS IN COUNSELING WITH THE NATIONAL COUNCIL OF THE BOY SCOUTS OF AMERICA FOR SUCH A REVISION OF THE BOY SCOUT PROGRAM AS TO MAKE IT UNOBJECTIONABLE ALSO AS FAR AS OUR CHURCH IS CONCERNED. The claim was made that these representatives of the Missouri Synod had been instructed to study the Boy Scout movement for "the purpose of determining whether our boys could affiliate with it." Their cooperation with the other Lutheran churches in the revision of the Boy Scout Manual, they felt, offered the best opportunity to effect such a revision "as would enable also our Lutheran boys to join this organization. The final result of these meetings was the provision that all religious features be left fully and completely to the respective churches." The Missouri Synod considered its cooperation with other bodies at these meetings "more or less incidental."

In regards to the Boy Scout program itself, the Missouri Synod felt that Scouting deals "only with the natural side of the body" and leaves "the religious and moral training of the boys in church troops" completely to the respective churches and that it "will make no attempt to direct" it. The Missouri Synod therefore resolved that "it be left to the individual congregation to decide, and that under the circumstances Synod may consider her interests sufficiently protected." But to the Wisconsin Synod this was over-simplification of the whole problem. It finds much deistic theology and unscriptural moralizing in the Scout program itself, irregardless of its application, whether in a church-sponsored troop, or a non-church troop. (Here the reader may refer to the Wisconsin Synod's publication, *Scouting in the Light of Scripture*, and *Testimony of a Former Scout*. Also, it is to be noted that many years ago the Wisconsin Synod congregations embarked on a program for both boys and girls to offer them the good things of Scouting but in a Christian and church-orientated setting. These programs are called the Lutheran pioneers—boy and girl.)

The sixth question had to do with the Missouri Synod's position regarding Romans 16:17, which states: *I urge you, brothers, to watch out for those who cause divisions and put obstacles in your way that are contrary to the teaching you have learned. Keep away from them. (NIV)* Did the Missouri Synod still hold to its interpretation of this passage as forbidding religious unionism...yes, even with fellow Lutherans? Missouri's convention reaffirmed, as scripturally correct, the use of Romans 16:17... "in the constitution of Synod, the synodical Catechism, and the Brief Statement." Furthermore the convention stated: "In this passage and in many others...Scripture warns against unionism and the tolerance of error and requires that we deny church fellowship to all who persist in false doctrine. Under church fellowship we include pulpit fellowship, altar fellowship, and prayer fellowship as defined by the synodical resolutions of 1944." The synod urged all pastors, teachers and laymen to study Romans 16:17 and the related texts. Furthermore, note was taken that "violations may occur due to the infirmity that still cleaves to the individual as well as to a church body."*

And so, with the Missouri Synod's answers to the six questions, matters

755

stood just about where they were before the questions were asked. Nothing was changed.

THE COMMON CONFESSION – 1950

At this point there was a new development called the "Common Confession." The American Lutheran Church did not remain true to its own words of despairing of attaining "Lutheran unity by way of additional formulations and reformulations." Its committee kept working with the Missouri Synod's committee and by 1950 had succeeded in drawing up a new document, which was adopted by both bodies the same year. In 1951 the Common Confession was submitted to the Wisconsin Synod to secure this body's consent and approval. Exhaustive study of it was made. The following report was adopted by the Wisconsin Synod:

...THAT WE INFORM THE LUTHERAN CHURCH-MISSOURI SYNOD THAT WE NOT ONLY FIND THE COMMON CONFESSION TO BE INADEQUATE...BUT THAT WE ALSO HOLD THAT THE ADOPTION OF THE COMMON CONFESSION BY THE LUTHERAN CHURCH-MISSOURI SYNOD INVOLVES AN UNTRUTH AND CREATES A BASICALLY UNTRUTHFUL SITUATION SINCE THIS ACTION HAS BEEN OFFICIALLY INTERPRETED AS A SETTLEMENT OF PAST DIFFERENCES WHICH ARE IN FACT NOT SETTLED.

...THAT WE ASK THE LUTHERAN CHURCH-MISSOURI SYNOD TO REPUDIATE ITS STAND THAT THE COMMON CONFESSION IS A SETTLEMENT OF THE DOCTRINES TREATED BY THE TWO COMMITTEES [MISSOURI/ALC]

...THAT WE DIRECT THE ATTENTION OF OUR SISTER SYNOD OF MISSOURI TO THE POSITION WHICH THE AMERICAN LUTHERAN CHURCH HAS TAKEN IN THE FRIENDLY INVITATION OF MARCH 4, 1947, WITH THE REMARK CONTENDING FOR "AN AREA WHERE THERE EXISTS AN ALLOWABLE AND WHOLESOME LATITUDE OF THEOLOGICAL OPINION ON THE BASIS OF THE TEACHINGS OF THE WORD OF GOD," AND THAT WE INDICATE TO THE LUTHERAN CHURCH-MISSOURI SYNOD THAT THIS POSITION OF THE AMERICAN LUTHERAN CHURCH CHALLENGES THE CLARITY AND THEREFORE THE AUTHORITY OF THE SCRIPTURES (PSALM 119:105). THIS CAN ONLY CAUSE CONFUSION AND DISTURBANCE IN THE CHURCH. THEREFORE NEGOTIATIONS SHOULD BE SUSPENDED.[46]

However, the Missouri Synod did not repudiate the Common Confession. In 1953 it reaffirmed its stand and proposed that until its next convention, to be held in 1956, the Wisconsin Synod study Part II of the Common Confession as the answer to that synod's objections. In reality, Part II had not even been officially adopted by the Missouri Synod. It was strange reasoning, then, that Part I was to be studied in connection with Part II!

At its 1951 Convention the Wisconsin Synod had resolved to inform...THE PRESIDENT OF THE LUTHERAN CHURCH-MISSOURI SYNOD...THAT, IF THE APPROPRIATE ACTION IN THE MATTER TREATED IN THIS REPORT IS NOT FORTHCOMING, AT LEAST THROUGH THE PRAESIDIUM OF THAT BODY, WE SHALL FEEL CONSTRAINED TO CARRY THE ISSUE TO THE SYNODICAL CONFERENCE AT ITS NEXT REGULAR CONVENTION.[47]

Not all was well within Missouri Synod ranks at this time. Many voices were heard from within speaking out against the Common Confession. This

756

writer can vividly recall the reaction to the Common Confession that was felt at the Missouri Synod's Springfield Seminary—a reaction led by Professor Walter Albrecht, who wrote his own criticism of the Common Confession and held open meetings for the faculty and student body in order to discuss the matter. There can be no doubt that this kind of negative reaction within Missouri's ranks had much to do with the decision later to put the Common Confession aside and not consider it "a functioning union document."

But the battle over the Common Confession was not over. It would be pressed by both sides for a time. At its 1953 Convention the Missouri Synod had these frank requests by the Wisconsin Synod to deal with:

(1) RESCIND THE FOLLOWING RESOLUTIONS: "THAT WE REJOICE AND THANK GOD THAT THE COMMON CONFESSION SHOWS THAT AGREEMENT HAS BEEN ACHIEVED IN THE DOCTRINES TREATED BY THE TWO COMMITTEES...AND BE IT FURTHER RESOLVED, THAT IF THE AMERICAN LUTHERAN CHURCH, IN CONVENTION ASSEMBLED, ACCEPTS IT, THE COMMON CONFESSION SHALL BE RECOGNIZED AS A STATEMENT OF AGREEMENT ON THESE DOCTRINES BETWEEN US AND THE AMERICAN LUTHERAN CHURCH."

(2) SUSPEND THE DOCTRINAL DISCUSSIONS WITH THE AMERICAN LUTHERAN CHURCH UNTIL THAT BODY IN CONVENTION CLEARLY AND UNEQUIVOCALLY HAS DECLARED ITSELF AGAINST UNIONISM AS DEFINED IN THE BRIEF STATEMENT AND HAS BEGUN TO PUT THIS PRINCIPLE INTO PRACTICE. [Reference is then made to the Sandusky Resolutions, the quotation from the Friendly Invitation, the declaration for Selective Fellowship, and the associations which the American Lutheran Church has continued to maintain (i.e. in the American Lutheran Conference and the National Lutheran Council) and new ones which it has recently entered.]

(3) REVERSE YOUR RESOLUTIONS ON SCOUTING AND RECONSIDER YOUR POSITION ON JOINT PRAYER, AS WELL AS YOUR ANSWER TO THE QUESTIONS OUR SYNOD ADDRESSED TO YOURS IN 1949. (The Convention's attention was also called to the fact that the Wisconsin Synod's representatives had met with representatives of the Missouri Synod and the other synods of the Synodical Conference for discussions in several areas.)

The letter which the Wisconsin Synod had addressed from its New Ulm Convention to the Missouri Synod's 1953 Houston Convention was presented to the delegates at Houston. Later, the Wisconsin Synod's Committee on Church Union reported:

IN GENERAL IT MAY BE SAID THAT OUR SEVERAL REQUESTS WERE COURTEOUSLY BUT DEFINITELY DECLINED.

In its action the Missouri Synod showed that a definite change had been made in its official stand on the matter of Joint Prayer. At one time it had considered the practice of entering into prayer at joint meetings attended by those not in doctrinal accord with it, unionistic. Not anymore, for it was resolved by the Convention...

THAT SYNOD DECLARES THAT IT DOES NOT CONSIDER "JOINT PRAYER" AT INTERSYNODICAL MEETINGS UNIONISTIC AND SINFUL, "PROVIDED SUCH PRAYER DOES NOT IMPLY DENIAL OF TRUTH OR SUPPORT OF ERROR."[48]

In the matter of Scouting the only resolution passed stated:

THAT THE MATTER OF SCOUTING SHOULD BE LEFT TO THE INDIVIDUAL CONGRE-

GATION TO DECIDE.

The Houston Convention in considering the misgivings expressed by the Norwegian Synod and the Wisconsin Synod, passed this resolution:

THAT WE RESPECTFULLY REQUEST ALSO OUR SISTER SYNODS IN THE SYNODICAL CONFERENCE, FOR PURPOSES OF STUDY TO TREAT PART I AND PART II OF THE COMMON CONFESSION AS ONE DOCUMENT.

Still, the Missouri Synod's 1953 Convention, while resolving to treat Part I and II as one document also stipulated:

...WITH THE UNDERSTANDING THAT PART II HAS NOT YET BEEN ADOPTED. (ADOPTION OF THIS DOCUMENT WAS TO BE SOUGHT AT THE 1956 MISSOURI SYNOD CONVENTION.)

In answering the Wisconsin Synod's objections to further negotiations with the ALC, the Missouri Synod stated:

PROGRESS TOWARD UNITY OF DOCTRINE HAS BEEN ACHIEVED THROUGH DISCUSSION ON THE BASIS OF THE WORD OF GOD BY REPRESENTATIVES OF THE AMERICAN LUTHERAN CHURCH AND THE LUTHERAN CHURCH-MISSOURI SYNOD, RESOLVED, (A) THAT THIS CONVENTION URGE THE COMMITTEE ON DOCTRINAL UNITY OF THE LUTHERAN CHURCH-MISSOURI SYNOD TO CONTINUE ITS DISCUSSIONS WITH THE REPRESENTATIVES OF THE AMERICAN LUTHERAN CHURCH. (Further meetings were then authorized.)[49]

THE CHARGE OF UNIONISM IS MADE AGAINST THE MISSOURI SYNOD

The report that was adopted by the Wisconsin Synod Convention held in Watertown, Wisconsin, in 1953 was sharp and pointed:

THE ISSUE THAT HAS OPENED THIS SERIOUS BREACH BETWEEN OUR SYNOD AND THE MISSOURI SYNOD AND THREATENED THE CONTINUANCE OF THE SYNODICAL CONFERENCE IS UNIONISM. UNIONISM IS THE UNDERLYING ISSUE IN THE CONTROVERSIES REGARDING THE CHAPLAINCY, COOPERATION WITH UNAFFILIATED CHURCH BODIES IN SERVICE CENTERS, PRAYER FELLOWSHIP AND SCOUTING. THE SAME UNIONISTIC SPIRIT IS OBSERVABLE IN THE ARRANGEMENTS THAT HAVE BEEN MADE FOR COMMUNION WITH LUTHERANS NOT IN FELLOWSHIP WITH US, UNDER THE EXCUSE OF EMERGENCY; IN NEGOTIATIONS WITH LODGES TO MAKE CHANGES IN THEIR RITUALS; AND IN COOPERATING IN VARIOUS OTHER AREAS WITH THE EXCUSE THAT SAFEGUARDS HAVE BEEN SET UP TO AVOID UNIONISM.

IN THIS MATTER OF UNIONISTIC PRACTICE MISSOURI HAS DEPARTED FROM THE POSITION THAT IT ONCE HELD, A POSITION THAT MADE IT A STRONGHOLD OF THE CHURCH AND A BANNER TO REPAIR TO, AND THAT WAS ONE OF THE STRONGEST LINKS THAT BOUND US TOGETHER IN THE SYNODICAL CONFERENCE. MISSOURI HAS BROKEN THAT LINK.[50]

A STATE OF CONFESSION

The 1953 Wisconsin Synod Convention went on to accuse the Missouri

Synod of bringing on...THE PRESENT BREAK IN RELATIONS THAT IS NOW THREATEN-
ING THE EXISTENCE OF THE SYNODICAL CONFERENCE AND THE CONTINUANCE OF OUR
AFFILIATION WITH THE SISTER SYNOD. The Convention listed as the cause of the
threatening break the Missouri Synod's reaffirmation of its acceptance of the
Common Confession; joint prayer; Scouting; the chaplaincy; the communion
agreement with the National Lutheran Council; cooperation with unorthodox
church bodies in matters clearly not in the field of externals; negotiating with
lodges and the Boy Scouts of America, with the plea that this gives opportunity
to bear witness, under the same plea taking part in unionistic religious programs and in the activities of unionistic church federations; negotiating for
purposes of union with a church body (the ALC) whose official position it is
that it is neither possible nor necessary to agree in all matters of doctrine, and
which contends for an "allowable and wholesome latitude of theological opinion
on the basis of the teachings of the Word of God."

The Wisconsin Synod then voted itself into a STATE OF CONFESSION
over against the Missouri Synod. At the same time, the Synod embarked upon
a course of thoroughly instructing its members as to the issues that were troubling the relationship between the two churches.

"MARK...AVOID" (ROMANS 16:17)

The fellowship matter had not improved by the time the 1955 Wisconsin
Synod Convention opened in Saginaw, Michigan. The sad state of affairs was
laid bare for the Convention by President Oscar J. Naumann in his opening address to the delegates:

DIFFERENCES IN PRACTICE HAVE INCREASED AND MULTIPLIED, MAKING OUR
MINISTRY, PARTICULARLY IN THE FIELD OF EVANGELICAL ADMONITION, EX-
TREMELY DIFFICULT. IT HAS BECOME EXTREMELY DIFFICULT TO CARRY ON IN-
TERSYNODICAL ADMONITION AND DISCIPLINE. I BELIEVE IT CAN TRUTHFULLY BE
SAID THAT WE HAVE BEEN GROWING APART INSTEAD OF BEING DRAWN CLOSER
TOGETHER. IT IS A FAIR OBSERVATION, I THINK, THAT AT TIMES SYNODICAL
LINES AND SYNODICAL PATRIOTISM HAVE BECLOUDED ISSUES AND HAVE OB-
SCURED THE FACT THAT WE WERE BRETHREN IN THE FAITH, AND THAT WE NOT
ONLY ARE BUT MUST BE OUR BROTHER'S KEEPER...IF, HOWEVER, IT WERE TRUE
AS WE HAVE BEEN CHARGED IN PRINT, IN LETTERS—BOTH SIGNED AND UN-
SIGNED—AND IN ORAL DISCUSSION, THAT OUR ACTION WAS PROMPTED BY HURT
FEELINGS, BY JEALOUSY, BY A SPIRIT OF SEPARATION, OR BY ANY OTHER HUMAN
VICE OR WEAKNESS, I WOULD WANT TO BE THE FIRST TO DISAVOW SUCH ACTION.
BUT ON THE CONTRARY, WE ARE CONVINCED THAT OUR POSITION NOT ONLY IN
DOCTRINE BUT ESPECIALLY IN THE APPLICATION OF DOCTRINE IN OUR LIVES AND
IN THE LIVES OF OUR MEMBERS, IS THE POSITION THAT THE EVANGELICAL
LUTHERAN SYNODICAL CONFERENCE HAD OCCUPIED EVER SINCE ITS ORGANI-
ZATION. THE DIFFERENCES THAT HAVE ARISEN BETWEEN US, WHICH WE HAVE
BEEN TRYING TO FACE HONESTLY AND SOBERLY, AND TO REMOVE IN AN EVAN-
GELICAL MANNER BY THE APPLICATION OF GOD'S HOLY WORD BROTHER TO
BROTHER, HAVE NOT BEEN REMOVED. THEY HAVE INCREASED. THINGS WE
CONSIDER CONTRARY TO GOD'S WORD HAVE BEEN DEFENDED WITH THE STATE-

MENT, "THAT PASSAGE DOES NOT APPLY IN THIS CASE." WE HAVE HEARD SO
OFTEN THE EXPRESSION, "SYNOD'S INTERESTS ARE SUFFICIENTLY SAFE-
GUARDED." MATTERS WHICH WE NAMED IN OUR RESOLUTIONS OF 1953,
WHICH WE CONSIDERED DANGEROUS TO OUR SOULS' WELFARE, DETERRENT
TO OUR GOSPEL MINISTRY, AND DETRIMENTAL TO OUR FELLOWSHIP IN THE
CONFERENCE, HAVE BEEN AND STILL ARE VIGOROUSLY DEFENDED. THE
CHARGES WHICH WE BROUGHT IN AN EFFORT TO DO OUR BROTHERLY DUTY
BEFORE GOD, HAVE BEEN DEFINITELY DENIED. WE HAVE REACHED THE
CONVICTION THAT THROUGH THESE DIFFERENCES DIVISIONS AND OFFENSES
HAVE BEEN CAUSED CONTRARY TO THE DOCTRINE WHICH WE HAVE
LEARNED. AND WHEN THAT IS THE CASE, THE LORD OUR GOD HAS A DEF-
INITE COMMAND FOR US: "AVOID THEM!" FOR THOSE OF US WHO HAVE BEEN
CLOSEST TO THESE PROBLEMS, IT APPEARS QUITE DEFINITE THAT WE MUST
NOW OBEY THE LORD'S WORD IN ROMANS 16:17. DEEPLY GRIEVED OVER
THE DEVELOPMENTS OF THE PAST YEARS, WITH HEARTS HEAVY AT THE SIGHT
OF A CRUMBLING FELLOWSHIP, AND AT THE SAME TIME AWARE OF THE PRES-
ENCE IN OUR SISTER SYNOD OF SO MANY WHO SHARE OUR POSITION, WE EX-
PRESSED OUT INNERMOST CONVICTIONS IN OUR PRELIMINARY REPORT OF
THE STANDING COMMITTEE ON MATTERS OF CHURCH UNION.[51]

This was strong language. This address by the president was followed
later by the report of the Standing Committee on Matters of Church Union.
In its report the Committee reviewed the matters as they then stood and
concluded:

IN OUR DEALINGS WITH OUT SISTER SYNOD WE HAVE BEEN EARNESTLY EN-
DEAVORING TO HEED THE SCRIPTURAL EXHORTATIONS TO PATIENCE AND
FORBEARANCE IN LOVE. WE HAVE, HOWEVER, ARRIVED AT THE FIRM CON-
VICTION THAT, BECAUSE OF THE DIVISIONS AND OFFENSES THAT HAVE BEEN
CAUSED, AND WHICH HAVE UNTIL NOW NOT BEEN REMOVED, FURTHER POST-
PONEMENT OF A DECISION WOULD BE A VIOLATION OF THE APOSTOLIC IN-
JUNCTION OF ROMANS 16:17 ...ON THE BASIS OF THESE CONSIDERATIONS
WE RECOMMENDED THE FOLLOWING RESOLUTION, WHICH WE HEREWITH
SUBMIT FOR STUDY BY OUR BRETHREN AND FOR SUBSEQUENT CONSIDERA-
TION AND ACTION BY THE SYNODICAL CONFERENCE. RESOLVED: THAT
WITH DEEPEST SORROW, TAKING NOTICE OF THE FACT THAT THE LUTHERAN
CHURCH-MISSOURI SYNOD IS CAUSING DIVISIONS AND OFFENCES CONTRARY
TO THE DOCTRINE WHICH WE HAVE LEARNED, WE, IN OBEDIENCE TO GOD'S
INJUNCTION TO AVOID SUCH, DECLARE THE FELLOWSHIP WHICH WE HAVE
HAD WITH SAID SYNOD TO BE TERMINATED.

In a supplementary report the Committee stated:

WE DEPLORE THE FACT THAT OUR TESTIMONY HAS NOT BEEN HEEDED BY
THE MISSOURI SYNOD. ON THE CONTRARY, WE FIND THAT OUR TESTIMONY
IS BEING OPENLY REPUDIATED BY MISSOURI SYNOD REPRESENTATIVES, AND
WE ARE NOW PUBLICLY BEING ACCUSED OF MISAPPLYING SCRIPTURE AND OF
BRINGING FALSE CHARGES AGAINST THE MISSOURI SYNOD. WE ALSO DE-
PLORE THE VEHEMENT TONE AND THE ASSERTION OF DR. JOHN W.
BEHNKEN, PRESIDENT OF THE LUTHERAN CHURCH-MISSOURI SYNOD, IN
HIS LAST TWO ARTICLES IN THE *LUTHERAN WITNESS* (JULY 19 AND AUGUST
2) THAT THERE IS NO BASIS FOR ANY OF THE CHARGES OF THE WISCONSIN

SYNOD: "WE DO NOT ADMIT THE CHARGES. ON THE CONTRARY, WE EM-
PHATICALLY DENY THEM."[52]

And so it had to be concluded that any gains that had been made
were in fact nullified.

ACTION TOWARD THE MISSOURI SYNOD IS POSTPONED

The matter of suspending fellowship with the sister synod was not resolved
at the 1955 Synod Convention. Rather, final action was deferred to a recessed
session in 1956. The resolution to be put before the recessed session was as fol-
lows:...THAT WHEREAS THE LUTHERAN CHURCH-MISSOURI SYNOD HAS CREATED DI-
VISIONS AND OFFENSES BY ITS OFFICIAL RESOLUTIONS, POLICIES, AND PRACTICES NOT
IN ACCORD WITH SCRIPTURE, WE, IN OBEDIENCE TO THE COMMAND OF OUR LORD IN
ROMANS 16:17-18, TERMINATE OUR FELLOWSHIP WITH THE LUTHERAN CHURCH-MIS-
SOURI SYNOD.[53]

Several members of the Floor Committee which drew up this resolution
made the statement to the Convention that they were of the conviction that the
reasons stated for delay do not warrant postponement of action upon the resolution. When the matter came up for vote in the Convention, a good number
of voting and advisory delegates asked to have their names recorded in
protest...AGAINST THE ADOPTION OF THAT PORTION OF THE RESOLUTION WHICH
CALLS FOR A FINAL VOTE ON THE TERMINATION OF FELLOWSHIP IN A RECESSED SES-
SION OF THE CONVENTION IN 1956 (see the Proceedings, pages 77-87).

When the recessed session was held in August 1956 at Watertown, Wisconsin, the delegates concurred in the suggestion of the synod's Standing Committee on Matters of Church Union, to hold in abeyance the judgment of the
Saginaw resolutions until the next convention, and it also resolved that the
Standing Committee on Matters of Church Union continue to evaluate any
further developments in these matters.

Following the 1956 Recessed Convention the Joint Union Committees of the
synods in the Synodical Conference met in several sessions. A program of discussion of areas of doctrine was adopted. But later, the Wisconsin Synod's
Committee felt constrained to report the following to the 1957 New Ulm Convention:

OVER AGAINST THE WILLINGNESS EXPRESSED IN THE PREMISE ADOPTED BY THE
JOINT UNION COMMITTEES "WITHOUT EQUIVOCATION AND EVASION TO COME TO
GRIPS WITH ALL THE ISSUES THAT HAVE ARISEN BETWEEN US" AND THE "FIRM
INTENTION TO EXPOSE AND CONDEMN ALL MATTERS CONTRARY TO THE WORD
OF GOD IN DOCTRINE AND LIFE WITH THE PURPOSE OF REMOVING WHAT IS NOT
IN KEEPING WITH THE WORD OF GOD," WE MUST RECOGNIZE THE DIFFICULTY
OF THE JOINT UNION COMMITTEES THUS FAR TO AGREE ON AN ANTITHETICAL
PREMISE, AND THE PROBLEM PRESENTED BY THE FACT THAT THE MISSOURI
SYNOD REPRESENTATIVES WERE NOT READY TO DECLARE THE ISSUES BETWEEN
US DIVISIVE.

SINCE THE NEGOTIATIONS OF THE JOINT UNION COMMITTEES HAVE NOT PRO-
GRESSED BEYOND THE FIRST AREA UNDER STUDY (SCRIPTURE AND ESCHATOL-
OGY), THE CONTROVERSIAL ISSUES STILL REMAIN WHOLLY UNRESOLVED AND

761

CONTINUE TO CAUSE OFFENSE.[54]

In the meantime, at its 1956 Convention the Missouri Synod passed new resolutions regarding the Common Confession, which were then interpreted by the Missouri Synod Praesidium in writing to mean:

(1)   THAT THE COMMON CONFESSION, PARTS I AND II, ONE DOCUMENT, REPRESENTED A SINCERE ATTEMPT ON THE PART OF SYNOD TO ACHIEVE UNITY OF DOCTRINE WITH THE AMERICAN LUTHERAN CHURCH, WHICH NATURALLY INCLUDED A SINCERE CONVICTION ON THE PART OF SYNOD THAT ALL DOCTRINAL DIFFERENCES WERE SETTLED AS FAR AS THE COMMON CONFESSION AS SUCH WAS CONCERNED. (ADMITTEDLY WE NEVER REACHED AN AGREEMENT IN MATTERS OF PRACTICE, WHICH ACCORDING TO SYNODICAL RESOLUTIONS HAD TO BE SETTLED, TOO, BEFORE FELLOWSHIP COULD BE ESTABLISHED.)

(2)   THAT, BECAUSE OF RECENT HISTORICAL DEVELOPMENTS,* THE COMMON CONFESSION WILL HENCEFORTH NOT BE REGARDED OR EMPLOYED AS A FUNCTIONING BASIC DOCUMENT TOWARD THE ESTABLISHMENT OF ALTAR AND PULPIT FELLOWSHIP WITH OTHER BODIES, WHICH ESTABLISHMENT OF ALTAR AND PULPIT FELLOWSHIP INCLUDES THE SETTLING OF DOCTRINAL DIFFERENCES, WHICH IS BASIC FOR SUCH FELLOWSHIP. *(Note: In spite of this statement, the Common Confession was not rescinded.)*[55]

UNREST IN THE WISCONSIN SYNOD

There was a growing feeling in the Wisconsin Synod, especially evident at this time, that the Missouri Synod, which had been marked as causing divisions and offenses contrary to God's Word, should be avoided. Many came to protest the delay in carrying out the judgments of the 1955 Saginaw Convention. The Nebraska District, meeting in May 1957, urged the synod to carry out the resolutions of the Saginaw Convention to "terminate our fellowship with The Lutheran Church-Missouri Synod." The wording of the Nebraska District's memorial was sharp and to the point:

THE LUTHERAN CHURCH-MISSOURI SYNOD, IN ITS ST. PAUL CONVENTION OF 1956, PASSED SPECIFIC RESOLUTIONS, "WHICH SHOW THAT THE SISTER SYNOD'S POSITION ON ISSUES SUCH AS SCOUTING, MILITARY CHAPLAINCY, AND PRAYER FELLOWSHIP, HAS NOT UNDERGONE ANY CHANGE"...IN SPITE OF REPEATED CONTINUED FRATERNAL ADMONITIONS, THE REAL ISSUES REMAIN WHOLLY UNRESOLVED. THE CONTINUANCE OF OUR SISTER SYNOD'S UNSCRIPTURAL PRACTICES IS CREATING CONSTANT OFFENSE; IT IS THREATENING TO DESTROY THE CHERISHED PURITY OF DOCTRINE AND PRACTICE OF THE WISCONSIN SYNOD; IT WILL UNDERMINE FAITH. 1 COR. 5:6 "KNOW YE NOT THAT A LITTLE LEAVENETH THE WHOLE LUMP?" (KJV) THEREFORE, SINCE THE LUTHERAN CHURCH-MISSOURI SYNOD TOLERATES, ADVOCATES, AND PERSISTS IN ERROR, AND SINCE IT IS OBVIOUS WE ARE NO LONGER WALKING TOGETHER, WE URGE OUR SYNOD TO CARRY OUT THE ABOVE-MENTIONED SAGINAW RESOLUTION.[56] (Note: the wording above contained in quotation marks is from the Evaluation of the Standing Committee on Church Union.)

Because of the number of protests which came to the Wisconsin Synod's officials regarding the failure to carry out the Saginaw resolutions, a special Protest Committee was created to study these documents.

762

CONTINUATION OF THE STATE OF
CONFESSION WITH THE MISSOURI SYNOD

The 1957 New Ulm Convention of the Wisconsin Synod did not resolve to terminate fellowship with the Missouri Synod. However, the Floor Committee's report did call for suspension of church fellowship with the sister synod: SINCE WE NOW FIND THAT THE LUTHERAN CHURCH-MISSOURI SYNOD STILL UPHOLDS RESOLUTIONS AND CONDONES PRINCIPLES AND PRACTICES WHICH DENY THE SCRIPTURAL TRUTH EXPRESSED IN ARTICLE 28 OF ITS OWN BRIEF STATEMENT OF DOCTRINE...WE FEEL CONSCIENCE-BOUND TO DECLARE PUBLICLY, THAT THESE PRINCIPLES, POLICIES AND PRACTICES CREATE A DIVISION BETWEEN OUR SYNODS WHICH THE LUTHERAN CHURCH-MISSOURI SYNOD ALONE CAN REMOVE. UNTIL THESE OFFENSES HAVE BEEN REMOVED, WE CANNOT FELLOWSHIP TOGETHER WITH THE LUTHERAN CHURCH-MISSOURI SYNOD AS ONE BODY, LEST OUR OWN WISCONSIN SYNOD BE AFFECTED BY THE SAME UNIONISTIC SPIRIT WHICH FINALLY WEAKENS AND DESTROYS ALL TRUE DOCTRINE AND LEADS TO INDIFFERENCE AND LIBERALISM CONCERNING SCRIPTURAL TRUTH; THEREFORE BE IT RESOLVED, THAT WE NOW SUSPEND CHURCH FELLOWSHIP WITH THE LUTHERAN CHURCH-MISSOURI SYNOD ON THE BASIS OF ROMANS 16:17, 18, UNTIL THE PRINCIPLES, POLICIES IN CONTROVERSY BETWEEN US HAVE RESOLVED IN A THOROUGHLY SCRIPTURAL AND MUTUALLY ACCEPTABLE MANNER.[57] This resolution was narrowly defeated, and in its place the Convention passed the following: RESOLVED, THAT WE CONTINUE OUR VIGOROUSLY PROTESTING FELLOWSHIP OVER AGAINST THE LUTHERAN CHURCH-MISSOURI SYNOD, BECAUSE OF THE CONTINUATION OF THE OFFENSES WITH WHICH WE HAVE CHARGED THE SISTER SYNOD, ROMANS 16:17,18...RESOLVED, THAT WE CONTINUE OUR DOCTRINAL DISCUSSIONS WITH THE UNION COMMITTEES OF THE SYNODS OF THE SYNODICAL CONFERENCE IN AN EFFORT TO RESTORE FULL UNITY ON THE BASIS OF THE WORD OF GOD....[58]

THE SEMINARY PRESIDENT RESIGNS

The failure of the Floor Committee's resolves to be adopted by the synod at New Ulm began a process of withdrawals from the Wisconsin Synod. The men who, over the ensuing years, suspended fellowship with the Wisconsin Synod did so because of their synod's failure to carry out its own resolution. The synod had marked the Missouri Synod as a causer of divisions and offenses; nevertheless, through several conventions the synod held in abeyance the avoiding of the Missouri Synod. This course of action laid a heavy burden on many consciences.

Already in 1955 Professor E. Reim had offered his resignation as professor and president of the synod's seminary. His resignation had not been accepted. With the subsequent failure by the Wisconsin Synod to suspend fellowship with the Missouri Synod both at the Recessed Convention in 1956 and at the 1957 New Ulm Convention, Professor Reim felt constrained to address the following letter to the Wisconsin Synod: DEAR BRETHREN: TWO YEARS AGO I MADE THE FOLLOWING STATEMENT TO THE 1955 CONVENTION OF OUR SYNOD, IN REGARD TO ITS ACTION IN MATTERS OF

UNION AT THAT TIME: "THE DECISION OF THE SYNOD TO CONTINUE ITS FELLOW-SHIP WITH THE LUTHERAN CHURCH-MISSOURI SYNOD PENDING A VOTE TO FOL-LOW THE CONVENTION OF THAT BODY IN 1956 (EVEN WHILE RECOGNIZING THAT THERE IS FULL REASON FOR SEPARATION NOW) COMPELS ME TO DECLARE THAT I CAN CONTINUE FELLOWSHIP WITH MY SYNOD ONLY UNDER CLEAR AND PUBLIC PROTEST. I HOPE AND PRAY THAT THE EVENTUAL DECISION CONCERNING OUR RELATIONS WITH THE LUTHERAN CHURCH-MISSOURI SYNOD WILL BE SUCH AS TO REMOVE THE OCCASION FOR THIS PROTEST."

LAST NIGHT'S ACTION OF THIS CURRENT (1957) CONVENTION IN REJECTING THE REPORT AND RESOLUTIONS OF ITS FLOOR COMMITTEE NOT ONLY DOES NOT RE-MOVE THE OCCASION FOR THIS PROTEST, BUT INCREASES AND CONFIRMS IT. I HAVE TRIED TO MAKE THIS PROTEST CLEAR AND STRONG TO THIS CONVENTION. SINCE IT HAS BEEN DISREGARDED NEVERTHELESS, I FIND MYSELF COMPELLED TO DISCONTINUE MY FELLOWSHIP WITH THE SYNOD. I HOPE AND PRAY THAT THE SYNOD MAY YET RETURN TO ITS FORMER WAYS AND TO FULL OBEDIENCE TO THE WORD OF GOD, SPECIFICALLY ROMANS 16:17, 18. I TRUST THAT YOU WILL RE-ALIZE THAT I TAKE THIS STEP, NOT IN ANGER, BUT IN DEEPEST SORROW, AND BE-CAUSE I AM CONSTRAINED BY THE WORD OF GOD.[59]

Two other pastors followed Professor Reim in his action. Another man placed himself in a state of selective fellowship, refusing the hand of fellowship to those who advocated the position which the synod made its own.

In the two years that followed the New Ulm Convention (prior to the 1959 Saginaw Convention), President Naumann, with the Standing Committee on Matters of Church Union, met a total of 18 days with the committee members of the other synods. The tangible results of these meetings were two doctrinal statements to be presented to the synods for approval: the final form of the statement on Scripture, and the statement on the Antichrist. Much time was also taken up discussing the doctrine of the Church and of Church Fellowship, primarily on the basis of the Wisconsin Synod's presentation.

It was reported to the Saginaw Convention in 1959:

ON THE WHOLE, MOST OF THE POINTS OF OUR PRESENTATION WERE NOT ONLY PERMITTED TO STAND WHEN THEY WERE INDIVIDUALLY DISCUSSED AND ELUCI-DATED BUT THEY WERE EVEN HIGHLY COMMENDED AS SCRIPTURALLY SOUND AND WELL EXPRESSED. STILL AT THE END OF THE DISCUSSION THE MISSOURI SYNOD REPRESENTATIVES WERE NOT READY TO ACKNOWLEDGE THE SCRIPTURAL CORRECTNESS OF THE BASIC POINT OF OUR WISCONSIN SYNOD PRESENTA-TION...THAT ALL JOINT EXPRESSIONS AND DEMONSTRATIONS OF A COMMON CHRISTIAN FAITH—CALL THEM CHURCH FELLOWSHIP OR BY ANOTHER TERM—ARE ESSENTIALLY ONE, THAT THEY INVOLVE A UNIT CONCEPT, AND THAT THEY ARE THEREFORE ALL GOVERNED BY ONE SET OF PRINCIPLES, NAMELY ON THE ONE HAND BY THE CONSIDERATION OF OUR DEBT OF LOVE TOWARD THE WEAK BROTHER, AND ON THE OTHER HAND BY THE LORD'S CLEAR INJUNCTION, ALSO FLOWING OUT OF LOVE, TO AVOID THE PERSISTENT ADHERENT OF FALSE DOC-TRINE AND PRACTICE.[60]

THE MISSOURI SYNOD CONTINUES
TO SEEK FELLOWSHIP WITH THE ALC

Meanwhile, at its San Francisco Convention, the Missouri Synod passed the following resolution regarding doctrinal discussions with the American Lutheran Church:

WHEREAS, THE AMERICAN LUTHERAN CHURCH, THE EVANGELICAL LUTHERAN CHURCH, AND THE UNITED EVANGELICAL LUTHERAN CHURCH ARE PLANNING THE COMPLETION OF THEIR MERGER IN 1960 [TO FORM THE AMERICAN LUTHERAN CHURCH], AND

WHEREAS, SYNOD HAS REPEATEDLY EXPRESSED ITS READINESS TO MEET WITH OTHER CHURCH BODIES FOR DOCTRINAL DISCUSSIONS; THEREFORE BE IT

RESOLVED, THAT THE COMMITTEE ON DOCTRINAL UNITY INVITE THE REPRESENTATIVES OF THE NEW THE AMERICAN LUTHERAN CHURCH (TALC) TO MEET FOR THE PURPOSE OF SEEKING A GOD-PLEASING UNITY AND FELLOWSHIP; AND BE IT FURTHER

RESOLVED, THAT THE SISTER SYNODS OF THE SYNODICAL CONFERENCE BE INVITED TO JOIN IN THIS ENDEAVOR.[61]

The Wisconsin Synod representatives at San Francisco had presented to the Floor Committee the unfeasibility of discussing doctrine with TALC as a Synodical Conference "while we ourselves have weighty unresolved issues."[62]

MOUNTING PROTEST IN THE WISCONSIN SYNOD
AGAINST CONTINUED FELLOWSHIP WITH THE
MISSOURI SYNOD

When the Synod met in Convention at Saginaw, Michigan, in August 1959 the Protest Committee reported:

A CONSIDERABLE VOLUME OF PROTEST REACHED THE FILES OF THE PROTEST COMMITTEE DURING THE PAST BIENNIUM. SINCE THERE ARE MANY, WE MIGHT SPEAK OF THEM AS BELONGING TO TWO GROUPS. THERE ARE, IN THE FIRST PLACE, THOSE WHICH PROTEST THE ACTION OF THE NEW ULM CONVENTION. THE COMMUNICATIONS BELONGING TO THIS GROUP ARE IN SOME CASES ANNOUNCEMENTS OF SEVERANCE OF FELLOWSHIP WITH THE SYNOD; OTHERS ARE FORMAL PROTESTS AGAINST THE 1957 RESOLUTION OF THE SYNOD; OTHERS CONTAIN RESIGNATIONS FROM CERTAIN OFFICIAL POSITIONS, PROMPTED, OF COURSE, BY THE INTERSYNODICAL PROBLEM; AND STILL OTHERS CONSIST IN EXPRESSIONS OF CONVICTIONS, MISGIVINGS, OR QUESTIONS CONCERNING THE PRESENT STATE OF AFFAIRS ON THE INTERSYNODICAL SCENE.[63]

Note was then taken that the other major group of communications raised objection to the Protest Committee's expressing approval of and quoting from "A Report to the Protest Committee" prepared by Professor C. Lawrenz upon request of the Standing Committee on Matters of Church Union.*

A memorial was received by the 1959 Saginaw Convention from the Nebraska District. The memorial closed thus:

RESOLVED, THAT WE SUSPEND CHURCH FELLOWSHIP WITH THE LUTHERAN CHURCH-MISSOURI SYNOD ON THE BASIS OF ROMANS 16:17-18, UNTIL THE

765

PRINCIPLES, POLICIES, PRACTICES IN CONTROVERSY BETWEEN US HAVE BEEN
RESOLVED IN A THOROUGHLY SCRIPTURAL AND MUTUALLY ACCEPTABLE MAN-
NER; AND BE IT FURTHER

RESOLVED, THAT WE DECLARE OURSELVES READY TO CONTINUE DISCUS-
SIONS WITH REPRESENTATIVES OF THE LUTHERAN CHURCH-MISSOURI SYNOD
WITH THE AIM AND HOPE OF REESTABLISHING UNITY OF DOCTRINE AND PRAC-
TICE.[64]

Other memorials which were received, some signed by several individuals,
also called for immediate suspension of fellowship with the Missouri Synod.

In its report to the 1959 Convention, the Floor Committee on Church Union
made a report that differed considerably in tone from those of former conventions. It did not call for suspension of fellowship by did urge the followings:

THAT IN OUR VIGOROUSLY PROTESTING FELLOWSHIP WITH THE LUTHERAN
CHURCH-MISSOURI SYNOD WE TESTIFY STRONGLY AGAINST THE OFFENSES
WHICH ARE STILL PREVALENT AND UNRESOLVED IN THE LUTHERAN CHURCH-
MISSOURI SYNOD AND REQUEST THAT BODY TO REMOVE THEM, AND TO REFRAIN
FROM CAUSING A WIDER BREACH BETWEEN THE MEMBERS OF THE SYNODICAL
CONFERENCE.

The above resolution followed a statement by the Floor Committee that recognized that many of the offenses of the Missouri Synod that have brought
about "the troubled conditions in the Synodical Conference (named in the 1955
Saginaw resolutions) have not been removed and have been aggravated..."[65]

Why didn't the Floor Committee at this time resolve to suspend fellowship
with the Missouri Synod, but instead put forth the following resolution to the
1959 Saginaw Convention? (Note: there were six parts to the resolution.)

A)   THAT WE EXPRESS OUR THANKS TO THE TRIUNE GOD THAT OUR CHURCH
UNION COMMITTEE COULD REPORT ON THESE MATTERS AS IT DID;

B)   THAT WE INSTRUCT OUR CHURCH UNION COMMITTEE UNDER THE GUID-
ANCE OF THE HOLY SPIRIT TO CONTINUE AND ACCELERATE THE DISCUSSIONS IN
THE JOINT UNION COMMITTEES TO BRING ABOUT COMPLETE UNITY OF DOC-
TRINE AND PRACTICE IN THE SYNODICAL CONFERENCE;

C)   THAT WE INSTRUCT OUR CHURCH UNION COMMITTEE TO CONTINUE ITS
EFFORTS IN THE JOINT UNION COMMITTEES UNTIL AGREEMENT ON DOCTRINE
AND PRACTICE HAS BEEN REACHED, OR UNTIL AN IMPASSE IS REACHED AND NO
SUCH AGREEMENT CAN BE BROUGHT ABOUT;

F)   ....THAT OUR CHURCH UNION COMMITTEE REQUEST THE JOINT UNION
COMMITTEES TO GIVE PRIMARY CONSIDERATION IN THEIR DISCUSSIONS TO THE
AREA OF FELLOWSHIP...[65]

The reasons for the Floor Committee's resolution, quoted in part above,
which once again put off the action of suspension of fellowship with the Missouri Synod were: (1) The Lutheran Church-Missouri Synod Doctrinal Unity
Committee's receptive attitude toward the Wisconsin Synod's Union Committee's testimony. (2) The discussions took place in a spirit of frankness and willingness to face all the issues confronting the synods. (3) The unifying power of
the Word of God had brought about agreement in the Statement on Scripture
adopted by The Lutheran Church—Missouri Synod and by the Wisconsin
Synod, and the Statement on the Antichrist had been adopted by all contin-
gents of the Joint Union Committees. (4) At the San Francisco meeting the

Missouri Synod had passed the resolution "calling for the use of every available means for proper supervision of doctrine and practice. (5) It was reported that disciplinary action had already been instituted against some who were teaching error in the Missouri Synod, and in some instances had been completed. (6) The Joint Union Committees were in the midst of discussing the presentations on Church Fellowship, in which area lay the problem of unionism, which had been troubling the Synodical Conference.[66]

THE JOINT UNION COMMITEES' STATEMENT REGARDING THE SCRIPTURES

At this point it would be helpful to quote briefly from this important statement. An article—actually a nine page Special Report—in the April 4, 1961 issue of the *Lutheran Witness* (published by the Missouri Synod) raised doubts in the minds of Wisconsin Synod officials that the synods of the Synodical Conference shared the same doctrine. Though all four synods of the Conference adopted the joint statement on Scripture, certain statements in the Special Report were not in harmony with it. This statement, for example, was very troubling to the Wisconsin Synod Committee: THE SCRIPTURES EXPRESS WHAT GOD WANTS THEM TO SAY AND ACCOMPLISH WHAT GOD WANTS THEM TO DO. IN THIS SENSE AND IN FULFILLMENT OF THIS FUNCTION THEY ARE INERRANT, INFALLIBLE, AND WHOLLY RELIABLE. When the recessed 46th Convention of the Conference was held in May 1961 the Missouri Synod representatives were approached on this matter. The Conference was then assured that the Missouri Synod was in full agreement with the Wisconsin Synod on the doctrine of Scripture. Here are excerpts from the Statement on Scripture:

WE BELIEVE AND TEACH THAT ALL SCRIPTURE (THAT IS, ALL THE CANONICAL BOOKS OF THE OLD AND NEW TESTAMENTS) IS GIVEN BY INSPIRATION OF GOD AND IS IN ITS ENTIRETY, IN ITS PARTS, AND IN ITS VERY WORDS INSPIRED BY THE HOLY SPIRIT...INSPIRATION MEANS, THEN, THAT MIGHTY ACT OF GOD WHEREBY HE SPOKE HIS WORD IN THE WORDS OF MEN AND MADE THEM THE EFFECTIVE AND FINAL VEHICLE OF HIS REVELATION...WE CONDEMN AND REJECT ANY AND ALL TEACHINGS AND STATEMENTS THAT WOULD LIMIT THE INERRANCY AND SUFFICIENCY OF SCRIPTURE; OR THAT DENY THE DIVINE AUTHORSHIP OF CERTAIN PORTIONS OF SCRIPTURE. INSPIRATION APPLIES NOT ONLY TO SUCH STATEMENTS AS SPEAK DIRECTLY OF CHRIST, BUT ALSO TO SUCH AS MAY SEEM VERY REMOTE (E.G. IN THE FIELD OF HISTORY, GEOGRAPHY, AND NATURE)...THE TERM "OPEN QUESTIONS" MAY LEGITIMATELY BE USED WHERE THE SCRIPTURE LANGUAGE LEAVES OPEN THE PRECISE SCOPE OF A PASSAGE, OR WHERE LINGUISTIC, TEXTUAL, OR HISTORICAL PROBLEMS MADE THE PERCEPTION OF THE INTENDED SENSE DIFFICULT. BUT WHERE SCRIPTURE HAS SPOKEN, THERE GOD HAS SPOKEN, WHETHER IT BE A CENTRAL DOGMA OR ON A PERIPHERAL POINT; WHERE SCRIPTURE HAS NOT SPOKEN, THE MATTER MUST FOREVER REMAIN OPEN...SCRIPTURE ALONE IS TO INTERPRET SCRIPTURE...SINCE SCRIPTURE IS IN ALL ITS PARTS AND IN ALL ITS WORDS THE INSPIRED WORD OF GOD, WE REJECT AND CONDEMN ANY USE OF THE PHRASE "TOTALITY OF SCRIPTURE" WHICH

TENDS TO ABRIDGE OR ANNUL THE FORCE OF ANY CLEAR PASSAGE OF SCRIP-
TURE. SIMILARLY WE REJECT THE USE OF ANY PHRASE WHICH MAKES ROOM
FOR THE IDEA THAT THE SCRIPTURE AS A WHOLE MAY BE REGARDED AS THE
WORD OF GOD, THOUGH IT IN MANY DETAILS IS REGARDED AS ONLY THE WORDS
OF MEN. WE REJECT AND CONDEMN "DEMYTHOLOGIZING" AS A DENIAL OF THE
WORD OF GOD. WHERE SCRIPTURE RECORDS AS HISTORICAL FACTS THOSE
EVENTS AND DEEDS WHICH FAR SURPASS THE ORDINARY EXPERIENCE OF MEN,
THAT RECORD MUST BE UNDERSTOOD LITERALLY, AS A RECORD OF FACTS; THE
MIRACULOUS AND MYSTERIOUS MAY NOT BE DISMISSED AS INTENDED TO HAVE
ONLY A METAPHORICAL OR SYMBOLICAL MEANING. *(Note: the Wisconsin Synod
at its 1959 Convention adopted this statement without a dissenting voice.)*[67]

THE STATEMENT REGARDING CHURCH FELLOWSHIP

This statement was presented by the Wisconsin Synod in the Joint Union
Committee meetings and was discussed but not adopted. Here are excerpts:
CHURCH FELLOWSHIP IS EVERY JOINT EXPRESSION, MANIFESTATION, AND
DEMONSTRATION OF THE COMMON FAITH IN WHICH CHRISTIANS ARE UNITED
WITH ONE ANOTHER...THROUGH THE BOND OF FAITH IN WHICH HE UNITES US
WITH ALL CHRISTIANS THE HOLY SPIRIT ALSO LEADS US TO EXPRESS AND MAN-
IFEST OUR FAITH JOINTLY WITH FELLOW CHRISTIANS ACCORDING TO OPPORTU-
NITY: AS SMALLER AND LARGER GROUPS ACTS 1:14,15; 2:41-47; GAL. 2:9; 2
COR. 9:2. (BEFORE GOD EVERY ACTIVITY OF OUR FAITH IS AT THE SAME TIME
FELLOWSHIP ACTIVITY IN THE COMMUNION OF SAINTS. 1 COR. 12; EPH. 4:11-
16; ROM. 12:1-8; 2 TIM. 2:19.)... WE MAY CLASSIFY THESE JOINT EXPRESSIONS
OF FAITH IN VARIOUS WAYS ACCORDING TO THE PARTICULAR REALM OF ACTIVITY
IN WHICH THEY OCCUR, E.G., PULPIT FELLOWSHIP, ALTAR FELLOWSHIP, PRAYER
FELLOWSHIP, FELLOWSHIP IN WORSHIP, FELLOWSHIP IN CHURCH WORK, IN MIS-
SIONS, IN CHRISTIAN EDUCATION, IN CHRISTIAN CHARITY. YET INSOFAR AS
THEY ARE JOINT EXPRESSIONS OF FAITH THEY ARE ALL ESSENTIALLY ONE AND
THE SAME THING, AND ARE ALL PROPERLY COVERED BY A COMMON DESIGNA-
TION, NAMELY, CHURCH FELLOWSHIP. CHURCH FELLOWSHIP SHOULD THERE-
FORE BE TREATED AS A UNIT CONCEPTION, COVERING EVERY JOINT EXPRESSION,
MANIFESTATION AND DEMONSTRATION OF A COMMON FAITH. HENCE SCRIPTURE
CAN GIVE THE GENERAL ADMONITION "AVOID THEM" WHEN CHURCH FELLOWSHIP
IS TO CEASE, ROM. 16:17...WEAKNESS OF FAITH IS IN ITSELF NOT A REASON
FOR TERMINATING CHURCH FELLOWSHIP, BUT RATHER AN INDUCEMENT FOR
PRACTICING IT VIGOROUSLY TO HELP ONE ANOTHER IN OVERCOMING OUR INDI-
VIDUAL WEAKNESSES. IN PRECEPT AND EXAMPLE SCRIPTURE ABOUNDS WITH
EXHORTATIONS TO PAY OUR FULL DEBT OF LOVE TOWARD THE WEAK...PERSIS-
TENT ADHERENCE TO FALSE DOCTRINE AND PRACTICE CALLS FOR TERMINATION
OF CHURCH FELLOWSHIP...THE "AVOID THEM" OF ROM. 16:17, 18 EXCLUDES
ANY CONTACT THAT WOULD BE AN ACKNOWLEDGEMENT AND MANIFESTATION
OF CHURCH FELLOWSHIP; IT CALLS FOR A CESSATION OF EVERY FURTHER JOINT
EXPRESSION OF FAITH...THOSE WHO PRACTICE CHURCH FELLOWSHIP WITH PER-
SISTENT ERRORISTS ARE PARTAKERS OF THEIR EVIL DEEDS...WE FIND IT TO BE
AN UNTENABLE POSITION...TO DISTINGUISH BETWEEN JOINT PRAYER WHICH IS

768

ACKNOWLEDGED TO BE AN EXPRESSION OF CHURCH FELLOWSHIP AND AN OCCA-
SIONAL JOINT PRAYER WHICH PURPORTS TO BE SOMETHING SHORT OF CHURCH
FELLOWSHIP...[WE FIND IT TO BE AN UNTENABLE POSITION] TO ENVISION FEL-
LOWSHIP RELATIONS (IN A CONGREGATION, IN A CHURCH BODY, IN A CHURCH
FEDERATION, IN A CHURCH AGENCY, IN A COOPERATIVE CHURCH ACTIVITY) LIKE
SO MANY STEPS OF A LADDER, EACH REQUIRING A GRADUALLY INCREASING OR
DECREASING MEASURE OF UNITY IN DOCTRINE AND PRACTICE.[68]

NO BREAK IN FELLOWSHIP IN 1959—
THE WISCONSIN SYNOD SUFFERS MORE LOSSES

In spite of the memorials and protests that it had received from dissident
members, the Wisconsin Synod in 1959 voted to continue in protesting fellowship with the Missouri Synod, adopting the report of its Floor Committee.

This action (or, term it inaction) by the synod caused many of those who had
written or voiced protests or had memorialized the synod, to the take their own
action. This meant not only suspending fellowship with the Missouri Synod but
also with their own synod. In leaving the Wisconsin Synod's fellowship, most
of the dissidents banded together to form a new Lutheran synod, which later
took the name, the Church of the Lutheran Confession (CLC). The first president was Pastor Paul Albrecht. The *Journal of Theology* was edited by Professor E. Reim, former president of the Wisconsin Lutheran Seminary. In
1960, 37 pastors and professors subscribed to the constitution of the new body.
By January, two more pastors had applied for membership in the CLC. *(See
the separate chapter, THE CHURCH OF THE LUTHERAN CONFESSION.)*

THE BREAK WITH THE MISSOURI
SYNOD FINALLY COMES

When the Thirty-Sixth Convention of the Wisconsin Synod convened in Milwaukee in August 1961, the delegates found themselves meeting in the same
building that had housed the Convention of the Synodical Conference earlier
that year. Fears and misgivings that had clouded the Synodical Conference
meeting lay even heavier over the auditorium of Wisconsin Lutheran High
School as the Wisconsin Synod delegates began to discuss the church union
matters.

Coming to a climax were all the talks and discussions which the Wisconsin
Synod had held with the Missouri Synod since 1939, in which the Wisconsin
Synod had maintained that the much larger sister synod was on an unscriptural course, a course which was at variance also with its own doctrinal statements. The Wisconsin Synod's Union Committee was constrained to report
that an impasse had been reached in drawing up the Statement on Fellowship.
The Convention Floor Committee drew up its report consisting of 12 Whereas
and 10 Resolves, which, adopted by the Convention, acknowledged the impasse
that had been encountered, and suspended fellowship with the Missouri Synod:
WHEREAS, THE WISCONSIN EVANGELICAL LUTHERAN SYNOD HAS LODGED

769

MANY ADMONITIONS AND PROTESTS WITH THE LUTHERAN CHURCH-MISSOURI SYNOD DURING THE PAST TWENTY YEARS TO WIN HER FROM THE PATH THAT LEADS TO LIBERALISM IN DOCTRINE AND PRACTICE (CF. PROCEEDINGS 1939, P. 159; 1941, P. 43F; 74FF; 1947, P. 104FF, 114F; 1949, P. 114FF; 1951, P. 110FF.; 1953, P. 95FF.), AND

WHEREAS, OUR ADMONITIONS HAVE LARGELY GONE UNHEEDED, AND THE ISSUES HAVE REMAINED UNRESOLVED,

WHEREAS, MANY OF THE POLICIES AND PRACTICES WHICH CALLED FORTH OUR ADMONITIONS WERE IN THE FIELD OF FELLOWSHIP, AND

WHEREAS, THE 1959 CONVENTION OF THE WISCONSIN EVANGELICAL LUTHERAN SYNOD THEREFORE GAVE ITS COMMISSION ON DOCTRINAL MATTERS THE DIRECTIVE "TO CONTINUE AND ACCELERATE THE DISCUSSIONS IN THE JOINT UNION COMMITTEES TO BRING ABOUT COMPLETE UNITY OF DOCTRINE AND PRACTICE IN THE SYNODICAL CONFERENCE...TO GIVE PRIMARY CONSIDERATION IN THEIR DISCUSSIONS TO THE AREA OF FELLOWSHIP...TO CONTINUE ITS EF-FORTS IN THE JOINT UNION COMMITTEES UNTIL AGREEMENT ON DOCTRINE AND PRACTICE HAS BEEN REACHED, OR UNTIL AN IMPASSE IS REACHED AND NO SUCH AGREEMENT CAN BE BROUGHT ABOUT"...AND

WHEREAS, THE COMMISSION HAS FAITHFULLY CARRIED OUT THIS DIRECTIVE BUT NOW REGRETFULLY REPORTS THAT DIFFERENCES WITH RESPECT TO THE SCRIPTURAL PRINCIPLES OF CHURCH FELLOWSHIP—DIFFERENCES WHICH IT HOLDS TO BE DIVISIVE—HAVE BROUGHT US TO AN IMPASSE...

WHEREAS, THE LUTHERAN CHURCH-MISSOURI SYNOD HAS NOT RETREATED FROM THE UNSCRIPTURAL POSITION LONG HELD BY IT AND ALSO EXPRESSED IN THE THEOLOGY OF FELLOWSHIP, PART II, BUT CONTINUES TO DE-FEND THAT POSITION AND CARRIES ON FELLOWSHIP PRACTICES WHICH CONFIRM THAT POSITION (E.G. THE TWO MEETINGS WITH THE NATIONAL LUTHERAN COUNCIL ON COOPERATIVE ACTIVITIES, JULY 7-9, 1960, AND NOVEMBER 18 AND 19, 1960, WITH A THIRD MEETING TO BE HELD OCTOBER 30-NOVEMBER 1, 1961; THE NATIONAL LUTHERAN EDUCATION CONFERENCE, JANUARY 8-10, 1961; THE CONFERENCE OF LUTHERAN PROFESSORS OF THEOLOGY, JUNE 5-7, 1961—ALL OF THESE INCLUDING CONFERENCE DEVOTIONS), AND

WHEREAS, WE RECOGNIZE OUR SACRED TRUST AND OBLIGATION TO "CON-TEND FOR THE FAITH ONCE DELIVERED UNTO THE SAINTS," AND ALSO TO GIVE VIGOROUS TESTIMONY ON CHURCH FELLOWSHIP BEFORE THE CHURCH AND THE WORLD...

RESOLVED: A) THAT WE NOW SUSPEND FELLOWSHIP WITH THE LUTHERAN CHURCH-MISSOURI SYNOD ON THE BASIS OF ROMANS 16:17, 18, WITH THE HOPE AND PRAYER TO GOD THAT THE LUTHERAN CHURCH-MISSOURI SYNOD WILL HEAR IN THIS RESOLUTION AN EVANGELICAL SUMMONS TO "COME TO HER-SELF" (LUKE 15:17) AND TO RETURN TO THE SIDE OF THE SISTER FROM WHOM SHE HAS ESTRANGED HERSELF...

RESOLVED, B) THAT UNDER CONDITIONS WHICH DO NOT IMPLY A DENIAL OF OUR PREVIOUS TESTIMONY WE STAND READY TO RESUME DISCUSSIONS WITH THE LUTHERAN CHURCH-MISSOURI SYNOD WITH THE AIM OF REESTABLISHING UNITY OF DOCTRINE AND PRACTICE AND OF RESTORING FELLOWSHIP RELATIONS, THESE DISCUSSIONS TO BE CONDUCTED OUTSIDE THE FRAMEWORK OF FELLOW-

SHIP.

In Resolution c), it was noted that judgment was not passed on the personal faith of the members of the Missouri Synod. Resolution d), stated a willingness to continue support of joint projects until "we can adjust to the new conditions brought about by the suspension of fellowship with The Lutheran Church-Missouri Synod."

RESOLVED, F) THAT THE ACTION TAKEN IN OUR RESOLUTION OF SUSPENSION DOES NOT APPLY TO OUR FELLOWSHIP RELATIONS WITH THE EVANGELICAL LUTHERAN SYNOD, THE SYNOD OF EVANGELICAL LUTHERAN CHURCHES (SELC=SLOVAK), THE EVANGELICAL LUTHERAN CHURCH OF AUSTRALIA, THE EVANGELICAL LUTHERAN (OLD LUTHERAN) CHURCH, AND THE IGREJA EVANGELICA LUTERANA DO BRASIL, AS WELL AS ANY OTHER CHURCH BODIES OUTSIDE THE SYNODICAL CONFERENCE WITH WHOM WE HAVE BEEN IN FELLOWSHIP.[69]

The vote to suspend fellowship with the Missouri Synod was 124 to 49. In the years that followed the synod's action taken in 1961, some of the pastors and others who had withdrawn from the synod asked to be readmitted into fellowship. There were approaches made to the synod by pastors and teachers, as well as by groups of concerned Christians from other Lutheran bodies (including the Missouri Synod, but not limited to it) who studied the confessional position of the Wisconsin Synod. Some of these asked for membership. In some cases rather large congregations saw fit to protest the course followed by the Missouri Synod and subsequently terminated their fellowship with that body.

THE WISCONSIN SYNOD AND OTHER LUTHERAN BODIES

THE WISCONSIN SYNOD AND THE CHURCH OF THE LUTHERAN CONFESSION (CLC)

Only a small group of pastors ultimately returned from the CLC to membership in the Wisconsin Synod. (*See the next chapter, THE CHURCH OF THE LUTHERAN CONFESSION, for more information.*)

Seeing that the Wisconsin Synod finally suspended fellowship with the Missouri Synod one might ask the question: What then still holds the Wisconsin Synod and the CLC apart? The two bodies are not now in a state of fellowship and, in fact, things look rather bad as far as establishing fellowship. In November 1962 the Wisconsin Synod's Study Committee met with representatives of the CLC to discuss the Wisconsin Synod's presentation on Church Fellowship. Over the years charges have been leveled against the Wisconsin Synod by the CLC, charges that are not considered valid by Wisconsin.

While it has been difficult to pinpoint actual differences in principle, the CLC asked for a review of the Wisconsin Synod's actions since the 1955 Convention "in order to demonstrate what the CLC representatives hold to be the Wisconsin Synod's position on Church Fellowship."[70] The Wisconsin Synod at the time declined to follow that route, no doubt spurred on by the CLC's contention that the Wisconsin Synod's position is unscriptural. In short, the CLC accuses the Wisconsin Synod of making admonition the prerequisite for apply-ing the "mark" and "avoid" of Romans 16:17. The CLC representatives took ex-ception to the following statement in the WELS statement on Church Fellowship: WE CAN NO LONGER RECOGNIZE AND TREAT AS CHRISTIAN BRETHREN THOSE WHO IN SPITE OF PATIENT ADMONITION PERSISTENTLY ADHERE TO AN ERROR IN DOCTRINE. THE CLC REPRESENTATIVES CONTENDED THAT PERSISTENT ADHER-ENCE TO ERROR DESPITE PATIENT ADMONITION IS NOT THE CRITERION BY WHICH WE JUDGE WHETHER WE ARE TO MARK AND AVOID THOSE WHO "DEMAND RECOGNITION FOR THEIR ERROR, AND MAKE PROPAGANDA FOR IT."

The CLC in its own statement "Concerning Fellowship" declares: WE FUR-THER BELIEVE, TEACH AND CONFESS THAT ESTABLISHED FELLOWSHIPS ARE TO BE TER-MINATED WHEN IT HAS BEEN ASCERTAINED THAT A PERSON OR GROUP THROUGH A FALSE POSITION IS CAUSING DIVISIONS AND OFFENSES IN THE CHURCH. The CLC further contends that the Wisconsin Synod erred by inserting admonition be-tween the "marking" and the "avoiding." The Wisconsin Synod has denied the charge.

THE WELS COMMISSION OFFERED SOME INTERPRETATIONS OF THE SECTIONS CHALLENGED THAT DID NOT CONFLICT WITH CORRESPONDING PARAGRAPH OF...[CONCERNING CHURCH FELLOWSHIP, CLC]. IT WAS SPECIFICALLY AF-FIRMED (1) THAT ADMONITION IS NOT A PREREQUISITE FOR, OR A DETERMINING FACTOR IN TERMINATING FELLOWSHIP; (2) THAT ADMONITION IS HELPFUL IN IDENTIFYING AN ERRORIST; AND (3) THAT IN CASES OF ERROR ARISING WITHIN A FELLOWSHIP ADMONITION IS THE NORMAL PROCEDURE INDICATED BY SCRIP-TURE.[71]

The CLC Board of Doctrine contended that an examination of past official statements is necessary to justify its understanding of the Theses.

At its 1969 Convention at New Ulm, Minnesota, the Wisconsin Synod's Commission reported that it had invited the CLC Board of Doctrine to a re-sumption of doctrinal discussions in a meeting at New Ulm on August 5, 1969, to discuss the principles of "weak brother" and "persistent errorist." The invi-tation, however, was declined. The following report was made to the Synod Convention:

IN [DECLINING THE INVITATION] THEY STATE THAT THEY "DEEM IT URGENT THAT BOTH SIDES SUBMIT TO THE NEED OF RESTORING UNITY BY FRANK AND HONEST CONFRONTATION WITH THE TRUTH, HISTORICAL AS WELL AS SCRIPTURAL, WITH-OUT FURTHER RECOURSE TO UNREALISTIC PROCEDURAL RESERVATIONS WHICH HAVE PROVED TO BE OBSTACLES TO PROMPT ATTAINMENT OF THE GOD-PLEASING OBJECTIVES OF OUR DISCUSSION."

IT IS THE WISH OF THE CLC THAT THE HISTORICAL EVENTS FROM 1955 TO 1961 BECOME THE SUBJECT MATTER OF SUCH DISCUSSIONS. OUR COMMISSION IS CONVINCED THAT A DISCUSSION OF THE BASIC PRINCIPLES OF CHURCH FELLOW-SHIP, WHICH COULD LEAD TO A COMMON BASIS FOR FURTHER DISCUSSION OF PAST EVENTS, IS THE ONLY PROPER AND EFFECTIVE WAY TO PROCEED. WITHOUT SUCH A COMMON BASIS OF SCRIPTURAL PRINCIPLES, EVEN AN AGREEMENT IN EVALUATING HISTORICAL EVENTS WOULD BE IMPOSSIBLE...UNDER THESE CIR-CUMSTANCES OUR COMMISSION ON DOCTRINAL MATTERS DOES NOT FIND IT-SELF IN A POSITION TO PLAN FURTHER DISCUSSION WITH THE BOARD OF

DOCTRINE OF THE CHURCH OF THE LUTHERAN CONFESSION.[72]
In 1972 representatives of the two bodies met in Milwaukee. It was reported
that in this meeting...
NO SCRIPTURAL WARRANT WAS GRANTED BY THE CLC REPRESENTATIVES FOR
A STATE OF CONFESSION IN DEALING WITH THE SITUATION IN WHICH ERROR IN
DOCTRINE OR PRACTICE HAS INFECTED A LARGE GROUP OF CONFESSIONAL
BRETHREN. THE WELS REPRESENTATIVES HELD, HOWEVER, THAT SUCH A
STATE OF CONFESSION IS FREQUENTLY CALLED FOR BEFORE TERMINATING FEL-
LOWSHIP WITH A GROUP THAT HAS BEEN INFECTED BY ERROR: (1) IN ORDER TO
OFFER OPPORTUNITY FOR DETERMINING WHAT THE CONFESSIONAL POSITION OF
THE GROUP FOR WHICH IT MUST BE HELD RESPONSIBLE REALLY IS... (2) TO
OFFER OPPORTUNITY TO BRING SCRIPTURAL TESTIMONY AGAINST ERROR INFECT-
ING THE GROUP TO THOSE BRETHREN WHO ARE NOT THEMSELVES ADVOCATING
AND PROPAGANDIZING THE ERRORS—BEFORE TREATING SUCH BRETHREN AS RE-
SPONSIBLE PARTAKERS OF THE ERROR OR FALSE PRACTICE INFECTING THEIR
GROUP.
The Wisconsin Synod representatives held that such procedure is called for
to satisfy the many scriptural injunctions quoted in their Church Fellowship
Statement bidding "us to exercise and make earnest effort to preserve the bond
of confessional fellowship, to help the weak and the confused." The explanation
was offered by the WELS committee that when the synodical resolutions of
that period before 1961 used the term "state of confession," it was not yet meant
to express a judgment tantamount to that of Romans 16:17. And here is where
the matter lay between the Wisconsin Synod and the Church of the Lutheran
Confession until the talks that occurred 1987-1990.
After these many years that the WELS and the CLC have remained apart,
the question is asked if there really is a doctrinal difference between the two
synods that justifies their failure to establish fellowship. The WELS would
answer, "No." The CLC would answer, "Yes." A main reason for the CLC to
accuse the WELS of having a different Doctrine of Fellowship—the point of
contention—is the issue of "admonishment" of the erring. The CLC points to
history and shows that the WELS continued to admonish the Missouri Synod
after it had come to the conclusion that Missouri was causing divisions and offenses contrary to sound scriptural doctrine. Instead of breaking fellowship
with Missouri, the WELS carried on admonition in a state of "protesting fellowship."
There is another matter that the CLC offers as a reason to believe that
WELS has a different Doctrine of Fellowship, one that is not scriptural. The
CLC returns repeatedly to a statement which Professor Carl Lawrenz (WELS)
made in "A Report to the Protest Committee" in 1958. The statement reads:
TERMINATION OF CHURCH FELLOWSHIP IS CALLED FOR WHEN YOU HAVE REACHED
THE CONVICTION THAT ADMONITION IS OF NO FURTHER AVAIL AND THAT THE ERRING
BROTHER OR CHURCH BODY DEMANDS RECOGNITION FOR THEIR ERROR. This statement came before the WELS at the 1959 Synod Convention. The Lawrenz
statement was challenged by a fairly large group of WELS pastors in a memorial titled, "A Call for Decision." Many of the signers of this memorial later
were instrumental in organizing the CLC. The memorial put forward this alternative wording: TERMINATION OF CHURCH FELLOWSHIP IS CALLED FOR WHEN

773

SCRIPTURAL CORRECTION HAS BEEN OFFERED AND REJECTED AND THE ERRING BROTHER OR CHURCH BODY HAVE CONTINUED IN THEIR ERROR DESPITE ADMONITION. THIS IS THE PERSISTENCE WHICH DISTINGUISHES AN ERRORIST (ROMANS 16:17, 18) FROM AN ERRING BROTHER (GALATIANS 2:11-14)." (*WELS Proceedings*, 1959, p. 210)

The CLC accuses the Lawrenz statement of assuming the need for clairvoyance, seeing into the future and being able to know that admonition would never do any good before breaking off the fellowship.

Because the issue of the role of admonition in terminating fellowship with an erring church body is very much involved in the controversy between the CLC on the one hand and the WELS and the ELS on the other hand, the focus of the last doctrinal talks held by the three bodies (1987-1990) was on the role of admonition in dealing with an erring church body, which admonition could possibly end in terminating fellowship with it. The three bodies reached the following agreement: ADMONITION CONTINUES UNTIL THE ERRING INDIVIDUAL OR GROUP EITHER REPENTS OF ITS ERROR AND TURNS AWAY FROM IT OR UNTIL IT SHOWS ITSELF TO BE PERSISTENT IN ITS ERROR BY ADHERING TO IT IN ITS PUBLIC DOCTRINE AND PRACTICE, BY DEMANDING RECOGNITION FOR IT, OR BY MAKING PROPAGANDA FOR IT AND TRYING TO PERSUADE OTHERS FOR IT.[73]

The three bodies agreed that admonition is necessary before a termination of fellowship, and accepted the following statement on the purpose and limited duration of admonition:

THE IMPERATIVE EKKLINATE [GREEK FOR "AVOID," ROMANS 16:17,18] CALLS FOR A CLEAN BREAK OF FELLOWSHIP WITH THOSE WHO PERSISTENTLY ADHERE TO ERROR. WHEN IT HAS BEEN ASCERTAINED THAT A PERSON OR CHURCH BODY IS CAUSING DIVISION AND OFFENSES...BY TEACHING CONTRARY TO HOLY SCRIPTURES, THE DIRECTIVE TO AVOID IS AS BINDING AS ANY WORD ADDRESSED TO US BY OUR SAVIOR IN HIS HOLY WORD. PLEADING A DEBT OF LOVE DARE NOT SERVE AS AN EXCUSE FOR PUTTING OFF A BREAK OF FELLOWSHIP WITH THOSE WHO HAVE SHOWN THEMSELVES TO BE NOT WEAK BRETHREN BUT PERSISTENT ERRORISTS...WE REJECT THE VIEW THAT THE DECISION TO CONTINUE OR DISCONTINUE ADMONITION AND PROCEED TO AVOID IS TO BE MADE ON THE BASIS OF A SUBJECTIVE HUMAN JUDGMENT OR CONJECTURE ABOUT THE POSSIBLE OUTCOME OF ADMONITION...WE REJECT THE VIEW THAT PERMITS THE USE OF HUMAN JUDGMENT TO PROLONG FELLOWSHIP WITH PERSISTENT ERRORISTS AS CONTRARY TO SCRIPTURE.[74]

The CLC requested a preamble, to deal with past statements of the respective synods and of individuals within them. The CLC proposed a preamble that would contain the following statement: ANY PREVIOUS EXPRESSION OR ACTIONS WHICH MAY NOT BE IN CONFORMITY WITH [THE JOINT STATEMENT] ARE HEREBY SET ASIDE AND REJECTED. It should be noted that the CLC representatives were troubled by the consistent use by the WELS of the expression "persistent errorist." The CLC felt that use of the word "persistent" contributed to the WELS' delay in terminating fellowshipwith the LCMS. While the CLC accepted the WELS' explanation of "persistent errorist," the CLC later had second thoughts about both the use of the term and the WELS' explanation of it.

Rather than accept the CLC preamble, the WELS offered a longer preamble, which included these words: THIS JOINT STATEMENT, THEREFORE, WHEN AC-

774

CEPTED BY OUR THREE CHURCH BODIES, SUPERCEDES ANY AND EVERY PREVIOUS STATEMENT THAT MIGHT BE OR MIGHT APPEAR TO BE IN CONFLICT WITH THIS DOCUMENT. ANY AND ALL SUCH CONFLICTING OR POSSIBLY CONFLICTING STATEMENTS ARE HEREWITH DISAVOWED.

The CLC preamble was thus rejected by the WELS. Years later, a WELS theologian gave the following explanation for this rejection:...BECAUSE WE IN WELS HAVE NEVER BEEN ABLE TO SEE THAT THERE HAD BEEN A CLEAR DIFFERENCE IN THE DOCTRINAL PRINCIPLES THEMSELVES BETWEEN THE CLC AND WELS. WHAT WE ADMIT IS THAT THERE WAS A DIFFERENCE CONCERNING THE APPLICATION OF THE CHURCH FELLOWSHIP DOCTRINE IN THE 1950S. DIFFERENT PEOPLE APPLIED THE DOCTRINAL PRINCIPLES DIFFERENTLY AT THE TIME IN KEEPING WITH THEIR CONSCIENCE, FOR WHICH EACH PERSON HAD TO BE RESPECTED...THE CLC, ON THE OTHER HAND, ASSUMES THAT BECAUSE THE ACTIONS OF PEOPLE WERE DIFFERENT IN THE 1950's, THERE MUST HAVE BEEN DIFFERENT DOCTRINAL PRINCIPLES. WHEN ASKED WHAT THE DOCTRINAL DIFFERENCE WAS, THE LAWRENZ STATEMENT OF 1958 IS QUOTED BY THE CLC AS PROOF OF FALSE DOCTRINE ON THE PART OF WELS.[75]

Regarding the Lawrenz statement of 1958 in "Report to the Protest Committee, a WELS theologian makes this admission:...(A)GAIN WE WOULD SAY IT HAS SHOWN ITSELF TO BE AN AMBIGUOUS STATEMENT OPEN TO VARYING INTERPRETATIONS. THEREFORE WE DON'T USE IT ANY MORE. HOWEVER, WE WOULD NOT BE ABLE TO CONDEMN IT AS FALSE DOCTRINE, BECAUSE WE CAN UNDERSTAND IT IN A PROPER WAY. AND, THE WAY IT HAS BEEN EXPLAINED BY ITS ORIGINAL AUTHOR AND ITS SUBSEQUENT WELS INTERPRETERS HAS SEEMINGLY BEEN IN AGREEMENT WITH THE PRINCIPLES OF THE CLC ITSELF.[76]

The same WELS writer contends: IT CAN BE ARGUED THAT THIS STATEMENT WAS INTENDED TO SAY NOTHING MORE THAN WHEN ERROR SHOWS UP IN A CHURCH BODY, ADMONITION WILL BE GIVEN TO THEM AS WEAK BROTHERS TO CORRECT THEM. IF ADMONITION IS REJECTED, THE CHURCH BODY WILL BE IDENTIFIED AS PERSISTENT ERRORISTS AND NOT WEAK BROTHERS. THEN FELLOWSHIP SHOULD BE BROKEN IMMEDIATELY. IN OTHER WORDS, COMING TO "THE CONVICTION THAT ADMONITION IS OF NO FURTHER AVAIL" IS THE SAME AS RECOGNIZING THAT ONE'S ADMONITION HAS BEEN REJECTED. WHEN WE IN WELS CONCLUDED THAT WE HAD REACHED AN "IMPASSE" WITH LCMS IN 1961, THIS SIMPLY MEANT WE RECOGNIZED THAT OUR ADMONITION HAD BEEN CLEARLY UNDERSTOOD AND REJECTED.[77]

In the Joint Statement drawn up in 1987-1990 by the three synods, the WELS representatives agreed with the following antithesis: WE REJECT THE VIEW THAT THE DECISION TO CONTINUE OR DISCONTINUE ADMONITION AND PROCEED TO AVOID IS TO BE MADE ON THE BASIS OF SUBJECTIVE JUDGMENT OR POSSIBLE OUTCOME OF THE ADMONITION.[78]

One would think that this agreement by the WELS would lay to rest the confusion and consternation caused by the Lawrenz statement in A Report to the Protest Committee in 1958. Especially so, when other statements by Professor Lawrenz and the WELS are also considered. The WELS writer quoted above points out: IN DISCUSSIONS WITH SIGNERS OF "A CALL FOR DECISION" C. LAWRENZ AND THE WELS REPRESENTATIVES INSISTED THAT WHAT THEY INTENDED WITH THE CONTESTED STATEMENT WAS NO DIFFERENCE THAN "A CALL FOR DECISION." THEY INSISTED THAT THE THESIS IS DEFENDED BY THE MEMORIAL, AND THE

PROPOSITION SET UP IN THEIR DOCUMENT WERE IDENTICAL IN SUBSTANCE.

Furthermore, the WELS representatives stated their willingness to amend the contested statement if it was misleading. (*Journal of Theology*, 1:3, June 1961, p. 42.) We remind the reader that Professor Lawrenz' contested statement has dropped out of use over the years, because it is subject to various interpretations and to misunderstanding.

So then, what finally happened to the 1987-1990 talks? The CLC broke off the negotiations with the WELS in 1990. In the words of Professor John Brug, "It's as though the CLC-WELS-ELS meeting had never taken place." The CLC maintains—in spite of the Joint Statement—that a doctrinal difference regarding Church Fellowship exists between the CLC and the WELS. The CLC keeps going back to the Lawrenz statement in A Report to the Protest Committee— a statement that is no longer in use in the WELS.

A CLC congregation in Albuquerque, NM, requested that the CLC state what the doctrinal difference is between the CLC and the WELS. In replying to this request, the CLC's 1994 Convention adopted the following statements:

WHEREAS, THE WELS, HAVING ALREADY "MARKED" THE LC-MS IN 1955 AS A CAUSER OF DIVISIONS AND OFFENSES, NEVERTHELESS AT ITS 1959 CONVENTION ADOPTED THE FOLLOWING PRINCIPLE ON THE TERMINATION OF CHURCH FELLOWSHIP: "TERMINATION OF CHURCH FELLOWSHIP IS CALLED FOR WHEN YOU HAVE REACHED THE CONVICTION THAT ADMONITION IS OF NO FURTHER AVAIL AND THAT THE ERRING BROTHER OR CHURCH BODY DEMANDS RECOGNITION OF ITS ERROR," AND

WHEREAS, THE CLC HOLDS TO THE SCRIPTURAL PRINCIPLE SET FORTH IN ITS OFFICIAL PUBLICATION, "CONCERNING CHURCH FELLOWSHIP," WHICH SAYS: "WE FURTHER BELIEVE AND TEACH THAT SUSPENSION OF AN ESTABLISHED FELLOWSHIP IS TO TAKE PLACE WHEN IT HAS BEEN ASCERTAINED THAT A PERSON OR GROUP IS CAUSING DIVISIONS AND OFFENSES THROUGH A FALSE POSITION IN DOCTRINE OR PRACTICE" THEREFORE, BE IT RESOLVED, THAT WE LET THE DOCTRINAL CONTRAST BETWEEN THESE TWO OFFICIAL STATEMENTS FROM THE RESPECTIVE CHURCH BODIES STAND AS OUR ANSWER TO THE MEMORIAL OF HOLY SPIRIT CONGREGATION OF ALBUQUERQUE, NM.[79]

The WELS sees the CLC as presenting an inadequate and even false characterization of the WELS Doctrine of Fellowship. The WELS also senses that the CLC downplays the issue of admonishing the errorist. Frankly stated, the WELS is of the opinion that the CLC attempts to manufacture a doctrinal difference where none exists.

The WELS representatives did not officially present the Joint Statement to the synod convention for adoption, because the CLC refused further discussions, thereby negating the reason to present the Joint Statement. However, the statement has been accepted by the WELS representatives, whose desire it is that it be used as the starting point in any future negotiations.

We close our discussion of the current situation (2007) between the CLC and the WELS with these words of Professor John F. Brug, Managing Editor of the *Wisconsin Lutheran Quarterly*, and professor of Systematic Theology at Wisconsin Lutheran Seminary:

If the CLC insists that the 1959 sentence [the Lawrenz statement] must mean what they say it means and not what the parallel WELS statements and explanations say it was intended to mean, it appears that an impasse has been reached and further discussion is of no avail.

It is sad that the talks which began so promisingly failed to produce concrete steps toward removing the division between the WELS and the CLC. It is doubly sad that CLC spokesmen are ignoring the Joint Statement and basing allegations of a doctrinal difference between the WELS and CLC on a caricature of the WELS position which WELS representatives could not accept as an accurate summary of their view. Readers who want to reach their own conclusion should read the WELS Reports and Memorials, 1993, pp. 232-241and the CLC Journal of Theology, December 1994, pp. 31-34, June 2000, pp. 41-50.[80]

In the following chapter, THE CHURCH OF THE LUTHERAN CONFESSION, the reader will be able to view the controversy between the WELS and the CLC from the latter synod's perspective.

THE WISCONSIN SYNOD AND THE SLOVAK SYNOD (SYNOD OF EVANGELICAL LUTHERAN CHURCHES)

It was only a matter of time following the breakup of the Synodical Conference in 1963 before the Wisconsin Synod would feel impelled to recognize that fellowship with the Slovak Synod would also have to be officially terminated. This occurred at the Saginaw Convention in 1967.

WHEREAS, THE SYNOD OF EVANGELICAL LUTHERAN CHURCHES, WHICH FOR MANY YEARS WAS IN FELLOWSHIP WITH THE WELS, HAS JOINED THE LUTHERAN COUNCIL IN THE USA, A NEWLY CONSTITUTED ORGANIZATION OF SYNOD OF CONFLICTING CONFESSIONAL POSITIONS, AND

WHEREAS, IT HAS BECOME EVIDENT FROM A RECENT OFFICIAL COMMUNICATION THAT THE SYNOD OF EVANGELICAL LUTHERAN CHURCHES NO LONGER HOLDS ITS FORMER SCRIPTURAL PRINCIPLES ON CHURCH FELLOWHIP, AND

WHEREAS, THE WELS, THROUGH ITS DOCTRINAL COMMISSION, HAS REPEATEDLY HELD DOCTRINAL DISCUSSIONS WITH THE SYNOD OF EVANGELICAL LUTHERAN CHURCHES, WITHOUT REACHING AGREEMENT; THEREFORE BE IT RESOLVED....B) THAT WE NOW SUSPEND FELLOWSHIP WITH THE SYNOD OF EVANGELICAL LUTHERAN CHURCHES ON THE BASIS OF ROMANS 16:17 WITH THE HOPE AND PRAYER THAT THE SYNOD OF EVANGELICAL LUTHERAN CHURCHES WILL HEAR IN THIS RESOLUTION AN EVANGELICAL SUMMONS TO COME TO HERSELF (LUKE 15:17) AND TO RETURN TO THE SIDE OF HER SISTER SYNOD FROM WHOM SHE HAS ESTRANGED HERSELF.[81]

THE WISCONSIN SYNOD AND THE EVANGELICAL LUTHERAN SYNOD (ELS—NORWEGIAN SYNOD)

While not establishing a synodical conference with the ELS, the Wisconsin Synod and the ELS enjoy a close fellowship.

To strengthen its fellowship ties with the Evangelical Lutheran Synod (ELS) the Commission on Inter-Church Relations meets every other year with the ELS Doctrine Committee. In the years that a meeting does not take place, the Evangelical Lutheran Confessional Forum, a meeting of church leaders from both synods, takes place. [Such as the forum held in October 2004.]

THE WISCONSIN SYNOD AND THE NATIONAL LUTHERAN COUNCIL (NLC), THE LUTHERAN COUNCIL IN THE USA (LCUSA), AND THE LUTHERAN WORLD FEDERATION (LWF)

The Wisconsin Synod consistently declined overtures to participate in discussions with the National Lutheran Council and later, with the Lutheran Council in the USA. It consistently refused to join these groups, and has also consistently refused to join the Lutheran World Federation. The outstanding reason for the synod's aloofness to these bodies is unionism. Wisconsin felt that membership in any of these groups would place it into fellowship with those who openly espouse doctrinal error and false church practice. The attitude of the Wisconsin Synod then and now is that for a church body to be involved in such groups is not simply cooperation in the area of "externals," but rather cooperation in actual church work—sharing of joint ventures, such as Christian mission work. When this is done the door is open to joint worship and fellowship among the member churches of such bodies, even though the participants are not agreed fully in matters of doctrine and practice. In other words, unionism becomes an accepted practice.

Perhaps a reply made by President Oscar J. Naumann in 1959 to an invitation to participate in talks with the National Lutheran Council will illustrate the Wisconsin Synod position regarding any participation with others in joint church work and fellowship: As we have replied to a previous similar invitation, so we wish to give expression once more to our convictions that true unity in doctrine and practice is the only God-pleasing basis for cooperation in spiritual work.[83]

1917-THE ORIGINAL DISTRICTS DISTRICTS ADDED AFTER 1917

1917-THE ORIGINAL DISTRICTS	DISTRICTS ADDED AFTER 1917
Southeastern District*	Pacific Northwest-1918
Western Wisconsin District*	Dakota-Montana-1920
Michigan District*	Arizona-California-1954
Minnesota District	South Atlantic-1973
Nebraska District	North Atlantic-1983
	South Central-1983

Footnotes for Chapter Thirty-Six

1 *American Heritage New Pictorial Guide To The United States*, Created and Designed by the Editors of American Heritage Magazine (New York, NY: Dell Publishing Co., Inc., 1965—by American Heritage Publishing Co., Inc.), p. 1322.

2 *American Heritage...*, p. 1323.

3 Conrad Bergendoff, *The Church of the Reformation—A Historical Survey of Lutheranism* (St. Louis, MO: Concordia Publishing House, 1967), p. 225.

4 A.P. Voss, Editor-in-Chief, *Continuing in His Word—The History of the Evangelical Joint Synod of Wisconsin and Other States* (Milwaukee, WI: Northwestern Publishing House, 1951—Prepared for publication at its Centenary by the Centennial Committee of the Joint Synod), p. 12.

5 Omar Bonderud and Ch. Lutz, Editors, *America's Lutherans* (Columbus, OH; Wartburg Press, 1955), p.

6 James M. Johnson, Editor for Chapter and Verse, writing in a Milwaukee Catholic Paper.

7 Voss, *Continuing in His Word...*, pp. 16, 17.

8 Voss, *Continuing in His Word...*, p. 17.

9 Voss, *Continuing in His Word...*, pp. 17, 18.

10 Voss, *Continuing in His Word...*, p. 23.

* After the suspended pastors were excluded from membership in the Michigan Synod they quickly organized themselves as the Evangelical Lutheran District of Michgan and maintained contact with the Joint Synod of Wisconsin and with the Synodical Conference.

11 *The Michigan District History* 1833-1970; "The Michigan District," an essay by Karl F. Krauss. (Copyright 1972 by the Michigan District, Wisconsin Ev. Lutheran Synod), pp. 6-9, the direct quote is from page 8.

12 *Michigan District History...*, pp. 10, 11, 15, 16.

13 Voss, *Continuing in His Word...*, p. 10.

14 Voss, *Continuing in His Word...*, p. 103, 104.

15 Voss, *Continuing in His Word...*, pp. 126, 127.

16 *American Heritage...* p. 883, Vol. 10.

17 *American Heritage...*, p. 881, Vol. 10.

18 *American Heritage...*, p. 676, Vol. 8.

19 Voss, *Continuing in His Word...*, p. 132.

20 Voss, *Continuing in His Word...*, p. 201.

21 *Report To The Twelve Districts, June 2004*, p. 75.

22 John A. Braun, *Together In Christ* (Milwaukee, WI: Northwestern Publishing House, 2000), p. 41.

23 *You And Your Synod—The Story of the Wisconsin Evangelical Lutheran Synod*, prepared for the WELS by the Board For Parish Education (Milwaukee, WI: Northwestern Publishing House, 1972), p. 135f.

24 Reported in...*Forward in Christ* magazine, Wisconsin Evangelical Lutheran Synod, formerly *Northwestern Lutheran*, February 2003, p. 2002, 2003. Milwaukee, WI 53222-4398.

25 *Report to the Twelve Districts, June 2002*, Wisconsin Evangelical Lutheran Synod, pp. 43,44.

26 *Report to the Twelve Districts, June 2002...*pp. 44,45.

27 The information concerning the Wisconsin Synod's foreign mission fields/global sister churches was partially provided by the following publications:

   Reports and Memorials, WELS' 58th Biennial Convention, 2005;

   Braun, *Together in Christ...; Report to the Twelve Districts,* June 2002;

   June 2004/*Forward In Christ magazine* (The Word From The WELS): January 2003, pp.

12,13; March 2003, pp. 14,15; April 2003, pp. 14,15; May 2003, pp. 12, 13; August 2003, p.

29; February 2004, p. 23; March 2004, p. 23; September 2005, p. 21; November 2005, p. 21.

28 *Reports and Memorials*, WELS' 58th Biennial Convention, 2005, p. 16.

29 *Report To The Twelve Districts, June 2004*, pp. 60,61.

30 *Report To The Twelve Districts, June 2004*, pp. 60-63.

31 *Forward...*, May 2000, p. 17.

32 *Forward...*, August 2004, p. 17.

33 *Report To The Twelve Districts*, June 2004, p. 75.

34 *Forward...*, May 2003, p. 23.

35 *Forward...*, May 2003, p. 23.

36 *2004 Yearbook, Wisconsin Evangelical Lutheran Synod* (Milwaukee, WI: Northwestern Publishing House, 2003), pp. 141-172.

37 "The Chaplaincy Question," Tract #11 of the series, *Continuing in His Word*. (Milwaukee, WI: Northwestern Publishing House, issued 1954), p. 8.

38 *Forward...*, June 2003, p. 26.

39 "Suspension of Relations With the Missouri Synod," a tract published by the Evangelical Lutheran Synod, p. 5.

40 "1938-1952", Tract #2 of the series *Continuing in His Word*, quoting the Proceedings of the Wisconsin Synod 1939 Convention, pp. 59-61. (Tract, p.3)

41 *Proceedings, 1946 Wisconsin Synod Convention*, pp. 112, 113.

42 *Proceedings, 1949...* p. 115.

43 *Proceedings, 1949...* pp. 115, 116.

44 *Proceedings, 1949...* p. 116.

45 *Proceedings, 1949...* pp. 116, 117.

* *Proceedings, 1951...* pp. 111-116

46 *Proceedings, 1951...* pp. 147-148

47 *Proceedings, 1951...* pp. 148.

48 *Proceedings, 1947 Missouri Synod Convention*, p. 517.

49 *Proceedings, 1953 Wisconsin Synod Convention*, p. 99-101.

50 *Proceedings, 1953..., pp. 103, 104.*

51 *Proceedings, 1955...*, pp. 13f.

52 *Proceedings, 1955...*, pp. 81.

53 *Proceedings, 1955...*, p. 86.

54 *Proceedings, 1957...*, p. 135.

* The term "historical developments"—The Missouri Synod Praesidium restricted this term to the ALC's action of probably uniting with the Evangelical Lutheran Church and the United Evangelical Lutheran Church.

55 *Proceedings, 1957...*, pp. 135.

56 *Proceedings, 1957...*, p. 75.

57 *Proceedings, 1957...*, pp. 143.

58 *Proceedings, 1957...*, pp. 144.

59 *Proceedings, 1957...*, pp. 144, 145.

60 *Proceedings, 1959...*, pp. 165.

61 *Proceedings, 1959...*, pp. 174.

62 *Proceedings, 1959...*, pp. 175.

63 *Proceedings, 1959...*, pp. 178.

* This report contained a statement regarding the timing of termination of fellowship which a sizable group of pastors objected to.

64 *Proceedings, 1959...*, pp. 180.

65 *Proceedings, 1959...*, pp. 195, 196.

65 *Proceedings, 1959...*, pp. 195, 196.

66 *Proceedings, 1959...*, pp. 193, 194.

67 *Proceedings, 1959...*, pp. 198-200.

68 *Proceedings, 1959...*, pp. 205-208.

69 *Proceedings*, 1961..., pp. ____.

70 *Proceedings*, 1965 (Wisconsin Synod)..., p.____.

71 *Proceedings, 1967...*, p. 280.

72 *Proceedings, 1969...*, p. 149.

73 *Wisconsin Lutheran Quarterly*, Vol. 98, No. 1, 2001 p. 59. Quoting *WELS Reports and Memorials*, 1993, p. 236.

74 *Wisconsin Lutheran Quarterly*, Ibid., p. 62. Quoting the Joint Statement.

75 *Wisconsin Lutheran Quarterly*, Ibid, pp. 62, 63.

76 *Wisconsin Lutheran Quarterly*, Ibid., p. 61.

77 *Wisconsin Lutheran Quarterly*, Ibid., pp. 58, 59.

78 *Wisconsin Lutheran Quarterly*, p. 60. Quoting *WELS Reports and Memorials*, 1993, p. 237.

79 *Wisconsin Lutheran Quarterly*, Ibid., pp. 63, 64. Quoting the *CLC Proceedings*, pp. 66, 67.

80 *Wisconsin Lutheran Quarterly*, Vol. 98, No. 1, 2001, p. 67.

81 *Proceedings*, 1967 Wisconsin Synod Convention, p.   .

82 *Reports and Memorials, WELS' 58th Biennial Convention (2005)*, p. 38.

83 *Proceedings*, 1959Wisconsin Synod Convention, p. 168.

CHAPTER THIRTY-SEVEN

CHURCH OF THE LUTHERAN CONFESSION (CLC) (1960 -)

CLC ROOTS ARE MAINLY IN THE WISCONSIN EVANGELICAL LUTHERAN SYNOD (WELS)

The Church of the Lutheran Confession (CLC) is one of the younger Lutheran bodies in the United States. It was legally incorporated in the State of Minnesota on December 23, 1960. Two other Lutheran church bodies were organized about the same time: The American Lutheran Church (TALC, later to be simply known as the American Lutheran Church or ALC the "new" one), April 22, 1960, and the Lutheran Church in America (LCA), June 28 to July 1, 1962. These two Lutheran bodies were giants in size compared with the CLC and were unions of existing Lutheran synods. The CLC, on the other hand, was organized especially by those pastors, teachers, and laymen of the Wisconsin Synod who were disturbed by the said synod's continuation of fellowship with the Missouri Synod. A small number who helped to organize the CLC came out of the Evangelical Lutheran Synod (ELS). Still fewer had their roots in the Lutheran Church-Missouri Synod (LC-MS).

SUMMARY OF THE WISCONSIN-MISSOURI CRISIS THAT RESULTED, AMONG OTHER EVENTS, IN THE FORMATION OF THE CHURCH OF THE LUTHERAN CONFESSION

(Refer also to the histories of the Wisconsin and Missouri Synods and to the history of the Evangelical Lutheran Synod)

The roots of this crisis go back into the later 1930's when the Wisconsin Synod began its campaign of admonition against what it saw as a liberalizing trend of its sister synod, whose fellowship it had cherished and enjoyed for many years. Missouri began to unilaterally negotiate in 1935 with the American Lutheran Church (ALC—the "old" one).

Five documents figure in these negotiations. First, was the ALC's Chicago Theses, drawn up in 1928 and later rejected by the Missouri Synod. Second, was Missouri's Brief Statement, drawn up in 1932, accepted by the synod and approved by the Wisconsin Synod and the Norwegian Synod (which later took the name, Evangelical Lutheran Synod [ELS]). The Brief Statement, however, was not accepted by the ALC. In spite of the fact that the two negotiating bodies did not accept the doctrinal statement of the other, they nevertheless entered into serious fellowship negotiations. Third, the ALC in 1938 found it necessary through its Doctrine Committee to supplement the Brief Statement with its own Declaration.

It was at this time that the Missouri Synod took a step which caused no little concern and even amazement within Synodical Conference circles. Without entering into fellowship with the ALC, Missouri declared its own Brief Statement, together with the ALC's Declaration, to be an acceptable doctrinal basis for future fellowship. The Wisconsin Synod in 1939 did not accept the Declaration, ruling the terms of this document "as not stating the truth clearly, nor excluding error, in the controverted doctrines." To top it off, the ALC earlier that year had reached an agreement at Pittsburgh (1940, the Pittsburgh Agreement) with representatives of the United Lutheran Church in America (ULCA) on the Doctrine of Inspiration. The Wisconsin Synod viewed the Doctrine of Inspiration as held in the Synodical Conference and in the ULCA, to be mutually exclusive.

Wisconsin was convinced that not two but only one document should be made the basis of fellowship, and that the proper course of action of two bodies seeking to establish fellowship is to hammer out jointly one clear, concise doctrinal statement that not only states the truth of Scripture, but also covers the controverted points of doctrine. And so, Wisconsin proceeded to request Missouri to break off discussions for the time being. Missouri, on the other hand, expressed its willingness to continue efforts to unite the Lutherans of this country.

Fourth, was a document called the Doctrinal Affirmation, which was produced in the early 1940's and amounted to the Brief Statement interspersed with statements from the ALC's Declaration. However, when this document was presented to the Missouri Synod's 1944 Convention, it was not accepted. Instead, it was referred to the members of the synod for study, with final vote

784

on the document to come in 1947. If the members accepted it, the Doctrinal Affirmation would supercede all previous documents. In 1946 the ALC rejected the Doctrinal Affirmation as generally not acceptable, and a year later issued "A Friendly Invitation." On the one hand the ALC reiterated its stand, accepting the Brief Statement together with the Declaration as a sufficient doctrinal basis for church fellowship. At that same time, however, the ALC made a statement which, to Wisconsin and many observers in Missouri as well, showed the true color and stripe of the ALC's doctrine of Scripture. That body declared that there is "an area where there exists an allowable and wholesome latitude of theological opinion on the basis of the teachings of the Word of God." Furthermore, the ALC committee termed the demand for a unified statement of doctrine as an absolute condition of fellowship, "a threat to evangelical liberty of conscience."

As far as Wisconsin was concerned, the first crack in Missouri's confessional wall appeared in 1938 when the 1938 Resolutions permitted the falsehood to stand that agreement in all doctrine is not necessary for fellowship. Wisconsin saw the crack widen as Missouri continued negotiations with the ALC, thus revealing a liberalizing trend, which admonition from both within and without the synod did not halt. Wisconsin was deeply concerned over the fact that there was evidence of more and more fellowship being carried on by Missouri, as well as by individuals within the synod—worshipping, praying, joint church work—with those with whom full agreement in doctrine and practice had not been reached. These practices were becoming less and less the exception and more and more the order of the day.

It was then that a fifth document appeared—a joint product of the committees of the LC-MS/ ALC. In 1950 the Common Confession was drawn up and accepted by both church bodies. Exhaustive study was made of this new document by Wisconsin, which then in 1951 adopted the following report:

...THAT WE INFORM THE LUTHERAN CHURCH-MISSOURI SYNOD THAT WE NOT ONLY FIND THE COMMON CONFESSION TO BE INADEQUATE...BUT THAT WE ALSO HOLD THAT THE ADOPTION OF THE COMMON CONFESSION BY THE LUTHERAN CHURCH-MISSOURI SYNOD INVOLVES AN UNTRUTH AND CREATES A BASICALLY UNTRUTHFUL SITUATION SINCE THIS ACTION HAS BEEN OFFICIALLY INTERPRETED AS A SETTLEMENT OF PAST DIFFERENCES WHICH ARE IN FACT NOT SETTLED.[1]

Wisconsin then asked that negotiations be suspended. Missouri, however, continued its part in the negotiations and helped produce the Common Confession Part II. In 1953 Wisconsin openly charged Missouri with unionism:

THE ISSUE THAT HAS OPENED THIS SERIOUS BREACH BETWEEN OUR SYNOD AND THE MISSOURI SYNOD AND THREATENED THE CONTINUANCE OF THE SYNODICAL CONFERENCE IS UNIONISM. UNIONISM IS THE UNDERLYING ISSUE IN THE CONTROVERSIES REGARDING THE CHAPLAINCY, COOPERATION WITH UNAFFILIATED CHURCH BODIES IN SERVICE CENTERS, PRAYER FELLOWSHIP AND SCOUTING. THE SAME UNIONISTIC SPIRIT IS OBSERVABLE IN THE ARRANGEMENTS THAT HAVE BEEN MADE FOR COMMUNION WITH LUTHERANS NOT IN FELLOWSHIP WITH US, UNDER THE EXCUSE OF EMERGENCY; IN NEGOTIATIONS WITH LODGES, TO MAKE CHANGES IN THEIR RITUALS; AND IN COOPERATION IN VARIOUS OTHER AREAS, WITH THE EXCUSE THAT SAFEGUARDS HAVE BEEN SET UP TO AVOID

UNIONISM.

IN THIS MATTER OF UNIONISTIC PRACTICE, MISSOURI HAS DEPARTED FROM THE POSITION THAT IT ONCE HELD, A POSITION THAT MADE IT A STRONGHOLD OF THE CHURCH AND A BANNER TO REPAIR TO, AND THAT WAS ONE OF THE STRONGEST LINKS THAT BOUND US TOGETHER IN THE SYNODICAL CONFERENCE. MISSOURI HAS BROKEN THAT LINK.[2]

The 1953 Convention of the Wisconsin Synod even went so far as to speak of "the present break in relations that is now threatening the existence of the Synodical Conference and the continuance of our affiliation with the sister Synod." Wisconsin then put itself into a State of Confession over against the Missouri Synod.

In 1955 the President of the Wisconsin Synod, Oscar J. Naumann, had to report to the Saginaw (Michigan) Convention that matters had not improved, that the differences in practice had increased and multiplied and that...

...IT HAS BECOME EXTREMELY DIFFICULT TO CARRY ON INTERSYNODICAL ADMONITION AND DISCIPLINE...WE HAVE BEEN GROWING APART INSTEAD OF BEING DRAWN CLOSER TOGETHER...MATTERS WHICH WE NAMED IN OUR RESOLUTIONS OF 1953 WHICH WE CONSIDERED DANGEROUS TO OUR SOUL'S WELFARE, DETERRENT TO OUR GOSPEL MINISTRY, AND DETRIMENTAL TO OUR FELLOWSHIP IN THE CONFERENCE, HAVE BEEN AND STILL ARE VIGOROUSLY DEFENDED...WE HAVE REACHED THE CONVICTION THAT THROUGH THESE DIFFERENCES DIVISIONS AND OFFENSES HAVE BEEN CAUSED CONTRARY TO THE DOCTRINE WHICH WE HAVE LEARNED. AND WHEN THAT IS THE CASE, THE LORD OUR GOD HAS A DEFINITE COMMAND FOR US: "AVOID THEM!" FOR THOSE OF US WHO HAVE BEEN CLOSEST TO THESE PROBLEMS, IT APPEARS QUITE DEFINITE THAT WE MUST NOW OBEY THE LORD'S WORD IN ROMANS 16:17. *(CLC Response: We note that Romans 16:17, 18 is quoted. In the same report the president said, "We implore the Holy Spirit to guide and direct us as we try to decide in the face of all the reports whether the Lord would have us apply His definite command 'Avoid them!' or whether we still have an unpaid debt of love to those whose fellowship we have cherished so many years."* --Proceedings, 1955 Wisconsin Synod, p. 14)*

The report given by President Naumann was later followed by the Report of the Standing Committee in Matter of Church Union, which summed up its position with the following resolution:

...THAT WITH DEEPEST SORROW, TAKING NOTICE OF THE FACT THAT THE LUTHERAN CHURCH-MISSOURI SYNOD IS CAUSING DIVISIONS AND OFFENSES CONTRARY TO THE DOCTRINE WHICH WE HAVE LEARNED, WE, IN OBEDIENCE TO GOD'S INJUNCTION TO AVOID SUCH, DECLARE THE FELLOWSHIP WHICH WE HAVE HAD WITH SAID SYNOD TO BE TERMINATED.[4]

WISCONSIN'S FAILURE TO SUSPEND
FELLOWSHIP WITH MISSOURI—THE CLIMAX

To those pastors and laymen and teachers who were later to withdraw from the Wisconsin Synod and organize themselves into the Church of the Lutheran Confession (CLC), the climax for the synod came in the 1955 "Saginaw Resolution," when the synod recognized that Missouri was causing divisions and offenses contrary to the Word of Truth, yet failed to terminate fellowship. Instead of voting to suspend fellowship with Missouri, the Wisconsin Synod rather resolved to defer final action to a recessed session in 1956. The following resolution was to be put before this recessed session:

...THAT WHEREAS THE LUTHERAN CHURCH-MISSOURI SYNOD HAS CREATED DIVISIONS AND OFFENSES BY ITS OFFICIAL RESOLUTIONS, POLICIES, AND PRACTICES NOT IN ACCORD WITH SCRIPTURE, WE, IN OBEDIENCE TO THE COMMAND OF OUR LORD IN ROMANS 16:17, TERMINATE OUR FELLOWSHIP WITH THE LUTHERAN CHURCH-MISSOURI SYNOD.[5] *(CLC Response: This began the delaying action on the part of the WELS. It continued until 1961...the obedience that was urged, instead became disobedience.)*

Several members of the Floor Committee which drew up this resolution made the public statement that they were of the conviction that the reasons stated for the delay did not warrant postponement of action upon the resolution, and a goodly number of voting and advisory delegates recorded their names in protest against calling the final vote in a recessed session.

When the recessed session was held the following year in Watertown, Wisconsin, the Wisconsin Synod's Standing Committee on Matters of Church Union recommended to the synod that it hold in abeyance the judgment of the Saginaw Resolutions (the application of Romans 16:17, 18 to the Missouri Synod) until the next convention. This would give the Joint Union Committees of the synods in the Synodical Conference time to meet for discussion. Several meetings were held, but by 1957 the report to the synod was again not favorable. It appeared that Missouri's representatives were not ready to come to grips with all the issues that had arisen between that synod and the Wisconsin Synod and in fact were not ready to even declare the issues divisive. Therefore, the Standing Committee on Matters of Church Union had to report: THE CONTROVERSIAL ISSUES STILL REMAIN WHOLLY UNRESOLVED AND CONTINUED TO CAUSE OFFENSE.[6]

The Floor Committee on Union Matters felt constrained to make the following statement to the 1957 Synod Convention.

...WE FEEL CONSCIENCE-BOUND TO DECLARE PUBLICLY, THAT THESE PRINCIPLES, POLICIES, AND PRACTICES, AND PRACTICES [OF THE MISSOURI SYNOD] CREATE A DIVISION BETWEEN OUR SYNODS WHICH THE LUTHERAN CHURCH-MISSOURI SYNOD ALONE CAN REMOVE.

The Convention Floor Committee on Union Matters offered the following resolution:

THAT WE NOW SUSPEND CHURCH FELLOWSHIP WITH THE LUTHERAN CHURCH-MISSOURI SYNOD ON THE BASIS OF ROMANS 16:17,18, UNTIL THE PRINCIPLE POLICIES, AND PRACTICES IN CONTROVERSY BETWEEN US HAVE RESOLVED IN A THOROUGHLY SCRIPTURAL AND MUTUALLY ACCEPTABLE MANNER...[7]

However, the 1957 Convention of the Wisconsin Synod, meeting in New Ulm, Minnesota, did not adopt the above resolution offered by the Floor Committee. The motion failed to carry by a standing vote 61 to 77, with eight delegates abstaining. Instead, it was resolved...

...THAT WE CONTINUE OUR VIGOROUSLY PROTESTING FELLOWSHIP OVER AGAINST THE LUTHERAN CHURCH-MISSOURI SYNOD, BECAUSE OF THE CON-

TINUATION OF THE OFFENSES WITH WHICH WE HAVE CHARGED THE SISTER SYNOD, ROMANS 16:17,18.[8] *(CLC Response: Again, note the contradiction! In spite of using the passage that calls for separation from a heterodox church, the WELS voted to continue in fellowship, albeit again, in a "protesting" fellowship. Efforts were made by the president to explain the contradiction. The reality is that in 1957 [as in conventions past] the WELS did not follow through with the required action against a body it had recognized as "causing divisions and offenses." A Protest Committee of the WELS stated in an apparent justification of the situation, "Timing and human judgment appear to be the basic sources of the difference of opinion in our circles concerning the problem at hand."—Proceedings, 1957 Wisconsin Synod, p. 147)*

The 1959 Saginaw (Michigan) Convention passed the following resolutions: THAT WE INSTRUCT OUR CHURCH UNION COMMITTEE UNDER THE GUIDANCE OF THE HOLY SPIRIT TO CONTINUE AND ACCELERATE THE DISCUSSION IN THE JOINT UNION COMMITTEES TO BRING ABOUT COMPLETE UNITY OF DOCTRINE AND PRACTICE IN THE SYNODICAL CONFERENCE...THAT WE INSTRUCT OUR CHURCH UNION COMMITTEE TO CONTINUE ITS EFFORTS IN THE JOINT UNION COMMITTEES UNTIL AGREEMENT ON DOCTRINE AND PRACTICE HAS BEEN REACHED, OR UNTIL AN IMPASSE IS REACHED AND NO SUCH AGREEMENT CAN BE BROUGHT ABOUT...Under Resolution No. 2. the following was adopted...THAT IN OUR VIGOROUSLY PROTESTING FELLOWSHIP WITH THE LUTHERAN CHURCH-MISSOURI SYNOD WE TESTIFY STRONGLY AGAINST THE OFFENSES WHICH ARE STILL PREVALENT AND UNRESOLVED IN THE LUTHERAN CHURCH-MISSOURI SYNOD AND REQUEST THAT BODY TO REMOVE THEM, AND TO REFRAIN FROM CAUSING A WIDER BREACH BETWEEN THE MEMBERS OF THE SYNODICAL CONFERENCE.[9]

In "A Report to the Protest Committee," prepared by Professor Carl Lawrenz, the following statement is made (which statement was requested by the Standing Committee on Matters of Church Union and adopted as its own): TERMINATION OF CHURCH FELLOWSHIP IS CALLED FOR WHEN YOU HAVE REACHED THE CONVICTION THAT ADMONITION IS OF NO FURTHER AVAIL AND THAT THE ERRING BROTHER OR CHURCH BODY DEMANDS RECOGNITION FOR THEIR ERROR.[10] *(CLC Response: By the 1959 Convention the official justification for lack of required action was: "Termination of church fellowship is called for when you have reached the conviction that admonition is of no further avail and that the erring brother or church body demands recognition for their error" [Report to the Protest Committee]. Instead of separation, the Church Union Committee was instructed to continue its efforts until an agreement was reached with the LC-MS, or "until an impasse is reached." No longer was action to be dictated by recognition of the false doctrine of a church body that the WELS had said was "causing division and offenses." Instead, the action would be based upon a subjective conclusion that discussions were at an impasse, or that "admonition is of no further avail." A memorial, or overture to the 1959 Convention entitled A CALL FOR DECISION forced the issue. This overture urged the WELS to terminate fellowship with the LC-MS. The overture was rejected. An exodus from the WELS that had begun earlier (1957) now became much larger. After the 1959 Convention, many who later formed the Church of*

788

the Lutheran Confession left the WELS for reasons of conscience.)
In regards to the above-mentioned memorial, A CALL FOR DECISION: This memorial was signed by 30 persons, many of whom later separated from the Wisconsin Synod. The teaching that doctrinal talks are to continue with an erring body until an impasse is reached or until an agreement is reached, is branded by the memorial "as false and unscriptural, and that the argument based upon it is rationalistic and untenable." Synod was asked to disavow it. Then follows what is put forth as "a true and correct statement of the doctrinal issue involved": TERMINATION OF CHURCH FELLOWSHIP IS CALLED FOR WHEN SCRIPTURAL CORRECTION HAS BEEN OFFERED AND REJECTED AND THE ERRING BROTHER OR CHURCH BODY HAVE CONTINUED IN THEIR ERROR DESPITE ADMONITION. THIS IS THE PERSISTENCE WHICH DISTINGUISHES AN ERRORIST (ROMANS 16:17,18) FROM AN ERRING BROTHER (GALATIANS 2:11-14).[11]

THE INTERSYNODICAL ISSUE BECOMES AN INTRASYNODICAL PROBLEM

The chipping off from the Wisconsin Synod began in 1956 when the first congregation broke away. After Wisconsin's 1957 and 1959 Convention, additional congregations, parts of congregations, individual pastors, professors, teachers, and individual members of congregations were compelled by their conscience to leave the Wisconsin Synod. The same process had been taking place—but to a lesser degree—in the Evangelical Lutheran Synod (ELS).

Those who separated from the Wisconsin Synod over the ensuing years did so because of said synod's failures to carry out its 1955 Saginaw Resolution. They were convinced in their consciences that this resolution—which charged the Missouri Synod with causing divisions and offenses, and subsequently declared a termination of fellowship with the Missouri Synod—truthfully and scripturally set forth the situation as it existed, as well as the proper action ("avoid them") to be taken by the Wisconsin Synod. However, neither in Wisconsin's 1956 Recessed Convention nor in the 1957 and 1959 Conventions did the Wisconsin Synod carryout its 1955 Saginaw Resolution.

Even the president of the synod's seminary found it necessary to leave both his post and his synod. Already in 1955 Professor Edmund Reim offered his resignation, but it was not accepted. Two years later, with the subsequent failure of the Wisconsin Synod at its New Ulm (Minnesota) Convention to suspend fellowship with the Missouri Synod, Professor Reim felt that he had been given no other choice but to resign. At this Convention the report and resolutions of the Floor Committee were rejected, which called for suspension of fellowship on the basis of Romans 16:17,18. The resolution was narrowly defeated, and in its place it was resolved to continue "our vigorously protesting fellowship over against The Lutheran Church-Missouri Synod..." The CLC would later—as we have seen in the CLC Responses—be critical of the Wisconsin Synod for this procedure of charging Missouri with causing divisions and offenses, and yet at the same time treating the members of said synod as weak brethren whom they admonished within the realm of fellowship. The CLC would point out that instead of admonishing Missouri within a state of fellowship, Wisconsin should have avoided—separated from—the sister synod.

789

FREE CONFERENCES EVOLVE
INTO THE "INTERIM CONFERENCE,"
WHICH BECOMES THE CLC

The withdrawals were chiefly from the Wisconsin and Evangelical Lutheran Synods. These withdrawals continued through 1961, when Wisconsin finally took action to suspend fellowship with Missouri. The individuals who left the WELS and the ELS because of what they considered to be a false admonition policy sought each other out and met in free conferences seeking mutual encouragement and edification. The first free conference was held in Lyons, Nebraska, in October 1957. This meeting was attended by seven pastors, one teacher, and a number of laymen. The second free conference was held in Mankato, Minnesota, in December of the same year. Not only were these meetings attended by some individuals who had already withdrawn from their synods, others who still maintained their memberships also attended.

Since there was much confusion regarding the doctrine of Fellowship as it had been interpreted and applied over the preceding 20 years, this small group agreed to conduct an intensive study of this doctrine. All interested parties were invited to participate freely. Thus the confessional document "Concerning Church Fellowship" was begun. In addition, since there had been misunderstanding in the Synodical Conference concerning the doctrine of Church and Ministry, a second document was started in order to clarify that matter. Both documents were later included in the confession of the CLC.

By the time of the second free conference about 12 congregations and pastors, one professor, and a number of teachers had withdrawn from synods in the Synodical Conference. Five such congregations were located in the Pacific Northwest. Another pastor and part of his congregation left the synod during the first part of 1958.

Meanwhile, the Board of Trustees of the Wisconsin Synod requested a meeting with Pastor M.J. Witt, who was serving a congregation in the State of Washington, and had separated from the synod. This meeting was held in Los Angeles in order to discuss a settlement in regard to the Japan property. Hachiman Dori Lutheran Church in Tokyo, formerly a mission of the Wisconsin Synod, had withdrawn together with their pastor, Fred Tiefel, from the synod. The mission itself continued discussions with the Wisconsin Synod, but later became the one foreign mission of the CLC. A dollar figure for the Japan property was mutually agreed upon. There was, of course the need to make payments in an orderly and God-pleasing way. The group thought of forming an association for the Japan Mission which would be responsible for making the regular payments.

And so, the group's need to secure the physical plant for the Tokyo mission, their need for one another, and their need to provide mutual encouragement of brothers in far-flung outposts, resulted in the second free conference of those who had withdrawn from their synods, or were in the process of withdrawing. This conference was held in Mankato, Minnesota, at Immanuel Lutheran Church in December 1957.

AT THIS MEETING MUTUAL PROBLEMS WERE DISCUSSED AND ENCOURAGEMENT WAS GIVEN. BUT OF PRIME IMPORTANCE AT THIS MEETING WAS THE PRESENTA-

790

TION OF THE EPITOME OF THE DOCTRINE OF FELLOWSHIP. AFTER A THOROUGH DISCUSSION AND CRITICISM, THE SCRIBE WAS SENT ON HIS WAY WITH THE ENCOURAGEMENT OF THE GROUP TO WRITE THE POSITION PAPER ON FELLOWSHIP ACCORDING TO THE OUTLINE.
THE CHEYENNE MEETING WAS HELD IN MAY 1958 AS A SEQUEL TO THE LYONS AND MANKATO MEETINGS. THE FIRST DRAFT OF THE ESSAY ON CHURCH FELLOWSHIP WAS THOROUGHLY REVIEWED AND EXAMINED IN THE LIGHT OF SCRIPTURE. CERTAIN CHANGES WERE PROPOSED, AND RECEIVED BY THE ESSAYIST. AFTER MORE POLISHING, THE DOCUMENT ON FELLOWSHIP ["CONCERNING CHURCH FELLOWSHIP"] WAS AGAIN READ AND THEN ACCEPTED AS TO ITS ESSENCE AT THE SPOKANE CONFERENCE IN AUGUST 1958.[12]
The essays on the doctrines of Church, Ministry, and the Authority of the Keys had been assigned to be written, and subsequently were delivered and accepted at meetings at Spokane, Washington, in 1958 and at Watertown, South Dakota, in 1960. Pastor M.J. Witt reports that the formal propositions on these doctrines were drawn up by Professor Edmund Reim and edited Professor Egbert Schaller.
The group takes a name:
AFTER A NUMBER OF FREE CONFERENCES, WHEN IT BECAME APPARENT IN WHICH DIRECTION THINGS WERE GOING, THE GROUP CALLED ITSELF THE "INTERIM CONFERENCE." THE NAME FIT THE SITUATION, SINCE AN INTERIM IS THE TIME BETWEEN TWO EVENTS. IN THIS CASE IT HAD REFERENCE TO THE TIME BETWEEN WITHDRAWING FROM ONE SYNODICAL ORGANIZATION AND PARTICIPATING IN THE FORMATION OF ANOTHER...AT THE CONFERENCE IN RED WING, MINNESOTA (AUGUST 1959), A COMMITTEE WAS APPOINTED TO WRITE A CONSTITUTION WHICH WOULD LEAD TO THE ORGANIZATION OF A NEW CHURCH BODY. THESE MEETINGS WERE FILLED WITH ZEAL AND ENTHUSIASM...IN JANUARY OF 1960 AT A CONFERENCE IN MANKATO MORE WORK WAS DONE ON THE CONFESSIONAL WRITINGS AND THE CONSTITUTION. AT THIS TIME DISCUSSION ALSO BEGAN ON A NAME FOR THE NEW GROUP.[13]
The next step was to formally organize the Interim Conference into a fullfledged Lutheran body. Lacking in size, the Conference made up for it in vigor and zeal. The Conference was determined that the new synod be based fully in the Scriptures and the Lutheran Confessions and thus that it be doctrinally sound.
THE TIME HAD COME FOR THE NEXT STEP. THE MEETING SCHEDULED FOR AUGUST OF 1960 AT WATERTOWN, SOUTH DAKOTA, BECAME THE CONSTITUTING CONVENTION. THIS WAS THE PLACE AND THE TIME FOR FORMAL ORGANIZATION TO TAKE PLACE. MUCH TIME WAS SPENT ON THE DOCUMENTS TO BE INCLUDED IN THE CONFESSIONAL ARTICLE OF THE CONSTITUTION. IN ADDITION TO THE USUAL DOCUMENTS FOUND IN THE CONFESSION OF AN ORTHODOX LUTHERAN CHURCH, CONCERNING CHURCH FELLOWSHIP AND THE YET UNFINISHED CHURCH AND MINISTRY WERE INCLUDED...THE ENTIRE CONSTITUTION WAS DISCUSSED, CHANGED, EDITED, AND FINALLY ADOPTED ON FRIDAY AFTERNOON, AUGUST 12. AT THAT MOMENT ALL THOSE PRESENT AROSE AND SANG THE TE DEUM LAUDAMUS AS AN EXPRESSION OF PRAISE AND JOY TO THE LORD FOR WHAT HAD BEEN ACCOMPLISHED IN HIS NAME... [O]PPORTUNITY WAS GIVEN TO THOSE PRESENT TO RECORD THEIR INDIVIDUAL ACCEPTANCE OF THE CONSTITU-

TION BY SIGNING THEIR NAMES TO IT. IN ORDER THAT CONGREGATIONS AND OTHER INDIVIDUALS MIGHT HAVE OPPORTUNITY TO JOIN THE NEW CHURCH BODY, IT WAS RESOLVED THAT THE CONSTITUTION BE PRINTED AND DISTRIBUTED TO ALL GROUPS AND INDIVIDUALS WHO HAD SHOWN AN INTEREST. TIME AND OPPORTUNITY TO READ AND TO STUDY THE CONSTITUTION HAD TO BE GIVEN...[T]HE CONVENTION RECESSED BY DECIDING TO MEET AGAIN IN JANUARY OF 1961, AT SLEEPY EYE, MINNESOTA. IN THE MEANTIME INCORPORATION ACCORDING TO THE LAWS OF MINNESOTA WAS COMPLETED ON DECEMBER 23, 1960...AT THE SLEEPY EYE CONVENTION THE MEMBERSHIP OF THE NEW CHURCH BODY WAS ESTABLISHED. THE CONVENTION REPORT LISTED THIRTY-FOUR CONGREGATIONS, SIXTY-SEVEN PASTORS AND PROFESSORS, TWENTY-ONE TEACHERS, AND SIX SEMINARY STUDENTS AS CHARTER MEMBERS. HOWEVER, APPLICATIONS FOR CHARTER MEMBERSHIP BY CONGREGATIONS AND PASTORS WERE RECEIVED UNTIL THE END OF THE AUGUST 1961 CONVENTION IN SPOKANE, WASHINGTON.[14]

The name, CHURCH OF THE LUTHERAN CONFESSION (CLC), was chosen on August 11, 1961 at the Spokane Convention. At this Convention the following officers were elected: President-Pastor Paul Albrecht, of Bowdle, South Dakota; Vice-president-Pastor M.J. Witt, of Spokane. Washington; Moderator-Pastor C.M. Gullerud, of Mankato, Minnesota; Secretary-Pastor Paul F. Nolting, of Sleepy Eye, Minnesota.

At the Spokane Convention in 1962 three more pastors and eight congregations were added as charter members of the CLC. Two congregations were received as confessional members.

The CLC was divided into five regional conferences: Eastern, Minnesota, Pacific Coast, West Central, and Wisconsin. Congregations according to states: ARIZONA-1; CALFORNIA-3; COLORADO-4; FLORIDA-1; GEORGIA-1; IDAHO-1; ILLINOIS-1; MICHIGAN-6; MINNESOTA-17; (INCLUDING 1 INSTITUTIONAL MISSIONARY AT ROCHESTER); MISSOURI-1; MONTANA-1; NEBRASKA-2; NEW MEXICO-1; NORTH CAROLINA-1; WASHINGTON-4; WISCONSIN-10 (SERVICES WERE ALSO PROVIDED FOR THE RETARDED AT MADISON); WYOMING-1. TOTAL OF 56 CONGREGATIONS. *(Note: The 2001-2002 CLC Directory lists 78 congregations and preaching stations in 21 states. Also, 1 congregation each in Alberta and British Columbia, Canada.)* The following official boards were established: Board of Trustees, Board of Doctrine, Board of Education, Board of Regents of Immanuel Lutheran College, Board of Missions, Book House Board.

THE CHURCH OF THE LUTHERAN CONFESSIONCONFESSIONAL LUTHERANISM

THE CLC'S STAND ON CERTAIN ISSUES

(Note: the offered Scripture passages are not included in the following quotations.)
The CLC:
1-ACCEPTS THE SCRIPTURES AS THE TOTALLY INSPIRED AND TOTALLY INERRANT WORD OF GOD...AND BELIEVES THAT THE CHIEF PURPOSE OF SCRIPTURE IS TO

MAKE WISE UNTO SALVATION.

2-HOLDS A "QUIA" SUBSCRIPTION TO THE LUTHERAN CONFESSIONS AS SET FORTH IN THE BOOK OF CONCORD OF 1850. [QUIA="BECAUSE" THE CONFESSIONS ARE A TRUE EXPOSITION OF THE SCRIPTURES.]

3-BELIEVES THAT THE TRIUNE GOD CREATED THE HEAVEN AND THE EARTH...CONSEQUENTLY, WE REJECT EVOLUTIONISM.

4-HOLDS TO THE HISTORIC LUTHERAN PRACTICE DRAWN FROM SCRIPTURE WITH RESPECT TO THE ROLE OF MEN AND WOMEN IN THE CHURCH. IT PROCLAIMS EQUALITY AT THE CROSS, AS SCRIPTURE DOES. IT REJECTS WOMAN SUFFRAGE WITHIN THE CHURCH AND THE ORDINATION OF WOMEN AS CONTRARY TO SCRIPTURE AND THUS SETS FORTH THE HISTORIC AND CORRECT LUTHERAN DOCTRINE AND PRACTICE DRAWN FROM SCRIPTURE.

5-IS COMMITTED TO THE HISTORIC LUTHERAN DISTINCTION BETWEEN LAW AND GOSPEL AS SET FORTH IN SCRIPTURE AND THE LUTHERAN CONFESSIONS AND ELUCIDATED BY CFW WALTHER IN LAW AND GOSPEL.

6-TEACHES JUSTIFICATION BY GRACE THROUGH FAITH IN CHRIST JESUS.

7-PRACTICES WITHOUT QUALIFICATION "CLOSED COMMUNION."

8-REJECTS THE CHURCH GROWTH MOVEMENT WITH ITS EMPHASIS ON NUMBERS, PROGRAMS, ETC. AND ITS CONSEQUENT DIMINUTION OF AND REJECTION OF THE MEANS OF GRACE.

9-EXPECTS ALL PASTORS, TEACHERS AND PROFESSORS TO TEACH IN ACCORD WITH THE SCRIPTURES AND THE LUTHERAN CONFESSIONS, DRAWN FROM THE SCRIPTURES. WE ARE ALL TO SPEAK THE SAME THING, BEING OF THE SAME MIND AND THE SAME JUDGMENT IN MATTERS OF DOCTRINE.

10-REJECTS AS SINFUL UNIONISM ANY JOINT RELIGIOUS ENDEAVORS WITH SUCH AS ARE NOT AGREED IN THE DOCTRINES OF SCRIPTURE. THIS INCLUDES ORGANIZATIONS IN WHICH RELIGIOUS ELEMENTS CONTRARY TO SCRIPTURE ARE AN ESSENTIAL PART OF THE ORGANIZATION (E.G. LODGES, SCOUTING).

11-REJECTS HOMOSEXUALITY AND ABORTION. WE WILL EXERCISE LOVE TOWARD SUCH AS ARE CAUGHT IN SUCH SINS, WITH THE INTENT TO CONVINCE THEM FROM THE SCRIPTURE OF THEIR SIN; WE WILL COMFORT THE PENITENT WITH THE GOSPEL, AS WELL AS LEND OUR SUPPORT TO THEM IN THEIR STRUGGLE AGAINST SUCH SINS.

12-BELIEVES THAT IN ALL MATTERS OF DOCTRINE AND FAITH WE ARE TO BE OF ONE MIND, BOUND BY THE SCRIPTURES...IN MATTERS NOT SET FORTH IN SCRIPTURE, THE CHRISTIAN IS FREE TO EXERCISE HIS CONSCIENCE AND WILL, BUT ALWAYS IN LOVE TOWARD AND CONSIDERATION FOR THE BRETHREN AND THE NEIGHBOR.

13-INSISTS ON THE SEPARATION OF CHURCH AND STATE.

14-TEACHES FROM SCRIPTURE THAT THERE IS A REAL HEAVEN AND A REAL HELL.

15-BELIEVES AND TEACHES THAT WHEN CHRIST RETURNS HE WILL JUDGE THE LIVING AND THE DEAD, AS IS CONFESSED IN THE APOSTOLIC CREED.

16-ADOPTS NO PARTICULAR BIBLE VERSION...THE SAME HOLDS TRUE WITH RESPECT TO A HYMNAL. HOWEVER, IN COMMON USE AMONG US IS THE OLD SYNODICAL CONFERENCE BOOK, THE LUTHERAN HYMNAL.

17-HAS TWO PUBLICATIONS, THE LUTHERAN SPOKESMAN, AND THE JOURNAL OF THEOLOGY,

18-PUTS EMPHASIS ON CHRISTIAN EDUCATION AT ALL LEVELS BEGINNING AT

793

THE ELEMENTARY LEVEL.

19-REJECTS THE CHARISMATIC MOVEMENT BUT BELIEVES THAT THE SPIRIT OF GOD WORKS ONLY THROUGH THE MEANS OF GRACE TO CONVERT TO FAITH AND TO CONFIRM IN FAITH. THE MARKS OF THE CHURCH ARE THE MEANS OF GRACE—THE GOSPEL IN WORD AND SACRAMENT. WHERE THE MEANS OF GRACE ARE PRESENT, GOD WILL HAVE HIS CHILDREN. THERE THE HOLY CHRISTIAN CHURCH IS FOUND, THE MEMBERS OF WHICH ONLY THE LORD, WHO READS THE HEART, KNOWS.

FINALLY, WE RECOGNIZE THAT INSISTENCE ON PURE DOCTRINE IS NOT FOR DOCTRINE'S SAKE ALONE, BUT BECAUSE THE CAUSE OF THE GOSPEL IS SERVED AND HEARTS TRULY COMFORTED ONLY WHEN THE DOCTRINE TAUGHT IS THAT COMMITTED UNTO US BY THE LORD THROUGH HIS WORD. OUR LORD HIMSELF SAYS, "IF YOU CONTINUE IN MY WORD THEN YOU ARE MY DISCIPLES INDEED. AND YOU SHALL KNOW THE TRUTH, AND THE TRUTH SHALL MAKE YOU FREE" (JOHN 8:31,32). THE FACT THAT THE LORD HAS HIS BELIEVERS IN WHATEVER FELLOWSHIP THE GOSPEL OF CHRIST IS STILL PROCLAIMED DOES NOT GIVE THE CHURCH LICENSE TO COMPROMISE SCRIPTURE AT ANY POINT. TO DO SO RUNS THE RISK OF LOSING THE TRUTH COMPLETELY. "SEPARATION FOR THE SAKE OF PRESERVATION" FAIRLY DESCRIBES OUR FELLOWSHIP PRINCIPLE.[15]

THE DOCTRINE STAND OF THE CLC

The Church of the Lutheran Confession is an orthodox Lutheran Church which subscribes without equivocation to the Holy Scriptures and the Lutheran Confessions. Under ARTICLE III: CONFESSIONS, we find the following statements of special interest:

A. WE ACCEPT WITHOUT RESERVATION THE CANONICAL SCRIPTURES OF THE OLD AND NEW TESTAMENTS AS THE VERBALLY INSPIRED WORD OF GOD...AND THEREFORE AS THE SOLE AND ONLY INFALLIBLE RULE OF DOCTRINE AND LIFE.

B. WE CONFESS THE *APOSTOLIC, NICENE,* AND *ATHANASIAN CREEDS* AND THE PARTICULAR SYMBOLS OF THE LUTHERAN CHURCH AS PUBLISHED IN THE *BOOK OF CONCORD OF 1580,* BECAUSE THEY ARE A TRUE EXPOSITION OF THE TEACHINGS OF THE WORD OF GOD (EMPHASIS ADDED).

C. WE SUBSCRIBE TO THE BRIEF STATEMENT OF 1932.

IN ADDITION...THE FOLLOWING DOCUMENTS: CONCERNING CHURCH FELLOWSIP, THESES ON THE RELATION OF SYNOD AND LOCAL CONGREGATION TO THE HOLY CHRISTIAN CHURCH, AND THESES ON THE MINISTRY OF THE KEYS AND THE PUBLIC MINISTRY.

Under Article II: PURPOSE, the following points is of special interest:

TO PROTECT THIS FELLOWSHIP AGAINST THE ENCROACHMENT OF ERROR AND UNIONISM THROUGH UNITED TESTIMONY AND DOCTRINAL DISCIPLINE.

Under ARTICLE VIII: SUPERVISION AND DISCIPLINE, the following is noted:

WHEN MEMBERS OF THIS BODY ARE CAUSING DIVISIONS AND OFFENSES CONTRARY TO THE DOCTRINE WHICH WE HAVE LEARNED, THE PRESIDENT, IN CONJUNCTION WITH THE VICE-PRESIDENT, SHALL BE HELD TO DECLARE A SUSPENSION OF FELLOWSHIP WITH THE OFFENDERS. IF THIS SHOULD INVOLVE

THE PASTOR OR TEACHER OF A CONGREGATION, SUCH A DECLARATION SHOULD
NOT BE MADE WITHOUT FULL CONSIDERATION HAVING FIRST BEEN GIVEN TO
THE RIGHTS OF THE LOCAL CONGREGATIONS AND SPECIFICALLY THE SANCTITY
OF THE CALL.

THE CLC'S STAND ON THE DOCTRINE
OF CHURCH FELLOWSHIP

Since the doctrine of Church Fellowship figures so prominently in the controversy that tore the Synodical Conference asunder and presently keeps the
Wisconsin Synod (as well as the Evangelical Lutheran Synod) and the Church
of the Lutheran Confession apart, it would be beneficial to at least touch upon
some of the statements presented in the CLC's "Concerning Church Fellowship." Of special interest are statements concerning the action of separating
from errorists, and the place of admonition in a doctrinal controversy.

(6) THOUGH THE MANNER OF SPEAKING MAY VARY, YET THE TRUTH SPOKEN
MUST BE EVER ONE AND THE SAME THING.

(7) THUS THE CHURCH TOLERATES NO DIVISIONS...ALL MEMBERS OF THE
CHURCH ARE TO SPEAK THE SAME THING. (1 COR. 1:10)

(8) IN SO FAR AS WE ARE MEMBERS OF THE CHURCH WE MAY SPEAK, CONFESS,
AND TEACH ONLY THE WORD. (1 PET. 4:11)

(9) WE ACCORDINGLY TEACH THAT THE HOLY SCRIPTURES DIFFER FROM ALL
OTHER BOOKS IN THE WORLD IN THAT THEY ARE THE WORD OF GOD...THE HOLY
MEN OF GOD WHO WROTE THE SCRIPTURES WROTE ONLY THAT WHICH THE
HOLY GHOST COMMUNICATED TO THEM BY INSPIRATION. (2 TIM. 3:16; 2 PET.
1:21)

(12) WE FURTHER BELIEVE THAT THIS INERRANT SCRIPTURE, WHICH IS THE
SOLE AUTHORITY FOR ALL DOCTRINE IN THE CHURCH, IS INVIOLABLE...THIS
QUALITY...SUFFERS AT THE HANDS OF ALL WHO IN THESE DAYS DESIRE LATI-
TUDE IN MATTERS OF DOCTRINE.

(13) NEITHER, DO WE BELIEVE, IS THERE ROOM FOR PRIVATE INTERPRETATION
OF SCRIPTURE ON THE BASIS OF ANY SUPPOSED AMBIGUITY OR UNCLARITY IN
THE DIVINE REVELATION...TO SAY THAT THE BIBLE IS UNCLEAR IS BLASPHEMY.

(14) [THUS]...ALL ABERRATIONS FROM HOLY SCRIPTURE ARE CONDEMNED.
FOR WHAT IS FALSE MAY NOT BE MIXED WITH TRUTH. (JER. 23:38, ETC.)

(15) IT WOULD BE TEMPTING OF THE HOLY GOD EVEN TO MAKE A DISTINCTION
BETWEEN SMALL AND GREAT ABERRATIONS.

(16) THIS THEN IS ALSO THE REASON WHY SCRIPTURE SO EMPHATICALLY AND
BLUNTLY DEMANDS THAT CHRISTIANS SEPARATE THEMSELVES FROM ALL WHO
DEVIATE IN THEIR DOCTRINAL POSITION FROM THE TRUTH OF GOD'S WORD.

(17) (A)LL CHRISTIANS ARE REQUIRED BY GOD TO DISCRIMINATE BETWEEN OR-
THODOX AND HETERODOX CHURCH BODIES, MATTHEW 5:15, TO HAVE CHURCH
FELLOWSHIP ONLY WITH ORTHODOX CHURCH BODIES, AND, IN CASE THEY HAVE
STRAYED INTO HETERODOX CHURCH BODIES, TO LEAVE THEM, ROMANS 16:17.
WE REPUDIATE UNIONISM, THAT IS, CHURCH FELLOWSHIP WITH THE ADHERENTS
OF FALSE DOCTRINE, AS DISOBEDIENCE TO GOD'S COMMAND, AS CAUSING DIVI-
SIONS IN THE CHURCH, ROMANS 16:17; 2 JOHN 9:10, AND AS INVOLVING THE

CONSTANT DANGER OF LOSING THE WORD OF GOD ENTIRELY, 2 TIMOTHY 2:17-21.

(18) THIS THEN IS A PURE OR ORTHODOX CHURCH WHICH ADHERES TO THE UNADULTERATED DOCTRINE OF GOD'S WORD AND ADMINISTERS THE SACRAMENTS ACCORDING TO THEIR DIVINE INSTITUTIONS...A CHURCH WHICH CONTRARY TO THE DIVINE ORDINANCE TOLERATES FALSE DOCTRINE IN ITS MIDST OR DEVIATES FROM THE DIVINE INSTITUTION IN THE ADMINISTRATION OF THE SACRAMENTS IS RIGHTLY CALLED AN IMPURE OR HETERODOX CHURCH.

(19) [HETERODOX CHURCH BODIES]...ARE NOT DESIRED BY GOD, BUT EXIST BY HIS PERMISSION ONLY. AND THEREBY WE DO NOT DENY THAT THERE ARE DEAR CHILDREN OF GOD IN HETERODOX CHURCHES.

(20) (A)LL CHRISTIANS ARE REQUIRED BY GOD TO DISCRIMINATE BETWEEN FALSE AND TRUE CHURCHES AS WELL AS TEACHERS (1 JOHN 4:1; MATTHEW 7:15)

(21) ....CHRISTIANS ARE REQUIRED TO HAVE CHURCH FELLOWSHIP ONLY WITH ORTHODOX CHURCH BODIES.

(23) FALSE TEACHING IS UNRIGHTEOUSNESS AND THERE CAN BE NO FELLOWSHIP WITH IT. FALSE DOCTRINE IS DARKNESS AND TRUE REVEALED DOCTRINE IS THE LIGHT OF THE WORLD...SCRIPTURE TEACHES THAT WE SHOULD COME OUT FROM AMONG THEM, THAT IS FROM THE ADHERENTS AND TEACHERS OF ERROR, AND BE SEPARATE.

(24) THAT THIS APPLIES TO ALL HETERODOX TEACHERS AND BODIES IS TAUGHT CLEARLY AND EXPLICITLY IN ROMANS 16:17. "NOW I BESEECH YOU, BRETHREN, MARK THEM WHICH CAUSE DIVISIONS AND OFFENSES (A CAUSE OF STUMBLING, SNARE TO ONE'S FAITH) CONTRARY TO THE DOCTRINE WHICH YE HAVE LEARNED; AND AVOID THEM."

(25) (F)ELLOWSHIP IS TO BE BASED ON ONE THING ONLY, THE DOCTRINE WHICH IS PROCLAIMED OR CONFESSED.

(27) WE THEREFORE BELIEVE AND TEACH THAT CHRISTIAN FELLOWSHIP IS BASED ONLY ON PROFESSION OF FAITH, BY WORD AND DEED (1 JOHN 4:2-3)

(28) (W)E DO NOT SEPARATE OURSELVES FROM THE CHILDREN OF GOD AMONG THE FALSE SECTS, BUT FROM THE SECTS AS SUCH. THE SECTS SEPARATE THESE DEAR CHILDREN OF GOD FROM US. WE BELIEVE THAT IT IS FOR THE BENEFIT OF THE TRUE BELIEVERS AMONG THE HETERODOX THAT WE ARE TO REFUSE FELLOWSHIP TO THESE CHURCHES.

(29) WE FURTHER BELIEVE, TEACH AND CONFESS THAT THERE ARE NO EXCEPTIONS TO THIS PRECEPT TO AVOID ALL FALSE TEACHERS AND THEIR ADHERENTS... "A LITTLE LEAVEN LEAVENETH THE WHOLE LUMP" (GALATIANS 5:9)

(33) WHERE PRIDE IN ONE'S SELF OR IN ONE'S PARTICULAR GROUPS IS THE MOTIVE FOR ISOLATION, THIS IS SINFUL AND SHOWS A GRAVE LACK OF UNDERSTANDING OF THE GOSPEL.

(42) (W)HEN OUR LORD JESUS CHRIST FORBIDS US TO EXERCISE CHURCH FELLOWSHIP WITH THOSE WHO DEVIATE IN THEIR TEACHINGS FROM THE WORD OF GOD...THEREBY ALL MANIFESTATIONS OF CHRISTIAN FELLOWSHIP ARE FORBIDDEN.

(44) THE PEOPLE WHO ADHERE TO FALSE TEACHING ARE TO BE SHUNNED AND AVOIDED...WHERE UNITY OF THE CONFESSED FAITH, UNITY IN THE WORD, IS

ABSENT, WE ARE FORBIDDEN TO PRACTICE ANY FELLOWSHIP.

(46) (E)STABLISHED FELLOWSHIPS OR EXISTING FELLOWSHIPS ARE TO BE TER-
MINATED WHEN IT HAS BEEN ASCERTAINED THAT A PERSON OR GROUP THROUGH
A FALSE POSITION IS CAUSING DIVISIONS AND OFFENSES IN THE CHURCH.

(48) THOUGH WE INSTRUCT WITH ALL LONG-SUFFERING IN DOCTRINE SUCH AS
THROUGH IGNORANCE HOLD ERRONEOUS OPINIONS AND BELIEFS, THIS IN NO
WISE RESTRICTS OR LIMITS THE AVOIDING OF THOSE WHO BY THEIR DEVIATIONS
"CAUSE DIVISIONS AND OFFENSES" IN THE CHURCH...THOSE CANNOT BE
TREATED AS "WEAK" BRETHREN WHO ARE PUBLICLY TEACHING THEIR ERRO-
NEOUS OPINIONS AS GOD'S TRUTH.

(51) THINKING THAT THEY ARE SERVING THE CAUSE OF TRUTH, MANY IN OUR
DAY HAVE MADE A SELECTION OF DOCTRINES WHICH THEY SAY ARE NECESSARY
FOR SAVING FAITH, AND RESTRICT THE PRINCIPLE OF SEPARATION TO THOSE
WHO IN SOME WAY DENY THE REDEMPTIVE WORK OF CHRIST. BUT ACTUALLY
THEY ARE SERVING THE CAUSE OF UNIONISM, NAMELY BY THEIR FELLOWSHIP
WITH THOSE WHO ERR IN ANY DOCTRINE OF SCRIPTURE...WE REPUDIATE SUCH
GROUPS AS SINFULLY UNIONISTIC...

(59) THE DISTINCTION BETWEEN FUNDAMENTAL AND NON-FUNDAMENTAL DOC-
TRINES HAS ITS PLACE, BUT THAT PLACE IS MOST CERTAINLY NOT IN THE QUES-
TION OF WHAT CONSTITUTES A SUFFICIENT BASIS FOR CHURCH
FELLOWSHIP...THEY ARE ALL DOCTRINES OF FAITH, I.E., DOCTRINES TO BE AC-
CEPTED IN FAITH.

(61) WE FURTHER REJECT THE TEACHING THAT FALSE TEACHERS AND
CHURCHES ARE TO BE AVOIDED ONLY WHEN THEY NO LONGER LISTEN TO ADMO-
NITION...WHEN ERRORISTS BY THEIR ADHERENCE TO THEIR ERRORS "CAUSE DI-
VISIONS AND OFFENCES" IN THE CHURCH, WE ARE TOLD BY THE HOLY GHOST
THROUGH THE APOSTLE PAUL IN ROMANS 16:17 TO AVOID THEM.

(63) (W)E FULLY BELIEVE IN DEALING PATIENTLY AND LOVINGLY WITH WEAK
BRETHREN. IN EVERY CONGREGATION THERE ARE CHRISTIANS WHO ARE STRONG
AND OTHERS WHO ARE WEAK...THUS THE CHURCH IS EVER BUSY AT THIS TASK
OF STRENGTHENING THE WEAK IN ITS MIDST, THE "TEACHING THEM TO OB-
SERVE"...BUT WE MOST ASSUREDLY OBJECT TO THIS, THAT THIS TEACHING AND
ADMONISHING FUNCTION BE OF NECESSITY CARRIED INTO THE PROCESS OF SEP-
ARATING FROM ERRORISTS.

(65) (A)NY CHRISTIAN OUGHT TO BE VERY SURE BEFORE HE WILL RAISE THE
CRY OF FALSE TEACHER. HE WILL MAKE CAREFUL INQUIRY AND ASCERTAIN EX-
ACTLY WHAT IS BEING TAUGHT BY THE SUSPECTED SPEAKER. THIS MAY REQUIRE
LITTLE OR MUCH TIME. IN THE CASE OF A PERSON OR GROUP WITH WHOM ONE
HAS BEEN IN FELLOWSHIP, IT WILL BY ITS NATURE INVOLVE AN ADMONITION,
OR SEVERAL ADMONITIONS. BUT WE EMPHATICALLY TEACH THAT THE ADMON-
ISHING PER SE AND BY ITSELF IS NOT AN ABSOLUTE MUST, A CONDITION SINE QUA
NON, FOR THE APPLICATION OF "AVOID THEM." AS WE HAVE SEEN, THERE MAY
BE YEARS OF ADMONITION BEFORE A PERSON IS REVEALED AS CAUSING DIVISIONS
AND OFFENSES BY HIS ERRORS, OR IT COULD BECOME CLEAR AT ONE MEETING
THAT THE BASIS FOR FELLOWSHIP BAS BEEN REMOVED BY ADHERENCE TO
ERROR. THE ARGUMENT THAT SEPARATION MUST BE DELAYED AS LONG AS THE
ERRORIST WILL LISTEN TO ADMONITION DOES NOT TAKE INTO ACCOUNT THAT

HE IS NOT ONLY LISTENING, BUT HE IS TEACHING HIS ERROR AT THE SAME TIME. (66) IF THE ERRORIST WOULD ALWAYS SUFFER ISOLATION FROM THE CHURCH, HE COULD BE INDUCED TO GIVE SERIOUS THOUGHT TO HIS ABERRATIONS.

(73) IN AN AGE NOTED FOR DOCTRINAL INDIFFERENCE...IT IS PARTICULARLY DAMAGING AND HARMFUL TO URGE THE PROPOSITION THAT ONE SHOULD NOT TERMINATE FELLOWSHIP UNTIL THE FALSE TEACHER OR FALSE CHURCH REFUSES TO LISTEN TO ADMONITION, SINCE IT IS CHARACTERISTIC OF ERRORISTS AND UNIONISTS, WHO BREATHE THE VERY AIR OF COMPROMISE, TO BE WILLING TO LEND AN EAR FOREVER, SO TO SPEAK, TO WHAT THEY TERM, "ANOTHER POINT OF VIEW."

(86) ON THE OTHER HAND, A CHURCH DOES NOT FORFEIT ITS ORTHODOX CHARACTER THROUGH THE CASUAL INTRUSION OF ERROR, PROVIDED THESE ARE COMBATED AND EVENTUALLY REMOVED BY MEANS OF DOCTRINAL DISCIPLINE, ACTS 20:30; 1 TIMOTHY 1:3.

(87) SOMETIMES, HOWEVER, THE ISSUE IS IN DOUBT, FOR ITS IS NOT CLEAR WHETHER THE ERROR HAS TAKEN SUCH A FIRM HOLD THAT IT HAS BECOME...PUBLIC DOCTRINE OF THE GROUPS, OR WHETHER IT IS BEING COMBATED SUCCESSFULLY AND ERADICATED. DURING SUCH A PERIOD OF STRIFE, AND IN ORDER TO MAKE HIS CONFESSION CLEAR, THE CHRISTIAN WILL BE COMPELLED PUBLICLY TO DISAVOW THE VARIOUS STATEMENTS ACTIONS AND POLICIES WHICH ARE NOT CONSISTENT WITH SCRIPTURE, BEFORE, HOWEVER, BREAKING THE ORGANIZATIONAL BOND.

(88) WHEN, HOWEVER SUCH A STATE OF PROTESTING FELLOWSHIP IS PROCLAIMED, BUT BUSINESS IS CARRIED ON AS USUAL, WITH THE INDIVIDUAL CONTINUING TO TREAT THE ERRORISTS AS THOUGH THEY ARE STILL FAITHFUL TEACHERS AND HEARERS OF THE WORD...THEN THAT USE OF THE EXPRESSION IS TO BE CONDEMNED AS A CLOAK OF UNIONISTIC ACTIVITY. WITHOUT THE APPROPRIATE ACTION IT BECOMES MERE LIP-SERVICE.[16]

THE POINT OF CONTROVERSY BETWEEN
THE CLC AND THE WISCONSIN SYNOD

Those who severed their connection with the Wisconsin Synod during the later years of said synod's controversy with the Missouri Synod, did so first of all because they recognized the Missouri Synod as "causers of divisions and offenses contrary to the doctrine" (Romans 16:17, 18), and secondly, because the Wisconsin Synod failed to carry out the resolutions of its own Standing Committee and the Convention Floor Committees, which repeatedly called for the synod to recognize the Missouri Synod as a causer of division and offenses and therefore to take the action to avoid her.

The area of disagreement between the two synods is not in the principle itself of separating from errorists. Both bodies agree to the necessity of separating from errorists. The Wisconsin Synod, early in its history, had learned from the Missouri Synod to take a solid stand against unionism of any form. Where then does the area of disagreement lie? Pastor Paul F. Nolting of the CLC in an essay titled "Mark...Avoid," written on the occasion of the tenth anniversary of the new body, summarized the area of disagreement as the members of the

798

CLC see it:

THE DISAGREEMENT REVOLVES ABOUT THE PROBLEM OF IDENTIFYING PEOPLE AS ERRORISTS WHEN THEY ARISE AMONG BRETHREN. THE WELS [WISCONSIN EV. LUTHERAN SYNOD] SEEMS TO CONTEND THAT THE DISAGREEMENT IS A MATTER OF HUMAN JUDGMENT AS TO WHEN THE CONVICTION OR JUDGMENT IS REACHED THAT THOSE WHO HAVE INTRODUCED ERROR COME UNDER THE INDICTMENT OF ROMANS 16:17,18—THAT IS, BECOME SUCH WHO ARE "CAUSING DIVISIONS AND OFFENSES" IN THE CHURCH AND SO MUST BE "AVOIDED." THE CLC CONTENDS THAT THE DISAGREEMENT IS NOT A MATTER OF HUMAN JUDGMENT AS TO WHEN BUT RATHER A MATTER OF DISAGREEMENT AS TO HOW A PERSON OR PERSONS ARE TO BE IDENTIFIED AS SUCH WHO ARE "CAUSING DIVISIONS AND OFFENSES," AND HENCE MUST BE "AVOIDED." DOCTRINE IS INVOLVED, NOT JUST HUMAN JUDGMENT.

The essayist then breaks the disagreement down into its component parts as the men of the CLC view it:

A)   INTRUSION OF ERROR—HOW? TOWARDS THE END OF THE 1939 TO 1961 PERIOD THE WELS WAS COMPELLED, BY DISSENT FROM HER OWN RANKS, TO JUSTIFY HER CONTINUED FELLOWSHIP WITH MISSOURI DESPITE MISSOURI'S ERRORS. THE WELS ASSUMED THE STANCE OF ADMONISHING MISSOURI AS WEAK BRETHREN. THUS THE WELS RETROACTIVELY TOOK THE POSITION THAT THE INTRUSION OF ERROR INTO ORTHODOX MISSOURI WAS DUE TO WEAKNESS AND/OR INADVERTENCE, AND THAT HENCE THE SITUATION CALLED FOR ADMONITION, WHICH INEVITABLY BECAME A LENGTHY PROCESS BECAUSE OF THE DIFFICULTY IN DEALING WITH A LARGE CHURCH BODY. THE CLC HAS LABELED THIS DIAGNOSIS AND PRESCRIBED CURE "THE WEAK BROTHER APPROACH." THE WELS THUS LABORED UNDER THE TENSION OF TWO CONFLICTING PRINCIPLES:

"...(T)HE GREAT DEBT OF LOVE WHICH THE LORD WOULD HAVE US PAY TO THE WEAK BROTHER, AND HIS CLEAR INJUNCTION TO AVOID THOSE WHO ADHERE TO FALSE DOCTRINE AND PRACTICE AND ALL WHO MAKE THEMSELVES PARTAKERS OF THEIR EVIL DEED."[17]   BUT THE INTRUSION OF ERROR INTO THE LONG-ESTABLISHED CONFESSIONAL POSITION OF AN ORTHODOX CHURCH BODY—OVER THE STRENUOUS PROTESTS OF SOME OF ITS OWN MEMBERS, DESPITE HER RECENT REJECTION OF ALL PREVIOUS EFFORTS TO ACHIEVE FELLOWSHIP WITHOUT UNITY, AND CONTRARY TO HER OWN RECENTLY REAFFIRMED CONFESSIONAL POSITION (BRIEF STATEMENT, 1932)—CAN HARDLY BE ATTRIBUTED TO EITHER WEAKNESS OR INADVERTENCE. THE 1938 CONVENTION OF MISSOURI, WHICH TOOK THE FIRST STEP TO BRIDGE THE GAP BETWEEN THE LCMS AND THE ALC AT THE EXPENSE OF THE TRUTH, ACTED WITH DELIBERATION AND RESPONSIBILITY. TO JUDGE OTHERWISE IS TO DISREGARD THE FACT OF THE CASE.

WE HOLD THAT "THE TREATMENT DUE A WEAK BROTHER IS ENTIRELY OUT OF PLACE WHEN DEALING WITH RESPONSIBLE LEADERS."[18]   IN 1938 MISSOURI TOOK A CALCULATED STEP AWAY FROM ITS FORMER CONFESSIONAL PLATFORM THAT AGREEMENT IN ALL THE DOCTRINES OF SCRIPTURE IS NECESSARY FOR FELLOWSHIP. IN 1969 THE GOAL OF FELLOWSHIP WITH TALC [THE AMERICAN LUTHERAN CHURCH] WAS ACHIEVED ON THE PLATFORM THAT FULL AGREEMENT IN ALL SCRIPTURAL DOCTRINE IS NOT NECESSARY. BEGINNING AT THE MID-FIFTIES, BUT THINKING RETROACTIVELY AND CONTINUING UNTIL 1961, THE

WELS DEALT WITH MISSOURI AS A "WEAK BROTHER." THIS APPROACH LED THE WELS ASTRAY.

B) INTRUSION OF ERROR—BY WHOM AND TO WHAT END? WHENEVER ERROR ARISES IN AN ORTHODOX CHURCH BODY, TWO QUESTIONS NEED TO BE ASKED: BY WHOM? AND, TO WHAT END? IF THE ERROR IS SPOKEN BY A "SIMPLE" (ROMANS 16:18) CHRISTIAN BECAUSE HE JUST DOESN'T KNOW OR IS CONFUSED OR MADE A SLIP OF THE TONGUE, THEN PATIENT ADMONITION IS CALLED FOR— WHICH TAKES THE FORM OF INSTRUCTION IN THE WORD OF TRUTH. SUCH A PERSON WAS "JUST TALKING." HE WASN'T TRYING TO INSTRUCT ANYONE OR GAIN A FOLLOWING. BUT WHEN TEACHERS IN THE CHURCH—EITHER CLERGY OR LAYMEN, AND WHEN DULY INFORMED CONVENTIONS AND RESPONSIBLE LEADERS OF CHURCH BODIES SPEAK ERROR, THE SITUATION IS DIFFERENT. SUCH SPEAK AS TEACHERS AND SPIRITUAL LEADERS WHOSE AIM IS ALWAYS TO GAIN A HEAR- ING, TO WIN DISCIPLES OR FOLLOWERS. THE LORD SAYS OF SUCH, "BEWARE!" ST. PAUL URGES US TO "AVOID" SUCH, LEST THEY "DECEIVE THE HEARTS OF THE SIMPLE"—THE COMMON MAN IN THE PEW AND THE CHILDREN. WISCONSIN FOL- LOWED AN APPROACH THAT LED THEM TO TREAT THE RESPONSIBLE LEADERS OF MISSOURI AS THOUGH THEY WERE LEARNERS, WEAK BRETHREN. FALSE PROPHETS FREQUENTLY GIVE EVERY APPEARANCE OF BEING WILLING TO LISTEN AND LEARN—PROVIDED THEY ARE LEFT FREE TO CONTINUE TEACHING THEIR ERRORS. THIS IS THE WAY OF THE UNIONIST, NOT THE WEAK BROTHER.

C) MARKING—ADMONITION? DOES THE "MARKING" THAT ST. PAUL URGES US TO DO IN ROMANS 16:17 INVOLVE ADMONITION? THE SIMPLE ANSWER IS, "NO." THE ROMANS PASSAGE IS THAT THOSE TEACHING AND PREACHING OTH- ERWISE THAN GOD'S WORD TEACHES BE AVOIDED—ISOLATED—FOR PROTEC- TION OF THE FLOCK. CONCERN FOR THE ERRORIST IS A SECONDARY MATTER. IN ACTUAL SITUATIONS THAT ARISE ADMONITION ORDINARILY PRECEDES THE "MARKING," BUT MAY BE INVOLVED IN THE "MARKING" TO THE EXTENT THAT IT IS NECESSARY TO ASCERTAIN WHETHER ONE IS, IN FACT, DEALING WITH PERSONS WHO ARE "CAUSING DIVISIONS AND OFFENSES" IN THE CHURCH OR WITH SUCH AS HAVE INADVERTENTLY FALLEN INTO ERROR.

IN THE HISTORICAL SITUATION OF THE WELS DEALING WITH THE LCMS FROM 1939-1961, ADMONITION WAS NOT USED MERELY TO ASCERTAIN WHETHER THE LCMS WAS, IN FACT TEACHING CONTRARY TO THE WORD OF GOD. A NEW PUR- POSE BECAME APPARENT. ADMONITION WAS DEEMED NECESSARY TO DETER- MINE WHETHER THE ERRING WOULD REPENT OF THEIR ERRORS OR PERSIST IN THEM. ONLY AFTER THIS EXERCISE OF ADMONITION DID THE WELS ARRIVE AT THE CONCLUSIVE JUDGMENT THAT THE LCMS WAS GUILTY OF "CAUSING DIVI- SIONS AND OFFENSES." THUS THE "MARKING" WAS, AND ACCORDING TO PRIN- CIPLE, IS TO BE ARTIFICIALLY DELAYED UNTIL THE OUTCOME OF THE PROCESS OF ADMONITION CAN BE DETERMINED. AND SO THE WELFARE OF THE "WOLF" IS PLACED AHEAD OF CONCERN FOR THE "SHEEP."

D) IDENTIFYING CAUSERS OF DIVISION. THE CLC CONTENDS THAT ST. PAUL URGES US SIMPLY TO KEEP THE EYE RIVETED ON ANYONE DEPARTING FROM SOUND DOCTRINE TO DETERMINE WHETHER OR NOT HE IS, IN FACT, PRO- FESSING, TEACHING, AND DEFENDING ERROR. IN THE CASE AT HAND THE WELS FINALLY, AFTER MORE THAN TWENTY YEARS, ARRIVED AT THE CONCLUSIVE JUDGMENT THAT MISSOURI IS GUILTY OF CAUSING DIVISIONS AND OFFENSES IN

THE CHURCH. HOW DID [THE WELS] ARRIVE AT THIS CONCLUSION? BY OB-
SERVING THE RESPONSE OF MISSOURI TO ALL [ITS] ADMONITION. (SEE THE
WHEREAS OF THE 1961 RESOLUTION). WHEN ALL EFFORTS AT ADMON-
ISHING WERE OF NO FURTHER AVAIL, WHEN [THE WELS] FAILED TO ACHIEVE
THE HOPED-FOR END, WHEN [THE WELS] REACHED AN "IMPASSE," THEN AND
THEN ONLY COULD AND WERE THE CAUSER OF DIVISIONS AND OFFENSES CON-
CLUSIVELY IDENTIFIED. SINCE THE DECISION WAS COMPLETELY A MATTER OF
HUMAN JUDGMENT, IT COULD NOT BUT BE—AS IT WAS—THE DECISION OF A MA-
JORITY. MORE THAN A QUARTER OF THE DELEGATES AT THE 1961 CONVENTION
STILL THOUGHT THE ADMONISHING SHOULD CONTINUE.

E)   MARKING, BUT NOT AVOIDING. THE QUESTION IS WHETHER ONE CAN
"MARK" A CHURCH BODY AS BEING GUILTY OF "CAUSING DIVISIONS AND OF-
FENSE," BUT YET CONTINUE ADMONISHING HER WITHIN THE BONDS OF FELLOW-
SHIP. THE OFFICIAL PROCEEDINGS OF THE CONVENTIONS OF THE WELS
EXHAUSTIVELY "MARKED" MISSOURI AS AN ERRING CHURCH BODY IN 1953—IN
FACT, EVER SINCE 1939—BUT CONTINUED ADMONISHING HER WITHIN THE
BONDS OF FELLOWSHIP UNTIL 1961. THIS COURSE OF ACTION WAS RATIONAL-
IZED AND DEFENDED ON THE GROUNDS THAT THE "MARKING" WAS NOT YET CON-
CLUSIVE, THAT THERE ALLEGEDLY WERE NEW "RAYS OF HOPE," THAT A "DEBT OF
LOVE" REMAINED TO BE PAID, AND THAT THE CONTINUING FELLOWSHIP WAS
"VIGOROUSLY PROTESTING." MANY PRESENT MEMBERS OF THE CLC PARTICI-
PATED IN THIS CONTRADICTION OF "MARKING," YET FELLOWSHIP. BUT THE CLC
HAS DISAVOWED THIS AS ERROR AND HAS RETURNED TO THE SIMPLE SCRIPTURAL
POSITION THAT THE "MARKING," ENJOINED IN ROMANS 17:17, IS TO BE FOL-
LOWED BY THE "AVOIDING"—WITHOUT A TIME LAPSE ALLOWING FOR A PROCESS
OF ADMONITION AND WITHOUT ARTIFICIALLY DELAYING THE OFFICIAL, CONCLU-
SIVE "MARKING."

F)   WHEN? OR HOW? BOTH THE WELS AND THE ELS HAVE ACCUSED THE
CLC OF ACTING HASTILY...THUS THE ENTIRE DISPUTE HAS BEEN MADE TO AP-
PEAR, AT ITS WORST, AS NOTHING MORE THAN IMPATIENCE AND RASHNESS ON
THE PART OF THE CLC OR, AT ITS BEST, AS A MERE DIFFERENCE IN HUMAN
JUDGMENT AS TO WHEN THE SEPARATION FROM MISSOURI SHOULD HAVE
TAKEN PLACE. THE WELS POINTS TO THE OBVIOUS FACT THAT THERE WAS NO
AGREEMENT IN THE CLC AS TO THE WHEN—SOME HAVING PLEADED FOR A
BREAK IN 1953, MORE IN 1955, WHILE MANY AGREED TO GO ALONG WITH THE
"ADMONITORY PROCESS" IN 1956, SOME LEAVING AFTER 1957, AND THE REST
AFTER 1959.

THE MEMBERS OF THE CLC FREELY CONFESS THAT THEY TOO WERE MISLED BY
THE FALSE EMPHASIS ON THE WHEN. HISTORICALLY SPEAKING, THE BREAK
SHOULD HAVE BEEN SOONER. BUT THE CLC CONTENDS THAT MAKING THE
WHEN THE BIG ISSUE HAS RESULTED IN TWO HARMFUL EFFECTS. FIRST, THE
WHOLE ISSUE HAS BEEN REDUCED TO THE REALM OF HUMAN JUDGMENT...SEC-
OND, THE FALSE EMPHASIS ON THE WHEN HAS BECOME A SMOKESCREEN
WHICH HAS COVERED A SMALL, BUT VITAL CHANGE IN THE DOCTRINE OF THE
TERMINATION OF FELLOWSHIP. THE REASON FOR TERMINATING FELLOWSHIP
HAS BEEN CHANGED FROM THE OBSERVABLE FACT THAT SOMEONE IS CAUSING
DIVISIONS AND OFFENSES, THAT IS PREACHING, TEACHING, AND DEFENDING
ERROR, TO A MAJORITY DECISION THAT THE ADMONISHING OF THE ERRING HAS

REACHED AN "IMPASSE."

FURTHER CONFESSION: IN ADDITION TO PERSONAL WEAKNESS IN INTERPER-
SONAL RELATIONS, WE CONFESS THAT MANY IN THE CLC WERE EITHER AC-
TIVELY OR PASSIVELY RESPONSIBLE FOR FORMING, IMPLEMENTING, SUPPORTING,
AND DEFENDING THE POLICIES THAT LED BOTH THE WELS AND THE ELS
ALONG A BYPATH THAT LED TO ERROR IN THE DOCTRINE OF THE TERMINATION
OF FELLOWSHIP. THIS SIN WE HAVE PRIVATELY AND PUBLICLY CONFESSED. IN
THIS MATTER WE DID SIN AGAINST THE MAJESTY OF GOD'S WORD. WE WERE
GUILTY OF LEADING OTHERS ASTRAY. WE PRAY FOR FORGIVENESS AND GRACE
TO BE FAITHFUL TO HIS WORD.[19]

THE CLC'S REACTION TO WISCONSIN'S ACTION OF
SUSPENDING FELLOWSHIP WITH MISSOURI

In 1960 the CLC was organized mainly by pastors, teachers, professors and laymen who had left the Wisconsin Synod for reasons of conscience, reacting to the continuation of fellowship (even though a "vigorously protesting" one) with the Missouri Synod. A year later the Wisconsin Synod in its August Convention resolved to suspend fellowship with the Missouri Synod. Would Wisconsin's action nullify the reason for the continued existence of this tiny, newly organized body? This writer must conclude that years of talks between the two bodies has not resulted in agreement over a basic issue that has arisen. That issue has been discussed above in Pastor Paul Nolting's essay, "Mark...Avoid." The CLC frankly accuses the Wisconsin Synod of dallying in the application of the "avoid" as it is commanded by St. Paul in Romans 16:17,18. Furthermore, the CLC accuses Wisconsin of bringing in admonition where admonition is not called for but where the act of "avoiding" is. In other words, the CLC points out that when one by closely observing a person or persons finds them to be causers "of divisions and offenses contrary to the doctrine," then the avoiding is to follow. If admonition is called for, it is to serve to identify the errorist. Once the errorist has been identified the "avoid" is to be practiced, while any admonition that is offered must be carried on outside the framework of fellowship. The order then is NOT mark, admonish, determine them to be persistent errorists (that an impasse in negotiations has been reached) and finally, avoid them. Nor does the CLC believe that admonition is necessarily required in all cases. If admonition within fellowship is called for then it is carried on BEFORE the judgment of Romans 16:17, 18 is applied.

True, the Wisconsin Synod in its 1956 recessed Convention voted to hold in abeyance the judgment of the 1955 Saginaw Convention resolution (which marked the Missouri Synod as causing divisions and offenses). A ray of hope had been held out. There would be intensified examination—it was hoped—of the situation by the Synodical Conference. But as it turned out, many observers were openly discouraged at the little time given in the Conference meetings to a discussion of the inter-synodical issues, while a large amount of time was given to nondoctrinal matters.

Be that as it may, the CLC—in the light of historical events—does not deem the recessed Convention's action of holding in abeyance the judgment of the

1955 Saginaw Resolution justified. One year later (1957) Wisconsin's Floor Committee again brought a resolution to the synod in convention, asking for suspension of fellowship with the Missouri Synod. This resolution failed to pass by only 16 votes.

The years that followed were agonizing ones for the Wisconsin Synod. Many protests came in to the synod against continuation of fellowship with a church body which showed itself to be erring. Congregations, portions of congregations, as well as individuals (Including pastors, teachers, professors, and laymen) were leaving the synod out of protest. Others, while remaining in membership, publicly protested the synod's actions. Finally, in 1961 the Wisconsin Synod in Convention concurred with the findings of its Floor Committee and voted to suspend fellowship with the Missouri Synod on the basis of Romans 16:17,18.

President Albrecht of the CLC in a pamphlet titled, "What Separates the CLC from Wisconsin?" pinpointed the unresolved issues between the two bodies:

WE CONSIDER THIS RESOLUTION A SINCERE AND HEROIC EFFORT ON THE PART OF WISCONSIN TO EXTRICATE HERSELF FROM THE WEB OF UNIONISM INTO WHICH HER RELATIONS WITH ERRORISTIC MISSOURI HAD DEGENERATED. WE REJOICED AND THANK GOD. THIS ACTION OF WISCONSIN AT ONCE GAVE RISE TO THE QUESTION: DOES WISCONSIN'S RESOLUTION SUSPENDING FELLOWSHIP WITH MISSOURI PAVE THE WAY FOR OUR RETURN TO THE FELLOWSHIP WHICH MOST OF US HAD ENJOYED FOR SO MANY YEARS?

President Albrecht then referred the reader to the action of the Spokane Convention of the CLC:

WE DO FEEL CONSTRAINED TO POINT OUT, HOWEVER, THAT THIS SUSPENSION OF FELLOWSHIP DOES NOT IN ITSELF REMOVE THE REAL ISSUES THAT ARE INVOLVED IN OUR RELATIONS WITH THE WISCONSIN SYNOD...DEVIATIONS [ON THE PART OF WISCONSIN] FROM THE SCRIPTURAL DOCTRINE OF CHURCH FELLOWSHIP, AND THE DOCTRINE OF THE CLARITY AND AUTHORITY OF THE SCRIPTURES, AS WELL AS INSTANCES OF VIOLATION OF THE SANCTITY OF THE CALL.

President Albrecht went on to explain what he and the CLC say to be deviations from the scriptural doctrine of Church Fellowship in the Wisconsin Synod:

FOR QUITE SOME TIME, WISCONSIN HAS PROCLAIMED AND DEFENDED THE POSITION THAT "TERMINATION OF CHURCH FELLOWSHIP IS CALLED FOR WHEN YOU HAVE REACHED THE CONVICTION THAT ADMONITION IS OF NO FURTHER AVAIL." (REPORT TO THE PROTEST COMMITTEE OF THE WISCONSIN SYNOD.) WISCONSIN'S PRACTICE HAS BEEN IN CONFORMITY WITH THIS UNSCRIPTURAL PRINCIPLE. WISCONSIN CONTINUED TO PRACTICE CHURCH FELLOWSHIP WITH MISSOURI LONG AFTER SHE HAD RECOGNIZED MISSOURI AS A CAUSER OF DIVISIONS AND OFFENSES CONTRARY TO THE DOCTRINE, UNDER THE PLEA THAT SHE HAD NOT YET REACHED THE CONVICTION THAT FURTHER ADMONITION WOULD BE FRUITLESS. THIS ABERRATION LED WISCONSIN SO FAR ASTRAY THAT THOSE WHO HAD BEEN CHARGED WITH THE DUTY OF DEALING WITH THE SISTER SYNOD FELLOWSHIPED WITH THAT SYNOD EVEN AFTER THEY HAD PUBLICLY DECLARED THAT AN IMPASSE HAD BEEN REACHED.

THE LORD SAYS, ROMANS 16:17: "NOW I BESEECH YOU, BRETHREN, MARK

THEM (THAT IS, TAKE CAREFUL NOTE OF THEM) WHICH CAUSE DIVISIONS AND OF-
FENSES CONTRARY TO THE DOCTRINE WHICH YE HAVE LEARNED, AND AVOID
THEM"—HAVE NO FELLOWSHIP WITH THEM, NOT TOMORROW NOR NEXT YEAR
OR WHEN YOU REACH THE CONVICTION THAT ADMONITION IS OF NO FURTHER
AVAIL, OR WHEN A MAJORITY OF CONVENTION DELEGATES REACHES THIS CON-
VICTION, BUT WHEN YOU SEE WHAT THEY ARE DOING.
WHEN WE SEEK TO UNDERSTAND WHAT THE LORD WOULD HAVE US DO WHEN
CONFRONTED WITH A SITUATION IN WHICH DIVISIONS AND OFFENSES CONTRARY
TO THE DOCTRINE ARE BEING CAUSED, WE DARE NEVER ASK: HOW WILL THE ER-
RORIST REACT TO BROTHERLY ADMONITION? OR, IS THERE STILL A FAINT RAY OF
HOPE THAT HE WILL RECOGNIZE HIS ERROR AND RETURN TO THE "OLD PATHS"?
WE CANNOT LOOK INTO ANY MAN'S HEART NOR DISCERN HIS FUTURE REACTIONS.
THE ONLY PROPER QUESTION IS: WHAT DO WE SEE AFTER WE HAVE TAKEN A
VERY CAREFUL LOOK? IF WE SEE CAUSERS OF DIVISIONS AND OFFENSES CON-
TRARY TO THE DOCTRINE WE HAVE LEARNED, THAT IS, IF WE SEE PEOPLE WHO
BY THE UNSCRIPTURAL POSITION WHICH THEY ACTUALLY HOLD AND PROCLAIM,
CAUSE DIVISIONS AND OFFENSES CONTRARY TO THE DOCTRINE, THEN THE
LORD'S INJUNCTION IS, "AVOID THEM!" NOT TOMORROW OR NEXT YEAR, BUT AT
ONCE. WHEN GOD HAS SPOKEN, THEN DELAY IS DISOBEDIENCE. (FOR THE
PLACE OF ADMONITION IN THE MUTUAL RELATIONS OF CHRISTIAN BRETHREN,
REFER TO "CONCERNING CHURCH FELLOWSHIP," PARAGRAPHS 63, 65, AND 72.)

According to President Albrecht and the CLC, the Wisconsin Synod had no
alternative but to suspend fellowship with the Missouri Synod in 1955, at
which time Missouri was clearly marked both by the President of the Wisconsin
Synod and by the synod itself as causers of divisions and offenses.

In his anniversary essay, "Mark...Avoid," Pastor Paul F. Nolting of the CLC
made this observation:

WE CONSIDER IT A TOKEN OF DIVINE GRACE THAT BOTH THE WELS AND THE
ELS HAVE FINALLY SEPARATED FROM HETERODOX MISSOURI. BUT THE QUES-
TION THAT STILL MUST BE FACED IS THIS: DID THEY SUSPEND FELLOWSHIP FOR
THE RIGHT REASON? THE CLC CHARGES, AND THAT REGRETFULLY, THAT IN
THE TWENTY-PLUS YEAR PERIOD FELLOWING 1938 THE INITIAL RESPONSE OF
TESTIFYING AGAINST THE ERRORS OF MISSOURI WAS GRADUALLY CHANGED INTO
A PROCESS OF ADMONISHING MISSOURI AS WEAK BRETHREN. THIS BECAME THE
ALL-ABSORBING CONCERN OF THE SYNOD. AS THE LEAVEN OF ERROR CONTIN-
UED ITS EVIL WORK, THE DOCTRINE OF FELLOWSHIP BECAME CORRUPTED—
SPECIFICALLY IN THE AREA OF TERMINATING AN EXISTING FELLOWSHIP. IF THIS
EVALUATION ACCURATELY REFLECTS THE FACTS OF HISTORY—AS WE ARE CER-
TAIN IT DOES—BOTH THE WELS AND THE ELS HAVE BECOME GUILTY OF FALSE
DOCTRINE WHILE SEPARATING FROM ERRING MISSOURI. IF THIS CHARGE
STANDS, THE LEAVEN OF ERROR IS CONTINUING TO WORK IN BOTH THE WELS
AND THE ELS.

THE PASTORAL CALL—AN ISSUE

The sanctity of the pastoral call was also made a point of issue between the
CLC and the Wisconsin Synod. The CLC maintains that there were instances

where congregations terminated pastoral calls and, in fact, where Wisconsin Synod officials gave official sanction to such action, when the only reason for the action was that the pastor in question had ceased to be a member of the Wisconsin Synod. The stand of the CLC is that a pastor's call should not be terminated because he for confessional reasons left the Wisconsin Synod. Rather, a pastor's call should be terminated only when there is "clear evidence of persistent adherence to false doctrine, a scandalous life, or willful neglect of duty." The synod may remove a pastor from the synod: only the congregation can terminate the pastor's call.

THE WISCONSIN SYNOD'S REACTION TO THE CHARGES MADE BY THE CLC—WELS/CLC TALKS

Over the years there have been meetings between the two bodies through their appropriate committees. In 1966 the Wisconsin Synod Commission on Doctrinal Matters reported that the CLC representatives took exception particularly to the following wording of the WELS statement on Church Fellowship: WE CAN NO LONGER RECOGNIZE AND TREAT AS CHRISTIAN BRETHREN THOSE WHO IN SPITE OF PATIENT ADMONITION PERSISTENTLY ADHERE TO AN ERROR IN DOCTRINE.

The report went on to state:

IT WAS CONTENDED BY THE CLC REPRESENTATIVES THAT PERSISTENT ADHERENCE TO ERROR DESPITE PATIENT ADMONITION IS NOT THE CRITERION BY WHICH WE JUDGE WHETHER WE ARE TO MARK AND AVOID THOSE WHO "DEMAND RECOGNITION FOR THEIR ERROR, AND MAKE PROPAGANDA FOR IT." THE WELS REFERENCE TO "PATIENT ADMONITION" AT THIS POINT IN THE STATEMENT, ACCORDING TO THE CLC REPRESENTATIVES, IS OUT OF PLACE WHEN SPEAKING OF THE TERMINATION OF CHURCH FELLOWSHIP, FOR THEREBY ADMONITION IS MADE A DETERMINING FACTOR OR PREREQUISITE IN THE APPLICATION OF ROMANS 16:17 AND ITS INJUNCTION TO AVOID.

Referring then to its own statement, "Concerning Church Fellowship," the CLC made this statement:

WE FURTHER BELIEVE, TEACH AND CONFESS THAT ESTABLISHED FELLOWSHIPS ARE TO BE TERMINATED WHEN IT HAS BEEN ASCERTAINED THAT A PERSON OR GROUP THROUGH A FALSE POSITION IS CAUSING DIVISIONS AND OFFENSES IN THE CHURCH.

The report of the Wisconsin Synod's Commission drew the following conclusion regarding the CLC's stand regarding termination of fellowship:

IN OTHER WORDS, THE ONLY PREREQUISITE, ACCORDING TO THE CLC REPRESENTATIVES, FOR APPLYING THE "AVOID" OF ROMANS 16:17 IS TO ASCERTAIN WHETHER A PERSON OR GROUP IS CAUSING DIVISIONS AND OFFENSES...OUR WISCONSIN SYNOD REPRESENTATIVES ON THE OTHER HAND HELD THAT WE FIND NO WARRANT FOR THE CONTENTION THAT THE EXPRESSION "PERSISTENT ADHERENCE TO FALSE DOCTRINE" SUPPORTS AN UNSCRIPTURAL POSITION WHEN USED TO DESCRIBE "CAUSING DIVISIONS AND OFFENSES." WE ALSO CALLED ATTENTION TO THE FACT THAT THE TERM "PERSISTENT" HAS LONG BEEN USED IN THE LUTHERAN CHURCH TO DESIGNATE THOSE "CAUSING DIVISIONS AND OF-

FENSES," E.G., THE "THESES ON OPEN QUESTIONS" OF 1868, ON THE BASIS OF WHICH THE WISCONSIN AND MISSOURI SYNODS HAD ESTABLISHED FELLOWSHIP.

WITH RESPECT TO OUR STATEMENT'S REFERENCE TO "PATIENT ADMONITION"..., WE POINTED OUT THAT THIS PARAGRAPH IS NOT AN ELABORATION SOLELY OF ROMANS 16:17, BUT CONCERNS ITSELF ALSO WITH OTHER PERTINENT SCRIPTURAL DIRECTIVES, EVEN AS THE MAIN THRUST OF OUR STATEMENT CONCERNS ITSELF WITH THE EXERCISE AND PRESERVATION OF THE PRECIOUS GIFT OF FELLOWSHIP RATHER THAN ITS TERMINATION. AND THOUGH WE RECOGNIZE OUR CHRISTIAN OBLIGATION OF ADMONISHING A BROTHER THAT HAS FALLEN INTO ERROR, WE DISAVOWED THE CONTENTION THAT WE HEREWITH MAKE ADMONITION A PREREQUISITE WHICH MUST IN ALL CASES PRECEDE THE AVOIDING OF ROMANS 16:17. WE LIKEWISE DISAVOWED ANY CONTENTION THAT WE INSERT ADMONITION BETWEEN THE MARKING AND AVOIDING OF ROMANS 16:17.

The Commission could also report that in its "Appraisal of the Wisconsin Synod's Presentation: 'Church Fellowship'" the CLC showed agreement with some sections (A and B: 1,2,3, as well as with the antithesis A, B, and C of the Theses). However, the "Appraisal" took exception to the "weak brother" approach that the Wisconsin Synod was accused of using.

Furthermore, in its report...

THE WELS COMMISSION OFFERED SOME INTERPRETATIONS OF THE SECTIONS CHALLENGED THAT DID NOT CONFLICT WITH CORRESPONDING PARAGRAPHS OF THE CCF (CONCERNING CHURCH FELLOWSHIP). IT WAS SPECIFICALLY AFFIRMED...(1) THAT ADMONITION IS NOT A PREREQUISITE FOR OR A DETERMINING FACT IN TERMINATING FELLOWSHIP, (2) THAT ADMONITION IS HELPFUL IN IDENTIFYING AN ERRORIST, AND (3) THAT IN CASES OF ERROR ARISING WITHIN A FELLOWSHIP, ADMONITION IS THE NORMAL PROCEDURE INDICATED BY SCRIPTURE. HOWEVER, THE CLC BOARD OF DOCTRINE CONTENDED THAT THE THESES AS THEY STAND, LEAVE ROOM FOR ERRORS THAT THE CLC FINDS IN PREVIOUS OFFICIAL PRONOUNCEMENTS.

THE CLC BOARD OF DOCTRINE CONTENDED THAT AN EXAMINATION OF PAST OFFICIAL STATEMENTS IS NECESSARY TO JUSTIFY ITS UNDERSTANDING OF THE THESES. THE WELS COMMISSION RESPONDED BY AGREEING TO RECEIVE THE ILLUSTRATIONS OFFERED FOR THEIR PRIVATE CONSIDERATION. BUT THE WELS COMMISSION STILL MAINTAINED THAT IF NO AGREEMENT IN PRINCIPLE IS ACHIEVED ON THE BASIS OF THE TWO PUBLISHED DOCUMENTS ALONE, PRECEEDING TO A THOROUGH DISCUSSION OF PAST OFFICIAL PRONOUNCEMENTS AND ACTIONS WOULD NOT SERVE ANY WHOLESOME PURPOSES.

The Commission on Doctrinal Matters had to report to the 1969 Wisconsin Synod Convention that recent attempts to conduct a joint meeting with the Board of Doctrine of the CLC had failed. The Commission was nevertheless asked to stand ready to enter upon meetings with the Board of Doctrine of the CLC to establish agreement on scriptural principles of church fellowship.

Reporting on a meeting which the Wisconsin Synod Commission had in July 1972 with the CLC Board of Doctrine, a summary was given of the discussion which had taken place on the matter of dealing between church bodies when error or false doctrine has arisen:

IN THIS CONNECTION REFERENCES WERE MADE TO OFFICIAL RESOLUTIONS, PAR-

TICULARLY OF THE WELS, ON THE BASIS OF A DOCUMENT DISTRIBUTED BY THE CLC REPRESENTATIVES. NO SCRIPTURAL WARRANT WAS GRANTED BY THE CLC REPRESENTATIVES FOR A STATE OF CONFESSION IN DEALING WITH THE SITUATION IN WHICH ERROR IN DOCTRINE OR PRACTICE HAS INFECTED A LARGER GROUP OF CONFESSIONAL BRETHREN (E.G., CONGREGATION OR SISTER SYNOD). THE WELS REPRESENTATIVES HELD, HOWEVER, THAT SUCH A STATE OF CONFESSION IS FREQUENTLY CALLED FOR BEFORE TERMINATING FELLOWSHIP WITH A GROUP THAT HAS BEEN INFECTED BY ERROR: (1) IN ORDER TO OFFER OPPORTUNITY FOR DETERMINING WHAT THE CONFESSIONAL POSITION OF THE GROUP FOR WHICH IT MUST BE HELD RESPONSIBLE REALLY IS (THIS MAY BECOME NECESSARY BECAUSE OF MUTUALLY EXCLUSIVE STATEMENTS, PRONOUNCEMENTS, [AND] RESOLUTIONS MADE IN SUCH A GROUP; BECAUSE OF CONFLICTING POSITIONS CONTENDING FOR MASTERY IN THIS GROUP, ONE OR THE OTHER OF WHICH MAY FOR GOOD REASONS BE CONSIDERED TO BE ONLY TEMPORARILY IN CONTROL); (2) TO OFFER OPPORTUNITY TO BRING SCRIPTURAL TESTIMONY AGAINST THE ERROR INFECTING THE GROUP TO THOSE BRETHREN WHO ARE NOT THEMSELVES ADVOCATING AND PROPAGANDIZING THE ERRORS—BEFORE TREATING SUCH BRETHREN AS RESPONSIBLE PARTAKERS OF THE ERROR OR FALSE PRACTICE INFECTING THEIR GROUP.

THE WELS REPRESENTATIVES HELD THAT SUCH PROCEDURE IS CALLED FOR TO SATISFY THE MANY SCRIPTURAL INJUNCTIONS QUOTED IN THEIR CHURCH FELLOWSHIP STATEMENT BIDDING US TO EXERCISE AND MAKE EARNEST EFFORT TO PRESERVE THE BOND OF CONFESSIONAL FELLOWSHIP, TO HELP THE WEAK AND CONFUSED.

The Wisconsin Synod representatives raised the question whether the CLC concept of "false teacher" and the WELS concept of "persistent errorist" perhaps actually have the same scope and would lend "to uniform fellowship practice whether dealing with an individual or with groups."

The WELS Commission made the following observation concerning the synod's use of the term "state of confession" during the period before 1961 to designate the synod's fellowship relation over against the Missouri Synod:...THE SYNODICAL RESOLUTIONS IN EFFECT DURING THAT PERIOD SHOULD MAKE IT QUITE EVIDENT THAT THE TERM "STATE OF CONFESSION" WAS NOT YET MEANT TO EXPRESS A JUDGMENT TANTAMOUNT TO THAT OF ROMANS 16:17. Nevertheless, several times in synodical conventions the term "causer of divisions and offenses"—and similar terms—was applied to the Missouri Synod.

From 1988 to 1992 representatives of the CLC, the WELS, and the ELS participated in a series of meetings and drew up what is called the "Joint Statement." This Statement, which was signed by the representatives of all three bodies, rejected...

...THE VIEW THAT THE DECISION TO CONTINUE OR DISCONTINUE ADMONITION AND PROCEED TO AVOID IS TO BE MADE ON THE BASIS OF A SUBJECTIVE JUDGMENT OR CONJECTURE ABOUT THE POSSBLE OUTCOME OF ADMONITION.

Also rejected...THE VIEW THAT PERMITS THE USE OF HUMAN JUDGMENT TO PROLONG FELLOWSHIP WITH PERSISTENT ERRORISTS CONTRARY TO THE PRINCIPLES OF SCRIPTURE.

In the view of the CLC, the WELS' consistent use of the expression "persistent errorist" was troubling. The CLC points out that historically that expres-

807

sion "was a catchword used with the WELS," which use contributed to the delay in terminating fellowship with the LC-MS. Though the CLC representatives accepted the verbal explanation of "persistent errorist" from the WELS, it was felt later on that subsequent words and actions of the WELS made acceptance of this expression ill advised.

It was proposed by the CLC representatives that a preamble be added to the "Joint Statement," and offered their version whose thrust was: ANY PREVIOUS EXPRESSIONS OR ACTIONS WHICH MAY NOT BE IN CONFORMITY WITH...[THE JOINT STATEMENT] ARE HEREBY SET ASIDE AND REJECTED (EMPHASIS ADDED).

The WELS representatives, however, rejected the CLC proposed preamble and countered with their own version, which said that when the Joint Statement is accepted by the three church bodies, it...SUPERCEDES ANY AND EVERY PREVIOUS STATEMENT THAT MIGHT APPEAR TO BE IN CONFLICT WITH THIS DOCUMENT. ANY AND ALL SUCH CONFLICTING OR POSSIBLY CONFLICTING STATEMENTS ARE HEREWITH DISAVOWED.

The CLC representatives in effect concluded that the WELS version of a preamble for the Joint Statement was weak in that it did not use the word "reject" concerning conflicting previous statements.

IN THE LUTHERAN CONFESSIONS AS WELL AS IN THE BRIEF STATEMENT DOCTRINES CONTRARY TO THE TRUTH ARE CLEARLY REJECTED. TO REJECT A CONTRARY DOCTRINE CLEARLY DECLARES THAT WHAT IS CONTRARY TO SCRIPTURE HAS NO STANDING WHATEVER WITH THE TRUTH. WITHOUT A CLEAR, UNEQUIVOCAL, AND UNAMBIGUOUS REJECTION OF PAST STATEMENTS CONTRARY TO SCRIPTURE, THE QUESTION WAS OPEN, NAMELY, WHAT IS THE POSITION OF THE WELS—THAT OF THE "FATHERS" OR THE EXPRESSIONS OF THE UNADOPTED JOINT STATEMENT?

The CLC further pointed out:

THE WELS MADE THE POINT THAT THEY DID NOT "WANT TO SIT IN JUDGMENT OF THE FATHERS." THEY DID NOT WANT TO USE THE STRAIGHTFORWARD PREAMBLE OF THE CLC THAT USED THE EXPRESSIONS "REJECT" AND "SET ASIDE." THEY PREFERRED THE WORDS "SUPERCEDE" AND "DISAVOW." UNDER THE CIRCUMSTANCES OF THE HISTORY, THE CLC JUDGED THAT CLEAR AND UNEQUIVOCAL WORDS SHOULD BE USED TO CONFIRM THAT THE HOPED FOR AGREEMENT WAS INDEED AN AGREEMENT AND SETTLEMENT OF DIFFERENCES.

The CLC faulted the WELS for its persistent use of the word "persistent":

THE USE OF THAT WORD SUBJECTED ANY ACTION OF SEPARATION FROM ERRORISTS TO HUMAN JUDGMENT, OR TO A DETERMINATION WHETHER OR NOT THE LC-MS WAS REALLY HETERODOX, OR INTENDED TO CONTINUE IN ITS ERRANT WAY. THE READER IS INVITED TO REREAD THE HISTORICAL REVIEW TO SEE FOR HIMSELF THAT WORDS AND FACTS CLEARLY SHOW THAT THE LC-MS HAD BEEN SHOWN CONCLUSIVELY TO BE HETERODOX. IF THE WELS DID NOT MEAN WHAT IT SAID, IT SHOULD HAVE WITHDRAWN THE CHARGE AGAINST THE LC-MS![20]

Finally then, as far as the CLC is concerned, the error of the WELS was not simply a matter of being tardy in separating from the LC-MS, but a matter of wrongly admonishing within the bonds of fellowship a church body that was already—yes, several times—recognized to be a causer of divisions and offenses contrary to the doctrine that the church has learned from God's Word, which church body should the have been avoided (Romans 16,17:18).

The uniting of the two synods in fellowship is not at this time in the offing. To the settlement of past differences the CLC believes addressing Wisconsin's doctrine of Church Fellowship in the light of past convention resolutions is pertinent. The Wisconsin Synod does not want the discussions to take such a course, but wants rather to seek agreement and thus fellowship on the basis of statements of principle. Thus a stalemate has developed. However, in the meantime there exists this AREA OF AGREEMENT, expressed by Pastor Paul Nolting of the CLC:

BOTH THE WELS AND THE ELS AND ALSO THE CLC AGREE THAT THE LORD WANTS ONLY HIS WORD PREACHED AND TAUGHT IN THE CHURCH, THAT ERROR MUST BE COMBATED WHEN IT ARISES, AND THAT THE WORD OF GOD DEMANDS THAT TRUE DISCIPLES SEPARATE FROM ANY AND ALL WHO "CAUSE DIVISIONS AND OFFENSES CONTRARY TO THE DOCTRINE WHICH YE HAVE LEARNED" (ROMANS 16:17).[21]

LUTHERAN FRATERNAL INSURANCE COMPANIES—DIFFERING ASSESSMENTS BY WELS AND CLC

We quote from a CLC informational brochure:

IN 2001 THE AID ASSOCIATION FOR LUTHERANS (AAL) MERGED WITH THE LUTHERAN BROTHERHOOD (LB) TO FORM THRIVENT, BECOMING "THE LARGEST FRATERNAL BENEFIT SOCIETY IN THE WORLD. (REFER: http:/www.thrivent.com/about us/history.html) WITH THE MERGER OF THESE COMPANIES IT IS NECESSARY FOR US TO EXAMINE THE NEW ORGANIZATION IN ORDER TO DETERMINE WHETHER OR NOT OUR VALID OBJECTIONS TO AAL/LB ARE STILL RELEVANT TO THRIVENT. AS BELIEVERS IN JESUS CHRIST WHO ENJOY THE FREEDOM OF THE GOSPEL WE DO NOT WANT TO LABEL ANYTHING AS SINFUL THAT IS NOT. ON THE OTHER HAND, WE DARE NOT GLOSS OVER SOMETHING THAT IS CONTRARY TO THE WORD OF GOD.

The CLC goes on to make this comparison between the WELS and ELS in their appraisal of Thrivent Financial for Lutherans organization:

ONE EXAMPLE OF THE CONTINUING DIFFERENCES [BETWEEN THE TWO CHURCH BODIES] HAS BEEN IN THE DIFFERENT ASSESSMENT AND ACTION REGARDING FRATERNAL INSURANCE COMPANIES. THE CLC HAS RECOGNIZED SUCH COMPANIES AS INVOLVING THEIR MEMBERS IN RELIGIOUS UNIONISM. THE WELS HAS NOT. WITH THE MERGER OF THE TWO LARGEST LUTHERAN FRATERNAL BENEFIT COMPANIES, IS THIS STILL AN ISSUE? OR HAVE THEY CHANGED THEIR PRACTICE?

THE OBJECTIONS OF THE CHURCH OF THE LUTHERAN CONFESSION REGARDING THE AAL CENTERED AROUND THEIR STATEMENT THAT, *When a Lutheran buys AAL Insurance protection, he also becomes a member of our fraternal family and automatically participates in projects which serve Lutherans and Lutheranism in special ways.* (1972 summer edition of "AAL Correspondent")

The name chosen for the merger, *Thrivent Financial for Lutherans* gives us our first clue that religious unionism continues to be business as usual in the new company... "As a fraternal [sic], Thrivent Financial is required by charter to limit membership to Lutherans, eligible family members and others who meet the eligibility rules." (http://thrivent.com/joinus/membership.html)

The following are statements made by Thrivent:

MISSION

THRIVENT FINANCIAL FOR LUTHERANS IS A FAITH-BASED MEMBERSHIP (EMPHASIS ADDED) ORGANIZATION CALLED TO IMPROVE THE QUALITY OF LIFE OF IT MEMBERS, THEIR FAMILIES, AND THEIR COMMUNITIES BY PROVIDING UNPARALLELED SOLUTIONS THAT FOCUS ON FINANCIAL SECURITY, WELLNESS AND CARING FOR OTHERS.

VISION

OUR VISION IS TO BE THE ORGANIZATION THAT LUTHERANS, LUTHERAN CONGREGATIONS AND LUTHERAN INSTITUTIONS SEEK FIRST WHEN PURSUING THEIR FINANCIAL GOALS. MORE THAN CREATING FINANCIAL SOLUTIONS, WE ADD THE UNIQUE CAPABILITY OF ENABLING LUTHERANS TO DEMONSTRATE THEIR CARE AND CONCERN FOR OTHERS.

OUR CORE VALUES

THRIVENT FINANCIAL WAS FOUNDED TO HELP LUTHERANS CARE FOR AND SUPPORT ONE ANOTHER IN TIME OF NEED, GUIDED BY THE PRINCIPLES OF THE CHRISTIAN FAITH. WE REMAIN COMMITTED TO THIS RICH FRATERNAL HERITAGE AS WE STRIVE TO ACHIEVE THE HIGHEST POSSIBLE GOOD FOR MEMBERS, STAFF AND SOCIETY. WE HOLD THESE VALUES TO BE ESSENTIAL AS WE WORK TO FULFILL OUR MISSION, VISION AND STRATEGIES.

CONCERNING THEIR "FRATERNAL PROGRAMS," THRIVENT NOTES:

AS THE COUNTRY'S LARGEST FRATERNAL BENEFIT SOCIETY, THRIVENT FINANCIAL FOR LUTHERANS DOES MORE THAN OFFER FINANCIAL SERVICES. WE OFFER HOPE AND HELP TO LUTHERANS, THEIR FAMILIES AND THEIR COMMUNITIES. FIND INFORMATION HERE ABOUT HOW YOU AND YOUR FAMILY CAN:

....

....

• FINANCIALLY HELP LUTHERAN CHURCHES, SCHOOLS AND ORGANIZATIONS.

So then, how does the CLC stand regarding members having membership in Thrivent for Lutherans?

NOTE WELL THE STATEMENT IN THE MISSION STATEMENT: "THRIVENT FINANCIAL FOR LUTHERANS IS A FAITH-BASED MEMBERSHIP ORGANIZATION." BY ITS OWN ADMISSION THRIVENT (AAL/LB) CONTINUES TO BE A PAN-LUTHERAN ORGANIZATION THAT PROUDLY LUMPS ALL OF ITS MEMBERS INTO ITS LUTHERAN FAMILY OF CONFESSION AND SUPPORT, REGARDLESS OF REAL, DOCTRINAL DIFFERENCES BETWEEN THE VARIOUS MEMBERS AND THE DIFFERENT LUTHERAN CHURCHES TO WHICH THEY BELONG. (ROMANS 16:17 IS THEN QUOTED) AVOIDING FALSE TEACHERS MEANS THAT WE REFUSE TO BE PARTNERS WITH THEM IN RELIGIOUS MATTERS. SIMPLY BUYING A PRODUCT FROM A COMPANY DOES NOT MAKE YOU A RELIGIOUS PARTNER WITH THEM. HOWEVER, MEMBERSHIP IN THRIVENT IS DIFFERENT. SINCE IT IS A FRATERNAL BENEFIT SOCIETY FOR LUTHERANS, YOUR MEMBERSHIP DOES MAKE YOU A RELIGIOUS PARTNER WITH THE WELS, LC-MS, AND ELCA.

....

...........WHEN YOU BELONG TO THIS KIND OF FRATERNAL SOCIETY, YOU ARE

810

NOT SIMPLY A CUSTOMER OF THE COMPANY, YOU ARE THE COMPANY, BY REA-
SON OF YOUR FRATERNAL MEMBERSHIP AND VOTING RIGHTS. THEREFORE, YOU
ARE RESPONSIBLE FOR HOW THE COMPANY'S PROFITS ARE SPENT, AND THAT
MAKES IT MUCH MORE THAN JUST A "BUSINESS ARRANGEMENT." THRIVENT FI-
NANCIAL FOR LUTHERANS CALLS ITSELF YOUR RELIGIOUS "BROTHER" IN MANY
WAYS—IN FACT, THAT'S WHAT THE WORD "FRATERNAL" MEANS.

....

....

THE QUESTION CAN BE SUMMARIZED IN THIS WAY: "IS IT PLEASING TO OUR LORD
TO BE A MEMBER OF A FRATERNAL SOCIETY THAT, IN ADDITION TO ITS OTHER AC-
TIVITIES, SUPPORTS AND PROMOTES FALSE TEACHERS?" THE ANSWER FROM
SCRIPTURE IS "NO," AND THAT IS WHY MEMBERSHIP IN FRATERNAL LUTHERAN
BENEFIT SOCIETIES, INCLUDING THRIVENT FINANCIAL FOR LUTHERANS, IS NOT
COMPATIBLE WITH OUR CHRISTIAN LIFE.[22]

MORE CLC FACTS

CHRISTIAN EDUCATION IN THE CLC—HUMBLE
BEGINNINGS FOLLOWED BY NOTEWORTHY PROGRESS

At the Interim Conference sessions held in Spokane in 1958, a concern for
educating the youth of the church was expressed. A group of laymen from Immanuel Lutheran Church in Mankato, Minnesota, invited the Conference to
aid them in planning an educational institution in which future pastors, teachers, and workers in the church could be trained. An offer of property and a
school building could only be considered by the Conference as a possible future
site to train workers.

The following year, the Interim Conference—meeting in January at
Mankato, Minnesota—considered opening a school, but since the group had
no constitution and was not incorporated, little could be done. The Conference
was informed that there were about 34 students interested in a Christian high
school education, and that there were 14 students who wanted to enroll in the
college and seminary. But while the Conference could not underwrite such a
venture into education at that time, it gave its blessing to any effort that Immanuel congregation could make toward providing a school, especially for the
training of pastors and teachers. Four members of Immanuel congregation
who owned a piece of property and a school building immediately offered them
to the project. A great number of Immanuel members contributed their time
and donated materials to remodel the building and to prepare it for classes.
The school building served the high school while the basement of Immanuel
Church provided space for college classes. The school was operated by a private
association of laymen and controlled by a Board of Directors from Immanuel
Lutheran Church. (The old frame country schoolhouse had been moved from
the country to an extensive plot of land in northwest Mankato.)[23]

PROVIDING HIGH SCHOOL, COLLEGE, AND SEMINARY EDUCATION

In the summer of 1959 Professor Robert Dommer was called by the Immanuel Lutheran School Board to head the high school department, and Mrs. Adlegunde Schaller was called as the second teacher in the high school. Professor Edmund Reim, who had served as president of the Wisconsin Synod Seminary, was called to head the college and seminary departments. Professors Martin Galstad was called to teach two periods in education. Later, an instructor for the athletic program was added. The Interim Conference pledged moral and financial support and promised to encourage young people to avail themselves of the facilities that were offered to them.

The school year started in the fall of 1959 with two students who wanted to prepare themselves as teachers in the parochial schools, and two students who wanted to continue their studies in the seminary. The college started the year with an enrollment of 17, and the high school with an enrollment of 24 students. During the summer of 1960 additions were made to the faculties. By the end of its third year the schools had an enrollment of 62 students.

RELOCATION OF THE SCHOOLS

At the Spokane Convention in 1961 an Expansion Committee was chosen to plan the relocation of the schools. In December 1962 the Ingram Estate, located in Eau Claire, Wisconsin, came to the attention of the Committee. The asking price was $85,000 and included 75 acres of land, a large mansion, an apartment annex, two barns, and a custodian's house. The Special Convention held at Messiah Church in Eau Claire in January 1963 voted to purchase this estate as the permanent campus for Immanuel Lutheran College. Though the very reasonable price of $85,000 was a huge sum to the members of the fledging synod, the membership response was positive and generous. During the summer, volunteer crews remodeled the buildings on the beautiful campus to make them usable for school purposes. The building and campus site were dedicated on September 1, 1963, when Immanuel Lutheran College was officially opened on its new campus. "Since that time two classroom buildings (1965 and 1970), a field house (1970), a girls' dormitory (1976), a boys' dormitory (1981), and thirteen professor homes have been added to the campus. In 1997 a large commons building was added to the campus, providing modern kitchen and dining facilities and expanded lounge space for the student body. The Sem House was relocated to make room for the new Commons, and now houses a museum of CLC history. The Seminary itself now meets in the Ingram mansion."[24]

THE SCHOOLS OF THE CLC— THE PICTURE IN LATER YEARS

Elementary schools=22; Secondary schools=2; Schools on the Eau Claire, Wisconsin, campus: Immanuel High School (coeducational boarding school), Immanuel Lutheran College (offers three degree programs), Immanuel

Lutheran Seminary (trains men for the Gospel Ministry. Doctrinally based on acceptance of the canonical writings of the Old and New Testaments as the verbally inspired Word of God, and unqualified subscription to the Lutheran Confessions of the *Book of Concord* as presenting the true teachings of the Word); number of teachers in the CLC=46, not counting those who both pastor and teach. (Information valid to November 22, 2000)

PUBLISHING

The work of publishing is carried on by the CLC BOOK HOUSE, Immanuel Lutheran College, 501 Grover Road, Eau Claire, WI 54701-7199. Publications include *Journal of Theology* (for those who teach the Word), *The Lutheran Spokesman* (a monthly magazine for the home), *Ministry by Mail* (weekly publication—sermons). A substantial library of video tape recordings of worship services is maintained by the Video Tape Ministry. Additional note: *The Journal of Theology* was begun in 1960 with Professor Edmund Reim as the first editor. *The Lutheran Spokesman* was begun in 1958 at Cheyenne, Wyoming, in mimeographed form and sponsored by Redeemer Congregation.

MISSION WORK—HOME MISSIONS

Most of the missionaries/pastors of the CLC at first had to work in secular employment to support themselves. For the most part the congregations of the newly formed synod were small. Emergency grants were given in some classes. Other missionaries were given a regular but meager subsidy. As the new synod faced the world, promising mission fields were before it but could be opened only if the missionary supported himself. As the synod grew, so did its home budget. In the ten years from 1961 to 1971 the budget grew from about $18,000 to about $72,000. And, of course, the financial picture for pastors and missionaries improved over time.

OUR MISSION PROGRAM HAS AIDED ALMOST HALF OF OUR EXISTING CLC CHURCHES AT SOME POINT IN THEIR HISTORY. WITH THE HELP OF SUBSIDY AND LOW INTEREST LOANS FROM OUR MISSION EXTENSION FUND, THEY HAVE BEEN ABLE TO CALL RESIDENT PASTORS, BUILD HOUSES OF WORSHIP, AND CARRY OUT THE LORD'S COMMISSION IN THEIR AREAS.[25]

MISSION WORK—FOREIGN MISSIONS

In the last two decades of the twentieth century the CLC has regularly pursued foreign contacts.

THE LORD HAS BLESSED US WITH OPPORTUNITIES NEVER DREAMED OF WHEN OUR CLC WAS ORGANIZED. IN 1979 A MISSIONARY-AT-LARGE PROGRAM WAS ESTABLISHED IN ORDER THAT NEW U.S. FIELDS COULD BETTER BE EXPLORED AND DEVELOPED FOR RESIDENT PASTORS. SINCE 1974 WE HAVE WITNESSED THE SPIRITUAL GROWTH AND DEVELOPMENT OF THE NIGERIAN CHURCH OF THE LUTHERAN CONFESSION. IN 1985 WE CALLED OUR FIRST OVERSEAS MISSIONARY

TO SOUTHERN INDIA TO ASSIST IN THE GOSPEL EFFORTS OF BRETHREN IN THE CHURCH OF THE LUTHERAN CONFESSION OF INDIA AND THE BHARATH EVANGELICAL LUTHERAN CHURCH. CONTACTS IN VERNON, BRITISH COLUMBIA, CANADA, BLOSSOMED INTO A CLC MISSION WITH GERMAN LANGUAGE SERVICES AND A FULL-TIME PASTOR IN 1997. SINCE THAT TIME THERE HAVE BEEN FURTHER CANADIAN CONTACTS. IN 1998 THE CLC CONVENTION ESTABLISHED FELLOWSHIP WITH THE INDEPENDENT LUTHERAN CONGREGATION OF PARIS, FRANCE.[26] HOWEVER, THIS FELLOWSHIP NO LONGER EXISTS, FOR THE CLC TERMINATED IT.

PROJECT KINSHIP to aid orphans in India was developed in 1983. A sponsorship program emerged whereby individuals or groups within the CLC could sponsor an orphan. The following year the CLC Convention authorized the construction of a building to house about 30 orphans.

THE CLC AND OTHER LUTHERAN BODIES

Affiliated Foreign Churches: NIGERIA-Nigerian Church of the Lutheran Confession (NCLC). INDIA-Church of the Lutheran Confession of India (CLCI), and Bharath Evangelical Lutheran Church (BELC)—both in South India. CONGO-Eglise Lutherienne de Confession du Congo (ELCC).

LATE STATISTICS FOR THE CLC (2003)

Congregations-74; Parish Pastors-64; Communicants-6365; Pre-Communicants-2025; Total Souls-8390; Contributions for home purposes-$4,999,122; Contributions for the CLC Missions-$690,027; Contributions for Special Purposes-$166,212; TOTAL CONTRIBUTIONS-$5,855,961; Average Contributed per Communicant-$920.

Footnotes for Chapter Thirty-Seven

1 *Proceedings, 1951 Wisconsin Synod Convention*, p. 147.

2 *Proceedings, 1953 Wisconsin Synod Convention*, pp. 103, 104

3 *Proceedings, 1955 Wisconsin Synod Convention*, p. 13.

* The CLC *Responses* are taken from "Yes, There Is Still A Difference" - The Continuing Difference Betwen the Church of the Lutheran Confession and the Wisconsin Ev. Lutheran Synod. By Pastor Daniel Fleischer (May 2005), a member of the CLC Board of Doctrine. Represents the position of the CLC.

4 *Proceedings, 1955 Wisconsin Synod Convention*, p. 79.

5 *Proceedings, 1955 Wisconsin Synod Convention*, p. 86.

6 *Proceedings, 1957 Wisconsin Synod Convention*, p. 143.

7 *Proceedings, 1957 Wisconsin Synod Convention*, p. 143.

8 *Proceedings, 1957 Wisconsin Synod Convention*, p. 144.

9 *Proceedings, 1959 Wisconsin Synod Convention,* pp. 195,196.

10 *Proceedings, 1959 Wisconsin Synod Convention,* pp. 178,210.

11 *Proceedings, 1959 Wisconsin Synod Convention,* p. 210.

12 M.J. Witt, "Ten Years of Grace," an essay celebrating the Tenth Anniversary of the CLC.

13 *This Is Your Church - The Church of the Lutheran Confession* (Eau Claire, WI: CLC Book House, Third Edition 2001). pp. 7,8.

14 *"This Is Your Church...,* p.p. 8,9.

15 An informational brochure titled, CHURCH OF THE LUTHERAN CONFESSION

16 *Concerning Church Fellowship—A Statement of Principle,* Revised Edition (Eau Claire, WI: The CLC Book House, 1961), pp. 7-9

17 A quote from, "The Scriptural Principles Concerning Church Fellowship," by Carl Lawrenz, an article in *Quarterlschrift,* Vol. 51, No. 4, (Milwaukee, WI: Northwestern Publishing House), p. 290.

18 A quote from, "Do the Recent Declarations of the ALC Warrant the Establishment of Fraternal Relations?" by John Meyer, an article in Quartalschrift, Vol. 36, No. 4, pp. 264, 268.

19 Paul F. Nolting, "Mark...Avoid," a printed Tenth Anniversary (CLC) Essay. First printing, October 1970; second printing, December 1970.

20 Fleischer, "Yes, There Is Still A Difference"..., pp. 6,7.

21 Nolting, "Mark...Avoid."

22 "Aid Associations for Lutherans/Lutheran Brotherhood—Is This Still An Issue?" An informational brochure of the CLC.

23 Information in this paragraph is taken from "This Is Your Church—The Church of the Lutheran Confession," p. 13.

24 *"This Is Your Church...,* p. 15.

25 *"This Is Your Church...,* p. 10, 11.

26 *"This Is Your Church...,* p. 11.

CHAPTER THIRTY-EIGHT

THE EVANGELICAL LUTHERAN SYNODICAL CONFERENCE OF NORTH AMERICA 1872 - 1967

FEDERATION OF CONSERVATIVE BODIES

THE MISSOURI SYNOD PROVIDED THE INITIATIVE FOR FORMING A NEW GENERAL BODY

THE GENERAL COUNCIL DID NOT SATISFY SOME SYNODS

The Evangelical Lutheran Synodical Conference of North America (or simply the Synodical Conference) was the fourth general body to be formed of Lutheran synods in America. Previous to 1872 there existed the General Synod (org. 1820), the United Synods in America (org. 1863), and the General Council (org. 1867). The following synods participated in the formation of the Synodical Conference in 1872: Missouri Synod, Wisconsin Synod, Joint Synod of Ohio, Illinois Synod, Norwegian Synod, and Minnesota Synod. (Regarding the Wisconsin Synod, note that in 1892 the General Evangelical Lutheran Synod of Wisconsin, Minnesota, Michigan and Other States was formed as a loose confederation of synods. In 1919 the Evangelical Joint Synod of Wisconsin and Other States was formed as a much more closely bound body.)

As early as 1856 Dr. C.F.W. Walther, founder of the Missouri Synod, proposed that free conferences be held in order to realize one United Evangelical Lutheran Church of North America. Dr. Walther called the free conferences at the time when "American Lutheranism" was being fostered within the liberal General Synod, whose confessional stand was quite unionistic. The Lutheran Confessions were not mentioned in the General Synod's constitution. Some of its members did, however, defend the *Augsburg Confession*. And so, Dr. Walther suggested in the Missouri Synod's theological journal, *Lehre Und Wehre*, the calling of free conferences of such Lutherans as subscribed to the *Unaltered Augsburg Confession* (U.A.C.) without reservation, to discuss the situation and to pave the way for a doctrinally united, truly Lutheran Church in North America. Having received encouragement from numerous replies, Walther published an invitation, signed by himself and four other men from St. Louis. It reads:

THE UNDERSIGNED MINISTERS OF THE EVANGELICAL LUTHERAN CHURCH IN THE UNITED STATES, WITH THE CONVICTION THAT THE UNITY AND THE WELL-BEING OF OUR LUTHERAN ZION WILL BE GREATLY ADVANCED THROUGH THE FREE EXPRESSION OF OPINION REGARDING THE VARIOUS INTERESTS OF OUR CHURCH IN THIS LAND BY BRETHREN WHO ARE UNITED IN FAITH, HEREWITH EXTEND AN INVITATION TO ALL MEMBERS OF THE EVANGELICAL LUTHERAN CHURCH IN THE UNITED STATES WHO HOLD THE *UNALTERED AUGSBURG CONFESSION* TO BE A TRUE PRESENTATION OF THE TEACHINGS OF THE WORD OF GOD TO MEET WITH THEM...IN A FREE AND BROTHERLY CONFERENCE CONCERNING THE STATUS AND NEEDS OF THE CHURCH IN AMERICA.[1]

Responding to this invitation, representatives from the Ohio, New York, Pennsylvania, and Missouri Synods met in conference over a period of years (1856-1859), but with no permanent result.

The General Council, which later came to be organized in 1867 as a protest against the unLutheran position of the General Synod, did not satisfy all conservative Lutherans, the reason being that it failed to take a clear and definite stand with regard to the so-called "Four Points" (Lodgery, Pulpit Fellowship, Altar Fellowship, and Chiliasm or Millennialism). The Missouri, Ohio, and Norwegian Synods refused to join the Council, and shortly afterwards the Wisconsin, Minnesota, and Illinois Synods—and somewhat later, the Michigan Synod—withdrew from that general body. These withdrawals were especially due to prompting by the Missouri Synod, which then proceeded to hold a number of conferences with likeminded synods—in 1867 and after, with Ohio; in 1868 with Wisconsin; in 1869 with Illinois; and repeatedly with the Norwegian Synod. Through this series of meetings, these synods found themselves to be in agreement in doctrine and practice. Discussions between the Missouri and Wisconsin Synods produced in 1868 the "Articles of Agreement" establishing altar and pulpit fellowship between the two bodies.

In order to affect a closer union the Ohio Synod in 1870 appointed a committee to confer with similar committees of other synods of the same confessional position. The representatives of the synod met twice in 1871 to adopt a draft for the proposed union, and declared that "the organization of a new general body along strictly confessional lines, free from all unionistic and lax practices, was necessary for the preservation and spread of Lutheran unity." [2] This resulted in the drafting of a constitution for a new general body.

It had been hoped that the General Council (1867) would fill the need for gathering together the confessional Lutheran synods in America. This hope, however, was not realized and so, on July 10-16, 1872, at Milwaukee, six synods holding to the *Unaltered Augsburg Confession* without reservation united to form the Evangelical Lutheran Synodical Conference of North America, known simply as the Synodical Conference. In addition to the above-mentioned synods, the Synod of Minnesota also took part—six synods in all. The organization was effected on the basis of the Constitution which had been drafted the previous year. Dr. Walther was elected as the first president. Other offices provided by the Constitution were those of secretary and treasurer. Besides Dr. Walther, early presidents included: Lehman (Ohio), H.A. Preuss (Norwegian), P.L. Larsen (Norwegian), J. Bading (Wisconsin), G. Gausewitz (Wisconsin), L. Fuerbringer (Missouri).

THE SYNODICAL CONFERENCE—
AN EXCLUSIVE FEDERATION

The Iowa Synod chose not to join the Conference because of that synod's stand on open questions, which the Conference disallowed. The Conference had strict fellowship principles. Concerning Romans 16:17 ("mark and avoid"), and Titus 3:10 (a divisive person is warned twice and then excluded from fellowship), and similar passages, the Conference accepted this statement (published in a memorandum):

IN THESE AND SIMILAR PASSAGES OF HOLY SCRIPTURE GOD EXPRESSLY AND EARNESTLY COMMANDS US NOT TO REMAIN IN CHURCH-BROTHERLY FELLOWSHIP WITH FALSE TEACHERS AND HERETICAL PEOPLE, MUCH LESS TO SEEK THEIR FELLOWSHIP OR TO ENTER IN UPON FRATERNAL ASSOCIATIONS. ON THE CONTRARY, WE ARE EARNESTLY AND AS A MATTER OF PRINCIPLE, TO FLEE FROM AND AVOID THEM.

The Conference was also clear in its opposition to the Masonic Lodge, prohibiting membership in it.

The Conference from its beginning was what could be termed an exclusive federation, for its growth was to be only on the basis of true Lutheran confessionalism. It had justified its founding as a fourth general Lutheran body because the synods involved could not with good conscience enter any of the others. From its beginning the Synodical Conference determined to "fight against any falsification of the Lutheran Confessions" and to make a "determined witness" against such matters as rationalism, unionism, and doctrinal indifference ("Justification For The Synodical Conference," 1871).

ORGANIZATION INTO STATE SYNODS WAS ENCOURAGED

In 1876, in order to preserve unity of spirit, the Conference resolved that the reports of the proceedings of the various districts and synods be exchanged, passed upon by committees and placed before the Synodical Conference. It also advised that all synods take steps toward organizing state synods, thus uniting in one organization all the congregations of the Conference within the respective state or territory—in effect, blurring synodical lines through consolidation. It also advised the establishing of one seminary and teacher's college. And so, through the years, some synods withdrew and others joined, while still others consolidated. Thus the Concordia Synod of Virginia, which joined the Conference in 1876, became a district of the Ohio Synod in 1877. The Illinois Synod consolidated with the Illinois District of the Missouri Synod in 1880, and the Missouri Synod organized the districts of Illinois, Iowa, Nebraska and Kansas, to eventually become state synods. However, this project of consolidation of congregations and educational institutions was later abandoned.

In 1881 the election controversy resulted in the withdrawal of the Ohio Synod from the Synodical Conference. Those who refused to go with Ohio formed the Concordia Synod in June 1882, with 14 pastors particpating. It became a member of the Synodical Conference at its next meeting. This small synod made the *Lutheran Witness* and the *Lutheraner* its official publications. Later, those members who did not join the English Missouri Synod in 1888 joined the Missouri Synod. The Norwegian Synod of the American Evangelical Lutheran Church, which today bears the name Evangelical Lutheran Synod (ELS), joined the Conference in 1920. This small Norwegian body was formed by those who disagreed with the "Madison Theses" or "Agreement" (which supposedly solved the election controversy) and thus would not take part in the merger of the Norwegian churches in 1917, which formed the Evangelical Lutheran Church (ELC)—as it came to be called. This tiny remnant of the old Norwegian Synod regarded themselves as the spiritual successor of that body (org. 1853). The English Synod of Missouri joined the Conference in 1888, merging later, in 1911, with the Missouri Synod. The Michigan Synod, having finally left the General Council, joined the Conference in 1892. The Nebraska District Synod (Wisconsin Synod) joined in 1906, and the Slovak Evangelical Lutheran Church (later called the Synod of Evangelical Lutheran Churches or Slovak Synod) joined the Conference in 1908.

THE 1871 CONSTITUTION

ARTICLE II-CONFESSION: [THE SYNODICAL CONFERENCE] ACKNOWLEDGES THE CANONICAL WRITINGS OF THE OLD AND NEW TESTAMENTS AS GOD'S WORD, AND THE CONFESSIONS OF THE EVANGELICAL LUTHERAN CHURCH OF 1580, CALLED THE "CONCORDIA," AS HER OWN.

ARTICLE III-AIM AND PURPOSE: THE EXTERNAL EXPRESSION OF THE SPIRITUAL UNITY OF THE RESPECTIVE SYNODS; MUTUAL STRENGTHENING IN BELIEF AND CONFESSION; FURTHERANCE OF UNITY IN TEACHING AND PRACTICE, AND THE ELIMINATION OF POTENTIAL OR THREATENING DISTURBANCES THEREOF; COM-

MON ACTIVITY FOR MUTUAL AIMS; THE ENDEAVOR TO FIX THE LIMITS OF THE SYNODS ACCORDING TO TERRITORIAL BOUNDARIES...THE CONSOLIDATION OF ALL LUTHERAN SYNODS OF AMERICA INTO A SINGLE, FAITHFUL, DEVOUT AMERICAN LUTHERAN CHURCH.

ARTICLE IV-AUTHORITY: THE SYNODICAL CONFERENCE IS SOLELY A COUNSELING BODY IN ALL MATTERS IN WHICH IT HAS NOT BEEN GRANTED POWER OF DECISION BY ALL THE CONSTITUENT SYNODS; THE ENTIRETY OF THE SYNODS ALONE CAN DECIDE CONCERNING THE RECEPTION OF CORPORATE CHURCH BODIES INTO THE SYNODICAL CONFERENCE...SUCH ADMISSION CAN TAKE PLACE ONLY THROUGH THE CONSENT OF ALL THE UNITED SYNODS; IT IS TO PROVIDE FOR THE HOLDING OF REGULAR JOINT PASTORAL CONFERENCES...NONE OF THE REPRESENTED SYNODS CAN ENTER INTO OFFICIAL CHURCH RELATIONS WITH OTHER CHURCH BODIES WITHOUT THE AGREEMENT OF ALL THE REPRESENTED SYNODS.

ARTICLE V-OBJECTS OF ACTIVITY: SPIRITUAL TEACHING AND PRACTICE; THE RELATION OF THE ENTIRE BODY AND THE INDIVIDUAL PARTS OF THE SAME TO OFFICIAL CHURCH ORGANIZATIONS OUTSIDE THE UNION; IMPORTANT EXTERNAL AND INTERNAL MATTERS, AS WELL AS MISSIONS FOR EMIGRANTS; MATTERS RELATING TO THE SICK AND THE ORPHANS; LUTHERAN LITERATURE IN GENERAL AND LUTHERAN TRACT PUBLICATION IN PARTICULAR; MATTERS CONCERNING THE EDUCATION OF PASTORS, SCHOOL-TEACHERS AND OTHERS.[3]

The Constitution was signed by representatives from: the Joint Synod of Ohio and Other States; the Synod of Missouri, Ohio and Other States; the Synod of Wisconsin and Other States; the Norwegian Synod; the Synod of Illinois and Other States; and the Synod of Minnesota.

GOVERNMENT OF THE SYNODICAL CONFERENCE

Voting members consisted in all pastors and lay delegates elected by their respective synods as official representatives. Advisory members were all members present, who were either members in good standing of the specific Synods, or who took part in the prior synodical meetings as congregational representatives.

Ministers and congregational representatives were to be in equal number. Each synod was entitled to at least four representatives, with further representation to be determined by the size of the voting membership. Meetings were held every two years.[4]

FELLOWSHIP PRACTICES

As has already been pointed out, the Synodical Conference was an exclusive federation employing strict fellowship practices. The fellowship practices of the Conference can be seen for example in the defense which Dr. Bente made in *Lehre Und Wehre* of the Conference's action of not practicing joint prayer at the free conference held in the early 1900's. He wrote:

THE PREREQUISITE FOR PRAYER FELLOWSHIP AND CHURCH FELLOWSHIP IS

821

UNITY OF FAITH. GOD HAS EXPRESSLY FORBIDDEN US TO PRACTICE CHURCH FELLOWSHIP WITH SUCH WITH WHOM WE ARE NOT UNITED IN THE TRUTH.

In another article he wrote:

IF ANYTHING IS CLEARLY TAUGHT IN THE SCRIPTURES, NOT ONLY INDIRECTLY, BUT DIRECTLY, THEN IT IS JUST THIS THAT WITH SUCH WHO CANNOT BE RE-GARDED AS WEAK IN UNDERSTANDING, BUT MUST BE CONSIDERED PERSISTENT ERRORISTS WE ARE NOT PERMITTED TO PRACTICE CHURCH AND BROTHER FEL-LOWSHIP.

Quoting Romans 16:17, Bente stated:

THE APOSTLE SPEAKS HERE OF PEOPLE IN THE ROMAN CONGREGATION WHO CAME UP WITH A DOCTRINE THAT DIFFERED FROM THE DOCTRINE THEY HAD HEARD FROM THE APOSTLES, WHO CLUNG TO THAT DOCTRINE, AND SOUGHT TO GAIN ADHERENTS FOR IT…AND WHAT IS THE COMMAND OF THE APOSTLE TO ALL CHRISTIANS IN REGARD TO SUCH FALSE TEACHERS? IS IT PERHAPS: PRAC-TICE PULPIT FELLOWSHIP, CHURCH FELLOWSHIP, ALTAR FELLOWSHIP WITH THEM, OR AT LEAST CONDUCT LITURGICAL PRAYER SERVICES WITH THEM? ON THE CONTRARY, HE SAYS: "AVOID THEM!"[5]

The fellowship practice of the Synodical Conference was revealed clearly in the document "Justification for A Synodical Conference" (1871):

WE ARE…ABOVE ALL IN COMPLETE AGREEMENT, THANKS BE TO GOD, THAT WE WILL KEEP THE TREASURE OF THE PURE DOCTRINE AS OUR HIGHEST GOOD AND DEAREST JEWEL. THIS PRICELESS TREASURE, TAKEN FROM THE WORD OF GOD AND SET DOWN IN THE DOCTRINAL WRITINGS OF OUR LUTHERAN CHURCH WE WILL KEEP AS A WHOLE AND IN EVERY DETAIL UNCHANGED AND UNCHANGE-ABLE. WITH GOD'S HELP WE WILL FAITHFULLY WITNESS AND FIGHT AGAINST ANY FALSIFICATION THEREOF. FURTHER…WE WILL MAKE A DETERMINED WIT-NESS AGAINST…RATIONALISM, UNIONISM, INDIFFERENCE AND EMOTIONALISM. WE WILL EQUALLY WITNESS AGAINST THE SPECIAL PLAGUES FROM WHICH LUTHERAN CHURCH POLITY SUFFERS IN MANY PLACES, E.G., THE ROMANIZING TENDENCIES IN THE TEACHING ABOUT THE MINISTRY, ABOUT THE CHURCH AND THE MEANS OF GRACE, CHILIASM, THE FALSE FREEDOM OF THEOLOGICAL RE-SEARCH IN THE SCRIPTURES AND IN THE DEVELOPMENT OF CHURCH DOCTRINE. AND THIS UNITY OF SPIRIT IN REGARD TO STRICT ADHERENCE TO DOCTRINE AND…OPPOSITION TO ALL DEVIATIONS FROM IT REPRESENTS THE DISTINCTIVE-NESS OF OUR ECCLESIASTICAL POINT OF VIEW AND OF THE CONSEQUENT TASK TO WHICH, BY THE GRACE OF GOD, WE CONSIDER OURSELVES CALLED…[6]

Clearly, the unity that the Synodical Conference promoted among Luther-ans in America was a oneness in spirit and profession concerning all scriptural truths.

THE PREDESTINATION OR ELECTION CONTROVERSY
(Gnadenmahl Streit)

The tragic controversy came on the scene in 1880, less than a decade after the founding of the Synodical Conference. The protagonists were Dr. C. F.W. Walther of the Missouri Synod, and Professor F.A. Schmidt of the Norwegian

Synod, both of whom were professors at the seminary of the Missouri Synod in St. Louis. The point of issue was the interpretation of the phrase *intuitu fidei* (in view of faith). Some held that the election of the individual by God was due to the person's faith, which God foresaw. Reconciliation was impossible, and to make matters worse, the members of the Conference began to take sides. Walther and the Missouri Synod were accused by the followers of Professor Schmidt of teaching a Calvinistic-slanted doctrine of Predestination—that God elected some to faith and salvation, but others he elected to remain in unbelief and be damned. Missouri denied that God's election unto salvation was "in view of faith," and on the other hand denied Schmidt's charges of Calvinism—e.g. that God must have elected some to damnation, and that God's grace is irresistible.

When the Missouri Synod adopted a set of thirteen theses on the doctrine of election in 1881, this had the effect of adding fuel to the fire, for the two sides of the controversy began to interpret and argue over these statements. The Joint Synod of Ohio even called Missouri's doctrine of Predestination a "new doctrine." The Missouri and Wisconsin Synods taught that God's election is the cause of faith in the individual. The Ohio Synod taught that it is not. Thus:

WE BELIEVE, TEACH, AND CONFESS THAT ELECTION TOOK PLACE *IN VIEW OF CHRIST'S MERIT APPREHENDED BY FAITH*, OR MORE BRIEFLY STATED BUT WITH THE SAME SENSE, *IN VIEW OF FAITH*. FAITH PRECEDES ELECTION IN THE MIND OF GOD.

As a result of the controversy, the Joint Synod of Ohio, finding that its leaders took up a position against Walther, withdrew from the Conference in 1881 and later sought fellowship with the Iowa Synod, which espoused "open questions." What finally forced the issue of the Joint Synod's withdrawal from the Conference was the action of the Missouri Synod forbidding its delegates to the Synodical Conference convention to confer with individuals who had accused the synod of Calvinism, or to regard as members of the Conference such synods as had charged Missouri with Calvinism.

Most of the members of the Norwegian Synod were aligned with Professor Schmidt, and so in 1883 this body, for the purpose of setting its own house in order, felt constrained to also withdraw from the Synodical Conference. After the Norwegians left the Conference their synod suffered a schism when the supporters of Schmidt formed the Anti-Missourian Brotherhood, with Schmidt as the leader.

With the turn of the century came a thrust to unite all the Norwegians in one body. But one of the matters standing in the way was the matter of the election controversy that had earlier divided the Norwegians and finally even caused a split. Efforts to surmount this difficulty culminated in the "Madison Agreement" or *Opgjør*. The "Agreement" actually allowed two forms of the doctrine of election and thus amounted to a compromise. The Synodical Conference did not waste time disagreeing with the content of this 1912 "Agreement" (or Compromise), which paved the way for the great Norwegian merger of 1917. (The reader may review the finer details of this document, and the controversy it caused, in the chapters of Norwegian Lutheranism.) The Synodical Conference charged that the "Agreement" was inconsistent since it taught both that election is "in view of faith"—that faith is the *cause* of the Christian's election

823

to salvation—while another part of the document taught that faith is the *result* of the Christian's election. The Missouri Synod went so far as to say that the union which formed the Evangelical Lutheran Church (1917) was based "on common blood rather than common Christian faith." Only a tiny portion of the former Norwegian Synod—the group which refused to accept the "Agreement" and remained out of the merger—rejoined the Synodical Conference in 1920, as was reported earlier.

FREE CONFERENCES: ATTEMPTS TO UNITE THE LUTHERANS

Between 1903 and 1906 a series of Intersynodical Conferences (free conferences) were held at which members of the Ohio and Iowa Synods met with men from the Synodical Conference. However, these conferences did not remove the differences which had so long divided the Synodical Conference synods from the rest of Lutheranism.

In 1916 conferences were again initiated, but on a smaller scale, leading to the appointment of the Intersynodical Committee, representing the Missouri, Wisconsin, Ohio, Iowa, and Buffalo Synods. Efforts to arrive at agreement extended into the twenties. By 1928 it seemed as though agreement had been reached through the "Chicago Theses;" nevertheless, in 1929 none of the synods officially accepted, but rather rejected, the Theses. By then three of the synods—Ohio, Iowa, Buffalo—were planning to merge to form the American Lutheran Church (1930).

The Missouri Synod rejected the Theses as not in fact settling the differences, especially in the doctrine of Conversation and Election. Missouri drew up a confession of its own, setting forth its doctrinal position in clear and unmistakable language. This confession, adopted in 1932, is known as the "Brief Statement" and was to serve as the basis for any further deliberation with those differing from the Missouri Synod in doctrine. After this body found the Chicago Theses to be unacceptable, the document no longer served any practical purpose. Following the merger of the Ohio, Iowa, and Buffalo Synods in 1930, the Missouri Synod continued to seek doctrinal agreement, and thisw as the beginning of much heartache to the members of the Wisconsin and Norwegian Synods, as well as to many conservatives within the synod itself. (Note: For a thorough discussion of this matter refer to the individual histories of these synods.)

THE NATIONAL LUTHERAN COMMISSION AND THE NATIONAL LUTHERAN COUNCIL

The National Lutheran Commission was organized in October 1917 by representatives of seven Lutheran bodies out of concern for the religious and moral well being of soldiers. Six other church bodies soon joined, and even the Synodical Conference agreed to coordination of effort. Historian Abdel Ross Wentz points out that this agency, which was born of emergencies of war, included virtually all Lutherans of America, and was the first organization to do so.[7]

Later, the National Lutheran Council (NLC) was organized by representatives of the participating bodies of the National Lutheran Commission. Only the Synodical Conference synods did not use the NLC as their agency of cooperation.[8] When the Council was formed at Chicago, September 6, 1918, the Synodical Conference sent a letter stating that it would not be possible for it to enter into complete cooperation with the proposed Council. In 1958 the NLC made overtures to the Missouri Synod to gain its support for the establishment of an agency of milder cooperative activities among Lutherans in this country. The Missouri Synod participated in a series of conferences and gave indication that it could seriously consider participating in a wider federation of Lutherans. The discussions carried on by the Inter-Lutheran Consultation—which included the American Lutheran Church, the Missouri Synod, and the United Lutheran Church in America (later took the name Lutheran Church in America), resulted in 1962 in a resolution to draw up the documents for a new Lutheran agency. In 1963 another synod of the Synodical Confernce, the Synod of Evangelical Lutheran Churches (Slovak)—the synod most closely allied with the Missouri Synod—also consented to join the Consultation. The proposed Constitution was approved by the Missouri Synod at its Detroit Convention in 1965. Upon acceptance also by the other bodies, the Constitution brought into being the Lutheran Council in the U.S.A. More will be said later of the Missouri Synod's participation in the NLC meetings.

MISSION WORK-HOME

The home mission work of the Synodical Conference was centered in the so-called "Black Belt" in the southern part of the United States. However, in 1946 the process was begun of having synodical districts take over the work of the Conference among Negroes in their territories.

The mission program of the Conference in the South was transferred to the Southern District of the Missouri Synod. The ownership of the Alabama Lutheran Academy-College at Selma, Alabama, was transferred to the Missouri Synod. Immanuel Lutheran College, Greensboro, North Carolina, was permanently closed, effective June 30, 1961 and the property sold.

MISSION WORK-AFRICAN

The African Continent really is huge. It has been pointed out that the U.S.A., Western Europe, China, and India can be superimposed on the African map and still have space left over. In 1937 Dr. and Mrs. Henry Nau arrived in Ibesikpo in West Africa, a tiny portion of a vast continent, to begin work among 18 congregations which had petitioned the Synodical Conference to bring them the Word. The plea was sent through Jonathan Udo Ekon, who at the time was studying at Immanuel Lutheran College, Greensboro, North Carolina. The work progressed, and in 1949 the seminary was opened. Then came the Lutheran High School, Lutheran Teachers Training College, and finally, in

1960, the two Lutheran Bible Institutes for the training of evangelists.

The early 1950's saw the opening of a Lutheran Hospital on the Cross River near Eket, which, in the early sixties, numbered some 137 beds, including a tubercular ward. In 1961 alone the medical staff tended to the needs of some 50,000 outpatients. In early 1957 the church made its first penetration of more distant provinces when it began bringing the gospel to the people of Ogoja, some 250 miles north of Uyo.[9]

The Nigerian Field (by 1962)

Churches	197
Communicant members	14,635
Preaching stations	7
Primary schools	87
Baptized members	35,606
American Missionaries	1
American Teachers	8
American Medical Staff	8
American Lay Workers	4
National Pastors	18
National Teachers	567
National Medical Workers	15

The Ghana field was to be the newest and last mission undertaken by the Synodical Conference with the Wisconsin and Norwegian Synods as members. The field had two established congregations.

By the time the Wisconsin and Norwegian Synods left the Synodical Conference in 1963, it had completed 26 years of labor in the African field. After 1963 and until the Synodical Conference was officially dissolved in 1967, the work in Nigeria and Ghana was conducted as a project of the Conference, with the responsibility, of course, in the hands of the Missouri Synod and the Slovak Synod. In 1962, in view of the imminent dissolution of the Conference, and in view of the Missouri Synod's willingness to take over the African work, the Wisconsin Synod recommended that "the dissolution committee in consultation with the Synodical Conference Missionary Board and possibly the missions themselves prepare recommendations to the Lutheran Synodical Conference regarding the disposition of all joint work."[10]

A COMMON HYMNAL FOR
THE SYNODICAL CONFERENCE

In 1930 the Intersynodical Committee on Hymnology and Liturgy was established at the request of the Missouri Synod. Its aim was to produce a common English Hymnal for use by the federation. The work of the Committee resulted in *The Lutheran Hymnal* of 1941, a revision of the *Evangelical Lutheran Hymnbook* of 1912. This hymnal continued in popular usage for many years, and still remains a favorite in some congregations of the former Synodical Conference bodies. In 1982 the Missouri Synod published its new hymnal, *Lutheran Worship*. The Wisconsin Synod later followed suite with its own hymnal, *Christian Worship-A Lutheran Hymnal*, in 1993.

THE AMERICAN LUTHERAN CONFERENCE (1930): AN OPPOSING FORCE TO THE SYNODICAL CONFERENCE

What had kept the Synodical Conference apart from other Lutherans was not only the unwavering stand it held on the doctrine of Election but also its insistence on unconditional doctrinal agreement—a full and complete agreement by the other bodies to the doctrinal position of the Conference—before church fellowship, or even cooperation in joint endeavors, could be entered upon. The Conference stood firm against unionism of every form.

Mention has already been made of the participation by the Missouri and Wisconsin Synods in an Intersynodical Committee which attempted to work out an agreement on doctrine to serve as the basis for fellowship and cooperation. The Intersynodical (Chicago) Theses was presented to the bodies. Far from serving as a uniting force, the Theses were the cause of a great deal of dissatisfaction and friction among the bodies. The Missouri Synod in 1929 soundly rejected them. Thus the reaction of the bodies to the Theses played its own part in keeping the two sides isolated and finally, in promoting the formation of the American Lutheran Conference the following year as an opposing force to the Synodical Conference. One of the elements missing from the Theses—an element Missouri considered essential—was a statement—at the beginning, outlining the controversy existing between the synods. There was also the failure to include all historical data in working out the Theses. Of special concern to the Missouri Synod was the move toward a closer union between the Ohio and Iowa Synods. Furthermore, Missouri considered the Madison Agreement or Settlement (regarding the election controversy) to be a compromise rather than a settlement of doctrinal differences. (Note: For a detailed study of the reactions by the Wisconsin and Missouri Synods, and the Norwegian Synod, to the doctrinal discussions and agreements worked out in the 1930's, refer to the chapters outlining the histories of these bodies as well as the histories of the synods comprising the American Lutheran Conference.)

Doctrinally, the American Lutheran Conference took its stand to the left of the Synodical Conference position, and to the right of that held by the United Lutheran Church.[11] The basis for this median doctrinal position was the Chicago Theses. Thus, by 1930 the Lutherans in America were enclosed in three bodies (except for a few small bodies: Lutheran Brethren, Eielsen Synod, Finnish Apostolic, and National Evangelical). Theses groupings were: United Lutheran Church in America (1918), Synodical Conference (1872), American Lutheran Conference (1930).

THE SYNODICAL CONFERENCE
AND THE BRESLAU SYNOD

In 1948 the Conference declared full fellowship with the Evangelical Lutheran Church—commonly called the Breslau Synod—in old Prussia. This action was taken on the basis of the fact that the Breslau Synod had arrived at full unity of faith with the Evangelical Lutheran Free Church and had entered into fellowship with it. For years the Evangelical Free Church had been in fellowship with the Synodical Conference. (Note: It would be of interest to the reader to refer to Dr. John W. Behnken's autobiography, *This I Recall*, Concordia Publishing House, St. Louis, for a discussion of the Lutheran Church in Germany and Behnken's personal experiences with this country following World War II.)

CRUCIAL YEARS FOR THE
SYNODICAL CONFERENCE

The events crucial to the very existence of the Synodical Conference began to take place already in the 1930's and snowballed in the '40's. The Wisconsin and Norwegian Synods raised objections to the Missouri Synod's continuation of negotiations with the American Lutheran Church. The two bodies had been negotiating on the basis of the Missouri Synod's Brief Statement and the ALC's Sandusky Resolutions. While negotiations were stopped momentarily, the two bodies resumed their meetings and by 1949 had jointly produced the "Common Confession"-Part I, later followed by Part II in 1952. Part II was not officially accepted by the Missouri Synod, and the Norwegians vigorously protested this venture of Missouri into unionism—as they labeled it—for they did not feel that the Common Confession really resolved the past doctrinal differences, nor that it dealt with such practical questions as lodgery. Furthermore, Missouri's two sister synods felt that the ALC had shown its stripe by associating through the American Lutheran Conference with other Lutheran bodies whose orthodoxy was much in question.

There were also other issues that caused the Wisconsin Synod and the Norwegians much concern. Among them: Missouri's participation in the governmental chaplaincy program, Missouri's decision to leave Scouting as an open matter to be decided within each congregation, Missouri's failure to discipline theological professors who taught error, and Missouri's cooperative activities with the National Lutheran Council.

The Missouri Synod's pursuit of a wider fellowship would result finally in the withdrawal of two of the four synods that made up the Synodical Conference, and finally in the dissolution of the Conference itself.

The years 1955 and 1963 were especially crucial ones for the Conference. In fact, they rang the death knoll for it. The Wisconsin Synod and the Norwegians were sharp in their attacks on the Common Confession, and were insistent in their demands that the Missouri Synod cease negotiations with the American Lutheran Church. There were sharp attacks also on Missouri's stand on the matter of joint prayer (revealed in its statements on prayer) and on its cooperation in certain endeavors with the National Lutheran Council. Furthermore, there was criticism of a host of individual cases where discipline was called for but not administered. But there were other matters also which, according to the two sister synods indicated that their beloved counterpart was departing from its former staunch stand on doctrine and church practice.

In 1955 the Wisconsin and Norwegian Synods officially stated their grievances against the Missouri Synod and took action to suspend fellowship with that body. The Norwegian Synod actually carried through that year with its resolutions of suspension, while retaining fellowship with those in sympathy with its position. It would be another six years, however, before the Wisconsin Synod would put its suspension resolutions into effect—a delay that resulted in a growing number of defections from its ranks.

In 1956 the Synodical Conference had to decide what measures to take in order to check the controversy. The Missouri Synod also acted. It stated that it no longer regarded the Common Confession as a "functioning union document for fellowship with the American Lutheran Church." Missouri stated that it wanted to discuss the issues involved with its sister synods, and suggested the drafting jointly of "one clear, comprehensive statement concerning doctrine and practice." Both the other synods responded favorably, and the Wisconsin Synod deferred acting on its resolutions of suspension of fellowship, even though President Oscar J. Naumann, in his opening address to the synod, indicated that the events that had transpired called for carrying out these resolutions.

In the Synodical Conference a Joint Union Committee was appointed to carry on the discussions and possibly produce a joint confession. But as time went on, the breach widened rather than narrowed, and in 1961 the Wisconsin Synod followed the earlier action of the Evangelical Lutheran Synod (by that time the name had been changed) in suspending fellowship with the Missouri Synod, until which time that body would come to her former self. In 1963 both synods withdrew from the Synodical Conference, for all practical purposes thereby ending its history. The Conference failed by less than a decade to celebrate its centennial.

A BRIEF HISTORY OF THE FINAL YEARS
OF THE SYNODICAL CONFERENCE

Although this history is given in detail in other chapters of this book dealing with the respective synods, nevertheless, it might be well to at least give some of the highlights here. Already in 1955 both the Convention Floor Committee and the Standing Committee in Matters of Church Union of the Wisconsin Synod affirmed that the Missouri Synod...

(A)   BY REAFFIRMING ITS ACCEPTANCE OF THE COMMON CONFESSION AS A "SETTLEMENT OF PAST DIFFERENCES WHICH ARE IN FACT NOT SETTLED"...AND
(B) BY ITS PERSISTENT ADHERENCE TO ITS UNIONISTIC PRACTICES (THE COMMON CONFESSION; JOINT PRAYER; SCOUTING; CHAPLAINCY; COMMUNION AGREEMENT WITH THE NLC; COOPERATION WITH UNORTHODOX CHURCHES IN MATTERS CLEARLY NOT IN THE FIELD OF EXTERNALS; NEGOTIATING WITH LODGES AND BOY SCOUTS OF AMERICA WITH THE PLEAS THAT THIS GIVES OPPORTUNITY TO

829

BEAR WITNESS, UNDER THE SAME PLEA TAKING PART IN UNIONISTIC RELIGIOUS PROGRAMS AND IN ACTIVITIES OF UNIONISTIC CHURCH FEDERATIONS; NEGOTI-ATING FOR THE PURPOSE OF UNION WITH A CHURCH BODY WHOSE OFFICIAL PO-SITION IS THAT IT IS NEITHER POSSIBLE NOR NECESSARY TO AGREE IN ALL MATTERS OF DOCTRINE AND WHICH CONTENDS FOR AN ALLOWABLE AND WHOLE-SOME LATITUDE OF THEOLOGICAL OPINION ON THE BASIS OF THE TEACHINGS OF THE WORD OF GOD) HAS BROUGHT ABOUT THE PRESENT BREAK IN RELATIONS, AND THAT OUR SYNOD, BOUND BY THE WORD OF GOD, SHOULD NOW DECLARE ITSELF ON THE MATTER WHICH IS NOW THREATENING THE EXISTENCE OF THE SYNODICAL CONFERENCE AND THE CONTINUANCE OF OUR AFFILIATION WITH THE SISTER SYNOD...[HOWEVER, THE WISCONSIN SYNOD DID NOT RESOLVE TO SUSPEND FELLOWSHIP THAT YEAR.][12]

The Norwegian Synod in its statement of suspension of fellowship in 1955 took exception to the 1938 St. Louis Articles of Union, which had been drawn up and accepted as the doctrinal basis for union with the ALC, and which both the Wisconsin Synod and the Norwegian Synod also petitioned the Missouri Synod to revoke–which petition went unheeded. The Norwegian Synod also took exception to the "Saginaw Resolution" of 1944 which attempted to draw a distinction between joint prayer and prayer fellowship. It took exception to the 1945 Chicago Statement signed by 44 Missouri Synod pastors and profes-sors, which "further weakened the bulwarks against unionism and laid down unscriptural principles for church fellowship." It should be noted that doctrinal discipline was not exercised and there was no requirement of retraction by the signers, although President John W. Behnken was very upset by their action. A Joint Committee—ten men from the signers and ten men appointed by Pres-ident Behnken—held a series of meetings, but no satisfactory solution was ar-rived at and the meetings were dropped. Later, the praesidium of the synod met with representatives of the Forty-Four resulting in agreement by the spokesmen of the signers to withdraw A Statement as a basis for further dis-cussion. The Praesidium of the synod agreed to a series of special study docu-ments to consider the issues that had been raised, to be prepared by men chosen by President Behnken. The Forty-Four, as an organized group, went out of existence.[13] The Norwegian Synod also took exception to both the agree-ment entered upon by the Missouri Synod with the National Lutheran Council and to the Common Confession of 1950, which Missouri helped to formulate.

In 1956 the Missouri Synod pleaded with the sister synods to accept "our fra-ternal expressions of concern" and urged the carrying out of the Conference resolution that: the issues which disturb the unity of the Synodical Conference be thoroughly discussed and considered on the basis of God's Word," in joint meetings of faculties, pastoral conferences (mixed), and smaller groups. Again, the Missouri Synod showed that it desired the formulation of a new document by all the synods in the Conference. At the same time, Missouri agreed "not to enter discussions or negotiations with other Lutheran synods without having informed the sister synods of the Synodical Conference of our intentions and without having invited and urged them to join with us in these discussions."[14]

In 1956 the Wisconsin Synod delayed in suspending fellowship with the Mis-souri Synod, while the Norwegians that same year resolved to continue its sus-pension of fellowship.

AN INVITATION FROM THE AUGUSTANA CHURCH AND THE ULCA TO THE MISSOURI SYNOD

In the meantime, in 1955, the Augustana Church and the United Lutheran Church in America invited the Missouri Synod to designate representatives to meet with commissions of those two bodies and with representatives of other Lutheran bodies as well, "to consider such an organic union as will give real evidence of our unity in the faith, and to proceed to draft a constitution and devise organizational procedures to effect union." Missouri, however, respectfully declined the invitation, but also resolved to express its willingness to meet with the ULCA and the Augustana Evangelical Lutheran Church with a view to resolve their differences. Missouri also asked that the other synods of the Synodical Conference be included in the invitation "when such deliberations are proposed."

PROGRESS, AND YET, ROADBLOCKS TO PRESERVING THE SYNODICAL CONFERENCE

The Joint Committees of the synods submitted to the 1958 Lakewood Synodical Conference Convention and to the constituent synods the following Statement on Scripture:

WE REJECT AND CONDEMN "DEMYTHOLOGIZING" AS A DENIAL OF THE WORD OF GOD. WHERE SCRIPTURE RECORDS AS HISTORICAL FACTS THOSE EVENTS AND DEEDS WHICH FAR SURPASS THE ORDINARY EXPERIENCE OF MEN, THAT RECORD MUST BE UNDERSTOOD LITERALLY, AS A RECORD OF FACTS; THE MIRACULOUS AND MYSTERIOUS MAY NOT BE DISMISSED AS INTENDED TO HAVE ONLY A METAPHORICAL OR SYMBOLICAL MEANING.[14]

To quote an observation by Aaberg of the Evangelical Lutheran Synod (Norwegian):

TWO SUBSEQUENT EVENTS REVEALED THE STATEMENT'S TIMELINESS. PROFESSOR MARTIN H SCHARLEMANN, A MEMBER OF THE FACULTY OF CONCORDIA SEMINARY, ST. LOUIS, PRESENTED SHORTLY THEREAFTER FOUR ESSAYS REGARDING SCRIPTURE, ALL OF WHICH CONTAINED FALSE DOCTRINE, AND THE ST. LOUIS FACULTY ITSELF ADOPTED "A STATEMENT ON THE FOR M AND FUNCTION OF SCRIPTURE," WHICH CALLED INTO QUESTION ITS POSITION IN REGARD TO INSPIRATION.[15]

The Synodical Conference was agreed on the doctrine of Scripture. Its agreement was tested in its joint study of the doctrine of the Antichrist. After somewhat discordant debate, agreement was reached that the papacy as it is known today, is the Antichrist and that it shall continue to the end of time, "whatever form or guise it may take."

A conclave of theologians was held in June 1959 at Oakland, California. Representatives were present also from Argentina, Australia, Brazil, Canada, England, Germany, India, and Japan. The conservatives found quite a few to shake hands with in the foreign delegation, and also with many daughter churches and districts of the Missouri Synod, who held to a more orthodox

831

stand than did the parent body.

In the 1959 San Francisco Convention of the Synodical Conference, a resolution was adopted that was a joy to the conservatives, for it required pastors, teachers, and professors to teach and act in harmony with formally adopted statements on doctrine and practice such as the Brief Statement.

What seemed to be progress toward unity in the Synodical Conference was halted by what has been termed "roadblocks erected by the Missouri Synod's Praesidium and Doctrinal Unity Committee."[16]   Actions which adversely affected; intersynodical relations within the Synodical Conference were the acceptance of the NLC invitation for discussion which could lead towards the expansion of cooperative activities, and the Missouri Synod Committee's presentation of its Theology of Fellowship to the Joint Committee of the Conference. This was Missouri's positional statement on the doctrine of Church Fellowship.

Missouri at first declined to accept the NLC's invitation. However, Dr. Behnken was later urged by the Doctrinal Unity Committee to accept it, and he ultimately gave in to their promptings. It would appear that Dr. Behnken was more disturbed by "bad public press" and hurt feelings outside the Synodical Conference, and more disturbed over the cries of protest within the circle of Missouri's liberals, than he was over the counsel of the conservatives both within and without his synod. Another consideration was that Dr. Paul Empie, Executive Director of the NLC, stated that while the Council could not engage in discussions involving church fellowship in the fullest sense of the term, it could and would most certainly examine with the Missouri Synod the doctrinal implications of cooperation between Christians.[17]   Therefore Missouri's Committee recommended to Dr. Behnken that he accept the invitation of the NLC "with the express purpose of bearing witness to our theological position."[18]

President Oscar J. Naumann of the Wisconsin Synod declined the NLC's invitation, but added this statement:

IF THE LORD OF THE CHURCH CROWNS OUR EFFORTS WITHIN THE SYNODICAL CONFERENCE WITH HIS BLESSINGS, AND THE VARIOUS EFFORTS PRESENTLY AIMED AT UNION AND MERGER MEET WITH SUCCESS, WE WOULD NOT BE ADVERSE TO CONSULTATION TO EXPLORE WHAT DIVIDES US AT PRESENT AND TO SEEK TO ESTABLISH TRUE UNITY IN DOCTRINE AND PRACTICE.[19]

Perhaps if Dr. Behnken would have followed a similar course in dealing with the NLC's invitation, the course of history for the Synodical Conference might have been altered, for at this time there was sharp division in the Joint Committee over the doctrine of Church Fellowship. The following was reported to the 1960 Milwaukee Synodical Conference Convention:

By far the largest amount of time during the past several meetings was devoted to a determined wrestling with the problems growing out of divergent views on fellowship, recognizing that there lay the single most formidable obstacle to a restoration of proper inter-synodical relations...Yet with profound perplexity and genuine grief it must be reported that a solution has thus far escaped the Joint Committee.[20]

And so, while there was a growing disagreement within the Conference's Joint Committee on the doctrine of Church Fellowship, the Missouri Synod aimed at discussions of this very doctrine with the NLC!

Needless to say, both the Wisconsin Synod and the Norwegians strongly objected to the Missouri Synod Committee's participation in the NLC meetings. Even President Paul Rafaj of the Slovak Synod appealed to the Joint Committee to first try to settle "our own differences and then go out and negotiate with other church bodies. If my house is on fire and the neighbor's house happens to be on fire at the same time, what would be my duty? Of course, first my own house, then the neighbor's."

In the recessed Synodical Conference Convention, May 17-19, 1961, a resolution was passed which in effect asked the Missouri Synod to suspend meetings with the NLC. However, the Missouri Committee, together with the synod praesidium, chose to continue meetings with the NLC. This decision no doubt caused considerable damage to the effort to restore unity in the Synodical Conference, if not scuttling the efforts altogether.

In their study of various doctrines involved in the dispute within the Synodical Conference, the Joint Committee finally tackled the one that lay as the biggest obstacle on the road to unity—the doctrine of Church Fellowship. The committees of both the Wisconsin Synod and the Norwegian Synod objected strongly to Part II of Missouri's presentation, "Theology of Fellowship," which had to do with principles governing the exercise of church fellowship. In their presentation, the faculties of the two Missouri Synod seminaries, who drew up the statement, condoned joint prayer with those who are not in confessional agreement, and also condoned prayer at civic functions.

Theodore A. Aaberg of the Evangelical Lutheran Synod (Norwegian) draws our attention to a point that should not be overlooked:

ALL OF THE PRESENTATIONS ON CHURCH FELLOWSHIP, INCLUDING THAT OF THE OVERSEAS BRETHREN, WITH THE SOLE EXCEPTION OF MISSOURI, HAD AS THEIR POSITION THAT CHURCH FELLOWSHIP IS TO BE EXERCISED ON THE BASIS OF A TRUE CONFESSION TO THE WORD OF GOD. [21]

In May 1960 the Wisconsin Synod Committee, at a meeting of the Joint Committee, announced that an impasse had been reached in the discussion on Church Fellowship, and thus its participation in the Joint Committee discussions was at an end. The same year, the Norwegian Synod Committee recommended to the parent body that it withdraw its participation. And so, the Joint Committee meetings were ended.

THE OVERSEAS BRETHREN TRIED THEIR HAND AT PRESERVING THE UNITY OF THE CONFERENCE

The conclave of theologians, which included the Overseas Brethren, met in Thiensville (Mequon), Wisconsin, during July 1960, but the conclave was not able to resolve the impasse. The Overseas Brethren asked that a committee representing them join the Joint Committee and study the four presentations on Church Fellowship, and also make its own contributions as well. This recommendation was accepted. In April 1961 a delegation came to the United States to present their evaluation of the papers on fellowship and to give their

833

own presentation. However, the presentation by the overseas Brethren did not change the course of history for the Conference, for none of the statements on Church Fellowship, including that of the Missouri Synod, were modified. And while a new forum for discussion was suggested—the formation of one Commission on Doctrine for the Synodical Conference, with Overseas Theologians serving on a consultative basis—this suggestion was not accepted by Wisconsin or by the Norwegians. Included in the above suggestion was the holding of the four fellowship statements in abeyance while the Doctrine of the Church was restudied. Finally, a statement would be formulated followed by the formulating of theses on Church Fellowship. While a recessed convention of the Conference was scheduled for 1961, the fact remains that primary time should have been set aside at the regular convention held in August 1960, for the purpose of setting the Synodical Conference's disparate doctrinal house in order. Yet, very little time, relatively speaking, was devoted to the issue disturbing the synods. Instead, joint work was planned covering the next two years. Budgets for spending joint monies were adopted. So little time and effort were given to the doctrinal issues that more then one pastor stood up to state his dissent to the procedure. A Wisconsin Synod pastor summed up the Synodical Conference sessions on the floor with the words, "I just wonder if we are trying to postpone something we are afraid to face?" A Missouri Synod pastor stated on the floor that the only thing the convention was doing regarding the union matter was "to pass the buck." During the discussion which concerned the matter of calling a recessed convention, Pastor Carl A. Gaertner of Dallas, first vice-president of Missouri's Texas District—with the thought in mind that the same delegates would be present at the recessed convention as were present at the 1960 Synodical Conference Convention—stated: "Many of us who have come here have a sense of frustration; when I come back I don't want to hear discussion of just a lot of committee reports. I want to have a chance to discuss the real issues that are involved, on the basis of the Word of God." A Wisconsin Synod layman from Morton Grove, Illinois, called attention to the fact that a special meeting of laymen at the convention had been called . He pointed out that at this meeting the one thing that was deplored was that laymen of the Missouri Synod were uninformed as regards issues threatening the continuance of fellowship.[22]

THE WISCONSIN SYNOD'S DECLARATION OF SUSPENSION OF FELLOWSHIP WITH MISSOURI

New storm clouds appeared on the scene for the Synodical Conference which brought even more overcast to an already dark and foreboding sky. The Missouri Synod's St. Louis faculty presented "A Statement On the Form and Function of Scripture," excerpts of which were printed in the *Lutheran Witness* in April 1961. A study of this document caused the Wisconsin Synod Commission on Doctrinal Matters to report to the recessed Synodical Conference Convention in 1961 that it was no longer certain that the Wisconsin and Missouri Synods were in agreement on the doctrine of Scripture. The report went on to make this significant statement:

...FOR UNLESS CERTAINTY THAT WE ARE AT ONE ON THE DOCTRINE OF SCRIP-
TURE AND REVELATION IS RESTORED, WE WOULD HAVE LOST THE BASIS FOR A
PROFITABLE DISCUSSION OF THE OTHER MATTERS IN CONTROVERSY BETWEEN
US, EVEN IF THERE WERE NO IMPASSE ON THE DOCTRINE OF FELLOWSHIP.[23]

It was at its own convention that year that the Wisconsin Synod declared a
suspension of fellowship with the Missouri Synod.

The reaction of the Evangelical Lutheran Synod to the St. Louis faculty document was also a very negative one. At their 1961 Convention, the Norwegians
declared:

IT IS EVIDENT THAT THE LUTHERAN SYNODICAL CONFERENCE IS NO LONGER
FUNCTIONING ACCORDING TO THE PRIME PURPOSE STATED IN ITS CONSTITUTION,
AND ITS EXISTENCE, AS ITS MEMBERSHIP IS PRESENTLY CONSTITUTED, IS NO
LONGER TRUTHFUL.

A resolution was then passed to...

...DIRECT A MEMORIAL TO THE 1962 CONVENTION OF THE LUTHERAN SYNODI-
CAL CONFERENCE TO INSTITUTE MEASURES TO DISSOLVE THE LUTHERAN SYN-
ODICAL CONFERENCE.[24]

When the Synodical Conference convened, November 13-15, 1962, at St.
James Lutheran Church, Chicago, the Evangelical Lutheran Synod and the
Wisconsin Synod did not partake in a joint opening service with the Missouri
and Slovak Synods, but joined together in their own communion service at St.
Paul's Church, a congregation of the ELS, located in Chicago.

The ELS president listed four evidences of a widening gap in the Synodical
Conference: (1) Public error in the Missouri Synod was not publicly repudiated
(some names were given). (2) Real doubt existed as to Missouri's position on
the doctrine of Scripture. (3) "Theology of Fellowship" represented a new and
false position. (4) Failure on the part of the Missouri Synod to carry out in synodical life good doctrinal statements.

Prior to this time the two sister synods had accused the Missouri Synod of
the following errors in the field of doctrine and practice: (1) Prayer Fellowship–
Missouri was accused of making an unscriptural distinction between prayer fellowship and joint prayer. (Joint prayer was used to designate prayers prayed
at Intersynodical meetings to ask God's blessings and guidance upon the deliberations and discussions of His Word.) Wisconsin accused Missouri of changing its position on Prayer Fellowship in 1944 when it came forth with this
distinction. (2) Fellowship meetings–Missouri allowed such meetings (i.e. with
church bodies not in fellowship with the Synodical Conference) in conferences
of seminary students, faculty members, editors of church papers and the like.
(3) Cooperating in mission activity—Missouri's Board for Missions in North
and South America was accused of joining the Division of American Mission of
the National Council of Churches in 1960. (4) Changing the application of Romans 16:17—Missouri was accused of applying the judgment spoken of in this
passage of Scripture to makers of divisions and offenses, but not to their victims—people who follow, perhaps blindly, the false teachers. (See: Four Statements on Fellowship, p. 40.) (5) Prayers at civic occasions—Missouri was
accused of calling these prayers a justifiable "public witness of the church's in-
tercession for all sorts and conditions of men and of the Christian's readiness

835

to participate in every work that promotes the weal of mankind." (See: Four Statements on Fellowship, p. 46.)[25]

The ELS called for dissolving the Synodical Conference, when it met in November 1962. After all, both the ELS and the Wisconsin Synod had suspended fellowship with the Missouri Synod, whose membership was by far the largest in the Conference. However, by a close 5-4 vote—the Missouri Synod and the Slovak Synod voting together on one side, and the Wisconsin Synod and the Norwegians voting together on the other side—the Conference was continued.[26]

The ELS in 1963 resolved to withdraw from membership in the Synodical Conference.[27] It also maintained an offer made in 1962 to meet with the Missouri Synod, but on strict rules which the Norwegians drew up, which included refraining from doctrinal discussion with any and all outside the Lutheran Synodical Conference while the synods strived for unity in their midst, except by common consent of the four synods...and...Missouri's practice would have to be brought into conformity with (the supreme demands of the marks of the Church: Word and Sacrament) and that while there had to be time in carrying out disciplinary action, there would have to be immediate public repudiation of those who publicly promoted error.

The Wisconsin Synod also withdrew from the Conference in 1963, with the Missouri Synod and the Slovak Synod (Synod of Evangelical Lutheran Churches) remaining members of the Conference. Joint work in missions among the Negroes in this country, and the work in Nigeria, was taken over by the Missouri and Slovak Synods.

DISSOLUTION OF THE
SYNODICAL CONFERENCE

The 1967 Missouri Synod Convention resolved to seek the dissolution of the Synodical Conference, pointing out that its continuation served "no useful purpose."[28]

The Synod of Evangelical Lutheran Churches (commonly designated Slovak Synod) in its convention the same year reached the same conclusion. And so, the funeral was held and the burial was carried out of an institution which had existed for more than 90 years as a bulwark of Lutheran confessionalism, whose very purpose was to bring about doctrinal unity based on Holy Scripture and the Lutheran Confessions, and to preserve this unity. "Can two walk together except they be agreed?" There was once a time when every synod in the Synodical Conference was of one heart with every other synod in the Conference on the issue of Church Fellowship and Prayer Fellowship, and on the matter of joint work. There had been long-standing agreement among the synods of the Conference that before there can be fellowship and prayer and joint work there first must come about total unity based on Scripture and the Lutheran Confessions. This included repudiation of every error. But those days came to an end when a seemingly greater challenge loomed on the horizon: that of uniting all Lutherans. In the face of so great a challenge and hope, doctrinal differences, as well as differences in church practice did not seem so important to many individuals. At the same time, voices were being heard in the Missouri

Synod that echoed more the doctrinal stand of the liberal side of Lutheranism than the traditional—even official—conservative stand of the Missouri Synod and the sister synods in the Conference. The doctrine of Scripture was especially under attack.

When situations such as these arise in the church, it would be good, especially for the religious leaders, to remember that scriptural doctrines, as well as church practice based on Scripture, are not the property of a committee of theologians nor the property of influential people in high places to barter and to buy and sell. Only when theologians can point their churches to the Scripture with the proverbial "It stands written," is the church safe from encroachment by man-made doctrines. It would be in place to remind all theologians who represent their churches in matters of doctrine and practice that only when God's Word is followed to the letter, upheld, defended, taught, and kept pure from every admixture of human rationalization, are the minds of men free from the bondage imposed by false doctrine. Willing, heartfelt obedience to God's Word is a wonderful liberating force, for its yields to God, to God's truth, and not to men. Martin Luther made this abundantly clear when he took his famed stand at the Diet of Worms. His bold and courageous stand, except for the grace of God, could have cost him his very life. Still, he testified that his conscience was bound by the Word of God and that he was a slave to no man. To be a slave of Scripture is to be free, free to choose the truth and reject error. Free to know truth and be blessed mightily by it—especially the truth of forgiveness of sins and salvation through Jesus Christ—at the same time, not to be bound by man-made teachings and traditions. Recall Jesus' promise: "If you hold to my teaching, you are really my disciples. Then you will know the truth, and the truth will set you free" (John 8:31. 32).

POSTSCRIPT

In August 1964 President Oscar J. Naumann of the Wisconsin Synod received a communiqué from the Synodical Conference Convention, which had been held in Ann Arbor, Michigan, the previous month. Both the Wisconsin Synod and the Evangelical Lutheran Synod were urged "to re-evaluate the opportunities and the challenges with which our Lord confronts them in unity with brethren"...and..."to reconsider the basis on which they withdrew from the Lutheran Synodical Conference"...and..."to rejoin the common task the common task of sound confessional Lutheranism through the agency of the Lutheran Synodical Conference."

The communiqué met with icy coldness from the Wisconsin Synod, which concluded:

IT IS OBVIOUS THAT THE SYNODICAL CONFERENCE DOES NOT CONSIDER AS ADEQUATE THE BASIS ON WHICH OUR SYNOD WITHDREW FROM THE SYNODICAL CONFERENCE. FAILURE ON THE PART OF THE SYNODICAL CONFERENCE TO REVEAL ITS REASONS FOR ASKING OUR SYNOD "TO RECONSIDER THE BASIS" FOR OUR WITHDRAWAL OFFERS NO SCRIPTURAL WARRANT ON OUR PART OF HEEDING THE REQUEST. MOREOVER, OUR COMMISSION IS NOT AWARE OF ANY CHANGE IN THE CONFESSIONAL POSITION OF THE MISSOURI SYNOD WHICH WOULD GIVE

WARRANT FOR OUR SYNOD "TO RECONSIDER THE BASIS" ON WHICH OUR SYNOD TOOK ACTION IN 1963. RATHER, THE CONFESSIONAL POSITION OF THE MISSOURI SYNOD SEEMS TO BE DETERIORATING NOT ONLY WITH RESPECT TO THE DOCTRINE OF CHURCH FELLOWSHIP, BUT WITH RESPECT TO THE DOCTRINE OF THE HOLY SCRIPTURES THEMSELVES...IN ADDITION, THE DOCTRINAL POSITION OF THE SYNOD OF EVANGELICAL LUTHERAN CHURCHES (SLOVAK SYNOD) IS LIKEWISE GIVING CAUSE FOR CONCERN...TO REVERSE OUR ACTION UNDER THE CIRCUMSTANCES FOR "THE SAKE OF SOUND CONFESSIONAL LUTHERANISM" WOULD NOT SERVE THE CAUSE INDICATED. IT WOULD HAVE THE OPPOSITE EFFECT. IT WOULD DESTROY THE SOUND CONFESSION MADE BY OUR SYNOD WHEN IN 1961 WE DECLARED THE BOND OF FELLOWSHIP WITH THE MISSOURI SYNOD SEVERED AND AGAIN IN 1963 WHEN WE WITHDREW FROM THE LUTHERAN SYNODICAL CONFERENCE.[29] (See the history of the Synod of Evangelical Lutheran Churches—communications between President Oscar J. Naumann and SELC.)

Footnotes for Chapter Thirty-Eight

1 *Lehre Und Wehre* (St. Louis, MO, 1856), pp. 186f. Quoted in "Fellowship Then and Now" (Milwaukee, WI: Northwestern Publishing House), pp. 7,8.

2 Erwin L. Lueker, Editor-in-Chief, *Lutheran Cyclopedia* (St. Louis, MO: Concordia Publishing House, 1954), p. 1030.

3 Richard C. Wolf, *Documents of Lutheran Unity in America* (Philadelphia, PA: Fortress Press, 1966) pp. 196, 197; Doc. #88.

4 Lueker, *Lutheran Cyclopedia*, p. 1030.

5 "Fellowship Then And Now" (Milwaukee, WI: Northwestern Publishing House), p. 18.

6 Wolf, *Documents...*, pp. 188, 189; Doc. #87.

7 Abdel Ross Wentz, *A Basic History of Lutheranism in America* (Philadelphia, PA: Muhlenberg Press, 1955), p. 302.

8 Wentz, *A Basic History...*, p. 305.

9 *The Proceedings of the 47th Convention of the Synodical Conference (1962).*

10 *The Proceedings of the 47th Convention of the Synodical Conference (1962)*, p. 66.

11 Wolf, *Documents...*, p. 339.

12 *Proceedings, 1955 Wisconsin Synod Convention*, p. 78.

13 John W. Behnken, *This I Recall* (St. Louis, MO: Concordia Publishing House, 1964), pp. 190-193.

14 *Proceedings, 1958 Synodical Conference Convention*, p. 44.

15 Theodore A. Aaberg, *A City Set On A Hill* (Published by Board of Publications Evangelical Lutheran Synod, Mankato, MN, 1968), page____.

16 Aaberg, *A City...*, p. 222.

17 Wolf, *Documents...*, p. 620.

18 Aaberg, *A City...*, p. 224.

19 *Proceedings, 1959 Wisconsin Synod Convention*, p. 168.

20 *Proceedings, 1960 Synodical Conference Convention*, p. 35.

21 Aaberg, *A City...*, p. 229.

22 The quotations of individuals were reported by the *Confessional Lutheran*, September 1960 issue.

23 *Proceedings, 1961 Wisconsin Synod Convention*, p. 186.

24 *Report 1961, of the Evangelical Lutheran Synod Convention*, p. 62.

25 These points were listed in *Fellowship Then and Now*, pp. 21-27. "Concerning the Impasse in the Intersynodical Discussion on Church Fellowship." Published by the Wisconsin Synod Commission on Doctrinal Matters. Originally published in 1961 in the *Northwestern Lutheran* as a series.

26 *The Lutheran Sentinel*. November 22, 1962, pp. 348, 349.

27 *Report, 1963, of the Evangelical Lutheran Synod Convention*, p. 48.

28 *Proceedings, 1967 Lutheran Church-Missouri Synod Convention*, p. 99.

29 *Proceedings 1965 Wisconsin Synod Convention*, pp. 281-283.

CHAPTER THIRTY-NINE

THE EVANGELICAL LUTHERAN CHURCH IN AMERICA (1988 -)

THE LUTHERAN MERGER THAT OUTSIZED THEM ALL

On January 1, 1988, the largest Lutheran body ever formed in the U.S.A. began its official operations in the Lutheran Center at 8765 W. Higgins Road. The Center comprises an 11 story office building newly purchased by the Evangelical Lutheran Church in America (ELCA) and located near the O'Hare Airport in greater Chicago. The coming together of two large Lutheran churches and one tiny Lutheran group was the result of negotiations and planning by a 70 member Commission, numerous task forces, and a Transition Team. The Commission for a New Lutheran Church was comprised of delegates from the 2.9 million member Lutheran Church in America (LCA), the 2.3 million member American Lutheran Church (ALC), and the 100.5 thousands member Association of Evangelical Lutheran Churches (AELC).

The 70 members of the Commission For a New Lutheran Church (CNLC) met 10 times in as many cities across the country, for a total of 44 days, which were spread over a period of five years, with two sessions held each year. These meetings took place from 1982 to 1986. On August 29, 1986, the three Lutheran groups cast their votes overwhelmingly for merging into one church

841

body under the name, the Evangelical Lutheran Church in America (ELCA). This body was legally constituted on April 30, 1987, but it did not become the legal successor to the three bodies until January 1, 1988. The merger produced a Lutheran church body that is fourth in size in comparison with other Protestant bodies.

(1) The largest of the merger churches, the LCA, was itself a merger in 1962 of the Augustana Lutheran Church (Swedish), the United Lutheran Church in America (German), the Finnish Evangelical Lutheran Church (Suomi Synod), and the America Evangelical Lutheran Church (Danish). Twenty-five percent of the LCA's membership was located in Pennsylvania. The LCA showed itself to be on the liberal side of Lutheranism, both in doctrine and polity.

(2) The new ALC dated from 1960 when a merger of the old ALC (German), the Evangelical Lutheran Church (ELC, Norwegian), and the United Evangelical Lutheran Church (UELC, Danish) was brought about. Three years later, the Lutheran Free Church (LFC) merged with the new ALC. The ALC bore the "moderate" label for its brand of theology and polity.

(3) The AELC was organized in 1976 by the moderate element of the Lutheran Church—Missouri Synod (LCMS), who left that synod after their liberal doctrinal stand was repudiated during the controversy that centered in most of the faculty of Concordia Seminary in St. Louis. Basic issues were the Doctrine of Inspiration and Inerrancy of Holy Scripture, combined with the seminary faculty's employment of the historical-critical method of biblical interpretation. It was in December 1976 that this moderate splinter group established themselves as a new but tiny Lutheran church body, numbering about 150 congregations and (at that time) about 75,000 members. The name, the Association of Evangelical Lutheran Churches (AELC) was chosen. This tiny new body immediately took its stand on the side of Lutheran unity. In the words of William Kohn, the president: WE ARE COMMITTED TO LUTHERAN UNITY. WE DO NOT KNOW HOW LONG WE WILL EXIST AS A SEPARATE CHURCH BODY [THE AELC WAS STRUGGLING TO SURVIVE], AND WE WILL CONTINUE TO EVALUATE OUR REASON FOR BEING IN THE LIGHT OF OUR OVERPOWERING CONCERN FOR GREATER LUTHERAN CONSOLIDATION.[1] The AELC immediately sought fellowship with the other Lutherans who were of like mind—the LCA and the ALC. Ten years later (1986) these three Lutheran bodies would vote to merge into one, the Evangelical Lutheran Church in America (ELCA).

THE INTRIGUING PROCESS THAT PRODUCED THE EVANGELICAL LUTHERAN CHURCH IN AMERICA

The process which formed the ELC merits more than passing attention. Therefore we intend to spend some time reviewing how this largest of all Lutheran churches in the U.S.A. came to be formed. No church body before it had been put together in the same manner that produced the ELCA. The theology, polity, and the sociological and political determinations of this body, evidence already in its formation, are important issues that need to be examined and evaluated. Furthermore, the bare fact that the merger that was produced encompasses such a large portion of people in the U.S.A. who claim to be *Lutheran*, and thus plays an important part in shaping the spiritual thinking, beliefs, lives, and eternal destinies of millions of people, begs careful study and review.

In pursuing the history of the formation of the ELCA we will rely heavily on Edgar R. Trexler's scholarly and absorbing book, *Anatomy of a Merger—People, Dynamics, and Decisions That Shaped The ELCA.* In detailing the efforts of so many people that went into forming this new Lutheran church, Trexler furnishes us with a careful step-by-step account of what took place in those 10 meeting that occurred over the five years from 1982 to 1986. Trexler was intimately associated with the process of merging the bodies. He was, at the time, editor of the *Lutheran* (LCA), and later became editor of the Lutheran, the magazine of the ELCA. As his blurb on the back cover of the book states: HE WAS PRESENT AT MEETINGS OF THE COMMITTEE ON LUTHERAN UNITY (1979-82), THE COMMISSION FOR A NEW LUTHERAN CHURCH (1982-1986) AND THE TRANSITION TEAM (1986-87) AND ATTENDED CONVENTIONS AND NUMEROUS OTHER GATHERINGS OF THE THREE PREDECESSOR CHURCH BODIES. (*Anatomy...*, back cover)

Before we move into the merger process that finally led to the formulation of the ELCA, we need to understand an important fact: the ALC had to experience a remarkable shift in its theology and in its polity in order to even agree to study the possibility of merging with the LCA. For example, there was a time when the ALC taught that confessional unity requires theological uniformity. There was a time when the ALC, old (1930) and new (1960) was conservative enough in its theology and practice to court the fellowship of the then conservative Missouri Synod (which today should probably be classified as moderate), and to actually realize this fellowship, beginning in 1969 and ending in 1977. During this period the ALC veered farther and farther to the left in its theology.

The Doctrines of the Inerrancy and Infallibility of Scripture had been issues that existed between the ALC—old and new—and the ULCA (which later morphed with 3 other bodies into the LCA) throughout the history of inter synodical negotiations. Recall that for years the ALC resisted inviting the ULCA into the American Lutheran Conference, because of that body's liberal position in doctrine and practice. Especially involved was the ULCA's treatment of the Doctrine of Scripture. After its introduction here in America, the historical-critical method, with its many attacks on the veracity, reliability and authority of Scripture had gained a solid foothold in the ULCA. It was accepted more slowly and less enthusiastically in the ALC, but gained momentum as time wore on.

While the old ALC declined organic union with the liberal ULCA for years, content instead to maintain ties to this body in matters of cooperation in joint endeavors, nevertheless pastors in the ALC more and more embraced historical criticism and a more liberal outlook on doctrine and practice. The new ALC (1960) gladly extended the hand of fellowship to the LCA, of which the ULCA had become a part in 1962.

In 1971 the ALC adopted, and in 1972 the LCA adopted the recommendations made by the Lutheran Council in the U.S.A. (LCUSA) in its study of

843

Lutheran unity. Both church bodies voted to appoint representatives to a Consultation on Lutheran Unity. The Consultation would seek structures, or, if necessary, parallel structures, in order to aid cooperation. Because its constitution committed the LCA to search for wider Lutheran unity, this body requested that structural unity be added to the Consultation's agenda. However, this request caused the Consultation's collapse, because of the Missouri Synod's membership on it. Missouri was not ready to engage in talks geared to structural unity, but to talks geared to cooperative endeavors.

In 1972 both the LCA and ALC underwent restructuring, which efforts were similar and widely regarded as stepping-stones toward the organic union of the two churches. However, due to the death of the ALC presiding bishop, Kent S. Knudsen, who was replaced by the vice president, David W. Preus, the outlook for speedy organic union of the two bodies was considerably dampened. After 13 years, the ALC merger was still not meshing smoothly, according to Preus, who felt it was too soon for his church to go through the merger process again. As Edgar R. Trexler points out in his book *Anatomy of a Merger*, the ALC...HAD ENDURED DISPUTES OVER SCRIPTURAL INTERPRETATION INVOLVING INERRANCY AND HAD OVERCOME A STRONG FEELING IN SOME PARTS OF OHIO AND OTHER FORMER ALC GERMAN BACKGROUND AREAS THAT MINNESOTANS, PRIMARILY EVANGELICAL LUTHERAN CHURCH LEADERS (NORWEGIAN), HAD TAKEN OVER THEIR CHURCH...ALL THE CHIEF EXECUTIVES OF THE NEW ALC EXCEPT ONE [WERE] SELECTED FROM THE ELC.[2] Preus felt that there was unity among Lutherans according to their common confession of faith and that there was no need to express this unity structurally.[3] As we shall observe later, Preus underwent a 180 degree turn, and came out on the side of structural unity, a merger of the two bodies (which later included the much smaller group, the Association of Evangelical Lutheran Churches).

Bringing about the ELCA proved to be a difficult, wearisome, often frustrating, sometimes infuriating and discouraging, as well as expensive undertaking. Formal merger negotiations took place from 1979 to 1987. Missing in the equation for success was the combined vision of the two previous presidents of the LCA and ALC—both influential men, whose separate ideas concerning merger meshed well with each other. These were Robert J. Marshall of the LCA and Kent S. Knutson of the ALC. Knutson died after a six-month struggle with Creutzfeld-Jacob disease. Marshall went on to serve as a member of the Commission for a New Lutheran Church (CNLC).[4]

In 1974 the LCA Convention recommended that the Standing Committee on Approaches to Unity meet with ALC representatives for discussion of possible organic unity. Finding this proposal agreeable, the ALC contributed members to the ALC/LCA Committee on Cooperation, which Joint Committee began meeting in 1977. In 1976 the LCA Convention directed the "LCA members on the (Joint) Committee to pursue the negotiations with the ALC with the goal of organic unity."[5]

At this point, enter a third party. Early in 1978 the AELC, firmly dedicated to the cause of Lutheran unity, issued "A Call to Union" to all Lutheran bodies of North America and invited interested parties to meet in the fall of 1979. The AELC's "A Call to Lutheran Union" asked the Lutheran bodies to commit to organic union without prior consideration of the process that would bring this about—a matter which the AELC felt could be worked out later. No mention was made of doctrinal discussions between the Lutheran bodies. Since the LCA was already committed to inter-Lutheran fellowship without the need for doctrinal discussions, and operating under the belief that "there must be room for theological diversity" among Lutherans in an organic union, this Lutheran body responded favorably and enthusiastically to the AELC proposal. However, the ALC response was just the opposite. Still, a four-year study plan was agreed upon and the rest is history—the creation of the Evangelical Lutheran Church in America by a merger of the LCA, ALC, and AELC.[6]

The AELC's proposed meeting did not come about. Instead, the conventions of the LCA and ALC asked the Joint Committee to "evaluate options for possible organizational structures for effective mission fulfillment..."[7] Three choices of organization were suggested for consideration, the last one being the creation of a single church body.[8]

The AELC accepted the invitation given it to join the Committee, which then was changed into the Committee on Lutheran Unity (CLU), which met for the first time January 22-23, 1979. The AELC—a struggling body—needed, for very practical reasons, to become a part of a larger group of Lutherans. Not intending to remain a separate body permanently, the AELC was eager to participate.

When Knutson of the ALC died, he was succeeded by David W. Preus, who at the time was not interested in merger. However, his views were apparently—as would later become evident—not shared by the vast majority of grass roots members in the ALC. Opposed at first to organic union, Preus, on the other hand, was satisfied with pulpit and altar fellowship and the adherence to the Lutheran Confessions shared by the ALC/LCA, considering it to be sufficient demonstration of Lutheran unity.[9] The AELC, however, pressed for union of the three bodies.

President Crumley of the LCA pressed for union too, especially on the basis of the LCA statement in its constitution that committed his church "to strive for the unification of all Lutherans." The LCA, it could be said, appeared to be obsessed with an urgent need and a longing desire for Lutheran union, whatever the cost. As it turned out, the three churches had "vastly different approaches" to the matter of structural options for a unified Lutheran Church.[10]

Four structural options were considered: (1) RETAINING THE PRESENT STRUCTURES; (2) CONSIDERATION OF A REGIONAL CHURCH WITH SMALL SYNODS; (3) DEVELOPING AUTONOMOUS REGIONAL CHURCHES; (4) CREATION OF A NATIONAL CHURCH.[11]

There were occasional flare-ups between the presidents of the two large bodies. Preus was at first adamant about a single church not being the only way to express oneness. He observed that there was no biblical mandate for a single organization for the church's life on earth...that unity has to do with a common confession, with sharing of sacraments and loving each other.[12] With what type of structure Lutheran unity should manifest itself was at first a big issue, engendering theological papers and discussions both in committees and in church conventions.

The Committee on Lutheran Unity (CLU) provided a 32 page as its report to the three church conventions meeting in 1980. The booklet contained a response form. It also contained structural options, theological perspectives—

845

their implications for structure, a summary of major developments in Lutheran unity, and suggestions on how to evaluate the structures.[13] The LCA Convention approved the report. So did the ALC (with one "no" vote) and the AELC with no "no" votes. The issue that was brought to the conventions in the report was whether or not to authorize a two year study process of organizational structures for Lutheran unity (or union). The conventions voted "yes." Having been adopted by the three bodies in convention in 1980, 156,000 copies of the booklet were sent to 53,000 parish leaders and clergy in November of the same year, and the congregations were instructed to study the booklet and to respond with their opinions and suggestions to their national churches.

In the spring of 1981 those who had been delegates to the three church's synod/district conventions were asked to study the booklet and complete an opinion poll regarding structural options, etc. Later, in the fall, the CLU would meet and consider the results. David Preus of the ALC was surprised to learn of the overwhelming favorable reaction in his church regarding the CLU report, which reaction indicated intense interest on the part of the ALC membership for pursuing Lutheran union.

In January 1981 the president of nine LCA, ALC, and AELC seminaries signed a document, a "Call to Lutheran Union Now," in which they stated their conviction "that the union of Lutheran churches in the United States at this time is not an option to be considered but an action to be taken."[14]

Still, David Preus of the ALC dragged his feet regarding having only one church, and promoted the possibilities for new joint activities. He concluded that very little would be added by a massive nationwide organizational restructuring. Meanwhile, Bishop Crumley of the LCA pushed for union of the three Lutheran church bodies.

And the results of the opinion polls being conducted in the three bodies? The reports of the LCA's 31 synods and the ALC's 19 district conventions revealed a firm enthusiasm by the grass roots element, who overwhelmingly favored merger. It appeared certain that a huge new church would be formed. Grass roots participation in the decision-making of the merger process—thus adhering to Bishop Crumley's request—was assured.[15]

In May 1981 ALC Presiding Bishop David W. Preus, speaking at the LCA Michigan Synod Convention, made his concession speech, in which he declared: SOME OF US HEAR DIFFERENT MUSIC WHEN PEOPLE TALK OF MERGER, BUT WITH THE ENTHUSIASM OF THE ALC AND OBVIOUSLY THE LCA I AM WILLING TO SAY, "LET'S GET AT IT."[16]

By August, Preus had completely swung over to the pro-merger side. Furthermore, every district, every synod of the three Lutheran bodies were in favor of uniting into one church. LCA delegates: 86.6% in favor; ALC delegates: 63.9% in favor; AELC delegates: 96% in favor. The "one church type structure" received the most votes. There would not be a mere enhanced cooperation of the three bodies in mutual projects; there would not be a federation-type union of the three (such as more or less constituted the ULCA); there would be a full-fledged consolidation or merger of three into one. And the poll also showed that the laity felt that they should "be involved in policy-forming decision making, and administration leadership at each 'level' of the church." Furthermore, the poll results sowed that missions and evangelism should be top priorities,

846

and that the churches should "get on with the union" as soon as possible, with continued grass roots involvement in the process.[17]

A tentative time line was suggested: 1982—The churches themselves in their respective conventions vote to commit to work to establish a new church body. 1984—A progress report to be made to each church convention. 1986—Approval or non-approval vote by each church regarding merging the three churches. 1987-1988—Constitution Convention for the new church.[18]

Next would come the merger commission of the proposed new church. The CLU, not being a merger commission, set about to establish one, which was named the "Commission For A New Lutheran Church" (CNLC). The term "new" would be employed again and again in the course of Commission meetings to define the goal toward which the commissioners were working. It was to be a distinctively new and different church from the three bodies which were from it—new, not a clone of the old. But would it be too "new" and too "different," to the point that people would feel like strangers in it? Time would tell.

As it turned out, the CNLC would be set up using a quota system, a heretofore–unused system for putting a church together. This mean that clergy/laity, male/female, racial/ethnic groups should have 31 members from the LCA and ALC and with eight members from the AELC, a total of 70 members. Adopted by the Commission, the principle of quotas was destined to be passed on to be a factor in deciding representation in the merger church itself. It certainly "would also bring different dynamics to the Commission's deliberations than any merger group had previously experienced."[19] An example of this were the caucuses regularly held by the women members of the Commission regarding issues up for discussion.

A note of interest: Lutheran Brotherhood would eventually contribute $98,822 to the CNLC to help cover expenses, and the Aid Association for Lutherans would contribute $95,804.[20]

The CLU, still in operation, agreed on the following wording of commitment to merger, to be used by the three bodies...to... "commit themselves to join in forming a new Lutheran church and to take all deliberate steps toward its earliest realization."[21] The following timetable was suggested for the CNLC: 1984—The three churches in convention to consider and respond to "a statement of theological understandings and ecclesiastical principles, and a narrative description of the new church." 1986—The three churches in convention to consider and respond to "the articles of incorporation of the new church, the constitution and bylaws of the new church, and be able to take action to cease functioning on December 31, 1987."[22]

On January 21, 1982, the CLU adopted its final report to the three churches, which would meet simultaneously in September of the same year to vote on it. The LCA would meet in Louisville, the ALC in San Diego, and the AELC in Cleveland. A telephone hookup would inform the three churches of the decision of the delegates of each convention to accept or reject the CLU's report, which amounted to a decision either to join or not to join the merger process to produce a "new" Lutheran Church. As we have already hinted, the positive outcome of the voting by the three conventions was pretty much assured.

During the summer of 1982 a group of conservative Lutherans—Lutherans Alert National (now known as the World Confessional Lutheran Association)—

some of whom had declined to participate in the 1960 ALC merger—advised congregations not to join the proposed new church. As it turned out, there were congregations in all three bodies which chose to not take part in the merger. More of this later.

The results of the voting by the three bodies concerning participation in the merger process to form one body out of the three was, in a way, anticlimactic, for a favorable vote had been strongly indicated. The CLU's recommendations were all accepted by the three churches in convention, which also then established the 70 member Commission For A New Lutheran Church (CNLC). The AELC voted 136 yes, 0 no; the LCA voted 611 yes, 11 no; the ALC voted 897 yes, 87 no.

The makeup of the 70 member Commission For a New Lutheran Church (CNLC) was as follows:

AELC: 5 men, 3 women (3 were clergy and 5 were lay....4 were minority)

ALC: 18 men, 13 women (14 were clergy and 17 were lay....5 were minority)

LCA: 19 men, 12 women (15 were clergy and 16 were lay....6 were minority)

The Commission would meet twice a year for five years. The first meeting was held at Madison, Wisconsin, September 27-29, 1982. The last meeting was held June 23-25, 1986, at Seattle, Washington. William Kennison, the president of the LCA's Wittenberg University, became the chairperson of the CNLC. He diligently worked to keep the Commission on track and to adhere to the timeline. Kinnison found his job to be both frustrating and rewarding. Various task forces, with one Commission member on each, were implemented. A Planning Committee, which turned out to be highly significant, and in fact the most powerful Committee, was elected by the CNLC.

BUMPS IN THE ROAD LEADING TO MERGER

The self-imposed quota system added to the many challenges and difficulties faced by the Commissioners as they went about their work. Experienced and inexperienced members served side by side, with the inexperienced unwilling for the experienced leaders to lead.[23]

Another bump in the road was the differing organizational styles of the LCA and ALC. The LCA tended to be systematic and precise, while the ALC tended to be pragmatic and casual.

There were a lot of bumps—some big and some not so big. There was distrust at first of one another. There was the question: Does a member of the CNLC represent his/her church body or the CNLC? Furthermore, there was simply too much to do and too little time to do it in, especially with the Commission becoming bogged down by certain issues, such as procedure. There was the issue of how to handle theological and sociological issues (two task forces were appointed). The Task Force on Theology had the task of laying a foundation for A Statement of Faith, the Nature of the Church and of the Ministry (which became a thorny issue for years to come). The Task Force on Society was given the task "to prepare a descriptive analysis of the political, economic, cultural, demographic and ethnic characteristics and trends into which the new church would be born."[24]

A big bump was the issue of biblical Inerrancy (and thus also Infallibility), which was a worry, since there was diversity among the bodies regarding these doctrines. The ALC Constitution described the Old and New Testaments...AS THE DIVINELY INSPIRE, REVEALED, AND INERRANT WORD OF GOD...THE ONLY INFALLIBLE AUTHORITY IN ALL MATTERS OF FAITH AND LIFE. Some in the ALC stayed with this statement, others did not. The LCA avoided identifying Scripture as inerrant and infallible. And, as we learned from our study of the controversy involving the St. Louis Seminary faculty (LCMS), many of whose members later led in the founding of the AELC, they were moderates who had a doctrine of Scripture highly subject to the whims of historical criticism. The CNLC ultimately adopted an understanding of the Word of God which stated: (1) THE WORD OF GOD, THROUGH WHOM GOD CREATED EVERYTHING, BECAME INCARNATE IN JESUS CHRIST, THROUGH WHOM FASHIONS A NEW CREATION. (2) THE WORD OF GOD IS THE MESSAGE FROM GOD AND ABOUT GOD, BOTH LAW AND GOSPEL, REVEALING JUDGMENT AND MERCY THROUGH WORD AND DEED BEGINNING WITH THE WORD IN CREATION, CONTINUING IN THE HISTORY OF ISRAEL, AND CENTERING IN ALL ITS FULLNESS IN THE PERSON AND WORK OF JESUS CHRIST. (3) AS A RECORD AND WITNESS OF GOD'S REVELATION, CENTERING IN JESUS CHRIST AND PROCLAIMING BOTH LAW AND GOSPEL, THE SACRED SCRIPTURES ARE THE WORD OF GOD, AUTHORITATIVE AS SOURCE OF THE CHURCH'S PROCLAMATION AND NORM FOR THE CHURCH'S LIFE AND FAITH. THESE SCRIPTURES ARE DIVINELY INSPIRED, FOR GOD'S SPIRIT SPOKE THROUGH THEIR AUTHORS. THE SAME SPIRIT SPEAKS TO US THROUGH THE SCRIPTURE. GIVEN BY GOD THEY ARE SUFFICIENT AND RELIABLE FOR BRINGING US THE TRUTH OF OUR SALVATION. THEY THEREBY PRESENT THE STANDARD FOR CHRISTIAN FAITH AND LIFE.[25] This understanding of the Doctrine of Scripture became the core of "A Statement of Faith," presented at the fourth CNLC meeting, held in Minneapolis in February 1984. Note how carefully the term "inerrant" is avoided.

And then there was an especially irritating bump in the road leading to the merger. The commissioners were unable to agree on the doctrines of the Ministry and the Nature of the Church. They passed this double problem on to the new church to resolve. Years into the life of the new church there still was not a doctrine of the Ministry. According to Trexler, "the status of full-time lay workers in the church defied decision." At issue, really, was how to classify the AELC's parochial school teachers. Bear in mind that the AELC came out of the Missouri Synod and so was naturally strongly imbued with the importance of Christian Day Schools. The AELC maintained that their teachers could be ordained, even though such ordination was not practiced. The IRS classified their teachers as ministers of religion. The AELC maintained "that God gave an overall ministry to the church that can be carried on in several forms ordained and otherwise." There are, then, ministers of the Word whom the congregation calls, and entrusts with specific duties. "Word and Sacrament ministry is one form of that ministry [the ELCA] believed, and an ordained diaconate could include teachers and deacons"... "The CNLC's dilemma was not whether to have two or three levels of ministry, but whether to expand the clergy roster in some way to accommodate teachers whom the AELC considered to be quasi-clergy."[26] After much discussion and entertaining motions regarding Ministry, the CNLC could not come up with a unanimous position on this doctrine, and so the motion that finally passed asked for continuing study.[27]

The Task Force on Society found its work to be daunting in its nature and eventually prepared a 302 page report giving "a descriptive analysis of the political, economic, social, cultural, demographic, and ethnic characteristics and trends into which the church would be born."[28] The new church would clearly be deeply involved in social/ethnic/political/justice concerns—an involvement that would earn the new church harsh criticism, even from its own membership, who claimed that the church's true work, evangelism/missions, was being shortchanged. There clearly would be a melding of church and state, rather than a clear-cut separation of the two in the ELCA.

Speaking of bumps in the road to merger, the business of quotas came up again and again and engendered sharp discussions and deep feelings. There was to be inclusiveness in the CNLC and in task forces and committees, and later in choosing officers and delegates of the merger church: 60/40 lay/clergy for assembly delegates and board members, 50/50 male/female; and 10% minority at ELCA assemblies, boards, and committees. The AELC's influence toward maintaining quotas was considerable. The above listed quotas were affirmed by the CNCL meeting in Los Angeles in 1984. The quota system remained unpopular in polls taken in the LCA and ALC, and there were continual efforts to have quota removed from the merger plans. However, the CNLC stubbornly held from on the issue. No doubt the quota system accommodated the continual, aggressive thrust of the feminine movement, which sought to protect the 50/50 male/female representation on all synod assemblies. Later on, the LCA bishops would seek to have quotas eliminated "for elective groups, except for 60/40 percent lay/clergy representation." Many in the LCA and ALC regarded the whole business of quotas as a big negative: undesirable, unrealistic, unbending, and legalistic.[29] Trexler sums up the far-reaching effect of the quota system on the new church in this way:

OF ALL THE "NEW" FEATURES, NONE HAD BROADER IMPACT THAN QUOTAS. ALL ACROSS THE CHURCH, EVERYONE HAD TO DEAL WITH THEM. CONGREGATIONS HAD TO SEND A MALE AND FEMALE DELEGATE TO SYNOD ASSEMBLIES; THE MEMBERS OF A SYNOD'S ASSEMBLIES, BOARDS, AND STAFFS WERE FORCED TO REFLECT THAT SYNOD'S OWN MEMBERSHIP; QUOTAS WERE ADHERED TO FOR NATIONAL ASSEMBLIES, BOARDS AND STAFF...

Though minority membership in the ELCA was less than 2%, nevertheless the quota system mandated a 10% minority quota in filling elective positions.

There was a total of 11 task forces, with 145 persons named to them by the CNLC. One member of the CNLC was on each task force. There were four additional groups, which hammered out a constitution and bylaws, considered legal matters, the church office site, and planning for a constituting convention. How to make sense of all the reports that came out of these groups? The answer lay in the Design Committee, which proved to be very powerful in the CNLC. The various reports were funneled to this Committee, which then coordinated them so that it could finally present a single structure for the new church to the three merging bodies. As it turned out, the ELCA would be a combination of traditional and new.[30] But things almost fell apart at the fourth meeting of the CNLC, which was held in February 1984 at Minneapolis. The commissioners, finding it hard to agree, ran into trouble trying to determine the "essential" content of their report which would be made to the 1984 conventions of the synods, districts and church bodies.

Then there were interest groups and thorny issues that had to be dealt with. For example: in late 1982 two conservative groups organized, whose focus was on Scripture and theology. About 500 "conservative evangelical Lutherans concerned about 'heresy and moral corruption'" were involved. The group, which called itself the Fellowship of Evangelical Lutheran Laity and Pastors" (FELLIP), made plans to "ensure that the new church would be evangelical in faith and life." The group wanted Scripture defined as "inerrant" and "infallible" and warned against what they labeled "ethical relativism." The group had in mind especially the church's acceptance of homosexual behavior and abortion.[31] Another conservative group, Friends for Biblical Lutheranism, organized in York, Pennsylvania. Their fear was that Scripture "is being eroded in the church." Because of this, the group wanted the new church's statement of Faith to describe Scripture as "eternally true and the norm for the faith and practice of the church."[32] These were doctrinal issues, and the CNLC seemed to shy away as much as possible from dealing with such matters. Long on working out practical matters, the CNLC was, on the other hand, short on dealing with theological issues. A WELS reviewer in the *Wisconsin Lutheran Quarterly* concludes that in all of the debates in the CNLC, at least reported by the author of *Anatomy of a Merger*,...THERE NEVER WAS A SERIOUS ATTEMPT AT SOLID STUDY OF THE SCRIPTURES ON THEOLOGICAL QUESTIONS LIKE BIBLICAL INERRANCY AND MINISTRY. SOME OF THE MOST HEATED DEBATES CENTERED ON EXTERNALS AND ADIAPHORA [THINGS NEITHER COMMANDED NOR FORBIDDEN IN SCRIPTURE].[33]

There were also social justice groups that formed, who then pushed for a serious consideration of justice issues. Inclusiveness of gays in the new church was on the agenda of some members of the merger bodies.

The statement on Scripture had to be revised by the CNLC and would be revised yet another time into this, its final form:

[2.02C] THE CANONICAL SCRIPTURES OF THE OLD AND NEW TESTAMENTS ARE THE WRITTEN WORD OF GOD. INSPIRED BY GOD'S SPIRIT SPEAKING THROUGH THEIR AUTHORS, THEY RECORD AND ANNOUNCE GOD'S REVELATION CENTERING IN JESUS CHRIST. THROUGH THEM GOD'S SPIRIT SPEAKS TO US TO CREATE AND SUSTAIN CHRISTIAN FAITH AND FELLOWSHIP FOR SERVICE IN THE WORLD. [2.03] THIS CHURCH ACCEPTS THE CANONICAL SCRIPTURES OF THE OLD AND NEW TESTAMENTS AS THE INSPIRED WORD OF GOD AND THE AUTHORITATIVE SOURCE AND NORM OF ITS PROCLAMATION, FAITH, AND LIFE.[34]

Where to locate the ELCA headquarters turned out to be somewhat of a thorny issue. Finally, the choice of cities was reduced to four: Chicago, Kansas City, Minneapolis, and Philadelphia. Milwaukee was a strong favorite for a while, until it was learned that the WELS had more members there then the three merging bodies combined. Finally, Chicago was chosen, but not everyone was happy with the choice.

The percentage of contributions to the pension fund for individual employees of congregations was a thorny issue. The ALC was content with 9%, while the LCA wanted the contribution raised to 12% (and repeatedly brought up the issue). The flap over the percentage amount to be contributed by congregations for their employees' pension continued to be an aggravation.

Defining the relation of the congregation to the national church was also a source of irritation, for it was difficult to reconcile the two different positions occupied by the LCA and ALC. The LCA Constitution reads: CONGREGATIONS FIND THEIR FULFILLMENT IN THE UNIVERSAL COMMUNITY OF THE CHURCH, AND THE UNIVERSAL CHURCH EXISTS IN AND THROUGH CONGREGATIONS. According to the LCA, church and congregation are not equal but "partners under the authority of Christ." The LCA had concerns of congregationalism in the new church— an influence of ALC theology and practice—and these concerns left the LCA fearing that this emphasis on the congregation would impinge on the ecumenicalism which was such a driving force in the LCA's theology and practice. The LCA bishops recommended reducing congregational authority. Their belief was that "the authority of the congregation is derived from the whole church and it is incorporated in the life of the whole church." The congregation is church but not the whole church. The ALC on the other hand emphasized the congregation more than the larger church, and maintained that "the universal church exists in and through the congregation." Bear in mind that the ELC (later a part of the new ALC) leaned heavily in the direction of congregational authority. As a part of the ALC, the ELC with its Norwegian heritage downplayed central authority, retaining a distrust toward the "absolute" authority that the State Church exerted on the Norwegians in the old country. This situation compelled many Norsks to emigrate to America to seek religious freedom here. And so, the ELC was a powerful force in the new ALC, which took the position that the national church is created by the congregations, which then are foundational to the national church and not the other way around.

On the Nature of the Church, the following words from the LCA Constitution were inserted into the proposed constitution for the new church at the CNLC's final meeting:...CONGREGATIONS FIND THEIR FULFILLMENT IN THE UNIVERSAL COMMUNITY OF THE CHURCH, AND THE UNIVERSAL CHURCH EXISTS IN AND THROUGH CONGREGATIONS. Furthermore, the church's "character and power" derives from...THE SANCTION AND REPRESENTATION OF ITS CONGREGATIONS AND FROM ITS INHERENT NATURE AS AN EXPRESSION OF A BROADER FELLOWSHIP OF THE FAITHFUL.[35]

Working on the Doctrine of the Ministry was not a smooth ride either for the members of the CNLC. It was like a thorn poking the commissioners throughout their tenure. Unable to reach an agreement on either the Church or the Ministry, the commissioners left to the new church the task of hammering out a statement acceptable to all parties. At Kansas City in September 1985 the following compromise on the Ministry issue was accepted: From 1988 (when the new church would begin functioning) to 1994, the new church would...RECEIVED ALL IN ANY SPECIALLY RECOGNIZED STATUS OF MINISTRY IN THE UNITING CHURCHES AND RETAIN THEM IN THAT STATUS ON THE CHURCH'S ("FROZEN") ROSTER. During these six years the church would conduct an intensive study to...DECIDE ON APPROPRIATE FORMS OF MINISTRY FOR ITS FUTURE. (According to Edgar Trexler, Lutherans in America had never agreed on a Doctrine of the Ministry.) The LCA saw evidences of "anti-clericalism," because pastors are not allowed to serve as president of the congregational council. Furthermore, LCA bishops felt that the addition of non-ordained persons (namely, AELC parochial school teachers) to the roll of "public ministers" weakened the "unique character" of the ordained ministry. And so, the stand the bishops took went against the policy of the AELC. In regards to the doctrine of the Ministry the LCA bishops also resented the course which the CNLC had set regarding the removal of pastors from the ministry. The CNLC made it difficult to remove pastors from the ministry for violating the church's Constitution and Bylaws, which move by the CNLC upset the bishops. It should be noted that in the 1991 Churchwide Assembly the ELCA adopted the rule that ministers can be removed from office for "willful disregard" of the new church's Constitution.[36]

The LCA bishops also took issue with the proposed church's ecumenical commitment, and proposed that it should be "more fully articulated." Several points were added to the new church's ecumenical commitment:...SEEK UNITY IN FAITH AND LIFE WITH ALL LUTHERANS WITHIN ITS BOUNDARIES....FOSTER CHRISTIAN UNITY BY PARTICIPATING IN ECUMENICAL ACTIVITY, CONTRIBUTING ITS WITNESS AND WORK AND COOPERATION WITH OTHER CHURCHES WHICH CONFESS GOD THE FATHER, SON, AND HOLY SPIRIT...DEVELOP RELATIONSHIPS WITH COMMUNITIES OF OTHER FAITHS FOR DIALOGUE AND COMMON ACTION...LIFT ITS VOICE IN CONCORD AND WORK IN CONCERT WITH FORCES FOR GOOD, SERVE HUMANITY, COOPERATING WITH CHURCHES AND OTHER GROUPS PARTICIPATING IN ACTIVITIES THAT PROMOTE JUSTICE, RELIEVE MISERY AND RECONCILE THE ESTRANGED.[37]

Meanwhile, David Preus, presiding bishop of the ALC (and a member of the CNLC), proposed that the Lutherans of the U.S. enter altar and pulpit fellowship with the Presbyterian Church (U.S.A.), the Reformed Church in America, and the Cumberland Presbyterian Church. Preus strove for "unity in reconciled diversity"—whatever that means. Preus favored continuing the "interim sharing" of Holy Communion with the Episcopal Church and also favored "pursuing with patience" the establishing of altar and pulpit fellowship with the Roman Catholic Church. Preus also wanted to continue searching out ecumenical relationships with other Christian Churches.[38]

The LCA Council, however, while welcoming intercommunion with the above listed churches on an individual member basis as opportunity allowed, on the other hand concluded that establishing "full communion" with these churches was not warranted at this time, for dialogues had not brought about the clarity that was needed on the nature of the presence of Christ in the Lord's Supper.[39]

David Preus of the ALC, on the other hand, reacted negatively to LCA President Crumley's exchanging letters with Pope John Paul II, feeling "that the letters tilted toward more relationship between the Lutherans and Roman Catholics than the dialogues had warranted." Crumley had also visited the Vatican twice.[40]

To sum up the described situation: The ALC at its Convention voted to recognize the Presbyterian Church (U.S.A.) and the Reformed Church in America as churches "in which the Gospel is proclaimed and the sacraments administered according to the ordinances of Christ." The ALC also approved the sharing of pastors and "occasional joint services" of communion. This new relationship was also approved by the AELC, the Presbyterian Church (U.S.A.) and the Reformed Church at their conventions.[41] The LCA was more cautious and adopted a proposal that stated its eagerness to work with the two Protestant churches "to provide jointly for occasional services of the Lord's Supper where appropriate and desirable and in accord with the disciplines of our several churches."[42] Of course, when the three bodies ended their separate existences on December 31, 1987,their relationships with the two Protestant churches also ended. New ecumenical relationships would have to be ironed out by the new church, something not immediately initiated. It is of interest here to note that at the LCA's final Convention, the LCA president, James R. Crumley, Jr., and the archbishop of Canterbury, Robert Runcie, communed each other.

And so, the old Galesburg Rule (Lutheran altars and Lutheran pulpits should be for Lutherans only) was considered a "ghost" that had stalked the ALC but had been laid to rest. The new rule now was "unity in reconciled diversity."[43]

There were indeed serious irritations and annoying bumps in the road that the three churches had to travel in order to become one. How serious these annoyances could become was seen at the final CNLC meeting. There, at Seattle in June 1986, the merger talks almost fell apart, for a strong feeling was held among the commissioners that the LCA bishops had waited to the last minute to express their concerns including a challenge of the CNLC's proposed constitution for the new church. Things were finally worked out through the efforts of Minnesota bishop, Herbert W. Chilstrom, a recognized conciliator, who gave the new body its name and later became its first bishop.

Perhaps a question is in order in regards to the irritations that were experienced by the commissioners in putting together the "new" church. Were the three merger churches each trying to produce a body that would be a clone of itself instead of seeking to form a church that would in fact be new? Another question that comes to mind: What can one expect, when meetings that are held to bring about a new church are not characterized by discussions and decisions based upon Holy Scripture? As Edgar Trexler's *Anatomy of a Merger* apparently indicates, theological discussions were not the first order of the day. The irritations experienced by the CNLC members would not cease when the new church actually came into being. As we shall soon see, there were rough days and even rough years ahead for the newly established ELCA.

At the meeting in Seattle in June 1986, the ALC Church Council endorsed most of the CNLC proposals, and these were points in conflict with LCA positions. However, the LCA Executive Council endorsed the merger proposals.

In the same year that the merger talks between the ALC, LCA, and AELC came to an end, and the CNLC offered its final report to the three bodies for a vote of acceptance or rejection, the three received a verbal slap from the faculty of Concordia Seminary in Fort Wayne, Indiana. The faculty requested the Missouri Synod to declare that the three synods are "no longer genuine Lutheran Churches from a traditional and confessional point of view." Furthermore, the faculty advised that after the formation of the new church "LCMS officials and members...avoid any actions or relationships tending to lend credibility to the new body as a Lutheran Church."[44] Years later, on the final day of Missouri's 2001 Convention, after an hour and a half debate, the delegates passed by a 706-343 vote a resolution that among other things recognized that the ELCA

854

is "not an orthodox Lutheran body." Earlier a report had been given by participants in the recent ELCA-LCMS theological dialogues. These dialogues reached an impasse after three sessions, when the 10 LCMS participants came to the conclusion that the ELCA is not orthodox, and the 10 ELCA participants returned the favor, concluding the same thing about the LCMS. More will be reported on the LCMS-ELCA relationship later.

THE MERGER PRODUCING
THE ELCA FINALLY ACCOMPLISHED

The year of decision had come, for the three Lutheran bodies were scheduled to meet in order to accept or reject the final report of the CNLC. Either a merger would be formed or three Lutheran bodies would continue their separate existences. The final CNLC meeting was held June 23-25, 1986, in Seattle, Washington, where the commissioners' final report was hammered out. The conventions of the three churches met on August 29 of the same year and voted overwhelmingly in favor of the agreement and plan of merger that the CNLC offered them. The LCA Executive Council had already endorsed the merger proposal and the ALC Church Council recommended approval of the merger plan to the church's convention delegates meeting in July. Here, then, is the final tally of votes by the three conventions regarding the agreement and plan of merger: LCA Convention, Milwaukee=640-29 in favor; ALC Convention, Minneapolis = 891-59 in favor; AELC Convention, Chicago = 137-0 in favor.

The Evangelical Lutheran Church in America (ELCA) was legally constituted on April 30, 1987, but became the legal successor to the LCA, ALC, and AELC on January 1, 1988, at 12:01 A.M. Central Standard Time, when the three predecessor bodies were dissolved into the ELCA. After the historic vote by the three churches in August 1986 they would continue their individual existence for another 16 months.[45]

The ELCA, the "new" Lutheran church that had been in planning for five years, came into existence as the 4th largest Protestant denomination in the United States. The Southern Baptist Convention, the United Methodist Church, and the National Baptist Convention were larger, in that order.

Yet to take place after the positive vote to merge, August 1986, was the vote by each body to accept the proposed constitution and bylaws. The Constituting Convention of the ELCA was held in Columbus, Ohio, April 30-May 3, 1987. The delegates to the Constituting Convention came a day earlier in order to take part in the closing conventions of the merger churches. During the Constituting Convention the following officers were elected: Bishop = Rev. Herbert W. Chilstrom (9 ballots were cast over two days); Vice President = Christine H. Grumm; Secretary = Rev. Lowel G. Almen; Treasurer = George E. Aker.

SOME STATISTICS INVOLVED IN THE MERGER

The merger produced a Lutheran body of 5.3 million members, 11, 174 congregations, 16,608 pastors, and 65 synods. The ALC owned 12 colleges and four seminaries; the LCA synods owned that body's seven seminaries and most

855

of its 18 colleges. There would by 64 geographical synods and 9 regions. In addition there would by the Slovak Zion Synod, a nongeographical synod with congregations widely distributed. CNLC operations cost $2,592,659. A total of $30,453,000 or $5.75 per baptized member would be needed for closing operations of the merger churches, transitioning to the new church, start-up costs for churchwide and synod structures, and cash flow for the new church.

DIVISIONS, COMMISSIONS, AND OFFICES OF THE ELCA

(In addition to four offices mentioned above. Dated to the reconfiguration of the ELCA by the 1991 Churchwide Assembly):[46]
Division for Global Missions
Division for Outreach
Division for Congregational Ministries
Division of Ministry
Division for Higher Education and Schools
Division for Church in Society
Department for Communication
Department for Ecumenical Affairs
Department for Research and Evaluation
Department for Human Resources
Office of the Treasurer
Department for Synodical Relations
Board of Pensions
Publishing House of the ELCA
Women of the Evangelical Lutheran Church in America
The Lutheran
ELCA Foundation
Conference of Bishops (staff provided by Department for Synodical Relations)

THE EVANGELICAL LUTHERAN CHURCH IN AMERICA: DISTINGUISHED IN U.S. LUTHERANISM BY ITS LIBERAL THEOLOGY AND PRACTICE—A CONSERVATIVE LUTHERAN PERSPECTIVE

THE ELCA AND THE BIBLE

The Lutheran bodies—large, medium, small, tiny—that remain apart from the merger that produced the ELCA, maintain a doctrine of Holy Scripture which many used to hold in the American Lutheran Church. An earmark of conservative Lutheranism is the belief that Holy Scripture, the Bible, is the

856

all-inspired, inerrant, infallible, and fully authoritative Word of the Triune God. While there were pastors and theologians in the ALC that held to this doctrine of Scripture, there were fewer and fewer that did so as time went on, with more and more accepting the historical-critical method of the Bible interpretation. By 1968 only 23% of the new ALC's clergy accepted the Bible's full inspiration and inerrancy.[47]   Nelson points out that by 1956, when the proposed constitution for the new ALC came up for a vote by the Evangelical Lutheran Church (ELC), several, if not most, of its professors of theology taught a view of Scripture that did not match the new ALC's constitutional statement which proclaimed the inerrancy of Scripture. And so, a neo-Lutheranism was being widely taught.[48]

When the new ALC was formed, the Doctrine of the Inerrancy of Scripture was confessed in the Constitution, but later it was surrendered in order for the ALC to become a part of the new Lutheran church, the ELCA. To quote David R. Barnhart, a conservative former LCA pastor: AND SO, AS THE MERGER OF THE THREE BODIES APPROACHED THE ALC SHOWED A DEFINITE CHANGE IN ITS THEOLOGY, FOR ITS CHURCH LEADERS WERE "READY TO ADOPT A MUCH LOWER VIEW OF THE BIBLE THAN PREVIOUSLY HAD BY THAT DENOMINATION AND ITS PREDECESSORS."[49] As Edgar Trexler reports in *Anatomy of A Merger*: ON THEOLOGICAL ISSUES ... "A MAJOR SECTION OF A STATEMENT OF FAITH AND AN UNDERSTANDING OF SCRIPTURE THAT AVOIDED INERRANCY WERE HAMMERED OUT" BY THE CNLC RATHER QUICKLY. "IT WAS A CLUE THAT THESE ISSUES WERE NOT THE CHIEF CONCERNS FACING THE CNLC."[50]

The wording of the ELCA Constitution is weak regarding Scripture, with the words "inerrant" and "infallible" purposely left out: (T)HE WORDS INERRANT AND INFALLIBLE CAN BE UNDERSTOOD IN WAYS THAT LEAD TO INTERPRETATIONS OF THE SCRIPTURES THAT ARE CONTRARY TO WHAT THE SCRIPTURES ARE AND WHAT THEY TEACH. THESE TERMS CAN BE USED IN A WAY THAT IMPLIES A PRECISION ALIEN TO THE MINDS OF THE AUTHORS OF THE SCRIPTURES AND THEIR OWN USE OF THE SCRIPTURES...THEY MAY ENCOURAGE ARTIFICIAL HARMONIZATIONS RATHER THAN SERIOUS WRESTLING WITH THE IMPLICATION OF SCRIPTURAL STATEMENTS WHICH SEEM TO DISAGREE. THEY MAY LEAD PEOPLE TO THINK THAT IF THERE IS ONE PROVEN ERROR IN THE BIBLE, HOWEVER MINOR, ITS WHOLE TEACHING IS SUBJECT TO DOUBT. THEREFORE, WE RECOMMEND THAT THE WORDS INERRANT AND INFALLIBLE NOT BE INCLUDED.[51] A writer in the *Wisconsin Synod Quarterly* draws this conclusion: IT HAS BEEN CORRECTLY STATED THAT THE PROBLEM WITH THE CONFESSION OF FAITH OF THE NEW ELCA IS NOT WITH WHAT IS SAID, BUT RATHER WITH WHAT IS NOT SAID.[52] The wording of the ELCA's Statement of Faith is such that both liberals and conservative forces can find shelter for their beliefs there.

The historical-critical method of interpreting Scripture has been thoroughly discussed in the Chapter *THE LUTHERAN CHURCH IN AMERICA (LCA)*. There it is pointed out that the historical-critical method rapidly gained a foothold in the ULCA (a predecessor of the LCA) and was also received by many in the ALC. This method was then passed on to the new Lutheran Church by these predecessor churches, and room was made to accommodate this method in the ELCA's theology. Furthermore, it has been thoroughly taught to the lay people of the merging churches: EVEN BEFORE THE MERGER BOTH THE LCA AND ALC HAD PROGRAMS TO INTRODUCE AND POPULARIZE THE HISTORICAL-CRITICAL

APPROACH TO SCRIPTURE AMONG THE LAITY. IN 1984 THE ALC PRODUCED A SERIES OF ESSAYS PUBLISHED UNDER THE COLLECTIVE TITLE *THE DOCTRINE OF THE WORD IN THE LUTHERAN CHURCH*. THIS DOCUMENT WAS SENT TO ALL CONGREGATIONS AS A PART OF THE PREMERGER EFFORT TO WIN ACCEPTANCE OF THE HISTORIC-CRITICAL METHOD. THE ALC'S SEARCH AND THE LCA'S WORD AND WITNESS PROGRAMS WERE OTHER EFFORTS TOWARD THIS GOAL. [Today, the Bible-study materials in the ELCA are based primarily on the historical-critical method of Bible interpretation.] PRIOR TO THE MERGER *THE LUTHERAN* AND *THE LUTHERAN STANDARD* PUBLISHED NUMEROUS ARTICLES TO INCREASE ACCEPTANCE OF THE HISTORICAL-CRITICAL METHOD AMONG THE LAITY.[53]

And so, the lay people of the ELCA are widely taught to place Scripture under intense "scientific" scrutiny in order to learn the truth, rather than simply trust the words of the inspired prophets, apostles, and evangelists (who also give us the words of Christ himself). Because of the "theological reconstruction" or the use of the historical-critical method, all Lutheran bodies were not merged to form the ELCA. The LCMS, WELS, ELS, CLC and other smaller Lutheran bodies remain aloof to what is actually a merger of the liberal or neo-Lutheran bodies in the U.S.A.

The direct results of the widespread employment of the historical-critical method in the ELCA are open attacks on—and even denials of—Scripture doctrines. This fact is clear to any person who seriously examines the writings of the ELCA's leaders and its theologians and dogmaticians in books and official publications. Furthermore, individuals and groups within the ELCA have been vocal in revealing their concerns about the direction in which ELCA's theology is headed. These negative appraisals furnish first-hand evidence of a theology gone awry in the ELCA. For example, in the February 1994 edition of *Lutheran Forum*, a magazine which calls itself "The Independent Voice for Lutherans," an editorial expressed this concern:

OUR CHURCH IS SEIZED BY A PROFOUND MALAISE AND A VIRTUAL COLLAPSE OF VISION. WE ARE AT SHARP ODDS WITH EACH OTHER ABOUT WHAT IT MEANS TO BE LUTHERAN. PEOPLE ARE FEARFUL ABOUT THE FUTURE, BATTERED BY THE WINDS AND WAVES OF MODERNITY, WORRIED WHETHER THEY CAN PASS ON THE FAITH TO THEIR CHILDREN. STUDIES OF CLERGY MORALE SHOW A FRIGHTENING DEGREE OF FRUSTRATION AND EXHAUSTION. THE FIRM COMMITMENTS THAT HAVE CHARACTERIZED LUTHERANISM IN THE PAST HAVE BEGUN TO WEAKEN ON ALL FRONTS. MAJOR DOCTRINAL AND MORAL TEACHINGS OF THE CHURCH ARE UNDER ATTACK. THE SACRED LITURGY IS MOCKED AS AN IMPEDIMENT. VALUABLE PARTS OF OUR HERITAGE IN CULTURE AND MUSIC ARE EMBARRASSING TO GOOD PEOPLE WHO OUGHT TO KNOW BETTER.

Furthermore, an advertisement appeared in the Lutheran Forum concerning a conference entitled, "Reclaiming the Bible for the Church." Sponsored by the *Center for Catholic and Evangelical Theology* and the *American Lutheran Publicity Bureau*, the Conference was scheduled to be held at St. Olaf College, Northfield, Minnesota, on June 6-8, 1994.

CONFERENCE PARTICIPANTS WILL ADDRESS THE GAP BETWEEN THE HISTORICAL-CRITICAL METHOD OF BIBLICAL STUDIES AND THE THEOLOGY OF THE CHURCH. HISTORICAL CRITICISM HAS NOT PROVEN TO BE A NEUTRAL METHODOLOGY. AND SYSTEMATIC THEOLOGY HAS LARGELY BYPASSED BIBLICAL EXEGE-

SIS, ALLYING ITSELF WITH PHILOSOPHICAL SYSTEMS OR, MORE RECENTLY, PSY-
CHOLOGICAL THEORIES.[54]

Four years earlier, on June 4-6, 1990, a major free conference, which dealt
with doctrinal decay in the ELCA, met at St. Olaf College. This earlier conference was sponsored by independent Lutheran Journals, *Dialog, Lutheran
Forum, Forum Letter, Lutheran Quarterly*. The invitation to the conference
was extended to "all who subscribe to the authority of the Word of God, as articulated by the ecumenical creeds and confessions of the Lutheran Church."
The purpose of the conference was "to deliberate and debate on key doctrinal
issues facing the Lutheran Church in the United States and ELCA in particular." More than 800 people responded. An observer to the conference later reported the following in the *Wisconsin Lutheran Quarterly* (theological journal
of the WELS):

THE CONFERENCE THEME, "A CALL TO FAITHFULNESS," EXPRESSED THE OR-
GANIZERS' DISTRESS AT THE THEOLOGICAL DIRECTION WHICH ELCA IS TAKING
AND THEIR DESIRE TO PRESERVE THE CONFESSIONAL INTEGRITY OF
LUTHERANISM....THE KEY ISSUES TO BE DISCUSSED: THE MINISTRY, THE ECU-
MENICAL DIRECTION OF ELCA AND LUTHERANISM IN AMERICA, THE MISSION
OF THE CHURCH, AND CHURCH AND SOCIETY....MANY OF THE SPEAKERS AT THE
CONFERENCE WERE PROMINENT ELCA THEOLOGIANS WHO HAVE LONG ADVO-
CATED DOCTRINAL POSITIONS WHICH DEPART DRASTICALLY FROM THE TEACH-
INGS OF SCRIPTURE AND THE POSITION OF THE LUTHERAN CONFESSIONS.
THE KEYNOTE ADDRESS ON "THE AUTHORITY OF GOSPEL, SCRIPTURE, AND
CONFESSION" WAS DELIVERED BY ROBERT JENSON OF ST. OLAF. HE SAID THAT
MANY WERE IN ATTENDANCE AT THE CONFERENCE "BECAUSE WE FEAR THAT
THE FAITHFULNESS OF OUR OWN CHURCH, OF LUTHERANISM IN NORTH AMER-
ICA, IS NOW DOUBTFUL"...ONE [SPEAKER] SAID, "WE ARE AT A MOMENT OF
TRUTH IN AMERICAN LUTHERANISM." ANOTHER WAS CRITICAL OF THE "PRAC-
TICED AMBIGUITY OF ECUMENICAL DISCUSSION." A PREACHER WARNED OF THE
"IMPENDING APOSTASY OF THE CHURCH."
....AN-
OTHER MATTER WHICH TROUBLED MANY OF THOSE IN ATTENDANCE WAS THE
LOSS OF BIBLICAL LITERACY AND LACK OF KNOWLEDGE OF DOCTRINE AMONG
MANY LUTHERAN MEMBERS. JENSON SAID, "IF I WERE TO POINT TO THE SINGLE
MOST ALARMING PORTENT OF UNFAITHFULNESS IN OUR CHURCH, I WOULD POINT
TO THE CONTENT OF OUR CHILDREN'S CATECHESIS [CATECHISM INSTRUCTION]."
JAMES KITTELSON, AUTHOR OF A RECENT WELL-RECEIVED BIOGRAPHY OF
LUTHER ASKED, "WHY IS IT THAT OUR CHILDREN DO NOT HAVE THE SMALL CAT-
ECHISM PUT INTO THEIR HANDS AND HEARTS?" HE CHARGED THAT WHAT WAS
BEING TAUGHT IN SOME PARISHES WAS "RANK HERESY."

The WELS reviewer asks the question:

"WHAT DID THESE THEOLOGIANS EXPECT FROM A CHURCH THAT WAS FOUNDED
ON THE BASIS OF A DELIBERATE REJECTION OF THE INERRANCY OF SCRIPTURE?"
THE ELCA MERGER WAS FOUNDED ON A CONFESSION OF THE "AUTHORITY" OF
THE GOSPEL WHICH REALLY REJECTED ANY BINDING AUTHORITY OF SCRIPTURE
OVER THE DOCTRINE OF THE CHURCH. UNPALATABLE TEACHINGS OF THE CON-
FESSIONS, SUCH AS THE DOCTRINE OF THE ANTICHRIST, WERE PUBLICLY DIS-
AVOWED IN SPITE OF ELCA'S PAPER ENDORSEMENT OF THE CONFESSIONS. A

859

GENERATION OF SEMINARIANS WAS FED POISONOUS CRITICAL VIEWS OF SCRIP-
TURE. POSITIONS OF LEADERSHIP IN THE CHURCH WERE PARCELED OUT ON THE
BASIS OF QUOTAS RATHER THAN ON THE BASIS OF THEOLOGICAL KNOWLEDGE
AND FAITHFULNESS TO SCRIPTURE.

....

The WELS reviewer draws the following conclusion:

MANY OF THE LEADING SPEAKERS OF THIS CONFERENCE, SUCH AS BRAATEN,
JENSON, FORDE, AND SPONHEIM, WERE ACCOMPLICES IN THE WRITING OF THE
TEXTBOOK *CHRISTIAN DOGMATICS*, WHICH SO FLAGRANTLY DENIES SO MANY
DOCTRINES OF SCRIPTURE AND THE LUTHERAN CONFESSIONS [see the Chapter
THE LUTHERAN CHURCH IN AMERICA for examples of doctrinal
aberrations]. THEY HAVE LONG USED SCRIPTURAL AND CONFESSIONAL LAN-
GUAGE IN THE SERVICE OF DOCTRINAL POSITIONS THAT ARE A GRIEVOUS DEPAR-
TURE FROM OUR LUTHERAN HERITAGE. THAT THEOLOGIANS SUCH AS THESE
ARE "CONFESSIONAL LUTHERANS" AND "DOCTRINAL CONSERVATIVES" IN ELCA
IS A SAD TOKEN OF THE DEGREE TO WHICH ELCA'S LEADERSHIP HAS ABAN-
DONED ITS LUTHERAN HERITAGE....ONLY REPENTANCE AND SUBMISSION TO
THE FULL TEACHING AUTHORITY OF SCRIPTURE OFFER ANY HOPE OF PULLING
ELCA BACK TOWARDS CONFESSIONAL LUTHERANISM.

The WELS reviewer also points out:

IT IS DOUBLY SAD THAT LUTHERANS WHO WANT TO BE FAITHFUL TO SCRIPTURE
ARE NOT READY TO HEED AND OBEY SCRIPTURE'S ADMONITION THAT THOSE WHO
LOVE GOD'S WORD MUST SEPARATE THEMSELVES FROM FALSE TEACHERS WHO
HAVE MOVED AWAY FROM THE BIBLICAL AND CONFESSIONAL FOUNDATION OF
THE CHURCH. WE FEAR THAT WORKING ZEALOUSLY TO GAIN NEW MEMBERS
FOR A CHURCH THAT HAS TURNED AWAY FROM THE PURE TRUTH OF GOD'S
WORD WILL PROVE TO BE A VERY FRUSTRATING TASK FOR THE MEMBERS OF THE
GREAT COMMISSION NETWORK.[55]

And now, to sum up the issue at hand: The leading doctrines of Scripture
have been obscured and corrupted by the ELCA's theologians and dogmaticians. Over and over, as shown in the Chapter *THE LUTHERAN CHURCH
IN AMERICA* the authors of *Christian Dogmatics*—edited by Braaten and Jenson—empty the basic doctrines of Scripture of their true meaning, and treat
Scripture itself as an unreliable source of doctrine, a book filled with error and
inconsistencies, a book that cannot stand up to scientific scrutiny, a book unreliable in its historical references. Braaten: THE ULTIMATE AUTHORITY OF CHRIS-
TIAN THEOLOGY IS NOT THE BIBLICAL CANNON AS SUCH, BUT THE GOSPEL OF JESUS
CHRIST TO WHICH THE SCRIPTURES BEAR WITNESS.

Tragically, in explaining the various points of Christian doctrine, a whole
new obscure jargon and confusing philosophical statements and vague conclusions are employed by ELCA theologians and dogmaticians, who at times do
not agree among themselves. In the volume *WELS AND OTHER LUTHER-
ANS* the following is noted:

WE CAN HARDLY JUSTIFY CALLING THE THEOLOGY OF THE TOP THEOLOGIANS OF
ELCA LUTHERAN OR EVEN CHRISTIAN....MANY IN ELCA BELIEVE IN SALVA-
TION DETACHED FROM THE HISTORICAL DEEDS OF CHRIST, SALVATION WHICH
CAN BE OBTAINED WITHOUT KNOWLEDGE OR FAITH IN CHRIST. IF BIBLICAL
CHRISTIANITY STILL EXISTS IN ELCA, IT IS FOUND IN THE PREACHING OF SOME

FAITHFUL PASTORS AND IN THE HEARTS OF GOD'S CAPTIVE PEOPLE. IT IS NOT FOUND IN THE TEACHING OF ITS CHIEF DOGMATICIANS.

The authors of *WELS and Other Lutherans* also point out: THE LEADING THEOLOGIANS OF THE ELCA HAVE NOT ONLY ABANDONED CONFESSIONAL LUTHERANISM. THEY ATTACK AND UNDERMINE EVEN THE MOST BASIC TEACHINGS OF CHRISTIANITY. ALTHOUGH THERE IS LIP SERVICE TO SCRIPTURE AND THE LUTHERAN CONFESSIONS, THE DOCTRINES WHICH THEY CONFESS ARE NOT MAINTAINED IN THE ELCA. IN THE REGULAR SERVICES AND INSTRUCTION, THE TEACHINGS OF SCRIPTURE ARE OFTEN OBSCURED BY AMBIGUITY OR BY FALSE STATEMENTS.[57]

The author of this last observation listened to 27 sermons preached in the ELCA and read devotions covering a six-month period in an ELCA home devotional booklet.

As far as the authority of Scripture is concerned in the ELCA, as it pertains to theology, it is pretty much limited to the gospel of Jesus Christ. As the authors of *WELS and Other Lutherans* point out: IN THE ELCA...THE BIBLE IS THE WORD OF GOD, NOT SO MUCH BECAUSE IT WAS GIVEN BY INSPIRATION OF GOD, BUT BECAUSE IT CONVEYS THE MESSAGE OF SALVATION.[58]

The theologians who authored *WELS and Other Lutherans*–the First Edition–also draw this conclusion: OVERALL, THERE IS NO VOICE LEFT FOR BIBLICAL LUTHERANISM AT THE OFFICIAL LEVEL [OF THE ELCA] OR THE SEMINARY LEVEL. And they also pointed out:...THE OFFICIAL DOCTRINAL POSITION OF ELCA LEAVES THE DOOR OPEN FOR THEOLOGIANS TO DEVELOP AND PROMOTE ALL SORTS OF DOCTRINAL DIVERSITY...LEADING THEOLOGIANS OF ELCA HAVE USED THIS FREEDOM TO OVERTHROW EVEN THE MOST BASIC DOCTRINES OF CHRISTIANITY. IN ELCA CONCERN FOR DOCTRINE OFTEN TAKES A BACKSEAT TO CHURCH AND WORLD POLITICS. ON THE ORGANIZATIONAL LEVEL OF ELCA THERE IS VIRTUALLY NO TESTIMONY REMAINING FOR CONFESSIONAL LUTHERANISM.[59]

These observations by conservative, confessional theologians of the Wisconsin Evangelical Lutheran Synod (WELS) were made after careful examination of ELCA theological and dogmatic writings in the light of Scripture and the Lutheran Confessions.

In regards to doctrine in the ELCA "taking a backseat to church and world politics," the following satirical words of an older ELCA pastor were recorded in the March/April issue of *Lutheran Partners* and indicate how out of place older pastors must at times feel when they appear to be too theological for the church today: NOBODY CARES WHAT YOUR THEOLOGY IS ANY MORE. WHEN I HEAR SOME SO-CALLED LUTHERANS TALK THEOLOGY, THEY SOUND LIKE SOUTHERN BAPTISTS. OTHERS SOUND LIKE ROMAN CATHOLICS. SOME EVEN SOUND LIKE UNITARIANS. AND THAT'S OKAY! NOBODY IN THE CHURCH MINDS THAT...YOU CAN THINK WHATEVER YOU WANT ABOUT THEOLOGICAL QUESTIONS, AND THAT'S OKAY. BUT...YOU BETTER HOLD THE RIGHT POSITION ON SOCIAL ISSUES OR YOU'RE IN BIG TROUBLE. NOBODY CARES MUCH ABOUT YOUR THEOLOGY, BUT YOU BETTER BE ON TARGET WITH YOUR POLITICS, OR WATCH OUT.[60]

Here is a list of books and publications which a person may obtain to study more carefully the official writings produced by the ELCA:

The Lutheran, Augsburg Fortress Press, 426 South Fifth Street, Box 1209, Minneapolis, MN 554440. Phone 800-446-6129 (Official magazine of the ELCA)

Christian Dogmatics, Carl E. Braaten and Robert W. Jensen, editors, (2 vols.), Augsburg Fortress Press (address above).

What's Going On Among the Lutherans? and *WELS and Other Lutherans, First and Second Editions*: all are published by Northwestern Publishing House (WELS), 1250 North 113th Street, Milwaukee, WI 53226-3284, Phone 800-662-6022.

Wisconsin Lutheran Quarterly (WELS), published by Northwestern Publishing House (address above).

Search Weekly Bible Studies (Adult Bible study program.) Contact Augsburg Fortress Press—address above.

The Christian News Encyclopedia, Volume I-V, *Christian News*, 684 Luther Lane, New Haven, Missouri 63068-2218; phone – 573-237-3110.

THE ELCA—DEEPLY COMMITTED TO ECUMENISM

One of the outstanding traits that distinguishes the ELCA from Lutheran bodies which did not join the merger—the conservative and moderate groups—is the ELCA's fervor (or to some, obsession) for ecumenism. Historically (consider the actions of the predecessor churches) and officially (consider the numerous actions taken by the Churchwide Assemblies) the ELCA is committed to reaching out to other Christian bodies worldwide for fellowship. In fact, already at the 1991 Churchwide Assembly a statement on ecumenism was drawn up, which was then approved overwhelmingly (919-67) by the delegates. This "Declaration of Ecumenical Commitment" contained the term "full communion" (i.e. with other churches) and described it as being rooted in agreement on essentials while allowing diversity in non-essentials. This document explains "full communion as including the following: a common confession of the Christian Faith; a mutual recognition of baptism and a sharing of the Lord's Supper; a mutual recognition and availability of ordained ministers; a common commitment to evangelism, witness, and service: common decision-making on critical issues; a mutual lifting of any condemnations that exist between churches."[61]

An even earlier example of the ELCA's fervor for ecumenism was the action taken by the delegates of the three merging churches meeting in the ELCA's Constituting Convention in Columbus, Ohio, April 30 to May 3, 1987. They quickly voted the ELCA into membership in the Lutheran World Federation, the National Council of Churches, and the World Council of Churches—liberal bodies all. At the same time, the delegates asked for a study of Lutheran-Reformed relations.

The ELCA Constitution provides a logical basis for the ELCA's ecumenical fervor: THIS CHURCH ACCEPTS THE UNALTERED AUGSBURG CONFESSION (1530) AS A TRUE WITNESS TO THE GOSPEL, ACKNOWLEDGING AS ONE WITH IT IN FAITH AND DOCTRINE ALL CHURCHES THAT LIKEWISE ACCEPT ALL THE TEACHINGS OF THE *UNAL-*

At this point it would be profitable to review three terms which are interconnected: ecumenism, pluralism, and minimalism. The three terms describe the ELCA's endeavors to unite all church bodies in "full fellowship."

ECUMENISM IS THE DRIVE TO UNITE ALL CHURCHES INTO ONE LARGE ORGANIZATION.

PLURALISM IS THE TOLERATION AND SIDE-BY-SIDE EXISTENCE OF VARIOUS AND CONFLICTING DOCTRINAL POSITIONS WITHIN A SINGLE CHURCH BODY. IN THE BROADER SENSE, IT REFERS TO THE BELIEF THAT THERE IS VALUE IN ALL RELIGIONS AND ALL SHOULD ENJOY EQUAL TOLERATION.

MINIMALISM IS THE VIEW THAT CHURCHES CAN AND SHOULD UNITE, OR AT LEAST HAVE FELLOWSHIP WITH ONE ANOTHER, ON THE BASIS OF A MINIMUM OF DOCTRINAL AGREEMENT. AN EXAMPLE OF SUCH LOWEST-COMMON-DENOMINATOR CONSENSUS IS THE WORLD COUNCIL OF CHURCHES' AGREEMENT ON THE PROPOSITION THAT JESUS CHRIST IS "LORD."[62]

In regards to the ELCA's quick entry into the ecumenical scene, it is of interest to note that soon after the formation of this new Lutheran church, the elected bishop, Dr. Herbert W. Chilstrom, left on a ten-day ecumenical pilgrimage that took him to Rome and Pope John Paul II; also to Istanbul, Moscow and London to meet with church leaders. Later, Chilstrom visited Geneva, Switzerland, where the offices of the World Alliance of Reformed Churches, the Lutheran World Federation, and the World Council of Churches are located. Dialog continues with various bodes, and we will note some of this effort to reach out to others shortly. Bear in mind as we consider this subject that the predecessor churches of the ELCA were led by men fully committed to ecumenism—Dr. Fry in the LCA and Dr. Schiotz in the ALC. Their enthusiasm for ecumenism has been shared by subsequent leaders, who have been successful in injecting it into the grass roots element of the ELCA.

Like one of its predecessors, the United Lutheran Church in America, the ELCA put forth much effort to dialogue with the Roman Catholic Church with the purpose to establish the bond of "full communion" with that body. At one point the ELCA was ready to capitulate to Rome's Doctrine of the Ministry but was rejected by Rome. The ELCA hoped that the removal of the mutual condemnation between Roman Catholics and Lutherans on Justification, which was planned for 1997, would reopen ecumenical discussions on other issues, including Ministry. But as reported in the *Wisconsin Lutheran Quarterly*:

ELCA'S POSITION IS UNTENABLE ON AT LEAST THREE COUNTS. IT HOPES TO FIND CONSENSUS WITH THE HISTORIC EPISCOPACY OF ROMAN CATHOLIC, ORTHODOX AND EPISCOPAL CHURCHES. AT THE SAME TIME ITS WANTS CONSENSUS WITH THE REFORMED CHURCHES, WHICH DO NOT HAVE THE HISTORIC EPISCOPACY. MEANWHILE, ELCA HAS NO OFFICIAL STATEMENT OF ITS OWN ON MINISTRY. [THIS LACK] ALLOWS ELCA TO FORGE ITS DOCTRINE AND PRACTICE ON MINISTRY WHILE SEEKING TO SATISFY ITS ECUMENICAL AMBITIONS. IT HOPES TO BE ABLE TO SATISFY BOTH FRONTS AND STILL END UP BEING A CHURCH BODY WHICH HOLDS TO HISTORIC LUTHERANISM...NOTICEABLY ABSENT IS ANY APPEAL TO THE SCRIPTURES.[63]

The *Wisconsin Lutheran Quarterly* reported that the 1997 Churchwide Assembly of the ELCA...

...DECLARED THAT THE DIFFERENCE IN THE DOCTRINE OF JUSTIFICATION BE-
TWEEN CATHOLICS AND LUTHERANS ARE NO LONGER A CAUSE FOR DIVISION OR
CONDEMNATION BETWEEN THE CHURCHES...BY A VOTE OF 958-25 THE ASSEM-
BLY ADOPTED A "JOINT DECLARATION ON THE DOCTRINE OF JUSTIFICATION,"
DECLARING THAT CONDEMNATIONS WHICH LUTHERANS HURLED AT ROMAN
CATHOLICS DURING THE 16TH CENTURY CONCERNING THE KEY LUTHERAN DOC-
TRINE OF JUSTIFICATION NO LONGER APPLY TO PRESENT CATHOLIC TEACHING
ON THIS TOPIC...HISTORICALLY LUTHERANS HAVE INSISTED THAT JUSTIFICA-
TION IS A FREE GIFT FROM GOD. ROMAN CATHOLICS HAVE INSISTED THAT GOOD
WORKS ARE PART OF THE PROCESS OF JUSTIFICATION. THE DECLARATION NEV-
ERTHELESS ASSERTS, *THE UNDERSTANDING OF THE DOCTRINE OF JUSTIFICA-
TION SET FORTH IN THIS DECLARATION SHOWS THAT A CONSENSUS IN THE BASIC
TRUTHS OF THE DOCTRINE OF JUSTIFICATION EXISTS BETWEEN LUTHERANS AND
CATHOLICS....THUS THE DOCTRINEAL CONDEMNATIONS OF THE 16TH CENTURY,
IN SO FAR AS THEY RELATE TO THE DOCTRINE OF JUSTIFICATION, APPEAR IN A
NEW LIGHT.* THE DOCUMENT DOES NOT CLAIM TO PRODUCE AN AGREEMENT ON
ALL ASPECTS OF THE DOCTRINE OF JUSTIFICATION BUT ONLY A "CONVERGENCE"
ON KEY POINTS.

THE DOCUMENT STATES (POINT 13)....*THE POST-VATICAN II ECUMENICAL DIA-
LOGUE HAS LED TO A NOTABLE CONVERGENCE CONCERNING JUSTIFICATION,
WITH THE RESULT THAT THIS JOINT DECLARATION IS ABLE TO FORMULATE A
CONSENSUS ON BASIC TRUTHS CONCERNING THE DOCTRINE OF JUSTIFICA-
TION...(POINT 15) IN FAITH WE TOGETHER HOLD THE CONVICTION THAT JUSTI-
FICATION IS THE WORK OF THE TRIUNE GOD. THE FATHER SENT HIS SON INTO
THE WORLD TO SAVE SINNERS...WE CONFESS TOGETHER THAT ALL PERSONS
DEPEND COMPLETELY ON THE SAVING GRACE OF GOD FOR THEIR SALVATION.*

However, the WELS theologians, writing in the *Wisconsin Lutheran Quarterly*, points out:

THIS, HOWEVER, HAS NEVER BEEN THE POINT OF DISAGREEMENT. CATHOLICS
AND LUTHERANS HAVE ALWAYS AGREED THAT WE ARE SAVED BY GRACE. THE
POINT OF DISAGREEMENT HAS ALWAYS BEEN WHETHER THE GRACE BY WHICH
OUR SINS ARE FORGIVEN IS A VERDICT OF GOD WHICH TAKES PLACE OUTSIDE OF
US OR IF IT INCLUDES ABILITY WHICH GOD PUTS INTO US [*GRATIA INFUSA*, IN-
FUSED GRACE], WHICH WE USE TO COMPLETE OUR JUSTIFICATION. Point num-
ber 27 of the above-mentioned document states: *The justification of
sinners is forgiveness of sins and being made righteous by justifying grace,
which makes us children of God.* Commenting on this statement, the
WELS theologian observes: POINT 27 CLEARLY PERMITS THE CATHOLIC BE-
LIEF THAT JUSTIFICATION IS BOTH FORGIVENESS OF SINS AND THE INNER RE-
NEWAL OF THE SINNER. IT IS BOTH BEING DECLARED RIGHTEOUS AND BEING
MADE RIGHTEOUS. THE REFERENCES TO...*Christ, who in his person is our
righteousness, the saving presence of God himself, and justification and re-
newal joined in Christ, who is present in faith...*ARE ALL DESIGNED TO
ALLOW THE VIEW OF OSIANDER, WHO TAUGHT THAT WE ARE JUSTIFIED BY
CHRIST DWELLING IN US, RATHER THAN BY THE VERDICT OF GOD WHICH TAKES
PLACE OUTSIDE OF US. OSIANDER'S DOCTRINE WAS REJECTED BY LUTHER AND
ALL OF HIS TRUE FOLLOWERS. THE JOINT STATEMENT THUS IS NOT A REAL RES-

OLUTION OF THE CRITICAL DIFFERENCE BETWEEN THE LUTHERAN AND CATHOLIC DOCTRINES OF JUSTIFICATION, BUT AN ATTEMPT TO HIDE THESE CRITICAL DIFFERENCES.

The WELS theologian concludes his remarks first with a reminder of what the new Catholic Catechism has to say on the Doctrine of Justification:

Justification includes the remission of sins, sanctification, and the renewal of the inner man (Par. 2019)...No one can merit the initial grace which is at the origin of conversion. Moved by the Holy Spirit, we can merit for ourselves and others all the graces needed to attain eternal life. (Par. 2017)

And so, the WELS theologian points out that nothing has changed from Luther's time to the present regarding the Doctrine of Justification.[64]

It was actually the hope of the ELCA that in 1997 the condemnations that the Lutherans and Roman Catholics have in the past issue against each other would be lifted and that full communion would be reached. This goal was not met.

The ELCA Churchwide Assembly had also scheduled for the year 1997 a discussion proposal which called for "full communion" with the following bodies: the Episcopal Church, the Presbyterian Church (U.S.A.), the United Church of Christ, and the Reformed Church in America. The ELCA educators, theologians, and officials, who met in February 1993, reacted to this proposal by stating that "ELCA can adopt both ecumenical initiatives with integrity and credibility."[65]

This conclusion drawn by these representatives of the ELCA was but a natural outcome to the ecumenical fervor that gripped the ELCA since its inception a few years earlier, a fervor that it inherited from the three bodies that merged to form it. Unity in doctrine and practice simply was not given priority in its ecumenical outreach to other church bodies, including non-Lutheran churches with whom it carried on dialogues.

The proposal to enter full communion with the above mentioned churches was based on a document titled "A Common Calling" (ALC). (It was also hoped that the ELCA could declare full communion with the Roman Catholic Church.) In studying the above document, the Missouri Synod concluded that it put forth "different modes of doing theology," that it dismissed entirely the "importance of consensus in both the understanding and meaning of doctrinal formulations and confessional statements," and that there was a policy to "agree to disagree."[66]

While the 1997 ELCA Churchwide Assembly voted 839-193 to approve full communion with the three Reformed churches, thus committing the churches to share communion, and to share in mission work and to develop procedures to allow clergy to cross denominational lines to serve pastorates, the proposal to establish full communion with the Episcopal Church was rejected (the measure failed by 6 votes). Mainly bothersome was the required commitment of the ELCA to the "historic episcopate" of the Episcopal Church. Under this episcopate only bishops can ordain candidates for the ministry or priesthood. Nevertheless the ELCA remained committed to establishing full communion with the Episcopal Church, as well as with others.[67]

Finally, in 1999, the ELCA in its Churchwide Assembly held in Denver, amicably, but intensely, debated the issue of full communion with the Episcopal

Church for three days and then gave its approval, with a vote of 716 to 317. The tipping of the vote came about with the help of a document, "Calling to Common Mission," which was written after the failure in 1997 to commit to full communion with the Episcopal Church. And so, the ELCA finally agreed to accept the historic episcopate concept "that those who ordain new pastors are from a line of bishops stretching back to the earliest days of the church."

In accommodating the ELCA's gesture to fellowship with them, the Episcopalians in turn agreed to suspend the 17th century rule defining who is a priest and accept all current ELCA pastors and bishops. In the offing would be the exchange of clergy. The ELCA is also committed to work together on future mission and service projects.[68]

About 31% of the 1999 delegates voted against the ELCA's resolution to establish "full communion" with the Episcopal Church. Further dissent surfaced after that. A pastoral letter sent out in March of 2000 acknowledged "that the 1999 resolution to adopt Called to Common Mission has caused 'deep concern and opposition' among some of the ELCA's members." The hope was expressed that the Conference of Bishops would be able to work with those of "diverse views"—including people in both the ELCA and the Episcopal Church—with the purpose of implementing the Called to Common Mission document. The notion was expressed that ways could be explored to allow exceptions to the requirement that in the ELCA a bishop must ordain pastors. Perhaps another ELCA pastor could be authorized to preside at an ordination. Dissenting members of the ELCA pointed out that in the Anglican Communion the historic episcopate is of the essence for a valid ministry and for true unity in the church. It isn't a mere matter of church polity or traditional practice.[69]

Also, at the 1999 ELCA Churchwide Assembly the delegates endorsed full communion with the Moravian Church in America (with only 11 no votes). While making these important decisions, which would affect the role of ELCA's clergy, this Lutheran body still lacked a doctrine of the Ministry. As stated before, the ELCA was, in effect, allowing its ecumenical efforts to define its doctrine of the Ministry—at least temporarily—which then it was free to change in order to fit the requirements of a particular ecumenical agreement.

By an overwhelming majority at the ELCA Churchwide Assembly in August 2005, (877-60) the delegates once again showed their lack of concern for steadfast adherence to conservative, confessional expression of scriptural doctrine (and thus also a lack of concern for conservative, confessional Lutheranism) by paving the way to engage in "Eucharistic sharing" between the ELCA and the United Methodist Church. What this means is that a Methodist can receive communion in the ELCA and vice versa. Full communion with the Methodist Church is the goal of this Eucharistic sharing. With the establishing of full communion between the two churches, a Methodist pastor could become the minister of an ELCA congregation and vice versa. The greater significance of the Assembly's action is this: the ELCA has once again taken a step toward the complete loss of its Lutheran identity.

In voting for full communion with Reformed churches and with the Episcopal Church, and in Eucharistic sharing with the United Methodist Church, the ELCA's delegates showed an open willingness to gloss over the differences in doctrine and practice that have ever existed between them. With the Reformed churches, it included such defining doctrines as the Real Presence (of Christ's body and blood in the Lord's Supper, a doctrine denied by the Reformed), and on the other hand, the teaching of a limited atonement (thus Jesus' sacrifice for sin was only for the believers, the saved, not for the entire world of sinners—a teaching of the Reformed that is denied by the Lutherans, who believe that Jesus died for the whole world of sinners). The aim of the ELCA has been mutual understanding and acceptance of each other's differences. And so, the ELCA Lutherans celebrate a unity in the church that is not true unity where all sides agree not to let their disagreements keep them apart. It is supposed unity based simply on mutual belief in the gospel, but even here there is disunity, for there are varied teachings regarding the gospel itself among the various denominations, and even within the ELCA itself. Some of the ELCA's theologians and pastors deny the cardinal doctrine of Scripture, the Blood Atonement of Christ for the sins of the world, and with it, the doctrine of Justification by Faith apart from the works of the law. Furthermore, the true gospel of Jesus Christ has in many instances been replaced to a great extent by the social gospel, including today's "liberation theology." And the ELCA is not alone among churches in having those members who denigrate the gospel of our Lord while exalting political and social endeavors. Finally, there are those in the ELCA and in other church bodies who teach "universalism" (everyone is saved whether or not they believe in Jesus Christ).

The ELCA seeks unity among churches by intercommunion, thus using the Lord's Supper as an area where various churches, who represent a variety of teachings and practices, can get together and practice fellowship—and in the process demonstrate their unity. Here the critical differences between the Reformed Church and the Lutheran Church regarding the Lord's Supper are overlooked. The authors of What's Going On Among the Lutherans? respond to this practice with the following weighty words of Dr. Theodore Schmauke, the president of the General Council (1903-18):

IS THE LORD'S SUPPER THE PLACE TO DISPLAY MY TOLERATION, MY CHRISTIAN SYMPATHY OR MY FELLOWSHIP WITH ANOTHER CHRISTIAN, WHEN THAT IS THE VERY POINT IN WHICH MOST OF ALL WE DIFFER, AND IN WHICH THE DIFFERENCES MEAN FOR ME EVERYTHING—MEANS FOR ME, THE RECEPTION OF MY SAVIOR'S ATONEMENT? IS THIS THE POINT TO BE SELECTED FOR THE DISPLAY OF CHRISTIAN UNION, WHEN IN FACT IT IS THE VERY POINT IN WHICH CHRISTIAN UNION DOES NOT EXIST?[70]

The liberal church bodies are all united in this manner: they do not possess and promote the whole truth of Scripture. In their rejection of scriptural truth, much of it is done through employing the historical-critical method or by minimizing the importance of doctrine or by substituting man-made teachings—in this they are united. David Preus, president of the ALC before it became a part of the ELCA spoke of "reconciled diversity"—thus unity in that. They are united in agreeing that their diverse theologies shall not keep them apart. They agree to acknowledge and tolerate diversity in doctrine, as well as in practice. In fact, the impression is given that diversity is actually a plus.

Finally, the authors of What's Going On Among the Lutherans? draw the following conclusion:

SINCE THOSE WHO ACCEPT HISTORICAL CRITICISM CAN NO LONGER ANSWER

WITH ANY REAL CERTAINTY THE QUESTION "WHAT IS TRUTH?" THEY ARE, IN A REAL SENSE, ALREADY UNITED. THEIR UNITY, THE UNITY OF THE MAINLINE CHURCHES, IS EXPRESSED MOST CLEARLY BY BRAATEN AND JENSON'S *CHRISTIAN DOGMATICS*, WHICH IS A REJECTION OF ALL THE BASIC DOCTRINES OF THE CHRISTIAN FAITH. IF THEY ARE UNWILLING TO REFUTE THE HERESY OF HISTORICAL CRITICISM, ONE MIGHT CONCLUDE THAT THEY MAY AS WELL STRIVE FOR ORGANIC UNION AND LEARN TO LIVE WITH THEIR DOCTRINAL CONFUSION BY "AGREEING TO DISAGREE." HOWEVER, THIS IS CONTRARY TO THE WILL OF GOD, AND THOSE WHO INDULGE IN THIS PRACTICE ARE GUILTY OF RELIGIOUS UNIONISM. IT IS FAR BETTER THAT THEY REMAIN SEPARATE. KRAUTH SAYS IT MOST SUCCINCTLY: "TRUTHFUL SEPARATION IS FAR BETTER THAN DISHONEST UNION, AND TWO CHURCHES ARE HAPPIER, AND MORE KINDLY IN THEIR MUTUAL RELATIONS, WHEN THEIR DIFFERENCES ARE FRANKLY CONFESSED, THAN WHEN THEY ARE CLOUDING WITH AMBIGUITIES AND DOUBLE MEANING THE REAL DIVERGENCES."[71]

To state the matter quite bluntly: In declaring church union, or at least church fellowship, without true doctrinal accord, the participants are involved in a blatantly untruthful situation that brings no glory to God and dishonors his holy Word. It is, simply stated, dishonest on a grand scale. Unity not based on mutual recognition and adherence to the truth is a fraudulent endeavor, no matter how "good" and how "fulfilled" it makes the participants feel. In the eyes of conservative, confessional Lutheranism, ecumenism is simply another word for unionism, and unionism is forbidden in Scripture (John 8:31-32, Matthew 28:20; 1 Corinthians 5:6; 1 Corinthians 1:10; Romans 16:17,18; Ephesians 4:3; 2 Thessalonians 2:15; 2 Thessalonians 3:14,15; 1 Timothy 6:3-5).

Dr J. Michael Reu of the old ALC gives one of the marks of unionism as the following:

A FORMULA OF UNIFICATION IS FOUND WHICH EACH OF TWO HITHERTO SEPARATE CHURCHES MAY ACCEPT BUT WHICH EACH OF THEM INTERPRETS DIFFERENTLY. AN EXTERNAL BOND IS FOUND FOR INTERNALLY DIVIDED GROUPS. WE FIND THIS ATTITUDE OF TOLERANCE QUITE FREQUENTLY AMONG UNIONISTS. IT IS OFTEN USED TO ASSUAGE A TROUBLED CONSCIENCE, ONE'S OWN AS WELL AS THAT OF OTHERS; FOR THE UNIONIST DECLARES THAT EVERY ONE MAY CONTINUE TO HOLD HIS OWN PRIVATE CONVICTIONS AND MERELY NEEDS TO RESPECT AND TOLERATE THOSE OF ANOTHER. THIS ATTITUDE IS TOTALLY WRONG, FOR IT DISREGARDS TWO IMPORTANT FACTORS: (A) IN TOLERATING DIVERGENT DOCTRINES ONE EITHER DENIES THE PERSPICUITY AND CLARITY OF THE SCRIPTURES, OR ONE GRANTS TO ERROR THE RIGHT TO EXIST ALONGSIDE OF TRUTH, OR ONE EVIDENCES INDIFFERENCE OVER AGAINST BIBLICAL TRUTH BY SURRENDERING ITS ABSOLUTE VALIDITY; AND (B) IN ALLOWING TWO OPPOSITE VIEWS CONCERNING ONE DOCTRINE TO EXIST SIDE BY SIDE, ONE HAS ENTERED UPON AN INCLINED PLANE WHICH OF NECESSITY LEADS EVER FURTHER INTO COMPLETE DOCTRINAL INDIFFERENCES, AS MAY PLAINLY BE SEEN FROM THE MOST CALAMITOUS CASE ON RECORD, VIZ., THE PRUSSIAN UNION. DOCTRINAL INDIFFERENCE IS AT ONCE THE ROOT OF UNIONISM AND ITS FRUIT. WHOEVER ACCEPTS, IN THEORY AS WELL AS IN PRACTICE, THE ABSOLUTE AUTHORITY OF THE SCRIPTURES AND THEIR UNAMBIGUOUSNESS WITH REFERENCE TO ALL FUNDAMENTAL DOCTRINES,

MUST BE OPPOSED TO EVERY FORM OF UNIONISM.[72]

Reverend Paul Fleischer, long-time president of the ultra-conservative Church of the Lutheran Confession, gives this timely reminder:

CHURCH HISTORY HAS SHOWN THAT, WHEN CHURCHES OR ENTIRE CHURCH BOD-IES BECOME GUILTY OF ERROR IN DOCTRINE AND PRACTICE, THE FAULT MOST OFTEN LIES WITH THE LEADERS. THE LEADERS OF THE VARIOUS LUTHERAN SYNODS WHICH UNITED TO FORM THE ELCA HAVE FOR YEARS BEEN ACTIVELY PROMOTING AN ECUMENISM WHICH ENCOURAGES ORGANIZATIONAL UNION WITH-OUT DOCTRINAL UNITY. THE CURRENT ELCA BISHOP [CHILSTROM] IS LEADING HIS NEW SYNOD DOWN THE SAME PATH. WE ARE NOT SURPRISED, THEREFORE, THAT MAINSTREAM LUTHERANISM IS CONTINUING ON THE UNIONISTIC PATH IT HAS BEEN TRAVELING. NOR SHOULD WE BE SURPRISED THAT, BEFORE LONG, IT WILL CLAIM UNION WITH ROME ITSELF. WE ARE ALIVE TO WITNESS SOME OF THE SADDEST DAYS IN THE HISTORY OF LUTHERANISM.[73]

CONFUSION IN THE ELCA REGARDING
THE CHURCH'S MISSION—THE SOCIAL GOSPEL

Early in the ELCA's history, concerns were expressed that the new church was lacking in zeal for Christian mission work, and that social and political concerns were engaging the attention and resources of the church in preference to the work of preaching the gospel of Jesus of Christ to the salvation of sinners, which is the work the church is commissioned by the Lord to do.

At the free conference held at St. Olaf College in Northfield, Minnesota, on June 4-6, 1990, only two and a half years after ELCA's inception, one of the major concerns that was expressed—which reportedly drew the greatest interest of any topic discussed at the conference—involved the ELCA's gospel mission endeavors. Consider the following expressed concern:

ANOTHER MAJOR CONCERN...WAS WHAT MANY SEE AS THE FAILURE OF THE MIS-SION DIVISION OF ELCA TO EMPHASIZE THE PROCLAMATION OF THE GOSPEL, THE GOOD NEWS OF SALVATION. THE MAIN SPEAKER HERE WAS CARL BRAATEN OF THE LUTHERAN SCHOOL OF THEOLOGY IN CHICAGO...HE WORRIED THAT THE CHURCH IS "SPENDING PRIME TIME ON CONCERNS FOR WHICH IT HAS NO UNIQUE COMPETENCE, BUT NEGLECTS THE ONE THING NEEDFUL WHICH ONLY THE CHURCH, AND NO OTHER AGENCY IN THE WORLD HAS BEEN COMMISSIONED TO ACCOMPLISH"...(H)E DECLARED, "I CANNOT SQUELCH THE CONVICTION THAT WE ARE ENGAGED IN A CHURCH STRUGGLE FOR THE TRUTH OF THE GOSPEL AND THE INTEGRITY OF THE CHURCH'S MISSION. WE DO NOT KNOW HOW MUCH TIME WE HAVE BEFORE GOD WILL TAKE THE GOSPEL OUT OF OUR FAITHLESS HANDS AND PASS IT ON TO THOSE WHO WILL COMMIT THEIR LIVES AS WITNESSES TO ITS TRUTH."

A further report informs us:

ABOUT 50 EVANGELICAL LUTHERAN CHURCH IN AMERICA PASTORS, MOSTLY IN MINNESOTA, HAVE FORMED THE GREAT COMMISSION NETWORK IN HOPES OF TURNING ELCA IN A MORE CONSERVATIVE DIRECTION. THIS GROUP SEEMS TO OFFER MORE HOPE FOR PROMOTING REAL GOSPEL WORK IN ELCA THAN THE FREE CONFERENCE [HELD AT ST. OLAF COLLEGE]. THE GROUP OPPOSES THE

ORDINATION OF AVOWED HOMOSEXUALS, ABORTION, SEX OUTSIDE OF MARRIAGE, DRUG ABUSE AND THE ELIMINATION OF MASCULINE REFERENCES TO GOD AND IS ALARMED BY THE TOLERATION OR EVEN PROMOTION OF SOME OF THESE CAUSES BY SOME IN ELCA. THEY ALSO EXPRESSED DISMAY OVER A RECENT POLL THAT SHOWED THAT 61 PERCENT OF ELCA MEMBERS DO NOT BELIEVE IN SALVATION BY GRACE ALONE...WE FEAR THAT WORKING ZEALOUSLY TO GAIN NEW MEMBERS FOR A CHURCH THAT HAS TURNED AWAY FROM THE PURE TRUTH OF GOD'S WORD WILL PROVE TO BE A VERY FRUSTRATING TASK FOR THE MEMBERS OF THE GREAT COMMISSION NETWORK.[74]

Edgar R. Trexler, who gave us a thorough account of how the ELCA merger was put together, reports toward the end of his book *Anatomy of a Merger* that humanization, development, liberation, wholeness, and justice were substituted by the new church for salvation, that justice issues, not missions, were holding it together.

In their thorough study of the ELCA in its early years, authors Patsy Leppien and J. Kincaid Smith drew the following conclusion:

IT IS SIGNIFICANT, AND YET THOROUGHLY CONSISTENT WITH THE DIRECTION THAT THE LIBERAL THEOLOGY HAS TAKEN, THAT THE ZEAL FOR MISSIONS IN THE ELCA HAS ALMOST ENTIRELY EVAPORATED IN RECENT YEARS. WRITING NOW FROM THE PERSPECTIVE OF LIBERAL, HETERODOX LUTHERANS, THE AUTHORS CONTINUE: ONCE THE SHIFT IN OUR THINKING TAKES PLACE AND WE SEE BEHIND THE MYTHICAL NOTIONS OF THE DIVINITY OF THE MAN JESUS CHRIST, PRIMITIVE IDEAS OF SPREADING A MESSAGE ABOUT A SPIRITUAL, OTHERWORLDLY REDEMPTION FROM SIN CAN BE SEEN AS MISSING THE AUTHENTIC MESSAGE OF THE MAN JESUS. JESUS MUST BE SEEN AS THE MAN FOR OTHERS, ESPECIALLY THE POOR AND DOWNTRODDEN. HIS CHIEF CONCERN [I.E. IN THE EYES OF THE LIBERALS WAS THE ELIMINATION OF POVERTY AND OPPRESSION.] [THUS IT FOLLOWS:]...CHRISTIANS SHOULD NOT SEEK TO "CONVERT" SINCERE FOLLOWERS OF OTHER RELIGIONS THAT ALSO TEACH LOVE AND CONCERN FOR MANKIND. INSTEAD, WE SHOULD JOIN OUR EFFORTS WITH THEIRS IN THE TRUE SPIRIT OF JESUS. OTHER RELIGIONS SINCERELY FOLLOWED ARE EQUALLY AS VALID AS CHRISTIANITY.

The authors point out that in their book they

...HAVE DOCUMENTED THE FACT THAT SOME LEADING THEOLOGIANS AND PROFESSORS OF THE EVANGELICAL LUTHERAN CHURCH IN AMERICA (ELCA) HAVE GONE SO FAR IN THEIR ACCEPTANCE OF THE LIBERAL THEOLOGY THAT THEY ATTACK THE DEITY OF CHRIST AND THE BIBLICAL REALITY OF HEAVEN AND HELL AND ALLOW FOR THE POSSIBILITY OF UNIVERSALISM, THE DOCTRINE THAT SOMEHOW ALL MEN WILL BE SAVED REGARDLESS OF WHAT THEY BELIEVE. IT NATURALLY FOLLOWS THAT IF CHRISTIANITY IS NO LONGER SEEN AS THE ONLY HOPE FOR MAN, THERE IS NO NEED TO CHANNEL THE CHURCH'S EFFORTS INTO REACHING THE ENTIRE WORLD WITH THE SAVING GOSPEL OF JESUS CHRIST. CONCERN FOR MAN'S SPIRITUAL NEEDS BECOMES OF SECONDARY IMPORTANCE. THIS NEW WAY OF THINKING HAS CHANGED THE MISSION EMPHASIS OF THE ELCA AND HAS LED TO A DEEP INVOLVEMENT IN A WIDE VARIETY OF SOCIAL AND POLITICAL ISSUES DESIGNED TO IMPROVE MAN'S EARTHLY CONDITIONS—NAMELY THE SOCIAL GOSPEL.

The authors make this further observation regarding ELCA and its employ-

870

ment of the Social Gospel:

EVIDENCE OF THE DRIFT OF THE ELCA AWAY FROM THE HISTORIC LUTHERAN UNDERSTANDING OF THE CHURCH'S MISSION TO THE SOCIAL GOSPEL CAN BE EASILY SEEN THROUGH THE OFFICIAL ELCA PUBLICATIONS. ANY ISSUE OF *THE LUTHERAN* CONTAINS AN ABUNDANCE OF ARTICLES THAT DEAL WITH THE SOCIAL-POLITICAL AGENDA THAT NOW DOMINATES ELCA MISSION ENDEAVORS. IN ADDITION, ELCA SUNDAY SCHOOL MATERIALS, ADULT BIBLE STUDY COURSES, AND BOOKS AND ARTICLES ARE FILLED WITH ENDLESS REFERENCES TO POVERTY, FREEDOM, PEACEMAKING, JUSTICE CONCERNS, LIBERATION, THE OPPRESSED, AND SO FORTH.

FURTHER PROOF OF THE DRIFT INTO THE SOCIAL-POLITICAL REALM IS PROVED BY THE PUBLICATION *WORKING FOR JUSTICE: A 1988 DIRECTORY OF LUTHERAN MINISTRIES.* THIS PUBLICATION LISTS "FIFTY LUTHERAN-AFFILIATED GROUPS, ORGANIZATIONS, NETWORKS, AGENCIES, COALITIONS, PROJECTS AND PROGRAMS ORIENTED TOWARD JUSTICE CONCERNS" AND DESCRIBES THE JUSTICE NETWORK IN THE LUTHERAN CHURCH (JNLC) AS A "NETWORK OF ORGANIZATIONS GATHERED TO ENSURE THAT JUSTICE IS CENTRAL TO THE LIFE AND MISSION OF THE LUTHERAN CHURCH."[76]

At this point we need to remind ourselves that the ELCA has involved itself in what is termed "liberation theology." This theology emphasizes man's material needs and the kingdom of God on earth. It is a theology that...INTERPRETS GOD AS THE ONE WHO FREES PEOPLE FROM ALL CONDITIONS OF LIFE THAT ENSLAVE. To the liberation theologian: THE KINGDOM OF GOD IS NOT JUST A STATE OF MIND BUT A PHYSICAL, SOCIAL, AND POLITICAL REALM IN WHICH GOD RULES AND GOD'S WILL FOR JUSTICE AND PEACE PREVAILS.[77] Quite simply, this theology teaches that the kingdom of God is not a spiritual kingdom, but an earthly kingdom. This, in spite of the fact that Jesus proclaimed that his kingdom is not of this world. Rather, the kingdom he emphasized is the rule of God's saving grace in human hearts through the gospel. The gospel's declaration of God's grace in human hearts through the gospel. The gospel's declaration of God's grace works faith in the heart, which then receives the forgiveness of sins, the peace with God, and the promise of everlasting life in heaven which Jesus' redeeming death on the cross has won for sinners, doomed by nature to eternal damnation. This is the gospel that every person on earth needs to hear. This is the gospel that Jesus has commissioned his church to preach to every creature. And this is the gospel which orthodox, confessional Lutheran churches are involved with in carrying out their great commission in the world. When people believe this gospel. Their hearts will also be attuned to the needs of others, and they will respond by doing what they can—as God enables them—to alleviate the suffering of others.

THE ELCA'S STAND ON THE
ISSUES OF SEXUAL MORALITY

The LCA took a liberal stand regarding the issue of homosexuality and brought this stand into the ELCA merger. Again, refer to the Chapter *THE LUTHERAN CHURCH IN AMERICA.* The leadership of the LCA—the synod bishops—pushed a pro-homosexual agenda. Passages of Scripture which clearly condemn homosexual conduct are given an altogether different meaning. It is claimed that the New Testament writers wrongly interpret what God had to say regarding homosexuality in the Old Testament and that is their reason for speaking out against it. Treating Scripture as it does, the ELCA welcomes into membership persons who are homosexual or lesbian in their sexual orientation and are even given the rite of ordination into the ministry, as long as they pledge to not engage in homosexual or lesbian conduct. (In 2007 this rule was somewhat relaxed, as we shall later observe.)

When three men from the Pacific Lutheran Seminary (ELCA), after they had been certified for ordination declared that they were homosexual, there were those who feared that the ELCA would be "soft" on homosexuality, and said so. The Conference of Bishops stated categorically that "persons of homosexual orientation who seek to be ordained or who are already ordained will be expected to refrain from homosexual practice." Two years later, two San Francisco congregations "ordained" two openly lesbian candidates. Both congregations were suspended from the ELCA for five years.[78]

The point, however, is that the ELCA does not regard homosexuality as a sin to be repented of, but a condition which Christians are to accept in love and understanding.

Regarding the policy of the ELCA as its concern homosexuality, an article in *Forum Letter*, an independent Lutheran Journal, brought the following comment from a WELS theologians, writing in the *Wisconsin Lutheran Quarterly*:

"IRRITATING THE CHURCH," THE TITLE OF A RECENT ARTICLE IN *FORUM LETTER*, SURELY RATES AS A CLASSIC EXAMPLE OF UNDERSTATEMENT. THE SUBJECT OF THE ARTICLE IS THE APPEARANCE OF A NEW DOCUMENT FROM THE ELCA YOUTH MINISTRY STAFF, ENTITLED "LET JUSTICE ROLL DOWN LIKE WATERS." AMONG THE DISCUSSIONS FOR YOUTH IS A TOPIC ON SEXUAL DIVERSITY BY A SELF-PROFESSED LESBIAN MEMBER OF THE ELCA HUMAN SEXUALITY TASK FORCE. THE STUDY AIMS TO COMBAT "HETEROSEXISM," THE BELIEF THAT PRACTICES OF HETEROSEXUALITY ARE THE ONLY ACCEPTED AND SANCTIONED EXPRESSIONS OF HUMAN SEXUALITY.

PASTOR TOM HORN, AUTHOR OF THE ARTICLE, CONCLUDES, "THIS IS THE LOWEST POINT TO WHICH ELCA HAS SUNK. IT IS ONE THING FOR ADULTS IN THE CHURCH TO FIND THEMSELVES READING THE PRODUCT OF AN IMBALANCED TASK FORCE ON SEXUALITY. IT IS ANOTHER TO INDOCTRINATE OUR YOUTH IN PRO-GAY IDEOLOGY"…ACCORDING TO THE ARTICLE, BISHOP CHILSTROM EXPRESSED UNCERTAINTY WHETHER ELCA WOULD AFFIRM THE TEACHING THAT SEXUAL INTERCOURSE BEFORE MARRIAGE AND HOMOSEXUAL BEHAVIOR ARE WRONG. HE REPORTEDLY EXPRESSED THE HOPE THAT ELCA WILL APPLY THE SAME PRINCIPLES TO THIS DECISION WHICH IT USED TO OPEN ORDINATION TO WOMEN AND THAT IT WILL EXPRESS A WARM WELCOME TO GAYS. NOTABLY ABSENT FROM THE ELCA DISCUSSION OF THE TOPIC IS THE WORD "REPENTANCE."[79]

After years of debating the matter of homosexuality, the ELCA again and again affirmed its desire to take a welcoming stance toward homosexuals. The Churchwide Assembly (Orlando) managed to define marriage as taking place between one man and one woman, therefore declining to authorized a churchwide rite for blessing same-sex couples. However, the recommendation in this matter was broad enough to allow for "local" approaches to "pastoral care" to homosexuals, including the blessing of homosexual couples. The matter is left up to individual pastors and congregations to act toward homosexual couples as they see fit in providing pastoral care.[80]

According to the New York Times, August 13, 2005, in an article titled "Lutherans Reject Plan to Allow Gay Clerics," Bishop Bouman reported that Lutheran churches in "most regions of the country" already perform same-sex blessings. He interpreted the vote in the Orlando Churchwide Assembly on the issue of authorizing a church-wide rite for blessing same-sex couples--which was turned down—as creating a little more public room for such ceremonies.

Writing in the *Wisconsin Lutheran Quarterly* (WLQ) the WELS commentator draws the following conclusion:

FOR MANY DELEGATES [TO THE CHURCHWIDE ASSEMBLY IN ORLANDO] HOMOSEXUALITY IS NO LONGER A SIN...HOMOSEXUALS, THEY INSIST, ARE MADE THAT WAY BY GOD...SADLY, THE ELCA IS NO LONGER CALLING SINNERS TO REPENTANCE. INSTEAD, SIN IS EXPLAINED AWAY, EXCUSED, AND JUSTIFIED...SINCE IT NO LONGER RECOGNIZES THAT THERE IS ABSOLUTE TRUTH IN SCRIPTURE, THE ELCA SEEMS INTENT ON DOING WHATEVER APPEARS TO BE MOST EXPEDIENT.[81]

No doubt not a few people in the ELCA itself would agree with this assessment. In fact, ELCA's stand on homosexuality is one of the "hot button" issues that has forced some pastors and individuals and congregations to disassociate themselves from the ELCA, or at least to take a vocal stand against that church's practice.

REGARDING HOMOSEXUALITY

Here then, is a quick review of the ELCA Churchwide Assembly actions regarding homosexuality and its immediate concerns affecting the church.

<u>1989</u> A year after it officially began functioning, the ELCA stated: "The Biblical understanding which the church affirms is that the normative settings for sexual intercourse is marriage." At the same time the ELCA decreed that "practicing homosexuals are excluded from the ordained ministry."

<u>1991</u> The ELCA Churchwide Assembly affirmed that gay and lesbian people are individuals created by God, who can participate fully in the life of the congregation. However, these relationships were not blessed by the church, nor were gays and lesbians in committed relationships allowed to be ordained or to remain in their clergy role.

<u>1993</u> A committee drafted a document on homosexuality which declared that the Bible does not condemn homosexual relationships and that homosexuality is a healthy part of human life. Unintentional premature publication of this statement caused an uproar of negative response within the ELCA.

<u>2001</u> The ELCA Churchwide Assembly approved this body's first churchwide study of homosexuality, based on biblical, theological, scientific, and practical considerations. A study report was mandated for 2003. It was decided that the ELCA Division for Ministry and The Division for

Church in Society prepare a timeline to conduct a joint denomination-wide study of the following two issues: (1) whether to ordain gay and lesbian clergy in committed relationships and (2) whether to create a church ritual to bless same-sex committed relationships. And so, the "Task Force for the Evangelical Lutheran Church in America Studies on Sexuality" was created by the Churchwide Assembly in 2001 and issued its report to the 2005 Churchwide Assembly.

2005 The Task Force's Studies on Sexuality gave its report, which recognized two main belief systems in the ELCA concerning homosexuality: (1) Homosexuality is seen a as sin, because it is always considered a sin where it is mentioned in the Bible. Thus homosexuality is viewed as contrary "both to scriptural witness and to God's creative design." (2) Homosexuality is a condition, not a choice, and recognizes that same-sex couples do form loving, committed, long-term relationships. The claim is made that Bible passages which address the issue of same-sex behavior—condemning it—did not address same-sex couples in committed relationships. The conclusion is reached that "all language excluding gay and lesbian persons in committed relationships is unjust and should be removed." The 2005 Assembly did not pass a motion to ordain homosexuals in committed relationships. The vote was almost half and half—for and against. (Passage required two-thirds majority.) According to WELS theologian John F. Brug, author of the Second Edition of *THE WELS AND OTHER LUTHERANS* (Northwestern Publishing House, Milwaukee WI, 2009) the action of this Assembly amounted to a settlement of the two views expressed by the Task Force. "This 'settlement' in effect recognized that no agreement was possible, so everyone should agree to live and let live. The church will give no explicit endorsement to same-sex relationships, but will not take steps to oppose or correct unscriptural principles. Loopholes are left open for 'local solutions'" (p. 116).

2007 Two years later the Churchwide Assembly pretty much left things as they were. However, the Assembly, which met in Chicago, adopted a resolution that made it possible for openly homosexual clergy in a committed relationship to retain their positions within the church. The resolution..."prays, urges, and encourages [its geographical synods], synodical bishops, and the presiding bishop to refrain from or demonstrate restraint in disciplining those rostered leaders in a mutual, chaste, and faithful committed same-gender relationship who have been called and rostered in this church." At the same time the Assembly rejected motions to explicitly permit the ordaining of gays churchwide. Brug concludes that this decision left the doctrinal position of the ELCA against homosexuality intact but made it a nonbinding practice (p. 110). Meanwhile bishops, pastors, congregations, and even synods in the ELCA, boldly and publicly take unscriptural stands in their promotion of homosexuality by calling on the ELCA to end the ban on ordination of sexually active gays and lesbians, and by calling for "a rite of blessing for same-gender committed relationships of lifelong fidelity. The call for such a rite of blessing has come from several areas of the ELCA. Already in 2000 the Milwaukee Synod of the ELCA granted permission to use a rite of blessing. One Milwaukee pastor had been doing so for the past five years.

The ELCA remains greatly divided on the subject of sexual morality, while the study to determine what should be the ELCA's doctrinal position re homosexuality—a study that has gone on for many years now—continues. Brug terms the ELCA study document a frontal attack on biblical-Christian morality that aims to overthrow the authority of Scripture as the only norm for establishing doctrine and morals (p. 119).

Conclusion: The ELCA finds itself in the quagmire of errant popular human, societal, and so-called scientific opinion regarding the morality of homosexuality. The reason is simple. The ELCA will not allow Holy Scripture to have the first and final word on the matter. Anyone who reads the scriptural references regarding homosexuality and approaches them with a reason held captive to God's verbally inspired, inerrant Word must reach the conclusion that homosexuality is a sin, even an abomination to God and a vile stench in his nostrils. But when the historical-critical method of Bible interpretation was widely accepted in the ELCA—which method of interpretation sets aside and even denies the divine authority and veracity of Holy Scriptures—then God's word is no longer looked to as the guiding light and determining factor in any discussions held in the ELCA on the much-debated topic of sexual morality. The result is that it doesn't really matter what God says; it's what agrees with the mores of the majority that counts. And so, the church is called upon to agree with and even to promote the prevailing moral views and values of an unregenerate society—which moral views and values change with the times. Yes, the church is made accountable to ever-changing public opinion and whim. Within the church the call goes out to the members to tolerate the opposing views of others and thus avoid the splintering of the church which opposing views can cause.

Finally—and tragically—this means that no one is called to repentance for the liberal, worldy, unscriptural sexual values they endorse and promote—values which are plainly and diametrically opposed to God's Word. And so, the homosexual lobby, with its disproportionate cloute—made possible in part by the much maligned quota system—continues to be a powerful source of irritation and division in the ELCA and forces the need to continue the search for a doctrinal stand on issues of sexual morality that everyone can live with without giving up their individual beliefs.

THE ELCA'S STAND ON ABORTION

The abortion issue has in its own way divided our country. People tend to be vocal on the subject—for or against abortion. It's no different within some church bodies. When the ELCA's Task Force on Abortion went public with its abortion statement it caused a flap by both pro-life and pro-choice factions in the ELCA by avoiding an "absolutist position," and extreme pro-life/pro-choice language. Abortion was termed a "positive option."

What is particularly troublesome in regard to differing opinions among Christians concerning abortion is that these opinions may not be based so much on God's Word, as on human conjecture, opinion, and biases. Any attempts by members of a church body to reach agreement on the abortion issue must be based on what God has to say concerning the sanctity of human life, the origin of human life, the respect we are to have for human life, the care we are to take of human life, and God's warnings against the taking of human life. The proper Christian attitude toward abortion, as toward homosexuality and the practice of sex outside of marriage, must be determined by what God has to say on these issues. Harmony can only come to the people of the ELCA when God's Word in its truth and purity is allowed to carry the day, and the full authority of Scripture is recognized and accepted.

Edgar Trexler in *Anatomy of a Merger* includes the following points from the Task Force on Abortion's statement:

...ABORTION COULD BE MORALLY RESPONSIBLE ONLY WHEN "CONTINUATION OF A PREGNANCY THREATENS THE WOMAN'S PHYSICAL LIFE"...WHEN A FETUS HAS "EXTREME ABNORMALITIES...WHICH WILL RESULT IN SEVERE SUFFERING AND EARLY DEATH...AND IF THE PREGNANCY OCCURS WHEN BOTH PARTIES DO NOT PARTICIPATE WILLINGLY IN SEXUAL INTERCOURSE" SUCH AS "CASES OF RAPE AND INCEST" AND IN "SITUATIONS WHERE WOMEN...HAVE NO CHOICE REGARD-ING SEXUAL INTERCOURSE AND LITTLE ACCESS TO CONTRACEPTIVE."[83]

The reviewer in the *Wisconsin Lutheran Quarterly*, after studying the ELCA's abortion statement, concludes that the ELCA generally opposes abortion and urges every woman with an unwanted pregnancy to carry her child to term and emphasizes the responsibility God's people have toward those women who do not choose to have abortions, and the children who are born as a result. The reviewer notes, however, that nothing really is condemned as sin in the abortion statement and that almost any position on abortion can find room under the statement's umbrella.[84]

DISCORD IN THE ELCA REGARDING THE USE OF MASCULINE TERMS FOR GOD

Another cause of discord in the ELCA is the support within this church body of a radical feminist agenda, which, among other things urges that masculine pronouns should be avoided when we speak of God. Some are removing the name of the Triune God from the formula of baptism and replacing it with more sexually inclusive titles. Thus, Father, Son, and Holy Spirit, are changed to Creator, Redeemer and Sanctifier in a suggested baptismal formula. Others in the ELCA refer to this tampering with Scripture as evidence of feminist theology. Elwyn Ewald of the AELC actually proposed to the Planning Committee when it was drawing up the ELCA's Confession of Faith, that the words "Father, Son, and Holy Spirit be dropped from the Confession in order to avoid sexually exclusive language." But since these are scriptural terms, his proposal was not accepted. Still, there has been continued debate in the ELCA concerning the use of the scriptural Trinitarian Formula in baptism.[85]

Consider carefully what took place at the Churchwide Assembly held in August 2005. The delegates adopted a new hymnal project. But many opposed the production of new hymnal, especially due to the drastic change in language that was proposed:

"MASCULINE" AND "AUTHORITARIAN" TITLES FOR GOD, SUCH AS "KING" AND "LORD," AND THE WORD "MAN" ARE TO BE CAREFULLY AVOIDED IN THIS NEW EFFORT. THE SAME IS TRUE FOR THE MALE PRONOUN "HE"...THE FEMINIST THEOLOGY THAT LED TO WOMEN'S ORDINATION 35 YEARS AGO HAS NOW DEMONSTRATED THE CONFIDENCE TO CHANGE BIBLICAL LANGUAGE. IN ADDITION TO THIS PROBLEM WITH THE NEW HYMNAL, THE ELCA'S ORDERS OF SERVICE BETRAY AN ALMOST TOTAL ABSENCE OF THE TEACHING OF ORIGINAL SIN.[86]

A ROUGH BEGINNING FOR THE ELCA— THORNY ISSUES

LACK OF A CLEAR DOCTRINE OF THE CHURCH

Edgar Trexler makes the following observation:

AS SIMPLE AS IT MAY SOUND, THE LACK OF AGREEMENT WITHIN THE COMMISSION FOR A NEW LUTEHRAN CHURCH ON THE NATURE OF THE CHURCH LURKED BEHIND MANY OF THE DIFFICULTIES [EXPERIENCED BY THE NEW CHURCH]. THE CONGREGATION/NATIONAL CHURCH DICHOTOMY—WHICH SHOWED UP IN REELING FINANCIAL SUPPORT, QUESTIONS ABOUT ECUMENICAL PERSPECTIVES, THE LINGERING UNCERTAINTY ABOUT MINISTRY, AND THE CHURCH'S REPRESENTATIVE PRINCIPLES [THE QUOTA SYSTEM]—WERE ROOTED IN ECCLESIOLOGY, THE DOCTRINE OF THE CHURCH.[87]

FAILURE OF FINANCING

This was the most troublesome issue facing the struggling new church. In spite of the fact that congregational giving within the ELCA was increasing, there was at first a deficit each year. Needless to say, the ELCA had to endure cuts in expenses and spending as well as staff layoffs. Some staff positions were canceled. The implementation of programs was stifled; some were dropped. The merger church was actually receiving considerably less income than the former churches would have received as separate entities prior to the merger. Congregations were simply not sending to the ELCA the proportion of their revenues that the ELCA needed. According to Trexler various explanations for this shortfall were given: dislodged loyalties, cumbersome structure, church is too large and too remote, lack of identity, the church has been taken over by ideological cliques. There was also the lack of the necessary feeling of interdependence and being a part of the larger church.[88]

LACK OF FOCUS AND OF VISION, AND LACK OF ADEQUATE LEADERSHIP

More than half of the first bishops of the ELCA had not been a bishop before, thus presenting a problem of inexperience in high places. It was observed that the great number of new staff produced a strangeness in the new church. There was lack of emphasis on retaining former staff and as a result the new church "gave away experienced resources." Tried and true methods from the "old" were left behind, "with lesser experienced people trying to replace them with something new."[89]

THE UNCERTAIN STATUS OF THE AELC
CHRISTIAN DAY SCHOOL TEACHERS

There were years of uncertainty as to what their status would be in the new church, and other lay professionals found themselves in the same boat with them.

THE QUOTA SYSTEM

There was much dissatisfaction with this system. This dissatisfaction was felt already while the merger was being worked out and continued after the merger was put in place. The wealth of experience, expertise, traditions of the former churches was to a great extent unemployed in the new church. This system also spawned "special interests versus the rest of the church."[90]   Recall again that the women commissioners on the CNLC regularly held their own caucuses. They planned to be a powerful voice, and they planned to be heard. Even long-time leaders like James R. Crumley, Jr., of New York (formerly LCA), condemned quotas as not serving the church well and that they should be discontinued. Before, he had defended them.[91]

A NEED FOR RESTRUCTURING
FELT SOON AFTER THE MERGER

Proposals for restructuring the new church were put forth on July 28, 1990, a little less than 2½ years after the ELCA began its official operations. The restructuring merged some divisions and commissions and otherwise streamlined the church, making it in the words of Bishop Herbert Chilstrom, "a tighter, leaner structure than we had at the time of the merger."[92]   Less cumbersome and certainly less expensive.

SLOW TO START NEW CONGREGATIONS,
AND LOSS OF MEMBERSHIP

The ELCA did manage to start new congregations immediately, but at a lower rate than it had anticipated. In 1988, its first year, the ELCA lost almost 37,000 members and close to 13,000 the next year. There was a gain of almost 2,000 members in 1990. The ELCA had a distinct goal of increasing minority membership by 10 percent in the first 10 years of its existence, but reaching toward this goal was a slow process.[93]

DISAGREEMENT OVER THE ECUMENICAL POLICY
OF THE ELCA AND ITS THEOLOGICAL TRENDS

The ecumenical scene in the ELCA produced tensions, some of which were caused by differences in ecumenical perspective/commitments by the former LCA and ALC.[94] In 1991, the *Wisconsin Lutheran Quarterly* recorded evidences of tensions within the ELCA over the ecumenical thrust of this body and the loss of Lutheran identification:

AT THE SAME TIME THAT MERGERS AND DIALOGUES, WHICH ARE TAKING THEIR TOLL OF GENUINE LUTHERAN DOCTRINE AND PRACTICE, ARE PRAISED AND PUBLICIZED, OTHERS WITHIN THE ELCA ARE LAMENTING THE LOSS OF LUTHERAN IDENTIFICATION. THREE SEPARATE ARTICLES IN THE *LUTHERAN FORUM* (FEBRUARY 1991) AND *DIALOG* (WINTER 1991) SERIOUSLY QUESTION THEOLOGICAL TRENDS IN THE ELCA. THE PLACE OF THEOLOGY IN THE ELCA BY GEORGE W. FORELL, PHILADELPHIA LUTHERAN SEMINARY, QUESTIONS THE CHURCH'S "REASONS FOR BEING A LUTEHRAN CHURCH IN THE 21ST CENTURY" IF IT DOES NOT SOON "STEER AWAY FROM THE LEAST COMMON DENOMINATOR, ECUMENISM, AND THE PROMOTION OF THE THEOLOGICAL 'FAD OF THE MONTH' AND BUILD ITS PROCLAMATION ON A CHRISTOCENTRIC EXPOSITION OF THE HOLY SCRIPTURES WITH THE HELP OF THE GREAT TRINITARIAN CREEDS AND THE CONFESSIONS OF THE LUTHERAN CHURCH."...SCOTT ICKERT...IN...THE USES OF THE LAW SENSES THAT HIS CHURCH HAS ADOPTED A COURSE WHICH IS IN "DANGER OF ABANDONING ITS VOCATION TO DISTINGUISH THE LAW AND THE GOSPEL, IF NOT CONVERTING THE GOSPEL INTO LAW"...Ted Peters of Pacific Lutheran Seminary in "The Battle over Trinitarian Language" protests the fact that ELCA members in any number have joined their voices with those who suggest that the use of "Father, Son, and Holy Spirit" is sexist language and argue for the use of Creator, Redeemer and Sanctifier as a viable substitute in baptisms.

There can be no doubt that the ELCA's close association with other church bodies has weakened and confused its stand on scriptural doctrines and on Lutheran confessionalism, and caused deeply felt irritations in those who want to remain faithful to Scripture and the Confessions.

THE SOCIETAL CONTEXT OF THE ELCA LAUNCHING

According to Edgar Trexler, there was a loss of confidence in large institutions, high degrees of individualism, gay-lesbian issues, high visibility and forthright demands by women and minorities, the appeal of fundamentalism to a harried populace—all of which worked against the ELCA having a smooth start.[96] There was also the problem of major turnovers in staff at the beginning.

The authors of *WELS And Other Lutherans* point out that the ELCA merger was driven by special interest groups which promoted sexual and political liberation.

THE QUOTA SYSTEM FOR SELECTING DELEGATES...ALLOWED SUCH GROUPS TO DOMINATE THE PLANNING COMMISSION AND THE FIRST GOVERNING BOARDS OF ELCA TO A DEGREE DISPROPORTIONATE TO THEIR STRENGTH WITHIN THE MEM-

BERSHIP OF THE ELCA.[97] IN REGARDS TO THE SPECIAL INTEREST GROUPS IN THE ELCA, IT IS POINTED OUT IN THE ABOVE LISTED VOLUME THAT THESE GROUPS OPERATE AS LOBBIES...WHOSE PRIMARY INTEREST IS NOT DOCTRINE, BUT THE PROMOTION OF CERTAIN POLITICAL, SOCIAL, RACIAL, OR SEXUAL GOALS...THEY...HAVE A VERY POWERFUL INFLUENCE IN THE MACHINERY OF ELCA.[98]

OPPOSITION TO THE DRAFT STATEMENTS ON SEXUALITY

These draft statements of 1991 and 1993, circulated by the Division for the Church in Society of the ELCA, resulted in a backlash from those in the ELCA who opposed the statements for apparently condoning homosexuality and extramarital sex by appealing to ELCA's membership to take a fresh and sympathetic look at these practices, while refraining to judge these actions if practiced in a loving, committed way. The statements have been described as an "act of war against the Christian faith," by ELCA pastor, Leonard Klein (February 3, 1992, issue of *Lutheran Forum*). A close look at the ELCA's Social Statement "The Church and Human Sexuality" (A Lutheran Perspective) brought out the following comments by a WELS theologian:

SIN IS NEVER DEFINED AS A TRANSGRESSION OF GOD'S REVEALED LAW, BUT AS THAT WHICH HARMS OUR NEIGHBOR...THE RESULT OF THIS DISMISSAL OF ANY MORAL ABSOLUTES EXCEPT "LOVE YOUR NEIGHBOR AND DO NOT HARM HIM" IS THAT PARTICULAR RELATIONSHIPS AND EXTERNAL ACTS SUCH AS HOMOSEXUAL RELATIONSHIPS OR LIVE-IN ARRANGEMENTS ARE NOT IN AND OF THEMSELVES WRONG SIMPLY BECAUSE GOD'S WORD CONDEMNS THEM, BUT ARE WRONG ONLY WHEN THEY ARE CARRIED OUT IN A SELF-GRATIFYING, ABUSIVE, OR UNLOVING WAY...MORAL CODES AND STANDARDS FOR THE PEOPLE OF GOD ARE SET MORE BY CONSENSUS OF THE CHRISTIAN COMMUNITY THAN BY THE CLEARLY REVEALED NORMS OF SCRIPTURE. BOUNDARIES SET IN SCRIPTURE FOR GOD-PLEASING SEXUAL BEHAVIOR AND RELATIONSHIPS AND FOR THE ROLES OF MAN AND WOMAN ARE ALL TO BE QUESTIONED AND FINALLY REJECTED AS HOPELESSLY OUT OF DATE FOR OUR ENLIGHTENED SOCIETY. PREFERENCES FOR MORAL BEHAVIOR SUCH AS ABSTINENCE BEFORE MARRIAGE AND LIFE-LONG COMMITMENT RATHER THAN DIVORCE ARE STRONGLY VOICED, BUT THEY OFTEN ARE PRESENTED AS THE BEST OF MANY OPTIONS.[99]

THE ELCA'S RELATIONSHIP WITH THE LUTHERAN CHURCH-MISSOURI SYNOD

Recall that in the 2001 Convention of the Missouri Synod, the delegates passed a resolution stating that the ELCA is "not an orthodox Lutheran church body." The dialogue that had been carried on with the ELCA theologians reached an impasse after three sessions. At the same convention it was announced that there are 34 LCMS school associations that have ELCA churches or churches of other denominations as members. And that seven of these schools have official "Affiliated School Status" in the ELCA together with "Recognized Service Organization" status in the LCMS. The convention delegates voted to allow existing schools to continue as they are, as long as they comply with LCMS standards, and with monitoring by the LCMS district presidents. The delegates also allowed new associations with ELCA congregations to be formed, but they cannot seek official status in the ELCA.

There was a strong floor committee resolution to end all joint pastoral ministry with ELCA. This would include the military chaplaincy and campus ministries. (It should be noted that ELCA military chaplains have attained high rank and leadership roles, which places them in close contact with LCMS chaplains.)

The ELCA and the LCMS have had cooperative agreements related to the military chaplaincy and carry out joint disaster-relief, development, and social-services work. The Convention, however, steered away from requiring a separation of the two church bodies in regards to the above mentioned enterprises. All such joint ministries were to be evaluated by the synod praesidium with a report to the next synod convention. At the same convention the delegates showed an eagerness to continue dialogues with the ELCA (and also with the Roman Catholic Church).

In 2003 the LCMS informed its people that renewed theologians talks and more frequent meetings of top leadership were in the offing between the ELCA and the LCMS. The LCMS Committee on Lutheran Cooperation (CLC) agreed to pursue discussions of issues that divide the two churches and to hold meetings twice a year.[101]

It should be noted that in 1998 the Missouri Synod Convention, while supporting the efforts of the heads of the two synods to meet for talks—which were not for the purpose to pursue unity between them, but to center especially on the ELCA's ecumenical actions at its Churchwide Assembly in Philadelphia in 1997—adopted the following resolutions: IN FAITHFULNESS TO GOD'S WORD AND THE LUTEHRAN CONFESSIONS, AND MOTIVATED BY OUR LOVE AND CONCERN FOR THE PEOPLE AND PASTORS OF THE ELCA, WE EXPRESS OUR DEEP REGRET AND PROFOUND DISAGREEMENT WITH THESE ACTIONS TAKEN BY THE ELCA. This resolutions was conveyed to Bishop Anderson of the ELCA.[102]

DISATISFACTION AND DEPARTURES

After the three church conventions voted "yes" to the merger proposal in 1986, there was yet another vote that had to be taken in the ALC. The ALC Constitution required that there be a referendum of the congregations, with a necessary two-thirds of the congregations favoring the Convention vote. This referendum extended over a period of six months, which then gave dissident groups, congregations, and pastors time to voice their opposition to the merger. Those on the conservative side of Christianity and Lutheranism in the ALC sent a letter to about 5,000 ALC clergy, in which they proposed the formation of the Association of American Lutheran Churches, thus providing an alternative Lutheran body for those—both congregations and pastors and individuals—who opposed joining the merger to form the ELCA, for those who had reservations, for those who wanted to carry on the ALC's positions on congregational authority, for those tired of debating secular issues at church conventions, for those desiring a church which commits its resources to evangelism and home and world missions.[103]

One of the leaders of the conservative group, Rev. James E. Minor, pastor of Calvary Ev. Lutheran Church in St. Paul, stressed that the new group will be a continuation of the conservative wing of the present ALC and would be structured on the ALC Constitution. Rev. Minor was critical of the new Lutheran Church's treatment of the Scriptures, because it did not refer to them as inerrant or infallible. On the other hand, his group believes the Bible it true from Genesis to Revelation, that the Bible's words are the inspired Word of God, and that the Bible is without error, solidly true and that we can rely on it. His group also favors local control of church property, and favors a congregation-centered structure. The group disagreed with the quota system and opposed the weakening of the ALC stand on abortion and homosexuality.

Edgar Trexler reports in *Anatomy of a Merger* that there were about 125 persons, representing 70 Congregations in 17 states, who voted at the October 20, 1986, meeting to go ahead with forming the new Lutheran body apart from the ELCA. Nevertheless, they agreed to cancel their plans if the ALC congregational vote did not ratify the ALC Convention action to join the ELCA.[104] There were also 10 representatives from LCA congregations in the group of dissidents. When the ALC announced the returns of the referendum, the will of the congregations was clearly to join the merger forming the ELCA. This, of course, spurred many of the dissidents to withdraw from their church body and to proceed to either join the American Association of Lutheran Churches (AALC) or the Association of Free Lutheran Congregations. The majority joined the latter church, rather than the AALC. Fifty-eight congregations, with 16,810 members withdrew from the ELCA merger in 1987, and in 1988, 12 congregations withdrew with 4,176 member. The following year four congregations with 1,187 members, and in 1990, seven congregations with 2,373 members, withdrew. ALC congregations=75; LCA congregations=3; AELC congregations=3. By the spring of 1991, 83 congregations were members of the AALC. There were also a couple dozen congregations connected in various ways to the AALC. Membership was primarily from the ALC. The AALC claims that it owes its origin to three strands of Lutheranism: orthodox, evangelical, and charismatic. The charismatic strand sets the AALC apart from most of the other Lutheran bodies.[105]

While there continues to be dissatisfaction within the ELCA regarding its doctrine, practice, focus, and numerous other issues (including moral), the dissidents for the most part choose to remain in the ELCA, with the purpose of changing the ELCA's course. The dissidents lack the cohesiveness that would facilitate their leaving the ELCA as a group in order to establish their own church body. They are a splintered group in the realm of defining Scripture and agreeing on scriptural doctrine.

Footnotes for Chapter Thirty-Nine
1 Edgar R. Trexler, *Anatomy of a Merger—People, Dynamics, and Decisions*

That Shaped the ELCA (Minneapolis, MN: Augsburg Fortress, 1991), p. 4.

2 Trexler, *Anatomy...*, p. 2.

3 Trexler, *Anatomy...*, p. 3.

4 Trexler, *Anatomy...*, p. 2.

5 Trexler, *Anatomy...*, p. 3.

6 Patsy A. Leppien and J. Kincaid Smith, *What's Going On Among the Lutherans?—A Comparison of Beliefs* (Milwaukee, WI: Northwestern Publishing House, 1992), p. 335.

7 Trexler, *Anatomy...*, p. 4.

8 Trexler, *Anatomy...*, p. 5.

9 Trexler, *Anatomy...*, p. 8.

10 Trexler, *Anatomy...*, p. 8.

11 Trexler, *Anatomy...*, p. 9.

12 Trexler, *Anatomy...*, pp. 12, 13.

13 Trexler, *Anatomy...*, p. 24.

14 Trexler, *Anatomy...*, p. 29.

15 Trexler, *Anatomy...*, p. 30.

16 Trexler, *Anatomy...*, p. 27.

17 Trexler, *Anatomy...*, p. 32.

18 Trexler, *Anatomy...*, p. 32.

19 Trexler, *Anatomy...*, p. 41.

20 Trexler, *Anatomy...*, p. 43.

21 Trexler, *Anatomy...*, p. 41, 42.

22 Trexler, *Anatomy...*, p. 42.

23 Trexler, *Anatomy...*, p. 51.

24 Trexler, *Anatomy...*, p. 66.

25 Trexler, *Anatomy...*, p. 59.

26 Trexler, *Anatomy...*, p. 63, 64.

27 Trexler, *Anatomy...*, p. 120.

28 Trexler, *Anatomy...*, p. 66.

29 Trexler, *Anatomy...*, p. 94.

30 Trexler, *Anatomy...*, p.72.

31 Trexler, *Anatomy...*, p. 87.

32 Trexler, *Anatomy...*, pp. 87, 88.

33 *Wisconsin Lutheran Quarterly*, Vol. 89, No. 4, 1992 (Milwaukee, WI: Northwestern Publishing House), p. 307.

34 Trexler, *Anatomy...*, p. 272.

35 Trexler, *Anatomy...*, p. 183.

36 Trexler, *Anatomy...*, p. 183.

37 Trexler, *Anatomy...*, p. 181.

38 Trexler, *Anatomy...*, p. 175.

39 Trexler, *Anatomy...*, p. 176.

40 Trexler, *Anatomy...*, p. 176.

41 Trexler, *Anatomy...*, p. 206.

42 Trexler, *Anatomy...*, p. 206.

43 Trexler, *Anatomy...*, p. 175.

44 Trexler, *Anatomy...*, p. 177.

45 Trexler, *Anatomy...*, p. 242.

46 Trexler, *Anatomy...*, p. 276.

47 Trexler, *Anatomy...*, p. 108.

48 Clifford E. Nelson, *Lutherans in North America—1914-1970* (Minneapolis, MN: Augsburg Publishing House, 1972), p. 164.

49 David E. Barnhart, *The Church's Desperate Need for Revival* (Egan, MN: Abiding Word Publications, 1986), p. 81.

50 Trexler, *Anatomy...*, p. 55.

51 *Wisconsin Lutheran Quarterly*, Vol. 89. No. 4, 1992, Ibid., p. 254.

52 *Wisconsin Lutheran Quarterly*, Vol. 89, No. 4, 1992, Ibid., p. 255.

53 John F. Brug, Edward C. Fredrich II, Armin W. Schuetze, *WELS and Other Lutherans: Lutheran Church Bodies in the USA* (Milwaukee, WIL Northwestern Publishing House, 1995, Fourth Printing 1998), p. 69.

54 *Wisconsin Lutheran Quarterly*, Vol. 91, No. 3, 1994, p. 226.

55 *Wisconsin Lutheran Quarterly*, Vol. 87, No. 4, 1990, pp. 304-307.

56 Carl E. Braaten and Robert W. Jenson, *Christian Dogmatics*, Vol. 1 (Philadelphia, PA: Fortress Press, 1987), p. 61.

57 Brug, Fredrich II, Schuetze, *WELS and Other Lutherans*, p. 55.

58 Brug, Fredrich II, Schuetze, *WELS and Other Lutherans*, p. 55.

59 Brug, Fredrich II, Schuetze, *WELS and Other Lutherans*, pp. 42, 68.

60 *Lutheran Partners*, March/April, 1988 (?).

61 *Wisconsin Lutheran Quarterly*, Vol. 94, No. 1, 1997, p.31-35.

62 *Wisconsin Lutheran Quarterly,* Vol. 88, No. 1, 1991, p.3-14.

63 *Wisconsin Lutheran Quarterly,* Vol. 92, No. 3, 1995, pp. 214, 215.

64 *Wisconsin Lutheran Quarterly,* Vol. 95, No. 1, 1998, pp. 45-47.

65 *Wisconsin Lutheran Quarterly,* Vol. 90, No. 4, 1993, pp. 304, 305.

66 *Wisconsin Lutheran Quarterly*, Vol. 92, No. 1, 1995, p.p. 58,59.

67 *Wisconsin Lutheran Quarterly*, Vol. 95, No. 1, 1998, pp. 48, 49.

68 *Wisconsin Lutheran Quarterly*, Vol. 97, No. 1, 2000, pp. 52, 53.

69 *Wisconsin Lutheran Quarterly*, Vol. 97, No. 3, 2000, pp. 211,212.

70 Leppien-Smith, *What's Going On...?* p. 357. Quoting Theodore E. Scmauk and C. Theodore Benze, *The Confessional Principle and the Confessions, as Embodying the Evangelical Confession of the Christian Church*, Philadelphia, PA: General Council Publication Board, 1911, pp. 905ff.

71 Leppien-Smith, *What's Going On...?* pp. 357, 358. Quoting Charles P. Krauth, *The Conservative Reformation and Its Theology*, Philadelphia, PA: The United Lutheran Publishing House, 1913, first edition, 1871, p. 326.

72 Leppien-Smith, *What's Going On...?*, p. 359. Quoting J. Michael Reu, *In the Interest of Lutheran Unity, Two Lectures*, Columbus, OH: Lutheran Book Concern, 1940, pp. 19, 20.

73 Paul Fleischer, "On Unity and Union or the ELCA and Bankrupt Lutheranism," July 1989 issue of the *Lutheran Spokesman*, p. 11. (Official magazine of the Church of the Lutheran Confession).

74 *Wisconsin Lutheran Quarterly*, Vol. 87, No. 4, 1990, pp. 304-307.

75 Trexler, *Anatomy...*, p. 251.

76 Leppien-Smith, *What's Going On...?* pp. 168, 175.

77 Leppien-Smith, *What's Going On...?*, p. 180.

78 Trexler, *Anatomy...*, pp. 247, 248.

79 *Wisconsin Lutheran Quarterly*, Vol. 90, No. 3, 1993, p. 225.

80 *Wisconsin Lutheran Quarterly*, Vol. 103, No. 1, 2006, pp. 54,55.

81 *Wisconsin Lutheran Quarterly*, Vol. 103, No. 1, 2006, pp. 54-57.

82 Trexler, *Anatomy...*, p. 250.

83 Trexler, *Anatomy...*, p. 250.

84 *Wisconsin Lutheran Quarterly*, Vol. 89, No. 1, 1992, pp. 64,65.

85 Brug, Fredrich II, Schuetze, *WELS and Other...*, p. 44.

86 *Wisconsin Lutheran Quarterly*, Vol. 103, No. 1, 2006, pp. 54,55.

87 Trexler, *Anatomy...*, p. 255.

88 Trexler, *Anatomy...*, p. 255.

89 Trexler, *Anatomy...*, p. 258.

90 Trexler, *Anatomy...*, p. 260.

91 Trexler, *Anatomy...*, p. 260.

92 Trexler, *Anatomy...*, p. 264.

93 Trexler, *Anatomy...*, pp. 248, 250.

94 Trexler, *Anatomy...*, pp. 249, 250

95 *Wisconsin Lutheran Quarterly*, Vol. 88, No. 3,1991, pp. 232, 233.

96 Trexler, *Anatomy...*, p. 24.

97 Brug, Fredrich II, Schuetze, *WELS and Other...*, p. 41.

98 Brug, *The WELS and Other...*, p. 70.

99 *Wisconsin Lutheran Quarterly*, Vol. 91, No. 2,1994, p.133,134.

100 *Wisconsin Lutheran Quarterly*, Vol. 99, No. 1, 2002, pp. 62, 63, 68.

101 *Wisconsin Lutheran Quarterly*, Vol. 100, No. 3, 2003, p. 224.

102*Wisconsin Lutheran Quarterly*, Vol. 96, No. 1, 1999, p. 58.

103 Trexler, *Anatomy...*, p. 207.

104 Trexler, *Anatomy...*, pp. 207, 208.

105 Brug, Fredrich II, Schuetze, *WELS and Other...*, p. 87.

ADDENDUM

A PARTIAL LISTING OF SMALL AND TINY LUTHERAN BODIES*

AMERICAN ASSOCIATION OF LUTHERAN CHURCHES (AALC)

In 1987, 68 congregations that didn't want to take part in the ELCA merger formed their own Lutheran body. This group was formed as a continuation of the conservative wing of the American Lutheran Church (ALC), structured on the ALC Constitution. A main bone of contention for the group who formed the AALC was the treatment accorded to Holy Scripture by the new Lutheran Church (ELCA), which did not refer to the Scripture as infallible or inerrant. There were other points of departure from the new Lutheran Church: the local congregation should retain control of church property; the AALC should be a congregation centered structure; there should be no quota system; there should be a strong stand against abortion and homosexuality. The AALC claims to be a convergence of three strands of Lutheranism: orthodox, evangelical, and charismatic.

By 1989 the new group counted 76 congregations and about 15,000 members. By May 1991 the AALC numbered 83 congregations, with roughly a couple of dozen other congregations associated in some way with it. The headquarters are located in the Twin Cities. The official publication is the *Evangel*. (See a brief accounting of this body toward the end of Chapter Thirty-nine.)

887

APOSTOLIC LUTHERAN CHURCH IN AMERICA

This small Finnish body is mentioned briefly toward the end of Chapter Twenty-eight, THE FINNS: THE FINNISH EVANGELICAL LUTHERAN CHURCH OF AMERICA (SUOMI SYNOD).
Also this Finnish body:

FINNISH NATIONAL CHURCH

This body became a part of the Lutheran Church—Missouri Synod. A brief history is included at the end of Chapter Twenty-eight, THE FINNS: THE FINNISH EVANGELICAL LUTHERAN CHURCH OF AMERICA (SUOMI SYNOD).

ASSOCIATION OF FREE LUTHERAN CONGREGATIONS (AFLC)

This is the largest of the smaller Lutheran bodies. The Association of Free Lutheran Congregations (AFLC) is a breakaway group from the former Lutheran Free Church (LFC). When the new American Lutheran Church was formed in 1960, the LFC declined to join it at that time. However, in 1963 this Scandinavian body, comprised mostly of Norwegians, officially joined the ALC. The dissident group within the LFC left this body a short time before its merger with the new ALC and organized themselves into the small but conservative Association of Free Lutheran Congregations in October 1962 at Thief River Falls, Minnesota. By the mid 1990s the original forty congregations had grown to 200 congregations and 175 pastors. The AFLC received a goodly number of dissident congregations that refused to take part in the ELCA merger. Over the years the AFLC has been a haven for congregations and pastors who withdrew from larger Lutheran bodies in order to identify with a more theologically conservative Lutheranism. The official journal of the AFLC is the *Lutheran Ambassador*. The AFLC seminary was founded in 1964 in the Twin Cities. The Bible School has a two-year program. World missions are conducted in Central/South America and India.

Five reasons were given by the dissident group for declining membership in the new ALC. (1) The ALC's membership in the Word Council of Churches. (2) The trend of merging bodies toward liberal theological positions and practices. (3) Church polity which moved from the Free Church's historic congregational form of government to a more centralized government. (4) The high church worship tradition within the membership of the ALC. (5) The lack of emphasis on the historic Free Church's practice of Christian piety.[1]

A summary of AFLC beliefs: (1) The Bible is inerrant and the authority in all areas of life. (2) The teaching and preaching of God's Word is the main task of the Church. The Word of God is to be taught and preached in such a way that the saints are built up in the faith and unbelievers see their need for salvation. (3) The congregation is the right form of the Kingdom of God on earth, with no authority over it but the Word and Spirit of God. (4) Christian unity is a spiritual concept and not a man-made organization or body such as the World Council of Churches, the National Council of Churches, etc. (5) Christians are to be different from the unbelievers and are to be a salt in the world (Pietism). This difference is to be reflected also in the work of the Christian congregations and the institutions of the church.[2]

CHURCH OF THE LUTHERAN BRETHREN

A brief history of this church body is included at the end of Chapter Fifteen THE SMALL EARLY GROUPS.

CHURCH OF THE LUTHERAN CONFESSION (CLC)

See Chapter Thirty-seven, THE CHURCH OF THE LUTHERAN CONFESSION. *(Note that an entire chapter has been devoted to this small Lutheran body because of the role it had in the great controversy within the Synodical Conference, which finally resulted in the WELS and the ELS suspending fellowship with the Missouri Synod and the eventual breakup of the Synodical Conference. Not only did the organizers of the CLC sever fellowship with the Missouri Synod, they also left the fellowship of the WELS and the ELS over the doctrine of Fellowship.)*

CONCORDIA LUTHERAN CONFERENCE

In 1951 members of the Lutheran Church—Missouri Synod who protested their synod's deviations from the historic fellowship principles and practices of the Synodical Conference formed the Orthodox Lutheran Conference. (Some members of the other Synodical Conference bodies also took part in this endeavor.) Then, in 1956, differences of opinion regarding fellowship principles among the members of the Conference caused some to withdraw and a year later organize the Concordia Lutheran Conference.

This body follows strict fellowship principles and thus remains isolated from other Lutherans. Membership is in the hundreds (baptized), in only a few congregations. Periodical: *Concordia Lutheran.*

EIELSEN SYNOD

This Norwegian body and its founder are portrayed in Chapter Fifteen, THE NORWEGIANS—THE SMALL EARLY GROUPS, the beginning of the chapter.

ESTONIAN EVANGELICAL LUTHERAN CHURCH

Organized during World War II era in Sweden. The United States District had about 7,000 members in the mid 1990s.

EVANGELICAL LUTHERAN FEDERATION (ELF)

This tiny group was organized in 1977. In the mid 1990s it numbered only five congregations—Indiana, New York, Ohio, and Washington. The ELF espoused an "exclusionary" lodge practice. The latest available headquarters address: President Ervin C. Dobberstein, P.O. Box 477, Kingston, Washington 98346.

FELLOWSHIP OF LUTHERAN CONGREGATIONS

Formed by members of the Lutheran Church—Missouri Synod in protest against liberal theological developments in that body. Organized in 1979 by Midwestern congregations. A tiny body of only a few congregations, numbering totally in the hundreds of baptized members. Official periodical: *The Voice*. Headquarters (latest): President Robert J. Lietz, 320 Erie St., Oak Park, Illinois 60302.

INTERNATIONAL LUTHERAN FELLOWSHIP

A tiny group of only a few congregations, dedicated to an international preaching of the gospel.

LATIVIAN EVANGELICAL CHURCH IN AMERICA

At first, a loose federation of Latvian Lutherans in this country was formed in the 1950's, which in the 1970s became a more centralized church body. At first there were contacts with the conservative Wisconsin Evangelical Lutheran Synod (WELS), but later the Latvians gravitated to the liberal side of Lutherans, joining the Lutheran Council in the USA (LCUSA), the Lutheran World Federation (LWF), and the World Council of Churches (WCC). It is of interest to note that the LCMS in its 2001 Convention declared fellowship with the Evangelical Lutheran Church of Latvia, (ELCL) a moderate church that once practiced the ordination of women and is a member of the Lutheran World Federation and is in fellowship with the Evangelical Lutheran Church of Latvia (ELCA), which the LCMS has branded as a heterodox church. The WELS has not declared fellowship with the ELCL. At about the same time that the LCMS was declaring fellowship with the ELCL, the WELS declared fellowship with the Confessional Lutheran Church of Latvia (CLCL). The CLCL "came into existence when some of its founding members were expelled from the ministry of the ELCL and members were driven from their church building because they wanted to practice closed communion and sound fellowship principles."[3]

LUTHERAN CHURCHES OF THE REFORMATION (LCR)

Members of the disbanded Orthodox Lutheran Conference and other like-minded Missouri Synod dissidents, in 1964 organized the Lutheran Churches of the Reformation. Like the Missouri Synod, the LCR holds adamantly to the doctrine that the congregation is the only God-ordained form of the church (contrary to Wisconsin Synod doctrine) and that pastoring the local congregation is the only God-ordained form of the gospel ministry. These Missouri Synod views on Church and Ministry were important factors in keeping the Wisconsin Synod and the LCR apart. This body remains very small. Periodicals: *One Accord* and *The Faithful Word* (a theological journal).

PROTÉSTANT CONFERENCE

The Protéstant Conference appeared on the scene in the 1920's as a protest movement within the Wisconsin Synod against certain actions taken by the Board of Education at Northwestern College, and against the suspension of two Fort Atkinson, Wisconsin, parochial school teachers who clashed with their pastor over the issue of lax discipline in the congregation. A conference paper also sparked controversy when the seminary faculty found doctrinal errors in it. The Protéstant Conference and the Wisconsin Synod have not been able to arrive at a peaceful solution of their differences. About three dozen pastors, teachers, and congregations were involved in forming the Conference. However, this dissident group at times found themselves at odds with each other, thus diminishing the ranks of the Conference. In the early 1990s there were fewer than ten congregations and fewer than 1,000 baptized members. Official publication: *Faith Life.*

WORLD CONFESSIONAL LUTHERAN ASSOCIATION (WCLA)

Formed in 1980 as the Conservative Lutheran Association, this group's roots go back to 1960 and the formation of the new American Lutheran Church. There were protests by the theologically conservative members against the departures by the ALC from the doctrine of the Inerrancy of Scripture. There were also protests against the acceptance of ecumenism by the ALC.

In 1984 the group adopted the name the World Confessional Lutheran Association. The WCLA did not appear to benefit from defections from the bodies in the ELCA merger. In the early 1990s there were ten congregations and fewer than 2000 baptized members.

The group operates Faith Lutheran Seminary in Tacoma, Washington. An introductory tract, "Our Faith" asserts:

THE WCLA ACCEPTS ALL THE CANONICAL BOOKS OF THE OLD AND NEW TES-
TAMENT AS A WHOLE AND IN ALL OF THEIR PARTS AS THE DIVINELY INSPIRED,
REVEALED, AND INERRANT WORD OF GOD, AND SUBMITS TO THEM AS THE ONLY
INFALLIBLE AUTHORITY IN ALL MATTERS OF FAITH AND LIFE.

THE WCLA ACCEPTS THE DOCTRINAL STATEMENTS OF THE CONFESSIONAL
LUTHERAN CHURCH; NAMELY THE *APOSTOLIC, NICENE,* AND *ATHANASIAN
CREEDS*; AND THE *UNALTERED AUGSBURG CONFESSION, THE SMALCALD AR-
TICLES,* AND *THE FORMULA OF CONCORD,* NOT INSOFAR AS, BUT BECAUSE THEY
ARE TRUE AND RELIABLE EXPOSITIONS OF THE HOLY SCRIPTURES.

THE WCLA ACKNOWLEDGES JESUS CHRIST AS HEAD AND LORD OF THE
CHURCH, AND ACCEPTS THE BIBLE, THE HOLY SCRIPTURES, AS THE INERRANT
REVELATION AND DIRECTIVE TO HIS PEOPLE.

The above are the truths, as enunciated by the WCLA, that are the reason
for its existence, truths this group contended for from the start, the issues upon
which all others hinged.

The WCLA states as its main purpose:

THE WCLA IS A COLLECTIVE BODY OF CONCERNED CHRISTIANS WHO DESIRE TO
RETAIN THE LUTHERAN DISTINCTIVES OF WORD ALONE, GRACE ALONE, FAITH
ALONE IN CHRIST ALONE AS THE HALLMARK OF THE TRUE CHRISTIAN CHURCH
ON EARTH.

THE INDIVIDUALS, CONGREGATIONS AND ASSOCIATED MINISTRIES MAKING UP
THE WCLA BELIEVE THAT THE DOCTRINE OF BIBLICAL INERRANCY IS OF VITAL
IMPORTANCE IN ACCOMPLISHING THIS GOAL. THESE PEOPLE ARE WORKING TO-
GETHER TO HELP ACHIEVE CHRIST'S "GREAT COMMISSION" IN THIS GENERA-
TION. (From: *Introducing the World Confessional Association*—a tract.)

Footnotes for Addendum

* Some of the information contained in the ADDENDUM is from *WELS
And other Lutherans*, written by John F. Brug, Edward C. Fredrich II, Armin
W. Schuetze, (Milwaukee, WI: Northwestern Publishing House, 1995), pp. 87-
99.

1 David R. Barnhart, *The Church's Desperate Need For Revival* (Eden
Prairie, MN: Viking Press, Inc., copyright by Abiding Word Minstries, Inc.,
1986), p. 68.

2 Barnhart, *The Church's Desperate Need...*, p. 68.

3 *Wisconsin Lutheran Quarterly*, Vol. 99, No. 1, 2002 (Milwaukee, WI:
Northwestern Publishing House), pp. 66, 67.

NOTE: For a more thorough coverage of the small and tiny Lutheran
bodies, refer to: John F. Brug, *The WELS And Other Lutherans—Second
Edition,* (Milwaukee, WI: Northwestern Publishing House, 2009, 1-800-
662-6022).

A CAUTION:

John F. Brug, a professor at the Wisconsin Lutheran Seminary in
Mequon, WI, who is the author of the *Second Edition* of the above men-

tioned book: *The WELS and Other Lutherans* and co-author of the *First Edition*, has a caution for those seeking comprehensive and accurate information regarding the small and tiny Lutheran bodies that have surfaced in recent decades: "There are constant additions and subtractions from the list of small Lutheran Church bodies...Almost every time I checked the web links, another group had come or gone. Also, statistical information on many of the smaller bodies is hard to come by...Some of the groups are more like parachurch organizations than organized synods. Their members may also be members of other church bodies...Some of these small groups may give quite different versions of the cause of the split and whether the departing party was removed or resigned." (*The WELS and Other Lutherans—Second Edition*, p. 174)

THE GENERAL SYNOD IN DIAGRAM

The G. S. was organized at Hagerstown, Md. Oct. 22, 1820 by: Penn. Min. (1748), N.Y. Min. (1786), No. Carolina Syn. (1803), and Syn. of Maryland and Virginia (1820)

(NOTE: numbers in parentheses are the dates of founding or organization)

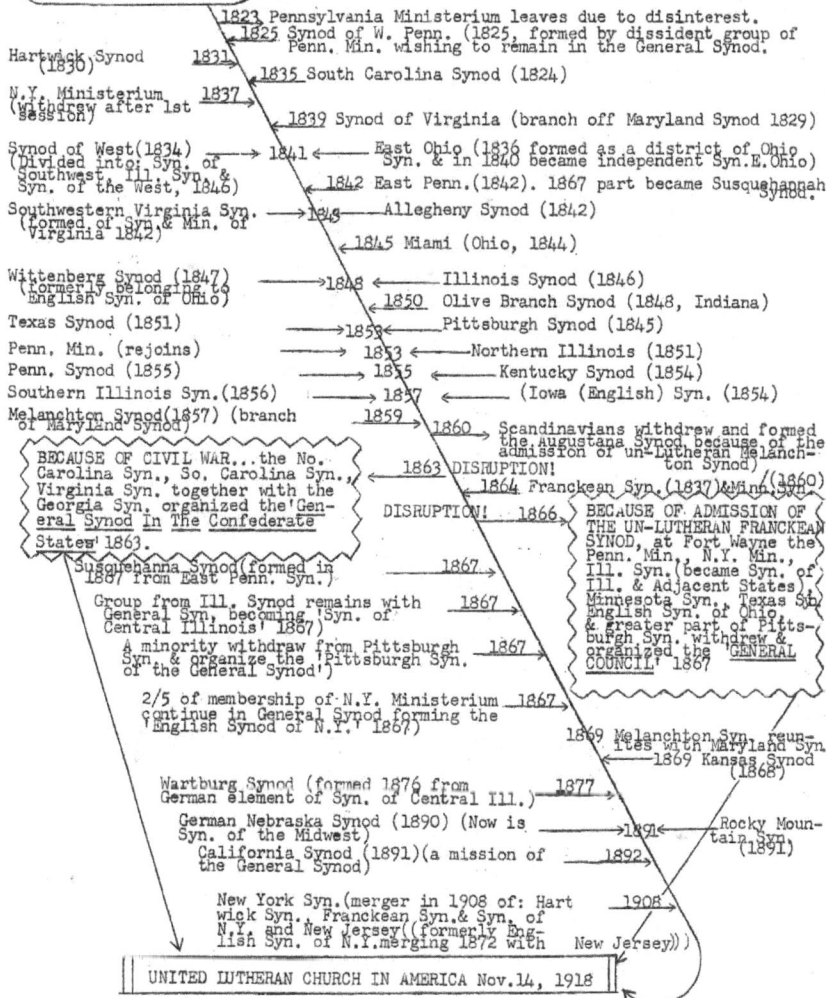

1823 Pennsylvania Ministerium leaves due to disinterest.

1825 Synod of W. Penn. (1825, formed by dissident group of Penn. Min. wishing to remain in the General Synod.

Hartwick Synod (1836)　1831

1835 South Carolina Synod (1824)

N.Y. Ministerium (withdrew after 1st session)　1837

1839 Synod of Virginia (branch off Maryland Synod 1829)

Synod of West (1834) (Divided into: Syn. of Southwest. Ill. Syn. & Syn. of the West, 1846)　→ 1841 ←　East Ohio (1836 formed as a district of Ohio Syn. & in 1840 became independent Syn. E. Ohio)

1842 East Penn. (1842). 1867 part became Susquehannah Synod.

Southwestern Virginia Syn. (formed of Syn. & Min. of Virginia 1842)　→ 1843 ← Allegheny Synod (1842)

1845 Miami (Ohio, 1844)

Wittenberg Synod (1847) (formerly belonging to English Syn. of Ohio)　→ 1848 ← Illinois Synod (1846)

1850 Olive Branch Synod (1848, Indiana)

Texas Synod (1851)　→ 1852 ← Pittsburgh Synod (1845)

Penn. Min. (rejoins)　→ 1853 ← Northern Illinois (1851)

Penn. Synod (1855)　→ 1855 ← Kentucky Synod (1854)

Southern Illinois Syn. (1856)　→ 1857 ← (Iowa (English) Syn. (1854)

Melanchton Synod (1857) (branch of Maryland Synod)　1859

1860 Scandinavians withdrew and formed the Augustana Synod, because of the admission of un-Lutheran Melanchton Synod)

BECAUSE OF CIVIL WAR...the No. Carolina Syn., So. Carolina Syn., Virginia Syn. together with the Georgia Syn. organized the 'General Synod In The Confederate States' 1863.

1863 DISRUPTION!

1864 Franckean Syn. (1837) (Min. (1860)

DISRUPTION! 1866

BECAUSE OF ADMISSION OF THE UN-LUTHERAN FRANCKEAN SYNOD, at Fort Wayne the Penn. Min., N.Y. Min., Ill. Syn. (became Syn. of Ill. & Adjacent States), Minnesota Syn., Texas Syn., English Syn. of Ohio & greater part of Pittsburgh Syn. withdrew & organized the 'GENERAL COUNCIL' 1867

Susquehanna Synod (formed in 1867 from East Penn. Syn.)

Group from Ill. Synod remains with General Syn. becoming 'Syn. of Central Illinois' 1867)　1867

A minority withdraw from Pittsburgh Syn. & organize the 'Pittsburgh Syn. of the General Synod')　1867

2/5 of membership of N.Y. Ministerium continue in General Synod, forming the 'English Synod of N.Y.' 1867)　1867

1869 Melanchton Syn. reunites with Maryland Syn. (1868)

1869 Kansas Synod

Wartburg Synod (formed 1876 from German element of Syn. of Central Ill.)　1877

German Nebraska Synod (1890) (Now is Syn. of the Midwest)　→ 1891 ← Rocky Mountain Syn. (1891)

California Synod (1891)(a mission of the General Synod)　1892

New York Syn. (merger in 1908 of: Hartwick Syn., Franckean Syn. & Syn. of N.Y. and New Jersey ((formerly English Syn. of N.Y. merging 1872 with New Jersey))　1908

UNITED LUTHERAN CHURCH IN AMERICA Nov. 14, 1918

THE GENERAL COUNCIL IN DIAGRAM

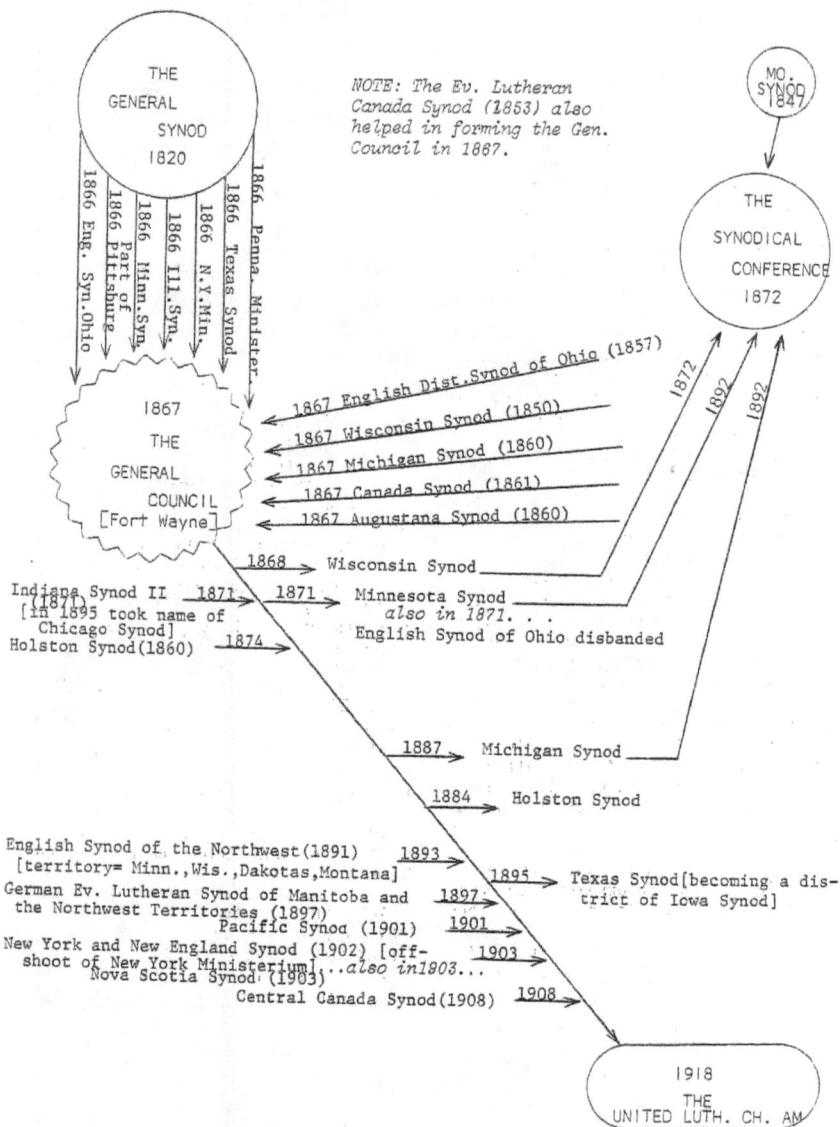

THE
GENERAL
SYNOD
1820

NOTE: *The Ev. Lutheran*
Canada Synod (1853) also
helped in forming the Gen.
Council in 1867.

MO.
SYNOD
1847

THE
SYNODICAL
CONFERENCE
1872

1866 Eng. Syn.Ohio
1866 Part of Pittsburg
1866 Minn.Syn.
1866 Ill.Syn.
1866 N.Y.Min.
1866 Texas Synod
1866 Penna. Minister.

1867
THE
GENERAL
COUNCIL
[Fort Wayne]

1867 English Dist.Synod of Ohio (1857)
1867 Wisconsin Synod (1850)
1867 Michigan Synod (1860)
1867 Canada Synod (1861)
1867 Augustana Synod (1860)

1872
1892
1892

1868 → Wisconsin Synod

Indiana Synod II 1871
(1871)
[In 1895 took name of
Chicago Synod]
Holston Synod(1860)   1874 →

1871 → Minnesota Synod
    also in 1871. . .
English Synod of Ohio disbanded

1887 → Michigan Synod

1884 → Holston Synod

English Synod of the Northwest(1891)   1893 →
[territory= Minn.,Wis.,Dakotas,Montana]
German Ev. Lutheran Synod of Manitoba and   1897 →
the Northwest Territories (1897)
Pacific Synod (1901)   1901 →
New York and New England Synod (1902) [off-
shoot of New York Ministerium]   1903 →
Nova Scotia Synod (1903) . . *also in1903. . .*
Central Canada Synod(1908)   1908 →

1895 → Texas Synod[becoming a district of Iowa Synod]

1918
THE
UNITED LUTH. CH. AM

THE WISCONSIN EVANGELICAL LUTHERAN SYNOD [IN DIAGRAM]

GERMAN EV. MINISTERIUM OF WIS.

MICHIGAN SYNOD   MINNESOTA SYNOD

(1850)

(1860)   (1860)

1867

1864

1867

Michigan Synod left
the Joint Synod
in 1896, rejoined
in 1909

(MICH. SYNOD)

WIS. SYNOD left G.C. 1868

MICH. SYNOD left G.C. 1887

MINN. SYNOD left G.C. 1871

GENERAL COUNCIL 1867

1867

GENERAL SYNOD 1820

1909

1866
Minnesota
Synod
withdrew
from G.S.

1892
Wisconsin Synod, Michigan Synod, and Minnesota
Synod become loosely federated, each keeping its
independence. Thus is formed the EV. LUTHERAN
JOINT SYNOD OF WIS., MINN., MICH. AND OTHER STATES

1904

(1901)

NEBRASKA
DISTRICT
SYNOD

*NOTE: In 1963, having
suspended fellowship
with the Missouri Synod
the Wis. Synod and the
Ev. Lutheran Synod(ELS)
withdrew from the Synod-
ical Conference and for
all practical purposes
it thus came to an end.*

(MISSOURI SYNOD)   1872

(MINN. SYNOD)   1892

(WIS. SYNOD)   1872

SYNODICAL CONFERENCE 1872 - 1963

1902 (SLOVAK SYNOD)

(MICH. SYNOD)   1892

1918 (EV. LUTHERAN SYNOD)
(Norwegian)

1917
A closer amalgamation of the District Synods
of the Joint Synod was brought about, forming
the EV. LUTHERAN JOINT SYNOD OF WISCONSIN, MINN-
ESOTA, MICHIGAN AND OTHER STATES

Over the years
more dis-
tricts

are
added

1959
New name is
adopted: WISCON-
SIN EV. LUTHERAN
SYNOD [WELS]

SELECTIVE BIBLIOGRAPHY

Aaberg Theodore A. *A City Set On A Hill*, Mankato, MN: 1968. Published by the Board of Publications of the Evangelical Lutheran Synod (ELS).

Adams, James E. *Preus of Missouri*. San Francisco, CA: Harper and Row, 1977.

Adams, James E. "The Seed of Schism: A Seminary in Exile." An article reprinted from *The Christianity Century*: "From Concordia to Seminex: A Seminary in Exile," March 6, 1974.

"Aid Association for Lutherans/Lutheran Brotherhood—Is This Still an Issue?" An informational brochure of the CLC. Eau Claire, WI: CLC Book House.

Aurandt, Paul. *Destiny*. New York, NY: Bantom Books, Inc., 1983 by Paulynne, Inc.

Baepler, Walter A. *A Century of Blessing—A History of Concordia Theological Seminary, Springfield, Illinois*. St. Louis, MO: Concordia Publishing House.

Baepler, Walter A. *A Century of Grace—A History of the Missouri Synod 1847-1947*. St. Louis, MO: Concordia Publishing House, 1947.

Baepler, Walter A. *History of the Lutheran Church in America* (up to the 1940's). Unpublished class notes, Concordia Theological Seminary, Springfield, IL. By permission.

Bainton, Roland H. *The Reformation of the Sixteenth Century*. Boston, MA: Beacon Press, 1953.

Barnhart, David R. *The Church's Desperate Need For Revival*. Eden Prairie, MN: Viking Press, Inc., 1986 by Abiding Word Ministries.

Becker, Siegbert W. "The Historical-Critical Method of Bible Interpretation." *Wisconsin Lutheran Quarterly*, Vol. 74, No. 1, 1977.

Behnken, John W. *This I Recall*. St. Louis, MO: Concordia Publishing House, 1964.

Bente, Frederick, *American Lutheranism*. 2 vols. St. Louis, MO: Concordia Publishing House, 1919.

Bente, Frederick, *Concordia Triglotta—Historical Introduction*. St. Louis, MO: Concordia Publishing House, 1921.

Bergendoff, Conrad. *The Church of the Lutheran Reformation—A Historical Survey of Lutheranism*. St. Louis, MO: Concordia Publishing House, 1967.

Boehmer, Heinrich, *Road to Reformation*. Philadelphia, PA: Muhlenberg Press, 1946.

Bonerud, Omar, and Charles Lutz, eds. *America's Lutherans*. Reprinted from *One* magazine. A chapter titled, "The Little Norse," by J.A.O. Preus, Jr. Columbus, OH: Wartburg Press, 1955.

Braaten, Carl E., and Robert W. Jenson, eds. *Christian Dogmatics*. 2 vols. Philadelphia, PA: Fortress Press, 1984.

Braun, John A. *Together in Christ—A History of the Wisconsin Evangeli-*

cal Lutheran Synod. Milwaukee, WI: Northwestern Publishing House, 2000.

Braun, Mark E. *A Tale of Two Synods—Events That Led to the Split Between the Wisconsin and Missouri Synods.* Milwaukee, WI: Northwestern Publishing House, 2006.

Brokoff, John R. "Morning Has Broken." *The Lutheran.* April 18, 1984. Minneapolis, MN: Augsburg Fortress. Official magazine of the ELCA.

Brug, John F., Edward C. Fredrich II, and Armin W. Schuetze. *WELS and Other Lutherans.* Milwaukee, WI: Northwestern Publishing House, 2006.

Buchheimer, L., ed. *Great Leaders and Great Events—Historical Essays on the Field of Church History.* St. Louis, MO: Concordia Publishing House.

Chilstrom, Herbert W. "A Pastoral Letter: The Church and the Homosexual Person." Bishop, Minnesota Synod, Lutheran Church in America (LCA), 1979.

Christian Worship—A Lutheran Hymnal. (A WELS hymnal) Milwaukee, WI: Northwestern Publishing House, 1993.

Church of the Lutheran Confession. An informational brochure. Eau Claire, WI: CLC Book House.

Clement, Arthur J. *The Pentecostals and Charismatics—A Confessional Lutheran Evaluation.* Milwaukee, WI: Northwestern Publishing House, 2000.

Clement, Arthur J. *Pentecost or Pretense?—An Examination of the Pentecostal and Charismatic Movements.* Milwaukee, WI: Northwestern Publishing House, 1981.

The Common Confession and Other Pertinent Documents. Issued by the Wisconsin Joint Synod. Milwaukee WI: Northwestern Publishing House.

"Concerning the Impasse in the Intersynodical Discussion on Church Fellowship." Published by the Wisconsin Synod Commission on Doctrinal Matters. Originally published in 1961 in the *Northwestern Lutheran,* as a series.

"Conservatives" Versus "Moderates." From: "Chronological Account of the Assumption and Use of Power During the Synodical Administration of J.A.O. Preus."

Continuing in His Word. A series of eleven tracts issued by the Conference of Presidents, The Evangelical Lutheran Joint Synod of Wisconsin and Other States. Milwaukee, WI: Northwestern Publishing House, 1954.

Deitz, Reginald W., and W. Kent Gilbert, eds. *Luther and the Reformation.* Philadelphia, PA: Muhlenberg Press, 1953.

Doctrinal Declarations—A Collection of Official Statements on the Doctrinal Position of Various Lutheran Synods in America. St. Louis, MO: Concordia Publishing House.

Doctrinal Statements of the WELS. Prepared by the Commission on Inter-Church Relations of the Wisconsin Evangelical Lutheran

Synod, 1997.

Dolak, George. *A History of the Slovak Evangelical Lutheran Church, 1902-1927.* St. Louis, MO: 1955.

"Entrenched Unionistic Practices—A Record of Unionistic Practice in the Lutheran Church-Missouri Synod." Article II: Meetings with the National Lutheran Council. Authorized by the Commission on Doctrinal Matters, the Wisconsin Ev. Lutheran Synod (WELS). Published, early 1960's.

Essays on the Lutheran Confession Basic to Lutheran Cooperation. 2 booklets of essays. Published jointly by the NLC and the Missouri Synod, 1961.

The Evangelical Catechism, American Edition. Trans. By Lawrence W. Denef. Minneapolis, MN: Augsburg Publishing House, 1982.

The Evangelical Lutheran Synod—Character, Doctrine, History, Mission. Printed by the Evangelical Lutheran Synod (ELS), 1977.

Evangelical Lutheran Synod Convention *Report*, 1963, 1952.

Everett, Arden, G. *Meet the Lutherans—Introducing the Lutheran Church in North America.* Rock Island, IL: Augustana Press, 1962 by Augustana Book Concern.

Empie, Paul C., and James I. McCord, eds. *Marburg Revisited.* Minneapolis, MN: Augsburg Publishing House.

"Faithful to Our Calling—Faithful to Our Lord." Doc.#1. St. Louis Concordia Seminary faculty majority.

"Fellowship Then and Now." Quoting *Lehre Und Wehre*, St. Louis, MO: 1856. Milwaukee, WI: Northwestern Publishing House.

Ferm, V. *The Crisis in American Lutheran Theology—A Study of the Issue Between American Lutheranism and Old Lutheranism, 1927.*

Fevold, Eugene L. "Trailblazers For the Church." *Lutheran Brotherhood/Bond.* June 1975.

Fink, W.J. *Lutheran Landmarks and Pioneers in America,* 1913.

Fleischer, Paul. "On Unity and Union or the ELCA and Bankrupt Lutheranism." *Lutheran Spokesman (CLC).* July 1989.

Forester, Walter O. *Zion on the Mississippi.* St. Louis, MO: Concordia Publishing House, 1953.

Forward in Christ. Formerly, *Northwestern Lutheran.* Official magazine of the WELS. May 2000; January, March, April, May, June, August, September 2003; March, June, August 2004; November 2005. Milwaukee, WI: Northwestern Publishing House.

Fricke, James A. *Formula of Concord—A Study for Bible Classes.* Milwaukee, WI: Northwestern Publishing House, 1979.

Graebner, A.L. *Geschichte der Lutherischen Kirche in America. Erster Theil.* St. Louis, MO, 1892.

Graebner, Theodore. *Church Bells in the Forest—A Story of Lutheran Pioneer Work on the Michigan Frontier 1840-1850.* St. Louis, MO: Concordia Publishing House, 1944.

Haapenen, Alfred. *Our Church. The Suomi Synod, the Finnish Evangelical Lutheran Church of America.* Hancock, MI: Finnish Book

Concern, 1945.

Hammerton, J.A. ed. *Universal World History.* Vol. 6. New York, NY: Wm. H. Wise and Co., 1937.

Heinecken, Martin J. *We Believe and Teach.* Philadelphia, PA: Fortress Press, 1980.

Henry, Carl F. H., ed. *Christianity Today,* Vol. 6, No. 20, July 6, 1962. Washington D.C.

Hetico, Robert P. *America's Lutherans (The Orphans are Three).* Reprinted from *One* magazine. Columbus, OH: Wartburg Press, 1955.

Hudson, Winthrop S. *The Story of the Christian Church.* New York, NY: Harper and Brothers, 1958 by Winthrop S. Hudson.

Jackson, Gregory L. *Catholic, Lutheran, Protestant—A Doctrinal Comparison of Three Christian Confessions.* St. Louis, MO: Martin Chemnitz Press. 1992 by Gregory L. Jackson. Printed by Leader Publishing Co., New Haven, MO.

Jacobs, Henry Eyster. *A History of the Evangelical Lutheran Church in the United States.* New York, NY: 1893, 1916, 1934.

Jensen, John M. *The United Evangelical Lutheran Church—An Interpretation.* Minneapolis, MN: Augsburg Publishing House, 1964.

Jersild, Paul. *Invitation to Faith.* Minneapolis, MN: Augsburg Publishing House, 1978.

Jeske, John C. "Amazing Grace—125 Years of It!" WELS Convention paper, February 13, 1974.

Jewett, Robert. "The Gospel As Heresy: Concordia Seminary in Exile." An article appearing in "From Concordia to Seminex: A Seminary in Exile": *A Christian Century* reprint. Material appeared: May 23, 1973; August 1, 1973; March 6, 1974; March 27, 1974; April 17, 1974.

Johnson, Marshall D. *Affirm Series, The Apostles Creed, Teacher's Guide.* Minneapolis, MN: Augsburg Publishing House, 1984.

Johnston, Johanna, and James L. Steffenson. *The Universal History of the World—Reformation and Exploration,* Vol. 8. New York, NY: Golden Press, 1966 by Western Publishing Co., Inc., and Librairie Hachette.

Kleeberg, M.A., and Gerhard Lemme. *In the Footsteps of Martin Luther.* Liscensed English Edition, first printing, 1966; second printing, 1968. St. Louis, MO: Concordia Publishing House. Trans. By Eric Hopka.

Knudsen, Johannes. *The Formation of the Lutheran Church in America.* Philadelphia, PA: Fortress Press, 1978.

Koelpin, Arnold J., ed. *No Other Gospel—Essays in Commemoration of the 400th Anniversary of the Formula of Concord 1580-1980.* Milwaukee, WI: Northwestern Publishing House, 1980.

Koenig, Richard E. "What's Behind the Showdown in the Lutheran Church-Missouri Synod?" Three articles published in the *Lutheran Forum,* an independent journal published by the America Lutheran Publicity Bureau: November 1972; February and

May 1973 issues.

Krause, Karl F. "The Michigan District." An essay in the *Michigan District History 1833-1970*. Copyright 1972 by the Michigan District of the WELS.

Krauth, Charles, P. *The Conservative Reformation and Its Theology*. Philadelphia, PA: The United Lutheran Publishing House, 1913; first edition, 1871.

Lenski, Gerhard E. *Stirring Scenes From the Life of Luther*. Columbus, OH: The Wartburg Press, 1935.

Leppien, Patsy A., and J. Kincaid Smith. *What's Going On Among the Lutherans?—A Comparison of Beliefs*. Milwaukee, WI: Nonwestern Publishing House, 1992.

Lindsell, Harold. *The Battle for the Bible*. Grand Rapids, MI: Zondervan Corporation, 1976.

Lueker, Erwin L., ed. *Lutheran Cyclopedia*. St. Louis, MO: Concordia Publishing House, 1954.

Lussky, Herbert O. *The Missouri Synod Laymen and Lutheran Union*. Second Edition. Evanston, IL: 1950.

The Lutheran Hymnal. A hymnal for the Synodical Conference bodies. St. Louis, MO: Concordia Publishing House, 1941.

Lutheran Worship. Prepared by the Commission on Worship of the Lutheran Church-Missouri Synod. St. Louis, MO: Concordia Publishing House, 1982.

Maddow, Ben. *A Sunday Between Wars—The Course of America Life From 1865-1917*. New York, London: W. W. Norton and Company, 1979.

"Mark...Avoid...Origin of the CLC." Coordinating Council of the Church of the Lutheran Confession. Eau Claire, WI: The CLC Book House, 1963.

Marquart, Kurt E. *Anatomy of an Explosion*. Grand Rapids: Baker Book House, 1978.

McGoldrick, James Edward. *Luther's English Connection*. Milwaukee, WI: Northwestern Publishing House, 1979.

McCurley, Foster R., Jr., and John Reumann. *Word and Witness*. LCA Adult Bible Study Program. Philadelphia, PA: Fortress Press, 1977.

Meuser, Fred W. *The Formulation of the American Lutheran Church*. Columbus, OH: Wartburg Press, 1958.

Mortensen, Enok. *Stories From Our Church*. Blair, NE: Lutheran Publishing House, 1952.

Mueller, John Theodore. *The Lutheran Confessions*. A Tract. St. Louis, MO: Concordia Publishing House.

Mundinger, Carl S. *Government in the Missouri Synod*. St. Louis, MO: Concordia Publishing House, 1947.

Nelson, Clifford E., and Eugene L. Fevold, *The Lutheran Church Among Norwegian-Americans*. 2 vols. Minneapolis, MN: Augsburg Publishing House, 1960.

Nelson, Clifford E. *Lutheranism in North America 1914-1970*. Minneapolis, MN: Augsburg Publishing House, 1972.

Nelson, Clifford E., ed. *The Lutherans in North America*. Philadelphia, PA: Fortress Press, 1975.

Neve, J.L. *A Brief History of the Lutheran Church in America*. Burlington, IA, 1903.

Nolting, Paul F. "Mark...Avoid!" A printed Tenth Anniversary (CLC) Essay. First printing, October 1970; second printing, December 1970. Eau Claire, WI: CLC Book House.

Nyholm, Paul C. *The Americanization of the Danish Lutheran Churches in America*. Minneapolis, MN: Augsburg Publishing House.

Olson, Osacr N. *The Augustana Lutheran Church in America 1860—1910*. From: *Lutherans in the U.S.A., 1956*.

Olson, Oscar N., and George W. Wickstrom, eds. *A Century of Life and Growth—1848 to 1948 Lutheran Augustana Synod*. Rock Island, IL: Augustana Book Concern, 1948.

Orvick, George M. *Our Great Heritage—A Popular History of the Evangelical Lutheran Synod*. Rock Island, IL: Augustana Book Concern, 1948.

Otten, Herman, ed. *A Christian Handbook on Vital Issues*. New Haven, MO: By *Christian News*, 1963-1973. Leader Publishing Co.

Otten, Herman, ed. *The Christian News Encyclopedia*. 5 vols. Washington, MO: Missourian Publishing Company.

Otten, Herman, ed. *Christian News*. New Haven, MO.

Our Relations With the Lutheran Church-Missouri Synod. Published by the Union Committee of the Norwegian Synod (now the Ev. Lutheran Synod).

Pieper, Francis. *Christian Dogmatics*. 4 vols. St. Louis, MO: Concordia Publishing House, 1950, 1951, 1953.

Polack, W.G. *The Building of a Great Church*. St. Louis, MO: Concordia Publishing House, 1926. (A Brief History of Our Lutheran Church in America.)

Polack, W.G. *The Story of Luther*. St. Louis, MO: Concordia Publishing House, 1931, 1934, 1941.

Qualben, Lars P. *A History of the Christian Church*. New York, NY: Thomas Nelson and Sons. Revised and reprinted 1942. Copyright, 1933.

Reim, Edmund C. *Where Do We Stand?—An Outline of the Wisconsin Position*. Published by the authority of the Committee on Tracts of the Wisconsin Synod. Milwaukee, WI: Northwestern Publishing House, 1950.

Reu, Michael J. *In the Interest of Lutheran Unity, Two Lectures*. Columbus, OH: Lutheran Book Concern.

Reumann, John. *Jesus in the Church's Gospels*. Philadelphia, PA: Fortress Press, 1968.

Rogness, Alvin N. "What Kind of Cooperation is Possible in View of the Discussions to Date?" An essay in *Toward Cooperation Among American Lutherans*. Published jointly by the NLC and the Missouri Synod, 1961.

Schmauk, Theodore E., and C. Theodore Benze. *The Confessional Principle and the Confessions, As Embodying the Evangelical Confession of the Christian Church.* Philadelphia, PA: General Council Publication Board.

Schruhl, Joe E. "Historical-Critical Method of Bible Interpretation." *The Christian News Encyclopedia,* No. 1, 1983.

Schwarz, Hans. *Beyond the Gates of Death: A Biblical Examination of Evidence for Life After Death.* Minneapolis, MN: Augsburg Publishing House, 1981.

Schwarz, Hans. *What Christians Believe.* Philadelphia, PA: Fortress Press, 1987.

Schwiebert, E.G. *Luther and His Times.* St. Louis, MO: Concordia Publishing House, 1950.

Scroggs, Robin. *Homosexuality in the New Testament.* Philadelphia, PA: Fortress Press, 1983.

Sentzke, Geert. *Finland—Its Church and Its People.* Helinski, Finland, 1963. *A Short History of the Association of Free Lutheran Congregations.* Also: *A Statement on the Historical Situation (AFLC).* Minneapolis, MN: Association of Free Lutheran Congregations, 3110 East Medicine Lake Blvd., Minneapolis, MN 55441.

Snell, Tee Loften. *The Wild Shores, America's Beginnings.* The national Geographic Society, 1974.

Stanford, Craig. *The Death of the Lutheran Reformation.* Fort Wayne, IN: Stanford Publishing, 1988.

Starr, Richard. *Speaking the Unspeakable! Homosexuality—A Biblical and Modern Perspective.* Milwaukee, WI: Northwestern Publishing House, 1987.

Steen, Inez. *The March of Faith.* Minneapolis, MN: Augsburg Publishing House, 1939.

Steffenson, James, L. *The Universal History of the World.* Vol. 7 *The Renaissance.* New York, NY: Golden Press, 1966 by Western Publishing Co., Inc., and Librairie Hachette.

Stephenson, George M. *The American Immigration Collection.* Arno Pussan: *The New York Times,* 1969. Copyright originally, 1932 by the University of Minnesota Press, Minneapolis, MN.

"Suspension of Relations with the Lutheran Church-Missouri Synod by the 38th Regular Convention of the Norwegian Synod, June 1955."

This Is Your Church—The Church of the Lutheran Confession. Eau Claire, WI: CLC Book House, Third Edition, 2001.

Tietjen, John. "Fact Finding or Fault Finding?" September 8, 1972.

Tietjen, John. *Memoirs In Exile—Confessional Hope and Institutional Conflict.* Minneapolis, MN: Augsburg Fortress Press.

Tillmanns, Walter G. "The First American Martyrs." *Liberty.* November/December 1969. Reprint from the *Lutheran Standard.* November 2, 1965.

Tjernagel, Neelak. *Henry VIII and the Lutherans—A Study of Anglo-Lutheran Relations from 15212 to 1547.* St. Louis, MO: Concordia Publishing House, 1965.

Trexler, Edgar R. Anatomy of a Merger—People, Dynamics, and Decisions That Shaped the ELCA. Minneapolis, MN: Augsburg Fortress Press, 1991.

Voss, A.P., ed. *Continuing in His Word—The History of the Evangelical Joint Synod of Wisconsin and Other States.* Prepared for publication at the Synod's Centenary by the Centennial Committee of the Joint Synod. Milwaukee, WI: Northwestern Publishing House, 1951.

Walther, C.F.W. *The Proper Distinction Between Law and Gospel.* Reproduced from the German Edition of 1897. St. Louis, MO: Concordia Publishing House. Translated by W.H.T. Dau, 1928.

Wentz, Abdel Ross. *A Basic History of Lutheranism in America.* Philadelphia, PA: Muhlenberg Press, 1955.

Wicke, Harold E. *A Catechism of Differences—A Popular Study of the Doctrine and Practice of the Various Lutheran Bodies in the United States.* Milwaukee, WI: Northwestern Publishing House, 1964. Third Edition.

Wisconsin Evangelical Lutheran Synod 2004 Yearbook. Milwaukee, WI: Northwestern Publishing House, 2003.

Witt, M.J. "Ten Years of Grace." An essay celebrating the Tenth Anniversary of the Church of the Lutheran Confession (CLC).

Wolf, Edmund Jacob. *The Lutherans in America.* New York, NY:, 1889.

Wolf, Richard C. *Documents on Lutheran Unity in America.* Philadelphia, PA: Fortress Press, 1966.

"Woman Suffrage in the Church." Report of the Commission on Theology and Church Relations of the Lutheran Church-Missouri Synod: a study mandated by the New York Convention, 1967, and presented to the Denver Convention, 1969.

"Yes, There is Still A Difference!" An informational brochure explaining the continuing differences between the CLC and the WELS. Eau Claire, WI: CLC Book House.

You and Your Synod—The Story of the Wisconsin Evangelical Lutheran Synod. Prepared for the WELS by the Board For Parish Education. Milwaukee, WI: Northwestern Publishing House, 1972.

INDEX

910

* 9 7 8 0 9 6 4 4 7 9 9 9 9 *